FOURTH EDITION

LOOKING AT
MOVIES

FOURTH EDITION

LOOKING

AT MOVIES

AN INTRODUCTION TO FILM

RICHARD BARSAM & DAVE MONAHAN

 W. W. NORTON & COMPANY
NEW YORK • LONDON

W. W. Norton & Company has been independent since its founding in 1923, when William Warder Norton and Mary D. Herter Norton first published lectures delivered at the People's Institute, the adult education division of New York City's Cooper Union. The firm soon expanded its program beyond the Institute, publishing books by celebrated academics from America and abroad. By midcentury, the two major pillars of Norton's publishing program—trade books and college texts—were firmly established. In the 1950s, the Norton family transferred control of the company to its employees, and today—with a staff of four hundred and a comparable number of trade, college, and professional titles published each year—W. W. Norton & Company stands as the largest and oldest publishing house owned wholly by its employees.

Editor: Peter Simon
Senior project editor: Thomas Foley
Senior production manager: Benjamin Reynolds
Assistant editor: Conor Sullivan
Editorial assistant: Quynh Do
Managing editor, college: Marian Johnson
Book design: Lissi Sigillo
Design director: Rubina Yeh
Marketing manager, fine arts: Nicole Albas
Media editors: Eileen Connell and Cassie del Pilar
Media designer: Jack Lamb
Associate editor, media: Laura Musich
Assistant editor, media: Carson Russell
Index by Cohen & Carruth, Inc.

Development Editor for the First Edition: Kurt Wildermuth
Authors photograph taken by Joshua Curry
Cover design: Leo Hageman

The text of this book is composed in Benton Modern Two
Composition by Jouve North America—Brattleboro, VT
Digital art file manipulation by Jay's Publishers Services
Manufacturing by Quad / Graphics—Taunton, MA

Library of Congress Cataloging-in-Publication Data

Barsam, Richard Meran.
    Looking at movies : an introduction to film / Richard Barsam and Dave Monahan.—4th ed.
        p. cm.
    Includes bibliographical references and index.

ISBN 978-0-393-91302-6 (pbk.)

    1.   Motion pictures. 2.   Cinematography. I.   Monahan, Dave. II.   Title.
    PN1994.B313 2013
    791.43—dc23
                                                                    2012031341

W. W. Norton & Company, Inc., 500 Fifth Avenue, New York, N.Y. 10110
                            wwnorton.com

W. W. Norton & Company Ltd., Castle House, 75/76 Wells Street, London W1T 3QT

1 2 3 4 5 6 7 8 9 0

About the Authors

RICHARD BARSAM (Ph.D., University of Southern California) is Professor Emeritus of Film Studies at Hunter College, City University of New York. He is the author of *Nonfiction Film: A Critical History* (rev. and exp. ed., 1992), *The Vision of Robert Flaherty: The Artist as Myth and Filmmaker* (1988), *In the Dark: A Primer for the Movies* (1977), and *Filmguide to "Triumph of the Will"* (1975); editor of *Nonfiction Film: Theory and Criticism* (1976); and contributing author to Paul Monaco's *The Sixties: 1960–1969* (Vol. 8 in the History of the American Cinema series, 2001) and *Filming Robert Flaherty's "Louisiana Story": The Helen Van Dongen Diary* (ed. Eva Orbanz, 1998). His articles and book reviews have appeared in *Cinema Journal*, *Quarterly Review of Film Studies*, *Film Comment*, *Studies in Visual Communication*, and *Harper's*. He has been a member of the Executive Council of the Society for Cinema and Media Studies and the Editorial Board of *Cinema Journal*, and he cofounded the journal *Persistence of Vision*.

DAVE MONAHAN (M.F.A., Columbia University) is an Associate Professor and Department Chair of Film Studies at the University of North Carolina, Wilmington. His work as a writer, director, and editor includes *Things Grow* (2010), *Ringo* (2005), *Monkey Junction* (2004), *Prime Time* (1996), and *Angels Watching Over Me* (1993). His work has been screened internationally in over fifty film festivals and has earned numerous awards, including the New Line Cinema Award for Most Original Film (*Prime Time*) and the Seattle International Film Festival Grand Jury Prize for Best Animated Short Film (*Ringo*).

Contents

To Students xiii

Preface xv

Acknowledgments xix

CHAPTER 1
Looking at Movies 1

Learning Objectives 2

Looking at Movies 2

What Is a Movie? 3

Ways of Looking at Movies 5

    Invisibility and Cinematic Language 7

    Cultural Invisibility 10

    Implicit and Explicit Meaning 11

    Viewer Expectations 13

    Formal Analysis 14

    Cultural and Formal Analysis in *Harry Potter* 22

Analyzing Movies 32

Screening Checklist: Looking at Movies 32

Questions for Review 33

Movies Described or Illustrated in This Chapter 33

CHAPTER 2
Principles of Film Form 35

Learning Objectives 36

Film Form 36

Form and Content 36

Form and Expectations 39

Patterns 42

Fundamentals of Film Form 46

    Movies Depend on Light 46

    Movies Provide an Illusion of Movement 47

    Movies Manipulate Space and Time in Unique Ways 49

Realism and Antirealism 56

    Verisimilitude 58

Cinematic Language 60

Analyzing Principles of Film Form 62

Screening Checklist: Principles of Film Form 62

Questions for Review 62

Movies Described or Illustrated in This Chapter 63

CHAPTER 3
Types of Movies 65

Learning Objectives 66

The Idea of Narrative 66

Types of Movies 70
   Narrative Movies 70
   Documentary Movies 70
   Experimental Movies 75

Hybrid Movies 82

Genre 83
   Genre Conventions 87
      Story Formulas 87
      Theme 88
      Character Types 88
      Setting 88
      Presentation 88
      Stars 90

Six Major American Genres 90
   Gangster 90
   Film Noir 93
   Science Fiction 96
   Horror 99
   The Western 102
   The Musical 105

Evolution and Transformation of Genre 108

What about Animation? 111

Analyzing Types of Movies 116
Screening Checklist: Types of Movies 116
Questions for Review 116
Movies Described or Illustrated in This Chapter 117

CHAPTER 4
Elements of Narrative 121

Learning Objectives 122

What Is Narrative? 122
   Characters 127
   Narrative Structure 131

The Screenwriter 136

Elements of Narrative 137
   Story and Plot 140
   Order 145
   Events 148
   Duration 149
   Suspense versus Surprise 153
   Repetition 154
   Setting 155
   Scope 156

Looking at Narrative: John Ford's Stagecoach 157
   Story, Screenwriter, and Screenplay 157
   Narration and Narrator 159
   Characters 160
   Narrative Structure 160
   Plot 161
      Order 161
      Diegetic and Nondiegetic Elements 161
      Events 162
      Duration 164
      Repetition 164
   Suspense 164
   Setting 164
   Scope 166

Analyzing Elements of Narrative 167
Screening Checklist: Elements of Narrative 167
Questions for Review 168
Movies Described or Illustrated in This Chapter 168

CHAPTER 5
Mise-en-Scène 171

Learning Objectives 172

What Is Mise-en-Scène? 172

Design 179

The Production Designer 180

Elements of Design 183

Setting, Decor, and Properties 183

Lighting 185

Costume, Makeup, and Hairstyle 187

International Styles of Design 194

Composition 202

Framing: What We See on the Screen 202

On-screen and Offscreen Space 204

Open and Closed Framing 204

Kinesis: What Moves on the Screen 208

Movement of Figures within the Frame 209

Looking at Mise-en-Scène 210

Tim Burton's *Sleepy Hollow* 211

Sam Mendes's *American Beauty* 215

Analyzing Mise-en-Scène 221

Screening Checklist: Mise-en-Scène 221

Questions for Review 222

Movies Described or Illustrated in This Chapter 222

CHAPTER 6
Cinematography 225

Learning Objectives 226

What Is Cinematography? 226

The Director of Photography 226

Cinematographic Properties of the Shot 228

Film Stock 229

Black and White 231

Color 234

Lighting 236

Source 237

Quality 238

Direction 238

Color 242

Lenses 244

Framing of the Shot 248

Implied Proximity to the Camera 248

Shot Types 250

Depth 252

Camera Angle and Height 259

Eye Level 259

High Angle 260

Low Angle 260

Dutch Angle 263

Aerial View 263

Scale 264

Camera Movement 265

Pan Shot 266

Tilt Shot 267

Dolly Shot 267

Zoom 268

Crane Shot 269

Handheld Camera 272

Steadicam 272

Framing and Point of View 274

Speed and Length of the Shot 275

Special Effects 279
  In-Camera, Mechanical, and Laboratory Effects 279
  Computer-Generated Imagery 280
Analyzing Cinematography 284
Screening Checklist: Cinematography 284
Questions for Review 285
Movies Described or Illustrated in this Chapter 285

Looking at Acting 327
  Barbara Stanwyck in King Vidor's *Stella Dallas* 331
  Michelle Williams in Derek Cianfrance's *Blue Valentine* 333
Analyzing Acting 336
Screening Checklist: Acting 336
Questions for Review 337
Movies Described or Illustrated in This Chapter 337

CHAPTER 7
Acting 287

Learning Objectives 288
What Is Acting? 288
  Movie Actors 289
The Evolution of Screen Acting 294
  Early Screen-Acting Styles 294
  D. W. Griffith and Lillian Gish 295
  The Influence of Sound 297
  Acting in the Classical Studio Era 299
  Method Acting 302
  Screen Acting Today 304
  Technology and Acting 309
Casting Actors 310
  Factors Involved in Casting 311
Aspects of Performance 314
  Types of Roles 314
  Preparing for Roles 316
  Naturalistic and Nonnaturalistic Styles 318
  Improvisational Acting 320
  Directors and Actors 321
How Filmmaking Affects Acting 322
  Framing, Composition, Lighting, and the Long Take 323
  The Camera and the Close-up 326
  Acting and Editing 327

CHAPTER 8
Editing 339

Learning Objectives 340
What Is Editing? 340
The Film Editor 342
  The Editor's Responsibilities 344
    Spatial Relationships between Shots 344
    Temporal Relationships between Shots 345
    Rhythm 351
Major Approaches to Editing: Continuity and Discontinuity 355
  Conventions of Continuity Editing 358
    Master Scene Technique 359
    Screen Direction 359
  Editing Techniques That Maintain Continuity 364
    Shot/Reverse Shot 364
    Match Cuts 364
    Parallel Editing 367
    Point-of-View Editing 368
  Other Transitions between Shots 368
    The Jump Cut 368
    Fade 368
    Dissolve 371
    Wipe 372
    Iris Shot 372
    Freeze-Frame 373
    Split Screen 374

Looking at Editing 375
    Fernando Meirelles and Kátia Lund's *City of God* 376
Analyzing Editing 384
Screening Checklist: Editing 385
Questions for Review 385
Movies Described or Illustrated in This Chapter 386

CHAPTER 9
Sound 387

Learning Objectives 388

What Is Sound? 388

Sound Production 390
    Design 390
    Recording 391
    Editing 392
    Mixing 393

Describing Film Sound 393
    Pitch, Loudness, Quality 393
    Fidelity 395

Sources of Film Sound 395
    Diegetic versus Nondiegetic 396
    On-screen versus Offscreen 397
    Internal versus External 398

Types of Film Sound 399
    Vocal Sounds 399
    Environmental Sounds 401
    Music 403
    Silence 409
    Types of Sound in Steven Spielberg's
        War of the Worlds 410

Functions of Film Sound 414
    Audience Awareness 415
    Audience Expectations 416

    Expression of Point of View 416
    Rhythm 418
    Characterization 419
    Continuity 420
    Emphasis 421

Sound in Orson Welles's *Citizen Kane* 423
    Sources and Types 424
    Functions 424
    Characterization 426
    Themes 428

Analyzing Sound 428

Screening Checklist: Sound 428

Questions for Review 429

Movies Described or Illustrated in This Chapter 429

CHAPTER 10
Film History 431

Learning Objectives 432

What Is Film History? 432

Basic Approaches to Studying Film History 433
    The Aesthetic Approach 433
    The Technological Approach 434
    The Economic Approach 434
    Film as Social History 434

A Short Overview of Film History 435
    Precinema 435
        Photography 435
        Series Photography 436
    1891-1903: The First Movies 437
    1908-1927: Origins of the Classical Hollywood Style—
        The Silent Period 440
    1919-1931: German Expressionism 443
    1918-1930: French Avant-Garde Filmmaking 445
    1924-1930: The Soviet Montage Movement 448

1927-1947: Classical Hollywood Style in Hollywood's Golden Age 450

1942-1951: Italian Neorealism 455

1959-1964: French New Wave 457

1947–Present: New Cinemas in Great Britain, Europe, and Asia 461

England and the Free Cinema Movement 462

Denmark and the Dogme 95 Movement 462

Germany and *Das neue Kino* 463

Japan and Postwar Filmmaking 464

China and Postwar Filmmaking 467

The People's Republic 468

Hong Kong 468

Taiwan 469

India 470

1965–1995: The New American Cinema 472

Analyzing Film History 477

Screening Checklist: Film History 477

Questions for Review 479

Movies Described or Illustrated in This Chapter 479

CHAPTER 11
Filmmaking Technologies and Production Systems 483

Learning Objectives 484

The Whole Equation 484

Film, Video, and Digital Technologies: An Overview 486

Film Technology 486

Video Technology 489

Digital Technology 489

Film versus Digital Technology 490

How a Movie Is Made 491

Preproduction 492

Production 493

Postproduction 494

The Studio System 495

Organization before 1931 495

Organization after 1931 496

Organization during the Golden Age 498

The Decline of the Studio System 500

The Independent System 501

Labor and Unions 503

Professional Organizations and Standardization 504

Financing in the Industry 505

Marketing and Distribution 507

Production in Hollywood Today 512

3-D Movies: Gimmick or Trend of the Future 515

Foreign Influences on Hollywood Films 516

Maverick Producers and Directors 517

Thinking about Filmmaking Technologies and Production Systems 518

Screening Checklist: Filmmaking Technologies and Production Systems 518

Questions for Review 519

Movies Described or Illustrated in This Chapter 519

For Further Viewing 520

Further Viewing 521

Academy Award Winners for Best Picture 521

Sight & Sound: Top Ten Best Movies of All Time 524

American Film Institute: One Hundred Greatest American Movies of All Time 525

Entertainment Weekly: One Hundred Greatest Movies of All Time 528

The Village Voice: One Hundred Best Films of the Twentieth Century 531

Glossary 535

Further Reading 549

Permissions Acknowledgments 573

Index 577

To Students

In 1936, art historian Erwin Panofsky had an insight into the movies as a form of popular art—an observation that is more true today than it was when he wrote it:

> If all the serious lyrical poets, composers, painters, and sculptors were forced by law to stop their activities, a rather small fraction of the general public would become aware of the fact and a still smaller fraction would seriously regret it. If the same thing were to happen with the movies, the social consequences would be catastrophic.[1]

Decades later, we would hardly know what to do without movies. They are a major presence in our lives and, like personal computers, perhaps one of the most influential products of our technological age. In fact, some commentators feel that movies are too popular, too influential, too much a part of our lives. Since their invention a little more than a hundred years ago, movies have become one of the world's largest industries and the most powerful art form of our time.

A source of entertainment that makes us see beyond the borders of our previous experience, movies have always possessed powers to amaze, frighten, and enlighten us. They challenge our senses, emotions, and intellect, pushing us to say, often passionately, that we love (or hate) them. Because they arouse our most public and private feelings—and can overwhelm us with their sights and sounds—it's easy to be excited by movies. The challenge is to join that enthusiasm with understanding, to say why we feel so strongly about particular movies. That's one reason why this book encourages you to go beyond movies' stories, to understand how those stories are told. Movies are not reality, after all—only illusions of reality—and

(as with most works of art) their form and content work as an interrelated system, one that asks us to accept it as a given rather than as the product of a process. But as you read this book devoted to looking at movies—that is, not just passively watching them, but actively considering the relation of their form and their content—remember that there is no one way to look at any film, no one critical perspective that is inherently better than another, no one meaning that you can insist on after a single screening. Indeed, movies are so diverse in their nature that no single approach could ever do them justice.

This is not a book on film history, but it includes relevant historical information and covers a broad range of movies; not a book on theory, but it introduces some of the most essential approaches to interpreting movies; not a book about filmmaking, but one that explains production processes, equipment, and techniques; not a book of criticism, but one that shows you how to think and write about the films you study in your classes.

Everything we see on the movie screen—everything that engages our senses, emotions, and minds—results from hundreds of decisions affecting the interrelation of formal cinematic elements: narrative, composition, design, cinematography, acting, editing, and sound. Organized around chapters devoted to those formal elements, this book encourages you to look at movies with an understanding and appreciation of how filmmakers make the decisions that help them tell a story and create

---

[1] Erwin Panofsky, "Style and Medium in the Motion Pictures," in *Film Theory and Criticism: Introductory Readings*, ed. Leo Braudy and Marshall Cohen, 5th ed. (New York: Oxford University Press, 1999), p. 280.

the foundation for its meaning. After all, in the real life of the movies, on the screen, it is not historians, theorists, or critics—important and valuable as their work is—but filmmakers who continually shape and revise our understanding and appreciation of film art.

The second century of movie history is well under way. The entire process of making, exhibiting, and archiving movies is fast becoming a digital enterprise, especially outside of the mainstream industry. As the technology for making movies continues to evolve, however, the principles of film art covered in this book remain essentially the same. The things you learn about these principles and the analytic skills you hone as you read this book will help you look at motion pictures intelligently and perceptively throughout your life, no matter which medium delivers those pictures to you.

Preface

Students in an introductory film course who read *Looking at Movies* carefully and take full advantage of the materials surrounding the text will finish the course with a solid grounding in the major principles of film form as well as a more perceptive and analytic eye. A short description of the book's main features follows.

An Accessible and Comprehensive Overview of Film

Recognized from its first publication as an accessible introductory text, *Looking at Movies* covers key concepts in films studies as comprehensively as possible, too. In addition to its clear and inviting presentation of the fundamentals of film form, the text discusses film genres, film history, and the relationship(s) between film and culture in an extensive but characteristically accessible way, thus providing students with a thorough introduction to the major subject areas in film studies.

Film Examples Chosen with Undergraduates in Mind

From its very first chapter, which features sustained analyses and examples from the *Harry Potter* series and Jason Reitman's *Juno* (2009), *Looking at Movies* invites students into the serious study of cinema via films that are familiar to them and that they have a reasonable chance of having experienced outside of the classroom prior to taking the course. Major film texts from the entire history of cinema are also generously represented, of course, but always with an eye to helping students see enjoyment and serious study as complementary experiences.

A Focus on Analytic Skills

A good introductory film book needs to help students make the transition from the natural enjoyment of movies to a critical understanding of the form, content, and meaning(s) of movies. *Looking at Movies* accomplishes this task in several different ways:

Model Analyses

Hundreds of illustrative examples and analytic readings of films throughout the book provide students with concrete models for their own analytic work. The sustained analyses in Chapter 1 of *Juno* and the *Harry Potter* series—films that most undergraduates will have seen and enjoyed but perhaps not viewed with a critical eye—discuss not only the formal structures and techniques of these films, but also their social and cultural meanings. These analyses offers students an accessible and jargon-free introduction to most of the major themes and goals of the introductory film course, and they show students that looking at movies analytically can start immediately—even before they learn the specialized vocabulary of academic film study.

Video Tutorials

A series of video "tutorials"—written, directed, and hosted by the authors—complement and expand upon the book's analyses. Ranging from 2 minutes to 15 minutes in length, these tutorials show students via moving-image media what the book describes and illustrates in still images. Helpful as a quick review of core concepts from the text, these tutorials also provide useful models for film analysis, thus helping students further develop their analytical skills.

"Screening Checklists"

Each chapter ends with an "Analyzing" section that includes a "Screening Checklist" feature. This series of leading questions prompts students to apply what they've learned in the chapter to their own critical viewing, in class or at home. Printable versions of these checklists are available on the *Looking at Movies* website, at wwnorton.com/movies.

The Most Visually Dynamic Text Available

Looking at Movies was written with one goal in mind: to prepare students for a lifetime of intelligent and perceptive viewing of motion pictures. In recognition of the central role played by visuals in the film-studies classroom, *Looking at Movies* includes an illustration program that is both visually appealing and pedagogically focused, as well as accompanying moving-image media that are second to none.

Hundreds of In-Text Illustrations

The text is accompanied by over 750 illustrations in color and in black and white. Nearly all of the still pictures were captured from digital or analog film sources, thus ensuring that the images directly reflect the textual discussions and the films from which they're taken. Unlike publicity stills, which are attractive as photographs but less useful as teaching aids, the captured stills throughout this book provide visual information that will help students learn as they read and—because they are reproduced in the aspect ratio of the original source—will serve as accurate reference points for students' analysis.

Five Hours of Moving-Image Media

The video supplements that accompany *Looking at Movies* offer five hours of two different types of content:

> The twenty-six video tutorials described above were specifically created to complement *Looking at Movies*, and they are exclu-

sive to this text. The tutorials guide students' eyes to see what the text describes, and because they are viewable in full-screen, they are suitable for presentation in class as "lecture launchers" as well as for students' self-study.

> A mini-anthology of twelve complete short films, ranging from 5 to 30 minutes in length, provides a curated selection of accomplished and entertaining examples of short-form cinema, as well as useful material for short in-class activities or for students' analysis. Most of the films are also accompanied by optional audio commentary from the filmmakers. This commentary was recorded specifically for *Looking at Movies* and is exclusive to this text.

Accessible Presentation; Effective Pedagogy

Among the reasons that *Looking at Movies* is considered the most accessible introductory film text available is its clear and direct presentation of key concepts, and its unique pedagogical organization. The first three chapters of the book—"Looking at Movies," "Principles of Film Form," and "Types of Movies"—provide a comprehensive yet truly "introductory" overview of the major topics and themes of any film course, giving students a solid grounding in the basics before they move on to study those topics in greater depth in later chapters.

In addition, pedagogical features throughout provide a structure that clearly signals to students the main ideas and primary goals of each chapter:

Learning Objectives

A checklist at the beginning of every chapter provides students with a brief summary of the core concepts to be covered in the chapter.

Extensive Captions

As in previous editions, each illustration in *Looking at Movies*, Fourth Edition, is accompanied by a caption that elaborates on a key concept or that guides students to look at elements of the film more analytically. These captions expand on the in-text presentation and reinforce students' retention of key terms and ideas.

"Analyzing" Sections

At the end of each chapter is a section that ties the terms, concepts, and ideas of the chapter to the primary goal of the book: honing students' own analytical skills. This short overview makes explicit how the knowledge students have gained in the chapter can move their own analytical work forward. A short "Screening Checklist" provides leading questions that students can ponder as they screen a film or scene.

"Questions for Review"

"Questions for Review" at the end of each chapter test students' knowledge of the concepts first mentioned in the "Learning Objectives" section at the beginning of the chapter.

Ebook Options

Looking at Movies is also available in two alternate ebook formats:

Inkling format

The first, delivered in the new Inkling environment (readable in Google Chrome or Apple Safari web browsers, and on the iPad), incorporates the video tutorials and other, custom-built, moving-image features into the text itself. The result is a seamless blending of the book and its exciting media supplements. For students and teachers who want to make the most of the digital reading experience, the Inkling format is the best ebook option.

Norton ebook format

The second ebook format, the Norton ebook, retains the look and layout of the print text, and offers some integration of the *Looking at Movies* media, but doesn't provide all of the dynamic features of the Inkling ebook. Offered at less than half the price of the printed text, this ebook option is best for students and teachers concerned principally about cost.

Writing about Movies

Written by Karen Gocsik (Executive Director of the Writing & Rhetoric Program at Dartmouth College) and the authors of *Looking at Movies*, this book is a clear and practical overview of the process of writing papers for film-studies courses. In addition to providing helpful information about the writing process, the new third edition of *Writing about Movies* also offers a substantial introduction-in-brief to the major topics in film studies, including an overview of the major film theories and their potential application to student writing, practical advice about note-taking during screenings and private viewings, information about the study of genre and film history, and an illustrated glossary of essential film terms. This inexpensive but invaluable text is available separately or in a significantly discounted package with *Looking at Movies*.

Chapter-by-Chapter Pedagogical Materials on the Web (wwnorton.com/movies)

Like the book, the *Looking at Movies* student website is clear, accessible, and focused on helping students become knowledgeable and analytically astute viewers of film. Among the site's features are multimedia quizzes that use still and moving-image prompts to reinforce and test student knowledge of core concepts, chapter outlines and learning objectives, timelines, printable versions of the "Screening Checklists" described above, a glossary with flashcard features, and more.

Resources for Instructors
Interactive Instructor's Guide

This online database provides instructors with free access to Norton's extensive collection of teaching resources. Instructors can search for and download the resources they need by topic and resource type and can integrate those resources into their own course materials. Subscribers to this service also receive automated alerts as new resources are made available.

Test Bank

Completely rewritten for this edition, each chapter of the test bank includes a "concept map," 60–65 multiple-choice and 10–15 essay questions (with sample answer guides). Questions are labeled by concept, question type, and difficulty.

Coursepacks for Learning Management Systems

Ready-to-use coursepacks for Blackboard and other learning management systems are available free of charge to instructors who adopt *Looking at Movies*. These coursepacks offer unique activities that reinforce key concepts, chapter overviews and learning objectives, quiz questions, streaming access to the video tutorials, questions about those tutorials and the short films, the complete test bank, lecture PowerPoint slides, art and figures from the text in PowerPoint and JPEG formats, and more.

A Note about Textual Conventions

Boldface type is used to highlight terms that are defined in the glossary at the point where they are introduced in the text. *Italics* are used occasionally for emphasis. References to movies in the text include the year the movie was released and the director's name. Members of the crew who are particularly important to the main topic of the chapter are also identified. For example, in the chapter on cinematography, a reference to *The Matrix* might look like this: Andy and Lana Wachowski's *The Matrix* (1999; cinematographer: Bill Pope). The movie lists provided at the end of each chapter identify films that are used as illustrations or examples in the chapter. In each case, only the movie title, year, and director are included. Other relevant information about the films listed can be found in the chapter itself.

Acknowledgments

Writing a book seems very much at times like the collaborative effort involved in making a movie. In writing this Fourth Edition of *Looking at Movies*, we are grateful to our excellent partners at W. W. Norton & Company. Chief among them is our editor, Pete Simon, who guided us in preparing this new edition with insightful ideas and a sure hand. Other collaborators at Norton were Thomas Foley, senior project editor; Benjamin Reynolds, senior production manager; Eileen Connell and Cassie del Pilar, e-media editors; Laura Musich, associate editor, media; Jack Lamb, media designer; Nicole Albas, marketer; and Quynh Do, editorial assistant. It has been a pleasure to work with such a responsive, creative, and supportive team.

Richard Barsam thanks the friends and colleagues who contributed suggestions for this edition, including Luis-Antonio Bocchi, Richard Koss, Vinny LoBrutto, and Renato Tonelli. Finally, I am grateful to Edgar Munhall for his interest, patience, and companionship.

Dave Monahan would like to thank the faculty, staff, and students of the Film Studies Department at the University of North Carolina, Wilmington. My colleagues Mariana Johnson, Shannon Silva, Andre Silva, Tim Palmer, Todd Berliner, Carlos Kase, Nandana Bose, Chip Hackler, Lou Buttino, Glenn Pack, and Sue Richardson contributed a great deal of expertise and advice. Nate Daniel and Alex Markowski deserve special thanks for their post-production help with this edition's new tutorials and other video assets. The film-studies students Leanne Entwistle and Chad Perz contributed to the new tutorial content as well, principally by scouring movies for new examples and illustrations.

I'd also like to thank my wife, Julie, and daughters, Iris and Elsa, for their patience, support, and encouragement.

Reviewers

We would like to join the publisher in thanking all of the professors and students who provided valuable guidance as we planned this revision. *Looking at Movies* is as much their book as ours, and we are grateful to both students and faculty who have cared enough about this text to offer a hand in making it better.

The following colleagues provided extensive reviews of the Third Edition and many ideas for improving the book in its Fourth Edition: Katrina Boyd (University of Oklahoma), James B. Bush (Texas Tech University), Rodney Donahue (Texas Tech University), Cable Hardin (South Dakota State University), Christopher Jacobs (University of North Dakota), Tammy A. Kinsey (University of Toledo), Bradford Owen (California State University, San Bernadino), W. D. Phillips (College of Staten Island/New York University), Michael Rowin (Hunter College, CUNY), and Nicholas Sigman (Hunter College, CUNY).

The transition from our Second Edition to the Third was an especially momentous revision, and we wish to acknowledge once more the following people, all of whom provided invaluable input during that important stage in the evolution of *Looking at Movies*: Donna Casella (Minnesota State University), John G. Cooper (Eastern Michigan University), Mickey Hall (Volunteer State Community College), Stefan Hall (Defiance College), Jennifer Jenkins (University of Arizona), Robert S. Jones

(University of Central Florida), Mildred Lewis (Chapman University), Matthew Sewell (Minnesota State University), Michael Stinson (Santa Barbara City College), and Michael Zryd (York University).

The following scholars and teachers responded to a lengthy questionnaire from the publisher several years ago, and their responses shaped the early editions of this book: Rebecca Alvin, Edwin Arnold, Antje Ascheid, Dyrk Ashton, Tony Avruch, Peter Bailey, Scott Baugh, Harry Benshoff, Mark Berrettini, Yifen Beus, Mike Birch, Robin Blaetz, Ellen Bland, Carroll Blue, James Bogan, Karen Budra, Don Bullens, Gerald Burgess, Jeremy Butler, Gary Byrd, Ed Cameron, Jose Cardenas, Jerry Carlson, Diane Carson, Robert Castaldo, Beth Clary, Darcy Cohn, Marie Connelly, Roger Cook, Robert Coscarelli, Bob Cousins, Donna Davidson, Rebecca Dean, Marshall Deutelbaum, Kent DeYoung, Michael DiRaimo, Carol Dole, Dan Dootson, John Ernst, James Fairchild, Adam Fischer, Craig Fischer, Tay Fizdale, Karen Fulton, Christopher Gittings, Barry Goldfarb, Neil Goldstein, Daryl Gonder, Patrick Gonder, Cynthia Gottshall, Curtis Green, William Green, Tracy Greene, Michael Griffin, Peter Hadorn, William Hagerty, John Harrigan, Catherine Hastings, Sherri Hill, Glenn Hopp, Tamra Horton, Alan Hutchison, Mike Hypio, Tom Isbell, Delmar Jacobs, Mitchell Jarosz, John Lee Jellicorse, Matthew Judd, Charles Keil, Joyce Kessel, Mark Kessler, Garland Kimmer, Lynn Kirby, David Kranz, James Kreul, Mikael Kreuzriegler, Cory Lash, Leon Lewis, Vincent LoBrutto, Jane Long, John Long, Jay Loughrin, Daniel Machon, Travis Malone, Todd McGowan, Casey McKittrick, Maria Mendoza-Enright, Andrea Mensch, Sharon Mitchler, Mary Alice Molgard, John Moses, Sheila Nayar, Sarah Nilsen, Ian Olney, Hank Ottinger, Dan Pal, Gary Peterson, Klaus Phillips, Alexander Pitofsky, Lisa Plinski, Leland Poague, Walter Renaud, Patricia Roby, Carole Rodgers, Stuart Rosenberg, Ben Russell, Kevin Sandler, Bennet Schaber, Mike Schoenecke, Hertha Schulze, David Seitz, Timothy Shary, Robert Sheppard, Charles Silet, Eric Smoodin, Ken Stofferahn, Bill Swanson, Molly Swiger, Joe Tarantowski, Susan Tavernetti, Edwin Thompson, Frank Tomasulo, Deborah Tudor, Bill Vincent, Richard Vincent, Ken White, Mark Williams, Deborah Wilson, and Elizabeth Wright.

Thank you all.

CHAPTER ONE

Looking at Movies

Looking at Movies

In just over a hundred years, movies have evolved into a complex form of artistic representation and communication: they are at once a hugely influential, wildly profitable global industry and a modern art—the most popular art form today. Popular may be an understatement. This art form has permeated our lives in ways that extend far beyond the multiplex. We watch movies on hundreds of cable and satellite channels. We buy movies online or from big-box retailers. We rent movies through the mail, and from Redbox machines at the supermarket. We TiVo movies, stream movies, and download movies to watch on our televisions, our computers, our iPads, and our smart phones.

Unless you were raised by wolves—and possibly even if you were—you have likely devoted thousands of hours to absorbing the motion-picture medium. With so much experience, no one could blame you for wondering why you need a course or this book to tell you how to look at movies.

After all, you might say, "It's just a movie." For most of us most of the time, movies are a break from our daily obligations—a form of escape, entertainment, and pleasure. Motion pictures had been popular for fifty years before even most filmmakers, much less scholars, considered movies worthy of serious study. But motion pictures are much more than entertainment. The movies we see shape the way we view the world around us and our place in that world. What's more, a close analysis of any particular movie can tell us a great deal

Movies shape the way we see the world No other movie featuring a homosexual relationship has earned the level of international critical acclaim and commercial success of *Brokeback Mountain* (2005). The film, made for a relatively paltry $14 million, grossed $178 million at the box office, eventually becoming the eighth highest-grossing romantic drama in Hollywood history. Academy Awards for Best Director (Ang Lee) and Best Adapted Screenplay (Diana Ossana and Larry McMurtry, from a short story by Annie Proulx) were among the many honors and accolades granted the independently produced movie. But even more important, by presenting a gay relationship in the context of the archetypal American West and casting popular leading men (Heath Ledger, Jake Gyllenhaal) in starring roles that embodied traditional notions of masculinity, *Brokeback Mountain* influenced the way many Americans perceived same-sex relationships and gay rights. No movie can single-handedly change the world, but the accumulative influence of cinema is undeniable.

about the artist, society, or industry that created it. Surely any art form with that kind of influence and insight is worth understanding on the deepest possible level.

And there is much more to movies than meets the casual eye . . . or ear, for that matter. Cinema is a subtle—some might even say sneaky—medium. Because most movies seek to engage viewers' emotions and transport them inside the world presented onscreen, the visual vocabulary of film is designed to play upon those same instincts that we use to navigate and interpret the visual and aural information of our "real life." This often imperceptible **cinematic language**, composed not of words but of myriad integrated techniques and concepts, connects us to the story while deliberately concealing the means by which it does so.

Yet behind this mask, all movies, even the most blatantly commercial ones, contain layers of complexity and meaning that can be studied, analyzed, and appreciated. This book is devoted to that task—to actively *looking at* movies rather than just passively watching them. It will teach you to recognize the many tools and principles that filmmakers employ to tell stories, convey information and meaning, and influence our emotions and ideas.

Once you learn to speak this cinematic language, you'll be equipped to understand the movies that pervade our world on multiple levels: as narrative, as artistic expression, and as a reflection of the cultures that produce and consume them.

What Is a Movie?

Now that we've established what we mean by looking at movies, the next step is to attempt to answer the deceptively simple question, What is a movie? As this book will repeatedly illustrate, when it comes to movies, nothing is as straightforward as it appears.

Let's start, for example, with the word *movies*. If the course that you are taking while reading this book is "Introduction to Film" or "Cinema Studies 101," does that mean that your course and this book focus on two different things? What's the difference between a *movie* and a *film*? And where does the word *cinema* fit in?

For whatever reason, the designation *film* is often applied to a motion picture that is considered by critics and scholars to be more serious or challenging than the *movies* that entertain the masses at the multiplex. The still loftier designation of *cinema* seems reserved for groups of films that are considered works of art (e.g., "French cinema"). The truth is, the three terms are essentially interchangeable. *Cinema*, from the Greek *kinesis* ("movement"), originates from the name that filmmaking pioneers Auguste and Louis Lumière coined for the hall in which they exhibited their invention; *film* derives from the celluloid strip on which the images that make up motion pictures were originally captured, cut, and projected; *movies* is simply short for motion pictures. Since we consider all cinema worthy of study, acknowledge that films are increasingly shot on formats other than film stock, and believe motion to be the essence of the movie medium, this book favors the term used in our title. That said, we'll mix all three terms into these pages (as evidenced in the preceding sentence) for the sake of variety, if nothing else.

To most of us, a movie is a popular entertainment, a product produced and marketed by a large commercial studio. Regardless of the subject matter, this movie is pretty to look at—every image is well polished by an army of skilled artists and technicians. The finished product, which is about two hours long, screens initially in movie theaters, is eventually released to DVD and Blu-ray, streaming, or pay-per-view, and ultimately winds up on television. This common expectation is certainly understandable; most movies that reach most English-speaking audiences have followed a good part of this model for three-quarters of a century.

And almost all of these ubiquitous commercial, feature-length movies share another basic characteristic: narrative. When it comes to categorizing movies, the narrative designation simply means that these movies tell fictional (or at least fictionalized) stories. Of course, if you think of narrative in its broadest sense, *every* movie that selects and arranges subject matter in a cause-and-effect sequence of events is employing a narrative structure. For all their creative flexibility, movies by their very nature must travel a straight line.

Narrative in documentary Just because a film is constructed from footage documenting actual events doesn't mean it can't tell a story. Luc Jacquet's *March of the Penguins* (2005) presents the Antarctic emperor penguins' annual cycle of courtship, breeding, and migration as a compelling and suspenseful narrative.

A conventional motion picture is essentially one very long strip of film stock. This linear quality makes movies perfectly suited to develop subject matter in a sequential progression. When a medium so compatible with narrative is introduced to a culture with an already well-established storytelling tradition, it's easy to understand how popular cinema came to be dominated by those movies devoted to telling fictional stories. Because these fiction films are so central to most readers' experience and so vital to the development of cinema as an art form and cultural force, we've made narrative movies the focus of this introductory textbook.

But keep in mind that commercial, feature-length narrative films represent only a fraction of the expressive potential of this versatile medium. Cinema and narrative are both very flexible concepts. Documentary films strive for objective, observed veracity, of course, but that doesn't mean they don't tell stories. These movies often arrange and present factual information and images in the form of a narrative, whether it be a predator's attempts to track and kill its prey, a creature in search of a mate, or a young animal's struggle to adapt to a hostile environment.

Even the most abstract experimental film may assemble images in an order that could be thought of as a kind of narrative. While virtually every movie, regardless of category, employs narrative in some form, cultural differences often affect exactly how these stories are presented. Narrative films made in Africa, Asia, and Latin America reflect storytelling traditions very different from the story structure we expect from films produced in North America and Western Europe. The unscripted, minimalist films by Iranian director Abbas Kiarostami, for example, often intentionally lack dramatic resolution, inviting viewers to imagine their own ending.[1] Sanskrit dramatic traditions have inspired "Bollywood" Indian cinema to feature staging that breaks the illusion of reality favored by Hollywood movies, such as actors that consistently face, and even directly address, the audience.[2]

Compared to North American and Western European films, Latin American films of the 1960s, like *Land in Anguish* (Glauber Rocha, 1967, Brazil) or *Memories of Underdevelopment* (Tomás Gutiérrez Alea, 1968, Cuba), are less concerned with individual character psychology and motivation, instead presenting characters as social types or props in a political allegory.[3] The growing influence of these and other even less conventional approaches, combined with emerging technologies that make filmmaking more accessible and affordable, have made possible an ever-expanding range of independent movies created by crews as small as a single filmmaker and shot on any one of a variety of film, video, and digital formats. The Irish director John Carney shot his musical love story *Once* (2006) on the streets of Dublin with a cast of mostly nonactors and a small crew using consumer-grade video cameras. American Oren Peli's homemade horror movie *Paranormal Activity* (2007) was produced on a miniscule $15,000 budget and was shot entirely from the point of view of its characters' camcorder. *Once* received critical acclaim and an Academy Award for best original song; *Paranormal Activity* eventually earned almost $200 million at

[1]Laura Mulvey, "Kiarostami's Uncertainty Principle," *Sight and Sound* 8, no. 6 (June 1998): 24–27.
[2]Philip Lutgendorf, "Is There an Indian Way of Filmmaking?" *International Journal of Hindu Studies* 10, no. 3 (December 2006): 227–256.
[3]Many thanks to Dr. Mariana Johnson of the University of North Carolina Wilmington for some of the ideas in this analysis.

Cultural narrative traditions The influence of Sanskrit dramatic traditions on Indian cinema can be seen in the prominence of staging that breaks the illusion of reality favored by Hollywood movies, such as actors that consistently face, and even directly address, the audience. In this image, Dr. Arya (Naseeruddin Shah), the villain of Rakesh Roshan's Bollywood blockbuster *Krrish* (2006), interrupts the action to taunt viewers face-to-face with the lies he will tell to conceal his crimes.

the box office, making it one of the most profitable movies in the history of cinema. Even further out on the fringes of popular culture, an expanding universe of alternative cinematic creativity continues to flourish. These noncommercial movies innovate styles and aesthetics, can be of any length, and exploit an array of exhibition options—from independent theaters to cable television to film festivals to Netflix streaming to YouTube.

No matter what you call it, no matter the approach, no matter the format, every movie is a motion picture: a series of still images that, when viewed in rapid succession (usually 24 images per second), the human eye and brain see as fluid movement. In other words, movies *move*. That essential quality is what separates movies from all other two-dimensional pictorial art forms. Each image in every motion picture draws upon basic compositional principles developed by these older cousins (photography, painting, drawing, etc.), including the arrangement of visual elements and the interaction of light and shadow. But unlike photography or painting, films are constructed from individual **shots**—an unbroken span of action captured by an uninterrupted run of a motion-picture camera—that allow visual elements to rearrange themselves and the viewer's perspective itself to shift within any composition.

And this movie movement extends beyond any single shot, because movies are constructed of multiple individual shots joined to one another in an extended sequence. With each transition from one shot to another, a movie is able to move the viewer through time and space. This joining together of discrete shots, or **editing**, gives movies the power to choose what the viewer sees and how that viewer sees it at any given moment.

To understand better how movies control what audiences see, we can compare cinema to another, closely related medium: live theater. A stage play, which confines the viewer to a single wide-angle view of the action, might display a group of actors, one of whom holds a small object in her hand. The audience sees every cast member at once and continuously from the same angle and in the same relative size. The object in one performer's hand is too small to see clearly, even for those few viewers lucky enough to have front-row seats. The playwright, director, and actors have very few practical options to convey the object's physical properties, much less its narrative significance or its emotional meaning to the character. In contrast, a movie version of the same story can establish the dramatic situation and spatial relationships of its subjects from the same wide-angle viewpoint, then instantaneously jump to a composition isolating the actions of the character holding the object, then **cut** to a **close-up** view revealing the object to be a charm bracelet, move up to feature the character's face as she contemplates the bracelet, then leap thirty years into the past to a depiction of the character as a young girl receiving the jewelry as a gift. Editing's capacity to isolate details and juxtapose images and sounds within and between shots gives movies an expressive agility impossible in any other dramatic art or visual medium.

Ways of Looking at Movies

Every movie is a complex synthesis—a combination of many separate, interrelated elements that form a coherent whole. A quick scan of this book's table of contents will give you an idea of just how many elements get mixed together to make a

[1]

[2]

[3]

[4]

[5]

[6]

The expressive agility of movies Even the best seats in the house offer a viewer of a theatrical production like Stephen Sondheim's *Sweeney Todd: The Demon Barber of Fleet Street* only one unchanging view of the action. The stage provides the audience a single wide-angle view of the scene in which the title character is reintroduced to the set of razors he will use in his bloody quest for revenge [1]. In contrast, cinema's spatial dexterity allows viewers of Tim Burton's 2007 film adaptation to experience the same scene as a sequence of fifty-nine viewpoints, each of which isolate and emphasize distinct meanings and perspectives, including Sweeney Todd's (Johnny Depp's) point of view as he gets his first glimpse of his long-lost tools of the trade [2]; his emotional reaction as he contemplates righteous murder [3]; the razor replacing Mrs. Lovett (Helena Bonham Carter) as the focus of his attention [4]; and a dizzying simulated camera move that starts with the vengeful antihero [5], then pulls back to reveal the morally corrupt city he (and his razors) will soon terrorize [6].

movie. Anyone attempting to comprehend a complex synthesis must rely on analysis—the act of taking something complicated apart to figure out what it is made of and how it all fits together.

A chemist breaks down a compound substance into its constituent parts to learn more than just a list of ingredients. The goal usually extends to determining how the identified individual components work together toward some sort of outcome: What is it about this particular mixture that makes it taste like strawberries, or grow hair, or kill cockroaches? Likewise, film analysis involves more than breaking down a sequence, a scene, or an entire movie to identify the tools and techniques that comprise it; the investigation is also concerned with the function and potential effect of that combination: Why does it make you laugh, or prompt you to tell your friend to see it, or incite you to join the Peace Corps? The search for answers to these sorts of questions boils down to one essential inquiry: What does it mean? For the rest of the chapter, we'll explore film analysis by applying that question to three very different movies: first, and most extensively, the 2007 independent film *Juno*, and then the blockbusters *Harry Potter and the Deathly Hallows,* Parts 1 and 2.

Unfortunately, or perhaps intriguingly, not all movie meaning is easy to see. As we mentioned earlier, movies have a way of hiding their methods and meaning. So before we dive into specific approaches to analysis, let's wade a little deeper into this whole notion of hidden, or "invisible," meaning.

Invisibility and Cinematic Language

The moving aspect of moving pictures is one reason for this invisibility. Movies simply move too fast for even the most diligent viewers to consciously consider everything they've seen. When we read a book, we can pause to ponder the meaning or significance of any word, sentence, or passage. Our eyes often flit back to review something we've already read in order to further comprehend its meaning or to place a new passage in context. Similarly, we can stand and study a painting or sculpture or photograph for as long as we require

in order to absorb whatever meaning we need or want from it. But up until very recently, the moviegoer's relationship with every cinematic composition has been transitory. We experience a movie shot—which is capable of delivering multiple layers of visual and auditory information—for the briefest of moments before it is taken away and replaced with another moving image and another and another. If you're watching a movie the way it's designed to be experienced, there's no time to contemplate any single movie moment's various potential meanings.

Recognizing a spectator's tendency (especially when sitting in a dark theater, staring at a large screen) to identify subconsciously with the camera's viewpoint, early filmmaking pioneers created a film grammar (or cinematic language) that draws upon the way we automatically interpret visual information in our real lives, thus allowing audiences to absorb movie meaning intuitively . . . and instantly.

The **fade-out/fade-in** is one of the most straightforward examples of this phenomenon. When such a transition is meant to convey a passage of time between scenes, the last shot of a scene grows gradually darker ("fades out") until the screen is rendered black for a moment. The first shot of the subsequent scene then "fades in" out of the darkness. The viewer doesn't have to think about what this means; our daily experience of time's passage marked by the setting and rising of the sun lets us understand intuitively that significant story time has elapsed over that very brief moment of screen darkness. A **low-angle shot** communicates in a similarly hidden fashion. When, near the end of *Juno* (Jason Reitman, 2007), we see the title character happily transformed back into a "normal" teenager, our sense of her newfound empowerment is heightened by the low angle from which this (and the next) shot is captured. Viewers' shared experience of literally looking up at powerful figures—people on stages, at podiums, memorialized in statues, or simply bigger than them—sparks an automatic interpretation of movie subjects seen from this angle as, depending on context, either strong, noble, or threatening.

This is all very well; the immediacy of cinematic language is what makes movies one of the most

Cinematic invisibility: low angle When it views a subject from a low camera angle, cinematic language taps our instinctive association of figures who we must literally "look up to" with figurative or literal power. In this case, the penultimate scene in *Juno* emphasizes the newfound freedom and resultant empowerment felt by the title character by presenting her from a low angle for the first time in the film.

pioneering Soviet filmmaker and theorist Sergei Eisenstein believed that every edit, far from being invisible, should be very noticeable—a clash or collision of contiguous shots, rather than a seamless transition from one shot to the next. Filmmakers whose work is labeled "experimental"—inspired by Eisenstein and other predecessors—embrace self-reflexive styles that confront and confound conventional notions of continuity. Even some commercial films use techniques that undermine invisibility: in *The Limey* (1999), for example, Hollywood filmmaker Steven Soderbergh deliberately jumbles spatial and chronological continuity, forcing the spectator to actively scrutinize the

visceral experiences that art has to offer. The problem is that it also makes it all too easy to take movie meaning for granted.

The relatively seamless presentation of visual and narrative information found in most movies can also cloud our search for movie meaning. In order to exploit cinema's capacity for transporting audiences into the world of the story, the commercial filmmaking process stresses a polished continuity of lighting, performance, costume, makeup, and movement to smooth transitions between shots and scenes, thus minimizing any distractions that might remind viewers that they are watching a highly manipulated, and manipulative, artificial reality.

Cutting on action is one of the most common editing techniques designed to hide the instantaneous and potentially jarring shift from one camera viewpoint to another. When connecting one shot to the next, a film editor will often end the first shot in the middle of a continuing action and start the connecting shot at some point in the same action. As a result, the action flows so continuously over the cut between different moving images that most viewers fail to register the switch.

As with all things cinematic, invisibility has its exceptions. From the earliest days of moviemaking, innovative filmmakers have rebelled against the notion of hidden structures and meaning. The

1

2

Invisible editing: cutting on action in *Juno* Juno and Leah's playful wrestling continues over the cut between two shots, smoothing and hiding the instantaneous switch from one camera viewpoint to the next. Overlapping sound and the matching hairstyles, wardrobe, and lighting further obscure the audience's awareness that these two separate shots were filmed minutes or even hours apart from different camera positions.

1

2

3

4

Invisible editing: continuity of screen direction
Juno's opening-credits sequence uses the title character's continuous walking movement to present the twenty-two different shots that comprise the scene as one continuous action. In every shot featuring lateral movement, Juno strolls consistently toward the left side of the screen, adding continuity of screen direction to the seamless presentation of the otherwise stylized animated sequence.

cinematic structures on-screen in order to assemble, and thus comprehend, the story. But most scenes in most films that most of us watch rely heavily on largely invisible techniques that convey meaning intuitively. That's not to say that cinematic language is impossible to spot; you simply have to know what you're looking for. And soon, you will. The rest of this book is dedicated to helping you to identify and appreciate each of the many different secret ingredients that movies blend to convey meaning.

And, luckily for you, motion pictures have been liberated from the imposed impermanence that helped create all this cinematic invisibility in the first place. Thanks to DVDs, Blu-rays, DVRs, and streaming video, you can now watch a movie much

the same way you read a book: pausing to scrutinize, ponder, or review as necessary. This relatively new relationship between movies and viewers will surely spark new approaches to cinematic language and attitudes toward invisibility. That's for future filmmakers, including maybe you, to decide. For now, these viewing technologies allow students of film like yourself to study movies with a lucidity and precision that was impossible for your predecessors.

But not even repeated DVD viewings can reveal those movie messages hidden by our own preconceptions and belief systems. Before we can detect and interpret these meanings, we must first be aware of the ways expectations and cultural traditions obscure what movies have to say.

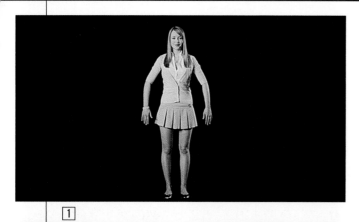

1

2

3

4

Exceptions to invisibility Even *Juno* deviates from conventional invisibility in a stylized sequence illustrating a high-school jock's secret lust for "freaky girls." As Juno's voice-over aside detailing Steve Rendazo's (Daniel Clark) fetish begins, the movie suddenly abandons conventional continuity to launch into a series of abrupt juxtapositions that dress a generic girl posed like a paper doll in a rapid-fire succession of eccentric accessories. The moment Juno's diatribe ends, the film returns to a smooth visual flow of events and images. While this sequence is far from "realistic," its ostentatious style effectively illustrates the trappings of teenage conformity and the ways that young women are objectified.

Cultural Invisibility

The same commercial instinct that inspires film-makers to use seamless continuity also compels them to favor stories and themes that reinforce viewers' shared belief systems. After all, the film industry, for the most part, seeks to entertain, not to provoke, its customers. A key to entertaining one's customers is to "give them what they want"—to tap into and reinforce their most fundamental desires and beliefs. Even movies deemed "controversial" or "provocative" can be popular if they trigger emotional responses from their viewers that reinforce yearnings or beliefs that lie deep within. And because so much of this occurs on an unconscious, emotional level, the casual viewer may be blind to the implied political, cultural, and ideological messages that help make the movie so appealing.

Of course, this cultural invisibility is not always a calculated decision on the part of the filmmakers. Directors, screenwriters, and producers are, after all, products of the same society inhabited by their intended audience. Oftentimes, the people making the movies may be just as oblivious of the cultural attitudes shaping their cinematic stories as the people who watch them.

Juno's filmmakers are certainly aware that their film—which addresses issues of abortion and pregnancy—diverges from the ways that movies traditionally represent family structures and teenage girls. In this sense, the movie might be seen as resisting common cultural values. But what they

Cultural invisibility in *Juno* An unrepentant former stripper (Diablo Cody) writes a script about an unrepentantly pregnant sixteen year old, her blithely accepting parents, and the dysfunctional couple to whom she relinquishes her newborn child. The resulting film goes on to become one of the biggest critical and box-office hits of 2007, attracting viewers from virtually every consumer demographic. How did a movie based on such seemingly provocative subject matter appeal to such a broad audience? One reason is that, beneath its veneer of controversy, *Juno* repeatedly reinforces mainstream, even conservative, societal attitudes toward pregnancy, family, and marriage. Although Juno initially decides to abort the pregnancy, she quickly changes her mind. Her parents may seem relatively complacent when she confesses her condition, but they support, protect, and advise her throughout her pregnancy. When we first meet Mark (Jason Bateman) and Vanessa (Jennifer Garner), the prosperous young couple Juno has chosen to adopt her baby, it is with the youthful Mark [1] that we (and Juno) initially sympathize. He plays guitar and appreciates alternative music and vintage slasher movies. Vanessa, in comparison, comes off as a shallow and judgmental yuppie. But ultimately, both the movie and its protagonist side with the traditional values of motherhood and responsibility embodied by Vanessa [2], and reject Mark's rock-star ambitions as immature and self-centered.

may not be as conscious of is the way their **protagonist** (main character) reinforces our culture's celebration of the individual. Her promiscuous, forceful, and charming persona is familiar because it displays traits we often associate with Hollywood's dominant view of the (usually male) rogue hero. Like Sam Spade, the Ringo Kid, Dirty Harry, and countless other classic American characters, Juno rejects convention yet ultimately upholds the very institutions she seemingly scorns. Yes, she's a smart-ass who cheats on homework, sleeps with her best friend, and pukes in her stepmother's decorative urn, yet in the end she does everything in her power to create the traditional nuclear family she never had. So even as the movie seems to call into question some of contemporary America's attitudes about family, its appeal to an arguably more fundamental American value (namely, robust individualism) explains in part why, despite its controversial subject matter, *Juno* was (and is) so popular with audiences.

Implicit and Explicit Meaning

As we attempt to become more skilled at looking at movies, we should try to be alert to the cultural values, shared ideals, and other ideas that lie just below the surface of the movie we're looking at. Being more alert to these things will make us sensitive to, and appreciative of, the many layers of meaning that any single movie contains. Of course, all this talk of "layers" and the notion that much of a movie's meaning lies below the surface may make the entire process of looking at movies seem unnecessarily complex and intimidating. But you'll find that the process of observing, identifying, and interpreting movie meaning will become considerably less mysterious and complicated once you grow accustomed to actively looking at movies rather than just watching them. It might help to keep in mind that, no matter how many different layers of meaning there may be in a movie, each layer is either implicit or explicit.

An **implicit meaning**, which lies below the surface of a movie's story and presentation, is closest to our everyday sense of the word *meaning*. It is an association, connection, or inference that a viewer makes on the basis of the **explicit meanings** available on the surface of the movie.

To get a sense of the difference between these two levels of meaning, let's look at two statements about *Juno*. First, let's imagine that a friend who hasn't seen the movie asks us what the film is *about*. Our friend doesn't want a detailed plot summary; she simply wants to know what she'll see if she decides to attend the movie. In other words, she is asking us for a statement about *Juno*'s explicit meaning. You might respond to her question by explaining: "The movie's about a rebellious but smart sixteen-year-old girl who gets pregnant and resolves to tackle the problem head on. At first, she decides to get an abortion; but after she backs off that choice, she gets the idea to find a couple to adopt the kid after it's born. She spends the rest of the movie dealing with the implications of that choice." This isn't to say that this is the *only* explicit meaning in the film, but we can see that it is a fairly accurate statement about one meaning that the movie explicitly conveys to us, right there on its surface.

Now what if our friend hears this statement of explicit meaning and asks, "Okay, sure, but what do you think the movie is trying to say? What does it *mean?*" In a case like this, when someone is asking in general about an entire film, he or she is seeking something like an overall message or a "point." In essence, our friend is asking us to *interpret* the movie—to say something arguable about it—not simply to make a statement of obvious surface meaning that everyone can agree on, as we did when we presented its explicit meaning. In other words, she is asking us for our sense of the movie's implicit meaning. One possible response might be: "A teenager faced with a difficult decision makes a bold leap toward adulthood but, in doing so, discovers that the world of adults is no less uncertain or overwhelming than adolescence." At first glance, this statement might seem to have a lot in common with our summary of the movie's explicit meaning, as, of course, it does—after all, even though a meaning is under the surface, it nonetheless has to relate to the surface, and our interpretation needs to be grounded in the explicitly presented details of that surface. But if you compare the two statements more closely, you can see that the second one is more interpretive than the first, more concerned with what the movie "means."

Explicit and implicit meanings need not pertain to the movie as a whole, and not all implicit meaning is tied to broad messages or themes. Movies convey and imply smaller, more specific doses of both kinds of meaning in virtually every scene. Juno's application of lipstick before she visits the adoptive father, Mark, is explicit information. The implications of this action—that her admiration for Mark is beginning to develop into something approaching a crush—are implicit. Later, Mark's announcement that he is leaving his wife and does not want to be a father sends Juno into a panicked retreat. On her drive home, a crying jag forces the disillusioned Juno to pull off the highway. She skids to a stop beside a rotting boat abandoned in the ditch. The discarded boat's decayed condition and the incongruity of a watercraft adrift in an expanse of grass are explicit details that convey implicit meaning about Juno's isolation and alienation.

It's easy to accept that recognizing and interpreting implicit meaning requires some extra effort, but keep in mind that explicit meaning

Explicit detail and implied meaning in *Juno* Vanessa is the earnest yuppie mommy-wannabe to whom Juno has promised her baby. In contrast to the formal business attire she usually sports, Vanessa wears an *Alice in Chains* T-shirt to paint the nursery. This small explicit detail conveys important implicit meaning about her relationship with her husband, Mark, a middle-aged man reluctant to let go of his rock-band youth. The paint-spattered condition of the old shirt implies that she no longer values this symbol of the 1990s grunge-rock scene and, by extension, her past association with it.

cannot be taken for granted simply because it is by definition obvious. Although explicit meaning is on the surface of a film for all to observe, it is unlikely that every viewer or writer will remember and acknowledge every part of that meaning. Because movies are rich in plot detail, a good analysis must begin by taking into account the breadth and diversity of what has been explicitly presented. For example, we cannot fully appreciate the significance of Juno's defiant dumping of a blue slushy into her stepmother's beloved urn unless we have noticed and noted her dishonest denial when accused earlier of vomiting a similar substance into the same precious vessel. Our ability to discern a movie's explicit meanings is directly dependent on our ability to notice such associations and relationships.

Viewer Expectations

The discerning analyst must also be aware of the role expectations play in how movies are made, marketed, and received. Our experience of nearly every movie we see is shaped by what we have been told about that movie beforehand by previews, commercials, reviews, interviews, and word of mouth. After hearing your friends rave endlessly about *Juno*, you may have been underwhelmed by the actual movie. Or you might have been surprised and charmed by a film you entered with low expectations, based on the inevitable backlash that followed the movie's surprise success. Even the most general knowledge affects how we react to any given film. We go to see blockbusters because we crave an elaborate special-effects extravaganza. We can still appreciate a summer movie's relatively simpleminded storytelling, as long as it delivers the promised spectacle. On the other hand, you might revile a high-quality tragedy if you bought your ticket expecting a lighthearted comedy.

Of course, the influence of expectation extends beyond the kind of anticipation generated by a movie's promotion. As we discussed earlier, we all harbor essential expectations concerning a film's form and organization. And most filmmakers give us what we expect: a relatively standardized cinematic language, seamless continuity, and a narrative organized like virtually every other fiction film

we've ever seen. For example, years of watching movies has taught us to expect a clearly motivated protagonist to pursue a goal, confronting obstacles and antagonists along the way toward a clear (and usually satisfying) resolution. Sure enough, that's what we get in most commercial films.

We'll delve more deeply into narrative in the chapters that follow. For now, what's important is that you understand how your experience—and, thus, your interpretation—of any movie is affected by how the particular film manipulates these expected patterns. An analysis might note a film's failure to successfully exploit the standard structures or another movie's masterful subversion of expectations to surprise or mislead its audience. A more experimental approach might deliberately confound our presumption of continuity or narrative. The viewer must be alert to these expected patterns in order to fully appreciate the significance of that deviation.

Expectations specific to a particular performer or filmmaker can also alter the way we perceive a movie. For example, any fan of actor Michael Cera's previous performances as an endearingly awkward adolescent in the film *Superbad* (Greg Mottola, 2007) and television series *Arrested Development* (2003–2006) will watch *Juno* with a built-in affection for Paulie Bleeker, Juno's sort-of boyfriend. This predetermined fondness does more than help us like the movie; it dramatically changes the way we approach a character type (the high-school athlete who impregnates his teenage classmate) that our expectations might otherwise lead us to distrust. Ironically, audience expectations of Cera's sweetness may have contributed to the disappointing box-office performance of *Scott Pilgrim vs. the World* (2010, Edgar Wright). Some critics proposed that viewers were uncomfortable seeing Cera play the somewhat vain and self-centered title character.

Viewers who know director Guillermo del Toro's commercial action/horror movies *Mimic* (1997), *Blade II* (2002), and *Hellboy* (2004) might be surprised by the sophisticated political and philosophical metaphor of *Pan's Labyrinth* (2006) or *The Devil's Backbone* (2001). Yet all five films feature fantastic and macabre creatures as well as social commentary. An active awareness of an audience's various

[1]

[2]

Expectations and character in *Juno* Audience reactions to Michael Cera's characterization of Juno's sort-of boyfriend, Paulie Bleeker, are colored by expectations based on the actor's perpetually embarrassed persona established in previous roles in the television series *Arrested Development* and films like *Superbad* [1]. We don't need the movie to tell us much of anything about Paulie—we form an almost instant affection for the character based on our familiarity with Cera's earlier performances. But while the character Paulie meets our expectations of Michael Cera, he defies our expectations of his character type. Repeated portrayals of high-school jocks as vain bullies, such as Thomas F. Wilson's iconic Biff in Robert Zemeckis's *Back to the Future* (1985) [2] have conditioned viewers to expect such characters to look and behave very differently than Paulie Bleeker.

expectations of del Toro's films would inform an analysis of the elements common to the filmmaker's seemingly schizophrenic body of work. Such an analysis could focus on his visual style in terms of production design, lighting, or special effects, or might instead examine recurring themes such as oppression, childhood trauma, or the role of the outcast.

As you can see, cinematic invisibility is not necessarily an impediment; once you know enough to acknowledge their existence, these potential blind spots also offer opportunities for insight and analysis. There are many ways to look at movies and many possible types of film analysis. We'll spend the rest of this chapter discussing the most common analytical approaches to movies. Since this book considers an understanding of how film grammar conveys meaning, mood, and information as the essential foundation for any further study of cinema, we'll start with **formal analysis**—that analytical approach primarily concerned with film **form**, or the means by which a subject is expressed. Don't worry if you don't fully understand the function of the techniques discussed; that's what the rest of this book is for.

Formal Analysis

Formal analysis dissects the complex synthesis of cinematography, sound, composition, design, movement, performance, and editing orchestrated by creative artists like screenwriters, directors, cinematographers, actors, editors, sound designers, and art directors, as well as the many craftspeople who implement their vision. The movie meaning expressed through form ranges from narrative information as straightforward as where and when a particular scene takes place to more subtle implied meaning, such as mood, tone, significance, or what a character is thinking or feeling.

While it is certainly possible for the overeager analyst to read more meaning into a particular visual or audio component than the filmmaker intended, you should realize that cinematic storytellers exploit every tool at their disposal and that, therefore, every element in every frame is there for a reason. It's up to the analyst to carefully consider the narrative intent of the moment, scene, or sequence before attempting any interpretation of the formal elements used to communicate that intended meaning to the spectator.

For example, the simple awareness that *Juno*'s opening shot [1] is the first image of the movie informs the analyst of the moment's most basic and explicit intent: to convey setting (contemporary

1

2

from a safe distance, as if the inanimate object might attack at any moment, adds to our implicit impression of Juno as alienated or off-balance. Our command of the film's explicit details alerts us to another function of the scene: to introduce the recurring **theme** (or **motif**) of the empty chair that frames—and in some ways defines—the story. In this opening scene, accompanied by Juno's voice-over explanation, "It started with a chair," the empty, displaced object represents Juno's status and emotional state, and foreshadows the unconventional setting for the sexual act that got her into this mess. By the story's conclusion, when Juno announces, "It ended with a chair," the motif—in the form of an adoptive mother's rocking chair—has been transformed, like Juno herself, to embody hope and potential.

All that meaning was packed into two shots spanning about twelve seconds of screen time. Let's see what we can learn from a formal analysis of a more extended sequence from the same film: Juno's visit to the Women Now clinic. To do so, we'll first want to consider what information the filmmaker needs this scene to communicate for viewers to understand and appreciate

middle-class suburbia) and time of day (dawn). But only after we have determined that the story opens with its title character overwhelmed by the prospect of her own teenage pregnancy are we prepared to deduce how this implicit meaning (her state of mind) is conveyed by the composition: Juno is at the far left of the frame and is tiny in relationship to the rest of the wide-angle composition. In fact, we may be well into the four-second shot before we even spot her. Her vulnerability is conveyed by the fact that she is dwarfed by her surroundings. Even when the scene cuts to a closer viewpoint [2], she, as the subject of a movie composition, is much smaller in frame than we are used to seeing, especially in the first shots used to introduce a protagonist. The fact that she is standing in a front yard contemplating an empty stuffed chair

LOOKING AT MOVIES
FILM ANALYSIS

DVD In this tutorial, Dave Monahan analyzes the "waiting room" scene from *Juno* and covers other key concepts of film analysis.

this pivotal piece of the movie's story in relation to the rest of the narrative. As we delve into material that deals with *Juno*'s sensitive subject matter, we must keep in mind that we don't have to agree with the meaning or values projected by the object of our analysis; one is not required to like a movie in order to learn from it. Our own values and beliefs will undoubtedly influence our analysis of any movie. Our personal views provide a legitimate perspective, as long as we recognize and acknowledge how they may color our interpretation.

Throughout *Juno*'s previous eighteen minutes, all information concerning its protagonist's attitude toward her condition has explicitly enforced our expectation that she will end her unplanned pregnancy with an abortion. She pantomimes suicide once she's forced to admit her condition; she calmly discusses abortion facilities with her friend Leah; she displays no ambivalence when scheduling the procedure. Approaching the clinic, Juno's nonchalant reaction to the comically morose pro-life demonstrator Su-Chin reinforces our aforementioned expectations. Juno treats Su-Chin's assertion that the fetus has fingernails as more of an interesting bit of trivia than a concept worthy of serious consideration.

The subsequent waiting-room sequence is about Juno making an unexpected decision that propels the story in an entirely new direction. A formal analysis will tell us how the filmmakers orchestrated multiple formal elements, including sound, composition, moving camera, and editing, to convey in thirteen shots and thirty seconds of screen time how the seemingly insignificant fingernail fac-

toid infiltrates Juno's thoughts and ultimately drives her from the clinic. By the time you have completed your course (and have read the book), you should be prepared to apply this same sort of formal analysis to any scene you choose.

The waiting-room sequence's opening shot [1] **dollies in** (the camera moves slowly toward the subject), which gradually enlarges Juno in frame, increasing her visual significance as she fills out the clinic admittance form on the clipboard in her hand [2]. The shot reestablishes her casual acceptance of the impending procedure, providing context for the events to come. Its relatively long ten-second **duration** sets up a relaxed rhythm that will shift later along with her state of mind. As the camera reaches its closest point, a loud sound invades the low hum of the previously hushed waiting room.

This obtrusive drumming sound motivates a somewhat startling cut to a new shot that plunges our viewpoint right up into Juno's face [3]. The sudden spatial shift gives the moment resonance and conveys Juno's thought process as she instantly shifts her concentration from the admittance form to this strange new sound. She turns her head in search of the sound's source, and the camera adjusts to adopt her **point of view** of a mother and daughter sitting beside her [4]. The mother's fingernails drumming on her own clipboard is revealed as the source of the tapping sound. The sound's abnormally loud level signals that we're not hearing at a natural volume level—we've begun to experience Juno's psychological perceptions. The little girl's stare into Juno's (and our) eyes helps to

1

2

[3]

[4]

[5]

establish the association between the fingernail sound and Juno's latent guilt.

The sequence cuts back to the already troubled-looking Juno [5]. The juxtaposition connects her anxious expression to both the drumming mother and the little girl's gaze. The camera creeps in on her again. This time, the resulting enlargement keys in our intuitive association of this gradual intensification with a character's moment of realization.

Within half a second, another noise joins the mix, and Juno's head turns in response [6].

The juxtaposition marks the next shot as Juno's point of view, but it is much too close to be her literal point of view. Like the unusually loud sound, the unrealistically close viewpoint of a woman picking her thumbnail reflects not an actual spatial relationship but the sight's significance to Juno [7]. When we cut back to Juno about a second later, the camera continues to close in on her, and her gaze shifts again to follow yet another sound as it joins the rising clamor [8].

A new shot of another set of hands, again from a close-up, psychological point of view, shows a woman applying fingernail polish [9]. What would normally be a silent action emits a distinct, abrasive sound.

When we cut back to Juno half a second later, she is much larger in the frame than the last few times we saw her [10]. This break in pattern conveys a sudden intensification; this is really starting to get to her. Editing often establishes patterns and rhythms, only to break them for dramatic impact.

[6]

[7]

8

9

10

Our appreciation of Juno's situation is enhanced by the way editing connects her reactions to the altered sights and sounds around her, as well as by her implied isolation—she appears to be the only one who notices the increasingly boisterous symphony of fingernails. Of course, Juno's not entirely alone—the audience is with her. At this point in the sequence, the audience has begun to associate the waiting-room fingernails with Su-Chin's attempt to humanize Juno's condition.

Juno's head jerks as yet another, even more invasive sound enters the fray [11]. We cut to another close-up point-of-view shot, this time of a young man scratching his arm [12]. At this point, another pattern is broken, initiating the scene's formal and dramatic climax. Up until now, the sequence alternated between shots of Juno and shots of the fingernails as they caught her attention. Each juxtaposition caused us to identify with both Juno's reaction and her point of view. But now, the sequence shifts gears; instead of the expected switch back to Juno, we are subjected to an accelerating succession of fingernail shots, each one shorter and louder than the last. A woman bites her fingernails [13]; another files her nails [14]; a woman's hand drums her fingernails nervously [15]; a man scratches his neck [16]. With every new shot, another noise is added to the sound mix.

This pattern is itself broken in several ways by the scene's final shot. We've grown accustomed to seeing Juno look around every time we see her, but this time, she stares blankly ahead, immersed in thought [17]. A cacophony of fingernail sounds rings in her

11

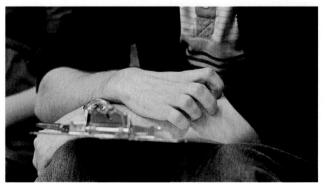

12

13

14

15

16

(and our) ears as the camera glides toward her for three and a half very long seconds—a duration six times longer than any of the previous nine shots. These pattern shifts signal the scene's climax, which is further emphasized by the moving camera's enlargement of Juno's figure [18], a visual action that cinematic language has trained viewers to associate with a subject's moment of realization or decision.

But the shot doesn't show us Juno acting on that decision. We don't see her cover her ears, throw down her clipboard, or jump up from the waiting-room banquette. Instead, we are ripped prematurely from this final waiting-room image and are plunged into a shot that drops us into a different space and at least several moments ahead in time—back to Su-Chin chanting in the parking lot [19]. This jarring spatial, temporal, and visual shift helps us feel Juno's own instability at this crucial narrative moment. Before we can get our bearings, the camera has pivoted right to reveal Juno bursting out of the clinic door in the

17

18

[19]

[20]

background [20]. She races past Su-Chin without a word. She does not have to say anything. Cinematic language—film form—has already told us what she decided and why.

Anyone watching this scene would sense the narrative and emotional meaning revealed by this analysis, but only a viewer actively analyzing the film form used to construct it can fully comprehend how the sophisticated machinery of cinematic language shapes and conveys that meaning. Formal analysis is fundamental to all approaches to understanding and engaging cinema—whether you're making, studying, or simply appreciating movies—which is why the elements and grammar of film form are the primary focus of *Looking at Movies*.

Alternative Approaches to Analysis

Although we'll be looking at movies primarily in terms of the forms they take and the nuts and bolts from which they are constructed, any serious student of film should be aware that there are many other legitimate frameworks for analysis. These alternative approaches analyze movies more as cultural artifacts than as traditional works of art. They search beneath a movie's form and content to expose implicit and hidden meanings that inform our understanding of cinema's function within popular culture as well as the influence of popular culture on the movies.

The preceding formal analysis demonstrated how *Juno* used cinematic language to convey meaning and tell a story. Given the right interpretive scrutiny, our case study film may also speak eloquently about social conditions and attitudes. For example, considering that the protagonist is the daughter of an air-conditioner repairman and a manicurist, and that the couple she selects to adopt her baby are white-collar professionals living in an oversized McMansion, a cultural analysis of *Juno* could explore the movie's treatment of class. An analysis from a feminist perspective could concentrate on, among other elements, the movie's depiction of women and childbirth, not to mention Juno's father, the father of her baby, and the prospective adoptive father. Such an analysis might also consider the creative and ideological contributions of the movie's female screenwriter, Diablo Cody, an outspoken former stripper and sex blogger. A linguistic analysis might explore the historical, cultural, or imaginary origins of the highly stylized slang spouted by Juno, her friends, even the mini-mart clerk who sells her a pregnancy test. A thesis could be (and probably has been) written about the implications of the T-shirt messages displayed by the film's characters or the implicit meaning of the movie's running-track-team motif. Some analyses place movies within the stylistic or political context of a director's career. *Juno*'s young director, Jason Reitman, has made only three other feature films. But even that relatively short filmography provides opportunity for comparative analysis: all of Reitman's movies take provocative political stances, gradually generate empathy for initially unsympathetic characters, and favor fast-paced expositional montages featuring expressive juxtapositions, graphic compositions, and first-person voice-over narration.

Another comparative analysis could investigate society's evolving (or perhaps fixed) attitudes toward "illegitimate" pregnancy by placing *Juno* in context with the long history of films about the subject, from D. W. Griffith's 1920 silent drama *Way*

[1]

[2]

[3]

[4]

[5]

[6]

Comparative cultural analysis A comparison of *Juno*'s treatment of unwanted pregnancy with other films featuring the same subject matter is but one of the many analytical approaches that could be used to explore cinema's function within culture, as well as the influence of culture on the movies. Such an analysis could compare *Juno* with American films produced in earlier eras, from [1] D. W. Griffith's dramatic *Way Down East* (1920), to [2] Preston Sturges's 1944 screwball comedy *The Miracle of Morgan's Creek*, to [3]

Roman Polanski's paranoid horror film *Rosemary's Baby* (1968). An alternate analysis might compare *Juno* with the other American films released in 2007 that approached the subject with a similar blend of comedy and drama: [4] Judd Apatow's *Knocked Up* and [5] Adrienne Shelly's *Waitress*. A comparative analysis of these movies' international contemporaries, such as [6] Cristian Mungiu's stark *4 Months, 3 Weeks and 2 Days* (2007), might reveal differences between American and European sensibilities.

Down East, which banished its unwed mother and drove her to attempted suicide, to Preston Sturges's irreverent 1944 comedy *The Miracle of Morgan's Creek* and its mysteriously pregnant protagonist, Trudy Kockenlocker (whose character name alone says a great deal about its era's attitudes toward women), to another mysterious, but ultimately far more terrifying, pregnancy in Roman Polanski's 1968 horror masterpiece *Rosemary's Baby*.

Juno is only one of a small stampede of recent popular films dealing with this seemingly ever-timely issue. A cultural analysis might compare and contrast *Juno* with its American contemporaries *Knocked Up* (Judd Apatow, 2007) and *Waitress* (Adrienne Shelly, 2007), both of which share *Juno*'s blend of comedy and drama, as well as a pronounced ambivalence concerning abortion, but depict decidedly different characters, settings, and stories. What might such an analysis of these movies (and their critical and popular success) tell us about our own particular era's attitudes toward women, pregnancy, and motherhood? *Knocked Up* is written and directed by a man, *Juno* is written by a woman and directed by a man, *Waitress* is written and directed by a woman. Does the relative gender of each film's creator affect those attitudes? If this comparative analysis incorporated Romanian filmmaker Cristian Mungiu's stark abortion drama *4 Months, 3 Weeks and 2 Days* (2007) or Mike Leigh's nuanced portrayal of the abortionist *Vera Drake* (2004), the result might inform a deeper understanding of the differences between European and American sensibilities.

An unwanted pregnancy is a potentially controversial subject for any film, especially when the central character is a teenager. Any extensive analysis focused on *Juno*'s cultural meaning would have to address what this particular film's content implies about the hot-button issue of abortion. By way of illustration, let's return to the clinic waiting room. An analysis that asserts *Juno* espouses a "pro-life" (i.e., anti-abortion) message could point to several explicit details in this sequence and to those preceding and following it. In contrast to the relatively welcoming suburban settings that dominate the rest of the story, the ironically named Women Now abortion clinic is an unattractive stone structure squatting at one end of an urban asphalt parking lot. Juno is confronted by clearly stated and compelling arguments against abortion via Su-Chin's dialogue: the "baby" has a beating heart, can feel pain, . . . and has fingernails. The clinic receptionist, the sole on-screen representative of the pro-choice alternative, is a sneering cynic with multiple piercings and a declared taste for fruit-flavored condoms. The idea of the fetus as a human being, stressed by Su-Chin's earnest admonishments, is driven home by the scene's formal presentation analyzed earlier.

On the other hand, a counterargument maintaining that Juno implies a pro-choice stance could state that the lone on-screen representation of the pro-life position is portrayed just as negatively (and extremely) as the clinic receptionist. Su-Chin is presented as an infantile simpleton who wields a homemade sign stating, rather clumsily, "No Babies Like Murdering," shouts "All babies want to get borned!" and is bundled in an oversized stocking cap and pink quilted coat as if dressed by an overprotective mother. Juno's choice can hardly be labeled a righteous conversion. Even after fleeing the clinic, the clearly ambivalent mother-to-be struggles to rationalize her decision, which she announces not as "I'm having this baby" but as "I'm staying pregnant." Some analysts may conclude that the filmmakers, mindful of audience demographics, were trying to have it both ways. Others could argue that the movie is understandably more concerned with narrative considerations than a precise political stance. The negative aspects of every alternative are consistent with a story world that offers its young protagonist little comfort and no easy choices.

Cultural and Formal Analysis in *Harry Potter*

The preceding discussion demonstrates that a popular mainstream entertainment like *Juno* offers ample material for analysis. But are popular movies worthy of this sort of scholarly attention? After all, isn't serious intellectual inquiry supposed to be reserved for art films—the more difficult and obscure, the better?

Although film scholars often do study unconventional movies that most people have never heard of, many of these same scholars pay special attention to blockbusters and other popular entertainments. Why do they do this? To begin with, they may seek the answer to an obvious question: why do audiences like this movie? Or, to take it a step further, they may try to analyze the movie's form, themes, and messages to better understand how those elements might explain the movie's popularity with contemporary audiences. But why is this sort of analysis important? Stated plainly: because movies are influential. The more consumers see a movie—or even just see the advertising and witness public reaction to its success—the more likely it is that that movie will exert some kind of effect on those consumers' culture. Any movie capable of influencing society is surely worth a closer look.

For example: few cinematic figures have been so ubiquitous for so long as Harry Potter. Since 2001, the *Harry Potter* franchise has produced eight hit films that together earned over $7 billion worth of worldwide ticket sales,[1] a staggering figure that doesn't even include the additional exposure and revenue generated by DVD, pay-per-view, streaming video, and other sales of the movies. Clearly, the *Harry Potter* series is an influential and important cultural phenomenon. But how can we even begin to explain its popularity?

To start with, the sheer scope of the series provides viewers a particular brand of narrative development unavailable in most movies or film series. If we stop to consider other well-known film series, few if any of them feature any significant figurative or literal character growth. Consider Frodo Baggins in *The Lord of the Rings* or Captain Jack Sparrow in *Pirates of the Caribbean* or even Luke Skywalker in the original *Star Wars* trilogy. Although they accomplish extraordinary feats in spectacular adventures, all of these leading characters act and look much the same from the first movie to the final installment. In contrast, Harry Potter and his classmates literally grow up on-screen. Watching (and anticipating)

LOOKING AT MOVIES
FILM ANALYSIS PART II: *HARRY POTTER*

DVD In this tutorial, Dave Monahan discusses cultural analysis and looks closely at the *Harry Potter* series.

Harry (Daniel Radcliffe), Hermione (Emma Watson), and Ron (Rupert Grint) develop from innocent children to moody adolescents to world-weary but resolute young adults provides viewers a participatory pleasure that compels them to see the next movie, as well as rewatch and compare earlier installments.

An analyst studying the appeal of the *Harry Potter* movies would likely examine the role nostalgia plays in the story and its visual presentation. Instead of computers, smart phones, or video games, the wizarding world of Harry Potter features puzzles, riddles, and Quidditch. Although the story is set in the 1990s, the movies' design schemes are a pastiche of more distant and romanticized pasts. The look of the Hogwarts boarding school and much of its eccentric faculty suggests the Middle Ages; many character costumes, including the Hogwarts school uniforms and the office attire favored by the Ministry of Magic, evoke fashions from the 1940s.

The visual associations with the World War II era are one piece of evidence that the series connects with audiences by tapping into a shared cultural and political experience. Lord Voldemort may not look like Adolf Hitler, but he does rule by fear, is bent on world domination, and exploits a racist ideal of "pure blood" to intimidate and

[1]*Source:* boxofficemojo.com

1

2

3

4

5

6

7

8

[1]

[2]

[3]

Harry Potter and World War II One reason that audiences were drawn to the *Harry Potter* films may be the movies' narrative, thematic, and visual references to World War II. Although most viewers were born long after Adolf Hitler was vanquished, the threat he posed to civilization had such a profound effect on our culture that Harry's struggle to stop a seemingly unstoppable tyrant bent on world domination still resonates with contemporary audiences. *Harry Potter and the Deathly Hallows: Part 1* (2010, David Yates) opens with the Minister of Magic, Rufus Scrimgeour (Bill Nighy), delivering a stirring public pledge "to continue to defend your liberty and repel the forces that seek to take it from you" that evokes the famous wartime speeches of British Prime Minister Winston Churchill [1]. Later in the same film, Harry discovers Voldemort's followers publishing "pure-blood" pamphlets that bear a chilling similarity to anti-Semitic Nazi propaganda [2]. The sets depicting Hogwarts in the aftermath of the battle scene in *Harry Potter and the Deathly Hallows: Part 2* (2011, David Yates) echo indelible war-era images of devastated European cities [3].

inspire his growing legions of followers. The fictional struggle against Voldemort has a trajectory similar to the historic struggle against Hitler: Complacency delays resistance until almost too late, but the forces of reason finally unite to stand up to the evil megalomaniac, who is ultimately undone by his own hubris.

Voldemort exploits the weaker characters' need to belong to the winning team; the character of Harry Potter appeals to an essential human longing to be special. A narrative analysis of the *Potter* films might explore Harry's place in a classical storytelling tradition. He is an ordinary boy suddenly revealed as a chosen one with extraordinary hidden talents and a special destiny. This secret savior is plucked from obscurity, undergoes training, and is tested by a series of increasingly dangerous challenges. In the end, our unlikely

hero defeats a seemingly invincible evil. This same description could be applied to characters at the heart of other recent popular serial adventures, including Neo in the *Matrix* movies and Luke Skywalker in the original *Star Wars* trilogy. Some scholars maintain that Jesus Christ belongs to the same narrative tradition; others may argue that the character type is in fact inspired by Christ's actual experience. Regardless of one's own religious beliefs, it's hard to deny that Harry

Familiarity and progression The eight *Harry Potter* films offer the rare opportunity to experience familiar characters' physical and emotional development over an extended period of time. For many viewers, especially those who grew up during the decade it took to produce every installment, watching (and rewatching) Harry, Ron, and Hermione's serialized adolescence can feel like paging through a family photo album. [1] *Harry Potter and the Sorcerer's Stone** (2001, Chris Columbus) (UK title: *Harry Potter and the*

Philosopher's Stone); [2] *Harry Potter and the Chamber of Secrets* (2002, Chris Columbus); [3] *Harry Potter and the Prisoner of Azkaban* (2004, Alfonso Cuarón); [4] *Harry Potter and the Goblet of Fire* (2005, Mike Newell); [5] *Harry Potter and the Order of the Phoenix* (2007, David Yates); [6] *Harry Potter and the Half-Blood Prince* (2009, David Yates); [7] *Harry Potter and the Deathly Hallows: Part 1* (2010, David Yates); [8] *Harry Potter and the Deathly Hallows: Part 2* (2011, David Yates).

Harry Potter as Christ figure Key narrative elements in the *Harry Potter* films may resonate with viewers familiar with Christian scripture. A ruthless despot attempts to destroy an innocent infant. Years later, the seemingly ordinary boy is revealed as a chosen one with a special destiny. He endures self-doubt and temptation; ultimately he must sacrifice himself and rise from the dead to save the world from evil. In *Harry Potter and the Deathly Hallows: Part 2*, the filmmakers visualize the allegory by flooding the scene following Harry's temporary death with white light. The look of the heavenly "King's Cross" station suggests a certain divine transcendence and differentiates the events portrayed there from the rest of the movie, which is literally and figuratively quite dark.

is a Christ figure of sorts. Perhaps this resemblance accounts for at least some of Harry's resonance with audiences. After all, he's not just anointed, questioned, betrayed, and redeemed. He also sacrifices himself, dies, and is resurrected. In the final film, Harry and Dumbledore's radiant reunion on a luminous train platform visually reinforces the comparison.

A cultural analysis of the Potter phenomenon might investigate if (and if so, how) these religious allusions influence the millions of viewers who have experienced the movies. Do audiences identify with Christian themes, or is the power of Potter purely narrative and cinematic? Many religiously-conservative critics of the series contend that the relationship between Harry Potter and Christianity is adversarial, not associative. They argue that the movies glamorize the occult and thus lure young people away from traditional religious values. Other observers argue that the fictional witchcraft of the *Potter* films is nothing more than an endorsement of imagination and individuality.

We go to the movies for many reasons: to immerse ourselves in stories; to identify with interesting characters; to be enlightened or moved or

simply distracted. But sometimes we also crave the kind of lavish visual extravaganza known as spectacle. Cinema's unique capacity for conjuring fantastic images and action has enticed audiences since the silent film era. The abundance of on-screen magic that the *Harry Potter* movies provide has almost certainly contributed to the series' commercial success. And that success was aided by fortuitous timing. The movie adaptations began at a time when the film industry was entering a digital revolution. As the story and characters grew increasingly sophisticated, so did special effects. Technology advanced to meet each new installment's demands for greater cinematic wizardry. The visual extravaganza culminates in *Harry Potter and The Deathly Hallows: Part 2*. The final episode delivers a roller-coaster chase sequence atop a runaway dragon, an epic battle sequence, a race to escape an animate (and animated) firestorm, and a wand duel to the death, all in 3-D.

Of course, it takes more than spectacle to satisfy millions of viewers—especially for eight consecutive movies. Some of the series' most engaging scenes employ a far more subtle approach to cinematic storytelling. Let's close this introduction with a formal analysis of an unassuming but effective scene created specifically for the film *Harry Potter and The Deathly Hallows: Part 1*.

Frustrated and exhausted by worry and jealousy, Ron has walked out—leaving Harry and Hermione to carry on without him. They're on the run, and their quest to find and destroy a series of enchanted objects (aka *horcruxes*) that safeguard the evil lord's soul is going nowhere. In this scene, an impromptu dance momentarily breaks the oppressive tension and reaffirms and defines Harry and Hermione's friendship.

The opening shot [1] is the widest—in other words, it shows us the most space. We see the interior of Harry and Hermione's dreary tent, as well as the literal (and figurative) distance between the troubled friends. The figures' relative small size in relation to the space between and around them helps convey a sense of vulnerability. Harry trudges to his chair and sits to face Hermione, who does not return his gaze. Instead, she stares at Ron's abandoned radio. Other than muffled wind and

[1]

[2]

[3]

[4]

creaking floorboards, the radio is all we hear. The reception is spotty and the speaker is tinny, but we can just make out the song "O Children" (by Nick Cave and The Bad Seeds).

Now that the mood and the state of the relationship have been established, the next shot [2] concentrates on Harry. He is large enough in the frame to allow us to easily read his defeated expression, and to register his stare at the offscreen Hermione. The camera creeps in on him, gradually increasing his size in the frame and thus lending significance to his expression. Something is on Harry's mind.

The next shot [3] confirms it. The scene shows us what Harry is thinking about, and looking at: Hermione, bigger in the frame and still hunched over Ron's radio, which is still playing "O Children."

The song's melancholy tone reinforces our characters' mood; the radio's thin sound and bad reception convey their isolation.

When we cut back to Harry [4], he reacts to what he (and we) just saw in the previous point-of-view shot. It's difficult to know exactly what he's feeling, but he seems agitated—a feeling reinforced by the intensifying effects of the creeping camera, the back-and-forth cutting, the progressively tighter framing, and the crackling radio.

The pattern continues as he stirs and the scene cuts back to a tightly framed, high-angle shot of Hermione. A moment after the shot begins, Harry steps into the foreground, momentarily obscuring Hermione [5a] before she reemerges and looks up to meet his implied gaze [5b]. Harry's sudden

5a

5b

[6a]

[6b]

[7a]

[7b]

[8]

looming appearance feels almost aggressive; the filmmakers are building tension and tickling our expectations. After all, we're watching two anxious teenagers alone in an isolated tent; maybe Ron's jealousy was justified after all.

Harry looks down at the offscreen Hermione at the beginning of the next shot [6a]. The camera starts on his face, then drifts down to his outstretched hand [6b]. We cut back to Hermione [7a], who considers the offer. This moment brings the scene to a turning point that is both tantalizing and disturbing. Several things happen at once to provoke our expectations: Hermione takes Harry's hand. As she stands, the camera follows her into a cozy composition in which the young witch and wizard stand face to face to share the frame for the first time since the scene's first shot [7b]. Where that opening image implied distance, this shot emphasizes intimacy. Harry removes Hermione's horcrux necklace (a gesture that propels us into the next equally intimate shot [8]). All of a sudden, Harry and Hermione are holding hands, staring into each others' eyes, and taking off each others' enchanted jewelry. This turn of events takes even those viewers who have read the books by surprise. This scene does not occur in the original novel. Could it be that Harry and Hermione are about to hook up?

And something is happening with the scene's sound to further stimulate this expectation. The wind and floorboard sounds disappear. What was once faint music drifting from a portable radio rises in volume and clarity until it dominates the sound track. "O Children" is no longer playing on the radio; it's emanating from the movie itself. The swelling music seems to embody the characters' escalating emotions.

The potential sexual intensity persists in the next shot as Harry tosses the horcrux on Hermione's bed and leads her, hand in hand into the foreground [9]. The cut to the next shot [10] provides a new angle on the couple as Harry coaxes Hermione to sway along to the still-swelling music. The pace of the sequence picks up as they begin to dance over the next four short shots: [11], [12], [13], and [14a].

Up until this point, the scene has maintained conventional continuity editing. Eye-line match cuts

9

10

11

12

13

14a

(when the direction a character looks corresponds with the angle of a point-of-view shot or another character's responding look) or cutting on action smoothes each transition from one shot to the next. Each shift to a new perspective has been orchestrated to keep the viewer neatly oriented in space and time.

Now the scene is about to shift gears, and the filmmakers use a shift in style to let us know it. The cut between shots 14b and 15 is a **jump cut**: a sudden "jump forward" in the action that intentionally defies our expectations of continuity. One moment, Harry is on the left side of the screen looking to the right toward Hermione [14b], but the cut pops him instantaneously into the middle of a twirl [15]. The next cut jumps forward again: suddenly it's

Hermione who's twirling [16]. It's as if the editor took a shot of the dance, snipped out a couple of pieces of the action, then stuck the remaining pieces back together again—which is essentially how most jump cuts are achieved. Defying the rules of continuity disorients the viewer, which is why this technique is often employed to convey chaos or confusion. But in this case, the technique defuses the tension and triggers a sort of giddy catharsis. With the aid of the music, the actors' playful performances, and the rapid pace of the action and cutting, the discontinuity transforms what appeared to be a somber seduction into a good-natured game. The lighthearted mood continues through the next eight cuts, five of which are jump cuts. Harry and Hermione's friendship has

[24]

[25a]

[25b]

[26]

[27]

been threatened, confirmed, and celebrated over the course of twenty-three shots, ending with shots [17–23].

When continuity returns, so does grim reality. Shot 24 flows into shot 25 with a match on action—that is, a transition that moves seamlessly from the action in one shot to a continuation of that action in the next shot. The shots show Harry and Hermione's whirling dance collapse into an affectionate, but strictly fraternal, hug in shots [24] and [25a]. These close-up shots let us see the characters' faces as they slow to a stop. The music fades along with their smiles as the gravity of their situation reasserts itself [25b]. Hermione walks out of shot 26, and the final image [27] is then a lingering close-up of Harry watching her go. The scene ends as it began: with our characters alone, outnumbered, and seemingly out of options.

Speaking of options, the previous examples illustrate only a few of the virtually limitless approaches available to advanced students and scholars interested in interpreting the relationship between culture and cinema. But before we can effectively interpret a movie as a cultural artifact, we must first understand how that artifact functions. To begin that process, we must return our focus to the building blocks of cinematic language, starting with the principles of film form, the subject of our next chapter.

Analyzing Movies

As we said at the beginning of the chapter, the primary goal of *Looking at Movies* is to help you graduate from being a spectator of movies—from merely *watching* them—to actively and analytically *looking at* them. The chapters that follow provide very specific information about each of the major formal components of film, information that you can use to write and talk intelligently about the films you view in class and elsewhere. Once you've read the chapter on cinematography, for example, you will have at hand the basic vocabulary to describe accurately the lighting and camera work you see on-screen.

As you read the subsequent chapters of this book, you will acquire a specialized vocabulary for describing, analyzing, discussing, and writing about the movies you see. But now, as a beginning student of film and armed only with the general knowledge that you've acquired in this first chapter, you can begin looking at movies more analytically and perceptively. You can easily say more than "I liked" or "I didn't like" the movie, because you can enumerate and understand the cinematic techniques and concepts the filmmakers employed to convey story, character state of mind, and other meanings. What's more, by cultivating an active awareness of the meanings and structures hidden under every movie's surface, you will become increasingly capable of recognizing the film's implicit meanings and interpreting what they reveal about the culture that produced and consumed it.

The following checklist provides a few ideas about how to start.

Screening Checklist: Looking at Movies

✔ Be aware that there are many ways to look at movies. Are you primarily interested in interpreting the ways in which the movie manipulates formal elements such as composition, editing, and sound to tell its story moment to moment, or are you concerned with what the movie has to say in broader cultural terms, such as a political message?

✔ Whenever you prepare a formal analysis of a scene's use of film grammar, start by considering the filmmakers' intent. Remember that filmmakers use every cinematic tool at their disposal; very little in any movie moment is left to chance. So before analyzing any scene, first ask yourself some basic questions. What is this scene about? After watching this scene, what do I understand about the character's thoughts and emotions? How did the scene make me feel? Once you determine what information and mood the scene conveyed, you'll be better prepared to figure out how cinematic tools and techniques were utilized to communicate the scene's intended meaning.

✔ Do your best to see beyond cinematic invisibility. Remember that a great deal of a movie's machinery is designed to make you forget you are experiencing a highly manipulated, and manipulative, artificial reality. One of the best ways to combat cinema's seamless presentation is to watch a movie more than once. You may allow yourself to be transported into the world of the story on your first viewing. Repeated viewings will give you the distance required for critical observation.

✔ On a related note, be conscious of the fact that you may be initially blind to a movie's political, cultural, and ideological meaning, especially if that meaning reinforces ideas and values you already hold. The greater your awareness of your own belief systems (and those you share with your culture in general), the easier it will be to recognize and interpret a movie's implicit meaning.

✔ Ask yourself how expectations shaped your reaction to this movie. Does it conform to the ways you've come to expect a movie to function? How did what you'd heard about this movie beforehand—through the media, your friends, or your professor—affect your attitude toward the film? Did your previous experience of the director or star inform your prior understanding of what to expect from this particular film? In each case, did the movie fulfill, disappoint, or confound your expectations?

✔ Before and after you see a movie, think about the direct meanings, as well as the implications, of its *title*. The title of Roman Polanski's *Chinatown* (1974) is a specific geographic reference, but once you've seen the movie, you'll understand that it functions as a metaphor for a larger body of meaning. Richard Kelly's *Donnie Darko* (2001) makes us wonder if Darko is a real name (it is) or if it is a not-so-subtle clue that Donnie has a dark side (he does). Try to explain the title's meaning, if it isn't self-evident.

Questions for Review

1. What do you think of when you hear the word *movie*? Has your perception changed since reading this chapter? In what ways?
2. How is the experience of seeing a movie different from watching a play? Reading a book? Viewing a painting or photograph?
3. Why has the grammar of film evolved to allow audiences to absorb movie meaning intuitively?
4. In what ways do movies minimize viewers' awareness that they are experiencing a highly manipulated, artificial reality?
5. What do we mean by *cultural invisibility*? How is this different from *cinematic invisibility*?
6. What is the difference between *implicit* and *explicit* meaning?
7. How might your previous experiences of a particular actor influence your reaction to a new movie featuring the same performer?
8. What are some of the other expectations that can affect the way viewers react to a movie?
9. What are you looking for when you do a formal analysis of a movie scene? What are some other alternative approaches to analysis, and what sorts of meaning might they uncover?

10. At this point, would you say that learning what a movie is all about is more challenging than you first thought? If so, why?

Movies Described or Illustrated in This Chapter

Back to the Future (1985). Robert Zemeckis, director.

Brokeback Mountain (2005). Ang Lee, director.

Edward Scissorhands (1990). Tim Burton, director.

4 Months, 3 Weeks and 2 Days (2007). Cristian Mungiu, director.

Harry Potter and the Chamber of Secrets (2002). Chris Columbus, director.

Harry Potter and the Deathly Hallows: Part 1 (2010). David Yates, director.

Harry Potter and the Deathly Hallows: Part 2 (2011). David Yates, director.

Harry Potter and the Goblet of Fire (2005). Mike Newell, director.

Harry Potter and the Half-Blood Prince (2009). David Yates, director.

Harry Potter and the Order of the Phoenix (2007). David Yates, director.

Harry Potter and the Prisoner of Azkaban (2004). Alfonso Cuarón, director.

Harry Potter and the Sorcerer's Stone (2001). Chris Columbus, director. (UK title: *Harry Potter and the Philosopher's Stone*.)

Juno (2007). Jason Reitman, director.

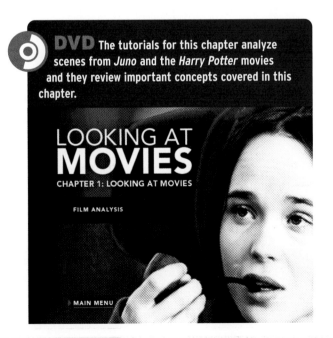

DVD The tutorials for this chapter analyze scenes from *Juno* and the *Harry Potter* movies and they review important concepts covered in this chapter.

Knocked Up (2007). Judd Apatow, director.

Krrish (2006). Rakesh Roshan, director.

Land in Anguish (1967). Glauber Rocha, director.

The Limey (1999). Steven Soderbergh, director.

March of the Penguins (2005). Luc Jacquet, director.

Memories of Underdevelopment (1968). Tomás Gutiérrez Alea, director.

The Miracle of Morgan's Creek (1944). Preston Sturges, director.

Once (2006). John Carney, director.

Paranormal Activity (2007). Oren Peli, director.

Rosemary's Baby (1968). Roman Polanski, director.

Scott Pilgrim vs. The World (2010). Edgar Wright, director.

Superbad (2007). Greg Mottola, director.

Sweeney Todd: The Demon Barber of Fleet Street (2007). Tim Burton, director.

Vera Drake (2004). Mike Leigh, director.

Waitress (2007). Adrienne Shelly, director.

Way Down East (1920). D. W. Griffith, director.

CHAPTER TWO

Principles of Film Form

Film Form

Chapter 1's analyses of scenes from *Juno* and the *Harry Potter* movies provided us with a small taste of how the various elements of movies work. We saw how the filmmakers coordinated performance, composition, sound, and editing to create meaning and tell a story. All of these elements were carefully chosen and controlled by the filmmakers to produce each movie's form.

If we've learned nothing else so far, we can at least now say with confidence that very little in any movie is left to chance. Each of the multiple systems that together become the "complex synthesis" that we know as a movie is highly organized and deliberately assembled and sculpted by filmmakers. For example, **mise-en-scène**, one elemental system of film, composes design elements such as lighting, setting, props, costumes, and makeup within individual shots. **Sound**, another elemental system, is organized into a series of dialogue, music, ambience, and effects tracks. **Narrative** is structured into acts that establish, develop, and resolve character conflict. **Editing** juxtaposes individual **shots** (the product of one uninterrupted run of the camera) to create **sequences** (a series of shots unified by theme or purpose), arranges these sequences into **scenes** (complete units of plot action), and from these scenes builds a movie. The synthesis of all of these elemental systems (and others not mentioned above) constitutes the overall form that the movie takes. We'll spend some time with each of these elemental formal systems in later chapters, but first let's take a closer look at the concept of form itself, beginning with the correlation between form and the content it shapes and communicates.

Form and Content

The terms *form* and *content* crop up in almost any scholarly discussion of the arts, but what do they mean, and why are they so often paired? To start with, we can define **content** as the subject of an artwork (what the work is about), and **form** as the means by which that subject is expressed and experienced. The two terms are often paired because works of art need them both. Content provides something to express; form supplies the methods and techniques necessary to present it to the audience.

And form doesn't just allow us to *see* the subject/content; it lets us see that content *in a particular way*. Form enables the artist to shape our particular experience *and interpretation* of that content. In the world of movies, form is **cinematic language:** the tools and techniques that filmmakers use to convey meaning and mood to the viewer, including lighting, mise-en-scène, cinematography, performance, editing, and sound . . . in other words, the content of most of this textbook.

If we consider the *Juno* scene analyzed in Chapter 1, the content is: *Juno in the waiting room*. We could be more specific and say that the content is

Form and content The *content* of the *Juno* waiting room scene analyzed in Chapter 1 is: Juno thinking about fingernails and changing her mind. As we saw in that analysis, a great deal of *form* was employed to shape our experience and interpretation of that content, including sound, juxtaposition, pattern, point of view, and the relative size of the subject in each frame.

Juno thinking about fingernails and changing her mind. The form used to express that subject and meaning includes decor, patterns, implied proximity, point of view, moving camera, and sound.

The relationship between form and content is central not just to our study of movies; it is an underlying concern in all art. An understanding of the two intersecting concepts can help us to distinguish one work of art from another or to compare the styles and visions of different artists approaching the same subject.

If we look at three sculptures of a male figure, for example—by Praxiteles, Alberto Giacometti, and Keith Haring, artists spanning history from ancient Greece to the present—we can see crucial differences in vision, style, and meaning (see the illustrations on page 38). Each sculpture can be said to express the same subject, the male body, but they clearly differ in form. Of the three, Praxiteles's sculpture, *Hermes Carrying the Infant Dionysus*, comes closest to resembling a flesh-and-blood body. Giacometti's *Walking Man* (1960) elongates and exaggerates anatomical features, but the figure remains recognizable as a male human. Haring's *Self Portrait* (1989) smooths out and simplifies the contours of the human body to create an even more abstract rendering.

Once we recognize the formal differences and similarities among these three sculptures, we can ask questions about how the respective forms shape our emotional and intellectual responses to the subject matter. Look again at the ancient Greek sculpture. Although there might once have been a living man whose body looked like this, very few bodies do. The sculpture is an idealization—less a matter of recording the way a particular man actually looked than of visually describing an ideal male form. As such, it is as much an interpretation of the

[1]

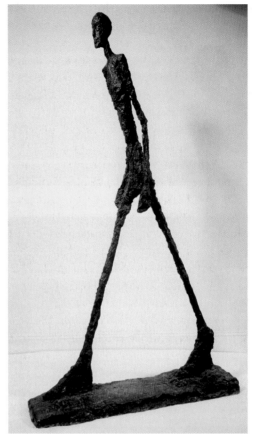

[2]

Form and content Compare these sculptures: [1] *Hermes Carrying the Infant Dionysus*, by Praxiteles, who lived in Greece during the fourth century BCE; [2] *Walking Man II*, by Alberto Giacometti (1901–1966), a Swiss artist; and [3] *Self Portrait*, by Keith Haring (1958–1990), an American. Although all three works depict the male figure, their forms are so different that their meanings, too, must be different. What, then, is the relationship between the form of an artwork and its content?

[3]

subject matter as, and thus no more "real" than, the other two sculptures. Giacometti's version, because of its exaggerated form, conveys a sense of isolation and nervousness, perhaps even anguish. Haring's sculpture, relying on stylized and almost cartoonlike form, seems more playful and mischievous than the other two. Suddenly, because of the different form each sculpture takes, we realize that the content of each has changed: they are no longer *about* the same subject. Praxiteles's sculpture is somehow about defining an ideal; Giacometti's seems to reach for something that lies beneath the surface of human life and the human form; and Haring's appears to celebrate the body as a source of joy. As we become more attentive to their formal differences, these sculptures become more unlike each other in their content, too.

Thus, form and content—rather than being separate things that come together to produce art—are instead two aspects of the entire formal system of a work of art. They are interrelated, interdependent, and interactive. Sometimes, of course, we might have good reasons, conceptually and critically, to isolate the content of a film from its form. It might be useful to do so when, say, comparing the rendition in Ridley Scott's *Black Hawk Down* (2001; screenwriter: Ken Nolan) of the 1993 U.S. military intervention in Somalia with a historical account of the same event. In such an analysis, issues of completeness, accuracy, and reliability would take

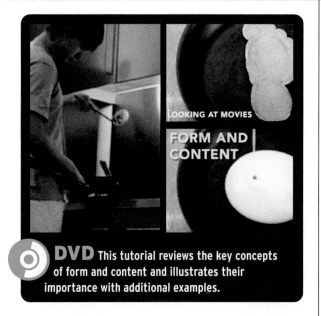

DVD This tutorial reviews the key concepts of form and content and illustrates their importance with additional examples.

precedence over formal qualities of the film, such as cinematography and editing. By focusing solely on content, however, we risk overlooking the aspects that make movies unique as an art form and interesting as individual works of art.

Form and Expectations

As we discussed in Chapter 1, our decision to see a particular movie is almost always based on certain expectations. Perhaps we have enjoyed previous work by the director, the screenwriter, or the actors; or publicity, advertisements, friends, or reviews have attracted us; or the genre is appealing; or we're curious about the techniques used to make the movie.

Even if we have no such preconceptions before stepping into a movie theater, we will form impressions very quickly once the movie begins, sometimes even from the moment the opening credits roll. (In Hollywood, producers and screenwriters assume that audiences decide whether they like or dislike a movie within its first ten minutes.) As the movie continues, we experience a more complex web of expectations, many of which may be tied to the narrative—the formal arrangement of the events that make up the story—and, specifically, to

Focusing on content On October 3, 1993, nearly a hundred U.S. Army Rangers parachuted into Mogadishu, the capital of Somalia, to capture two men. Their mission was supposed to take about an hour, but they ended up in a fifteen-hour battle, the longest sustained ground attack involving American soldiers since the Vietnam War. Two U.S. Black Hawk helicopters were destroyed; eighteen Americans and hundreds of Somalis were killed; military and civilian casualties numbered in the thousands. Whereas its source, Mark Bowden's best-selling nonfiction book of the same title, was a minute-by-minute account of the firefight, Ridley Scott's narrative film *Black Hawk Down* (2001) re-creates events by dramatically condensing the action into 144 minutes. Clearly, the book and the movie differ in their form, and we might have interesting discussions about their differences. But for many viewers, the primary concern is the *content* of both book and movie. What relationship does each work bear to the facts? What would it mean, in this case, to say that the movie is better than the book or vice versa?

Formal expectations and *The Searchers* Directors can subvert our most basic expectations of film form to dramatic effect. We have been conditioned to assume that the subject (or narrative focus) of any shot will be the largest or most noticeable element in the frame. At the point in John Ford's *The Searchers* (1956) illustrated here, the movie has devoted most of its screen time to Ethan Edward's (John Wayne) thus-far fruitless five-year search for his kidnapped niece Debbie (Natalie Wood). Ford lends resonance to the climactic point at which the searchers and their objective are finally (albeit briefly) reunited by reversing our formal expectations for such an important dramatic moment. As Ethan and his exasperated partner, Martin (Jeffrey Hunter), argue, the all-important Debbie appears not as the composition's featured visual element, but as a tiny figure in the background, distinguishable only by her movement across the stark sky and sand. Even though she is barely a speck on the screen, Debbie instantly becomes the focus of our attention. This unexpected formal approach allows the audience to spot the search's goal long before Ethan and Martin do, which creates suspense as we await her long-delayed arrival, anticipate her volatile uncle's reaction, and ask the story's central question one last time: Will the searchers ever find Debbie?

our sense that certain events produce likely actions or outcomes.

We've learned to expect that most movies start with a "normal" world, which is altered by a particular incident, that in turn compels the characters to pursue a goal. And once the narrative begins, those expectations provoke us to ask predictive questions about the story's outcome, questions we will be asking ourselves repeatedly and waiting to have answered over the course of the film.

The nineteenth-century Russian playwright Anton Chekhov famously said that when a theater audience sees a character produce a gun in the first act, they expect that gun to be used before the play ends. Movie audiences have similar expectations. In the Coen brothers' 2010 version of *True Grit*, the villain Tom Chaney threatens young Mattie Ross: "That pit is one hundred feet deep and I will throw you in it." From that moment on, our interpretation of events is colored by the suggestion that Mattie is destined for the abyss. Later, when her would-be rescuer LeBoeuf says in passing, "Mind your footing, there is a pit here," our expectations are reinforced. We can't help but suppose that somebody is going down that hole. Screenwriters often organize a film's narrative structure around the viewer's desire to learn the answers to such central questions as, Will Dorothy get back to Kansas? or Will Frodo destroy the ring?

In Sam Mendes's *American Beauty* (1999; screenwriter: Alan Ball), the very first scene introduces us to two of the film's central characters—Jane Burnham (Thora Birch), the daughter of Lester Burnham (Kevin Spacey); and Ricky Fitts (Wes Bentley), the charismatic marijuana dealer and video artist who lives next door—in a manner that plants the idea that Ricky will kill Lester. The scene opens with Jane on-screen being videotaped by Ricky, whom we can hear but not see. Jane complains about her father, calling him a "horny geekboy" rather than a "role model," and she concludes that "someone really should put him out of his misery." Ricky, still offscreen, asks, "Want me to kill him for you?" After a moment's pause, Jane looks straight into the camera and replies, "Yeah, would you?" This scene (and the one that immediately follows, in which Lester tells us in a voice-over that "in less than a year, I'll be dead") shapes our expectations during the rest of the movie.

As we learn more about Ricky's rebellious and idiosyncratic nature, we wonder whether he may be capable of using a deadly weapon at some point. Our suspense is heightened as we learn more about Ricky's father, Frank Fitts (Chris Cooper), a gung-ho, physically abusive marine colonel who collects Nazi memorabilia. The complications mount as Ricky and Lester strike up a friendly rapport and as Jane's mother, Carolyn Burnham (Annette Bening), starts brandishing a gun, implying that she will use it to kill the husband she despises. At each point, we adjust our expectations about the final outcome, even as we know (because Lester has told us) what that outcome will be.

Director Alfred Hitchcock treated his audiences' expectations in ironic, even playful, ways—sometimes using the gun, so to speak, and sometimes not—and this became one of his major stylistic traits. Hitchcock used the otherwise meaningless term *MacGuffin* to refer to an object, document, or secret within a story that is of vital importance to the characters, and thus motivates

[1]

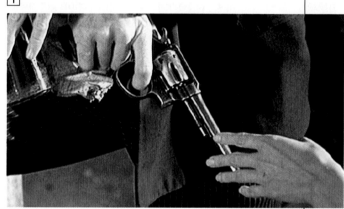

[2]

Expectations in *Bonnie and Clyde* Much of the development and ultimate impact of Arthur Penn's *Bonnie and Clyde* (1967) depends on the sexual chemistry between the title characters [1], established through physical expression, dialogue, and overt symbolism. Early in the film, Clyde (Warren Beatty), ruthless and handsome, brandishes his gun threateningly and phallically [2]. Attracted by this display and others, the beautiful Bonnie (Faye Dunaway) is as surprised as we are when Clyde later rebuffs her obvious sexual attraction to him (at one point, he demurs, "I ain't much of a lover boy"). We may not like this contradiction, but it is established early in the film and quickly teaches us that our expectations will not always be satisfied.

their actions and the conflict, but that turns out to be less significant to the overall narrative than we might at first expect.[1] In *Psycho* (1960; screenwriter:

[1]Hitchcock discusses the MacGuffin in François Truffaut, *Hitchcock*, rev. ed. (New York: Simon & Schuster, 1984), pp. 137–139.

Joseph Stefano), for example, Marion Crane (Janet Leigh) believes that the $40,000 she steals from her employer will help her start a new life. Instead, her flight with the money leads to the Bates Motel, the resident psychopath, and Marion's death. The money plays no role in motivating her murderer; in fact, the killer doesn't seem to know it exists. Once the murder has occurred, the money—a classic MacGuffin—is of no real importance to the rest of the movie. With the death of our assumed protagonist, Hitchcock sends our expectations in a new and unanticipated direction. The question that drew us into the narrative—Will Marion get away with embezzlement?—suddenly switches to Who will stop this murderously overprotective mother? As anyone who has seen *Psycho* knows, this narrative about-face isn't the end of the director's manipulation of audience expectations.

Even as the narrative form of a movie is shaping and sometimes confounding our expectations, other formal qualities may perform similar functions. Seemingly insignificant and abstract elements of film such as color schemes, sounds, the length of shots, and the movement of the camera often cooperate with dramatic elements to either heighten or confuse our expectations. One way they do this is by establishing patterns.

Patterns

Instinctively, we search for patterns and progressions in all art forms. The more these meet our expectations (or contradict them in interesting ways), the more likely we are to enjoy, analyze, and interpret the work.

The penultimate scene in D. W. Griffith's *Way Down East* (1920; scenario: Anthony Paul Kelly), one of the most famous chase scenes in movie history, illustrates how the movies depend on our recognition of patterns. Banished from a "respectable" family's house because of her scandalous past, Anna Moore (Lillian Gish) tries to walk through a blizzard but quickly becomes disoriented and wanders onto a partially frozen river. She faints on an ice floe and, after much suspense, is rescued by David Bartlett (Richard Barthelmess)

just as she is about to go over a huge waterfall to what clearly would have been her death.

To heighten the drama of his characters' predicament, Griffith employs parallel editing—a technique that makes different lines of action appear to be occurring simultaneously. Griffith shows us Anna on the ice [1], Niagara Falls [2], and David jumping from one floe to another as he tries to catch up with her [4]. As we watch these three lines of action edited together (in a general pattern of ABCACBCABCACBC), they appear simultaneous. We assume that the river flows over Niagara Falls and that the ice floe that Anna is on is heading down that river. It doesn't matter that the actors weren't literally in danger of going over a waterfall or that David's actions did not occur simultaneously with Anna's progress downriver on the floe. The form of the scene, established by the pattern of parallel editing, has created an illusion of connections among these various shots, leaving us with an impression of a continuous, anxiety-producing drama.

The editing in one scene of Jonathan Demme's *The Silence of the Lambs* (1991; screenwriter: Ted Tally) takes advantage of our natural interpretation of parallel action to achieve a disorienting effect (see page 44). Because earlier in the movie Demme has already shown us countless versions of a formal pattern in which two elements seen in separation are alternated and related (ABABAB), we expect that pattern to be repeated when shots of the serial killer Buffalo Bill (Ted Levine) arguing with his intended victim in his basement are intercut with shots of the FBI team preparing to storm a house. We naturally assume that the FBI has targeted the same house in which Buffalo Bill is going about his grisly business. When the sequence eventually reveals that the FBI is, in fact, attacking a different house, the pattern is broken, thwarting our expectations and setting in motion the suspenseful scene that follows.

Parallel editing is not the only means of creating and exploiting patterns in movies, of course. Some patterns are made to be broken. The six consecutive underwater shots that open Terrence Malick's *The New World* (2005) establish a pattern of peace and affinity (see page 45). Each shot conveys a

[3]

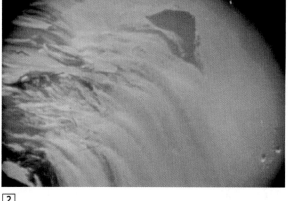
[2]

[4]

[1]

Parallel editing in *Way Down East* Pioneering director D. W. Griffith risked the lives of actors Lillian Gish and Richard Barthelmess to film *Way down East*'s now classic "ice break" scene—a scene that builds suspense by exposing us to a pattern of different shots called *parallel editing*. Griffith shot much of the blizzard and ice-floe footage along the Connecticut River, then edited it together with studio shots and scenes of Niagara Falls. Gish, thinly dressed, was freezing on the ice and was periodically revived with hot tea. Although the dangers during filming were real enough, the "reality" portrayed in the final scene—a rescue from the certain death that would result from a plunge over Niagara Falls—is wholly the result of Griffith's use of a pattern of editing that has by now become a standard technique in narrative filmmaking.

harmonious fusion of indigenous people and their natural environment: fish glide past the camera; a smiling Pocahontas runs her hand across the shimmering surface; Algonquin natives swim hand in hand; Pocahontas glides upward trailing a stream of air bubbles. The accumulative effect of this AAAAAA pattern is quietly powerful—it repeatedly reinforces a feeling of slow-motion tranquility. But the sequence's most expressive moment comes just when this pleasant pattern is broken. The seventh shot rises from the blue waters to cinematically signal the Virginia Company's intrusion into the Algonquin paradise. The underwater A shots were infused with blue; this open-air B shot is dominated by shades of brown. The opening A sequence featured close-framed human subjects; this pattern-breaking B shot is a wide angle of three large European ships. Everything has suddenly changed: the light, the framing, the content, the world.

The preceding examples offer a taste of how important patterns can be to our experience and interpretation of movies. Narrative patterns provide an element of structure, ground us in the

[1]

[2]

[3]

[4]

[5]

[6]

Patterns and suspense Filmmakers can use patterns to catch us unawares. In *The Silence of the Lambs* (1991), Jonathan Demme exploits our sense that when shots are juxtaposed, they must share a logical connection. After FBI agents surround a house, an agent disguised as a deliveryman (Lamont Arnold) rings the doorbell [1]; a bell rings in the serial killer Buffalo Bill's (Ted Levine) basement [2]; Bill reacts to that ring [3], leaves behind the prisoner he was about to harm, goes upstairs, and answers his front door, revealing not the deliveryman we expect to see but Clarice Starling (Jodie Foster) [4]. As agents storm the house they've been staking out [5], Clarice and Bill continue to talk [6]. The agents have entered the wrong house, Clarice is now alone with a psychopath, and our anxiety rises as a result of the surprise.

1

2

3

4

5

6

7

Breaking patterns for dramatic effect The six consecutive underwater shots that open Terrence Malick's *The New World* (2005) establish a pattern of tranquility and affinity. Each shot conveys a harmonious fusion of indigenous people and their natural environment. The seventh shot rises from the blue waters to break the pattern and thus cinematically signal the Virginia Company's intrusion into the Algonquin paradise. Everything has suddenly changed: the light, the framing, the content, the world.

familiar, or acquaint us with the unfamiliar; repeating them emphasizes their content. Shot patterns can convey character state of mind, create relationships, and communicate narrative meaning. As we shall see in later chapters, nonnarrative patterns such as the repetition of a familiar image or a familiar sound effect (or motif from the movie's musical score) are also important components of film form.

Fundamentals of Film Form

The remaining chapters in this book describe the major formal aspects of film—narrative, mise-en-scène, cinematography, acting, editing, sound—to provide you with a beginning vocabulary for talking about film form more specifically. Before we study these individual formal elements, however, we shall briefly discuss three fundamental principles of film form:

> Movies depend on light.
> Movies provide an illusion of movement.
> Movies manipulate space and time in unique ways.

Movies Depend on Light

Light is the essential ingredient in the creation and consumption of motion pictures. Movie images are made when a camera lens focuses light onto either film stock or a video sensor chip. Movie-theater projectors and video monitors all transmit motion pictures as light, which is gathered by the lenses and sensors in our own eyes. Movie production crews—including the cinematographer, the gaffer, the best boy, and many assorted grips and assistants—devote an impressive amount of time and equipment to illumination design and execution. Yet it would be a mistake to think of light as simply a requirement for a decent exposure. Light is more than a source of illumination; it is a key formal element that film artists and technicians carefully manipulate to create mood, reveal character, and convey meaning.

One of the most powerful black-and-white films ever made, John Ford's *The Grapes of Wrath* (1940), tells the story of an Oklahoma farming family forced off their land by the violent dust storms that plagued the region during the Great Depression of the 1930s. The eldest son, Tom Joad (Henry Fonda), returns home after serving a prison sentence, only to find that his family has left their farm for the supposedly greener pastures of California. Tom and an itinerant preacher named Casy (John Carradine), whom he has met along the way, enter the Joad house, using a candle to help them see inside the pitch-black interior. Lurking in the dark, but illuminated by the candlelight (masterfully simulated by cinematographer Gregg Toland), is Muley Graves (John Qualen), a farmer who has refused to leave Oklahoma with his family. As Muley tells Tom and Casy what has happened in the area, Tom holds the candle so that he and Casy can see him better, and the contrasts between the dark background and Muley's haunted face, illuminated by the flickering candle, reveal their collective state of mind: despair. The unconventional direction of the harsh light distorts the characters' features and casts elongated shadows looming behind and above them. The story is told less through words than through the overtly symbolic light of a single candle. Muley's flashback account of the loss of his farm reverses the pattern. The harsh light of the sun that, along with the relentless wind, has withered his fields beats down upon Muley, casting a deep, foreshortened shadow of the ruined man across his ruined land. Such sharp contrasts of light and dark occur throughout the film, thus providing a pattern of meaning.

Perhaps it would be useful to draw a distinction between the luminous energy we call light and the crafted interplay between motion-picture light and shadow known as lighting. Light is responsible for the image we see on the screen, whether photographed (shot) on film or video, caught on a disc, created with a computer, or, as in animation, drawn on pieces of celluloid known as cels. Lighting is responsible for significant effects in each shot or scene. It enhances the texture, depth, emotions, and mood of a shot. It accents the rough texture of a cobblestoned street in Carol Reed's *The Third Man* (1949), helps to extend the illusion of depth in Orson Welles's *Citizen Kane* (1941), and emphasizes a character's subjective feelings of

apprehension or suspense in such film noirs as Billy Wilder's *Double Indemnity* (1944). In fact, lighting often conveys these things by augmenting, complicating, or even contradicting other cinematic elements within the shot (e.g., dialogue, movement, or composition). Lighting also affects the ways in which we see and think about a movie's characters. It can make a character's face appear attractive or unattractive, make the viewer like a character or be afraid of her, and reveal a character's state of mind.

These are just a few of the basic ways that movies depend on light to achieve their effects. We'll continue our discussion of cinema's use of light and manipulation of lighting later (Chapter 6 includes information and analysis of lighting's aesthetic role in cinematography; Chapter 11 covers how motion-picture technologies capture and utilize light). For now, it's enough to appreciate that light is essential to both movie meaning and the filmmaking process itself.

Movies Provide an Illusion of Movement

We need light to make, shape, and see movies, but it takes more than light to make *motion* pictures. As we learned in Chapter 1, movement is what separates cinema from all other two-dimensional pictorial art forms. We call them "movies" for a reason: the movies' expressive power derives in large part from the medium's fundamental ability to move. Or, rather, they *seem* to move. As we sit in a movie theater, believing ourselves to be watching a continuously lit screen portraying fluid, uninterrupted movement, we are actually watching a quick succession of twenty-four individual still photographs per second. And as the projector moves one of these images out of the frame to bring the next one

1

2

3

4

5

6

Lighting and character in *Atonement* Filmmakers often craft the interplay between illumination and shadow to imply character state of mind. The tragic romance of *Atonement* (2007; director: Joe Wright; cinematographer: Seamus McGarvey) hinges on the actions of a precocious thirteen year old, Briony Tallis (Saoirse Ronan). Lives are irrevocably altered when Briony's adolescent jealousy prompts her to accuse the housekeeper's son Robbie of rape. As events unfold, a series of different lighting designs are employed to enhance our perception of Briony's evolving (and often suppressed) emotions as she stumbles upon Cecilia and Robbie making love in the library [1], catches a startled glimpse of her cousin's rape [2], accuses Robbie of the crime [3], guiltily retreats upon Robbie's arrival [4], contemplates the consequences of her actions [5], and observes Robbie's arrest [6].

in, the screen goes dark. Although the movies are distinguished from other arts by their dependence on light and movement, we spend a good amount of our time in movie theaters sitting in complete darkness, facing a screen with nothing projected on it at all!

The movement we see on the movie screen is an illusion, made possible by two interacting optical and perceptual phenomena: persistence of vision and the phi phenomenon. **Persistence of vision** is the process by which the human brain retains an image for a fraction of a second longer than the eye records it. You can observe this phenomenon by quickly switching a light on and then off in a dark room. Doing this, you should see an afterimage of the objects in the room, or at least of whatever you were looking at directly when you switched the light on. Similarly, in the movie theater we see a smooth flow of images and not the darkness between frames. Thus, the persistence of vision gives the *illusion of succession*, or one image following another without interruption. However, we must also experience the *illusion of movement*, or figures and objects within the image changing position simultaneously without actually moving.

The **phi phenomenon** is the illusion of movement created by events that succeed each other rapidly, as when two adjacent lights flash on and off alternately and we seem to see a single light shifting back and forth. The phi phenomenon is related to **critical flicker fusion,** which occurs when a single light flickers on and off with such speed that the individual pulses of light fuse together to give the illusion of continuous light. (Early movies were called *flicks* because the projectors that were used often ran at slower speeds than were necessary to sustain this illusion; the result was not continuous light, but a flickering image on-screen. The most acute human eye can discern no more than fifty pulses of light per second. Because the shutters of modern projectors "double-flash" each frame of film, we watch forty-eight pulses per second, close enough to the limit of perception to eliminate our awareness of the flicker effect.) The movie projector relies on such phenomena to trick us into perceiving separate images as one continuous image; and because each successive image differs only slightly from the one that precedes it, we perceive **apparent motion** rather than a series of jerky movements.

The most dazzling contemporary films, such as Andy and Lana Wachowski's *The Matrix* (1999), exploit these properties of cinematic movement to create kinetic excitement that makes the impossible look totally possible. How do they do this? Special effects, involving the most advanced computer technology in both hardware and software, play a large role in creating this virtual reality. Indeed, seamlessly integrated to create the film's virtual realm, special effects reportedly constitute 20 percent of *The Matrix*. But such sophisticated effects would not be possible without the simple illusions just discussed. Much of what we regard as the absolute cutting edge of moviemaking technology capitalizes on these illusions, especially the speeding up or slowing down of movement to achieve the desired effects.

In making *The Matrix*, the filmmakers initially discovered that a number of the necessary action sequences might not be possible, because they required motion to be captured at exceptionally high speeds. That is, to create the illusion of such slow motion, the camera would have had to speed up beyond its capacity. Working with engineers, the filmmakers developed new technology in a process that resembled sequence photography experiments from the earliest days of motion-picture photography. For example, a scene in which Neo (Keanu Reeves) is fired at by another protagonist in the virtual world was shot not by one motion-picture camera, but by 120 still cameras mounted in a roller coaster-style arc and snapping single images in a computer-driven, rapid-fire sequence. The resulting effect allows dramatic action, such as dodging a barrage of bullets, to appear in exaggerated slow motion, while the swooping moving camera seems to circumnavigate this stylized slo-mo subject at normal "real time" speed.

Movies Manipulate Space and Time in Unique Ways

Some of the arts, such as architecture, are concerned mostly with space; others, such as music,

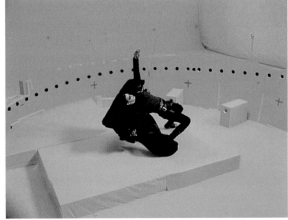

1

2

3

Movement in *The Matrix* For Andy and Lana Wachowski's *The Matrix* (1999), special-effects supervisors Steve Courtley and Brian Cox employed a setup much like that used by early pioneers of serial photography (see Chapter 10). They placed 120 still cameras in an arc and coordinated their exposures using computers. The individual frames, shot from various angles but in much quicker succession than is possible with a motion-picture camera, could then be edited together to create the duality of movement (sometimes called *bullet time*) for which *The Matrix* is famous. The camera moves around a slow-motion subject at a relatively fast pace, apparently independent of the subject's stylized slowness. Despite its contemporary look, this special-effects technique is grounded in principles and methods established during the earliest years of motion-picture history.

are related mainly to time. But movies manipulate space and time equally well and are thus both a spatial and a temporal art form. Movies can move seamlessly from one space to another (say, from a room to a landscape to outer space), or make space move (as when the camera turns around or away from its subject, changing the physical, psy-chological, or emotional relationship between the viewer and the subject), or fragment time in many different ways. Only movies can record real time in its chronological passing as well as subjec-tive versions of time passing—slow motion, for example, or extreme compression of vast swaths of time.

On the movie screen, space and time are relative to each other, and we can't separate them or perceive one without the other. The movies give time to space and space to time, a phenomenon that art historian and film theorist Erwin Panofsky describes as the *dynamization of space* and the *spatialization of time*.[2] To understand this principle of "co-expressibility," compare your experiences of space when you watch a play and when you watch a movie. As a spectator at a play in the theater, your relationship to the stage, the settings, and the actors is *fixed*. Your perspective on these things is determined by the location of your seat, and everything on the stage remains the same size in relation to the entire stage. Sets may change between scenes, but within scenes the set remains, for the most part, in place. No matter how skillfully constructed and painted the set is, you know (because of the clear boundaries between the set and the rest of the theater) that it is not real and that when actors go through doors in the set's walls, they go backstage or into the wings at the side of the stage, not into a continuation of the world portrayed on the stage.

By contrast, when you watch a movie, your relationship to the space portrayed on-screen can be flexible. You still sit in a fixed seat, but the screen images move: the spatial relationships on the screen may constantly change, and the film directs your gaze. Suppose, for example, that during a scene in which two characters meet at a bar, the action suddenly flashes forward to their later rendezvous at an apartment, then flashes back to the conversation at the bar, and so on; or a close-up focuses your attention on one character's (or both characters') lips. A live theater performance can attempt versions of such spatial and temporal effects,[3] but a play can't do so as seamlessly, immediately, persuasively, or intensely as a movie can. If one of the two actors in that bar scene were to back away from the other and thus disappear from the screen, you would perceive her as moving to another part of the bar—that is, into a continuation of the space already established in the scene. You can easily imagine this movement because of the fluidity of movie space, more of which is necessarily suggested than is shown.

The key to the unique power of movies to manipulate our sense of space is the motion-picture camera, particularly its lens. We identify with this lens, for it determines our perception of cinematic space. Indeed, if we didn't automatically make this identification—assuming, for example, that the camera's point of view is a sort of roving, omniscient one with which we are supposed to identify—movies would be almost incomprehensible. The key to understanding our connection to the camera lens lies in the differences between how the human eye and the camera eye see. The camera eye perceives what's placed before it through a series of different pictures (shots), made with different lenses, from different camera positions and angles, using different movements, under different lighting, and so on. Although both the camera eye and the human eye can see the movements, colors, textures, sizes, and locations of people, places, and things, the camera eye is more selective in its view. The camera frames its image, for example, and can widen and foreshorten space. Through camera positioning, the lens can record a close-up, removing from our view the surrounding visual context that we see in real life, no matter how close we get to an object. In short, the camera mediates between the exterior (the world) and the interior (our eyes and brains).

We use the term **mediation,** a key concept in film theory, literally to mean the process by which an agent, structure, or other formal element, whether human or technological, transfers something from one place to another. No matter how straightforward the mediation of the camera eye may seem, it always involves selection and manipulation

[2]Erwin Panofsky, "Style and Medium in the Motion Pictures," in *Film Theory and Criticism: Introductory Readings*, 5th ed., ed. Leo Braudy and Marshall Cohen (New York: Oxford University Press, 1999), pp. 281–283.

[3]Film director Ingmar Bergman demonstrated spatial manipulation in his 1970 stage production of Henrik Ibsen's *Hedda Gabler* (1890), in which a spotlight left only the actor's face or lips visible, thus creating a kind of close-up; and Arthur Miller's *Death of a Salesman* (1949), in which past and present intermingle within scenes, demonstrates temporal manipulation.

[2]

[1]

[4]

[3]

[6]

[5]

Manipulating space in *The Gold Rush* Film editing can convince us that we're seeing a complete space and a continuous action, even though individual shots have been filmed in different places and at different times. In Charles Chaplin's *The Gold Rush* (1925), an exterior shot of the cabin [1] establishes the danger that the main characters only slowly become aware of [2]. As the cabin hangs in the balance [3], alternating interior and exterior shots [4-6] accentuate our sense of suspense and amusement.

of what is seen. This is what mediation as a concept implies. Unlike a video surveillance camera or a webcam, the motion-picture camera eye is not an artless recorder of "reality." It is instead one of a number of expressive tools that filmmakers use to influence our interpretation of the movie's meaning.

Cinema's ability to manipulate space is illustrated in Charles Chaplin's *The Gold Rush* (1925). This brilliant comedy portrays the adventures of two prospectors: the "Little Fellow" (Chaplin) and his nemesis, Big Jim McKay (Mack Swain). After many twists and turns of the plot, the two find themselves sharing an isolated cabin. At night, the winds of a fierce storm blow the cabin to the brink of a deep abyss. Waking and walking about, the Little Fellow slides toward the door (and almost certain death). The danger is established by our first seeing the sharp precipice on which the cabin is located and then by seeing the Little Fellow sliding toward the door that opens out over the abyss. Subsequently, we see him and Big Jim engaged in a struggle for survival, which requires them to maintain the balance of the cabin on the edge of the abyss.

The suspense exists because individual shots—one made outdoors, the other safely in a studio—have been edited together to create the illusion that they form part of a complete space. As we watch the cabin sway and teeter on the cliff's edge, we imagine the hapless adventurers inside; when the action cuts to the interior of the cabin and we see the floor pitching back and forth, we imagine the cabin perched precariously on the edge. The experience of these shots as a continuous record of action occurring in a complete (and realistic) space is an illusion that no other art form can convey as effectively as movies can.

The manipulation of time (as well as space), a function of editing, is handled with great irony, cinematic power, and emotional impact in the "Baptism and Murder" scene in Francis Ford Coppola's *The Godfather* (1972). This five-minute scene consists of thirty-six shots made at different locations. The primary location is a church where Michael Corleone (Al Pacino), the newly named godfather of the Corleone mob, and his wife, Kay (Diane Keaton), attend their nephew's baptism. Symbolically, Michael is also the child's godfather. Coppola cuts back and forth between the baptism; the preparations for five murders, which Michael has ordered, at five different locations; and the murders themselves.

Each time we return to the baptism, it continues where it left off for one of these cutaways to other actions. We know this from the continuity of the priest's actions, Latin incantations, and the Bach organ music. This continuity tells us not only that these actions are taking place simultaneously, but also that Michael is involved in all of them, either directly or indirectly. The simultaneity is further strengthened by the organ music, which underscores every scene in the sequence, not just those that take place in the cathedral—music that picks up in pitch and loudness as the sequence progresses, rising to particular climaxes as the murders are committed. As the priest says to Michael, "Go in peace, and may the Lord be with you," we are left to reconcile this meticulously timed, simultaneous occurrence of sacred and criminal acts.

Many of the examples we shared earlier in this chapter to illustrate pattern, cinematic space, and the relationship between form and content can also teach us something about how movies manipulate time. *The Matrix*'s "bullet time" effect is dazzling because we have not yet grown accustomed to seeing two time references share the same screen simultaneously. Neo and his attacker's bullets are presented in stylized slow motion that expands our experience of a moment in time (and is often used to lend violence or action a balletic grace). Yet the moving camera capturing Neo's dodging dance glides at a conventional speed that we associate with "real time." The parallel action sequences in *The Silence of the Lambs, Way down East*, and *The Godfather* are evidence of cinema's ability to use crosscutting to represent multiple events occurring at the same instant. Some movies, like *City of God* (2002; directors: Fernando Meirelles and Kátia Lund), do parallel action one better, using a split screen to actually show the concurrent actions simultaneously.

Movies frequently rearrange time by organizing story events in nonchronological order. Orson

Split screen and simultaneous action Most movies use crosscutting techniques like parallel action to represent more than one event occurring at the same moment. The audience experiences only one event at a time, but the repeated crosscutting implies simultaneity. *City of God* (2002; directors: Fernando Meirelles and Kátia Lund) sometimes breaks with convention and splits the screen into multiple frames in order to present a more immediate depiction of simultaneous action.

Welles's *Citizen Kane* (1941) and Todd Haynes's *I'm Not There* (2007) both begin their exploration of a life with that character's death and, for the rest of the film, shuffle the events leading up to that opening conclusion. Movies like *Atonement* (2007; director: Joe Wright) reorder time to present events from multiple perspectives and depict character memory. A number of films, most famously Christopher Nolan's *Memento* (2000) and Gaspar Noé's *Irréversible* (2002), transpose time by presenting their stories in scene-by-scene reverse chronological order. All of these approaches to rearranging time allow filmmakers to create new narrative meaning by juxtaposing events in ways linear chronology does not permit.

John Woo's 1989 action extravaganza *The Killer* maintains conventional chronology but utilizes many other expressive manipulations of time to tell its story of a kind-hearted assassin (Yun-Fat Chow) and the relentless cop (Danny Lee) determined to capture him. Each of the film's many gun battle scenes features elegant slow-motion shots of either the antihero or one of his unfortunate rivals delivering or absorbing multiple bullets. The slow motion invites the audience to pause and

savor an extended moment of stylized violence. The sequences also employ occasional bursts of fast motion that have the opposite effect. These sudden temporal shifts allow Woo and film editor Kung Ming Fan to choreograph cinematic patterns and rhythms that give their fight scenes a dizzying kinetic energy that borders on the outrageous.

Woo expands the audience's experience of time at key points in the story by fragmenting the moment preceding an important action. The film's climactic gunfight finds the hit man and the cop allied against overwhelming forces. The sequence begins with several shots of an army of trigger-happy gangsters bursting into the isolated church where the unlikely partners are holed up. The film extends the brief instant before the bullets fly with a series of twelve shots, including a panicked bystander covering her ears, a priest crossing himself, and the cop and killer exchanging tenacious glances. The accumulation of these time fragments holds us in the moment far longer than the momentum of the action could realistically allow. The sequence's relative stasis establishes a pattern that is broken by the inevitable explosion of violence. Later, a brief break in the combat is punctuated by a **freeze-frame** (in which a still image is shown on-screen for a period of time), another of Woo's time-shifting trademarks. Bloodied but still breathing, the newfound friends emerge from the bullet-ridden sanctuary. The killer's fond glance at the cop suddenly freezes into a still image, suspending time and motion for a couple of seconds. The

Manipulating time in *The Killer* (*Opposite*) The world-weary title character in John Woo's *The Killer* (1989) is an expert assassin attempting to cash in and retire after one last hit. Woo conveys the hit man's reluctance to kill again by expanding the moment of his decision to pull the trigger. Film editor Kung Ming Fan fragments the dramatic pause preceding the action into a thirty-four-shot sequence that cuts between multiple images of the intended target [1], the dragon-boat ceremony he is officiating [2, 3], and the pensive killer [4, 5]. The accumulation of all these fragments extends what should be a brief moment into a tension-filled fifty-two seconds. When the killer finally does draw his weapon, the significance of the decision is made clear by the repetition of this action in three shots from different camera angles [6–8]. The rapid-fire repetition of a single action is one of cinema's most explicit manipulations of time.

cop's smiling response is prolonged in a matching sustained freeze-frame. As you may have guessed, *The Killer* is an odd sort of love story. With that in mind, we can see that these freeze-frames do more than manipulate time; they visually unite the two former foes, thus emphasizing their mutual admiration.

Realism and Antirealism

All of the unique features of film form described in the preceding discussion combine to make it possible for filmmakers to create vivid and believable worlds on the screen. Although not every film strives to be "realistic," nearly all films attempt to immerse us in a world that is depicted convincingly on its own terms. Moving-picture technology arose primarily from attempts to record natural images through photography, but it also was shaped by similar attempts in painting and literature. That is, the realist impulse of the visual arts—recording the visible facts of people, places, and social life for a working-class and growing middle-class audience—helped inspire the first motion pictures. However, it very soon became clear that movies could be used to create antirealist as well as realist worlds.

Between 1895 and 1905, the French filmmakers Auguste and Louis Lumière and Georges Méliès established the two basic directions that the cinema would follow: the Lumières' **realism** (an interest in or concern for the actual or real, a tendency to view or represent things as they really are) and Méliès's **antirealism** (an interest in or concern for the abstract, speculative, or fantastic). Although in the following years a notion evolved that a movie was either realistic or fantastic, in fact movies in general and any movie in particular can be both. Today, many movies mix the real and the fantastic—especially those in the science-fiction, action, and thriller genres.

Realism is a complex concept, in part because it refers to several significant and related ideas. Most of us believe that the world really exists, but we don't agree about the level on which it exists. Some people trust in their senses, experiences, thoughts,

[1]

[2]

[3]

Mixing the real and the fantastic *Donnie Darko* (2001; director: Richard Kelly) shifts back and forth between showing a realistic depiction of the life of Donnie Darko (Jake Gyllenhaal) and his fantastic take on it. Darko is an intelligent, sensitive, and schizophrenic teenager who is seeing a therapist, and his normal suburban family blames his aberrant behavior on his failure to take his medication. When he is in control, he seems to be the only student in the class who understands the reading assignment [1]. When he is most troubled and loses control, he stares into a mirror, looking deranged [2], and then listens to the voice of a huge, demonic, imaginary rabbit [3], who encourages him to commit crimes. Donnie's motivating belief is in some kind of time travel, and just as the story ends, it curves back on itself to before the time it actually started. The movie asks more questions than it answers and leaves the viewer with a provocative vision of how thin the line between the real and the fantastic can be.

[1]

[2]

Technology and the appearance of realism Movies as diverse as the stark drama *L'Enfant* (2005; directors: Jean-Pierre Dardenne and Luc Dardenne; cinematographer: Alain Marcoen) and the apocalyptic horror film *Cloverfield* (2008; director: Matt Reeves; cinematographer: Michael Bonvillain) create a sense of realism by employing camera formats and techniques that audiences associate with "reality." *L'Enfant* [1] is shot with a relatively smooth handheld technique on light-sensitive (and, therefore, "grainy") 16mm film stock for a look that resembles that of professional documentary films. *Cloverfield* [2] goes several steps further, shooting in a shaky handheld style and degrading the video image to resemble amateur home movies—the ultimate in unvarnished reality footage.

and feelings. Others trust in a variety of historical, political, sociological, economic, and philosophical theories to provide a framework for understanding. Still others rely on a combination of both approaches. Realism in the movies basically overrides these approaches and implies that the world it depicts looks, sounds, and moves like the real world. It is also a way of treating subject matter that reflects everyday life. Realistic characters are expected to do things that conform to our experiences and expectations of real people. Artists in every medium, however, make choices about what aspects of "reality" to depict and how to depict them. Realism, no matter how lifelike it might appear, always involves mediation and, thus, interpretation. In the ways it is created and the ways it is perceived, realism is a kind of illusion.

If the characteristics listed here are one way to define realism in the movies, then we can define antirealism as a treatment that is against or the opposite of realism. We can illustrate the difference between realism and antirealism by contrasting two portrait paintings. The first, *The Hon. Frances Duncombe* by the eighteenth-century English painter Thomas Gainsborough, realistically depicts a recognizable woman. Its form is *representational*, meaning that it represents its subject in a form that conforms to our experiences and expectations of how a woman looks. The overall composition of the painting and the placement of the figure emphasize unity, symmetry, and order. If you were to see the painting firsthand, you would notice that Gainsborough worked with light, rapid brushstrokes and that he used delicate colors. Compare this with a second portrait, *Nude Descending a Staircase, No. 2*, by the twentieth-century French artist Marcel Duchamp, who worked in the styles of cubism, futurism, dadaism, and surrealism.

Even in the largest sense of portraiture, Duchamp's work may not represent, to most people, a recognizable woman. Duchamp has transformed a woman's natural appearance (which we know from life) into a radically altered form of sharp angles and fractured shapes. Clearly, the twentieth-century painting is less representational than its eighteenth-century predecessor. We say "less representational" because although its form is not completely recognizable, Duchamp's representation has sufficient form for us to at least identify it as a human being. If you were to see this painting firsthand, you would notice that the figure of the woman suggests an overall flatness, rather than the round, human quality of Gainsborough's figure, and that the brushstrokes and the colors are bold, rather than delicate.

[1]

[2]

Realism versus antirealism [1] *The Hon. Frances Duncombe* (1777), a realistic portrait painted by Thomas

Gainsborough; [2] *Nude Descending a Staircase, No. 2* (1912), the antirealistic work of Marcel Duchamp.

Verisimilitude

Whether a movie is realistic, antirealistic, or a combination of the two, it can achieve a convincing appearance of truth, a quality that we call **verisimilitude**. Movies are verisimilar when they convince you that the things on the screen—people, places, what have you, no matter how fantastic or antirealistic—are "really there." In other words, the movie's vision seems internally consistent, giving you a sense that in the world on-screen, things could be just like that. Of course, you can be convinced by the physical verisimilitude of the world being depicted and still be unconvinced by the "unreality" of the characters, their portrayal by

the actors, the physical or logical implausibility of the action, and so on.

In addition, audiences' expectations concerning "reality" change over time and across cultures. A movie made in Germany in the 1930s may have been considered thoroughly verisimilar by those Germans who viewed it at the time but may seem utterly unfamiliar and perhaps even unbelievable to contemporary American viewers. Films that succeed in seeming verisimilar across cultures and times often enjoy the sort of critical and popular success that prompts people to call them timeless.

Some of the most popular and successful movies of all time convincingly depict imaginative or

[1]

[2]

Lumiére/Méliès Whether presenting a scene from everyday life, as in Louis Lumière's *Employees Leaving the Lumière Factory* (1895) [1], or showing a fantastical scenario, as in Georges Méliès's *A Trip to the Moon* (1902) [2], motion pictures were recognized from the very beginning for their ability to create a feeling of *being there*, of seeing something that could actually happen. The Lumière brothers favored what they called *actualités*—mini-documentaries of scenes from everyday life; Méliès made movies directly inspired by his interest in magicians' illusions. Yet both the Lumières and Méliès wanted to portray their on-screen worlds convincingly.

supernatural worlds and events that have little or nothing in common with our actual experiences. For example, Victor Fleming's *Gone with the Wind* (1939) treats the American South of the Civil War as a soap opera rather than important history; Steven Spielberg's *Jurassic Park* (1993) almost convinces us that the dinosaur amusement park of the title really exists, just as Andy and Lana Wachowski's *The Matrix* (1999) makes us believe in an imaginary place below the surface of our everyday lives where everything is as bad as it possibly can be; and John Lasseter's *Toy Story* (1995), a feature-length animation, brings us into the world of children's toys through a saturation of detail (when Woody walks on Andy's bed, for example, we can even see his foot indentations on the comforter).

Verisimilitude and the viewing experience

Verisimilitude plays a large role in the viewers' relationship with *Let the Right One In* (2008, Tomas Alfredson) [1]. The authenticity of the bleak suburban apartment complex and its inhabitants brings an urgency to the horror and the camaraderie the adolescent vampire character inflicts on her new friends and neighbors. On the other hand, much of the fun of watching *Kick-Ass* (2010, Matthew Vaughn) [2] must be credited to the action extravaganza's gleeful disregard for verisimilitude. The characters and performances are larger than life, the situations are absurd, and the violence is outlandish.

[1]

[2]

In Ridley Scott's *Gladiator* (2000), people, places, and things look, sound, and move in ways that are believable and even convincing, not because they are true to our experiences but because they conform to what common knowledge tells us about how life might have been lived and how things might have looked in the ancient world. More to the point, *Gladiator* adheres to the cinematic conventions established by previous movies about the ancient world—dozens of them, ranging from Fred Niblo's *Ben-Hur: A Tale of the Christ* (1925) to William Wyler's remake of *Ben-Hur* (1959) to Stanley Kubrick's *Spartacus* (1960)—and thus satisfies our individual experiences with the subject matter of the film.

Cinematic Language

By cinematic language—a phrase that we have already used a few times in this book—we mean the accepted systems, methods, or conventions by which the movies communicate with the viewer. To fully understand cinema as a language, let's compare it with another, more familiar form of language—the written one you're engaged with this instant. Our written language is based, for the purpose of this explanation, on words. Each of those words has a generally accepted meaning; but when juxtaposed and combined with other words into a sentence and presented in a certain context, each can convey meaning that is potentially far more subtle, precise, or evocative than that implied by its standard "dictionary" definition.

Instead of arranging words into sentences, cinematic language combines and composes a variety of elements—for example, lighting, movement, sound, acting, and a number of camera effects—into single shots. As you work your way through this book, you will learn that most of these individual elements carry conventional, generalized meanings. But when combined with any number of other elements and presented in a particular context, that element's standardized meaning grows more individuated and complex. And the integrated arrangement of all of a shot's combined elements provides even greater expressive potential. Thus, in cinema, as in

the written word, the whole is greater than the sum of its parts. But the analogy doesn't end there. Just as authors arrange sentences into paragraphs and chapters, filmmakers derive still more accumulated meaning by organizing shots into a system of larger components: sequences and scenes. Furthermore, within sequences and scenes a filmmaker can juxtapose shots to create a more complex meaning than is usually achieved in standard prose. As viewers, we analyze cinematic language and its particular resources of expression and meaning. If your instructor refers to the *text* of a movie or asks you to *read* a particular shot, scene, or movie, she is asking you to apply your understanding of cinematic language.

The conventions that make up cinematic language are flexible, not rules; they imply a practice that has evolved through film history, not an indisputable or "correct" way of doing things. In fact, cinematic conventions represent a degree of agreement between the filmmaker and the audience about the mediating element between them: the film itself. Although filmmakers frequently build upon conventions with their own innovations, they nonetheless understand and appreciate that these conventions were themselves the result of innovations. For example, a dissolve between two shots usually indicates the passing of time but not the extent of that duration, so in the hands of one filmmaker it might mean two minutes, and in the hands of another, several years. Thus, you will begin to understand and appreciate that the development of cinematic language, and thus the cinema itself, is founded on this tension between convention and innovation.

In all of this, we identify with the camera lens. The filmmaker (here in this introduction we use that generic term instead of the specific terms *screenwriter, director, cinematographer, editor*, etc., that we shall use as we proceed) uses the camera as a maker of meaning, just as the painter uses the brush or the writer uses the pen: the angles, heights, and movements of the camera function both as a set of techniques and as expressive material, the cinematic equivalent of brushstrokes or of nouns, verbs, and adjectives. From years of looking at movies, you are already aware of how cinematic

Cinematic Language Looking at this single image, without even knowing what movie it is from or anything about the various characters pictured in the frame, we can immediately infer layers of meaning and significance. If we think of cinematic language as akin to written language, we can think of this single image from Cary Fukunaga's *Jane Eyre* (2011) as a richly layered "sentence" that communicates by combining and arranging multiple visual elements (or "words" in this analogy), that include lighting, composition, depth, design, cinematography, and performance.

language creates meaning: how close-ups have the power to change our proximity to a character or low camera angles usually suggest that the subject of the shot is superior or threatening.

All of the following chapters of this book will expand on this introduction to the language of cinema; and although they will focus mainly on the conventional meanings and methods of that language, you will also see exceptions. Soon you will understand how these and other elements of cinematic language help set movies apart from the other arts. Even as the technology used to make and display movies continues to evolve, the principles of film art covered in this book will remain essentially the same, and the knowledge and skill you acquire by reading this book will help you look at motion pictures intelligently and perceptively throughout your life, no matter which medium delivers those pictures to you.

Using cinematic conventions, filmmakers transform experiences—their own, others', purely imaginary ones, or some combination of all three—into viewing experiences that can be understood and appreciated by audiences. In addition to bringing our acceptance and understanding of conventions to looking at movies, we bring our individual experiences. Obviously, these experiences vary widely from person to person, not only in substance but also in the extent to which each of us trusts them. Personal observations of life may not be verifiable, quantifiable, or even believable, yet they are part of our perception of the world. They may reflect various influences, from intellectual substance to anti-intellectual prejudice; as a result, some people may regard gladiator movies as more meaningful than scholarly books on the subject. Thus, both cinematic conventions and individual experiences play significant roles in shaping the "reality" depicted by films.

Analyzing Principles of Film Form

At this early stage in your pursuit of actively looking at movies, you may still be wondering just what exactly you are supposed to be looking for. For starters, you now recognize that filmmakers deliberately manipulate your experience and understanding of a movie's content with a constant barrage of techniques and systems known as film form and that this form is organized into an integrated cinematic language. Simply acknowledging the difference between form and content, and knowing that there is a deliberate system at work, is the first step toward identifying and interpreting how movies communicate with viewers. The general principles of film form discussed in this chapter can now provide a framework to help you focus your gaze and develop deeper analytical skills. The checklist below will give you some specific elements and applications of form to watch out for the next time you see a film. Using this and subsequent screening checklists, you can turn every movie you watch into an exercise in observation and analysis.

Screening Checklist: Principles of Film Form

✔ A useful initial step in analyzing any movie is to distinguish an individual scene's content from its form. Try to first identify a scene's subject matter: What is this scene about? What happens? Once you have established that content, you should consider how that content was expressed. What was the mood of the scene? What do you understand about each character's state of mind? How did you perceive and interpret each moment? Did that understanding shift at any point? Once you know what happened and how you felt about it, search the scene for those formal elements that influenced your interpretation and experience. The combination and interplay of multiple formal elements that you seek is the cinematic language that movies employ to communicate with the viewer.

✔ Do any narrative or visual patterns recur a sufficient number of times to suggest a structural element in themselves? If so, what are these patterns? Do they help you determine the meaning of the film?

✔ Do you notice anything particular about the movie's presentation of cinematic space—what you see on the screen? Lots of landscapes or close-ups? Moving or static camera?

✔ Does the director manipulate our experience of time? Is this condensing, slowing, speeding, repeating, or reordering of time simply practical (as in removing insignificant events), or is it expressive? If it is expressive, just what does it express?

✔ Does the director's use of lighting help to create meaning? If so, how?

✔ Do you identify with the camera lens? What does the director compel you to see? What is left to your imagination? What does the director leave out altogether? In the end, besides showing you the action, how does the director's use of the camera help to create the movie's meaning?

Questions for Review

1. How and why do we differentiate between form and content in a movie, and why are they relevant to one another?
2. What expectations of film form can filmmakers exploit to shape an audience's experience?
3. What is parallel editing, and how does it utilize pattern?
4. In what other ways do movies use patterns to convey meaning? How do they create meaning by breaking an established pattern?
5. How do the movies create an illusion of movement?
6. How does a movie manipulate space?
7. How do movies manipulate time?
8. What is the difference between realism and antirealism in a movie, and why is verisimilitude important to them both?
9. What is meant by cinematic language? Why is it important to the ways that movies communicate with viewers?
10. Why do we identify with the camera lens?

DVD The tutorial for this chapter reviews the importance of form and content and features additional examples and illustrations.

LOOKING AT
MOVIES
CHAPTER 2:
PRINCIPLES OF FILM FORM

FORM AND CONTENT

▶ MAIN MENU

Studyspace Go to wwnorton.com/movies to test and expand your knowledge of the key concepts in this chapter.

Movies Described or Illustrated in This Chapter

American Beauty (1999). Sam Mendes, director.
Atonement (2007). Joe Wright, director.
Black Hawk Down (2001). Ridley Scott, director.
Bonnie and Clyde (1967). Arthur Penn, director.
Citizen Kane (1941). Orson Welles, director.
City of God (2002). Fernando Meirelles and Kátia Lund, directors.
Cloverfield (2008). Matt Reeves, director.
Donnie Darko (2001). Richard Kelly, director.
Employees Leaving the Lumière Factory (1895). Louis Lumière.
L'Enfant (2005). Jean-Pierre Dardenne and Luc Dardenne, directors.
Gladiator (2000). Ridley Scott, director.
The Godfather (1972). Francis Ford Coppola, director.
The Gold Rush (1925). Charles Chaplin, director.
Gone with the Wind (1939). Victor Fleming, director.
The Grapes of Wrath (1940). John Ford, director.
Heist (2001). David Mamet, director.
Henry V (1989). Kenneth Branagh, director.
Irréversible (2002). Gaspar Noé, director.
Jane Eyre (2011). Cary Fukunaga, director.
Juno (2007). Jason Reitman, director.
Kick-Ass (2010). Matthew Vaughn, director.
The Killer (1989). John Woo, director.
Let The Right One In (2008). Tomas Alfredson, director.
The Matrix (1999). Andy Wachowski and Lana Wachowski, directors.
Memento (2000). Christopher Nolan, director.
The New World (2005). Terrence Malick, director.
Psycho (1960). Alfred Hitchcock, director.
The Searchers (1956). John Ford, director.
The Silence of the Lambs (1991). Jonathan Demme, director.
The Third Man (1949). Carol Reed, director.
A Trip to the Moon (1902). Georges Méliès, director.
True Grit (2010). Joel Coen and Ethan Coen, directors.
Way down East (1920). D. W. Griffith, director.

CHAPTER THREE

Types of Movies

In this chapter, we will discuss the three major types of movies: narrative, documentary, and experimental. Within narrative movies, we will look at the subcategory of genre films, and we will explore six major American film genres in particular. Finally, we will look at a technique—animation—that is often discussed as if it were a type but that is actually used to make movies of all types.

The Idea of Narrative

The word *narrative* is much more than simply a general classification of a type of film. As you will soon see, depending on when and how we use the term, *narrative* might mean several slightly different things. Since we will be using the term *narrative* in a variety of ways throughout and beyond our exploration of the three essential types of movies, let's discuss some of the ways to approach the term.

When it comes to cinema, nothing is absolute. In the world of movies, a narrative might be a type of movie, the story that a particular film tells, the particular system by which a fictional story is structured, or a concept describing the sequential organization of events presented in almost any kind of movie. Once you become familiar with these different ways of looking at narrative, you will be able to recognize and understand almost any usage that you come across.

A narrative is a story. When we think of any medium or form—whether it's a movie, a joke, a commercial, or a news article—that tells a story, we consider that story a narrative. Journalists will often speak of finding the narrative in a news item, be it coverage of a city-council meeting, a national election, or an Olympic swimming competition. By this, they mean that under the facts and details of any given news item is a story. It is up to the reporter to identify that story and organize his reporting in such a way as to elucidate that narrative. Journalists do this because we are a story-telling species. We use stories to arrange and understand our world and our lives. So, of course, news articles are not the only place you'll find narrative. Scientists, songwriters, advertisers, politicians, comedians, and teachers all incorporate narrative into the ways they frame and present information. This semester, you will likely hear your professor refer to the narrative of a particular movie. Depending on the context she uses, she might be talking about the story that the film tells, whether that movie is a science-fiction film or a documentary about science.

Narrative is a type of movie. Our most common perception of the word *narrative* is as a categorical term for those particular movies devoted to conveying a story, whether they are works of pure fiction like J. J. Abrams's *Super 8* (2011) or a fictionalized version of actual events such as *The King's Speech* (2010; director: Tom Hooper). As we have made clear in previous chapters, these narrative films are the focus of this book. We'll discuss the narrative film as a type of movie (along with experimental and documentary films) later in this chapter.

Narrative is a way of structuring fictional or fictionalized stories presented in narrative films. Storytelling is a complicated business, especially when one is relating a multifaceted story involving multiple characters and conflicts over the course of two hours of screen time. Besides being a general term for a story or for a kind of movie, *narrative* is often used to describe the way that movie stories are constructed and presented in order to engage, involve, and orient an audience. This narrative structure—which includes exposition, rising action, climax, falling action, and denouement—helps filmmakers manipulate the viewer's cinematic experience by selectively conforming to or diverging from audience expectations of storytelling. Chapter 4 is devoted to this aspect of narrative.

Narrative is a broader concept that both includes and goes beyond any of these applications. Narrative can be defined in a broader conceptual context as any cinematic structure in which content is selected and arranged in a cause-and-effect sequence of events occurring over time. Any time a filmmaker consciously chooses and organizes material so that one event leads to another in a recognizable progression, that filmmaker is employing narrative in its most basic sense. In this case, narrative is not simply the telling of a fictional story, it is a structural quality that nearly every movie possesses, whether it's an avant-garde art film, a documentary account of actual events, or a blockbuster Hollywood fantasy.

Movies do not have to arrange events in conventional order to employ narrative organization. In *21 Grams* (2003), director Alejandro González Iñárritu and screenwriter Guillermo Arriaga arrange the events comprising the intersecting stories of ex-convict Jack (Benicio Del Toro), dying heart patient Paul (Sean Penn), and recovering cocaine addict Cristina (Naomi Watts) in a sequence motivated more by causality than chronology. A sequence in which Paul receives a heart transplant and Cristina loses her family propels the movie into a scene in which Paul approaches Cristina after he tracks her down as the person who saved his life by donating her recently deceased husband's heart. This personal connection is followed by the moments immediately preceding the death of Cristina's husband, the tragedy that will ultimately bring these two lost souls together. The next scene presents a devastated Jack resolving to turn himself in after leaving the scene of an accident that killed a man and his two daughters, knowing full well that his confession could send him back to prison. These events occur over time but are not connected by it. The scene-to-scene causality in this case is not motivated by chronology, but from the remorse, vulnerability, and sacrifice that bind the central characters. This particular approach to narrative demands a greater level of participation from viewers, who must actively engage the movie to recognize the connections presented and reassemble events into a chronology that will allow them to fully comprehend the story.

Although nonfiction filmmakers shooting documentary footage obviously can't always control the unstaged events happening before their cameras, contemporary documentary filmmakers often exploit their ability to select and arrange material in a cause-and-effect sequence of events. This very deliberate process may begin even before cameras roll. *Murderball* (2005) directors Henry Alex Rubin and Dana Adam Shapiro surely recognized the narrative potential of an international competition when they chose the months leading to the Paralympic Games in Athens, Greece, to chronicle a team of paraplegic wheelchair rugby players. Although the movie documents the off-court struggles of a variety of subjects, the film's events are very deliberately structured around the intense rivalry between Team USA star player Mark Zupan and Joe Soares, former Team USA member and now captain of Canada's team. Like a fictional sports film, *Murderball* reaches its climax in a suspenseful showdown between the two rival teams.

The nonfiction filmmaker's selective role is even more apparent in the Academy Award–winning documentary *Born into Brothels* (2004; directors: Zana Briski and Ross Kauffman). The film's events are structured around codirector Briski's explicitly stated intent to use photography to reach and ultimately rescue the children of prostitutes in Calcutta's red-light district. The film's events are arranged in a cause-and-effect structure strikingly similar to that of a conventional fiction movie, with the filmmakers themselves not only selecting and arranging events, but actively participating in them. Briski engages the children first by photographing

[3]

[1]

[4]

[2]

[5]

One thing leads to another The most elemental way of looking at narrative is as a cinematic structure that arranges events in a cause-and-effect sequence. This causality is the basic organizing structure of most movie narratives. Consider the principal events in one of the best-known movies of all time: *Star Wars* (1977; director: George Lucas): A starship is boarded by repressive Empire forces. The princess passenger records a plea for help on an android, which escapes to a desert planet. The roving android is captured by scavenging Jawas, who sell it to the farm family of Luke Skywalker, who discovers the message, which sends him in search of Obi-Wan Kenobi, who teaches him the way of the Force and accompanies him on a mission to rescue the princess. One event leads to another and another and another. Decisions are made, which lead to actions, which have consequences, which motivate reactions, which cause subsequent decisions, actions, and consequences. And so it goes. The viewer engages with this logical progression, anticipating probable developments, dreading some and hoping for others.

them, then by teaching them to take their own photographs. She works to convince the sex workers to allow her greater access to their children. As the children's talents emerge, she takes them on photo-taking expeditions to the beach and the zoo, and eventually stages a series of public exhibitions of their work. As the children grow in confidence and ability, the sequence of events builds to a conclusion that engaged and gratified mainstream audiences, as well as the Academy of Motion Picture Arts and Sciences, which awarded the film an Oscar for Best Documentary Film. Those documentary filmmakers who strive to avoid influencing the events they record still exert a great deal of narrative influence during the editing process.

Even experimental, or avant-garde, movies, most of which endeavor to break from the formulas and conventions of more mainstream narrative and documentary films, employ narrative according to our most general definition of the concept, despite being more concerned with innovation and experimentation than accessibility and entertainment.

The complex process of making movies discourages purely random constructions; filmmakers

[1]

[6]

[3]

[4]

[5]

[2]

Causal minimalism A fiction movie need not have a traditional goal-driven plot to be considered narrative. Richard Linklater's *Slacker* (1991) has no central character, no sustained conflict, and tells no single story: yet it employs a structure very much built upon cause-and-effect connections, however tenuous, between the young bohemians that drift in and out of the movie. Beginning with a man getting off a bus (played by Linklater himself), the camera follows one character to another, drifting through a succession of over a hundred individual participants as they cross paths in Austin, Texas. Each encounter leads to the next and so forth in an extended exercise in causal minimalism.

engaged with planning, capturing, selecting, and arranging footage tend to create sequences that grow logically in some way. The linear nature of motion pictures lends itself to structures that develop according to some form of progression, even if the resultant meaning is mostly impressionistic. Thus, nearly every movie, regardless of the label by which it is categorized, employs at least a loose interpretation of narrative.

Types of Movies

Films can be sorted according to a variety of systems. The film industry catalogs films according to how they are distributed (theatrical, television, straight to DVD, streaming, etc.); or how they are financed (by established studios or independent producers); or by their MPAA rating. Film festivals frequently separate entries according to running time. Film-studies curricula often group films by subject matter, the nation of origin, or the era or organized aesthetic movement that produced them.

The whole idea of breaking down an art form as multifaceted as motion pictures into strict classifications can be problematic. Although most movies fall squarely into a single category, many others defy exact classification by any standard. This is because cinematic expression exists along a continuum; no rule book enforcing set criteria exists. Throughout the history of the medium, innovative filmmakers have blurred boundaries and defied classification. Since this textbook is interested primarily in understanding motion-picture *form*, the categories of films that we will discuss below—narrative, documentary, and experimental—are focused on the filmmaker's intent and the final product's relationship with the viewer.

Narrative Movies

As we learned earlier, the primary relationship of a narrative film to its audience is that of a storyteller. Narrative films are so pervasive, so ingrained in our culture, that prior to reading this book, you may have never stopped to consider the designation *narrative film*. After all, to most of us, a narra-

tive movie is just a movie. We apply a label only to documentary or experimental films—movies that deviate from that "norm."

What distinguishes narrative films from these other kinds of movies, both of which also tell stories or utilize other formal aspects of narrative, is that narrative films are directed toward fiction. Even those narrative movies that purport to tell a true story, such as David Fincher's *The Social Network* (2010), adjust the stories they convey so as to better serve those principles of narrative structure that filmmakers use to engage and entertain audiences. Events are added or removed or rearranged; characters are composited: actors (who are usually more attractive than the actual participants they play) add elements of their own persona to the role. Audiences may be attracted to movies marketed as "based on a true story" perhaps because of the perception of immediacy or relevance that such a label imparts. But the truth is that very few "true stories" can deliver the narrative clarity and effect that audiences have come to expect from narrative films.

No matter what the source, typical narrative films are based on screenplays in which nearly every behavior and spoken line are predetermined. The characters are played by actors delivering dialogue and executing action in a manner that not only strives for verisimilitude, but also facilitates the technical demands of the motion-picture production process. These demands include coordinating their activity with lighting design and camera movement, and performing scenes out of logical chronological sequence. This action typically takes place in artificial worlds created on studio soundstages or in locations modified to suit the story and technical demands of production. The primary purpose of most narrative films is entertainment, a stance motivated by commercial intent.

Many narrative films can be broken down still further into categories known as genres. We'll explore that subject later in the chapter.

Documentary Movies

We might say that narrative film and documentary film differ primarily in terms of allegiance. Narrative film begins with a commitment to dramatic

[1]

[2]

[3]

Narrative commonality Even those narrative films bearing an overt ideological message or a dark theme are designed to engage an audience with a story. A twisted formal exercise like David Lynch's *Mulholland Dr.* (2001) [1], an earnest political thriller like Stephen Gaghan's *Syriana* (2005) [2], and an animated crowd-pleaser like Gore Verbinski's *Rango* (2011) [3], all deliver different messages and are each designed to appeal to a different audience. But they all employ the same narrative structures and techniques designed to transport viewers into a story, get them invested in the characters, and make them care about the end results, despite knowing up front that none of it is real.

storytelling: documentary film is more concerned with the recording of reality, the education of viewers, or the presentation of political or social analyses. In other words, if we think of a narrative movie

as fiction, then the best way to understand documentary film is as nonfiction.

But it would be a mistake to think that simply because documentary filmmakers use actual people, places, and events as source material, their films always reflect objective truth. Whatever their allegiance, all documentary filmmakers employ storytelling and dramatization to some degree in shaping their material. If they didn't, their footage might end up as unwatchably dull as a surveillance video recording everyday comings and goings. As the subsequent chapters will repeatedly illustrate, all elements of cinematic language—from the camera angle to the shot type to the lighting to the sound mix—color our perceptions of the material and are, thus, subjective to some degree. And no documentary subject that knows she is being filmed can ever behave exactly as she would off camera. So the unavoidable act of making the movie removes the possibility of a purely objective truth. And truth, of course, is in the eye of the beholder. Every documentary filmmaker has a personal perspective on the subject matter, whether she entered the production with a preexisting opinion or developed her point of view over the course of researching, shooting, and editing the movie. The informed documentary viewer should view these mediating factors thoughtfully, always trying to understand the ways in which the act of cinematic storytelling and the filmmaker's attitude toward the people and events depicted affect the interpretation of the truth up on the screen.

These complicating factors may have influenced film critic John Grierson, who originally coined the term *documentary* in 1926 to delineate cinema that observed life. Some time after he'd started making documentaries himself, Grierson described the approach as the "creative treatment of actuality." Robert J. Flaherty's pioneering documentary *Nanook of the North* (1922) demonstrates the complex relationship between documentary filmmaking and objective truth. Flaherty's movie included authentic "documentary" footage but also incorporated a great deal of staged reenactments. He reportedly encouraged the Inuit subjects to use older, more "traditional" hunting and fishing techniques for the film instead of their then-current practices.

However, no one who watches *Nanook* could argue that the film's portrayal of the Inuit and their nomadic northern lifestyle is a complete failure. The challenge for the viewer is to untangle *Nanook*'s nonfiction functions from its dramatic license, to view its anthropology apart from its artifice. Such a task requires a broad appreciation of both the movie and its subject from cinematic, historical, and scientific perspectives. We tend to assume that a wide separation exists between fact and fiction, historical reality and crafted story, truth and artifice. The difference, however, is never absolute in any film.

Historically, documentary films have been broken into four basic approaches: factual, instructional, persuasive, and propaganda. **Factual films,** including *Nanook of the North*, usually present people, places, or processes in straightforward ways meant to entertain and instruct without unduly influencing audiences. Early examples include some of the first movies made. In 1896, audiences marveled at the Lumière brothers' short, one-shot films documenting trains arriving, boats leaving, and soldiers marching off to the front. (At that time, the spectacle of moving images impressed viewers as much as, or more than, any particular subject matter.) More recent documentaries that could fall into the factual-documentary classification include Patrick Creadon's *Wordplay* (2006), an appreciation of the people who create and complete crossword puzzles.

Instructional films seek to educate viewers about common interests, rather than persuading them to accept particular ideas. Today, these movies are most likely to teach the viewer basic skills like cooking, yoga, or golf swings. They are not generally considered worthy of study or analysis.

Persuasive films were originally called *documentary films* until the term evolved to refer to all nonfiction films. The founding purpose of persuasive documentaries was to address social injustice, but today any documentary concerned with presenting a particular perspective on social issues or with corporate and governmental injustice of any kind could be considered persuasive. Director Davis Guggenheim's motivation in adapting Al Gore's global warming lecture into the documentary *An Inconvenient Truth* (2006) was not to simply entertain or inform audiences, but to persuade them to do something about climate change. Michael Moore's darkly humorous, self-aggrandizing documentaries take the persuasive documentary a step further. His confrontational and provocative movies address a series of left-of-center political causes, including health care (*Sicko*, 2007), gun control (*Bowling for Columbine*, 2002), and the Bush administration's role in the Iraq War (*Fahrenheit 9/11*, 2004).

When persuasive documentaries are produced by governments and carry governments' messages, they overlap with **propaganda films,** which systematically disseminate deceptive or distorted information. The most famous propaganda film ever made, Leni Riefenstahl's *Triumph of the Will* (1935), records many events at the 1934 Nuremberg rally of Germany's Nazi party and, thus, might mistakenly be considered a "factual" film. After all, no voice-over narration or on-screen commentator preaches a political message to the viewer. But through its carefully crafted cinematography and editing, this documentary presents a highly glori-

Nanook of the North Robert J. Flaherty's *Nanook of the North* (1922), a pioneering nonfiction film, gave general audiences their first visual encounter with Inuit culture. Its subject matter made it significant (and successful), and its use of narrative film techniques was pathbreaking. Flaherty edited together many different kinds of shots and angles, for example, and directed the Inuit through reenactments of life events, some of which—hunting with spears—were no longer part of their lives.

Triumph of the Will The most accomplished (and notorious) propaganda film of all time, Leni Riefenstahl's *Triumph of the Will* (1935), is studied by both historians and scholars of film. Much of the blocking of the 1934 Nuremberg Nazi rally was crafted specifically with the camera in mind. [1] Riefenstahl, wearing a white dress and helping to push the camera, films a procession during the rally. [2] Taken from a distant perspective, this shot conveys many concepts that the filmmaker and the Nazis wanted the world to see: order, discipline, and magnitude.

fied image of Adolf Hitler and his Nazi followers for the consumption of non-German audiences before World War II.

Over a century of documentary innovation has blurred the distinctions between these four historical categories. Most documentary movies we consider worthy of study today are hybrids that combine qualities of two or more of these foundational approaches to nonfiction filmmaking. This versatility is one reason that documentary is enjoying a renaissance unprecedented in the history of cinema.

Barbara Kopple's *Harlan County USA* (1976) is an example of the nonfiction filmmaking style known as **direct cinema**. While many documentaries include on-screen or over-the-shoulder interviewers having conversations with subjects (in the segments on television's *60 Minutes*, for example), direct-cinema documentaries eschew interviewers and even limit the use of narrators. Instead of having voice-over narration to encourage the audience's indignation about the crime, scandal, or corruption being exposed, direct cinema involves the placement of small portable cameras and sound-recording equipment in an important location for days or weeks, recording events as they occur. The resulting documentary may never include a question from an interviewer; instead, it enables the audience to overhear conversations and interactions as they happen. *Harlan County USA* documents a yearlong Kentucky coal miners' strike in 1973–74. Risking her life and the lives of her crew, Kopple aligned herself with the United Mine Workers of America, who were intimidated and sometimes shot at by strikebreakers for the Eastover Mining Company. During the film, Kopple's cameras begin to focus on the coal miners' wives, who encourage, cajole, and chastise their men to maintain the strike,

[1]

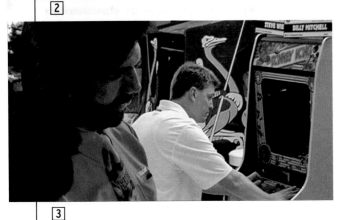

[2]

[3]

walk the picket lines, and hold their families and communities together. While direct cinema can help reveal a subject in profound and unexpected ways, this technique may not remove the narrative voice and perspective as much as hide it or transfer its function to the more "invisible" power of other filmmaking systems. The editing process, for example, can include and exclude materials, ironically juxtapose people, events, and ideas, and arrange and order reality to suit the filmmaker's perspective.

Documentary filmmakers continue to employ conventional formal elements such as interviews, voice-over narration, and archival footage in innovative ways to create new and compelling nonfiction forms. Director Ken Burns seeks to bring history alive by presenting historical documents, archival photographs, painterly location shots, and posed artifacts to public-television audiences in a formalized style very different from the handheld "fly on the wall" perspective offered by direct-cinema documentaries. He has been known to film thousands of historical photographs in his signature manner, where the camera glides and the framing tightens; such "dramatic" camera movements emphasize details and link them to the narration and historical observations. Burns's use of the effect became so ubiquitous that Apple computers incorporated it into their home-movie-

Documentary storytelling Many documentary filmmakers select subjects that offer potential narrative development. The resulting movie may be considered factual, or even persuasive in some ways. But the content need not be "important." Rather, the movie's primary intent is to entertain and involve audiences with the struggles of goal-driven protagonists. The efforts of a hapless but relentless Wisconsin filmmaker to marshal the resources and support necessary to complete a low-budget horror film is the subject of Chris Smith's *American Movie* (1999) [1]. S. R. Bindler's *Hands on a Hard Body* (1997) follows twenty-four desperate contestants through a grueling and often dehumanizing endurance contest to win a new pickup truck [2]. Seth Gordon's *The King of Kong: A Fistful of Quarters* (2007) explores the strange, obsessive world of classic-arcade-game enthusiasts by chronicling the efforts of high-school math teacher Steve Wiebe's attempts to achieve the official world-record score in Donkey Kong, despite the efforts of the competitive gaming establishment to preserve that distinction for their hero, Billy Mitchell [3].

[1]

[2]

Direct cinema Documentaries made in the style known as direct cinema attempt to immerse the viewer in an experience as close as is cinematically possible to witnessing events as an invisible observer. Direct-cinema films like Albert and David Maysles's *Grey Gardens* (1975; with codirectors Ellen Hovde and Muffie Meyer) seek to avoid conventional documentary techniques such as interviews and voice-over narration, and instead rely on very small crews and lightweight, handheld camera and sound equipment to capture the action as unobtrusively as possible. As they filmed *Grey Gardens*, the Maysleses observed that their extroverted subject "Little Edie" Beale was becoming increasingly more interested in performing for the filmmakers than in ignoring their presence. Some direct-cinema purists may have discouraged or deleted her behavior, but the Maysleses recognized Edie's need for recognition, and the delusions that fueled it, as a crucial part of her reality. The filmmakers acknowledged their own role in the situation by incorporating their own image (as captured in a mirror) into the movie.

editing software iMovie and openly identified it as the "Ken Burns Effect."

Many documentaries investigate events that happened in the past, but some of these cinematic investigations are more personal than historical. The approach of films like Andrew Jarecki's *Capturing the Friedmans* (2003) rejects presenting a single "factual" interpretative stance in favor of offering a more ambiguous range of often-conflicting accounts. *Capturing the Friedmans* explores accusations of child molestation leveled at Arnold Friedman and his teenage son, Jesse, from multiple perspectives through a collage of home movies, archival media coverage, and interviews with both family members and alleged victims.

Director Errol Morris incorporates cinematic techniques normally associated with highly stylized narrative and experimental films into the typically spartan documentary form. *Fast, Cheap & Out of Control* (1997) implies profound associations between his seemingly diverse subjects—a topiary gardener, a lion tamer, a robotics researcher, and a scientist studying naked mole rats—by intercutting interviews of all four men and lacing the movie with artfully crafted extreme close-ups, beautiful slow-motion effects, footage from old adventure films, abstracted reenactments, and original music by Caleb Sampson. Morris is famous for conducting his interviews using an Interrotron, a device of his own invention that projects the director's face onto a glass plate placed over the camera lens. The apparatus allows the subject to address responses directly into the lens, which establishes direct eye contact with the viewer.

Experimental Movies

Experimental is the most difficult of all types of movies to define with any precision, in part because experimental filmmakers actively seek to

Exit Through the Gift Shop The Academy Award nominated documentary *Exit Through the Gift Shop* (2010; director: Banksy), tests the boundaries between observation and exploitation, fiction and nonfiction. What begins as a rambling archive of street art shot by a somewhat incompetent enthusiast named Theirry Guetta turns into a movie about Guetta himself when one of his subjects (the mysterious and wildly successful artist known as Banksy) appropriates the footage, takes over the camera, and turns Guetta into a pseudo-celebrity called Mr. Brainwash. Banksy uses his considerable clout to influence the art world and his subject, and records the results as the fame-hungry Guetta (and a small army of paid assistants) mounts a huge exhibit of new artworks credited to Mr. Brainwash. Is Mr. Guetta Banksy's dupe or his wily collaborator? Is this movie art, or is the entire premise a hoax designed as a critique of art? Can a movie be a documentary when the filmmaker actively manipulates the people and events he documents? Does the precise nature of truth matter, so long as the results are entertaining? Parsing these questions is a part of the experience of watching *Exit Through the Gift Shop*.

defy categorization and convention. For starters, it's helpful to think of experimental cinema as that which pushes the boundaries of what most people think movies are—or should be. After all, *avant-garde*, the term originally applied to this approach to filmmaking, comes from a French phrase used to describe scouts and pathfinders who explored ahead of an advancing army, implying that avant-garde artists, whether in film or another medium, are innovators who lead, rather than follow, the pack. The term *experimental* falls along these same lines. It's an attempt to capture the innovative spirit of an approach to moviemaking that plays with the medium, is not bound by established traditions, and is dedicated to exploring possibility. Both *avant-garde* and *experimental* (and other

terms) are still used to describe this kind of movie. But since *experimental* is the word most commonly used, is appropriately evocative, and is in English, let's stick with it.

In response to the often-asked question "What is an experimental film?" film scholar Fred Camper offers six criteria that outline the basic characteristics that most experimental films share. While no criterion can hope to encapsulate an approach to filmmaking as vigorously diverse as experimental cinema, a summarization of Camper's list of common qualities is a good place to start:

1. *Experimental films are not commercial.* They are made by single filmmakers (or collaborative teams consisting of, at most, a few artists) for very low budgets and with no expectation of financial gain.
2. *Experimental films are personal.* They reflect the creative vision of a single artist who typically conceives, writes, directs, shoots, and edits the movie by him- or herself with minimal contributions by other filmmakers or technicians. Experimental film credits are short.
3. *Experimental films do not conform to conventional expectations of story and narrative cause and effect.*
4. *Experimental films exploit the possibilities of the cinema* and, by doing so, often reveal (and revel in) tactile and mechanical qualities of motion pictures that conventional movies seek to obscure. Most conventional narrative films are constructed to make audiences forget they are watching a movie, whereas many experimental films repeatedly remind the viewer of the fact. They embrace innovative techniques that call attention to, question, and even challenge their own artifice.
5. *Experimental films critique culture and media.* From their position outside the mainstream, they often comment on (and intentionally frustrate) viewer expectations of what a movie should be.
6. *Experimental films invite individual interpretation.* Like abstract expressionist paint-

ings, they resist the kind of accessible and universal meaning found in conventional narrative and documentary films.[1]

Because most experimental films do not tell a story in the conventional sense, incorporate unorthodox imagery, and are motivated more by innovation and personal expression than by commerce and entertainment, they help us understand in yet another way why movies are a form of art capable of a sort of motion-picture equivalent of poetry. Disregarding the traditional expectations of audiences, experimental films remind us that film—like painting, sculpture, music, or architecture—can be made in as many ways as there are artists.

For example, Michael Snow's *Wavelength* (1967) is a 45-minute film that consists, in what we see, only of an exceedingly slow zoom lens shot through a loft. Although human figures wander in and out of the frame, departing at will from that frame or being excluded from it as the camera moves slowly past them, the film is almost totally devoid of any human significance. Snow's central concern is space: how to conceive it, film it, and encourage viewers to make meaning of it. *Wavelength* is replete with differing qualities of space, light, exposures, focal lengths, and printing techniques, all offering rich possibilities for how we perceive these elements and interpret their meaning. For those who believe that a movie must represent the human condition, *Wavelength* seems empty. But for those who believe, with D. W. Griffith, that a movie is meant, above all, to make us see, the work demonstrates the importance of utterly unconventional filmmaking.

Su Friedrich's experimental films also "make us see," but in different ways. Friedrich's *Sink or Swim* (1990) opens abstractly with what seems to be scientific footage—a microscope's view of sperm cells, splitting cells, a developing fetus—inexplicably narrated by a young girl's voice recounting the mythological relationship between the goddess Athena and her father, Zeus. As the movie's remaining

Experimental film: style as subject Among many other random repetitions and animations, Fernand Léger and Dudley Murphy's *Ballet Mécanique* (1924) repeatedly loops footage of a woman climbing stairs. This action lacks completion or narrative purpose and instead functions as a rhythmic counterpart to other sections of the film, in which more abstract objects are animated and choreographed in (as the title puts it) a "mechanical ballet."

[1]Fred Camper, "Naming, and Defining, Avant-Garde or Experimental Film" (n.d.), http://www.fredcamper.com/Film/Avant GardeDefinition.html.

[1]

[2]

[3]

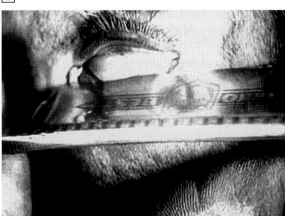

[4]

Experimental film: image as shock Luis Buñuel and Salvador Dalí collaborated to produce *An Andalusian Dog* (1929), one of the most famous experimental films. Through special effects, its notorious opening sequence can be summarized in four shots: [1] the title, "Once upon a time . . . ," which, under the circumstances, is an absurd use of the classic beginning of a nursery story; [2] an image of a man (who has just finished sharpening his straight razor); [3] an image of the hand of a differently dressed man holding a razor near a woman's eyeball with the implication that he will slit it; and [4] an image of a slit eyeball. There is no logic to this sequence, for the woman's eye is not slit; rather the slit eyeball appears to belong to an animal. The sequence is meant to shock the viewer, to surprise us, to make us "see" differently, but not to explain what we are seeing.

25 segments unfold, the offscreen girl narrator shifts from mythological accounts of paternal relationships to third-person accounts of episodes between a contemporary girl and her father. The episodes are illustrated with candid documentary footage, often featuring men and girls at play, and with what appear to be home movies, edited in a way that obscures their origins. The footage sometimes enforces the narration's mood and content but just as often conflicts with the girl's story or combines with it so that additional meaning is imparted to both image and spoken word. As the successive layers are revealed, what began as an apparent abstract exercise reveals itself as an autobiographical account of the filmmaker's troubled relationship with her distant and demanding father. Ironically, this experimental approach ultimately delivers a more emotionally complex and

involving experience than most conventional narrative or documentary treatments of similar subject matter.

While *Wavelength* explores cinematic space and *Sink or Swim* focuses on personal expression, other experimental films are primarily concerned with the tactile and communicative qualities of the film medium itself. These movies scavenge found footage—originally created by other filmmakers for other purposes—and then manipulate the gleaned images to create new meanings and aesthetics not intended by the artists or technicians who shot the original footage.

To create *Tribulation 99: Alien Anomalies under America* (1992), his feature-length satire of paranoid conspiracy theories, Craig Baldwin collected thousands of still and moving images from a wide variety of mostly vintage sources, including educational films, scientific studies, and low-budget horror movies. By combining, superimposing, and sequencing selected shots, and overlaying the result with ominous text and urgent voice-over narration, Baldwin changes the image context and meaning, thus transforming the way audiences interpret and experience the footage.

Experimental filmmaker Martin Arnold also manipulates preexisting footage to alter the viewer's interpretation and experience with a method that is in many ways the reverse of Baldwin's frenetic collage approach. Arnold's most famous film, *Passage à l'acte* (1993), uses only one sequence from a single source: a short, relatively mundane breakfast-table scene from Robert Mulligan's narrative feature *To Kill a Mockingbird* (1962). Using an optical printer, which allows the operator to duplicate one film frame at a time onto a new strip of film stock, Arnold stretched the 34-second sequence to over 11 minutes by rhythmically repeating every moment in the scene. The result forces us to see the familiar characters and situation in an entirely new way. What was originally an innocent and largely inconsequential exchange is infused with conflict and tension. Through multiple and rapid-fire repetitions, a simple gesture such as putting down a fork or glancing sideways becomes a hostile or provocative gesture, a mechanical loop, or an abstract dance. Like many experimental films, *Passage à l'acte* deliberately challenges the viewer's ingrained expectations of narrative, coherence, continuity, movement, and forward momentum. The resulting experience is hypnotic, musical, disturbing, fascinating, and infuriating.

It's easy to assume that films that test the audience's expectations of how a movie should behave are a relatively recent phenomenon. But the truth is that filmmakers have been experimenting with film form and reception since the very early days of cinema. In the 1920s, the first truly experimental movement was born in France, with its national climate of avant-garde artistic expression. Among the most notable works were films by painters: René Clair's *Entr'acte* (1924), Fernand Léger and Dudley Murphy's *Ballet mécanique* (1924), Marcel Duchamp's *Anémic cinéma* (1926), and Man Ray's *Emak-Bakia* (1926). These films are characterized uniformly by their surreal content, often dependent on dream impressions rather than objective observation; their abstract images, which tend to be shapes and patterns with no meaning other than the forms themselves; their absence of actors performing within a narrative context; and their desire to shock not only our sensibilities but also our morals. The most important of these films, the surrealist dreamscape *An Andalusian Dog* (1929), was made in France by the Spanish filmmaker Luis Buñuel and the Spanish painter Salvador Dalí. Re-creating the sexual nature of dreams, this film's images metamorphose continually, defy continuity, and even attack causality—as in one scene when a pair of breasts dissolves into buttocks.

Although an alternative cinema has existed in the United States since the 1920s—an achievement of substance and style that is all the more remarkable in a country where filmmaking is synonymous with Hollywood—the first experimental filmmakers here were either European-born or influenced by the French, Russians, and Germans. The first major American experimental filmmaker was Maya Deren, whose surreal films—*Meshes of the Afternoon* (1943), codirected with her husband, Alexander Hammid, is the best known—virtually established alternative filmmaking in this country. Deren's work combines her interests in various fields, including film, philosophy, ethnography, and dance,

[1]

[2]

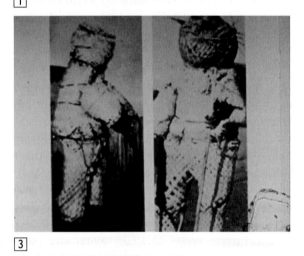

[3]

[4]

[5]

Rearranged footage A sequence in Craig Baldwin's *Tribulation 99: Alien Anomalies under America* (1992) presents successive images of Mayan carvings [1], Lucha Libre masked wrestlers [2], natives in ceremonial woven suits [3], hooded prisoners [4], and nature footage of snakes [5] to illustrate the narration's breathless claim that displaced aliens hiding below the earth's surface have been forced to mate with reptiles. The power of editing to create meaning through juxtaposition allowed Baldwin to mutate his seemingly random collection of images of wildly disparate origins into a cohesive, if bizarre, story of the malevolent aliens emerging from their subterranean lair to attempt world domination.

and it remains the touchstone for those studying avant-garde movies.

Concerned with the manipulation of space and time, which, after all, is the essence of filmmaking,

Deren experimented with defying continuity, erasing the line between dream and reality. She used the cinematic equivalent of **stream of consciousness,** a literary style that gained prominence in the 1920s in the hands of such writers as Marcel Proust, Virginia Woolf, James Joyce, and Dorothy

Manipulated footage Naomi Uman's *Removed* (1999) employs a reductive approach to found-footage filmmaking that made audiences reinterpret and reexamine previously existing footage. She used nail polish and bleach to remove the female character from the emulsion of all 10,000 frames of a 7-minute pornographic movie. The result forces the viewer to experience the objectification of women in a literal—or at least graphic—sense. The film's female character appears as an animated blank space, which is physically manipulated by the male actors.

Richardson and that attempted to capture the unedited flow of experience through the mind. In *Meshes*, Deren is both the creative mind behind the film and the creative performer on the screen. She takes certain recognizable motifs—a key, a knife, a flower, a telephone receiver, and a shadowy figure walking down a garden path—and repeats them throughout the film, each time transfiguring them into something else. So, for example, the knife evolves into a key and the flower into a knife. These changing motifs are linked visually but also structurally. Deren's ideas and achievements bridge the gap between the surrealism of the French avant-garde films and such dream-related movies as Alain Resnais's *Last Year at Marienbad* (1961), Federico Fellini's *8½* (1963), Ingmar Bergman's *Persona* (1966), and Luis Buñuel's *The Milky Way* (1969).

Greatly influenced by Deren's work, an American underground cinema emerged in the 1950s and has since favored four subgenres—the formal, the self-reflexive, the satirical, and the sexual—each of which tends to include aspects of the lyrical approach so typical of Deren. Works of pure form include John Whitney's early experiments with computer imagery in such films as *Matrix I* and *Matrix II* (both 1971); Shirley Clarke's *Skyscraper* (1960), one of several lighthearted, abstract tributes to city life; Peter Kubelka's *Arnulf Rainer* (1960), which created its images through abstract dots; Jordan Belson's *Allures* (1961), using abstract color animation; Robert Breer's *Fist Fight* (1964), which combines animation, images of handwriting, and other material; and Ernie Gehr's *The Astronomer's Dream* (2004), in which he speeds up the images so much that they become vertical purple lines.

Self-reflexive films, meaning those that represent their own conditions of production (movies, in other words, about movies, moviemaking, moviemakers, and so on), include Hans Richter's *Dreams That Money Can Buy* (1947), in the spirit of surrealism; Stan Brakhage's five-part *Dog Star Man* (1962–64), whose lyricism is greatly influenced by Deren's work; Bruce Baillie's *Mass for the Dakota Sioux* (1964), which combines a lyrical vision and social commentary; Hollis Frampton's *Zorn's Lemma* (1970), a complex meditation on cinematic structure, space, and movement; and Michael Snow's *Wavelength* (1967), which we already discussed.

Films that take a satirical view of life include James Broughton's *Mother's Day* (1948), on childhood; Stan van der Beek's *Death Breath* (1964), an apocalyptic vision using cartoons and other imagery; Bruce Conner's *Marilyn Times Five* (1973), which makes its comic points by compiling stock footage from other sources; and Mike Kuchar's *Sins of the Fleshapoids* (1965), an underground look at the horror genre.

Satirical and sexual films often overlap, particularly in their portrayal of sexual activities that challenge conventional ideas of "normality." Examples of these include Kenneth Anger's *Scorpio Rising* (1964), an explicit homosexual fantasy that is tame by today's standards; Jack Smith's *Flaming Creatures* (1963), a major test case for pornography laws; and many of Andy Warhol's films, including *Lonesome Cowboys* (1968). The directors who made these films tended to be obsessed, as was Deren, with expressing themselves and their subconscious through cinematic forms and images.

These days, movies that seem to be in direct opposition to Camper's experimental film criteria dominate our culture. Popular cinema is largely commercial, universal, and narrative. When most of us think of movies, we picture movies that conceal their artifice, reinforce viewer expectations, and seek a common, accessible interpretation.

While purely experimental cinema rarely penetrates into the mainstream, this highly personal and innovative approach to cinematic expression continues to thrive on the fringes of popular culture. A grass-roots "microcinema" subculture has grown out of the affordability and accessibility of digital video formats, personal computer–based editing systems, and video-hosting Web sites like YouTube and Vimeo. Most film festivals, from the most influential international competitions to the smallest local showcases, feature experimental programs. Many prestigious film festivals specializing in experimental cinema, such as the Ann Arbor Film Festival, attract hundreds of submissions and thousands of patrons each year. International organizations like Flickr provide experimental filmmakers with an online venue to share and promote their work. Peripheral Produce and Invisible Cinema are among a growing number of companies and cooperatives that distribute experimental film and video compilations on DVD. Many art museums consider experimental applications of cinematic principles a fine-art form worthy of public display along with painting and sculpture. Artists such as Bill Viola and Matthew Barney have attracted great attention to their avant-garde video installations, which change the traditional ways in which viewers experience and interact with moving images.

And, finally, while truly experimental films rarely if ever reach mass audiences, experimental approaches to narrative construction, visual style, and editing techniques do often find their way into movies made by filmmakers sympathetic to the avant-garde's spirit of invention. Many of the Hollywood directors incorporating experimental techniques developed a taste for unconventional innovation in film school or art school, or while honing their craft on music videos, commercials, and independent art films. These filmmakers include David Lynch (*Inland Empire*, 2006), Spike Jonze (*Where the Wild Things Are*, 2009); Michel Gondry (*The Science of Sleep*, 2006), Richard Linklater (*A*

Scanner Darkly, 2006), and Charlie Kaufman (*Synecdoche, New York*, 2008). Experimental sensibilities have emerged in a growing number of mainstream productions, from Christian Wagner's wildly kinetic editing in Tony Scott movies like *Man on Fire* (2004) and *Domino* (2005), to the simulated found-footage sequence that opens each episode of the HBO dramatic series *True Blood* (2008).

Hybrid Movies

The flexibility of film form has made cross-pollination among experimental, documentary, and narrative approaches an inevitable and desirable aspect of cinematic evolution. The resulting hybrids have blurred what were once distinct borders among the three primary film-type categories. For example, Roger Beebe's experimental movie *The Strip Mall Trilogy* (2001) documents a mile-long stretch of strip malls in Florida but so isolates and abstracts the images that he evokes meanings that

Documentary/narrative fusion Larry Charles's *Borat: Cultural Learnings of America for Make Benefit Glorious Nation of Kazakhstan* (2006) pushes the documentary/narrative marriage to its extreme by placing the fictional character of Borat (Sacha Baron Cohen) in real-life situations with people who were led to believe that they (and Borat) were the subjects of a documentary about a foreign reporter's exploration of American culture. The result functions as both documentary and narrative: we experience a very deliberately structured character pursuing a clearly defined goal, but that pursuit is punctuated with a series of spontaneous explosions of authentic human behavior provoked and manipulated by Borat/Cohen and captured by a documentary film crew.

[1]

[2]

Film-type fusion Perhaps the film that best exemplifies the fusion of narrative, documentary, and experimental film types is William Greaves's *Symbiopsychotaxiplasm: Take One* (1968). Greaves employed three camera crews and instructed the first crew to shoot only the series of actors performing the scripted scene, the second crew to film the first crew shooting the scene [1], and the third to shoot the entire multileveled production as well as anything else they judged footage-worthy going on around them. The edited film frequently uses split screen to present several of its multiple layers simultaneously [2]. Greaves intentionally provoked his various crews and casts with vague or contradictory directions until what amounts to a civil war erupted as some of the film professionals involved began to question the director's intentions and methods. Greaves, who functioned as the director of the actors as well as a sort of actor himself in the dual layers of documentary footage, made sure that every aspect of the ensuing chaos—including private crew meetings criticizing the project—was captured on film and was eventually combined into an experimental amalgam that breaks down audience expectations of narrative and documentary, artifice and reality.[2]

rowing works in both directions. Contemporary directors such as Jean-Pierre and Luc Dardenne (*The Kid with a Bike,* 2011), Lance Hammer (*Ballast,* 2008), Darren Aronofsky (*The Wrestler,* 2008), Zack Godshall (*Lord Byron,* 2011), and Kelly Reichardt (*Meek's Cutoff,* 2010) use small crews, natural lighting, handheld cameras, and nonactors (alongside deglamorized professionals) to lend their gritty narrative films the sense of authentic realism associated with documentary aesthetics and techniques.[3]

Genre

Our brief survey of documentary and experimental cinema demonstrates that both of these primary types of movies can be further divided into defined

transcend any architectural or anthropological investigation of commercial suburban development. Ray Tintori's narrative movie *Death to the Tinman* (2007) most certainly tells a story, but does so with narration, cinematography, performance, and production-design stylings that subvert audience expectations as only an experimental film can.

We've already discussed the importance of narrative to many documentary films. A growing number of narrative feature films that incorporate documentary techniques demonstrate that the bor-

[2]Amy Taubin, "*Symbiopsychotaxiplasm*: Still No Answers," Criterion Collection DVD Liner Notes: (December 5, 2006), http://www.criterion.com/current/posts/460.

[3]Many thanks to Dr. James Kruel and University of North Carolina Wilmington professors Shannon Silva, Andre Silva, and Dr. J. Carlos Kase for some of the ideas in this analysis.

subcategories. These distinctions are both useful and inevitable. Any art form practiced by ambitious innovators and consumed by a diverse and evolving culture can't help but develop in multiple directions. When filmmakers and their audiences recognize and value particular approaches to both form and content, these documentary or experimental subcategories are further differentiated and defined. And the moment such a distinction is accepted, filmmakers and viewers will begin again to refine, revise, and recombine the elements that defined the new categorization in the first place.

Genre refers to the categorization of narrative films by the stories they tell and the ways they tell them. Commonly recognized movie genres include the Western, horror, science fiction, musical, and gangster film. But this is far from a complete list. The film industry continues to make action movies, biographies (biopics), melodramas, thrillers, romances, romantic comedies, fantasy films, and many others that fall within some genre or subgenre category.

A long list like that may lead you to believe that all films are genre movies. Not so. A quick scan of the movies in theaters during a single week in 2011 reveals many narrative films that tell stories and employ styles that don't fit neatly into any existing genre template. The nongenre titles filling out the top fifteen box-office leaders during the week of June 24, 2011, for example, included *Midnight in Paris* (Woody Allen), *The Tree of Life* (Terrence Malick), *Bad Teacher* (Jake Kasdan), *Mr. Popper's Penguins* (Mark Waters), and *Judy Moody and the NOT Bummer Summer* (John Schultz). And genre is certainly not the only way that narrative movies are classified. The film industry breaks down films according to studio of origin, budget, target audience, and distribution patterns. Moviegoers often make viewing decisions according to the directors and/or stars of the films available. Film scholars may categorize and analyze a movie based on a wide range of criteria, including its specific aesthetic style, the artists who created it, its country or region of origin, the apparent ideologies expressed by its style or subject matter, or the particular organized cinematic movement from which it emerged.

Cinema of ideas All cinema is about ideas—many about the idea of cinema itself—and there are many ways to approach making one. Some filmmakers find nothing more challenging than making a movie about an idea for its own sake. With *The Tree of Life* (2011), writer/director Terrence Malick gently deals with such abstract ideas as life and death, love, family, joy and sorrow, the flow of time, and whether or not eternity exists. Its visual impact, produced by vivid images of our natural world, creates an overlaying structure, under which he gently tucks a beautifully realized account of one family's life in the 1950s American Southwest, thus letting us experience the universe and the individual. But its principal purpose, like that of all cinema, is to make us see and help us understand its ideas.

Unlike these film movements (such as French New Wave or Dogme 95), in which a group of like-minded filmmakers consciously conspire to create a particular approach to film style and story, film genres tend to spring up organically, inspired by shifts in history, politics, or society. Genres are often brought about inadvertently—not through any conscious plan, but rather because of a cultural need to explore and express issues and ideas through images and stories. Many classic genres, including Westerns, horror, and science fiction, emerged in literature and evolved into cinematic form during the twentieth century. Others, such as the musical, originated on the Broadway and vaudeville stages before hitting the screen. Some, like the gangster film, were born and bred in the cinema. Cultural conditions inspire artists to tell certain kinds of stories (and audiences to respond to them), the nature of those narratives motivates certain technical and aesthetic approaches, and eventually the accumulation of like-minded movies is detected, labeled, studied, and explicated by cinema scholars.

[1]

[2]

[3]

Genre study Scholars find genre films to be especially rich artifacts that can reveal a great deal about the culture that produced and consumed them, as well as about the filmmakers who made them. What does Martin Scorsese, a director associated with gangster films such as *Mean Streets* (1973) [1], and *Goodfellas* (1990) [2], do with a musical like *New York New York* (1977) [3]? What do the forty-eight or so thrillers that Alfred Hitchcock produced in a prolific fifty-year span tell us about the evolution of our popular culture, film style, the movie business . . . and Hitchcock himself?

And, of course, academic scholars are not the only movie lovers who find it useful to categorize films by genre. Genre has a significant effect on how audiences choose the movies they attend, rent, or purchase. Movie reviewers often critique a film based on how it stacks up against others in its genre. Most movie-rental retailers organize movies according to genre (along with more general catchall classifications like drama and comedy). Online and newspaper theater listings include a movie's genre alongside its rating, running time, and show time. Of the aforementioned fifteen top-grossing movies for the weekend of June 24, 2011, at least nine could be considered genre films: *The Green Lantern* (Martin Campbell), *X-Men: First Class* (Matthew Vaughn), and *Thor* (Kenneth Branagh) are all part of the action movie subgenre dedicated to comic book adaptations; *Fast Five* (Justin Lin) is a full-blown action movie; *Super 8* (J. J. Abrams) is a science-fiction thriller; and *Pirates of the Caribbean: On Stranger Tides* (Rob Marshall) updates the classic swashbuckler movie. Two top-grossing animated kid's movie sequels have adopted action film subgenres: *Kung Fu Panda 2* (Jennifer Yuh) is a martial arts film, and *Cars 2* (John Lasseter and Brad Lewis) is a spy thriller. There's no official name for the emerging genre that places anthropomorphized celebrity-voiced animals in straightforward, goal-driven plots that speak to children's fears of (among other things) parental abandonment. But this particular kind of movie has been around since *Dumbo* (1941; director: Ben Sharpsteen) and lives on this particular weekend in the form of *Rio* (Carlos Saldanha).

Since genre labels allow us to predict with reasonable certainty what sort of movie to expect, these classifications don't just help audiences make their viewing choices; the people that finance movies often must account for genre when deciding which projects to bankroll.

Genres offer familiar story formulas, conventions, themes, and conflicts, as well as immediately recognizable visual icons, all of which together provide a blueprint for creating and marketing a type of film that has proven successful in the past. Studios and distributors can develop genre-identified stars, select directors on the basis of proven proficiency in a particular genre; piggyback on the success of a previous genre hit; and even recycle props, sets, costumes, and digital backgrounds. Just as important, the industry counts on genre to predict ticket sales, presell markets, and cash in on recent trends by making films that allow consumers to predict they'll like a particular movie. In other words: give people what they want, and they will buy it. This simple economic principle helps us understand the phenomenal growth of the movie industry from the 1930s on, as well as the mind-numbing mediocrity of so many of the movies the industry produces. The kind of strict adherence to genre convention driven solely by economics often yields derivative and formulaic results.

If genre films are prone to mediocrity, why are so many great filmmakers drawn to making them? The beginning of the answer can be found, of all places, in a statement by the Nobel Prize–winning poet T. S. Eliot, who wrote: "When forced to work within a strict framework, the imagination is taxed to its utmost—and will produce its richest ideas." Eliot was talking about poetry, but the same concept can be applied to cinema. Creatively ambitious writers and directors often challenge themselves to create art within the strict confines of genre convention. A genre's so-called rules can provide a foundation upon which the filmmaker can both honor traditions and innovate change. The resulting stories and styles often expertly fulfill some expectations while surprising and subverting others as the filmmaker references, refutes, and revises well-established cultural associations. Genre has intrigued so many of our greatest American and European filmmakers that many entries in the canon of important and transformative movies are genre films. *The Godfather* (1972; director: Francis Ford Coppola), *Goodfellas* (1990; director: Martin Scorsese), and *Bonnie and Clyde* (1967; director: Arthur Penn) are all gangster films; Stanley Kubrick's *2001: A Space Odyssey* (1968) is science fiction; Carol Reed's *The Third Man* (1949) and even Jean-Luc Godard's

Genre masterpieces Not all genre movies are disposable formula pictures churned out for the indiscriminate masses. Many of cinema's most revered films are also genre movies. Stanley Kubrick's *2001: A Space Odyssey* (1968) incorporates virtually every standard science-fiction genre element, including speculative setting, special effects, and a decided ambivalence toward the benefits of technology. Yet Kubrick's skills as a storyteller and stylist make 2001 a work of art that transcends conventional attitudes toward genre movies.

Breathless (1960) could be considered film noir; Woody Allen's *Annie Hall* (1977) is a romantic comedy; John Ford's *The Searchers* (1956) is a Western, as is Sergio Leone's *The Good, the Bad and the Ugly* (1966); Stanley Donen and Gene Kelly's *Singin' in the Rain* (1952) is a musical; David Lean's *Lawrence of Arabia* (1962) is a biography and a war movie and an epic.

But audiences don't like just the classic films that transcend genre conventions. Genre films have been prevalent since the earliest days of cinema because, contrary to popular perceptions, most movie viewers value predictability over novelty. Elements of certain genres appeal to us, so we seek to repeat an entertaining or engaging cinema experience by viewing a film that promises the same surefire ingredients. There is a certain pleasure that comes from seeing how different filmmakers and performers have rearranged and interpreted familiar elements, just as there is an exhilarating pleasure to be found in an unexpected deviation from the anticipated path. To put this relationship into gastronomic terms: the most common pizza features a flour-based crust topped with tomato sauce and mozzarella cheese, but it's the potential variety within that familiar foundation that has made pizza one of America's favorite foods.

A less obvious but perhaps more profound explanation for the persistent prevalence of genre lies in the deep roots genre has in our society. Remember that any given genre naturally emerges and crystallizes not because Hollywood thinks it'll sell, but because it gives narrative voice to something essential to our culture. The film industry may ultimately exploit a genre's cultural resonance, but only after cultural conditions motivate enough individual artists and viewers to create the genre in the first place. No studio executive or directors' club decided to invent horror movies out of thin air. Horror movies exist because of our collective fear of death and the human psyche's need for catharsis. Westerns enact and endorse aspects of American history and the human condition that Americans have needed to believe about themselves. We go to these movies not only to celebrate the familiar, but to enforce fundamental beliefs and passively perform cultural rituals. As our world evolves and audience perspectives change, genre movies adapt to reflect these cultural shifts. A Western made during the can-do patriotism of World War II is likely to express its themes differently than one produced at the height of the Vietnam War.

Genre Conventions

Movie genres are defined by sets of conventions—aspects of storytelling such as recurring themes and situations, setting, character types, and story formula, as well as aspects of presentation and visual style such as decor, lighting, and sound. Even the movie stars associated with a particular genre can be considered one of these defining conventions. Keep in mind that these conventions are not enforced; filmmakers don't follow mandated genre checklists. While every movie within any particular genre will incorporate some of these elements, few genre movies attempt to include every possible genre convention.

Story Formulas The way a movie's story is structured—its plot—also helps viewers determine what genre it belongs to. For example, gangster films—from Howard Hawks's *Scarface* (1932) to Ridley Scott's *American Gangster* (2007)—tend to share a plot structure in which an underprivileged and disrespected immigrant joins (or forms) an organized crime syndicate, works his way to the top with a combination of savvy, innovation, and ruthlessness, becomes corrupted by his newfound power and the fruits of his labors, and, as a result, is betrayed, killed, or captured.

Romantic comedy plots are structured around characters in love as they couple, break up, and reconnect. When they first meet, the two characters (usually a man and a woman) are at odds. They fall in love in spite of—or sometimes because of—this seeming incompatibility, then must overcome obstacles to their relationship in the form of misunderstandings, competing partners, social pressures, or friction caused by the aforementioned incompatibility. Eventually the romance will appear doomed, but one half of the couple will realize they are meant for each other and make a grand gesture that reunites the romantic duo.

Theme A movie's *theme* is a unifying idea that the film expresses through its narrative or imagery. Not every genre is united by a single, clear-cut thematic idea, but the Western comes close. Nearly all Westerns share a central conflict between civilization and wilderness: settlers, towns, schoolteachers, cavalry outposts, and lawmen stand for civilization; free-range cattlemen, Indians, prostitutes, outlaws, and the wide-open spaces themselves fill the wilderness role. Many classic Western characters exist on both sides of this thematic conflict. For example, the Wyatt Earp character played by Henry Fonda in John Ford's *My Darling Clementine* (1946) is a former gunfighter turned lawman turned cowboy turned lawman. He befriends an outlaw but falls in love with a schoolteacher from the east. Early Westerns tend to sympathize with the forces of civilization and order, but many of the Westerns from the 1960s and 1970s valorize the freedom-loving outlaw, cowboy, or Native American hero.

Gangster films from Howard Hawks's *Scarface* (1932) to Ridley Scott's *American Gangster* (2007) are shaped by three well-worn, but obviously resonant, themes: rags to riches; crime does not pay; absolute power corrupts absolutely. The thematic complexity made possible by the tension between these aspirational and moralistic ideas can provide the viewer a more meaningful experience than one might expect from a genre dedicated to career criminals.

Character Types While most screenwriters strive to create individuated characters, genre films are often populated by specific character "types." Western protagonists personify the tension between order and chaos in the form of the free-spirited but civilized cowboy or the gunslinger turned lawman. Female characters also personify this tension, but only on one side or the other—as schoolmarm or prostitute, only rarely as a combination of both. Other Western character types include the cunning gambler, the greenhorn, the sidekick, and the settler. John Ford packed nearly every Western character type into a single wagon in his classic Western *Stagecoach* (1939). The horror and science-fiction film antagonist is almost always some form of "other"—a being utterly different than the

movie's protagonist (and audience) in form, attitude, and action. Many of these movie monsters are essentially large, malevolent bugs—the more foreign the villain's appearance and outlook, the better. When the other is actually a human, he often wears a mask designed to accentuate his otherness.

Setting Setting—where a movie's action is located and how that environment is portrayed—is also a common genre convention. Obviously, Westerns are typically set in the American West, but setting goes beyond geography. Most classic Westerns take place in the 1880s and 1890s, an era of western settlement when a booming population of Civil War veterans and other eastern refugees went west in pursuit of land, gold, and cattle trade. The physical location of Monument Valley became the landscape most associated with the genre, not because of any actual history that occurred there, but because the scenic area was the favorite location of the prolific Western director John Ford. Since science-fiction films are speculative and, therefore, look forward rather than backward, they are usually set in the future; sometimes in space, sometimes in futuristic earth cities, sometimes in a postapocalyptic desolation, but almost always in an era and place greatly affected by technology. While gangster films are almost always urban in setting, horror films seek the sort of isolated locations—farms, abandoned summer camps, small rural villages—that place the genre's besieged protagonists far from potential aid.

Presentation Many genres feature certain elements of cinematic language that communicate tone and atmosphere. For example, horror films take advantage of lighting schemes that accentuate and deepen shadows. The resulting gloom helps to create an eerie mood, but horror films are more than just dark; filmmakers use the hard-edged shadows as a dominant compositional element to convey a sense of oppression, distort our sense of space, and conceal narrative information. Film noir, a genre that also seeks to disorient the viewer and convey a sense of unease (although for very different thematic and narrative reasons), employs many of the same lighting techniques.

Ironically, science-fiction films use the latest high-tech special effects to tell stories that warn against the dehumanizing dangers of advanced technology. In fact, the genre is responsible for many important special effect innovations, from the miniatures and matte paintings that made possible the futuristic city of Fritz Lang's *Metropolis* (1927), to the motion-control cameras and rotoscope animation that launched the spaceships of Stanley Kubrick's *2001: A Space Odyssey* (1968), to the special "virtual camera system" director James Cameron and his *Avatar* (2009) team used to capture actors' expressions and actions as the first step in a revolutionary technical process that transformed the film's cast into aliens inhabiting an all-digital world.

Westerns, a genre clearly associated with setting, feature a great many exterior shots that juxtapose the characters with the environment they inhabit. The human subject tends to dominate the frame in most movie compositions, but many of these Western exterior shots are framed so that the "civilized" characters are dwarfed by the overwhelming expanse of wilderness around them.

Movies in the action genre often shoot combat (and other high-energy action) from many different angles to allow for a fast-paced editing style that presents the action from a constantly shifting perspective. These highly fragmented sequences subject the viewer to a rapid-fire cinematic simulation of the amplified exercise presumably experienced by the characters fighting on-screen.

Gangster plot elements Francis Ford Coppola's *The Godfather* trilogy (1972–90), perhaps the most famous gangster film series, includes many plot elements common to the genre, including the protagonist's humble origins and his rise to power through a combination of astute management and ruthless violence. But Coppola incorporated genre innovations that differentiated *The Godfather* movies from more typical gangster films. For example, the protagonist, Michael (Al Pacino), is an unwilling crime boss forced into syndicate leadership by circumstances and birthright. The plot elements of a humble origin and the rise to power are presented as flashbacks featuring not Michael, but his father, the man whose death propels Michael into a life of organized crime. Finally, Michael is unusual in that he attains power and prestige but is not destroyed (physically, at least) by corruption and greed.

Stars Even the actors who star in genre movies factor into how the genre is classified, analyzed, and received by audiences. In the 1930s and 1940s, actors worked under restrictive long-term studio contracts. With the studios choosing their roles, actors were more likely to be "typecast" and identified with a particular genre that suited their studio-imposed persona. Thus, John Wayne is forever identified with the Western, Edward G. Robinson with gangster films, and Boris Karloff with horror. These days, most actors avoid limiting themselves to a single genre, but several contemporary actors have become stars by associating themselves almost exclusively with action films. Arnold Schwarzenegger, Chuck Norris, Steven Seagal, and others have benefited from the genre's preference for physical presence and macho persona over acting ability. That's not to say that no genre stars can act. In fact, an actor who has become identified with one genre will often receive extra attention and accolades for performing outside of it. For example, Bill Murray became a star while acting in screwball comedies, but his subtle performances in the dramas *Lost in Translation* (2003; director: Sofia Coppola) and *Broken Flowers* (2005; director: Jim Jarmusch) made him an actor worthy of movie critics' praise.

Compiling an authoritative list of narrative genres and their specific conventions is nearly impossible, especially within the confines of an introductory textbook. There are simply too many genres, too much cinematic variety and flexibility, and too little academic consensus to nail every (or any) genre down definitively. That said, the next section offers a closer look at six major American genres to help you begin to develop a deeper understanding of how genre functions.

Six Major American Genres
Gangster

The gangster genre is deeply rooted in the concept of the American dream, which states that anyone, regardless of how humble his origins, can succeed. For much of its history, America's wealth and political power have been primarily wielded by succes-sive generations of a white, Anglo-Saxon, highly educated, and Protestant ruling class. American heroes like Daniel Boone, leaders like Andrew Jackson and Abraham Lincoln, and popular novelists like Horatio Alger, Jr., challenged this tradition of power by birthright; their example gave rise to the notion that anyone with intelligence and spunk can rise to great riches or power through hard work and bold action. The nation's expanding population of working-class American immigrants were eager to embrace this rags-to-riches mythology.

By the turn of the twentieth century, pulp-fiction accounts of the American West had already established the hero as an outsider who lives by his wits and is willing to break the rules in order to achieve his goals. Two historical events provided the remaining ingredients needed to turn these working-class notions into what we know now as the gangster genre. First, the Eighteenth Amendment to the Constitution—passed in 1919—banned the manufacture, sale, and transport of alcohol. This ill-advised law empowered organized crime, which expanded to capitalize on the newfound market for the suddenly forbidden beverages. Many of the criminal entrepreneurs who exploited this opportunity were Irish, Italian, and Jewish immigrants. What's more, Prohibition legitimized unlawful behavior by making outlaws out of common citizens thirsty for a beer after quitting time. As a result, common people—many of them immigrants themselves—began to identify with the bootleggers and racketeers, and to see them as active protagonists who take chances, risk the consequences, and get results—all surefire elements of successful cinema heroes. The stock market crash in 1929 and the resulting economic depression further cemented the public's distrust of authority (i.e., banks and financiers) and the allure of the gangster.

In this specific cultural context, American audiences began to question the authority of discredited institutions such as banks, government, and law enforcement, which fed their fascination with the outlaws who bucked those systems that had failed the rest of society. As the Depression deepened, the need for vivid, escapist entertainment increased. Hollywood was the ideal conduit for this emerging zeitgeist; the result was the gangster film.

Multigenre stardom With striking performances in Francis Ford Coppola's *Peggy Sue Got Married* (1986) and Joel and Ethan Coen's *Raising Arizona* (1987) [1], Nicolas Cage also began his career identified with screwball comedy. He then spent years reestablishing himself as a dramatic actor before being awarded an Oscar for his portrayal of a suicidal alcoholic in the grimly realistic *Leaving Las Vegas* (1995; director: Mike Figgis) [2] and then suddenly emerged as an action hero in a string of blockbusters that began with Michael Bay's *The Rock* (1996) and has continued into the present day with recent action extravaganzas like Oxide Pang Chun and Danny Pang's *Bangkok Dangerous* (2008) [3].

1

2

3

Just as the gangster film emerged, however, the film industry adopted a production code that forbade movies from explicitly engaging audience sympathy with "crime, wrongdoing, evil or sin." As a result, while early gangster films were among the most violent and sexually explicit movies of their time, the central conflicts and themes that they explored were often at odds with one another. For example, the stories were centered around outlaw entrepreneurs who empowered themselves, bucked the establishment, and grabbed their piece of the pie; yet, by the end of the story, this theme of success would give way to a "crime does not pay" message in which the enterprising hero is finally corrupted by his hunger for power and, thus, defeated by forces of law and order. In many of these films, violent crime was both celebrated and condemned. Movies that had audiences sympathizing with criminals (or at least their goals) at the start would ultimately turn an exhilarating rags-to-riches story of empowerment into a cautionary tale of the consequences of blind ambition. Central characters would achieve their goal only to be killed either by the law or their own equally ruthless subordinates. Along the way, audiences enjoyed the vicarious thrills of a daring pursuit of power, as well as the righteous satisfaction of seeing order restored.

While modern gangster narratives have expanded to include a wide range of stories set within the milieu of organized crime, classic gangster plots typically follow this rags-to-riches-to-destruction formula. The protagonist is initially powerless and sometimes suffers some form of public humiliation that both emphasizes his vulnerability and motivates his struggle for recognition. (This humiliation can come at the hands of a governing institution or the ruling gang organization; often, the ensuing conflict pits the gangster hero against both the law and the criminals currently in control.) The hero gains status and eventually grabs power and riches through ingenuity, risk taking, and a capacity for violence. While most gangster protagonists are killers, their initial victims (such as the thugs responsible for the protagonist's initial humiliation) are usually portrayed as deserving of their fate. This pattern shifts as the hero reaches his goal to rule the criminal syndicate. His ambition clouds his vision; he becomes paranoid and power-hungry, and begins to resemble his deposed adversaries. Before he self-destructs, he often destroys—figuratively or literally—characters that represent his last remaining ties to the earnest go-getter that began the story. Frequently, the protagonist expresses last-minute regret for what he has become, but by then it is almost always too late.

More sympathetic secondary characters often serve to humanize the gangster antihero. While the doomed protagonist is nearly always male, the secondary characters that provide a tenuous connection to the Old World values that he must sacrifice on his climb up the ladder usually take the form of a mother or sister. The only other female character typical to the genre is either a fellow criminal or a sort of gangster groupie known as a moll. Whereas the protagonist's mother loves him for his potential humanity, the gangster moll loves him for his potential power and wealth. She is a symbol of his aspirations—an alluring veneer concealing a rotten core.

He may also have a sidekick—a trusted companion from the old neighborhood—who makes the journey with him. This friend may be responsible for giving the protagonist his first break in the business, only to be later eclipsed by the hero. He is often instrumental in the protagonist's downfall—either as a betrayer or as a victim of the central character's greed and lust for power.

Antagonists come in two forms: law-enforcement agents and fellow gangsters. In stark contrast to portrayals in traditional procedurals, the police in gangster movies are portrayed as oppressors who are corrupt, incompetent, or both. They are sometimes in league with the gangster antagonist, the current kingpin who lacks the imagination or courage of our hero. His overthrow is often one of the first major obstacles the protagonist must overcome. Of course, the ultimate antagonist in many gangster movies is the protagonist himself.

According to an urban legend, when the gangster Willie Sutton was asked why he robbed banks, he replied, "Because that's where the money is." The same sort of logic explains the setting of the vast majority of gangster films. Movies about organized crime are set in urban locations because organized crime flourishes primarily in large cities. The particulars of the setting evolve as the plot progresses. The story usually opens in a slum, develops on the mean streets downtown, then works its way upward into luxury penthouses.

In contrast to most movie stars, the actors most closely associated with early gangster films were diminutive and relatively unattractive. The authority that actors like Edward G. Robinson and James Cagney conveyed on-screen was made all the more powerful by their atypical appearance. (In another blow to Hollywood logic, Cagney—whose gangster

The antihero The gangster movie provided the cinema with some its first antiheroes. These unconventional central characters pursue goals, overcome obstacles, take risks, and suffer consequences—everything needed to propel a compelling narrative—but they lack the traditional "heroic" qualities that engage an audience's sympathy. While he may not be courteous, kind, and reverent, he is almost always smart (if uneducated), observant, and brave. More than anything, the gangster-hero is driven by an overwhelming need to prove himself. This need motivates his quest for power, fame, and wealth . . . and almost always proves to be the tragic flaw that brings about his inevitable downfall. In the final moments of Raoul Walsh's *White Heat* (1949), the psychopathic protagonist Cody Jarrett (James Cagney) declares "top of the world, Ma!" before blowing himself to bits rather than submitting to the policemen who have him surrounded.

portrayals were among the most brutal in cinema history—was equally beloved as a star of happy-go-lucky musicals.)

Other notable gangster films include *Little Caesar* (1931; director: Mervyn LeRoy); *The Public Enemy* (1931; director: William A. Wellman); *Scarface* (1932; director: Howard Hawks); *White Heat* (1949; director: Raoul Walsh); *Touchez pas au grisbi* (1954; director: Jacques Becker); *Rififi* (1955; director: Jules Dassin); *Bonnie and Clyde* (1967; director: Arthur Penn); *Le Samouraï* (1967; director: Jean-Pierre Melville); *Battles without Honor or Humanity* (1973; director: Kinji Fukasaku); *Scarface* (1983; director: Brian De Palma); *Once upon a Time in America* (1984; director: Sergio Leone); *The Krays* (1990; director: Peter Medak); *Miller's Crossing* (1990; director: Joel Coen); *Reservoir Dogs* (1992; director: Quentin Tarantino); *Sonatine* (1993; director: Takeshi Kitano); *Road to Perdition* (2002; director: Sam Mendes); *City of God* (2002; directors: Fernando Meirelles and Kátia Lund); and *Mesrine: Killer Instinct* and *Mesrine: Public Enemy #1* (2008; director: Jean-François Richet).

Film Noir

In the early 1940s, the outlook, tone, and style of American genre films grew decidedly darker with the emergence of film noir (from the French for "black film"), a shift clearly denoted by its name. Not that movies hadn't already demonstrated a cynical streak. The gangster movies that surfaced in the previous decade featured antiheroes and less-than-flattering portrayals of our cities and institutions. World War I, Prohibition, and the Great Depression began the trend toward more realistic—and, thus, bleaker—artistic and narrative representations of the world, as evidenced in the written word of the time. Pulp-fiction writers like Dashiell Hammett had been publishing the hard-boiled stories that formed the foundation of film noir since the early 1930s. In fact, had it not been for the efforts of Hollywood and the U.S. government during World War II, film noir might have come along sooner. Instead, gung-ho war movies were designed to build support for the war effort, and lighthearted musicals and comedies were produced to provide needed distractions from overwhelming world events. Yet the same war that helped delay the arrival of film noir also helped give birth to the new genre by exposing ordinary Americans to the horrors of war. Whether in person or through newsreels and newspapers, troops and citizens alike witnessed death camps, battlefield slaughters, the rise of fascism, and countless other atrocities. Many of the genre's greatest directors, including Otto Preminger, Billy Wilder, and Fritz Lang, were themselves marked by the hardship and persecution that they experienced before leaving war-torn Europe for Hollywood. Others, like Samuel Fuller, fought as American soldiers. The atomic bomb that ended the war also demonstrated that not even a nation as seemingly secure as the United States was safe from its devastating power. The financial boom that the war effort had generated ended abruptly as the soldiers returned home to a changed world of economic uncertainty. Film noir fed off the postwar disillusionment that followed prolonged exposure to this intimidating new perspective.

In part because many of the early noir movies were low-budget "B" movies (so called because they often screened in the second slot of double features), the genre was not initially recognized or respected by most American scholars. Its emphasis on corruption and despair was seen as an unflattering portrayal of the American character. It was left to French critics—some of whom went on to make genre films of their own—to recognize (and name) the genre.

In fact, the American critic Paul Schrader (himself a filmmaker who has written and directed noir films) feels that film noir is not a genre at all. He claims that "film noir . . . is not defined, as are the Western and gangster genres, by conventions of setting and conflict, but rather by the more subtle qualities of tone and mood."[4] Regardless of how it is classified, film noir has continued to flourish long past the events that provoked its birth, in part because of a universal attraction to its visual and narrative style and a lasting affinity for its

[4]Paul Schrader, "Notes on *Film Noir*" (1972), in *Film Noir Reader*, ed. Alain Silver and James Ursini (New York: Limelight, 1996), pp. 53–64.

outlook. Like the eggs for which they are named, the hard-boiled characters in film noir have a tough interior beneath brittle shells. The themes are fatalistic, the tone cynical. Film noir may not be defined by setting, but noir films are typically shot in large urban areas (such as Chicago, New York, or Los Angeles) and contain gritty, realistic night exteriors, many of which were filmed on location, as opposed to the idealized and homogenized streets built on the studio back lot.

Like his counterpart in the gangster movie, the film-noir protagonist is an antihero. Unlike his gangster equivalent, he rarely pursues or achieves leadership status. On the contrary, the central noir character is an outsider. If he is a criminal, he's usually a lone operator caught up in a doomed attempt at a big score or a wrongdoer trying to elude justice. The private detectives at the center of many noir narratives operate midway between lawful society and the criminal underworld, with associates and enemies on both sides of the law. They may be former police officers who left the force in either disgrace or disgust; or they may be active but isolated police officers ostracized for their refusal to play by the rules. Whatever his profession, the noir protagonist is small-time, world-weary, aging, and not classically handsome. He's self-destructive and, thus, fallible, often suffering abuse on the way to a story conclusion that may very well deny him his goal and will almost certainly leave him unredeemed. All this is not to say that the noir protagonist is weak or unattractive. Ironically, the world-weary and wisecracking noir antihero is responsible for some of cinema's most popular and enduring characters. Humphrey Bogart was just a middle-aged character actor before his portrayal of the private detective Sam Spade in John Huston's *The Maltese Falcon* (1941) made him a cultural icon.

World War II expanded opportunities for women on the home front who took over the factory jobs and other responsibilities from the men who left to fight in Europe and the Pacific. Perhaps as a reflection of men's fear or resentment of these newly empowered women, film noir elevated the female character to antagonist status. Instead of passive supporting players, the femme fatale (French for

[1]

[2]

Fatalism in film noir Film-noir movies sometimes present information and events in a way that heightens the audience's sense that the hard-luck protagonist is doomed from the moment the story opens. Director and screenwriter Billy Wilder pushed this technique to the extreme in two of his most famous noir movies, both of which reveal the demise of the protagonist. The first moments of *Double*

Indemnity (1944) open with antihero Walter Neff (Fred MacMurray) stumbling wounded into his office to confess to the murder he will spend the rest of the story trying to get away with [1]. *Sunset Boulevard* (1950) goes one step further. The entire film is narrated in first-person voice-over by a protagonist (William Holden) presented in the opening scene as a floating corpse [2].

"deadly woman") role cast women as seductive, autonomous, and deceptive predators who use men for their own means. As a rule, the femme fatale is a far smarter—and, thus, formidable—opponent for the protagonist than other adversarial characters, most of whom are corrupt and violent but are not necessarily a match for the hero's cynical intelligence.

More than virtually any other genre, film noir is distinguished by its visual style. The name *black film* references not just the genre's attitude, but its look as well. Noir movies employ lighting schemes that emphasize contrast and create deep shadows that can obscure as much information as the illumination reveals. Light sources are often placed low to the ground, resulting in illumination that distorts facial features and casts dramatic shadows. Exterior scenes usually take place at night; those interior scenes set during the day often play out behind drawn shades that cast patterns of light and shadow, splintering the frame. These patterns, in turn, combine with other diagonal visual elements to create a compositional tension that gives the frame—and the world it depicts—a restless, unstable quality.

Film-noir plot structure reinforces this feeling of disorientation. The complex (sometimes incomprehensible) narratives are often presented in nonchronological or otherwise convoluted arrangements. Plot twists deprive the viewer of the comfort of a predictable plot. Goals shift, and expectations are reversed; allies are revealed to be enemies (and vice versa); narration, even that delivered by the protagonist, is sometimes unreliable. Moral reference points are skewed: victims are often as corrupt as their persecutors; criminals are working stiffs just doing their job. Paradoxically, this unsettling narrative complexity is often framed by a sort of enforced predictability. Fatalistic voice-over narration telegraphs future events and outcomes, creating a sense of predetermination and hopelessness for the protagonist's already lost cause.

1

2

3

Modern film noir While many modern noir films, such as Curtis Hanson's *L.A. Confidential* (1997), set their stories in places and times that directly reference the classic noir films of the 1940s, others offer a revised genre experience by relocating noir's thematic, aesthetic, and narrative elements to contemporary times and atypical locations. Rian Johnson's *Brick* (2005) [1] takes place within the convoluted social strata of a suburban high school. Joel Coen's *Fargo* (1996) [2] unfolds on the frozen prairies of rural North Dakota and the snow-packed Minneapolis suburbs. Erik Skjoldbjærg's *Insomnia* (1997) [3] trades ominous shadows for the unrelenting light of the midnight sun in a village above the Arctic Circle.

Other notable film-noir movies include *The Maltese Falcon* (1941; director: John Huston); *Laura* (1944; director: Otto Preminger); *Scarlet Street* (1945; director: Fritz Lang); *Detour* (1945; director: Edgar G. Ulmer); *The Big Sleep* (1946; director: Howard Hawks); *The Postman Always Rings Twice* (1946; director: Tay Garnett); *The Killers* (1946; director: Robert Siodmak); *Out of the Past* (1947; director: Jacques Tourneur); *The Naked City* (1948; director: Jules Dassin); *Criss Cross* (1949; director: Robert Siodmak); *Asphalt Jungle* (1950; director: John Huston); *D.O.A.* (1950; director: Rudolph Maté); *Panic in the Sreets* (1950; director: Elia Kazan); *Ace in the Hole* (1951; director: Billy Wilder); *Pickup on South Street* (1953; director: Samuel Fuller); *The Hitch-Hiker* (1953; director: Ida Lupino); *Kiss Me Deadly* (1955; director: Robert Aldrich); *Sweet Smell of Success* (1957; director: Alexander Mackendrick); *Touch of Evil* (1958; director: Orson Welles); *Chinatown* (1974; director: Roman Polanski); *After Dark, My Sweet* (1990; director: James Foley); *The Last Seduction* (1994; director: John Dahl); *The Usual Suspects* (1995; director: Bryan Singer); *Lost Highway* (1997; director: David Lynch); *Memento* (2000; director: Christoper Nolan); *The Man Who Wasn't There* (2001; director: Joel Coen); *Sin City* (2005; directors: Frank Miller and Robert Rodriguez); *The Square* (2008; director: Nash Edgerton); and *Broken Embraces* (2009; director: Pedro Almodovar).

Science Fiction

It seems logical to think of science fiction as being speculative fantasy about the potential wonders of technological advances. But most science-fiction films are not really about science. If we tried to prove the "science" that most sci-fi films present, much of it would be quickly exposed as ridiculous. Instead, the genre's focus is on humanity's relationship with science and the technology it generates. Science fiction existed as a literary genre long before movies were invented. The genre began in the early nineteenth century as a reaction to the radical societal and economic changes spurred by the industrial revolution. At that time, the introduction of new technologies such as the steam engine dramatically changed the way Americans and Europeans worked and lived. What were once rural agrarian cultures were quickly transformed into mechanized urban societies. Stories are one way that our cultures process radical change, so it didn't take long for the anxiety unleashed by this explosion of technology to manifest itself in the form of Mary Shelley's 1818 novel *Frankenstein; or, The Modern Prometheus*. The subtitle makes evident the novel's theme: in Greek mythology, Prometheus is the Titan who stole fire from Zeus and bestowed this forbidden and dangerous knowledge on mortals not yet ready to deal with its power. Shelley's "monster" represents the consequences of men using science and technology to play God.

Those of you familiar with twentieth-century movie versions may think of *Frankenstein* as a horror story. The genres are indeed closely related through their mutual exploitation of audience fears; it is the source of the anxiety that is different. Horror films speak to our fears of the supernatural and the unknown, whereas science-fiction movies explore our dread of technology and change. Both genres have their roots in folklore that articulates the ongoing battle between human beings and everything that is other than human. In ancient folklore, this other was anthropomorphized into monsters (trolls, ogres, etc.) that inhabited (and represented) the wilderness that humans could not control. Ironically, the same advances in science and technology that allowed cultures to explain away—and, thus, destroy—all of these old monsters have given voice to the modern folklore of science fiction. For most of us, science is beyond our control. Its rapid advance is a phenomenon that we didn't create, that we don't entirely comprehend, and that moves too fast for us to keep up with. So when it comes to science fiction, the other represents—directly or indirectly—this technological juggernaut that can help us but also has the power to destroy us or at least make us obsolete.

All this is not to say that science is an inherently negative force or even that anxiety dominates our relationship with technology. We all love our computers, appreciate modern medicine, and marvel at the wonders of space exploration. But conflict is an essential element of narrative. If everything is perfect, then there's no story. And unspoken, even

[1]

[2]

The other in science fiction Science-fiction films often emphasize a malevolent alien's "otherness" by modeling its appearance on machines or insects. The benevolent visitors in Steven Spielberg's popular science-fiction film *Close*

Encounters of the Third Kind (1977) [1] look much more reassuringly humanoid than the hostile invaders his collaborators created for *War of the Worlds* (2005) [2].

unconscious, concerns are at the root of a great deal of artistic expression.

Science-inspired anxiety is behind the defining thematic conflict that unites most science-fiction movies. This conflict can be expressed many ways, but for our purposes let's think of it as technology versus humanity or science versus soul.[5] This theme is expressed in stories that envision technology enslaving humanity, invading our minds and bodies, or bringing about the end of civilization as we know it. The antagonist in these conflicts takes the form of computers like the infamous HAL in Stanley Kubrick's *2001: A Space Odyssey* (1968); robots or machines in films like Ridley Scott's *Blade Runner* (1982), the Wachowski's *The Matrix* series (1999–2003), and James Cameron's *Terminator* movies (1984–2003); and mechanized, dehumanized societies in Fritz Lang's *Metropolis* (1927), Jean-Luc Godard's *Alphaville* (1965), and George Lucas's *THX 1138* (1971).

Alien invaders, another common science-fiction antagonistic "other," are also an outgrowth of our innate fear of the machine. As soon as humankind was advanced enough to contemplate travel outside the earth's orbit, we began to speculate about the possibility of life on other planets. Our fear of the unknown, combined with our tendency to see

Earth as the center of the universe, empowered this imagined other as a threatening force, endowed with superior destructive technology, bent on displacing or enslaving us. The otherness of the most malevolent aliens is emphasized by designing their appearance to resemble machines or insects. In contrast, the science-fiction movies that reverse expectations and portray alien encounters in a positive light typically shape their extraterrestrials more like humans—or at least mammals. One need look no further than *Star Wars'* comfortably fuzzy Chewbacca (as opposed to Imperial storm troopers and Jabba the Hutt) for evidence of this tradition.

While most science-fiction movies stress the otherness of the antagonist, the opposite is true for the sci-fi protagonist. Science-fiction heroes are often literally and figuratively down-to-earth. They tend to be so compassionate and soulful that their essential humanity seems a liability . . . until their indomitable human spirit proves the key to defeating the malevolent other.

Because science-fiction narratives often deal with what-ifs, the setting is frequently speculative. If those sci-fi movies are set in the present day, they often heighten the dramatic impact of invasive aliens or time travelers. Most commonly, the genre places its stories in a future profoundly shaped by advances in technology. This allows filmmakers to hypothesize future effects of contemporary cultural, political, or scientific trends. These speculative settings may be high-tech megacities or postapocalyptic

[5]Per Schelde, *Androids, Humanoids, and Other Science Fiction Monsters: Science and Soul in Science Fiction Films* (New York: New York University Press, 1993).

Science fiction and special effects James Cameron's *Avatar* (2009) puts a new spin on the science-fiction genre by presenting humans as the cold-blooded alien invaders using superior technology to threaten an unspoiled world and its compassionate natives. The planet's symbiotic creatures and spectacular landscapes were created using the most sophisticated digital technology in the history of cinema. Ironically, the movie genre founded on audience's dread of technology also happens to depend heavily on viewers' attraction to high-tech special effects. The speculative spectacle that audiences expect of science fiction means that most films in the genre feature elaborate sets, costumes, makeup, computer animation, and digital effects.

ruins. In movies like Ridley Scott's *Blade Runner* (1982), the setting suggests a combination of both. Of course, outer space is also a popular science-fiction setting for obvious reasons. In many of these examples, the technology-versus-humanity theme is presented in part by dramatizing the consequences of science taking us places we don't necessarily belong—or at least in which we are not physically and spiritually equipped to survive. Science-fiction films made before the 1970s tended to feature sterile, well-ordered, almost utopian speculative settings. Movies like Scott's *Alien* (1979), with its grimy industrial space-barge interiors, reversed that trend by presenting a future in which living conditions had degraded, rather than evolved.

The following list includes some notable science-fiction films: *A Trip to the Moon* (1902; director: Georges Méliès); *Things to Come* (1936; director: William Cameron Menzies); *The Day the Earth Stood Still* (1951; director: Robert Wise); *It Came from Outer Space* (1953; director: Jack Arnold); *Forbidden Planet* (1956; director: Fred M. Wilcox); *Invasion of the Body Snatchers* (1956; director: Don Siegel); *On the Beach* (1959; director: Stanley Kramer); *Village of the Damned* (1960; director: Wolf Rilla); *Fahrenheit 451* (1966; director: François Truffaut); *Solaris* (1972; director: Andrei Tarkovsky); *The Man Who Fell to Earth* (1976; director: Nicolas Roeg); *Stalker* (1979; director: Andrei Tarkovsky); *Mad Max 2* (1981; director: George Miller); *Nausicaä* (1984; director: Hayao Miyazaki); *Brazil* (1985; director: Terry Gilliam); *The Fly* (1986; director: David Cronenberg); *Akira* (1988; director: Katsuhiro Ôtomo); *Until the End of the World* (1991; director: Wim Wenders); *Ghost in the Shell* (1995; director: Mamoru Oshii); *Twelve Monkeys* (1995; director: Terry

Gilliam); *Gattaca* (1997; director: Andrew Niccol); *Starship Troopers* (1997; director: Paul Verhoeven); *The Iron Giant* (1999; director: Brad Bird); *Donnie Darko* (2001; director: Richard Kelly); *Children of Men* (2006; director: Alfonso Cuarón); *Wall-E* (2008; director: Andrew Stanton); *Avatar* (2009; director: James Cameron); *Moon* (2009; director: Duncan Jones); and *District 9* (2009; director: Neill Blomkamp).

Horror

Like science fiction, the horror genre was born out of a cultural need to confront and vicariously conquer something frightening that we do not fully comprehend. In the case of horror films, those frightening somethings are aspects of our existence even more intimidating than technology or science: death and insanity. Both represent the ultimate loss of control and a terrifying, inescapable metamorphosis. In order to enact any sort of narrative conflict with either of these forces, they must be given a tangible form. And, like horror's sister genre, sci-fi, that form is the "other." Death takes the shape of ghosts, zombies, and vampires—all of which pose a transformative threat to the audience. The only thing scarier than being killed or consumed by the other is actually becoming the other. So it makes sense that the werewolves, demonic possessions, and homicidal maniacs that act as cinematic stand-ins for insanity also carry the threat of infection and conversion.

We could hypothesize that early, primitive religions—even the source of some modern religions—derive from the same essential human need to demystify and defeat these most basic fears. But the difference between movies and religious rituals is the intensity and immediacy that the cinema experience provides. Sitting in a darkened movie theater staring at oversized images of the other, movie viewers are immersed in a shared ritual that exposes them to dread, terror, and, ultimately, catharsis. We vicariously defeat death (even if the protagonist does not), because we survive the movie and walk back into our relatively safe lives after the credits roll and the lights come up. We experience the exhilaration of confronting the dreaded other without the devastating consequences.

Germany, with its strong tradition of folklore and more developed engagement with the darker aspects of existence (thanks in part to the devastation of World War I), created the first truly disturbing horror movies. Robert Wiene's *The Cabinet of Dr. Caligari* (1920) sees the world through the distorted perspective of a madman; F. W. Murnau's expressionist Dracula adaptation, *Nosferatu, a Symphony of Horror* (1922), associates its other with death and disease. The United States embraced the genre with the release of *Dracula* (1931; director: Tod Browning), and thus began Hollywood's on-again, off-again relationship with the horror film. A golden age of Hollywood horror followed, with the monster others at its center taking top billing: *Frankenstein* (1931; director: James Whale); *The Mummy* (1932; director: Karl Freund); and *The Wolf Man* (1941; director: George Waggner).

With the return of prosperity and the end of World War II, the classic "monster"-based horror film faded into mediocrity and relative obscurity until a new generation of audiences with their own fears resurrected the genre. Foreign and independent studios updated and moved beyond the original monster concept with low-budget productions created for the B-movie and drive-in markets. Horror did not return to the mainstream until veteran British directors Alfred Hitchcock and Michael Powell, both of whom were associated with very different motion-picture styles, each unleashed his own disturbing portrait of an outwardly attractive young serial killer. By subverting audiences' expectation of the other, Hitchcock's *Psycho* (1960) and Powell's *Peeping Tom* (1960) shocked audiences and revolutionized the horror genre. Ever since, as our culture's needs and attitudes change, and global awareness of real-life atrocities multiplies, horror has evolved to become one of cinema's most diverse and fluid genres.

A typical horror narrative begins by establishing a normal world that will be threatened by the arrival of the other. This monster must be vanquished or destroyed in order to reestablish normalcy. Often, the protagonist is the only person who initially recognizes evidence of the threat. Because

[1]

[2]

The infectious other One reason we go to horror movies is to confront our fear of death and insanity, as well as the anxiety that arises out of our ultimate inability to control either condition. As a result, the other that fills the role of antagonist often carries the threat of infection and transformation. The raging zombies in Danny Boyle's *28 Days Later . . .* (2002) [1] are former humans changed into mindless killing machines by a runaway virus. Hideo Nakata's *Ringu* (1998) and Gore Verbinski's 2002 American remake, *The Ring* [2], contaminate via a videotape that transforms viewers into hideously contorted corpses by converting their trusted televisions into portals of evil.

the other is so far removed from normalcy, the protagonist may reject her own suspicions before she experiences the other more directly and announces the menace to those around her. When her warnings are ignored, the central character is directly targeted by the other. She must either enlist help or face the monster on her own. In the end, the protagonist may destroy the other—or at least appear to. Horror narratives tend to feature resurrections and other false resolutions. Originally, these open endings were meant to give the audience

one last scare; now, they are just as likely intended to ensure the possibility of a profitable sequel.

This basic horror plot structure offers a number of typical variants: the protagonist may actually be directly or indirectly responsible for summoning the other, a violation that places even greater responsibility on her to restore the normal world. The protagonist may also have to enlist the help of a mentor or apprentice, or even sacrifice herself, in order to defeat the antagonistic other. Sometimes the protagonist actually becomes the other. She becomes infected and attempts to deny, and then hide, her encroaching transformation. She may pursue a solution, but ultimately faces the decision to either destroy herself or face a complete metamorphosis. Oftentimes, as in similar science-fiction stories, she is somehow saved by the power of her own humanity.

This protagonist is often a loner, someone socially reviled who must save the community that rejects her. We identify with her because she is (initially, at least) unusually fearful, a weakness that allows us the greatest possible identification with her struggle. This characteristic is certainly not limited to horror films. Many movie narratives center on flawed characters because they create high stakes and allow for the kind of character development that satisfies audiences.

While a significant number of horror-film antagonists are one-dimensional killing machines, many of these others are actually more compelling characters than the protagonists charged with destroying them. Vampires fascinate us because they can be as seductive as they are terrifying. Other monsters, such as Frankenstein's monster or his progeny, Edward Scissorhands, may actually display more humanity than the supposedly threatened populace. And, yes, the malevolent father in Stanley Kubrick's *The Shining* (1980) and Freddy Krueger of Wes Craven's *A Nightmare on Elm Street* (1984) may be evil, but they have undeniable personality. Even the masked, robotic killers at the center of the *Halloween* and *Friday the 13th* slasher franchises offer more complex histories and motives than their relatively anonymous victims.

Horror-movie settings tend to fall into two categories. The first is the aforementioned "normal world"—a hyperordinary place, usually a small town threatened by invasion of the other. This setting casts the protagonist as the protector of her beloved home turf and violates our own notions of personal safety. Other horror films set their action in remote rural areas that offer potential victims little hope for assistance. A related horror setting places the central character in a foreign, often exotic, environment that lacks the security of the familiar. The alien customs, language, and landscape disorient the protagonist (and the audience) and diminish any hope for potential support. And, as you may have guessed, regardless of where horror stories are located, they almost invariably stage their action at night.

Besides tapping into our instinctive fears, night scenes lend themselves to the chiaroscuro lighting—the use of deep gradations of light and shadow within an image—that most horror-movie cinematography depends upon. This lighting style emphasizes stark contrasts, with large areas of deep shadow accented with bright highlights. The light is often direct or undiffused, which creates well-defined shadows and silhouettes, and low-key, meaning the dense

shadows are not abated by additional "fill" lights. Horror-genre lighting is sometimes cast from below, an angle of illumination not typical of our everyday experience. The result is the distorted facial features and looming cast shadows known on film sets as "Halloween lighting." Viewer's perceptions are often made still more disoriented with the use of canted camera angles that tilt the on-screen world off balance. Horror-film staging also exploits the use of offscreen action and sound that suggests the presence of peril but denies the audience the relative reassurance of actually keeping an eye on the antagonist.

Some notable horror films include *Freaks* (1932; director: Tod Browning); *Bride of Frankenstein* (1935; director: James Whale); *Cat People* (1942; director: Jacques Tourneur); *Black Sunday* (1960; director: Mario Bava); *The Innocents* (1961; director: Jack Clayton); *Carnival of Souls* (1962; director: Herk Harvey); *The Birds* (1963; director: Alfred Hitchcock); *Kaidan* (1964; director: Masaki Kobayashi); *Rosemary's Baby* (1968; director: Roman Polanski); *Night of the Living Dead* (1968; director: George Romero); *The Exorcist* (1973; director: William Friedkin); *The*

Horror-movie settings Most horror stories unfold in settings that isolate potential victims from potential help. Dario Argento's *Suspiria* (1977) goes one step further by placing the young protagonist, Suzy (Jessica Harper), in an unusually creepy ballet academy in rural Italy. As a

newcomer and the only American student, Suzy is not only isolated from the relative security of a populated area, but must face considerable danger alone, without allies, in unfamiliar surroundings.

Halloween lighting in *Bride of Frankenstein* Like film noir, the horror genre utilizes a style of lighting (referred to as low-key, or chiaroscuro, lighting) that emphasizes stark contrasts between bright illumination and deep shadow. These shadows are used to create unsettling graphic compositions, obscure visual information, and suggest offscreen action. Lighting a subject from below, a technique often referred to as "Halloween lighting," distorts a subject's features by reversing the natural placement of shadows.

Texas Chain Saw Massacre (1974; director: Tobe Hooper); *Carrie* (1976; director: Brian De Palma); *The Omen* (1976; director: Richard Donner); *Dawn of the Dead* (1978; director: George A. Romero); *Phantasm* (1979; director: Don Coscarelli); *The Evil Dead* (1981; director: Sam Raimi); *Poltergeist* (1982; director: Tobe Hooper); *Evil Dead II* (1987; director: Sam Raimi); *Hellraiser* (1987; director: Clive Barker); *The Silence of the Lambs* (1991; director: Jonathan Demme); *Braindead* (1992; director: Peter Jackson); the TV miniseries *The Kingdom* (1994; directors: Lars von Trier and Morton Arnfred); *Scream* (1996; director: Wes Craven); *Ringu* (1998; director: Hideo Nakata); *The Blair Witch Project* (1999; directors: Daniel Myrick and Eduardo Sánchez); *The Sixth Sense* (1999; director: M. Night Shyamalan); *The Others* (2001; director: Alejandro Amenábar); *28 Days Later . . .* (2002; director: Danny Boyle); *Shaun of the Dead* (2004; director: Edgar Wright); *Nightwatch* (2004; director: Timur Bekmambetov); *Rec* (2007; directors: Jaume Balagueró and Paco Plaza); *Paranormal Activity* (2007;

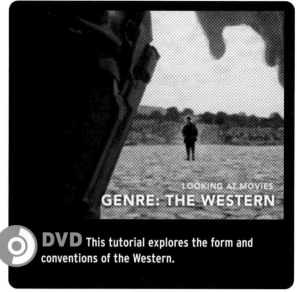

DVD This tutorial explores the form and conventions of the Western.

director: Oren Peli); *Let the Right One In* (2008; director: Tomas Alfredson); and *Drag Me to Hell* (2009; director: Sam Raimi).

The Western

Like most of the major genres, the Western predates the invention of motion pictures. The exploration and settlement of the western United States has fascinated European Americans since the frontier was just a few hundred miles inland from the eastern coast. Set in 1757 and published in 1826, James Fenimore Cooper's *The Last of the Mohicans* is widely considered the first popular novel to explore the tension between the wilderness and encroaching civilization. But the considerably less reputable literature most responsible for spawning the Western movie didn't come along until about twenty-five years later. Dime novels (so called because of their cheap cost), short novellas written for young men and semiliterates, delivered sensational adventures of fictional cowboys, outlaws, and adventurers, as well as wildly fictionalized stories starring actual Western figures. By the 1870s, stage productions and traveling circuslike shows featuring staged reenactments of famous battles and other events capitalized on the growing international fascination with the American West. Movies wasted no time getting into the act. Some of the earliest motion pictures were Westerns, including Thomas Edison's 46-second, one-shot vignette *Cripple Creek Bar-Room Scene* (1899) and Edwin S. Porter's groundbreaking *The Great Train Robbery* (1903).

American history inspired the Western, but the genre's enduring popularity has more to do with how Americans see and explain themselves than with any actual event. Westerns are a form of modern mythology that offers narrative representations of Americans as rugged, self-sufficient individuals taming a savage wilderness with common sense and direct action. The concept of the frontier as a sort of societal blank slate is at the heart of this mythology. The Wild West is a land of opportunity—both a dangerous, lawless country in need of taming and an expansive territory where anyone with the right stuff can reinvent himself and start a new life. The mythology label does not mean that these notions cannot be true. It simply acknowledges that certain aspects of the history of the American West have been amplified and modified to serve a collective cultural need.

Earlier in the chapter, we discussed the civilization-versus-wilderness conflict that provides the Western's thematic framework. The tension produced by this conflict is an essential ingredient in virtually every Western narrative. The wilderness can take the form of antagonistic forces in direct conflict with the civilizing settlers, such as the Apache Indians in John Ford's *The Searchers* (1956) and *Stagecoach* (1939), or the free-range cattleman of George Stevens's *Shane* (1953). Or it can manifest itself in more metaphorical terms. The wilderness of Ford's *3 Godfathers* (1948), for example, takes the form of the outlaw protagonists' self-interest, which is put in direct opposition with the civilizing effects of social responsibility when the bandits discover an infant orphaned in the desert.

But this sort of duality was nothing new. Many Western characters reverse or combine the thematic elements of order and chaos. Lawmen in movies like Clint Eastwood's *Unforgiven* (1992) are antagonists, and often even a lawman protagonist is a former outlaw or gunfighter. Cowboys—quintessential Western characters—also embody

[1]

[2]

Wilderness and civilization Although many Western narratives favor the forces of order, the outlaw is not always the bad guy. Revisionist Westerns like George Roy Hill's *Butch Cassidy and the Sundance Kid* (1969) mourn the inevitable loss of freedom that accompanies the civilization of the frontier. In that movie, and in many others that reconsidered Western mythology, the protagonists are good-natured outlaws [1]; the righteous avenging posse (presented as a faceless "other" in a technique borrowed from the horror and science-fiction genres) is the dreaded antagonist [2].

the blurred borders between the Western's thematic forces. Cowboys may fight the Indians, but they are also symbols of rootless resisters of encroaching development. Whatever his particular stance and occupation, the Western hero is typically a man of action, not words. He is resistant—or at least uncomfortable—with the trappings of civilization, even in those common cases where he serves as a civilizing agent. *Shane*'s gunfighter protagonist sacrifices himself to defend the homesteader, but he rides off into oblivion, rather than settling down and taking up a plow himself. The actors associated with the genre reflect the quiet power of the laconic characters they repeatedly play. Whereas gangster icons such as James Cagney are compact and manic, Western stars, from the silent era's William S. Hart through Henry Fonda and John Wayne and on up to Clint Eastwood, are outsized but relatively subdued performers.

All of the tertiary character types found in Westerns have a role to play in this overarching conflict between the wild and settled West. Native Americans are both ruthless savages and noble personifications of dignity and honor. Prostitutes are products of lawlessness but often long for marriage and family. Schoolmarms are educated and cultured, yet are irresistibly drawn to the frontier and the men who roam it. The greenhorn character may be sophisticated back East, but he is an inexperienced bumbler (and, as such, a perfect surrogate for the viewer) when it comes to the ways of the West. His transformation into a skilled cowboy/ gunfighter/lawman embodies the Western ideal of renewal.

More than any genre, the American Western is linked to place. But the West is not necessarily a particular place. The genre may be set on the prairie, in the mountains, or in the desert. But whatever the setting, the landscape is a dominant visual and thematic element that represents another Western duality: it's a deadly wilderness of stunning natural beauty. Because setting is of such primary importance, Westerns are dominated by daylight exterior shots and scenes. As a result, Westerns were among the first films to be shot almost exclusively on location. (When the Hollywood noir classic *Sunset Boulevard* needs to get a film-industry character

Character duality in the Western Western protagonists often embody both sides of the genre's thematic conflict between wilderness and civilization. Clint Eastwood's *Unforgiven* (1992) stars Eastwood himself as Bill Munny, a farmer and father enlisted as a hired gun on the basis of his faded (and dubious) reputation as a former gunslinger. Munny resists violent action until the murder of his friend and partner, Ned (Morgan Freeman), reawakens the ruthless desperado within him [1]. Johnny Depp's character in Jim Jarmusch's allegorical Western *Dead Man* (1995) begins his journey west as a hopelessly meek and inept accountant, but is gradually transformed into a deadly outlaw by both the figurative and literal wilderness [2].

out of town, it gets him a job on a Western.) The Western landscape is not limited to background information. The big skies and wide-open spaces are used to symbolize both limitless possibility and an untamable environment. For this reason, Westerns favor extreme long shots in which the landscape dwarfs human subjects and the primitive outposts of civilization.

The following list contains important Westerns: *The Iron Horse* (1924; director: John Ford); *Tumbleweeds* (1925; director: King Baggot); *The Big Trail* (1930; director: Raoul Walsh); *Destry Rides Again* (1939; director: George Marshall); *The Ox-Bow Incident* (1943; director: William A. Wellman); *Duel in the Sun* (1946; director: King Vidor); *Fort Apache* (1948; director: John Ford); *Red River* (1948; directors: Howard Hawks and Arthur Rosson); *She Wore a Yellow Ribbon* (1949; director: John Ford); *The Gunfighter* (1950; director: Henry King); *Winchester '73* (1950; director: Anthony Mann); *The Naked Spur* (1953; director: Anthony Mann); *Johnny Guitar* (1954; director: Nicholas Ray); *3:10 to Yuma* (1957; director: Delmer Daves); *Forty Guns* (1957; director: Samuel Fuller); *Man of the West* (1958; director: Anthony Mann); *Lonely Are the Brave* (1962; director: David Miller); *The Man Who Shot Liberty Valance* (1962; director: John Ford); *Major Dundee* (1965; director: Sam Peckinpah); *Hombre* (1967; director: Martin Ritt); *Once upon a Time in the West* (1968; director: Sergio Leone); *Will Penny* (1968; director: Tom Gries); *The Wild Bunch* (1969; director: Sam Peckinpah); *Little Big Man* (1970; director: Arthur Penn); *McCabe & Mrs. Miller* (1971; director: Robert Altman); *Silverado* (1985; director: Lawrence Kasdan); *Dances with Wolves* (1990; director: Kevin Costner); *The Ballad of Little Jo* (1993; director: Maggie Greenwald); *Dead Man* (1995; director: Jim Jarmusch); *The Missing* (2003; director: Ron Howard); *Appaloosa* (2008; director: Ed Harris); and *True Grit* (2010; directors: Ethan Coen and Joel Coen).

The Musical

The musical tells its story using characters that express themselves with song and/or dance. The actors sing every line of dialogue in a few musicals, such as Jacques Demy's *The Umbrellas of Cherbourg* (1964), and those musicals from the 1930s featuring Fred Astaire and Ginger Rogers focus more on dancing than singing. But, for the most part, musicals feature a combination of music, singing, dancing, and spoken dialogue.

Unlike many genres, the musical film genre was not born out of any specific political or cultural moment or preexisting literary genre. But musical performance was already a well-established entertainment long before the invention of the movie camera. The long-standing traditions of religious pageants, opera, operetta, and ballet all present narrative within a musical context. Musical comedies similar in structure to movie musicals were popular on British and American stages throughout much of the nineteenth century.

So it was inevitable that the dazzling movement, formal spectacle, and emotional eloquence inherent in musical performance would eventually join forces with the expressive power of cinema. But two hurdles stood in the way of the union. First, the

Civilization and wilderness This archetypal scene from John Ford's *My Darling Clementine* (1946) demonstrates the tension (and inevitable attraction) between encroaching civilization and the wide-open Wild West that lies at the heart of most Western-genre narrative conflicts. Deadly gunfighter turned reluctant lawman Wyatt Earp (Henry Fonda) escorts Clementine (Cathy Downs), a refined and educated woman from the East, to a community dance held in the bare bones of a not-yet-constructed church surrounded by desert and mountains.

Backstage and integrated musicals Early Hollywood musicals like Harry Beaumont's *The Broadway Melody* (1929) [1] constructed their narratives around the rehearsal and performance of a musical stage show, a setting that provided an intriguing backdrop, narrative conflict, and a context that allowed the characters to sing and dance without testing verisimilitude. Within a few years, integrated musicals like Rouben Mamoulian's *Love Me Tonight* (1932) [2] proved that audiences were already willing to accept characters who burst into song in everyday situations, such as a tailor (Maurice Chevalier) who sings an ode to romantic love as he measures a customer for a suit.

early film industry had to create a workable system for recording and projecting sound—a process over twenty-five years in the making. The next obstacle had less to do with mechanical engineering and more with audience perceptions. Because the new medium of motion-picture photography was closely associated with documentation and, thus, naturalism, the idea of otherwise realistic scenarios suddenly interrupted by characters bursting into song didn't seem to fit with the movies. Therefore, cinema had to establish a context that would allow for musical performance but still lend itself to relatively authentic performances and dramatic situations, as well as spoken dialogue.

The first major movie to incorporate extended synchronized sound sequences provided the solution. Alan Crosland's *The Jazz Singer* (1927) was a backstage musical. This kind of film placed the story in a performance setting (almost always Broadway), so that the characters were singers and dancers whose job it was to rehearse and stage songs anyway. By placing its narrative in this very specific setting, this early musical incarnation established some of the genre's most fixed plot and character elements. Backstage-musical stories typically revolved around a promising young performer searching for her big show-business break, or a talented singer/dancer protagonist pressured by a love interest or family member to leave show business, or a struggling company of singers and dancers determined to mount a big show. Many backstage narratives managed to combine two or more of these standard storylines. These musicals had their own set of character types, including the hard-bitten producer, the gifted ingenue, the insecure (i.e., less talented) star, and the faltering veteran with a heart of gold.

One might assume that since the backstage musical's songs were all performed as either rehearsals or productions within the framework of an externalized Broadway show, these songs would be missing the emotional power provided by a direct connection to the character's lives. But in practice, the lyrics and context were usually presented in such a way as to underscore the performing character's state of mind or personal situation.

Backstage musicals had only been around for a few years when so-called integrated musicals like

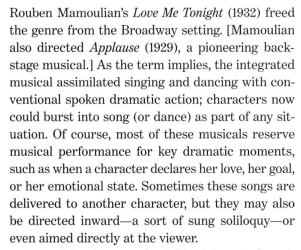

Contemporary musicals Bill Condon's *Dreamgirls* (2006) is set within a backstage musical situation that allows for staged performance of some musical numbers [1]. But a significant amount of the movie's most meaningful music is delivered in the style of the integrated musical: offstage and in character [2]. Julie Taymor's *Across the Universe* (2007) and Phyllida Lloyd's *Mamma Mia!* (2008) [3] represent a relatively new approach to the genre, one in which all of the music expresses character emotions and contributes to the narrative despite the fact that none of it was originally written for the movie. Both musicals select familiar songs from the catalogs of popular supergroups (the Beatles and ABBA, respectively) and create narratives to suit the appropriated music.

Rouben Mamoulian's *Love Me Tonight* (1932) freed the genre from the Broadway setting. [Mamoulian also directed *Applause* (1929), a pioneering backstage musical.] As the term implies, the integrated musical assimilated singing and dancing with conventional spoken dramatic action; characters now could burst into song (or dance) as part of any situation. Of course, most of these musicals reserve musical performance for key dramatic moments, such as when a character declares her love, her goal, or her emotional state. Sometimes these songs are delivered to another character, but they may also be directed inward—a sort of sung soliloquy—or even aimed directly at the viewer.

Part of the pleasure of watching integrated musicals comes from the potentially dramatic shifts in tone and style required to move between dramatic and musical performance. Audiences have learned to appreciate the stylistic prowess required to balance these two seemingly incompatible entertainments, along with the whimsy or poignancy such combinations are capable of generating. Only in a musical can downtrodden factory workers erupt into a celebratory tune, as in Lars von Trier's

Dancer in the Dark (2000), or a gang of rebellious college students sing and dance their way into a drunken, stoned stupor, as in Julie Taymor's *Across the Universe* (2007). The integrated musical, as these examples illustrate, freed the genre from the Broadway backdrop and allowed the musical to apply its unique stylings to a virtually limitless range of stories, characters, and settings. While traditional musicals still tend to use the romantic comedy for their narrative template, contemporary movies have mixed the musical with a variety of other genres and cinema styles. Director Trey Parker has created credible musicals within the context of an extended *South Park* episode (*South Park: Bigger, Longer & Uncut*, 1999), a Michael Bay–style action movie performed by marionettes (*Team America: World Police*, 2004), and the only prosecuted case of cannibalism in United States history (*Cannibal! The Musical*, 1996). The genre dominated animated features from Walt Disney studios for almost sixty years. Even television programs have gotten into the act: *The Simpsons*, *Scrubs*, *Xena: Warrior Princess*, and *Buffy the Vampire Slayer* have all created special musical episodes.

Notable musicals include *Le Million* (1931; director: René Clair); *The Three Penny Opera* (1931; director: G. W. Pabst); *42nd Street* (1933; director: Lloyd Bacon); *Footlight Parade* (1933; director: Lloyd Bacon); *Swing Time* (1936; director: George Stevens); *The Wizard of Oz* (1939; director: Victor Fleming); *Yankee Doodle Dandy* (1942; director: Michael Curtiz); *Meet Me in St. Louis* (1944; director: Vincente Minnelli); *On the Town* (1949; directors: Stanley Donen and Gene Kelly); *An American in Paris* (1951; director: Vincente Minnelli); *Singin' in the Rain* (1952; directors: Stanley Donen and Gene Kelly); *The Band Wagon* (1953; director: Vincente Minnelli); *French Cancan* (1954; director: Jean Renoir); *A Star Is Born* (1954; director: George Cukor); *Oklahoma!* (1955; director: Fred Zinnemann); *The King and I* (1956; director: Walter Lang); *West Side Story* (1961; directors: Jerome Robbins and Robert Wise); *The Music Man* (1962; director: Morton DaCosta); *The Sound of Music* (1965; director: Robert Wise); *The Jungle Book* (1967; director: Wolfgang Reitherman); *Cabaret* (1972; director: Bob Fosse); *Jesus Christ Superstar* (1973; director: Norman Jewison); *Grease* (1978; director: Randal Kleiser); *Hair* (1979; director: Milos Forman); *Blood Wedding* (1981; director: Carlos Saura); *Pennies from Heaven* (1981; director: Herbert Ross); *Moulin Rouge!* (2001; director: Baz Luhrmann); *Chicago* (2002; director: Rob Marshall); *Teacher's Pet* (2004; director: Timothy Björklund); and *Rent* (2005; director: Chris Columbus).

Evolution and Transformation of Genre

Filmmakers are rarely satisfied to leave things as they are. Thus, as with all things cinematic, genre is in constant transition. Writers and directors, recognizing genre's narrative, thematic, and aesthetic potential, cannot resist blending ingredients gleaned from multiple styles in an attempt to invent exciting new hybrids. The seemingly impossible marriage of the horror and musical genres has resulted in a number of successful horror-musical fusions, including Jim Sharman's *The Rocky Horror Picture Show* (1975), Frank Oz's *Little Shop of Horrors* (1986), and Takashi Miike's *The Happiness of the Katakuris* (2001). Antonia Bird melded horror with another unlikely genre partner, the Western, for her 1999 film *Ravenous*. Sometimes the hybridization takes the form of a pastiche, as in Quentin Tarantino's *Kill Bill* cycle (*Vol. 1*, 2003; *Vol. 2*, 2004), films that borrow not only from the Japanese *chambara* (sword-fighting) genre but from many Hollywood genres, including the Western, musical, thriller, action, horror, and gangster. Guillermo del Toro's *Hellboy* franchise combines horror, action, romance, fantasy, and science fiction.

And genres develop inwardly as well. Subgenres occur when areas of narrative or stylistic specialization arise within a single genre. Thus, Westerns can be divided into revenge Westerns, spaghetti Westerns, bounty-hunter Westerns, cattle-drive Westerns, gunfighter Westerns, cavalry Westerns, and so on. Zombie movies, slasher flicks, vampire films, the splatter movie, and torture porn are but a few of the many manifestations of the horror genre.

To understand how complex a single genre can become, let's consider comedy. Movies are categorized as comedies because they make us laugh, but we quickly realize that each is unique because it is funny in its own way. Comedies, in fact, prove why movie genres exist. They give us what we expect, they make us laugh and ask for more, and they make money, often in spite of themselves. As a result, the comic genre in the movies has evolved into such a complex system that we rely on defined subgenres to keep track of comedy's development.

The silent-movie comedies of the 1920s—featuring such legends as Max Linder, Charlie Chaplin, Buster Keaton, Roscoe "Fatty" Arbuckle, Harry Langdon, and Harold Lloyd, many of whom worked for producer Mack Sennett—were known as slapstick comedies because aggression or violent behavior, not verbal humor, was the source of the laughs. (The term *slapstick* refers to the two pieces of wood, hinged together, that clowns used to produce a sharp sound that simulated the sound of one person striking another.)

Although after the arrival of sound movie comedy continued the sight gags of the slapstick tradition (Laurel and Hardy, the Marx Brothers, W. C. Fields), it also increasingly relied on verbal wit.

[1]

[2]

The romantic vampire Ever since Bela Lugosi first portrayed *Dracula* in Todd Browning's 1931 film, forbidden desire has been an essential ingredient of the vampire movie [1]. In recent years, much of the horror has been drained from the subgenre as audiences have fully embraced the vampire as a romantic figure. Films like *The Twilight Saga: Eclipse* (2010; director: David Slade) [2] and television series like HBO's *True Blood* feature attractive vampires who are ambivalent about their sinister appetites and dark powers, a contradiction that makes them irresistible to their mortal companions.

Through the 1930s, a wide variety of subgenres developed: comedy of wit (Ernst Lubitsch's *Trouble in Paradise*, 1932); romantic comedy (Rouben Mamoulian's *Love Me Tonight*, 1932), screwball comedy (Frank Capra's *It Happened One Night*, 1934), farce (any Marx Brothers movie), and sentimental comedy, often with a political twist (Frank Capra's *Meet John Doe*, 1941).

By the 1940s, comedy was perhaps the most popular genre in American movies, and it remains that way today, although another group of subgenres has developed, most in response to our changing cultural expectations of what is funny and what is now permissible to laugh at. These include light sex comedies (Billy Wilder's *Some Like It Hot*, 1959), gross-out sex comedies (Bobby and Peter Farrelly's *Stuck on You*, 2003), and neurotic sex comedies (almost any Woody Allen movie), as well as satire laced with black comedy (Stanley Kubrick's *Dr. Strangelove or: How I Learned to Stop Worrying and Love the Bomb*, 1964), outrageous farce (Mel Brooks's *The Producers*, 1968, and Susan Stroman's musical remake, 2005), and a whole subgenre of comedy that is associated with the comedian's name: Alec Guinness, Jacques Tati, Jim Carrey, Whoopi Goldberg, and Will Ferrell, to name but a few.

The recent wave of what film critic Stephen Holden calls the "boys-will-be-babies-until-they-are-forced-to-grow-up school of arrested-development comedies"[6] seems to have spawned the beginnings of a new comic subgenre. These genre contenders (many of which are directed or produced by the disconcertingly prolific Judd Apatow) include *The 40 Year Old Virgin* (2005; director: Judd Apatow); *Knocked Up* (2007; director: Judd Apatow); *Superbad* (2007; director: Greg Mottola); *Pineapple Express* (2008; director: David Gordon Green); and Todd Philips's *The Hangover* (2009) and *The Hangover Part II* (2011). Women characters broke into this formerly all-male subgenre in 2011 with the hit *Bridesmaids* (director: Paul Feig).

On one hand, as a form of cinematic language, genres involve filmic realities—however stereotyped—that audiences can easily recognize and understand, and that film distributors can market (e.g., "the scariest thriller ever made"). On the other hand, genres evolve, changing with the times and adapting to audience expectations, which are in turn influenced by a large range of factors—technological, cultural, social, political, economic, and so on. **Generic transformation** is the process by which a particular genre is adapted to meet the expectations of a

---

[6]Stephen Holden, "Those Darn Kidults!: The Menace of Eternal Youth," *New York Times* (November 7, 2008).

changing society. Arguably, genres that don't evolve lose the audience's interest quickly and fade away.

The Western, perhaps the most American of all genres, began to fade away in the 1960s. With certain exceptions—including Kevin Costner's *Dances with Wolves* (1990), Clint Eastwood's *Unforgiven* (1992), and the Coen brothers' *True Grit* (2011)—the Western no longer had the same appeal that it had for previous generations of movie audiences. Part of the explanation was that most Westerns were out of touch with reality, made by directors who ignored the roles played by Native Americans and women in the development of this country; that they relied instead on the fatigued nature of the good guys/bad guys conflict and equally tired myths about the West; and that they ended up creating a world that might as well have come from outer space.

Just when we thought that the Western was dead—for all practical purposes, meaning severely diminished box-office appeal—it was transformed in an original way in Ang Lee's *Brokeback Mountain* (2005). The director remains true to Annie Proulx's short story, on which the screenplay is based, but what he transforms is our fixed idea of the conventions of the Western. Gone is the conflict between the white man and the Native Americans on the frontier, the saloon, and the shootout on Main Street. Gone is the cowboy, with his apparently sexless existence, high moral purpose, and uncanny sense of nature. In place of these traditional Western elements, against a background of spectacular Western scenery (a staple of all Westerns), Lee gives us the story of two ranch hands who fall in love with one another. In Ang Lee's process of generic transformation, he has revived some of the elements of the Western to tell a story that is not about sex, but rather about loneliness, love, heartbreak, and, ultimately, sorrow—elements borrowed from yet other genres, notably the melodrama and romance.

Brokeback Mountain is set in the Wyoming of the 1960s, where and when its transformation of the traditional "boy meets girl" romance would have been even less acceptable than it would be in many parts of the country today. Even though some viewers recognized homoerotic longing in such classic Westerns as Howard Hawks's *Red River* (1948) and

Mixed genre The screenwriter, director, and producer Joss Whedon has made a career of blending seemingly incompatible genres. *Buffy the Vampire Slayer* [1], which began as a 1992 feature film (written by Whedon, directed by Fran Rubel Kuzui) before being adapted to a long-running television series (1997–2003), injects horror into an otherwise conventional high-school melodrama. The title character is a cheerleader whose popularity is threatened when she discovers that she is destined to save the world from a plague of vampires. *Firefly*, which began as a short-lived television series before being concluded in the 2005 feature film *Serenity* [2], is rife with Western archetypes, including righteous renegades, pitiless bounty hunters, earnest greenhorns, noble prostitutes, and gritty pioneers threatened by ruthless savages. But this Western is set in space: the frontier is a distant ring of outlying planets, and the outlaws ride spaceships more often than horses. The oppressive high-tech Alliance that constantly threatens the romantic independence of the brigand protagonists represents both the civilizing forces that oppose the Western's wide-open wilderness, as well as the menace of technology run amok behind the typical science-fiction antagonist.

George Roy Hill's *Butch Cassidy and the Sundance Kid* (1969), this was not a dominant theme in those movies. Today, in a culture where grappling with one's sexual identity is a staple of books and television talk shows but very few movies, *Brokeback Mountain* demonstrates that generic transformation can work in very powerful ways not only to expand the original concept of the Western genre, but also, in this case, to encourage the viewer to think more about the subject.

And new genres continue to emerge. For example, blockbuster franchises like Jon Favreau's *Iron Man* movies and Christopher Nolan's *Dark Knight* series, as well as lower-budget entries like *Kick-Ass* (2010; director: Matthew Vaughn) and *Scott Pilgrim vs. the World* (2010; director: Edgar Wright), are all comic-book movies, a rapidly emerging genre that has grown darker and more effects-laden since the modern genre's birth in Richard Donner's *Superman* (1978). Any movie that resonates with audiences and inspires imitators that turn a profit could be the beginning of another new movie genre.

What about Animation?

Animation is regularly classified as a distinct type of motion picture. Even the Academy Awards separates the top honor for narrative feature films into "Best Picture" and "Best Animated Feature" categories. It is undeniable that animated films look different than other movies. But it is important to recognize that, while animation employs different mechanisms to create the multitude of still images that motion pictures require, animation is just a different form of moviemaking, not necessarily a singular type of movie. In a recent interview, director Brad Bird (*Ratatouille, The Incredibles, The Iron Giant*) stresses that process is the only difference between animation and filmmaking that relies on conventional photography. Bird explains: "Storytelling is storytelling no matter what your medium is. And the language of film is also the same. You're still using close ups and medium shots and long shots. You're still trying to introduce the audience to a character and get them to care."[7] In fact, animation techniques have been employed to make every type of movie described in this chapter. We are all familiar with animated narrative feature films; the animation process has been applied to hundreds of stories for adults and children, including examples from every major genre described earlier. In addition, a long tradition of experimental filmmaking consists entirely of abstract and representational animated images. Even documentaries occasionally utilize animation to represent events, ideas, and information that cannot be fully realized with conventional photography. Brett Morgen recreated undocumented courtroom scenes for portions of his documentary *Chicago 10* (2007); Ari Folman's war memoir *Waltz with Bashir* (2008) claims to be the first fully animated feature-length documentary.

While there are countless possible types and combinations of animation, three basic types are used widely today: hand-drawn, stop-motion, and digital. To create hand-drawn animation, animators draw or paint images that are then photographed one frame at a time in a film camera. Since 24 frames equal 1 second of film time, animators must draw 24 separate pictures to achieve 1 second of animation.

In 1914, Winsor McCay's classic animation *Gertie the Dinosaur* required over 5,000 drawings on separate sheets of paper.[8] The difficulty of achieving fluid movement by perfectly matching and aligning so many characters and backgrounds led, the next year, to the development of cel animation. Animator Earl Hurd used clear celluloid sheets to create single backgrounds that could serve for multiple exposures of his main character. Thus, he needed to draw only the part of the image that was in motion, typically the character or a small part of the character. Although the highly flammable celluloid first used for this process has now been replaced by acetate, this type of animation is still called "cel" animation. Until the advent of digital animation, this method was used to create nearly all feature-length animated films.

Stop-motion records the movement of objects (toys, puppets, clay figures, or cutouts) with a

---

[7]Brad Bird, interview with Elvis Mitchell, *The Business*, KCRW Public Radio (May 5, 2008).

[8]Charles Solomon and Ron Stark, *The Complete Kodak Animation Book* (Rochester, N.Y.: Eastman Kodak Co., 1983), p. 14.

[1]

[3]

[2]

Alternative animation Animation isn't just for narrative. *Waltz with Bashir*, Ari Folman's 2008 documentary portraying soldiers' recollections of the Lebanon war of 1982, uses animation to visualize his interview subjects' memories, dreams, and hallucinations [1]. The artist Oskar Fischinger began experimenting with abstract animation in 1926 [2]. The fifty avant-garde movies he animated, including *Motion Painting No. 1* (1947), influenced generations of animators and experimental filmmakers. Influential filmmakers like Jan Svankmejer and his stylistic progeny Stephen and Timothy Quay (better known as the Brothers Quay) employ stop-motion animation to create dark, surreal experimental movies like the Quays' *The Comb* (1990) [3].

motion-picture camera; the animator moves the objects slightly for each recorded frame. The objects moved and photographed for stop-motion animation can be full-scale or miniature models, puppets made of cloth or clay, or cutouts of other drawings or pictures. Underneath some figures are armatures, or skeletons, with fine joints and pivots, which hold the figures in place between the animators' careful manipulations. Though more sophisticated types of stop-motion animation are available, many animators still use this method because it is relatively inexpensive and quick to produce.

Among the first American stop-motion films was *The Dinosaur and the Missing Link: A Prehistoric Tragedy* (1915), by Willis O'Brien, who went on to animate stop-motion dinosaurs for Harry O. Hoyt's live-action adventure *The Lost World* (1925), then added giant apes to his repertoire with Merian C.

Cooper and Ernest B. Schoedsack's *King Kong* (1933) and Schoedsack's *Mighty Joe Young* (1949). Inspired by O'Brien's work on *King Kong*, Ray Harryhausen set out at thirteen to become a stop-motion animator and is now most famous for his work on Don Chaffey's *Jason and the Argonauts* (1963), a Hollywood retelling of the ancient Greek legend. (O'Brien's and Harryhausen's work established a continuing tradition of using animation to create special effects for incorporation into live-action feature films.) Feature-length animated narrative films that use this technique include Nick Park's *Wallace & Gromit in The Curse of the Were-Rabbit* (2005), Wes Anderson's *Fantastic Mr. Fox* (2009), and Tim Burton's *Frankenweenie* (2012).

Digital animation, which may begin with drawings, storyboards, puppets, and all the traditional tools of theater and animation, uses the virtual world of computer-modeling software to generate the animation. John Lasseter's *Toy Story* (1995), produced by Pixar, was the first feature-length digitally animated film. A commercial and critical success, it humanized computer animation and obliterated the fear that computer animation was limited to shiny, abstract objects floating in strange worlds. *Toy Story*'s focus on plastic toys, however, helped disguise the limitations of early digital-animation techniques. Six more years of development enabled digitally animated movies such as Andrew Adamson and Vicky Jenson's *Shrek* (2001) to present compelling characters with visually interesting skin, hair, and fur.

The production of digitally animated features begins with less costly traditional techniques that allow filmmakers to test ideas and characters before starting the difficult and expensive computer-animation process. Thus, in the early phases, filmmakers use sketches, storyboards, scripts, pantomime, puppets, models, and voice performances to begin developing stories and characters. By creating a digital wire-frame character with virtual joints and anchor points, digital animators use technology to do some of the same work that stop-motion animators do by hand. Typically, a clay model is created and then scanned into the computer with the use of a digital pen or laser scanner. Animal and human actors can be dressed in black suits with small white circles attached to joints and extremities, allowing for "motion capture" of the distinctive movement of the actors. The advanced motion-capture technologies developed to animate the Na'vi natives in *Avatar* blur the line between animation and live action.

In digital animation, animators manipulate virtual skeletons or objects frame by frame on computers. To clothe the wire-frame figures with muscle, skin, fur, or hair, the animators use a digital process called texture mapping. Digital animators also "light" characters and scenes with virtual lights, employing traditional concepts used in theater and film. Specialists work on effects such as fire, explosions, and lightning. Compositing is the process of bringing all these elements together into one frame, while rendering is the process by which hundreds of computers combine all the elements at high resolution and in rich detail. Because the backgrounds, surface textures, lighting, and special effects require a tremendous amount of computer-processing power, animators typically work with wire-frame characters and with unrendered backgrounds until all elements are finalized, at which point a few seconds of screen time may take hundreds of computers many hours to render. Although the process is extremely expensive and labor-intensive, digital animation's versatility and aesthetic potential have made it the method of choice for studio-produced feature animation. Aardman Animations, the Claymation production company behind the popular *Wallace & Gromit* movies, designed their project *Flushed Away* (2006; directors: David Bowers and Sam Fell) with the stop-motion plasticine look of their popular *Wallace & Gromit* characters but created every frame of the film on a computer.

After a string of traditionally animated failures, ending with Will Finn and John Sanford's *Home on the Range* (2004), Walt Disney studios announced that it would no longer produce hand-drawn features. Ironically, Pixar mastermind John Lasseter has now assumed the position of chief creative executive at Disney, and this king of digital animation has announced plans to revive the studio's hand-drawn tradition. The move comes as no surprise to those familiar with Lasseter, who began his career drawing cel animation and is a vocal proponent of the hand-drawn animation of Japanese master Hayao Miyazaki, the director of the Disney-distributed Academy Award–winning *Spirited Away* (2001) and the Oscar-nominated *Howl's Moving Castle* (2004).

With the release of Hironobu Sakaguchi and Moto Sakakibara's *Final Fantasy: The Spirits Within* (2001), audiences were introduced to the most lifelike digitally animated human characters to date. To create these sophisticated representations, the filmmakers used an elaborate process (since dubbed "performance capture") whereby actors perform scenes in motion-capture ("mocap") suits that record millions of pieces of data that computers use to render the motion of CGI characters on-screen.

Persepolis While digital animation now dominates the animated movie market, hand-drawn films like *Persepolis* (2007) still garner popular and critical attention. Marjane Satrapi's memoir of her childhood and adolescence in Iran and Paris (codirected with Vincent Paronnaud) broke with commercial animation practices by combining its adult subject matter with graphic, mostly black-and-white drawings that emphasized a two-dimensional universe.

This process was so time consuming and expensive that it contributed to the failure of the film's production company. Nonetheless, *Final Fantasy* set the standard for digitally animated human characters. But for many animators and audiences, "realistic" figures are not necessarily the ideal. In 2004, the stylized characters in Pixar's blockbuster *The Incredibles* (director: Brad Bird) trumped the motion-capture-guided "lifelike" figures in Robert Zemeckis's *The Polar Express* in both box-office and critical response.

Although there are many other potential reasons that audiences and analysts preferred *The Incredibles*, the key issue for many critics was an unsettling feeling that they couldn't shake while watching the characters in *The Polar Express*—a feeling that the whole thing wasn't heartwarming or endearing, but was instead simply creepy. Among fans of computer-generated imagery, there was considerable debate about why, exactly, *The Polar Express* left so many viewers feeling weird and uncomfortable rather than filled with the holiday spirit. Eventually, on blogs and Listservs all over the Internet, a consensus was reached: *The Polar Express* had fallen into the "uncanny valley."

The uncanny valley is a theoretical concept first described in 1970 by a Japanese robotics engineer, Masahiro Mori. It states that the closer an object (a robot, an animated character) comes to resembling a human being in its motion and appearance, the more positive our emotional response to that object becomes until suddenly, at some point of very close (but not perfect) resemblance, our emotional response turns from empathy to revulsion. This revulsion or uneasiness, Mori says, is the result of a basic human tendency to look for anomalies in the appearance of other human beings. When an object such as a robot or an animated character is so anthropomorphic that it is nearly indistinguishable from a human being, we monitor the appearance of that object very closely and become extremely sensitive to any small anomalies that might identify the object as not fully human. For whatever reason, these anomalies create in many people a shudder of discomfort, similar in effect to the feeling we have when we watch a zombie movie or see an actual corpse. In both cases, what we see is both human and not fully human, and the contradiction produces a very negative reaction. As a result, viewers found it easy to identify and sympathize with the highly stylized characters in *The Incredibles* but responded to the much more realistic figures in *The Polar Express* with unease and discomfort.

All this is not to say that animation and photographed "reality" can't get along. Animation has been incorporated into live-action movies since the 1920s. Today, many traditionally photographed movies integrate computer-generated animation into characters, backgrounds, and special effects. Animated characters like Gollum in Peter Jackson's *Lord of the Rings* trilogy (2001–3) or Optimus Prime in Michael Bay's *Transformers: Dark of the Moon* (2011) routinely interact on-screen with flesh-and-blood performers.

This now-commonplace intrusion into conventional motion pictures is only one example of the animation explosion made possible by the recent emergence of new technologies and growing audience demand. As a result, a dozen animated narrative features were given a major theatrical release in the United States in 2011. Countless more forgo the movie-house release and go straight to DVD.

The uncanny valley If a filmmaker strives for a very high level of verisimilitude in computer-generated characters, as Robert Zemeckis did in *The Polar Express* (2004), he may risk taking the humanlike resemblance too far, causing viewers to notice every detail of the characters' appearance or movement that doesn't conform to the way real human beings actually look or move. Our emotional response to these "almost human" characters will, therefore, be unease and discomfort, not pleasure or empathy—a negative reaction known as "the uncanny valley."

Network and cable television stations, including at least one dedicated entirely to cartoons, broadcast hundreds of animated series, specials, and advertisements. The video-game market exploits animation to create animated characters and situations that allow the viewer an unprecedented level of interaction. Viewers have always been drawn to cinema's ability to immerse them in environments, events, and images impossible in daily life. Animation simply expands that capacity.

Analyzing Types of Movies

This chapter's broad survey of the different types of movies should make clear that movies are divided into narrative, documentary, and experimental (and animation) categories, and that each of these has evolved a great variety of ways to express ideas, information, and meaning. What's more, the longer cinema is around, the more ways filmmakers find to borrow, reference, and blend elements from other types in order to best serve their own vision. Now that you have studied the various ways that movies are differentiated and classified, you should be able to identify what basic type or genre a movie belongs to, recognize how the movie utilizes the elements of form and content particular to its film type, and appreciate and understand those times when the filmmakers incorporate styles and approaches rooted in other film types.

Screening Checklist: Types of Movies

✔ If the film is a documentary, is it factual, instructional, persuasive, or propaganda–or a blend of two or more of these documentary approaches? Consider the movie's relationship with the spectator and with relative truth. Does it appear to be attempting to present events and ideas in as objective a manner as is cinematically possible, or does it make a specific persuasive argument? What elements of form or content lead you to this conclusion?

✔ Look for ways in which the documentary employs narrative. Are the events portrayed selected and organized so as to tell a story?

✔ Ask yourself how this movie compares to other documentary films you've seen. Think about your formal expectations of nonfiction movies: talking-head interviews, voice-over narration, archival footage, etc. Does this movie conform to those expectations? If not, how does it convey information and meaning in ways that are different from a typical documentary?

✔ To analyze an experimental movie, try to apply Fred Camper's criteria for experimental cinema. Which of the listed characteristics does the movie seem to fit, and from which does it diverge?

✔ Remember that experimental filmmakers often seek to defy expectations and easy characterization. So consider effect and intent. How does the movie make you feel, think, or react? Do you think the filmmaker intended these effects? If so, what elements of form and content contribute to this effect?

✔ When watching an experimental film, be especially aware of your expectations of what a movie should look like and what the movie experience should be. If the movie disappoints or confounds your expectations, do your best to let go of what you've been conditioned to assume, and try to encounter the movie on its own terms. Remember that many experimental movies, unlike documentaries and narrative films, are open to individual interpretation.

✔ Since most of the movies that you study in your introductory film class will be narrative films, you should ask whether a particular film can be linked with a specific genre and, if so, to what extent it does or does not fulfill your expectations of that genre.

✔ Be aware that many movies borrow or blend elements of multiple genres. Look for familiar formal, narrative, and thematic genre elements, and ask yourself how and why this film uses them.

Questions for Review

1. What are the four related ways we can define the term *narrative*?

2. What are the main differences among the three basic types of movies?

3. What are the four basic approaches to documentary cinema? How are these approaches blended and reinterpreted by contemporary documentary filmmakers?

4. What is direct cinema, and how does it differ in approach and technique from

a conventional interview-based documentary?

5. What are Fred Camper's six characteristics most experimental films share?

6. What is a hybrid movie? What are some of the ways that documentary, narrative, and experimental movies intersect?

7. What is genre? How does genre affect the way movies are made and received?

8. What are the six sets of conventions used to define and classify film genres?

9. What are the formal and narrative elements common to each of the six movie genres described in the chapter?

10. How does animation differ from the other three basic types of movies?

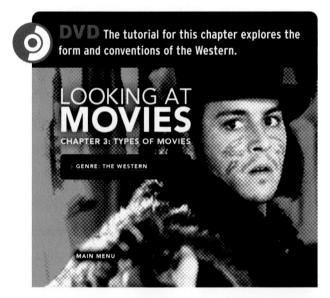

DVD The tutorial for this chapter explores the form and conventions of the Western.

LOOKING AT MOVIES
CHAPTER 3: TYPES OF MOVIES

GENRE: THE WESTERN

MAIN MENU

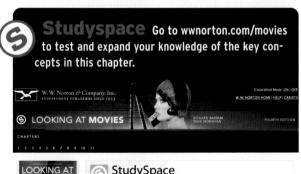

Studyspace Go to wwnorton.com/movies to test and expand your knowledge of the key concepts in this chapter.

StudySpace
Your Place for a Better Grade

1 StudySpace tells you what you know

2 Shows you what you still need to review

3 Gives you an organized study plan to master the material

Movies Described or Illustrated in This Chapter

Across the Universe (2007). Julie Taymor, director.
Alien (1979). Ridley Scott, director.
Alphaville (1965). Jean-Luc Godard, director.
American Gangster (2007). Ridley Scott, director.
American Movie (1999). Chris Smith, director.
An Andalusian Dog (1929). Luis Buñuel, director.
Applause (1929). Rouben Mamoulian, director.
Avatar (2009). James Cameron, director.
Ballast (2008). Lance Hammer, director.
Ballet mécanique (1924). Fernand Léger and Dudley Murphy, directors.
Blade Runner (1982). Ridley Scott, director.
Bonnie and Clyde (1967). Arthur Penn, director.
Borat: Cultural Learnings of America for Make Benefit Glorious Nation of Kazakhstan (2006). Larry Charles, director.
Born into Brothels (2004). Zana Briski and Ross Kauffman, directors.
Bowling for Columbine (2002). Michael Moore, director.
Breathless (1960). Jean-Luc Godard, director.
Brick (2005). Rian Johnson, director.
Bride of Frankenstein (1935). James Whale, director.
The Broadway Melody (1929). Harry Beaumont, director.
Brokeback Mountain (2005). Ang Lee, director.
Broken Flowers (2005). Jim Jarmusch, director.
Buffy the Vampire Slayer (1992). Fran Rubel Kuzui, director.
Butch Cassidy and the Sundance Kid (1969). George Roy Hill, director.
The Cabinet of Dr. Caligari (1920). Robert Wiene, director.
Cannibal! The Musical (1996). Trey Parker, director.
Capturing the Friedmans (2003). Andrew Jarecki, director.
Chicago 10 (2007). Brett Morgen, director.
Close Encounters of the Third Kind (1977). Steven Spielberg, director.
The Comb (1990). Stephen Quay and Timothy Quay, directors.
Cripple Creek Bar-Room Scene (1899). Director unknown.
Dancer in the Dark (2000). Lars von Trier, director.

Dead Man (1995). Jim Jarmusch, director.

Death to the Tinman (2007). Ray Tintori, director.

The Dinosaur and the Missing Link: A Prehistoric Tragedy (1915). Willis H. O'Brien, director.

Double Indemnity (1944). Billy Wilder, director.

Dracula (1931). Tod Browning, director.

Dreamgirls (2006). Bill Condon, director.

Dumbo (1941). Ben Sharpsteen, director.

Exit Through the Gift Shop (2010). Banksy, director.

Fahrenheit 9/11 (2004). Michael Moore, director.

Fargo (1996). Joel Coen, director.

Fast, Cheap & Out of Control (1997). Errol Morris, director.

Final Fantasy: The Spirits Within (2001). Hironobu Sakaguchi and Moto Sakakibara, directors.

Flushed Away (2006). David Bowers and Sam Fell, directors.

Frankenstein (1931). James Whale, director.

Gertie the Dinosaur (1914). Winsor McCay, director.

The Godfather (1972). Francis Ford Coppola, director.

Goodfellas (1990). Martin Scorsese, director.

The Good, the Bad and the Ugly (1966). Sergio Leone, director.

Grey Gardens (1975). Ellen Hovde, Albert Maysles, David Maysles, and Muffie Meyer, directors.

Hands on a Hard Body (1997). S. R. Bindler, director.

Harlan County USA (1976). Barbara Kopple, director.

Home on the Range (2004). Will Finn and John Sanford, directors.

Howl's Moving Castle (2004). Hayao Miyazaki, director.

An Inconvenient Truth (2006). Davis Guggenheim, director.

Insomnia (1997). Erik Skjoldbjærg, director.

Jason and the Argonauts (1963). Don Chaffey, director.

The Jazz Singer (1927). Alan Crosland, director.

Kill Bill: Vol. I (2003). Quentin Tarantino, director.

Kill Bill: Vol. II (2004). Quentin Tarantino, director.

King Kong (1933). Merian C. Cooper and Ernest B. Schoedsack, directors.

The King of Kong: A Fistful of Quarters (2007). Seth Gordon, director.

Kung Fu Panda (2008). Mark Osborne and John Stevenson, directors.

L.A. Confidential (1997). Curtis Hanson, director.

Lawrence of Arabia (1962). David Lean, director.

Leaving Las Vegas (1995). Mike Figgis, director.

Lost in Translation (2003). Sofia Coppola, director.

The Lost World (1925). Harry O. Hoyt, director.

Love Me Tonight (1932). Rouben Mamoulian, director.

The Maltese Falcon (1941). John Huston, director.

Mamma Mia! (2008). Phyllida Lloyd, director.

Mean Streets (1973). Martin Scorsese, director.

Meshes of the Afternoon (1943). Maya Deren and Alexander Hammid, directors.

Metropolis (1927). Fritz Lang, director.

Mighty Joe Young (1949). Ernest B. Schoedsack, director.

Motion Painting No. 1 (1947). Oskar Fischinger, director.

Mulholland Dr. (2001). David Lynch, director.

The Mummy (1932). Karl Freund, director.

Murderball (2005). Henry Alex Rubin and Dana Adam Shapiro, directors.

My Darling Clementine (1946). John Ford, director.

Nanook of the North (1922). Robert J. Flaherty, director.

A Nightmare on Elm Street (1984). Wes Craven, director.

Nosferatu, a Symphony of Horror (1922). F. W. Murnau, director.

Passage à l'acte (1993). Martin Arnold, director.

Peeping Tom (1960). Michael Powell, director.

Persepolis (2007). Marjane Satrapi and Vincent Paronnaud, directors.

The Polar Express (2004). Robert Zemeckis, director.

Psycho (1960). Alfred Hitchcock, director.

Raising Arizona (1987). Joel Coen, director.

Rango (2011). Gore Verbinski, director.

Ravenous (1999). Antonia Bird, director.

Removed (1999). Naomi Uman, director.

The Ring (2002). Gore Verbinski, director.

Ringu (1998). Hideo Nakata, director.

Scarface (1932). Howard Hawks, director.

Serenity (2005). Joss Whedon, director.

Shane (1953). George Stevens, director.

The Shining (1980). Stanley Kubrick, director.

Shrek (2001). Andrew Adamson and Vicky Jenson, directors.

Sicko (2007). Michael Moore, director.

Singin' in the Rain (1952). Stanley Donen and Gene Kelly, directors.

Sink or Swim (1990). Su Friedrich, director.

Slacker (1991). Richard Linklater, director.

Slumdog Millionaire (2008). Danny Boyle, director.

Snow White and the Seven Dwarfs (1937). David Hand, director; Walt Disney, producer.

South Park: Bigger, Longer & Uncut (1999). Trey Parker, director.

Spirited Away (2001). Hayao Miyazaki, director.

Stagecoach (1939). John Ford, director.

Star Wars (1977). George Lucas, director.

The Strip Mall Trilogy (2001). Roger Beebe, director.

Sunset Boulevard (1950). Billy Wilder, director.

Suspiria (1977). Dario Argento, director.

Symbiopsychotaxiplasm: Take One (1968). William Greaves, director.

Syriana (2005). Stephen Gaghan, director.

Team America: World Police (2004). Trey Parker, director.

The Third Man (1949). Carol Reed, director.

3 Godfathers (1948). John Ford, director.

THX 1138 (1971). George Lucas, director.

Toy Story (1995). John Lasseter, director.

The Tree of Life (2011). Terrence Malick, director.

Tribulation 99: Alien Anomalies under America (1992). Craig Baldwin, director.

Triumph of the Will (1935). Leni Riefenstahl, director.

28 Days Later . . . (2002). Danny Boyle, director.

21 (2008). Robert Luketic, director.

21 Grams (2003). Alejandro González Iñárritu, director.

The Twilight Saga: Breaking Dawn, Part 1 (2010). Bill Condon, director.

The Twilight Saga: Eclipse (2010). David Slade, director.

2001: A Space Odyssey (1968). Stanley Kubrick, director.

The Umbrellas of Cherbourg (1964). Jacques Demy, director.

Unforgiven (1992). Clint Eastwood, director.

Wallace & Gromit in The Curse of the Were-Rabbit (2005). Nick Park and Steve Box, directors.

Waltz with Bashir (2008). Ari Folman, director.

War of the Worlds (2005). Steven Spielberg, director.

Wavelength (1967). Michael Snow, director.

White Heat (1949). Raoul Walsh, director.

The Wolf Man (1941). George Waggner, director.

Wordplay (2006). Patrick Creadon, director.

The Wrestler (2008). Darren Aronofsky, director.

CHAPTER FOUR

Elements of Narrative

After reading this chapter, you should be able to

✔ know the relative meaning of the terms narrative, narration, and narrator.

✔ understand the function of the camera narrator, a first-person narrator, and a third-person narrator.

✔ recognize and understand the function of omniscient and restricted narration.

✔ distinguish characters by their complexity, their motivation, and their role in the narrative.

✔ understand how narrative structure functions, including the concepts of character goal and need, inciting incident, obstacles, stakes, crisis, and climax.

✔ differentiate between the story and the plot of a movie.

✔ know the difference between diegetic and nondiegetic elements of a movie's plot.

✔ understand the importance of the order (chronological or nonchronological), significance, and duration of plot events.

✔ understand the three kinds of relationships between screen duration and story duration.

What Is Narrative?

We've already gotten a good start on exploring the question, "What is narrative?" in Chapters 1 and 3. Among other things, we begin this chapter dedicated to the subject having already learned the following:

> A narrative is a story.
> Narrative movies are fiction films, as opposed to other movie modes, such as documentary or experimental.
> At the broadest conceptual level, narrative is a cinematic structure in which the filmmakers have selected and arranged events in a

cause-and-effect sequence occurring over time.

> When we think of it that way, almost all movies, even documentaries and experimental films, employ some level of narrative.
> In fact, narrative permeates more than just the world of movies—it infuses our culture and our lives. Whether we're describing a sporting event, relating a dream, recalling a memory, or telling a joke, we humans tend to order events so as to convey meaning and engage the recipient.
> Because story and storytelling are so ingrained in our everyday lives, including the movies we watch, it's all too easy to take narrative for granted.

In order to better recognize and understand how it works, we'll first need to break narrative down into the various components that contribute to telling a cinematic story. Let's start with two closely related (and potentially confusing) terms: *narration* and *narrator*.

Narration is the *act of telling* the story. The **Narrator** is *who or what tells* the story. In other words, the *narrator* delivers the *narration* that conveys the *narrative*. Filmmakers employ different approaches to the concept of narrator (who or what tells the story) and narration (how that story

LOOKING AT MOVIES

NARRATORS, NARRATION, AND NARRATIVE

DVD This tutorial discusses the relationships among narration, narrators, and narrative.

is told) to shape the viewer's experience of the narrative (the story itself).

In every movie, the camera is the primary narrator. Its narration consists of the many visual elements it captures and arranges in every composition in every shot. A narrative moment in Alfred Hitchcock's *Notorious* (1946; screenwriter: Ben Hecht) offers an easy example. In the previous scene, we have seen the Nazi conspirator Alexander Sebastian (Claude Rains) discover that his wife, Alicia (Ingrid Bergman), is a U.S. government spy. Naturally, he tells his mother, and she begins brainstorming ways to discreetly eliminate his unfaithful spouse. A shot in the next scene begins focused on the betrayed husband as he urges his wife to drink her coffee. The camera drifts down from his smirking face and across the breakfast table until Alicia's coffee cup fills the screen. When she picks it up, the camera follows it to her lips. As Alicia begins to drink, the camera moves over to feature her scheming mother-in-law contentedly stitching her needlepoint. The next shot shows Alicia rubbing her forehead and looking decidedly under the weather. Throughout the sequence, the *camera narrator* tells us that Alicia's coffee is poisoned by selecting what we see and shaping when and how we see it. In other words, the camera tells the story.

And, of course, other cinematic elements contribute to the narration. The lighting, set design, makeup, and performances in each shot, as well as the associations achieved through the juxtaposition of images, all contribute to our engagement with the narrative. Maybe it would be more accurate to state that in every movie, the filmmakers and their creative techniques constitute the primary narrator. Nonetheless, it is a little more streamlined to think of all that as "the camera".

And "the camera" isn't always a movie's only narrator. Some movies use more than one narrator to deliver the narration. This narration can be in the form of a *character's* particular perspective on the narrative's events.

A **first-person** narrator is a character in the narrative who typically imparts information in the form of **voice-over** narration, which is when we hear a character's voice *over* the picture without actually seeing the character speak the words. This technique of a character speaking to the audience allows us to *hear* one narration—from the first-person character narrator—while simultaneously *watching* the narration provided by our narrator camera.

The combination of these narrator partners may be relatively straightforward, such as in Danny Boyle's *Trainspotting* (1996; screenwriter: John Hodge), when the first-person voice-over primer to heroin addiction delivered by Renton (Ewan McGregor) plays over the opening sequences depicting the lives of the addicts that populate the story.

A richer, more complex experience of the narrative is possible when the first-person narration contrasts somehow with what we see on-screen. The first-person narrators of writer/director Terrence Malick's first two films (*Badlands*, 1973, and *Days of Heaven*, 1978) are naive and sometimes deluded young women who attempt to rationalize and even romanticize events and actions we can see for ourselves. The conflict between what the camera is telling us and the perspective provided by the first-person narrator can expand our relationship with the narrative beyond anything a camera alone can deliver.

And some movies push this relationship even further. These films don't limit the first-person narrative to voice-over narration. Instead, the first-person narrator character interrupts the narrative to deliver **direct-address** narration directly to the audience, thus breaking the "fourth wall" that traditionally separates the viewer from the two-dimensional fiction on-screen.

Ferris Bueller's Day Off (1986; director/screenwriter: John Hughes) features a charismatic slacker who seduces his fellow characters as well as his audience. Ferris (Matthew Broderick) frequently pauses the on-screen action to gaze into our eyes and charm us with his own personal take on the story he inhabits. Ferris Bueller follows in the footsteps of other smooth-talking scoundrels who break the fourth wall, most notably Tony Richardson's *Tom Jones* (1963; screenwriter: John Osborne) and Lewis Gilbert's *Alfie* (1966; screenwriter: Bill Naughton). Other direct-address narration is more confrontational. Michel Haneke's *Funny Games* (2007; screenwriter: Haneke) challenges the viewer

[1]

[2]

[3]

[4]

The camera as narrator The camera (and everything that implies) is the primary narrator in every film. In this moving camera shot from Alfred Hitchcock's *Notorious*, the camera shows us the Nazi conspirator Alexander urging his wife Alicia to drink her coffee [1], moves to fill the screen with a close-up of her cup [2], follows it to her lips [3], and then turns to connect the action to her vengeful mother-in-law [4]. The next shot features Alicia holding her throbbing head [5]. The camera has told us a story: *Alexander and his mother are poisoning Alicia.*

[5]

to endure a brutal game of cat and mouse played by a pair of psychotic young men. After they take a young family hostage, the attackers goad their victims to wager on their own survival. When their prey try to refuse the bet, one of the attackers turns to confront the audience with a string of questions: "I mean, what do you think? Do you think they stand a chance? You're on their side, aren't you? Who are you betting on, huh?" By breaking the fourth wall in this way, Haneke forces the audience to acknowledge our participation in the violence. The filmmaker implies that, in watching this senseless cruelty, we're complicit in it.

Sometimes the voice-over narrator isn't even someone in the movie. Voice-over narration can also be expressed by a voice imposed from outside of the narrative. Standing at a remove from the action allows this **third-person narrator** to provide information not accessible to a narrator who is also a participant in the story. Like the author of the story, the third-person narrator knows all and can thus provide objective context to any situation.

Wes Anderson's *The Royal Tenenbaums* (2001) opens with a third-person voice-over relating the history of a family of eccentric geniuses delivered in the dispassionate tone of a documentary reporter. But even this seemingly remote narrator (voiced by Alec Baldwin) provides more than just information. The deadpan delivery layers a sort of literary seriousness over an extended series of comic scenes detailing the family's brilliant successes and staggering failures. Later, the third-person narrator interjects to let us into a character's head at a crucial narrative moment. Royal Tenenbaum, a manipulative con man, has wormed his way back into his estranged family by pretending to be dying of cancer. When he is caught in the lie, his non-apology is predictably slick: "Look, I know I'm going to be the bad guy on this one, but I just want to say that the last six days have been the best six days of probably my whole life." As the words leave his lips, he pauses as if momentarily confused. The third-person narrator speaks up to illuminate the situation: "Immediately after making this statement, Royal realized that it was true." All this goes to show that movies can use a number of possible narrators—even combina-

Multiple narrators in *Stranger Than Fiction* In Marc Forster's *Stranger than Fiction* (2006; screenwriter: Zack Helm), the third-person narrator doesn't just help *tell* the story—it becomes a player in the narrative itself. Harold Crick (Will Farrell) hears the voice-over narrating his own story and learns that his character is slated for an imminent demise. His goal of finding the source of the narration and changing his own tragic ending forms the basis of the rest of the story. As the story progresses, we meet the depressed novelist crafting Harold's destiny. Does knowing the character who wrote it make the narration first person, or is the novel's text a third-person narrator that exists apart from the novelist character? Or is it narration at all if a character can hear it? Participating in these inconsistencies is part of the fun—and playful strangeness—of *Stranger Than Fiction*.

tions of narrators. Likewise, movies employ more than one approach to *narration*.

Narration can be **omniscient,** meaning it knows all and can tell us whatever it wants us to know. Omniscient narration has *unrestricted* access to all aspects of the narrative. It can provide *any* character's experiences and perceptions, as well as information that *no* character knows. An omniscient camera shows the audience whatever it needs to in order to best tell the story.

An espionage thriller like *Notorious* involves deception, double crosses, and mixed motives. To fully exploit the intrigue, the camera narrator must show us what is going on with multiple characters and situations. We watch Alicia uncover evidence in the wine cellar proving her husband's Nazi plotting while he hosts a party in oblivious bliss upstairs. We see him plot her death after he learns she's an American spy. We writhe with frustration watching her fellow agent (and love interest) blame

[1]

[2]

[3]

Narrators In *The Royal Tenenbaums* (2001), the camera narrator tells us the story by displaying evidence of the children Royal abandoned, as well as the slick con man himself as he delivers what we assume to be the latest in a string of manipulative lies [1]. But the narrative deepens when the third-person voice-over interjects to tell the audience that he's telling the truth this time. Mattie Ross (Hailee Steinfeld) helps tell the story of the 2010 version of *True Grit* in a couple of ways. The camera shows us the character's image and actions on-screen, and her first-person narration (as spoken by Mattie as an elderly woman) is delivered in voice-over [2]. The sadistic home invader Paul (Michael Pitt) in *Funny Games* takes a more direct approach when he breaks the fourth wall to confront his audience with direct-address narration [3].

her disheveled appearance on a hangover, when we know that all she's been drinking is poisoned coffee. A large part of the pleasure in experiencing such a story comes from knowing more than the characters and anticipating what will happen if and when they learn the whole truth.

Another Hitchcock movie, *Rear Window* (1954; screenwriter: John Michael Hayes), tells the story of Jeff Jeffries (James Stewart), a man of action stuck in his apartment in a wheelchair recovering from a badly broken leg. To amuse himself, Jeff begins spying on his neighbors. The recreational snooping suddenly takes a dark turn when he witnesses what may—or may not be—a murder.

For the viewer, the pleasure of watching Jeff slowly unravel the mystery depends on being restricted to his incomplete understanding of the events unfolding outside his rear window. As a result, Hitchcock chose **restricted narration**, which limits the information it provides the audience to things known only to a single character. This approach encourages the audience to identify with the character's singular perspective on perplexing and frightening events—and invites us to participate in the gradual unlocking of the narrative's secrets.

Steven Soderbergh's *The Limey* (1999; screenwriter: Lem Dobbs) uses a similar approach. For most of the film, the camera narrator restricts the narration. We see and hear only the thoughts, memories, perspectives, and experiences available to the character of Wilson (Terrence Stamp), as he doggedly pursues the mystery behind the death of his daughter. In fact, as the narrative progresses, the viewer gradually realizes that the movie's highly stylized editing is not conveying the story events as they happened, but as they are recalled by Wilson on his way back to England after the mystery has been solved. It's a sort of visual first-person narration without voice-over.

Of course, nothing in cinema is absolute. Many films shift between restricted and omniscient narration depending on the needs of the story. Movies like *The Limey* enforce restricted narration for most of the story, only to switch to omniscient narration when it serves the narrative to expand our view on the action. For those few times that the

Restricted narration in *Black Swan* Restricted narration makes watching *Black Swan* both excruciating and ultimately cathartic. The audience must endure every moment of the story locked inside the increasingly unreliable perspective of Nina (Natalie Portman), a prima ballerina, as the pressures of her role drive her insane. For many viewers, the ultimate experience of sharing Nina's transcendent final performance makes enduring her breakdown worthwhile.

narrative demands that the audience witness events outside Wilson's experience, the narration temporarily shifts into omniscient mode.

The deeper you look, the more complex and expressive cinema gets. But the general concepts at the foundation of cinematic storytelling are pretty straightforward. Just remember: **the narrative** is the story; **narration** is the act of telling the story; the **narrator** is who or what tells the story. In other words: the *narrator* delivers the *narration* that conveys the *narrative*.

Characters

Whether it's a pregnant teenager trying to find suitable parents to adopt her baby or a hobbit seeking to destroy an all-powerful ring, virtually every film narrative depends upon two essential elements: **a character** pursuing **a goal**.

The nature of that pursuit depends on the character's background, position, personality, attitudes, and beliefs. These traits govern how the character reacts to opportunities and problems, makes decisions, acts upon those decisions, and deals with the consequences of those actions. The allies and adversaries (all of whom have traits of their own) that the character attracts are influenced by these traits, as are all interactions between these other various characters. And that pursuit, and all the decisions, actions, consequences, relationships, and interactions that intersect and influence it, is the story.

Imagine how different the story of the original *Star Wars* series would have been if Luke Skywalker had been cautious, devoutly religious, and privileged, instead of the reckless orphaned farm boy skeptic who stumbles upon Princess Leia's holographic rescue plea? Or in the case of the Harry Potter series, what if Ron Weasley, the insecure and unrefined product of a large rambunctious wizard family, had been the boy who lived, instead of the instinctive and strong-willed neglected orphan Harry Potter? Better still, what if the earnest, intelligent, overachieving child-of-muggles Hermione was the *girl* who lived? Even if the goal remained the same in each of these hypothetical narratives, the character's traits would inspire choices and behavior that would lead them to a different path, and thus tell a different story.

The profound effect characters have on narrative comes in handy. After all, there are only so many stories in the world—consider how many movies sound interchangeable when reduced to a short description—but character traits may be assembled in infinite combinations. Each new character makes possible a different take on the same old story. Think of all the love stories or murder mysteries you've watched. The individual personalities falling in love and/or solving (and committing) crimes play a large part in keeping those archetypal narrative approaches fresh. The directors, actors, cinematographers, and designers responsible for putting the characters and their story onscreen build upon the characterizations in the screenplay to develop how exactly each character looks, speaks, and behaves in the movie.

Of course, some characters are more complicated than others. In literature, complex characters are known as **round characters**. They may possess numerous subtle, repressed, or even contradictory traits, which can change significantly over the course of the story—sometimes surprisingly so. Because they display the complexity we associate with our own personalities, we tend to see round characters as more life-like. In contrast, relatively

[1]

[2]

Round and flat characters in *Precious* Different types of stories, and even different roles within the same story, call for different approaches to character traits, behavior, and development. *Precious: Based on the Novel "Push" by Sapphire* (2009; director: Lee Daniels; screenwriter: Geoffrey Fletcher) features two remarkable characters: the illiterate teenager Precious (Gabourey Sidibe) and her abusive mother Mary (Mo'Nique). Each character is captivating in her own way, and the actresses who played them were both rightfully praised for their powerful performances. But the narrative requires that Mary be a flat character clearly defined by malicious anger and an inability to change [1]. In contrast, Precious must be a round character to drive a narrative built around revelation and transformation. At first glance, Precious appears to be slow-witted and apathetic, but as the story peels away at the layers of her complex personality, we (and Precious herself) learn that she's capable of imagination, ambition, bravery, intelligence, and insight [2].

uncomplicated **flat characters** exhibit few distinct traits and do not change significantly as the story progresses.[1] This doesn't mean that one character classification is any more legitimate than the other. Different types of stories call for different approaches to character traits, behavior, and development.

For example, the flamboyant Jack Sparrow (Johnny Depp) is entertaining enough to drive the spectacular success of the *Pirates of the Caribbean* franchise; no one could call his character boring. But with Jack, what we see is what we get. His character is clearly and simply defined, and at the end of every installment he remains the same lovable scoundrel he was in the opening scene. The *Pirates of the Caribbean* movies benefit from Jack's flat character.

The coming-of-age drama *An Education* (2009; director: Lone Scherfig; screenwriter: Nick Hornby) calls for a round character. Jenny Mellor (Carey Mulligan) is a complicated adolescent—she's smart but naive; she's both ambitious and insecure; she rebels against the same authorities whose approval she craves. Jenny falls in love with a charming older man who introduces her to a glamorous new lifestyle of concerts, art auctions, martinis, and sex. She quickly blossoms into a cosmopolitan sophisticate with no use for anything as inane as school. But she does receive an education when David turns out to be a thief and a con man—a married con man at that. Jenny enters the story as a bright girl and leaves it as a wise woman.

Of course, as with most things in the movies, round and flat characters exist, not in absolutes, but along a continuum that adjusts according to narrative and cinematic needs. Some characters are rounder than others, and vice versa. And flat characters are no more limited to crowd-pleasing blockbusters than are round characters confined to sophisticated dramas.

No one could call the hyperkinetic and provocative *Black Swan* (2010; director: Darren Aronofsky; screenwriter: Mark Heyman) a simplistic movie. Natalie Portman's powerful performance as Nina, a ballerina driven to madness by her quest to inhabit

[1]E. M. Forster, *Aspects of the Novel* (New York: Harcourt, Brace, 1927), pp. 103–118.

a demanding role, deserved the critical and popular acclaim it received. Yet in many ways, Nina could be considered a flat character. Her traits are straightforward; she's a fearful, driven perfectionist. Throughout her excruciating journey to the final performance, even as she (apparently) physically transforms, Nina stubbornly clings to the same insecurities and flaws that she carried into the story. Her final direct-address declaration is evidence of her inability to change.

On the other hand, Flynn Rider, the handsome singing rogue who costars in the popular animated children's movie *Tangled* (2010; directors: Nathan Greno and Byron Howard; screenwriter: Dan Fogelman) would have to be considered at least somewhat rounded. After all, he has a hidden past that complicates our original assessment of his behavior and intentions. The character we originally perceive as a heartless thief is revealed to be a wounded orphan with a love of reading. Over the course of the story, narrative events change him from a vain and manipulative thief to a caring and honest (albeit still vain) prince charming.

Whatever the shape of the character, narrative cannot exist if that character does not have a goal. The goal does not just give the character something to do (although that activity is important), it also gives the audience a chance to participate in the story by creating expectations that viewers want to either see fulfilled or surprised. More on that later—for now let's stick to how that goal affects our character.

The primary character who pursues the goal is known as the **protagonist**. The protagonist is sometimes referred to as the hero (or heroine), but this term can be misleading, since engaging narratives do not necessarily depend on worthy goals or brave and sympathetic characters. As Harry Potter or Frodo Baggins can attest, it's certainly not a liability if the audience happens to like or admire the protagonist. But as long as the protagonist actively pursues the goal in an interesting way, the viewer cannot help but become invested in that pursuit, and by extension, the story.

Seemingly unsympathetic protagonists chasing less than noble goals are sometimes called **antiheroes**: Walter Neff is a cocky insurance agent whose quest is to murder his lover's husband so he can have her body—and her inheritance—all to himself. Walter's no Boy Scout, but when watching *Double Indemnity* (1944; director: Billy Wilder; screenwriters: Wilder and Raymond Chandler), it's tough not to root for him to get away with murder. Mark Zuckerberg doesn't kill anyone, but he does manipulate and cheat and alienate his friends in order to make Facebook a social media juggernaut (and show up his ex-girlfriend). However, while watching David Fincher's *The Social Network* (2010, screenwriter: Aaron Sorkin), we take some pleasure in Zuckerberg's triumphs and can't help but pity him for the price he pays.

In fact, impeccable characters are rare in modern movies. Narrative craves imperfect characters because those imperfections provide obstacles, another essential building block of storytelling. We'll discuss obstacles in the narrative structure section. For now, simply consider that a romance about a shy, awkward boy in love with the head cheerleader is likely to be much more interesting than a love story between the two most beautiful and popular kids in school. Character imperfections and flaws also give characters room to grow. As the previous discussion of round and flat characters indicated, character development is central to many movie narratives.

In *Precious,* based on the novel *Push* by Sapphire, the title character's struggle to escape her violent mother and learn to read transforms her from a numbed victim into an assertive and expressive young woman. Precious's character development makes watching this often-harrowing movie a satisfying and rewarding narrative experience. On the other end of the entertainment spectrum, part of the pleasure of seeing *Kung Fu Panda* (2008, directors: Mark Osborne and John Stevenson; screenwriter: Jonathan Aibel) is Po's progress from a hapless buffoon to a skilled master of his own unique martial art style.

It's easy to understand what motivates these protagonists to pursue their goals. Precious is abused by her mother and inspired by her new teacher. Po's training is likewise prompted by both positive and negative reinforcement: he admires his kung fu master, dreams of glory, and knows he

Character development in *District 9* Progression is an essential narrative element, and the changes a character undergoes, especially when those changes involve some level of personal growth, are one of the most satisfying progressions movies have to offer. Neill Blomkamp's dystopian science-fiction thriller *District 9* (2009, screenwriters: Blomcamp and Terri Tachell) explores the themes of racism and xenophobia with a story about the forced relocation of unwanted alien squatters. The posturing protagonist Wikus (Sharlto Copley) gets what's coming to him when his meddling results in his own inexorable transformation into one of the very aliens he persecuted. But it is the interior changes Wikus experiences that give his story meaning. The more he looks like a monster, the more human he becomes.

must face a deadly adversary. Most narrative relies on this character motivation. If the viewer doesn't believe or understand a character's actions, the story's verisimilitude, and thus the audience's identification with the protagonist's efforts, will be compromised. We believe and connect with Mattie Ross's quest to track down Tom Chaney in the Coen brothers' *True Grit* (2010; written and directed by Joel and Ethan Coen) because we know that he killed her father. Sonny Wortzik (Al Pacino), the protagonist of Sidney Lumet's *Dog Day Afternoon* (1975; screenwriter: Frank Pierson), robs a bank (or tries to) because he needs money to pay for his lover's sex-change operation. We might not agree with Sonny's goal or his methods, but understanding the impulse behind his actions allows us to engage in his story.

Some storytellers use expectations of clear character motivation against their audience in order to create a specific experience of the narrative. In David Lynch's *Blue Velvet* (1986; screenwriter: Lynch), Frank Booth's heinous behavior includes huffing a strange gas, stroking a swatch of velvet, and blurting "mommy" before assaulting his sex slave. Frank's bizarre behavior isn't motivated in a way that we can easily identify, but his bizarre actions only deepen our fascination with this disturbing movie's vivid mystery.

Characters are frequently motivated by basic psychological needs that can profoundly influence the narrative—even when the character is oblivious of the interior motivation directing his or her behavior. This character need often supports the pursuit of the goal. In John G. Avildson's classic boxing picture *Rocky* (1976, screenwriter: Sylvester Stallone), the title character *wants* to win the big fight, but it is his *need* for self respect that compels him to train hard and endure extraordinary physical punishment on his difficult road to the final bell of the championship bout. The narrative goes to great lengths to establish Rocky's need to regain his self respect. The movie spends 54 minutes detailing Rocky's pathetic existence and degraded social status before he is offered a goal in the form of a serendipitous shot at a title fight. In the end, Rocky loses the big fight, but the audience still feels rewarded because his gutsy performance proves that he has fulfilled his need.

Sometimes, a story may gain a level of complexity by endowing a character with a need that is, in fact, in direct conflict with his goal. C. C. Baxter (Jack Lemmon), the protagonist of Billy Wilder's *The Apartment* (1960; screenwriters: Wilder, I. A. L. Diamond), is a lonely man who works crunching numbers at a huge insurance company. C. C. *needs* love, but he *wants* to be a big shot. Sick of being a lowly cog in the company machine, C. C. does everything possible to achieve his goal of being promoted to an executive position, including letting his supervisors use his apartment as a base for their illicit affairs. C. C. is disheartened when he discovers that Fran (Shirley MacLaine), the office elevator operator he very much likes, is the mistress his boss Mr. Sheldrake (Fred MacMurray) has been entertaining in C. C.'s apartment. But C. C. continues to pursue his goal, even after he discovers the

Goals and needs The intersection of narrative and character provides for a wide range of narrative structures and outcomes. Not every movie must have a happy ending, and the stories that do provide a happy ending are not always dependent on the protagonist achieving his or her goal. In *Rocky*, the ending is satisfying even though the underdog boxer loses the heavyweight match, because his gutsy performance gives him back the self-respect he was missing at the beginning of the story. Ultimately, the audience identifies with Rocky's psychological need even more than his goal of defeating the mighty Apollo Creed.

jilted Fran dying of a drug overdose in a suicide attempt. As he nurses Fran back to health, C. C.'s need for love progressively complicates his pursuit of corporate power. Ultimately, Sheldrake rewards C. C.'s discretion with the long-coveted job promotion, and our hero must choose between his goal and his need.

For the purposes of clarity, we've focused our discussion of character on the protagonist. But, of course, most stories require a number of players, and many of these secondary characters, including those who support or share the protagonist's objective, as well as those who oppose it, may have their own goals and needs. Typically, the traits and storylines of these characters are not as developed as that of our protagonist. These characters' primary function is to serve the narrative by helping to move the story forward or flesh out the motivations of the protagonist.

Narrative Structure

The narrative structure employed by the movies is very similar to the way that events are organized by novelists, short-story writers, playwrights, comedians, and other storytellers. In all these cases, the basic formula that has evolved is calculated to engage and satisfy the receiver of the story.

The use of the word *formula* can be misleading. Just because most stories follow the same general progression, narrative is not a single simple recipe. Like pizza, one of the many beauties of narrative structure is its very malleability. We all know a pizza when we see it, but very few pies look or taste exactly the same. Once the chef knows the basic formula and the purpose of each individual ingredient, she has a certain amount of creative freedom when creating her own personal concoction—as long as it still tastes good when it comes out of the oven. Just as good cooks know when and how to bend the rules, so do the most effective cinematic storytellers recognize how to adjust narrative structure to serve their own particular style and story.

In order to organize story events into a recognizable progression, some screenwriters break the narrative into three acts, or sections; others prefer to divide the action into five acts; others—particularly television writers—employ a seven-act structure. Not that it really matters to the audience. Our experience of the story as a continuous sequence of events is not affected by any particular screenwriter's organizational approach to partitioning the narrative development.[2]

For our purposes, we might as well keep it simple. Most narratives can be broken into three basic pieces that essentially function as the beginning, middle, and end of the story. Each section performs a fundamental narrative task. The first act sets up the story; the second (and longest) act develops it; the third act resolves it. Of course, nothing as expressive and engaging as cinematic storytelling can be quite *that* simple. Each of these narrative components involves a few moving parts.

To begin with, the setup in the first act has to tell us what kind of a story we're about to experience by establishing the **normal world**. A movie's first few minutes lay out the rules of the universe that we will inhabit (or at least witness) for the next

[2]David Howard and Edward Mabley, *The Tools of Screenwriting* (New York: St. Martin's Griffin, 1981), p. 24.

couple of hours. Once the viewer knows whether she has entered a world of talking dogs or wartime chaos—or whatever the case may be—she'll know how to appraise and approach the events to come. The viewer's expectations of the story also depend on learning the movie's tone. Is she about to watch a grim drama, a whimsical fantasy, or something else altogether? It's up to the events and situations presented in the first act to let her know.

Character, which we already know to be the linchpin of the story, must also be established. The narrative will often begin by revealing something about the protagonist's current situation, often by showing him engaged in an action that also reveals some of those essential character traits we discussed earlier in the chapter.

For example, in the Coen brothers' *The Big Lebowski* (1988; screenwriters: Joel and Ethan Coen), we first meet Jeff Lebowski (Jeff Bridges)—known to his friends as The Dude—as he shuffles into a supermarket dairy section dressed in sunglasses, pajama shorts, flip-flops, and a well-worn bathrobe. The Dude scrutinizes the assortment like a connoisseur in a wine cellar, then cracks open a carton of half and half to sniff the contents. In the next shot, he pays for his selection with a check for 69 cents.

Before we even learn his name, we know that The Dude is a free spirit who plays by his own rules. He's a slob, is not necessarily smart, and is certainly not ambitious—but he does have standards. Thus we already possess some of the essential information we'll need to anticipate and appreciate his particular response to the events and situations the narrative is about to present. We have been initiated into the story's comic, absurdist tone and are also becoming acquainted with the movie's normal world: Jeff Lebowski inhabits a decidedly unglamorous Los Angeles sprawl of dilapidated bungalows, strip malls, and bowling alleys.

Now that the character and his world have been established, it's time to get the story started. For this to happen, something must occur to change that normal world. The inciting incident (also known as the **catalyst**) presents the character with the goal that will drive the rest of the narrative.

Establishing the normal world The first scene of the Coen brothers' cult movie *The Big Lebowski* tells us what we need to know in order to understand and evaluate the narrative and its inhabitants. This offbeat comedy features a protagonist (Jeff Bridges) who wears a bathrobe in public, samples half and half in the supermarket, and writes checks for 69 cents. We are now armed with an understanding of the character that will help us appreciate The Dude's particular response to the situations the story presents to him.

In The Dude's case, the inciting incident happens the moment he gets home from the supermarket. Two thugs ambush him, shove his head in the toilet, and demand a large amount of missing money. It turns out that it's a case of mistaken identity—they're looking for a much richer Jeffrey Lebowski. To demonstrate his displeasure with this revelation, one of the attackers urinates on The Dude's beloved rug. The next day, our scruffy little Lebowski goes to see the big Lebowski about getting his rug replaced—and the story has begun.

Most inciting incidents and the resulting character goals are easy to spot. In *Black Swan*, Nina the ballerina is offered a chance at the lead role in *Swan Lake*, so she resolves to dance the part to perfection. When Tom Chaney guns down Mattie Ross's father in Fort Smith, Arkansas, in *True Grit*, the young girl swears vengeance. Dorothy, the protagonist of *The Wizard of Oz* (1939; director: Victor Fleming; screenwriter: Noel Langley), realizes that there's no place like home after a tornado deposits her among the munchkins.

Not all goals are this straightforward. Some goals shift—Luke Skywalker sets off to rescue a princess but winds up taking on the Death Star. The Dude sets off to replace a rug and winds up a pawn in someone else's mystery. The goal changes every day for William James, the danger-addicted protagonist of Kathryn Bigelow's Iraq war drama *The Hurt Locker* (2008; screenwriter: Mark Boal)—but it's always the same goal: defuse the bomb before it explodes. Ultimately, James's toughest battle is with his own inner demons.

Whatever the goal, the nature of the pursuit depends on the individual character. Nina trains, panics, and sprouts black feathers. Mattie gets on the first train to Fort Smith and scours the frontier town for a lawman with true grit. Dorothy follows the Yellow Brick Road. This active pursuit of the goal signals the beginning of the second act.

The moment Dorothy is off to see the Wizard, the audience begins to ask themselves what screenwriters call the central question: will she ever get back to Kansas? Whether the question whispers within our subconscious mind or we shout it at the screen, it is this expectation, this impulse to learn what happens and how it happens, that keeps us engaged with the narrative. We need to know if Nina will learn to let go and embrace the Black Swan inside her—and hold on to her sanity. We must find out if the spunky teenager Mattie can actually manage to wrangle Rooster Cogburn and track down the elusive Tom Chaney. We want to see if Rocky can beat the odds and defeat Apollo Creed to become heavyweight champ.

Naturally, in most cases, we want the answer to the central question to be yes. The irony, however, is that if the goal is quickly and easily attained, our story is over. This is where conflict comes in. Narrative depends on obstacles to block, or at least impede, our protagonist's quest for the goal. The person, people, creature, or force responsible for obstructing our protagonist is known as the **antagonist**. Sometimes, the identity and nature of the antagonist are clear-cut. The Wicked Witch is obviously the antagonist of *The Wizard of Oz* because she sets the scarecrow on fire, conjures a field of sleep-inducing poppies, and imprisons Dorothy. But we have to be careful with this term because, while most movies have a single—or at least primary—protagonist, the nature of the antagonist is much more variable. In *The Big Lebowski*, The Dude is

beaten and bamboozled by a host of oddballs who each use him for his or her own obscure purposes. One might say that the fugitive Tom Chaney is the antagonist of *True Grit*. After all, he gunned down Mattie's beloved father. But he doesn't even appear on-screen until two-thirds into the movie. Before she discovers (and is taken hostage by) Chaney, Mattie's obstacles are imposed by mostly well-meaning characters concerned for the safety of the plucky young heroine. So, just as not every protagonist is a hero, not every antagonist is necessarily a villain. The imposing ballet director in *Black Swan* intimidates and manipulates Nina, but he also sincerely wants her to succeed. The restricted narration makes it difficult to determine any actual malice on the part of Nina's gifted understudy. Even the dark forces represented by Nina's apparent hallucinations play a role in pushing her toward greatness. Nina's greatest adversary is herself.

The antagonist need not even be human. Opposition and obstacles are supplied by a persistent shark in Steven Spielberg's *Jaws* (1975; screenwriters: Peter Benchley and Carl Gottleib); the harsh elements and isolation of the Andes mountains in Frank Marshall's *Alive* (1993; screenwriter: John Patrick Shanley); and a very stubborn rock in Danny Boyle's *127 Hours* (2010; screenwriters: Boyle and Simon Beaufoy).

Whatever the source, obstacles are the second act's key ingredient. Let's take a closer look at *127 Hours* to see how obstacles help construct and drive the narrative. We'll start with a quick look at the setup in the first act: in the opening scene, the way the protagonist Aron Ralston (James Franco) packs establishes that he is a loner and an experienced, if overconfident, outdoorsman. As he scrambles around his spartan apartment throwing climbing gear and provisions into a day bag, he doesn't bother to locate his missing Swiss Army knife and ignores a call from his sister. Now that the narration has conveyed some of Aron's flaws, he has some room to grow, and we're prepared to chart and appreciate his development as the adventure unfolds.

Aron ventures into the desert wilds of the remote Canyonlands National Park. Along the way, he reaffirms his character traits by luring two novice

Plot points in *The Social Network* Screenwriting specialist Syd Field describes "plot points" as significant events that turn the narrative in a new direction.[3] For example, the development of the *Social Network* narrative is profoundly influenced by Eduardo Saverin's (Andrew Garfield) decision to contribute a crucial algorithm to his friend Mark Zuckerberg's first social networking experiment [1]. The plot point sets up a major narrative development that leads to Eduardo's involvement in Mark's enterprise, his eventual betrayal, and his fervent attempts for credit and compensation. Likewise, the moment when Sean Parker (Justin Timberlake) discovers an early version of "The Facebook" certainly qualifies as a plot point [2]. The intervention of the slick entrepreneur drives the explosive success of Facebook, while simultaneously alienating Zuckerberg from faithful friends like Eduardo.

hikers to an exhilarating but dangerous plunge into an underground pool before leaving them behind to trek still deeper into the wilderness. In the process of descending a deep slot canyon, Aron dislodges a small boulder. The man and the rock both tumble

---

[3]This description and elements of Figure 4.1 are based on Syd Field, *Screenplay: The Foundations of Screenwriting*, rev. ed. (New York: Delta, 2005), pp. 19–30.

down the narrow ravine. When they meet again at the bottom, the rock pins Aron's arm to the canyon wall. This sudden event gives our protagonist a goal, supplies the story with conflict and an antagonist, and begins the second act.

The next hour of the movie will be devoted to Aron's struggle to free himself. That struggle can be broken down into the series of obstacles he encounters. Aron will overcome some of them, circumvent others, and surrender to still more. Obviously, his tightly wedged arm is Aron's greatest obstacle. He attempts to yank it loose, he uses his cheap multi-tool to try to chip away at the rock, and he builds a pulley system with his climbing ropes. Nothing works.

Aron must confront other obstacles as well. When he drops his multi-tool, he retrieves it with a long stick gripped between his toes. He defeats the freezing night temperatures by wrapping his climbing ropes around his legs. He rations his water. As time goes on, Aron must also deal with memories, hallucinations, hopelessness, and regret.

And each time an attempt to dislodge the rock fails or a new obstacle presents itself, the audience asks itself the central question: will Aron free himself and survive? When his water runs out and he begins to lose his grip on reality, a positive outcome seems increasingly unlikely and the question takes on greater urgency.

This is because the **stakes are rising**. In other words, the deeper we get into the story, the greater the risk to our protagonist. What begins as a possibility of getting lost progresses to the dangers of being trapped, which develops into what appears to be certain death. Of course, the ultimate magnitude of the stakes depends on the movie. By the end of *Bridesmaids* (2011; director: Paul Feig), Lillian and Annie may lose their friendship forever. If Harry doesn't stop he-who-must-not-be-named in *Harry Potter and the Deathly Hallows: Part 2* (2011; director: David Yates; screenwriter: Steve Kloves), the entire world will be enslaved by death eaters.

The stakes are rising because the obstacles are becoming increasingly difficult for our protagonist to navigate. Over the course of the second act, narrative typically builds toward a peak, a breaking point of sorts, as the conflict intensifies and the

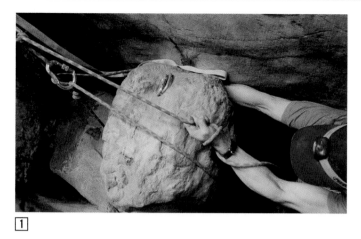

[1]

[2]

[3]

[4]

Narrative obstacles in *127 Hours* Before the Aron Ralston character can finally achieve his narrative goal, he must first engage a series of obstacles. He tries (almost) every possible method of freeing his arm from the stubborn rock pinning it to a remote canyon wall [1], insulates himself from freezing temperatures with his otherwise useless climbing rope [2], and retrieves his dropped multi-tool with his toes [3]. The crisis comes when Aron must take dramatic action or die. [4]

goal remains out of reach. This **rising action**, and the tension it provokes, enhances our engagement with the ongoing narrative. As the stakes and action rise in *127 Hours*, Aron undergoes character development. He reevaluates his selfish and solitary lifestyle, appreciates his family, and mourns a squandered relationship. In fact, Aron's encounters with memory provide some of the movie's most meaningful moments.

Eventually, our protagonist must face a seemingly insurmountable obstacle, and our story must reach a turning point and work its way toward resolution and the third and final act. This narrative peak is called the **crisis**. The goal is in its greatest jeopardy, and an affirmative answer to the central question seems all but impossible. In Aron Ralston's case, he's on the verge of death and out of options—almost.

The **climax** comes when the protagonist faces this major obstacle. In the process, usually the protagonist must take a great risk, make a significant sacrifice, or overcome a personal flaw. As the term implies, the climax tends to be the most impressive event in the movie. Aron breaks the bone in his trapped arm, and then saws through what's left with a very dull blade. At the crisis

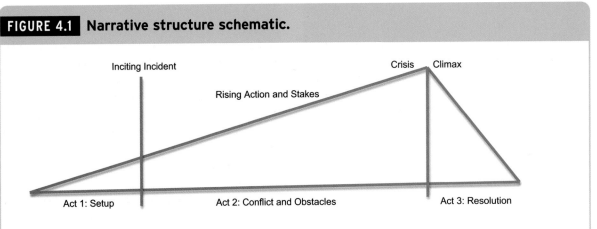

FIGURE 4.1 Narrative structure schematic.

Inciting Incident

Rising Action and Stakes

Crisis   Climax

Act 1: Setup   Act 2: Conflict and Obstacles   Act 3: Resolution

Narrative structure is typically characterized by a three-act structure. The first act establishes character, setting, and tone, then introduces a goal with an inciting incident. The second act is structured around the protagonist's pursuit of the goal and the conflict and obstacles that must be confronted before the goal is either gained or lost at the peak of the rising action and stakes. The narrative then falls as the third act resolves the conflict, wraps up ongoing storylines, and gives the viewer a chance to either celebrate or mourn the dramatic result. Diagrams like this are helpful in visualizing a standard structure, but we should keep in mind that the shape any story takes is as flexible as the filmmakers want it to be.

point of *Star Wars: Episode IV—A New Hope* (1977; director/screenwriter: George Lucas), Luke Sky-walker's fellow fighter pilots have been decimated and the Death Star is within range of the rebel stronghold, so Luke uses the Force to drop a pro-ton torpedo into the evil Empire's exposed orifice. At the climax of *Black Swan*, Nina realizes she's been stabbed (by herself—it's complicated), but she dances onto the stage and gives the perform-ance of her career.

Once the goal is either gained or lost, it's time for the **resolution**—the third act of falling action, in which the narrative wraps up loose ends and moves toward a conclusion. For some protagonists, the struggle continues well into this final act. After being trapped for 127 hours and amputating his own arm, Aron must still strike out in search of help. In *True Grit*, the recoil from the rifle that dispatches Chaney propels Mattie into a snake pit. She has to endure being bitten on the arm by rattlesnakes and carted across the prairie to a distant doctor. But sooner or later, virtually every story resolves the conflict and allows the audience a chance to celebrate and/or

contemplate the final score before the credits roll. We see footage showing the real-life Aron Ralston (yes, it's a true story) as an active hiker with a wife and child. Luke, in blissful ignorance of his family history, enjoys a kiss from the princess. Surrounded by her adoring director and fellow dancers, the black swan declares her perfection. An elderly (and one-armed) Mattie pays homage to the crusty U.S. marshal whose true grit saved her life. Rocky hugs his girlfriend. The Dude abides—and bowls.

The Screenwriter

The screenwriter is responsible for coming up with this story, either from scratch or by adapting another source, such as a novel, play, memoir, or news story. He or she (or they) builds the narrative structure and devises every character, action, line of dialogue, and setting. And all this must be man-aged with the fewest words possible. Screenplay format is precisely prescribed—right down to page margins and font style and size—so that each script page represents one minute of screen time. The best screenwriters learn to craft concise but vivid descriptions of essential information so as to provide the director, cinematographer, designers, and actors a practical foundation that informs the collaborative creative process necessary to adapt the script to the screen. Many scripts are even described and arranged to take a step beyond written storytelling and suggest specific images, juxtapositions, and sequences. No rules determine how an idea should be developed or an existing literary property should be adapted into a film script, but the process usually consists of several stages, involving many rewrites. Likewise, no rule dictates the number of people who are eventually involved in the process. One person may write all the stages of the screenplay or may collaborate from the beginning with other screenwriters; sometimes the director is the sole screenwriter or co-screenwriter.

Before the breakdown of the Hollywood studio system and the emergence of the independent film, each of the major studios maintained its own staff of writers, to whom ideas were assigned depending on the particular writer's specialty and experience. Each writer was responsible by contract to write a specified number of films each year. Today, the majority of scripts are written in their entirety by independent screenwriters (either as write-for-hires or on spec) and submitted as polished revisions. Many other screenplays, especially for movies created for mass appeal, are written by committee, meaning a collaboration of director, producer, editor, and others, including *script doctors* (professional screenwriters who are hired to review a screenplay and improve it). Whether working alone or in collaboration with others, a screenwriter has significant influence over the screenplay and the completed movie and, thus, its artistic, critical, and box-office success.

When the director is also the screenwriter—and, thus, genuinely an auteur—there is a higher likelihood that the screenplay will reflect and convey a consistent vision. This is true of films by directors such as François Truffaut, Werner Herzog, Chantal Akerman, Joel and Ethan Coen, Woody Allen, Akira Kurosawa, John Ford, and Satyajit Ray, to name a very few.

Despite the widespread existence of seminars, books, and software programs that promise to teach the essentials of screenwriting overnight, becoming a professional screenwriter requires the possession of innate talents and skills that can be enhanced by experience. Such skills include understanding the interaction of story, plot, and narrative; being able to write visually (meaning not only putting a world on the page, but also foreseeing it on the screen); and being able to create characters and dialogue. Screenwriters must understand the conventions and expectations of the various genres, work within deadlines that are often unreasonable, and be able to collaborate, particularly with the producer and director, and to anticipate that their original ideas may be extensively and even radically altered before the shooting starts. In addition to creating a compelling story, engaging plot, and fascinating characters, screenwriters must have a solid understanding of what is marketable. Finally, if they are presenting a finished screenplay, it must conform to industry expectations regarding format and style.

Elements of Narrative

Narrative theory (sometimes called *narratology*) has a long history, starting with Aristotle and continuing with great vigor today. Aristotle said that a good story should have three sequential parts: a beginning, a middle, and an end—a concept that has influenced the history of playwriting and screenwriting. French New Wave director Jean-Luc Godard, who helped to revolutionize cinematic style in the 1950s, agreed that a story should have a beginning, a middle, and an end but, he added, "not necessarily in that order." Given the extraordinary freedom and flexibility with which cinema can handle time (especially compared to the limited ways in which the theater handles time), the directors of some of the most challenging movies ever made—including many contemporary examples—would seem to agree with Godard.

Script to screen In *Pulp Fiction* (1994), the mob hit man Vinnie (John Travolta) has inadvertently caused his bosses' mistress Mia (Uma Thurman) to overdose on pure heroin. Desperate to revive her, he drags her seemingly lifeless body to the drug dealer Lance (Eric Stoltz) who sold him the drugs in the first place. In this scene, Vince attempts to revive Mia with a shot of adrenaline injected directly into her heart. The stakes are high: if she dies, he dies. Writer/director Quentin Tarantino's screenplay provides more than plot and dialogue. Screenwriters use the script format to isolate and order images and actions on the page to suggest shot-by-shot cinematic storytelling. A long line of creative collaborators—from director to designers to cinematographer to actors to editors—build upon the narrative foundation supplied by the original screenplay. As we can see from this example, the moment-by-moment presentation has evolved and expanded somewhat along the journey from written word to edited images, but the essential narrative impulse remains intact.

The shots are presented in sequence as they appear in the completed film; the notations below [1, 5, 6, 4, 7, 3, 8, 9, 10] indicate the portion of the original script depicted in each shot.

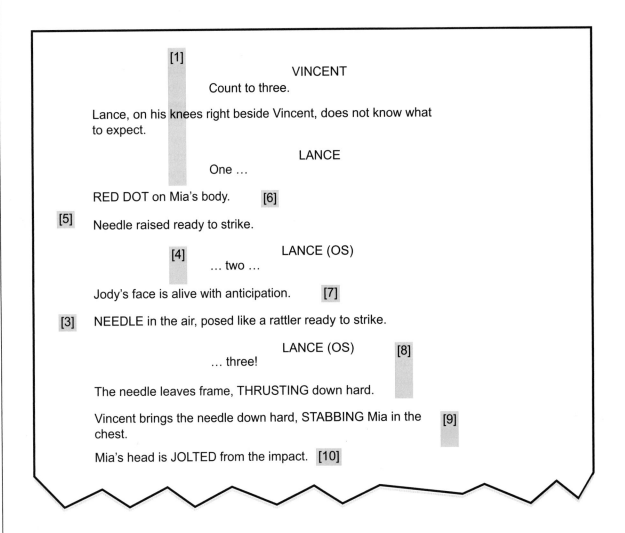

[1]

VINCENT
Count to three.

Lance, on his knees right beside Vincent, does not know what to expect.

LANCE
One …

RED DOT on Mia's body.   [6]

[5]   Needle raised ready to strike.

[4]   LANCE (OS)
… two …

Jody's face is alive with anticipation.   [7]

[3]   NEEDLE in the air, posed like a rattler ready to strike.

LANCE (OS)   [8]
… three!

The needle leaves frame, THRUSTING down hard.

Vincent brings the needle down hard, STABBING Mia in the   [9]
chest.

Mia's head is JOLTED from the impact.   [10]

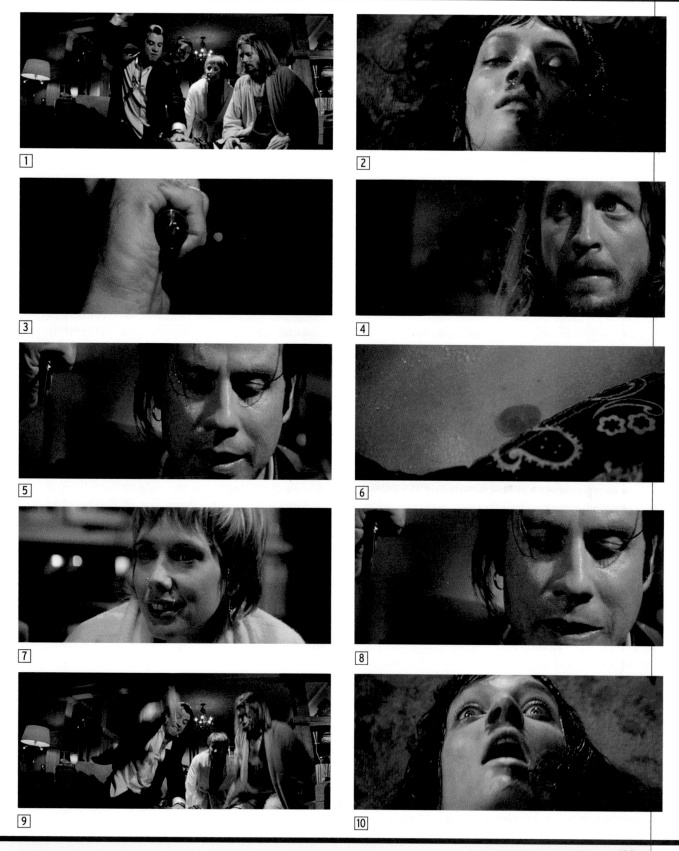

The complexities of narratology are beyond the scope of this book,[4] but we can begin our study by distinguishing between two fundamental elements: story and plot.

Story and Plot

Although in everyday conversation we might use the words *story* and *plot* interchangeably, they mean different things when we write and speak about movies. A movie's **story** consists of (1) all the narrative events that are explicitly presented on-screen plus (2) all the events that are implicit or that we infer to have happened but are not explicitly presented. The total world of the story—the events, characters, objects, settings, and sounds that form the world in which the story occurs—is called its **diegesis**, and the elements that make up the diegesis are called **diegetic elements**.

In the first scene of *The Social Network* we see Mark Zuckerberg (Jesse Eisenberg) and Erica Albright (Rooney Mara) sitting together in a crowded bar. They are having a heated conversation—at least it's heated on one side. Mark is chattering a rapid-fire monologue involving SAT scores in China and rowing crew; Erica is struggling to clarify what exactly he's talking about. Everything we experience in this scene is part of the movie's diegesis, including the other bar patrons and the muffled dissonance of the crowd's chatter mixed with the White Stripes' "Ball and Biscuit" playing on an unseen jukebox. Of course, we pay special attention to what the featured characters say and how they look saying it. From this explicitly presented information, we are able to infer still more story information that we have not witnessed on-screen. They've been here a while—their beers are half empty and they're in the middle of an ongoing conversation—and they're a couple. Watching their interaction, we can even guess the nature and duration of Mark and Erica's relationship. As the conversation intensifies, we can pick up on still more implicit information. Mark is obsessed with getting into a prestigious student club—his intensity implies that he is not exactly popular with the elite crowd. We learn Mark is going to Harvard and that he looks down on Erica for merely attending lowly (in his eyes) Boston University. The tone of her angry retort about Mark's Long Island roots lets us imagine a relatively humble upbringing that might be fueling his need for prestige. The story includes everything in the diegesis, every event and action we've seen on-screen, as well as everything we can infer from watching those events.

The **plot** consists of the specific actions and events that the filmmakers select and the order in which they arrange those events so as to effectively convey the narrative to the viewer. In this scene, what the characters do on-screen is part of the *plot*, including when Erica breaks up with Mark and stalks off, but the other information we infer from their exchange belongs exclusively to the *story*.

The distinction between plot and story is complicated by the fact that in every movie, the two concepts overlap and interact with one another. Let's continue exploring the subject by following the jilted Mark as he slinks out of the bar and makes his way back to his dorm. In this sequence, we hear the diegetic sounds of evening traffic, the tread of Mark's sneakers, and the muted chatter of his fellow pedestrians. We watch Mark trudge past the pub, trot across a busy street and down a crowded sidewalk, and jog across campus. As we can see in Figure 4.2, these *explicitly presented events*, and every image and sound they produce, are included in the intersection of story and plot.

But remember that story also incorporates those events *implied* by what we see (and hear) on-screen. In the case of this particular sequence, that might involve the portions of Mark's journey that were not captured in any of the shots used to portray his journey. In addition, everything we infer from these images and sounds, from the supremacy of the great university to the sophistication of the young scholars strolling its campus, is strictly story. The

[4]This discussion of narrative theory adapts material from, and is indebted to, Seymour Chatman, *Story and Discourse: Narrative Structure in Fiction and Film* (Ithaca, N.Y.: Cornell University Press, 1978) and *Coming to Terms: The Rhetoric of Narrative in Fiction and Film* (Ithaca, N.Y.: Cornell University Press, 1990). Other works of contemporary narrative theory are recommended in the bibliography at the end of this book.

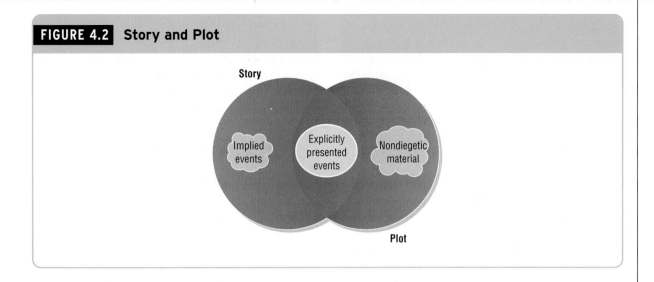

plot concerns only those portions of his journey necessary to effectively convey the Ivy League setting and the narrative idea of Mark's hurrying faster and faster the closer he gets to the sanctuary of his dorm room.

But the plot provides more than simply this particular arrangement of these specific events. Plot also includes **nondiegetic elements**: those things that we see and hear on the screen that come from outside the world of the story, such as score music (music not originating from the world of the story), titles and credits (words superimposed over the images on-screen), and voice-over comments from a third-person voice-over narrator.

For example: back in the bar, moments after Erica storms out, music begins to play over the shot of Mark alone at the table. This music is different than the White Stripes song we heard in the background earlier in the scene. Whereas that *diegetic* music came from a jukebox from within the world of the story, this new music is *nondiegetic* score music that the filmmakers have imposed onto the movie in order to add narrative meaning to the sequence. The music begins as lilting piano notes that help convey the sadness Mark feels after getting unexpectedly dumped. Deeper, darker notes join the score as the music continues over Mark's journey home, allowing us to sense the thoughts of vengeance intruding on Mark's hurt feelings. As he

trots up the steps to his dorm, a title announces the time and place of our story: Harvard University *Fall 2003*. These nondiegetic elements—score music and titles—are not part of the story. But they are an important piece of the plot: the deliberate selection and arrangement of specific events and elements the filmmakers employ to deliver the narrative.

A new sequence begins when Mark arrives home and cracks open a beer and his laptop. The

[1]

[2]

[3]

[4]

[5]

Plot and story in *The Social Network* The deliberate structure of selected events, as well as nondiegetic elements such as a rhythmic musical score and titles marking the passage of time, comprise the *plot* that delivers the *story* of Mark Zuckerberg's social networking epiphany. Causality guides the filmmakers' plot choices: Mark gets a diabolical idea [1], downloads dormitory resident photos [2], uses computer code and an algorithm to create an online game comparing relative female hotness [3], which rapidly escalates into an Internet sensation [4] that crashes the Harvard network—which delights Mark [5]. The specific events and their particular arrangement are plot; the events, along with other actions and meaning they imply but don't show, are the story.

next eight minutes of *The Social Network* depict his discovery of the Internet's latent power to enthrall and connect its users.

The *story* conveyed in those eight minutes includes the following: still stinging from Erica's rejection, Mark blogs a blistering critique of his new ex-girlfriend. Then, an offhand comment from one of his roommates gives Mark an idea. What if he could create a way for other students to compare pairs of female Harvard students and vote on which woman is hotter? Mark hacks into each of the university's dormitory "Face Book" photo ros-ters and downloads every possible female resident photo. His friend Eduardo (Andrew Garfield), having read Mark's blog, drops by to console him and winds up getting pressured into creating an algorithm to automatically select and pair photos, then collate and come up with new pairings based on the results. Mark and Eduardo write the necessary code, and "Facemash" goes up on the campus network. Students all across Harvard discover and play and recommend Facemash. The explosion of online participation crashes the university's computer network.

Every event implied by the previous description, including every line of code Mark must write, every gathering happening across campus, every student who plays Facemash, every relative hotness vote they cast, and every roommate cheering them on or reacting with disgust are part of that *story*.

The filmmakers use *plot* to tell us that story. We can't possibly see every line of code, every game of Facemash, every campus activity interrupted and enlivened by the new Internet sensation. So specific events and elements are selected and ordered to present the cause and effect chain of events that enables the audience to experience and understand the narrative. Our engagement with the story on-screen is enhanced by the nondiegetic elements the plot layers onto this specific sequence of selected events, including a pulsating musical score and occasional titles announcing the time as the phenomenon spreads.

And, of course, the story and the plot overlap. Every event explicitly presented on-screen, and every diegetic sound generated by those events, qualifies as both story *and* plot.

The relationship between plot and story is important to filmmakers and to the audience. From the filmmaker's perspective, the story exists as a precondition for the plot, and the filmmaker must understand what story is being told before going through the difficult job of selecting events to show on-screen and determining the order in which they will be presented. For us as viewers, the story is an abstraction—a construct—that we piece together as the elements of the plot unfold before us on-screen, and our impressions about the story often shift and adjust throughout the movie as more of the plot is revealed. The plots of some movies—classic murder mysteries, for example—lead us to an unambiguous sense of the story by the time they are done. Other movies' plots reveal very little about the causal relationships among narrative events, thus leaving us to puzzle over those connections, to construct the story ourselves. As you view movies more critically and analytically, pay attention not only to the story as you have inferred it, but also to how it was conveyed through its plot. Understanding this basic distinction will help you appreciate and analyze the overall form of the movie more perceptively.

To picture the relationship between plot and story slightly differently, and to become more aware of the deliberate ways in which filmmakers construct plots from stories, you might watch a number of different movies that tell a story with which you are familiar—for example, Walt Disney's *Cinderella* (1950; screenwriters: Ken Anderson et al.), Frank Tashlin's *Cinderfella* (1960, starring Jerry Lewis; screenwriter: Tashlin), Garry Marshall's *Pretty Woman* (1990, starring Julia Roberts; screenwriter: J. F. Lawton), Andy Tennant's *Ever After* (1998, starring Drew Barrymore; screenwriters: Susannah Grant, Tennant, and Rick Parks), and John Pasquin's *Miss Congeniality 2: Armed and Fabulous* (2005, starring Sandra Bullock; screenwriters: Marc Lawrence, Katie Ford, and Caryn Lucas)—all of which rely on the basic story structure of the well-known fairy tale. This sort of critical comparison will enable you to see more clearly how the plots differ, how the formal decisions made by the filmmakers have shaped those differences, and how the overall form of each movie alters your perception of the underlying story. When James Cameron planned to make a movie about the sinking of the HMS *Titanic*, he had to contend with the fact that there were already three feature films on the subject, as well as numerous television movies and documentaries. Moreover, everyone knew the story. So he created a narrative structure that was based on a **backstory**, a fictional history behind the situation extant at the start of the main story: the story of Rose Calvert's diamond. That device, as well as a powerful romantic story and astonishing special effects, made his *Titanic* (1997) one of the greatest box-office hits in history.

Through plot, screenwriters and directors can provide structure to stories and guide (if not control) viewers' emotional responses. In fact, a particular plot may be little more than a sequence of devices for arousing predictable responses of concern and excitement in audiences. We accept such a plot because we know it will lead to the resolution of conflicts, mysteries, and frustrations in the story.

Literary adaptations have inspired the movies since they were invented and remain a vital source of movie narratives. For example, over 250 movies—many of them masterpieces in their own

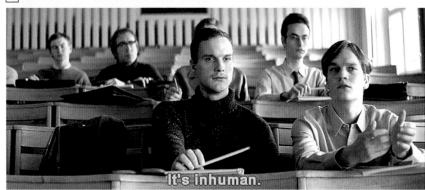

when they know in advance that the movie is not in English. Unfortunately, this bias means that many great movies never reach audiences outside of major metropolitan areas. Nonetheless, most film lovers would rather be distracted by reading subtitles than by an imposed and often awkward imposition of one performance onto another.

In director-screenwriter Florian Henckel von Donnersmarck's *The Lives of Others* (2006), which explores the repressive surveillance of East German citizens by the Ministry of State Security (known as the Stasi), language is unusually important. Spying or wiretapping activities were ubiquitous in East Germany in the 1980s, and people were often jailed or murdered for what they said. Thus, it was essential for the movie to have subtitles that conveyed precisely what the characters were saying so that the viewer could follow the story and evaluate the moral dilemma that is at its heart. Fortunately, its subtitles are succinct, clear, and as faithful as they can be to the original German. Indeed, they are so good that the scriptwriter might have had eventual subtitling in mind when he wrote it.

Narrative in foreign films The narratives of most movies we see depend on language—the spoken language of dialogue and narration—but we are presented with a different viewing situation when the movie is shot in a foreign language. In that case, we have to rely either on subtitles or rerecording (also known as dubbing). Subtitles, which provide a visual translation into English of a film's dialogue or narration, are usually displayed at the bottom of the screen. Rerecording involves actors (sometimes the actual actors we see on the screen, but more likely other professional actors who are fluent in spoken English) who watch the footage, synchronize their delivery as closely as possible to the lip movements of the actor on the screen, and reread the lines. Obviously, rerecording provides a more accurate account of the film's language, but the process— which often obscures a significant portion of the original performance—is also expensive, so subtitling remains the standard, particularly with those foreign films that have a limited release in the United States and, thus, cannot bear the cost of rerecording. The challenge with subtitling is to provide, in a limited graphic way, a viable summary of what is being said on the screen. However, in an effort to have the subtitles match the action on the screen, the subtlety, idiom, and nuance inherent in spoken language are often, and of necessity, neglected by the person supervising their preparation. While subtitles (or close-captioned devices in selected theaters) are essential for hearing-impaired viewers, most American mainstream audiences avoid subtitled movies

In the scene pictured here, the movie must make it clear that the Stasi routinely used surveillance and torture to achieve its goals. It does this by intercutting between two events: an earlier one in which Stasi officer Gerd Wiesler (Ulrich Mühe) conducts a lengthy interrogation of a prisoner (unidentified), who finally begs, "Please, let me sleep!" [1] and a later one in which Wiesler explains his methods to students and one of them, Benedict Lehmann (Ludwig Blochberger, *right*), speaks out against the practice of sleep deprivation, saying "It's inhuman" [2]. The explicit, objective language in both scenes is clearly conveyed in the subtitles. After Lehmann's remark, we see Wiesler marking an "X" next to the man's name on his class roster, a gesture full of implications. Wiesler then tells the class that torture is sometimes necessary to get a prisoner to tell the truth. These subtitled images convey the moral dilemma that is at the heart of this film.

Narrative form and the biopic A biographical movie, or biopic, provides particularly rich opportunities to ask why the filmmakers chose to tell the story the way they did. After all, the facts of the main character's life are objectively verifiable and follow a particular order. But storytellers' shaping of the material, the form that the facts take, determines how compelling the movie is dramatically, how interesting it is cinematically, and what it ultimately means.

Movie audiences love boxing movies, such as Clint Eastwood's *Million Dollar Baby* (2004), Martin Scorsese's *Raging Bull* (1980), and David O. Russell's *The Fighter* (2010; screenwriters: Scott Silver, Paul Tamsay, and Eric Johnson), a boxing drama based on the true story of Micky Ward (Mark Wahlberg) and his brother Dicky (Christian Bale). The narrative relies on facts about their upbringing in a working-class Boston neighborhood, their manipulation by a scheming mother-cum-manager (Melissa Leo), and most spectacularly, Dicky's descent into crack cocaine addiction and eventual imprisonment. Dicky—once a champion, and then Micky's trainer—is now a loser and an obstacle to his brother's success in the ring. On his own, Micky comes from behind and becomes a winner, but by recounting the almost simultaneous fall of his brother, the screenwriters have chosen a darker way to tell the story. *The Fighter* encourages us to analyze this narrative choice: Is the conflict between the brothers central to Micky's eventual winning of a welterweight title?

right—have been made from Shakespeare's plays, and producers continue to find imaginative ways of bringing other literary classics (e.g., *Beowulf* or *The Iliad*) to the screen. In the last few years alone, cinematic adaptations have been made of the works of such distinguished writers as Raymond Carver (*Jindabyne*, 2006; director: Ray Lawrence), Ian McEwan (*Atonement*, 2007; director: Joe Wright), Philip K. Dick (*A Scanner Darkly*, 2006; director: Richard Linklater), Gabriel García Márquez (*Love in the Time of Cholera*, 2007; director: Mike Newell), D. H. Lawrence (*Lady Chatterley*, 2006; director: Pascale Ferran), and, of course, Shakespeare.

Today, publishers of all kinds are bringing their books to the screen by forming partnerships with movie production companies. For example, Marvel Comics has done this in order to retain aesthetic and financial control over its characters and stories, such as those in Jon Favreau's *Iron Man* movies. This gives them a larger share of the money paid for film rights, as well as a larger cut of the box-office sales, and additional revenues from DVDs, cable TV, and other media. Authors whose books are adapted under these partnerships also have more influence on choosing the screenwriters and even actors.

Peter Jackson's *Lord of the Rings* trilogy (2001–3), while faithful to the spirit of J. R. R. Tolkien's novels, is very different from the books; movies are, by their nature, different from the books on which they are based. Jackson's trilogy is a lavish visual interpretation of Tolkien's literary vision, and thus its mythical world is different from the one each of us imagines as we read those books.

Jackson relies heavily on action scenes, which are exciting, and special effects, which are wondrous. And he had to eliminate or combine certain characters and details in order to manage the vast amount of source material. However, it is the ending—as happy a Hollywood ending as in *The Wizard of Oz*—that challenges us. You are no doubt familiar enough with quest movies to expect that, in the end, the good protagonist will defeat the evil antagonist and that the hero's quest will reach a satisfactory conclusion. In contrast to Tolkien's much darker and more pessimistic ending, that is exactly what happens in Jackson's version. In the movie's last segment, Frodo continues his journey as he boards a ship with his mentors and sails away, and Sam returns to find that the shire is almost exactly as he left it, just as Dorothy finds Kansas pretty much as she left it. We assume that Sam will live "happily ever after," the conclusion of all fairy tales.

Order

Bringing order to the plot events is one of the most fundamental decisions that filmmakers make about relaying story information through the plot. Unlike

Adaptation of literary sources [1] David Lean's *Great Expectations* (1946; screenwriters: Anthony Havelock-Allan, Lean, Cecil McGivern, Ronald Neame, and Kay Walsh) takes place, as Dickens's novel does, in nineteenth-century England. The young protagonist (John Mills, *left*), a student in London named Pip (as in the novel), confronts his previously anonymous benefactor, Magwitch (Finlay Currie). [2] Fifty-two years later, Alfonso Cuarón's version of the same story (*Great Expectations*, 1998; screenwriter: Mitch Glazer) is set in contemporary America. Finn (Ethan Hawke, *right*), a painter in New York City, confronts his previously anonymous benefactor, Arthur Lustig (Robert De Niro). An analysis of the differences between these two adaptations of the same novel can lead you to a deeper appreciation of the power of filmmakers' decisions regarding plot specifically and film form more generally.

story order, which necessarily flows chronologically (as does life), plot order can be manipulated so that events are presented in nonchronological sequences that emphasize importance or meaning or that establish desired expectations in audiences. Many of the movies that puzzle but delight audiences—Danny Boyle's *Trainspotting* (1996; screenwriter: John Hodge), Christopher Nolan's *Memento* (2000; screenwriters: Christopher and Jonathan Nolan), or Michel Gondry's *Eternal Sun-*

shine of the Spotless Mind (2004; screenwriters: Charlie Kaufman, Gondry, and Pierre Bismuth)—are built on risky moves by the filmmakers to scramble plot order or play with it in such a way that discerning the underlying story can be one of the audience's chief sources of interest and enjoyment. If any of these movies' plots had presented the story information in strict chronological order, viewers might have found these films much less challenging.

Like many other aspects of filmmaking, conventions of plot order have been established and challenged over the course of film history. For example, Orson Welles and Herman J. Mankiewicz, the co-screenwriters of *Citizen Kane* (1941), adopted an approach to plot order so radical for its time that it actually bewildered many viewers with its unconventional narrative style and structure. The movie's plot consists of nine sequences, five of which are flashbacks. The second of these sequences, the "News on the March" newsreel, grounds us by presenting Kane's (Welles) life in a reasonably chronological line; but Mr. Thompson (William Alland), the newsreel reporter, does not conduct his search for the meaning of "Rosebud" chronologically. His investigation is a kind of detective story, and Welles and Mankiewicz incorporate ellipses (gaps and jumps) into the narrative to make the film's form another kind of detective story. That is, just as Thompson tries to assemble clues about Kane's life into a solution of that life's mystery, so we must, even as we watch, fill in plot details and give it order. *Citizen Kane* presented techniques, ideas, and demands on an audience that are now a standard part of film vocabulary, yet at the time audiences were unprepared for the challenge of taking in and working with so many audio and visual facts so quickly.

However challenging it was for its time, the plot structure of *Citizen Kane* has been so influential that it is now considered conventional. Among the many movies that it influenced is Quentin Tarantino's *Pulp Fiction* (1994; screenwriters: Tarantino and Roger Avary). The plot of *Pulp Fiction*, which is full of surprises, is constructed in a nonlinear way and fragments the passing of time. We might have to see the movie several times before being able to say, for instance, at what point—in the plot and in the story—Vincent Vega (John Travolta) dies.

Plot order in *Citizen Kane* To provide a straightforward account of Charles Foster Kane's life and help viewers get their bearings within a highly unconventional plot order, Orson Welles's *Citizen Kane* (1941) begins with a fictionalized mini-documentary. "News on the March" is a satire on the famous weekly newsreel series *The March of Time* (1935–51), which was shown in movie theaters and which mixed location footage with dramatic reenactments. Using this culturally familiar narrative device as an anchor for the rest of the movie, Welles tried to ensure that viewers wouldn't lose their way in the overall plot.

By contrast, Gaspar Noé's *Irréversible* (2002; screenwriter: Noé), which takes place within the span of one day, begins with an appalling revenge murder, after which the plot order—much of the action is equally violent—unfolds in reverse. The movie's overall form is also aggressive. The spinning, swooping camera work is disorienting; the handheld camera gives it a documentary look that is nullified by the fact that it is an intensely subjective account of two men's vengeance; and each episode unfolds in an uninterrupted long take. We have to ask why, aside from the novelty and shock value, Noé has chosen to tell the story in reverse chronological order and to use these other techniques; why does he believe that these stylistic aspects are more suited to telling his story than conventional narrative techniques? Because the work stands on its own, he does not have to answer these questions. Nonetheless, there appears to be a disconnect between the story and plot of his movie.

Christopher Nolan's *Memento* (2000), a puzzle movie like M. Night Shyamalan's *The Sixth Sense*

Complex plot structures Since *Citizen Kane*, some movies have tended toward increasingly complex plot structures, including Bryan Singer's *The Usual Suspects* (1995; screenwriter: Christopher McQuarrie). Its dense, dark story involves five suspects in a police lineup, one of whom—Roger "Verbal" Kint (Kevin Spacey, *right*)—narrates parts of the intricate nonlinear structure. In this image, Kint undergoes an unusually intense interrogation from U.S. Customs Agent Dave Kujan (Chazz Palminteri). Kint's playfulness and inventiveness during this ordeal make him a highly unusual suspect, especially when it turns out that he has made up almost all of the story, including the identity of the puzzling Keyser Söze, who proves to be as much of an enigma as Charles Foster Kane. Movie buffs will recognize that the title is an allusion to "Round up the usual suspects," the often-quoted remark made by Captain Louis Renault (Claude Rains) at the conclusion of *Casablanca* (1942; director: Michael Curtiz; screenwriters: Julius J. Epstein, Philip G. Epstein, and Howard Koch). The Writers Guild of America, West, ranked *Casablanca* as number 1 in their list of the 101 greatest screenplays (probably more for its romanticism and eternal popularity with audiences, since it is not a particularly complex screenplay). *The Usual Suspects* ranked number 35. Nonetheless, movies with complex plot structures remain very popular among movie buffs and often attain cult status.

(1999) or Bryan Singer's *The Usual Suspects* (1995), is a far more successful experiment with plot order than the other two. The story itself is fairly superficial; it's the telling that counts. Nolan alternates black-and-white sequences—which move forward in chronological order in telling the story—with color sequences that move backward in an order that confuses chronology. Like Noé's *Irréversible*, *Memento* ends with the story's beginning—a structure that creates surprise and suspense, and challenges the audience's expectations of movie narrative. And like *Citizen Kane*, *Memento* asks us to pay close attention to story and plot, challenges our basic assumptions of how we experience and remember what we have done, and literally requires us to put the pieces of the puzzle together. If you have the time and patience to do that, you'll find that the puzzle is remarkably well constructed.

In Akira Kurosawa's *Rashomon* (1950; screenwriters: Kurosawa and Shinobu Hashimoto), we see an innovative variation on the idea of plot order. The same story—the rape of a woman—is told from four different points of view: a bandit, the woman, her husband, and a woodcutter (the only witness of the rape). Kurosawa's purpose shows us that we all remember and perceive differently, thus challenging our notions of perception and truth. This approach has influenced many other movies, including an American remake, Martin Ritt's *The Outrage* (1964, based on Kurosawa and Hashimoto's original screenplay) and Bryan Singer's *The Usual Suspects* (1995; screenwriter: Christopher McQuarrie). Spanish director-screenwriter Jorge Sánchez-Cabezudo's solemn and macabre film *The Night of the Sunflowers* (2006) plays with Kurosawa's idea, amplifying its moral complexity by presenting its six-part plot in six overlapping, nonchronological sections told from six different points of view. The movie culminates in a dramatic crescendo in which the director succeeds in putting all the pieces together.

Despite these experiments with the chronology of plot events, most narrative films follow a more or less chronological order.

In discussions of plot order, you will often hear the term *backstory*, the experiences of a character or the circumstances of an event that supposedly have occurred before the start of the movie's narrative. Movies like *Irréversible* and *Memento* utilize a variation on this narrative convention by telling the narrative in reverse chronological order, thus structuring the plot entirely of backstory.

Events

In any plot, events have a logical order, as we've discussed, as well as a logical hierarchy. Some events are more important than others, and we infer their relative significance through the director's selec-

Plot order in *Memento* In Christopher Nolan's *Memento* (2000), Leonard Shelby (Guy Pearce) suffers from a disorder that prevents him from forming short-term memories. To remember details of his life, he takes Polaroid snapshots, jots notes on scraps of paper, and even tattoos "The Facts" on his body. The movie's two-stranded plot order, both chronological and reverse chronological, likewise challenges us to recall what we've seen and how the parts fit together.

tion and arrangement of details of action, character, or setting. This hierarchy consists of (1) the events that seem crucial to the plot (and thus to the underlying story) and (2) the events that play a less crucial or even subordinate role.

The first category includes those major events or branching points in the plot structure that force characters to choose between or among alternate paths. Ridley Scott's *Gladiator* (2000; screenwriters: David Franzoni, John Logan, and William Nicholson) recounts three stages in the life of Maximus (Russell Crowe) as he moves from general to slave, slave to gladiator, and gladiator to savior of the Roman people. Soon after the film opens, Emperor Marcus Aurelius (Richard Harris) dies, a major event that forces the main character to escape the guards of the succeeding emperor, Commodus (Joaquin Phoenix), or be killed by them. Each following stage in the plot turns on such events, which force Maximus to face similar choices.

The second category includes those minor plot events that add texture and complexity to characters and actions but are not essential elements within the narrative. The love that Lucilla (Connie Nielsen), Commodus's sister, has long felt for Maximus—before he was married, during his marriage, and after his wife was murdered by Com-

[1]

[2]

Hierarchy of events in *Gladiator* In Ridley Scott's *Gladiator* (2000), the death of Emperor Marcus Aurelius (Richard Harris) [1] instantly transforms the fortunes of General Maximus (Russell Crowe) for the worse, setting the plot in motion. Lucilla's (Connie Nielsen) love for Maximus [2] informs the plot through a series of subordinate circumstances, which produce a crucial event near the end.

modus's guards—creates subordinate events. Her love surfaces at key moments, troubling and tempting Maximus; but because other things are more important to him, he is not forced to make a decision based on his feelings for her. These minor or subordinate events enrich and complicate the diegesis (the world of the story) in a narrative film, but no single such event is indispensable to the story. When filmmakers make decisions about which scenes to cut from a film during the editing phase, they generally look for minor events that, for one reason or another, don't contribute enough to the overall movie. As a critical viewer of movies, you can use this hierarchy of events in diagramming a plot (as a practical way of understanding it) or charting a course of the major and minor events confronting the characters.

Duration

Events, in life and in the movies, take time to occur. **Duration** is this length of time. When talking about narrative movies specifically, we can identify three specific kinds of duration: **story duration** is the amount of time that the implied story takes to occur; **plot duration** is the elapsed time of those events within the story that the film explicitly presents (in other words, the elapsed time of the plot); and **screen duration** is the movie's running time on-screen. In *Citizen Kane*, the plot duration is approximately one week (the duration of Thompson's search), the story duration is more than seventy years (the span of Kane's life), and the screen duration is 1 hour 59 minutes, the time it takes us to watch the film from beginning to end without interruption.

These distinctions are relatively simple in *Citizen Kane*, but the three-part relation of story, plot, and screen duration can become quite complex in some movies. Balancing the three elements is especially complex for a filmmaker because the screen duration is necessarily constrained by financial and other considerations. Movies may have become longer on average over the years, but filmmakers still must present their stories within a relatively short span of time. Because moviegoers generally regard films that run more than three hours as too long, such movies risk failure at the box office. Figure 4.3 illustrates the relationship between story duration and plot duration in a hypothetical movie. The story duration in this illustration—one week—is depicted in a plot that covers four discrete but crucial days in that week.

The relationships among the three types of duration can be isolated and analyzed, not only in the context of the entire narrative of the film, but also within its constituent parts—in scenes and sequences. In these smaller parts, however, the relationship between plot duration and story duration generally remains stable; that is, in most mainstream Hollywood movies, the duration of a plot event is assumed to be equivalent to the duration of the story event that it implies. At the level of scenes (a sequence of related shots), the more interesting relationship is usually between screen duration and

---

FIGURE 4.3 Duration: Story versus Plot

Imagine a hypothetical movie that follows the lives of two people over the course of one week, starting with the moment that they first move into an apartment together as a couple and ending with their parting of ways seven days later.

Story duration = 1 week

| Day 1 | Day 3 | Day 5 | Day 7 |

Plot duration = 4 days out of that week

Although the movie's implied story duration is one week, the events that are explicitly part of the plot of the movie take place during four discrete days within that week (the plot duration). Day 1 in the plot shows the couple moving and settling in. Day 3 shows them already squabbling. Day 5 shows the misguided couple getting ready for and throwing a housewarming party that concludes with a disastrous (but hilarious) argument. Day 7 shows them moving out and then having an amicable dinner over which they agree that the only way they can live with each other is by living apart.

FIGURE 4.4 Duration: Plot versus Screen

One portion of the plot in this hypothetical movie involves the housewarming party thrown by our ill-fated couple. The implied duration of this event (the plot duration) is four hours—from 8:00 in the evening to midnight of day 5.

8:00 PM   Midnight

Day 5

Plot duration = 4 hours

Although the implied duration of the plot event is 4 hours, the actual duration on-screen of the shots that cover this 4-hour event is only 10 minutes (the screen duration). As you can see below, those 10 minutes are divided among 15 discrete shots, each of which features a specific event or discussion at the party.

Screen duration = 15 individual shots = 10 minutes

---

plot duration. We can generally characterize that relationship in one of three ways: (1) in a **summary relationship**, screen duration is shorter than plot duration; (2) in **real time**, screen duration corresponds directly to plot duration; and (3) in a **stretch relationship**, screen duration is longer than plot duration.

Both stretch and summary relationships are established primarily through editing techniques (discussed in detail in Chapter 8). The summary relationship is very familiar and occurs much more frequently in mainstream movies than do the other two. The summary relationship is depicted in Figure 4.4, which illustrates one scene in our hypothetical movie; the screen duration of this scene is 10 minutes, but the implied duration of the plot event is 4 hours. In Terrence Malick's *Days of Heaven* (1978; screenwriter: Malick), a 30-second sequence of time-lapse cinematography shows the seeds of a wheat plant germinating under the soil, the wheat grass sprouting, and its tips turning a golden color. This haunting shot, which is a metaphor for the more gradual changes that occur on farms in the cycle from planting to germination to harvest, depicts in a very short time on the screen a growth period that lasts much longer. In *Citizen Kane*, Welles depicts the steady disintegration of Kane's first marriage to Emily Norton (Ruth Warrick) through a rapid montage of six shots at the breakfast table that take two minutes on the screen but depict seven years of their life together. Through changes in dress, hairstyle, seating, and their preferences in newspapers, we see the couple's relationship go from amorous passion to sarcastic hostility. Summary relationships are essential to telling movie stories, especially long and complicated ones.

Because it is less common than summary, the stretch relationship is often used to highlight a plot event, stressing its importance to the overall narrative. A stretch relationship can be achieved by special effects such as slow motion, particularly when a graceful effect is needed, as in showing a reunited couple running slowly toward one another. It can also be constructed by editing techniques. The "Odessa Steps" sequence in Sergei Eisenstein's *Battleship Potemkin* (1925; screenwriters: Nina Agadzhanova, Nikolai Aseyev, Eisenstein, and Sergei Tretyakov) uses editing to stretch out the plot duration of the massacre so that our experience of it on-screen lasts longer than it would have taken to occur in reality. Eisenstein does this because he wants us to see the massacre as an important and meaningful event, as well as to increase our anxiety and empathy for the victims.

The real-time relationship is the least common of the three relationships between screen duration and plot duration, but its use has always interested and delighted film buffs. Many directors use real time within films to create uninterrupted "reality" on the screen, but directors rarely use it for entire films. Fred Zinnemann's *High Noon* (1952; screenwriter: Carl Foreman) and Alfred Hitchcock's *Rope* (1948; screenwriter: Arthur Laurents) are two outstanding films that present a real-time relationship between screen and plot duration. In *Rope*, Hitchcock used the long take (discussed further in Chapter 6)—an unedited, continuous shot—to preserve real time. One roll of motion-picture film can record approximately 11 minutes of action, and thus Hitchcock made an 80-minute film with ten shots that range in length from 4 minutes 40 seconds to 10 minutes.[5] Six of the cuts between these shots are virtually unnoticeable because Hitchcock has the camera pass behind the backs of people or furniture and then makes the cut on a dark screen; four others are ordinary hard cuts from one person to another. Even these hard cuts do not break time or space, so the result is fluid storytelling in which the plot duration equals the screen duration of 80 minutes.

In most traditional narrative movies, cuts and other editing devices punctuate the flow of the narrative and graphically indicate that the images occur in human-made cinematic time, not seamless real time. As viewers, we think that movies pass before us in the present tense, but we also understand that cinematic time can be manipulated through editing, among other means. As we accept these manipulative conventions, we also recognize that classic Hollywood editing generally goes out of its way to avoid calling attention to itself. Furthermore, it attempts to reflect the natural mental processes by which human consciousness moves back and forth between reality and illusion, shifting between past, present, and future.

Abel Gance's masterpiece *Napoléon* (1927; screenwriter: Gance) not only exhibits each of the relationships between duration and plot that have just been described, but also includes some of the

[5]Various critics have said that each shot in *Rope* lasts 10 minutes, but the DVD release of the film shows the timings (rounded off) to be as follows: opening credits, 2:09; shot 1, 9:50; shot 2, 8:00; shot 3, 7:50; shot 4, 7:09; shot 5, 10:00; shot 6, 7:40; shot 7, 8:00; shot 8, 10:00; shot 9, 4:40; shot 10, 5:40; closing credits, 00:28.

[1]

[2]

[3]

[4]

[5]

[6]

Summary relationship A sequence in Martin Scorsese's *Raging Bull* (1980; screenwriters: Paul Schrader and Mardik Martin) covers three years (story duration) in a few minutes (screen duration). Black-and-white shots of Jake La Motta's (Robert De Niro) most significant boxing matches from 1944 to 1947 are intercut with color shots from home movies that show La Motta and his second wife, Vickie (Cathy Moriarty), during the early years of their marriage.

most dazzling technical innovations in film history. The legendary French director's handling of time, speed, and movement builds dramatically on D. W. Griffith's earlier experiments in awakening us to the manifold possibilities of the cinematic medium for manipulating both time and space. With astonishing fluidity, Gance jumps forward and backward in time, so that a moment in the present is frequently related to events that preceded it and often foreshadows the events that will follow. For example, in the famous snowball sequence near the beginning of the film, Napoléon's participation in a schoolyard snowball fight becomes a genuine battle—on one hand, to restore the young man's reputation among his stupid, class-conscious schoolmates and, on the other, to point toward his destiny as a military genius. To extend his control over *Napoléon*'s cinematic time, Gance introduced

Real-time relationship Mike Figgis's *Timecode* (2000; screenwriter: Figgis) offers a dramatic and daring version of real time. Split into quarters, the screen displays four distinct but overlapping stories, each shot in one continuous 93-minute take (the length of an ordinary digital videocassette), uninterrupted by editing.

the Polyvision process, which used three synchronized cameras (and three synchronized projectors) to put three different actions on the screen simultaneously, as in a triptych, or to spread one vast composition across three screens. *Napoléon* concludes with not only such a triptych, but also, within each panel, a rapid recapitulation of footage seen previously in the film—again a fluid demonstration of the symbolic continuity of past, present, and future.

Suspense versus Surprise

It is important to distinguish between suspense, which has been mentioned in the preceding discussions, and surprise. Although they are often confused, suspense and surprise are two fundamentally different elements in the development of many movie plots. Alfred Hitchcock mastered the unique properties of each, taking great care to ensure that they were integral to the internal logic of his plots. In a conversation with French director François Truffaut, Hitchcock explained the terms:

> We are now having a very innocent little chat. Let us suppose that there is a bomb underneath this table between us. Nothing happens, and then all of a sudden, "Boom!"
>
> There is an explosion. The public is *surprised*, but prior to this surprise, it has seen an absolutely ordi-

nary scene of no special consequence. Now, let us take a *suspense* situation. The bomb is underneath the table and the public *knows* it, probably because they have seen the anarchist place it there. The public is *aware* that the bomb is going to explode at one o'clock and there is a clock in the decor. The public can see that it is a quarter to one. In these conditions this same innocuous conversation becomes fascinating because the public is participating in the scene. The audience is longing to warn the characters on the screen: "You shouldn't be talking about such trivial matters. There's a bomb beneath you and it's about to explode!"

> In the first scene we have given the public fifteen seconds of *surprise* at the moment of the explosion. In the second we have provided them with fifteen minutes of *suspense*. The conclusion is that whenever possible the public must be informed. Except when the surprise is a twist, that is, when the unexpected ending is, in itself, the highlight of the story.[6]

Because there are no repeat surprises, we can be surprised in the same way only once. As a result, a **surprise**, a being taken unawares, can be shocking, and our emotional response to it is generally short-lived. By contrast, **suspense** is a more

[6]Alfred Hitchcock, qtd. in François Truffaut, *Hitchcock*, rev. ed. (New York: Simon & Schuster, 1984), p. 73.

Surprise versus suspense Billy Wilder's *Some Like It Hot* (1959; screenwriters: Wilder and I. A. L. Diamond) concerns two musicians who witness a mob murder, disguise themselves as women, and leave town to work in an all-woman band. Although their attempts to maintain this disguise are frustrated by their desires for the women who surround them, they persist through a series of hilarious turns that heighten the suspense. When will they be discovered? What will happen as a result? Eventually, a rich millionaire, Osgood Fielding III (Joe E. Brown, *left*) falls in love with Jerry/Daphne (Jack Lemmon, *right*), who frantically explains to Osgood that they can't marry because they are both men. As a surprise to cap the suspense, Osgood simply shrugs his shoulders and makes one of the greatest comebacks in movie history: "Well, nobody's perfect."

drawn-out (and, some would say, more enjoyable) experience, one that we may seek out even when we know what happens in a movie. Suspense is the anxiety brought on by a partial uncertainty: the end is certain, but the means is uncertain. Or, even more interestingly, we may know both the result and the means by which it's brought about, but we still feel suspense: we know what's going to happen and we want to warn and protect the characters, for we have grown to empathize with them (though we can intellectually acknowledge the fact that they aren't "real" people).

Repetition

The **repetition**, or number of times, with which a story element recurs in a plot is an important aspect of narrative form. If an event occurs once in a plot, we accept it as a functioning part of the narrative's progression. Its appearance more than once, however, suggests a pattern and thus a higher level of importance. Like order and duration, then, repetition serves not only as a means of relaying story information, but also as a signal that a particular event has a meaning or significance that should be acknowledged in our interpretation and analysis.

Story events can be repeated in various ways. A character may remember a key event at several times during the movie, indicating the psychological, intellectual, or physical importance of that event. The use of flashbacks or slow-motion sequences tends to give a mythical quality to memory, making the past seem more significant than it might actually have been. For example, in Atom Egoyan's *The Sweet Hereafter* (1997; screenwriter: Egoyan), Mitchell Stephens (Ian Holm) is so troubled by his teenage daughter's drug addiction that he tries to put it out of his mind by frequently visualizing more pleasant memories of her as a child. In another form of repetition, the director relies on editing to contrast past and present.

The **familiar image** is defined by film theorist Stefan Sharff as any image (audio or visual) that a director periodically repeats in a movie (with or without variations) to help stabilize its narrative. By its repetition, the image calls attention to itself as a narrative (as well as visual) element. Theoretically, the composition and framing of such images should remain the same, although variations on these elements are frequently used as long as they preserve the integrity of the original image. An example of the rhythmic use of identical images occurs in Eisenstein's repetition of a set of images (steps, soldiers, mother holding baby, mother with baby in carriage, woman shot in stomach, woman with broken glasses, etc.) in the "Odessa Steps" sequence of *Battleship Potemkin*. Other movies rely on our familiarity with the original image to make variations in it that we will recognize. In Howard Hawks's *Red River* (1948; screenwriters: Borden Chase and Charles Schnee), the familiar image is that of "Groot" Nadine (Walter Brennan) in the driver's seat of a stagecoach, which is repeated many times in order to emphasize his importance to the journey, as well as to connect him to the actions of other characters.

Some familiar images are symbols, particularly those where a material object represents something abstract. Just for starters, think of the Grail cross in *Indiana Jones and the Last Crusade*, the gold in *The Treasure of the Sierra Madre*, Leonardo's paintings in *The Da Vinci Code*, the black bird in *The Maltese Falcon*, or the extraordinary cars that James Bond drives in the many movies devoted to his exploits. In *Volver* (2006), director Pedro Almodóvar uses frequent shots of wind turbines in the Spanish landscape as a symbol to help us understand the meaning of the title, a Spanish word that means "turn," "return," or "revolution," as in a circle turning. On the literal level, the story itself turns on the theme of the "sins of the fathers"—the cycle of genetic or behavioral influences that pass from one generation to the next (here, it's the sins of the mothers).

Setting

The **setting** of a movie is the time and place in which the story occurs. It not only establishes the date, city, or country, but also provides the characters' social, educational, and cultural backgrounds and other identifying factors vital for understanding them, such as what they wear, eat, and drink. Setting sometimes provides an implicit explanation for actions or traits that we might otherwise consider eccentric, because cultural norms vary from place to place and throughout time. Certain genres are associated with specific settings—for example, Westerns with wide-open country, film noirs with dark city streets, and horror movies with creepy houses.

In addition to providing us with essential contextual information that helps us understand story events and character motivation, setting adds texture to the movie's diegesis, enriching our sense of the overall world of the movie. Terrence Malick's *Days of Heaven* (1978; screenwriter: Malick) features magnificent landscapes in the American West of the 1920s. At first, the extraordinary visual imagery seems to take precedence over the narrative. However, the settings—the vast wheat fields and the great solitary house against the sky—directly complement the depth and power of the narrative, which is concerned with the cycle of the seasons, the work connected with each season, and how fate, greed, sexual passion, and jealousy can lead to tragedy. Here, setting also helps to reveal the characters' states of mind. They are from the Chicago slums, and once they arrive in the pristine wheat fields of the West, they are lonely and alienated from themselves and their values. They cannot adapt and thus end tragically. Here, setting is destiny.

Other films tell stories closely related to their international, national, or regional settings, such as the specific neighborhoods of New York City that form the backdrop of many Woody Allen films. But think of the many different ways in which Manhattan has been photographed, including the many film noirs with their harsh black-and-white contrasts; the sour colors of Martin Scorsese's *Taxi Driver* (1976; screenwriter: Paul Schrader); or the bright colors of Alfred Hitchcock's *North by Northwest* (1959; screenwriter: Ernest Lehman).

Settings are not always drawn from real-life locales. An opening title card tells us that F. W. Murnau's *Sunrise: A Song of Two Humans* (1927; screenwriter: Carl Mayer) takes place in "no place and every place"; Stanley Kubrick's *2001: A Space Odyssey* (1968; screenwriters: Kubrick and Arthur C. Clarke) creates an entirely new space–time continuum; and Tim Burton's *Charlie and the Chocolate Factory* (2005; screenwriter: John August) creates

Setting in science fiction Based on Philip K. Dick's science-fiction novel *Do Androids Dream of Electric Sheep?* (1968), Ridley Scott's *Blade Runner* (1982) takes place in 2019 in an imaginary world where cities such as Los Angeles are ruled by technology and saturated with visual information. In most science-fiction films, setting plays an important part in our understanding of the narrative, so sci-fi filmmakers spend considerable time, money, and effort to make the setting come to life.

the most fantastic chocolate factory in the world. The attraction of science-fiction films such as George Lucas's *Star Wars* (1977; screenwriter: Lucas) and Ridley Scott's *Blade Runner* (1982; director's cut released 1992; screenwriters: Hampton Fancher and David Webb Peoples) is often attributed to their almost totally unfamiliar settings. These stories about outer space and future cities have a mythical or symbolic significance beyond that of stories set on Earth. Their settings may be verisimilar and appropriate for the purpose of the story, whether or not we can verify them as "real."

Scope

Related to duration and setting is **scope**—the overall range, in time and place, of the movie's story. Stories can range from the distant past to the narrative present, or they can be narrowly focused on a short period, even a matter of moments. They can take us from one galaxy to another, or they can remain inside a single room. They can present a rather limited perspective on their world, or they can show us several alternative perspectives. Determining the general scope of a movie's story—understanding its relative expansiveness—can help you piece together and understand other aspects of the movie as a whole.

For example, the *biopic*, a film about a person's life—whether historical or fictional—might tell the story in one of two ways: through one significant episode or period in the life of a person, or through a series of events in a single life, sometimes beginning with birth and ending in old age. Biopics remain one of the great staples of movie production. Think of the variety of subjects in these recent movies: the notorious Australian criminal Mark Brandon Read in *Chopper* (2000; director and screenwriter: Andrew Dominik), the British anti-slavery advocate William Wilberforce in *Amazing Grace* (2006; director: Michael Apted; screenwriter: Stephen Knight), gay activist Harvey Milk in *Milk* (2008; director: Gus Van Sant; screenwriter: Dustin Lance Black), English poet John Keats in *Bright Star* (2009; directors and screenwriters: Robert Epstein and Jeffrey Friedman), King George VI in *The King's Speech* (2010; director: Tom Hooper; screenwriter: David Seidler), or Marilyn Monroe in *My Week with Marilyn* (2011; director: Simon Curtis; screenwriter: Adrian Hodge).

Many war films have been limited in scope to the story of a single battle; others have treated an entire war. Steven Spielberg's *Saving Private Ryan* (1998; screenwriter: Robert Rodat) covers two stories happening simultaneously: the larger story is that of the June 1944 D-Day invasion of Normandy, involving the vast Allied army; the more intimate story, and the one that gives the film its title, presents what happens from the time the U.S. government orders Private Ryan (Matt Damon) to be removed from combat to the time it actually happens. Both stories are seen from the American point of view, perceptually and politically.

By contrast, Ken Annakin, Andrew Marton, and Bernhard Wicki's *The Longest Day* (1962; screenwriters: Romain Gary, James Jones, David Pursall, Jack Seddon, and Cornelius Ryan) relates the D-Day invasion to what was happening in four countries—the United States, France, England, and Germany—though also from the perspective of American politics. Thus, its scope is broader, enhanced by the viewpoints of its large cast of characters. Although Terrence Malick's *The Thin Red Line* (1998; screenwriter: Malick) focuses on the American invasion of the Japanese-held Pacific

Scope Bernardo Bertolucci's *The Last Emperor* (1987; screenwriters: Mark Peploe and Bertolucci) recounts the comparatively small story of the title character, China's Pu Yi (John Lone), against the political changes enveloping China as it moved from monarchy to communism from 1908 to 1967. Even though the two stories occur simultaneously and are related causally, the expansive scope of the historical epic takes precedence over the story of the emperor's life.

island of Guadalcanal, it ultimately uses the historical setting as a very personal backdrop for a meditation on war and its horrors.

Looking at Narrative: John Ford's *Stagecoach*

To better understand how these foundations and elements of narrative work together in a single movie, let's consider how they're used in John Ford's *Stagecoach* (1939; screenwriter: Dudley Nichols). This movie is regarded by many as *the* classic Western, not only for its great entertainment value, but also for its mastery of the subjects discussed in this chapter.

Story, Screenwriter, and Screenplay

The story of *Stagecoach* is based on a familiar convention (sometimes called the "ship of fools") in which a diverse group of people—perhaps passengers traveling to a common destination or residents of a hotel—must confront a common danger and, through that experience, confront themselves, both as individuals and as members of a group.

These people (male and female; weak and strong; from different places, backgrounds, and professions; and with dissimilar temperaments) have either been living in, or are passing through, the frontier town of Tonto. Despite a warning from the U.S. Cavalry that Apache warriors, under the command of the dreaded Geronimo, have cut the telegraph wires and threatened the settlers' safety, this group boards a stagecoach to Lordsburg. In charge of the coach is Buck Rickabaugh (Andy Devine), the driver, and Marshal Curly Wilcox (George Bancroft), who is on the lookout for an escaped prisoner called the Ringo Kid (John Wayne). The seven passengers include (1) Lucy Mallory (Louise Platt), the aloof, Southern-born, and (as we later learn) pregnant wife of a cavalry officer whom she has come west to join; (2) Samuel Peacock (Donald Meek), a liquor salesman; (3) Dr. Josiah Boone (Thomas Mitchell), a doctor who still carries his bag of equipment, even though he has been kicked out of the profession for malpractice and now is being driven out of Tonto for drunkenness; (4) Mr. Hatfield (John Carradine), a Southern gambler, who is proud of the fact that he served in Lucy's father's regiment in the Civil War and leaves Tonto to serve as her protector on the trip; (5) Henry Gatewood (Berton Churchill), the Tonto bank president, who is leaving town with a mysterious satchel that we later learn contains money he stole from his bank; and (6) Dallas (Claire Trevor), a good-hearted prostitute, who has been driven out of town by a group of Tonto's righteous women. The seventh passenger, Ringo, has been heading for Lordsburg to avenge his father's murder, but when his horse becomes lame outside Tonto, he stops the stagecoach and is arrested by the marshal before he boards. Each passenger has personal reasons for leaving Tonto (or, in Ringo's case, prison) and making the perilous journey. Lucy, Hatfield, Gatewood, and Peacock all have specific purposes for traveling to Lordsburg; Dallas and Dr. Boone are being forced to leave town; and the Ringo Kid has a grudge to settle.

The screenwriter Dudley Nichols, a veteran of working with Ford, based the screenplay on the story "Stage to Lordsburg," written by Ernest Haycox, who specialized in fiction based on Western themes.[6] Although this story is fiction, Ford usually sought to anchor his Western movies in historical reality by giving them a date; he does not do that in *Stagecoach*. Since Geronimo and his Apaches were

[1]

[2]

[3]

[5]

[4]

[6]

The cast of characters in *Stagecoach* [1] Buck Rickabaugh (Andy Devine, *left*) and Marshal Curly Wilcox (George Bancroft); [2] Dallas (Claire Trevor) and Henry Gatewood (Berton Churchill); [3] the Ringo Kid (John Wayne); [4] Gatewood and Lucy Mallory (Louise Platt); [5] Samuel Peacock (Donald Meek, *left*) and Dr. Josiah Boone (Thomas Mitchell); and [6] Mr. Hatfield (John Carradine).

most active between 1881 and 1886 in their encounters with the U. S. Army, we can locate the action sometime in this period. Haycox's story provides a basic plot and characters, but Ford and Nichols recognized in it the basis for a new kind of Hollywood Western, and made many alterations. They retained most characters, but added two new ones (Doc Boone and Gatewood) and changed all their names. Significantly, while Haycox had the Ringo character board the stagecoach with everyone else in Tonto, Nichols made him an escaped prisoner, thus strengthening the group of outcasts and contributing to the class consciousness that is at the heart of the story. Catering to the audience's expectations, Ford provides a spectacular Indian fight, but its true strength lies not only in its magnificent imagery, but also in the screenplay's sharp psychological portraits of vivid characters and pointed social commentary. At the end of the movie, we expect that Ringo, having gotten his revenge, will return to jail to complete his sentence. And we know that, after his release, Ringo and Dallas plan to be married and live on his ranch across the border. Nichols made a significant addition to the story by giving it a happy ending—the couple escape into the night—and having Doc Boone utter the movie's cynical last words: "Well, they're saved from the blessings of civilization."

Narration and Narrator

As was typical of John Ford's style throughout his career, he relies on visual images and dialogue, not a narrator, to tell the *Stagecoach* story. His narration is provided by an omniscient camera that sees and knows everything and can tell us whatever it wants us to know. You see this, for example, in the exterior shots of Geronimo on the hill, Gatewood robbing his own safe, the stagecoach racing across the territory, and the Luke Plummer scene. This camera has unrestricted access to all aspects of the narrative and, as a result, can provide the experiences and perceptions of any character, as well as information that no character knows. You see this in the medium and close-up shots of characters under stress. Ford's camera shows the audience whatever it needs to in order to best tell the story. Although the movie uses neither narrator nor interior monologue, it features one especially interesting use of an auditory point of view when Lucy, a cavalry wife, is the first to recognize the bugle announcing the cavalry's impending arrival during the Apache attack. The situation is dire. She is praying, and Hatfield, who intends to shoot her so that she won't be captured by the Apaches, has pointed his revolver at her head. Just before he can pull the trigger, he is struck by an Apache bullet. Hearing the bugle at that moment, her face reacts with great emotion as she says, "Do you hear it? It's a bugle. They're blowing the charge." With a cut to the cavalry riding to save the stagecoach, the movie reaches its turning point. This powerful moment manipulates our expectations (we believe that Hatfield will perform the mercy killing), conventions of the Western genre (we would expect the Cavalry to

Auditory point of view as narration in *Stagecoach*
Upon hearing the cavalry bugle and knowing that help is near, Lucy reacts with great emotion. This is a key turning point in the journey from Tonto to Lordsburg, and the arrival of the Cavalry means—or at least the members of the stagecoach party hope it means—that the travelers will end their journey safely.

[6]Both the story and the screenplay are in Dudley Nichols, *Stagecoach: A Film by John Ford and Dudley Nichols* (New York: Simon & Schuster, 1971). See also Edward Buscombe's excellent analysis of the film in *Stagecoach* (London: British Film Institute, 1992), to which I am indebted.

announce itself directly, not through a fragile woman's perception), and diegesis (particularly the characterization and explicitly presented events). Lucy, unwittingly, becomes one of the heroes of the movie.

When he needs to show that the characters do not form a community—for example, at the noontime lunch stop at Dry Fork, where underlying tensions flare up because Ringo has seated Dallas at the same table as Lucy—Ford establishes and reinforces ideological and emotional differences by alternating between (1) shots from an omniscient point of view and (2) shots from the characters' subjective points of view. As a result, the space at the dinner table, even though it is physically larger, is as socially and morally restricted as the space inside the stagecoach. The pattern of editing here establishes the camera's presence as narrator, the social stratification within the group, Lucy's inflexibility, Hatfield's protectiveness, and Gatewood's pretentiousness. But it also reveals Ringo's kindness, Dallas's vulnerability, and Ford's sympathy for them, which engages our sympathy.

Characters

All the characters inside the stagecoach—Dallas, Ringo, Hatfield, Peacock, Gatewood, Dr. Boone, and Lucy—are major, because they make the most things happen and have the most things happen to them. Dallas, Ringo, Dr. Boone, and Lucy are round characters: three-dimensional, possessing several traits, and unpredictable. The flat characters—one-dimensional, possessing one or very few discernible traits, and generally predictable—include Hatfield, Peacock, and Gatewood. But Gatewood is somewhat more complicated. We know that when the Apaches cut the telegraph wires in the opening scene, they severed all communication between Tonto and Lordsburg. (Although the telephone was invented in 1876, it hadn't yet reached Tonto.) This incident helps to get the story underway, and is also the reason the marshal later realizes that Gatewood is guilty, since, as he enters the stagecoach, he claims to have "just" gotten a telegram. Buck Rickabaugh and Marshal Wilcox, riding on the bench at the exterior front of the coach, are essentially minor (and flat) characters; they play less important roles and usually function as a means of moving the plot forward or of fleshing out the motivations of the major characters.

Ringo is the primary protagonist, with a goal to revenge his family and a (conflicting) need to find love and settle down. But you could argue that all of the passengers are protagonists, for they all have a common goal: Lordsburg. The primary antagonist, for everyone on this journey, is Geronimo, even though he and his warriors appear on the screen briefly. One of the many things that makes *Stagecoach*'s narrative so interesting is that, while Geronimo is responsible for many of the narrative obstacles, much of the story's conflict originates in disputes between the characters who share a common goal. For Ringo, the Plummers are the antagonists. They loom large in the story, but do not appear on-screen until just before the movie ends.

Narrative Structure

The narrative structure employed by the screenwriter follows the familiar three-act paradigm established earlier in this chapter. The first act, or setup, establishes the world of Tonto, presented as a typical frontier town: rough, prosperous, and ruled by a formidable force of social prejudice, the Ladies Law and Order League. The daily stagecoach, a lifeline to the outer world, stops for passengers, mail, news, and other necessities. In spite of the U. S. Cavalry's warning about Geronimo and his troops, all its passengers have a reason for going to Lordsburg. Thus, there are several inciting incidents: some want to leave (Mr. Hatfield, Mr. Gatewood), some are forced to leave (Doc Boone and Dallas), some are just passing through (Mrs. Mallory, Mr. Samuel Peacock), and some are just doing their jobs (Buck Rickabaugh, the stagecoach driver, and Curly Wilcox, the marshal). Ringo has his own reason for going to Lordsburg: revenge.

In the second act, we see what's at stake: delay and danger. While the characters share a common goal, Lordsburg, they each have traits that color and shape their pursuits of it. However, there are major obstacles to their pursuit of this goal: Geronimo cuts the telegraph wires, the Cavalry Scout leaves them, the interior of the stagecoach is cramped and uncomfortable, and there are no fresh horses at the way station. In addition, there are social divisions among the passengers (so-called polite society versus the outcasts), Lucy Mallory's delivery of a baby, and, of course, the Apaches' attack. In addition to these, Ringo has his own personal obstacles. Curly arrests him and takes his gun. Dallas tries to stop him from confronting the murderous Plummers, whom he must face even though he has only three bullets left. Ringo must convince Curly to give him ten minutes to say goodbye to Dallas. He not only overcomes these obstacles, but also sets an example of courage during the Apache attack with his willingness to sacrifice himself for the good of the group in successfully bringing the rampaging stagecoach horses under control. Hero that he is, he also gets lucky when the Cavalry arrives to bolster the gutsy gunplay and determination he (and some others) use to fend off the Apaches. The group's crisis is averted, and the stagecoach proceeds toward Lordsburg. But Ringo's crisis is his showdown with the Plummers. He overcomes this seemingly insurmountable obstacle with guts and eagle-eye shooting. Doc Boone tries to help by relieving Luke Plummer of his shotgun, but his girlfriend supplies him with one just before the gunfight.

In the third act, with Ringo's crisis solved, there are several resolutions: Gatewood is arrested, Mrs. Mallory implicitly asks Dallas's forgiveness, Mr. Mallory is all right, and Mr. Peacock has survived the Apache attack. But Doc, Curly, and Ringo and Dallas, especially, have another resolution. Doc stands up to the Plummers, but doesn't stop drinking; Ringo tells Dallas that he doesn't care about her past; Curly quietly lets Ringo elude his obligation to return to jail; and Ringo and Dallas ride off into the night.

Plot

The plot of *Stagecoach* covers the two-day trip from Tonto to Lordsburg and is developed in a strictly chronological way without flashbacks or flashforwards. The events follow one another coherently and logically, and their relations of cause and effect are easy to discern. Balance, harmony, and unity are the principal keys to understanding the relationship between the story and the plot. Indeed, the eminent French film theorist and critic André Bazin notes that

> *Stagecoach* (1939) is the ideal example of the maturity of a style brought to classic perfection. John Ford struck the ideal balance between social myth, historical reconstruction, psychological truth, and the traditional theme of the Western mise en scène. None of these elements dominated any other. *Stagecoach* is like a wheel, so perfectly made that it remains in equilibrium on its axis in any position.[7]

Order As already noted, Ford maintains strict chronological order in using the journey to structure the story events. The journey provides both chronological and geographical markers for dividing the sequences. Furthermore, it reveals a clear pattern of cause and effect created primarily by each character's desire to go to Lordsburg on this particular day. That pattern proceeds to conflict (created both by internal character interaction and by the external Apache attack, which frustrates the characters' desires), reaches a turning point (the victory over the Apaches), and concludes with a resolution (Ringo's revenge on the Plummers, whose testimony had put him in prison, and his riding off a free man with the woman he loves). Otherwise, the plot order is not manipulated in any way.

Diegetic and Nondiegetic Elements The diegetic elements are everything in the story except the opening and closing titles and credits and the background music, all of which are, of course, nondiegetic. One very important formal element in *Stagecoach* is American folk music, including the song "Bury Me Not on the Lone Prairie," most often heard in connection with Buck and representing his justifiable fears of dying on the range; a honky-tonk piano in the bar; and a symphonic score mixing many familiar folk tunes. The film's main theme is Stephen Foster's classic ballad

[7]André Bazin, "Evolution of the Western," in *What Is Cinema?* trans. Hugh Gray, 2 vols. (Berkeley: University of California Press, 1967–71), II, p. 149.

"Jeanie with the Light Brown Hair." A song about remembering the past, perhaps with regret or loss, it is closely associated with the Old South and evokes the memories of Lucy Mallory and Hatfield: the devastating Civil War, the uncertain westward movement, the fragmented western territories, and, in all of this, a yearning for a simpler time and a woman with light brown hair.

Events The major events in *Stagecoach*—those branching points in the plot structure that force characters to choose between or among alternate paths—include (in the order of the plot):

> the passengers' decision to leave Tonto in spite of the Cavalry's warning about Geronimo and his troops [1].

> Marshal Wilcox's decision to let Ringo join the party [2].

> the passengers' vote to leave the Dry Fork station for Lordsburg, even though a relief unit of cavalry has not yet arrived [3].

> Dr. Boone's willingness to sober up and deliver the baby [4].

> Dallas's decision at the Apache Wells station to accept Ringo's proposal [5].

> the group's decision to delay departure from Apache Wells until Lucy has rested from childbirth and is ready to travel [6].

> Ringo's attempt to escape at Apache Wells [7].

> the passengers' decision at the burned-out ferry landing to try to reach Lordsburg, even though they realize that an Apache attack may be imminent [8].

Major events in *Stagecoach* These twelve images illustrate the major events in John Ford's *Stagecoach* (characters are listed from left to right): [1] Peacock, Curly, Hatfield, Lucy; [2] Buck, Curly, Ringo, cavalry captain; [3] Dallas, Ringo, Lucy, Buck, Curly, Peacock, Gatewood, Hatfield; [4] Curly, Peacock, Ringo; [5] Ringo and Dallas; [6] Gatewood, Buck, Curly, Hatfield, Peacock; [7] Ringo; [8] Buck, Curly, Dallas, Ringo; [9] Ringo; [10] cavalry flag bearer and bugler; [11] Ringo and Curly; [12] Curly, Ringo, and Dallas.

5

9

6

10

7

11

8

12

Ringo's willingness to risk his life to bring the coach under control as the Apaches attack [9].

the arrival of the cavalry soon after the Apache attack has begun [10].

Marshal Wilcox's decision to reward Ringo's bravery by allowing him ten minutes of freedom in which to confront the Plummers [11].

the marshal's decision to set Ringo free [12].

The minor plot events that add texture and complexity to characters and events but are not essential elements within the narrative include (in plot order) the Apaches' cutting of the telegraph wires; Gatewood's anxiety about getting to Lordsburg no matter what happens along the route; Peacock's anxiety over Dr. Boone's helping himself to his stock of liquor; Buck's wavering enthusiasm for driving the stagecoach against the odds; Lucy's, Hatfield's, and Gatewood's demonstrations of their self-perceived social superiority, especially at the lunch table at Dry Fork; Hatfield's attempt to defend Lucy from Apache attack, which results in his being shot; Marshal Wilcox's distribution of weapons to the travelers for their self-defense during the Apache attack; Wilcox's arrest of Gatewood for embezzlement; and Ringo's successful killing of the three Plummer brothers.

Duration The story duration includes what we know and what we infer from the total lives of all the characters (e.g., Lucy's privileged upbringing in Virginia, marriage to a military officer, current pregnancy, and the route of her trip out west up until the moment the movie begins). The plot duration includes the time of those events within the story that the film chooses to tell—here the two days of the trip from Tonto to Lordsburg. The screen duration, or running time, is 96 minutes.

Repetition Although no story events recur in *Stagecoach*, character traits both recur (e.g., Gatewood's insensitive desire to keep moving, no matter what, puts in danger both individuals and the group as a whole) and are transformed as a result of the journey (e.g., Lucy tenderly acknowledges Dallas's invaluable assistance during childbirth: "Dallas, if there's ever anything I can do for . . ."). Ford also repeats a three-part editing pattern some dozen times in the movie: (shot 1) a *long shot* of the stagecoach rolling along the plain; (shot 2) a *two-shot* of Curly and Buck on the driver's seat; (shot 3) a *middle shot* or *close-up* of the passengers inside. We could broadly consider the recurrences of this series of shots as repetitions of familiar images.

Suspense

In this period, it took two days for a fast stagecoach to make the trip from Tonto to Lordsburg, and the plot follows this two-day trip chronologically. However, the pace also serves other functions. The fear first expressed in the opening moments at mention of the name Geronimo intensifies the suspense of the imminent Indian attack, thus providing a decisive crisis during which the characters respond to the challenges and rigors of the trip and reveal their true selves. Will Lucy stop acting like a spoiled rich woman? Will Dr. Boone sober up in time to deliver her child? Will Dallas accept Ringo's proposal? Because we know little of their origins, we must trust in what we see of their current surroundings, as well as their interactions with each other and with the community (both the community of Tonto and the "community" that develops on the journey).

Setting

The story takes place in settings constructed in Hollywood—the interiors and exteriors of two towns and the stagecoach—and on actual locations in the spectacular Monument Valley of northern Arizona. Beautiful and important as Monument Valley and other exterior shots are to the film, the shots made inside the stagecoach as it speeds through the valley are essential to developing other themes in the movie. As the war with the Apaches signifies the territorial changes taking place outside, another drama is taking place among the passengers. In journeying through changing scenery, they also change through their responses to the dangers they face and their relations with, and reactions to, one another. This may be a wilderness, but the settlers have brought from the East and the

South their notions of social respectability and status. Thus, as the film begins in Tonto, they enter the stagecoach in the descending order of their apparent importance within the film's social scale:

Gatewood, the banker, is a highly respected social pillar of Tonto.

Lucy, the transient army wife, is a respected Southern aristocrat.

Hatfield, the transient gambler, seems to be a gentleman.

Peacock, the transient whiskey salesman, is barely acceptable.

Dr. Boone has been run out of town by the Law and Order League.

Dallas, a prostitute, has also been run out of town.

Ringo, an escaped convict, has no social status.

However, after the challenges and conflicts of the two-day trip, Ford reverses this order of importance as the characters leave the coach in Lordsburg:

Ringo becomes the hero through his heroic defense of the stagecoach.

Dallas becomes the heroine by showing dignity in the face of humiliation and compassion in helping to deliver Lucy's baby.

Dr. Boone is redeemed when he sobers up and delivers Lucy's baby.

Peacock does not change.

Hatfield is redeemed by chivalrously dying to defend Lucy.

Lucy, still aloof, nonetheless acknowledges Dallas's kindness.

Gatewood is apprehended as a bank thief.

Settings in *Stagecoach* [1] The main street of Tonto, where the horses are being attached to the stagecoach before the journey begins. [2] The stagecoach, with its cavalry escort, entering the first phase of the journey. [3] The Apache attack on the stagecoach. [4] The main street of Lordsburg, where residents watch the stagecoach arrive.

There is plenty of irony in these changes. At the end of the trip, the pretentious, overbearing Gatewood becomes the prisoner, while Ringo—who is guarded by the marshal and feared by some of the passengers because he is an escaped convict—becomes the hero. Dallas's compassion takes precedence over Lucy's cold, haughty manner, and so on.

Scope

The story's overall range in time and place is broad, extending from early events—Dallas orphaned by an Indian massacre and the comparatively more pleasant childhood that Lucy enjoyed in Virginia—to those we see on-screen. And although we look essentially at the events on the two days that it takes the stagecoach to go from Tonto to Lordsburg, we are also aware of the larger scope of American history, particularly the westward movement, Ford's favorite subject. Made right before the start of World War II in Europe, *Stagecoach* presents a historical, social, and mythical vision of American civilization in the 1880s. Ford looked back at the movement west because he saw that period as characterized by clear, simple virtues and values. He viewed the pioneers as establishing the traditions for which Americans would soon be fighting: freedom, democracy, justice, and individualism.

One of the social themes of the movie is *manifest destiny*, a term used by conservative nationalists to explain that the territorial expansion of the United States was not only inevitable, but also ordained by God. In that effort, embodied in the westward movement, the struggle to expand would be waged against the Native Americans. In his handling of the story, Ford strives to make a realistic depiction of settlers' life in a frontier town and the dangers awaiting them in the wilderness. Although scholars differ in interpreting the politics of Ford's vision, particularly as it relates to his depictions of whites and Native Americans (depictions that vary throughout his many movies), here his Apaches, just like the white men, are both noble (in their struggle) and savage (in war). Whether this particular story actually happened is not the point. As we understand American history, it could have hap-

pened. Ford accurately depicts the Apaches as well as the settlers—the stakes are high for each group—and though the cavalry rather theatrically arrives to save the stagecoach party, both sides suffer casualties and neither side "wins." In fact, Ringo's heroism during the Indian attack permits the stagecoach party to reach Lordsburg safely and earns him the freedom to avenge the deaths of his father and brother. That, of course, is one of the movie's personal themes: Ringo's revenge.

However, Ford sees many sad elements in the westward expansion: the displacement of the Native Americans, the migration of discriminatory social patterns from the East and South to the West, the establishment of uncivilized towns, and the dissolution of moral character among the settlers. These issues are related to the setting in which the story takes place. Here and in his other Westerns, Ford created his own vision of how the West was won. Most critics recognize that this vision is part real and part mythical, combining as it does the retelling of actual incidents with a strong overlay of Ford's ideas on how people behaved (or should have behaved).

One of Ford's persistent beliefs is that civilization occurs as a result of a genuine community built—in the wilderness—through heroism and shared values. In Ford's overall vision, American heroes are always fighting for their rights, whether the fight is against the British, the Native Americans, or the fascists. Precisely because the beauty of Monument Valley means so many different things to different people, it becomes a symbol of the many outcomes that can result from exploration, settlement, and the inevitable territorial disputes that follow. But there seems little doubt that Ford himself is speaking (through Dr. Boone) at the end of the film. As Ringo and Dallas ride off to freedom across the border, Dr. Boone utters the ironic observation, "Well, they're saved from the blessings of civilization."

Dr. Boone's "civilization" includes the hypocritical ladies of Tonto, who force him and Dallas to flee the town; the banker, Gatewood, who pontificates about the importance of banks—"What's good for the banks is good for the country"—while embezzling $50,000 from a payroll meant for miners; and the culture of violence in towns such as Lordsburg. In the 1930s, when *Stagecoach* was made, President Franklin D. Roosevelt singled out the banks as a major cause of the Great Depression and increased the government's regulatory power of them, so we can see that Gatewood (who is not in the original story) gives the movie contemporary political relevance. In the year after he made *Stagecoach*, in his adaptation of John Steinbeck's *The Grapes of Wrath* (1940)—which tells the story of a dispossessed family journeying through dangerous country to reach a place of safety—the director again put himself fundamentally against the rich and powerful and on the side of the poor and weak.

Analyzing Elements of Narrative

Most of us can hardly avoid analyzing the narrative of a movie after we have seen it. We ask, "Why did the director choose *that* story?" "Why did he choose to tell it in *that* way?" "What does it mean?" At the simplest level, our analysis happens unconsciously while we're watching a movie, as we fill in gaps in events, infer character traits from the clues or cues we receive, and interpret the significance of objects. But when we're actively *looking at* a movie, we should analyze their narratives in more precise, conscious detail. The following checklist provides a few ideas about how you might do this.

Screening Checklist: Elements of Narrative

✔ Who is the movie's protagonist? What factors and needs motivate or complicate their actions? Can you characterize each of them according to their depth (round characters versus flat) and motivation?

✔ What is the narration of the movie? Does it use a narrator of any kind?

✔ What are the differences among omniscient, restricted, and unrestricted narration?

✔ Carefully reconstruct the narrative structure of the movie. What is the inciting incident? What goal does the protagonist pursue? How does the protagonist's need influence that pursuit? What obstacles (including the crisis) does the protagonist encounter, and how does she engage them?

✔ Keep track of nondiegetic elements that seem essential to the movie's plot (voice-overs, for example). Do they seem natural and appropriate to the film, or do they appear to be "tacked on" to make up for a shortcoming in the overall presentation of the movie's narrative?

✔ Are the plot events presented in chronological order? What is the significance of the order of plot events in the movie?

✔ Keep track of the major and minor events in the movie's plot. Are any of the minor events unnecessary to the movie overall? If these events were removed from the movie, would it be a better movie? Why?

✔ Are there scenes that create a noticeable summary relationship between story duration and screen duration? Do these scenes complement or detract from the overall narrative? Are you given all the information about the underlying story that you need in these scenes to understand what has happened in the elapsed story time?

✔ Do any scenes use real time or a stretch relationship between story duration and screen duration? If so, what is the significance of these scenes to the overall narrative?

✔ Is any major plot event presented on-screen more than once? If so, why do you think the filmmaker has chosen to use repetition of the event?

✔ How do the setting and the scope of the narrative complement the other elements?

Questions for Review

1. What is the difference between narration and narrator?
2. What are the differences between omniscient and restricted narration?
3. What are the differences between (a) the camera narrator and a first-person narrator and (b) a first-person narrator and a third-person narrator?
4. Can a major character be flat? Can a minor character be round? Explain your answer.
5. What is the climax, and how does it relate to the protagonist's pursuit of the goal?
6. How (and why) do we distinguish between the story and the plot of a movie?
7. What is meant by the diegesis of a story? What is the difference between diegetic and nondiegetic elements in the plot?
8. What are major and minor events each supposed to do for the movie's plot?
9. Which of the following is the most common relationship of screen duration to story duration: summary relationship, real time, or stretch relationship? Define each one.
10. What is the difference between suspense and surprise? Which one is more difficult for a filmmaker to create?

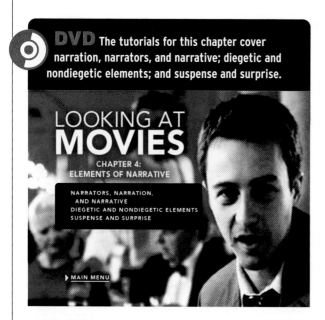

DVD The tutorials for this chapter cover narration, narrators, and narrative; diegetic and nondiegetic elements; and suspense and surprise.

Movies Described or Illustrated in This Chapter

The Apartment (1960). Billy Wilder, director.
Badlands (1973). Terrence Malick, director.
Battleship Potemkin (1925). Sergei Eisenstein, director.
The Big Lebowski (1988). Joel Coen, director.
The Birds (1963). Alfred Hitchcock, director.
Black Swan (2010). Darren Aronofsky, director.
Blade Runner (1982). Ridley Scott, director.
Blue Velvet (1986). David Lynch, director.
Citizen Kane (1941). Orson Welles, director.
Days of Heaven (1978). Terrence Malick, director.
District 9 (2009). Neill Blomkamp, director.
Dog Day Afternoon (1975). Sidney Lumet, director.
Dogville (2003). Lars von Trier, director.
Double Indemnity (1944). Billy Wilder, director.
An Education (2009). Lone Scherfig, director.
Ferris Bueller's Day Off (1986). John Hughes, director.
The Fighter (2010). David O. Russell, director.
Funny Games (2007). Michel Haneke, director.
Gladiator (2000). Ridley Scott, director.
Great Expectations (1946). David Lean, director.
Great Expectations (1998). Alfonso Cuarón, director.
The Hurt Locker (2008). Kathryn Bigelow, director.
Iron Man (2008). Jon Favreau, director.
Irréversible (2002). Gaspar Noé, director.
Kung Fu Panda (2008). Mark Osborne and John Stevenson, directors.
The Last Emperor (1987). Bernardo Bertolucci, director.
The Last Laugh (1924). F. W. Murnau, director.

The Limey (1999). Steven Soderbergh, director.

The Lives of Others (2006). Florian Henckel von Donnersmarck, director.

The Longest Day (1962). Ken Annakin, Andrew Marton, and Bernhard Wicki, directors.

The Lord of the Rings trilogy (2001–03). Peter Jackson, director.

The Maltese Falcon (1941). John Huston, director.

Memento (2000). Christopher Nolan, director.

Napoléon (1927). Abel Gance, director.

The Night of the Sunflowers (2006). Jorge Sánchez-Cabezudo, director.

Notorious (1946). Alfred Hitchcock, director.

127 Hours (2010). Danny Boyle, director.

One Wonderful Sunday (1947). Akira Kurosawa, director.

The Outrage (1964). Martin Ritt, director.

Precious: Based on the Novel "Push" by Sapphire (2009). Lee Daniels, director.

Pulp Fiction (1994). Quentin Tarantino, director.

Raging Bull (1980). Martin Scorsese, director.

Raiders of the Lost Ark (1981). Steven Spielberg, director.

Rashomon (1950). Akira Kurosawa, director.

Rear Window (1954). Alfred Hitchcock, director.

Red River (1948). Howard Hawks, director.

Rocky (1976). John G. Avildson, director.

Rope (1948). Alfred Hitchcock, director.

The Royal Tenenbaums (2001). Wes Anderson, director.

Saving Private Ryan (1998). Steven Spielberg, director.

Scarface (1932). Howard Hawks, director.

The Social Network (2010). David Fincher, director.

Some Like It Hot (1959). Billy Wilder, director.

Stagecoach (1939). John Ford, director.

Star Wars: Episode IV—A New Hope (1977). George Lucas, director.

Stranger Than Fiction (2006). Marc Forster, director.

The Sweet Hereafter (1997). Atom Egoyan, director.

Tangled (2010). Nathan Greno and Byron Howard, directors.

The Thin Red Line (1998). Terrence Malick, director.

Trainspotting (1996). Danny Boyle, director.

True Grit (2010). Joel Coen and Ethan Coen, directors.

2001: A Space Odyssey (1968). Stanley Kubrick, director.

The Usual Suspects (1995). Bryan Singer, director.

Volver (2006). Pedro Almodóvar, director.

The Wizard of Oz (1939). Victor Fleming, director.

CHAPTER FIVE

Mise-en-Scène

What Is Mise-en-Scène?

The French phrase mise-en-scène (pronounced "meez-ahn-sen") means literally "staging or putting on an action or scene" and thus is sometimes called *staging*. In the critical analysis of movies, the term refers to the overall look and feel of a movie—the sum of everything the audience sees, hears,[1]

and experiences while viewing it. A movie's mise-en-scène subtly influences our mood as we watch, much as the decor, lighting, smells, and sounds can influence our emotional response to a real-life place.

The two major visual components of mise-en-scène are design and composition. **Design** is the process by which the look of the settings, props, lighting, and actors is determined. Set design, décor, prop selection, lighting setup, costuming, makeup, and hairstyle design all play a role in shaping the overall design. **Composition** is the organization, distribution, balance, and general relationship of actors and objects within the space of each shot. The visual elements of mise-en-scène are all crucial to shaping our sympathy for, and understanding of, the characters shaped by them. As you consider how a movie's mise-en-scène influences your thoughts about it, ask yourself if what you see in a scene is simply appealing decor, a well-dressed actor, and a striking bit of lighting, or if these elements have a distinctive significance to your understanding of the narrative, characters, and action of the movie. Keep in mind that the director has a reason—related to the overall vision for the movie—for each thing put into a shot or scene (figures, objects, decor, landscaping, etc.), but each of these things does not necessarily have a meaning in and by itself. It is the combination of elements within the frame that provides the overall meaning to the shot or scene.

Although every movie has a mise-en-scène, in some movies the various elements of the mise-en-scène are so powerful that they enable the viewer to experience the aura of a place and time. A list of such films, chosen at random, might include historical spectacles such as Sergei Eisenstein and Dmitri Vasilyev's *Alexander Nevsky* (1938) or Andrei Tarkovsky's *Andrei Rublev* (1966); conventional dramas such as Stephen Frears's *My Beautiful Laundrette* (1985) or John M. Stahl's *Leave Her to Heaven* (1945); or the evocation of an unfamiliar place or culture, such as Satyajit Ray's *The Music Room* (1958), Bernardo Bertolucci's *The Last Emperor* (1987), Lars von Trier's *Dogville* (2003), or

[1] As a scholarly matter, some critics and instructors, including us, consider sound to be an element of mise-en-scène. Other scholars consider mise-en-scène to be only the sum of *visual* elements in a film. Because of its complexity, we will discuss

sound separately in Chapter 9. In this chapter, we will focus on the wholly visual aspects of mise-en-scène: on those filmmaking techniques and decisions that determine the placement, movement, and appearance of objects and people on-screen.

Guillermo del Toro's *Pan's Labyrinth* (2006). These movies challenge us to *read* their mise-en-scène and to relate it directly to the ideas and themes that the director is developing. Let's take a similar look at two such movies: Todd Haynes's *Far from Heaven* (2002) and Luchino Visconti's *The Leopard* (1963).

In *Far from Heaven* (production designer: Mark Friedberg), a melodrama about Cathy Whitaker's (Julianne Moore) personal and social problems, director Todd Haynes uses the style of such Hollywood women's melodramas as Michael Curtiz's *Mildred Pierce* (1945) and Douglas Sirk's *Imitation of Life* (1959)—a style in which mise-en-scène is absolutely essential to the director's defining (and our understanding) of character and action. But Haynes's story, set in the 1950s, couldn't have been told in those years: it's about Cathy, a "perfect" wife, mother, and community member; a husband who leaves her for a man; and the black man with whom she falls in love. Once Haynes establishes the ideas of perfection, regularity, and predictability (reinforced by periodic references to the changes of the seasons as reflected in the trees), he returns again and again to setting key moments of the action in the Whitakers' Connecticut house, located in a white suburb rife with racial prejudice. But the excellence of Cathy's house, clothes, appearance, entertaining, and civic activities is only surface perfection, because once it is shattered by her husband's confession that he loves a man, it quickly falls apart, leaving Cathy in limbo.

Another dimension to mise-en-scène also contributes to our responses to a movie: how its surfaces, textures, sights, and sounds "feel" to us. There's nothing particularly surprising about this. Think about how real-life environments affect your emotions. For people who have lived in a rural or suburban environment their whole lives, for example, their first visit to a large city is a memorable experience that triggers an emotional response. That response flows directly from what we might call the city's mise-en-scène: the scale of the buildings, the proportion of steel and concrete to trees and grass, the appearance and demeanor of the people walking the streets, and the multitude of sounds. If you have ever experienced a city, your

Mise-en-scène creates a sense of triumph in *Pan's Labyrinth* This movie, which might be a political fable in the appearance of a fairy tale, or the other way around, is, however we interpret it, a work of cinematic magic. It tells the tale of a young Spanish girl, Ofelia (Ivana Baquero), who in a former life was Princess Moanna of the Underground Realm. As the movie begins, the year is 1944 and the location Spain, then under the harsh rule of the Fascist dictator Francisco Franco. As her daily life becomes intolerable, Ofelia escapes into her world of fantasy and undertakes a set of challenges that, should she succeed, will enable her to return to her father's realm. Like other movies in the quest genre (e.g., the *Lord of the Rings* trilogy), this involves magical tools and weapons and encounters with highly imaginative creatures, including a kindly faun (who may or may not be the Pan of ancient myths), a hideous toad, and the equally hideous Pale Man, a child-eating monster. Guillermo del Toro, a director who is very active in the design of his movies, and Eugenio Caballero, the art director, employ an exquisite combination of extraordinary makeup, animatronics, and computer-generated special effects to create creatures and the corps of fairies who lead and protect Ofelia in her activities. When she fulfills the challenges, she is transformed into the Princess Moanna and reunited with her father and mother. Here, in this splendid image of gold and red, we see Ofelia (*back to the camera*) and (*left to right*) the queen on her pillared throne, Pan stepping toward us (look closely and you'll see two tiny fairies on his left), the king on his throne, and an empty throne waiting for the princess. Complicating one's interpretation is the unmistakable Christian imagery: the stained-glass rose window in the background, the pillars that in a cathedral would be topped by statues of saints, the massive wooden columns defining an altarlike space, and (out of range in this illustration) rows of pews filled with people who joyously applaud this family reunion.

memory of it is at least partly filled with impressions of these sorts of details.

Similarly, nearly every movie immerses us in its mise-en-scène. When the mise-en-scène in a movie creates a feeling completely in tune with the

Far from Heaven uses mise-en-scène to reinforce characters and themes The surface perfection of Cathy Whitaker (Julianne Moore, *center*) is reflected in her annual New Year's Eve party: the house is tastefully decorated, the guests are well dressed, and Cathy is a lovely hostess. But the party is all hers, because her husband, Frank (Dennis Quaid, *sitting*), is already drunk.

movie's narrative and themes, we may not consciously notice it; it simply feels natural. French director René Clair said that the highest level of artistic achievement in movie design is reached when "the style relates so closely to that of the work itself that the audience pays no special attention to it."[2] That description fits the memorable Greenwich Village setting of Alfred Hitchcock's *Rear Window* (1954; art directors: Joseph MacMillan Johnson and Hal Pereira). As the title credits roll, three bamboo shades rise, as if they were a curtain to reveal the stage beyond—an almost completely enclosed backyard space. The mise-en-scène is tightly controlled, and everything is photographed from the stationary point of view of L. B. Jefferies (James Stewart), a photographer who is sidelined with a broken leg in a wheelchair. As the camera next pans across the backyard in the early morning, we see the backs of the various structures that surround the open space: a glass-walled studio, a couple of brick apartment houses, and a

small two-story house. An alley next to the house leads to the street beyond. It's located in the middle of New York City and, except for the alley, is isolated from the hubbub of street traffic. Within the first minutes, we have learned that this enclosed space embodies a world of differences: different structures, different tenants, and different lives. The tenants perceive that they live in a world of privacy, acting as if no one were watching; but (through Jefferies's eyes) we see them engaged in such private activities as shaving, getting out of bed, and dressing. Jefferies sees that in this enclosed space there are hidden, subtle clues that help him to solve the murder mystery at the heart of Hitchcock's narrative.[3]

Italian director Luchino Visconti's *The Leopard* (1963; production designer: Mario Garbuglia) is an example of a film whose mise-en-scène perfectly complements its narrative and themes. The movie explores the gradual submergence and transformation of the aristocracy in Sicily after the unification of Italy, in 1861. More than anyone else in his family, Prince Don Fabrizio Salina (Burt Lancaster) makes sincere efforts to adjust to the emerging middle class, but at the same time he continues to enjoy the rituals he has always loved—masses in the family chapel, lavish banquets, travel to his other houses, and fancy balls. The 45-minute ball sequence (out of 185 minutes total), in fact, is the movie's set piece. Its length makes it more or less extraneous to the overall sequence of events in the movie, but its gorgeous surface beautifully reveals the social change beneath.

Visconti immerses us in the atmosphere of the ball: the grand rooms in the candlelit palazzo; the formalities of arrival and welcome; the ladies in elegant gowns and gentlemen in white-tie or military attire; the champagne and the food; the music; the room with a dozen chamber pots; the excitement of the young and the boredom of some of their elders; the endless gossiping and flirting; and the dancing

[2]Qtd. in Léon Barsacq, *Caligari's Cabinet and Other Grand Illusions: A History of Film Design*, rev. and ed. Elliott Stein, trans. Michael Bullock (Boston: New York Graphic Society, 1976), p. vii.

[3]For a superb analysis of the mise-en-scène and a fascinating account of the set's design and construction, see James Sanders, *Celluloid Skyline: New York and the Movies* (New York: Knopf, 2001), pp. 228–241.

[1]

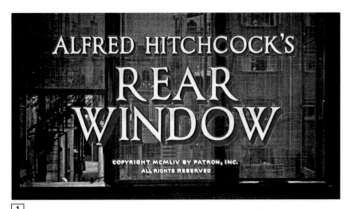

[2]

[3]

[4]

Impressive mise-en-scène for Hitchcock's *Rear Window* In *Rear Window*, director Alfred Hitchcock literally sets the stage by raising three bamboo window blinds one by one as the credits roll [1]. The principal mise-en-scène of the movie looks very much like a stage set; in fact, the single set was built to actual size—rising five stories—and filled one of the biggest soundstages on the studio lot. When completed, it included thirty-one individual apartments, twelve of them fully furnished, around a central courtyard [2], creating a memorable likeness of Greenwich Village in the early 1950s. The scope of this wonderful set permits the main character—Jeff Jefferies (James Stewart), who is temporarily immobilized in a wheelchair—to observe the activities of most of his neighbors. Indeed, there is little else he can do with his time. What we see is what he sees. Jeff

becomes particularly interested in a married couple, seen here in their large apartment [3]. Lars Thorwald is in the kitchen (*left*) preparing a meal for his wife, a nagging invalid, who is in the bedroom (*right*). Over the next few days, Jeff will become preoccupied with Thorwald's behavior. His suspicions eventually lead to the police arresting Thorwald for the murder of his wife. There are also less suspenseful things to occupy Jeff's voyeurism. Part of this courtyard complex is a small house with a terrace [4], where Jeff sees a young woman—Miss Torso, a dancer—entertaining several male friends. At the same time, the expansive set enables him to look through a passageway (*far left*) at people walking on a street. The street lamp and the human activity not only add the illusion of spatial depth, but also confirm that there is a world outside the courtyard.

of quadrilles, mazurkas, and waltzes. Visconti's care with the minute details of the decor, costumes, and characters' relationship to this environment is true to the time, space, and rhythm of life in the period.

The prince wanders from room to room, greeting old friends, reflecting on change. His only moment

of real engagement in this sweepingly romantic ball is the powerful moment when he dances a waltz with Angelica (Claudia Cardinale), the fiancée of Tancredi (Alain Delon), the prince's nephew. The daughter of a crude but wealthy bourgeois, Angelica is unquestionably the most beautiful woman in the room, and the prince's dance with her is a sign to everyone at the ball of just how far the society has been transformed. He blesses the marital union as he accedes to the larger societal change. You can see and hear this transformation occurring, just as you can almost feel the silken texture of the gowns and the wall coverings and almost taste the wine and the food. Visconti's moving camera and changing angles bring us into the action and make us a participant, yet his control of the compositional elements keeps us focused on the main character. Throughout *The Leopard*, Visconti helps us to understand not only how his mise-en-scène has been constructed but also how it guides our reading of the scene's meaning. That room of colors, rituals, and music is a perfect lens through which to understand the change both inside and outside.

However, not all movies offer a mise-en-scène that successfully complements the movie's narrative and themes. Others overwhelm us with design, including Andy and Larry Wachowski's *The Matrix* (1999; production designer: Owen Paterson), Martin Scorsese's *Gangs of New York* (2002; production designer: Dante Ferretti), Michael Polish's *Northfork* (2003; production designers: Brandee Dellaringa, Del Polish, and Ichelle Spitzig), and Christopher Nolan's *The Dark Knight* (2008; production designer: Nathan Crowley). Baz Luhrmann's *Moulin Rouge!*

An overpowering mise-en-scène in *Moulin Rouge!*
The Moulin Rouge nightclub in Paris is *all* mise-en-scène: fabulous sets and costumes, spectacular production numbers, and beautiful dancers. Baz Luhrmann's interpretation of the nightclub's famous cancan dance is different from any other version ever seen on the screen, giving a contemporary twist to the swirling dancers, colorful costumes, and uninhibited choreography of the original.

(2001; production designer: Catherine Martin) aspired to reinvent the Hollywood musical for the twenty-first century, trying to match the inventiveness and spectacle of earlier high points of the genre, including Francis Ford Coppola's visionary musical *One from the Heart* (1982; production designer: Dean Tavoularis). Luhrmann blended these influences and others into a pastiche of musical references from many periods, movies, and styles. But the result has provoked some viewers to ask how much is too much

Mise-en-scène as perfect complement to narrative in *The Leopard* Luchino Visconti, one of the world's great masters of mise-en-scène, was at the height of his creative powers when he made *The Leopard*. Practically every setting, particularly the interiors of Prince Salina's palaces, is characterized by opulence and color. The rebellious activities in the streets outside are equally colorful. When Giuseppe Garibaldi, intent on unifying Italy and Sicily, swept through Sicily with his red-shirted forces [1], the aristocracy was overwhelmed. Princess Salina faints in her parlor as she hears the news, the orange flowers ironically echoing the rebellion outside [2]. But life goes on: the prince reads aloud to his family in a sumptuous parlor, notable for the muted browns and purple tones [3]; supper is served in a magnificent dining room with walls covered in alternating orange and green fabrics [4]; the prince relaxes in his study with its red leather sofa, books bound in red, and red velvet draperies [5]; the family travels by coach through the comparatively barren landscape to their mountaintop

palace [6], where Angelica, in a shocking pink dress, wanders through some of its abandoned rooms [7]. But it is in the 45-minute ballroom sequence that Visconti creates a virtual microcosm of how aristocratic Sicilian life has been altered in this time of great social transformation. This still image [8] from a sequence full of movement—swirling dancers, officers in splendid military uniforms with gold braid, active guests, and an almost constantly moving camera—features three of the principals: Tancredi (Alain Delon), in the far-left background in white-tie formal dress; Angelica (Claudia Cardinale), in a beautiful white gown; and Prince Don Fabrizio Salina (Burt Lancaster), dancing a waltz in the left middle ground. All of this is in a ballroom that has never changed, its walls covered by gold brocade fabric and lit entirely by candles. The prince stoically accepts the social changes, including the marriage of Angelica, who comes from a family of new wealth, and Prince Tancredi, his nephew, for his motto is "Things will have to change in order that they remain the same."

1

2

3

4

5

6

7

8

[1]

[2]

Stanley Kubrick tightly controls mise-en-scène in Eyes Wide Shut Two types of finely controlled mise-en-scène in Stanley Kubrick's *Eyes Wide Shut* (1999): [1] In this indirect-point-of-view shot, we see through the eyes of Dr. William Harford (Tom Cruise, not pictured) as he is brought before a ritualistic tribunal. Painterly framing concentrates our attention and thus accentuates the scene's harrowing, hallucinatory effects. Every particular in this image—the elaborate architecture, the beautiful masks and cloaks, the color scheme, the staging—makes clear that Harford is headed into the center of power within this cinematic underworld. [2] In contrast, a scene in which Harford

searches for a costume in New York City's Greenwich Village seems natural, chaotic, even haphazard—but this illusion has been constructed as carefully as every other one in the movie. Here, the darkly clad Harford is the focal point amid more visual information than we can absorb. We note the urgency of his quest, not the details of the surroundings. (In fact, Kubrick filmed the Greenwich Village scenes not in his native New York but on sets in his adopted home, London. That the street names and shop names do not correspond to real ones in New York alerts sharp-eyed viewers to the sets' artificiality.)

before the mise-en-scène overwhelms the narrative with overripe colors, swirling movements (of characters and camera), manic editing, and non-naturalistic acting. The movies can create the most imaginative spectacles, but when those spectacular effects do not help to tell the story, viewers are left with cinematic fireworks and little else.

The creation of a movie's mise-en-scène is nearly always the product of very detailed planning of each shot in the movie. Planning a shot involves making advance decisions about the placement of people, objects, and elements of decor on the set; determining their movements (if any); setting up the lighting; figuring out the camera angles from which they will be photographed; determining the initial framing of the shot; choreographing the movement of the cam-

era during the shot (if any); and creating the sounds that emanate from the shot. Mise-en-scène is the result of all that planning.

To be sure, impressive aspects of a movie's mise-en-scène can occur by chance, without planning, whether through an act of nature (a sudden rainstorm, for example), an actor's deviating from the script, or some other accident. Although some directors display strict control of mise-en-scène and some don't, they generally collaborate with their teams to control every aspect of it. Consciously and deliberately put there by someone, staged for the camera, mise-en-scène happens because directors and their creative colleagues have envisioned it.

You should find the term *mise-en-scène* useful for explaining how all the formal elements of cinema contribute to your interpretation of a film's meanings. Indeed, the more familiar you become with film history, the more you will see that mise-en-scène can be used to distinguish the work of many great directors noted for their consummate manipulation of cinematic form from each other and from filmmakers whose mastery of mise-en-scène is less impressive. The work of some directors—Tim Burton, Sergei Eisenstein, John Ford, Howard Hawks, Alfred Hitchcock, Buster Keaton, Stanley Kubrick, Fritz Lang, Kenji Mizoguchi, F. W. Murnau, Max Ophüls, Yasujiro Ozu, Otto Preminger, Nicholas Ray, Satyajit Ray, Jean Renoir, Josef von Sternberg, Erich von Stroheim, and Orson Welles, to name a few—calls our attention to scope as well as to detail, to light as well as to shadow, to action as well as to nuance.

Although mise-en-scène can be highly personal and can help us distinguish one director's work from another's, it can also be created through a predetermined formula, as it was, for instance, by the studios during the classical Hollywood studio era, when, typically, each studio had its own look. In addition, there is the powerful influence that genre formulas can have on the mise-en-scène of individual films within that genre. Every director of a new film within a genre understands the pressure to make the mise-en-scène of that film correspond to the viewers' expectations of that genre. Nonetheless, each new film within a genre offers some new twist on the preceding formula, and those new twists may be the product of just a single collaborator's efforts.

Design

Sometimes the way the actors, setting, and decor in a movie look is the most powerful impression we take away from a first viewing. But design involves more than first impressions. Whatever its style and ultimate effect may be, design should help express a movie's vision; create a convincing sense of times, spaces, and moods; suggest a character's state of mind; and relate to developing themes. Ideally, a movie's design should be appropriate to the narrative. So if the narrative strives to be realistic, then

The twenty-second-century world of *Avatar* Here we see Na'vi people as well as the human hybrids known as avatars in a jungle setting that was designed and lit to suggest an underwater realm. It is, in fact, one of the many ethereal jungle locations in the movie.

its look should have that quality too (as, for example, in Elia Kazan's *On the Waterfront* (1954; art director: Richard Day). If its story is fantastic, then its design should mirror and complement the fantasy (Stuart Craig's production designs for all of the *Harry Potter* films to date are good examples). If a movie is of a particular genre, then its design should be suited to that genre. Every good designer knows that the Western needs open skies, the film noir relies on shadowy rooms, and horror movies must have creepy, expressionistic effects. That does not imply the use of design clichés, as you can easily prove to yourself by watching a few great Westerns. A movie's design should also be transparent, capable of transmitting light so that the audience can clearly see the actors, settings, objects, etc. within each setting. The director counts on a team of professionals to design the look of the movie with these important criteria in mind. Chief among these professionals is the production designer.

The challenge for the designers of James Cameron's *Avatar* (2009)—Rick Carter, Robert Stromberg, and Kim Sinclair—was to create a detailed vision of Pandora. Carter, the team's leader, designed a number of science-fiction movies, including Steven Spielberg's *Jurassic Park* (1993) and *War of the Worlds* (2005). The extraterrestrial world of Pandora is populated by the blue-faced, thin-bodied Na'vi, a race that is physically superior to the technologically superior military and business interests that are mining valuable minerals in the area. Amid floating mountains, lush jungles, and cascading waterfalls fly and gallop some of the most imaginative and gorgeous airborne and earthbound creatures ever seen on the screen. Using the most advanced cinematic technology to date—including Cameron's Reality Camera System (which combines two cameras in a single camera body to create a heightened depth perception for the viewer)—the **motion capture** system, and other innovative visual effects, the designers created a world so awe-inspiring that their colleagues awarded them the Oscar for Best Art Direction.

The Production Designer

Generally one of the first collaborators that a director hires, the **production designer** works closely with the director, as well as with the director of photography, in visualizing the movie that will appear on the screen. The production designer is both an artist and an executive, responsible for the overall design concept, the look of the movie—as well as individual sets, locations, furnishings, props, and costumes—and for supervising the heads of the many departments that create that look. These departments include

> art (the design personnel responsible for sketching out the movie's look, including sketch artists, painters, and computer-graphics specialists)
> costume design and construction
> hairstyling
> makeup
> wardrobe (maintaining the costumes and having them ready for each day's shooting)
> location (personnel responsible for finding appropriate locations, for contracting for their use, and for coordinating the logistics necessary for transporting the cast and crew back and forth between the studio and the locations)
> properties (personnel responsible for finding the right piece of furniture or object for a movie, either from a studio's own resources

or from specialized outside firms that supply properties)
> carpentry
> set construction and decoration
> greenery (real or artificial greenery, including grass, trees, shrubs, and flowers)
> transportation (supplying the vehicles used in the film)
> visual effects (digital postproduction effects)
> special effects (mechanical effects and in-camera optical effects created during production)

During shooting, the production designer also works closely with the camera and lighting crews.

The title *production designer* is a relatively new one. In the classical Hollywood studio system of the 1930s, each studio had an art department headed by an executive (called the **art director**) who, in addition to creating and maintaining the studio's distinctive visual style, took full screen credit and any awards the film received for art direction. The art department collaborated with the other departments that bore any responsibility for a film's visual look. The supervising art director, though nominally in charge of designing all the studio's films, in fact assigned an individual art director to each movie. Most art directors were trained in drafting or architecture, and this brought to their work a fundamental understanding of how to draw and how to construct a building. In addition to having a thorough knowledge of architecture and design, art directors were familiar with decorative and costume styles of major historical periods and were acquainted with all aspects of film production. As a result, the most accomplished art directors worked closely with film directors in a mutually influential and productive atmosphere.[4]

---

[4]Despite their importance to the production process, most art directors worked in relative obscurity. Cedric Gibbons, supervising art director at MGM for thirty-two years, was the one art director for much of the twentieth century that the general public knew by name, not only because the quality of MGM's style was so high but also because he was nominated forty times for the Academy Award for Art Direction, an honor he won eleven times.

By the 1960s, the title *production designer*, which we shall use, began to replace the title *art director*.[5] This shift in title wasn't merely a matter of ego or whim; it signaled an expansion of this important executive's responsibilities. In reality, yesterday's art director might not recognize the scope of responsibilities of today's production designer, because the technological advances in all phases of production, as well as the increasing domination of computer-generated special effects, have completely changed the way that movies are made. Nonetheless, while today's production designers face more complicated challenges than their predecessors, their fundamental responsibility remains the same: to assist in realizing the overall look of a film.[6]

Design begins with the intensive previsualization done by the director and production designer—imagining, thinking, discussing, sketching, planning—that is at the core of all movies. If the collaboration succeeds, the production designer inspires the director to understand not only how the characters, places, objects, and so on will look, but also the relationships among these things. Responsible for everything on the screen except the actors' performances, the production designer helps create visual continuity, balance, and dramatic emphasis; indeed, the production designer "organizes the narrative through design."[7] Of course, the production designer's control over the final appearance of the movie is limited to a certain extent by the cinematographer's decisions about how to shoot the film.

The director and the production designer control, to paraphrase film theorist V. F. Perkins, everything we see *within* the image;[8] yet when they have different ideas about what a movie should look like, the design details can take precedence over the narrative and alter the relationship of the movie's formal elements. In all likelihood, this happened in Werner Herzog's *Invincible* (2001; production designer: Ulrich Bergfelder), where some scenes are so beautiful they break your heart yet seem to exist for their own sake, not to further our understanding of the powerful story. Or Raoul Ruiz's *Klimt* (2006; production designers: Rudi Czettel and Katharina Wöppermann), a biopic of the Austrian painter Gustav Klimt, where the mise-en-scène, which accurately reflects the color and vibrancy of Klimt's paintings, is such a visual triumph that it makes the weak narrative all the more incomprehensible. Wes Anderson's *The Darjeeling Limited* (2007; production designer: Mark Friedberg) is a goofy, oddly touching movie about three brothers who are traveling together in India in an attempt to bond, against the odds, with one another. The designer has paid meticulous attention to trains, clothes, luggage, personal belongings, and customs, but this is not sufficient to bolster the narrative or give meaning to it.

What about production design in animated films, which consist primarily, if not completely, of computer-generated imagery? While the relationship between the director and the production designer remains the same, the production designer and his staff have even greater control over the mise-en-scène and the entire look of the film than they could possibly have in nonanimated films. So, for example, in Brad Bird and Jan Pinkava's *Ratatouille* (2007; production designer: Harley Jessup), which has the visual perfectionism associated with Pixar Studios, the visual re-creation of Paris is magnificent, an integration of story and spectacle that recalls Vincente Minnelli's classic musical *An American in Paris* (1951; art directors: E. Preston Ames and Cedric Gibbons).

[5]Actually, the title *production designer* was first used to acknowledge William Cameron Menzies's contributions to *Gone with the Wind* (1939), but it came into common use only in the 1960s. Menzies had drawn every shot of *Gone with the Wind*, and those meticulous drawings held the production together through four directors, many writers, and constant interventions by the producer, David O. Selznick. Before that—and through the 1950s—the credit title *art director* was generally used; in fact, Menzies won the first two Academy Awards for Art Direction, for movies made in 1927 and 1928.
[6]See Cathy Whitlock and the Art Directors Guild, *Designs on Film: A Century of Hollywood Art Direction* (New York: HarperCollins, 2010).
[7]Charles Affron and Mirella Jona Affron, *Sets in Motion: Art Direction and Film Narrative* (New Brunswick, N.J.: Rutgers University Press, 1995), p. 12.

[8]V. F. Perkins, *Film as Film: Understanding and Judging Movies* (New York: Penguin, 1972), p. 74.

Many art directors have become directors. Mitchell Leisen, for example, who began his career designing films for Cecil B. DeMille and Ernst Lubitsch, who was the director of a long string of stylish studio films between 1934 and 1967. The Leisen style was pure glamour in interiors, clothes, and cars, as seen in the over-the-top Art Deco look of *Easy Living* (1937; art directors: Hans Dreier and Ernst Fegté). Edgar G. Ulmer, who began his career designing several of the classic German Expressionist films—including F. W. Murnau's *The Last Laugh* (1924) as well as Murnau's Hollywood debut film, *Sunrise: A Song of Two Humans* (1927)—directed some fifty movies, most of which have cult status, including *The Black Cat* (1934). From his early career as an art director, Alfred Hitchcock learned much about creating visual and special effects, such as the powerful expressionist settings and lighting in *Number Seventeen* (1932; art director: Wilfred Arnold). William Cameron Menzies was both a movie director (the futuristic *Things to Come* (1936; art director: Vincent Korda) and a designer, whose most significant achievement was designing the entire production of Victor Fleming's *Gone with the Wind* (1939). Vincente Minnelli, who

began his career as a theater designer, directed a host of lavish MGM musicals and dramas, all of which had outstanding production values (supervised by Cedric Gibbons, with whom Minnelli had legendary quarrels), including *Meet Me in St. Louis* (1944; art directors: Gibbons, Lemuel Ayers, and Jack Martin Smith) and *Lust for Life* (1956; art directors: Gibbons, Preston Ames, and Hans Peters). Ridley Scott began his career as a set designer for England's BBC television and has directed a series of visually stylish films, including *Prometheus* (2012). David Fincher, who began his career doing special effects and went on to do music videos for Madonna and other artists, has since directed *Se7en* (1995), *Fight Club* (1999), and *The Girl with the Dragon Tattoo* (2011).

Many directors make detailed drawings and storyboards to assist the production designer in fulfilling their vision. For example, the movies of Mexican director Guillermo del Toro are known, among other things, for the gruesome-looking beasts that populate them, including *Pan's Labyrinth* (2006; production designer: Eugenio Caballero), *Hellboy* (2004; production designer: Stephen Scott), and *Hellboy II: The Golden Army* (2008; production

[1] [2]

From director's drawing to screen For *Hellboy II: The Golden Army*, director Guillermo del Toro made a clear drawing of how he thought Abe Sapien should appear [1]; in [2], you see how he actually looks on the screen. Obviously, this drawing was valuable to production designer Stephen Scott's on-screen conception.

designer: Scott). The "Hellboy" creatures—which resemble images from science fiction, Japanese anime, and horror movies—originated in Mike Mignola's Dark Horse comic books, but del Toro sketched his own preproduction take on them. These meticulous drawings are accompanied by annotations that he enters in his diaries.

Elements of Design

During the process of envisioning and designing a film, the director and production designer (in collaboration with the cinematographer) are concerned with several major elements. The most important of these are (1) setting, decor, and properties; (2) lighting; and (3) costume, makeup, and hairstyle.

Setting, Decor, and Properties

The spatial and temporal setting of a film is the environment (realistic or imagined) in which the narrative takes place. In addition to its physical significance, the setting creates a mood that has social, psychological, emotional, economic, and cultural significance.

Perhaps the most important decision that a filmmaker must make about setting is to determine when to shoot on location and when to shoot on a set. In the first two decades of moviemaking, the first preference was to shoot in exterior locations for both authenticity and natural depth. But location shooting proved expensive, and the evolution of larger studios made possible interiors (or sets) that were large, three-dimensional spaces that permitted the staging of action on all three planes and that could also accommodate multiple rooms. Interior shooting involves the added consideration of decor—the color and textures of the interior decoration, furniture, draperies, and curtains—and properties (or *props*)—objects such as paintings, vases, flowers, silver tea sets, guns, and fishing rods that help us understand the characters by showing us their preferences in such things.

A movie set is not reality but a fragment of reality created as the setting for a particular shot, and it must be constructed both to look authentic and to photograph well. The first movie sets were no different from theater sets: flat backdrops erected, painted, and photographed in a studio, observed by

Design of literary adaptations Sir Arthur Conan Doyle's universally popular detective stories featuring Sherlock Holmes have been the source, in one way or another, of nearly fifty movies. Although these stories are set in the Victorian England of the late nineteenth century, some of these films (including serious, comic, and animated adaptations) take place in modern settings. The look of Guy Ritchie's 2009 version (*Sherlock Holmes*)—despite its complex chase and fight scenes, a modern element not foreseen by Doyle—remains within the Victorian milieu. Sarah Greenwood, production designer, and Katie Spencer, set decorator, were able to use existing English locations as well as computer-generated imagery to create a replica of Holmes's world of which even Doyle would have approved. The brilliant, neurotic, and vain Holmes is famous for his elaborately messy apartment, with its profusion of books, scientific equipment, and works of art: the true haunt of a brilliant man of many interests. In this image, Dr. Watson (Jude Law), accompanied by his fiancée, Mary Morstan (Kelly Reilly), discover Holmes (Robert Downey, Jr.) hanging from the ceiling. Holmes has not taken his life but instead is testing a theory of how his antagonist, Lord Blackwood, could have escaped a hanging. The design does justice to the author's literary vision and recalls yet another of Holmes's traits: his diabolical sense of humor.

For a contemporary update on the legendary stories, you should compare this Hollywood version to the BBC-TV series, *Sherlock* (2010–2013; various directors). Set in modern London, in what is now a comparatively classless society, production designer Arwel Jones relies on settings that depict actual locations. And by contrast to the traditional depiction of Holmes as a detective who relies almost completely on his intuition, the new Holmes (played by Benedict Cumberbatch), still a brilliant thinker, also relies heavily on all sorts of digital technology including Twitter, interactive maps, social networks, and the Internet.

the camera as if it were a spectator in the theater. Indoor lighting was provided by skylights and artificial lights. (Outdoors, filmmakers often left natural settings unadorned and photographed them realistically.) The first spectacular sets to be specifically

DVD In this tutorial, Dave Monahan looks at setting in classic and contemporary films that have been influenced by German Expressionism.

Movie sets are designed for the benefit of the camera When a movie scene is shot in a studio (as opposed to an actual location outside the studio), the crew making a movie can give us the illusion of a whole room or building when, in fact, only those aspects of a set that are necessary for the benefit of the camera are actually built. David Fincher's *The Social Network* (2010; production designer: Donald Graham Burt) was shot on actual locations in Massachusetts, Maryland, California, and England as well in the Hollywood studio of Columbia Pictures. This set was designed and constructed to be a life-size representation of the Winklevoss brothers' dormitory rooms at Harvard, but as you can see, the principal room is missing its fourth wall, and lighting equipment is suspended from the ceiling (out of camera range). The wall with the window on the left clearly indicates that no shots will be made of the outside of the building in which this room is supposed to be. The camera is in the middle foreground, and through careful framing of each shot, the cinematographer will capture images that make us think that this is an actual room. But fake as it is, the designers and decorators were meticulous about little details, which one of the actors said helped him to better understand the characters and situation. The DVD release of *The Social Network* includes a supplementary disc that is, by comparison with other such bonus features, unusually thorough in its detailed account of the film's making.

constructed for a film were made in Italy; and with Giovanni Pastrone's epic *Cabiria* (1914; no credits for art director or costume designer), "the constructed set emerged completely developed and demanding to be imitated."[9] Indeed, it was imitated in D. W. Griffith's *Intolerance* (1916), which featured the first colossal outdoor sets constructed in Hollywood. Other directors soon began to commission elaborate sets constructed as architectural units out of wood, plaster, and other building materials or created from drawings that were manipulated by optical printers to look real. (Today, computers and computer-generated imagery [CGI] have replaced optical printers.)

The old Hollywood studios kept back lots full of classic examples of various types of architecture that were used again and again, often with new paint or landscaping to help them meet the requirements of a new narrative.[10] Today, the Universal Studios theme park in Hollywood preserves some of the sets from those lots. Sometimes, however, filmmakers construct and demolish a set as quickly as possible to keep the production on schedule. Only those aspects of a set that are necessary for the benefit of the camera are actually built, whether to scale (life-size) or in miniature, human-made or computer-modeled. For example, the exterior front of a house may look complete, with bushes and flowers, curtains in the windows, and so on, but there may be no rooms behind that facade. Constructed on a **soundstage**—a windowless, soundproofed, professional shooting environment that is usually several stories high and can cover an acre or more of floor space—will be only the minimum parts of the rooms needed to accommodate the actors and the movement of the camera: a corner, perhaps, or three sides.

[9]Affron and Affron, *Sets in Motion*, p. 12.
[10]See Stephen Binger, et al., *M-G-M: Hollywood's Greatest Backlot* (Solana Beach, Calif.: Santa Monica Press, 2011).

[1]

[2]

[3]

First spectacular movie sets created for *Cabiria*
Produced over six months at a cost equivalent to $2 million today, Giovanni Pastrone's *Cabiria* (1914) is regarded by many as the greatest achievement of the era of Italian blockbusters (roughly from 1909 through 1914). Its settings were the most complex and elaborate, yet they were created for a motion picture and, along with location shooting in Tunisia, Sicily, and the Alps, helped convince audiences that they were witnessing history in action (in this case, the Second Punic War between Rome and Carthage, which raged from 218 to 201 BCE). Italian pioneers of set design were later recruited by Hollywood producers and directors—including D. W. Griffith—to produce even more convincing (and expensive) backdrops for epic historical dramas. Three images give an idea of Pastrone's attempt at historical accuracy: [1] the Temple of Moloch; [2] Hannibal (Emilio Vardannes) and his troops crossing the Alps; and [3] Princess Sophonisba (Italia Almirante-Manzini) with her pet leopard, which is drinking milk.

On the screen, these parts will appear, in proper proportions to one another, as whole units. Lighting helps sustain this illusion. In *Citizen Kane* (1941; art directors: Van Nest Polglase and Perry Ferguson), Orson Welles, like many others before him, was determined to make his sets look more authentic and thus photographed them from high angles (to show four walls) and low angles (to include both ceilings and four walls). In *The Shining* (1980; production designer: Roy Walker), Stanley Kubrick mounted a special camera (called a Steadicam) on a wheelchair that could follow Danny (Danny Lloyd) on his Big Wheel to provide the boy's close-to-the-floor view of the Overlook Hotel sets, which included ceilings, rooms with four walls, and a seemingly endless series of corridors.

Lighting During the planning of a movie, most production designers include an idea of the lighting in their sketches. When the movie is ready for shooting, these sketches help guide the cinematographer in coordinating the camera and the lighting. Light is not only fundamental to the recording of images on film but also has many important functions in shaping the way the final product looks, guiding our eyes through the moving image and helping to tell the movie's story. Light is an essential element in drawing the composition of a frame and realizing that arrangement on film. Through highlights, light calls attention to shapes and textures; through shadows, it may mask or conceal things. Often, much of what we remember about a film is its expressive style of lighting faces, figures,

[1]

[2]

Stark black-and-white lighting emphasizes a struggle between good and evil In these images from *The Night of the Hunter*, which film critic Pauline Kael correctly calls "one of the most frightening movies ever made," the lighting underscores universal childhood fears. Before going to bed, John (Billy Chapin, *left*) is telling a story to his sister, Pearl (Sally Jane Bruce). Raised with the Bible in a fundamentalist home, he recounts a prophetic biblical tale that parallels the children's current situation. Just as he says, "The bad man came back," we see the ominous shadow of Harry Powell (Robert Mitchum) fall on the bedroom window, right [1]. These innocent children are deeply affected by his dark, menacing presence in their warm, cozy bedroom. Later, confronting—almost trapping—John in a narrow hallway, Powell (*left*) informs the boy [2] that he will soon marry their mother and become their stepfather. Throughout the movie, elaborately staged, lit, and photographed shots contrast light and dark to reinforce the impending evil that is to change these children's lives.

surfaces, settings, or landscapes. Both on a set and on location, light is controlled and manipulated to achieve expressive effects; except in rare instances, there is no such thing as wholly "natural" lighting in a movie.

The cinematographer Stanley Cortez said that in his experience only two directors understood the uses and meaning of light: Orson Welles and Charles Laughton.[11] Both directors began their careers on the stage in the 1930s, when theatrical lighting had evolved to a high degree of expressiveness. One of the great stage and screen actors of the twentieth century, Laughton directed only one film, *The Night of the Hunter* (1955; art director: Hilyard Brown), an unforgettable masterpiece of sus-

pense. For his cinematographer, he chose Cortez, a master of **chiaroscuro**—the use of deep gradations and subtle variations of lights and darks within an image.

Cortez once remarked that he "was always chosen to shoot weird things,"[12] and *The Night of the Hunter* is a weird film in both form and content. Its story focuses on Harry Powell (Robert Mitchum), an itinerant, phony preacher who murders widows for their money. His victims include the widow of a man who stole $10,000 to protect his family during the Depression, hid the money inside his daughter's doll, and swore both of his children to secrecy. After Harry marries and murders their widowed mother, the children flee, ending up at a farm down-

[11]See Charles Higham, "Stanley Cortez," in *Hollywood Cameramen: Sources of Light* (London: Thames & Hudson in association with the British Film Institute, 1970), p. 99.

[12]Stanley Cortez, qtd. ibid. p. 102.

LOOKING AT MOVIES

LIGHTING AND FAMILIAR IMAGE IN THE NIGHT OF THE HUNTER

DVD This tutorial analyzes lighting in Charles Laughton's *The Night of the Hunter* (1955).

river kept by Rachel Cooper (Lillian Gish), a kind of fairy godmother devoted to taking in homeless children. When Harry tracks down the kids and begins to threaten the safety of Rachel and her "family," Rachel sits on her porch, holding a shotgun to guard the house, while Harry, lurking outside, joins her in singing a religious hymn, "Lean on Jesus." Laughton uses backlighting that has a hard quality associated with the evil, tough Harry, but he also uses it on Rachel—not to equate her with his evil, but to intimate that she is a worthy adversary for him. Later in the same scene, she is suddenly lit differently—softer light, from a different direction, creates a halo effect through light behind her—because at this moment in the movie the director wants to emphasize not her resolve or her ability to stand up to Harry, but her purity of spirit.

The story and emotional tones of Fernando Meirelles and Kátia Lund's *City of God* (2002; cinematographer: César Charlone), to cite another example, are closely linked with the movie's use of light. The codirectors and production designer, Tulé Peak, work with the contrasts between bright sunlight on the beach, the various kinds of lighting in the houses and apartments in the Brazilian slums, and in a climactic moment in the movie, in a crowded disco. The lighting in the disco is true to

the source: the flickering spangles that come from the revolving mirrored ball high above the dancers; spotlights that are moved restlessly; banks of bright lights to which the camera returns again and again rhythmically, increasing our awareness that the situation is getting out of control. During this scene, Benny (Phellipe Haagensen), a drug dealer who has decided to go straight, is murdered by Neguinho/Bluckie (Rubens Sabino) after a heated quarrel. The pulsating strobe lighting ramps up the chaos of the scene, and although it is perfectly natural to the world of the disco, it underscores the violent struggle between Benny's desire to get out of the terrible world in which he has been involved in order to lead a good life and the evil forces that want to stop him from accomplishing his goal.

Costume, Makeup, and Hairstyle During the years of the classical Hollywood studio system, an actor's box-office appeal depended on that individual's ability to project a screen image that audiences would love. Makeup and hair were the two most personal aspects of that image. The studios frequently took actors with star potential and "improved" their looks by having their hair dyed and restyled, their teeth fixed or replaced, or their noses reshaped or sagging chins tightened through cosmetic surgery. Such changes were based on each studio's belief that its overall look included a certain "ideal" kind of beauty, both feminine and masculine. To that end, each studio had the right to ask actors under contract to undergo plastic or dental surgery to improve their images on and off the screen. Today's audiences have learned to love actors for their individual looks and styles, not for their conformity to ideals determined by the studios, which, as a result, led to the typecasting of actors in certain kinds of roles with which they became identified. An actor's ability to break out of stereotyped casting, when possible, was often due to the work of members of the studio's design staff who gave the actor a new look.

Today's actors, unfettered by rigid studio contracts, tend to play a wider variety of roles than they would have in the 1930s and 1940s. Although the actors' range and skill are important in making these different roles believable, perhaps even more

[2]

[1]

[3]

Expressive lighting in *City of God* Lighting plays a powerful role in establishing the setting (as well as character and mood) in Fernando Meirelles and Kátia Lund's *City of God* (2002), a violent story of constantly changing moods that is told with equally rapid changes in style. [1] For a playful day on the beach, the lighting is bright sunlight, probably intensified by reflectors. [2] For a drug deal in a decaying slum building, the strong sunlight is filtered through a brick screen into the creepy hallway. [3] Strobe lights and reflections underscore the rapidly developing chaos at a disco party.

important is the work of the art departments' professional staff to render the actors' appearance appropriate to the role. For example, Charlize Theron, a very versatile actor who has won multiple awards for her talent, has taken on many different parts, often changing her appearance (through costume, makeup, and hairstyle) to suit the roles. Theron has played Aileen Wuornos, a mentally ill prostitute who brutally kills seven of her clients in Patty Jenkins's *Monster* (2003); Gilda Bessé, a French Resistance fighter against the Nazis in John Duigan's *Head in the Clouds* (2004); the rebellious title character in Karyn Kusama's science-fiction thriller *Æon Flux* (2005); a police detective in Paul Haggis's *In the Valley of Elah* (2007), a provocative film about the aftereffects of the Iraq war on some U.S. soldiers; and in a **cameo** role, the character known as Woman in John Hillcoat's *The Road* (2009), about survival in a postapocalyptic world. Without the changes brought by costume, makeup, and hairstyle, she easily appears as her beautiful self in such films as Niki Caro's *North Country* (2005), Peter Berg's *Hancock* (2008), Guillermo Arriaga's *The Burning Plain* (2008), and Ivan Reitman's *Young Adult* (2011).

Costume   The setting of a film generally governs the design of the **costumes** (the clothing worn by an actor in a movie, sometimes known as *wardrobe*), which can contribute to that setting and suggest specific character traits, such as social station, self-image, the image that the character is trying to project for the world, state of mind, overall situation, and so on. Thus, costumes are another element that help tell a movie's story. When the setting is a past era, costume designers may need to undertake extensive research to ensure authenticity. Even with such research, however, the costumes in historical films often do not accurately depict such details as women's necklines, breast shapes, and waistlines. Hats tend to look more contemporary and undergarments more lavish than they would have historically. Designing costumes for a movie set in the contemporary world is equally rigorous, perhaps even more so. Because the characters will wear clothes similar to our own, the designer understands that we will read these

1

2

3

4

Costume, makeup, and hairstyle Charlize Theron has created a memorable list of characters, ranging from comic and delightful to disturbing and tragic. No matter what role she plays, she manages to personify the character largely because of her acting talent, but also because of the artists who helped create her screen image. [1] In *Monster*, she plays Aileen Wuornos, a serial murderer, who is here driving frantically away from the scene of a near-accident. For this role, she put on weight, her makeup artists covered her face with freckles, and she wore a shabby wig. [2] In *Æon Flux*, a science-fiction thriller, she has an entirely different look: an asymmetrical black wig, perfectly applied eyeliner, and sculpted, black eyebrows all add to the mysteriousness of her character. [3] She plays a young French aristocrat who becomes the lover of a Nazi officer in *Head in the Clouds*, a political thriller set in the turmoil of late-1930s Europe. In such

a role, we would expect her to be chic and sophisticated, and she does not disappoint, appearing here with a carefully coiffed wig, sculpted eyebrows, bright red lipstick and fingernails, and a neatly tailored suit. [4] In *North Country*, there are times when Theron, in the role of Josey Aimes, looks much as she does in real life. As one of few women working at a Minnesota mine, Josey rebels against the pervasive sexual harassment and eventually wins a landmark class action suit that changed the workplace forever. Here, at the trial and under pressure from the prosecuting attorney, she creates a distinctive impression with a casual wig and light, unobtrusive makeup. She is hated by most of the townspeople, who owe their livelihood to the mine, and she is the victim of witnesses who lie, yet she projects the image of an honest woman with a mission.

costumes more closely and interpret them on the basis of our experiences. The same can be said of makeup and hair design.

Although verisimilitude is a factor in costume design, there are other factors—style, fit, condi-tion, patterns, and color of the clothing—that can also define and differentiate characters. In Tim Burton's *Edward Scissorhands* (1990; costume designer: Colleen Atwood; makeup designer: Ve Neill), Edward's (Johnny Depp) outsider status

1

2

3

4

The importance of costume design in *Alice in Wonderland* Tim Burton's adaptation of the classic story *Alice in Wonderland* (2010) is rendered with live action and computer-animated characters, all wearing whimsical costumes. John Tenniel's original drawings for Lewis Carroll's *Alice's Adventures in Wonderland* and *Through the Looking Glass* were in black and white, but Burton's conception is in full, rich color, very much in the tradition of his other highly imaginative movies, including *Edward Scissorhands* (1990) and *Charlie and the Chocolate Factory* (2005). Colleen Atwood won an Oscar for her design of the costumes,

including those of the principal characters: [1] the Red Queen (Helena Bonham Carter), [2] the White Rabbit (voiced by Michael Sheen), [3] the Mad Hatter (Johnny Depp) and Alice (Mia Wasikowska), and [4] the White Queen (Anne Hathaway). Each of these costumes reinforces the uniqueness of the characters for whom they were created. But even costumes as good as these cannot exist by themselves. They are part of the film's larger world, particularly its overall production design (by Robert Stromberg) and the decoration of its sets (by Karen O'Hara). Both Stromberg and O'Hara also won Oscars for their achievements.

and otherness are emphasized by his costume and makeup. Other characters' traits, such as conformity, sexual neediness, and brutality are also portrayed through makeup and costume.

Two movies with brilliant costumes created for memorable actors impersonating other celebrities are Gus Van Sant's *To Die For* (1995; costume

designer: Beatrix Aruna Pasztor), in which Nicole Kidman plays a delusional, driven "dumb blond" (almost a Marilyn Monroe imitation) who wants more than anything to be a TV star. Her costumes—pastel outfits that make her seem cute and cuddly—represent her vision of herself, but in fact she is a scheming backstabber who will do anything to get ahead. In Brian W. Cook's *Color Me Kubrick* (2005; costume designer: Vicki Russell), a somewhat true story, John Malkovich plays Alan Conway, who until he was caught and jailed, masqueraded as movie director Stanley Kubrick in order to pick up young men in gay bars. In the first example, we are so familiar with Monroe's persona that it's a delight to see how she might have looked on the other side of stardom; in the second example, because Kubrick was a well-known recluse (and not known to be gay), the costume designer had free rein to create outrageous costumes for his impersonator.

Historical films tend to reflect both the years they hope to represent and the years in which they were created. Nonetheless, they shape our ideas of historical dress. For example, although Walter Plunkett's clothing designs for Victor Fleming's *Gone with the Wind* (1939; production designer: William Cameron Menzies) are often quite anachronistic, audiences usually see them as truly reflecting what people wore during the Civil War. Even though we have plenty of evidence to show what people wore in the mid-1800s, Vivien Leigh's appearance as Scarlett O'Hara only approximates how a woman of her social class might have dressed. Still, the costume design in *Gone with the Wind* often supports the narrative very well. Scarlett's green dress made from a curtain plays a major role in one scene and tells us a great deal about her character: the green reminds us of her Irish background, and the use of curtains reminds us of her newfound practicality and frugality. Ann Roth's costumes for Anthony Minghella's *Cold Mountain* (2003), another movie about the Civil War, were based not only on diligent research but also on her belief that costumes help an actor to create character by restricting—or facilitating—movement. For Joseph L. Mankiewicz's *Cleopatra* (1963), Irene Sharaff created spectacular costumes for Elizabeth Taylor that were basically contemporary gowns designed to accentuate the actress's beauty; experts agree that they bear very little resemblance to the elaborate styles of the late Greco-Roman period.

When a film involves the future, as in science fiction, the costumes must both reflect the social structure and values of an imaginary society and look the way we expect "the future" to look. Ironically, these costumes almost always reflect historical influences. The characters may live on other planets, but the actors' costumes recall, for example, the dress of ancient Greeks and Romans (as in Richard Marquand's *Star Wars VI: Return of the Jedi*, 1983; costume designers: Aggie Guerard Rodgers and Nilo Rodis-Jamero), Asian samurai and geisha (as in Daniel Haller's *Buck Rogers in the 25th Century*, 1979; costume designer: Jean-Pierre Dorléac), or medieval knights and maidens (as in Leonard Nimoy's *Star Trek III: The Search for Spock*, 1984; costume designer: Robert Fletcher).

The movies have always been associated with the greatest style and glamour. Beautiful clothes worn by beautiful people attract audiences, and since the earliest years filmmakers have invested considerable effort and expense in costume design. Giovanni Pastrone's Italian epic *Cabiria* (1914) was the first major film in which costumes were specifically designed to create the illusion of an earlier period (in this case, the Second Punic War, 218–201 BCE), and it influenced D. W. Griffith when he made *The Birth of a Nation* (1915; costume designer: Robert Goldstein) and *Intolerance* (1916; costume designer: Clare West, uncredited)—both notable for their authentic costumes. The first, concerned with the Civil War, featured Ku Klux Klan robes that helped provoke the public outrage against the film; the second told stories set in four different periods in history, each requiring its own costumes, some of which, as in the Babylon sequence, were researched carefully and realized extravagantly. Prior to those films, actors wore their own clothes, whether or not those garments were appropriate for the setting of a film. During the 1920s, costume design became a serious part of the glamour of such stars as Gloria Swanson (in Erich von Stroheim's *Queen Kelly*, 1929), Theda Bara (in J. Gordon Edwards's *Cleopatra*, 1917), and Clara Bow (in Clarence G. Badger's *It*, 1927).

In the 1930s, with the studio and star systems in full swing, Hollywood began to devote as much attention to costume as to setting. One measure of the impact of such fashionable design work was that the public bought huge quantities of copies of the clothing originally created for movie stars. Yet Hollywood has tended to regard costume design less seriously than some of the other design areas in film. From its establishment in 1928, the Academy of Motion Picture Arts and Sciences gave awards for art direction, but it did not establish awards for costume design until 1948.

Makeup Traditionally, whether films took place in modern or historical settings, stars' makeup invariably had a contemporary look. This approach to makeup preserved the stars' images and also led to new beauty products being developed that actors could advertise, enabling female consumers to use the makeup worn by their favorite stars. In fact, the history of the commercial makeup industry roughly parallels the history of the movies. The single most important person in the manufacture of movie makeup was Max Factor. In 1908, he began supplying wigs and makeup to the small movie studios cropping up around Los Angeles. In the early 1920s, makeup was usually the responsibility of

the actors, but Factor standardized makeup procedures and thus created the position of makeup designer. His products became the industry standard. Through research, Max Factor & Company continued to provide new forms of makeup to meet the challenges created by new camera lenses, lighting, and film stocks, especially color film, which required a very different approach to makeup than that required by black-and-white film. The most important names in the history of makeup design

[1]

[2]

The expressive power of makeup For Christopher Nolan's *The Dark Knight* (2008), a large team of makeup artists and hairstylists created the look of two remarkable characters. [1] The Joker (Heath Ledger) is a psychopathic criminal with a sick sense of humor, green hair and a purple suit. But it's his face makeup that is most remarkable—that great, gashed red mouth, created through facial painting and prosthetics—a darkly comic deformation and a visual parallel to the character's dual traits of sadistic humor and true evil. In contrast, [2] Harvey Dent (Aaron Eckhart) appears normal in the first part of the movie as the handsome district attorney who attempts to eliminate organized crime from Gotham City. But toward the end, in a climactic struggle, Dent's face is badly burned by an explosion rigged by the Joker, and he is then known as "Two-Face." This horrifying face was created by a digital makeup process, which essentially allowed the designers to remove half of Eckhart's face from a digital image and replace it with their creation.

Design of historical dramas In W. S. Van Dyke's *Marie Antoinette* (1938; costume designer: Adrian), one of the most lavish costume epics ever made, the French queen (Norma Shearer) looks as glamourous as a movie star; Adrian, the designer, did everything within his power to embellish Shearer's screen image rather than make her resemble the queen, whose comparatively plain face is familiar from many paintings and other representations.

are those of George Westmore and his six sons; succeeding generations of the Westmore family have continued to dominate the field.

Although many directors favor makeup that is as natural as possible, we tend to notice makeup design when it helps create an unusual or fantastic character: Boris Karloff as the Monster in James Whale's *Frankenstein* (1931; makeup designer: Jack P. Pierce); the self-transformation through science of Fredric March from the mild Dr. Jekyll into the evil side of his own character, the lustful and hideous Mr. Hyde, in Rouben Mamoulian's *Dr. Jekyll and Mr. Hyde* (1931; makeup designer: Wally Westmore); James Cagney as the great silent-screen actor Lon Chaney in Joseph Pevney's *Man of a Thousand Faces* (1957; makeup designers: Bud Westmore and Jack Kevan); the ape-men in Stanley Kubrick's *2001: A Space Odyssey* (1968; makeup designer: Stuart Freeborn); or the varied creatures in the *Lord of the Rings* trilogy (makeup designer: Peter King).

Hairstyle During the studio years, hairstyles were based on modified modern looks rather than on the period authenticity favored in costumes. Exceptions to this rule—such as Bette Davis's appearing as Queen Elizabeth I with shaved eyebrows and hairline in Michael Curtiz's *The Private Lives of Elizabeth and Essex* (1939) and with a bald head in the same role in Henry Koster's *The Virgin Queen* (1955)—are rare, because few studios were willing to jeopardize their stars' images. The idea of achieving historical accuracy in hairstyle was completely undercut in the late 1930s, when the studios developed a "Hollywood Beauty Queen" wig serviceable for every historical period. This all-purpose wig was worn by, among many others, Norma Shearer in W. S. Van Dyke's *Marie Antoinette* (1938) (see illustration on page 192) and Glynis Johns in Norman Panama and Melvin Frank's medieval comedy *The Court Jester* (1955). Generic as this wig was, hairstylists could obviously cut and style it to conform

[1]

[2]

Hairstyles Because putting stars before the camera in hairstyles from, say, the Greek or Roman period, the Middle Ages, or even eighteenth-century France could threaten an actor's image with the public, American studios in the 1930s devised the "Hollywood Beauty Queen" (HBQ) wig, which could be cut and styled in a manner that was usually most flattering to the wearer. [1] The stylized HBQ wigs Vivien Leigh wore as Scarlett O'Hara in *Gone with the Wind* (1939) were, according to experts, more suggestive of the 1930s than the 1860s, the period in which the story is set. [2] The HBQ wig worn by Maid Jean (Glynis Johns) in *The Court Jester* (1955), however, has been styled more in keeping with the 1950s than the Middle Ages, and although Hubert Hawkins (Danny Kaye) is presumably wearing his own hair, he also looks very contemporary.

to the requirements of the individual production. Thus one hairstyle served to depict two different characters at two different times in history.

In fact, until the 1960s, actors in almost every film, whether period or modern, were required to wear wigs designed for the film for reasons both aesthetic and practical. In shooting out of sequence, in which case continuous scenes can be shot weeks apart, it is particularly difficult to re-create colors, cuts, and styles of hair. Once designed, a wig never changes, ensuring, at least, that an actor's hair won't be the source of a continuity "blooper." Such aspects of continuity are the responsibility of the **script supervisor**, who once kept a meticulous log of each day's shooting. Today, script supervisors use a tiny **video assist camera**, which is mounted in the viewing system of the film camera and provides instant visual feedback, enabling them to view a scene (and thus compare its details with those of surrounding scenes) before the film is sent to the laboratory for processing. Although hairstylists receive screen credit, the Academy of Motion Picture Arts and Sciences has never recognized hair design as a craft within its awards system. However, hair design is so important in today's styles that many actors have their own hairdressers under personal contract.

International Styles of Design

Although there are as many styles of design as there are production designers, there are arguably only two fundamental styles of film design: the realistic and the fantastic. These two styles were established in France in the very first motion pictures. The Lumière brothers pioneered the nonfiction film, shooting short, realistic depictions of everyday activities. Georges Méliès created the fictional film, using illusions he had learned in the theater. As Méliès employed all kinds of stage tricks, mechanisms, and illusions, he invented a variety of cinematic effects. In so doing, he also invented the film set, and thus we can consider him the first art director in film history.

In Russia, after the 1917 revolution, the avantgarde constructivists and futurists reshaped the entire concept of cinema: what it is, how it is shot, how it is edited, and how it looks. The great Russian filmmakers of the 1920s and 1930s—Dziga Vertov, Lev Kuleshov, Sergei Eisenstein, Vsevolod I. Pudovkin, and Aleksandr Dovzhenko—were influenced by two seemingly contradictory forces: (1) the nonfiction film, with its "documentary" look, and (2) a highly dynamic style of editing. Their films—masterpieces both of cinematic design and of political propaganda involving so-called socialist realism—combined highly realistic exterior shots with an editing rhythm that, ever since, has affected the handling of cinematic time and space.

In 1922, Russian artists working in Paris introduced scenic conventions from the Russian realistic theater to French cinema and also experimented with a variety of visual effects influenced by contemporary art movements—cubism, dadaism, surrealism, and abstractionism. In the following decades, the look of the Russian film changed in many ways, including an increased use of art directors, studio and location shooting, and constructed sets and artificial lighting. Notable are Isaak Shpinel's designs for two great Eisenstein films—*Alexander Nevsky* (1938), whose medieval helmets, armor, and trappings for horses rival any historical re-creation ever seen on the screen, and *Ivan the Terrible: Parts I* and *II* (1944, 1958)—and, much later, Yevgeni Yenej and Georgi Kropachyov's designs for two Shakespearean films: Grigori Kozintsev's adaptations of *Hamlet* (1964) and *King Lear* (1971). This version of *Hamlet*, in particular, is noteworthy for being filmed at Kronborg Castle in Elsinore, Denmark; the director uses its mighty staircases for highly choreographed movement and the sounds and sights of the surrounding sea for emotional effect.

However, most important early developments in art direction took place in Germany. Expressionism, which emerged in the first decades of the twentieth century, influenced almost every form of German art, including the cinema. Its goal was to give objective expression to subjective human feelings and emotions through the use of such objective design elements as structure, color, or texture; it also aimed at heightening reality by relying on such nonobjective elements as symbols, stereotyped characters, and stylization. In German cinema, in the years immediately following World War I,

[1]

[2]

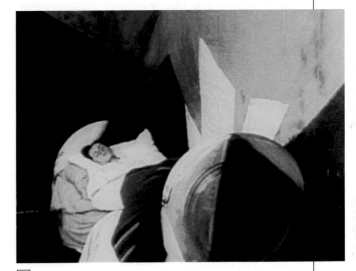

[3]

[4]

Expressionism Highly stylized sets and **intertitles (insert titles)** added to the radical look of *The Cabinet of Dr. Caligari*, as in the following examples taken from the 1996 release of the restored movie. Image [1] is an abstract graphic intertitle—"The Annual Fair in Holstenwall"—tinted in beige, white, and brown; it immediately precedes image [2], an icy blue-tinted drawing that exaggerates the shape and height of the mountain town. Image [3] is also an abstract graphic—"Night"—tinted white, gray, and green, which precedes [4], another icy blue-tinted shot of a man asleep in his bed. In a convention used throughout the movie, the walls behind his bed are not actual walls but a painted image of them in a distorted perspective tinted in black, white, and gray. Rose-colored tints are used in other images. Such conventions ushered in an era of expressionist cinematography, design, and mise-en-scène in the United States and elsewhere. That influence is clear in, for example, Charles D. Hall's designs for James Whale's *Frankenstein* (1931) and *Bride of Frankenstein* (1935), Jack Otterson's designs for Rowland V. Lee's *Son of Frankenstein* (1939), Van Nest Polglase and Perry Ferguson's designs for Orson Welles's *Citizen Kane* (1941), and the designs of countless film noirs.

[1]

[2]

The powerful influence of German Expressionist design   The color design of *The Cabinet of Dr. Caligari* influenced many movies, including Dario Argento's *Suspiria* (1977; production designer: Giuseppe Bassan). The plot of this popular slasher movie concerns Suzy Bannion (Jessica Harper), a young American ballet student who is studying at a supposedly prestigious German dance academy. She soon realizes that life there is not what she expected, for it includes murders, bizarre behavior, weird apparitions and noises, and an erratic director and ballet mistress. When Suzy investigates, she learns that a witches' coven rules the house and that they have tagged her for murder. Much like *Caligari*, in which Wiene used hand-tinted colors to externalize emotions, Argento saturated his shots (fifty-seven years after *Caligari*) with deep Technicolor reds and blues. In [1], these colors transform Suzy's paranoid fears into a surrealist stage setting. In [2], we see her escape this claustrophobic mise-en-scène as it collapses around her.

expressionism gave rise to a new approach to composition, set design, and directing. The object was to create a totally unified mise-en-scène that would increase the emotional impact of the production on the audience.

Expressionist films were characterized by extreme stylization in their sets, decor, acting, lighting, and camera angles. The grossly distorted, largely abstract sets were as expressive as the actors, if not more so. To ensure complete control and free manipulation of the decor, lighting, and camera work, expressionist films were generally shot in the studio even when the script called for exterior scenes—a practice that was to have an important effect on how movies were later shot in Hollywood. Lighting was deliberately artificial, emphasizing deep shadows and sharp contrasts; camera angles were chosen to emphasize the fantastic and the grotesque; and the actors externalized their emotions to the extreme.

The first great German Expressionist film was Robert Wiene's *The Cabinet of Dr. Caligari* (1920), designed by three prominent artists (Hermann Warm, Walter Reimann, and Walter Röhrig) who used painted sets to reflect the anxiety, terror, and madness of the film's characters and thus reflected psychological states in exterior settings. *Dr. Caligari* gave space—interior and exterior—a voice. Its highly experimental and stylized setting, decor, costumes, and figure movement influenced the design of later German silent classics such as F. W. Murnau's *Nosferatu* (1922) and Fritz Lang's *Destiny* (1921), *Siegfried* (1924), *Kriemhild's Revenge* (1924), and *Metropolis* (1927). The influence of expressionist design is evident in such genres as horror movies, thrillers, and film noirs, and many films have paid homage to the expressionist style, including James Whale's *Frankenstein* (1931; art director: Charles D. Hall) and Woody Allen's *Shadows and Fog* (1992; production designer: Santo Loquasto).

While the expressionist film was evolving, the Germans developed a realist cinema (known as *Kammerspielfilm*), the masterpiece of which is F. W. Murnau's *The Last Laugh* (1924; production designer: Edgar G. Ulmer). This film radically changed the way shots were framed, actors were blocked, and sets were designed and built thanks mainly to Murnau's innovative use of the moving camera and the subjective camera. His "unchained camera" freed filmmakers from the limitations of a camera fixed to a tripod; his subjective camera used the camera eye as the eyes of a character in the film so that the audience saw only what the character saw. These new developments intensified the audience's involvement in events on-screen, extended the vocabulary by which filmmakers could tell and photograph stories, and thus influenced the conception and construction of sets.

From the 1920s on, Hollywood's idea of design became aesthetically more complex and beautiful as foreign-born directors and art directors were hired by the studios (e.g., Alfred Hitchcock, Erich von Stroheim, F. W. Murnau) or, in the early 1930s, fled the Nazis and went to work in California (Karl Freund, Fritz Lang, Billy Wilder). Viennese-born von Stroheim—like D. W. Griffith and Orson Welles, a director, screenwriter, designer, and actor—was a master of realistic design in such movies as *Queen Kelly* (1929; art director: Harold Miles). His demands for full-scale sets and lavish interiors cost millions to realize, a factor—in addition to his egotistical and tyrannical behavior on the set—that led to his early retirement.

One need look no further than the extraordinary settings and costumes for *Queen Kelly* to understand von Stroheim's reputation as a perfectionist. In one scene, a banquet is given to announce a royal wedding. Most directors would have used a medium shot to show the splendidly dressed royal couple-to-be and enough guests sitting near them to suggest a much larger party. Not von Stroheim. After the announcement, he cuts to a reaction shot of the dinner guests, a very long shot that includes perhaps 100 people (guests and servants, all extras, appropriately costumed) in a lavish hall and a magnificent banquet table set with huge candelabra, china, silver, serving pieces, and flowers. The movie's producer and star, the legendary Gloria Swanson, said of this scene's extravagant cost, "Real caviar, real champagne to be sure."[13] Von Stroheim had a major influence on movie realism in general and, as can be seen in movies as diverse as Elia Kazan's *On the Waterfront* (1954; production designer: Richard Day), Sergei Bondarchuk's *War and Peace* (1967; production designers: Mikhail Bogdanov, Aleksandr Dikhtyar, Said Menyalshchikov, and Gennadi Myasnikov), and Martin Scorsese's *The Age of Innocence* (1993; production designer: Dante Ferretti).

Other pioneering art directors who emigrated from Europe to Hollywood include German-born

---

[13]See the interview with Gloria Swanson on the Kino Video DVD release of the movie (2003).

1

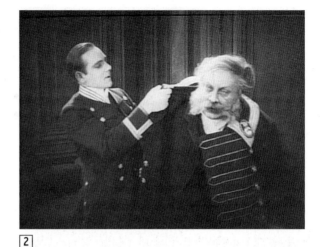

2

3

4

Camera use in *The Last Laugh* F. W. Murnau's *The Last Laugh* (1924) is one of the most poignant, yet ultimately happy, movies ever made. Emil Jannings plays an aging, weary hotel doorman who is demoted to the job of men's washroom porter; in the process, he is stripped of his magnificent uniform coat and given a simple white jacket to wear. Because the character has no name, we can assume that he is "everyman." With great sensitivity to this man's predicament, Murnau pays careful attention to camera point of view as he photographs the character's descent from a job of great dignity to one of humiliation. The drama begins when the hotel manager notices that the doorman is so weary that he has to sit down and rest. [1] From the manager's point of view, the camera looks through the glass revolving doors and sees the resplendent doorman formally greeting a guest; however, the manager has previously decided that the doorman is too old and tired to continue bearing these responsibilities. [2] Later, in the manager's

office, from the manager's point of view, we see an assistant remove the doorman's symbolic coat—a shameful moment in which the old man's pride is stripped away from him, like the skin being flayed from an animal. [3] Still later, because the doorman does not want to be seen by anyone now, Murnau uses an objective camera to show us his descent to the basement to begin his new position; notice that, in contrast to image [1], the former doorman cowers in fear of being seen. [4] Once he is in the new job, because he is tired and weary here (just as he was when the manager decided to demote him), the former doorman dozes while holding a towel for a hotel guest, from whose point of view (through a mirror) this shot is photographed. Thus, with the exception of image [3], we see only what the characters see. The movie's title refers to the fact that, at the last moment, the doorman (through a plot twist you'll have to see to appreciate) becomes a rich man, returns to the hotel to dine, and has the last laugh.

Narrative drives design in *Queen Kelly* Ideally, the director and production designer (or art director) collaborate on creating a design scheme that is appropriate to the narrative. The art director for Erich von Stroheim's *Queen Kelly* (1929)—essentially a storybook romance—was nominally Harold Miles, but it's clear that von Stroheim, the consummate perfectionist, had his usual say about the overall look of the mise-en-scène. His extravagance forced producer-star Gloria Swanson to fire him. It was further obvious to the studio that, in the midst of the transition to sound, he was no longer in touch with what audiences wanted. Here, the work of the art director serves the narrative with designs that are both appropriate and visually inseparable from it.

Hans Dreier, whose design career includes such memorable achievements as Rouben Mamoulian's *Dr. Jekyll and Mr. Hyde* (1931) and Billy Wilder's *Sunset Boulevard* (1950; co–art director: John Meehan), and Irish-born Cedric Gibbons, who supervised MGM's impressive art department for thirty-two years and, as supervisor, received screen credit as art director for hundreds of movies, even though his staff (who received other screen credit) did the actual work. He won eleven Oscars for Best Art Direction and was responsible for the studio's rich, glossy look in such movies as Edmund Goulding's *Grand Hotel* (1932), Ernst Lubitsch's *The Merry Widow* (1934), and W. S. Van Dyke's *Marie Antoinette* (1938).[14] German-born Robert Siodmak had a distinctive talent for making great movies with

[14]For a list of movies notable for their design, see "A Canon for Art Direction" in Affron and Affron *Sets in Motion,* pp. 210–211.

The Third Man As already noted, many great movies, including Orson Welles's *Citizen Kane* (1941), owe visual and even thematic debts to Robert Wiene's *The Cabinet of Dr. Caligari* (1920). Among them is Carol Reed's hugely influential thriller *The Third Man* (1949; art directors: Vincent Korda, Joseph Bato, and John Hawkesworth). In this masterpiece of design and mise-en-scène, a pulp writer, Holly Martins (Joseph Cotten), finds himself in a shadowy, angular, mazelike Vienna. Because Martins's investigation into the mysterious death of a long-lost friend yields as much deceit as truth, the city becomes not just a backdrop but a kind of major character, the troubled Martins's alter ego. The film's climactic chase scene—set in the labyrinthine sewer system, with bright lights revealing the sweating tunnel walls and police officers splashing through the dark waters—is one of the most memorable nightmare visions in movie history. That Harry Lime, the subject of the police chase, is played by Orson Welles has led some viewers to regard *The Third Man* as an homage to both *Dr. Caligari* and Welles's *Citizen Kane* (1941). Indeed, because of its characteristically Wellesian "look," some other viewers mistakenly think Welles directed it.

MGM's superlative look, including *The Spiral Staircase* (1945; art directors: Albert S. D'Agostino and Jack Okey), a suspenseful murder mystery set in a very stylish, elaborate Victorian mansion.

The list of great Hollywood art directors and production designers is a long one, and it's impossible to include all of them. However, the names of certain production designers stand out. Mark-Lee Kirk (Orson Welles's *The Magnificent Ambersons*, 1942), Richard Sylbert (Roman Polanski's *Chinatown*, 1974), Ken Adam (Stanley Kubrick's *Barry Lyndon*, 1975), Tim Yip (Ang Lee's *Crouching Tiger, Hidden Dragon*, 2000), Grant Major (Peter Jackson's

Lord of the Rings trilogy, 2001–3), Gemma Jackson (Marc Forster's *Finding Neverland*, 2004), Sarah Greenwood (Joe Wright's *Atonement*, 2007), Dante Ferretti (Anthony Minghella's *Cold Mountain*, 2003), and Jack Fisk (Paul Thomas Anderson's *There Will Be Blood*, 2007) are all recognized as exceptional practitioners of the designer's craft.

British films of the 1930s and 1940s were in most instances indistinguishable in look from Hollywood films, but the two major exceptions were the films directed by Alfred Hitchcock and those designed by Vincent Korda. Because of his background as a designer, Hitchcock created films that were always unusually stylish, including such early works as the first version of *The Man Who Knew Too Much* (1934), *Sabotage* (1936), and *The Lady Vanishes* (1938). Korda's distinctive, lavish style can be seen in Ludwig Berger, Michael Powell, and Tim Whelan's *The Thief of Bagdad* (1940), a colorful adaptation of an Arabian Nights tale, and in most of the films produced by London Films, which was headed by Korda's brother Alexander, including the historical epics *The Private Life of Henry VIII* (1933) and *Rembrandt* (1936). In addition, Vincent Korda helped design the sets for designer-director William Cameron Menzies's stylish science-fiction film *Things to Come* (1936) and was one of several designers on Carol Reed's *The Third Man* (1949), set in a decadent Vienna after World War II and perhaps the most stylish of all black-and-white movies in the film-noir style. Michael Powell and Emeric Pressburger, as creative partners, coproduced and codirected a body of major films that reflect serious attention to design elements, including *The Life and Death of Colonel Blimp* (1943; production designer: Alfred Junge), *Black Narcissus* (1947; production designer: Junge), and *The Red Shoes* (1948; production designer: Hein Heckroth).

Italian Neorealism, developed during World War II, influenced how cinema worldwide handled both narrative and design (or, in this case, absence of design). Its use of nonprofessional actors, handheld cameras, and location sets all diverged strongly from the practices of studio-bound productions, even those shot on location, and opened the door for new styles in Europe, India, and Hollywood. Its humanism and concerns with social con-

Italian Neorealism Vittorio De Sica's *The Bicycle Thieves* (1948) is perhaps the best-loved movie from Italy's neorealist period, in part because its simple story speaks to many people by focusing on the details and chance events of ordinary lives. As Antonio Ricci (Lamberto Maggiorani) and his son Bruno (Enzo Staiola) pursue an old man who can identify the thief of Antonio's bicycle, for example, a rainstorm delays them and enables the old man to get away. The rainstorm was real, and the scene was filmed on location.

ditions during and after the war broke away from conventional movie narrative and established a "new realism" in both story and style in the early films of Roberto Rossellini (*Rome, Open City*, 1945), Vittorio De Sica (*Shoeshine*, 1946, and *The Bicycle Thieves*, 1948), Michelangelo Antonioni (*L'Avventura*, 1960), and Federico Fellini (*I Vitelloni*, 1953).

Shooting in "real" locations—a seeming lack of design—actually reflects the work of an art director or a production designer who makes a well-orchestrated selection of streets and buildings, and produces a very definite look and feel—a mise-en-scène as recognizable as the most elaborately designed picture. This approach has been very influential on the design of countless films in Hollywood, where after 1950, the increasing production of stories set in real locations owed much to the postwar Italian cinema. It was also notably influential in India, where Satyajit Ray, that country's most distinctive stylist, was deeply influenced by *The Bicycle Thieves* in making his classic "Apu" trilogy: *Pather Panchali* (1955), *The Unvanquished* (1956), and *The World of Apu* (1959).

One type of Japanese mise-en-scène A distinctive feature of many of Yasujiro Ozu's movies, including *Late Spring* (1949; art director: Tatsuo Hamada), from which this image is taken, is the low but level camera angle that seems to imply the presence of a houseguest sitting on a traditional Japanese floor mat. The resulting mise-en-scène is intimate, relaxed, and generally very still.

Art direction and design are very important elements in the films of the three Japanese directors best known in the West: Akira Kurosawa, Kenji Mizoguchi, and Yasujiro Ozu. Yoshirô Muraki and Shinobu Muraki's design brings visual simplicity and dramatic power to Kurosawa's *Ran* (1985), for example. In Mizoguchi's *Sansho the Bailiff* (1954), Kisaku Ito and Shozaburo Nakajima's beautiful design is both poetic and realistic. Design credits seldom appear on Ozu's films, but we can discern a consistent visual style, austere and beautifully balanced in composition, in many of his films, including *An Autumn Afternoon* (1962) and *Late Spring* (1949). This style is based in part on Japanese culture itself—on the way Ozu's contemporaries lived, designed their houses and furniture, and ate their meals—and is, therefore, not exportable.

In India, the films of Satyajit Ray, who was successful as a graphic designer before he turned to film directing, are noted for their adherence to the principles of Italian Neorealism, particularly the emphasis on shooting in real locations. But Ray was also influenced by the movies of Jean Renoir and John Ford, which is one reason his movies stand out from the traditional Indian cinema, which—like that of Japan or China—mostly reflects the uniqueness of its culture and therefore is not particularly influential on the filmmaking of other countries. Ray is highly esteemed by audiences and his fellow film directors for his mastery of design details that reveal setting, a character's state of mind, and mood in such films as *The Music Room* (1958), *The Goddess* (1960), *Charulata* (1964), and *The Home and the World* (1984).

Chinese films display diverse visual styles. In the People's Republic of China, distinctive directors include Kaige Chen (*Yellow Earth*, 1984) and Yimou Zhang, whose films *Red Sorghum* (1987) and *Raise the Red Lantern* (1991) exploit color in impressive ways. In Hong Kong, a new cinema emerged in the 1960s characterized by its focus on the local Cantonese culture and on technological sophistication rather than style. Its distinctive achievements include Ann Hui's political *Ordinary Heroes* (1999), Hark Tsui's epic *Peking Opera Blues* (1986), and John Woo's superviolent *The Killer* (1989), a strong influence on director Quentin Tarantino and others.

Several important directors have emerged from Taiwan, including Edward Yang, whose *That Day, on the Beach* (1983) reflects Antonioni's austere style, and Hsiao-hsien Hou, whose *A City of Sadness* (1989) adheres to a more traditional Chinese cinematic style. Most famous internationally is Ang Lee, whose early films include *The Wedding Banquet* (1993) and *Eat Drink Man Woman* (1994). Since crossing over into mainstream Western film production, Lee has made movies set in utterly disparate worlds: *Sense and Sensibility* (1995), based on the 1811 novel by English writer Jane Austen; *The Ice Storm* (1997), based on the 1994 novel by American writer Rick Moody; and *Crouching Tiger, Hidden Dragon* (2000), which tells a Chinese love story in the highly kinetic style reminiscent of Hong Kong martial-arts films. Each of these movies displays a mastery of the principles of production design.

Apart from such postmodern filmmaking efforts as the Danish Dogme 95 movement (with its location shooting, handheld cameras, and natural light), most contemporary movie design tends to strive for the seamless integration of studio and natural settings. And with the exception of highly popular and hugely successful science-fiction and fantasy movies, the majority of today's stories involve recognizable people wearing recognizable clothes and moving through recognizable settings. The design work, however, is as challenging and involved as it was during the classical studio era, and the results, created with sophisticated technologies, are no less impressive.

Composition

Composition is part of the process of visualizing and planning the design of a movie. More precisely, composition is the organization, distribution, balance, and general relationship of stationary objects and **figures** (any significant things that move on the screen—people, animals, objects) as well as of light, shade, line, and color within the frame. Ensuring that such organization helps develop a movie's narrative and meanings requires much thought and discussion, so filmmakers use drawings and models—general sketches of the look of overall scenes, specific set designs, costume designs, storyboards for particular shot sequences, and so on—to aid them in visualizing each shot and achieving a unified whole. As filmmakers visualize and plan each shot, they must make decisions about two aspects of composition: **framing** (what we see on the screen) and **kinesis** (what moves on the screen).

This is true whether the movie strives for verisimilitude or fantasy. Certain visionary directors are known for making shots that resemble the canvas of an enormous painting and in doing so, they pay impressive amounts of attention to all aspects of composition. Such directors, to name only a few, include David Lynch (*The Elephant Man*, 1980; *Blue Velvet*, 1986; and *Mulholland Dr.*, 2001), Terry Gilliam (*Brazil*, 1985; *Fear and Loathing in Las Vegas*, 1998; and *The Brothers Grimm*, 2005), Roy Andersson (*World of Glory*, 1991; and *Songs from the Second Floor*, 2000), and Francis Ford Coppola (*One from the Heart*, 1982; and *Apocalypse Now Redux*, 2001 [director's cut of *Apocalypse Now*, 1979]).

Composition is important because it helps to ensure the aesthetic unity and harmony of the movie as well as to guide our looking—how we read the image and its component parts and, particularly, how we interpret the characters' physical, emotional, and psychological relationships to one another. Composition can produce a flat image, one in which figures and objects are arranged and photographed in the foreground of the screen, or an image that has the illusion of depth.

Framing: What We See on the Screen

The frame is the border between what the filmmaker wants us to see and everything else—the dimensions of height and width that provide the shape of the movie's images. However, unlike the static frame around a painting, the frame around a motion-picture image can move and thus change its point of view (this process of **reframing** results from what is called a **moving frame**). The movie frame is therefore not merely a container for a movie's visual elements, but is itself an important and dynamic visual element.

Framing also implies **point of view (POV)**. At times, the framing seems to present us with the point of view of a single character (subjective POV). At other times, the framing implies a view that seems to be coming from no one in particular (omniscient POV). However, sometimes the framing can be so

LOOKING AT MOVIES

COMPOSING THE FRAME

DVD In this tutorial, Dave Monahan discusses the core principles of composition within the frame.

varied that it creates a desirable ambiguity, one in which viewers are required to reach their own conclusions about the moral issues at hand. For example, Krzysztof Kieslowski's *The Decalogue* (1989; cinematographer: Slawomir Idziak; art director: Ewa Smal) is composed of ten one-hour films, each of which is devoted to a contemporary interpretation of one of the biblical commandments. The film pays particular attention to the point of view of the camera that visually narrates each of the stories. Kieslowski, a Catholic who experienced the Communist-controlled Poland of the 1960s and 1970s, was not overtly religious and thus he does not espouse any particular doctrinal interpretation of the commandments, leaving interpretation to the viewer.

Thou Shalt Not Kill (1990), the fifth film, is perhaps the most demanding of the series, both because it deals with a murder so random and horrifying that it provokes our strongest moral outrage and because Kieslowski's approach to the framing, which employs both traditional and innovative techniques, creates the sense of a coldly "objective" perspective on the crime even as it reveals subjective points of view. Kieslowski achieves this effect by shooting the actors and settings from a variety of angles, using a very close framing so that we become intimate with all of the characters, and shifting the camera's point of view so that, for example, as the murder is about to take place, we see shots of the murderer coiling a rope around his fist while drinking a cup of coffee and flirting with two young girls, hailing a taxi, staring at the driver's face in the rearview mirror, calmly looking out the window, and then murdering the driver. In other words, we see (1) the murderer's objective actions as observed by the camera, as if it were a documentary movie, including his garroting the driver, bludgeoning him, and dragging him to the riverside, where he smashes his face with a rock; (2) facial expressions that reveal some of the murderer's subjective thoughts; and (3) reaction shots of the driver as he picks up the passenger, discusses a change of route that leads him onto a deserted road

[1]

[2]

Composition and mise-en-scène Two shots from William Wyler's *The Best Years of Our Lives* (1946; art directors: Perry Ferguson and George Jenkins) illustrate the relationship between composition and mise-en-scène. In the movie, the lives of three veterans are intertwined, and triangular compositions reinforce that theme visually. [1] Early in the film, Fred Derry (Dana Andrews, *top*), Al Stephenson (Fredric March, *lower right*), and Homer Parrish (Harold Russell, *lower left*) return home after serving in World War II. Their tight physical grouping in the nose of a bomber reflects the tight emotional bond that they have only recently established. [2] Much later, a similar tripoint pattern establishes a different relationship among the men. Here, a shot in Butch's bar has Derry using the phone in the background with a noticeable gap between Stephenson and Parrish, reflecting the new and estranged relationship. Time has changed their lives, and the same old patterns have different meanings within the larger context.

where he is killed. At other times, the scene begins with the murderer in one corner of the frame, so that we see what he's seeing, and then the camera reframes so that he is central to the action. Because he has no apparent motive, we are appalled at the extraordinary brutality that we see. Even he seems shocked by what he has done. Obviously, the director's choices in such techniques as camera angle, framing, and camera movement contribute to our reactions, but they do not lead those reactions in one way or another. In fact, the continual use of reflections in windows and mirrors makes us wonder which images to trust.

On-screen and Offscreen Space How filmmakers envision the look of a film and how the camera interprets that vision depend on the fundamental fact that cinematic seeing *is* framing. The frame of the camera's **viewfinder** (the little window you look through when taking a picture) indicates the boundaries of the camera's point of view. To demonstrate for yourself the difference between the camera's point of view and your everyday vision, put your hands together to form a rectangular frame, then look through it using one eye. If you move it to the left or the right, move it closer or farther away from your face, or tilt it up or down, you will see instantly how framing (and moving the frame) changes what you see.

Because the frame is dynamic, it often makes us aware of the **offscreen space** outside the frame as well as the **on-screen space** inside it. As the frame moves, it presents on the screen details that were previously offscreen, thus prompting us to be aware of the dynamic between offscreen and on-screen spaces. As the film theorist Noël Burch first suggested, the entire visual composition of a shot depends on the existence of both on-screen and offscreen spaces; both spaces are equally important to the composition and to the viewer's experience of it.[15] Burch divides offscreen space into six segments: the four infinite spaces that lie beyond the four borders of the frame; the spaces beyond the movie

settings, which call our attention to entrances into and exits from the world of the frame; and the space behind the camera, which helps the viewer define the camera's point of view and identify a physical point beyond which characters may pass. Offscreen space has power, as Burch emphasizes: "The longer the screen remains empty, the greater the resulting tension between screen space and off-screen space and the greater the attention concentrated on off-screen space as against screen space."[16] In any movie—a verisimilar one, in particular—most shots depend on both on-screen and offscreen space, and our awareness of their interdependence reinforces the illusion of a larger spatial world than what is contained in any single frame.

In *Chinatown* (1974; production designer: Richard Sylbert), Roman Polanski uses offscreen space to accentuate the suspense of the second meeting between the prying detective J. J. Gittes (Jack Nicholson) and the menacing tycoon Noah Cross (John Huston) at the house of Evelyn Mulwray (Faye Dunaway), who is both Cross's daughter and Gittes's client. Cross is a ruthless man who will do anything to keep his loathsome personal life and corrupt public activities from further notice, and Gittes knows he's now in danger when Cross arrives at the house. As the scene begins no one is in the frame, but a puff of cigarette smoke enters the left side of the frame and lets us know that Gittes is waiting there. This may be one of the rare instances when a puff of smoke can produce a powerful reaction from the viewers. Although it's been put there for a reason, its meaning is more metaphorical than literal: a transitional moment of vagueness before a powerful confrontation between two antagonists. Cross steps onto the front porch, enters the house, crosses the foyer, appears on the terrace, looks offscreen at Gittes, and says, "Oh, there you are," as if he weren't prepared for the meeting. Gittes then enters the frame, and their conversation begins.

Open and Closed Framing The first and most obvious function of the motion-picture frame is to control our perception of the world by enclosing

---

[15]Noël Burch, *Theory of Film Practice*, trans. Helen R. Lane (1973; repr., Princeton, N.J.: Princeton University Press, 1981), p. 25.

[16]Ibid.

On-screen and offscreen space in *Chinatown*
[1] Because of the smoke from his cigarette (*screen left*), we know that J. J. Gittes (Jack Nicholson) is in the space depicted here, and not being able to see him accentuates the suspense in this climactic scene from Roman Polanski's *Chinatown* (1974). [2] Noah Cross (John Huston) enters, looking for Gittes, and sees him offscreen left. [3] Gittes enters the frame and begins their conversation.

what we see within a rectangular border, generally wider than it is high. Because it shapes the image in a configuration that does not allow for peripheral vision and thus does not conform to our visual perception, we understand framing as one of the many conventions through which cinema gives form to what we see on the screen. Film theorist Leo Braudy, one of many writers to study the relation-ship between cinematic arrangement and viewer perception, distinguishes between open and closed films (or forms) as two ways of designing and representing the visible world through framing it, as well as two ways of perceiving and interpreting it.

Each of these cinematic worlds—open and closed—is created through a system of framing that should remain fairly consistent throughout the film so as not to confuse the viewer. The **open frame** is designed to depict a world where characters move freely within an open, recognizable environment, and the **closed frame** is designed to imply that other forces (such as fate; social, educational, or economic background; or a repressive government) have robbed characters of their ability to move and act freely. The open frame is generally employed in realistic (verisimilar) films, the closed frame in antirealistic films. In the realistic, or verisimilar, film, the frame is a "window" on the world—one that provides many views. Because the "reality" being depicted changes continuously, the movie's framing changes with it. In the antirealistic film, the frame is similar to the frame of a painting or photograph, enclosing or limiting the world by closing it down and providing only one view. Because only that one view exists, everything within the frame has its particular place. As with all such distinctions in film analysis, these differences between open and closed frames aren't absolute; they are a matter of degree and emphasis (as shown in Table 5.1).

Who or what decides whether a movie is "open" or "closed"? Sometimes it's the director; at other times, it's the narrative; in most movies, it's both. Directors choose the open frame to enable their characters to act freely, to come and go within the film's world. John Ford's *My Darling Clementine* (1946) is not only shot with an open frame, but concludes in open-ended ambiguity. In one sense, its characters (Wyatt Earp and company) face an existentialist dilemma: whether to live as uncivilized, lawless barbarians or to become lawful members of a civilized community. The town of Tombstone, set among the vast expanses of Monument Valley, can go one way or the other, depending upon the actions of individuals who live there. Ford seems to favor community, family, and organized religion; his

1

2

3

4

5

6

7

8

On-screen and offscreen space in *Stagecoach*

(*Opposite*) In John Ford's *Stagecoach* (1939; art director: Alexander Toluboff), a scene set in the noontime lunch stop at Dry Fork illustrates social division among the characters through the use of on-screen and offscreen spaces. [1] The scene opens by establishing the location, showing two of the room's four walls. Following this establishing shot, a series of cuts fills in parts of the room not seen here. [2] Revealing a third wall but keeping us oriented by showing the chairs and part of the table, this shot takes us to what had been offscreen space and remains marginal territory, where Ringo (John Wayne) and Dallas (Claire Trevor) interact before he seats her at the table. [3] Opposed to Ringo and Dallas, on the other side of the room, are Gatewood (Berton Churchill, *seated left*), Hatfield (John Carradine, *standing right*), and Lucy (Louise Platt, *seated right*)—three characters who consider themselves socially superior to the others. [4] From yet another perspective we see the room's fourth wall and Lucy, who stares coldly and haughtily at [5] Dallas, who yields no ground. [6] When Ringo defies the anger rising across the table (a reinforcement of his position in image [2]), [7] Hatfield escorts Lucy away from Dallas (a reinforcement of their position in image [3]) to [8] the opposite end of the table, which we see from an entirely new perspective. Thus an area that had been largely offscreen, hardly registering, takes prominence, especially in contrast to the brightly lit, vacant, and exposed end of the table.

hero, Earp, arrives in the lawless town, becomes the sheriff, establishes civic order, and then departs for his own personal reasons. This seems to be an ambiguous ending. It's noteworthy that both Kurosawa and Ford first attempted to be painters, an art in which everything has its place and is enclosed within a frame. Although they both became film directors, their painting experience probably influenced their masterful sense of composition and attention to detail within the frame.

Directors choose the closed frame when their stories concern characters who are controlled by outside forces and do not have the freedom to come and go as they wish. Design elements frequently drive the story's development. Good examples include almost any Alfred Hitchcock movie (e.g., *Dial M for Murder*, 1954), Carol Reed's *The Third Man* (1949), Kelly Reichardt's *Wendy and Lucy* (2008) and *Meek's Cutoff* (2011), or King Vidor's silent classic *The Crowd* (1928).

Darren Aronofsky's *Black Swan* (2010) is a closed movie in which the design and framing are

TABLE 5.1	Open and Closed Frames	
	Open	**Closed**
Visual characteristics	Normal depth, perspective, light, and scale. An overall look that is realistic, or verisimilar.	Exaggerated and stylized depth; out of perspective; distorted or exaggerated light and shadow; distorted scale. An overall look that is not realistic, or verisimilar.
Framing the characters	The characters act. They may move freely in and out of the frame. They are free to go to another place in the movie's world and return.	The characters are acted upon. They are controlled by outside forces and do not have the freedom to come and go as they wish. They have no control over the logic that drives the movie's actions.
Relationship of characters to design elements	The characters are more important than the sets, costumes, and other design elements. The design elements support the development of character and story.	Design elements call attention to themselves and may be more important than the characters. Design elements drive the story's development.
The world of the story	The world of the story is based on reality. It changes and evolves, and the framing changes with it. The frame is a window on this world.	The world of the story is self-contained; it doesn't refer to anything outside of itself. It is rigid and hierarchical: everything has its place. The frame is similar to a painting.

Source: Adapted from Leo Braudy, *The World in a Frame: What We See in Films* (1976; repr., Chicago: University of Chicago Press, 1984).

more important than the characters. The highly melodramatic story concerns a young ballet dancer, Nina Sayers (Natalie Portman), an artist with great technique who cannot become a prima ballerina until she realizes her soul as a dancer. In this case, that means fighting her demons, primarily her psychotic view of her world and colleagues. Her struggle occurs within a production design that is very claustrophobic; virtually all of its major scenes are shot in interiors: backstage, stage, dressing room, corridors, and Nina's bedroom at home. Despite her ambitions and her talent, Nina (as well as the other young dancers) seems caught in this labyrinth of spaces that defines their world. Indeed, they are trapped in a world where their success is often determined more by destiny than talent. While some of the dancers are comfortable with this reality, those who aren't try to destroy it at their peril. Thomas Leroy (Vincent Cassel), the hard-driving director of the ballet company, controls the repetitive rehearsals with an iron hand, calling our attention to the movie director's manipulation of the students' confining world.

An interesting paradox occurred when two different directors from different countries—Jean Renoir (France) and Akira Kurosawa (Japan)—each made their own cinematic adaptation of Russian writer Maxim Gorky's play *The Lower Depths* (1902). Gorky's work gives a pessimistic, dark view of lower-class Russians who share a boarding house, the principal setting of the play. In his 1936 version, Renoir, who generally favors the open frame, sets the story in a Parisian flophouse and allows his characters to move freely in and out of the frame as well as out of the house and into the city beyond. Kurosawa, in his 1957 version, sets the story in seventeenth-century Japan and, like Gorky, keeps the action inside the house. Renoir emphasizes that man's life is left to free will and chance, while Kurosawa allows his characters little freedom. Renoir's open frame is more relevant to the modern audience, while Kurosawa's relatively closed frame seems claustrophobic by contrast, perhaps reflecting the hierarchical society of the time.

The formulaic nature of these distinctions does not mean that you should automatically categorize movies that you see and analyze as open or closed, for there will be no profit in that. Instead, you can recognize the characteristics of each type of film (as described in Table 5.1), and you can be aware that certain directors consistently depict open worlds (Jean Renoir, John Ford, Robert Altman) while others are equally consistent in making closed ones (Alfred Hitchcock, Stanley Kubrick, Lars von Trier).

Kinesis: What Moves on the Screen

Because the movies move in so many ways, our perception of kinesis (movement) in a movie is influenced by several different factors at once—including the use of music in an otherwise static scene. But we perceive movement mainly when we see (1) the movement of objects and characters within the frame and (2) the apparent movement of the frame itself (the moving frame). Although their particular applications will differ depending on the specific work, both types of movement are part of any movie's composition and mise-en-scène.

Of course, all movies move, but some move more than others and differently. The kinetic quality of many movies is determined by their genre: action pictures, cartoons, and comedies tend to include more and faster movement than do love stories or biographical films. Many great films—Carl Theodor Dreyer's *The Passion of Joan of Arc* (1928), Robert Bresson's *Diary of a Country Priest* (1951), Yasujiro Ozu's *Tokyo Story* (1953), and Michelangelo Antonioni's *The Outcry* (1957), for example—use little movement and action. That lack of action represents not only a way of looking at the world (framing it) but also an approach to the movie's narrative and themes.

Which movie, then, is the more cinematic—one that moves all the time or one that moves hardly at all? Because kinetic power is only one of the inherent creative possibilities of movies, not an essential quality of every movie, we can answer this question only by examining the relationships among the movement, narrative, and overall mise-en-scène. In this way, we can determine what movement is appropriate and furthermore what movement works to control perceptions. To condemn *Tokyo*

Kinesis in action films Throughout the history of film—from the swashbuckling of Hollywood legend Douglas Fairbanks to the cinematic portrayals of Shakespeare's Hamlet by Laurence Olivier, Mel Gibson, Kenneth Branagh, and many others, to the movie careers of martial artists such as Bruce Lee and Jackie Chan—old-fashioned swordplay has always been one of the most exciting forms of movement on-screen. Ang Lee's *Crouching Tiger, Hidden Dragon* (2000), a contemporary update of Hong Kong sword-and-sorcery movies, combines martial arts with elaborate choreography. In playing the nobleman's-daughter-turned-warrior, Jen Yu, shown here in one of many fight sequences, actress Ziyi Zhang used her training in dance as well as her martial-arts skills.

Story's lack of movement when compared to the frenetic movement in, say, Yimou Zhang's *Hero* (2002; production designers: Tingxiao Huo and Zhenzhou Yi) is equivalent to condemning Shakespeare for not writing in the style of contemporary playwright Harold Pinter. In other words, the comparison is unfair to both sides.

Movement of Figures within the Frame

The word *figure* applies to anything concrete within the frame: an object, an animal, a person. The most important figure is usually the actor, who is cast, dressed, made up, and directed for the film and thus is a vital element in the composition and resulting mise-en-scène. Figures can move in many ways: across the frame (in a horizontal, diagonal, vertical, or circular pattern), from foreground to background (and vice versa), or from on and off the screen. A character can float weightlessly in outer space, as Frank Poole (Gary Lockwood) does in Stanley Kubrick's *2001: A Space Odyssey* (1968); dance without danger to himself up a wall and across the ceiling, as Tom Bowen (Fred Astaire)

does in Stanley Donen's *Royal Wedding* (1951); or break free from leg braces and run like the wind, defying a childhood spinal problem and gravity itself, as the title character, played by Tom Hanks, does in Robert Zemeckis's *Forrest Gump* (1994). These and other kinds of figure movement—which can be as prosaic or as poetic as the story requires—not only show where a character is moving, but how (on foot, in a vehicle, through the air in a fight), and sometimes (explicitly or implicitly) also why.

The director and his team must plan the positions and movements of the actors and the cameras for each scene and, in rehearsals, familiarize the cast and camera operators with their plan—a process known as **blocking.** In the early stages of blocking, the director often places pieces of tape on the floor to indicate the position of the camera and the actors; once crew and cast are familiar with their positions, the tape is removed. In designing a film, another essential element to be considered is how all the figures move within the space created to tell the story, as well as how they are placed in relation to each other. The physical placement of characters

[1]

[2]

[3]

Movement of figures within the frame Movies can make anything and anyone move in any way the story calls for. All three movements in the images here are in the realm of the unbelievable. [1] Astronaut Frank Poole (Gary Lockwood)—betrayed by an onboard computer that severs his lifeline—floats weightlessly to his death in *2001: A Space Odyssey* (1968). [2] Expressing his love for a woman, Tom Bowen (Fred Astaire) in *Royal Wedding* (1951) dances his way up a wall and eventually across the ceiling. [3] Forrest Gump (Tom Hanks), in the movie of that name (1994), acts from complete willpower to shed his leg braces and run free.

can suggest the nature and complexity of whatever relationship may exist between them, and thus their placement and proximity are relevant to our understanding of how the composition of a shot helps to create meaning. (Analyzing placement and proximity is the study of *proxemics*.)

Ordinarily, close physical proximity implies emotional or other kinds of closeness. Federico Fellini's *I Vitelloni* (1953; cinematographers: Carlo Carlini, Otello Martelli, and Luciano Trasatti; production designer: Mario Chiari) goes against this convention by employing a very rigorous compositional plan that involves placing the characters in symmetrical proximity. In one memorable shot, Fellini suggests group indolence by seating each character at a separate café table, with half of them facing in one direction and the other half facing in the other. In *Love and Death* (1975; cinematographer: Ghislain Cloquet; production designer: Willy Holt), a low comedy about life's big issues, director Woody Allen shows that physical proximity between two characters can also mean the absence of romantic closeness. On the night before he is to fight a duel, Boris (Woody Allen) asks Sonja (Diane Keaton) to marry him. They are very tightly framed in the shot, and he starts intoning a nonsensical monologue: "To die before the harvest, the crops, the grains, the fields of rippling wheat—all there is in life is wheat." The shot continues as she, looking offscreen left, confesses her innermost feelings about him; and although he does not seem to hear what she is saying, his reaction is to mug all sorts of exaggerated facial reactions as he mumbles more nonsense about wheat. As he does with so many other aspects of film, Allen manipulates proxemics for brilliant comic effect.

Looking at Mise-en-Scène

The better the fit between mise-en-scène and the rest of a movie's elements, the more likely we are to take that mise-en-scène for granted. A movie's mise-en-scène may be so well conceived that it seems merely something there for the cinematographer to film rather than the deliberately produced result of labor by a team of artists and craftspeople. A fully realized mise-en-scène plays a crucial role in creating the illusion of naturalness that encourages our enjoyment of movies as spectators. But we must consciously resist that illusion if we hope to graduate from being spectators to being students of film, people who look at movies rather than just watch them. Looking at mise-en-scène critically does not mean taking the fun away from movies. You may still have as much fun as you like with (or is the better word *in*?) *The Matrix* (1999) while realizing that everything you see, hear, and feel in it was put there for a purpose.

Let's look closely at two movies in which mise-en-scène produces a rich viewing experience: Tim Burton's *Sleepy Hollow* (1999) and Sam Mendes's *American Beauty* (1999).

Tim Burton's *Sleepy Hollow*

Tim Burton is a director who has created imaginative fantasies that reveal great visual ingenuity and a wicked sense of humor. His movies are always a treat to look at, and they offer abundant opportunities for analyzing their design and mise-en-scène, even when these aspects do not always serve the narrative well. Among his most successful movies are *Batman* (1989), *Edward Scissorhands* (1990), *Ed Wood* (1994), *Sleepy Hollow* (1999), *Planet of the Apes* (2001), *Charlie and the Chocolate Factory* (2005), *Sweeney Todd: The Demon Barber of Fleet Street* (2007), and *Alice in Wonderland* (2010).

The highly stylized reimagining of Washington Irving's tale "The Legend of Sleepy Hollow" (1819–20) so totally transforms its source that, in effect, it leaves the text behind; it emphasizes instead the director's stunning vision and his production team's meticulous realization of that vision. The story concerns the efforts of Ichabod Crane (Johnny Depp), a forensic scientist, to solve three murders in the village of Sleepy Hollow where the victims were beheaded. The ending is so muddled that we don't really know if he succeeds, but at least he escapes with his head. The movie's unified design plan and mise-en-scène create the correct times, places, and moods—according to Burton's vision— and go beyond the superficial to reveal characters, provide the appropriate settings for the extraordi-

Mise-en-scène creates *Sleepy Hollow*'s unified look
[1] *Sleepy Hollow*'s primary palette, tending toward slate-gray and bluish-gray, and the overcast, forbidding look used in most of the outdoor shots enhance our sense of the mystery and danger lurking within the village. [2] Punctuating this overall grayness are magnificent homages to classic horror films, including a windmill straight out of James Whale's *Frankenstein* (1931).

nary action of the film, and develop its themes. Burton's overall goal in production design seems to have been to make this film as weird and scary as possible. Verisimilitude has nothing to do with it. Although Washington Irving's story describes the valley of Sleepy Hollow as a place filled with rippling brooks, cheerful birdcalls, and unchanging tranquility, Burton's version of Sleepy Hollow is dark and foreboding from the start. The visual presentation of the village is clearly inspired by the design vocabularies of horror and gothic movies.

Such movies include James Whale's *Frankenstein* (1931), which ends with an angry mob trapping the Monster in a windmill that they set afire. Burton similarly places the spectacular climax of his film in an ominous windmill, where Ichabod Crane lures the Headless Horseman (Christopher Walken), whose mysterious powers save him from death in the fiery explosion. In addition, Burton draws on Mario Bava's visually sumptuous vampire movie *Black Sunday* (1960), Roman Polanski's *The Fearless Vampire Killers* (1967), and films from Britain's Hammer Studios (the foremost producer of gothic horror films in movie history), whose style was characterized by careful attention to detail—including, of course, lots of blood—in such films as Terence Fisher's *The Curse of Frankenstein* (1957) and *Horror of Dracula* (1958). Burton also pays homage to the horror genre by casting Christopher Lee, who plays the Creature in *The Curse of Frankenstein*, as the Burgomaster in *Sleepy Hollow*.

Sleepy Hollow features many of the prominent characteristics of the horror and gothic genres, including

> a spooky setting—the almost colorless village of Sleepy Hollow and the creepy woods that surround it.
> a forensic scientist, Ichabod Crane (played by Johnny Depp, an actor whose fey style has added much to several of Burton's movies), forced to struggle with a demonic antagonist (or perhaps the illusion of one), the Headless Horseman (Christopher Walken).
> a seemingly virginal heroine who dabbles in witchcraft—Katrina Anne Van Tassel (Christina Ricci)—and her wicked stepmother, Lady Mary Van Tassel (Miranda Richardson), the wife of the lord of the manor who moonlights as a witch.
> various other eccentric and deranged locals.

In addition, there are glimpses of the spirit world and other frightening, mysterious, and supernatural events.

Burton and his collaborators were also inspired by the visual style of the eighteenth-century British artists William Hogarth and Thomas Rowlandson. In such works as *A Rake's Progress* (1732–35), Hogarth created a series of anecdotal pictures (similar to

[1]

[2]

[3]

Different characters in *Sleepy Hollow* require different looks [1] Baltus Van Tassel (Michael Gambon, *standing left*) is among the many characters in *Sleepy Hollow* who might have stepped out of period paintings. Indeed, most of the village's residents seem stuck in an antiquated, vaguely European style of dress. [2] By contrast, the darkly and sleekly dressed Ichabod Crane (Johnny Depp) is a "modern" American man of science, here wearing the ambitious but wonderful instrument that he has designed to perform forensic inspections. [3] In a flashback, the "Hessian" (Christopher Walken), who in death will become the Headless Horseman, is all spikes and sharp angles, looking very much like the vampire in F. W. Murnau's classic *Nosferatu* (1922).

movie storyboards) that had both a moral and a satirical message. Rowlandson created an instantly recognizable gallery of social types, many of whom seem to have served as models for the characters we meet at Van Tassel's mansion. When Crane steps into the house, a "harvest party" is taking place, and the guests are dancing, drinking, and quietly talking. The color palette changes from the exterior gloom to soft browns, grays, greens, and blacks. The interior colors are very subdued but warmed by a patterned tile floor, orange jack-o'-lanterns, candles, and firelight. (Here, as throughout the movie's interior scenes, candles seem to be the principal source of illumination.) Baltus Van Tassel (Michael Gambon) wears a suit of beautiful dark-green velvet decorated with gold brocade, under which his cream-colored silk shirt is fastened with a bow; unlike many of the other men, he does not wear a wig. His beautiful, younger wife, Lady Mary Van Tassel, wears an elaborate gown of yellow silk velvet decorated with an overlaid pattern in cut brown velvet. Her hair is swept back from her high forehead. The Van Tassels' dress and manner leave no question as to who heads society in Sleepy Hollow.

In a scene that could have come straight from Hogarth, Crane is introduced to the other ranking members of the community. We are in Van Tassel's study, with its muted green wallpaper, leather chairs, books, portraits, Oriental carpet, blazing fire on the hearth, and candles mounted in wall sconces. Each man in the scene is striking in dress and manner. The Reverend Steenwyck (Jeffrey Jones) wears the most distinctive wig in the movie, and Magistrate Samuel Philipse (Richard Griffiths), seen pouring the contents of his flask into his teacup, has the stock red face of a drinking man that one sees so often in portraits of British aristocrats by George Romney, another of Hogarth's contemporaries.

Rick Heinrichs, the production designer, said of the design scheme for the village, "One of the things we were trying to do was inspire a sense of scary portentousness in the village. I think it's different from Irving's Sleepy Hollow which is described as a dozing Dutch farming community. If our Sleepy Hollow is asleep, it's a fitful sort of sleep,

[1]

[2]

[3]

Contrasting colors emphasize narrative contrasts in *Sleepy Hollow* Blood-red sealing wax [1] and blood spattered on a menacing jack-o'-lantern [2] are the sorts of bold design details that stand out against *Sleepy Hollow's* generally muted palette, as seen in the "harvest party" scene [3], in which Katrina Anne Van Tassel (Christina Ricci, *blindfolded*) first encounters Ichabod Crane (Johnny Depp). Note, in contrast to the smiling children on the right, the jack-o'-lantern in the upper left corner, echoing the sour expression on the face of Crane's eventual romantic rival, Brom Van Brunt (Casper Van Dien, *center*).

with nightmares."[18] *Sleepy Hollow* is clearly a closed film that depicts a singular, self-enclosed world in which almost everyone and everything are held in the grip of powerful personal, societal, and supernatural forces. Director Tim Burton is of course the strongest, most controlling force in this world.

To create this gloomy atmosphere, Burton and his collaborators use a muted, even drab, color palette, punctuated here and there by carefully placed bright details. (The only consistent deviation is in the sequences depicting Crane's dreams of his mother.) As the movie begins with prologue and title credits, however, the dominant color is not muted, but the red of dripping wax being used to seal a last will and testament—a red so evocative that we momentarily mistake it for blood. After sealing his will, Peter Van Garrett (Martin Landau, in an uncredited performance), a pale figure wearing a pale yellow silk jacket, flees by carriage with the Headless Horseman in pursuit. The Horseman lops off the head of the coachman and then of Van Garrett, whose blood spatters all over an eerie orange pumpkin head mounted on a stake. Decapitation, a central theme of *Sleepy Hollow*, produces lots of blood, and blood continually spurts throughout the movie in the murders committed by the Horseman as well as in self-inflicted wounds and the gory examinations of dead bodies.

As Ichabod Crane travels by a closed, black carriage between New York City and Sleepy Hollow in the opening scene of the film, we are introduced to the principal color palette of late fall and early winter: gray river, gray wintry skies, trees almost barren of leaves, and rime on the ground. As day turns to twilight, Crane arrives at the village entrance, marked by two pillars topped by stone stags' heads, and walks down the road through the village and across the fields to the Van Tassel mansion. The entire scene appears to have been shot in black and white, rather than color, for Crane's extremely pale face provides the only color here, signifying, as we have already learned in theory but will now learn in fact, that the townspeople are drained of all life by their fear of the Horseman. Completely skeptical of what he considers the "myth" of the Horseman, Crane wears black and looks pallid, perturbed, and wary throughout the early part of the movie.

The village, the movie's most elaborate outdoor set, was constructed in England in a style that Heinrichs calls "Colonial Expressionism"; it includes a covered wooden bridge, church, general store, midwife's office, tavern, notary public, blacksmith, bank, mill house, warehouses, and several residences. Even the houses are scary, with their gray facades, doors, and shutters. Recalling English and Dutch architecture of the seventeenth and eighteenth centuries, many of these exteriors were also duplicated inside London studios, where heavy layers of artificial fog and smoke and controlled lighting helped create the illusion of a dark, misty valley under a leaden sky.

This meticulously created mise-en-scène encourages us not only to escape into the past but also to suspend our disbelief. On this ground, two worlds collide: one is represented by Crane, a "modern" criminal investigator using the latest technology (most of it of his own invention); the other is represented by the community of Sleepy Hollow, which itself ranges from the rich to the poor, all afraid of the Headless Horseman. Burton tells the story in part through fantastic objects and details, including Crane's notebook containing his drawings and notes, various forensic instruments, and peculiar eyeglasses; Katrina's book of witchcraft and evil-eye diagrams, over which an ominous spider creeps; the fairy-tale witch's cave deep in the forest and her potions made of bats' heads and birds' wings; the mechanical horse used to propel the Horseman through the village and surrounding woods; the "Tree of Death," where the Horseman lives between murders; the windmill, where he almost meets his end; and the fountain of blood at the climactic moment, when the Horseman's head is restored to him and he returns to life. Impressionist, even expressionist, much of what we see in this creepy place, with its frightening inhabitants and their eccentric costumes and hairstyles, was created through special effects.

Although it is necessary to be precise in analyzing all of the design elements in a single scene or

[18]Rick Heinrichs, qtd. in Denise Abbott, "Nightmare by Design," *Hollywood Reporter*, international ed., 361, no. 49 (February 29–March 6, 2000):S-6.

[1]

[2]

Expressive details define characters in *Sleepy Hollow* In a movie as brilliantly stylized as Tim Burton's *Sleepy Hollow*, one in which the story hangs on the struggle between superstition and reason, many of the characters are defined in part by their costumes, makeup, or the props with which they are associated. For example, [1] Katrina Van Tassel's (Christina Ricci) book, *A Compendium of Spells, Charms and Devices of the Spirit World*, associates her clearly with the witchcraft that bedevils Sleepy Hollow, while [2] Ichabod Crane's (Johnny Depp) wonderful eyeglasses and bag of medical instruments, including some of his own devising, tell the town's inhabitants, as well as the movie's viewers, that he is a man of science.

clip from a movie, we can only generalize in discussing them in a movie as stylistically rich as *Sleepy Hollow*. Throughout, however, Burton's mise-en-scène reflects a fairly consistent use of framing and camera movement. Reinforcing the closed nature of the movie, the frame is tightly restricted on the characters being photographed. Even many shots of the landscape are equally tight, providing little sense of the sky above or even the

earth below; and when they do, the sky is invariably overcast.

The lighting creates a very moody atmosphere. The exterior lighting—where mist, chimney smoke, and flashes of lightning are constant motifs—is slightly less dim than the interior lighting, which is provided seemingly by candles and firelight. The total impact of the design elements in *Sleepy Hollow* is that they produce distinct emotional responses in the viewer that perfectly complement our emotional responses to the narrative's twists and turns. We are repelled by the superstitious fears of the entire community and are made uncomfortable by the conspiracy among the townspeople to hide the secret of the Horseman, and the mise-en-scène reinforces our discomfort even as it mesmerizes our eyes.

Sam Mendes's *American Beauty*

American Beauty (1999; production designer: Naomi Shohan), about two families in crisis, the Burnhams and the Fittses, is essentially a verisimilar movie, totally different from the fantastic world of *Sleepy Hollow*. But it is also subtly satirical, and its overall mise-en-scène is central to making us aware of its satirical slant. The director and production designer use many aspects of their design scheme to define characters and comment on various aspects of contemporary American society, including consumerism and corporate culture, violence, puritanical sexual mores, mindless patriotism, self-empowerment jargon, peer pressure, drug use, unemployment, loneliness, and discrimination. These details are integral elements in an overall vision, patiently creating and revealing the characters while establishing the context for their lives and conflicts. *American Beauty* is a movie whose total mise-en-scène makes us laugh and feel terrified at the same time.

The Burnham family includes Lester (Kevin Spacey), an advertising salesman who quits his job in an attempt to free himself from the limits of middle-class life; his wife, Carolyn (Annette Bening), a real-estate agent who is a perfectionist; and Jane (Thora Birch), their teenage daughter, who coolly regards her parents as "gross."

The film opens with a moving aerial shot that establishes the classic suburban scene of tree-lined streets in an upper-middle-class neighborhood. Another overhead shot, this one inside Lester and Carolyn's bedroom, sets the scene of the Burnhams' loveless marriage. We see Lester just before the alarm clock awakens him, alone in a big bed, flanked by two identical end tables. Next, we see him masturbating in the shower ("This will be the high point of my day. It's all downhill from here"), followed by a shot of a perfect rose growing outside and then another of Carolyn cutting the rose from its stem. Roses are traditionally symbols of love, but Carolyn's decisive use of the scissors pointedly underscores her emasculating behavior toward her husband.

The design creates a recognizable time and place, but it is also highly symbolic in establishing and developing the movie's themes. The Burnham and Fitts families live in what the movies have often tried to make us believe is a "typical" neighborhood. In keeping with this type of film—one that explores bright domestic surfaces and murky angst-filled depths and, in so doing, strips away many aspects of the American dream—the exterior shots are bathed in clear, abundant sunlight, making everything look new, bright, and welcoming. The interiors of both houses are frequently dimly lit: at the Burnhams' house, it's likely by design, but at the Fittses', it underscores the gloominess of their family life. Unlike the lighting in *Sleepy Hollow*, however, this lighting does not call attention to itself or have much effect on the composition of scenes.

The Burnhams live in a two-story white house, surrounded by a white picket fence, with blue shutters and a bright red door. Bright red is used prominently throughout the movie: for that red door, Carolyn's red roses, Lester's fantasies of his daughter's friend Angela (Mena Suvari) in a bathtub filled with red rose petals, his red car, and—almost the last thing we see in the film—Lester's blood splattered on the white kitchen wall.

Inside, the house looks "perfect" in the choice and maintenance of its decor. For example, the kitchen, where Carolyn prepares "nutritious but savory meals," is immaculate. Everything has a

[1]

[2]

Details within a shot help to create mood in *American Beauty* Lester and Carolyn Burnham's estrangement is established early in *American Beauty* by simple shots such as these two images. [1] Lester (Kevin Spacey), alone in bed and shot from above, is clearly wearied by his life. [2] Carolyn (Annette Bening), meanwhile, decisively snips a rose in bloom and eerily inspects it. Clearly, these visual elements are important figuratively as well as literally.

place, and Carolyn has no doubt placed everything exactly where she wants it. Cooking pans hang over the island work space, a bowl of ripe fruit provides healthy snacks, small appliances are lined up neatly on the counters, dish towels are folded and hung, no dirty dishes linger in the sink, no messages are fastened with magnets to the refrigerator door. Whereas Carolyn thinks it's lovely to listen to Frank Sinatra during dinner, Jane calls it "elevator music," and Lester calls it "Lawrence Welk shit." In fact, Carolyn is so much in control of her environment that, as Lester tells us, "the handle of her gardening shears matches her gardening clogs—and that's no accident!"

The Fittses, who have recently moved in next door, include Colonel Frank Fitts (Chris Cooper), a marine obsessed with guns, discipline, and gay

[1]

[2]

American Beauty uses color for symbolic emphasis
The color red appears often in *American Beauty*, [1] sometimes subtly punctuating a shot, as in this image of the Burnhams' home, and [2] sometimes dominating the frame, as in this image from one of Lester's many fantasies about Angela (Mena Suvari).

people; his disturbed, unresponsive wife, Barbara (Allison Janney); and their teenage son, Ricky (Wes Bentley), who is part student, part drug dealer, part poet (he shoots moody videos featuring dead birds and plastic bags in the wind), and even though his father abuses him terribly, the most stable and happy person in the film. The Fittses' is a more modest house, also immaculately kept, no doubt reflecting Frank's military background. They appear to be less materialistic and have not tried to keep up with the Burnhams—their chairs are covered in plastic, Barbara does not bring home a second income—and they have no pretensions to style. Inside Frank's den, a locked cabinet holds a gun collection and a dinner plate from Hitler's private

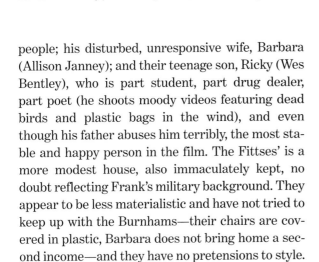

[1]

[2]

An attractive house in *American Beauty* cannot conceal the marital disharmony inside The members of the Burnham family are surrounded by a picture-perfect decor that many Americans dream of. This aspect of the mise-en-scène makes the psychological distance between them all the more striking. They have attained the outward appearances of the American dream, but at what cost?
[1] The decor of the Burnhams' dining room reflects Carolyn's pretensions to formality: drapes, curtains, framed pictures, a tablecloth (with place mats to protect it), candles, and each person seated in a specific place at the table. Somewhat oddly, though, the floor is bare (a touch of coldness?).
[2] When Lester has been drinking beer and then attempts to make love to Carolyn on the sofa, she worries that he will spill the beer. [3] In the ensuing argument, this element of decor provides a defining moment for them both. Carolyn shrieks, "It's a $4,000 sofa upholstered with Italian silk!" to which Lester responds, "This isn't life—it's just *stuff!*"

[3]

[1]

[2]

[3]

Stern, dark decor in *American Beauty* reflects a family's dysfunctional state Like the Burnhams next door, the Fitts family is plagued by dysfunction. The dark and stern decor of their house reflects the family's state of mind, which is largely dictated by the father, Colonel Frank Fitts. [1] Barbara (Allison Janney), Frank (Chris Cooper), and Ricky (Wes Bentley) Fitts watch a military movie on TV (Colonel Fitts's choice of entertainment in all likelihood). [2] Jane Burnham (Thora Birch) holds a plate from Colonel Fitts's basement collection of Nazi memorabilia, a chilling reminder of Fitts's brutal repression of his son, Ricky. [3] Barbara sits alone in the dining room staring blankly ahead, nearly dead to the world.

china service. Ricky pretends that he buys his state-of-the-art audio and video equipment with money earned from a job working for a caterer, not from the drugs he sells—a perfect indicator that all is not what it seems in these lives.

Clothing also helps us understand these characters. Carolyn Burnham, who is always beautifully coiffed and made up, wears the sort of "power" out-fits favored by some professional women, except when she strips down to her slip to clean a house she hopes to sell that day, ironic behavior considering the badly dressed yokels to whom she shows it. By contrast, Barbara Fitts, who never seems to leave the house, instead sits at the kitchen and dining room tables in a near-catatonic state, has dark circles under her eyes and wears drab clothing.

Clothing can reveal a character's personality
Clothing, makeup, and hairstyle in *American Beauty* complement our sense of each character's personality. Ricky (Wes Bentley) [1], wearing a white shirt and tie, strikes stylish

Angela (Mena Suvari) [2, *left*] as a "weirdo," but Jane (Thora Birch) [2, *right*], whose style is inspired by alternatives to name-brand fashion, sees something in Ricky (maybe the knit hat is a tip-off) that intrigues her.

[1]

[2]

Once he has quit his job, Lester wears jeans when he is relaxing and next to nothing when he is working out with weights in his garage. His goal is to "look good naked," as he tells the gay couple who lives next door. These men, by the way, meet Carolyn Burnham's standards: "I *love* your tie . . . that *color*," she tells one of them. Both men are successful professionals, yet they upset Colonel Fitts when they present him with a welcome basket and tell him that they are "partners," which, at first, he understands to mean business partners.

Frank Fitts wears white T-shirts and pressed khakis, an outfit as close as he can get to a uniform without actually wearing one. The serious, confident Ricky—who probably makes more money, from dealing drugs, than anyone else in the movie—looks decidedly different from his fellow high-school students, wearing a white shirt, tie, dark pants, dark sweater, and dark ski cap. Jane looks down-to-earth, like the rest of the students, wearing simple T-shirts, pants, and sweaters. She usually wears a strand of beads, has on a little lipstick, and pulls her hair back in a ponytail. Angela, who has delusions about her attractiveness and potential as a model, appears somewhat more sophisticated than Jane and the other young women at school, wearing heavy makeup, sporting a shoulder bag, wearing her blonde hair long, and smoking cigarettes. She thinks Ricky is a weirdo and asks Jane, "Why does he dress like a Bible salesman?"

American Beauty is an open film, one in which the characters have free will, even though it usually results in behavior that is out of control. The meticulous framing and consistently moving camera are two very important elements in establishing the mise-en-scène. To begin with, the film is shot in widescreen format, meaning that the frame is a rectangle, the perfect shape for revealing the design and furnishings of an entire room. Director Mendes and Conrad Hall—one of Hollywood's greatest cinematographers—invariably place two or more characters in the middle of this format, thereby emphasizing relationships, or use the zoom lens to highlight the characters in the frame. Characters frequently walk in and out of the frame, reminding us of the offscreen space. The framing most frequently adopts an omniscient POV, but this perspective is punctuated by subjective-POV framing that implicates us in voyeuristic moments, such as Lester's first vision of Angela during a cheerleading routine or the many scenes in which Ricky uses his video camera.

Voyeurism is clearly a theme of *American Beauty*; in fact, it is the source of the bond that forms between Ricky and Jane: their friendship begins when Ricky photographs Jane from his window, first secretly, then openly, and finally with her complete cooperation. At one point, she even uses the camera herself. Ricky is on the left side of the screen, but his image is being fed by the video camera to a monitor on the right side (see image [4] on the next page). Thus, we not only have his movies within the larger movie, but both of these movies use screens within screens—wall mirrors in the houses, rearview mirrors in cars, and windows—to reflect what they are shooting.

The acting in *American Beauty* is as notably consistent as the design; all the characters are edgy and strung out, some of them more than others. The only sure thing in these lives, the only "American beauty," is death, and Ricky, who finds beauty in photographing dead birds, smiles knowingly after looking into the dead Lester's eyes. What he sees there, however, is left for us to decide. Perhaps that red door is a warning—that, to paraphrase Dante, we should abandon any hope when entering this particular vision of suburban hell.

[1]

[2]

[3]

[4]

Different settings in *American Beauty* provoke different behaviors from different characters In *American Beauty*, male and female gazes play a central role in the developing drama. [1] Lester Burnham's (Kevin Spacey) overheated imagination turns Angela's (Mena Suvari) cheerleading performance into a seductive striptease performed only for his benefit. [2] Lester reacts with dumbfounded amazement at Angela's charms. [3] Meanwhile, Lester's daughter, Jane (Thora Birch), has attracted fellow student Ricky Fitts (Wes Bentley), who is shooting footage of her in his bedroom. [4] When Jane gets tired of telling Ricky how much she hates her father, she grabs the video camera and turns her gaze on him as he tells her about his past. [5] The bond between Jane and Ricky is sealed when he shares with her a poignant and poetic film of a simple, random occurrence: a plastic bag floating on a breeze.

[5]

Analyzing Mise-en-Scène

This chapter has introduced the major elements that together form any film's mise-en-scène. You should now understand that the term *mise-en-scène* denotes all of those elements taken together—the overall look and feel of the film—and that mise-en-scène plays a crucially important role in shaping the mood of the film. Using what you have learned in this chapter, you should be able to characterize the mise-en-scène of any movie (or any shot) in precise terms, referring to the framing, composition in depth, the lighting, the setting, the design and use of objects, and the placement and appearance of characters.

Screening Checklist: Mise-en-Scène

✔ As you watch the film or clip, be alert to the overall design plan and mise-en-scène and to your emotional response to them. Are you comforted or made anxious by them? Are your senses overwhelmed or calmed by what you see on-screen?

✔ Identify the elements of the mise-en-scène that seem to be contributing the most to your emotional response.

✔ Does the design in the movie or clip create the correct times, spaces, and moods? Does it go beyond surfaces and relate to developing themes?

✔ Be alert to the framing of individual shots, and make note of the composition within the frame. Where are figures placed? What is the relationship among the figures in the foreground, middle ground, and background?

✔ Is the framing of this film or clip open, or is it closed? How can you tell? What is the effect of this framing on your understanding of the narrative and characters?

✔ Does the use of light in the movie or clip call attention to itself? If so, describe the effect that it has on the composition in any shot you analyze.

✔ Does the film or clip employ lots of movement? Very little movement? Describe how the use of movement in the film or clip complements or detracts from the development of the narrative.

✔ Note the type of movement (movement of figures within the frame or movement of the frame itself) in important shots and describe as accurately as possible the effect that that movement has on the relationships among the figures in the frame.

✔ Does the movie's design have a unified feel? Do the various elements of the design (the sets, props, costumes, makeup, hairstyles, etc.) work together, or do some elements work against others? What is the effect either way?

✔ Was achieving verisimilitude important to the design of this film or clip? If so, have the filmmakers succeeded in making the overall mise-en-scène feel real, or verisimilar? If verisimilitude doesn't seem to be important in this film or clip, what do you suspect the filmmakers were attempting to accomplish with their design?

✔ How does the design and mise-en-scène in this movie or clip relate to the narrative? Is it appropriate for the story being told? Does it quietly reinforce the narrative and development of characters? Does it partly determine the development of narrative and characters? Does it render the narrative secondary or even overwhelm it?

Questions for Review

1. What is the literal meaning of the phrase *mise-en-scène*? What do we mean by this phrase more generally when we discuss movies?

2. What are the two major visual components of mise-en-scène?

3. Does a movie's mise-en-scène happen by accident? If not, what or who determines it?

4. What are the principal responsibilities of the production designer?

5. Name and briefly discuss the major elements of cinematic design.

6. What is composition? What are the two major elements of composition?

7. What is the difference between the static frame and the moving frame?

8. Why do most shots in a film rely on both on-screen and offscreen spaces?

9. What are the essential differences between the open frame and the closed frame?

10. What are the two basic types of movement that we see on-screen?

DVD The tutorials for this chapter cover setting, lighting, and composition within the frame. An additional feature called *Drawing the Coke* looks at the Lumiere brothers' short "actualite" to demonstrate the importance of mise-en-scène even at the very beginning of film history.

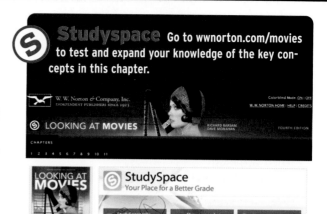

Movies Described or Illustrated in This Chapter

Æon Flux (2005). Karyn Kusama, director.

The Age of Innocence (1993). Martin Scorsese, director.

Alice in Wonderland (2010). Tim Burton, director.

American Beauty (1999). Sam Mendes, director.

An American in Paris (1951). Vincente Minnelli, director.

Avatar (2009). James Cameron, director.

The Bad Sleep Well (1960). Akira Kurosawa, director.

The Best Years of Our Lives (1946). William Wyler, director.

Black Swan (2010). Darren Aronofsky, director.

Buck Rogers in the 25th Century (1979). Daniel Haller, director.

The Cabinet of Dr. Caligari (1920). Robert Wiene, director.

Cabiria (1914). Giovanni Pastrone, director.

Chinatown (1974). Roman Polanski, director.

Citizen Kane (1941). Orson Welles, director.

City of God (2002). Fernando Meirelles and Kátia Lund, directors.

Color Me Kubrick (2005). Brian W. Cook, director.

Crouching Tiger, Hidden Dragon (2000). Ang Lee, director.

The Crowd (1928). King Vidor, director.

The Darjeeling Limited (2007). Wes Anderson, director.

The Dark Knight (2008). Christopher Nolan, director.

The Decalogue (1989). Krzysztof Kieslowski, director.

Edward Scissorhands (1990). Tim Burton, director.

Eyes Wide Shut (1999). Stanley Kubrick, director.

Far from Heaven (2002). Todd Haynes, director.

Forrest Gump (1994). Robert Zemeckis, director.

Gone with the Wind (1939). Victor Fleming, director.

Head in the Clouds (2004). John Duigan, director.

Hellboy (2004). Guillermo del Toro, director.

Hellboy II: The Golden Army (2008). Guillermo del Toro, director.

Hero (2002). Yimou Zhang, director.

Intolerance (1916). D. W. Griffith, director.

Invincible (2001). Werner Herzog, director.

Klimt (2006). Raoul Ruiz, director.

The Last Laugh (1924). F. W. Murnau, director.

Late Spring (1949). Yasujiro Ozu, director.

The Leopard (1963). Luchino Visconti, director.

Love and Death (1975). Woody Allen, director.

The Lower Depths (1936). Jean Renoir, director.

The Lower Depths (1957). Akira Kurosawa, director.

Marie Antoinette (1938). W. S. Van Dyke, director.

Monster (2003). Patty Jenkins, director.

Moulin Rouge! (2001). Baz Luhrmann, director.

My Darling Clementine (1946). John Ford, director.

The Night of the Hunter (1955). Charles Laughton, director.

North Country (2005). Niki Caro, director.

On the Waterfront (1954). Elia Kazan, director.

Pan's Labyrinth (2006). Guillermo del Toro, director.

Queen Kelly (1929). Erich von Stroheim, director.

Ratatouille (2007). Brad Bird and Jan Pinkava, directors.

Rear Window (1954). Alfred Hitchcock, director.

Shadows and Fog (1992). Woody Allen, director.

Sherlock Holmes (2009). Guy Ritchie, director.

The Shining (1980). Stanley Kubrick, director.

Sleepy Hollow (1999). Tim Burton, director.

The Social Network (2010). David Fincher, director.

Stagecoach (1939). John Ford, director.

Star Trek III: The Search for Spock (1984). Leonard Nimoy, director.

Star Wars VI: Return of the Jedi (1983). Richard Marquand, director.

Suspiria (1977). Dario Argento, director.

The Third Man (1949). Carol Reed, director.

To Die For (1995). Gus Van Sant, director.

I Vitelloni (1953). Federico Fellini, director.

Young Adult (2011). Ivan Reitman, director.

CHAPTER SIX

Cinematography

After reading this chapter, you should be able to

✔ describe the differences among a shot, a setup, and a take.

✔ understand the role that a director of photography plays in film production.

✔ describe the basic characteristics of the cinematographic properties of a shot: film tock, lighting, and lenses.

✔ understand the basic elements of composition within the frame, including implied proximity to the camera, depth, camera angle and height, scale, and camera movement.

✔ define the *rule of thirds*.

✔ describe any shot in a movie by identifying

• its proximity to its subject.
• the angle of the camera.
• the nature of camera movement, if any, within the shot.
• the speed and length of the shot.

✔ understand the ways in which special effects are created and the various roles that special effects play in movies.

What Is Cinematography?

Cinematography is the process of capturing moving images on film or a digital storage device. The word comes to us from three Greek roots—*kinesis*, meaning "movement"; *photo*, meaning "light"; and *graphia*, meaning "writing"—but the word was coined only after motion pictures themselves were invented. Cinematography is closely related to still photography, but its methods and technologies clearly distinguish it from its static predecessor. This chapter introduces the major features of this unique craft.

Although cinematography might seem to exist solely to please our eyes with beautiful images, it is in fact an intricate language that can (and in the most complex and meaningful films, does) contribute to a movie's overall meaning as much as the story, mise-en-scène, and acting do. The cinematographer (also known as the director of photography, or DP) uses the camera as a maker of meaning, just as the painter uses the brush or the writer uses the pen: the angles, heights, and movements of the camera function both as a set of techniques and as expressive material, the cinematic equivalent of brushstrokes or of nouns, verbs, and adjectives. So, in order to make an informed analysis and evaluation of a movie, we need to consider whether the cinematographer, in collaboration with the other filmmakers on the project, has successfully harnessed the powers of this visual language to help tell the story and convey the meaning(s) of the movie. As director Satyajit Ray puts it, "There is no such thing as good photography *per se*. It is either right for a certain kind of film, and therefore good; or wrong—however lush, well-composed, meticulous—and therefore bad."[1]

The Director of Photography

Every aspect of a movie's preproduction—writing the script, casting the talent, imagining the look of the finished work, designing and creating the sets and costumes, and determining what will be placed in front of the camera and in what arrangement and manner—leads to the most vital step: representing the mise-en-scène on film or video. Although what we see on the screen reflects the vision and design of the filmmakers as a team, the director of photography is the primary person responsible for transforming the other aspects of moviemaking into moving images.

Freddie Young, who won Best Cinematography Oscars for three David Lean movies—*Lawrence of Arabia* (1962), *Doctor Zhivago* (1965), and *Ryan's Daughter* (1970)—defines the DP's job within the overall process of film production:

> [The cinematographer] stands at the natural confluence of the two main streams of activity in the production of a film—where the imagination meets the reality of the film process.

[1]Satyajit Ray, *Our Films, Their Films* (1976; repr., New York: Hyperion, 1994), p. 68.

Setting up a shot On an interior setting for *The Social Network* (2010), director David Fincher (*left*) and cinematographer Jeff Cronenweth (*center*)—aided by an unidentified camera operator or technician (*right*)—work with a video-assist camera to set up a shot. Fincher and Cronenweth also worked together on *Fight Club* (1999) and *The Girl with the Dragon Tattoo* (2011). Cronenweth was nominated for an Oscar for Best Cinematography on *The Social Network*.

Imagination is represented by the director, who in turn is heir to the ideas of the scriptwriter, as he is to those of the original author of the story. Three minds, and three contributing sources of imagination have shaped the film before the cameraman can begin to visualize it as a physical entity.[2]

In the ideal version of this working relationship, the director's vision shapes the process of rendering the mise-en-scène on film, but the cinematographer makes very specific decisions about how the movie will be photographed.

When the collaboration between the director and the cinematographer has been a good one, the images that we see on-screen correspond closely to what the director expected the DP to capture on film. As cinematographer John Alton explains,

The screen offers the advantage of an ability (although we do not always utilize it) to photograph the story from the position from which the director thinks the audience would like to see it. The success of any particular film depends a great deal upon the ability of the director to anticipate the desires of the audience in this respect. . . .

. . . [T]he director of photography visualizes the picture purely from a photographic point of view, as determined by lights and the moods of individual sequences and scenes. In other words, how to use angles, set-ups, lights, and camera as means to tell the story.[3]

As cinematographers translate visions into realities, however, they follow not inflexible rules but rather conventions, which are open to interpretation by the

[2]Freddie Young and Paul Petzold, *The Work of the Motion Picture Cameraman* (New York: Hastings House, 1972), p. 23.

[3]John Alton, *Painting with Light* (1949; repr., Berkeley: University of California Press, 1995), p. 33.

artists entrusted with them. "You will accomplish much more," advises Gregg Toland—the cinematographer famous for such classics as John Ford's *The Grapes of Wrath* (1940), William Wyler's *The Best Years of Our Lives* (1946), and Orson Welles's *Citizen Kane* (1941)—"by fitting your photography to the story instead of limiting the story to the narrow confines of conventional photographic practice. And as you do so you'll learn that the movie camera is a flexible instrument, with many of its possibilities still unexplored."[4]

Many cinematographers succeed in "fitting [the] photography to the story." For example, in *The Lives of Others* (2006; director: Florian Henckel von Donnersmarck), the cinematographer Hagen Bogdanski, employs a flat lighting scheme and color palette to portray an ugly world of surveillance in which citizens are fearful, paranoid, and humiliated into submission to the Stasi, the secret police in Communist East Germany in the 1980s. Todd Louiso's *Love Liza* (2002) concerns the anguish of a man (played by Philip Seymour Hoffman) whose wife has killed herself. Lisa Rinzler, the cinematographer, influenced by German Expressionist movies, observes him from a 360-degree tracking shot and from striking angles shot with bold lighting to depict the emotional torment and physical clumsiness with which he confronts his despair.

The three key terms used in shooting a movie are *shot, take,* and *setup.* A **shot** is (1) one uninterrupted run of the camera and (2) the recording on film, video, or other medium resulting from that run. A shot can be as short or as long as necessary, with the obvious condition that it not exceed the time limitations of the medium on which the moving images are being recorded. The term **take** refers to the number of times a particular shot is taken. A **setup** is one camera position and everything associated with it. Whereas the shot is the basic building block of the film, the setup is the basic component of the film's production process and the component on which the director and the cinematographer spend the most time collaborating.

The cinematographer's responsibilities for each shot and setup (as well as for each take) fall into four broad categories:

1. cinematographic properties of the shot (film stock, lighting, lenses)
2. framing of the shot (proximity to the camera, depth, camera angle and height, scale, camera movement)
3. speed and length of the shot
4. special effects

Although these categories necessarily overlap, we will look at each one separately. In the process, we will also examine the tools and equipment involved and what they enable the cinematographer to do.

In carrying out these responsibilities, the DP relies on the assistance of the **camera crew**, who are divided into one group of technicians concerned with the camera and another concerned with electricity and lighting. The camera group consists of the **camera operator**, who does the actual shooting, and the **assistant camerapersons** (ACs). The **first AC** oversees everything having to do with the camera, lenses, supporting equipment, and the material on which the movie is being shot. The **second AC** prepares the **slate** that is used to identify each scene as it is shot, files camera reports, and when film stock is being used, feeds that stock into magazines that are then loaded onto the camera. The group concerned with electricity and lighting consists of the **gaffer** (chief electrician), **best boy** (first assistant electrician), other electricians, and **grips** (all-around handypersons who work with both the camera crew and the electrical crew to get the camera and lighting ready for shooting).

Cinematographic Properties of the Shot

The director of photography controls the cinematographic properties of the shot, those basics of motion-picture photography that make the movie

---

[4]Gregg Toland, "How I Broke the Rules in *Citizen Kane*," in *Focus on Citizen Kane*, ed. Ronald Gottesman (Englewood Cliffs, N.J.: Prentice-Hall, 1971), p. 77. For an excellent account of how many contemporary cinematographers consider their art and craft, see Roger Clarke and Edward Lawrenson, "Talking Shop," in the special cinematography issue of *Sight & Sound* (April 2009): 18–26.

In Cold Blood: serendipity creates an unforgettable shot Although the director of photography must maintain strict control over the cinematographic properties of a movie's shots, every great cinematographer must also be alert to moments when an unplanned situation happens on the set that could make a shot even better than planned. In a climactic scene of *In Cold Blood* (1967; director: Richard Brooks), based on Truman Capote's masterpiece, cinematographer Conrad Hall took advantage of a chance observation—the juxtaposition of rain running down a window with a condemned murderer's last-minute remembrance of his father—to create a memorable moment of cinema. Just before his execution for the brutal murders of a Kansas family, Perry Smith (Robert Blake) remembers his father. As he moves toward the window and looks out at the prison yard, heavy rain courses down the window, making it appear that he is crying. With the strong exterior lights directed at Smith's face, cinematographer Conrad Hall explains that he found the setup for this shot when he realized that this situation "created these avenues for the bright light outside to come in. . . . It was an accident I saw, and used, and capitalized on the moment." This just helps to prove that a great shot can be the result of careful planning or, as in this case, serendipity.

image appear the way it does. These properties include the film stock, lighting, and lenses. By employing variations of each property, the cinematographer modifies not only the camera's basic neutrality, but also the look of the finished image that the audience sees.

Film Stock

The cinematographer is responsible for choosing a recording medium for the movie that has the best chance of producing images corresponding to the director's vision. Among the alternatives available are film stocks of various sizes and speeds, videotape, and direct-to-digital media. A skilled cinematographer must know the technical properties and cinematic possibilities of each option and must be able to choose the medium that is best suited to the project as a whole.

Even though more movies are being shot on digital media with each passing year, the majority of feature films are still shot on traditional **film stock**. The two basic types of film stock—one to record images in black and white, the other to record them in color—are completely different and have their own technical properties and cinematic possibilities. Film stock is available in several standard **gauges** (widths measured in millimeters): 8mm, Super 8mm, 16mm, 35mm, 65mm, 70mm, as well as special-use formats such as IMAX, which is ten times bigger than a 35mm frame. (65mm film is used in the camera and then printed on 70mm film, which is used for projection; the additional space holds the sound track.) Before the advent of camcorders, 8mm and Super 8mm were popular gauges for amateurs (for home movies). Many television or student movies, as well as low-budget productions, are shot on 16mm. Most professional film productions use either 16mm or 35mm. Generally, the wider the gauge, the more expensive the film and, all other factors being equal, the better the quality of the image.

Another variable aspect of film stock is its **speed** (or exposure index)—the degree to which it is light-sensitive. Film stocks that are extremely sensitive to light and thus useful in low-light situations are called fast; those that require a lot of light are called slow. There are uses for both slow and fast film stock, depending on the shooting environment and the desired visual outcome. Fast films are grainy (as larger grains of light-sensitive material need less light to record an image with a fast shutter speed), whereas slow films are fine-grained and require either a slow shutter speed, more light, or both. When a film's look must uniquely match the demands of the story, cinematographers will mix film stocks (e.g., Oliver Stone's *Natural Born Killers*, 1994; cinematographer: Robert Richardson or Tom Tykwer's *Run Lola Run*, 1998; cinematographer: Frank Griebe) or intentionally use the wrong chemicals to process film stocks to achieve the desired look, as in David O. Russell's *Three Kings* (1999; cinematographer: Newton Thomas Sigel).

Which stock is right for a particular film depends on the story being told. With only a few outstanding exceptions, however, virtually all movies are now shot in color, for that is what the public is accustomed to and therefore expects. As Figure 6.1 shows, when Hollywood began to use color film stock, only 1 percent of the feature releases from major studios in 1936 were in color. The growth of color production slowed during World War II because all film stock, especially color, was in short supply, but by 1968 virtually all feature releases were in color.

Although color can heighten the surface realism (if not the verisimilitude) and the spectacle of many stories, it is not suitable for all films. For example, films in the expressionist or film-noir styles are deliberately conceived to be shot in black and white; it's almost impossible to imagine anyone having shot F. W. Murnau's *Nosferatu* (1922), John Ford's *The Informer* (1935), or Fritz Lang's *The Big Heat* (1953) in color. During the 1970s and 1980s, certain television executives tried to "improve" the "old" movies they were showing on television with the process of **colorization**: using digital technology, they "painted" colors on movies meant by the

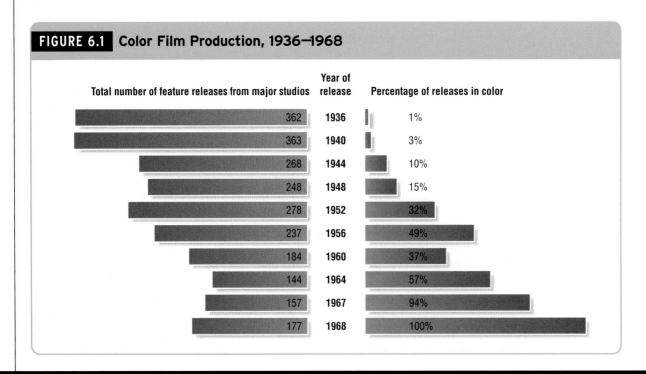

FIGURE 6.1 Color Film Production, 1936–1968

Total number of feature releases from major studios	Year of release	Percentage of releases in color
362	1936	1%
363	1940	3%
268	1944	10%
248	1948	15%
278	1952	32%
237	1956	49%
184	1960	37%
144	1964	57%
157	1967	94%
177	1968	100%

original filmmakers to be seen in black and white. The unimpressive results were limited by the state of computer graphics at the time, but even though computer technology has improved since then, the practice has abated. Many viewers, even those who grew up with color movies, could see that colorization was not an improvement for movies that had been shot in black and white. Film artists breathed a sigh of relief once it became clear that colorization was a failed experiment.

Although today the default choice for feature-film production is color, the period from 1940 to 1970 was a time during which the choice between color and black and white needed to be carefully considered, and many films shot in color during that period might have been even stronger if they had been shot instead in black and white. John Ford's *The Searchers* (1956; cinematographer: Winton C. Hoch), a psychological Western that is concerned less with the traditional Western's struggle between good and evil than with the lead character's struggle against personal demons, might have been an even more powerful film had it been shot in black and white instead of color. Doing so might have produced a visual mood, as in film noir, that complemented the darkness at the heart of the movie's narrative. Instead, the choice of color film stock for *The Searchers* seems to have been inspired by industry trends at the time—designed to improve flagging box-office receipts—rather than by strictly artistic criteria.

Ironically, audiences who had grown to love Ford's black-and-white movies set in Monument Valley reacted badly to his first color feature set there: *She Wore a Yellow Ribbon* (1949; cinematographer: Winton C. Hoch). The vibrant colors they were seeing in this movie and in *The Searchers*—the reds and browns of the earth, the constantly changing blues of the sky—accurately captured the appearance of Monument Valley in real life, but for viewers whose expectations were shaped by Ford's earlier movies, such as *Stagecoach* (1939), Monument Valley existed only in black and white. In color, *The Searchers* is magnificent; we can only guess at what it might have been in black and white.

Black and White   Black-and-white movies are not pictures that lack color, for black and white (and

the range in between) *are* colors. Contemporary movies with exceptionally good black-and-white cinematography include *Good Night, and Good Luck* (2005; director: George Clooney; cinematographer: Robert Elswit), the animated feature *Persepolis* (2007; directors: Marjane Satrapi and Vincent Paronnaud), *Sin City* (2005; directors: Frank Miller and Robert Rodriguez; cinematographer: Robert Rodriguez), Darren Aronofsky's *Pi* (1998; cinematographer: Matthew Libatique), Joel Coen's *The Man Who Wasn't There* (2001; cinematographer: Roger Deakins), and *Dark Days* (2000), a documentary directed and shot by Marc Singer. Although black-and-white film stock offers compositional possibilities and cinematographic effects that are impossible with color film stock, today it is used almost exclusively for nonprofessional productions. Because of its use in documentary films (before the 1960s) and in newspaper and magazine photographs (before the advent of color newspaper and magazine printing), we have ironically come to associate black-and-white photography and cinematography with a stronger sense of gritty realism than that provided by color film stock. But the distinct contrasts and hard edges of black-and-white cinematography can express an abstract world (that is, a world from which color has been abstracted or removed) perfectly suited for the kind of morality tales told in Westerns, film noirs, and gangster films. In fact, although many excellent color films have been made in these same genres—such as Roman Polanski's neo-noir *Chinatown* (1974; cinematographer: John A. Alonzo) or Quentin Tarantino's gangster film *Pulp Fiction* (1994; cinematographer: Andrzej Sekula)—we generally view their distinctive black-and-white predecessors as the templates for the genres.

Movies shot in black and white can also have moral or ethical implications. In theater throughout the ages, black-and-white costumes have been used to distinguish, respectively, between the "bad" and "good" characters. In the Western and film-noir genres, this has been a familiar pattern. In *The Seventh Seal* (1957; cinematographer: Gunnar Fischer), set in the Middle Ages, Swedish director Ingmar Bergman uses high-contrast black-and-white cinematography to articulate a conflict

[1]

[1]

[2]

Black and white versus color *Stagecoach* [1], made in 1939, was the first film that John Ford shot in Arizona's Monument Valley. Bert Glennon's black-and-white cinematography in *Stagecoach* provided a portrayal of the Old West that was different from Winton C. Hoch's depiction using color cinematography in *The Searchers* (1956) [2], one of the last films that Ford shot in Monument Valley. Although the expressive photography was state of the art in both films, the use of black and white and of color was not a matter of aesthetics but was dictated by industry standards.

between those who are devout Christians (dressed most often in white or gray costumes) and those nonbelievers who have only doubt and despair (dressed in black). But his color scheme goes beyond costuming to encompass distinct contrasts in lighting (both artificial and natural), settings (interior and exterior), and the chess pieces in a

Black and white in *The Seventh Seal* In the climactic battle between the allegorical figure of Death (Bengt Ekerot, *left*) and Antonius Block, the Knight (Max von Sydow, *right*) in *The Seventh Seal* (1957; cinematographer: Gunnar Fischer), director Ingmar Bergman dresses both men in dark costumes but uses light and chess figures to distinguish between them [1]. Light from the upper left streams across the image, illuminating the Knight's blond-white hair, the Christian cross on his sword, and his chess pieces. There is just enough ambient light to outline the pale white face of the figure Death, shrouded in his hood. While this lighting and color strategy raises our expectations, we soon see that, in the chess game against Death, the Knight loses. The concluding shot [2] is one of the most iconic images in film history: Death leading the Knight and his squire, wife, and friends in a solemn dance of death. Again, notice Bergman's use of black and white: the dark-clad figures move upward on the mountain between the black earth and the white clouds. Death unites all.

climactic game in which the figure of Death (in a black cowl) plays with black pieces, while the Knight, who has returned from the Crusades to find his country ravaged by the Black Plague, plays with white pieces.

Tonality—the system of tones—is the distinguishing quality of black-and-white film stock. This system includes the complete range of tones from black to white. Anything on the set—furniture, furnishings, costumes, and makeup—registers in these tones. Even when a film is shot in black and white, it is customary to design its settings and costumes in color. Black-and-white cinematography achieves its distinctive look through such manipulation of the colors being photographed and through the lighting of them. During the height of the classical Hollywood studio system, set and costume designers worked in close collaboration with directors of photography to ensure that the colors used in their designs produced the optimal varieties of tones in black and white. Their goal was to ensure a balance of "warm" and "cold" tones to avoid a muddy blending of similar tones. Sometimes the colors chosen for optimal tonality on film were unattractive, even garish, on the set. Audiences were none the wiser, however, because they saw only the pleasing tonal contrasts in the final black-and-white movie.

Manipulation of tonal range makes black-and-white movies visually interesting, but that isn't all it does. For good or ill, tonality in black-and-white films often carries with it certain preconceived interpretations (e.g., black = evil, white = good). As simplistic, misleading, and potentially offensive as these interpretations may be, they reflect widespread cultural traditions that have been in effect for thousands of years. The earliest narrative films, which greatly appealed to immigrant audiences (most of whom could neither read nor speak English), often relied on such rough distinctions to establish the moral frameworks of their stories. Later, even though both audiences and cinematography became more

Tonal range This shot from Fred Zinnemann's *High Noon* (1952; cinematographer: Floyd Crosby) illustrates the tonal range possible in black-and-white cinematography: from absolute white (in the shirt), through a series of grays, to absolute black (in the bottom of the hat's brim). For the purposes of explanation, this illustration includes only six tones out of the complete range. Note that although he is the movie's protagonist, Marshal Will Kane (Gary Cooper) wears a black hat—typically, in less sophisticated morality tales, the symbolic mark of the bad guy.

Black-and-white tonality The opening scene of Alexander Mackendrick's *Sweet Smell of Success* (1957; cinematographer: James Wong Howe) takes place near midnight in Times Square, which is alive with activity. The thousands of incandescent and neon lights create a brash black-and-white environment in which the space lacks both depth and shadows. The people packed on the streets are members of a crowd, not individuals. In other movies, such bold blacks and whites might suggest the contrast of good and evil, but the lighting here gives no clue as to which is which.

sophisticated, these distinctions held together the narratives of countless films in diverse genres.

After tonality, the next thing we notice about black-and-white films is their use of, and emphasis on, texture and spatial depth within their images. The cinematographer can change the texture of an image by manipulating shadows and can control the depth of the image by manipulating lighting and lenses. The best-loved black-and-white movies employ such visual effects to underscore and enhance their stories. Looking at the work of cinematographer James Wong Howe on Alexander Mackendrick's *Sweet Smell of Success* (1957), for example, we are immediately struck by how his deft manipulation of tone, texture, and spatial depth have captured the sleazy allure of New York City's once notorious Times Square, and how the look of this movie is absolutely essential to its story of urban menace, corruption, and decay.

Color Although almost all movies today are shot in color, for nearly sixty years of cinema history color was an option that required much more labor, money, and artistic concession than black and white did. Color movies made prior to 1960 were typically elaborate productions, and the decisions to use color were made with the expectation from producers that the movies would justify the expense with impressive box-office returns. To gain a better understanding of the period prior to 1968, when color was not necessarily the default choice, let's take a moment to review briefly the history of color-film technology.

Although full-scale color production began only in the late 1930s, it was possible to create color images soon after the movies were invented, in 1895. The first methods were known as **additive color systems** because they added color to black-and-white film stock. These processes included hand-coloring, stenciling, tinting, and toning, but because they were so tedious, at first only selected frames were colored. Nonetheless, impressive achievements were made by such pioneers as Thomas A. Edison, Georges Méliès, Edwin S. Porter, and the filmmakers at Pathé Frères.

Hand-coloring involved the use of dyes applied directly by hand to the print to be projected, and stenciling, by contrast, was a complex, machine-driven process that enabled a film to use six different colors. However, the most common techniques were tinting and toning. Tinting consisted of dyeing the base of the film so that the light areas appeared in color; this technique provided shots or scenes in which a single color set the time of day, distinguished exterior from interior shots, created an emotional mood, or otherwise affected the viewer's perception. D. W. Griffith used this technique very effectively in such films as *Broken Blossoms* (1919; cinematographer: G. W. Bitzer), as did Robert Wiene in *The Cabinet of Dr. Caligari* (1920; cinematographer: Willy Hameister). Toning, a chemical process distinct from tinting, offered greater aesthetic and emotional control over the image by coloring the opaque parts of an image to a general color. Tinting and toning were often used together to extend the color of a single image.

As imaginative as these processes are, they do not begin to accurately reproduce the range of colors that exists in nature. Further experimentation with additive color processing resulted in a crude two-color additive process that used two complementary colors, usually red-orange and blue-green. Kinemacolor, an early process, used persistence of vision and a faster frame-per-second rate to simulate color in a lengthy documentary, *With Our King and Queen Through India* (1912). In 1915, the Technicolor Corporation introduced a similar two-color additive process, used effectively in aesthetic terms for the first time in Chester M. Franklin's *The Toll of the Sea* (1922; cinematographer: J. A. Ball), available on DVD, and a good example of the progress made to this point. This process was also used to photograph Albert Parker's impressive epic *The Black Pirate* (1926; cinematographer: Henry Sharp).

By the early 1930s, the additive process—with its technological difficulties and their economic consequences—had given way to a two-color **subtractive color system**, which was later refined to a three-color subtractive process introduced in 1932 for cartoons and 1934 for live-action features. The subsequent development of modern color cinematography is based on this subtractive system. How does it work in theory? Very basically, color results from the physical action of different light waves on our eyes and optical nervous system, meaning that we perceive these different wavelengths of energy as different colors. Of these colors, three are primary—red, green, and blue; mixing them can produce all the other colors in the spectrum, and when added together they produce white. The subtractive process takes away unwanted colors from the white light. So when one of the additive primary colors (red, green, blue) has been removed from the spectrum on a single strip of film, what remains are the complementary colors (cyan, magenta, yellow). How does it work in practice? Technicolor works by simultaneously shooting three separate black-and-white negatives through three light filters, each representing a primary color. These three color-separation negatives are then superimposed and printed as a positive in natural color. Thus the final color results from the removal of certain color components from each of the three emulsion layers. The first films to be made with the subtractive process were Walt Disney's short "Silly Symphony" cartoons *Flowers and Trees* (1932) and *The Three Little Pigs* (1933)—both directed by Burt Gillett—and Pioneer Pictures' live-action film *La Cucaracha* (1934; director: Lloyd Corrigan). The first feature-length film made in the three-color subtractive process was Rouben Mamoulian's *Becky Sharp* (1935; cinematographer: Ray Rennahan).

Making a Technicolor movie was complicated, cumbersome, and cost almost 30 percent more than comparable black-and-white productions. The Technicolor camera, specially adapted to shoot three strips of film at one time, required a great deal of light. Its size and weight restricted its movements and potential use in exterior locations. Furthermore, the studios were obliged by contract to employ Technicolor's own makeup, which resisted melting under lights hotter than those used for shooting black-and-white films, and to process the film in Technicolor's labs, initially the only place that knew how to do this work.

For all these reasons, in addition to a decline in film attendance caused by the Great Depression, producers were at first reluctant to shoot in color. By 1937, however, color had entered mainstream Hollywood production; by 1939 it had proved itself

much more than a gimmick in movies such as Victor Fleming's *Gone with the Wind* (cinematographer: Ernest Haller), *The Wizard of Oz* (cinematographer: Harold Rosson), and John Ford's *Drums along the Mohawk* (cinematographers: Bert Glennon and Ray Rennahan), all released that year.

In 1941, Technicolor introduced its Monopack—identical to Kodak's Kodachrome color-reversal film—a multilayered film stock that could be used in a conventional camera. Because the bulky three-strip camera was no longer necessary, Technicolor filming could now be done outdoors. Eventually, Kodak's rival Eastman Color system—a one-strip film stock that required less light, could be used in any standard camera, and could be processed at lower cost—replaced Technicolor. This single-strip process, developed by Kodak and used also by Fuji and Agfa, remained the standard color film stock in use until 2010, when Kodak ceased color film processing. But just as Hollywood took several years to convert from silent film to sound, so too the movie industry did not immediately replace black-and-white film with color. During the 1950s, Hollywood

Gone with the Wind and color filmmaking Victor Fleming's *Gone with the Wind* (1939; cinematographer: Ernest Haller) marked a turning point in Hollywood film production, ushering in an era of serious filmmaking in color. Its vibrant and nostalgic images of the antebellum South delighted audiences and earned it a special commendation at the 1939 Academy Awards for "outstanding achievement in the use of color for the enhancement of dramatic mood."

used color film strategically, like the **widescreen aspect ratio**, to lure people away from their television sets and back into theaters. (See "Framing of the Shot," pages 248–275.)

Now that color film dominates, a new naturalism has become the cinematographic norm, where what we see on the screen looks very much like what we would see in real life. By itself, however, color film stock doesn't necessarily produce a naturalistic image. Film artists and technicians can manipulate the colors in a film as completely as they can any other formal element. Ultimately, just like its black-and-white counterpart, color film can capture realistic, surrealistic, imaginary, or expressionistic images.

Much of Stanley Kubrick's *Barry Lyndon* (1975; cinematographer: John Alcott), for example, employs a color palette that reflects its temporal setting very well; it's the world of soft pastels and gentle shadows depicted in the paintings of such eighteenth- and nineteenth-century artists as Thomas Gainsborough, William Hogarth, and Adolph von Menzel. However, this palette wasn't achieved merely by pointing the camera in a certain direction and accurately recording the colors found there. Instead, the filmmakers specifically

Colors reflect and change lives in the movies In Gary Ross's *Pleasantville* (1998; cinematographer: John Lindley), a comic fable about the role of color in our lives, two contemporary teenagers (played by Reese Witherspoon and Tobey Maguire, *left* to *right*) are magically transported back into the world of a black-and-white television series called *Pleasantville,* set in 1958. Finding the town as realistically conformist, small-minded, and opposed to change as many small towns were in the late 1950s, they set about liberating their classmates and families. As they introduce love, sex, knowledge, modern art, self-expression, and freedom to the repressed black-and-white town, color begins to appear— slowly at first and then spreading as if it were a contagious disease. The town rebels, stages a witch hunt, and passes a law against all kinds of freedom, but the genie is out of the bottle, and color is there to stay.

manipulated the images through careful planning art direction, and technical know-how to render the naturally occurring colors in more subtle and "painterly" shades.

In a different vein, the interplay of fantasy and reality is brilliantly and vibrantly conveyed in Federico Fellini's first color film, *Juliet of the Spirits* (1965; cinematographer: Gianni Di Venanzo), through the use of a rich, varied, and sometimes surreal palette. To underscore the movie's theme, Fellini and Di Venanzo often interrupt seemingly naturalistic scenes with bursts of intense and dreamlike color. The effect is disorienting but magical, much like dreams themselves.

Lighting

During preproduction, most designers include an idea of the lighting in their sketches, but in actual production, the cinematographer determines the lighting once the camera setups are chosen. Ideally,

Evocative use of color Because we experience the world in color, color films may strike us as more realistic than black-and-white films. Many color films, however, use their palettes not just expressively, but also evocatively. For Stanley Kubrick's *Barry Lyndon* (1975), cinematographer John Alcott has helped convey both a historical period and a painterly world of soft pastels, gentle shading, and misty textures.

Reflector boards Many scenes of John Ford's *My Darling Clementine* (1946; cinematographer: Joe MacDonald) were shot in the sunny desert terrain of Monument Valley in Arizona and Utah. But as this photo shows, a large bank of reflector boards was used when the sunshine was insufficient or when the director wanted to control the lighting.

Suggestive use of lighting In Billy Wilder's comedy *Some Like It Hot* (1959; cinematographer: Charles Lang, Jr.), the beam from a spotlight suggestively doubles as a virtual neckline for Marilyn Monroe during her famous performance of "I Wanna Be Loved by You." As he often did during his long career as a screenwriter and director, Wilder was playfully testing the boundaries of Hollywood moviemaking—seeing what he could get away with.

the lighting shapes the way the movie looks and helps tell the story. As a key component of composition, lighting creates our sense of cinematic space by illuminating people and things, creating highlights and shadows, and defining shapes and textures. Among its properties are its source, quality, direction, and style.

Source There are two sources of light: natural and artificial. Daylight is the most convenient and economical source, and in fact the movie industry made Hollywood the center of American movie production in part because of its almost constant sunshine. Even when movies are shot outdoors on clear, sunny days, however, filmmakers use reflectors and artificial lights because they cannot count on nature's cooperation. And even if nature does provide the right amount of natural light at the right time, that light may need to be controlled in various ways, as the accompanying photograph of reflector boards being used in the filming of John Ford's *My Darling Clementine* (1946) shows.

Artificial lights are called *instruments* to distinguish them from the light they produce. Among the many kinds of these instruments, the two most basic are **focusable spotlights** and **floodlights**, which produce, respectively, hard (mirrorlike) and soft (diffuse) light. A focusable spotlight can pro-

duce either a hard, direct spotlight beam or a more indirect beam. When it is equipped with black metal doors (known as *barn doors*), it can be used to cut and shape the light in a variety of ways. In either case, it produces distinct shadows. Floodlights produce diffuse, indirect light with very few to no shadows. The most effective floodlight for

Softening shadows Outdoor shots in direct sunlight pose a risk of casting harsh shadows on actors' faces. This shot from James Cameron's *Titanic* (1997; cinematographer: Russell Carpenter) shows the effect of using a reflector board to soften shadows and to cast diffuse light on the bottom of the chin and the nose and under the brow, thus giving Leonardo DiCaprio's face a softer, warmer look on-screen.

filmmaking is the softlight, which creates a very soft, diffuse, almost shadowless light.

Another piece of lighting equipment, the **reflector board**, is not really a lighting instrument because it does not rely on bulbs to produce illumination. Essentially, it is a double-sided board that pivots in a U-shaped holder. One side is a hard, smooth surface that reflects hard light; the other is a soft, textured surface that provides a softer fill light. Reflector boards come in many sizes and are used frequently, both in interior and especially in exterior shooting; most often they are used to reflect sunlight into shadows during outdoor shooting.

Quality The quality of light on a character or situation is a very important element in helping a movie tell its story. Quality refers to whether the light is hard (shining directly on the subject, creating crisp details and a defined border and high contrast between illumination and shadow) or soft (diffused so that light hits the subject from many slightly varying directions, softening details, blurring the line between illumination and shadow, and thus decreasing contrast). We can generally (but not always) associate hard, high-contrast lighting featuring deep shadows (known as *low-key lighting*) with serious or tragic stories and soft, even lighting (*high-key lighting*) with romantic or comic stories.

The way the cinematographer lights and shoots an actor invariably suggests an impression of the character to the audience. A good example of how the quality of lighting can affect how we look at and interpret characters in a scene can be found in Orson Welles's *Citizen Kane* (1941; cinematographer: Gregg Toland). When Kane (Welles) first meets and woos Susan Alexander (Dorothy Comingore), the light thrown on their respective faces during close-up shots reveals an important distinction between them. Susan's face, lit with a soft light that blurs the border between illumination and shadow, appears youthful and naive. In contrast, Kane's face is lit with a hard and crisp light, making him appear older and more worldly.

Direction Light can be thrown onto a movie actor or setting (exterior or interior) from virtually any direction: front, side, back, below, or above. By direction, we also mean the angle of that throw, for the angle helps produce the contrasts and shadows that suggest the location of the scene, its mood, and the time of day. As with the other properties of lighting, the direction of the lighting must be planned ahead of time by the cinematographer in cooperation with the art director so that the lighting setup achieves effects that complement the director's overall vision.

The effects possible with any one lighting setup are extensive, but not limitless. If anything, the pioneering work of one cinematographer may make such an impression on moviegoers and filmmakers alike that it limits the freedom of subsequent filmmakers to use the same lighting setup in different ways. In other words, as with most other aspects of filmmaking, lighting is subject to conventions. Perhaps the best-known lighting convention in feature filmmaking is the **three-point system**. Employed extensively during the Hollywood studio era (1927–47), the three-point system was used to cast a glamourous light on the studios' most valuable assets during these years—their stars—and it remains the standard by which movies are lit today.

The three-point system employs three sources of light, each aimed from a different direction and position in relation to the subject: key light, fill light, and backlight. The backlight is the least

[1]

[2]

Lighting and setting A good way to understand the importance of how lighting influences our impressions of the setting is to compare the quality of two movies that were filmed in the same setting. Both Alexander Mackendrick's *Sweet Smell of Success* (1957; cinematographer: James Wong Howe) and Woody Allen's *Manhattan* (1979; cinematographer: Gordon Willis) use the Queensboro Bridge (or 59th Street Bridge, made famous in Simon and Garfunkel's song of the same name) for a key scene. Both scenes are shot at night in the environs of the bridge.

[1] This scene from *Sweet Smell of Success* takes place outside a nightclub located on a street that runs alongside and below the bridge. In this image, Sidney Falco, the unscrupulous assistant to J. J. Hunsecker, the city's most powerful gossip columnist, has just planted drugs in the coat of Steve Dallas, an innocent jazz guitarist who wants to marry Hunsecker's sister, Susan. We see Falco (Tony Curtis, *left*) confirming the setup with NYPD Lieutenant Harry Kello (Emile Meyer, *right*) and one of his assistants (unidentified

actor, *center*). Hunsecker has ordered Falco, as well as Kello, whom he controls, to make Dallas the victim of this scheme to keep the musician from marrying his sister. Shadows are deep, and the streetlights cast sharp pools of light on streets wet with rain. This atmosphere is made even more menacing by the noisy sounds of the bridge traffic overhead.

[2] In *Manhattan*, two of the typically self-deprecating New Yorkers that populate Allen's movies—Isaac Davis (Woody Allen) and Mary Wilkie (Diane Keaton)—meet for the second time at a cocktail party, desert their dates and leave together, and take a joyous walk through the streets, which ends on a bench in Sutton Square, a quiet, elegant neighborhood a few blocks closer to the river than the site of the scene in image [1], but close enough that this scene is also set alongside and below the bridge. The world of *Sweet Smell of Success* could be a million miles away. The bridge stretches above the two characters and across the frame, its supporting cables twinkling with lights, the early morning sky soft and misty behind. The only sounds are the lovers' voices and George and Ira Gershwin's romantic ballad "Someone to Watch over Me." Woody Allen is no starry-eyed fool, but the Manhattan in this movie is all romance, soft lights, and human relationships that (mostly) end happily.

[1]

[2]

Soft versus hard lighting Gregg Toland's use of lighting in *Citizen Kane* (1941) creates a clear contrast between Charles Foster Kane (Orson Welles) [1] and Susan Alexander (Dorothy Comingore) [2] that signals important differences between them in age (Kane is 45; Alexander is 22) and experience.

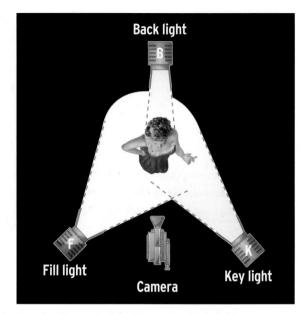

Three-point lighting In the history of over-the-top mise-en-scène, few directors surpass Josef von Sternberg. *The Scarlet Empress* (1934; cinematographer: Bert Glennon), a ravishing, high-camp historical drama, is also the director's visual tribute to the allure of Marlene Dietrich, who plays Russian empress Catherine the Great. Von Sternberg consistently photographs her with three-point lighting that accentuates her exquisite beauty. In this example, notice how the key light, positioned to the side and slightly below the actor, casts deep shadows around her eyes and on her right cheek; the fill light, which is positioned at the opposite side of the camera from the key light, softens the depth of the shadows created by the brighter key light; and the backlight (a von Sternberg trademark in lighting Dietrich), which is positioned behind and above, lighting both sides of the actor, not only creates highlights along the edges of her hair but also separates her from the background and thus increases the appearance of three-dimensionality in the image.

essential of these three sources. The overall character of the image is determined mainly by the relationship between the key and fill lights. The **key light** (also known as the *main*, or *source, light*) is the primary source of illumination and therefore is customarily set first. Positioned to one side of the camera, it creates hard shadows. The **fill light**, which is positioned at the opposite side of the camera from the key light, adjusts the depth of the shadows created by the brighter key light. Fill light may also come from a reflector.

The primary advantage of three-point lighting is that it permits the cinematographer to adjust the relationship and balance between illumination and shadow—the balance between the key and fill lights—a balance known as the **lighting ratio**. When little or no fill light is used, the ratio between bright illumination and deep shadow is very high; the effect produced is known as **low-key lighting**. Low-key lighting produces the overall gloomy atmosphere that we see in horror films, mysteries,

High-key lighting George Lucas's use in *THX 1138* (1971; cinematographers: Albert Kihn and David Myers) of an austere setting and intense white lighting that creates a shadowless environment is as chilling as the futuristic society it records. This society has outlawed sexual relations and controls inhabitants with a regimen of mind-changing drugs. Those who rebel are thrown into a prison that is a vast, white void.

psychological dramas, crime stories, and film noirs, where its contrasts between light and dark often imply ethical judgments.

High-key lighting, which produces an image with very little contrast between the darks and the lights, is used extensively in dramas, musicals, comedies, and adventure films; its even, flat illumination does not call particular attention to the subject being photographed. When the intensity of the fill light equals that of the key light, the result will be the highest of high-key lighting: no shadows at all.

You may have noticed that these terms—*low-key lighting* and *high-key lighting*—are counterintuitive: we increase the contrasts to produce low-key lighting and decrease them to produce high-key lighting. The cinematographer dims the fill light to achieve a higher ratio and contrast between shadow depth and illumination, and intensifies the fill light to lower the ratio and contrast.

The third source in three-point lighting is the **backlight**, usually positioned behind and above the subject and the camera and used to create highlights along the edges of the subject as a means of separating it from the background and increasing its appearance of three-dimensionality (such highlights are also known as *edge lights* or *rim lights*). In exterior shooting, the sun is often used as a backlight. Although it is less important to the three-point system than key light and fill light, backlight can be used on its own to achieve very expressive effects. One effect is to create depth in a shot by separating a figure from the background, as in the projection-room scene in Orson Welles's *Citizen Kane* (1941; cinematographer: Gregg Toland), in which Mr. Rawlston (Philip Van Zandt) and Jerry Thompson (William Alland) are outlined by the strong backlight from the projector.

Lighting from underneath a character (sometimes called *Halloween lighting*) creates eerie, ominous shadows on the actor's face by reversing the normal placement of illumination and shadow. This sort of lighting is especially appropriate in the horror genre, as in James Whale's *Bride of Frankenstein* (1935; cinematographer: John J. Mescall), in which the lighting thrown on Dr. Pretorius (Ernest Thesiger) from below accentuates the diabolical nature of his scientific ambitions.

Lighting thrown on a character from above can be used for many different effects, but a common result is to make a character appear vulnerable, or—in the example from Francis Ford Coppola's

Backlighting Backlighting can provide a dramatic sense of depth, especially when it is the sole light source, as in the projection-room scene in Orson Welles's *Citizen Kane* (1941; cinematographer: Gregg Toland). The intensity of light coming from the projection booth's windows provides clear visual cues to the depth of the on-screen space by creating a deep shadow in the foreground, a bright focus in the middle ground, and murky gray in the background. The shape of the beams of light—receding to a vanishing point behind the wall—not only contributes to our sense of depth but also accentuates the two main characters in the scene: Jerry Thompson (William Alland, *left*), the reporter who prepared the "News on the March" sequence, and his boss, Mr. Rawlston (Philip Van Zandt, *right*).

Lighting from below In this scene from *Bride of Frankenstein* (1935; cinematographer: John J. Mescall), Dr. Pretorius (Ernest Thesiger), with lighting cast from below, watches his monstrous creation come to life.

Lighting from above In the opening scene of Francis Ford Coppola's *The Godfather* (1972; cinematographer: Gordon Willis)—the wedding reception of his daughter Connie—Don Vito Corleone (Marlon Brando) responds to a request from one of the guests, Signore Bonasera, an undertaker, who asks Corleone to arrange the murder of two men who beat his daughter. Don Corleone listens impassively as lighting from above puts his eyes in deep shadow, emphasizing his power and mystique. He at first gently rebukes Bonasera for not paying him respect in the preceding years, but because it is traditional to grant requests on a daughter's wedding day, he finally grants the favor. Bonasera understands the magnitude of his debt and that he will one day be called upon to repay the favor.

The Godfather (1972; cinematographer: Gordon Willis) shown in the accompanying photo—threatening and mysterious.

Color   Color is another property of light. Perhaps its most important technical aspect is color temperature, a characteristic of visible light that is important in cinematography. Any light source will emit various light rays from the color spectrum. The absolute temperature of these rays is registered on the Kelvin scale, a measure of the color quality of the light source. The movie camera does not see color the way the human eye does and thus sometimes seems to exaggerate colors. We may see an object as white, but it may turn out to look very blue or orange on the screen. Understanding the temperature of a color enables a cinematographer during shooting (or laboratory technicians in the post-production phase) to correct the color and achieve the desired look. One way to balance color

is to match the sensitivity of the film stock to the color temperature of the light source. Another way is through the use of a camera filter, an optical element (usually a transparent sheet of colored glass or gelatin) placed in front of the lens that alters the light by cutting out distinct portions of the color spectrum as it passes to be registered on the film stock.

The overall style of a film is determined by its **production values**, or the amount and quality of human and physical resources devoted to the image. This includes specific decisions regarding the various properties of light we have just discussed. During the height of the classical Hollywood studio era, studios distinguished themselves from each other by adopting distinctive lighting styles and production values: for example, somber, low-key lighting in black-and-white pictures from Warner Bros.; sharp, glossy lighting in the films from 20th Century Fox; and bright, glamourous lighting for MGM's many color films, especially the musicals. The studios cultivated (and in many cases enforced) their distinct styles with an eye to establishing brand identities, and the filmmakers working for them were expected to work within the limits of the company style.

Cinematographers working within the constraints of a well-established genre often find that their decisions about lighting style are at least partly determined by the production values and lighting styles of previous films in that genre. Film-noir lighting, for example, conventionally uses high-contrast white-and-black tones to symbolize the opposing forces of good and evil. The very name *film noir* (*noir* means "black" in French) implies that lighting style is an important aspect of the genre. Filmmakers working within a genre with well-established conventions of lighting must at least be aware of those conventions.

Of course, the lighting conventions that define a genre can be altered by daring and imaginative filmmakers. For example, cinematographer John Alton deviates from the film-noir lighting formula in Anthony Mann's *T-Men* (1947) in order to develop a sense of moral ambiguity rather than a hard-edged distinction between good (light) and evil

[1]

[2]

[3]

[4]

Aspects of lighting in *Dogville* [1] Grace (Nicole Kidman) provokes Jack. [2] Grace faces the sunlight. [3] Grace, in profile, is transfixed by the sunlight.

[4] Grace turns toward Jack, astonished at how easy it was to bring light into darkness.

(darkness). A hard-edged crime story about U.S. Treasury Department agents' successful busting of a counterfeit ring, *T-Men* incorporates many shots made in near-total darkness—a black so deep that sometimes you can barely see the action. Bright lighting occasionally punctuates this gloom, but the overall tendency is to place everyone—cops and counterfeiters alike—in a dark and murky atmosphere. Alton lit his sets for mood rather than for making them completely visible to the viewer, and with this approach he rewrote the textbook on film-noir lighting. In doing this, he also changed the expectations traditionally raised by film-noir lighting in order to direct and complicate our interpretation of the film's narrative.

The various aspects of lighting—its source, quality, direction, and color—work together with other elements to determine the overall mood and meaning of a scene. Lars von Trier's *Dogville* (2003; cinematographer: Anthony Dod Mantle), a misanthropic

vision of the United States in the Depression-era 1930s, is set in a town of the same name that is located high on a plateau and populated by selfish, bored losers and miscreants. Grace (Nicole Kidman) arrives out of nowhere as a "gift" to the town's residents, whose primary reactions to her presence involve humiliating and torturing her, even as she does their chores to seek their acceptance. What is this place? Who is Grace? Why is she treated as an outsider? Lighting helps us answer these questions. The town's setting is a schematic design constructed on a vast, dark studio floor and often photographed from a very high angle that permits us to see its entire layout and total isolation from the surrounding countryside (which we never see). However, in contrast to the high-key lighting that floods the overall set with an even light, the scene we are considering (which takes place in one of the "houses" outlined on the floor) uses expressively lit close-ups to record a turning point in the action.

Grace is frustrated by her lot in life and tries to provoke Jack McKay (Ben Gazzara) into taking a more open view of the world, which is ironic, since he is blind. We are in McKay's residence, where the window is heavily draped to emphasize his condition. The scene opens with Grace sitting in a chair as she taunts Jack, telling him that she's walked outside and noticed the windows: "It must be a wonderful view." The lighting that illuminates her is a classic example of three-point lighting (image [1] on page 243): Grace is on the right side of the frame, in semiprofile; the light is falling on her from no identifiable source, highlighting her left cheek and the ridge of her nose; her heavily made-up eyes are in the shadows of her bangs. From this lighting, we clearly see that she is determined to get somewhere with her provocation; in addition to encouraging Jack to "see" more of the world, she may also be making sexual overtures toward him.

Next, Grace boldly takes the liberty of pulling open the drapes. Standing with her back toward us and holding the drapes apart with her widespread arms, she faces bright, almost surreal, sunlight and trees (significantly, there is little other greenery in the town) as the background music builds in a soft crescendo that suggests both spiritual and sexual release [2]. The reflection of her brightly lit face in the window accentuates the passage from darkness to light. She then turns, transfixed by the light: her profile, in the far right of the frame, faces directly left and toward the sunlight, which is evenly thrown onto her face; her lips are open in an ecstatic expression; the remaining two-thirds of the screen is dark [3]. Finally, she turns toward Jack, the bright sunlight behind her (an excellent example of backlighting), her face now in shadows, but her parted lips continue to underscore her sense of astonishment at how easy it was to bring light into darkness—a microcosm of her larger hope of achieving acceptance in Dogville [4]. As the scene ends, Jack remains trapped in his blindness. It is Grace, not Jack, who is able to see the light.

Lenses

In its most basic form, a camera **lens** is a piece of curved, polished glass or other transparent material. As the "eye" of the camera, its primary function is to bring the light that emanates from the subjects in front of the camera (actors, objects, or settings) into a focused image on the film, tape, or other sensor inside the camera. This was as true of the lens in the fifteenth-century camera obscura (in which the sensor was the wall on which the image was seen) as it is of the lenses of today.

The basic properties shared by all lenses are aperture, focal length, and depth of field. The **aperture** of a lens is usually an adjustable **iris** (or diaphragm) that limits the amount of light passing through a lens. The greater the size of the aperture, the more light it admits through the lens. The **focal length** of the lens is the distance (measured in millimeters) from the optical center of the lens to the focal point on the film stock or other sensor when the image is sharp and clear (in focus). Focal length affects how we perceive perspective—the appearance of depth—in a shot, and it also influences our perception of the size, scale, and movement of the subject being shot. The four major types of lenses are designated by their respective focal lengths:

1. The **short-focal-length lens** (also known as the wide-angle lens, starting as low as 12.5mm) produces wide-angle views. It makes the subjects on the screen appear

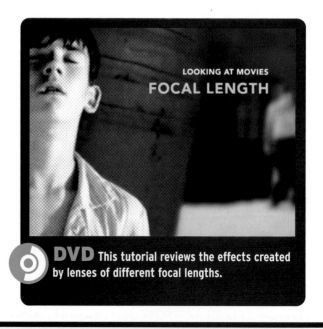

DVD This tutorial reviews the effects created by lenses of different focal lengths.

Short-focal-length lens This shot from Stanley Kubrick's *Dr. Strangelove* (1964; cinematographer: Gilbert Taylor) comically reinforces our sense of the powerlessness of Group Captain Lionel Mandrake (Peter Sellers, *facing the camera*) as he meets with his superior officer, Brigadier General Jack D. Ripper (Sterling Hayden). The resulting wide-angle composition makes Mandrake look almost like a toy doll standing on the powerful general's desk.

Middle-focal-length lens This shot from Billy Wilder's *Sunset Boulevard* (1950; cinematographer: John F. Seitz) includes the movie's three principal characters (*from left to right*): Max von Mayerling (Erich von Stroheim), with his back to us in the near left foreground; Norma Desmond (Gloria Swanson); and Joe Gillis (William Holden), in the middle ground facing us. A small orchestra is in the background. The middle-focal-length lens used to make this shot keeps the three principal subjects in normal focus, and the overall image corresponds to our day-to-day experience of depth and perspective.

Long-focal-length lens This image from Stanley Kubrick's *Barry Lyndon* (1975; cinematographer: John Alcott) shows the flattening effect of a long-focal-length lens. The marching soldiers' forward progress seems more gradual as a result.

2. The **long-focal-length lens** (also known as the telephoto lens; focal lengths ranging from 85mm to as high as 500mm) brings distant objects close, makes subjects look closer together than they do in real life, and flattens space and depth in the process. Thus, it alters the subject's movement, so that a subject moving from the background toward the camera might appear to be barely moving at all.

3. Although the short and long extremes are used occasionally to achieve certain visual effects, most shots in feature films are made with a **middle-focal-length lens**—from 35mm to 50mm—often called the *normal lens*. Lenses in this range create images that correspond to our day-to-day experience of depth and perspective.

4. The **zoom lens**—also called the *variable-focal-length lens*—permits the cinematographer to shrink or increase the focal length

farther apart than they actually are, and because this lens elongates depth, characters or objects moving at a normal speed from background to foreground through this stretched depth might appear to be moving faster than they actually are.

in a continuous motion and thus simulates the effect of movement of the camera toward or away from the subject. However, it does not actually move through space but simply magnifies the image.

Short-focal-length, long-focal-length, and middle-focal-length lenses all have fixed focal lengths and are known as **prime lenses**, but zoom lenses are in their own category. Both prime and zoom lenses have their specific optical qualities, and because they are thought to produce sharper images, prime lenses are generally used more than zoom lenses. In the hands of an accomplished cinematographer, the zoom lens can produce striking effects, but when it is used indiscriminately, as it often is by less skilled filmmakers, it not only feels artificial to an audience but can unintentionally disorient viewers. As with all other aspects of cinematography, the lens used must be appropriate for the story being told.

Depth of field is a property of the lens that permits the cinematographer to decide what **planes**, or areas of the image, will be in focus. As a result, depth of field helps create emphasis either on one or more selected planes or figures or on the whole image. The term *depth of field* refers to the distances in front of a camera and its lens in which the subjects are in apparent sharp focus. The short-focal-length lens offers a nearly complete depth of field, rendering almost all objects in the frame in focus. The depth of field of the long-focal-length lens is generally a very narrow range, and it leaves the background and foreground of the in-focus objects dramatically out of focus. In the middle-focal-length lens, the depth of field keeps all subjects in a "normal" sense of focus.

In virtually all shooting, cinematographers keep the main subject of each shot in sharp focus to maintain clear spatial and perspectival relations within frames. One option available to cinematographers, however, is a **rack focus** (also known as *select focus*, *shift focus*, or *pull focus*)—a change of the point of focus from one subject to another. This technique guides our attention to a new clearly focused point of interest while blurring the previous subject in the frame (see the illustration on page 247).

Zoom lens In making *The Hurt Locker* (2008; cinematographer: Barry Ackroyd), director Kathryn Bigelow wanted viewers to experience the Iraq war as if they were virtually involved in it. Thus, she had her camera team use lightweight Super 16mm cameras that gave them the mobility and flexibility to enter into the action and take viewers with them. One of these cameras was fitted with a zoom lens to allow its operator multiple perspectives on a scene within one shot. Overall, the movie is concerned with the highly dangerous work of a team that identifies and disables enemy roadside bombs and similar incendiary weapons. Here, the team, learning that a UN facility is apparently in danger of some kind of attack, orders the immediate evacuation of people from the building. In this shot, the camera lens begins with an extreme long shot [1] and then immediately shifts to a shorter focal length to put us among the coalition soldiers leading the frightened workers to safety [2]. The rapid, fluid movement of the lens between a neutral observation point and the people rushing toward the camera increases our involvement with the military forces and workers. In subsequent zoom lens shots, we see the weapons team make surveillance of the immediate area, shoot a suspicious man, and disarm a vehicle loaded with bombs, thus preventing an explosion.

[1]

[2]

Rack focus In this shot from Guillermo del Toro's *The Devil's Backbone* (2001; cinematographer: Guillermo Navarro), the camera uses depth of filed to guide our attention from one subject to another. When the shot begins, the lens is focused on the background where the villainous Jacinto (Eduardo Noriega) scans the orphanage courtyard for stray witnesses [1]. The lens then shifts focus to the foreground so that Jacinto's elusive prey, the orphan Jamie (Ìñigo Garcés), snaps into sharp relief [2].

TABLE 6.1 Types of Images Produced by Different Lenses

Type of Lens	Characteristics of Images Produced by Aperture, Focal Length, and Depth of Field
Prime lenses Short-focal-length lens (wide-angle lens)	• Produces wide-angle views. • Makes subjects appear farther apart than they actually are. • Through its nearly complete depth of field, renders almost all objects in the frame in focus.
Long-focal-length lens (telephoto lens)	• Produces deep-angle views. • Brings distant objects close. • Flattens space and depth. • Makes subjects look closer together than they actually are. • Narrow depth of field leaves most of the background and fore-ground of the in-focus objects dramatically out of focus.
Middle-focal-length lens (normal lens)	• Produces images that correspond to our day-to-day experience of depth and perspective. • Keeps all subjects in a normal sense of focus.
Zoom lens Zoom lens (variable-focal-length lens)	• Produces images that simulate the effect of movement of the camera toward or away from the subject. • Rather than actually moving through space, merely magnifies the image. • Can make a shot seem artificial to an audience.

The images you see on the screen are produced by a complex interaction of optical properties associated with the camera lens. Table 6.1 provides a ready reference on how the different lenses discussed here produce different images.

Framing of the Shot

Framing is the process by which the cinematographer determines what will appear within the borders of the image during a shot. Framing turns the comparatively infinite sight of the human eye into a finite movie image—an unlimited view into a limited view. This process requires decisions about each of the following elements: the proximity to the camera of main subjects, the depth of the composition, camera angle and height, the scale of various objects in relation to each other, and the type of camera movement, if any.

At least one decision about framing is out of the cinematographer's hands. Although a painter can choose any size or shape of canvas as the area in which to create a picture—large or small, square or rectangular, oval or round, flat or three-dimensional—cinematographers find that their choices for a "canvas" are limited to a small number of dimensional variations on a rectangle. This rectangle results from the historical development of photographic technology. Nothing absolutely dictates that our experience of moving images must occur within a rectangle; however, because of the standardization of equipment and technology within the motion-picture industry, we have come to know this rectangle as the shape of movies.

The relationship between the frame's two dimensions is known as its **aspect ratio** (Fig. 6.2), the ratio of the width of the image to its height. Each movie is made to be shown in one aspect ratio from beginning to end. The most common aspect ratios are

- ❯ 1.33:1 Academy (35mm flat)
- ❯ 1.66:1 European widescreen (35mm flat)
- ❯ 1.85:1 American widescreen (35mm flat)
- ❯ 2.2:1 Super Panavision and Todd-AO (70mm flat)
- ❯ 2.35:1 Panavision and CinemaScope (35mm anamorphic)
- ❯ 2.75:1 Ultra Panavision (70mm anamorphic)

Feature-length widescreen movies were made as early as 1927—the most notable being Abel Gance's spectacular *Napoléon* (1927)—and in Hollywood, the Fox Grandeur 70mm process very effectively enhanced the epic composition and sweep of Raoul Walsh's *The Big Trail* (1930; cinematographer: Arthur Edeson). Until the 1950s, when the widescreen image became popular, the standard aspect ratio for a flat film was the Academy ratio of 1.33:1, meaning that the frame is 33 percent wider than it is high—a ratio corresponding to the dimensions of a single frame of 35mm film stock. Today's more familiar widescreen variations provide wider horizontal and shorter vertical dimensions. Most commercial releases are shown in the 1.85:1 aspect ratio, which is almost twice as wide as it is high. Other widescreen variations include a 2.2:1 or 2.35:1 ratio when projected.[5]

Architectural elements—such as arches, doorways, and windows—are frequently used to mask a frame. A person placed between the camera and its subject can also mask the frame, as in the opening of John Ford's *The Searchers* (see page 362). In Mike Nichols's *The Graduate* (1967; cinematographer: Robert Surtees), during her initial seduction scene of Ben Braddock (Dustin Hoffman), Mrs. Robinson (Anne Bancroft) sits at the bar in her house and raises one leg onto the stool next to her, forming a triangle through which Ben is framed or, perhaps, trapped. Despite these modest attempts to break up the rectangular movie frame into other shapes through frames within the frame, movies continue to come to us as four-sided images that are wider than they are tall.

Implied Proximity to the Camera

From our earlier discussion of mise-en-scène (see Chapter 5), we know that in the vast majority of movies, everything we see on the screen—including

[5]In shooting for television broadcast, cinematographers are increasingly using the 1.78:1 aspect ratio, which can be seen on a home TV set with a format of 16:9, universal for HDTV.

FIGURE 6.2 Basic Aspect Ratios

1.33:1

1.85:1

2.35:1

subjects within a shot and their implied proximity to each other—has been placed there to develop the narrative's outcome and meaning. Our interpretations of these on-screen spatial relationships happen as unconsciously and automatically as they do in everyday life.

To get a sense of the importance of proximity, imagine yourself on a crowded dance floor at a club or party. Among all the other distracting things in your field of vision, you see an attractive person looking at you from the opposite end of the room. You may assign that person some significance from that distance, but if that same person walks up to you, virtually filling your field of vision, then the person suddenly has much greater significance to you and may provoke a much more profound reaction from

Architectural mask in *The Book of Eli* In this image, the Denzel Washington character is isolated in an architectural mask formed by an opening under a destroyed highway in Albert and Allen Hughes's sci-fi thriller *The Book of Eli* (2010), a movie that contains several other excellent examples of this technique.

Masking in *The Graduate* Mike Nichols's *The Graduate* (1967; cinematographer: Robert Surtees) features one of the most famous (and amusing) maskings of the frame in movie history. As the scene ends, Ben Braddock (Dustin Hoffman), framed in the provocative bend of Mrs. Robinson's (Anne Bancroft) knee, asks, "Mrs. Robinson, you're trying to seduce me . . . aren't you?"

Frames within the frame Some Japanese filmmakers experiment with the Western conventions of framing, not only by presenting more information within the frame, but also by using frames within the frame. The composition of the image preceding this one from Kyoshi Kurosawa's *Charisma* (1999) deliberately directs the viewer's eye: the window to the left is dark, the tree trunk draws our eyes to the right, the fallen window screen eliminates a window we don't see. These elements subconsciously tell us to concentrate our attention on the window in the upper right corner. What happens next alerts us not to follow such suggestions lightly because what we don't know is that the police have trapped a suspect, holding a hostage, in the room behind the window on the upper left. They storm the apartment, through the room on the upper right, and shoot and kill both men in the adjacent room.

you. Regardless of the outcome of this encounter, you have become visually involved with this person in a way that you wouldn't have if the person had remained at the other end of the room.

Similarly, the implied proximity of the camera to the subjects being shot influences our emotional involvement with those subjects. Think of how attentive you are during a close-up of your favorite movie actor or how shocked you feel when, as in Gore Verbinski's horror movie *The Ring* (2002; cinematographer: Bojan Bazelli), an actor moves quickly and threateningly from a position of obscurity in the background to a position of vivid and terrifying dominance of the frame. We all have favorite scenes from horror films that have shocked us in this way, violating and then virtually erasing the distance between us and the screen. Of course, nearness is not the only degree of proximity that engages our emotions. Each of the possible arrangements of subjects in proximity to each other and to the camera has the potential to convey something meaningful about the subjects on-screen, and thankfully, most of those meanings come to us naturally.

Shot types The names of the most commonly used shots employed in a movie—*extreme long shot, long shot, medium long shot, medium shot, medium*

close-up, close-up, and *extreme close-up*—refer to the implied distance between the camera lens and the subject being photographed. Since the best way to remember and recognize the different types of shots is to think in terms of the scale of the human

LOOKING AT MOVIES

SHOT TYPES AND IMPLIED PROXIMITY

DVD In this tutorial, Dave Monahan explores the concept of implied proximity and its relationship to various shot types.

body within the frame, we'll describe them in terms of that scale. The illustrations are from Tom Hooper's *The King's Speech* (2010; cinematographer: Danny Cohen). Historically, the story is familiar: King George V dies in 1936, and his son David accedes to the throne as Edward VIII; but his romantic relationship with and desire to marry Wallis Simpson, a twice-divorced American, leads to his abdication and the accession of his brother Albert ("Bertie"), the Duke of York, to the throne as George VI. The psychological and emotional effects of his royal upbringing add depth to the story. As a boy, Bertie developed a serious stammer due to the apparent bullying of his father and was therefore unprepared to handle the speaking engagements required of the king, both in person and over the radio. With the encouragement of his wife, he meets a relatively unknown speech therapist, Lionel Logue, who uses a series of experimental vocal, physical, emotional, and psychological techniques that eventually make it possible for the future king to speak fluently and confidently in public.

- In the **extreme long shot** (**XLS** or **ELS**), typically photographed at a great distance, the subject is often a wide view of a location, which usually includes general background

information. When used to provide such an informative context, the XLS is also an **establishing shot**. Even when human beings are included in such a shot, the emphasis is not on them as individuals but on their relationship to the surroundings. Image [1] shows Sandringham House, an immense country house used by the British royal family. Although there are several people on the terrace, the function of the shot is to identify the house and its grandeur.

- The **long shot** (**LS**) generally contains the full body of one or more characters (almost filling the frame, but with some of the surrounding area above, below, and to the sides of the frame also visible). In image [2], the archbishop and other officials of Westminster Abbey, standing amid the abbey's splendid surroundings, discuss the preparation for the inauguration of King George VI.

- A **medium long shot** (**MLS**) is neither a medium shot nor a long shot, but one in between. It is used to photograph one or more characters, usually from the knees up, as well as some of the background. This indispensable shot permits the director to place two characters in conversation and to shoot them from a variety of angles, as in image [3], where we see a meeting between the future king (Colin Firth, *left*) and his speech therapist, Lionel Logue (Geoffrey Rush, *right*), in Logue's studio. Because of the wide use of the MLS in Hollywood movies, the French call this shot the *plan Américain* (American shot).

- The **medium shot** (**MS**), somewhere between the long shot and the close-up, usually shows a character from the waist up. The MS is the most frequently used type of shot because it replicates our human experience of proximity without intimacy; it provides more detail of the body than the LS does. Unlike the close-up, the MS can include several characters, but it reveals more nuance in the characters' faces than can be captured in the MLS. Image [4] is a typical medium shot of Mrs. Wallis Simpson (Eve Best) greeting the duke and duchess of York at a cocktail party at a royal country house. Because she is not a member of the royal family, she is not officially entitled to take the role of host; nonetheless, her face registers her self-confidence.

- In a **close-up** (**CU**), the camera pays very close attention to the subject, whether it is an object or a person, but it is most often used in close-ups of actors' faces. Although it traditionally shows the full head (sometimes including the shoulders), it can also be used to show another part of the body, such as a hand, eye, or mouth. When focused on a face, the CU can provide an exclusive view of the character's emotions or state of mind, yet it can also show a face lacking emotion or thought. In image [5] we see George VI successfully deliver a radio speech in September 1939 informing the nation that Great Britain has declared war on Germany. It is, for him, a moment of personal and professional triumph, won through his evident determination and the efforts of his mentor.
- The **medium close-up** (**MCU**) shows a character from approximately the middle of the chest to the top of the head. It provides a view of the face that catches minor changes in expression and provides some detail about the character's posture. Image [6] portrays speech therapist Lionel Logue as he begins his sessions with the future king of England.
- An **extreme close-up** (**XCU** or **ECU**), a powerful variation on the CU, is produced when the camera records a very small detail of the subject. Comparing images [5] and [7], you can see that focusing on the future king's mouth and his aggressive repetition of the word "father" show how eager he is to break the psychological hold his father maintains on him.
- Note: you can more accurately label various shots according to the number of people in them. As is obvious, a **two-shot** contains two characters, a **three-shot**, three characters, and a group shot, more than three people.

Depth

Because the image of the movie screen is two-dimensional and thus appears flat (except for movies shot with 3-D cinematography), one of the most compelling challenges faced by cinematographers has been how to give that image an illusion of depth. From the earliest years of film history, filmmakers have experimented with achieving different illusions of depth. D. W. Griffith was a master at using huge three-dimensional sets in such movies as *Intolerance* (1916; cinematographer: G. W. Bitzer). A more sustained effort to make the most of deep-space composition began in the late 1920s. Many directors and cinematographers during this decade, especially those who were directing musicals with large casts and big production budgets, experimented with the technique of creating lines of movement from background to foreground to foster the illusion of depth.

For example, in *Applause* (1929; cinematographer: George Folsey), Rouben Mamoulian created spatial depth by organizing a line of burlesque

Shot types [1] **Extreme long shot** An extreme long shot of the exterior of Sandringham House, from which King George V delivers his annual Christmas address, humiliating his son in the process. [2] **Long shot** A long shot of the interior of Westminster Abbey, where the archbishop of Canterbury and other church officials discuss the forthcoming inauguration of King George VI. [3] **Medium long shot** A medium long shot of the interior of Lionel Logue's studio. The physical distance between the Duke of York and his mentor reflects both royal protocol and the duke's reluctance to undertake therapy. [4] **Medium shot** A medium shot showing Mrs. Wallis Simpson greeting guests at Balmoral House, acting, quite characteristically, as if she owned the place. [5] **Close-up shot** In this close-up shot, we see (and of course hear) King George VI, having overcome his stammer through diligent therapy, deliver the most important radio address of his reign, one that galvanized people's support of him. [6] **Medium close-up shot** In this medium close-up shot, at the outset of the future king's lessons, we see Lionel Logue, his mentor, a figure whose poise and confidence are evident throughout the movie. [7] **Extreme close-up shot** In this extreme close-up shot, we see one aspect of speech therapy: The Duke of York's repeatedly saying the word "father" as if to make the king's intimidation of him vanish from his consciousness.

1

2

3

4

5

6

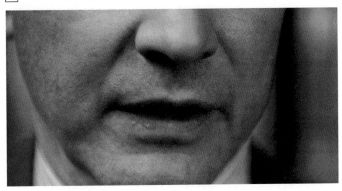

7

[1]

[2]

Depth From the earliest years of film history, filmmakers have experimented with achieving different illusions of depth. [1] Rouben Mamoulian created a very effective illusion of spatial depth in *Applause* (1929; cinematographer: George Folsey) by organizing a line of burlesque dancers to move from the stage in the back of the image, across the runway that bisects the audience in the middle of the image, to the viewer, sitting, presumably, in the right-hand corner of the foreground of the screen. Even though it was not yet possible to maintain clear focus from the foreground to background, the illusion of depth is there. [2] Three years later, in his dazzling comedy *Trouble in Paradise* (1932; cinematographer: Victor Milner), Ernst Lubitsch adhered to the traditional method of the time: suggesting depth by using an LS, placing the two main characters in the foreground plane and leaving the remainder of the image in a soft-focus background. In both of these examples, the cinematic space is arranged to draw the viewer's eyes either away from or toward the background.

dancers to move from the stage in the back of the image, across the catwalk that ran through the audience in the middle of the image, to the viewer, sitting, presumably, in the right-hand corner of the foreground of the screen. Director Mervyn LeRoy achieved a more elaborate effect with Busby Berkeley's choreography in *Gold Diggers of 1933* (1933).

Although these elaborately choreographed scenes reveal progress toward the goal of creating a cinematic image with greater depth, during the 1930s the traditional method of suggesting cinematic depth was to use an LS and place significant characters or objects in the foreground or middle-ground planes and then leave the remainder of the image in a soft-focus background. The filmmaker could also reverse this composition and place the significant figures in the background of the image with a landscape, say, occupying the foreground

and middle ground. Thus, in both of these examples the cinematic space is arranged to draw the viewer's eyes toward or away from the background. With such basic illusions, our eyes automatically give depth to the successive areas of the image as they seem to recede in space.

Also during the 1930s, however, various cinematographers experimented with creating a deeper illusion of space through cinematographic rather than choreographic means. Of these cinematographers, none was more important than Gregg Toland, who was responsible for bringing the previous developments together, improving them, and using them most impressively in John Ford's *The Long Voyage Home* (1940) and soon after in Orson Welles's *Citizen Kane* (1941). By the time he shot these two films, Toland had already rejected the soft-focus, one-plane depth of the established

Deep-focus cinematography and deep-space composition in _Citizen Kane_ Gregg Toland built on the work of previous directors, such as Allan Dwan, one of the most formally innovative of early film directors, who used deep-space composition in _The Iron Mask_ (1929; cinematographers: Warren Lynch and Henry Sharp), a silent swashbuckler featuring Douglas Fairbanks. Dwan could open up any shot into a complex, three-dimensional space with strategically placed foreground, middle ground, and background figures or objects. Similarly, in this beautiful deep-space composition from Orson Welles's _Citizen Kane_ (1941), Toland exploits all three planes of depth along a line that draws our eye from screen right to screen left. In the foreground, we see the reporter Mr. Thompson (William Alland) in a closed telephone booth; in the middle ground, outside the booth, we see the headwaiter of the El Rancho nightclub; and in the background, Susan Alexander Kane (Dorothy Comingore), the subject of Thompson's visit. Each character is photographed in clear focus in a unified setting, yet each is in a separate physical, psychological, and emotional space.

Deep-space composition An excellent example of the expressive potential of deep-space composition can be found in Alfred Hitchcock's _Notorious_ (1946; cinematographer: Ted Tetzlaff). Alicia Huberman (Ingrid Bergman), an American counterspy working in Brazil to discover enemy secrets, marries Alexander Sebastian (Claude Rains), a German spy, at the request of her government. Sebastian and his mother, Madame Konstantin (Leopoldine Konstantin), eventually discover Alicia's duplicity, and in this scene they have already begun to kill her by poisoning her coffee. As Alicia complains of feeling ill, Madame Konstantin places a small cup on the table near her, putting it in the immediate foreground of the frame. The tiny cup, no more than a few inches tall, appears almost as large as Alicia's head in the middle ground, heightening the menace facing her and raising the level of suspense.

Hollywood style; experimented with achieving greater depth; created sharper black-and-white images; used the high-powered Technicolor arc lights for black-and-white cinematography; used Super XX film stock, which produced a clearer image and was four times faster than previously available black-and-white stock; coated his lenses (to cut down glare from the lights); and used a camera equipped with a **blimp** so that he could work in confined spaces.

In _Citizen Kane_, these methods came together in two related techniques: a deliberate use of (1) **deep-space composition**, a total visual composition that places significant information or subjects on all three planes of the frame and thus creates an illusion of depth, coupled with (2) **deep-focus cinematography**, which, using the short-focal-length lens, keeps all three planes in sharp focus. Deep-space composition permits the filmmaker to exploit the relative size of people and objects in the frame to convey meaning and conflict.

Toland's pioneering work on _Citizen Kane_ had a profound influence on the look of subsequent movies and helped to distance Hollywood even further from the editing-centered theories of the Russian formalist directors (e.g., Sergei Eisenstein); Toland also brought American moviemaking closer

[1]

[2]

[3]

[4]

Use of deep-space composition in *The Little Foxes*
At the climax of William Wyler's *The Little Foxes* (1941; cinematographer: Gregg Toland), Horace (Herbert Marshall) responds to his wife's tirade [1], begins having a heart attack, and rises [2] while Regina (Bette Davis) remains rigidly in place [3], offering Horace no help as he staggers to his death in the background, helpless and out of focus [4].

to the realism of such European directors as Jean Renoir. French film critic André Bazin emphasizes that deep-focus cinematography "brings the spectator into a relation with the image closer to that which he enjoys with reality" and "implies, consequently, both a more active mental attitude on the part of the spectator and a more positive contribution on his part to the action in progress."[6] In preserving the continuity of space and time, deep-

[6]André Bazin, "The Evolution of the Language of Cinema," in *What Is Cinema?* trans. Hugh Gray, 2 vols. (Berkeley: University of California Press, 1967–71), I, pp. 35–36.

focus cinematography seems more like human perception.

Toland also understood that a scene involving deep-space composition did not necessarily have to be shot with deep-focus cinematography, as he demonstrated in William Wyler's *The Little Foxes* (1941). Perhaps the best example is found in a scene in which Regina Giddens (Bette Davis) confronts her severely ill husband, Horace Giddens (Herbert Marshall), a man she detests for his overall opposition to her scheming brothers and their plan to expand her family's wealth by exploiting cheap labor. The sequence takes place in their parlor after

Horace has returned home from a long hospital stay for treatment of his serious heart condition. When Regina asks him to put more funds into strengthening the family enterprise, he tells her that he has changed his will, leaving her nothing but bonds, which, he does not realize, members of the family have already stolen for the same purpose. Realizing that a man she despises has unknowingly trapped her in a difficult and illegal situation, Regina retaliates by telling him that she has always hated him. During her tirade, Horace has the first seizures of a heart attack. While attempting to take his medicine, he drops the bottle; when he asks Regina to get the spare bottle upstairs, she makes the decision to let him die and sits perfectly still as he staggers toward the stairs and collapses. As Horace struggles toward the stairs behind Regina, who is in the foreground, he grows progressively more out of focus, but he and his actions certainly are significant subject material. He goes out of focus for a specific reason—he is dying—and the shot is still very much deep-space composition but not deep focus. Even though he is out of focus in the deep background of the frame, Horace remains significant to the outcome of the story.

The coupling of deep-space composition and deep-focus cinematography is useful only for scenes in which images of extreme depth within the frame are required because the planning and choreography required to make these images are complex and time-consuming. Most filmmakers employ less complicated methods to maximize the potential of the image, put its elements into balance, and create an illusion of depth. Perhaps most important among these methods is the compositional principle known as the **rule of thirds**. This rule, like so many other "rules" in cinema, is a convention that can be adapted as needed. It takes the form of a grid pattern that, when superimposed on the image, divides it into horizontal thirds representing the foreground, middle ground, and background planes and into vertical thirds that break up those planes into further elements. This grid assists the designer and cinematographer in visualizing the overall potential of the height, width, and depth of any cinematic space.

You can watch the rule of thirds in action in a motion picture by placing four strips of ¼-inch masking tape on your television screen (to conform to the interior lines in the grid) and then looking at any movie being shown in the standard Academy aspect ratio (1.33:1). The lines will almost invariably intersect those areas of interest within the frame to which the designer and cinematographer wish to draw your attention. Simple as it is, the rule of thirds takes our natural human ability to create balance and gives it an artistic form. Furthermore, it helps direct our eyes to obvious areas of interest within a cinematic composition, reminding us yet again that movies result from a set of deliberate choices.

The rule of thirds, like other filmmaking conventions, is not a hard-and-fast law. Compositions that consciously deviate from the rule of thirds can be effective too, especially when they contrast with other compositions in the same film. In Stanley Kubrick's *Spartacus* (1960; cinematographer: Russell Metty), for example, the opening title sequence rejects the rule of thirds in favor of a series of perfectly centered compositions that complement the narrative and that contrast with the classically composed shots throughout the rest of the film.

Another common deviation from the rule of thirds is any shot that places the action extremely close to the camera, thus offering little or no visual depth. This is perhaps the most effective method for the filmmaker to indicate that this action is the most important thing at the moment—for example, at a turning point or climax. Such a composition occurs in the final shot of Lewis Milestone's *The Strange Love of Martha Ivers* (1946; cinematographer: Victor Milner).

Sometimes a filmmaker both uses the rule of thirds and partially rejects it in a single shot. Such shots are generally composed in depth, presenting one part of the action in the foreground and another, equally important part in either the middle ground or background. The shot may begin looking like a classically composed shot that is following the rule of thirds but then, because of the movement of several objects in the frame on all three planes, becomes less balanced and more complex. Such a shot is complex for a reason: the

The rule of thirds The rule of thirds applies to interior as well as exterior cinematography, particularly in genres such as the Western, where wide-open spaces figure significantly in a movie's meaning. Kit (Martin Sheen), the protagonist of Terence Malick's *Badlands* (1973; cinematographers: Tak Fujimoto, Steven Lamer, and Brian Probyn), takes to the road on a violent killing spree, accompanied by his girlfriend Holly (Sissy Spacek). Although not a Western per se, the movie is an American classic both for its focus on the serial killers that are now, unfortunately, part of our culture and its widescreen depiction of the flat, deep badlands between the Dakotas and the Canadian border. In this image, Kit (with his arms looped over his rifle) takes stock of himself on the eve of his final spree. The rising moon occupies the deep background plane of the image; the dust-filled air of the landscape dominates the middle ground. Kit is walking toward us in the foreground, looking something like a scarecrow (an object that is frightening, but not dangerous). This character, isolated in the natural grandeur, gives no hint of what evil he will do tomorrow.

filmmaker is probably attempting to call special attention to the relationship between the action in the foreground and that in the middle ground or background in order to establish a theme or to convey a number of narrative ideas simultaneously. In the long shot from Terrence Malick's *Days of Heaven* (1978; cinematographer: Néstor Almendros) pictured on the next page, composition of this sort establishes a very important hierarchical relationship between the characters in the foreground and the character (represented by his distant and visually aloof mansion) in the background.

In addition to helping filmmakers achieve distribution and balance in the general relationship of what we see on the screen, the rule of thirds helps cinematographers ensure that compositions flow appropriately from one shot to another. Without

LOOKING AT MOVIES
CAMERA ANGLES

DVD This tutorial examines the various types of camera angles and their effects on viewers.

Composition with limited depth In the final scene of Lewis Milestone's *The Strange Love of Martha Ivers* (1946; cinematographer: Victor Milner), Walter O'Neil (Kirk Douglas) points a gun at Martha Ivers (Barbara Stanwyck), who places her thumb over his finger on the trigger and causes the gun to fire, killing her. The camera eye's proximity to the actors' bodies produces an image with no depth—just the beautifully balanced composition of their hands on the gun next to her waistline.

Composition in depth in *Days of Heaven* This shot from Terrence Malick's *Days of Heaven* (1978; cinematographer: Néstor Almendros) establishes complex relationships, both spatially and thematically. The workers in the foreground are, as the direction of the woman's glance toward the house implies, curious about their employer, but they are physically (and culturally) removed from him. His house looms deep in the background, and although it is necessarily small within the frame, we can tell that it represents the position of power, mainly because it occupies the very edge of the high ground. Underscoring this relationship, the employer's agent walks (*left*) around the front of the car to explain that the workers are forbidden to go near the house.

that visual consistency, the editor will be unable to establish continuity—though he or she may choose to preserve graphic discontinuity as part of telling the story. For the viewer, such visual continuity suggests meanings through the placement and interrelationships of figures on the screen.

Camera Angle and Height

The camera's **shooting angle** is the level and height of the camera in relation to the subject being photographed. For the filmmaker, it is another framing element that offers many expressive possibilities. The normal height of the camera is eye level, which we take for granted because that's the way we see the world. Because our first impulse as viewers is to identify with the camera's point of view—and because we are likely to interpret any deviation from an eye-level shot as somehow different—filmmakers must take special care to use other basic camera angles—high angle, low angle, Dutch angle, and aerial view—in ways that

are appropriate to and consistent with a movie's storytelling.

The phrases *to look up to* and *to look down on* reveal a physical viewpoint and connote admiration or condescension. In our everyday experience, a high angle is a position of power over what we're looking at, and we intuitively understand that the subject of a high-angle view is inferior, weak, or vulnerable in light of our actual and cultural experiences. A filmmaker shooting from a high angle must be aware of this traditional interpretation of that view, whether or not the shot will be used to confirm or undermine that interpretation. Even a slight upward or downward angle of a camera may be enough to express an air of inferiority or superiority.

Eye Level An **eye-level shot** is made from the observer's eye level and usually implies that the camera's attitude toward the subject being photographed is neutral. An eye-level shot used early in a movie—as part of establishing its characters, time, and place—occurs before we have learned the

Eye-level shot In John Huston's *The Maltese Falcon* (1941; cinematographer: Arthur Edeson), this eye-level shot, used throughout the initial meeting of Miss Wonderly (Mary Astor) and Sam Spade (Humphrey Bogart), leads us to the false belief that the facts of their meeting are "on the level."

full context of the story, so we naturally tend to read its attitude toward the subject as neutral. Thus when Miss Wonderly (Mary Astor) introduces herself to Sam Spade (Humphrey Bogart) at the beginning of John Huston's *The Maltese Falcon* (1941; cinematographer: Arthur Edeson), the director uses an omniscient eye-level camera to establish a neutral client–detective relationship that seems to be what both characters want. This effect deliberately deceives us, as we learn only later in the film when we discover that Miss Wonderly is not the innocent person she claims to be (as the eye-level angle suggested).

By contrast, an eye-level shot that occurs in *The Grifters* (1990; cinematographer: Oliver Stapleton), comes later in the movie, after the director, Stephen Frears, has established a narrative context for interpreting his characters and their situation. From the beginning of the film, we know that Lilly Dillon (Anjelica Huston) and her son, Roy (John Cusack), are grifters, or con artists. After an eight-year estrangement they meet again, but each still regards suspiciously everything the other says or does. The eye-level shot reveals the hollow dialogue and tension of their reunion and is thus ironic, since they know, as we do, that their relationship is off balance (not "on the level").

High Angle A **high-angle shot** (also called a *high shot* or *down shot*) is made with the camera above the action and typically implies the observer's sense of superiority to the subject being photographed. In Rouben Mamoulian's *Love Me Tonight* (1932; cinematographer: Victor Milner), Maurice Courtelin (Maurice Chevalier) finally admits to Princess Jeanette (Jeanette MacDonald) that he is not an aristocrat, but rather an ordinary tailor. Although the princess loves him, she runs from the room in confusion, and the camera looks down on Maurice, who is now left to assess his reduced status with the symbolic measuring tape in his hands.

Sometimes, however, a high-angle shot can be used to play against its traditional implications. In Alfred Hitchcock's *North by Northwest* (1959; cinematographer: Robert Burks), one of the villains, Phillip Vandamm (James Mason), tells his collaborator, Leonard (Martin Landau), that he is taking his mistress, Eve Kendall (Eva Marie Saint), for a trip on his private plane. Vandamm knows that Kendall is part of an American spy ring that has discovered his selling of government secrets to the enemy, and he plans to kill her by pushing her out of the aircraft. As he speaks, the crane-mounted camera rises to a very high angle looking down at the two men, and Vandamm concludes, "This matter is best disposed of from a great height. Over water." The overall effect of this shot depends completely on this unconventional use of the high angle: it does not imply superiority, but rather emphasizes Vandamm's deadly plan. Its ironic, humorous effect depends as well on James Mason's wry delivery of these lines.

Low Angle A **low-angle shot** (or *low shot*) is made with the camera below the action and typically places the observer in the position of feeling helpless in the presence of an obviously superior force, as when we look up at King Kong on the Empire State Building or up at the shark from the underwater camera's point of view in *Jaws*. In Spike Lee's *Do the Right Thing* (1989; cinematographer:

[1]

[1]

[2]

[2]

High-angle shot [1] In this scene from Rouben Mamoulian's *Love Me Tonight* (1932; cinematographer: Victor Milner), the high-angle shot has the traditional meaning of making the subject seem inferior. After Maurice Courtelin (Maurice Chevalier) admits that he is not an aristocrat but rather an ordinary tailor, the camera looks down on him as he is left to assess his future with a symbolic measuring tape in his hands. [2] This shot from Alfred Hitchcock's *North by Northwest* (1959; cinematographer: Robert Burks), although taken from a high angle, makes Phillip Vandamm (James Mason) and Leonard (Martin Landau), who are planning to murder Vandamm's mistress by pushing her out of his private airplane, appear even more menacing than they have up to this point.

Low-angle shot Two faces, both shot at low angle, convey two different meanings. [1] A low-angle shot of Radio Raheem (Bill Nunn) from Spike Lee's *Do the Right Thing* (1989; cinematographer: Ernest Dickerson) puts us in the position of Sal (Danny Aiello, *not pictured*), a pizzeria owner who is intimidated and angered by his boom box-carrying customer. [2] In Stanley Kubrick's *The Shining* (1980; cinematographer: John Alcott), a low-angle shot from an omniscient point of view reveals the depth of Wendy's (Shelley Duvall) panic and despair.

Ernest Dickerson), Radio Raheem (Bill Nunn), who both entertains and intimidates the neighborhood by playing loud music on his boom box, appears menacing when photographed from a low, oblique angle during a confrontation with Sal (Danny Aiello), the owner of the neighborhood pizzeria.

However, filmmakers often play against the expectation that a subject shot from a low angle is menacing or powerful. In Stanley Kubrick's *The Shining* (1980; cinematographer: John Alcott), Wendy (Shelley Duvall) discovers a manuscript that suggests her husband, Jack (Jack Nicholson),

[1]

[2]

[3]

[4]

Camera angles in *M* This scene from Fritz Lang's *M* (1931; cinematographer: Fritz Arno Wagner)—in which an innocent man becomes the object of a crowd's suspicions—uses eye-level, low-angle, and high-angle shots to provide a context for us to distinguish real threats from perceived ones. [1] A neutral (and accidental) meeting between a short man and a little girl occurs in a context of suspicion (the city of Berlin has suffered a number of child murders in a short span of time). [2] The short man's perspective, an exaggerated low-angle shot, makes the question "Why were you bothering that kid?" even more ominous than the man's tone of voice makes it. [3] A high-angle shot from the perspective of a tall man who has brusquely asked, "Is that your kid?" reinforces the short man's modest stature and relative powerlessness. [4] Here we return to an LS as the short man protests his innocence and a crowd—soon to be a mob—gathers round.

is insane, and a low-angle shot emphasizes her anxiety, fear, and vulnerability. The shot also reminds us that the visual and narrative context of an angle affects our interpretation of it. The shot places Jack's typewriter in the foreground, thus making it appear very large, which implies its power over her and the threatening nature of what she is seeing (even before it is revealed to us). The low angle also

denies us the ability to see what is going on behind her at a moment in which we fear (and expect) the newly mad Jack to creep up behind her—thus elevating the suspense and making a character seen in extreme low angle appear more vulnerable than any high-angle shot could have.

In most scenes, obviously, different angles are used together to convey more complex meanings.

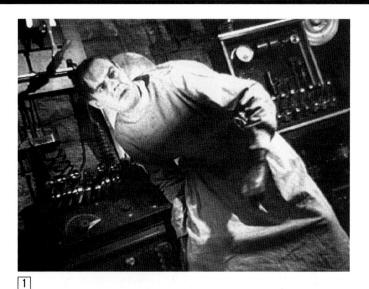

[1]

[2]

Dutch-angle shot In *Bride of Frankenstein* (1935; cinematographer: John J. Mescall), director James Whale uses Dutch-angle shots to enhance the campy weirdness of the lab work in this film [1]. This scene culminates in one of the most famous Dutch-angle shots of all time—that of the Bride (Elsa Lanchester) first seeing the Monster [2].

Neil Jordan's *The Crying Game* (1992; cinematographer: Ian Wilson), for example, uses alternating camera angles to convey and then resolve tensions between two characters. The scene begins with a confrontation between Fergus (Stephen Rea), an IRA gunman, and Jody (Forest Whitaker), a British-born black soldier whom Fergus and his terrorist cohorts have taken hostage. Power, race, and politics separate them, as confirmed by an alternating use of high- and low-angle shots from the perspectives of both characters during their dialogue. They start to relax when Jody shows Fergus a picture of his "wife," and by the time Jody talks about his experiences as a cricket player, they are speaking as men who have much in common—a transition that is signaled by a series of shots taken at eye level. These final shots help demonstrate that the men have more in common than their differences had at first suggested.

Dutch Angle In a **Dutch-angle shot** (also called a *Dutch-tilt shot* or *oblique-angle shot*), the camera is tilted from its normal horizontal and vertical position so that it is no longer straight, giving the viewer the impression that the world in the frame is out of balance.[7] Two classic films that use a vertiginously tilted camera are John Ford's *The Informer* (1935; cinematographer: Joseph H. August) and Carol Reed's *The Third Man* (1949; cinematographer: Robert Krasker). For the sequence in *Bride of Frankenstein* (1935; cinematographer: John J. Mescall) in which Dr. Frankenstein (Colin Clive) and Dr. Pretorius (Ernest Thesiger) create a bride (Elsa Lanchester) for the Monster (Boris Karloff), director James Whale creates a highly stylized mise-en-scène—a tower laboratory filled with grotesque, futuristic machinery—that he shoots with a number of Dutch angles. The Dutch angles accentuate the nature of the doctors' unnatural actions, which are both funny and frightening.

Aerial View An **aerial-view shot** (or *bird's-eye-view shot*), an extreme type of point-of-view shot, is

[7]The adjective *Dutch* (as in the phrases *Dutch uncle*, *Dutch treat*, and *Dutch auction*) indicates something out of the ordinary or, in this case, out of line. This meaning of *Dutch* seems to originate with the English antipathy for all things Dutch at the height of Anglo-Dutch competition during the seventeenth century. I am grateful to Russell Merritt for clarifying this for me.

taken from an aircraft or very high crane and implies the observer's omniscience. A classic example of the aerial view comes, naturally enough, from Alfred Hitchcock's *The Birds* (1963; cinematographer: Robert Burks). After showing us standard high-angle shots of a massive explosion at a gas station, the director cuts to a high aerial shot (literally a bird's-eye view) in which the circling birds seem almost gentle in contrast to the tragedy they have just caused below. Hitchcock said he used this aerial shot to show, all at once, the gulls massing for another attack on the town, the topography of the region, and the gas station on fire. Furthermore, he did not want to "waste a lot of footage on showing the elaborate operation of the firemen extinguishing the fire. You can do a lot of things very quickly by getting away from something."[8]

Scale

Scale is the size and placement of a particular object or a part of a scene in relation to the rest—a relationship determined by the type of shot used and the position of the camera. Scale may change from shot to shot. From what you learned in the preceding sections, it should be clear that the type of shot affects the scale of the shot *and* thus the effect and meaning of a scene. In *Jurassic Park* (1993; cinematographer: Dean Cundey), as in most of his movies, Steven Spielberg exploits scale to create awe and delight. The director knows that we really want to see dinosaurs—the stars of the film, after all—and he slowly builds our anticipation by delaying this sight. When he introduces the first dinosaur, he maximizes—through the manipulation of scale and special-effects cinematography—the astonishment that characters and viewers alike feel.

At Jurassic Park, jeeps carrying the group arrive on a grassy plain, clearly establishing the human scale of the scene. But Drs. Grant (Sam Neill) and Sattler (Laura Dern), preoccupied with scientific talk, take a moment to realize that Hammond (Richard Attenborough) has just introduced

[8]Alfred Hitchcock, qtd. in François Truffaut, *Hitchcock*, rev. ed. (New York: Simon & Schuster, 1985), pp. 292–294.

[1]

[2]

Scale In Steven Spielberg's *Jurassic Park* (1993; cinematographer: Dean Cundey), [1] the reaction of Dr. Sattler (Laura Dern, *left*) and Dr. Grant (Sam Neill, *right*) to their first dinosaur sighting prepares us for an impressive image on-screen, and we are not disappointed. In placing the reaction before the action itself, Spielberg heightens the suspense of the scene. [2] The scale of the apatosaurus is exaggerated by the framing of this shot, too, which implies that the beast is so gargantuan that it can't fit into the frame.

them to a live dinosaur, as benign as it is huge, which looks down upon them. ELSs make the dinosaur seem even taller. When the dazed Grant asks, "How did you do this?" Hammond replies, "I'll show you." It's impossible to forget what Spielberg then shows us: not just the first dinosaur, but also a spectacular vista in which numerous such creatures move slowly across the screen. Creating a sense of wonder is one of Spielberg's stylistic trademarks, and his use of scale here does just that as it also helps create meaning. Because this is a science-fiction film, we are prepared for surprises when we are introduced to a world that is partly recognizable and partly fantastic. Once the dinosaurs make their actual appearance, we know that humans, however powerful in their financial and scientific pursuits, are now small in comparison and therefore highly vulnerable.

Of course, the scale of small objects can be exaggerated for meaningful effect too, as in the example from Alfred Hitchcock's *Notorious* (1946) mentioned earlier (see page 255). When a tiny cup (or any other small object) looms larger than anything else in the frame, we can be sure that it is important to the film's meaning.

Camera Movement

Any movement of the camera within a shot automatically changes the image we see because the elements of framing that we have discussed thus far—camera angle, level, height, types of shots, and scale—are all modified when the camera moves within that shot. The moving camera, which can photograph both static and moving subjects, opens up cinematic space, and thus filmmakers use it to achieve many effects. It can search and increase the space, introduce us to more details than would be possible with a static image, choose which of these details we should look at or ignore, follow movement through a room or across a landscape, and establish complex relationships between figures in the frame—especially in shots that are longer than the average. It allows the viewer to accompany or follow the movements of a character, object, or vehicle, as well as to see the action from a character's point of view. The moving camera leads the viewer's eye or focuses the viewer's attention and, by moving into the scene, helps create the illusion of depth in the flat screen image. Furthermore, it helps convey relationships: spatial, causal, and psychological. When used in this way, the moving camera adds immeasurably to the director's development of the narrative and our understanding of it.

Within the first decade of movie history, D. W. Griffith began to exploit the power of simple camera movement to create associations within the frame and, in some cases, to establish a cause-and-effect relationship. In *The Birth of a Nation* (1915; cinematographer: G. W. Bitzer), within one shot he establishes a view of a Civil War battle, turns the camera toward a woman and small children on a wagon, and then turns back to the battle. From that instinctive, fluid camera movement we understand the relationship between the horror of the battle and the misery that it has created for innocent civilians. Of course, Griffith could have cut between shots of the battle and the bystanders, but breaking up the space and time with editing would not achieve the same subtle effect as a single shot does.

In the 1920s, German filmmakers took this very simple type of camera movement to the next level, perfecting fluid camera movement within and between shots. In fact, F. W. Murnau, who is associated with some of the greatest early work with the moving camera in such films as *The Last Laugh* (1924; cinematographer: Karl Freund) and *Sunrise: A Song of Two Humans* (1927; cinematographers: Charles Rosher and Karl Struss), referred to it as the *unchained camera,* thereby suggesting that it has a life of its own, with no limits to the freedom with which it can move. Since then, the moving camera has become one of the dominant stylistic trademarks of a diverse group of directors, including Orson Welles, Max Ophüls, Jean Renoir, Martin Scorsese, Otto Preminger, Lars von Trier, Terrence Malick, and Pedro Almodóvar.

Almodóvar uses the moving camera throughout *Talk to Her* (2002; cinematographer: Javier Aguirresarobe), perhaps most effectively at the very beginning of the movie. After a brief prologue photographed at a dance performance, we see a close-up of Benigno Martín (Javier Cámara) going about his work while he talks about this performance to someone we do not see. Although we don't yet know for certain where he works, we get a clue from his collarless blue shirt, one often worn by hospital nurses or orderlies. As the camera moves down from his face, we see that he is manicuring someone's nails, probably a woman's, but we don't yet know her identity or if she is interested in the story he is telling her. Still within the first shot, the camera moves to the right and reframes to a close-up of a woman lying in a bed, her eyes closed and a serene look on her face.

The gradual unfolding of the context of this scene grabs our interest and prompts us to ask, as each new detail is revealed by the moving camera, more questions about the relationship between these two people. After a series of shots immediately following this first one, we come to understand that the woman is Alicia (Leonor Watling), a young ballet student who has been in a coma in this hospital for four years, and that she is totally unaware of what is happening to and around her. Benigno, a respected member of the hospital staff, has fallen in love with her—a doomed endeavor it would seem, considering that he is homosexual and she is unlikely to recover. Throughout this complex story, Almodóvar uses the most subtle moving camera shots to reveal the psychological relationship between Benigno and Alicia.

The smoothly moving camera helped change the way movies were made and also the ways in which we see and interpret them. But before the camera was capable of smooth movement, directors and their camera operators had to find ways to create steady moving shots that would imitate the way the human eye/brain sees. When we look around a room or landscape or see movement through space, our eyes dart from subject to subject, from plane to plane, and so we "see" more like a series of rapidly edited movie shots than a smooth flow of information. Yet our eyes and brain work together to smooth out the bumps. Camera motion, however, must itself be smooth in order for its audience to make sense of (or even tolerate) the shots that result from that motion. The moving camera can also create suspense and even fear, as in Roman Polanski's *Rosemary's Baby* (1968; cinematographer: William Fraker), where the camera moves through a luxurious Manhattan apartment, peering around corners or into rooms just enough to keep you on the edge of your seat without letting you see what you know (or think you know) is there.

There are exceptions, of course: during the 1960s, nonfiction filmmakers began what was soon to become a widespread use of the handheld camera, which both ushered in entirely new ways of filmmaking, such as *cinéma vérité* and direct cinema, and greatly influenced narrative film style. For the most part, however, cinematographers strive to ensure that the camera does not shake or jump while moving through a shot. To make steady moving shots,

DVD In this tutorial, Dave Monahan demonstrates the various types of camera movement.

the camera is usually mounted on a tripod, where it can move on a horizontal or vertical axis, or on a dolly, crane, car, helicopter, or other moving vehicle that permits it to capture its images smoothly.

The basic types of shots involving camera movement are the pan, tilt, tracking, dolly, and crane shots, as well as those made with the Steadicam, the handheld camera, or the zoom lens. Each involves a particular kind of movement, depends on a particular kind of equipment, and has its own expressive potential.

Pan Shot   A **pan shot** is the horizontal movement of a camera mounted on the gyroscopic head of a stationary tripod. This head ensures smooth panning and tilting and keeps the frame level. The pan shot offers us a larger, more panoramic view than a shot taken from a fixed camera; guides our attention to characters or actions that are important; makes us aware of relationships between subjects that are too far apart to be shown together in the frame; allows us to follow people or objects; and attempts to replicate what we see when we turn our heads to survey a scene or follow a character. Pan shots are particularly effective in settings of great scope, such as the many circus scenes in Max Ophüls's *Lola Montès* (1955; cinematographer: Christian Matras) or the ballroom sequence in

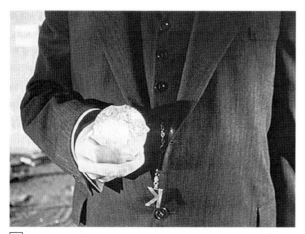

Tilt shot In Orson Welles's *Citizen Kane* (1941; cinematographer: Gregg Toland), the camera presents the first half of this shot [1], then tilts upward to present the second half [2]. Of course, Welles could have shown us both halves, even Kane's entire body, within one static frame. The camera movement directs our eyes, however, and makes the symbolism unmistakable.

Orson Welles's *The Magnificent Ambersons* (1942; cinematographer: Stanley Cortez), where he used several pan shots that moved almost 360 degrees.

Tilt Shot A tilt shot is the vertical movement of a camera mounted on the gyroscopic head of a stationary tripod. Like the pan shot, it is a simple movement with dynamic possibilities for creating meaning. Orson Welles makes excellent use of this shot in *Citizen Kane* (1941; cinematographer: Gregg Toland). When Susan Kane (Dorothy Comingore) finally summons the psychological and emotional strength to leave her tyrannical husband, he reacts by destroying her bedroom. At the peak of his violent rage, he seizes the glass globe with an interior snow scene; the camera tilts upward from the ball to Kane's (Welles) face; he whispers "Rosebud" and leaves the room. The tilt links the roundness and mystery of the glass ball with Kane's round, bald head; furthermore, it reminds us that the first place we saw the glass ball was on Susan's dressing table in her rooming-house bedroom, thus further linking the meaning of *Rosebud* with her.

Dolly Shot A dolly shot (also known as a tracking shot or traveling shot) is one taken by a camera fixed to a wheeled support, generally known as a dolly. The dolly permits the cinematographer to make noiseless moving shots. When a dolly runs on tracks, the resulting shot is called a tracking shot. The dolly shot is one of the most effective (and consequently most common) uses of the moving camera. When the camera is used to dolly in on (move toward) a subject, the subject grows in the frame, gaining significance not only through being bigger in the frame but also through those moments in which we actually see it growing bigger.

This gradual intensification effect is commonly used at moments of a character's realization and/or

A dolly in action Camera operators race alongside a speeding chariot on a dolly during the filming of Ridley Scott's *Gladiator* (2000; cinematographer: John Mathieson).

decision, or as a point-of-view shot of what the character is having a realization about. The scene in Hitchcock's *Notorious* (1946), in which Alicia Huberman (Ingrid Bergman) realizes that she is being poisoned via the coffee (see page 255), uses both kinds of dolly-in movements, as well as other camera moves that explicitly illustrate cause and effect (the camera moves from the coffee to Bergman at the moment she complains about not feeling well, for example).

The **dolly-out** movement (moving away from the subject) is often used for slow disclosure, which occurs when an edited succession of images leads from A to B to C as they gradually reveal the elements of a scene. Each image expands on the one before, thereby changing its significance with new information. A good example occurs in Stanley Kubrick's *Dr. Strangelove or: How I Learned to Stop Worrying and Love the Bomb* (1964; cinematographer: Gilbert Taylor) when—in a succession of images—the serious, patriotic bomber pilot is revealed to be concentrating not on his instruments, but on an issue of *Playboy* magazine instead.

Tracking shot In Jean Renoir's *The Grand Illusion* (1937; cinematographer: Christian Matras), the contradictory aspects of Captain von Rauffenstein's (Erich von Stroheim) life are engagingly and economically captured by the long tracking shot that catalogs the objects in his living quarters. The pistol on top of a volume of Casanova's memoirs is an especially telling detail: von Rauffenstein is a lover and a fighter.

A **tracking shot** is a type of dolly shot that moves smoothly with the action (alongside, above, beneath, behind, or ahead of it) when the camera is mounted on a wheeled vehicle that runs on a set of tracks. Some of the most beautiful effects in the movies are created by tracking shots, especially when the camera covers a great distance. Director King Vidor used an effective lateral tracking shot in his World War I film *The Big Parade* (1925; cinematographers: John Arnold and Charles Van Enger) to follow the progress of American troops entering enemy-held woods. This shot, which has a documentary quality to it because it puts us in motion beside the soldiers as they march into combat, has been repeated many times in subsequent war films.

Jean Renoir used the moving camera to create the feeling of real space, a rhythmic flow of action, and a rich mise-en-scène. In *The Grand Illusion* (1937; cinematographer: Christian Matras), Renoir's brilliant film about World War I, we receive an intimate introduction to Captain von Rauffenstein (Erich von Stroheim), the commandant of a German prison camp, through a long tracking shot (plus four other brief shots) that reveals details of his life.

Zoom The zoom is a lens that has a variable focal length, which permits the camera operator during shooting to shift from the wide-angle lens (short focus) to the telephoto lens (long focus) or vice versa without changing the focus or aperture settings. It is not a camera movement per se because it is the optics inside the lens that move in relation to each other and thus shift the focal length, yet the zoom can provide the illusion of the camera moving toward or away from the subject. One result of this shift is that the image is magnified (when shifting from short to long focal length) or demagnified by shifting in the opposite direction.

That magnification is the essential difference between **zoom-in** and dolly-in movements on a subject. When dollying, a camera actually moves through space; in the process, spatial relationships between the camera and the objects in its frame shift, causing relative changes in position between on-screen figures or objects. By contrast, because a zoom lens does not move through space, its depiction of spatial relationships between the camera and its subjects does not change. All a zoom shot does is magnify the image.

The result of zoom shots, as we've noted before, can be "movement" that appears artificial and self-conscious. Of course, there are dramatic, cinematic, and stylistic reasons for using this effect, but for the most part, the artificiality of the zoom (and the fact that viewers naturally associate the zoom effect with its overuse in amateur home videos) makes it a technique that is rarely used well in professional filmmaking. When the zoom shot *is* used expressively, however, it can be breathtaking. In *Goodfellas* (1990; cinematographer: Michael Ballhaus), during the scene in which Henry Hill (Ray Liotta) meets Jimmy Conway (Robert De Niro) in a diner, director Martin Scorsese achieves a memorable effect with the moving camera and the zoom lens. He tracks *in* (while moving the zoom lens *out*) and tracks *out* (while moving the zoom lens *in*) to reflect Henry's paranoid, paralyzed state of mind. As the camera and lens move against one another, the image traps Hill inside the hermetic world of the mob and us inside a world of spatial disorientation in an ordinary diner.

Crane Shot   A crane shot is made from a camera mounted on an elevating arm that is, in turn, mounted on a vehicle capable of moving under its own power. A crane may also be mounted on a vehicle that can be pushed along tracks to smooth its movement. The arm can be raised or lowered to the degree that the particular crane permits. Shots made with a crane differ from those made with a camera mounted on a dolly or an ordinary track (each of which is, in theory, capable only of horizontal or vertical movement) because the crane has the full freedom of horizontal and vertical movement, as well as the capability of lifting the camera high off the ground. Thus, a filmmaker can use a crane to shoot with extraordinary flexibility. As equipment for moving the camera has become more versatile, crane shots have become more commonplace.

Any list of memorable crane shots would have to include the shot in Victor Fleming's *Gone with the*

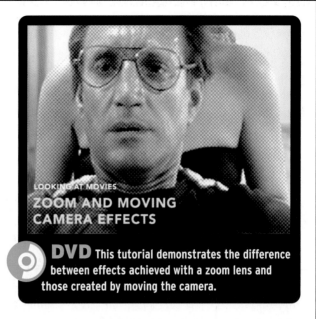

LOOKING AT MOVIES
ZOOM AND MOVING CAMERA EFFECTS

DVD This tutorial demonstrates the difference between effects achieved with a zoom lens and those created by moving the camera.

Wind (1939; cinematographer: Ernest Haller) in which the camera soars up over ground near the Atlanta railroad station to reveal the hundreds of Civil War dead and the smooth, graceful shot in Alfred Hitchcock's *Notorious* (1946; cinematographer: Ted Tetzlaff) in which the camera swoops down alongside a staircase and across a crowded ballroom. Another, more contemporary, crane shot can be seen in Oliver Stone's *Alexander* (2004; cinematographer: Rodrigo Prieto), the Macedonian warrior Alexander the Great (Colin Farrell) looks up to see the eagle that is his personal symbol. The camera soars up to assume the eagle's point of view and then looks down over the field on which Alexander and his troops will shortly fight the Persians.

Looking at camera movement: *Touch of Evil*
Perhaps the most impressive crane shot in movie history occurs at the opening of Orson Welles's *Touch of Evil* (1958; cinematographer: Russell Metty). The scene takes place at night in Los Robles, a seedy town on the U.S.–Mexico border. After the Universal International logo dissolves from the screen, we see a close-up of a man's hand swinging toward the camera and setting a timer that will make the bomb he holds explode in about three minutes. The camera pans left to reveal two figures approaching the camera from the end of a long interior corridor; the

[1]

[2]

[3]

[4]

[5]

[6]

[7]

[8]

The crane shot in *Touch of Evil* These stills from the opening crane shot in Orson Welles's *Touch of Evil* (1958; cinematographer: Russell Metty) show the progress of the camera over a wide-ranging space through a continuous long shot that ends only at the point where the car blows up [1–7].

A reaction shot of Mike and Susan Vargas (Charlton Heston and Janet Leigh) follows [8], and as the Vargases run toward the site of the explosion, the mystery at the heart of the movie begins to unfold.

bomber, Manelo Sanchez (Victor Millan), runs left into the frame, realizes that these people are his targets, and runs out of the frame to the right as the camera pans right to follow him. He places the bomb in the trunk of a luxurious convertible, the top of which is down, and disappears screen right just as the couple enters the frame at top left; the camera tracks backward and reframes to an LS.

As the couple gets into the car, the camera (mounted on a crane that is attached to a truck) swings to an extreme high angle. The car pulls forward alongside a building and turns left at the front of the building as the camera reaches the roof level at its back. We momentarily lose sight of the car, but the camera, which has oriented us to where the car is, merely pans left and brings it back into the frame as it moves left across an alley into a main street. The camera cranes down to an angle slightly higher than the car, which has turned left and now heads toward the camera on a vertical axis moving from background to foreground. When the car pauses at the direction of a policeman, who permits other traffic to cross in the foreground on a horizontal axis, the camera begins tracking backward to keep the car in the frame. The camera continues to track backward, reframes to an XLS, and pans slightly to the left. The car stops at an intersection.

A man and a woman ("Mike" Vargas, a Mexican narcotics agent played by Charlton Heston, and Susan Vargas, whom he has just married, played by Janet Leigh) enter the intersection at screen right and continue across the street as the camera lowers to an eye-level LS. The car turns left onto the street on which the Vargases are walking, and they scurry to get out of its way as the car moves out of the frame. They continue walking with the camera tracking slightly ahead of them; it keeps them in the frame as they pass the car, which is now delayed by a herd of goats that has stopped in another intersection. The camera continues to track backward, keeping the couple and the car in the frame; this becomes a deep-space composition with the car in the background, crossway traffic in the middle ground, and the Vargas couple in the foreground. The Vargases reach the kiosk marking the entrance to the border crossing and pass it on the right, still walking toward the camera, which now

rises, reframing into a high-angle LS that reveals the car driving past the left side of the kiosk. The frame now unites the two couples (one in the car, the other walking) as they move forward at the same time to what we, knowing that the bomb is in the car, anticipate will be a climactic moment.

The camera stops and reframes to an MS with the Vargases standing on the right and the car stopped on the left. While a border agent begins to question the newlyweds, soon recognizing Vargas, a second agent checks the car's rear license plate. The agents and Vargas discuss smashing drug rings, but Vargas explains that he and his wife are crossing to the American side so that his wife can have an ice cream soda. Meanwhile, the driver of the targeted car, Mr. Linnekar (actor not credited), asks if he can get through the crossing. The Vargases walk out of the frame, continuing the discussion about drugs, then apparently walk around the front of the car and reenter the frame at the left side; the camera pans slightly left and reframes the Vargases, border agents, and Linnekar and Zita (Joi Lansing), his companion.

After a few moments of conversation, the Vargases walk away toward the back and then left of the frame; the car moves slowly forward, and Zita complains to one of the guards—in a moment of delicious black humor—that she hears a "ticking noise." As the car leaves the frame, the camera pans left to another deep-focus composition with the Vargases in the background, two military policemen walking from the background toward the camera, and pedestrians passing across the middle ground. The camera tracks forward and reframes to an MS; the Vargases embrace as the bomb explodes. Startled, they look up and see the car in flames.

The final two shots in this extraordinary sequence are first, a rapid zoom-in on the explosion and second, a low-angle, handheld shot of Vargas running toward the scene. These shots, more self-conscious and less polished than the preceding, fluid crane shots, cinematically and dramatically shift the tone from one of controlled suspense to out-of-control chaos that changes the normal world and sets the scene for the story's development. This is also an excellent example of how movies exploit the establishment and breaking of narrative forms.

With extraordinary virtuosity, Welles has combined nearly all types of shots, angles, framings, and camera movements. He accomplishes the changes in camera height, level, angle, and framing by mounting the camera on a crane that can be raised and lowered smoothly from ground level to an extreme high angle, reframed easily, and moved effortlessly above and around the setting (parking lot, market arcade, street, intersections, and border inspection area). Here the moving camera is both unchained and fearless, a thoroughly omniscient observer as well as a voyeur, particularly in its opening observations of the bomber. But what is the function of this cinematographic tour de force? Is it just one of Welles's razzle-dazzle attempts to grab the audience's attention, or does it create meaning?

The answer, of course, is that it has both purposes. Its virtuosity astonishes but with a point. In addition to witnessing the inciting device for the plot, we learn that Los Robles is a labyrinth of activity, lights, shadows, and mysteries and that the destinies of Linnekar, Zita, Vargas, and Susan are in some way tangled. The odd and extreme camera angles (at both the beginning and the end of the scene) reinforce the air of mystery and disorient us within the cinematic space. All the while, the bold black-and-white contrasts pull us into the deep shadows of vice, corruption, and brutal crime.

Handheld Camera   The last two shots in the scene from *Touch of Evil* (1958) described in the previous section were made with a handheld camera, a small, portable, lightweight instrument that is held by the camera operator during shooting. At one time, handheld cameras were limited to 8mm or 16mm film stock, but now they can handle a variety of film gauges. In contrast to the smooth moving camera shots that we have been discussing, the inherent shakiness of the handheld camera can be exploited when a loss of control, whether in the situation or in the character's state of mind, is something the filmmaker wants to convey to the viewer. *Touch of Evil* does just that, with an elaborately choreographed and fluid moving camera sequence suddenly interrupted by an explosion, which is photographed with a shaky handheld. We feel that the world has changed because the way we see the world has shifted so dramatically.

However, the uses of the handheld camera go beyond that. After nearly fifty years of viewing news coverage of unfolding events, nonfiction films in the direct cinema style, and reality television shows, audiences have been conditioned to associate the look of handheld camera shots with documentary realism—that is, with the assumption that something is really happening and the photographer (and therefore the viewer) is there. Narrative feature films can take advantage of that intuitive association to heighten or alter our experience of a particular event, such as the attack on the military base in Stanley Kubrick's *Dr. Strangelove or: How I Learned to Stop Worrying and Love the Bomb* (1964; cinematographer: Gilbert Taylor), the influential documentary-style of cinematographer Haskell Wexler in such movies as Milos Forman's *One Flew over the Cuckoo's Nest* (1975) and John Sayles's *Matewan* (1987), or the astonishing, disorienting handheld shots of cinematographer Oliver Wood in Paul Greengrass's *The Bourne Supremacy* (2004). Other movies that make effective use of the handheld camera include Stefan Ruzowitzky's *The Counterfeiters* (2007; cinematographer: Benedict Neuenfels), Matt Reeves's *Cloverfield* (2008; cinematographer: Michael Bonvillain), and John Carney's *Once* (2006; cinematographer: Tim Fleming).

Steadicam   From the beginning of the movies, movie cameras (handheld as well as those mounted on tripods, dollies, or other moving devices) have

Handheld camera   The handheld camera is used to great advantage in keeping the viewer disoriented during Paul Greengrass's high-action thriller *The Bourne Supremacy* (2004; cinematographer: Oliver Wood), as in this shot of Jason Bourne (Matt Damon) trying to elude the pursuing police.

allowed filmmakers to approach their subjects, as when they move in for close-ups. But the handheld camera frequently produces a jumpy image, characteristic of avant-garde filmmaking and usually not acceptable in the mainstream. So mainstream filmmakers embraced the **Steadicam**, a device attached to the operator's body that steadies the camera, avoids the jumpiness associated with the handheld camera, and is now much used for smooth, fast, and intimate camera movement. The Steadicam system, which is perfectly balanced, automatically compensates for any movements made by the camera operator, whether in running downstairs, climbing a hill, or maneuvering in tight places where dollies or tracks cannot fit.

The Steadicam is used so frequently that it has all but ceased to call attention to itself. But there are many great, exhilarating uses of this device that are worth remembering, including the work of Garrett Brown, the Steadicam operator on Stanley Kubrick's *The Shining* (1980; cinematographer: John Alcott), perhaps the most memorable being the long sequence that follows Danny Torrance's (Danny Lloyd) determined tricycle ride through the halls of the Overlook Hotel. This sequence may have influenced Matías Mesa, the Steadicam operator on Gus Van Sant's *Elephant* (2003; cinematographer: Harris Savides), whose Steadicam-mounted camera unobtrusively follows the wanderings of students in the corridors of their high-school buildings.

Another memorable example is Larry McConkey's Steadicam shot of Henry and Karen (Ray Liotta and Lorraine Bracco) entering the Copacabana in Martin Scorsese's *Goodfellas* (1990; cinematographer: Michael Ballhaus). As in *The Shining*, the camera stays behind the subjects as they enter the club's rear entrance and move through the kitchen and various service areas, where everyone knows and greets Liotta's character, to the club's main room, where a table is set up for the couple near the stage. This Steadicam sequence is very different from the one used in *The Shining*. In the Kubrick film, the Steadicam (mounted on a wheelchair) takes us on a dizzying ride through the hotel's labyrinthine halls, echoing the actual labyrinth in the garden and emphasizing the intense mystery of the story. We are left breath-

The smoothest-moving camera The Steadicam, invented in the early 1970s, is not a camera but rather a steadying mechanism on which any motion-picture camera can be mounted. In this image of the Steadicam Ultra2 model,[9] the operator wears a harness that is attached to an arm which is connected to a vertical armature, here with the camera at the top and a counterbalance weight at the bottom. Unlike the handheld camera, this mechanism isolates the operator's movements from the camera, producing a very smooth shot even when the operator is walking or running quickly over an uneven surface.

[9]Steadicam and Ultra2 are trademarks of the Tiffen Company.

less at the end of it. In the *Goodfellas* sequence, however, the Steadicam leads the viewer, like a guide, as we follow a brash, young gangster trying to impress his future wife as they enter the glamourous world of a New York nightclub.

Framing and Point of View

As the preceding discussion has illustrated, the framing of a shot—including the type of shot and its depth, camera angle and height, scale, and camera movement—has several major functions. In the most basic sense, framing controls what we see (explicitly, what is on the screen; implicitly, what we know has been left out) and how we see it (up close, far away, from above or below, and so on). Framing also calls attention to the technique of cinematography, allowing us to delight in the variety of possibilities that the director and cinematographer have at their disposal. It also implies point of view (POV), which can mean the POV of the screenwriter, director, one or more characters, or the actual POV of the camera itself. Of course, all of these POVs can be used in any one movie.

The camera's POV, the eyes through which we view the action, depends on the physical position from which the camera shoots. In most movies, the camera is omniscient: virtually able to go anywhere and see anything, either at average human eye level or above it. Eye-level, high, and low shooting angles, however, raise questions of objectivity and subjectivity; sometimes, as we have seen, directors use them to play against our expectations, to control or mislead us. In looking at movies, we experience frequent shifts in the camera's POV. The dominant neutral POV gives us the facts and background that are the context in which the characters live. The **omniscient POV** shows what the omniscient camera sees, typically from a high angle; a **single character's POV**, in which the shot is made with the camera close to the line of sight of a character (or animal or surveillance camera), shows what that person would be seeing of the action; and the **group POV** shows us what a group of characters would see at their level.

Julian Schnabel's *The Diving Bell and the Butterfly* (2007; cinematographer: Janusz Kaminski) is a

LOOKING AT MOVIES
POINT OF VIEW

DVD This tutorial explores point of view and framing.

highly concentrated example of a movie shot from the mental and visual POV of a single character. Jean-Dominique Bauby (Mathieu Amalric), the editor of a French magazine, suffered a massive stroke that has left him almost totally paralyzed (he can use one of his eyes), yet able to maintain his sense of humor (often black), remember and think, hear from one ear, move his face and head a little, and most important to his therapy, use his left eyelid to blink for communication (one blink = yes; two = no). He also narrates the film through his interior monologue. (That monologue actually comes from the book that Bauby "wrote" by blinking his eyes for each letter to a collaborator who put the words on paper.) What's relevant here in terms of cinematography is that much of the film is shot from the position and angle of his left eye—what he calls "the only window to my cell." (There are also extreme close-up shots of his eye from a distance of a few inches away.) The images that Bauby and the viewer see simultaneously and identically are blurred, flickering, and bleached out. Bauby is in an extreme position, and the director and cinematographer have chosen a frame that is equally extreme. This movie's visual style meets the needs of this story, which is not a record of impending death but rather the saga of Bauby's highly determined process of rebirth. The movie's consistent use of this POV might seem gimmicky with a different narrative, but here it rightly puts the emphasis on that character's eye, the "I" of his narration, and, of course, the camera's eye.

Consider a very fast and active scene in Alfred Hitchcock's *The Birds* (1963; cinematographer: Robert Burks), in which a classic use of camera angle and point of view establishes and retains the viewer's orientation as the townspeople of Bodega Bay become increasingly agitated because of random attacks by birds (see the photo spread on page 276). During one such attack, frightened people watch from the window of a diner as a bird strikes a gas-station attendant, causing a gasoline leak that results in a tragic explosion. Chief among these spectators are Melanie Daniels (Tippi Hedren) and Mitch Brenner (Rod Taylor).

The basic pattern of camera angles alternates between shots from a high angle in the restaurant, looking out and down, to those from eye level, looking from the exterior through the window of the restaurant. These alternating points of view give the sequence its power. How does Hitchcock's use of alternating points of view create meaning in the sequence? It shows us (not for the first time) that the birds really do maliciously attack unsuspecting people. It also demonstrates that, at least in this cinematic world, people close to an impending tragedy—people like Mitch, Melanie, and the man with the cigar—can do virtually nothing to stop it.

Two other interesting movies that employ a single character's POV are Robert Montgomery's *Lady in the Lake* (1947; cinematographer; Paul C. Vogel)—perhaps the first movie in whch the camera gives the illusion of looking through a character's eyes—and Gaspar Noé's *Enter the Void* (2010; cinematographer: Benoît Debie), which includes dazzling camera work as the story is shot from a first-person viewpoint with psychedelic imagery reflecting the drug culture depicted.

Speed and Length of the Shot

Up to this point, we have emphasized the spatial aspects of how a shot is composed, lit, and photographed. But the image we see on the screen has both spatial *and* temporal dimensions. Its length can be as important as any other characteristic. Although a shot is one uninterrupted run of the camera, no convention governs what that length should be. Before the arrival of sound, the average shot lasted about five seconds; after sound arrived, that average doubled to approximately ten seconds. Nonetheless, a shot can (and should) be as long as necessary to do its part in telling the story.

By controlling the length of shots, not only do filmmakers enable each shot to do its work—establish a setting, character, or cause of a following event—but they also control the relationship of each shot to the others and thus to the rhythm of the film. The length of any shot is influenced by three factors: the screenplay (the amount of action and dialogue written for each shot), the cinematography (the duration of what is actually shot), and the editing (what remains of the length of the actual shot after the film has been cut and assembled).

Here we will concentrate on the second of these factors: the relationship between cinematography and time. What kind of time does the camera record? As you know from Chapter 4, when we see a movie, we are aware of basically two kinds of time: real time, time as we ordinarily perceive it in life outside the movie theater; and cinematic time, time as it is conveyed to us through the movie. Through a simple adjustment of the camera's motor, cinema can manipulate time with the same freedom and flexibility that it manipulates space and light.

Slow motion decelerates action by photographing it at a rate greater than the normal 24 fps (frames per second) so that it takes place in cinematic time less rapidly than the real action that took place before the camera. One effect of slow motion is to emphasize the power of memory, as in Sidney Lumet's *The Pawnbroker* (1964; cinematographer: Boris Kaufman), in which Sol Nazerman (Rod Steiger), a pawnbroker living in the Bronx, remembers pleasant memories in Germany before the Nazis and the Holocaust. Martin Scorsese frequently uses slow motion to suggest a character's heightened awareness of someone or something. In *Taxi Driver* (1976), for example, Travis Bickle (Robert De Niro) sees in slow motion what he considers to be the repulsive sidewalks of New York;

1

10

3

4

6

2

5

8

7

9

Types of shots in *The Birds* (*Opposite*) In this action-packed scene from *The Birds* (1963; cinematographer: Robert Burks), Alfred Hitchcock orients us by manipulating types of shots, camera angles, and points of view. It includes [1] an eye-level medium close-up of Melanie (Tippi Hedren) and two men, who [2] see a gas-station attendant hit by a bird; [3] an eye-level medium shot of Melanie and another woman, who, through high-angle shots such as this close-up [4], watch gasoline run through a nearby parking lot; [5] a slightly low-angle close-up of a group warning a man in the parking lot, seen in this high-angle long shot [6], not to light his cigar, though he doesn't hear the warning; [7] the resulting explosion and fire, seen in a long shot from high angle; and [8] Melanie watching the fire spread to the gas station [9], which the birds observe from on high [10].

and in *Raging Bull* (1980), Jake La Motta (De Niro) fondly remembers his wife, Vickie (Cathy Moriarty), in slow motion. Both films were shot by cinematographer Michael Chapman. Finally, slow motion can be used to reverse our expectations, as in Andy and Larry Wachowski's *The Matrix* (1999; cinematographer: Bill Pope), where Neo (Keanu Reeves) dodges the bullets shot by Agent Smith (Hugo Weaving) while shooting back with a spray of slow-motion bullets as he does cartwheels on the walls—a scene made possible, of course, with advanced special-effects techniques.

By contrast, **fast motion** accelerates action by photographing it at less than the normal filming rate, then projecting it at normal speed so that it takes place cinematically more rapidly. Thus, fast motion often depicts the rapid passing of time, as F. W. Murnau uses it in *Nosferatu* (1922; cinematographers: Fritz Arno Wagner and Günther Krampf), an early screen version of the Dracula story. The coach that Count Orlok (Max Schreck) sends to fetch his agent, Hutter (Gustav von Wangenheim), travels in fast motion, and although this effect may seem silly today, its original intent was to place us in an unpredictable landscape. In *Rumble Fish* (1983; cinematographer: Stephen H. Burum), director Francis Ford Coppola employs fast-motion, high-contrast, black-and-white images of clouds moving across the sky to indicate both the passing of time and the unsettled lives of the teenagers with whom the story is concerned. In *Requiem for a Dream* (2000; cinematographer: Matthew Libatique), director Darren Aronofsky uses fast motion to sim-

ulate the experience of being high on marijuana—an effect also used by Gus Van Sant in *Drugstore Cowboy* (1989; cinematographer: Robert D. Yeoman).

Perhaps no modern director has used and abused slow and fast motion, as well as virtually every other manipulation of cinematic space and time, more than Godfrey Reggio in his *Qatsi* trilogy: *Koyaanisqatsi* (1982; cinematographer: Ron Fricke); *Powaqqatsi* (1988; cinematographers: Graham Berry and Leonidas Zourdoumis); and *Nagoyqatsi* (2002; cinematographer: Russell Lee Fine). Although Reggio's sweeping vision of the cultural and environmental decay of the modern world is lavishly depicted in poetic, even apocalyptic, images, he often relies too heavily on manipulation to make his point.

Whereas the average shot lasts ten seconds, the **long take** can run anywhere from one to ten minutes. (An ordinary roll of film runs for ten minutes, but specially fitted cameras can accommodate longer rolls of film that permit takes of anywhere from fourteen to twenty-two minutes.) One of the most elegant techniques of cinematography, the long take has the double potential of preserving both real space and real time. Ordinarily, we refer to a sequence as a series of edited shots characterized by inherent unity of theme and purpose. The long take is sometimes referred to as a *sequence shot* because it enables filmmakers to present a unified pattern of events within a single period of time in one shot. However, with the exception of such extraordinary examples as the opening of Orson Welles's *Touch of Evil* (1958; discussed earlier), the long take is rarely used for a sequence filmed in one shot. Instead, even masters of the evocative long take—directors such as F. W. Murnau, Max Ophüls, Orson Welles, William Wyler, Kenji Mizoguchi, and Stanley Kubrick—combine two or more long takes by linking them, often unobtrusively, into an apparently seamless whole.

Coupled with the moving camera, the long take also eliminates the need for separate setups for long, medium, and close-up shots. It permits the internal development of a story involving two or more lines of action without use of the editing technique called *crosscutting* that is normally employed to tell such a story. Furthermore, if a solid sense of cause and effect is essential to developing a sequence, the long take permits both the cause and the effect to be recorded in one take.

Conventional motion-picture technology limited the fluid long take that these directors were striving for, but digital technology has enabled a director to achieve it. Using a Steadicam fitted with a high-definition video camera, Russian director Aleksandr Sokurov made *Russian Ark* (2002; cinematographer: Tilman Büttner), a 96-minute historical epic filmed in one continuous shot—the longest unbroken shot in film history.

A very effective use of a long take combined with a close-up occurs in Jonathan Glazer's *Birth* (2004; cinematographer: Harris Savides), a thriller that skirts the boundaries between the believable and the absurd. Anna (Nicole Kidman), a young widow, is torn between memories of her husband, Sean, and her obsession with a ten-year-old boy, also named Sean (Cameron Bright), who claims to be the reincarnation of her dead husband. At a concert that she attends with her fiancé, Joseph (Danny Huston), Anna listens intently to a selection from an opera that is concerned partly with the incestuous relationship between two mythical characters. This theme obviously invades Anna's thoughts, as does her unnerving sexual attraction to young Sean. Cinematographer Savides devotes a full two minutes to a long take of Kidman's face, capturing the subtle shifts in her expression in a way that seems inspired by cinematographer Rudolph Maté's adoration of the face of Maria Falconetti in Carl Theodor Dreyer's *The Passion of Joan of Arc* (1928; see page 326). On one hand, Savides's haunting, long take is a declaration

1

2

3

4

The long take and the close-up Great cinematographers love great female beauty, as demonstrated by these four images from Jonathan Glazer's *Birth* (2004), in which cinematographer Harris Savides holds the camera steady on Nicole Kidman's face for two minutes. The slight changes in her expression and the position of her head, eyes, and lips as she listens to music that absorbs her attention reveal, however slightly, the depth of her thoughts.

of love for an actor's face (one of the prime purposes of the close-up); but on the other hand, the length of the shot gives Kidman the time to convey the depth of Anna's thoughts without the use of dialogue or overt action.

Special Effects

Cinema itself is a special effect, an illusion that fools the human eye and brain into perceiving motion. **Special effects** (abbreviated **SPFX or FX**) is a term reserved for technology that creates images that would be too dangerous, too expensive, or in some cases, simply impossible to achieve with the traditional cinematographic materials that we have already discussed. As spectacular as SPFX technologies and their effects can be, however, the goal of special-effects cinematography is generally to create verisimilitude—an illusion of reality or a believable alternative reality—within the imaginative world of even the most fanciful movie. Special-effects expert Mat Beck says, "The art of visual effects is the art of what you can get away with, which means you really have to study a lot about how we perceive the world in order to find out how we can trick our perceptions to make something look real when it isn't."[10]

In-Camera, Mechanical, and Laboratory Effects

The ability of movies to create illusion has always been one of their major attractions for audiences. Indeed, the first special effect appeared in Alfred Clark's *The Execution of Mary Stuart* in 1895 (cinematographer: William Heise), the year the movies were born. To depict the queen's execution, Clark photographed the actor in position, stopped filming and replaced the actor with a dummy, then started the camera and beheaded the dummy. (Incidentally, this film involved another kind of illusion: a man, Robert Thomae, played Queen Mary.)

[10]Mat Beck, qtd. in "Special Effects: Titanic and Beyond," *Nova*, produced for PBS by the Science Unit at WGBH Boston, November 3, 1998.

From that point forward, special effects appeared regularly in the films of Georges Méliès, the great illusionist, who used multiple exposures and stop-motion animation. Edwin S. Porter's *The Great Train Robbery* (1903) featured matte and composite shots, and J. Searle Dawley's *Rescued from an Eagle's Nest* (1908; cinematographer: Porter) included a mechanical eagle, created by Richard Murphy, that was the forerunner of "animatronic" creatures in contemporary films. By the mid-1920s, extraordinary effects were featured in such films as Fritz Lang's *Metropolis* (1927; cinematographers: Karl Freund, Günther Rittau, and Walter Ruttmann), for which designer Otto Hunte created the city of the future in miniature on a tabletop; Cecil B. DeMille's first version of *The Ten Commandments* (1923; cinematographers: Bert Glennon, J. Peverell Marley, Archie Stout, and Fred Westerberg), in which technicians could part the Red Sea because it was made of two miniature slabs of Jell-O;[11] and the first of four versions of *The Lost World* (1925; cinematographer: Arthur Edeson), directed by Harry O. Hoyt. The special effects in *The Lost World* were the work of Willis H. O'Brien, who went on to create the special effects in Merian C. Cooper and Ernest B. Schoedsack's *King Kong* (1933; cinematographers: Edward Linden, J. O. Taylor, Vernon L. Walker, and Kenneth Peach), in which the giant ape terrorizing New York City from the top of the Empire State Building was, in fact, a puppet.

Until the advent of computer-generated imagery, in the 1960s, such illusions were accomplished in essentially three ways: through **in-camera effects** created in the production camera (the regular camera used for shooting the rest of the film) on the original negative, through **mechanical effects** that create objects or events mechanically on the set and in front of the camera, and through **laboratory effects** created on a fresh piece of film stock.

Although computer-generated graphics and animation have virtually eclipsed the way special

[11]DeMille's 1956 version of the parting of the Red Sea (cinematographically engineered by Loyal Griggs) cost $2 million—the most expensive special effect up to that time—and involved matte shots, miniatures, 600 extras, and a 32-foot-high dam channeling tens of thousands of gallons of water.

Early special effects For Fritz Lang's *Metropolis* (1927; cinematographers: Karl Freund, Günther Rittau, and Walter Ruttmann), a pioneering science-fiction film, the city of the future was a model created by designer Otto Hunte. Special-effects photography (coordinated by Eugen Schüfftan, who developed trick-shot techniques that are still in use today) turned this miniature into a massive place on-screen, filled with awe-inspiring objects and vistas.

effects are now made, as you study and analyze SPFX in movies from the past it is helpful to know how the principal types were made. Traditionally, the first category—in-camera effects—has included such simple illusory effects as fade, wipe, dissolve, and montage. (Although these are shots in themselves, together with editing they create transitional effects or manipulate time; for definitions and examples, see "Conventions of Continuity Editing" in Chapter 8.) Other in-camera effects include split screen, superimposition, models and miniatures, glass shots, matte paintings, in-camera matte shots, and process shots.

The second category—mechanical effects—includes objects or events that are created by artists and craftspeople and placed on the set to be photographed. There are, of course, endless examples of such special effects, including the different Frankenstein masks used in the many movies featuring that character, such as Mel Brooks's *Young Frankenstein* (1974; cinematographer: Gerald Hirschfeld; makeup artist: Edwin Butterworth). Other mechanical creatures include the beast in

Ishirô Honda's Japanese cult film *Godzilla* (1954; cinematographer: Masao Tamai; special effects: Sadamasa Arikawa) and the menacing shark in Steven Spielberg's *Jaws* (1975; cinematographer: Bill Butler; special effects: Robert A. Mattey and Kevin Pike).

In the third category—laboratory effects—are more complicated procedures, such as contact printing and bipack, as well as blowups, cropping, pan and scan, flip shots, split-screen shots, and day-for-night shooting. These complex technical procedures are outside the scope of this book, but you can find complete information on them in the books by Raymond Fielding, Bruce Kawin, and Ira Konigsberg listed in the bibliography at the back of this book.

Computer-Generated Imagery

Since its first use in film in the early 1970s, computer-generated imagery (**CGI**) has transformed the motion-picture industry, particularly the making of animated, fantasy, and science-fiction movies. During the subsequent forty years, CGI improved so rapidly that the major films that used it during that time now seem almost as old-fashioned as the process shot. (A **process shot** is made of action in front of a rear-projection screen that has on it still or moving images for the background.) Yet certain achievements are memorable for innovations that are landmarks in the development of CGI. Stanley Kubrick's *2001: A Space Odyssey* (1968; special-effects designer and director: Kubrick; supervisors: Wally Veevers, Douglas Trumbull, Con Pederson, and Tom Howard; cinematographer: Geoffrey Unsworth) was the first film to seamlessly link footage shot by the camera with that prepared by the computer, and now some four decades later, its look continues to amaze audiences. Indeed, it set a standard of technical sophistication, visual elegance, integration with the story, and power to create meaning that remains unsurpassed.

Other CGI landmarks include Steven Lisberger's *TRON* (1982; cinematographer: Bruce Logan), which, through comparatively simple

Modern special effects The special effects in Stanley Kubrick's *2001: A Space Odyssey* (1968; special-effects designer: Kubrick; supervisors: Wally Veevers, Douglas Trumbull, Con Pederson, and Tom Howard; cinematographer: Geoffrey Unsworth) took up more than 60 percent of the movie's production budget and required nearly eighteen months to complete. These SPFX, representing the state of the art at the time, add to the movie's cinematic beauty and philosophical depth. Early in the movie, Dr. Heywood R. Floyd, an American scientist, is dispatched via shuttle to Clavius, a U.S. base on the moon, to investigate reports of unusual happenings there. Here we see a pod, launched from the shuttle, as it approaches its final landing via a platform moving down a red-lit shaft into the base's quarters. Douglas Trumbull, whose technological contributions to the art of the movies were acknowledged by a special Oscar in 2012, was also responsible for the astonishing effects in Steven Spielberg's *Close Encounters of the Third Kind* (1977), Ridley Scott's *Blade Runner* (1982), and Terence Malick's *The Tree of Life* (2011).

SPFX, transports a computer hacker inside a computer; the *Star Wars* trilogy, consisting of *Star Wars* (1977; director: George Lucas; cinematographer: Gilbert Taylor), *The Empire Strikes Back* (1980; director: Irvin Kershner; cinematographer: Peter Suschitzky), and *Return of the Jedi* (1983; director: Richard Marquand; cinematographer: Alan Hume); Barry Levinson's *Young Sherlock Holmes* (1985; cinematographers: Stephen Goldblatt and Stephen Smith), which, in the "Glass Man" sequence, created a new standard for image resolution by laser-scanning the image directly onto the film stock; and James Cameron's *The Abyss* (1989; cinematographer: Mikael Salomon), which won the 1989 Oscar for Best Visual Effects, marking Hollywood's official embrace of the new technologies. Cameron's other movies, including *Terminator 2: Judgment Day* (1991; cinematographer: Adam Greenberg) and *Titanic* (1997; cinematographer: Russell Carpenter) were equally innovative.

In 1993, Steven Spielberg's *Jurassic Park* (cinematographer: Dean Cundey) became an instant classic with its believable computer-generated dinosaurs, and Cundey's work on Brad Silberling's *Casper* (1995) introduced the first computer-generated lead and talking figure. In 1988, Robert Zemeckis's *Who Framed Roger Rabbit* (cinematographer: Dean Cundey) combined computer-generated imagery with actual settings and characters, so cartoon-like images entered the real world. Zemeckis reversed that pattern in *Forrest Gump* (1994; cinematographer: Don Burgess) by using CGI to insert footage of Gump (Tom Hanks) into real footage of Presidents Richard Nixon and Lyndon Johnson and former Beatle John Lennon.

In the last ten years, the major CGI achievements have been even more astonishing. Andy and Lana

A wholly convincing cyber-character The character of Davy Jones (Bill Nighy, *center*) flanked by his equally frightening shipmates, made its debut in Gore Verbinski's *Pirates of the Caribbean: Dead Man's Chest* (2006; visual effects: John Knoll, Hal Hickel, Charles Gibson, and Allen Hall). A creation of the most advanced special effects—including 3-D computer-generated imagery and motion capture technology—he is a wholly convincing cyber-character, both human and inhuman. Jones, a physically and morally hideous creature, uses his many supernatural powers to inflict cruelty on virtually everyone with whom he comes in contact. His head resembles an octopus, with long tentacles forming a "beard"; he lacks a nose, breathing through a tentacle on the left side of his face, and has surprisingly blue eyes. He appears again in the third film of the *Pirates of the Caribbean* series, Verbinski's *At World's End* (2007), in which he is killed.

Wachowski's *The Matrix* (1999; cinematographer: Bill Pope) used still cameras to photograph actors in flight from all angles and then digitized them into moving images to replicate what might have been a shot from a moving camera if any moving camera were capable of such complex work. The sequels—*The Matrix Reloaded* and *The Matrix Revolutions* (both 2003), also directed by the Wachowskis and photographed by Bill Pope—continued to introduce new CGI techniques. In this new world, movies are more likely to be set in wholly imaginary places such as those depicted in Peter Jackson's *Lord of the Rings* trilogy (2001–3; cinematographer: Andrew Lesnie). So it was refreshing to see CGI used to re-create ancient Rome in Ridley Scott's *Gladiator* (2000; cinematographer: John Mathieson).

Much of the research and development that makes so many of these movies possible comes from George Lucas's special-effects company Industrial Light & Magic, where the visual-effects supervisor, Stefen Fangmeier, was behind the technology that made possible some of the movies mentioned here—including *Terminator 2: Judgment Day* (1991) and *Casper* (1995)—as well as the impressive historical re-creation of the world of the eighteenth-century British navy in Peter Weir's *Master and Commander: The Far Side of the World* (2003; cinematographer: Russell Boyd). With the increasing complexity of CGI and the investment in human and technical resources required for its production, independent companies—whose artists and technicians usually work in consultation with the director, production designer, and director of photography—have become increasingly responsible for creating these effects. This artistry, now virtually a separate industry within the film industry, is expensive, but it has achieved astonishingly realistic effects at costs acceptable to producers. In addition to Industrial Light & Magic, other principal CGI firms are Pixar Animation Studios (now a part of Walt Disney), Blue Sky Studios (Fox), and Pacific Data Images (Dream Works SKG).

Motion capture (also known as motion tracking or mocap) is a specific CGI effect in which a live-action subject wears a bodysuit fitted with reflective markers that allows a computer to record each movement as digital images; this is then translated, with as much manipulation as desired, into models on which the screen figures are based. When the images include facial contours and expressions, the process is called *performance capture*. These techniques are used to create virtual reality in animated, experimental, and feature movies, as well as in video games. Hironobu Sakaguchi and Moto Sakakibara's *Final Fantasy: The Spirits Within* (2001; cinematographer: Sakakibara), the first major motion picture to use the technique to generate all of its "cast," broke new ground in the world of special effects by featuring characters that—while convincingly human in features and motions—were entirely computer-generated. Other movies followed, including Peter Jackson's *Lord of the Rings* trilogy (2001–3; cinematographer: Andrew Lesnie), in which the character of Gollum was created by motion capture; Robert Zemeckis's *The Polar Express* (2004; cinematographers: Don Burgess and Robert Presley); and *Beowulf* (2007; cinematographer: Robert Presley). Motion capture and performance capture, as well as rotoscoping—another version of motion and performance capture in which animators trace over live-action film movement for use in animated sequences—constitute a provocative sign of what might happen to the design and production of movies in years to come.

Director David Fincher's *The Curious Case of Benjamin Button* (2008; cinematographer: Claudio Miranda) raises another issue related to motion and performance capture: actors' credits. The story is about a man who is born old and grows younger, and Brad Pitt, who plays the lead character, insisted on appearing as Button from old age to infancy. Since the handsome actor is relatively young, Fincher relied on electronic special effects to create the illusion of Button's reverse aging. To accomplish this, Fincher first photographed every facial expression of which Pitt was capable. This provided the base from which 150 visual artists created images reflecting the decrease in Button's aging (i.e., skin and hair) over the years. Second, Fincher photographed a group of "body actors"—actors whose bodies substitute for the credited actor—playing the younger and older Button. Images of Pitt's digitally altered face were then electronically inserted onto those body images to create the finished product. We know that many artists worked in the service of this single actor/character and that Pitt and six other actors actually played Benjamin Button. We also recognize that acting involves both facial expressions and physical movements, but the complex process used here raises a question: who deserves the credit for creating the character of Benjamin Button? While all seven actors are listed in the movie's credits, only Pitt was nominated for an Academy Award for Best Actor in a Leading Role. But the "actor" in this case is an electronic compilation.

Wherever special effects take movie production in the future, there is the ever-present danger that all the SPFX in action, adventure, and science-fiction films will dazzle us but do little to increase our understanding of the world we live in or the drama of human life.

Analyzing Cinematography

This chapter has provided an overview of the major components of cinematography—the process by which a movie's mise-en-scène is recorded onto film or some other motion-picture medium. More than just a process, however, cinematography is very much a language through which directors and their collaborators (most notably, directors of photogra-phy) can convey meaning, transmit narrative information, and influence the emotional responses of viewers. Now that you know something about the basic cinematographic tools available to filmmakers, you can pay greater attention to the particulars of this language while looking at movies.

Screening Checklist: Cinematography

✔ Determine whether or not the cinematographic aspects of the film—the qualities of the film stock, lighting, lenses, framing, angles, camera movement, and use of long takes—add up to an overall look. If so, try to describe its qualities.

✔ Take note of moments in the film in which the images are conveying information that is not reflected in characters' action and dialogue. These moments are often crucial to the development of a movie's themes, narrative, and meaning.

✔ Are special effects used in the film? To what extent? Are they appropriate to, and effective in, telling the story? Are they effective in making something look real when it isn't?

✔ Keep track of instances in which the film uses shots other than the medium shot (MS)—for instance, extreme close-ups (ECUs) or extreme long shots (ELSs). What role are these shots playing in the film?

✔ Also keep track of camera angles other than eye-level shots. If there are high- or low-angle shots, determine whether or not they are POV shots. That is, is the high or low angle meant to represent another character's point of view? If so, what does the angle convey about that character's state of mind? If not, what does it convey about the person or thing in the frame?

✔ As you evaluate crucial scenes, pay attention to the composition of shots within the scene. Are the compositions balanced in a way that conforms to the rule of thirds, or are the elements within the frame arranged in a less "painterly" composition? In either case, try to describe how the composition contributes to the scene overall.

✔ Can you determine whether the colors of a shot or scene have been artificially manipulated through the use of color filters, different film stocks, or chemical or digital manipulation in order to create a mood or indicate a state of mind?

✔ Pay attention to camera movement in the film. Sometimes camera movement is used solely to produce visual excitement or to demonstrate technological virtuosity on the part of the filmmaker. Other times it is playing an important functional role in the film's narrative. Be alert to these differences, and take note of meaningful uses of camera movement.

✔ Note when the cinematography calls attention to itself. Is this a mistake or misjudgment on the filmmakers' part, or is it intentional? If intentional, what purpose is served by making the cinematography so noticeable?

Questions for Review

1. What are the differences among a setup, a shot, and a take?
2. A cinematographer depends on two crews of workers. What is each crew responsible for?
3. How the lighting for any movie looks is determined, in part, by its source and direction. Explain these terms and the effect each has on the overall lighting.
4. What are the four major lenses used on movie cameras? What is the principal characteristic of the image that each lens creates?
5. In terms of proximity to the camera, what are the three most commonly used shots in a movie? What is the principle by which they are distinguished?
6. What is the rule of thirds?
7. The movie camera can shoot from various angles. What are they? What does each imply in terms of meaning? Do these implications always hold true?
8. What are the basic types of camera movement?
9. What is a long take? What can it achieve that a short take cannot? What is the difference between a long take and a long shot?

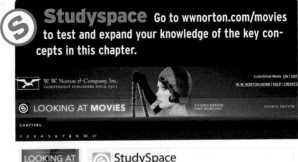

10. Special effects create images that might not be possible with traditional cinematography. What are the basic ways to create special effects?

Movies Described or Illustrated in This Chapter

2001: A Space Odyssey (1968). Stanley Kubrick, director.
The Abyss (1989). James Cameron, director.
Applause (1929). Rouben Mamoulian, director.
Barry Lyndon (1975). Stanley Kubrick, director.
Badlands (1973). Terence Malick, director.
The Birds (1963). Alfred Hitchcock, director.
Birth (2004). Jonathan Glazer, director.
The Birth of a Nation (1915). D. W. Griffith, director.
The Book of Eli (2010). Albert Hughes and Allen Hughes, directors.
The Bourne Supremacy (2004). Paul Greengrass, director.
Bride of Frankenstein (1935). James Whale, director.
Charisma (1999). Kyoshi Kurosawa, director.
Citizen Kane (1941). Orson Welles, director.
Cloverfield (2008). Matt Reeves, director.
The Counterfeiters (2007). Stefan Ruzowitzky, director.
The Crying Game (1992). Neil Jordan, director.
The Curious Case of Benjamin Button (2008). David Fincher, director.
Days of Heaven (1978). Terrence Malick, director.
The Diving Bell and the Butterfly (2007). Julian Schnabel, director.
Dogville (2003). Lars von Trier, director.

DVD The tutorials for this chapter provide more information about lighting, shot types, camera angles, lenses, moving camera effects, and point of view.

LOOKING AT MOVIES

CHAPTER 6: CINEMATOGRAPHY

LIGHTING
SHOT TYPES AND IMPLIED PROXIMITY
CAMERA ANGLES
POINT OF VIEW
ZOOM AND MOVING CAMERA EFFECTS
THE MOVING CAMERA
FOCAL LENGTH

MAIN MENU

Do the Right Thing (1989). Spike Lee, director.

Dr. Strangelove or: How I Learned to Stop Worrying and Love the Bomb (1964). Stanley Kubrick, director.

Drugstore Cowboy (1989). Gus Van Sant, director.

Gladiator (2000). Ridley Scott, director.

The Godfather (1972). Francis Ford Coppola, director.

Gone with the Wind (1939). Victor Fleming, director.

Goodfellas (1990). Martin Scorsese, director.

The Graduate (1967). Mike Nichols, director.

The Grand Illusion (1937). Jean Renoir, director.

The Grifters (1990). Stephen Frears, director.

High Noon (1952). Fred Zinnemann, director.

The Hurt Locker (2008). Kathryn Bigelow, director.

In Cold Blood (1967). Richard Brooks, director.

Juliet of the Spirits (1965). Federico Fellini, director.

Jurassic Park (1993). Steven Spielberg, director.

The King's Speech (2010). Tom Hooper, director.

Koyaanisqatsi (1982). Godfrey Reggio, director.

The Little Foxes (1941). William Wyler, director.

The Lives of Others (2006). Florian Henckel von Donnersmarck, director.

Lola Montès (1955). Max Ophüls, director.

The Lord of the Rings trilogy (2001–3). Peter Jackson, director.

Love Liza (2002). Todd Louiso, director.

Love Me Tonight (1932). Rouben Mamoulian, director.

M (1931). Fritz Lang, director.

The Maltese Falcon (1941). John Huston, director.

Manhattan (1979). Woody Allen, director.

The Matrix (1999). Andy Wachowski and Larry Wachowski, directors.

Nagoyqatsi (2002). Godfrey Reggio, director.

North by Northwest (1959). Alfred Hitchcock, director.

Nosferatu (1922). F. W. Murnau, director.

Notorious (1946). Alfred Hitchcock, director.

The Passion of Joan of Arc (1928). Carl Theodor Dreyer, director.

Philadelphia (1993). Jonathan Demme, director.

Pirates of the Caribbean: Dead Man's Chest (2006). Gore Verbinski, director.

Pleasantville (1998). Gary Ross, director.

Powaqqatsi (1988). Godfrey Reggio, director.

Raging Bull (1980). Martin Scorsese, director.

Requiem for a Dream (2000). Darren Aronofsky, director.

Return of the Jedi (1983). Richard Marquand, director.

Rosemary's Baby (1968). Roman Polanski, director.

Rumble Fish (1983). Francis Ford Coppola, director.

The Scarlet Empress (1934). Josef von Sternberg, director.

The Searchers (1956). John Ford, director.

The Seventh Seal (1957). Ingmar Bergman, director.

The Shining (1980). Stanley Kubrick, director.

The Social Network (2010). David Fincher, director.

Some Like It Hot (1959). Billy Wilder, director.

Stagecoach (1939). John Ford, director.

The Strange Love of Martha Ivers (1946). Lewis Milestone, director.

Sunset Boulevard (1950). Billy Wilder, director.

Sweet Smell of Success (1957). Alexander Mackendrick, director.

Talk to Her (2002). Pedro Almodóvar, director.

The Third Man (1949). Carol Reed, director.

THX 1138 (1971). George Lucas, director.

Titanic (1997). James Cameron, director.

T-Men (1947). Anthony Mann, director.

Touch of Evil (1958). Orson Welles, director.

Trouble in Paradise (1932). Ernst Lubitsch, director.

2001: A Space Odyssey (1968). Stanley Kubrick, director.

The King's Speech (2010). Tom Hooper, director. Pictured: Colin Firth.

CHAPTER SEVEN

Acting

After reading this chapter, you should be able to

✔ Explain how the coming of sound into the movie industry affected acting.

✔ Describe how movie acting today differs from that of the classical studio era.

✔ Explain why the relationship between the actor and the camera is so important.

✔ Describe the criteria used to cast actors.

✔ Explain the differences between naturalistic and nonnaturalistic movie acting.

✔ Define *improvisational acting*.

✔ Explain the potential effects on acting of framing, composition, lighting, shot types, and shot lengths.

What Is Acting?

When Richard M. Nixon was president of the United States, the public generally regarded him as a cold, calculating politician. So when Anthony Hopkins played him in Oliver Stone's *Nixon* (1995), many were astonished at the depth of humanity they saw on-screen. Hopkins persuaded audiences that Nixon had unexpected dimensions, turning him into a far more sympathetic character. Stone achieved a similar result with Josh Brolin's portrayal of President George W. Bush in *W* (2008).

Screen acting of this kind is an art, one in which an actor uses imagination, intelligence, psychology, memory, vocal technique, facial expressions, body language, and an overall knowledge of the filmmaking process to realize, under the director's guidance, the character created by the screenwriter. The performance and effect of that art can seem mysterious and magical when we're enjoying a movie, and acting turns out to be even more complex than we might at first assume.

Our initial interest in a movie is almost always sparked by the actors featured in it. As the critic Pauline Kael said, "I think so much of what we respond to in fictional movies is acting. That's one of the elements that's often left out when people talk theoretically about the movies. They forget it's the human material we go to see."[1] The power of some actors—Angelina Jolie or George Clooney, for example—to draw an audience is frequently more important to a movie's financial success than any other factor. For this reason, some observers regard screen actors as mere commodities, cogs in a machine of promotion and hype designed only to generate revenue. Although even the most accomplished screen actors can be used as fodder for promotional campaigns, such a view overlooks the many complex and important ways that skillful acting can influence the narrative, style, and meanings of a film. Writer-director-producer-actor Orson Welles, who questioned nearly every other aspect of filmmaking dogma, firmly believed in the importance of acting: "I don't understand how movies exist independently of the actor—I truly don't."[2]

Despite its central importance, acting is also the aspect of filmmaking over which directors have the least precise control. Directors may describe literally what they want from their principal collaborators—for example, screenwriters or costume designers—but they can only suggest to actors what they want. That becomes quite different when directors-screenwriters such as Joel and Ethan Coen write parts specifically for the actors whom they hope to cast. This has led to memorable performances—for example, by Frances McDormand in *Fargo* (1996), Javier Bardem in *No Country for Old Men* (2007), and John Malkovich in *Burn after Reading* (2008)—in which the director, screenwriter, and actor enjoy an unusually close collaboration. However, screen actors, or at least experienced screen actors, know that the essential relationship is between them and the camera—not between them and the director or even the audience. Actors interpret the director's guidance in the area between them and the lens—an intimate and narrowly defined space that necessarily concentrates much of the actors' energy on their faces. Through composition, close-ups, camera angles and movements, and

[1]Leonard Quart, "I Still Love Going to Movies: An Interview with Pauline Kael," *Cineaste* 25, no. 2 (2000): 10.
[2]Orson Welles and Peter Bogdanovich, *This Is Orson Welles*, ed. Jonathan Rosenbaum (New York: HarperCollins, 1992), p. 262.

The camera and the actor English film actor Michael Caine has compared the movie camera to an impossibly attentive lover who "hangs on your every word, your every look; she can't take her eyes off you. She is listening to and recording everything you do, however minutely you do it."[3] That appears to be exactly what the camera is doing in this expressive close-up of Caine as Thomas Fowler in Phillip Noyce's *The Quiet American* (2002). The business and art of Hollywood moviemaking intersect when "bankable" stars such as Michael Caine (and, in this example, his costar Brendan Fraser, left, back to camera) take on challenging, unglamorous roles that transcend their physical attractiveness.

other cinematic techniques, movie actors always come closer to the audience, and appear larger, than actors on the stage do.

The camera makes possible an attention to detail that was impossible before the invention of cinema, mainly because stage acting forced actors to project their voices and their gestures to the back of the theater. Screen acting, as an experience, can be as tight and intimate as examining a painting at arm's length. As American screen actor Joan Crawford put it, "A movie actor paints with the tiniest brush."[4]

Movie Actors

The challenges facing movie actors in interpreting and pretending to be their characters, and the responsibilities involved in performing those characters on the screen, are very different from the challenges and responsibilities facing stage actors.

[3]Michael Caine, *Acting in Film: An Actor's Take on Movie Making* (New York: Applause, 1990), p. 4.
[4]Joan Crawford, qtd. in Lillian Ross and Helen Ross, *The Player: A Profile of an Art* (New York: Simon & Schuster, 1962), p. 66.

Stage actors convey their interpretations of the characters they play directly to the audience through voice, gesture, and movement. By contrast, movie actors, using gesture and movement—and voice since the coming of sound—convey their characters directly to the camera. In turn, that camera is the single element that most radically differentiates the movie actor's performance. Stage actors play to a large audience and must project the voice so that it can be heard throughout the theater, and avoid the soft speech, subtle facial expressions, or small gestures that are fundamental tools of the movie actor.

Stage actors, who must memorize their lines, have the advantage of speaking them in the order in which they were written, which, in turn, makes it much easier to maintain psychological, emotional, and physical continuity in a performance as the play proceeds. By contrast, movie actors, who are subject to the shooting schedule—which, for budgetary and logistical reasons, determines that most shots are made out of the sequence in which they appear in the screenplay—learn only those lines that they need for the moment. Therefore, movie actors bear the additional burden, particularly on their memory, of creating continuity between related shots, even though the shots may have been made days, weeks, or even months apart.

Toward the goal of maintaining continuity (as we will discuss in Chapter 8), editing is a major factor in putting shots together and thus helping to create the performance. During the presentation of a play, the stage actor performs each scene only once; during the shooting of a movie, the actor may be asked to do many takes before the director is satisfied with the performance. Before a shot is made, the movie actor must be prepared to wait, sometimes for long periods, while camera, lighting, or sound equipment is moved or readjusted; the stage actor faces no such delays or interruptions.

Although the theater and the movies are both collaborative arts, once the curtain goes up, stage actors need not think much about the backstage crew, for the crew will perform scenery or lighting changes according to a fixed schedule. Movie actors, however, while playing directly to the camera, are always aware of dozens of people standing around just outside the camera's range, doing their jobs but also watching and listening to everything the actors do. Some of the people are there because they have to be (e.g., the director, script supervisor, cinematographer, sound recordist, makeup artist, hairstylist); others are there waiting to make the necessary changes in scenery, properties, or lighting required for the next shot. Over the years, some temperamental actors have succeeded in having removed from the set all but the most essential personnel, but that is an exception to conventional practice. Traditionally, however, movie sets have been closed to visitors, particularly the media.

Although there are many types of actors—probably as many types as there are actors themselves—we can, for the purposes of this discussion, identify four key types:

1. actors who take their personae from role to role (personality actors)
2. actors who deliberately play against our expectations of their personae
3. actors who seem to be different in every role (chameleon actors)
4. actors, often nonprofessionals or people who have achieved success in another field (sports or music, for example), who are cast to bring verisimilitude to a part

In our everyday lives, each of us creates a persona, the image of character and personality that we want to show the outside world. For movie actors, those personae are their appearance and mannerisms of moving and delivering dialogue—unique creations that are consistent at least on some level from role to role and from performance to performance. Actors' personae are usually (but not always) rooted in their natural behavior, personality, and physicality. Current actors defined by their personae include Tom Cruise, Cameron Diaz, and Will Smith. Paul Giamatti is not, by Hollywood standards, a leading man, yet in Richard J. Lewis's *Barney's Version* (2010), this actor—whose persona might be described as an overweight, balding, neurotic but likable loser—channels these attributes and attitudes in a way that makes us care about his character, Barney Panofsky. Even more versatile

LOOKING AT MOVIES
PERSONA AND PERFORMANCE

DVD This short tutorial discusses the importance of persona to our experience of acting performances.

actors—not just those who are popular action or comedy stars—rely on persona, including Susan Sarandon, Sean Penn, Morgan Freeman, Jack Nicholson, William H. Macy, Chris Cooper, Ewan McGregor, and Benicio Del Toro.

For many movie actors, the persona is the key to their career, as well as an important part of film marketing and why we choose particular movies over others. One reason audiences go to movies is to see a certain kind of story. That's a big part of what the concept of genre is all about. You go to a romantic comedy, an action movie, a horror film, or a comic-book adaptation because you know what to expect and you want what you expect. Having made your choice on the basis of story, you should get familiar and appealing narrative structures, cinematic conventions, character types, dramatic situations, and payoffs.

The same thing goes for persona-identified actors like Tom Cruise. He's not only good-looking, but he projects an interesting balance of arrogance and vulnerability that appeals to many viewers. When you go to a Tom Cruise movie (the kind where the star's name is the most important factor in your choice), you have an expectation of the kind of performance he's going to give you, based on his persona, and you expect to see that performance,

Cate Blanchett's complete transformation as Bob Dylan In *I'm Not There* (2007; director: Todd Haynes), Cate Blanchett transforms her glamorous self into Jude, a skinny, ragged, androgynous folksinger at the beginning of his career: Bob Dylan. In this image, Jude is responding to an obnoxious British journalist who questions his motives in switching from acoustic to electric guitar in 1965. To understand how accomplished Blanchett's portrayal is, compare her Dylan with the real Dylan as he appears in D. A. Pennebaker's *Dont Look Back* (1967) or Martin Scorsese's *No Direction Home: Bob Dylan* (2005).

that persona, within the context of a certain kind of story. Part of the fun comes from seeing that persona in different kinds of movies, enjoying your favorite persona interacting with a particular role or genre. So part of the reason you might go to see Cruise in Stanley Kubrick's *Eyes Wide Shut* (1999) is to see what he makes of Dr. William Harford, a Manhattan physician facing serious sexual and moral issues; or, in Michael Mann's *Collateral* (2004), how he portrays Vincent, a hit man; how he pushes the vulnerable side of his persona and unfortunately becomes the stereotype of a concerned dad in Steven Spielberg's *War of the Worlds* (2005); or how he manages to sustain a fresh portrayal of the character of IMF agent Ethan Hunt in each movie in the *Mission Impossible* series (1996, 2000, 2006, 2011).

Sometimes an actor with a familiar, popular persona takes on a role that goes against what we expect—for example, Jack Nicholson as Warren Schmidt in Alexander Payne's *About Schmidt* (2002) or Cate Blanchett as Jude in Todd Haynes's *I'm Not There* (2007). A major factor affecting our enjoyment of actors in such roles is not just the role, but the strange sensation of seeing an actor whose persona we have come to know well play a totally different sort of role—in Nicholson's case, the normally crafty, strong, menacing man as a powerless, mundane, befuddled, and cuckolded insurance salesman. In Blanchett's career, we are astonished to see an actor known for her regal beauty—in such roles as Queen Elizabeth I in Shekhar Kapur's *Elizabeth* (1998) or Lady Galadriel in Peter Jackson's *The Lord of the Rings* trilogy (2001–3)—undergo a complete physical transformation as Jude, one of six different interpretations, by six different actors, of Bob Dylan in Todd Haynes's *I'm Not There* (2007). Blanchett, famous for her ability to change her distinctly Australian accent to meet the needs of any role—speaking the Queen's English as Elizabeth and Galadriel, or with a flat, locale-less accent as a Susan Jones, a California housewife in Alejandro González Iñárritu's *Babel* (2006)—hits the mark squarely with her interpretation of Dylan's twangy, midwestern speech. In creating her gender-bending portrait of a diffident, slightly androgynous-looking singer, she uses every technique in the actor's stock besides her voice: movements and gestures, wig, makeup, eyeglasses, costumes, and props.

On the other side of the acting scale is the chameleon actor—named for the lizard that can make quick, frequent changes in its appearance in response to the environment. Chameleon actors adapt their look, mannerisms, and delivery to suit the role. They surprise us as persona actors when they are cast, as Jack Nicholson or Charlize Theron, in a role we do not expect—one that extends their range. Take, for example, Jeff Bridges, who often looks so different in roles that he's unrecognizable at first: Starman/Scott Hayden in John Carpenter's *Starman* (1984), Preston Tucker in Francis Ford Coppola's *Tucker: The Man and His Dream* (1988), Obadiah Stane in John Favreau's *Iron Man* (2008), or Rooster Cogburn in Ethan and Joel Coen's *True Grit* (2010). Indeed, along with such multitalented colleagues as Leonardo DiCaprio, Brad Pitt, and Christian Bale, he is a marvel of flexibility.

Johnny Depp, an actor who makes quick and frequent changes in the roles he plays, has reached star status without any fixed persona. Although he's earned the reputation as the ideal *nonnaturalistic* actor for such Tim Burton movies as *Edward Scissorhands* (1990), *Sweeney Todd: The Demon Barber of Fleet Street* (2007), *Alice in Wonderland* (2010), and *Dark Shadows* (2012), he's also played an astonishing range of very different roles, such as Raoul Duke/Hunter S. Thompson in

[1]

[2]

[3]

The versatile Johnny Depp A contemporary actor of style and substance, Johnny Depp has exhibited impressive flexibility both in the roles he chooses and the techniques he employs to convey his characters' often complex emotional lives. [1] As Gilbert in Lasse Hallström's moving drama *What's Eating Gilbert Grape* (1993), he plays a man who tenderly looks after Arnie (Leonard DiCaprio, *left*), his younger brother with a developmental disability. [2] In Mike Newell's *Donnie Brasco* (1997), in a complete change of pace, Depp plays an FBI agent who, under the alias Donnie Brasco, infiltrates a New York crime family. Benjamin "Lefty" Ruggiero (Al Pacino), a minor gang member who's going nowhere in the mob, makes Donnie his protégé with the hope that he'll be successful. In this image, Lefty tells Donnie (*right*) that if he successfully kills an adversary he'll be a "made man" (i.e., a full-fledged member of the gang). Donnie knows that he's betrayed Lefty and that when this assignment is over, Lefty will be arrested. Depp masterfully shows how Donnie undergoes a fascinating psychological change, slowly becoming attracted to a life of crime rather than fighting it, but ultimately remaining true to his real job. Lasse Hallström's romantic comedy *Chocolat* (2000) is a slight tale about two free spirits who find themselves in a very conservative French village, some of whose inhabitants regard them as undesirable. Depp is Roux, a roguish, Irish "river rat," seen here [3] with Vianne (Juliet Binoche), a French chocolate maker. Their affair doesn't amount to much, but this is a role that Depp was born to play, and he makes the most of it, Irish accent and all.

Terry Gilliam's *Fear and Loathing in Las Vegas* (1998); the cocaine king George Jung in Ted Demme's *Blow* (2001); Sir James Matthew Barrie, the author of *Peter Pan*, in Marc Forster's *Finding Neverland* (2004); Lord Rochester, the seventeenth-century English poet, in Laurence Dunmore's *The Libertine* (2004); and gangster John Dillinger in Michael Mann's *Public Enemies* (2009). In the current phase of his career, among other roles, he's played the over-the-top character of Captain Jack Sparrow in the *Pirates of the Caribbean* series: *The Curse of the Black Pearl* (2003), *Dead Man's Chest* (2006), *At World's End* (2007), and *On Stranger Tides* (2011). Gore Verbinski directed the first three films and Rob Marshall, the last. These swashbuckling pirate comedies have had enormous success with audiences, but many critics feel that Depp has compromised his overall achievement as an actor with this role.

Finally, there is the nonprofessional actor—someone who has achieved success in another field who is cast to bring verisimilitude to a part. Examples include football great Brett Favre playing himself in Bobby and Peter Farrelly's *There's Something about Mary* (1998); rap star Eminem playing Jimmy "B-Rabbit" Smith, Jr., a rapper whose rise to superstar status parallels his own, in Curtis Hanson's *8 Mile* (2002); fashion designer Isaac Mizrahi playing an art director in Woody Allen's *Hollywood Ending* (2002); and rapper 50 Cent playing Marcus, a character loosely based on his own life, in Jim Sheridan's *Get Rich or Die Tryin'* (2005). With these actors essentially playing themselves, there is very little distinction between the person and the part.

Whereas previous generations of stage actors knew that their duty was to convey emotion through recognized conventions of speech and gesture (mannerisms), screen actors have enjoyed a certain freedom to adopt individual styles that communicate emotional meaning through subtle—and highly personal—gestures, expressions, and varieties of intonation. American screen actor Barbara Stanwyck credited director Frank Capra with teaching her that "if you can think it, you can make the audience know it. . . . On the stage, it's mannerisms. On the screen, your range is shown in your eyes."[5] In addition, many different types of inspiration fuel screen acting; many factors guide actors toward their performances in front of the camera.

Consider American movie actor Sissy Spacek, who has been nominated six times for the Academy Award for Best Actress in a Leading Role and who won for her performance as country singer Loretta Lynn in Michael Apted's *Coal Miner's Daughter* (1980). We might say that Spacek's appearance—diminutive figure; pale red hair; large, open, very blue eyes; sharp, turned-up nose; abundant freckles; and Texas twang—has destined her to play a certain type of role: a sweet, seemingly simple and frail, but ultimately strong, perhaps strange and even otherworldly woman. Spacek brings out the depths within her characters, however, making each unique, believable, and easy to connect with or at least care about.

Depending on what the role calls for, Spacek can make herself look plain (avoiding makeup and hairstyling) or beautiful. Between the ages of twenty-four and twenty-seven, she played three characters in their teens, all childlike and somewhat naive. In Terrence Malick's *Badlands* (1973), she plays Holly, whose unemotional narration, taken from her flat yet poetic diary entries, contrasts markedly with her physical passion for Kit (Martin Sheen), a murderer who takes her on a horrifying odyssey. In Brian De Palma's *Carrie* (1976), a horror movie based on a novel by Stephen King, she plays the title character, a lonely, misunderstood teenager raised by a fundamentalist mother, tormented by her conceited schoolmates, and possessing the telekinetic ability to perform vengeful acts. In Robert Altman's *3 Women* (1977), she plays Pinky Rose, perhaps the most enigmatic of these three characters: vulnerable, unsophisticated, sensitive to what others think of her, and clumsy, but also shrewd in getting what she wants and psychologically haunted by what seems to be a dream of the past. Spacek's recent roles, each character and performance distinct from the others, include Ruth Fowler in Todd Field's *In the Bedroom* (2001), Alice Aimes in Niki Caro's

[5]Barbara Stanwyck, qtd. in *Actors on Acting for the Screen: Roles and Collaborations*, ed. Doug Tomlinson (New York: Garland, 1994), p. 524.

North Country (2005), and Maggie in Hunter Hill and Perry Moore's *Lake City* (2008).

Spacek recalls how three very different directors helped bring out these three very different types of screen performance:

> From Terry Malick I learned how to approach a character. . . . With Terry you feel an incredible intimacy. We spent a lot of time just talking about our lives, remembering things that help you to tie the character [to] your own life. . . . Bob [Altman] works by bringing elements together, not expecting anything—he brings things together to capture the unexpected. Brian [De Palma] approaches films more like a science project. With Brian I learned to work with the camera. . . . [E]verything was storyboarded. . . . You can act your guts out and the camera can miss it. But one little look, if you know how it's going to be framed, can have a thousand times more impact.[6]

Each directorial style requires something different from actors. Malick, encouraging actors to identify with characters, promotes a style loosely referred to as method acting. Altman, favoring spontaneity and unpredictability in actors' performances, encourages improvisation. De Palma, choosing neither of these two roads, pushes his actors to see their performances from a cinematographic point of view, to explicitly imagine how their gestures and expressions will look on-screen. In so doing, he essentially encourages actors to think more than to feel, to perform their roles almost as if they are highly skilled technicians whose main task is to control one aspect of the mise-en-scène (performance), much as set designers control the look and feel of sets, sound mixers control sound, directors of photography control cinematography, and so on.

No matter what type a movie actor is—how definite or changeable the persona is, how varied the roles are, how successful the career is—we tend to blur the distinction between the actor on-screen and the person offscreen. The heroes of today's world are performers—athletes, musicians, actors—and a vast media industry exists to keep them in the public eye and to encourage us to believe that they are every bit as fascinating in real life as they are on the screen. Inevitably, some movie actors become rich and famous without having much art or craft in what they do. Essentially, they walk through their movies, seldom playing any character other than themselves. Fortunately, for every one of these actors there are many more talented actors who take their work seriously; try, whenever possible, to extend the range of roles that they play; and learn to adapt to the constantly shifting trends of moviemaking and public taste. One definition of great acting is that it should look effortless—an achievement that takes talent, training, discipline, experience, and hard work. It also takes the skills necessary for dealing with the pressures that range from getting older (and thus becoming more apt to be replaced by a younger, better-looking actor) to fulfilling a producer's expectation that you will succeed in carrying a multimillion-dollar production and making it a profitable success.

As we continue this discussion of acting, remember that it is not actors' personal lives that count but rather their ability to interpret and portray certain characters. In today's world, where the media report actors' every offscreen activity, especially indiscretions, maintaining the focus required for good acting poses a challenge. Although the media have always done this, the behavior of some of today's actors is not only more reckless, but also, is seldom covered up by a studio's public-relations department as was done in Hollywood's golden age.

The Evolution of Screen Acting

Early Screen-Acting Styles

The people on the screen in the very first movies were not actors but ordinary people playing themselves. The early films caught natural, everyday actions—feeding a baby, leaving work, yawning, walking up and down stairs, swinging a baseball bat, sneezing—in a simple, realistic manner, and "acting" was simply a matter of trying to ignore the presence of the camera as it recorded the action. In the early

[6]Sissy Spacek, qtd. ibid., p. 518.

1900s, filmmakers started to tell stories with their films and thus needed professional actors. Most stage actors at the time scorned film acting, however, and refused to take work in the fledgling industry.

Therefore, the first screen actors were usually rejects from the stage or fresh-faced amateurs eager to break into the emerging film industry. Lack of experience (or talent) wasn't the only hurdle facing them. Because no standard language of cinematic expression or any accepted tradition of film direction existed at the time, these first actors had little option but to adopt the acting style favored in the nineteenth-century theater and try to adapt it to their screen roles. The resulting quaint, unintentionally comical style consists of exaggerated gestures, overly emphatic facial expressions, and a bombastic mouthing of words (which could not yet be recorded on film) that characterized the stage melodramas popular at the turn of the twentieth century.

In 1908, the Société Film d'Art (Art Film Society), a French film company, was founded with the purpose of creating a serious artistic cinema that would attract equally serious people who ordinarily preferred the theater. Commercially, this was a risky step, not only because cinema was in its infancy but also because, since the sixteenth century, the French had seen theater as a temple of expression. Its glory was (and remains) the Comédie-Française, the French national theater, and to begin its work at the highest possible level, the Société Film d'Art joined creative forces with this revered organization, which agreed to lend its actors to the society's films. In addition, the society commissioned leading theater playwrights, directors, and designers, as well as prominent composers, to create its film productions.

Sarah Bernhardt (1844–1923), revered by her public as *la divine Sarah*, was the first great theatrical actor to appear in a movie, Clément Maurice's *Le Duel d'Hamlet* (*Hamlet*, 1900, 2 mins.), a short account of Hamlet's duel with Laertes. She appeared in at least seven features, the most important of which is *Les Amours d'Elisabeth, Reine d'Angleterre* (*Queen Elizabeth*, 1912, 44 mins.), directed by Henri Desfontaines and Louis Mercanton and produced by the Société Film d'Art.

As interesting as it is to see one of the early twentieth century's greatest actors as Elizabeth I, it is even more interesting to observe how closely this "canned theater" resembled an actual stage production. The space we see is that of the theater, limited to having actors enter and exit from stage left or right, not that of the cinema, where characters are not confined to the physical boundaries imposed by theater architecture. For all her reputed skill, Bernhardt's acting could only echo what she did on the stage. Thus we see the exaggerated facial expressions, strained gestures, and clenched fists of late-nineteenth-century melodrama. Although such artificiality was conventional and thus accepted by the audience, it was all wrong for the comparative intimacy between the spectator and the screen that existed even in the earliest movie theaters.

Despite its heavy-handed technique, *Queen Elizabeth* succeeded in attracting an audience interested in serious drama on the screen, made the cinema socially and intellectually respectable, and therefore encouraged further respect for the industry and its development. What remained to be done was not to teach Sarah Bernhardt how to act for the camera, but to develop cinematic techniques uniquely suitable for the emerging narrative cinema, as well as a style of acting that could help actors realize their potential in this new medium.

D. W. Griffith and Lillian Gish

American film pioneer D. W. Griffith needed actors who could be trained to work in front of the camera, and by 1913 he had recruited a group that included some of the most important actors of the time: Mary Pickford, Lillian and Dorothy Gish, Mae Marsh, Blanche Sweet, Lionel Barrymore, Harry Carey, Henry B. Walthall, and Donald Crisp. Some had stage experience, some did not. All of them earned much more from acting in the movies than they would have on the stage, and all enjoyed long, fruitful careers (many lasting well into the era of sound films).

Because the cinema was silent during this period, Griffith worked out more-naturalistic movements and gestures for his actors rather than training their voices. The longer stories of such feature-length films as *The Birth of a Nation* (1915), *Intolerance* (1916), *Hearts of the World* (1918), and *Broken Blossoms* (1919) gave the actors more screen time and therefore more screen space in which to develop their characters. Close-ups required them to be more aware of the effect that their facial expressions would have on the audience, and actors' faces increasingly became more important than their bodies (although, in the silent comedies of the 1920s, the full presence of the human body was virtually essential for conveying humor).

Under Griffith's guidance, Lillian Gish invented the art of screen acting. Griffith encouraged her to study the movements of ordinary people on the street or in restaurants, to develop her physical skills with regular exercise, and to tell stories through her face and body. He urged her to watch the reactions of movie audiences, saying, "If they're held by what you're doing, you've succeeded as an actress."[7] Gish's performance in *Broken Blossoms* (1919) was the first great film performance by an actor. Set in the Limehouse (or Chinatown) section of London, the movie presents a very stylized fable about the love of an older Chinese merchant, Cheng Huan (Richard Barthelmess), for an English adolescent, Lucy Burrows (Gish). Lucy's racist father, the boxer Battling Burrows (Donald Crisp), beats her for the slightest transgression. Enraged by her friendship with the merchant, Burrows drags her home, and when Lucy hides in a tiny closet, he breaks down the door and beats her so savagely that she dies soon after.

The interaction of narrative, acting, extremely confined cinematic space, and exploitation of the audience's fears gives this scene its beauty, power, and repulsiveness. Seen from various angles within the closet, which fills the screen, Lucy clearly cannot escape. Hysterical with fear, she finally curls up

Lillian Gish in *Broken Blossoms* Lillian Gish was twenty-three when she played the young girl Lucy Burrows in D. W. Griffith's *Broken Blossoms* (1919). It was, incredibly, her sixty-fourth movie, and she gave one of her long career's most emotionally wrenching performances.

as her father breaks through the door. At the end, she dies in her bed, forcing the smile that has characterized her throughout the film. Terror and pity produce the cathartic realization within the viewer that Lucy's death, under these wretched circumstances, is truly a release.

In creating this scene, Gish invoked a span of emotions that no movie audience had seen before and few have seen since. Her performance illustrates the qualities of great screen acting: appropriateness, expressive coherence, inherent thoughtfulness/emotionality, wholeness, and unity. Amazingly, the performance resulted from Gish's own instincts—her sense of what was right for the climactic moment of the story and the mise-en-scène in which it took place—rather than from Griffith's direction:

> The scene of the terrified child alone in the closet could probably not be filmed today. To watch Lucy's hysteria was excruciating enough in a silent picture; a sound track would have made it unbearable. When we filmed it I played the scene with complete lack of restraint, turning around and around like a tortured

[7]Lillian Gish, with Ann Pinchot, *Lillian Gish: The Movies, Mr. Griffith, and Me* (Englewood Cliffs, N.J.: Prentice-Hall, 1969), pp. 97–101; quotation, p. 101. See also Jeanine Basinger, *Silent Stars* (New York: Knopf, 1999).

animal. When I finished, there was a hush in the studio. Mr. Griffith finally whispered: "My God, why didn't you warn me that you were going to do that?"[8]

Gish gives a similar, powerful performance—her character shoots the man who raped her—in Victor Sjöström's *The Wind* (1928), and her work in confined spaces influenced such later climactic scenes as Marion Crane's (Janet Leigh) murder in the shower in Alfred Hitchcock's *Psycho* (1960) and Jack Torrance's (Jack Nicholson) attempt to get out of a bathroom in which he is trapped in Stanley Kubrick's *The Shining* (1980).

With the discovery and implementation of the principles of screen acting, Gish (and her mentor, Griffith) also influenced excellent performances by her contemporaries, including Emil Jannings in F. W. Murnau's *The Last Laugh* (1924) and Janet Gaynor and George O'Brien in Murnau's *Sunrise: A Song of Two Humans* (1927), Gibson Gowland in Erich von Stroheim's *Greed* (1924), and Louise Brooks in G. W. Pabst's *Pandora's Box* (1929).

The Influence of Sound

It was not long after Griffith and Gish established a viable and successful style of screen acting that movie actors were faced with the greatest challenge yet: the conversion from silent to sound production. Instead of instantly revolutionizing film style, the coming of sound in 1927 began a period of several years in which the industry gradually converted to this new form of production (see Chapter 9). Filmmakers made dialogue more comprehensible by developing better microphones; finding the best placements for the camera, microphones, and other sound equipment; and encouraging changes in actors' vocal performances. Initially, they encased the camera, whose overall size has changed relatively little since the 1920s, in either a bulky soundproof booth or the later development known as a **blimp**—a soundproofed enclosure,

Early sound-film acting Sound technicians on the earliest sound films were challenged with recording the actors' voices with stationary microphones, which restricted their movements. This problem was solved later with microphones suspended on **booms** outside the camera's range and capable of moving to follow a character's movements. Looking backward, the classic movie musical *Singin' in the Rain* (1952; Stanley Donen and Gene Kelly, directors) found nothing but humor in the process of converting movie production to sound. In the background of this image, we see a reluctant and uncooperative actor— Lina Lamont (Jean Hagen, *right*), next to Don Lockwood (Gene Kelly, *left*)—who has had a microphone concealed in the bodice of her gown. This device is connected by wire to the loudspeaker in the glass booth in the foreground, where the exasperated director and sound recordist discover that it has recorded only Miss Lamont's heartbeat. Obviously, they'll have to find a different microphone placement if they want to hear her voice. And if you've seen the movie, you know that her voice is so bad that she could not in any case make the transition to sound movies.

somewhat larger than a camera, in which the camera may be mounted so that its sounds do not reach the microphone.

Such measures prevented the sounds of the camera's mechanism from being recorded, but also restricted the freedom with which the camera— and the actors—could move. Actors accustomed to moving around the set without worrying about speaking now had to curtail their movements inside the circumscribed sphere where recording took place. Furthermore, technicians required time

[8]Gish, *Lillian Gish,* p. 200. For another version of how this scene was prepared and shot, see Charles Affron, *Lillian Gish: Her Legend, Her Life* (New York: Scribner, 2001), pp. 125–131.

to adjust to the recording equipment, which restricted their movements as well. Eventually, technicians were able to free the camera for all kinds of movement and to find ways of recording sound that allowed the equipment and actors alike more mobility.

As monumental as the conversion to sound was—in economic, technological, stylistic, and human terms—Hollywood found humor in it, making it the subject of one of the most enjoyable of all movie musicals: Stanley Donen and Gene Kelly's *Singin' in the Rain* (1952), which vividly and satirically portrays the technical difficulties of using the voice of one actor to replace the voice of another who hasn't been trained to speak, trying to move a camera weighted down with soundproof housing, and forcing actors to speak into microphones concealed in flowerpots. As film scholar Donald Crafton writes, "Many of the clichés of the early sound cinema (including those in *Singin' in the Rain*) apply to films made during this period: long static takes, badly written dialogue, voices not quite in control, poor-quality recording, and a speaking style with slow cadence and emphasis on 'enunciated' tones, which the microphone was supposed to favor."[9]

How did the "talkies" influence actors and acting? Although sound enabled screen actors to use all their powers of human expression, it also created a need not only for screenplays with dialogue but also for dialogue coaches to help the actors "find" their voices and other coaches to help them master foreign accents. The more actors and the more speaking that a film included, the more complex the narrative could become. Directors had to make changes too. Before sound, a director could call out instructions to the actors during filming; once the microphone could pick up every word uttered on the set, directors were forced to rehearse more extensively with their actors, thus adopting a technique from the stage to deal with screen technology. Though many actors and directors could not make the transition from silent to sound films, others emerged from silent films ready to see the addition of sound less as an obstacle than as the means to a more complete screen verisimilitude.

An innovative production from this period is Rouben Mamoulian's *Applause* (1929; sound-recording technician: Ernest Zatorsky). After several years of directing theater productions in London and New York, Mamoulian made his screen-directing debut with *Applause*, which is photographed in a style that mixes naturalism with expressionism. From the opening scene, a montage of activity that plunges us into the lively world of burlesque, the film reveals Mamoulian's mastery of camera movement. But when the camera does not move, as in the many two-shots full of dialogue, we can almost feel the limited-range microphone boom hovering over the actors, one step beyond the use of flowerpots. In contrast to the vibrant shots with the moving camera, these static shots are lifeless and made even more confusing by the loud expressionist sounds that overwhelm ordinary as well as intimate conversations.

Obviously, such limitations have an impact on how we perceive the acting, which is *Applause*'s weak point throughout. In all likelihood because Mamoulian knew that symphonies of city sounds and noises would be the main impression of many scenes, the actors have little to say or do. However, the movie remains interesting because of a new technique in sound recording that Mamoulian introduced and that soon became common practice. Earlier, all sound in a particular shot had been recorded and manipulated on a single sound track. Mamoulian persuaded the sound technicians to record overlapping dialogue in a single shot using two separate microphones and then to mix them together on the sound track. When April Darling (Joan Peers), her head on a pillow, whispers a prayer while her mother, Kitty (Helen Morgan), sits next to her and sings a lullaby, the actors almost seem to be singing a duet—naturally, intimately, and convincingly.[10]

The conversion to sound, a pivotal moment in film history that simultaneously ruined many acting

---

[9]Donald Crafton, *The Talkies: American Cinema's Transition to Sound, 1926–1931* (New York: Scribner, 1997), p. 14.

[10]In his next films, Mamoulian made other innovations in sound, including the sound flashback in *City Streets* (1931) and the lavish use of contrapuntal sound in the opening of *Love Me Tonight* (1932).

careers while creating others, has long fascinated movie fans. And it has been treated with pathos as well as humor in movies other than those discussed here, including Billy Wilder's *Sunset Boulevard* (1950) and Michel Hazanavicius's *The Artist* (2011).

Acting in the Classical Studio Era

From the early years of moviemaking, writes film scholar Robert Allen, "the movie star has been one of the defining characteristics of the American cinema."[11] Most simply, a movie star is two people: the actor and the character(s) he or she has played. In addition, the star embodies an image created by the studio to coincide with the kinds of roles associated with the actor. That the star also reflects the social and cultural history of the period in which that image was created helps explain the often rapid rise and fall of stars' careers. But this description reveals at its heart a set of paradoxes, as Allen points out:

> The star is powerless, yet powerful; different from "ordinary" people, yet at one time was "just like us." Stars make huge salaries, yet the work for which they are handsomely paid does not appear to be work on the screen. Talent would seem to be a requisite for stardom, yet there has been no absolute correlation between acting ability and stardom. The star's private life has little if anything to do with his or her "job" of acting in movies, yet a large portion of a star's image is constructed on the basis of "private" matters: romance, marriage, tastes in fashion, and home life.[12]

British actor Dirk Bogarde drew a further distinction between film stars—"people with extrovert personalities and the sparkling quality that puts the glamour, the glitter and the 'stardust' into a very tough work-a-day job"—and film actors—"people who without being great extrovert personalities or looking particularly glamorous . . . have

been trained in the craft of acting and . . . [are] sound knowledgeable technicians."[13]

The golden age of Hollywood, roughly from the 1930s until the 1950s, was the age of the movie star, and acting in American movies generally meant "star acting." During this period, the major studios gave basic lessons in acting, speaking, and movement; but because screen appearance was of paramount importance, they were more concerned with enhancing actors' screen images than with improving their acting.

During this period, when the studio system and the star system went hand in hand, the studios had almost complete control of their actors. Every six months, the studio reviewed an actor's standard seven-year **option contract**: if the actor had made progress in being assigned roles and demonstrating box-office appeal, the studio picked up the option to employ that actor for the next six months and gave him or her a raise; if not, the studio dropped the option, and the actor was out of work. The decision was the studio's, not the actor's. Furthermore, the contract did not allow the actor to move to another studio, stop work, or renegotiate for a higher salary. In addition to those unbreakable terms, the contract had restrictive clauses that gave the studio total control over the star's image and services; it required an actor "to act, sing, pose, speak or perform in such roles as the producer may designate"; it gave the studio the right to change the name of the actor at its own discretion and to control the performer's image and likeness in advertising and publicity; and it required the actor to comply with rules covering interviews and public appearances.[14]

These contracts turned the actors into the studios' chattel. To the public, perhaps the most fascinating thing about making actors into stars was the process of changing their names. Marion Morrison became John Wayne, Issur Danielovitch Demsky became Kirk Douglas, Julia Jean Mildred Frances Turner became Lana Turner, and Archibald Leach became Cary

[11]For a study of stars in Hollywood from which this section liberally draws, see Robert C. Allen and Douglas Gomery, *Film History: Theory and Practice* (New York: Knopf, 1985), pp. 172–189, quotation, p. 174 (reprinted as Robert C. Allen, "The Role of the Star in Film History [Joan Crawford]," in *Film Theory and Criticism: Introductory Readings*, 5th ed., ed. Leo Braudy and Marshall Cohen [New York: Oxford University Press, 1999], pp. 547–561).
[12]Allen and Gomery, p. 174.

[13]Dirk Bogarde, qtd. in John Coldstream, *Dirk Bogarde: The Authorised Biography* (London: Weidenfeld & Nicolson, 2004), p. 223.
[14]Tino Balio, *Grand Design: Hollywood as a Modern Business Enterprise*, 1930–1939 (New York: Scribner, 1999), p. 145.

Grant. Name and image came first, with acting ability often considered secondary to an actor's screen presence or aura, physical or facial beauty, athletic ability or performance skills, or character "type." Although many stars were also convincing actors, capable of playing a variety of parts (e.g., Bette Davis, Henry Fonda, Barbara Stanwyck, Jimmy Stewart), surprisingly little serious attention was paid to screen acting. As Charles Affron observes:

> An almost total absence of analytical approaches to screen acting reflects the belief that screen acting is nothing more than the beautiful projection of a filmic self, an arrangement of features and body, the disposition of superficial elements. Garbo is Garbo is Garbo is Garbo. We mortals are left clutching our wonder, and victims of that very wonder, overwhelmed by our enthusiasm and blinded by the light of the star's emanation.[15]

Of course, movie stars were not the only acting talent in golden-age Hollywood. In his study of Hollywood's golden-age business practices, Tino Balio writes that there were four classes of performers: *supporting players*, who had small parts, worked for a brief period of time, had a simple contract (if any) for each role, and did not receive screen credit; *stock players*, who formed a large talent pool, had short-term contracts, received from $50 to $350 per week, and often had screen credit; *featured players*, who performed principal roles, had annual contracts that specified the minimum and maximum number of pictures, received a specified salary, and were given screen credit; and *movie stars*, "the elite class."[16] (See "Types of Roles" on page 314.) In her comprehensive study *The Star Machine*, Jeanine Basinger offers a list of observations of what a movie star is:

> A star has exceptional looks. Outstanding talent. A distinctive voice that can easily be recognized and imitated. A set of mannerisms. Palpable sexual

appeal. Energy that comes down off the screen. Glamour. Androgyny. Glowing health and radiance. Panache. A single tiny flaw that mars their perfection, endearing them to ordinary people. Charm. The good luck to be in the right place at the right time (also known as just plain good luck). An emblematic quality that audiences believe is who they really are. The ability to make viewers "know" what they are thinking whenever the camera comes up close. An established type (by which is meant that they could believably play the same role over and over again). A level of comfort in front of the camera. And, of course, "she has something," the bottom line of which is "it's something you can't define."[17]

Today, film acting has become the subject of new interest among theorists and critics in semiology, psychology, and cultural studies who wish to study acting as an index of cultural history and an aspect of ideology.[18] This approach stresses that stars are a commodity created by the studio system through promotion, publicity, movies, criticism, and commentary. As Richard Dyer notes, "Stars are involved in making themselves into commodities; they are both labour and the thing that labour produces. They do not produce themselves alone."[19] Such analyses tend to emphasize the ways in which culture makes meaning rather than the art and expressive value of acting, the ways in which actors make meaning.

Materialistic as it was, the star system dominated the movie industry until the studio system collapsed, at which time it was replaced by a similar industrial enterprise powered essentially by the same motivation of making profits for its investors. However, because every studio had its own system, creating different goals and images for different stars, there was no typical star. For example, when Lucille Fay

[15]Charles Affron, *Star Acting: Gish, Garbo, Davis* (New York: Dutton, 1977), p. 3. See also Roland Barthes, "The Face of Garbo," in *Film Theory and Criticism*, ed. Braudy and Cohen, pp. 536–538; Alexander Walker, *Stardom: The Hollywood Phenomenon* (New York: Stein and Day, 1970); and Leo Braudy, "Film Acting: Some Critical Problems and Proposals," *Quarterly Review of Film Studies* (February 1976): 1–18.
[16]Balio, p. 155.

[17]Jeanine Basinger, *The Star Machine* (New York: Knopf, 2007), pp. 3–4.
[18]See Richard Dyer, *Stars*, new ed. (London: British Film Institute, 1998); and his *Heavenly Bodies: Film Stars and Society* (New York: St. Martin's Press, 1986). See also Richard deCordova, "The Emergence of the Star System in America," *Wide Angle* 6, no. 4 (1985): 4–13; Carole Zucker, ed., *Making Visible the Invisible: An Anthology of Original Essays on Film Acting* (Metuchen, N.J.: Scarecrow Press, 1990); and Christine Gledhill, *Stardom: Industry of Desire* (New York: Routledge, 1991).
[19]Dyer, *Heavenly Bodies,* p. 5.

What makes a movie star? Jeanine Basinger's list of observations on what makes a movie star could have been written about Cary Grant, for her criteria fit him perfectly. Regarded by the public, as well as critics and colleagues, as the finest romantic comedian actor of his time, the handsome actor was often cast as a glamorous, high-society figure in a series of 1930s screwball comedies, including George Cukor's *The Philadelphia Story* (1940). In this image, Grant's wide-open handsome face and laid-back manner mask the charming wiles of a man who succeeds in remarrying a former wife, played by Katharine Hepburn. He played against some of Hollywood's most glamorous stars, including Mae West, Marlene Dietrich, Audrey Hepburn, Ingrid Bergman, Doris Day, and Grace Kelly. Long before the birth of the independent production system, Grant was unique among Hollywood actors by not signing a studio contract but rather controlling every aspect of his career himself, including the directors and actors he wanted to work with and the roles he wanted to play. Perhaps the high point of his career was working with Alfred Hitchcock on *Suspicion* (1941), *Notorious* (1946), *To Catch a Thief* (1955), and *North by Northwest* (1959), films in which he still plays a lighthearted rogue. His assets—sleek good looks, ease, lack of self-consciousness, physical grace, and natural comic sense—make him one of the great movie actors of all time; some say the greatest.

LeSueur (also known early in her career in the theater as Billie Cassin) went to Hollywood in 1925, MGM decided that her name must be changed and that her image would be that of an ideal American "girl." Through a national campaign conducted by a fan magazine, the public was invited to submit names; the first choice, "Joan Arden," was already being used by another actress, so Lucille LeSueur became Joan Crawford, a name to which she objected for several years but which became synonymous with the public's idea of a movie star—indeed, one proclaimed by MGM to be a "star of the first magnitude."[20]

Crawford's career soon took off, reaching a high level of achievement in the mid-1930s, when she became identified with the "woman's film." Subsequently, in a long series of films, she played women who, whether by family background or social circumstances, triumphed over adversity and usually paid a price for independence. No matter what happened to them, her characters remained stylish and distinctive in their looks—chic, self-generated survivors. Like many other stars, Crawford became indelibly associated with the roles she played. Yet she received little serious acclaim for her acting until the mid-1940s, when she left MGM for Warner Bros. For Michael Curtiz's *Mildred Pierce* (1945), her first film there, Crawford won the Academy Award for Best Actress in a Leading Role—her only Oscar, although she received two more nominations. After her success at Warner Bros., Crawford worked for various major studios and independents, shedding her image as the stalwart, contemporary American woman. Sometimes her performances were excellent, as in Curtis Bernhardt's *Possessed* (1947), David Miller's *Sudden Fear* (1952), and, costarring with Bette Davis, Robert Aldrich's *What Ever Happened to Baby Jane?* (1962).

Davis was a star of another sort, leading a principled and spirited fight against the studio and star systems' invasion into virtually every aspect of actors' personal and professional lives. In fact, Davis's career (from 1931 to 1989) comes as close to any as demonstrating these systems at their best and worst. In the mid-1930s, when she walked out of Warner Bros. demanding better roles, the studio successfully sued her for breach of contract. Though she returned to work rewarded by increased respect, a new contract, and better roles, her career sagged after World War II, for she had reached her early forties, an age at which female actors are seldom offered good parts. Ironically, playing just such a

[20]See Richard Oulahan, "A Well-Planned Crawford," *Life* 56 (February 21, 1964), pp. 11–12.

[1]

[2]

The movie star Elizabeth Taylor epitomizes what we mean by the term *movie star*: talent, beauty, sex appeal, and a glamour that dazzled the world. As a child star, the product of the studio system, she appeared in such movies as *Lassie Come Home* (1943) and *National Velvet* (1944). As a teenager, she came to prominence as Angela Vickers in [1] George Stevens's *A Place in the Sun* (1951), a romantic but tragic melodrama. During her most fruitful period—the 1950s and 1960s—she starred in such movies as George Stevens's *Giant* (1956), Richard Brooks's *Cat on a Hot Tin Roof* (1958), Joseph L. Mankiewicz's *Suddenly, Last Summer* (1959), and

Daniel Mann's *BUtterfield 8* (1960). Her career took a brief downward spin with Mankiewicz's *Cleopatra* (1963), one of the most lavish, expensive, and unsuccessful films of all time. A survivor, she recovered in two impressive roles: Martha [2] in Mike Nichols's *Who's Afraid of Virginia Woolf?* (1966) and Katharina in Franco Zeffirelli's *The Taming of the Shrew* (1967). In all, Elizabeth Taylor appeared in more than 50 films and was awarded three Oscars as Best Actress. Long after she quit her acting career, she remained a star, lending her name and reputation to raising hundreds of millions of dollars for AIDS research and other humanitarian causes.

character—an older stage actress in danger of losing roles because of her age—she triumphed in Joseph L. Mankiewicz's *All about Eve* (1950), generally regarded as her greatest performance. During her long career, Davis was nominated eleven times for the Oscar for Best Actress in a Leading Role, winning for Alfred E. Green's *Dangerous* (1935) and William Wyler's *Jezebel* (1938). Nominations for an Oscar as Best Actor in a Leading Role involve a peer-review process in which only actors vote. Davis's record of nominations is exceeded only by Meryl Streep's (thirteen nominations), Katharine Hepburn's (twelve), and Jack Nicholson's (eight).

Method Acting

During the studio years, movie acting and the star system were virtually synonymous. Although acting styles were varied, the emphasis was on the star's persona and its effect at the box office—on the product, not the process of acting. And as pro-

duction processes were regularized, so too was acting. That's not to say that screen acting in the 1930s and 1940s was formulaic or unimaginative; quite the contrary. On Broadway, however, stage actors were becoming acquainted with a Russian technique that became known as Method acting. Method acting did not make a major impact on Hollywood until the 1950s, but it marks a significant point in the evolution of screen acting from the studio system's reliance on "star acting" in the 1930s and 1940s to a new style in which actors draw on their own personal experiences and feelings in an attempt to become the character.

What Americans call *Method acting* was based on the theory and practice of Konstantin Stanislavsky, who cofounded the Moscow Art Theater in 1897 and spent his entire career there. Developing what became known as the **Stanislavsky system** of acting, he trained students to strive for realism, both social and psychological, and to bring their own past experiences and emotions to their roles. This intense psychological preparation required the actors' conscious efforts to tap their unconscious selves. On one hand, they had to portray living characters onstage; on the other, they could not allow their portrayals to detract from the acting ensemble and the play as a whole and as written text.

Stanislavsky's ideas influenced the Soviet silent-film directors of the 1920s—Sergei Eisenstein, Aleksandr Dovzhenko, Lev Kuleshov, and Vsevolod I. Pudovkin—all of whom had learned much from D. W. Griffith's work. But they often disagreed about acting, especially about how it was influenced by actors' appearances, and by editing, which could work so expressively both for and against actors' interpretations.

Among this group, Pudovkin, whose *Film Acting* (1935) was one of the first serious books on the subject, has the most relevance to mainstream movie acting today. Although he advocates an explicitly Stanislavskian technique based on his observations of the Moscow Art Theater, he writes from the standpoint of film directors and actors working together. Because film consists of individual shots, he reasons, both directors and actors work at the mercy of the shot and must strive to make acting (out of sequence) seem natural, smooth, and flowing while maintaining expressive coherence across the shots. He recommends close collaboration between actors and directors, with long periods devoted to preparation and rehearsal. He also advises film actors to ignore voice training because the microphone makes it unnecessary, notes that the close-up can communicate more to the audience than overt gestures can, and finds that the handling of "expressive objects" (e.g., Charlie Chaplin's cane) can convey emotions and ideas even more effectively than close-ups can.

Outside the Soviet Union, Stanislavsky's books *My Life in Art* (1924) and *An Actor Prepares* (1936) had a lasting impact. In the mid-1930s, Stella Adler studied privately with him in Moscow—perhaps the first American actor to do so. Soon after, she returned to New York and taught principles of Method acting to members of the experimental Group Theatre, including Elia Kazan. In 1947, Kazan, now a director, helped found the Actors Studio in New York City. In 1951, Kazan was replaced by

[1]

[2]

Elia Kazan and Method acting Elia Kazan is notable, among many other things, for directing two of the iconic Method-acting achievements: [1] Marlon Brando's as Terry Malloy in *On the Waterfront* (1954)—here we see Kazan (*center*) and Brando (*right*) on location during the filming—and [2] James Dean's as Cal Trask, a troubled teenager, in *East of Eden* (1955).

Lee Strasberg, who alienated many theater people, including Kazan, Adler, Arthur Miller, and Marlon Brando. Today, the studio is guided by three alumni: Ellen Burstyn, Harvey Keitel, and Al Pacino. In 1949, Adler went her own way, founding the Stella Adler Studio of Acting, where Marlon Brando was her most famous and successful student.

These teachers loosely adapted Stanislavky's ideas—not only his principle that actors should draw on their own emotional experiences to create characters but also his emphasis on the importance of creating an ensemble and expressing the subtext, the nuances that lay beneath the lines of the script. The naturalistic style that they popularized (and called **Method acting**, more popularly known as *the Method*) encourages actors to speak, move, and gesture not in a traditional stage manner but just as they would in their own lives. Thus it is an ideal technique for representing convincing human behavior on the stage and on the screen. The Method has led to a new level of realism and subtlety, influencing such actors as Marlon Brando, Montgomery Clift, James Dean, Robert De Niro, Faye Dunaway, Robert Duvall, Morgan Freeman, Gene Hackman, Dustin Hoffman, Dennis Hopper, Holly Hunter, Harvey Keitel, Walter Matthau, Paul Newman, Jack Nicholson, Al Pacino, Sidney Poitier, Jon Voight, and Shelley Winters.[21]

To understand Method acting, you have to see it. Fortunately, there are some wonderful examples, including James Dean's three movie roles—Cal Trask in Elia Kazan's *East of Eden* (1955), Jim Stark in Nicholas Ray's *Rebel without a Cause* (1955), and Jett Rink in George Stevens's *Giant* (1956)—and Marlon Brando's equally legendary performances as Stanley Kowalski in Elia Kazan's *A Streetcar Named Desire* (1951)—reprising the stage role that made him famous—and as Terry Malloy in Kazan's *On the Waterfront* (1954). Other notable performances, out of many, include those given by Paul Newman as Eddie Felson in Robert Rossen's *The Hustler* (1961), Shelley Winters as Charlotte Haze Humbert in Stanley Kubrick's *Lolita* (1962), and Faye Dunaway as Evelyn Cross Mulwray in Roman Polanski's *Chinatown* (1974). Each of these performances exhibits the major characteristics of Method acting: intense concentration and internalization on the actor's part (sometimes mistaken for discomfort); low-key, almost laid-back delivery of lines (sometimes described as mumbling); and an edginess (sometimes highly neurotic) that suggests dissatisfaction, unhappiness, and alienation. In directing *The Misfits* (1961), with a script by playwright Arthur Miller, John Huston (not a Method director) must have been bewildered by the range of acting talent in front of his camera: Clark Gable,

a traditional Hollywood star in any sense of the word, one who could be counted on to always deliver a reliable performance; Thelma Ritter, an equally seasoned supporting player who invariably played the role of a wisecracking sidekick; and several Method actors (Eli Wallach, Montgomery Clift, and Marilyn Monroe), whose performances, by contrast with the rest of the cast, seem out of touch and clumsy. Absent here is the ensemble Method acting obvious in Elia Kazan's movies.

No matter what school or style of acting is involved, it is clear that memorable acting results from hard work, skill, imagination, and discipline.

Screen Acting Today

From the earliest years, the development of movie acting has relied on synthesizing various approaches, including those already discussed. Contemporary actors employ a range of physically or psychologically based approaches, with some action stars, like Arnold Schwarzenegger or Jamie Foxx, relying entirely on physical effect, while others like Bruce Willis, relying both on physical prowess and a very defined persona that has evolved from his early wise-guy days to a more world-weary persona. Directors also take different approaches toward actors. Robert Altman, for example, who is particularly good at capturing the mood of an ensemble of actors within a narrative, encourages improvisation and the exploration of individual styles. Joel Coen, in contrast, tends to regard acting as a critical component of the highly stylized mise-en-scène within the often cartoonlike movies that he creates with his brother, Ethan.

In Altman's *The Player* (1992), Tim Robbins plays Griffin Mill, a Hollywood producer, at once emotively and satirically. He uses his big, open face and charming manner to draw us into Mill's professional and existential crises, then turns edgy enough to distance us as Mill becomes a murderer and ruthless careerist. In Altman's *Kansas City* (1996), Jennifer Jason Leigh delivers an emotional hurricane of a performance as the cheap, brassy, tough Blondie O'Hara, a Jean Harlow wannabe. Her scowl, furrowed brow, rotten teeth under big red lips, and screeching-cat voice leave no room for

[21]See Carole Zucker, "An Interview with Lindsay Crouse," *Post Script: Essays in Film and the Humanities* 12, no. 2 (Winter 1993): 5–28. See also Foster Hirsch, *A Method to Their Madness: The History of the Actors Studio* (New York: Norton, 1984), and Steven Vineberg, *Method Actors: Three Generations of an American Acting Style* (New York: Schirmer, 1991).

Contemporary star power Unlike some actors who become movie stars almost overnight, Robert Downey, Jr. began to appear in avant-garde movies directed by his father at the age of five. Working in the independent era, he was able to choose a range of roles that revealed his extraordinary talent. Downey's breakthrough as a major performer came with Richard Attenborough's *Chaplin* (1992), for which he received an Oscar nomination as Best Actor. He continued to demonstrate his remarkable versatility in serious roles in Robert Altman's *Short Cuts* (1993), Oliver Stone's *Natural Born Killers* (1994), Richard Loncraine's *Richard III* (1995), and Michael Hoffman's *Restoration* (1995). Between 1996 and 2001, his acting career faltered because of his drug abuse, and—with the exception of his role in Curtis Hanson's *Wonder Boys* (2000)—he was cast in relatively unimportant projects. He returned to serious roles, deserving serious attention, in such movies as George Clooney's *Good Night, and Good Luck* (2005), Dito Montiel's *A Guide to Recognizing Your Saints* (2006), Steven Shainberg's *Fur: An Imaginary Portrait of Diane Arbus* (2006), and David Fincher's *Zodiac* (2007). Soon after, he began playing two completely different characters: Tony Stark in Jon Favreau's *Iron Man* (2008) and *Iron Man 2* (2010) and Sherlock Holmes in Guy Ritchie's *Sherlock Holmes* (2009) and *Sherlock Holmes: A Game of Shadows* (2011). In this image, we see Downey as the brilliant, cool, arrogant, and intense Tony Stark, aka Iron Man.

the kind of gently ironic distance that Robbins creates in *The Player*.

In Coen's *The Hudsucker Proxy* (1994), however, both Robbins and Leigh tailor their performances to fit the madcap mood and mannered decor of an Art Deco screwball comedy. Indeed, part of the movie's appeal lies in watching an ensemble of actors working in this style. Channeling Cary Grant and Rosalind Russell in Howard Hawks's *His Girl Friday* (1940) and Spencer Tracy and Katharine Hepburn in Walter Lang's *Desk Set* (1957), Robbins plays Norville Barnes, a goofy mailroom clerk who

becomes company president, and Leigh plays Amy Archer, a hard-boiled, wisecracking newspaper reporter. Robbins and Leigh's zany comic interaction fits perfectly in Coen's jigsaw puzzle, which lovingly pays tribute to an era when movie style often transcended substance.

Today, actors struggle to get parts and to create convincing performances, and like their earlier counterparts, seldom have the chance to prove themselves across a range of roles. Once typecast—that is, cast in particular kinds of roles because of their looks or "type" rather than for their acting talent or experience—they continue to be awarded such parts as long they bring in good box-office receipts. No star system exists to sustain careers and images, but now, as in earlier periods of movie history, some individuals use films to promote themselves—like music stars, sports stars, or other celebrities who sometimes appear in a movie or two, but leave no mark on the history of film acting.

The transition from studio production to independent production has markedly affected the livelihood of actors and the art of acting. The shape of the average career has fundamentally changed; because fewer major movies appear each year, actors supplement film work with appearances on television shows, in advertisements, and in theater. (Salaries and contractual benefits, such as residual payments for television reruns, provide excellent financial security.) In addition, because today the average movie is a comedy targeted at—indeed, mass-marketed to—the under-thirty audience (and a comedy relying on physical humor, often of a scatological nature, rather than verbal wit), fewer quality roles are available to actors.

Some extremely versatile actors—Chris Cooper, Russell Crowe, Benicio Del Toro, Johnny Depp, Leonardo DiCaprio, Samuel L. Jackson, Nicole Kidman, John Malkovich, Julianne Moore, Kevin Spacey, and Hilary Swank, to name a few—have, with two or three successful films, become stars quickly. The greater their drawing power at the box office, the greater the urgency to promote them to top rank and cast them in more films. As independent agents, however, they can contract for one film at a time and thus hold out for good roles rather than having to make a specific number of films for a given

Stardom: then and now Bette Davis, an actor who became a legend for playing strong-willed and often neurotic female characters, was in top form as Leslie Crosbie in *The Letter* (1940). In the movie's electric opening scene, she pumps five bullets into her lover [1], then pleads self-defense in court. It represents another successful collaboration between Davis and director William Wyler, with whom she also worked on *Jezebel* (1938) and *The Little Foxes* (1941). Nicole Kidman, a legend in her own time, is famous, like Davis, for her professionalism and versatility. Unlike Davis, however, she has had almost total control of her career and thus has been far more adventurous in the roles she chooses to play, resulting in a filmography of considerable depth and range. She is well known for her willingness to take risks in highly individual movies, such as Robert Benton's *The Human Stain* (2003), Noah Baumbach's *Margot at the Wedding* (2007), and Steven Shainberg's *Fur: An Imaginary Portrait of Diane Arbus* (2006), a fictional account of the famous photographer's life. At a turning point in her career—she was 43, an age when most actresses have trouble securing good roles—Kidman costarred with Aaron Eckhart in John Cameron Mitchell's *Rabbit Hole* (2010), an important drama about an upper-middle-class suburban couple trying to deal with the death of their two-year-old son in a car accident. The movie avoids the tragedy itself in order to focus on the couple's very different attempts to put their marriage back together. In image [2], Kidman's distinctive "blank face" allows the audience to "write" whatever it wants on her conflicting day-to-day responses to her personal grief and to a marriage going somewhat recklessly to pieces. She wants to move on; her husband wants to keep everything that reminds him of the boy. With performances as moving as this one—for which she received an Oscar nomination as Best Actress—Kidman's career shows no sign of slowing down.

[1]

[2]

studio. In addition, these newcomers can negotiate a new salary for each film, and they routinely make more money from a single picture than some of the greatest stars of classical Hollywood made in their entire careers. Furthermore, they usually work under their own names. But because audience reaction, and not a studio's publicity office, maintains their status, such actors often face highly unpredictable futures.

Let's look more closely at the careers and earnings of two of the most important and popular movie stars in history: Bette Davis, who was at the top during the studio era, and Nicole Kidman, who is at the top today. Although they are both well regarded for their professional approach to performances in a range of film genres—including melodrama, comedy, historical and period films, and romantic dramas—there are significant differ-

ences in their careers that result from the different production systems in which each worked (see Chapter 11, "Filmmaking Technologies and Production Systems").

Bette Davis (1908–1989), who began her movie career on Broadway, went to Hollywood at the age of twenty-two and, over a career that spanned fifty-two years, appeared in eighty-nine movies, fifty-nine of them under contract to Warner Bros. Her breakthrough role was in John Cromwell's *Of Human Bondage* (1934); she won her first Oscar as Best Actress in a Leading Role in 1936 and again in 1939, when she reached the peak of her career in William Wyler's *Jezebel* (1938). She sued Warner Bros. in an attempt to get better roles in better pictures (she was forced, by contract, to make a lot of mediocre films) but lost her case. (In essence, Davis had to fight for what actors of Kidman's generation take for granted: the right to pick the roles they want to play.) However, Davis did get better roles (and rejected some juicy ones she shouldn't have, including *Mildred Pierce* [1945] and *The African Queen* [1951]) and was so well paid in the 1940s that she was known around Hollywood as the fourth Warner brother. The years between 1939 and 1945 were marked by major successes—Edmund Goulding's *Dark Victory* (1939), Michael Curtiz's *The Private Lives of Elizabeth and Essex* (1939), William Wyler's *The Letter* (1940) and *The Little Foxes* (1941), Irving Rapper's *Now, Voyager* (1942) and *The Corn Is Green* (1945)—but by 1950, her studio career was over. As one of the first freelancers in the independent system, she revived her career with her greatest performance (Joseph L. Mankiewicz's *All about Eve*, 1950). However, she was then 41, the "barrier" year that usually relegates women actors to character parts, of which she had her share, including Robert Aldrich's *What Ever Happened to Baby Jane?* (1962). Her career went downhill, although there were still a few good movies and loyal fans; her penultimate role was a very moving performance in Lindsay Anderson's *The Whales of August* (1987), and—a demanding perfectionist to the end—she walked off the set of her final film just before she died. Bette Davis, a name synonymous with Hollywood stardom, ranked second (after Katharine Hepburn) on the American Film Institute's poll of the greatest female actors.

While Bette Davis is an icon of movies past, Nicole Kidman is a screen legend for today, an actress who—unconstrained by a studio contract—is free to choose her roles. She has worked with a variety of directors, including Gus Van Sant, Jane Campion, Stanley Kubrick, Baz Luhrmann, and Stephen Daldry. Where Davis had some say over her directors (all of whom were studio employees), Kidman has worked with outsiders, insiders, kings of the megaplexes, and avant-garde experimenters. Kidman (b. 1967) began her movie career in Australia at the age of fifteen and has since made thirty-eight films (as of 2009), all independently produced. Her breakthrough movie was Tony Scott's *Days of Thunder* (1990), after which her career took off in such films as Gus Van Sant's *To Die For* and Joel Schumacher's *Batman Forever*

(1995), Jane Campion's *The Portrait of a Lady* (1996), Stanley Kubrick's *Eyes Wide Shut* (1999), Baz Luhrmann's *Moulin Rouge!* (2001), and Stephen Daldry's *The Hours* (2002), for which she won the Oscar as Best Actress in a Leading Role for her portrayal of Virginia Woolf. Another turning point came in 2003, when she made three different movies with three very different directors: Lars von Trier's *Dogville*, Robert Benton's *The Human Stain*, and Anthony Minghella's *Cold Mountain*. Kidman is willing to tackle serious melodrama (Sydney Pollack's *The Interpreter*, 2005), light comedy (Nora Ephron's *Bewitched*, 2005), edgy, experimental concepts (Steven Shainberg's *Fur: An Imaginary Portrait of Diane Arbus*, 2006), comic drama (Noah Baumbach's *Margot at the Wedding*, 2007), and fantasy films (Chris Weitz's *The Golden Compass*, 2007). When Bette Davis turned forty-one, her career (despite her success that year with *All about Eve*) began its downward spiral. Ironically, Kidman, now forty-four, remains at the peak of her career, although there is no way to predict whether she will continue to get roles worthy of her experience and talent.

Let's consider their earning power. In her career, we estimate that Bette Davis earned approximately $6 million, which, in today's money, is about $10 million.[22] Until 1949, her salary was set by contract; her highest studio earnings were $208,000 for the years 1941–43. Her highest poststudio earnings came with her last movie, for which she was paid $250,000. Kidman made $100,000 on her first movie and today receives $17.5 million per picture. During the first twenty-five years of her ongoing movie career, Kidman has earned $230 million. That's twenty-three times what Davis earned over an entire fifty-two-year career! Davis worked under a Warner Bros. contract, and the studio kept the lion's share of profits from her films. Kidman is free to negotiate the terms of her salary and her share of the profits for her movies, terms that are determined by a far more complicated equation than a

[22]The figures cited here are based, in part, on information provided by newspaper and magazine articles and by the online database pro.imdb.com and do not include fees for television acting, advertising work, DVD sales, etc.

[1]

[2]

A durable Hollywood legend In a career spanning forty-six years and 180 movies, John Wayne starred in war movies, romantic comedies, and historical epics, but he is best known for his roles as the hero in great Westerns, particularly those directed by John Ford and Howard Hawks. His first starring role, at the age of twenty-three, was as a winsome young scout in Raoul Walsh's *The Big Trail* (1930), a spectacular epic of a wagon train going west, shot in the widescreen Grandeur process [1]. Wayne's last film, at sixty-seven, was Don Siegel's *The Shootist* (1976), in which he plays an aging gunslinger ("shootist") dying of cancer, out to settle some old scores [2]. Wayne himself was to die of cancer three years after he completed it.

[1]

[2]

An icon of the new Hollywood Working wholly within today's independent system of movie production, an actor like Jeff Bridges does not have the security of a studio contract or of developing and perpetuating a legendary character, such as John Wayne did. Nonetheless, Bridges has earned universal respect as one of Hollywood's most talented, resilient actors. His characters have become legendary: Ernie in John Huston's *Fat City* (1972), Nick Kegan in William Richert's *Winter Kills* (1979), [1] Starman/Scott Hayden in John Carpenter's *Starman* (1984), Jeffrey "The Dude" Lebowski in Joel Coen's *The Big Lebowski* (1998), Obadiah Stone in Jon Favreau's *Iron Man* (2008), and [2] Rooster Cogburn in Joel and Ethan Coen's *True Grit* (2010), a character first developed by John Wayne in the 1969 film of the same name. To date, Bridges has made 65 films, earned six Oscar nominations (three for supporting and three for leading roles), and won Best Actor as Bad Blake in Scott Cooper's *Crazy Heart* (2009).

studio contract. These estimates do not include fees for television acting, advertising work, DVD sales, etc. Stars of Davis's era made far less money from advertisements than, say, Kidman, who is the face in Chanel's print and television campaigns, for which she earns millions each year. The most revealing indicator that separates the "old" from the "new" Hollywood, as far as actors are concerned, is clearly the freedom to choose roles and negotiate earnings.

Earnings are keyed to an actor's popularity with audiences. There are two basic ways of measuring this popularity: box-office receipts or popularity polls. Among the popularity polls, the Harris Poll, conducted by a leading market-research company, is probably as reliable as any poll of America's favorite movie stars. Below is the result of the 2008 poll[23] in ranked order: (1) Denzel Washington, (2) Tom Hanks, (3) Johnny Depp, (4) Julia Roberts, (5) Will Smith, (6) John Wayne, (7) (tie) Matt Damon, (8) (tie) Sean Connery, (9) Sandra Bullock, and (10) Bruce Willis. Consider the profile of this group: two African Americans are on the list, one of whom is the most popular of all; considering that women constitute the bulk of the movie audience, it's remarkable that only two women are on the list; there are considerable differences in the roles played by the three top males; Sean Connery, seventy-nine in 2009, seems to have retired from a full-time career (perhaps he's here because audiences will never forget his James Bond); the predominance of action movies is reflected in the inclusion of three action-movie stars (Bruce Willis, Will Smith, and Matt Damon); John Wayne died in 1979.

Indeed, John Wayne has been on Harris's top-ten list every year since he died. An actor of many parts, he is as durable a Hollywood legend as has ever existed. Wayne's a far better actor than many people give him credit for being. He was indelibly linked to the Western and, in private life, to right-wing politics, and a representative on-screen of a kind of American male virtue that many people admire. Wayne is an acting icon who has a solid place in American cultural ideology.[24] While the people who were polled here neglected to vote for many fine and popular actors, the results represent the unpredictability of Hollywood fame, if only for its sixth-place ranking of an actor who made his last movie—Don Siegel's excellent *The Shootist*—in 1974. That's stardom!

Technology and Acting

As discussed in Chapter 6, "Cinematography," for every advance in the world of special effects, the narrative and the acting that propels it lose some of their importance. Movies such as Stanley Kubrick's *2001: A Space Odyssey* (1968) and Steven Spielberg's *E.T. the Extra-Terrestrial* (1982) made us familiar, even comfortable, with nonhuman creatures that

[23]http://www.aceshowbiz.com/news/view/00013502.html (accessed September 25, 2008).
[24]See Garry Willis, *John Wayne's America: The Politics of Celebrity* (New York: Simon & Schuster, 1997).

had human voices and characteristics; John Lasseter, Ash Brannon, and Lee Unkrich's *Toy Story 2* (1999), with its shiny, computer-generated graphics, took this process another step forward.

With technology now revolutionizing filmmaking, will actors be replaced by digitally created "synthespians" (a name coined by the digital-effects expert Jeffrey Kleiser, who with Diana Walczak created the first synthespian for the 1988 short *Nestor Sextone for President*)? Yes and no. Today's computer-generated "actors" in Hironobu Sakaguchi and Moto Sakakibara's *Final Fantasy: The Spirits Within* (2001), Andrew Niccol's *S1mOne* (2002), and Robert Zemeckis's *The Polar Express* (2004) seem to be another stage in this evolution. George Lucas, as successful and influential as anyone in the industry, appears, as a director, to be more interested in perfecting digital technology than in directing actors and developing a character's emotions. For example, he "directed" the CGI character Jar Jar Binks (voice of Ahmed Best) to interact with live actors in three of his *Star Wars* movies: *The Phantom Menace* (1999), *Attack of the Clones* (2002), and *Revenge of the Sith* (2005). However, this strategy turned out to be particularly unpopular with his *Star Wars* fans, many of whom demanded that the character be eliminated from future movies. Nonetheless, the CGI character of Gollum (voice of Andy Serkis) in Peter Jackson's *The Lord of the Rings* trilogy (2001–3) is a fully realized character created in a very different way from a typical Lucas cardboard cutout.

Computer-generated characters might even meet with the fate of some of the other innovations that Hollywood has periodically employed to keep the world on edge, such as the short-lived Sensurround, which relied on a sound track to trigger waves of high-decibel sound in the movie theater, making viewers feel "tremors" during Mark Robson's *Earthquake* (1974), or the even shorter-lived Odorama process, involving scratch-and-sniff cards, for John Waters's *Polyester* (1981). Indeed, the use of computer technology to replace actors is one side effect of our current fascination with virtual reality. Although the evolving film technology may enable filmmakers to realize their most fantastic visions, we should remember, as film theorist André Bazin

"Synthespians" The future of movie acting is unlikely to be changed significantly by the recent development of synthespians: characters created not by human beings but by computer-generated imagery. Such on-screen figures can be convincing—such as the avatars digitally created to interact with the Na'vi, the blue-skinned humanoids in James Cameron's *Avatar* (2010)—but that is because they do not represent recognizable human beings and we accept them for the imaginative creations that they are.

What happens, though, when a movie director is faced with casting actors to play real-life identical twins, as was David Fincher in casting the actors who played the Winklevoss twins in *The Social Network* (2010)? Since Aaron Sorkin's screenplay is a fictional account of a true incident, it would have been acceptable to alter the story and cast actors as fraternal rather than identical twins. Instead, they cast Armie

Hammer and Josh Pence, respectively, in the roles of the identical Winklevoss twins, Cameron and Tyler. Throughout their scenes, Hammer acted alongside Pence, and through the postproduction use of motion-capture technology and digital grafting of Hammer's face onto Pence's, they appear on the screen as identical twins, as you can see in the image here (left to right, Hammer as Cameron, Pence as Tyler). Using two different actors in these roles allows the actors to develop characters with two different personalities; using digital grafting ensures the facial similarity necessary for depicting identical twins. While the result is totally convincing in this specific situation, there aren't many movies about identical twins. You can study the process by which this was achieved by watching *The Lot* on Disk Two, "The Supplements," accompanying the DVD release of the movie.

has so persuasively argued, that such developments may extend and enrich the illusions that the movies create at the expense of the film artists themselves, including directors, designers, cinematographers, editors, *and* actors.[25]

Casting Actors

Casting is the process of choosing and hiring actors for a movie, and there are various ways to do it. Although casting usually takes place during pre-

production after the script has been written, it may also occur during development if scripts are written for specific actors. In the studio system, each studio ran its casting department and thus tended to restrict casting to its own actors. Today, professional casting directors work under contract to independent producers and also have their own professional association, the Casting Society of America (CSA). Casting can be done either by professionals hired for a particular film or by a casting agency. In either case, the people in charge generally work closely with the producer, director, and screenwriter when first determining casting needs. To aid in the initial selection of candidates, they maintain files of actors' résumés and photographs.

[25]André Bazin, "The Myth of Total Cinema," in *What Is Cinema?* trans. Hugh Gray, 2 vols. (Berkeley: University of California Press, 1967–71), I, pp. 17–22.

Similarly, there is no one way for actors to find out about parts that they may want to play. Producers, directors, screenwriters, or casting directors may alert agents or contact actors directly. Audition calls may be published in trade papers such as *Variety, The Hollywood Reporter*, and *Back Stage*, or word may spread through networks of movie professionals.

Regardless of actors' experience, they may be asked to read for parts, either alone or with other actors, or to take **screen tests** (trial filmings). If they are chosen for the part, negotiations will, in most cases, be handled by their agents, but if they belong to one of the actors' unions—the Screen Actors Guild (SAG) or the American Federation of Television and Radio Artists (AFTRA)—the conditions of their participation will be governed by union contract.

New approaches to casting are helping to foster the growth of today's independent filmmaking. For example, casting leading actors in major roles focuses the attention of distributors and audiences alike on movies that they may otherwise overlook. Laura Linney (who earned an Oscar nomination for her work) and Philip Seymour Hoffman brought prestige to Tamara Jenkins's *The Savages* (2007), as did Robert Downey, Jr., and Dianne Wiest to Dito Montiel's *A Guide to Recognizing Your Saints* (2006). Woody Allen and his casting director routinely pack his small movies with rosters of stars. Allen has a huge following among sophisticated urban audiences, but it's hard to imagine that general audiences would flock to his *Vicky Cristina Barcelona* (2008) if its cast had not included Javier Bardem, Scarlett Johansson, and Penélope Cruz.

Factors Involved in Casting

The art of casting actors takes many factors into account. In theory, the most important considerations are the type of role and how an actor's strengths and weaknesses relate to it. In reality, casting—like every other aspect of movie production—depends, in one way or another, on the budget and expected revenues. Here, gender, race, ethnicity, and age also come into play. The American film industry has tended to produce films with strong, white, male leads. In the 2008 Harris Poll cited above, six of the ten actors fit this description, and two are African Americans. Other significant changes are affecting the evolution of male casting. Between the 1930s and the 1990s, the typical American leading man was often a strong, square-jawed actor with an attractive physique (Clark Gable, Cary Grant, Gary Cooper, Steve McQueen, Sean Connery, Robert Redford, and Russell Crowe, for example). Today, however, many leading men are younger and have softer faces and wiry bodies (Tobey Maguire, Orlando Bloom, Jake Gyllenhaal, Leonardo DiCaprio).[26]

It is also true, however, that today gender, race, ethnicity, and age have become important issues in the movies, as in other areas of American popular culture. Both the characters depicted on the screen and the actors playing them have grown more diverse, particularly in terms of race and ethnicity, and this diversification has, in turn, changed the people who make movies, the audiences for movies, and the financing that makes them possible. Twenty years ago, to see a movie about African Americans meant waiting for the next Spike Lee release, and anyone wanting to see a mainstream movie about Hispanic, Latino, or Asian Americans was generally out of luck. By contrast, now every week—depending, of course, on the distribution of movies in a particular part of the country—audiences can choose from a range of movies that reflect contemporary North America's social diversity in the stories they tell and the filmmakers and actors who made them. Here, the industry has learned that significant profits can be gained by targeting film releases to different demographics.

For decades, movie producers intentionally contradicted social reality by casting actors who are not of a certain race or ethnicity to portray that race or ethnicity: Richard Barthelmess as Cheng Huan in D. W. Griffith's *Broken Blossoms* (1919; see "D. W. Griffith and Lillian Gish," earlier in this chapter), Luise Rainer as O-Lan in Sidney Franklin's *The Good Earth* (1937), Marlon Brando as

[26]See Sharon Waxman, "Hollywood's He-Men Are Bumped by Sensitive Guys; Six-Pack Abs Not Required for New Masculine Ideal," *New York Times* (July 1, 2004), sect. E, p. 1, 5.

[1]

[2]

[3]

The faces of contemporary casting The diversity of contemporary film actors is apparent whenever we go to the cineplex to see the latest releases. Among the most popular actors working today are [1] Denzel Washington, seen here in his role as Ben Marco in Jonathan Demme's *The Manchurian Candidate* (2004); [2] Jennifer Lopez, shown here as Charlie in Robert Luketic's *Monster-in-Law* (2005); and [3] Antonio Banderas, here playing the role of Carlos Rueda in Christopher Hampton's *Imagining Argentina* (2003).

Sakini in Daniel Mann's *The Teahouse of the August Moon* (1956), and Mickey Rooney as Mr. Yunioshi in Blake Edwards's *Breakfast at Tiffany's* (1961), to name just a few. The practice is nearly but not completely extinct today. In Julian Schnabel's *Before Night Falls* (2000), for example, Sean Penn plays a dark-skinned Cuban, Cuco Sanchez; the somewhat darker-skinned Johnny Depp plays both Bon Bon, a transvestite, and Lieutenant Victor, a Cuban military officer. An even more striking example was the casting of Anthony Hopkins as a light-skinned African American in Robert Benton's *The Human Stain* (2003)—a decision that struck many critics as a critical casting error.

The long-standing explanation for this custom among movie executives was that they could not find the appropriate actors. Instead, they gave such all-purpose actors as Anthony Quinn, an Irish Mexican, roles of different races and ethnicities. Using costume, makeup, and accents to change himself, Quinn played a Spaniard, an Italian, a Greek, a Frenchman, an Arab, and a Native American, while Alec Guinness, a great British actor famous for his facility in international accents, played an Indian, an Arab, and a Scotsman. Laurence Olivier played an equally diverse set of roles on the stage and screen, including Shakespeare's Moor, Othello. This does not mean that Quinn, Guinness, and Olivier took these roles because they could not get other work; or that they did not look or sound appropriate in these roles, which they most often did; or even that actors should be limited to roles matching their own genders, races, ethnicities, or ages (since acting is, after all, about the creation of a character). But it is clear that producers simply felt more comfortable casting roles in this manner, that minority actors were disqualified as a result, and that, absent public opposition, the custom continued unabated.

Such barriers were not always in place—or at least not so firmly. Beginning in the 1920s, in reaction to the stereotyping of African Americans in D. W. Griffith's *The Birth of a Nation* (1915), some African Americans strove to make their own films. Producer, director, and exhibitor Oscar

Casting *Gandhi* In Richard Attenborough's *Gandhi* (1982), the English actor Ben Kingsley plays the Indian political and spiritual leader Mahatma Mohandas K. Gandhi (1869-1948) from his youth until his assassination. Born Krishna Bhanji, the son of an Indian doctor and an English fashion model, Kingsley looks so much like Gandhi and inhabits the role so completely that, for many viewers, the two men are inextricably linked.

"This door tonight has been opened" In Martha Coolidge's *Introducing Dorothy Dandridge* (1999), Halle Berry plays Dandridge, who is shown here starring as the title character in Otto Preminger's *Carmen Jones* (1954). For her role in that film, which featured an all-black cast, Dandridge was the first black woman to receive an Academy Award nomination for Best Actress in a Leading Role; Grace Kelly received the Oscar that year (for her performance in George Seaton's *The Country Girl*). Nearly fifty years later, Halle Berry became the first African American woman to win the Academy Award for Best Actress for her performance in Marc Forster's *Monster's Ball* (2001). Berry began her acceptance speech, "This moment is for Dorothy Dandridge, Lena Horne, Diahann Carroll . . . and it's for every nameless, faceless woman of color that now has a chance because this door tonight has been opened."

Micheaux was the most prominent among the leaders of this effort. Although he made about forty feature films, only ten survive. And although Hollywood also tried appealing to the African American audience with all-black musicals, its efforts were few and disappointing. From the beginning, however, Hollywood drew many actors from various racial backgrounds.

In the 1930s, the great comic actor Stepin Fetchit was the first African American to receive featured billing in the movies. Butterfly McQueen, Louise Beavers, and Hattie McDaniel (who won an Oscar for Best Actress in a Supporting Role for her performance in Victor Fleming's *Gone with the Wind*, 1939) all had durable careers playing such demeaning stereotypes as maids and mammies. Paul Robeson, a great actor and singer on the Broadway stage, was featured in several movies, most notably Dudley Murphy's *The Emperor Jones* (1933), James Whale's *Show Boat* (1936), and Julien Duvivier's *Tales of Manhattan* (1942). In the 1950s, Sidney Poitier and Dorothy Dandridge became the first African American movie stars. Poitier has enjoyed an extraordinarily successful career, but Dandridge was not so fortunate. She began by playing stereotypical African American roles in twenty-one movies and was later nominated for the Oscar for Best Actress for her leading role in Otto Preminger's sumptuous musical production

Carmen Jones (1954) but her career ended abruptly after starring (opposite Poitier) in Preminger's *Porgy and Bess* (1959), which despite garnering positive reviews, was a box office failure.

Among the African Americans who have since become stars are Pearl Bailey, Halle Berry, Diahann Carroll, Bill Cosby, Laurence Fishburne, Jamie Foxx, Morgan Freeman, Pam Grier, Samuel L. Jackson, James Earl Jones, Eddie Murphy, Will Smith, Denzel Washington, and Forest Whitaker. Among the many Hispanic, Latino, and Asian stars are Antonio Banderas, Javier Bardem, Joan Chen, Dolores del Rio, José Ferrer, Raul Julia, Nancy Kwan, Fernando Lamas, Li Gong, Lucy Liu, Jennifer Lopez, Keye Luke, Toshirô Mifune, Alfred Molina, Ricardo Montalban, Maria Montez, Rita Moreno, Haing S. Ngor, Edward James Olmos,

Cesar Romero, Lupe Velez, Anna May Wong, and Yun-Fat Chow.

Native Americans, too, have suffered the indignities of either being stereotypically cast—usually as the "bad guys" in movies depicting the "Old West"—or of having non-Indians play Native American parts. Notable actors in such cross-racial casting include Douglas Fairbanks (*The Half-Breed*, 1916; director: Allan Dwan), Pierce Brosnan (*Grey Owl*, 1999; director: Richard Attenborough), Sal Mineo (*Cheyenne Autumn*, 1964; director: John Ford), and Henry Brandon (*The Searchers*, 1956; director: John Ford). However, Ford also cast genuine Native Americans in Indian roles in his films, including Chief Big Tree—who appeared in *The Iron Horse* (1924), *Drums along the Mohawk* (1939), and *She Wore a Yellow Ribbon* (1949)—and Many Mules, an Apache, who plays the Apache antagonist, Geronimo, in *Stagecoach* (1939). Native American actors who have taken major roles as Native Americans include Eddie Spears (*Black Cloud,* 2004; director: Rick Schroder), Adam Beach (*Smoke Signals*, 1998; director: Chris Eyre), Russell Means (*The Last of the Mohicans*, 1992; director: Michael Mann), and Irene Bedard (*The New World*, 2005; director: Terrence Malick). Native American actors who play a variety of roles include Graham Greene (*Breakfast with Scot*, 2007; director: Laurie Lynd) and Gary Farmer (*California Indian*, 2008; director: Timothy Andrew Ramos). Many other movies have cast Native Americans in speaking roles as well as extras, including Arthur Penn's *Little Big Man* (1970), Kevin Costner's *Dances with Wolves* (1990), Terrence Malick's *The New World* (2005), and Charles Howard Thomas's *Morning Song Way* (2006). Native American directors include Chris Eyre (*Smoke Signals*, 1998), Zacharias Kunuk (*The Fast Runner*, 2001), Sterlin Harjo (*Four Sheets to the Wind*, 2007), and Sherman Alexie (*The Business of Fancydancing*, 2002).

Traditionally, because audiences have shown little interest in films about women older than forty-five, the American industry has produced few of them. Some women older than this cutoff—Joan Crawford, Bette Davis, Angela Lansbury, Shirley MacLaine, Debbie Reynolds, Elizabeth Taylor, Shelley Winters—have taken roles as stereotyped eccentrics, where the camp value of their performances translates into the triumphant statement "I'm still here!" Furthermore, audiences love it when a great star from a former era makes a rare comeback, as Gloria Swanson did in Billy Wilder's *Sunset Boulevard* (1950). But even though many excellent movies have featured older male actors—Henry Fonda, Jack Lemmon, Walter Matthau, Jason Robards, Jimmy Stewart, Spencer Tracy—the apparent bias against older female actors remains a box-office fact and thus a reality of casting in Hollywood. By contrast, the British seem to lack such prejudices, for their actors—including Judi Dench, Alec Guinness, Helen Mirren, Laurence Olivier, Peter O'Toole, Joan Plowright, Vanessa Redgrave, Ralph Richardson, Margaret Rutherford, and Maggie Smith—generally work as long as they can. Their popularity in the United States may say something about American audiences' cultural stereotypes—namely, that they'll accept and even expect aging, as long as it happens to other people.

Complicating the issue of age is the ability of young actors, in part through the magic of makeup, to play characters older than themselves: think of Jane Fonda as writer Lillian Hellman in Fred Zinnemann's *Julia* (1977), Leonardo DiCaprio as Howard Hughes in Martin Scorsese's *The Aviator* (2004), or Frank Langella as the CBS network boss in George Clooney's *Good Night, and Good Luck* (2005). Or they can play characters who mature on-screen from youth to old age, as did Orson Welles in his own *Citizen Kane* (1941), Dustin Hoffman as Jack Crabb in Arthur Penn's *Little Big Man* (1970), Ben Kingsley in Richard Attenborough's *Gandhi* (1982), and Robert Downey, Jr. in Attenborough's *Chaplin* (1992). In the standard variation on this approach, two or more actors play the same character during different stages of the character's life, as Kate Winslet and Gloria Stuart did in James Cameron's *Titanic* (1997).

Aspects of Performance

Types of Roles

Actors may play major roles, minor roles, character roles, cameo roles, and walk-ons. In addition, roles may be written specifically for bit players, extras, stuntpersons, and even animal performers. Actors who play **major roles** (also called *main, featured*, or *lead roles*) become principal agents in helping to move the plot forward. Whether stars or newcomers, they appear in many scenes and—ordinarily, but not always—receive screen credit preceding the title.

In the Hollywood studio system, major roles were traditionally played by stars such as John Wayne, whose studios counted on them to draw audiences regardless of the parts they played. Their steadfastness was often more important than their versatility as actors, although Wayne surprises us more often than we may admit. One of the strengths of the studio system was its grooming of professionals in all its creative departments, including actors at all levels, from leads such as Henry Fonda and Katharine Hepburn to character actors such as Thelma Ritter and Andy Devine—best remembered as, respectively, the wisecracking commentator on "Jeff's" (James Stewart) actions in Alfred Hitchcock's *Rear Window* (1954) and the Ringo Kid's (John Wayne) loyal friend in John Ford's *Stagecoach* (1939). Indeed, one of the joys of looking at movies from this period comes from those character actors whose faces, if not names, we always recognize: Mary Boland, Walter Brennan, Harry Carey, Jr., Ray Collins, Laura Hope Crews, Gladys George, Marjorie Main, Butterfly McQueen, Una O'Connor, Franklin Pangborn, Erskine Sanford, and Ernest Thesiger, to name a distinctive few out of hundreds.

Stars may be so valuable to productions that they have **stand-ins**, actors who look reasonably like them in height, weight, coloring, and so on and who substitute for them during the tedious process of preparing setups or taking light readings. Because actors in major roles are ordinarily not hired for their physical or athletic prowess, **stuntpersons** double for them in scenes requiring special skills or involving hazardous actions, such as crashing cars, jumping from high places, swimming, and riding (or falling off) horses. Through special effects, however, filmmakers may now augment actors' physical exertions so that they appear to do their own stunts, as in Andy and Larry Wachowski's *The Matrix* (1999) and McG's *Charlie's Angels* (2000).

In effect, the computer becomes the stunt double. Nonetheless, ten stunt boxers were cast for Clint Eastwood's *Million Dollar Baby* (2004), indicating, at least, that some activities cannot be faked on the screen, particularly activities that could cause damage to an actor's looks or other serious injuries.

Actors who play **minor roles** (or *supporting roles*) rank second in the hierarchy. They also help move the plot forward (and thus may be as important as actors in major roles), but they generally do not appear in as many scenes as the featured players. They may hold **character roles**, which represent distinctive character types (sometimes stereotypes): society leaders, judges, doctors, diplomats, and so on. **Bit players** hold small speaking parts, and **extras** usually appear in nonspeaking or crowd roles and receive no screen credit. **Cameos** are small but significant roles often taken by famous actors, as in Robert Altman's Hollywood satire *The*

The importance of minor roles In John Huston's *The Maltese Falcon* (1941), Humphrey Bogart stars as the hard-boiled private eye Sam Spade. Gladys George has a small part as Iva Archer, Spade's former lover and the widow of his business partner, Miles Archer (Jerome Cowan). In this scene, George delivers a strongly emotional performance, against which Bogart displays a relative lack of feeling that fills us in on relations between the characters. Stars' performances often depend on the solid and even exceptional work of their fellow actors. The unusually fine supporting cast in this movie includes Hollywood greats Mary Astor, Peter Lorre, and Sydney Greenstreet, who received an Oscar nomination for Best Actor in a Supporting Role.

Character actors Although Franklin Pangborn was never a household name, his face was instantly recognizable in the more than 200 movies he made over a career that spanned four decades. With his intimidating voice and fastidious manners, he was best known for playing suspicious hotel clerks, imperious department-store floorwalkers, and sourpuss restaurant managers. Here he's the threatening bank examiner J. Pinkerton Snoopington in the W. C. Fields classic *The Bank Dick* (1940; director: Edward F. Cline).

Player (1992), which features appearances by sixty-five well-known actors and personalities. **Walk-ons** are even smaller roles, reserved for highly recognizable actors or personalities. As a favor to his friend Orson Welles, with whom he'd worked several times before, Joseph Cotten played such a role in Welles's *Touch of Evil* (1958), where he had a few words of dialogue and literally walked on and off the set.

Animal actors, too, play major, minor, cameo, and walk-on roles. For many years, Hollywood made pictures built on the appeal of such animals as the dogs Lassie, Rin Tin Tin, Asta, and Benji; the cat Rhubarb; the parakeets Bill and Coo; the chimp Cheeta; the mule Francis; the lion Elsa; the dolphin Flipper; and the killer whale Willy. Most of these animals were specially trained to work in front of the camera, and many were sufficiently valuable that they, like other stars, had stand-ins for setups and stunt doubles for hazardous work. Working with animal performers often proves more complicated than working with human actors. For example, six Jack Russell terriers, including three puppies, played the title character in Jay Russell's *My Dog Skip* (2000), a tribute to that indomitable breed.

Preparing for Roles

In creating characters, screen actors begin by synthesizing basic sources, including the script, their own experiences and observations, and the influences of other actors. They also shape their understanding of a role by working closely with their director. This collaboration can be mutually agreeable and highly productive, or it can involve constant, even tempestuous, arguments that may or may not produce what either artist wants. Ideally, both director and actor should understand each other's concept of the role and, where differences exist, try to agree on an approach that is acceptable to both. Director Sidney Lumet, known for his keen understanding of how actors work, recognizes that acting is a very personal thing. He writes: "The *talent* of acting is one in which the actor's thoughts and feelings are instantly communicated to the audience. In other words, the 'instrument' that the actor is using is himself. It is *his* feelings, *his* physiognomy, *his* sexuality, *his* tears, *his* laughter, *his* anger, *his* romanticism, *his* tenderness, *his* viciousness, that are up there on the screen for all to see." He emphasizes that the difference between the actor who merely duplicates a life that he or she has observed and the actor who *creates* something unique on the screen "lies in the degree of the actor's personal revelation."[27]

Different roles have different demands, and all actors have their own approaches, whether they get inside their characters, get inside themselves, or do further research. Bette Davis, whose roles were often assigned her by studios, said, "It depends entirely on what the assignment happens to be. . . . [But] I have never played a part which I did not feel was a person very different from myself."[28] Jack Lemmon, a Method actor who generally chose his own roles, explained, "It's like laying bricks. You

[27]Sidney Lumet, *Making Movies* (New York: Knopf, 1995), pp. 59–60.
[28]Bette Davis, "The Actress Plays Her Part," in *Playing to the Camera: Film Actors Discuss Their Craft*, ed. Bert Cardullo, Harry Geduld, Ronald Gottesman, and Leigh Woods (New Haven, Conn.: Yale University Press, 1998), pp. 177–185, quotation, p. 179.

start at the bottom and work up; actually I guess you start in the middle and work to the outside."[29]

Building a character "brick by brick" is an approach also used by Harvey Keitel and John Malkovich, who might have varied this approach slightly when he played himself in Spike Jonze's *Being John Malkovich* (1999). Liv Ullmann and Jack Nicholson believe that the actor draws on the subconscious mind. Ullmann says, "Emotionally, I don't prepare. I think about what I would like to show, but I don't prepare, because I feel that most of the emotions I have to show I know about. By drawing on real experience, I can show them."[30] In describing his work with director Roman Polanski on *Chinatown* (1974), Nicholson says that the director "pushes us farther than we are conscious of being able to go; he forces us down into the subconscious—in order to see if there's something better there."[31] Jodie Foster works from instinct, doing what she feels is right for the character.[32] To create The Tramp, Charlie Chaplin started with the character's costume: "I had no idea of the character. But the moment I was dressed, the clothes and the make-up made me feel the person he was."[33] Alec Guinness said that he was never happy with his preparation until he knew how the character walked; Laurence Olivier believed that he would not be any good as a character unless he "loved" him;[34] and Morgan Freeman says that some of his preparation depends on the clothes he is to wear.[35]

Olivier, one of the greatest stage and screen actors of the twentieth century, defined acting in

Olivier's *Henry V* Laurence Olivier in the first screen adaptation of *Henry V* (1944); this very popular film, produced during a troubled time (World War II), was uniformly praised for the quality of its acting. The many previous screen adaptations of Shakespeare's plays had been mainly faithful records of stage productions, but Olivier's film, his first as a director, benefited from his understanding of cinema's potential as a narrative art, his extensive acting experience, his deep knowledge of Shakespeare's language, and his sharp instincts about the national moods in Great Britain and the United States. *Henry V* received an Oscar nomination for Best Picture, and Olivier received a nomination for Best Actor in a Leading Role as well as an Oscar for his outstanding achievement as actor, producer, and director for bringing *Henry V* to the screen.

various ways, including as "convincing lying."[36] Although Olivier stands out for the extraordinary range of the roles he undertook, on both stage and screen, and for his meticulous preparation in creating them, this remark suggests that he had little patience with theories of acting. Indeed, when asked how he created his film performance as the king in *Henry V* (1944; director: Olivier), he replied simply, "I don't know—I'm England, that's all."[37] Olivier had made this film to bolster British morale during the last days of World War II, and thus he wanted Henry V to embody traditional British values.

[29]Jack Lemmon, "Conversation with the Actor," ibid., pp. 267–275, quotation, p. 267.

[30]Liv Ullmann, "Conversation with the Actress," ibid., pp. 157–165, quotation, p. 160.

[31]See the entry on Jack Nicholson, in *Actors on Acting for the Screen*, ed. Tomlinson, pp. 404–407, quotation, p. 405.

[32]See the entry on Jodie Foster, ibid., pp. 196–197.

[33]Charles Chaplin, *My Autobiography* (New York: Simon & Schuster, 1964), p. 260.

[34]See the entry on Alec Guinness in *Actors on Acting for the Screen*, ed. Tomlinson, pp. 232–233; and Laurence Olivier, *Confessions of an Actor: An Autobiography* (1982; repr., New York: Penguin, 1984), pp. 136–137.

[35]From an interview with James Lipton, "James Lipton Takes on Three," on Disc 2 ("Special Features") in the widescreen DVD release of *Million Dollar Baby* (2004).

[36]Olivier, p. 20.

[37]Laurence Olivier, qtd. in Donald Spoto, *Laurence Olivier: A Biography* (New York: HarperCollins, 1992), pp. 111–112.

The great silent-era director F. W. Murnau emphasized intellect and counseled actors to restrain their feelings, to *think* rather than *act*. He believed actors to be capable of conveying the intensity of their thoughts so that audiences would understand. Director Rouben Mamoulian gave Greta Garbo much the same advice when she played the leading role in his *Queen Christina* (1933). The film ends with the powerful and passionate Swedish queen sailing to Spain with the body of her lover, a Spanish nobleman killed in a duel. In preparing for the final close-up, in which the queen stares out to sea, Garbo asked Mamoulian, "What should I be thinking of? What should I be doing?" His reply: "Have you heard of *tabula rasa*? I want your face to be a blank sheet of paper. I want the writing to be done by every member of the audience. I'd like it if you could avoid even blinking your eyes, so that you're nothing but a beautiful mask."[38] Is she remembering the past? Imagining the future? With the camera serving as an apparently neutral mediator between actress and audience, Garbo's blank face asks us to transform it into what we hope or want to see.

Naturalistic and Nonnaturalistic Styles

We have all seen at least one movie in which a character, perhaps a whole cast of characters, is like no one we have ever met nor like anyone we *could* ever meet. Either because the world they inhabit functions according to rules that don't apply in our world or because their behaviors are extreme, such characters aren't realistic in any colloquial sense of the word. But if the actors perform skillfully, we are likely to accept the characters as believable within the context of the story. We might be tempted to call such portrayals *realistic,* but we'd do better to use the term *naturalistic.*

Actors who strive for appropriate, expressive, coherent, and unified characterizations can render their performances naturalistically and/or nonnaturalistically. Screen acting appears naturalistic

when actors re-create recognizable or plausible human behavior for the camera. The actors not only look like the characters should (in their costume, makeup, and hairstyle) but also think, speak, and move the way people would offscreen. By contrast, nonnaturalistic performances seem excessive, exaggerated, even overacted; they may employ strange or outlandish costumes, makeup, or hairstyles; they might aim for effects beyond the normal range of human experience; and they often intend to distance or estrange audiences from characters. Frequently, they are found in horror, fantasy, and action films.

What Konstantin Stanislavsky was to naturalistic acting, German playwright Bertolt Brecht was to nonnaturalistic performance. Brecht allied his theatrical ideas with Marxist political principles to create a nonnaturalistic theater. Whereas Stanislavsky strove for realism, Brecht believed that audience members should not think they're watching something actually happening before them. Instead, he wanted every aspect of a theatrical production to limit the audience's identification with characters and events, thereby creating a psychological distance (called the **alienation effect** or **distancing effect**) between them and the stage. The intent of this approach is to remind the audience of the artificiality of the theatrical performance.

Overall, this theory has not had much influence on mainstream filmmaking; after all, unlike theater, cinema can change—as often as it wants—the relationship between spectators and the screen, alternately alienating them from or plunging them into the action. However, we do see this approach when actors step out of character, face the camera, and directly address the audience (a maneuver, more common in theater than cinema, that is called *breaking the fourth wall*—the imaginary, invisible wall that separates the audience from the stage). Although it is a device that can destroy a movie if used inappropriately, breaking the fourth wall works effectively when audience members are experiencing things as the character does *and* the character has the self-confidence to exploit that empathy.

In the late 1920s in Berlin, Brecht discovered Peter Lorre, who later became one of the most dis-

---

[38]Rouben Mamoulian, qtd. in Tom Milne, *Rouben Mamoulian* (Bloomington: Indiana University Press, 1969), p. 74.

tinctively stylized actors on the American screen. They worked closely together on several stage productions at the same time that Lorre was preparing the lead role of Hans Beckert, a child murderer, in Fritz Lang's *M* (1931). Lorre's magnificent performance, particularly in the final scene—one of the most emotional in movie history—reflects the influence of Brecht's theories and directing. Lorre creates a duality—Beckert and the actor detached from the character who comments on his actions—and while it is not pure direct address (he is addressing a "jury" in a kangaroo court), we are absolutely riveted by the power and strangeness of his conception of the role.

Tom Edison (Paul Bettany) frequently addresses his idealistic views directly to the viewer in Lars von Trier's *Dogville* (2003), which in overall style owes much to Bertolt Brecht's influence. In Max Ophüls's *Lola Montès* (1955), the Circus Master (Peter Ustinov) addresses the circus audience, of which, we understand, we are members. For comic effect, Tom Jones (Albert Finney) breaks the fourth wall in Tony Richardson's *Tom Jones* (1963), as does Alfie (Michael Caine) in Lewis Gilbert's *Alfie* (1966) and (played by Jude Law) in Charles Shyer's 2004 remake. Various characters speak directly to the viewer in Spike Lee's *Do the Right Thing* (1989). There is a much more solid tradition of direct address in the European theatrical cinema of such directors as Jean-Luc Godard, Chantal Akerman, and Eric Rohmer, among others.

In Buddy Giovinazzo's *No Way Home* (1996), Tim Roth gives a naturalistic performance as Joey, a slow but principled young man who is just out of prison. He has taken the rap for an assault he did not commit and returns to Staten Island to find that the people who framed him and circumstances in the community are just as rotten as they were when he left. Determined not to associate with his low-life brother and former friends or return to a life of crime, he boards a bus and heads for undiscovered country. In Boaz Yakin's *Fresh* (1994), Sean Nelson naturalistically plays the title character—a young, black Brooklynite working as a courier for a dope dealer between going to school and looking out for his older sister. In Tim Burton's *Edward Scissorhands* (1990), Johnny Depp gives a nonnatu-

⟦1⟧

⟦2⟧

Naturalistic versus nonnaturalistic performances
Naturalistic and nonnaturalistic performances sometimes overlap, but these categories help us relate actors' contributions to a filmmaker's overall vision. [1] In *Knocked Up* (2007), Seth Rogen's naturalistic performance as a reformed slacker becomes part of director Judd Apatow's clear-eyed depiction of the consequences of unprotected sex. Here, Rogen tells his pregnant girlfriend, who has decided to keep their baby, that he's ready to do whatever it takes to support her. He then congratulates himself by saying "awesome" in recognition of his newfound maturity. [2] Johnny Depp's nonnaturalistic performance as the title character in *Edward Scissorhands* (1990) enables director Tim Burton to draw us into the exaggerated, downright weird world of this story. Burton's film is about fantasy, the way things might be in that world. Nelson's and Depp's performances differ widely, but they suit their respective movies. Imagine how out of place either character would be in the other's world!

ralistic performance as the title character, a kind of Frankenstein's monster—scary, but benevolent—created by a mad inventor who died before his work was finished. Edward lives in a deteriorating Gothic castle on a mountaintop that overlooks a nightmarishly pastel suburb, to which he eventually moves. The decor and costumes identify him immediately as a metaphor for the ultimate outsider. But the challenge to Depp as an actor is not only to acknowledge just how different he appears to others ("hands," scars, makeup, hairstyle), which he does in a very self-conscious and often comic manner (e.g., using his hands to shred cabbage for cole slaw), but also to humanize this character so that he can be accepted as a member of the community.

Improvisational Acting

Improvisation can mean extemporizing—that is, delivering lines based only loosely on the written script or without the preparation that comes with studying a script before rehearsing it. It can also mean playing through a moment, making up lines to keep scenes going when actors forget their written lines, stumble on lines, or have some other mishap. Of these two senses, the former is most important in movie acting, particularly in the poststudio world; the latter is an example of professional grace under pressure.

Improvisation can be seen as an extension of Stanislavsky's emphasis that the actor striving for a naturalistic performance should avoid any mannerisms that call attention to technique. Occupying a place somewhere between his call for actors to bring their own experiences to roles and Brecht's call for actors to distance themselves from roles, improvisation often involves collaboration between actors and directors in creating stories, characters, and dialogue, which may then be incorporated into scripts. According to film scholar Virginia Wright Wexman, what improvisers

> seem to be striving for is the sense of discovery that comes from the unexpected and unpredictable in human behavior. If we think of art as a means of giving form to life, improvisation can be looked at as one way of adding to our sense of the liveliness of art, a means of avoiding the sterility that results from rote recitations of abstract conventional forms.[39]

[39]Virginia Wright Wexman, "The Rhetoric of Cinematic Improvisation," *Cinema Journal* 20, no. 1 (Fall 1980): 29. See also Maurice Yacowar, "An Aesthetic Defense of the Star System in Films," *Quarterly Review of Film Studies* 4, no. 1 (Winter 1979): 48–50.

Improvisation "You talkin' to me? . . . You talkin' to me?" Screenwriter Paul Schrader wrote no dialogue for the scene in Martin Scorsese's *Taxi Driver* (1976) in which Travis Bickle (Robert De Niro) rehearses his dreams of vigilantism before a mirror. Prior to filming, De Niro improvised the lines that now accompany this well-known moment in film history, a disturbing, darkly comic portrait of an unhinged mind talking to itself.

For years, improvisation has played a major part in actors' training, but it was anathema in the studio system—where practically everything was preprogrammed—and it remains comparatively rare in narrative moviemaking. Actors commonly confer with directors about altering or omitting written lines, but this form of improvisation is so limited in scope that we can better understand it as the sort of fertile suggestion making that is intrinsic to collaboration. Although certain directors encourage actors not only to discover the characters within themselves but also to imagine what those characters might say (and how they might act) in any given situation, James Naremore, an authority on film acting, explains that even great actors, when they improvise, "tend to lapse into monologue, playing from relatively static, frontal positions with a second actor nearby who nods or makes short interjections."[40]

Among the director-actor collaborations that have made improvisation work effectively are Bernardo Bertolucci and Marlon Brando (*Last Tango in Paris*, 1972); Robert Altman and a large

[40]James Naremore, *Acting in the Cinema* (Berkeley: University of California Press, 1988), p. 45.

company of actors (*Nashville*, 1975; *Short Cuts*, 1993; *Gosford Park*, 2001); Mike Leigh and various actors (*Life Is Sweet*, 1991; *Naked*, 1993; *Topsy-Turvy*, 1999; *All or Nothing*, 2002); and John Cassavetes and Gena Rowlands (*Faces*, 1968; *A Woman under the Influence*, 1974; *Gloria*, 1980).

The Cassavetes–Rowlands collaboration is particularly important and impressive, not only for what it accomplished but also for the respect it received as an experimental approach within the largely conventional film industry. "John's theory," Rowlands explains,

> is that if there's something wrong, it's wrong in the writing. If you take actors who can act in other things and they get to a scene they've honestly tried to do, and if they still can't get it, then there's something wrong with the writing. Then you stop, you improvise, you talk about it. Then he'll go and rewrite it—it's not just straight improvisation. I'm asked a lot about this, and it's true, when I look at the films and I *see* that they look improvised in a lot of different places where I know they weren't.[41]

Improvised acting requires directors to play even more active roles than if they were working with prepared scripts because they must not only elicit actors' ideas for characters and dialogue but also orchestrate those contributions within overall cinematic visions. Ultimately, directors help form all contributions, including those of actors. Nearly all directors who employ improvisation have the actors work it out in rehearsal, then lock it down for filming, perhaps radically changing their plans for how such scenes will be shot. This is how, for example, Martin Scorsese and Robert De Niro worked out the originally silent "You talkin' to me?" scene in *Taxi Driver* (1976). Unless directors and actors have talked publicly about their work, we seldom know when and to what extent improvisation has been used in a film. Because we know that Cassavetes prepared his actors with precise scripts that they refined with extensive improvisational exercises, by studying the original script we can

[41]Gena Rowlands in *Actors on Acting for the Screen*, ed. Tomlinson, p. 482.

prepare to look for the improvisation, to judge its usefulness, and to determine whether improvised performances seem convincing or, ironically, less convincing than scripted ones.

Directors and Actors

Directors and actors have collaborated closely since the days when D. W. Griffith established screen acting with Lillian Gish. Inevitably, such relationships depend on the individuals: what each brings to his or her work, what each can do alone, and what each needs from a collaborator. Such different approaches taken by different directors in working with actors are as necessary, common, and useful as the different approaches taken by different actors as they prepare for roles.

Some veterans of the studio system, such as William Wyler and George Cukor, are known as "actors' directors," meaning that the directors inspire such confidence they can actively shape actors' performances. Although Wyler may have enjoyed the trust of Bette Davis, Fredric March, Myrna Loy, Barbra Streisand, and other notable actors, the atmosphere on the set was considerably tenser when Laurence Olivier arrived in Hollywood for his first screen role, Heathcliff in Wyler's *Wuthering Heights* (1939). Olivier had already earned a considerable reputation on the London stage and was frankly contemptuous of screen acting, which he thought serious actors did only for the money. Wyler, on the other hand, was one of Hollywood's great stylists, a perfectionist who drove actors crazy with his keen sense of acting and love of multiple takes. Everyone on the set perceived the tension between them. Wyler encouraged Olivier to be patient in responding to the challenges involved in acting for the camera, and eventually Olivier overcame his attitude of condescension to give one of his greatest film performances.

In developing his relationships with actors, director John Ford encouraged them to create their characters to serve the narrative. He preferred to work with the same actors over and over, and his working method never changed. John Wayne, who acted in many of Ford's films and has been described as the director's alter ego, said Ford gave direction "with his entire personality—his facial expressions, bending his eye. He didn't verbalize. He wasn't articulate, he couldn't really finish a sentence. . . . He'd give you a clue, just an opening. If you didn't produce what he wanted, he would pick you apart."[42] Newcomers faced a challenge in getting it right the first time. Similarly, Otto Preminger, the director of *Laura* (1944), was so predictably cruel to his actors that he was known as Otto the Ogre.

However rigid Ford's approach may at first seem, we find it in similarly fruitful collaborations between Rouben Mamoulian and Greta Garbo, Josef von Sternberg and Marlene Dietrich, John Huston and Humphrey Bogart, William Wyler and Bette Davis, François Truffaut and Jean-Pierre Léaud, Akira Kurosawa and Toshirô Mifune, Satyajit Ray and Soumitra Chatterjee, Martin Scorsese and Robert De Niro, Spike Lee and Denzel Washington, and Tim Burton and Johnny Depp. These directors know what they want, explain it clearly, select actors with whom they work well, and then collaborate with them to create movies that are characterized in part by the seamless line between directing and acting. Alexander Mackendrick, the director of the classic *Sweet Smell of Success* (1957), was once asked how to get an actor to do what he needed him to do. "You don't," he said. "What you do is try to get him to *want* [emphasis added] what you need."

By contrast, the line that *can* exist between directing and acting is evident in the work of director Alfred Hitchcock, who tends to place mise-en-scène above narrative, and both mise-en-scène and narrative above acting. Hitchcock's movies were so carefully planned and rehearsed in advance that actors were expected to follow his direction closely, so that even those with limited talent (e.g., Tippi Hedren in *The Birds*, 1963; and Kim Novak in *Vertigo*, 1958) gave performances that satisfied the director's needs.

On the other hand, Stanley Kubrick, who was as rigidly in control of his films as Hitchcock, was more flexible. When directing *Barry Lyndon* (1975), a film in which fate drove the plot, Kubrick gave his principal actors—Ryan O'Neal and Marisa Berenson—almost nothing to say and then moved them about his sumptuous mise-en-scène like pawns on a chessboard. When working with a more open story, however, he encouraged actors to improvise in rehearsal or on the set. The results included such memorable moments as Peter Sellers's final monologue as Dr. Strangelove (and the film's last line, "*Mein Führer*, I can walk!") and Jack Nicholson's manic "Heeeere's Johnny!" before the climax of *The Shining* (1980). Malcolm McDowell in *A Clockwork Orange* (1971) and Tom Cruise and Nicole Kidman in *Eyes Wide Shut* (1999) are also said to have worked out their performances in improvisations with the director. Perhaps the most extreme example is director Werner Herzog, who, in directing *Heart of Glass* (1976), hypnotized the entire cast each day on the set to create what he called "an atmosphere of hallucination, prophecy, visionary and collective madness."

How Filmmaking Affects Acting

Actors must understand how a film is made, because every aspect of the filmmaking process can affect performances and the actors' contributions to the creation of meaning. At the same time, audiences should understand what a movie actor goes through to deliver a performance that, to their eyes, seems effortless and spontaneous. Here are some of the challenges an actor faces.

Although there are certain exceptions, most production budgets and schedules do not have the funds or the time to give movie actors much in the way of rehearsal. Thus, actors almost always perform a character's progression entirely out of sequence, and this out-of-continuity shooting can also force those who are being filmed in isolation to perform their parts as though they were interacting with other people. When these shots are edited together, the illusion of togetherness is there, but the actors must make it convincing. Actors must time their movements and precisely hit predetermined marks on the floor so that a moving camera and a focus puller know where they will be at every

[42]John Wayne, qtd. in Joseph McBride, *Searching for John Ford: A Life* (New York: St. Martin's Press, 2001), p. 299.

moment; they must often direct their gaze and position their body and/or face in unnatural-feeling poses to allow for lighting, camera position, and composition. These postures usually appear natural on-screen but don't feel natural to the actors performing them on the set.

Movie actors must repeat the same action/line/emotion more than once—not just for multiple takes from a single setup but also for multiple setups—which means that they may perform the close-up of a particular scene an hour after they performed the same moment for a different camera position. Everything about their performance is fragmented, and thus they must struggle to stay in character. Finally, actors are sometimes required to work with acting and dialogue coaches, physical trainers, and stunt personnel. For all the reasons listed here, delivering a convincing screen performance is very challenging.

In the following chapters we will examine editing and sound and the ways they relate to acting and meaning. Here we'll look briefly at how acting is affected by framing, composition, lighting, and the types and lengths of shots.

Framing, Composition, Lighting, and the Long Take

Framing and composition can bring actors together in a shot or keep them apart. Such inclusion and exclusion create relationships between characters, and these in turn create meaning. The physical relation of the actors to each other and to the overall frame (height, width, and depth) can significantly affect how we see and interpret a shot.

The inciting moment of the plot of Orson Welles's *Citizen Kane* (1941) and one of the principal keys to understanding the movie—for many viewers, its most unforgettable moment—occurs when Charles Foster Kane's (Welles) mother, Mary Kane (Agnes Moorehead), signs the contract that determines her son's future. It consists of only six shots, two of which are long takes. Relying on design, lighting, cinematography, and acting, Welles creates a scene of almost perfect ambiguity.

In designing the scene, Welles puts the four principal characters involved in the incident in the same frame for the two long takes but, significantly, divides the space within this frame into exterior and interior spaces: a young Charles (Buddy Swan) is outside playing with the Rosebud sled in the snow, oblivious to how his life is being changed forever; while Mary, her husband, Jim (Harry Shannon), and Walter Parks Thatcher (George Coulouris) are in Mrs. Kane's boardinghouse (image [2]) for shots 1 through 3 (images [1 to 5] on page 324) and outside for shot 4 (image [6]). In shot 3 (image [4]), this division of the overall space into two separate physical and emotional components is dramatically emphasized after Mary signs the contract and Jim walks to the background of the frame and shuts the window, symbolically shutting Charles out of his life and also cutting us off from the sound of his voice. Mary immediately walks to the same window and opens it, asserting her control over the boy by sharply calling "Charles!" before going out to explain the situation to him.

The two long takes carry the weight of the scene and thus require the adult actors to work closely together in shot 3 (image [4]) and with the boy in shot 4 (image [6]). They begin inside the house as a tightly framed ensemble confronting one another across a small table—their bodies composed and their faces lighted to draw attention to the gravity of the decision they are making—and continue outdoors, where these tensions break into the open as young Charles learns of his fate.

The lighting also helps create the meaning. Lamps remain unlit inside the house, where the atmosphere is as emotionally cold as the snowy landscape is physically cold. Outside, the light is flat and bright; inside, this same bright light, reflected from the snow, produces deep shadows. This effect appears most clearly after the opening of shot 3, when Mary Kane turns from the window and walks from the background to the foreground. As she does, lighting divides her face, the dark and light halves emphasizing how torn she feels as a mother in sending Charles away.

To prepare for the long take, Welles drilled his actors to the point of perfection in rehearsals, giving them amazing things to do (such as requiring Moorehead to pace up and down the narrow room)

1

2

3

4

5

6

7

8

and then letting this preparation pay off in moments of great theatrical vitality. Look closely, for example, at the performance of Agnes Moorehead, with whom Welles had worked in radio productions.[43] Moorehead knew exactly how to use the tempo, pitch, and rhythm of her voice to give unexpected depth to the familiar melodramatic type she plays here. In the carefully designed and controlled setting—the long room, dividing window, and snowy exterior—Mrs. Kane, whose makeup, hairstyle, and costume are those of a seemingly simple pioneer woman, reveals herself to be something quite different. She is both unforgettably humane as she opens the window and calls her son sharply to the destiny she has decreed and—given that her only business experience has been in running a boardinghouse—surprisingly shrewd in obviously having retained Thatcher to prepare the contract that seals this moment. In fact, this is one of the few scenes in the movie in which a female character totally dominates the action—not surprising, for it is a scene of maternal rejection.

As Mary Kane throws open the window, she cries out, "Charles!" in a strained, even shrill, voice that reveals her anxiety about what she is doing; yet a moment later, sounding both tender and guilty, she tells Thatcher that she has had Charles's trunk packed for a week. Should we read the cold mask of her face as the implacable look of a woman resigned to her decision or as a cover for maternal feelings? (image [7]) Does it reflect the doubt, indecision, and dread any person would feel in such a situation? Is it the face of sacrifice? Is it all of these possibilities and more? And how should we read Charles, who, in the span of a moment, goes from playful to wary to angry to antagonistic? (image [8].)

Although the downtrodden Jim Kane protests his wife's actions, when Thatcher coolly informs him that he and his wife will receive $50,000 per year, he feebly gives in, saying, "Well, let's hope it's all for the best"—a remark that invariably, as it should, provokes laughter from viewers. And Thatcher, wearing a top hat and dressed in the formal clothes of a big-city banker, sends contradictory signals. He's precise in overseeing Mrs. Kane's signature, dismissive of Mr. Kane, fawning as he meets Charles, and angry when Charles knocks him to the ground. In encouraging this kind of richly nuanced acting, and its resulting ambiguity, Welles shifts the challenge of interpretation to us.

As this scene shows, the long take, used in conjunction with deep-focus cinematography, provides directors and actors with the opportunity to create scenes of greater-than-usual length as well as broader and deeper field of composition. In addition, the long take encourages ensemble acting that calls attention to acting, not editing between shots. Although we tend to think of actors and their performances as acts of individual creativity, we should not neglect the fact that one actor's performance often very much depends on another's. Indeed, it may rely on an ensemble, or group, of actors.[44]

Ensemble acting—which emphasizes the interaction of actors, not the individual actor—evolved as a further step in creating a verisimilar mise-en-scène for both the stage and the screen. Typically experienced in the theater, ensemble acting is used less in the movies because it requires the provision of rehearsal time that is usually denied to screen actors. However, when a movie director chooses to use long takes and has the time to rehearse the actors, the result is a group of actors working

[43]Welles reportedly called Agnes Moorehead "the best actor I've ever known"; qtd. in Simon Callow, *Orson Welles: The Road to Xanadu* (New York: Viking, 1995), p. 512.

[44]Further study of the long take should consider the work of the great Japanese director Kenji Mizoguchi, notably the Lake Biwa episode in *Ugetsu* (1953). Other notable uses of the technique can be seen in Jean-Pierre Melville's *Le Doulos* (1962), which includes a virtuoso eight-minute single shot; Werner Herzog's *Woyzeck* (1979); Lisandro Alonso's *Los Muertos* (2004), where most of the movie is divided into very long takes; and Pedro Costa's *Colossal Youth* (2006), where real time and very long takes are the norm. *Avalanche* (1937), a work by Japanese director Mikio Naruse, includes a sequence of very brief shots that are edited together so seamlessly that they provide the visual equivalent of a single long take.

together continuously in a single shot. Depending on the story and plot situation, this technique can intensify the emotional impact of a specific plot situation by having all of the involved characters on the screen at the same time.

As with so many other innovations, Orson Welles pioneered ensemble acting in *Citizen Kane* (1941) and *The Magnificent Ambersons* (1942), and its influence was quickly seen in the work of other directors, notably William Wyler in *The Little Foxes* (1941) and *The Best Years of Our Lives* (1946). Other excellent examples of ensemble acting can be found in Akira Kurosawa's *The Lower Depths* (1957), Fred Schepisi's *Last Orders* (2001), Clint Eastwood's *Mystic River* (2003), Peter Weir's *Master and Commander: The Far Side of the World* (2003), Peter Jackson's *The Lord of the Rings* trilogy (2001–3), and Stephen Daldry's *The Hours* (2002). Two examples of impressive acting by an ensemble of child

Acting and the close-up Carl Theodor Dreyer's *The Passion of Joan of Arc* (1928) vividly and unforgettably illustrates the power of the close-up. Most of this silent movie's running time is taken up with contrasting close-ups of Joan (played by Maria Falconetti, a French stage actress who never again appeared on film) and of her many interrogators during the course of her trial. As Joan is questioned, mocked, tortured, and finally burned at the stake, we witness an entire, deeply moving story in her face. Thus we respond to a single character's expressions as they are shaped by the drama and the camera.

actors are Lasse Hallström's *My Life as a Dog* (1985) and Jacob Aaron Estes's *Mean Creek* (2004).

The Camera and the Close-up

The camera creates a greater naturalism and intimacy between actors and audience than would ever be possible on the stage, and thus it serves as screen actors' most important collaborator. Nowhere is the camera's role—that is, its effect on the actor's role—more evident than in a close-up. The true close-up isolates an actor, concentrating on the face; it can be active (commenting on something just said or done, reminding us who is the focus of a scene) or passive (revealing an actor's beauty). Thus, actors' most basic skill is understanding how to reveal themselves to the camera during the close-up.

All great movie actors understand, instinctively or from experience, what to do and not do with their faces when the camera moves in. They must temporarily forget their bodies' expressive possibilities, must stand as close to the camera as they would to a person in real life, must smoothly balance their voices because of the closeness of the microphone, and must focus on the communicative power of even the slightest facial gesture.

Close-ups can shift interpretation to the viewer, as in the two-minute-long close-up of Anna (Nicole Kidman) in Jonathan Glazer's *Birth* (2004; see page 278), or they can leave little room for independent interpretation, as in Marlene Dietrich's opening scene as Amy Jolly in Josef von Sternberg's *Morocco* (1930; cinematographer: Lee Garmes). On the deck of a ship bound for Morocco, the mysterious and beautiful Amy drops her handbag. A sophisticated, older Frenchman—Monsieur La Bessiere (Adolphe Menjou)—kneels at her feet to retrieve her things and then offers to assist her in any way he can when she arrives at her destination. In a relatively quick close-up, Amy looks off into space and tells him she will not need any help. Design elements further distance us from the actress and the character: Dietrich wears a hat with a veil, and thus the shot is "veiled by the 'Rembrandt' light, by the fog, by the lens, and by the diaphanous

Artistic collaboration and the close-up In *Morocco* (1930), Marlene Dietrich's beautiful face is made to appear even more haunting and enigmatic by director Josef von Sternberg's mise-en-scène and Lee Garmes's black-and-white cinematography. Dietrich, too, instinctively understood the kind of lighting and camera placement that was right for her role and the narrative as well as for the glamorous image she cultivated in all her movies. In this MCU, she stands on the deck of a ship at night and appears distant, almost otherworldly, as she is bathed in soft, misty "Rembrandt lighting." One half of her face is bright, part of the other half is in shadow. Her face is further framed and softened by her hat and veil and by shooting her against a background that is out of focus. In all likelihood, Garmes also placed thin gauze fabric over the lens to further soften the image. This is the first appearance of Dietrich's character in the movie, so we know little about her but can already discern that she is not only alluring but mysterious. But one thing we know for sure: the Dietrich face, as it appeared on the screen, was the conscious creation of the actress, director, and cinematographer.

fabric."[45] Although we do not yet know who Amy is, what she does, or why she's going to Morocco, we certainly understand La Bessiere's interest.

Close-ups can also reveal both the process of thinking and the thoughts at its end. In a close-up during the climactic moment of John Ford's *The Searchers* (1956), Ethan Edwards (John Wayne) transforms from a hateful to a loving man as he halts his premeditated attempt to murder his niece, Debbie (Natalie Wood) and instead lifts her to the safety of his arms. The shot doesn't give us

[45]Naremore, *Acting in the Cinema*, p. 141.

time to analyze why he has changed his mind—only to see the results of that change.

In a bar scene in Elia Kazan's *On the Waterfront* (1954), Terry Malloy (Marlon Brando), playing the tough guy, tells Edie Doyle (Eva Marie Saint) his philosophy: "Do it to him before he does it to you." Up to this point, he has remained aloof after witnessing the mob's murder of Edie's brother, an attitude he continues to display until Edie, who is trying to do something about the corruption on the waterfront, asks for his help. Stopped in his tracks, Terry sits down, and a series of close-ups reveals the shakiness of his unfeeling posture. In a soft, caring, but slightly nervous voice (in this bar setting, surrounded by other tough guys, he's a little self-conscious of being tender with a woman), he tells her, "I'd like ta help"—thus revealing to her, the camera, and the audience a more sensitive man under the macho mannerisms.

Acting and Editing

Because a screen actor's performance is fragmented, the editor has considerable power in shaping it. We've already emphasized that the actor is responsible for maintaining the emotional continuity of a performance, but even the most consistent actor delivers slightly different performances on each take. Editors can patch up mistakes by selecting, arranging, or juxtaposing shots to cover the error. They control the duration of an actor's appearance on the screen and how that time is used. When aspects of an actor's performance that was originally deemed acceptable appear in the editing stage to interrupt the flow of the narrative, the development of the character, or the tone of the movie, the editor, in consultation with the director, can dispense with it completely by leaving that footage on the cutting-room floor. In short, the editor can mold a performance with more control than most directors and even the actors themselves can.

Looking at Acting

Given all the elements and aspects in our discussion of an actor's performance, how do we focus our attention on analyzing acting? Before we look at

LOOKING AT MOVIES
EDITING AND PERFORMANCE IN SNAPSHOT

DVD This tutorial examines the effect that editing can have on our perception of actors' performances.

some recognized criteria, let's discuss how we can bring our own experiences to the task. An actor's performance on the screen is not only what we see and hear but also includes many intangibles and subtleties. That alone makes the analysis of acting much more challenging. Breaking down and cataloging other elements of cinematic language—whether narrative, mise-en-scène, production design, or cinematography—and using that information to analyze their usefulness and effectiveness is much easier than analyzing acting. Yet acting (perhaps second only to narrative) is the component most people use to assess movies. We feel an effective, natural, moving performance in a more direct way than other cinematic aspects of most films, and we feel both qualified and compelled to judge films by their performances.

What accounts for this sense of entitlement? Why are we so fixated on actors? Why do we so frequently judge the quality of the movie by the (often intangible) quality of their performances? There are several reasons. First, although cinematic language has a considerable effect on the way we look at a movie, we also identify with characters and, of course, with the actors who inhabit those characters. Second, we identify with characters who pursue a goal. We get involved with this pursuit—one that is driven by and embodied by the actors who

inhabit the characters—because a movie narrative is constructed to exploit what most involves us. We don't even have to like the characters as long as we believe them. Third, we identify with characters because of our own behavior as people. Although cinematic language draws from our instinctive responses to everyday visual and audio information, we don't consciously notice and process it as much as we do human behavior. We are people watchers by nature, necessity, and desire. We are constantly analyzing behavior. When you say hello to a friend or ask a professor a question or order a cup of coffee from a waiter, you are noticing and processing and reacting to human behavior. Is the friend happy? Does the professor think you're stupid? Is the waiter paying attention?

Finally, our identification with characters and the actors who play them has something to do with the fact that we too behave in a way that is consistent with our general character or state of mind, and beyond that, we are also engaged in role-playing. You present yourself differently, depending on where you are, what's going on, and whom you're with. You behave differently with a police officer than you do with your mother or your professor, differently with a new friend than with an old one.

These are some of the reasons why we react as we do to actors and acting. But how do we analyze performance? What are the criteria of a good performance? In their everyday moviegoing, people tend to appreciate acting very subjectively. They like an actor's performance when he or she looks, speaks, and moves in ways that confirm their expectations for the character (or type of character). Conversely, they dislike a performance that baffles those expectations.

This approach, though understandable, can also be limiting. How many of us have sufficient life experiences to fully comprehend the range of characters that appear on the screen? What background do we bring to an analysis of the performance of Humphrey Bogart as a cold-blooded private eye in John Huston's *The Maltese Falcon* (1941); Carlo Battisti as a retired, impoverished bureaucrat in Vittorio De Sica's *Umberto D.* (1952); Giulietta Masina as a childlike circus performer in Federico Fellini's *La Strada* (1954); Toshirô Mifune as a Japanese

[1]

[2]

Assessing acting performances [1] Toshirô Mifune in the death scene of Lord Washizu in Akira Kurosawa's *Throne of Blood* (1957) and [2] Holly Hunter in Jane Campion's *The Piano* (1993), a performance for which she won the Academy Award for Best Actress in a Leading Role. To analyze an actor's performance, we need to consider its context—the particular movie in which it appears. Kurosawa's film draws on a specific genre—the *jidai-geki*, or historical drama—that is traditionally full of action; Campion's film draws on history but focuses more on psychology than on action. Thus, Mifune uses ritualized, nonnaturalistic facial expressions and body language; and Hunter, who speaks only in voice-over, appears more naturalistic, inner-directed, *muted* (subdued).

warlord (based on Shakespeare's *Macbeth*) in Akira Kurosawa's *Throne of Blood* (1957); Marlon Brando as a Mafia don in Francis Ford Coppola's *The Godfather* (1972); Holly Hunter as a mute Victorian relocated from Scotland to New Zealand in Jane Campion's *The Piano* (1993); Sissy Spacek as

the mother of a murdered son in Todd Field's *In the Bedroom* (2001); Brad Pitt as the leader of a male aggression movement in David Fincher's *Fight Club* (1999); or Philip Seymour Hoffman as author Truman Capote in Bennett Miller's *Capote* (2005)?

Movie acting may be, as legendary actor Laurence Olivier once said, the "art of persuasion."[46] Yet it is also a formal cinematic element, one as complex as design or cinematography. To get a sense of how movie acting works on its own and ultimately in relation to the other formal elements, we need to establish a set of criteria more substantial than our subjective feelings and reactions.

Because every actor, character, and performance in a movie is different, it is impossible to devise standards that would apply equally well to all of them. Furthermore, different actors, working with different directors, often take very different approaches to the same material, as you can judge for yourself by comparing the many remakes in movie history. Within the world of a particular story, your goal should be to determine the quality of the actor's achievement in creating the character and how that performance helps tell the story. Thus, you should discuss an actor's specific performance in a specific film—discussing, say, Peter Sellers's acting in Hal Ashby's *Being There* (1979) as it serves to create the character of Chance and tell the story of that film without being influenced by expectations possibly raised by your having seen Sellers in other movies.

In analyzing any actor's performance, you might consider the following:

> *Appropriateness.* Does the actor look and act naturally like the character he or she portrays, as expressed in physical appearance, facial expression, speech, movement, and gesture? If the performance is nonnaturalistic, does the actor look, walk, and talk the way that character might or should?
>
> Paradoxically, we expect an actor to behave as if he or she were *not* acting but were simply living the illusion of a character we can accept within the context of the

[46]Olivier, *Confessions of an Actor*, p. 51.

movie's narrative. Such appropriateness in acting is also called *transparency*, meaning that the character is so clearly recognizable—in speech, movement, and gesture—for what he or she is supposed to be that the actor becomes, in a sense, invisible. Most actors agree that the more successfully they create characters, the more we will see those characters and not them.

> *Inherent thoughtfulness or emotionality*. Does the actor convey the character's thought process or feelings behind the character's actions or reactions? In addition to a credible appearance, does the character have a credible inner life?

An actor can find the motivations behind a character's actions and reactions at any time before or during a movie's production. They may come to light in the script (as well as in any source on which it is based, such as a novel or play), in discussions with the director or with other cast members, and in spontaneous elements of inspiration and improvisation that the actor discovers while the camera is rolling. No matter which of these aspects or combinations of them delineate the character's motivation, we expect to see the actor reflect them within the character's consciousness or as part of the illusion-making process by which the character appears. Another way of saying this is that characters must appear to be vulnerable to forces in the narrative—capable of thinking about them and, if necessary, changing their mind or feelings about them.

> *Expressive coherence*. Has the actor used these first two qualities (appropriateness and inherent thoughtfulness/emotionality) to create a characterization that holds together?

Whatever behavior an actor uses to convey character, it must be intrinsic, not extraneous to the character, "maintaining not only a coherence of manner, but also a fit between setting, costume, and behavior."[47]

[47]Naremore, *Acting in the Cinema*, p. 69.

When an actor achieves such a fit, he or she is playing in character. Maintaining expressive coherence enables the actor to create a very complex characterization and performance, to express thoughts and reveal emotions of a recognizable individual without veering off into mere quirks or distracting details.

> *Wholeness and unity*. In spite of the challenges inherent in most film productions, has the actor maintained the illusion of a seamless character, even if that character is purposely riddled with contradictions?

Whereas expressive coherence relies on the logic inherent in an actor's performance, wholeness and unity are achieved through the actor's ability to achieve aesthetic consistency while working with the director, crew, and other cast members; enduring multiple takes; and projecting toward the camera rather than to an audience. However, wholeness and unity need not mean uniformity. The point is this: as audience members we want to feel we're in good hands; when we're confused or asked to make sense of seemingly incoherent elements, we want to know that the apparent incoherence happened intentionally, for an aesthetic reason, as part of the filmmakers' overall vision. For example, if a given character suddenly breaks down or reveals himself to be pretending to be somebody he isn't, the actor must sufficiently prepare for this change in the preceding scenes, however he chooses, so that we can accept it.

To begin applying these criteria, let's examine the work of two very distinctive, successful actors: Barbara Stanwyck as Stella Dallas in King Vidor's *Stella Dallas* (1937) and Michelle Williams in Derek Cianfrance's *Blue Valentine* (2010). In these roles, both actors play strong, assertive women and bring a significant amount of physicality to their portrayals. However, in looking at these two movies and analyzing them, we must remember that they are separated by a wide chronological and cultural gap and take into consideration how those elements influence the narrative and acting.

Each actor started in the movies in a different way. Stanwyck, who was born Ruby Stevens in Brooklyn in 1907, started on the Broadway stage and went to Hollywood at the age of twenty-one. The studios changed her name (*Stanwyck* has the vaguely British aura that Hollywood admired—all the more amusing considering that Ms. Stevens never really lost her New York accent). Overall, she made more than a hundred movies and was nominated four times for the Oscar for Best Actress in a Leading Role: for her work in *Stella Dallas*, Howard Hawks's *Ball of Fire* (1941), Billy Wilder's *Double Indemnity* (1944), and Anatole Litvak's *Sorry, Wrong Number* (1948). She never won.

Michelle Williams is one of a younger generation of actors—including Carey Mulligan (Lone Scherfig's *An Education*, 2009), Jennifer Lawrence (Debra Granik's *Winter's Bone*, 2010), and Jessica Chastain (Terence Malick's *The Tree of Life*, 2011)—who are enriching the art of acting. Williams was born in Kalispell, Montana, in 1980, and was raised in San Diego, California, where, after completing the ninth grade, she quit school to pursue an acting career. Between 1993 and 1998, she appeared in various television productions, including *Dawson's Creek*. With her gamine-like features, she began her movie career with comedies—Andrew Fleming's *Dick* and Jamie Babbitt's *But I'm a Cheerleader*, both 1999—before moving on to serious drama with Erik Skjoldbjærg's *Prozac Nation* (2001). Between 1999 and 2010, 11 years, she'd completed 21 movies. She is best known for her portrayals of intelligent, determined women, including Emily in Thomas McCarthy's *The Station Agent* (2003); Alma in Ang Lee's *Brokeback Mountain* (2005), for which she was nominated for an Oscar as Best Supporting Actress; Wendy in Kelly Reichardt's *Wendy and Lucy* (2008); and Emily in Reichardt's *Meek's Cutoff* (2010). She was nominated for an Oscar as Best Actress in *Blue Valentine*.

Barbara Stanwyck in King Vidor's *Stella Dallas*

Stella Dallas, based on Olive Higgins Prouty's 1923 novel of the same title, tells the story of a brassy, scheming, but charming young woman from a

Barbara Stanwyck in *Stella Dallas* In King Vidor's *Stella Dallas* (1937)—a melodramatic weeper that in Hollywood's golden age was also considered a "woman's movie"—the title character is a loving mother who sacrifices everything for her daughter's happiness. In this image, Stella (Barbara Stanwyck, *right*) arranges for her ex-husband and his fiancée, Helen Morrison (Barbara O'Neil, *left*) to raise her daughter, Laurel (Anne Shirley), as their own. Despite the obvious differences between the two women, they are united in their maternal concerns. Stanwyck received an Oscar nomination for Best Actress in a Leading Role; Shirley, for Best Actress in a Supporting Role. To compare their performances to other actors' handling of the same roles, see Henry King's *Stella Dallas* (1925), starring Belle Bennett and Lois Moran, and John Erman's *Stella* (1990), starring Bette Midler and Trini Alvarado.

working-class family who is openly derided by members of the middle and upper middle classes but who has married Stephen Dallas (John Boles), a socially prominent man.[48] Although they have a daughter, Laurel (Anne Shirley), the Dallases separate when they realize that their social and educational backgrounds are too different for them to be happy together.

[48]*Stella Dallas* has been of interest to many feminist critics; see E. Ann Kaplan, "The Case of the Missing Mother: Maternal Issues in Vidor's *Stella Dallas*" and Linda Williams, "'Something Else besides a Mother': *Stella Dallas* and the Maternal Melodrama"—both in *Feminism and Film*, ed. E. Ann Kaplan (New York: Oxford University Press, 2000), pp. 466–478, 479–504.

Stella is a formidable character for any actress to attempt, but Stanwyck beautifully meets the challenge of balancing the character's nonnaturalistic and naturalistic qualities. On one hand, Stella is loud and overdressed in clothes of her own making; on the other, she is a tender mother who sacrifices everything for her daughter's happiness. After Stephen has returned to his former fiancée, Helen Morrison (Barbara O'Neil), Stella visits Helen, offering to divorce Stephen if he and Helen will marry and raise Laurel as their own. Stella wears a gaudy fur coat, ridiculous hat, and fussy blouse. Her blunt way of speaking, mannish walk, and nervous fidgeting with her hands set her apart completely from the elegant, cultured, simply dressed, and well-groomed Helen.

When Laurel becomes engaged to marry Richard Grosvenor (Tim Holt), Stella is pleased that her daughter will achieve the upper-middle-class married life that has eluded her, but she realizes that she will be an embarrassment to Laurel. She pretends to leave the country but instead stands outside the New York townhouse in which the marriage takes place, watching the ceremony through a big window. All the movie's major themes culminate here in the Depression-era contrasts between those born to wealth and those born to work; in the contrast between the warm, secure interior and the cold, rainy exterior, where envious strangers grab a quick glimpse at what's going on inside before being hurried along; and in the contrast between Laurel in her white wedding dress and her mother, who is dressed plainly.

Indeed, although she is wearing her usual heavy makeup, Stella's appearance has changed. Having always set herself apart from the ordinary, she now wears clothes that help her blend into the crowd—a cloth coat with fur trim and a simple felt hat—and she is not wearing jewelry. Stanwyck called this her favorite scene in the movie: "I had to indicate to audiences, through the emotions shown by my face, that for Stella joy ultimately triumphed over the heartache she had felt."[49] We do not know whether

1

2

Stella Dallas finds elusive happiness Not invited to the wedding of her daughter, Laurel, Stella Dallas (Barbara Stanwyck), in the eponymously named movie (1937), stands in the street watching the ceremony through a window. Stanwyck called this her favorite scene, no doubt because she masterfully shows the range of emotions raised by this bittersweet moment. In a close-up [1], with tears in her eyes, Stella bites almost unconsciously on a handkerchief, smiling through her tears. A moment later, in a long shot [2], she walks away, still chewing on the handkerchief. Despite director King Vidor's indignation about the social barriers that prevented her happiness, Stella is triumphant that her daughter has found what eluded her. It's the kind of performance that helped to make Barbara Stanwyck one of Hollywood's most enduring stars.

[49]Barbara Stanwyck, qtd. in Ella Smith, *Starring Miss Barbara Stanwyck* (New York: Crown, 1974), p. 99.

Stanwyck arrived at this interpretation intuitively or at Vidor's suggestion.

Let's look more closely at what Stanwyck expresses facially and through gestures with a handkerchief, which film scholar James Naremore, borrowing Russian director Vsevolod Pudovkin's term, calls an "expressive object."[50] As the wedding progresses, Vidor cuts between long and middle shots of the interior from Stanwyck's point of view and middle shots and close-ups of Stanwyck's face—a classic method for emphasizing the contrasts inherent in the scene.

As the ceremony begins, Stella's face is open and curious, but what is she thinking? Within the narrative context, it must be how happy she is to be there. As Richard places the ring on Laurel's hand, however, Stella runs through a range of emotions. She smiles tenderly, she shudders slightly, tears well up in her eyes, and finally she swallows hard to suppress her emotion. When a police officer asks the crowd to disperse, Stella asks for another minute, the only time she speaks in the scene, which otherwise is underscored by the kind of highly charged music intended to make the audience cry. After the officer gives Stella extra time to see the bride and groom kiss, Stanwyck brings the handkerchief into play. Looking like she's about to lose control of her emotions, she slowly lifts the handkerchief as though to wipe away tears. Instead, she puts a corner of it in her mouth and, like a child, begins to chew and suck on it. She looks down in a moment of perfect maternal happiness, then looks up, her eyes shining and brimming with tears.

Vidor then cuts to a long shot of Stanwyck walking confidently toward the camera, looking fulfilled and swinging the handkerchief back and forth freely. As she crumples the handkerchief into her hand, squares her shoulders, and straightens her posture, the film ends. This is the sort of tearjerking ending that made Hollywood's "women's films" so popular, and Stanwyck's performance is consistent not only with the character she plays but also with the melodramatic narrative. She gives us Stella's range of character between tough and sensitive, but with her final self-confident stride, she also emphasizes the fulfillment in a mother's dream of seeing her daughter happily married.

Ultimately, Stanwyck's performance transcends the story's melodrama. In her natural physical appearance, movements, and gestures (especially with the handkerchief); expressive coherence (aided by our belief that Stella is doing the right thing); and emotional consistency (alternating feelings of happiness and sorrow, determination and doubt), Stanwyck remains true to the good-hearted character that she has been building from the first scene.

Michelle Williams in Derek Cianfrance's *Blue Valentine*

Blue Valentine is a story about a marriage that was off course from the beginning, a union of Cindy (Michelle Williams), a talented, promising young woman, and Dean (Ryan Gosling), a romantic who is contented with only being her husband, not striving for more. His love for her is genuine, hers isn't, and it's clear from almost the beginning that she is not committed. It is basically a two-person story that requires two superb actors to handle the characters' development from needy teenagers to disillusioned parents. She's a pre-med student living at home and looking after her aging grandmother; he works for a moving company. He may be a high school dropout, but he doesn't lack intelligence, sensitivity, or a desire to be a good husband and father. But it doesn't help their situation that she's running away from her unhappy parents, that he hasn't seen his parents in some time, that their child was fathered by Cindy's high school boyfriend, or that she attempted to abort it before agreeing to start a family with Dean.

They move to rural Pennsylvania, where she works as an aide in a doctor's office and he as a house painter, a job that he jokingly says allows him to starting drinking at eight in the morning. She soon becomes disillusioned with him and their life together. From the marriage to the ultimate breakup, their situation changes dramatically, and the movie charts those changes through frequent

[50]See Naremore's excellent discussion of this scene in *Acting in the Cinema*, pp. 86–87, quotation, p. 85.

Cindy and Dean are married Cindy and Dean's wedding takes place in the office of a justice of the peace. She wears a white lace dress and cries tears of joy as she looks up at Dean and repeats the vows. The couple has taken a great risk in getting married, but they are happy as they begin their life together. The director chose to shoot all scenes of the couple's past on film stock, and the bright light flooding the office fades the colors of her face and Dean's jacket (*right*), making the image look old, as was intended.

flashbacks that show her falling for his boyish charm and promise of a life together to the nasty fight that ends it all. Their happy memories of the time before they were married are contrasted to a climactic weekend spent in the "Future Room" of a theme motel, an arrangement that Dean hopes will rekindle their love. When it doesn't, he provokes an ugly argument at the doctor's office where she works as a nurse; consequently, she is fired, and he walks off into the distance, with their young daughter begging him to come back, as the movie ends.

Such a story—so unlike *Stella Dallas* and so recognizable in our time—requires two actors who can truthfully convince us of the characters' range of intellect and emotions as they watch their marriage crumble. Williams and Gosling were so committed to bringing the story to the screen that they served as the film's executive producers. Thus they helped to formulate the process by which the movie would be shot. Indeed, this is an excellent example of how filmmaking affects acting, especially in a low-budget, independent movie such as *Blue Valentine*. The actors and director agreed that the film would be made in three stages. As we've already

1

2

The marriage falls apart Two incidents, among others, indicate that Cindy and Dean's marriage is falling apart. In image [1], Cindy, upset when their pet dog is killed by a passing car, watches stoically as Dean buries the body in their yard. It's an omen of what's to come, just as Dean's attempt to rekindle their marriage in the "Future Room" of a motel backfires. Soon, looking haggard in image [2], Cindy has one last fight with Dean. She's determined not to give in to his pleas for another chance and, within minutes, he walks out of her life. The use of digital cinematography for these scenes gives them the real-life look of a documentary film.

noted, the movie relies heavily on continual flashbacks that contrast the first part of this couple's relationship, which was happy, with the last part, which was not. So the first stage was to shoot those happy scenes, all together, with seldom more than one take for each. There were no rehearsals. And the director, Derek Cianfrance, chose to shoot on traditional film stock because it lends a romantic quality to the footage. The second stage began when the two principal actors—joined by Faith Wladyka, who plays Frankie, their daughter—spent a month "living" their parts in the house used for the actual shooting. (They simulated this marriage here only during the day, returning to their real-life homes at night.) In this unusual mode of working, they ripped apart the happy years, determining what they would have been like in the subsequent years, and then improvised much of the dialogue for the next stage of shooting. The third stage was to shoot the marriage as it dissolves, this time on digital media, which is bright and clinical in its look, contrasting markedly from the film footage. Here, the director shot many takes. Intercutting both kinds of footage gives the movie a discernible texture that helps the viewer separate past from present. Also, to emphasize the status of the marriage, you'll notice that in the first part of the film, the cinematographer almost always uses two-shots with the couple together in the frame, and in the second part, shoots them in separate frames.

Blue Valentine is the director's second feature film—Cianfrance's previous experience was mostly with television documentaries—and while he uses a unique method of creating the film, he also intuitively understands how to let Williams and Gosling work together to create their characters. They built on mutual trust, spent eight hours a day living together in a fully functional house, where Gosling and Williams—like Dean and Cindy—did nothing but bicker with each other. After a month, they were all ready to shoot "the present" and were so fully prepared in their parts that they didn't have to act.

In her role as Cindy in *Blue Valentine*, Williams uses her intelligence and insight to create a character who is determined to make the best of her life, but whose stoic acceptance of reality prevails until she can stand it no longer. The director takes this strong story—of which he is a coscreenwriter—and lets it run an emotional course that is clearly established by the spontaneous interaction of the two principal actors. Its measured pace builds slowly to the ultimate blowup. Of the two characters, many viewers will find Gosling to be the more sympathetic. He emphasizes Dean's loyalty, sense of humor, kind heart, and genuine but failed efforts to understand his wife's unhappiness. He makes it clear that Dean is incapable of evolving or changing. Like the cigarette that is perpetually dangling from his lower lip, he's predictable. But while Cindy is the more determined of the two to reverse her discontent, she does it at the cost of destroying Dean. It's a raw story, hard to watch in the rawness of its emotions and in its ambiguous ending. Shattered, Dean walks off; Cindy is now a single mother with no job and an uncertain future. But she has not been defeated.

Using those characteristics that we have just defined as key to analyzing an actor's performance, we can see that Williams looks and acts naturally, as we would expect of the character that she defines. Cindy keeps a messy house and takes little notice of her appearance, but she is engaged in something more important: balancing her tender empathy for Dean with her strong resolve to change her life. At first, their sexual life together seems satisfactory, but she soon regards it mechanically and then with resentment. They're both caring parents, but Dean works harder at it than she does. She's initially and passively resentful of Dean's lack of ambition, and then, in despair, challenges him to be more than he is (or could be). Williams conveys the thought process and feelings behind Cindy's actions and reactions primarily through gesture and physical movement: you can feel her physical resentment for her husband when he tries to make love to her. And the dialogue, which was improvised, has the honest rawness to be convincing. The frequent flashbacks to happier times require the actors to break the unity of their performances to accommodate the changes that have occurred between them then and now. Williams registers these changes more than Gosling—because he doesn't change—and we see them in her appearance, voice, and mannerisms. In high school, she's a sweet, passive kid, foolishly in love with the wrong man. Williams finds great joy in Cindy's singing and dancing in the street with Dean and to dressing up for their wedding. But in later life, there is little joy, and she makes Cindy into a hard, resentful, unforgiving woman. Shooting as they did, Williams (and Gosling) was faced with difficult challenges in maintaining expressive coherence. Ultimately, she creates a characterization that has the wholeness of its contradictory parts.

Finally, there's a truthfulness that comes with her seemingly effortless performance, a naturalness that only a born actor can create. Williams not only looks and acts like such a character in physical appearance, facial expression, speech, movement, and gesture but also understands—and can make us understand—all kinds of feelings, ranging from vulnerability to strength.

Stella Dallas and *Blue Valentine*: two different movies—both concerned with strong, natural women confronted by social barriers—and two different actors—both playing with strong emotion. Which is the better performance? Look at them, apply the criteria you've learned here, and decide for yourself.

Analyzing Acting

Because our responses to actors' performances on-screen are perhaps our most automatic and intuitive responses to any formal aspect of film, it is easy to forget that acting is as much a formal component of movies—something made—as mise-en-scène, cinematography, and editing are. And yet, acting is clearly something that must be planned and shaped in some manner; the very fact that films are shot out of continuity demands that actors approach their performances with a rigor and consciousness that mirrors the director's work on the film as a whole. This chapter has presented several different things to think about as you watch film acting from this point forward. Using the criteria described in the previous section, remaining sensitive to the context of the performances, and keeping the following checklist in mind as you watch, you should be able to incorporate an intelligent analysis of acting into your discussion and writing about the movies you screen for class.

Screening Checklist: Acting

✔ Why was this actor, and not another, cast for the role?

✔ Does the actor's performance create a coherent, unified character? If so, how?

✔ Does the actor look the part? Is it necessary for the actor to look the part?

✔ Does the actor's performance convey the actions, thoughts, and internal complexities that we associate with natural or recognizable characters? Or does it exhibit the excessive approach we associate with nonnaturalistic characters?

✔ What elements are most distinctive in how the actor conveys the character's actions, thoughts, and internal complexities: body language, gestures, facial expressions, language?

✔ What special talents of imagination or intelligence has the actor brought to the role?

✔ How important is the filmmaking process in creating the character? Is the actor's performance overshadowed by the filmmaking process?

✔ Does the actor work well with fellow actors in this film? Do any of the other actors detract from the lead actor's performance?

✔ How, if at all, is the actor's conception of the character based on logic? How does the performance demonstrate expressive coherence?

✔ Does the actor's performance have the expressive power to make us forget that he or she is acting? If it does, how do you think the actor achieved this effect?

Questions for Review

1. How is movie acting today different from movie acting from the 1930s through the 1960s?
2. Why is the relationship between the actor and the camera so important in making and looking at movies?
3. How did the coming of sound influence movie acting and actors?
4. What's the difference between movie stars and movie actors? Why do some critics emphasize that movie stars are a commodity created by the movie industry?
5. What factors influence the casting of actors in a movie?
6. How are naturalistic and nonnaturalistic movie acting different?
7. What is improvisational acting?
8. How do framing, composition, lighting, and the long take affect the acting in a movie?
9. Given the range of techniques available to movie actors, why do we say that their most basic skill is understanding how to reveal themselves to the camera during the close-up?
10. What do you regard as the most important criteria in analyzing acting?

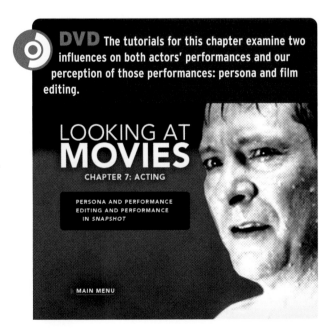

Movies Described or Illustrated in This Chapter

About Schmidt (2002). Alexander Payne, director.
Apocalypse Now (1979). Francis Ford Coppola, director.
Applause (1929). Rouben Mamoulian, director.
Avatar (2010). James Cameron, director.
The Big Trail (1930). Raoul Walsh, director.
Birth (2004). Jonathan Glazer, director.
Blow (2001). Ted Demme, director.
Blue Valentine (2010). Derek Cianfrance, director.
Broken Blossoms (1919). D. W. Griffith, director.
Burn after Reading (2008). Ethan Coen and Joel Coen, directors.
Carrie (1976). Brian De Palma, director.
Chinatown (1974). Roman Polanski, director.
Chocolat (2000). Lasse Hallström, director.
Citizen Kane (1941). Orson Welles, director.
Coal Miner's Daughter (1980). Michael Apted, director.
Collateral (2004). Michael Mann, director.
Donnie Brasco (1997). Mike Newell, director.
East of Eden (1955). Elia Kazan, director.
Edward Scissorhands (1990). Tim Burton, director.
Ed Wood (1994). Tim Burton, director.
Eyes Wide Shut (1999). Stanley Kubrick, director.
Fargo (1996). Joel Coen, director.
Finding Neverland (2004). Marc Forster, director.
Giant (1956). George Stevens, director.
The Godfather (1972). Francis Ford Coppola, director.
Henry V (1944). Laurence Olivier, director.
The Hudsucker Proxy (1994). Joel Coen, director.

I'm Not There (2007). Todd Haynes, director.

Iron Man (2008). Jon Favreau, director.

Kansas City (1996). Robert Altman, director.

The King's Speech (2010). Tom Hooper, director.

Knocked Up (2007). Judd Apatow, director.

Le Duel d'Hamlet (1900). Clément Maurice, director.

Les Amours d'Elisabeth, Reine d'Angleterre (1912). Henri Desfontaines and Louis Mercanton, directors.

Lolita (1962). Stanley Kubrick, director.

M (1931). Fritz Lang, director.

The Misfits (1961). John Huston, director.

Morocco (1930). Josef von Sternberg, director.

No Country for Old Men (2007). Ethan Coen and Joel Coen, directors.

No Way Home (1996). Buddy Giovinazzo, director.

On the Waterfront (1954). Elia Kazan, director.

The Passion of Joan of Arc (1928). Carl Theodor Dreyer, director.

The Philadelphia Story (1940). George Cukor, director.

A Place in the Sun (1951). George Stevens, director.

The Player (1992). Robert Altman, director.

Queen Christina (1933). Rouben Mamoulian, director.

Rabbit Hole (2010). John Cameron Mitchell, director.

Rebel without a Cause (1955). Nicholas Ray, director.

The Savages (2007). Tamara Jenkins, director.

The Searchers (1956). John Ford, director.

Singin' in the Rain (1952). Stanley Donen and Gene Kelly, directors.

The Shootist (1976). Don Siegel, director.

Sleepy Hollow (1999). Tim Burton, director.

The Social Network (2010). David Fincher, director.

Starman (1984). John Carpenter, director.

Stella Dallas (1937). King Vidor, director.

A Streetcar Named Desire (1951). Elia Kazan, director.

Sweeney Todd: The Demon Barber of Fleet Street (2007). Tim Burton, director.

True Grit (2010). Joel and Ethan Coen, directors.

Vicky Cristina Barcelona (2008). Woody Allen, director.

What's Eating Gilbert Grape? (1993). Lasse Hallström, director.

Who's Afraid of Virginia Woolf? (1966). Mike Nichols, director.

CHAPTER EIGHT

Editing

What Is Editing?

Editing, the basic creative force of filmmaking, is the process of selecting, arranging, and assembling the essential components of a movie—visual, sound, and special effects—to tell a story in a unique way. The director and his on-set collaborators capture those elements, but it is the editor who shapes them into the movie you experience. The editor controls what you see, when you see it, its speed and pace, and what you understand and feel about all this. Indeed, editing is what distinguishes the movies from the other dramatic and visual arts, a point that cannot be overemphasized. It involves far more than an assembly process, for film editing controls the creative and expressive power of the movies.

Film editor and scholar Ken Dancyger distinguishes among the technique, the craft, and the art of editing. The technique (or method) involves cutting the desired shots from the exposed roll of film or digital storage device and then joining them together so that they form a continuous whole. Before digital editing, this manual and often tedious process was called **cutting** and **splicing**, because the editor used scissors to sever the shots from the roll of film before using glue or tape to splice them together. Editors were responsible primarily for visual images. With digital editing, the work is simpler, cleaner, and easier to manage, and editors are now frequently responsible for editing all elements of the film, including the visual, sound, and special effects elements. The craft (skill) is the ability to join shots and produce a meaning that does not exist in either one of them individually. The art of editing, Dancyger declares, "occurs when the combination of two or more shots takes meaning to the next level—excitement, insight, shock, or the epiphany of discovery."[1] That is the essence of editing.

The basic building block of film editing is the **shot** (as defined in Chapter 6), and its most fundamental tool is the cut. Each shot has two explicit values: the first value is determined by what is within the shot itself; the second value is determined by how the shot is situated in relation to other shots. The first value is largely the responsibility of the director, cinematographer, production designer, and other collaborators who determine what is captured on film. The second value is the product of editing.

The early Soviet film theorist and filmmaker Lev Kuleshov reputedly demonstrated the fundamental power of editing by producing a short film (now lost, unfortunately) in which an identical shot of an expressionless actor appeared after each of these shots: a dead woman, a child, and a dish of soup. The audience viewing this film reportedly

[1]Ken Dancyger, *The Technique of Film and Video Editing: Theory and Practice*, 2nd ed. (Boston: Focal Press, 1997), pp. xiv–xv.

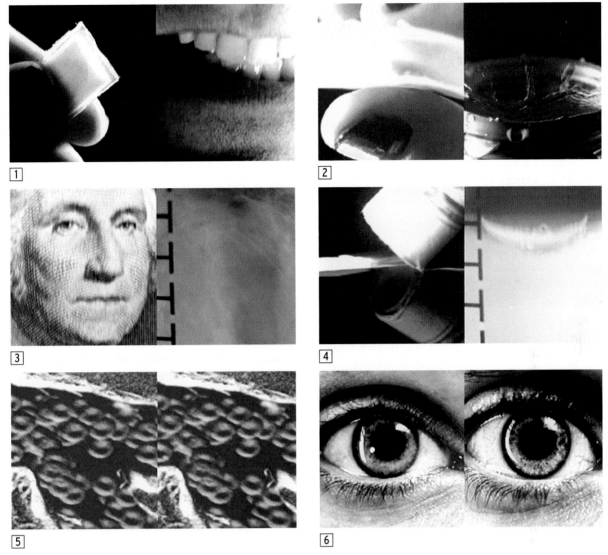

1 2 3 4 5 6

The power of editing These images, taken from a roughly half-minute sequence from Darren Aronofsky's *Requiem for a Dream* (2000; editor: Jay Rabinowitz), illustrate the potential power of film editing. As pictures are juxtaposed—in this case, literally placed side by side using an editing technique called *split screen*—the meaning of one affects the meaning of the other. That is, together the shots influence our creation of their meaning, and their combined meaning then affects how we see the following two halves, whose meaning undergoes a transformation similar to that of the first two, and so on. This interpretive process goes on through the sequence, into the following shot, the following sequence, and ultimately the entire movie. Our creation of meaning proceeds from increment to increment, though at a much faster rate of calculation than this caption can convey.

All of these images, in this context, relate to drug use. Focusing on minute details of the rituals of drug use, the sequence seeks to approximate the characters' frantic experience and to represent the perceptual changes that accompany their intake of narcotics. Through the language of editing, Aronofsky has given us a fresh look at a phenomenon that is often portrayed in clichéd and unimaginative ways.

As an experiment, try to imagine different juxtapositions of these same images, taken not in sequence but in isolation. Outside the context of drugs, what might George Washington's image on a dollar bill next to a widened, bloodshot eye mean? What might gritting teeth next to that reddish flow mean? For that matter, to what use might someone, maybe the creator of television commercials or public-service messages, put each image alone?

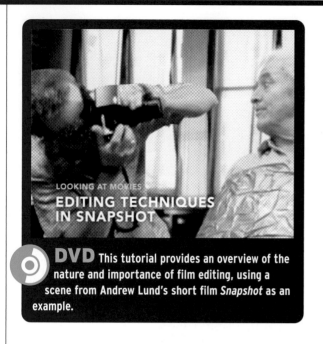

assumed that the actor was reacting to each stimulus by changing his expression appropriately—showing sorrow (for the dead woman), tenderness (for the young child), and hunger (for the food)—when in fact his expression remained the same.

This tendency of viewers to interpret shots in relation to surrounding shots is the most fundamental assumption behind all film editing. Editing takes advantage of this psychological tendency in order to accomplish various effects: to help tell a story, to provoke an idea or a feeling, or to call attention to itself as an element of cinematic form. No matter how straightforward a movie may seem, you can be sure that (with very rare exceptions) the editor had to make difficult decisions about which shots to use and how to use them.

The Film Editor

The person primarily responsible for such decisions is the film editor.[2] In theory, the bulk of the film editor's work occurs after the director and collaborators have shot all of the movie's footage. In fact, in many major film productions, the editor's responsibilities as a collaborator begin much earlier in the process. During preproduction and production—even from the moment the movie is conceived—an editor may make suggestions to the director and cinematographer for composition, blocking, lighting, and shooting that will help the editing itself. Editors literally work behind the scenes, but their contributions can make the difference between artistic success and artistic failure, between an ordinary movie and a masterpiece.

A good film editor must be focused, detail-oriented, well organized, disciplined, able to work alone for long stretches of time, and willing to take as much time as necessary to fulfill the director's vision. Throughout their work, film editors must collaborate with the director and be resilient enough to withstand the producer's interference. In short, a good editor practices a rigorous craft. Even in a well-planned production, one for which the director has a clear vision of what to shoot and how it will look, the editor will face countless difficult decisions about what to use and what to cut.

That has always been the case, but today's movies run longer and contain more individual shots than movies did fifty years ago, so the editor's job has become more involved. For example, a typical Hollywood movie made in the 1940s and 1950s runs approximately 1 to 1½ hours long and is composed of about 1,000 shots; today's movies typically run between 2 and 3 hours, but because they consist of approximately 2,000 to 3,000 shots, they have a faster tempo than earlier films had. That factor alone increases the editor's work of selecting and arranging the footage. It is not uncommon for the ratio between unused and used footage in a Hollywood production to be as high as 20 to 1, meaning that for every "1" minute you see on the screen, 20 minutes of footage has been discarded. The postproduction problems that really challenge editors, however—the ones we some-

---

[2]For a documentary that explores editing through interviews with many leading editors (including Thelma Schoonmaker, Mathilde Bonnefoy, George Lucas, and Sarah Flack), see *Edge Codes.com: The Art of Motion Picture Editing* (2004; director: Alex Shuper). Edge codes (also called edge numbers or footage numbers) are the numbers printed along the edge of film stock and the magnetic sound track to assist the editors in locating images quickly and matching audio and visual images.

Editing thousands of feet of footage for *Shine a Light* A remote-controlled, crane-mounted camera (*right*) was one of eighteen cameras used to record a 2008 Rolling Stones concert for Martin Scorsese's *Shine a Light* (2008).

The editor, David Tedeschi, met the overwhelming challenge of creating a record from the thousands of feet of footage recorded by those cameras. The result is one of the most vibrant, yet intimate, rock movies ever made.

times read about in the press—tend to inflate this ratio of unused to used footage to extremes.

Perhaps the best-known extreme example is Francis Ford Coppola's *Apocalypse Now* (1979). Working for two years, Walter Murch and his editorial team eventually shaped 235 hours of footage into a (mostly) coherent movie that runs 2 hours 33 minutes (resulting in a ratio of unused to used footage of just under 100 to 1). Sifting through the mountain of footage to find the best shots, making thousands of little decisions along the way, Murch and his team gave narrative shape to what many people at the time—including, occasionally, Coppola himself—considered a disaster of directorial self-indulgence. Twenty-two years later, Coppola asked Murch and his team to restore 49 minutes that they had originally cut; that version, known as the "director's cut," was released in 2001 as *Apocalypse Now Redux*.

Clearly, the creative power of the editor comes close to that of the director. But in most mainstream film productions, that creative power is put in service of the director's vision. "One gives as much as possible," says film editor Helen van Dongen, "as much as is beneficial to the final form of the film, without overshadowing or obstructing the director's intentions. . . . The editor working with a great director can do no better than discover and disclose the director's design."[3]

Consider, for example, the challenges faced by David Tedeschi, the editor of Martin Scorsese's *Shine a Light* (2008), which documents two Rolling Stones concerts in New York. Robert Richardson, the director of photography, supervised eighteen camera operators and dozens of camera assistants and lighting technicians. The editor was faced with

[3]Helen van Dongen, qtd. in Richard Barsam, "Discover and Disclose: Helen van Dongen and *Louisiana Story*," in *Filming Robert Flaherty's "Louisiana Story": The Helen van Dongen Diary*, by Helen Durant, ed. Eva Orbanz (New York: Museum of Modern Art, 1998), p. 86.

selecting and arranging the thousands of feet of live footage that, in the finished movie, is intercut with archival footage of the group's career. [Similar challenges face the editor of any large concert movie, such as Michael Wadleigh's *Woodstock* (1970), of which Scorsese was an editor.] If any one word could describe the Rolling Stones, it's probably the *energy* generated by the band's propulsive rhythms and stage movements. Mick Jagger rarely stops moving, which is a delight for audiences but a major challenge for camera operators and editors who have to contain him within the frame. With multiple cameras—stationary, moving, handheld—producing footage from many different angles and positions—on the stage, in the audience, in the balcony, backstage—the editor had to edit that footage so as to maintain on the screen, insofar as possible, the continuity and energy of Jagger's movements on the stage. Tedeschi cuts with grace and ease, managing, almost miraculously, to keep the star of the show on full screen when he was singing, thus preserving the integrity of each song, as well as cutting to other musicians and the audience. *Shine a Light* was released in standard 70mm as well as the IMAX format, the size of which magnifies every shot. There's no hiding a weak cut when the image is 72 feet wide and 53 feet high (and sometimes even larger). The cinematographers capture the Rolling Stones' essential energy, and the editor repackages it and keeps it going for the two-hour length of the movie.

The Editor's Responsibilities

The film editor has both stylistic and technical responsibilities in the telling of a movie's story. He or she is an artist, a full partner in creating a movie's expressive qualities. In terms of technique, the editor is responsible for managing the following aspects of the final film:

> spatial relationships between shots
> temporal relationships between shots
> the overall rhythm of the film

Let's examine these responsibilities more closely.

Spatial Relationships between Shots One of the most powerful effects of film editing is the creation of a sense of space in the mind of the viewer. When we are watching any single shot from a film, our sense of the overall space of the scene is necessarily limited by the height, width, and depth of the film frame during that shot. But as other shots are placed in close proximity to that original shot, our sense of the overall space in which the characters are moving shifts and expands. The juxtaposition of shots within a scene can cause us to have a fairly complex sense of that overall space (something like a mental map) even if no single shot discloses more than a fraction of that space to us at a time.

For example, as the opening titles roll in Kimberly Peirce's *Boys Don't Cry* (1999; editor: Lee Percy), through a short sequence of tightly framed shots we see cars dangerously passing one another on a rural highway, the exterior of a trailer park, an interior of a trailer where Teena Brandon (Hilary Swank) is getting a haircut to make her look like a teenage boy, the exterior of a skating rink, and finally the refashioned young woman inside introducing herself to her female blind date as "Brandon." The shots themselves and the manner in which they are edited introduce the space clearly, tightly, and unambiguously. These shots also introduce characters, mood, and conflict. The foreboding mood is established by the steady rhythm of the editing and the equally steady drumbeat on the sound track. There seems to be no turning back for Teena, and as a result, we sense that a conflict may arise over this young woman's identification of her gender.

The power of editing to establish spatial relationships between shots is so strong, in fact, that there is almost no need for filmmakers to ensure that there is a real space whose dimensions correspond to the one implied by editing. Countless films—especially historical dramas and science-fiction films—rely heavily on the power of editing to fool us into perceiving their worlds as vast and complete even as we are shown only tiny fractions of the implied space. Because our brains effortlessly make spatial generalizations from limited visual information, George Lucas was not required, for example, to build an entire to-scale model of the *Millennium Falcon* to convince us that the characters in *Star Wars* are flying (and moving around within) a vast spaceship. Instead, a series of cleverly composed shots filmed on carefully designed (and relatively small) sets could, when edited together, create the illusion of a massive, fully functioning spacecraft.

In addition to painting a mental picture of the space of a scene, editing manipulates our sense of spatial relationships among characters, objects, and their surroundings. For example, the placement of one shot of a person's reaction (perhaps a look of concerned shock) after a shot of an action by another person (falling down a flight of stairs) immediately creates in our minds the thought that the two people are occupying the same space, that the person in the first shot is visible to the person in the second shot, and that the emotional response of the person in the second shot is a reaction to what has happened to the person in the first shot. The central discovery of Lev Kuleshov, the Soviet film theorist mentioned at the beginning of this chapter, was that these two shots need not have any actual relationship at all to one another for this effect to take place in a viewer's mind. The effect of perceiving such spatial relationships even when we are given minimal visual information or when we are presented with shots filmed at entirely different times and places is sometimes called the *Kuleshov effect*.

LOOKING AT MOVIES
THE KULESHOV EXPERIMENT

DVD In this tutorial, Dave Monahan attempts to re-create the Kuleshov effect.

Temporal Relationships between Shots We have already learned that the plot of a narrative film is very often shaped and ordered in a way that differs significantly from the film's underlying story. In fact, the pleasure that many contemporary movies give us has its source in the bold decisions made by some filmmakers to manipulate the presentation of the plot in creative and confusing ways. Films such as Christopher Nolan's *Memento* (2000; editor: Dody Dorn), Spike Jonze's *Adaptation* (2002; editor: Eric Zumbrunnen), or Michel Gondry's *Eternal Sunshine of the Spotless Mind* (2004; editor: Valdis Óskarsdóttir) are interesting in part because their plots are presented in a fragmented, out-of-order fashion that we as viewers must reshuffle in order to make sense of the underlying story. But even in more traditional narrative films in which the plot is presented in a more or less chronological manner, editing is used to manipulate the presentation of plot time on-screen.

For example, **flashback** (the interruption of chronological plot time with a shot or series of shots that show an event that has happened earlier in the story) is a very common editing technique. Used in virtually all movie genres, it is a traditional storytelling device that typically explains how a situation or character developed into what we see at the present time.

The flashback can be as stimulating as it is in Orson Welles's *Citizen Kane* (1941; editor: Robert Wise), where our sense of Charles Foster Kane is created by the memories of those who knew him, or as straightforward as Walter Neff's (Fred MacMurray) on-screen narration of Billy Wilder's classic film noir *Double Indemnity* (1944; editor, Doane Harrison); in fact, the flashback is frequently used in film noir. It can also serve as the backbone for the structure of a complicated narrative, as in Alain Resnais's *Hiroshima mon amour* (1959; editors: Jasmine Chasney, Henri Colpi, and Anne Sarraute) or Quentin Tarantino's *Pulp Fiction* (1994; editor: Sally Menke).

Much less common than the flashback is the **flash-forward**, the interruption of present action by a shot or series of shots that shows images from the plot's future. Often, flash-forwards reflect a character's desire for someone or something, a

[1]

[2]

[1]

[2]

Flashbacks can help to develop characters Director
Terrence Malick makes a poignant use of flashbacks in *The
Thin Red Line* (1998; editors: Billy Weber, Leslie Jones, Saar
Klein), his epic account of a crucial World War II battle in
Asia. He knows that the depiction of soldiers—from Homer's
Iliad to the movies—often includes their longing for home,
wives, and family, a longing for safety and peace—and Malick
uses a series of such flashbacks to develop the characters of
Pvt. John Bell (Ben Chaplin) and his wife, Marty (Miranda
Otto). The flashbacks emphasize how war has interrupted
their deep, idyllic emotional and sexual relationship. In image
[1], talking to Cpl. Geoffrey Fife (Adrien Brody, *left*), Bell says
that he never touched another woman and wouldn't feel the
desire to do so; this is followed by a flashback to a romantic,
nighttime image [2] of Marty staring out their bedroom
window, as if longing for him. Such an interpretation would
be romantic, but Bell soon receives a letter from Marty
saying that she is tired of waiting for him and wants a
divorce so that she can marry a man with whom she has
fallen in love. Here, the flashback is used ironically, to
contrast John's illusions about the past—virtually his reason
for living and fighting in the war—with the reality of the
present wartime conditions.

premonition of something that might happen, or
even a psychic projection. Flash-forward is a problematic element in any film that strives for realism
because it implies that the characters in the film
are somehow seeing the future. Once employed,
flash-forward sends the signal that the movie we

Flash-forward clues us in on a murder yet to happen
The flash-forward creates an ironic context in Sydney
Pollack's *They Shoot Horses, Don't They?* (1969; editor:
Fredric Steinkamp), a melodrama about the marathon dance
contests that were a fad in the 1930s during the Great
Depression. Gloria (Jane Fonda) and Robert (Michael
Sarrazin)—who meet and agree to dance together in the
competition—want to win this grueling ordeal for the prize
money and are seemingly in it until the bitter end, or almost.
They are ill-matched: Gloria is a self-destructive aspiring
actress; Michael, who was deeply affected as a boy by seeing
a horse shot after breaking its leg, is the more optimistic.
The colorful contest is punctuated several times with highly
stylized flash-forwards—shot in an entirely different mise-en-
scène and color—depicting Robert in jail or at his trial for
murder. They suggest that there is more to this easygoing
young man than we expect. In image [1], we see the couple,
physically and emotionally exhausted from an ordeal that has
run for more than 1,000 hours; image [2] is a flash-forward to
Robert being sentenced to murder. We don't know if this trial
really happened—the blue-gray image seems expressionistic,
even surreal—and we don't know whom he has murdered.
Soon, the couple—who have fallen for one another—walk
out, disillusioned that the contest is dishonest. In the final
scene, Gloria takes a pistol from her purse and attempts to
kill herself; unable to pull the trigger, she asks Robert to do
it—and he does! The flash-forwards, eerie as they are,
foreshadow an action that contradicts everything we know
about Robert, whose final words are those of the title.

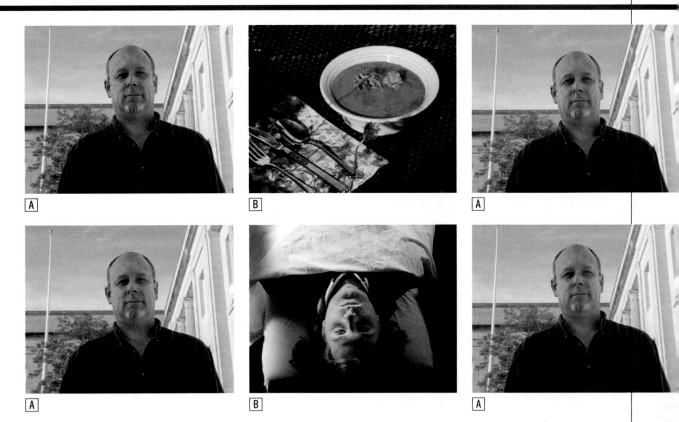

A   B   A

A   B   A

The Kuleshov effect In the 1920s, Soviet film pioneer Lev Kuleshov conducted an experiment to investigate editing's ability to create new meaning. He juxtaposed a shot of an actor wearing a neutral expression and looking offscreen with a number of other shots and then screened them in sequence for a test audience. When the viewers watched a series of shots like the ABA sequence above (from the DVD tutorial re-creation of Kuleshov's experiment), they interpreted the character in shot A as looking at the soup and assumed he was hungry. When shown a sequence using the same shot of the expressionless actor but juxtaposed instead with the image of a dead man, viewers assumed a relationship between the character and the corpse and felt the actor was expressing grief or remorse. With this simple experiment, Kuleshov demonstrated a creative capacity of film editing that is still utilized by editors: the juxtaposition of images can create new meaning not present in any single shot by itself.

are watching is at least partly fantastical and that we should be ready to suspend our disbelief.

The most common manipulation of time through editing is **ellipsis**, an omission between one thing and another. In a quotation, for example, an ellipsis mark (. . .) signifies the omission of one or more words. In filmmaking, an ellipsis generally signifies the omission of time—the time that separates one shot from another. Ellipsis in movies is first and foremost a practical tool; it economizes the presentation of plot, skipping over portions of the underlying story that do not need to be presented on-screen to be understood or inferred. But its use requires the filmmaker to have carefully established the time, place, location, characters, and action so that viewers are able not only to follow what they see but also to make the intuitive inferences that fill in the material that was left out. This is what happens in Gus Van Sant's *Drugstore Cowboy* (1989; editors: Mary Bauer and Curtiss Clayton) when a policeman asks Bob (Matt Dillon), a heroin addict, "Are you going to tell us where you hid the drugs, or are we going to have to tear the place apart bit by bit?" When the next shot shows Bob's house torn apart, the cut implies an ellipsis of time, and it presents us with everything we need to know about the period of story time that has elapsed.

The effect of an ellipsis on viewers is determined by how much story time is implied between shots

[3]

[1]

[2]

Ellipsis causing disorientation Steven Soderbergh's *Erin Brockovich* (2000; editor: Anne V. Coates) demonstrates how an ellipsis can be used to cause the viewer's momentary disorientation. A sharp cut leads from [1] Erin Brockovich's car being hit broadside to [2] Ed Masry (Albert Finney) being told by his secretary (Conchata Ferrell) that Brockovich is waiting to see him. Next [3], Masry is seen greeting Brockovich (Julia Roberts), who is wearing a neck brace. Images [2] and [3] take place sequentially; although we don't know how much time has elapsed between images [1] and [2], it was at least enough to permit Brockovich to get the brace and make an appointment to see a lawyer.

as well as by the manner in which the editing makes the transition from the first shot to the second. In some cases, such as the example from *Drugstore Cowboy* just mentioned, an ellipsis can seem very natural and may signal a straightforward cause-and-effect relationship. In others, an ellipsis may span a much longer period of implied story time, or the transition may be so unexpected and sudden that the effect on viewers is shock or disorientation.

For example, in Steven Soderbergh's *Erin Brockovich* (2000; editor: Anne V. Coates), the title character (played by Julia Roberts), while driving away from an unsuccessful job interview, is hit broadside. We don't see what happens as the immediate result of this incident, for there is a sharp elliptical cut to a scene in which lawyer Ed Masry (Albert Finney) arrives at his office and is told by his secretary that a woman named Erin Brockovich is waiting to see him: "car accident; not her fault, she says." When he enters his office, he sees Erin wearing a neck brace. However, we don't know how much time has elapsed between the accident and this meeting.

Playing with time, and particularly with ellipses of all kinds, has become one of Soderbergh's stylistic trademarks. In *The Limey*, the time and space of the entire movie are edited to be disorienting. The engine that drives the narrative is a continual use of the ellipsis for shock and/or disorientation. England and California are constantly juxtaposed, as are the present, past, and future, and memory, imagination, flashbacks, and flash-forwards. Some shots identify characters in full frames; others do not. We are never sure where or when the action is taking place. However, the cumulative progress of disorientation eventually leads us to put the pieces together, to see repeating patterns, and to become oriented.

Whether sudden and unexpected or seemingly natural, ellipses are also frequently used to provide an instant, sometimes comic, resolution to a situation. In *Out of Sight* (1998; editor: Anne V. Coates), for example, director Soderbergh tells the story of an improbable romance between two highly attractive people: Jack Foley (George Clooney), a notorious bank robber, and Karen Sisco (Jennifer Lopez),

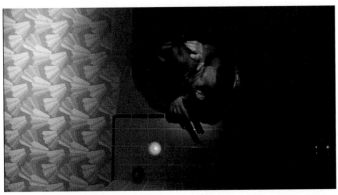

[1]

[2]

Ellipsis for comic effect An ellipsis shortens the time between two actions, but it can also have comic implications. In Steven Soderbergh's *Out of Sight* (1998; editor: Anne V. Coates), [1] Karen Sisco (Jennifer Lopez), a federal marshal, starts out to nab an escaped convict, Jack Foley (George Clooney), but instead is pulled into a bathtub and kisses him. While she may be romantically overwhelmed, note that she still has her gun firmly in hand. [2] A quick cut, an obvious ellipsis, shows her later in a hospital bed with a nasty bruise on her forehead. Considering that she thinks little about being in a bathtub with a convicted felon, we might reach various fanciful conclusions—until we remember that she was put in that hospital earlier in the movie for another reason.

a federal marshal. Sisco has witnessed Foley and a buddy bust out of prison, and they take her hostage, but she escapes. The next day, she learns that Foley is in Miami, and, with gun in hand, she enters his hotel room and discovers him relaxing in the bathtub. As she bends over him with her gun pointed at his head, he pulls her into the water on top of him, she lays down the gun, and they kiss.

There is a quick cut, and an obvious ellipsis, for the next shot is of Sisco's father standing over her

in a hospital bed with a dark bruise on her forehead. From earlier in the movie, we know that she got to the hospital as a result of a car crash that occurred during her escape from Foley and his buddy. However disorienting this ellipsis may be, it is also funny because, in such romantic comedies, it is conventional for opposites to fall for one another, perhaps even to become partners in crime, à la Bonnie and Clyde, whose portrayals on the screen (in Arthur Penn's *Bonnie and Clyde*, 1967) Sisco and Foley have previously discussed with admiration.

Another method for controlling the presentation of time in a film is **montage**. *Montage*—from the French verb *monter*, "to assemble or put together"— is French for "editing." French film theorist André Bazin defines montage as "the creation of a sense or meaning not proper to the images themselves but derived exclusively from their juxtaposition."[4] In the former Soviet Union in the 1920s, *montage* referred to the various forms of editing that expressed ideas developed by Eisenstein, Kuleshov, Vertov, Pudovkin, and others. In Hollywood, beginning in the 1930s, *montage* designates a sequence of shots, often with superimpositions and optical effects, that shows a condensed series of events. For example, a montage of flipping calendar pages was a typical (if trite) way to show the passage of time. In Wes Anderson's *Rushmore* (1998; editor: David Moritz), after the headmaster identifies Max Fischer (Jason Schwartzman) as "one of the worst students we've got," a twenty-one-shot montage unexpectedly shows Max as the key person in virtually every club at the school.

The hilarious *Team America: World Police* (2004; editor: Tom Vogt), an irreverent comedy from director Trey Parker (creator of *South Park*), has more targets than it can possibly reach in 97 minutes, but it hits dead right on the montage technique. At the end of the movie, Spottswoode (voice of Daran Norris), the sinister mastermind of Team America, believes that his protégé, Gary Johnston (voice of Parker), is the man to thwart the plan of Kim Jong Il (voice of Parker) to use weapons of

[4]André Bazin, *What Is Cinema?* ed. and trans. Hugh Gray, 2 vols. (Berkeley: University of California Press, 1967–1971), I, p. 25.

mass destruction to end the world. The problem is that Spottswoode has to make a complete soldier of Johnston in "*very little time*." Johnston naively asks, "How are we gonna do that?" and Spottswoode replies, "I think I know *just* what we need." Thus begins a musical sequence called "Montage!"—set to a lively disco beat—in which a time-condensing montage sequence (using many split screens) is accompanied by lyrics breathlessly announcing the technique and style of the conventional montage sequence:

> . . . show us the passage of time—we're gonna need a montage!

> . . . show a lot of things that are happening at once to remind everyone of what's going on

. . . with every shot, show a little improvement; to show it all would take too long—that's called a montage!

. . . even *Rocky* had a montage

and

. . . always fadeout in a montage; if you fadeout, it seems more time has passed in a montage.

This sequence provides an excellent example of a montage as it simultaneously satirizes action movies. The "Montage!" song itself was borrowed from *South Park*.

In order for these various editorial manipulations of time to be understandable to viewers, editors must employ accepted conventions of editing

Montage Although these still shots do not convey the pace of the lively lyrics in the "Montage!" sequence of Trey Parker's *Team America: World Police* (2004; editor: Tom Vogt), imagine a driving disco beat accompanying these images of Spottswoode overseeing the process by which Gary Johnston is being made into a complete soldier: close-up of Johnston [1], Johnston practicing on the firing range [2], running on a treadmill [3], lifting weights [4], and engaging in karate with Spottswoode [5].

to signal the transitions from shot to shot. Luckily, our minds are able to understand these conventions and to infer correctly the progression of plot and story from them, even when the plot is presented in nonchronological order and is riddled with ellipses. It's not entirely clear why our brains are able to do this, but for the sake of film history, it's a good thing. As Walter Murch puts it,

> When you stop to think about it, it is amazing that film editing works at all. One moment we're on top of Mauna Kea and—*cut!*—the next we're at the bottom of the Mariana Trench. The instantaneous transition of the cut is nothing like what we experience as normal life, which seems to be one continuous shot from the moment we wake until we close our eyes at night. It wouldn't have been surprising if film editing had been tried and then abandoned after it was found to induce a kind of seasickness. But it doesn't: we happily endure, in fact even enjoy, these sudden transitions for which nothing in our evolutionary history seems to have prepared us.[5]

Rhythm Among other things, editing determines the **duration** of a shot. Thus, it controls the length of time you can look at each shot and absorb the information within it. An editor can control the rhythm (or beat) of a film—the pace at which it moves forward—by varying the duration of the shots in relation to one another and thus control the speed (tempo) and accents (stress or lack of it on certain shots). Sometimes the editing rhythm allows us time to think about what we see; other times it moves too quickly to permit thought.

The musical analogy is useful, but only to a point, because a movie serves a narrative, while rhythm seldom does. However, there are some landmarks in the development of movie editing—among them the "Odessa Steps" sequence in Sergei Eisenstein's *Battleship Potemkin* (1925; editors: Grigori Akesandrov and Eisenstein), the diving sequence in Leni Riefenstahl's *Olympia* (1938; editor: Riefenstahl), Jean-Luc Godard's *Breathless*

(1960; editors: Cécile Decugis and Lila Herman), Andy and Larry Wachowski's *The Matrix* (1999; editor: Zach Staenberg), and Tom Tykwer's *Run Lola Run* (1998; editor: Mathilde Bonnefoy)—in which the editing (its patterns, rhythms, etc.) seem almost to take precedence over the narrative. A movie narrative has its own internal requirements that signal to the editor how long to make each shot and with what rhythm to combine those shots. Many professional editors say that they intuitively reach decisions on these matters.

What happens, however, when the rhythm is imposed autocratically before a film is made? To find out, you might look at Jørgen Leth and Lars von Trier's *The Five Obstructions* (2003; editors: Daniel Dencik, Morten Højbjerg, and Camilla Skousen). In the movie, von Trier, one of the founders of the Danish Dogme movement, views Leth's 12-minute film *The Perfect Human* (1967) and, in an interesting reversal of roles—Leth was one of von Trier's idols—"orders" the older director to remake the film five times, each version tightly controlled by limitations ("obstructions") that he specifies. The first version is to be composed of single shots of no more than twelve frames, each shot appearing for approximately one-half of a second on the screen. The result, a charming look at Cuba, closely resembles a television advertisement or an MTV spot.

Of course, the images "tell" a kind of story simply by the rhythm that links them, but this rigid imposition of a fixed rhythm makes traditional editing—and thus traditional storytelling—impossible. Why? Because editing requires the editor to make decisions about shot length, rhythm, emphasis, and the like; von Trier's formula (as successfully applied by Leth) ties the editor's hands and puts all of the decision making in the mind of the viewer. Looking at *The Five Obstructions*, we can understand the value of experimentation, particularly for those who prefer intellectual schematics to be applied to art.

Experimentation in editing does not have to be formulaic, as demonstrated by Mathilde Bonnefoy, the editor of Tom Tykwer's *Run Lola Run* (1998). Bonnefoy handles the editor's traditional tasks—fixing the duration and frequency of shots, thus

[5]Michael Ondaatje, *The Conversations: Walter Murch and the Art of Editing Film* (New York: Knopf, 2002), p. 49.

controlling the film's emphasis on a person, setting, or object—with such a sense of joy that the movie is more about the editing than about the narrative. In the opening sequence, Lola (Franka Potente) receives a phone call from her boyfriend, Manni (Moritz Bleibtreu), who implores her to help him return $100,000 to the criminal gang for which he works. If he does not do so in 20 minutes, the gang will kill him. Lola hangs up, imagines what her task will involve, and then sets off, running through the rooms of her apartment, down the stairs, and out into the city streets.

Although the principal action is composed of shots of Lola running, there are breaks in that rhythm for scenes of other action that introduce several of the characters relevant to Lola's quest. Tykwer uses a constantly moving camera, live and animated footage, time-lapse cinematography, slow motion and fast motion, different camera positions and angles, hard cuts, dissolves, jump cuts, and ellipses. Accents within the shots create their own patterns: different camera angles and heights, changes in the direction from which we see Lola's run on the screen (e.g., left to right, right to left, toward us, away from us, or diagonal across the frame). Underscoring the resulting visual rhythm is an equally exciting sound track: basically, the familiar disco beat scored for a synthesizer, piano, and percussion, with accents of glass breaking and camera shutters clicking, and Lola's voice repeating, "I wish I was a . . . ," and other voices chanting "Hey, hey, hey."

Together, editing and sound create the steady pace of Lola's run, make us empathize with her dilemma, and establish suspense (will Lola get the money? will she save Manni?) that continues until the last moment of the film. Editor Bonnefoy's handling of the complex rhythms in this scene not only dazzles us with its pacing, but also maintains the focus on what Lola is doing and why. The editing of this movie—its rhythm in particular—has been especially influential on such films as Paul Greengrass's *The Bourne Supremacy* (2004; editors: Richard Pearson and Christopher Rouse).

The tempo of a movie can also be strictly measured in slow rather than fast terms, as it is in another Tykwer work, *Heaven* (2002; editor:

Mathilde Bonnefoy), a moral fable-cum-thriller based on a script by the great Polish director-writer Krzysztof Kieslowski. Here the action—a bomb going off in the wrong place, a woman admitting responsibility for placing it, a police officer falling in love with the woman because of her sense of moral duty, the destruction of critical evidence by a corrupt police captain, a jailbreak and flight from the police—all takes place at a very deliberate pace established by a piano and violin score that is heard in virtually every shot in the movie. The music and editing are not only measured in tempo but are also devoid of accents, causing the viewer to wonder when something is going to happen that will break that tempo, signal a turning point, or provide a climax. Then, in the final moment, in a burst of gunfire, the two fugitives seize a helicopter and rise slowly toward heaven until they are out of sight—a moment of elation that contrasts with the previously unwavering tempo established by the rhythms of both the editing and the music.

Varying the duration and rhythm of shots guides our eyes just as varying the rhythm in jazz guides the almost involuntary tapping of our fingers or feet as we listen to it. When the rhythms of the visual and aural images match up, this is obvious, but when the visual images move with a rhythm that has little or nothing to do with the sound, we intuitively recognize and react to that rhythm. In the scene where the gulls attack a gas station attendant in *The Birds* (1963; see page 276 in Chapter 6), director Alfred Hitchcock and his editor, George Tomasini, masterfully use the rhythm of editing to build up excitement. If you attempt to tap the

Patterns in *Battleship Potemkin* (opposite) Soviet filmmaker and theorist Sergei Eisenstein helped pioneer the expressive use of patterns in movies using a dynamic form of editing called *montage*. Eisenstein's montage during the "Odessa Steps" sequence of *Battleship Potemkin* (1925; editors: Grigori Aleksandrov and Eisenstein) brings violence to a climax in both what we see and how we see it. After Cossacks fire [1] on a young mother [2], she collapses [3], sending her baby's carriage rolling [4]; an older woman reacts [5] to the carriage's flight down a series of steps [6], and a student cries out [7] as the carriage hits bottom [8]. The pattern of movement from shot to shot accentuates the devastating energy of the content of this scene.

Rhythm in editing In Tom Tykwer's *Run Lola Run* (1998; editor: Mathilde Bonnefoy), the title character (played by Franka Potente) [1] receives word that her boyfriend, Manni (Moritz Bleibtreu) [2], is in a dire situation—a matter of money and time [3], which is running out. Close-ups show

Lola facing facts [4] and imagining the possibilities [5]. Finally, she has no choice but to run for help [6]. From here on, the pace and rhythm of the editing will match the pace and rhythm of dramatic developments and Lola's sometimes split-second decision making.

rhythm with your finger at each of the thirty-nine cuts in the scene, you'll find that you're able to keep a discernible rhythm at first, but as the scene reaches its climax, you'll find that you can barely keep pace with the cuts.

The choices that an editor makes regarding the rhythm of scenes can, in turn, create larger patterns of shot duration. These patterns can be built

and broken for dramatic emphasis and impact, as in Sergio Leone's *Once upon a Time in the West* (1968; director's-cut DVD version released 2003; editor: Nino Baragli). During the opening title and credits, the editor has created a sequence of almost 15 minutes that is extraordinary for the patterns both of what we see (an isolated railroad station on the prairie where three desperate-looking characters are waiting for a train to arrive) and of what we hear (an equally extraordinary montage of sounds, the slow, steady rhythm of which establishes an ominous mood).

These visual and aural images establish a slow, deliberate pattern of duration, sound, and movement. The shots of waiting for the train's arrival last a very long time, made to seem even longer by the views of the vast prairie on the widescreen format, but they feature little or no action or movement by the characters. With this long sequence, Leone calls our attention to the **content curve**, which in terms of cinematic duration is the point at which we have absorbed all we need to know in a particular shot and are ready to see the next shot. Because we get very little information from this sequence, ordinarily we would expect the director to use shots of a shorter duration and to cut more quickly from one to the next. However, Leone frustrates our expectations by not cutting and traps us in each shot, making us wait along with the bored desperadoes.

The montage of natural sounds in Leone's opening sequence in this film has a different rhythm from that of the visual images; its purpose is to underscore the tedium of the wait. The duration of each sound is shorter than the duration of the shots, and what we hear are repetitions of the same sounds: wind, squeaking windmill, footsteps, telegraph machine, water dripping, fly buzzing, knuckles cracking, and silence. Suddenly this pattern, pace, and mood are broken by a shot—taken from a camera positioned underneath the tracks—of a train speeding toward the station. The pattern of editing speeds up, with cuts between close-ups of three men loading their guns; the train approaching at dramatic angle, its sounds now taking precedence over the others; and finally the train coming to a stop at a right angle to the screen, in front of the camera, wheels grinding to a halt and whistle blowing. In a moment, the train departs, leaving behind Harmonica (Charles Bronson).

The short, abrupt change in editing associated with the train's arrival takes on added significance because of Harmonica, who is to become one of the heroes of the film. In completing this scene, Leone returns to the overall pattern established in this sequence, with slow, quiet, static shots of the four-way face-off between Harmonica and the desperadoes building up to a rapid-fire shooting sequence (in terms of both the action being filmed and the camera shots that are capturing it) in which every gunman, even Harmonica, catches a bullet.

Major Approaches to Editing: Continuity and Discontinuity

Because the editing of most contemporary narrative movies is made to be as inconspicuous as possible, the process and the results of editing may not be apparent to people unfamiliar with filmmaking. In the editing of such movies, the point is to tell the story as clearly, efficiently, and coherently as possible. This style of editing, called **continuity editing**, is certainly the most prevalent in mainstream filmmaking, and it's the sort of editing that we'll spend most of this chapter discussing. Continuity editing seeks to achieve logic, smoothness, sequential flow, and the temporal and spatial orientation of viewers to what they see on the screen. It ensures the flow from shot to shot; creates a rhythm based on the relationship between cinematic space and cinematic time; creates filmic unity (beginning, middle,

LOOKING AT MOVIES
THE EVOLUTION OF EDITING:
CONTINUITY AND CLASSICAL CUTTING

DVD This tutorial explores the history of the major innovations in continuity (or classical) editing in early cinema.

1

2

3

5

4

6

7

8

9

10

Continuity editing in *Casablanca*, a classic Hollywood movie Ten frames from a sequence in *Casablanca* illustrate continuity editing. [1] The sequence opens with an interior shot of Rick's Café Americain; [2] inside, a moving camera pans across the main room, showing its customers and well-known piano player; [3] this diverse crowd includes an Arab customer, smoking a water pipe, and his waiter; [4] a man complains to a friend that all he does is wait, that he will never get out of Casablanca; [5] a woman, obviously in need of cash, sells her diamonds for less than they are worth; [6] two men, apparently spies or criminals, quietly discuss some impending event while they are watchful of those around them; [7] a refugee (*left*) buys an exit visa for a very large sum of cash; [8] the camera pans past a group of Asians at a table to an Englishman having a drink at the bar; [9] a female member of a large party asks the waiter to ask Rick to have a drink with them and is told that he never drinks with customers; and [10] a medium close-up of a hand approving a customer's charge; we see the bold signature "Rick" as the camera pans up to a middle shot of Rick Blaine (Humphrey Bogart). This sequence, flowing smoothly and rhythmically from shot to shot, shows that each shot has a meaning that is directly related to those that precede and follow it. The sequence tells us exactly where we are, establishes the customers' unique problems, and suggests that at least one person, Rick, who runs his café with an iron hand, may be able to solve them. Indeed, Rick will hold in his grasp the fate of several major characters.

and end); and establishes and resolves the characters' problems.

In short, continuity editing tells a story as clearly and coherently as possible, as in this example (on pages 356–357) from Michael Curtiz's *Casablanca* (1942: editor: Owen Marks). The movie opens by explaining that, prior to the outbreak of World War II, the French Moroccan city of Casablanca was a major rendezvous for Europeans seeking exit visas that would permit them to flee the Nazi offensive. In an atmosphere of intrigue over the buying and selling of such visas, there is civil unrest, including murder, as a major Nazi official arrives in town. The continuity editing, represented by this panel of images, establishes that Rick's Café Americain is an elegant, sophisticated rendezvous for everyone, a place for all nationalities and languages, and that its proprietor, Rick Blaine (Humphrey Bogart), is and will be at the center of the story.

But this is not the only approach to film editing. **Discontinuity editing** breaks the rules of continuity editing by seeking to achieve transitions between shots that are not smooth, continuous, or coherent. It permits a filmmaker to make abrupt shifts between shots, resulting in mismatches in the location of characters or objects, the direction or speed of movement, mise-en-scène, lighting, camera angles, or even colors. Instead of invisibly propelling the film forward, unlike continuity editing, it calls attention to itself as an element of cinematic form. It was pioneered by Soviet filmmakers (see Chapter 10, "1924-1930: The Soviet Montage Movement," page 448) and greatly influenced the French New Wave directors, including Jean-Luc Godard in *Breathless* (1960). It has become a standard tool of today's filmmakers.

Like the tension between realism (verisimilitude) and antirealism more generally, continuity and discontinuity are not absolute values but are instead tendencies along a continuum. An average Hollywood movie may exhibit continuity in some parts and discontinuity in others, even if the overall tendency of the movie is toward classical continuity. Similarly, an avant-garde film that is mostly discontinuous can include scenes that employ continuity editing. We don't need to look any further than Michel Gondry's *Eternal Sunshine of the Spot-*

LOOKING AT MOVIES
THE EVOLUTION OF EDITING: MONTAGE

DVD This tutorial explores montage and discontinuity editing in Sergei Eisentein's film *The Battleship Potemkin*.

less Mind (2004; editor: Valdis Óskarsdóttir) or Fernando Meirelles and Kátia Lund's *City of God* (2002; editor: Daniel Rezende)—to cite just two cases—to find examples that use both of these major approaches to editing as well as many of the specific tools of editing described in this chapter.

Conventions of Continuity Editing

Continuity editing, now the dominant style of editing throughout the world, seeks to achieve logic, smoothness, sequential flow, and the temporal and spatial orientation of viewers to what they see on the screen. As with so many conventions of film production, the conventions of continuity editing remain open to variation, but in general, continuity editing ensures that

> what happens on the screen makes as much narrative sense as possible.
> screen direction is consistent from shot to shot.
> graphic, spatial, and temporal relations are maintained from shot to shot.

The two fundamental objectives of continuity editing are to establish coverage of the scene through the master scene technique and to maintain screen direction through the 180-degree system.

Master Scene Technique This technique is based on the principle of **coverage**, meaning that a scene is photographed with a variety of individual shots, running from the general to the specific (long shot/medium shot/close-up), and taken from various distances and angles; in other words, all the shots that comprise the cinematography of that scene. Coverage is, at heart, a strategy employed specifically with the editing in mind. Usually, directors begin shooting a single scene with a long shot (sometimes known as the **master shot**) that covers the characters and action in one continuous take. The master scene technique then proceeds to covering the scene with whatever additional shots (medium shots, close-ups, etc.) the editor might need to create the finished scene. Covering the action in this comprehensive way gives the editor the tools, as well as the creative freedom, to choose the shot types and angles needed to tell the story as effectively as possible.

Typically, an editor starts a scene or sequence of shots with the master shot in order to establish location, situation, spatial relationships, and so on, then cuts in on various subjects as the drama and action dictate, regularly cutting back to the master to reacquaint viewers with location, what's happening, who's doing it, and how the characters are positioned in relation to one another.

Although some of today's mainstream directors are far more experimental with continuity (we discuss several in this chapter) and do not always adhere to the conventions of the master scene technique, note that those conventions are common in films in which place is paramount, such as Westerns. For example, John Ford opens *The Searchers* (1956; editor: Jack Murray) with a master shot of spectacular Monument Valley framed in the doorway of a darkened house. The point of view is that of Martha Edwards (Dorothy Jordan), who has an instinct that someone is outside, coming to her house. This orients and prepares us to understand the following shots. She steps out on her porch and—in an extreme long shot—soon sees a horseman riding in her direction. An exterior shot shows us the isolation of her house in the vast landscape, and we will soon learn why she has had this intuition and why this horseman is so important in her life.

Martha is joined by her husband, Aaron (Walter Coy), and their children, by which time they sense also that the lone rider is Ethan Edwards (John Wayne), her husband's brother. In a few shots of great economy, Ford establishes that Ethan has been away for a long period of time but that, somehow, his home is here. These shots establish two motifs—the vastness of the desert valley and the intimacy of the pioneer home—that Ford will develop throughout the movie.

Screen Direction In the early years of cinema, the evolution of films containing many shots from a variety of angles (especially those containing the types of action shot that occur in a chase scene) demanded that filmmakers find a way to maintain consistent **screen direction**, the direction of a figure's or object's movement on the screen. The fundamental result of their search—established as early as 1903 and used with occasional inconsistencies (often for deliberate comic purposes) until about 1912, when filmmakers first began to adhere to it—is the **180-degree system** (also called the *180-degree rule*, the **axis of action**, the *imaginary line*, and the *line of action*).

The axis of action, an imaginary horizontal line between the main characters being photographed, determines where the camera should be placed to preserve screen direction and thus one aspect of continuity (Fig. 8.1). Once this axis of action is determined, the camera must remain on the same side of the line. The resulting shots orient the viewer within the scene, ensure consistent screen direction across and between cuts, and establish a clear sense of the space in which the action occurs (because something, an object or person, remains consistent in the frame to identify the relations between sequential spaces). The axis of action shifts, though, as the characters move within the frame and as the camera moves.

To summarize, in reaching the goals of continuity, the 180-degree system depends on three factors working together in any single shot: (1) the action in a

1

2

3

4

5

6

7

8

Discontinuity editing in *Breathless* Consider this panel of the movie's opening images: [1] man A leaning against a storefront background; [2] woman B, against another background, who points her chin to signify something to someone; [3] man A seems oblivious of the woman; [4] woman B gestures more emphatically; [5] man C and woman D exit a car, located against a third background; [6] another shot of A against the storefront; [7] a shot of woman B, again beckoning, with man C and woman D moving away into the background; [8] man A, folding his newspaper and apparently getting ready to move; [9] a boat in a harbor, confusing because no spatial relationship was established between the previous shots and this one; [10] man A hot-wiring the car seen in [5], the first time we can reliably associate him with his accomplice, woman B; [11] woman B hurrying toward someone or something; [12] woman B asking the man, who is now in the stolen car, to take her with him. He has no further use for her and speeds away. Discontinuity editing has become a familiar convention, so this sequence may not

seem as surprising as it did when the film was first released some 50 years ago. Yet because Godard does not orient us to the time or place of the action (see "Master Scene Technique," page 359) and disregards the 180-degree line, the sequence still confuses us because we don't know the place, time, identity of the four characters, their surroundings, or their relationship to them. Although [12] reveals that the woman is an accomplice to the man's theft of the car, we have no sense of where the narrative is going from here. *Breathless* continues to tell the story of the man, Michel (Jean-Paul Belmondo), a charming but ruthless criminal who, within a few minutes, will kill a policeman and, once in Paris, will lie and steal cars or whatever else he needs whenever necessary. Eventually the police hunt him down and kill him as he tries to escape. The opening sequence helps us to understand the story, for it establishes that he seems sinister, uses people, and takes life as it comes. Equally important, the director trusts us to put the pieces together.

scene must move along a hypothetical line that keeps the action on a single side of the camera; (2) the camera must shoot consistently on one side of that line; and (3) everyone on the production set—particularly the director, cinematographer, editor, and actors—must understand and adhere to this system.

This means that in a scene of dialogue, say, in which character A is on the left and character B is on the right, the viewer is oriented to that spatial relationship between them because the camera stays on one side of the imaginary line; however, if the camera crosses the imaginary line between the

1

3

5

2

4

6

The master scene technique These six shots from the opening of John Ford's *The Searchers* (1956; editor: Jack Murray) very economically establish both the place and some of the themes of this complex movie: the vastness of the desert valley in which Aaron and Martha Edwards's home is situated; the intimacy of family life in this isolated spot; and the return home of Ethan Edwards, who became a mercenary soldier in the Civil War after his brother married Martha, who nonetheless still yearns for Ethan, as he does for her. [1] Martha (Dorothy Jordan), framed in the doorway, looks out at Monument Valley in the background; [2] she stands on the porch; [3] she shields her eyes to try to focus on someone approaching; [4] Ethan Edwards (John Wayne) rides toward the house; [5] Martha is joined by her husband, Aaron (Walter Coy), and their children; finally, [6] the two brothers meet for the first time in years.

FIGURE 8.1 The 180-Degree System

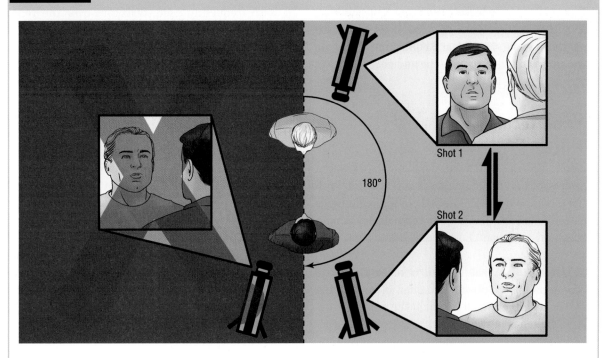

Shots 1 and 2 are taken from positions within the same 180-degree space (green background). When viewers see the resulting shots on-screen, they can make sense of the actors' relative positions to one another. If a camera is placed in the opposite 180-degree space (red background), the resulting shot reverses the actors' spatial orientation and thus cannot be used in conjunction with either shot 1 or shot 2 without confusing the viewer.

characters and moves to a position 180 degrees opposite its original position, the position of the characters in the image is reversed: character A is now on the right, character B is on the left.

Screen direction can also suggest meaning in an abstract or symbolic way. For example, the earlier discussion of *Run Lola Run* described how Lola runs against a deadline. If you study the patterns of her running, you'll see that she actually does run *against* time by continuously going in a counter-clockwise pattern. Thus, the screen movement and rhythm of editing reinforce the major theme: her need to beat the clock if she's going to save her boyfriend's life.

The 180-degree system remains a convention (not a rule) that can be broken if the director desires. Sometimes, for example, the director might wish to

LOOKING AT MOVIES
THE 180-DEGREE RULE

DVD This tutorial illustrates the 180-degree system by analyzing its use in a scene from Alfred Hitchcock's *Vertigo*.

use a **reverse-angle shot** (one in which the angle of shooting is opposite to that in a preceding shot) or to dolly or zoom out to include more people or actions. But if the director asks the cinematographer to cross the line, the shooting and editing must be done carefully so as not to confuse the audience.

Editing Techniques That Maintain Continuity

In addition to the fundamental building blocks—the master shot and maintaining screen direction with the 180-degree system—various editing techniques are used to ensure that graphic, spatial, and temporal relations are maintained from shot to shot.

Shot/Reverse Shot A **shot/reverse shot**, one of the most common and familiar of all editing patterns, is a technique in which the camera (and editor) switches between shots of different characters, usually in a conversation or other interaction. When used in continuity editing, the shots are typically framed over each character's shoulder to preserve screen direction. Thus, in the first shot the camera is behind character A, who is looking right, and records what character B says to A; in the second shot, the camera is behind character B, who is looking left, and records that character's response.

Michael Mann's *The Insider* (1999; editors: William Goldenberg, David Rosenbloom, and Paul Rubell) provides a good example. In one of their first discussions, Dr. Wigand (Russell Crowe) and Mr. Bergman (Al Pacino) are sitting in the closed confines of Wigand's car. As their conversation begins, Wigand is on the right of the frame, in the driver's seat, and Bergman is in the front passenger's seat, the imaginary line being the backs of the seats. But as you first might expect, the scene is not shot through the windshield. Instead, the camera shoots Wigand through the window adjacent to Bergman and vice versa. Although the two characters are essentially facing the windshield, they continually turn to face the other and maintain eyeline contact. The conversation is tense and perfectly suited to this closed, conspiratorial space.

The shot/reverse shot is one of the most fundamental of all filmmaking conventions, and because it is so frequently used, directors over the years have developed many variations on its basic technique. Besides playing an essential role in maintaining continuity, the shot/reverse shot helps ease some of the logistical challenges of making a movie. For example, this editing technique fools our eyes by bringing together two characters on the screen that could have been photographed in completely different locations or at completely different times. Thus, we are reminded that a movie is not shot in the order we see it on the screen and that the editor has the power to make it appear that it was.

Match Cuts **Match cuts**—those in which shot A and shot B are matched in action, subject, graphic content, or two characters' eye contact—help create a sense of continuity between the two shots. There are several kinds of match cuts. Technically, they are identical; the differences between them are in what is depicted.

David Lean's *Lawrence of Arabia* (1962; editor: Anne V. Coates) features a match cut that is legendary in film history. Call it elliptical, poetic, or simply brilliant, it both wows us and moves the story forward. T. E. Lawrence (Peter O'Toole) receives a charge to make a perilous journey from Mr. Dryden (Claude Rains), a British officer in Cairo; as he does so, he lights Dryden's cigarette, holds the match up and watches the flame burn closer and closer to his fingers (he enjoys such pain), responds to Dryden's skepticism about the assignment by saying, "No, Dryden, it's going to be fun," and blows out the match. The editor cuts to the rising of the sun above the desert horizon, thus "matching" two flares of light in two different places and time. Film critic Anthony Lane writes, "It was a moment that Steven Spielberg saw at the age of fifteen, and which, he says, ignited his determination to make films. If you don't *get* this cut, if you think it's cheesy or showy or over the top, and if something inside you doesn't flare up and burn at the spectacle that Lean has conjured, then you might as well give up the movies."[6]

---

[6]Anthony Lane, "Master and Commander: Remembering David Lean," *The New Yorker* (March 31, 2008), p. 116.

Legendary match cut in *Lawrence of Arabia* Director David Lean and his editor, Anne V. Coates, created a legendary match cut in *Lawrence of Arabia* (1962) by literally cutting from a shot of a match flame [1] to a shot of the sun rising on the desert [2]. Although Lean wrote, "I am not *absolutely* convinced that the match incident is worth the footage involved [less than a minute],"[7] once you've seen it, you'll no doubt disagree. To make this shot even more interesting, Lean created a sound bridge to link the two images. He said: "I thought Lawrence should blow out the match, and I wanted the sound to blow in the desert. What I did was this. He [Peter O'Toole, who plays T. E. Lawrence in the film] holds up the match and he blows. Now, I laid the first half of the blow over Peter and last half over the sunrise in the desert, so that the blow noise carried from his close-up over to the long shot. He was still blowing on the long shot. If I'd had him blow out the match and after the sound had faded I cut to the long shot, it wouldn't have had the same effect."[8]

Match-on-Action Cut

A **match-on-action cut** shows us the continuation of a character's or object's motion through space without actually showing us the entire action. It is a fairly routine editorial technique for economizing a movie's presentation of movement. Of course, the match-on-action cut has both expressive and practical uses.

Graphic Match Cut

In a **graphic match cut**, the similarity between shots A and B is in the shape and form of what we see. In this type of cut, the shape, color, or texture of objects matches across the edit, providing continuity. The prologue of Stanley Kubrick's *2001: A Space Odyssey* (1968; editor: Ray Lovejoy) contains a memorable example of a graphic match cut in which the action continues seamlessly from one shot to the next: a cut that erases millions of years, from a bone weapon of the Stone Age to an orbiting craft of the Space Age. The weapon and the spacecraft match not only in their tubular shapes but also in their rotations.

Alfred Hitchcock gives us another classic example of the graphic match cut in *Vertigo* (1958; editor: George Tomasini) when John "Scottie" Ferguson (James Stewart) places a necklace around the neck of Judy Barton (Kim Novak). This action occurs in a sequence: a medium shot of Barton and Ferguson in front of a mirror as Ferguson fastens the necklace followed by a dolly-in right to a close-up of him looking at her reflection; cut to a dolly-in to a close-up of the necklace on Barton's neck followed by the match cut to a dolly-out from a close-up of a similar necklace in a portrait.

Graphic matches often exploit basic shapes—squares, circles, triangles—and provide a strong visual sense of design and order. For example, at the end of the shower murder sequence in *Psycho* (1960; editor: George Tomasini), Hitchcock matches two circular shapes: the eye of Marion Crane (Janet Leigh), tears streaming down, with the round shower drain, blood and water washing down—a metaphorical visualization of Marion's life ebbing away.

Eye-line Match Cut

An **eye-line match cut** joins shot A, in which a person looks at someone off-screen, and shot B, the object of that gaze looking back. In Irving Rapper's *Now, Voyager* (1942; editor: Warren Low), Jerry Durrance (Paul Henreid) lights two cigarettes, one for him, the other for Charlotte Vale (Bette Davis). As he hands one to her and

[7]Lean, qtd. ibid., p. 116.
[8]Lean, qtd. in Kevin Brownlow, *David Lean: A Biography* (New York: St. Martin's, 1996), pp. 471–472.

[1]

[2]

Match-on-action cut   Near the conclusion of John Ford's *Stagecoach* (1939; editors: Otho Lovering and Dorothy Spencer), the Ringo Kid (John Wayne) intends to avenge the murder of his father by the Plummer gang by shooting those responsible for it: Luke Plummer and his two brothers. In an attempt to avert what might not turn out the way Ringo plans it, Doc Boone (Thomas Mitchell) enters a bar in

Lordsburg with the intention of persuading Luke Plummer to give up his shotgun. There follows an excellent match-on-action shot. In image [1], he points to a bottle of whiskey, says "Can I have that?" and Luke slides it across the bar toward him. In image [2], he catches the bottle and pours himself a drink.

[1]

[2]

[3]

Graphic match cut in *2001: A Space Odyssey*   In the opening scene of Stanley Kubrick's *2001: A Space Odyssey* (1968; editor: Ray Lovejoy), in which an ape-man [3] rejoices in his newfound weaponry, a bone, by tossing it into the air [4], at which point it becomes technology of a far more sophisticated kind [5]. This astonishing leap of space and time introduces several of the movie's principal themes: the relativity of time, the interaction of inventiveness and aggressiveness, and the desire of the human race to conquer the unknown.

[1]

[2]

Eye-line match cut in *Now, Voyager* As we know from looking at "old" movies, everyone smoked in them. For one thing, tobacco companies paid the studios to feature stars with cigarettes, cigars, or pipes; for another, public censorship of smoking was decades away. Today, it's seldom that we see stars smoking on-screen, but in early years Bette Davis was Hollywood's most memorable smoker. In Irving Rapper's *Now, Voyager* (1942; editor: Warren Low), the affair

between Charlotte Vale (Davis) and Jerry Durrance (Paul Henreid) is repeatedly punctuated by his signature custom of lighting two cigarettes and giving one to her. In the eye-line match cut pictured here, as Charlotte asks for Jerry's help, he says, "Shall we just have a cigarette on it?" This signals the viewer that he will do all she asks, even if it means that their relationship is going up in a puff of smoke.

looks into her eyes, an eye-line match cut joins a shot of her eyes looking into his, the culmination of an intensely romantic moment that, ironically, ends their relationship.

Parallel Editing Parallel editing (or **crosscutting**) is the cutting together of two or more lines of action that occur simultaneously at different locations.

Joel Coen's *Raising Arizona* (1987; editor: Michael R. Miller) uses crosscutting to link several simultaneous actions: Hi (Nicolas Cage) fleeing the police after robbing a convenience store; the police chasing him; his enraged wife, Ed (Holly Hunter), rescuing him from the police; the hapless clerk at the convenience store reacting to Hi's robbery; and a pack of runaway dogs also pursuing Hi. The complex choreography of this scene, accentuated by the brilliant crosscutting, creates a hilarious comic episode.

Intercutting is the editing of two or more actions that take place at different locations and/or different times but give the impression of one scene. Director Steven Soderbergh uses intercutting to foretell the outcome of a cozy scene in *Out of*

Sight (1998; editor: Anne V. Coates). We met Jack Foley (George Clooney) and Karen Sisco (Jennifer Lopez) earlier in this chapter; she's a federal marshal, he's an escaped convict. They meet under circumstances that have to be seen to be believed. Soon these circumstances separate them, and then they meet again, this time in a hotel bar, where they recount their meeting. By intercutting their conversation (in present time) with shots of them undressing (in future time), we know the predictable outcome even before it happens. There is something matter-of-fact, even comic, about this scene, which pays tribute to a similar scene in Nicolas Roeg's thriller *Don't Look Now* (1973).

Parallel editing permits us to experience at least two sides of related actions, and it has long been a very familiar convention in chase or rescue sequences (as we saw earlier in D. W. Griffith's *Way down East* [1920]; see page 43). Intercutting brings together two directly related actions, often slowing them down or speeding them up, and sometimes omitting some action that might have occurred between the two actions, thus also creating a sort of ellipsis.

Point-of-View Editing **Point-of-view editing** is the process of editing different shots together in such a way that the resulting sequence makes us aware of the perpective or point of view of a particular character or group of characters. Most frequently, it starts with an objective shot of a character looking toward something offscreen and then cuts to a shot of the object, person, or action that the character is supposed to be looking at.

In *Rear Window* (1954; editor: George Tomasini), Hitchcock uses this editing technique, alternating between subjective and omniscient shots in an ABABAB pattern. As we watch the temporarily sidelined photographer L. B. "Jeff" Jefferies (James Stewart) sitting near the window of his apartment and watching the activities of his neighbors, one of whom he believes has committed a murder, we begin to realize that this movie is partly about what constitutes the boundaries of our perceptions and how ordinary seeing can easily become snooping, even voyeurism.

To emphasize this concept, one of the movie's principal design motifs is the frame within a frame—established when we see the opening titles framed within a three-panel window frame in which blinds are raised automatically to reveal the setting outside. Similarly, Jefferies, immobilized in his chair by a broken leg, has his vision limited by the height and position of his chair, as well as by the window frame. This frame within a frame (or inner frame) is used throughout the movie, determining—along with the point-of-view editing— what we see and further defining the idea of perception that is at the movie's core.

Other Transitions between Shots

The Jump Cut The **jump cut**, made popular by French New Wave directors of the 1960s, presents an instantaneous reverse or advance in the action—a sudden, perhaps illogical, often disorienting ellipsis between two shots caused by the absence of a portion of the film that would have provided continuity. Because such a jump in time can occur either on purpose or because the filmmakers have failed to follow continuity principles, this type of cut has sometimes been regarded more

Point-of-view editing in *Rear Window* (opposite) Alternating subjective and omniscient shots in Alfred Hitchcock's *Rear Window* (1954; editor: George Tomasini): [1, 3, 5, 7] From his wheelchair, L. B. "Jeff" Jefferies (James Stewart) observes his neighbors: [2] a dancer (Georgine Darcy), known as Miss Torso; [4] a sculptor (Jesslyn Fax), known as Miss Hearing Aid because she adjusts hers to silence the noise of Miss Torso's dancing; [6] a songwriter (Ross Bagdasarian); and [8] Lars Thorwald (Raymond Burr) and his wife, Anna (Irene Winston).

as an error than as an expressive technique of shooting and editing.

In *Taxi Driver* (1976; editors: Tom Rolf and Melvin Shapiro), director Martin Scorsese, who often makes unconventional use of cinematic conventions, uses a jump cut, not to advance an action—the more familiar procedure—but to reverse and repeat it.

The jump cut and the freeze-frame (which we'll discuss later) had an important influence on the New American Cinema of the 1960s, including Arthur Penn's *Bonnie and Clyde* (1967; editor: Dede Allen) and Sam Peckinpah's *The Wild Bunch* (1969; editor: Lou Lombardo), by introducing new cinematic techniques to supplant the conventions that had dominated filmmaking since the 1930s.

Fade The **fade-in** and **fade-out** are transitional devices that allow a scene to open or close slowly. In a fade-in, a shot appears out of a black screen and grows gradually brighter; in a fade-out, a shot grows rapidly darker until the screen turns black for a moment. Traditionally, such fades have suggested a break in time, place, or action.

Fades can be used within a scene, as in John Boorman's *The General* (1998; editor: Ron Davis). Martin Cahill, aka "The General" (Brendan Gleeson), is one of Dublin's most notorious criminals, as famous for his audacious capers as he is for his ability to outwit the police. In one scene, he enters the house of a wealthy couple when almost everyone is asleep and steals several valuable items. The scene opens with a fade-in and closes with a fade-out; in between are eleven brief segments, each separated by a fade-out or fade-in. Cahill's stealth and self-confidence are underscored by the almost buoyant rhythm of these fades, and his evident arrogance

[1]

[2]

[3]

[4]

Point-of-view editing in *The Night of the Hunter* In Charles Laughton's *The Night of the Hunter* (1955; editor: Robert Golden), Harry Powell (Robert Mitchum) confronts Rachel (Lillian Gish) [1], who is providing refuge for the children he seeks. As one of the children (Pearl, played by

Sally Jane Bruce) enters the scene [2], she drops a doll containing something very valuable to Harry and runs to him. Harry, clearly more interested in the doll than in Pearl, betrays his true interest by looking directly at the doll [3], as we see in the shot of the doll that follows [4].

and satisfaction are echoed on the sound track: Van Morrison's "So Quiet in Here," which contains the lyric "This must be what paradise is like, so quiet in here, so peaceful in here." The fades convey both the passage of time and the character's thoughts.

Since editing conventions are not rules, variations are welcome, especially in the hands of a master filmmaker like Ingmar Bergman. In his *Cries and Whispers* (1972; editor: Siv Lundgren), he not only shoots the fades in color but also uses them between scenes of past and present. In this dreamlike movie, Agnes (Harriet Andersson) is

dying, attended by her two sisters, Karin (Ingrid Thulin) and Maria (Liv Ullmann), and a servant, Anna (Kari Sylwan). Color is central to understanding the fades and the film, for the predominant reds hold a key to its meanings, suggesting the cycles of life, love, and death with which the story is concerned. Whole rooms are painted red, and the plot, which moves back and forth across the lives of these women, is punctuated with frequent fades to a completely blood-red screen (sometimes the next scene begins with a fade-in from such a red screen).

[1]

[2]

[3]

[4]

Reverse jump cut in *Taxi Driver* In this scene, Travis Bickle (Robert De Niro) is acting out his plans to take revenge on the evils of a society that sickens him. Talking to an imaginary adversary, he repeats the same warning twice. This is captured in two shots, which are deliberately separated here into four images so that you can see the character's movements. In image [1] he faces screen left and turns (within the shot) to [2] face the camera. At this point, a jump cut takes us back to where he started, and again Bickle is photographed [3] facing screen left and turning [4] to face the camera. (Remember that the reverse jump occurs between two shots, not four.) The effect of this cut is to call attention to Bickle's cool preparation and determination.

Dissolve Also called a *lap dissolve*, the **dissolve** is a transitional device in which shot B, superimposed, gradually appears over shot A and begins to replace it midway through the process. Like the fades described in the preceding section, the dissolve is essentially a transitional cut, primarily one that shows the passing of time or implies a connection or relationship between what we see in shot A and shot B. But it is different from a fade in that the process occurs simultaneously on the screen, whereas a black screen separates the two parts of the fade. Fast dissolves can imply a rapid change of

time or a dramatic contrast between the two parts of the dissolve. Slow dissolves can mean a gradual change of time or a less dramatic contrast.

In John Ford's *My Darling Clementine* (1946; editor: Dorothy Spencer), a dissolve establishes a thematic connection between its parts. In the first scene, on the prairie outside of Tombstone, Wyatt Earp (Henry Fonda) and his brothers discuss the troublemakers who have killed their younger brother. After a fast dissolve to the wide-open town of Tombstone, we instinctively understand that the troublemakers might be there. This dissolve makes

[2]

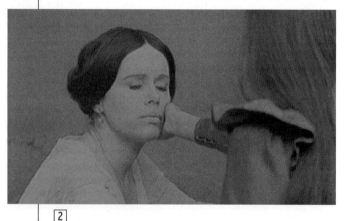

[3]

[1]

an important connection for our understanding of Earp, who quells a ruckus in a saloon and, as a result, is made the town's sheriff.

Wipe   Like the dissolve and the fade, the **wipe** is a transitional device—often indicating a change of time, place, or location—in which shot B wipes across shot A vertically, horizontally, or diagonally to replace it. A line between the two shots suggests something like a windshield wiper. A soft-edge wipe is indicated by a blurry line; a hard-edge wipe, by a sharp line. A jagged line suggests a more violent transition.

Although the device reminds us of early eras in filmmaking, directors continue to use it. Such diverse movies as Lewis Milestone's original version of *Ocean's Eleven* (1960; editor: Philip W. Anderson), George Lucas's *Star Wars* (1977; editors: Richard Chew, Paul Hirsch, and Marcia Lucas), and Guy Ritchie's *Snatch* (2000; editor: Jon Harris) continue to make imaginative use of this transitional technique.

Iris Shot   An **iris shot** appears on the screen in two ways: the **iris-out** begins with a large circle that closes in around the subject, while the **iris-in** begins with a small circle and expands to a partial or full image. It is both a shot and an editing technique because it functions as a transition to the next shot and thus involves an editor's decision. (Because it is named for the iris diaphragm, which controls the amount of light passing through a camera lens, it is usually circular, but can be any shape.) Filmmakers can create it in the camera, with special effects, or with a *mask*. The obvious function of the iris is to draw our attention to a particular place on the screen, thus emphasizing what we see there.

Fade-in and fade-out   In *Cries and Whispers* (1972; editor: Siv Lundgren), Ingmar Bergman builds the emotional intensity of his story by cutting back and forth between scenes of the past and the present and ending most of those scenes with a fade-out to a blood-red screen. Bergman has said that he thinks of red as the color of the human soul, but it also functions here as a symbolic system that has much to do with the film's focus on women. Just before this brief scene, Agnes (Rosanna Mariano, playing her as a child) has been hiding behind a curtain watching her mother (Liv Ullmann, who also plays Agnes's sister); when her mother sees Agnes, she summons the girl to her side. Agnes fears that she will be reprimanded, but instead Bergman gives us a moment of great simplicity and tenderness that unfolds in three shots: [1] Agnes touches her mother; [2] her mother is moved by the caress; [3] the image fades to the blood-red screen. Can we find words to explain the purpose of this fade-out to red?

[1]

[2]

Iris-in and iris-out Volker Schlöndorff's *The Tin Drum* (1979; editor: Suzanne Baron) contains an excellent sequence of two iris shots that single out a character and denote the passing of time in her life. The character, Anna, the narrator's mother, sells her farm produce in the municipal market. In an iris-in to a full-screen image, we see the young, prosperous Anna (Tina Engel) selling freshly killed geese [1]. This image quickly irises-out; then (with a superimposition of [2]) there is an iris-in of the older Anna (Berta Drews), who, during the First World War, has only turnips to sell. Thus, this succession of iris shots not only encompasses the passing of time, the aging of a principal character, and the narrator's vibrant memories, but also the changing economic and social circumstances of Germany before and during the war.

Freeze-Frame

The **freeze-frame** (also called *stop-frame or hold-frame*) is a still image within a movie, created by repetitive printing in the laboratory of the same frame so that it can be seen without movement for whatever length of time the filmmaker desires. It stops time and functions somewhat like an exclamation point in a sentence, halting our perception of movement to call attention to an image. In Alfonso Cuarón's *Y tu mamá*

Iris-out shot for comic emphasis In Gus Van Sant's *To Die For* (1995; editor: Curtiss Clayton), Nicole Kidman plays Suzanne Stone Maretto, a clueless woman who wants to be a celebrity so badly that she'll do anything, eventually including murder, to get there. At a low point in her unhappy marriage to Larry (Matt Dillon), her husband uncharacteristically tries to take control of the situation by proposing that she abandon her pipe dreams and help him implement a plan to improve the image of his father's restaurant, where he works. Her head is swimming with ideas of becoming the next hot thing on television, and she stares incredulously as he emphasizes that they are a family. Family is the last thing on Suzanne's mind, so, through an iris-out, reflecting her mental point of view, she cuts him down to size, providing a microscopic view of a man for whom she has nothing but contempt.

también (2001; editors: Cuarón and Alex Rodríguez), it is used to emphasize an important moment of passage in a young man's life. Julio Zapata (Gael García Bernal) has just felt what he calls "great pain" at learning of his best friend's getting the advantage over him with a woman they both desire. He retreats to a swimming pool. In an overhead shot, we see him sink underwater through a surface covering of brown leaves, a traditional symbol of the change that comes with autumn; the screen freezes as we hear a rooster crowing, underscoring Julio's realization of change.

Cuarón uses the freeze-frame here, in all likelihood, to pay homage to one of the most famous uses of the freeze-frame: the conclusion of François Truffaut's *The 400 Blows* (1959; editor: Marie-Josèphe

[3]

[2]

[1]

Freeze-frame Freeze-frames are often used to underscore a significant emotional change in a character—to "freeze" time, as it were, for the character's reflection on what's happening. In the final moments of François Truffaut's *The 400 Blows* (1959; editor: Marie-Josèphe Yoyotte), Antoine Doinel (Jean-Pierre Léaud), having escaped from reform school, arrives at a beach. Doinel runs along the shore, the camera following, until he abruptly turns and heads straight toward the camera. The freeze-frame [1] that ends the movie clearly doesn't tell us where Doinel goes next, but it conveys just how unsure he feels, here and now, about the possibilities that surround him. In Alfonso Cuarón's *Y tu mamá también* (2001; editors: Cuarón and Alex Rodríguez), Julio Zapata (Gael García Bernal) feels "great pain" at learning of his best friend's betrayal in having sex with an older woman whom Julio adores, and he sinks below the surface of the leaf-filled swimming pool [2] to think about it. [3] During this freeze-frame from Martin Scorsese's *Goodfellas* (1990; editors: Thelma Schoonmaker and James Y. Kwei), we actually hear young Henry Hill (Christopher Serrone) tell us what he thinks of his father's beating him for being a truant from school and working for the mob: "I didn't care. The way I saw it, everybody takes a beating sometimes." At roughly the same age as the other two boys described here, Henry has the greater self-realization at this moment of epiphany in his life.

Yoyotte). The poignant freeze-frame close-up of young Antoine Doinel (Jean-Pierre Léaud) that concludes the movie not only stops his movement on a beach, but also points toward the uncertainty of his future. In both examples, the freeze-frame ironically underscores a significant emotional change in the characters depicted.

Martin Scorsese uses the freeze-frame in *Goodfellas* (1990; editors: Thelma Schoonmaker and James Y. Kwei) to show a character who actually acknowledges an emotional change as it is happening. The scene begins with young Henry Hill (Christopher Serrone) doing odd jobs for the mob, his offscreen narration telling us that this makes him feel like a grown-up. At home, when Henry lies about his school attendance, his father (Beau Starr) savagely beats him with a belt. During an unusually long freeze-frame (15 seconds) that suspends the beating, Henry continues his narration, and then the violence resumes. The effect is ironic: while the film "stops" the violence (as Henry's mother cannot) so that we linger on its wrath, the boy continues his narration in a matter-of-fact voice suggesting his awareness that domestic violence and mob violence are now part of his life.

Split Screen The **split screen**, which has been in mainstream use since Phillips Smalley and Lois Weber's *Suspense* (1913), produces an effect that is similar to parallel editing in its ability to tell two or more stories at the same cinematic time, whether or not they are actually happening at the same time or even in the same place. Among its most familiar uses is to portray both participants in a telephone conversation simultaneously on the screen. Unlike parallel editing, however, which cuts back and forth between shots for contrast, the split screen can tell multiple stories within the same frame.

The split screen was used by other early filmmakers (e.g., D. W. Griffith and Erich von Stroheim), but never on the scale or with the technical ingenuity displayed by Buster Keaton in *The Play House* (1921), for which he invented a process (later, the industry standard) that split the screen into nine slivers of space. Buster plays all the parts, including actors, stagehands, and audience; he does drag and a dazzling imitation of a monkey. At one point, he portrays nine characters on the screen at once.

In *Napoléon* (1927; editor: Gance), Abel Gance introduced Polyvision, a multiscreen technique, as in the epic pillow fight between the young Napoléon (Vladimir Roudenko) and other boys in their school dormitory. The fight begins on a single screen; continues on a screen split into four equal parts, then on one split into nine equal parts; reaches its climax on a single screen with multiple, superimposed full-size images; and ends, as it began, on a single screen.

The split screen has figured prominently in other films, including Norman Jewison's *The Thomas Crowne Affair* (1968; editors: Hal Ashby, Byron Brandt, Ralph E. Winters), in which the editors cut between many small screens, which expand to fill the entire screen and then return to their smaller place within the composition; Gus Van Sant's *To Die For* (1995; editor: Curtis Clayton), in which there are 1, then 4, and then 64 screens near the end of the movie; Mike Figgis's *Timecode* (2000; editor: uncredited), in which the screen is divided into quarters that simultaneously show four different 90-minute shots (see the image on page 153); and Hans Canosa's *Conversations with Other Women* (2005; editor: Canosa), a movie shot so that the footage could be edited into a work consisting entirely of split screens. In *The Rules of Attraction* (2002; editor: Sharon Rutter), a dark satire about college life, sex, and love, director Roger Avary uses various editing techniques, including the split screen, to emphasize people who want to be together, or think they do, but never make it.

The split screen as would-be matchmaker *The Rules of Attraction* is about several pairs of people who want, or think they want, to be together but haven't learned the so-called "rules of attraction." Sean Bateman (James Van Der Beek) receives love notes from an anonymous admirer whom he believes to be Lauren Hynde (Shannyn Sossamon), simply because he's in love with her. And Lauren is attracted to Sean, but backs off when she discovers him in bed with her roommate. In fact, the letters were written by a desperate young woman who kills herself after a series of encounters in which Sean pays no attention to her. Both Sean and Lauren plan to attend a special Saturday tutorial, and in a long, lyrical sequence of shots, edited into a split screen, we follow him (on the left) and her (on the right) as they walk from their dorms across the campus and into the classroom building. Here, in one image from the sequence, Sean walks toward us, as does Lauren, who's just learned that the professor has canceled the session. Still in split screens, the two meet at the corner where the two hallways join, these long shots becoming two close-ups that fill each screen. After they talk briefly, recognizing each other's names and finding a few things they have in common, a special editing effect literally pulls the two together in medium shot in a single frame. This suggests that editing can be a match-maker—that they might become a couple after all—but that never happens.

Looking at Editing

When you watch a movie, you *see* the mise-en-scène, design, and acting, you *hear* the dialogue, music, and sound effects, but you *feel* the editing, which has the power to affect you directly or indirectly. Good editing—editing that produces the filmmakers' desired effects—results from the editor's intuition in choosing the right length of each shot, the right rhythm for each scene, the right moment for cutting to create the right spatial, temporal, visual, and rhythmic relationships between shots.

You can most effectively analyze an editor's contributions to a film by examining individual scenes and trying to understand how their parts—the shots that make up those scenes—fit together. One useful tool for helping you to see the parts clearly and to analyze their relationship to the whole is to create a shot-analysis chart similar to the one shown in Table 8.1 (pages 378–380). By carefully noting details about each shot in a sequence—including its length, the type of shot it is (long, medium, close-up, etc.), and details about the action included in the shot—you can "map" a scene to get a better sense of its shape and rhythm.

In the example we've provided in Table 8.1, which lays out the shots in the famous scene from D. W. Griffith's *The Birth of a Nation* (1915; editors: Griffith, Joseph Henabery, James Smith, Rose Smith, and Raoul Walsh) that re-creates the assassination of Abraham Lincoln, we can see that the scene consists of thirty-nine shots running just under 3½ minutes. Perhaps the first thing we notice about this sequence of shots is that they are all fairly short. The average length of a shot in this scene is approximately 5 seconds, and no shot lasts longer than 14 seconds. The effect of all of these short shots is a heightening of dramatic tension, an effect that is especially important when the action in the scene is already known to the audience (obviously, everyone watching the film knows that Abraham Lincoln will be shot in the head by the end of the scene). Looking at the descriptions of each shot, we can also see that Griffith rarely carries the action over from shot to shot, but instead presents a cumulative series of details from different viewpoints. According to British film editor and director Karel Reisz, who has written extensively on editing, this style of editing has two advantages:

> Firstly, it enables the director to create a sense of depth in his narrative: the various details add up to a fuller, more persuasively life-like picture of a situation than can a single shot, played against a constant background. Secondly, the director is in a far stronger position to guide the spectator's reactions, because he is able to choose what particular detail the spectator is to see at any particular moment. . . .

Shots from the assassination scene in *The Birth of a Nation* (*opposite*) [1] is from shot 21, [2] is from shot 22, [3] is from shot 32, [4] is from shot 33, [5] is from shot 38, and [6] is from shot 39.

Griffith's fundamental discovery, then, lies in his realisation that a film sequence must be made up of incomplete shots whose order and selection are governed by dramatic necessity.[9]

As an innovator of film form, Griffith cared not only about what happened within shots but also about what happened between shots. Through cinematography, Griffith constructed credible visual representations of the sights surrounding the assassination of Lincoln at Ford's Theatre and re-created the actions of the assassination as faithfully as was possible at the time. But the realistic tableaux and choreography that Griffith constructed within the shots come alive only because of his editing of these shots, which makes us feel the fateful pace of the impending tragedy.

Now, let's look closely at a contemporary film to see how editing has evolved (or not) since Griffith's time.

Fernando Meirelles and Kátia Lund's *City of God*

City of God (2002), codirected by Fernando Meirelles and Kátia Lund and edited by Daniel Rezende, also relies on editing to tell its story. But the filmmakers take a very different approach from Griffith's. The movie opens with a section entitled "Chasing the Chicken." The film's title and credits appear over this sequence, beginning with "A Film by Fernando Meirelles" and then running for 3 minutes, 7 seconds until the movie's second section begins. The movie, set in a violent, drug-ridden quarter of Rio de Janeiro, is narrated from the point of view of Rocket (Alexandre Rodrigues). In this opening sequence, we are introduced to Rocket

[9]Karel Reisz and Gavin Millar, *The Technique of Film Editing*, 2nd ed. (London: Focal Press, 1968), pp. 22, 24.

TABLE 8.1 The Assassination Sequence from *The Birth of a Nation*

INTERTITLE: *"And then, when the terrible days were over and a healing time of peace was at hand . . . came the fated night of 14th April, 1865."*

Two short scenes follow: Benjamin Cameron (Henry B. Walthall) fetches Elsie Stoneman (Lillian Gish) from the Stonemans house and they leave together. Next seen in a theater, they are attending a special gala performance at which President Lincoln is to be present. The performance has already begun.

INTERTITLE: *Time: 8:30*
The arrival of the President, Mrs. Lincoln, and party.

Shot	Description	Length (sec.)	Type of Shot*
1	Lincoln's party as, one by one, they reach the top of the stairs inside the theater and turn off toward the president's box. Lincoln's bodyguard comes up first, Lincoln last.	7	MS
2	The president's box, viewed from inside the theater. Members of Lincoln's party appear inside.	4	MS
3	President Lincoln, outside his box, giving up his hat to an attendant.	5	MS
4	The president's box [as in shot 2]. Lincoln appears in the box.	4	MS
5	Elsie Stoneman and Ben Cameron sitting in the auditorium. They look up toward Lincoln's box, then start clapping and rise from their seats.	7	MS
6	View from the back of the auditorium toward the stage. The president's box is to the right. The audience, backs to the camera, are standing in foreground, clapping and cheering the president.	3	LS
7	The president's box [as in shot 4]. Lincoln and Mrs. Lincoln bow to the audience.	3	MS
8	As in shot 6.	3	LS
9	The president's box [as in shot 7]. Lincoln enters the box and sits down.	5	MS
INTERTITLE: *Mr. Lincoln's personal bodyguard takes his post outside the Presidential box.*			
10	After coming into the passage outside the box and sitting down, the bodyguard starts rubbing his knees impatiently.	10	MS
11	View from the back of the auditorium toward the stage. The play is in progress, but the audience stands and greets the president.	5	LS
12	The president's box [as in shot 9]. Lincoln takes his wife's hand and acknowledges the audience's greeting.	9	MS
13	Standing, the audience waves white handkerchiefs at the president.	4	MLS

*CU = close-up; LS = long shot; MLS = medium long shot; MS = medium shot

14	Closer view of the stage. The play continues.	10	MLS
	INTERTITLE: *To get a view of the play, the bodyguard leaves his post.*		
15	Bodyguard [as in shot 10]. He is clearly impatient.	4	MS
16	Close view of the stage [as in shot 14].	2	MLS
17	The bodyguard [as in shot 15]. He gets up and puts his chair away behind a side door.	6	MS
18	As in shot 6, the theater viewed from the back of the auditorium. Camera is shooting toward the box of Lincoln's party [next to Lincoln's box] as the bodyguard enters and takes his place. [This shot is framed exactly as shot 6, but a closing-iris effect is added to isolate our gaze toward the bodyguard arriving at the box.]	3	LS
19	Within a circular mask, we see a closer view of the action of shot 18. The bodyguard takes his place in the box. The closing iris of the previous shot is repeated in this closer shot, consolidating continuity.	5	MS
	INTERTITLE: *Time: 10:13 Act III, Scene 2*		
20	A general view of the theater from the back of the auditorium; a diagonal mask leaves only Lincoln's box visible.	5	LS
21	Elsie and Ben. Elsie points to something in Lincoln's direction.	6	MS
	INTERTITLE: *John Wilkes Booth*		
22	The head and shoulders of John Wilkes Booth seen in an iris shot.	3	MS
23	As in shot 21, Elsie looks in Lincoln's direction.	6	MS
24	As in shot 22, Booth.	2.5	MS
25	View showing both Lincoln's box and the one next to it, with Booth waiting by the door.	5	MLS
26	As in shot 24, Booth.	4	MS
27	As in shot 14, close view of the stage.	4	MLS
28	Close view of Lincoln's box. Lincoln smiles approvingly at the play. He makes a gesture with his shoulders as if he were cold and starts to pull a shawl over his shoulders.	8	MS
29	As in shot 22, Booth moves his head up in the act of rising from his seat.	4	MS
30	Shot 28 continued. Lincoln finishes pulling on his shawl.	6	MS
31	As in shot 20, the theater viewed from the back of the auditorium. The mask spreads to reveal the whole theater.	4	LS

Shot	Description	Length (sec.)	Type of Shot*
32	As in shot 19, within a circular mask, the bodyguard, enjoying the play, with Booth leaving that box, right behind the bodyguard.	1.5	MS
33	Booth comes through the door at the end of the passage outside Lincoln's box. He stoops to look through the keyhole into Lincoln's box. He pulls out a revolver and braces himself for the deed.	14	MS
34	Booth cocks the revolver.	3	CU
35	Shot 33 continued. Booth comes up to the door, has momentary difficulty in opening it, then steps into Lincoln's box.	8	MS
36	As in shot 28, close view of Lincoln's box. Booth appears behind Lincoln.	5	MS
37	As in shot 14, the stage. The actors are performing.	4	MLS
38	As in shot 36; Booth shoots Lincoln in the back. Lincoln collapses. Booth climbs onto the side of the box and jumps over onto the stage.	5	MS
39	Booth on the stage. He throws up his arms and shouts.	3	LS

INTERTITLE: *"Sic Semper Tyrannis!"* ("thus always to tyrants"—motto of the State of Virginia)

Note: John Wilkes Booth, who assassinated President Lincoln on Good Friday, April 14, 1865, was an actor who won wide acclaim for his Shakespearean roles. He was also an ardent Confederate sympathizer who hated the president. After he shot Lincoln and jumped to the stage, fracturing his leg in the process, he shouted, *"Sic Semper Tyrannis!"*—adding, as Griffith does not, "The South is avenged."

Source: Chart prepared by Emanuel Leonard and Gustavo Mercado, revised from material in Karel Reisz and Gavin Millar, *The Technique of Film Editing*, 2nd ed. (London: Focal Press, 1968), pp. 20–22.

and Li'l Zé (Leandro Firmino da Hora), a drug lord who has murdered Rocket's brother and for whom violence is an everyday thing. The tension between the two young men—exacerbated by Rocket's desire to free himself from the drugs, gangs, and violence and pursue a career as a photographer—establishes one of the existential challenges faced by all the young people in this movie.

This brief section exemplifies several of the movie's major themes: the violence and lawlessness of the city, the struggle to escape it, and the hopelessness that plagues most of the people who live there. That so much should be established in a sequence that runs underneath the credits is both a familiar cinematic convention and a reminder to watch every movie carefully from the moment it begins.

"Chasing the Chicken" is comprised of two parts. For the purposes of discussion, we'll call the first "The Preparation" (1 minute, 9 seconds), because it focuses on the various activities of preparing a chicken stew, including slaughtering several chickens. We'll call the second part "The Chase" (2 minutes, 8 seconds), because one of the chickens escapes its apparent fate and provokes a wild chase through the neighborhood. The imagery of the chickens is an allegory for the film's attitude toward human captivity and hope for escape. Rocket believes that murder is the fate of anyone who tries to escape this living hell in this city. Yet *this* chicken—whom the camera and the editing quickly make into a "character" with whom we empathize—actually escapes! Let's look more closely at these two parts of the opening sequence to see how the editing, in particular, helps to tell the story.

Part 1, "The Preparation," is a montage composed of hundreds of repeated shots—primarily

[1]

[2]

[3]

***City of God*: editing in Part 1, "The Preparation"** In [1], a man sharpens a knife (notice the dismembered chicken claw in the background); in [2], a man beheads a chicken with a knife; and in [3], we meet the chicken that is the "star" of this sequence. (Here, you should remember the principle of the Kuleshov experiment: two or more juxtaposed shots need not have any actual relationship to one another for meaning to occur when they are juxtaposed.) We're watching the action, but in another sense we're also watching the chicken as she watches the same action. We assume that she sees the knife being sharpened and one of her fellow birds being killed, and as a result of the editing of these two shots, understands her possible fate. The chicken's state of mind (her instinct for survival) is conveyed in [3], in which she stretches her neck and head and rapidly moves her eyes. She appears to be nervous and very aware of her possible fate. In subsequent shots, she loosens the string that holds her captive and calmly walks away. We feel comfortable identifying the chicken's state of mind in this way because that is suggested by the editing. It seems to be the conclusion the editor wants us to reach.

close-ups from handheld cameras—including a man sharpening a knife; chickens waiting to be slaughtered and put into the pot; men playing musical instruments; people dancing, cleaning vegetables, making drinks, and lighting gas flames under the pot. If this were all that was going on here in terms of content, you might think you were watching documentary footage of these activities. But an analysis of the editing shows that there is much more here than that. Instead of cataloging all the shots here (as we did with the sequence in *The Birth of a Nation*), we will look for patterns in the editing that make meanings. For example, repetitive shots of a man sharpening a knife (taken from different camera angles) form a pattern that raises our expectations about the future use of that

knife—whether it will be in cooking or violence against others.

Suddenly, Li'l Zé, who we are seeing for the first time, appears on the screen saying, "Fuck, the chicken's got away! Go after that chicken, man!" We don't have time to wonder why he would care so much about one escapee, but we soon realize that it's the chase—precisely, winning the chase—that matters, not the chicken.

In Part 2, "The Chase," a group of boys and girls (teenage and younger) begins the chase. When we see that many of them are carrying guns, we have our first clue that there may be violence. In fact, they are members of Li'l Zé's gang. The chase begins in the yard from which the chicken escaped and ends in a confrontation with the police in

4

5

CINEMATOGRAFIA **CÉSAR CHARLONE**, A. B. C.

6

***City of God*: editing in Part 2, "The Chase"** This part of the scene begins with a shot of the chicken running through the streets [4], probably taken with a Steadicam from a ground-level point of view; the cut is to a low-angle shot of the armed gang running after the bird [5]: the editor then cuts to another shot of the chicken, ahead of its pursuers [6]. Not just in these three shots, but throughout this part of the sequence, the continuity cutting, going back and forth between shots of the chicken and of its pursuers, maintains screen direction from shot to shot. Although pace of the editing here remains rapid, to convey the urgency of the pursuit, it is not as rapid as the cutting of "The Preparation." However, this is not traditional continuity cutting, because—like the chase sequences in the movies that make up the *Bourne* cycle (2002-7)—it's highly fragmented and contains many otherwise jarring spatial leaps that do not stress a smooth flow from one shot to the next. Yet we accept it as one continuous, coherent action.

another part of the neighborhood. In between, there is a great deal of the gang's frenzied running after the bird. The cinematography includes overhead shots that show the area in which the chase is taking place, moving shots from a handheld camera as the gang (and the camera operators) run through the streets, and ground-level shots from the chicken's point of view. Since the chicken is running through a maze of lanes and alleyways, the director uses middle and long shots (some of them high angle) to give us a wider perspective on the chase and to verify the forward movement of its direction. The bird is running for its life, and the camera work and editing make sure we don't forget that. The continuity editing makes all this action coherent.

The editor now cuts away from the chase (an editing convention as old as the movies themselves) to introduce Rocket and begin a sequence of parallel action, cutting between Rocket and Li'l Zé. Unaware of the chase, Rocket and a friend are strolling through the area. Rocket says that he'll risk his life to get a good photograph; although we wonder what he means, we later learn that he is interested equally in the drug dealers, the armed children, and the corrupt police. He hopes that by getting photographs of any of them, he could get a good job at a newspaper. This is a comparatively calm moment in which the camera remains stationary in a long take. The editor now cuts back to Li'l Zé and the chase. His gang has only one thing on its mind—to obey the order to get the chicken—and as they rampage through the streets, they use their guns to threaten anyone in their path. Li'l Zé pulls his gun on a street vendor but does not shoot. Sud-

[7]

[8]

[9]

***City of God*: final confrontation** The shot that introduces Rocket (left) and a friend [7] is of relatively long duration and slower rhythm than the immediately preceding entrance of the gang leader. The friend says to Rocket, "If Li'l Zé catches you, he'll kill you," to which Rocket responds, "Yeah, well, he's gotta find me first." In the next shot [8], Li'l Zé (*second from right*) enters the frame in slow motion, brandishing his gun and a big smile. After several more shots (not shown here) that establish the space, he spots Rocket [9] and orders him to capture the chicken.

denly, the scene turns surreal as every kid seems armed. Meanwhile, the chicken has outwitted them, sometimes flying short distances that put a gap between it and the pursuers. A police van passes over the chicken, and again the chicken escapes death. All of these shots—and the way they are edited—keep us focused on the gang plunging down the streets after the chicken and the chicken's miraculous survival. The action reaches its climax as Li'l Zé and his gang meet up with Rocket. The shot of Li'l Zé's entrance into the frame is shot in slow motion, and the subsequent short shots build in an escalating rhythm. He struts like he's already won, calls Rocket a "melonhead" and a "fag," and orders him to "get that chicken."

In contrast to the shots of Rocket, which are relatively stable and of longer duration, the shots of Li'l Zé are heavily fragmented; made with a hand-held camera, they emphasize his instability. The parallel action also allows us to experience each element in a new, heightened way. When we are with Rocket, our experience of his actions is colored by our fear that this calm, likeable guy must be about to encounter the seemingly bloodthirsty Li'l Zé. Likewise, our time with Li'l Zé isn't just about catching the chicken, but also waiting for the inevitable collision with Rocket.

Rocket, realizing that he has no choice in the matter, gently tries to capture the bird as the gang, brandishing its guns and itching for violence, looks on. Anyone who has ever tried to catch a bird understands Rocket's predicament, and the editing builds suspense around the tense moment. Meanwhile, the cops arrive on the scene, jumping from their cars with machine guns. A standoff occurs: the cops at the background of the frame, Rocket in the middle ground, and the gang in the foreground. Everyone but Rocket has a gun; his weapon, a camera, is hanging around his neck. He recognizes the dangerous spot he's in, and his thoughts appear in a subtitle: ". . . in the City of God, if you run away, they get you, and if you stay, they get you too. It's been that way ever since I was a kid." As the camera circles Rocket, suggesting that he's trapped, the editor allows him to "escape" by using a match-on-action cut to a shot of a much younger Rocket moving in a circle. This ends the movie's first sequence.

To understand the editing of any movie, we need to answer these three questions:

1. What action occurs in the scene under analysis?
2. How has the scene been photographed?
3. What editing pattern holds the shots together?

If we know the answers to these questions, we can reach conclusions about the editing. As for the first question, we have described the basic action of this sequence and how it establishes several of the movie's major themes. Second, we have briefly summarized its cinematographic plan, which includes the use of a moving handheld camera and furtive camera angles, and reflects the bold, you-are-there graphic style of the documentary cinema. Third, the key elements of the editing pattern that hold all this footage together are fast and slow motion, freeze-frames, **swish pans**, and a montage influenced by the editing principles of the Soviet silent cinema. (Elsewhere in the movie, the editor uses the split screen, fast fade-ins/fade-outs, and superimpositions.)

Finally, what conclusions do we reach about the editing? First, we see that the editor's goal was to create a highly formal structure, one in which the cinematic conventions used are suited to the depiction of a violent youth/drug culture. These conventions add up to a coherent formal whole, with none being more (or less) important than the others. Second, the editor grabs and holds our attention on the violence. Third, the filmmakers, who are not out to make us squirm with disgust at the squalor and violence or feel guilty about the injustice of this Brazilian city—ironically called the "City of God"—make us not only see but *feel* the life depicted on the screen.

Analyzing Editing

When we watch a movie, we see the mise-en-scène, design, and acting; we hear the dialogue, music, and sound effects; but we feel the editing, which has the power to affect us directly or indirectly. Good editing—editing that produces the filmmakers' desired effects—results from the editor's intuition in choosing the right length of each shot, the right rhythm of each scene, the right moment for cutting to create the right spatial, temporal, visual, and rhythmic relationships between shots A and B. In answer to the question "What is a good cut?" Walter Murch says,

> At the top of the list is Emotion . . . the hardest thing to define and deal with. *How do you want the audience to feel?* If they are feeling what you want them to feel all the way through the film, you've done about as much as you can ever do. What they finally remember is not the editing, not the camerawork, not the performances, not even the story—it's how they felt.[11]

As a viewer, you can best understand the overall effects of an editor's decisions by studying a film as a creative whole. But you can most effectively analyze an editor's contributions to a film by examining individual scenes, paying attention to the ways in which individual shots have been edited together. Indeed, the principles of editing are generally most evident within the parts that make up the whole.

[11]*Walter Murch, In the Blink of an Eye: A Perspective on Film Editing* (Los Angeles: Silman-James Press, 1995), p. 18.

Questions For Review

1. What is editing? Why is it regarded as a language?

2. What is the basic building block of film editing? What is film editing's fundamental tool?

3. What are the film editor's principal creative and technical responsibilities?

4. What is continuity editing? What does it contribute to a movie?

5. What is the purpose of the 180-degree system? How does it work?

6. What is discontinuity editing? Given the dominance of continuity editing in mainstream filmmaking, what role does discontinuity editing usually play?

7. Name and describe the various types of match cuts.

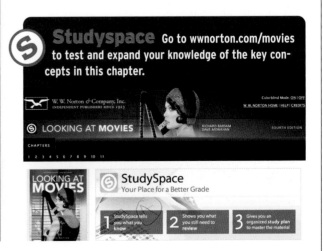

DVD The tutorials for this chapter demonstrate the techniques and importance of editing, discuss the major historical innovations in early cinematic editing, and illustrate two key concepts: the so-called "Kuleshov effect" and the 180-degree system.

LOOKING AT **MOVIES**

CHAPTER 8: EDITING

THE EVOLUTION OF EDITING:
   CONTINUITY AND
   CLASSICAL CUTTING
THE EVOLUTION OF EDITING:
   MONTAGE
THE KULESHOV EXPERIMENT
THE 180 DEGREE RULE
EDITING TECHNIQUES
   IN *SNAPSHOT*

▶ MAIN MENU

Studyspace Go to wwnorton.com/movies to test and expand your knowledge of the key concepts in this chapter.

8. How does the match cut differ from and compare to parallel editing?

9. What is a jump cut? What is the typical effect of a jump cut on a viewer?

10. Given the magnitude of the editor's overall responsibility during the postproduction stage of filmmaking, why is it considered desirable, if not essential, that the editor also collaborate during the preproduction phase?

Movies Described or Illustrated in This Chapter

Adaptation (2002). Spike Jonze, director.

Apocalypse Now (1979). Francis Ford Coppola, director.

Battleship Potemkin (1925). Sergei Eisenstein, director.

The Birth of a Nation (1915). D. W. Griffith, director.

Breathless (1960). Jean-Luc Godard, director.

The Cabinet of Dr. Caligari (1920). Robert Wiene, director.

A Canterbury Tale (1944). Michael Powell and Emeric Pressburger, directors.

Casablanca (1942). Michael Curtiz, director.

City of God (2002). Fernando Meirelles and Kátia Lund, directors.

Conversations with Other Women (2005). Hans Canosa, director.

Cries and Whispers (1972). Ingmar Bergman, director.

Don't Look Now (1973). Nicolas Roeg, director.

Drugstore Cowboy (1989). Gus Van Sant, director.

Erin Brockovich (2000). Steven Soderbergh, director.

The Five Obstructions (2003). Jørgen Leth and Lars von Trier, directors.

The 400 Blows (1959). François Truffaut, director.

The General (1998). John Boorman, director.

Goodfellas (1990). Martin Scorsese, director.

Heaven (2002). Tom Tykwer, director.

The Insider (1999). Michael Mann, director.

Lawrence of Arabia (1962). David Lean, director.

Memento (2000). Christopher Nolan, director.

My Darling Clementine (1946). John Ford, director.

Napoléon (1927). Abel Gance, director.

The Night of the Hunter (1955). Charles Laughton, director.

Now, Voyager (1942). Irving Rapper, director.

Once upon a Time in the West (1968; director's-cut DVD version released 2003). Sergio Leone, director.

Out of Sight (1998). Steven Soderbergh, director.

The Play House (1921). Buster Keaton, director.

Psycho (1960). Alfred Hitchcock, director.

Rear Window (1954). Alfred Hitchcock, director.

Requiem for a Dream (2000). Darren Aronofsky, director.

The Rules of Attraction (2002). Roger Avary, director.

Run Lola Run (1998). Tom Tykwer, director.

Rushmore (1998). Wes Anderson, director.

The Searchers (1956). John Ford, director.

Shine a Light (2008). Martin Scorsese, director.

Stagecoach (1941). John Ford, director.

Taxi Driver (1976). Martin Scorsese, director.

Team America: World Police (2004). Trey Parker, director.

They Shoot Horses, Don't They? (1969). Sydney Pollack, director.

The Thin Red Line (1998). Terence Malick, director.

The Thomas Crown Affair (1968). Norman Jewison, director.

Timecode (2000). Mike Figgis, director.

The Tin Drum (1979). Volker Schlöndorff, director.

To Die For (1995). Gus Van Sant, director.

2001: A Space Odyssey (1968). Stanley Kubrick, director.

Y tu mamá también (2001). Alfonso Cuarón, director.

The Hurt Locker (2008). Kathryn Bigelow, director; Paul Ottosson, sound designer.

CHAPTER NINE

Sound

What Is Sound?

The movies engage two senses: vision and hearing. Although some viewers and even filmmakers assume that the cinematographic image is paramount, what we hear from the screen can be at least as significant as what we see on it, and sometimes what we hear is more significant. Director Steven Spielberg says, "The eye sees better when the sound is great." Sound—talking, laughing, singing, music, and the aural effects of objects and settings—can be as expressive as any of the other narrative and stylistic elements of cinematic form. What we hear in a movie is often technologically more complicated to produce than what we see. In fact, because of the constant advances in digital technology, sound may be the most intensively creative part of contemporary moviemaking. Spielberg, for one, has also said that, since the 1970s, breakthroughs in sound have been the movie industry's most important technical and creative innovations. He means

not the sort of gimmicky sound that takes your attention away from the story being told—"using the technology to show off"—but rather sound used as an integral storytelling element.[1]

As the success of action movies and 3-D animated features grows each year, sound and music are playing a larger role in telling their stories. For one thing, these movies are often visual spectacles that require an equally spectacular sound track. For another, they usually feature nonrealistic heroes, whose characterization requires every sound element—narration, dialogue, sound effects, and music—to make them come alive. Sound has played a very important role in helping to define Harry Potter, Spider-Man, Shrek—in the series of films devoted to them—or Woody and Buzz Lightyear and their friends in the *Toy Story* movies. Likewise, where would such characters as James Bond, Benjamin Button, Superman, Indiana Jones, or Jamal Malik be without sound to establish their worlds and adventures? Without a powerful sound design that is an integral part of the movie's artistic vision, both the story and the characters would be less fascinating.

Christopher Nolan's *Inception* (2010) is a case in point. As seems appropriate for a science-fiction action movie about the creative powers of the human mind—how our thoughts and dreams create imaginary worlds—the story is complex and intellectually challenging. And the sound design, which shifts seamlessly between imagination and reality, and our perceptions of them, is equally caught up in its own intricacies. Richard King is responsible for the memorable sound editing of *Inception* and many other distinguished movies, including *War of the Worlds* (2005; discussed later in this chapter). His style produces sound that is multilayered and deeply textured, incorporating a bold and aggressive mix of sounds and music that complement the vivid visual and special effects. Virtually all of the sounds were produced in the studio, including the incredible sounds of the weapons, vehicles, explosions, and scenes of destruction.

---

[1]Rick Lyman, "A Director's Journey into a Darkness of the Heart," *New York Times* (June 24, 2001), sec. 2, p. 24.

Sound as meaning *Inception* is about an illegal espionage project that enters the subconscious minds of its targets to gain valuable information. Dominic Cobb (Leonardo DiCaprio, *right*), the leader of the team, has hired Ariadne (Ellen Page, *left*), a gifted young architecture student, to design labyrinthine dreamscapes for this work, but she (like the viewer) is still in the learning stage. In this image, they sit in a Parisian café that is part of a larger street scene exploding all around them. Ariadne (like the viewer) is astonished to see that they sit unhurt while the perceivable world is destroyed around them, but then Ariadne awakens in the design studio to realize that she has been dreaming this episode. The action is crafted with such visual and aural detail that everything we see—flower pots, people, wine glasses, tables, chairs, automobiles—explodes in its own unique way and with its own unique sound. Every sight and sound image has been created and implanted in Ariadne's dream to show her (and the viewer) the power of the "dreams within dreams" project in which she is now a key player. Richard King, the sound designer and editor, and his sound mixers (Lora Hirschberg, Gary A. Rizzo, and Ed Novick) won Oscars for the movie's richly textured sound design.

Stanley Kubrick's *The Shining* (1980; sound: Dino Di Campo, Jack T. Knight, and Winston Ryder) opens with a series of helicopter point-of-view shots that, without the accompanying sound, might be mistaken for a TV commercial. In these shots, we see a magnificent landscape, a river, and then a yellow Volkswagen driving upward into the mountains on a winding highway. Whereas we might expect to hear a purring car engine, car wheels rolling over asphalt, or the passengers' conversation, instead we hear music: an electronic synthesis by composers Wendy Carlos and Rachel Elkind of the Dies Irae, one of the most famous Gregorian chants, which became the fundamental music of the Roman Catholic Church. The Dies Irae (literally, "the day of wrath") is based on Zephaniah 1:14–16, a reflection on the Last Judgment, and is one section of the Requiem Mass, or Mass for the Dead. Experiencing the shots together with the sound track, we wonder about the location, the driver, and the destination.

What we hear gives life to what we see and offers some clues to its meaning. The symbolic import and emotional impact of this music transforms the footage into a movie pulsating with portentous energy and dramatic potential. Once we identify this music, we suspect that it is warning us that something ominous is going to happen before the movie ends. Thus forewarned, we are neither misled nor dissatisfied.

The sound in the scenes just described (or in any movie scene) operates on both physical and psychological levels. For most narrative films, sound provides cues that help us form expectations about meaning; in some cases, sound actually shapes our analyses and interpretations. Sound calls attention not only to itself but also to silence, to the various roles that each plays in our world and in the world of a film. The option of using silence is one crucial difference between silent and sound films; a sound film can emphasize silence, but a silent film has no option. As light and dark create the image, so sound and silence create the sound track. Each property—light, dark, sound, silence—appeals to our senses differently.

In terms of film history, the transition to sound, which began in 1927, brought major aesthetic and technological changes in the way movies were written, acted, directed, and screened to the public (see Chapters 10 and 11). After the first few sound movies, where sound was more of a novelty than a formal element in the telling of the story, a period of creative innovation helped integrate sound—vocal sounds, environmental sounds, music, and silence—into the movies. The results of this innovation can be seen and heard in some of the great movies of the 1930s, including King Vidor's *Hallelujah!* (1929; sound: Douglas Shearer), Rouben Mamoulian's *Applause* (1929; sound: Ernest Zatorsky), G. W. Pabst's *Westfront 1918* (1930; sound: W. L. Bagier Jr.), Fritz Lang's *M* (1931; sound: Adolf Jansen), and Ernst Lubitsch's *Trouble in Paradise* (1932; no sound credit). Comparing one or more of these movies to several silent classics will help you to understand how profoundly sound changed the movies.

Like every other component of film form, film sound is the product of very specific decisions by the filmmakers. The group responsible for the sound in movies—the **sound crew**—generates and controls the sound physically, manipulating its properties to produce the effects that the director desires. Let's look more closely at the various aspects of sound production controlled by the sound crew.

Sound Production

Sound production consists of four phases: design, recording, editing, and mixing. Although we might suppose that the majority of sounds in a movie are the result of recording during filming (such sounds are called *production sounds*), the reality is that most film sounds are constructed during the postproduction phase (and thus are called *postproduction sounds*). But before any sounds are recorded or constructed, the overall plan for a movie's sound must be made. That planning process is called *sound design*.

Design

Sound design, or creating the sound for a film, has in the past been the responsibility of a sound crew composed of the artists and technicians who record, edit, and mix its component parts into the **sound track**. In conventional filmmaking with film stock, the sound track is a narrow band to one side of the image on which the sound is recorded. In digital filmmaking, depending on the recording method being used, the sound track basically consists of a digital code being placed somewhere on the digital recording medium. (Sound recorded with the Dolby system, which reduces background noise and enhances fidelity, further requires a theater equipped with a Dolby playback system.)

As motion-picture sound has become increasingly innovative and complex, the result of comprehensive sound design, the role of the sound designer has become more well known. Given its name by film editor Walter Murch—the sound designer for such movies as Francis Ford Coppola's *The Conversation* (1974) and *Apocalypse Now* (1979), and Anthony Minghella's *The English Patient* (1996) and *Cold Mountain* (2003)—sound design combines the crafts of editing and mixing and, like them, involves matters both theoretical and practical.[2] Although many filmmakers continue to understand and manipulate sound in conventional ways, sound design has produced major advances in how movies are conceived, made, viewed, and interpreted. Prior to the 1970s, the vast majority of producers and directors thought about sound only after the picture was shot. They did not design films with sound in mind and frequently did not fully recognize that decisions about art direction, composition, lighting, cinematography, and acting would ultimately influence how sound tracks would be created and mixed. They considered sound satisfactory if it could distract from or cover up mistakes in shooting and create the illusion that the audience was hearing what it was seeing. They considered sound great if it was loud, either in ear-splitting sound effects or in a heavily orchestrated musical score.

[2]Randy Thom, "Designing a Movie for Sound" (1998), www.filmsound.org/articles/designing_for_soundelder.htm (accessed February 4, 2006).

By contrast, the contemporary concept of sound design rests on the following basic assumptions:

> Sound should be integral to all three phases of film production (preproduction, production, and postproduction), not an afterthought to be added in postproduction only.
> A film's sound is potentially as expressive as its images.
> Image and sound can create different worlds.
> Image and sound are co-expressible.

A sound designer treats the sound track of a film the way a painter treats a canvas. That is, for each shot, after all the necessary sounds are identified in terms of the story and plot, the designer starts by laying in all the background tones (different tones equal different colors) to create the support necessary for adding the specific sounds that help the scene to function. According to Tomlinson Holman (the creator of Lucasfilm's THX technology), "Sound design is the art of getting the right sound in the right place at the right time."[3] Today, many directors—Joel Coen and David Lynch, among others—are notable for their comprehensive knowledge and expressive use of sound.

Prior to the wide acceptance of sound design, the responsibilities for sound were divided among recording, rerecording, editing, mixing, and sound-effects crews; these crews sometimes overlapped but often did not. In attempting to integrate all aspects of sound in a movie, from planning to postproduction, the sound designer supervises all these responsibilities—a development that was initially resented by many traditional sound specialists, who felt their autonomy was being compromised. It is now conventional for sound designers (or supervising sound editors) to oversee the creation and control of the sounds (and silences) we hear in movies. They are, in a sense, advocates for sound.

During preproduction, sound designers encourage directors and other collaborators to understand that what characters hear is potentially as significant as what they see—especially in point-of-view shots, which focus characters' (and audiences') attention on specific sights or sounds. Sound designers encourage screenwriters to consider all kinds of sound; working with directors, they indicate in shooting scripts what voices, sounds, or music may be appropriate at particular points. They also urge their collaborators to plan the settings, lighting, cinematography plan, and acting (particularly the movement of actors within the settings) with an awareness of how their decisions might affect sound. During production, sound designers supervise the implementation of the sound design. During postproduction, after the production sound track has been cut along with the images, they aid the editing team. But although their results may far exceed the audience's expectations of clarity and fidelity, sound designers keep their eyes and ears on the story being told. They want audiences not only to regard sound tracks as seriously as they do visual images but also to interpret sounds as integral to understanding those images.

Recording

The process of recording sound for the movies is very similar to the process of hearing. Just as the human ear converts sounds into nerve impulses that the brain identifies, so the microphone converts sound waves into electrical signals that are then recorded and stored. The history of recording movie sound has evolved from optical and magnetic systems to the digital systems preferred in today's professional productions. The **digital format** offers greater flexibility in recording, editing, and mixing and thus is fast becoming the standard. Of the various types of film sound (which will be described later in the chapter), dialogue is the only type typically recorded during production. Everything else is added in the editing and mixing stages of postproduction.

The recording of production sound is the responsibility of the production sound mixer and a team of assistants, which includes, on the set, a sound recordist, a sound mixer, a microphone **boom** operator, and gaffers (in charge of the power supply, electrical connections, and cables). This team must

[3]Tomlinson Holman, *Sound for Film and Television* (Boston: Focal Press, 1997), p. 172.

place and/or move the microphones so that the sound corresponds to the space between actors and camera and the dialogue will be as free from background noise as possible. **Double-system recording** is the standard technique of recording film sound on a medium separate from the picture. At one time, sound was recorded directly on the film, but now the various media used to record sound include digital audiotape, compact discs, or computer hard drives. This system, which synchronizes sound and image, allows both for maximum quality control and for the manifold manipulation of sound during postproduction editing, mixing, and synchronization. Once the sound has been recorded and stored, the process of editing it begins.

Editing

The editor is responsible for the overall process of editing and for the sound crew, which consists of a supervising sound editor, sound editors (who usually concentrate on their specialties: dialogue, music, or sound effects), sound mixers, rerecording mixers, sound-effects personnel, and Foley artists. The editor also works closely with the musical composer or those responsible for the selection of music from other sources. In the editing room, the editor is in charge, but producers, the director, screenwriters, actors, and the sound designer may also take part in the process. In particular, the producer and director may make major decisions about editing.

The process of editing, of both pictures and sounds, usually lasts longer than the shooting itself. Sound editing takes up a great deal of that time, because a significant portion of the dialogue and all of the sound effects and music are created and/or added during postproduction. Included in this process is adding Foley sounds (discussed later in the chapter) for verisimilitude and emphasis and creating and layering ambience with traffic, crowd voices, and other background sounds.

Filmmakers first screen the **dailies** (or rushes), which are synchronized picture/sound work prints of a day's shooting; select the usable individual shots from among the multiple takes; sort out the

ADR in action For the American version of Hayao Miyazaki's animated movie *Spirited Away* (2001), it was necessary to rerecord the characters' voices using English-speaking actors and the ADR (automatic dialogue replacement) system. Here, Jason Marsden (the voice of Haku), standing in front of a microphone and holding his script, lip-synchs his lines to coordinate with the action on the monitor in the background.

outtakes (any footage that will not be used); log the usable footage in order to follow it easily through the rest of the process; and decide which dialogue needs recording or rerecording and which sound effects are necessary. **Rerecording** of sound first recorded on the set (sometimes called *looping* or *dubbing*) can be done manually (with the actors watching the footage, synchronizing their lips with it, and rereading the lines) or, more likely today, by computer through **automatic dialogue replacement (ADR)**—a faster, less expensive, and more technically sophisticated process.

If ambient or other noises have marred the quality of the dialogue recorded during photography, the actors are asked to come back, view the scene in question, and perform the dialogue again as closely as possible. When an acceptable rerecording take has been made, an ADR editor inserts it into the movie. Finally, the sound-editing team synchronizes the sound and visual tracks. There can be a certain amount of overlap between the sound editing and mixing stages, facilitated by the fact that the entire editing and mixing process is now done digitally.

Mixing

Mixing is the process of combining different sound tracks onto one composite sound track synchronous with the picture. Each type of sound occupies an individual sound track. *Mixing* is used in several different ways. Here the term refers to a single element (one track for vocals, one for sound effects, one for music, etc.) that can be combined in a multitrack sound design. However, the term is also familiarly used to describe a compilation of music included in a movie and typically released for consumers on a CD.

The number of sound tracks used in a movie depends on the kind and amount of sound needed to tell each part of the story; thus, filmmakers have an unlimited resource at their disposal. No matter how many tracks are used, they are usually combined and compressed during the final mixing. Working with their crew, sound mixers adjust the loudness and various aspects of sound quality; filter out unwanted sounds; and create, according to the needs of the screenplay, the right balance of dialogue, music, and sound effects. The result may be an "audio mise-en-scène" that allows the filmmaker and the viewer to distinguish between background and significant elements that are arranged in relation to one another.

This process resembles the typical recording process for popular music, in which drums, bass, guitars, vocals, and so on are recorded separately and then mixed and adjusted to achieve the desired acoustic quality and loudness. The ideal result of sound mixing is clear and clean—that is, whatever the desired effect is, the audience will hear it clearly and cleanly. Even if what the filmmakers want is distorted or cluttered sound, the audience will hear that distortion or clutter perfectly.

With this background on the four basic stages of sound production—the basics of what goes on during sound design, recording, editing, and mixing—we're ready now to look more closely at the actual characteristics that make up the sounds we hear in real life as well as in the movies.

Describing Film Sound

When talking or writing about a movie's sound, you should be able to describe a sound in terms of its perceptual characteristics (determined by its pitch, loudness, quality, and fidelity), its source (where it comes from), and its type (vocal or musical, for example). To that end, let's take a closer look at the perceptual characteristics of sound.

Pitch, Loudness, Quality

The perceptual and physical characteristics of sound are linked as illustrated in Table 9.1. The following

---

TABLE 9.1	Connections between the Perceptual and Physical Characteristics of Sound
Perceptual Characteristics (what we perceive in sound) →	**Physical Characteristics** ← (what constitutes the sound)
Pitch → (or level) Described as *high* or *low*.	← **Frequency** (or speed—that is, the number of sound waves produced per second)
Loudness → (or volume or intensity) Described as *loud* or *soft*.	← **Amplitude** (or degree of motion within the sound wave)
Quality → (or timbre, texture, or color) Described as *simple* or *complex*.	← **Harmonic content** (or texture resulting from a single sound wave or a mix of sound waves)

discussion explains in detail what the table shows in summary form.

The **pitch** (or level) of a sound can be high (like the screech of tires on pavement), low (like the rumble of a boulder barreling downhill), or somewhere between these extremes. Pitch is defined by the **frequency** (or speed) with which it is produced (the number of sound waves produced per second). Most sounds fall somewhere in the middle of the scale, but the extremes of high and low, as well as the distinctions between high pitch and low pitch, are often exploited by filmmakers to influence our experience and interpretation of a movie.

In Victor Fleming's *The Wizard of Oz* (1939; sound: Douglas Shearer), the voice of the "wizard" has two pitches—the high pitch of the harmless man behind the curtain and the deep, booming pitch of the magnificent "wizard"—each helping us to judge the trustworthiness of the character's statements. Similarly, in the "all work and no play" scene in Stanley Kubrick's *The Shining* (1980), the pitch of the accompanying music changes from low to high to underscore Wendy's (Shelley Duvall) state of mind as she discovers Jack's (Jack Nicholson) writing (the low pitch corresponds to her anxiety and apprehension; the high pitch signals that her anxiety has turned into sheer panic).

Sound propagates through the air in a wave that is acted upon by factors in the physical environment. Think of this as analogous to the wave that ripples outward when you throw a rock into a pond—a wave that is acted upon by the depth and width of the pond. The **loudness** (or volume or intensity) of a sound depends on its **amplitude**, the degree of motion of the air (or other medium) within the sound wave. The greater the amplitude of the sound wave, the harder it strikes the eardrum and thus the louder the sound. Again, although movies typically maintain a consistent level of moderate loudness throughout, filmmakers sometimes use the extremes (near silence or shocking loudness) to signal something important or to complement the overall mood and tone of a scene. In *The Shining*, during the scene in which Wendy and Jack argue and she strikes him with a baseball bat, Kubrick slowly increases the loudness of all the sounds to call attention to the growing tension.

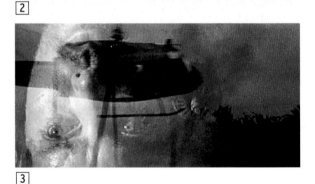

Exploiting the perceptual and physical characteristics of sound Francis Ford Coppola's *Apocalypse Now* (1979; sound designer: Walter Murch) opens with horrific images of war and continues with a scene of a very agitated Captain Benjamin L. Willard (Martin Sheen) in his Saigon hotel room. The first words in his voice-over narration—"Saigon. Shit!"—introduce the movie's counterintuitive logic. Between missions, Willard is distraught, not because he has not returned home to the United States, but because he is "still only in Saigon." The jungle is where he really wants to be. Intercut with shots of Willard, here seen upside down, are shots of his ceiling fan, the jungle, helicopters, napalm fires, and so on—all of which are represented in a ferocious and hugely ambitious sound track that combines sonic details, noise, dialogue, voice-over, and music. Together, pictures and sound prepare us for many of the movie's key themes, including the hellishness and surreality of the Vietnam War, the devastating power of military technology to destroy human beings and natural resources, and the complex roles within 1960s American society of countercultural forces such as rock music, drugs, and psychedelia.

The **quality** (also known as timbre, texture, or color) of a sound includes those characteristics that enable us to distinguish sounds that have the same pitch and loudness. In music, the same note played at the same volume on three different instruments (say, a piano, violin, and oboe) will produce tones that are identical in frequency and amplitude but very different in quality. The sound produced by each of these instruments has its own **harmonic content**, which can be measured as wavelengths. In talking about movie sounds, however, we do not need scientific apparatus to measure the harmonic content because most often we see what we hear.

In the opening sequence of Francis Ford Coppola's *Apocalypse Now* (1979; sound designer: Walter Murch), the sound comes from many sources—including helicopters, the fan in a hotel room, explosions, jungle noises, a smashed mirror, the Doors' recording of "The End," voice-over narration, and dialogue—each of which contributes its own qualities to an overall rich texture. Although many of these sounds are distorted or slowed down to characterize both the dreamlike, otherworldly quality of the setting and Captain Benjamin L. Willard's (Martin Sheen) state of mind, they have been recorded and played back with such accuracy that we can easily distinguish among them.

Nonfaithful sound In *Mean Streets* (1973; sound mixer: Don Johnson), Martin Scorsese uses nonfaithful sound when Charlie (Harvey Keitel), after making love to Teresa (Amy Robinson, *back to the camera*), playfully points his fingers at her as if they were a gun and pulls the "trigger." We hear a gunshot, but there is no danger, for this is just a lovers' quarrel.

Fidelity

Fidelity is a sound's faithfulness or unfaithfulness to its source. Ang Lee's *The Ice Storm* (1997; sound-effects designer: Eugene Gearty) faithfully exploits the sounds of a violent ice storm to underscore the tragic lives of two dysfunctional Connecticut families, the Hoods and the Carvers. At the climax of the movie, in the midst of the storm, Lee meticulously observes the phenomena and records the sounds of icy rain as it falls on the ground or strikes the windows of houses and cars, icy branches that crackle in the wind and crash to the ground, and the crunch of a commuter train's wheels on the icy rails. As the marriage of Ben and Elena Hood (Kevin Kline and Joan Allen), which is already on the rocks, completely falls apart, the ice storm has a powerful, even mystical, effect on the lives of these characters, and its harsh breaking sounds not only serve as a metaphor for their frail lives, but also provide an audibly faithful reminder of the power of nature.

An excellent early example of a sound effect that is not faithful to its source occurs in Rouben Mamoulian's *Love Me Tonight* (1932; sound: M. M. Paggi). During the farcical scene in which "Baron" Courtelin (Maurice Chevalier) tells Princess Jeanette (Jeanette MacDonald), whom he is wooing, that he is not royalty but just an ordinary tailor, pandemonium breaks out in the royal residence. As family and guests flutter about the palace singing of this deception, one of the princess's old aunts accidentally knocks a vase off a table. As it hits the floor and shatters, we hear the offscreen sound of a bomb exploding, as if to suggest that the aristocratic social order is under attack.

Sources of Film Sound

By *source*, we mean "the location from which a sound originates." Obviously, as mentioned already, most of the sounds heard in a movie literally originate from postproduction processes. But when we talk about source, we're speaking of the implied origin of that sound, whether it's a production sound or a postproduction sound. For example, the sound of footsteps that accompany a shot of a character

TABLE 9.2	Sources of Movie Sound	
	Diegetic Sound	Nondiegetic Sound
Spatial and temporal awareness		
Produces spatial awareness	X	
Produces temporal awareness	X	X
Source of sound		
Internal	X	
External	X	
On-screen	X	X
Offscreen	X	X
Simultaneous	X	
Nonsimultaneous	X	X

Diegetic sound in action In John Schlesinger's *Midnight Cowboy* (1969), right after stepping in front of an oncoming car (which screeches to a halt and honks its horn), "Ratso" Rizzo (Dustin Hoffman, *right*) interrupts his conversation with Joe Buck (Jon Voight, *left*) to shout one of the most famous movie lines of all time: "I'm walkin' here!" Even surrounded by everyday Manhattan pedestrian and traffic noise, Rizzo's nasal voice and heavy "Noo Yawk" accent help characterize him as the extremely eccentric and comic foil to Buck, a new and unseasoned arrival in the big city.

walking along a sidewalk may have been constructed by Foley artists in a sound studio after filming was completed, but the source of that sound is implied to be on-screen—created by the character while walking.

The descriptive terms that are used to describe the source of a movie sound are *diegetic* or *nondiegetic*, *on-screen* or *offscreen*, and *internal* or *external*. Table 9.2 summarizes how these terms relate to each other, and the discussion that follows provides the details.

Diegetic versus Nondiegetic

As you know from the "Story and Plot" section in Chapter 4, the word *diegesis* refers to the total world of a film's story, consisting perceptually of figures, motion, color, and sound. **Diegetic sound** originates from a source within a film's world; **nondiegetic sound** comes from a source outside that world. Most diegetic sound gives us an awareness of both the spatial and the temporal dimensions of the shot from which the sound emanates; most nondiegetic sound has no relevant spatial or temporal dimensions. For example, the electronic music that plays during the opening sequence of

Stanley Kubrick's *The Shining* (1980) is completely nondiegetic: we're not supposed to assume that the music is coming from the sky, or playing on the car radio, or coming from any location in the scene on-screen (see page 389).

Diegetic sound can be either internal or external, on-screen or offscreen, and recorded during production or constructed during postproduction. The most familiar kind of movie sound is diegetic, on-screen sound that occurs simultaneously with the image. All of the sounds that accompany everyday actions and speech depicted on-screen—footsteps on pavement, a knock on a door, the ring of a telephone, the report from a fired gun, ordinary dialogue—are diegetic.

Nondiegetic sound is offscreen and recorded during postproduction, and it is assumed to be inaudible to the characters on-screen. The most familiar forms of nondiegetic sound are musical scores and narration that is spoken by a voice that does not originate from the same place and time as the characters on the screen. When Redmond Barry (Ryan O'Neal) attracts the attention of the countess of Lyndon (Marisa Berenson) in Stanley Kubrick's *Barry Lyndon* (1975; sound: Robin Gregory and Rodney Holland) during a visually magnificent scene

[2]

[1]

Incongruous nondiegetic sound emphasizes an incongruous scene Inappropriate and out-of-place things are responsible for much of the comedy in Alfred Hitchcock's extremely lighthearted thriller *North by Northwest* (1959; sound: Franklin Milton). Mount Rushmore provides one of the movie's most incongruous—and therefore comic—settings as the expensively dressed and perfectly coiffed Eve Kendall (Eva Marie Saint) and Roger Thornhill (Cary Grant) attempt to escape their pursuer and defy death by climbing all over the national monument. Bernard Herrmann, who wrote scores for seven Hitchcock films and is considered the quintessential Hitchcock composer, uses lively Spanish dance music here. (The same music provides the "Overture" under Saul Bass's title sequence.) Perfectly irrational in this setting, the music seems to come from some other world entirely, signaling that the situation's improbability is part of the fun.

accompanied by the equally memorable music from the second movement of Franz Schubert's Trio no. 2 in E-flat Major (D. 929, op. 100) for violin, cello, and piano, the instrumentalists are nowhere to be seen; furthermore, we do not expect to see them. We accept, as a familiar convention, that this kind of music reflects the historical period being depicted but does not emanate from the world of the story.

Nondiegetic music is used comically in Alfred Hitchcock's *North by Northwest* (1959; sound: Franklin Milton; music: Bernard Herrmann) when we see Roger Thornhill (Cary Grant) and Eve Kendall (Eva Marie Saint) climbing across the presidential faces sculpted on Mount Rushmore and hear Bernard Herrmann's fandango score, music that is not only nondiegetic but also completely absurd given the danger facing these two characters.

The standard conventions of diegetic and nondiegetic sound may be modified for other effects. In Bobby and Peter Farrelly's *There's Something about Mary* (1998; supervising sound editor: Michael J. Benavente), for example, the "chorus" troubadour, Jonathan (Jonathan Richman), exists outside the story, which makes him and his songs nondiegetic even though we can see him. The Farrellys play with this concept by having Jonathan get shot accidentally in the climactic scene and thus become part of the story.

On-screen versus Offscreen

On-screen sound emanates from a source that we can see. **Offscreen sound**, which can be either diegetic or nondiegetic, derives from a source that we do not see. When offscreen sound is diegetic, it consists of sound effects, music, or vocals that emanate from the world of the story. When nondiegetic, it takes the form of a musical score or narration by someone who is not a character in the story. Note that on-screen and offscreen sound are also referred to, respectively, as simultaneous and nonsimultaneous sound. **Simultaneous sound** is diegetic and on-screen; **nonsimultaneous sound** occurs familiarly when a character has a mental flashback to an earlier voice that recalls a conversation or a sound that identifies a place. We recognize the sound too because its identity has previously been established in the movie.

Somewhere between on-screen and offscreen sound is **asynchronous sound**. We are aware of it when we sense a discrepancy between the things heard and the things seen on the screen. It is either a sound that is closely related to the action but not precisely synchronized with it or a sound that either anticipates or follows the action to which it belongs.

Because we cannot see its source, asynchronous sound seems mysterious and raises our curiosity and expectations. Thus it offers creative opportunities for building tension and surprise in a scene.

Asynchronous sound was used expressively in some of the first sound movies by such innovators as King Vidor, Rouben Mamoulian, and René Clair. For example, in his classic *Le Million* (1931), director René Clair uses asynchronous sound for humorous effect when we see characters scrambling to find a valuable lottery ticket and hear the sounds of a football game. Another classic example (with a variation) occurs in Alfred Hitchcock's *The 39 Steps* (1935; sound: A. Birch). A landlady enters a room, discovers a dead body, turns to face the camera, and opens her mouth as if to scream. At least, that's what we expect to hear. Instead, as she opens her mouth, we hear the high-pitched sound of a train whistle, and then Hitchcock cuts to a shot of a train speeding out of a tunnel. The sound seems to come from the landlady's mouth, but this is in fact an asynchronous sound bridge linking two simultaneous actions occurring in different places (see page 417).

Most movies provide a blend of offscreen and on-screen sounds that seems very natural and verisimilar, leading us to almost overlook the distinction between them. Some uses of sound, however, call attention to themselves; for example, when a scene favors offscreen sounds or excludes on-screen sounds altogether, we usually take notice. The total absence of diegetic, on-screen sound where we expect it most can be disturbing, as it is in the concluding, silent shots of a nuclear explosion in Sidney Lumet's *Fail-Safe* (1964; sound: Jack Fitzstephens); or comic, as it is at the conclusion of Stanley Kubrick's *Dr. Strangelove or: How I Learned to Stop Worrying and Love the Bomb* (1964; sound: John Cox), when the otherwise silent nuclear explosion is accompanied by nondiegetic music (Vera Lynn singing "We'll Meet Again").

In Robert Bresson's *A Man Escaped* (1956; sound: Pierre-André Bertrand), a member of the French Resistance named Lieutenant Fontaine (François Leterrier) is being held in a Nazi prison during World War II. Once he has entered the prison, he never sees outside the walls, although he remains very much aware, through offscreen sound, of the world outside. In fact, sounds of daily life—church bells, trains, trolleys—represent freedom to Fontaine.

Internal versus External

An **internal sound** occurs whenever we hear what we assume are the thoughts of a character within a scene. The character might be expressing random thoughts or a sustained monologue. In the theater, when Shakespeare wants us to hear a character's thoughts, he uses a soliloquy to convey them, but this device lacks verisimilitude. Laurence Olivier's many challenges in adapting *Hamlet* for the screen included making the title character's soliloquies acceptable to a movie audience that might not be familiar with theatrical conventions. Olivier wanted to show Hamlet as both a thinker whose psychology motivated his actions and a man who could not make up his mind. Thus in his *Hamlet* (1948; sound: Harry Miller, John W. Mitchell, and L. E. Overton), Olivier (as Hamlet) delivered the greatest of all Shakespearean soliloquies—"To be, or not to be"—in a combination of both spoken lines and **interior monologue**. This innovation influenced the use of internal sound in countless other movies, including subsequent cinematic adaptations of Shakespeare's plays.

External sound comes from a place within the world of the story, and we assume that it is heard by the characters in that world. The source of an external sound can be either on-screen or offscreen. In John Ford's *My Darling Clementine* (1946; sound: Eugene Grossman and Roger Heman Sr.), Indian Charlie (Charles Stevens, uncredited) is drunk and shooting up the town of Tombstone. The townspeople are afraid of Charlie, and the sheriff (actor uncredited) resigns rather than confront him, so Wyatt Earp (Henry Fonda)—who is both on- and offscreen during the scene—is appointed sheriff and takes it upon himself to stop the chaos that Charlie has created.

The scene effectively combines both on- and offscreen sounds. The characters (and the viewer) hear the offscreen sounds of Charlie shooting his gun inside the saloon followed by the offscreen sounds of women screaming; then the women appear on-screen as they run from the saloon with

Charlie right behind them, still shooting his gun. When Earp, on-screen, starts to enter the building through an upstairs window, we hear the offscreen screams of the prostitutes who are in the room as he says, "Sorry, ladies." Offscreen, Earp confronts Charlie and conks him on the head, for we hear the thud of Charlie falling to the saloon floor. This is followed by an on-screen shot of Earp dragging Charlie out of the saloon to the waiting crowd. This use of sound not only demonstrates Earp's courage and skill but also treats his serious encounter with Charlie with a comic touch.

Types of Film Sound

The types of sound that filmmakers can include in their sound tracks fall into four general categories: (1) vocal sounds (dialogue and narration), (2) environmental sounds (ambient sound, sound effects, and Foley sounds), (3) music, and (4) silence. As viewers, we are largely familiar with vocal, environmental, and musical sounds. Vocal sounds tend to dominate most films because they carry much of the narrative weight, environmental sounds usually provide information about a film's setting and action, and music often directs our emotional reactions. However, any of these types of sound may dominate or be subordinate to the visual image, depending on the relationship that the filmmaker desires between sound and visual image.

Vocal Sounds

Dialogue, recorded during production or rerecorded during postproduction, is the speech of characters who are either visible on-screen or speaking offscreen—say, from an unseen part of the room or from an adjacent room. Dialogue is a function of plot because it develops out of situations, conflict, and character development. Further, it depends on actors' voices, facial expressions, and gestures and is thus also a product of acting. Expressing the feelings and motivations of characters, dialogue is one of the principal means of telling a story. In most movies, dialogue represents what we consider ordinary speech, but dialogue can also be highly artificial.

Internal sound in *Hamlet*

To be, or not to be; that is the question:
Whether 'tis nobler in the mind to suffer
The slings and arrows of outrageous fortune,
Or to take arms against a sea of troubles,
And, by opposing, end them.[4]

Few lines cut deeper into a character's psyche or look more unflinchingly into the nature of human existence, and yet it's not hard to imagine how ineffective these well-known lines might be if simply recited at a camera. In his *Hamlet* (1948), actor-director Laurence Olivier fuses character and psyche, human nature and behavior, by both speaking his lines and rendering them, in voice-over, as the Danish prince's thoughts while simultaneously combining, in the background, music and the natural sounds of the sea. Olivier's version of *Hamlet* was the first to apply the full resources of the cinema to Shakespeare's text, and his innovativeness is especially apparent in the sound.

During the 1930s, screwball comedies invented a fast, witty, and often risqué style of dialogue that was frankly theatrical in calling attention to itself. Among the most exemplary of these films are Ernst Lubitsch's *Trouble in Paradise* (1932; screenwriters: Grover Jones and Samson Raphaelson), Howard Hawks's *Bringing Up Baby* (1938; screenwriters: Dudley Nichols and Hagar Wilde), and Preston Sturges's *The Lady Eve* (1941; screenwriters: Sturges and Monckton Hoffe), each of which

[4]William Shakespeare, *The Tragedy of Hamlet, Prince of Denmark*, act 3, scene 1.

must be seen in its lunatic entirety to be fully appreciated but nonetheless provides countless rich individual exchanges. Today the screwball-comedy genre has been transformed in such movies as Nora Ephron's *You've Got Mail* (1998) and Joel Coen's *Intolerable Cruelty* (2003). David Mamet, who writes and directs his own movies (e.g., *The Spanish Prisoner*, 1997; and *Heist*, 2001), is noted for dialogue that calls attention to itself with its sharp, terse, and often profane characteristics.

Movie speech can take forms other than dialogue. For example, French director Alain Resnais specializes in spoken language that reveals a character's stream of consciousness, mixing reality, memory, dream, and imagination. In Resnais's *Providence* (1977; screenplay: David Mercer; sound: René Magnol and Jacques Maumont), Clive Langham (John Gielgud), an elderly novelist, drinks heavily as he drifts in and out of sleep. Through the intertwining strands of his interior monologue, we learn of his projected novel—about four characters who inhabit a doomed city—and of his relationships with members of his family, on whom his fictional characters are evidently based. Langham's monologue and dialogues link the fantasy to the reality of what we see and hear; in this way, sound objectifies what is ordinarily neither seen nor heard in a movie.

Narration, the commentary spoken by either offscreen or on-screen voices, is frequently used in narrative films, where it may emanate from a third-person narrator (thus not one of the characters) or from a character in the movie. In the opening scene of Stanley Kubrick's *The Killing* (1956; sound: Rex Lipton and Earl Snyder), when Marvin Unger (Jay C. Flippen) enters the betting room of a racetrack, a third-person narrator describes him for us. This offscreen narrator knows details of Unger's personal life and cues us to the suspense of the film's narrative.

In Terrence Malick's *Badlands* (1973; sound: Maury Harris), the character of Holly (Sissy Spacek) narrates the story in first-person voice-over, helping us understand her loneliness, her obsession with Kit (Martin Sheen), her participation in a series of brutal murders, and her inability to stop. This technique enhances our appreciation of her character because rather than simply reinforcing what we are seeing, Holly's understanding and interpretation of events differ significantly from ours. She thinks of her life with Kit as a romance novel rather than a pathetic crime spree.

In *The Magnificent Ambersons* (1942; sound: Bailey Fesler and James G. Stewart), Orson Welles uses both offscreen and on-screen narrators. Welles himself is the offscreen, omniscient third-person narrator who sets a mood of romantic nostalgia for the American past while an on-screen "chorus" of townspeople—a device that derives from Greek drama—gossip about what is happening, directly offering their own interpretations. Thus, the townspeople are both characters and narrators.

Multiple voice-over narrators are also used effectively in two movies where such narration underscores the solitude and stress of characters living in small towns: Paolo and Vittorio Taviani's *Padre Padrone* (1977; sound: Petrantonio Federico, Giovanni Sardo, and Adriano Taloni), a documentary-like account of the lives of sheepherders in the Sardinian countryside, and Atom Egoyan's *The Sweet Hereafter* (1997; sound design: Steve Munro). Egoyan's eloquent, disturbing movie concerns the fatal crash of

On-screen narration Billy Wilder's *Double Indemnity* (1944; sound: Stanley Cooley and Walter Oberst) uses on-screen narration in a unique way. Walter Neff (Fred MacMurray), a corrupt insurance investigator, is pictured here recording his confession of murder on an office Dictaphone. His story leads to flashbacks that fill us in on events leading to that confession.

a school bus and its aftereffects on the townspeople who have lost children. Two principal characters voice the narration—the bus driver Dolores Discolt (Gabrielle Rose) and Nicole Burnell (Sarah Polley), a teenager who survived the crash. In scenes where these two are giving sworn testimony, Egoyan brilliantly employs the contrasts between the women in age, experience, and honesty. Since we have seen the crash in flashback, we know that Dolores gives an accurate account of the last moments before the crash; however, Nicole, who has promised to tell the truth but is determined to cover up her incestuous relationship with her father, deliberately lies as she accuses the bus driver of speeding and causing the crash. Nicole's narration is made all the more haunting because she reads (both on-screen to two children and offscreen to underscore the narrative) from the Robert Browning translation of *The Pied Piper of Hamelin* (1888), the legendary German folktale about a piper, masquerading as a rat catcher, who lures a town's children to their death in a river. Although there are parallels between this story and the movie narrative, Nicole's voice-over at the movie's conclusion shows that she has mixed fiction and fact, truth and lies. Angry about what life has handed her—an abusive father and an accident that has crippled her for life—she reads the fictional account of a "strange and new . . . sweet hereafter" and lies not only to conceal the secret and save her father from the consequences but also to prevent him from gaining damages from a lawsuit. The sound of her innocent, pure voice reading the grim folktale masks a tragedy as powerful as the bus crash itself.

Environmental Sounds

Ambient sound, which emanates from the ambience (or background) of the setting or environment being filmed, is either recorded during production or added during postproduction. Although it may incorporate other types of film sound—dialogue, narration, sound effects, Foley sounds, and music—ambient sound should not include any unintentionally recorded noise made during production, such as the sounds of cameras, static from sound-recording equipment, car horns, sirens, footsteps, or voices from outside the production. Filmmakers regard these sounds as an inevitable nuisance and generally remove them electronically during postproduction. Ambient sound helps set the mood and atmosphere of scenes, and it may also contribute to the meaning of a scene.

Consider the ambient sound of the wind in John Ford's *The Grapes of Wrath* (1940; sound: Roger Heman, Sr. and George Leverett). Tom Joad (Henry Fonda), who has just been released from prison, returns to his family's Oklahoma house to find it empty, dark, and deserted. The low sound of the wind underscores Tom's loneliness and isolation and reminds us that the wind of dust-bowl storms reduced the fertile plains to unproductive waste and drove the Joads and other farmers off their land. In Satyajit Ray's "Apu" trilogy—*Pather Panchali* (1955), *The Unvanquished* (1956), and *The World of Apu* (1959)—recurrent sounds of trains establish actual places, times, and moods, but they poetically express characters' anticipations and memories as well. These wind and train sounds, respectively, are true to the physical ambience of Ford's and Ray's stories, but filmmakers also use symbolic sounds as a kind of shorthand to create illusions of reality. In countless Westerns, for example, tinkling pianos introduce us to frontier towns; in urban films, honking automobile horns suggest the busyness (and business) of cities.

Sound effects include all sounds artificially created for the sound track that have a definite function in telling the story. All sound effects, except those made on electronic equipment to deliberately create electronic sounds, come from "wild" recordings of real things, and it is the responsibility of the sound designer and the sound crew to pick and combine these sounds to create the hyperreality of the film's sound track. (*Wild recording* is any recording of sound not made during synchronous shooting of the picture.) In Ray's *Pather Panchali* (sound: Bhupen Ghosh), two children, Apu (Subir Bannerjee) and Durga (Uma Das Gupta), find their family's eighty-year-old aunt, Indir Thakrun (Chunibala Devi), squatting near a sacred pond and think she is sleeping. As Durga shakes her, the old woman falls over, her head hitting the ground with a hollow sound—a diegetic, on-screen sound effect—that evokes death.

Sound effects in *Raging Bull* The boxing film against which all others are measured, Martin Scorsese's *Raging Bull* (1980; sound: Frank Warner)—based on former middleweight champion Jake La Motta's memoir of the same title—fully employs every aspect of filmmaking technology as it re-creates the experience of being in the ring. Close-ups don't get much more vivid than this one, in which La Motta's (Robert De Niro) glove slams into and breaks fighter Tony Janiro's (Kevin Mahon) nose; blood spurts and sweat flies. The image moves from powerful to unbearable, however, when accompanied by the Foley sounds of impact, collapse, and explosion.

A special category of sound effects—**Foley sounds**—was invented in the 1930s by Jack Foley, a sound technician at Universal Studios. There are two significant differences between Foleys and the sound effects just described. The first is that traditional sound effects are created and recorded "wild" and then edited into the film, whereas Foleys are created and recorded in sync with the picture. To do this, the technicians known as Foley artists have a studio equipped with recording equipment and a screen on which to view the movie as they create sounds in sync with it. The second difference is that traditional sound effects can be taken directly from a library of prerecorded effects (e.g., church bells, traffic noises, jungle sounds) or created specifically for the movie. By contrast, Foley sounds are unique. As an example of the latter, the sound technicians working on Peter Jackson's *The Lord of the Rings: The Fellowship of the Ring* (2001; sound designer: David Farmer) needed the sounds of arrows shooting through the air, so they set up stationary microphones in a quiet graveyard and shot arrows past the mikes to record those sounds.

Foley artists use a variety of props and other equipment to simulate everyday sounds—such as footsteps in the mud, jingling car keys, the rustling of clothing, or cutlery hitting a plate—that must exactly match the movement on the screen. Such sounds not only fill in the soundscape of the movie and enhance verisimilitude but also convey important narrative and character information. Although these sounds match the action we see on the screen, they can also exaggerate reality—both loud and soft sounds—and thus may call attention to their own artificiality. Generally, however, we do not consciously notice them, so when they are truly effective, we cannot distinguish Foley sounds from real sounds.

Music and dancing in *Slumdog Millionaire* Although this social and romantic drama, which presents a harrowing view of growing up in modern India, is a far cry from the generic Hollywood musical, it ends happily as the hero, Jamal, wins the grand prize in a TV game show and is reunited with his childhood sweetheart, Latika, who has escaped her criminal captor. To celebrate, the movie concludes with a musical extravaganza of the entire cast—led by Latika (Freida Pinto, in yellow, *left*) and Jamal Malik (Dev Patel, in blue shirt, *right*)—dancing and singing "Jai Ho" on the platforms of the Bombay train station. This scene, made memorable by its vibrant sounds, provides a very creative background for the closing credits.

In Martin Scorsese's *Raging Bull* (1980; sound: Frank Warner), brutal tape-recorded sounds from boxing matches are mixed with sounds created in the Foley studio, with many different tracks—including a fist hitting a side of beef, a knife cutting into the beef, water (to simulate the sound of blood spurting), animal noises, and the whooshes of jet airplanes and arrows—all working together to provide the dramatic illusion of what, in a real boxing match, would be the comparatively simpler sound of one boxer's gloves hitting another boxer's flesh.

Today's movies are particularly rich in their uses of sound. That includes musicals: Bill Condon's *Dreamgirls* (2006); fantasy adventure films: Peter Jackson's *King Kong* (2005) or Michael Bay's *Transformers: Revenge of the Fallen* (2009); war films: Kathryn Bigelow's *The Hurt Locker* (2008); dramas: Danny Boyle and Loveleen Tandan's *Slumdog Millionaire* (2008) or Tom Hooper's *The King's Speech* (2010); or animated features: Andrew Stanton's *WALL-E* (2008). The artistry involved in using all the various sources and types of sound has perma-nently established the role of the sound designer and exponentially increased the number of sound-related job titles—and therefore new employment—in the field of movie sound, all of which is reflected in the large number of sound artists and techni-cians receiving screen credit. Furthermore, it has made necessary the invention and development of new equipment for sound recording, editing, and mixing and has also brought change to many the-aters, which have had to install expensive new equip-ment to process the superb sound made possible by the digital revolution.

Music

Although music is used in many distinct ways in the movies, in this discussion we are concerned principally with the kind of music that Royal S. Brown, an expert on the subject, describes as "dra-matically motivated . . . music composed more often than not by practitioners specializing in the art to interact specifically with the diverse facets of the filmic medium, particularly the narrative."[5] Such music can be classical or popular in style, written specifically for the film or taken from music previously composed for another purpose, written by composers known for other kinds of music (e.g., Leonard Bernstein, Aaron Copland, Philip Glass, and Igor Stravinsky) or by those who specialize in movie scores (e.g., Elmer Bernstein, Carter Burwell, Georges Delerue, Bernard Herrmann, Ennio Morricone, David Raksin, Miklós Rózsa, Tôru Takemitsu, and John Williams, among many others), or music played by characters in the film or by offscreen musicians, diegetic or nondiegetic. The first film score was written by French composer Camille Saint-Saëns for the 1908 movie *The Assassination of the Duke de Guise* (codirectors: André Calmettes and Charles Le Bargy).

Some of Hollywood's most prolific contemporary composers were formerly rock musicians: Oingo Boingo's Danny Elfman has scored many Tim Burton movies, including *Corpse Bride* (2005); Devo's Mark Mothersbaugh, another prolific composer, scored Catherine Hardwicke's *Lords of Dogtown* (2005) and Wes Anderson's *The Life Aquatic with Steve Zissou* (2004). Songwriter and singer Randy Newman, equally prolific, scored Gary Ross's *Seabiscuit* (2003) and Jay Roach's *Meet the Fockers* (2004). Jonny Greenwood, the lead guitarist of the English alternative rock group Radiohead, is also the composer of the unearthly, beautiful score for Paul Thomas Anderson's *There Will Be Blood* (2007).

Like other types of sound, music can be intrinsic, helping to tell the story, whether it pertains to plot, action, character, or mood; indeed, music plays an indispensable role in many movies. Perhaps the most familiar form of movie music is the large symphonic score used to set a mood or manipulate our emotions.[6] Few old-Hollywood films were without a big score by masters of the genre such as Max Steiner (who scored Victor Fleming's *Gone with the Wind*, 1939). Although recent movies

have relied mainly on less ambitious scores, they are still used when large stories call for them, including Ridley Scott's *Gladiator* (2000; composers: Hans Zimmer and Lisa Gerrard); Peter Jackson's *The Lord of the Rings* trilogy (2001–3; composer: Howard Shore); Ang Lee's *Brokeback Mountain* (2005) and Alejandro González Iñárritu's *Babel* (2006) (both scored by composer Gustavo Santaolalla); Joe Wright's *Atonement* (2007) and Cary Fukunaga's *Jane Eyre* (2011) (both scored by composer Dario Marianelli); James Cameron's *Avatar* (2009; composer: James Horner); Terence Malick's *The Tree of Life* (2011; composer: Alexandre Desplat); and the *Harry Potter* movies (2001-11; various directors; composers include John Williams [films 1-3], Patrick Doyle [4], Nicholas Hooper [5-6], and Alexandre Desplat [7-8]).

Movie music can be equally effective when it creates or supports ideas in a film, as in Orson Welles's *The Tragedy of Othello: The Moor of Venice* (1952; music: Alberto Barberis and Angelo Francesco Lavagnino; 1999 sound-restoration supervisor: John Fogelson; 1999 music-restoration supervisor: Michael Pendowski). Welles takes a deterministic view of Othello's fate, but he depicts the two central characters, Othello (Welles) and Desdemona (Suzanne Cloutier), as being larger than life, even as they are each destined for an early death.

Accompanying their funeral processions is a musical score that leaves no question that these tragic circumstances are the result of fate. In fact, in their cumulative power the sights and sounds express the inexorable rhythm of all great tragedies. The complex musical score covers several periods and styles, but to most ears it resembles medieval liturgical music. Deep, hard, dirgelike piano chords combine with the chanting of monks and others in the processions, spelling out (even drawing us into) the title character's inevitable deterioration and self-destruction.

For John Curran's *We Don't Live Here Anymore* (2004), a dark melodrama about marital infidelities, composer Michael Convertino has written a score that builds with the suspense and establishes the mood of anxiety that hangs over everyone involved. By contrast, Don Davis's score for Andy and Lana Wachowski's *The Matrix* (1999) uses the

---

[5]Royal S. Brown, *Overtones and Undertones: Reading Film Music* (Berkeley: University of California Press, 1994), p. 13.

[6]See Larry M. Timm, *The Soul of Cinema: An Appreciation of Film Music* (New York: Simon & Schuster, 1998), ch. 1.

Music and ideas In the funeral procession that opens Orson Welles's *The Tragedy of Othello: The Moor of Venice* (1952), the composers, Alberto Barberis and Angelo Francesco Lavagnino, use heavy piano chords, insistent drums, and a chorus to underscore the director's interpretation that fate was the cause of the deaths of Othello (Welles) and Desdemona (Suzanne Cloutier).

sounds of brass and percussion instruments and songs by the Propellerheads and Rage against the Machine to match the world of the story's synthetic technological environment. Davis also scored the music for the two sequels (*The Matrix Reloaded* and *The Matrix Revolutions*, both 2003).

Irony often results from the juxtaposition of music and image because the associations we bring when we hear a piece of music greatly affect our interpretation of a scene. Take, for example, composer Ennio Morricone's juxtaposition of "Ave Maria" with shots of Brazilian natives and missionary priests being slaughtered by Portuguese slave traders in Roland Joffé's *The Mission* (1986), Quentin Tarantino's use of Stealers Wheel's carefree, groovy "Stuck in the Middle with You" to choreograph the violent cop-torture scene in *Reservoir Dogs* (1992), or Pier Paolo Pasolini's *Accatone* (1961), where the director contrasts urban gang violence with themes from the *St. Matthew Passion* by Johann Sebastian Bach. Perhaps the boldest experiment in juxtaposing music and image occurs in Sergei Eisenstein's *Alexander Nevsky* (1938), which depicts

the thirteenth-century conflict between Crusader knights and the Russian people. Here, using a complex graph, the director integrated Sergei Prokofiev's original musical score, note by note, with the visual composition, shot by shot. This mathematical and theoretically rigorous experiment results, at its best, in a sublime marriage of aural and visual imagery, which has been influential, particularly on such epic movies as Stanley Kubrick's *Spartacus* (1960) and Irvin Kershner's *The Empire Strikes Back* (1980).

Neil Jordan makes a more sustained use of such juxtaposition in *The Crying Game* (1992), a political and psychological thriller that is also a frank, revealing movie about loneliness, desire, and love. Its music helps underscore the surprises in its story. Fergus (Stephen Rea) is interested in Dil (Jaye Davidson), who appears to be an attractive black woman until Dil reveals that he is a transvestite. The personal and political plot twists are too complicated to discuss in this context, but Fergus falls in love with Dil and, because of his love, takes a prison rap for him. At the end of the movie, Dil is visiting Fergus in prison, and as the camera pulls back to the final fade-out and closing credits, we hear Tammy Wynette and Billy Sherrill's country-Western classic "Stand by Your Man," sung by Lyle Lovett. (This irony would be missed if the viewer did not stay for the credits, which today increasingly include music or other information vital to understanding the overall movie.) It's funny and touching at the same time, but especially ironic in light of the music under the opening credits: Percy Sledge singing the African American classic "When a Man Loves a Woman" (by Cameron Lewis and Andrew Wright), the perfectly ironic introduction—although we do not know it at the time—to this story of desperate love.

Among directors, Tom Tykwer is notable for his use of music to enhance the pace, or tempo, of *Run Lola Run* (1998; music: Reinhold Heil, Johnny Klimek, and Tykwer), in which the relentless rhythm of the techno-music matches the sped-up, almost surreal pace of the action. Significantly, this music does not change with developments in the action, so it takes on a life of its own. Indeed, any action movie with many exciting chase sequences,

[1]

[2]

[3]

[4]

[5]

[6]

Songs inspire a movie Miraculous things happen, and people and events connect in unexpected ways, throughout Paul Thomas Anderson's *Magnolia* (1999; sound designer: Richard King). Part of what inspired Anderson in writing his screenplay was hearing then-unreleased recordings by American pop-rocker Aimee Mann. In some cases, connections between the songs and the narrative are explicit, as when the lyrics to "Deathly"—"Now that I've met you / Would you object to / Never seeing each other again"—become a line of dialogue: "Now that I've met you, would you object to never seeing me again?" At the film's emotional climax, [1] Claudia Wilson Gator (Melora Walters), [2] Jim Kurring (John C. Reilly), [3] Jimmy Gator (Philip Baker Hall), [4] Quiz Kid Donnie Smith (William H. Macy), [5] "Big Earl" Partridge (Jason Robards, *left*) and his nurse, Phil Parma (Philip Seymour Hoffman, *right*), and [6] Stanley Spector (Jeremy Blackman)—all in different places and different situations—sing along with Mann's "Wise Up."

such as Paul Greengrass's *The Bourne Supremacy* (2004; composer: John Powell), could become routine if the music did not change significantly to suit the participants, location, and outcome of each chase. In *The Bourne Supremacy*'s spectacular chase through Moscow traffic, Jason Bourne (Matt Damon), whose own musical theme is played by a bassoon, successfully eludes the Russian police but not before many vehicles are destroyed. The sound in this scene is a very expressive mix of ambient sounds, Foley sounds, sound effects, and Powell's score. Indeed, it's impossible to disentangle these elements. The loud sounds of sirens, screeching tires, shattered glass, gunshots, and revving car engines accentuate the violent action, while the music, which is softer in volume, is a full orchestral score mixed with Russian folk themes and electronic sounds, including techno-music. The chase ends with a final smashup and silence.

Many directors use music to provide overall structural unity or coherence to a story, as in Otto Preminger's psychological thriller *Laura* (1944;

Great music, bad boy One of the principal concerns of Stanley Kubrick's *A Clockwork Orange* (1971; sound editor: Brian Blamey), the loss of moral choice through psychological conditioning, is developed by a focus on [1] Alex (Malcolm McDowell), a worthless, violent character, here staring at [2] a poster of the German classical/Romantic composer Ludwig van Beethoven. Alex's only good trait is his love for Beethoven's Ninth Symphony—especially the setting, in its finale, of Friedrich von Schiller's "Ode to Joy," music that represents all that is most noble in the human spirit. Here, however, this music is used ironically to underscore Alex's desire to preserve his freedom to do what he wants (which consists mostly of violent acts) even though society tries to socialize him away from these acts (using a fascistic treatment that attempts to turn him into a "clockwork orange"). In the somewhat muddled world of this controversial film, we're supposed to be glad that Alex is still sufficiently human to embrace Beethoven *and* resist brainwashing.

composer: David Raksin), about which Royal S. Brown writes:

> Almost every piece of music, diegetic and nondiegetic, heard in the film either is David Raksin's mysteriously chromatic fox-trot tune or else grows out of it, particularly in the nondiegetic backing. The detective (Dana Andrews) investigating Laura's "murder" turns on a phonograph: it plays "Laura." The journalist throws a party for Laura once she has "returned from the dead": the background music is "Laura." But the way in which the melody travels back and forth between the diegetic and the nondiegetic, making that distinction all but meaningless, likewise reinforces the overall obsessiveness.[7]

A movie such as Stephen Daldry's *The Hours* (2002), which tells a story spanning some eighty years in three different settings with three different women, presents a unique challenge to a musical composer to find some way to unify all these elements. The movie's narrative concerns the different ways these three women are affected by Virginia Woolf's 1925 novel *Mrs. Dalloway*, including the novelist herself (played by Nicole Kidman) in the 1920s; an American housewife, Laura Brown (Julianne Moore), in the 1940s; and a New York professional woman, Clarissa Vaughan (Meryl Streep), in the present. Therefore, one might expect a tripartite musical score with one distinct sound for each historical period and location, and perhaps even a distinct theme for each principal character. However, composer Philip Glass chooses a very different course.

A New Age classical composer with minimalist tendencies, Glass links the three stories with recurring musical motifs played by a chamber orchestra of a pianist and five string players. To create further unity among the lives of the three women, Glass emphasizes the bond that Woolf's novel has created among them by avoiding music from the periods in which they lived. The tensions in the score pull between the emotional and cerebral, underscoring the tensions that the characters experience in this psychological melodrama.

[7]Brown, p. 86.

Diegetic music Debra Granik's *Winter's Bone* (2010) is a horrific narrative film that shows how methamphetamine abuse destroys the lives of people in the rural Ozarks. Actor Jennifer Lawrence gives a brilliant performance as Ree Dolly, a teenager who takes charge and tries to keep her family together under the worst of circumstances. Her efforts are hampered by local traditions of patriarchy, secrecy, and resistance to authority, but in this image, when she listens to local bluegrass musicians, including Merideth Sisco singing "High on a Mountain," she momentarily forgets the strife. Here, a traditional folk song not only offers her and the others a moment of peace but also reveals a creative side of their culture.

Finally, film music may emanate from sources within the story—a television, a radio or stereo set, a person singing or playing a guitar, an orchestra playing at a dance. For example, Ridley Scott's *Black Hawk Down* (2001) depicts a complex and failed attempt by a group of U.S. Army Rangers to depose a Somalian warlord, a conflict between Americans and African Muslims. For this film, composer Hans Zimmer decided against writing the sort of score we hear in other classic war movies, such as Coppola's *Apocalypse Now* (1979; composers: Carmine and Francis Ford Coppola) or Oliver Stone's *Platoon* (1986; composer: Georges Delerue).

Instead of using familiar classical themes for theatrical effect, Zimmer relies heavily on diegetic music that emanates from soldiers' radios, street musicians, or mosques. Thus the score juxtaposes Western and African music, Irish tunes, and songs by Elvis Presley and popular groups such as Alice in Chains, Stone Temple Pilots, and Faith No More on the one hand, and traditional Muslim prayer music and chants, mournful piano and strings,

African pop music, and tribal drums on the other. At times, such as the beginning of the attack on the marketplace, Zimmer fuses elements of both. His "score" goes beyond music to include many sound effects that function as rhythmic elements (e.g., the constant hum of military and civilian vehicles, the beating of helicopter rotor blades, the voices of American soldiers and African crowds). In this expanded sense of a musical score, Zimmer and Jon Title, the sound designer, worked together to create an original, seamless entity in which there are few distinctions between music and other sounds. Of course, at times in *Black Hawk Down* music is just music and sound effects are just sound effects. But the major achievement here is the fusion of sounds.

With this score, Zimmer does not make conflict appear to be the work of godlike warriors (such as the helicopter gunships in *Apocalypse Now*) but rather conveys the hell of war, reinforces the bond among the soldiers, and helps us understand the agony they suffer on each other's behalf. Near the end, we hear his "Leave No Man Behind," a beautiful tapestry of piano and strings that includes familiar patriotic musical motifs, and his soft, martial arrangement of the heartbreaking Irish ballad "Minstrel Boy," sung by Joe Strummer and the Mescaleros. This score, derived from many sources—both diegetic and nondiegetic—is not background music but central to portraying the movie's almost unbearable tension.

Although a movie's characters and its viewers hear diegetic music, which can be as simple as sound drifting in through an open window, only viewers hear nondiegetic music, which usually consists of an original score composed for the movie, selections chosen from music libraries, or both. John Carney's *Once* (2006; score: Glen Hansard and Markéta Irglová) is a contemporary love story about a "Guy" (Glen Hansard) and a "Girl" (Markéta Irglová). Its song lyrics virtually replace the meager dialogue. The story is simple enough: boy meets girl, boy sings to girl, girl helps boy to perfect his songs, boy gets music contract and leaves girl to make his first recording. Its goofy charm is almost completely dependent upon this diegetic music.

Nondiegetic music is recorded at the very end of the editing process so that it can be matched accurately to the images. In recording an original score, the conductor and musicians work on a specially equipped recording stage, which enables them to screen the film and tailor every aspect of the music's tempo and quality to each scene that has music (similar to the way that Foley sounds are created). Further adjustments of the sounds of individual musicians, groups of musicians, or an entire orchestra are frequently made after these recording sessions and before the final release prints are made. Similar efforts are made to fit selections taken from music libraries with the images that they accompany.

The sound of silence In *Uncle Boonmee Who Can Recall His Past Lives* (director: Apichatpong Weerasethakul), there is silence everywhere in the Thai settings. In this tranquil image, Boonmee (Thanapa Saisaymar, *right*) and his sister-in-law Jen (Jenjir Pongpas, *left*) are sampling honey harvested at Boonmee's farm. With the exception of a few words, the only sound we hear is the soft hum of the bees and some distant ambient sound, perhaps a gentle wind or small river. This aesthetic pervades the entire movie, especially in the scenes where ghosts from Boonmee's family appear. Of course, we cannot call it a "silent film," but it powerfully demonstrates how to tell a story primarily with visual images.

Silence

As viewers, we are familiar with all the types of film sound that have been described in this chapter, but we may be unfamiliar with the idea that silence can be a sound. Paradoxically, silence has that function when the filmmaker deliberately suppresses the vocal, environmental, or musical sounds that we expect in a movie. When so used, silence frustrates our normal perceptions. It can make a scene seem profound or even prophetic. Furthermore, with careful interplay between sound and silence, a filmmaker can produce a new rhythm for the film—one that calls attention to the characters' perceptions. *The Silence before Bach* (2007; sound: Albert Manera), a film by the legendary Spanish Surrealist director Pere Portabella, does just that. It's a feast for the ears and eyes, providing an avant-garde filmmaker's look at how the music of Bach and the contemporary world might interact.

Classic directors such as Ingmar Bergman (e.g., *Wild Strawberries*, 1957) and Michelangelo Antonioni (e.g., *The Red Desert*, 1964) control their own sound designs, imaginatively using silence to evoke the psychological alienation of their characters. Akira Kurosawa's *Dreams* (1990; sound: Kenichi Benitani) consists of eight extremely formal episodes, each based on one of the director's dreams. The third episode, "The Blizzard," tells of four mountain climbers trapped in a fierce storm. We hear what they hear when they are conscious, but when they are exhausted and near death, they (and we) hear almost nothing.

As the episode begins, we hear the climbers' boots crunching the snow, their labored breathing, and the raging wind. They are exhausted, but the leader warns them that they will die if they go to sleep. Nonetheless, they all lie down in the snow. The previous loud sounds diminish until all we hear is the low sound of the wind. Then, out of this, we hear the sweet, clear, high sounds of a woman singing offscreen. The leader awakens to see a beautiful woman on-screen—the specter of Death—who says, "The snow is warm. . . . The ice is hot." As she covers the leader with shimmering fabrics, he drifts in and out of sleep, trying to fight her seductive powers—all in silence.

Ultimately, Death fails to convince the leader to give up. When it's clear that he has regained his consciousness and strength, he is able to hear the loud storm again. Death disappears, accompanied by wind and thunder. Perhaps her beauty has given the leader the courage to resist death and thus save the group. The other men awaken; they, of course, have not seen or heard any of this. We then hear muted trumpets, horns, and Alpine music—all nondiegetic sounds signifying the climbers' victory over the weather and death. Ironically, when they awaken in the bright sunshine, the climbers recognize that they have slept in the snow only a few yards away from the safety of their base camp. What is the meaning of this dream? Perhaps that life equals consciousness and, in this instance, awareness of sound.

While movies such as *Dreams*, Jean-Pierre Melville's *Le Cercle Rouge* (1970), or Patrice Chéreau's *Gabrielle* (2005) are important for calling our attention to the imaginative use of silence, no other contemporary movie has done this better than Joel and Ethan Coen's *No Country for Old Men* (2007; sound designer: Craig Berkey). Although Carter Burwell is credited for the score, there are only 16 minutes of music on the sound track of this tense, bloody thriller. Likewise, there is very little dialogue. In this absence, the sound effects are particularly striking and memorable: gunshots, the prairie winds, car doors slamming and engines roaring, the scrape of a chair or footsteps in a creepy hotel, and the beeping tracking device that facilitates the movie's violent ending. When long sections of a movie are as conspicuously silent as this one, audiences automatically are obliged, perhaps ironically, to listen more carefully. However, unlike the approach in many thrillers, where sound creates suspense and even helps the audience to anticipate what might happen, we don't have that to guide us here. Indeed, many of the movie's characters also have to strain to hear and identify sounds. With *No Country for Old Men*, Lance Hammer's *Ballast* (2008; sound designer: Kent Sparling)—another outstanding movie with little dialogue, music, or sound effects—suggests a reawakened interest in telling a story primarily with visual images.

In *Uncle Boonmee Who Can Recall His Past Lives* (2010; sound Richard Hocks), the acclaimed Thai director Apichatpong Weerasethakul has made a film about reincarnation that may also seek to transform cinema itself by emphasizing silence rather than sound. Significantly, it won the Palme d'Or for the best feature film at the 2010 Cannes Film Festival, and it is like nothing you have ever seen or heard on the screen. The story, based on the Buddhist belief in reincarnation, is about Boonmee, who is dying of a kidney disease and who believes that he can see ghosts from his past. His belief is powerful enough to call forth apparitions of his wife, with whom he has a discussion of the afterlife. It's all very matter-of-fact, with superimposed images of the dead appearing on the screen. Thus, we (and some other characters) see her too, just as she was in life. One ghost returns reincarnated as a monkey, another as a catfish. The director's radical vision involves a careful observation of ordinary life in scenes shot in long takes and real time and using a very austere sound design. He does not reject sound, for we hear the standard types of film sound, all of them diegetic, including vocal sounds (some dialogue, a short offscreen interior monologue, monks' prayers), music (from a TV melodrama, a stringed instrument), and environmental sounds of all kinds, including jungle noises, insects, water, and rainfall. Indeed, the combination of long takes in which there is little action and the soft, low tones of these sounds is hypnotic. Perhaps ironically, the overwhelming and calming silence of this place defines it. The silence of the perceivable world and the afterworld is Weerasethakul's most powerful sound.

Types of Sound in Steven Spielberg's *War of the Worlds*

Let's take a close look at how important sound is to one movie in particular: Steven Spielberg's *War of the Worlds* (2005; sound designer: Richard King; musical score: John Williams). To do this, we'll catalog the types of sounds we hear in the movie. Because the sound design of this movie is so complex, it would be impossible to identify every sound that we hear, but the following discussion will provide a sense of the numerous types of sound incorporated into the overall sound design.

The movie begins with shots of protoplasm as seen through a microscope, accompanied by the deep, soothing voice of the narrator (Morgan Freeman) speaking the opening lines of H. G. Wells's 1898 novel *The War of the Worlds*, on which the screenplay was loosely based:

> No one would have believed in the last years of the nineteenth century that this world was being watched keenly and closely by intelligences greater than man's and yet as mortal as his own; that as men busied themselves about their various concerns they were scrutinised and studied, perhaps almost as narrowly as a man with a microscope might scrutinise the transient creatures that swarm and multiply in a drop of water.

The ominous nature of this text, along with the grave voice of the narrator, lets us know that we're in for a thrilling story. Furthermore, these few lines establish the basis of the sound design. Those "intelligences greater than man's" inhabit the colossal tripods, which make thunderous noises. By contrast, humankind is a puny thing, prone to making incredulous assumptions about what is happening and then whimpering or crying about it. Big/little, loud/soft: that's the pattern underscoring this conflict.

As the action begins with Ray Ferrier (Tom Cruise) working at a New Jersey container port, we hear the ambient sounds of this industrial operation: traffic in and around the area; the television in Ray's apartment (bringing an ominous news report of violent lightning strikes in Ukraine); and dialogue between Ray, his ex-wife Mary Ann (Miranda Otto), and their children (Rachel, played by Dakota Fanning, and Robbie, played by Justin Chatwin), who are spending the weekend with their father. From this point on, however—when the movie rapidly enters the surreal world of the story—the majority of the sounds we hear are the work of sound engineers and technicians: the violent lightning storm that incites the action, sudden winds that make the laundry flap wildly on the line, shattering glass as a baseball breaks a window, the earthquake that splits the streets and enables the giant tripods to emerge, electrical flashes that emanate from the tripods, and the sounds of explosions, falling debris, shattered glass, and people being vaporized as the tripods wreak havoc. There are

Sounds introduce conflict At the beginning of Steven Spielberg's *War of the Worlds* (2005; sound designer: Richard King), we hear loud, high-pitched sounds (accompanying eerie atmospheric effects) and realize that something terrible is going to happen. Here, Ray Ferrier (Tom Cruise) and his daughter, Rachel (Dakota Fanning), brave the roaring winds to watch the darkening skies.

The tripods' warning For the first time, Ferrier sees and hears the foghornlike warning "voice" of the tripods. He and his neighbors, who do not yet understand what's happening, seem stunned by the tripods—as much by their massive size as by their ill-portending sounds.

also implied sounds, such as what Robbie is listening to on his iPod, which we cannot hear.

As the crisis in this New Jersey town worsens, we are overwhelmed by the sounds of fires, explosions, bridges and highways collapsing, and the screeching tires of the car as Ray drives frantically out of town. When Ray and his children reach the temporary safety of his ex-wife's new house, there are more light and lightning storms, heavy winds, and the sounds of a jet aircraft crashing on the front lawn. Many of these sounds were produced in the Foley lab.

Flight from terror Ferrier (at the wheel of a van that he has stolen) and his two children (who are hiding from danger on the floor of the car) flee their New Jersey town as it is destroyed by the tripods. Notable here are the sound effects of crumbling steel bridges, vaporizing concrete highways, and debris falling everywhere.

Panic The tripods cause a whirlpool that capsizes a ferry overcrowded with people trying to escape. Sounds here include the hornlike "voices" of the tripods, the screams of the crowd (those still on deck and those who have fallen or dived into the river), the buckling steel of the ferryboat, underwater sounds, and John Williams's musical score.

During a lull before the tripods appear again, we hear more ambient sounds: Rachel's shrill screams, a radio report on the status of the emergency broadcast system, a passing convoy of army tanks and trucks, and car horns in the heavy traffic as the Ferriers approach a ferry on the Hudson River. At the ferry landing we hear the deafening roar of a freight train as it passes in the night, the jangling of the warning bells at the train's crossing, a female ferry employee shouting instructions through a

megaphone, and the ferry's deep-sounding horns. The crowd there is furious at Ray for having a car in which to escape and begins to attack it; we hear loud crowd noises, individual voices, gunshots, and the sounds of the car's windows being smashed. In the midst of this pandemonium, Rachel looks up to the sky and hears geese honking as they fly by—a classic omen of the horror to come. There is very little music in this part of the film (the rising action of the plot), but we hear from a radio somewhere the sound of Tony Bennett singing "If I Ruled the World." Since viewers know that a new demonic force now rules the world, it's a particularly ironic use of music.

The Ferriers manage to get on the ferryboat, but their escape is thwarted when the boat is caught in a whirlpool and capsizes, throwing cars and passengers overboard. The sounds of this action are faithful and vivid. We also see and hear people thrashing underwater as they seek safety. By now, the tripods are on the scene, their huge tentacles (with their own peculiar noises) grabbing people out of the Hudson and gobbling them up into their nasty "mouths." Of course, the three members of the Ferrier family escape all of this.

On the riverbank, we see an Armageddon-like scene—what might be the final conflict between the tripods and humanity—and hear the sounds of the massive tripods crashing through the landscape, army tanks firing missiles at them, and helicopters and fighter jets above also firing missiles and dropping bombs. The scene is complete chaos, with ambient noises of the crowds rushing back and forth. In the midst of all this, Robbie Ferrier pleads with his father for independence and escapes into the fray.

As the crowds disperse, and a semblance of quiet and order return, Ray and Rachel are welcomed into the basement of a nearby farmhouse by Harlan Ogilvy (Tim Robbins). Soon the sounds of his sharpening a large blade provide another omen that the battle is not yet over and that this man may also become an evil force with which Ray will need to reckon. Actually, we suspect that Ogilvy is a murderer and that Ray and Rachel are in harm's way, but in fact he just wants to annihilate the tripods.

Armageddon As the tripods attack the fleeing crowds and devastate the landscape, military jets and missiles fail in their attempts to subdue them. We hear the sounds of the tripods and the chaos they create, aircraft, music, and various electronic sounds that add to the doomsday atmosphere.

Farmhouse refuge Rachel and her father take shelter in the house of Harlan Ogilvy (Tim Robbins, *far right*). Their initial meeting is a moment of comparative quiet that is rare for this movie; all we hear is Harlan's soft voice and the offscreen sounds of distant battles being fought outside.

The basement is full of sounds that further establish the imminent evil: scurrying rats; the soft, whirring sound of a tripod's tentacle as it searches the labyrinth of rooms; rippling water that is pooling there; and the sounds of the stealthy grasshopperlike creatures that have also emerged from inside the tripods. Meanwhile, as Rachel continues to scream, her father attempts to calm her by singing; she sings also. But Harlan has now decided to take on the tripods himself—an act that Ray knows will prove to be fatal for him and his daughter—so Ray kills Harlan (offscreen), apparently beating him to death with a shovel, as indicated by the accompanying heavy drumlike sound.

When Ray and his daughter emerge from the basement, they are confronted with a desolate landscape and an entire arsenal of eerie sounds associated with the tripods and other creatures. For an instant all is quiet (a rare moment in this very noisy movie), and then the tripods strike again with all the familiar sounds we have come to expect. Ray attempts to hide in a car, which is smashed by the tripods; Rachel and Ray scream as they are grabbed separately by the tentacles that are swirling everywhere like giant snakes.

It is already clear, though, that the Ferriers can withstand anything, and fulfilling that expectation, they once again escape, to Boston, where the tripods self-destruct in violent explosions and fire-

works. We hear the last sputtering bursts of flame, the gushing red fluid, and the last gasps of the creatures. At the conclusion, as leaves blow across a Boston street (reminding us of the winds in New Jersey at the beginning of this adventure), Rachel and Robbie reunite with their mother, who has been visiting her own mother for the weekend. We hear somber piano music and sad horns as the camera surveys the dead landscape.

As for the musical score, even though written by John Williams, the most famous composer of film music alive today, the fright that is at the heart of the story is realized more effectively with sound effects than with music. Contrary to our expectations (if we are, in fact, familiar with Williams's other work), Williams neither creates a musical theme for each of the major characters—although there is a recurring, low-key motif for the tripods—nor leaves us with one of his memorable "wall of sound" experiences. We are frightened when we see the unfamiliar tripods, and Williams underscores that fear with atonal music, but he also understands that what we see in this movie demands a level of sound effects that necessarily assigns music a secondary role.

It's interesting to compare Steven Spielberg's movie adaptation of *The War of the Worlds* with Orson Welles's classic radio adaptation. Spielberg spent some $135 million to make the movie and employed hundreds of artists and technicians in the

Rachel captured As her father screams, "No! No!" a tentacle of one of the tripods swoops down and captures Rachel. Other sounds include Rachel's screams and the ominous, insistent musical score that suggests the inevitability of this incident.

Home, devastated home At the conclusion of Spielberg's *War of the Worlds*, Ray, his daughter, Rachel, and his son, Robbie, are reunited with the children's mother. The soft, muted horns suggest a happy ending, but as Ray and his family tearfully celebrate their reunion, the camera reveals the full extent of the havoc that the alien invaders have wrought. Whatever future the Ferriers may have is uncertain.

fields of sound and special effects. Welles's budget (estimated at $2,000) paid for his eleven-person radio cast, small crew, and studio orchestra. We cannot easily compare a blockbuster movie released in 2005 with a radio show broadcast in 1938, not only because of the differences in the two media, but also because the radio audience then was less media-savvy than movie audiences of today are. But for anyone who has turned off the lights and

listened to Welles's production—the most famous of all radio broadcasts—it's clear how he was able to convince millions of people in the audience that aliens had actually landed and that humankind was in mortal danger. At some level, Spielberg instinctively understood this, because, like Welles, ultimately he created fright through sound.

Functions of Film Sound

Primarily, sound helps the filmmaker tell a movie's story by reproducing and intensifying the world that has been partially created by the film's visual elements. A good sound track can make the audience aware of the spatial and temporal dimensions of the screen, raise expectations, create rhythm, and develop characters. Either directly or indirectly, these functions provide the viewer with cues to interpretation and meaning. Sounds that work directly include dialogue, narration, and sound effects (often Foley sounds) that call attention (the characters' or ours) to on- or offscreen events.

In John Ford's *My Darling Clementine* (1946; sound: Eugene Grossman and Roger Heman, Sr.), "Doc" Holliday (Victor Mature) tosses his keys noisily on the hotel desk to underscore his desire to leave town if Clementine (Cathy Downs) won't keep her promise to leave before him. In Charles Laughton's *The Night of the Hunter* (1955; sound: Stanford Houghton), Harry Powell (Robert Mitchum) covets the large sum of money that he knows is hidden somewhere around the farm. His stepchildren, John (Billy Chapin) and Pearl (Sally Jane Bruce), have kept the money hidden inside Pearl's doll, but Pearl is too young to understand what's going on and has cut two of the bills into figures that she calls "Pearl" and "John." When Harry comes out of the house to tell the children that it's bedtime, they quickly restuff the crackling bills into the doll. Although we hear this sound, Harry doesn't; but a moment later, in a small but easily missed visual moment in the wide frame, we see and hear the two "Pearl" and "John" bills blowing across the path toward Harry. This ominous coincidence adds tension to the scene because we fear that Harry will surely hear it too, look down, and discover the children's secret. Happily, at least for the moment, he doesn't. The sound effects in both of these films were created by Foley artists.

Sounds that function indirectly help create mood and, thus, may help the audience interpret scenes subconsciously. Tomlinson Holman, a sound expert, points out that viewers differentiate visual elements in a movie far more easily and analytically than they do sound elements. The reason is that they tend to hear sound as a whole, not as individual elements. Filmmakers can take advantage of viewers' inability to separate sounds into constituent parts and use sound to manipulate emotions, often via the musical score. In *Bride of Frankenstein* (1935; composer: Franz Waxman), director James Whale uses low-pitched music to accentuate the terror of the scene in which a lynch mob pursues the Monster (Boris Karloff) through the woods. In Steven Spielberg's *Jaws* (1975), composer John Williams uses four low notes as the motif for the shark—the sound of fear being generated in an otherwise placid environment.

Whether direct or indirect, sound functions according to conventions, means of conveying information that are easy to perceive and understand.

Audience Awareness

Sound can define sections of the screen, guide our attention to or between them, and influence our interpretation. *Once upon a Time in the West* (1968; sound engineers: Fausto Ancillai, Claudio Maielli, and Elio Pacella), Sergio Leone's masterfully ironic reworking of the Western genre, begins with a scene at the Cattle Corner railroad stop somewhere in the Arizona desert. This scene is notable for an overall mise-en-scène that emphasizes the isolation of the location and the menacing behavior of three desperadoes waiting for a man called Harmonica (Charles Bronson) to arrive on the Flagstone train. Within that setting, the director and his sound engineers have created a memorable audio mise-en-scène for the opening scene, running approximately 14 minutes. This sequence utilizes various diegetic sounds that we perceive as emanating from very specific points on and off the screen.

[1]

[2]

Sound that defines cinematic space The tapestry of sounds that underscores the opening of Sergio Leone's *Once upon a Time in the West* (1968; sound engineers: Fausto Ancillai, Claudio Maielli, and Elio Pacella) is based on recurring sounds (squeaking windmill) [1], sounds heard only once (whimpering dog), sounds that advance the narrative (an approaching train), sounds that emphasize the tension of the situation in which three desperadoes wait for a train (buzzing fly, dripping water), and sounds that remind us of the outside world (the clackety-clack of the telegraph—until it is disabled by one of the desperadoes) [2].

It's worth studying this scene both for its montage of sounds and for the convincing way in which it pinpoints their sources. This sound tapestry is composed almost entirely of sound effects: a creaking door inside the crude station, the scratch of chalk as the station agent writes on a blackboard, a squeaking windmill, the clackety-clack of a telegraph machine, water slowly dripping from the ceiling, a man cracking his knuckles, various animals and insects (a softly whimpering dog, loudly buzzing fly, and chirping bird in a cage), the distant sound of a train approaching and the closer sounds of its chugging steam engine, the music from Harmonica's harmonica, and the sounds of the shootout in which Harmonica swiftly kills the three waiting desperadoes.

We see and hear clearly the source of each of these sounds. Because we are in the desert, there is no background sound per se (with the exception of the sound of the train approaching); at two brief moments we hear voices and, at the end, only a hint of Ennio Morricone's musical score. This sound design not only helps us distinguish the individual sounds, but also helps us understand how they are arranged in relation to one another. Furthermore, it creates a brooding suspense and raises fundamental questions about the narrative and characters: Who are these desperadoes? Who are they waiting for? Why do they seem to betray Harmonica the moment he arrives? Why does he kill them?

In addition to directing our attention to both the spatial and temporal dimensions of a scene, as in *Once upon a Time in the West*, sound creates emphasis by how it is selected, arranged, and (if necessary) enhanced. In Robert Altman's *The Player* (1992; sound: Michael Redbourn), sound helps us eavesdrop on the gossip at one table in a restaurant and then, even more deliberately, takes us past that table to another in the distance where the protagonist is heading and where the gossip will be confirmed. Because the scene takes place on the terrace of an exclusive restaurant in Beverly Hills—the guests all seem to be in the motion-picture business—the sound makes us feel as if we're among them, able to see the rich and famous come and go and, more relevant here, able to hear what they're saying, even if they think they aren't being overheard.

Audience Expectations

Sounds create expectations. For example, in a scene between a man and a woman in which you hear quiet music, the sounds of their movements, and a subtle sound of moving clothes, you might expect intimacy between the characters. However, in a similar scene in which the characters are not moving and you cannot hear their clothes—and instead you hear the harsh sound of traffic outside or a fan in the room—you might expect something other than intimacy. Sound also requires precise timing and coordination with the image. For example, when a simple scene of meeting in a doorway is accompanied by a musical chord, we know that the

incident is significant, whether or not we know how it will evolve. But in a scene where a small boy is taken away by a bad guy at a carnival, and we hear only the carnival music and loud crowd sounds, and then see the look of terror on the parents' faces when they realize their child is gone, dramatic music is probably not needed.

When a particular sound signals an action and that sound is used repeatedly, it plays on our expectations. In Ridley Scott's *Alien* (1979; sound: Jim Shields), sound (along with visual effects) plays an impressive role in helping to create and sustain the suspenseful narrative. This science-fiction/horror movie tells the story of the crew of a commercial spacecraft that takes on board an alien form of "organic life" that ultimately kills all but one of them, Lieutenant Ellen Ripley (Sigourney Weaver).

One device used to sustain this suspense is the juxtaposition of the familiar "meow" sounds made by Ripley's pet cat, Jonesy, against the unfamiliar sounds made by the alien. After the alien disappears into the labyrinthine ship, three crew members— Ripley, Parker (Yaphet Kotto), and Brett (Harry Dean Stanton)—attempt to locate it with a motion detector. This device leads them to a locked panel, which, when opened, reveals the cat, which hisses and runs away from them. Because losing the cat is Brett's fault, he is charged with finding it by himself. We hear his footsteps as he proceeds warily through the craft, calling "Here, kitty, kitty . . . Jonesy, Jonesy," and we are relieved when Brett finds the cat and calls it to him. Before the cat reaches Brett, however, it sees the alien behind him, stops, and hisses. Alerted, Brett turns around, but he is swiftly killed by the creature. This sound motif is repeated near the end of the film, when Ripley prepares to escape on the craft's emergency shuttle but is distracted by the cat's meow.

Expression of Point of View

By juxtaposing visual and aural images, a director can express a point of view. In countless movies, for example, the sounds of big-city traffic—horns honking, people yelling at one another, taxis screeching to a halt to pick up passengers—express the idea that these places are frenetic and unlivable. Similarly, when

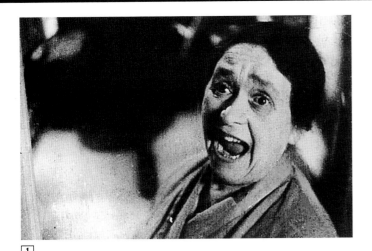

1

2

Sound that thwarts audience expectations A classic example of sound thwarting audience expectations occurs in Alfred Hitchcock's *The 39 Steps* (1935; sound: A. Birch). A landlady (actor not credited) enters a room, discovers a dead body, turns to face the camera, and opens her mouth as if to scream [1]. At least, that's what we expect to hear. Instead, as she opens her mouth we hear a sound that resembles a scream but is slightly different—a sound that, because it is out of context, we may not instantly recognize. Immediately, though, Hitchcock cuts to a shot of a train speeding out of a tunnel [2], and the mystery is solved: instead of a scream, we have heard the train whistle blaring a fraction of a second before we see the train.

a movie is set in other distinct environments—seashore, desert, mountain valley—the natural sounds associated with these places (the placid, turbulent, and stormy rhythms of the sea; or the howling winds of the desert sands; or the cry of a lone wolf in an otherwise peaceful valley) reflect the director's point of view of landscape and often as well the thoughts or emotional mood of the characters.

Alfred Hitchcock is a master of expressing his point of view through sound. In *The Birds* (1963), for example, one of the few of his movies that does not have background music, Hitchcock uses a design of electronic bird sounds (by Remi Gassmann and Oskar Sala) to express his point of view about the human chaos that breaks out in an unsuspecting town that has been attacked by birds. Bernard Herr-mann, who composed the scores for many Hitchcock movies, including *Psycho* (1960), was the uncredited sound designer on this one. It is a highly stylized sound track, consisting of a juxtaposition of natural sounds and computer-generated bird noises. Elisabeth Weis, an authority on film sound, writes:

> [In] *The Birds*, screeches are even more important than visual techniques for terrorizing the audience during attacks. Indeed, bird sounds sometimes replace visuals altogether. . . . Hitchcock carefully manipulates the sound track so that the birds can convey terror even when they are silent or just making an occasional caw or flutter. . . . Instead of orchestrated instruments there are orchestrated sound effects. If in *Psycho* music sounds like birds, in *The Birds* bird sounds function like music. Hitchcock even eliminates music under the opening titles in favor of bird sounds.[8]

Directors of visionary movies—those that show the past, present, or future world in a very distinctive, stylized manner—rely extensively on sounds of all kinds, including music, to create those worlds. In *2001: A Space Odyssey* (1968), where the world created comes almost totally from his imagination, Stanley Kubrick uses sounds (and the absence of them) to help us experience what it might be like to travel through outer space. The barks and howling

[8]Elisabeth Weis, *The Silent Scream: Alfred Hitchcock's Sound Track* (Rutherford, N.J.: Fairleigh Dickinson University Press, 1982), pp. 138–139.

of the apes in the prologue reflect Kubrick's point of view that aggression and violence have always been a part of the world—indeed, that such behavior removes the distinction between such concepts as *primitive* and *civilized*. The sounds of switches, latches, and doorways on the space shuttles have a peculiar hollow sound all their own. The electronic sounds emanating from the monolith reflect its imposing dignity, but also mirror the awe and fear of the astronauts who approach it.

Although Werner Herzog usually shoots his visionary movies with direct sound (meaning that it is recorded on-site), he frequently augments that sound with haunting musical scores by the German group Popol Vuh. These sounds, as well as Herzog's very deliberate use of silence, are part of what elevates such films as *Aguirre: The Wrath of God* (1972), *Nosferatu the Vampyre* (1979), and *The Enigma of Kasper Hauser* (1974) beyond being mere poetic movies to being philosophical statements about human life. *Aguirre* recounts the failed attempt of Don Lope de Aguirre (Klaus Kinski), a sixteenth-century Spanish explorer, to conquer Peru and find the fabled city of El Dorado. From the opening to the closing moments of this extraordinary movie, it is clear that Aguirre is mad. Indeed, Kinski's performance as Aguirre leaves no doubt that he is possessed by ruthless ambition and greed.

Herzog's style is frequently called "hallucinatory" (as well as "visionary") because it produces a feeling in the viewer of being somewhere between fantasy and reality, which is exactly where Aguirre is. In the opening scene, in which Aguirre and his forces slowly descend a steep mountainside toward a river, most of the action is shot in real time, helping us to understand just how arduous and dangerous the expedition will be. The primary sounds are people's low voices, footsteps on the path, and Popol Vuh's minimalist score, which mixes electronic and acoustic sources with choral monotones. This music makes clear Herzog's view of the futility of Aguirre's quest. Thus at the end, when Aguirre is alone on a drifting raft spinning slowly out of control on the river (photographed impressively from a helicopter, which, of course, we do not hear), we are not surprised to hear this musical score again—

except that now Aguirre too seems to understand the futility of his quest. This reuse of music reinforces the prophetic nature of the director's point of view.

Rhythm

Sound can add rhythm to a scene whether accompanying or juxtaposed against movement on the screen. In *Citizen Kane* (1941; sound: Bailey Fesler and James G. Stewart), in the comic scene in which Kane moves into the *Inquirer* office, Orson Welles uses the rhythms within overlapping dialogue to create a musical composition—one voice playing off another in its pitch, loudness, and quality (see "Sound in Orson Welles's *Citizen Kane*" later in this chapter). In Atom Egoyan's *The Sweet Hereafter* (1997; sound: Steve Munro), two conversations overlap, joined in time but separated in on-screen space: Wendell and Risa Walker (Maury Chaykin and Alberta Watson) talk with each other while Mitchell Stevens (Ian Holm) speaks with his daughter, Zoe (Caerthan Banks), on a cell phone.

A **montage** of sounds is a mix that ideally includes multiple sources of diverse quality, levels, and placement and usually moves as rapidly as a montage of images. Such a montage can also be orchestrated to create rhythm, as in the famous opening scene of Rouben Mamoulian's *Love Me Tonight* (1932; sound: M. M. Paggi)—one of the first films to use sound creatively—in which the different qualities of sounds made by ordinary activities establish the "symphony" that accompanies the start of the day in an ordinary Parisian neighborhood.

Jean-Pierre Jeunet and Marc Caro pay homage to Mamoulian's sound montage in *Delicatessen* (1991; sound: Jérôme Thiault). One comic scene in the film functions like a piece of music, with a classic verse-chorus-verse-chorus-verse-chorus pattern. When a butcher, Monsieur Clapet (Jean-Claude Dreyfus) makes love to his mistress, Mademoiselle Plusse (Karin Viard), the mattress and frame of the bed squeak noisily and in an increasing rhythm that matches their increasing ardor. As the tempo increases, we expect the scene to end climactically.

Playing on our expectations, though, Jeunet and Caro cut back and forth between the lovers and other inhabitants of the building, who hear the squeaking bed and subconsciously change the rhythm of their daily chores to keep time with the sounds' escalating pace. The sequence derives its humor from the way it satisfies our formal expectations for closure (the sexual partners reach orgasm) but frustrates the tenants, who just become exhausted in their labors.

On a far grander scale—commensurate with the scope of the story—Francis Ford Coppola's *Apocalypse Now* (1979; sound designer: Walter Murch) includes a mix of more than 140 sound tracks during the exciting, horrifying helicopter assault on the beach of a Vietcong stronghold (see page 420); prominent in the mix is "Ride of the Valkyries" from Richard Wagner's opera *Die Walküre* (1856). In a later film about Vietnam, Oliver Stone's *Platoon* (1986; sound designer: Gordon Daniel), the personal hatreds that divide a platoon are underscored by a montage that includes the roar of the helicopters, voices of frightened men, screams of the dying, and repeated excerpts from composer Samuel Barber's grief-stricken Adagio for Strings (1936).

Characterization

All types of sound—dialogue, sound effects, music—can function as part of characterization. In Mel Brooks's *Young Frankenstein* (1974; sound: Don Hall), when Frau Blücher's (Cloris Leachman) name is mentioned, horses rear on their hind legs and whinny. It becomes clear in context that she is so ugly and intimidating that even horses can't stand to hear her name, so for the rest of the movie, every time her name is mentioned, we hear the same sounds.

In *Jaws* (1975; sound: John R. Carter), Steven Spielberg uses a sound effect to introduce Quint (Robert Shaw), the old shark hunter. When Quint enters a community meeting called in response to the first killing of a swimmer by the shark, he draws his fingernails across a chalkboard to show his power and bravery: he is affected neither by a sound that makes most people cringe nor, by extension, by the townspeople or sharks. We might also observe that this sound is as abrasive as Quint is.

Musical themes are frequently associated with a character's thoughts, as in Lasse Hallström's *My Life as Dog* (1985), where Björn Isfalt's score reflects the melancholic state of mind of a boy yearning for his dead mother, or in Joseph L. Mankiewicz's *The Ghost and Mrs. Muir* (1947), where Bernard Herrmann's score reflects a widow's loneliness in an isolated house on a cliff overlooking the sea. Musical themes can also help us to understand the setting in which characters live. Miranda July's *Me and You and Everyone We Know* (2006) is an offbeat indie feature that tells the overlapping stories of a diverse group of people living in Los Angeles and looking for love, affection, or whatever they can find. These people—young, old, married, single, black, Hispanic, and white—are poignant in their somewhat goofy yearnings, and Michael Andrews's whimsical musical score—including solo guitar, solo piano, solo organ, pop songs, and a hymn—reflects their casual lifestyles and provides the perfect comment on their activities. Animals can also be identified by a significant musical theme, as with John Williams's memorable one for Hedwig, Harry's owl in the *Harry Potter* series.

Musical themes often identify characters, occurring and recurring on the sound track as the characters make their entrances and exits on the screen. But music can also underscore characters' insights. In Sam Mendes's *American Beauty* (1999; composer: Thomas Newman), for example, Lester Burnham (Kevin Spacey) is having a midlife crisis. Although a wide variety of diegetic popular music helps identify the musical tastes of the Burnham family, it is an original theme that helps identify and sustain Lester's longing for a different life, literally a "bed of roses"—roses being the symbol of Lester's lust for his daughter's friend Angela (Mena Suvari). Lying on his bed, having this fantasy—shots of rose petals floating on him are intercut with shots of Angela naked among the rose petals on the ceiling above him—we hear a peaceful theme played by a Javanese gamelan orchestra. The repetitiveness and quality of this music emphasize Lester's mood of wanting to escape to another world.

[1]

[2]

[3]

[4]

[5]

[6]

Sound and characterization The opening montage in Francis Ford Coppola's *Apocalypse Now* (1979; sound designer: Walter Murch) sets a high visual and sonic standard. But Coppola and his collaborators meet and perhaps exceed that standard during the "Helicopter Attack" scene, in which the lunatic Lieutenant Colonel Kilgore (Robert Duvall, *standing*, in image [6]) leads a largely aerial raid on a Vietnamese village. Accompanying horribly magnificent images of destruction and death are the sounds of wind, footsteps, gunfire, explosions, airplanes, helicopters, crowd noise, shouting, dialogue, and Richard Wagner's "Ride of the Valkyries." Although the grand operatic music gives unity, even a kind of dignity, to the fast-moving, violent, and disparate images, what it mostly accomplishes is to underscore Kilgore's megalomania.

Continuity

Sound can link one shot to the next, indicating that the scene has not changed in either time or space. **Overlapping sound** carries the sound from a first shot over to the next before the sound of the second shot begins. Charles Laughton's *The Night of the Hunter* (1955; sound: Stanford Houghton) contains an effective sound bridge: Harry Powell (Robert Mitchum), a con man posing as an itinerant preacher, has murdered his wife, Willa (Shelley Winters), placed her in an automobile, and driven it into the river. An old man, Birdie Steptoe (James Gleason), out fishing on the river, looks down and discovers the crime.

Through shot A, an underwater shot of great poetic quality in which we see Willa in the car, her

Music supporting characterization Richard (John Hawkes) and Christine (Miranda July) are just two of the endearing characters looking for love in *Me and You and Everyone We Know*. When they meet initially, nothing clicks—at least not for Richard—but later they discover that they live in the wacky world of LA and view it in the same detached way. The musical score does not create a theme for them; instead, it echoes their casual way of living and loving.

floating hair mingling with the reeds, we hear Harry singing one of his hymns; that music bridges the cut to shot B, where Harry, continuing to sing, is standing in front of their house looking for his stepchildren. Hearing Harry's hymn singing over Willa's submerged body affects the meaning of this scene in two ways: it both adds to the shot's eerie feeling of heavenly peace (with her gently undulating hair, diffused light, etc.) associated with what should be a grisly image and connects Harry directly to the murder. In addition, the fact that he sounds calm, satisfied, even righteous reinforces the interpretation that he sees his killings as acts of God. When the picture catches up with the sound to reveal Harry calmly stalking the murdered woman's children, the dramatic tension is increased as a result of the association between Harry and Willa's body that the sound bridge has reinforced.

Joel Coen's *The Man Who Wasn't There* (2001; sound designer: Eugene Gearty), a dark, twisted neo-noir film, contains a smoothly edited sequence of fifteen shots, thirteen of which are linked by overlapping, nondiegetic bits of a Beethoven piano sonata and two of which show Ed Crane (Billy Bob Thornton) listening to Rachael Abundas (Scarlett Johansson) playing the sonata (diegetic music). In

the midst of a life filled with conflict and tragedy, Ed has found "peace" listening to Rachael play this particular sonata, and this sequence is made all the more peaceful by its lyrical theme. But Carter Burwell, the movie's composer, must have chosen this sonata—no. 8 in C Minor, op. 13—for its subtitle, *Pathétique*, a pointedly ironic reminder that Crane sees himself as a loser, as does everyone else.

Overlapping sound can also be used to link and provide unity between disparate scenes, as in Roy Andersson's *You, the Living* (2007; sound: Jan Alvemark, Günther Friedhoff, Robert Sörling), a very stylish black comedy composed of 50 long takes and set in Sweden, which uses lively music and sound bridges that help the story move and make sense.

Emphasis

A sound can create emphasis in any scene—that is, can function as a punctuation mark—when it accentuates and strengthens the visual image. Although some movies treat emphasis as if it were a sledgehammer, others handle it more subtly. In Peter Weir's *The Truman Show* (1998; sound: Lee Smith), Truman Burbank (Jim Carrey) unknowingly has lived his entire life in an ideal world that is in fact a fantastic television set contained within a huge dome. When after thirty years he realizes the truth of his existence, he overcomes his fear of water and attempts to sail away. To deter him, the television producer orders an artificial storm, which temporarily disables Truman, but the sun comes out, he wakes up, and continues his journey, thinking he is free. Suddenly the boom of one of his sails pierces the inside of the great dome with a sound that is unfamiliar to him—indeed, one of the most memorable sounds ever heard in a movie. His first reactions are shock, anguish, and disbelief. How could there be an "end" to the horizon?

Distinct as this sound is, it has nothing of the sledgehammer effect. Rather, it underscores Truman's quiet, slow epiphany of who and where he is. His next reaction is the awareness that something is very wrong with his world. Cautiously touching the dome's metal wall, he says, "Aah," indicating a further insight into his situation. He walks along

[1]

[2]

[3]

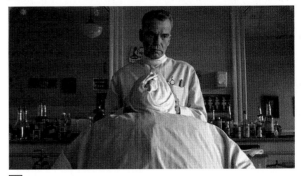

[4]

[5]

Overlapping music A fifteen-shot sequence in Joel Coen's *The Man Who Wasn't There* (2001; sound designer: Eugene Gearty) documents a futile attempt by Ed Crane (Billy Bob Thornton) to find a man who has swindled him out of $10,000. The sequence is one of many in the movie that show the decent but ineffectual Crane coming to grips with his life as an ordinary barber while his wife and everyone else around him set higher goals. The sequence is underscored with the nondiegetic and diegetic sounds of Beethoven's *Pathétique* piano sonata. Here are five shots from the middle of the sequence: Crane [1] tries to locate Creighton Tolliver, the swindler (played by Jon Polito), by phone; [2] checks the man's business card; and [3] listens to Rachael "Birdy" Abundas (Scarlett Johansson), a teenage neighbor, playing a Beethoven piano sonata. [4] Rachael's father, Walter (Richard Jenkins), also listens. [5] Crane is back at his job in the barber shop. When he says, "How could I have been so stupid," we understand the appropriateness of the filmmakers' choice of this Beethoven sonata to underscore his self-insight.

the edge of the "horizon," mounts a surreal staircase, pauses for a moment to talk with the show's producer, and finally walks through an exit door to the first free day of his life. The unique sound of the boom piercing the metal dome—underscored by the chord progressions of Burkhard Dallwitz's score—is nothing like the ordinary sound of a boat bumping against a dock. And although it is a real sound, it is not a natural one. This is a symbolic sound that both emphasizes Truman's captivity and heralds his liberation from a world of illusion.

In Adrian Lyne's version of *Lolita* (1997; sound: Michael O'Farrell), the sexual ambiguity of a confrontation between Humbert Humbert (Jeremy Irons) and his nemesis, Clare Quilty (Frank Langella), is punctuated by the insistent sound of an electric bug zapper. In action movies, such as *Sin*

City (2005; directors: Frank Miller and Robert Rodriguez; sound designer: Paula Fairfield), the sounds of violent action are greatly emphasized so that fists hit with a bone-crunching "thunk" and cars crash with a deafening noise. The same exaggerated emphasis applies to many animated movies, in which the violence is loud but usually harmless.

Sound in Orson Welles's *Citizen Kane*

During the 1930s, the first decade of sound in film, many directors used sound as an integral part of their movies. Their innovations were all the more significant because most of them had little or no prior background in sound. Between 1933 and 1938, Orson Welles established himself as one of the most creative innovators in American radio broadcasting. Before Welles, radio broadcasting had been a wasteland lacking in creativity, but Welles approached the medium the way he approached the theater and, later, the movies: experimenting and making things different.

As always, Welles was a one-man show: writer, director, producer, actor. As writer, he specialized in making modern adaptations of classic literary works; as producer, he cast famous stage and movie actors, generally saving the most important part for himself; and as director, he orchestrated voices, sound effects, narration, and music in a complex mix that had never been tried before, at least on the scale that he created. There was no commercial television broadcasting at the time, and Welles understood the power of pure sounds, without images, to entertain, educate, and engage listeners. He also understood the power of radio to shock people, as his notorious 1938 production of H. G. Wells's *The War of the Worlds* proved. Indeed, it was the awesome imagination behind that one radio broadcast that not only made Orson Welles world-famous overnight, but also was instrumental in his recruitment by Hollywood.

Welles's complex sound design for *Citizen Kane* (1941; sound: Bailey Fesler and James G. Stewart) is a kind of deep-focus sound in that it functions much like deep-focus cinematography. Indeed, we can, with confidence, call Welles the first sound designer in American film history because of the comprehensive way in which he used sound to establish, develop, and call our attention to the meanings of what we see. In this discussion we will look more closely at the impressive uses of sound in the party scene that celebrates Kane's acquisition of the *Chronicle* staff for the *Inquirer*. In addition to the combined staff of reporters, musicians, waiters, and dancers, the principal characters are Charles Foster Kane (Welles), Mr. Bernstein (Everett Sloane), and Jed Leland (Joseph Cotten). The setting for the party is the *Inquirer*'s offices, which have been decorated for the occasion. The room is both deep and wide, designed to accommodate the deep-focus cinematography. Welles made his complicated sound design possible by covering the ceilings with muslin, which concealed the many microphones necessary to record the multiple sounds as the scene was shot.

We hear these multiple sounds simultaneously, distinctly, and at the proper sound levels in relation to the camera's placement, so that the farther we are from the sound, the softer and less distinct the sound becomes. When Bernstein and Leland are

[1]

[2]

Sound mise-en-scène The mise-en-scène of this party scene from Orson Welles's *Citizen Kane* (1941; sound: Bailey Fesler and James G. Stewart) clearly reflects what's going on—both visually and aurally. Leland (Joseph Cotten) and Bernstein (Everett Sloane) are talking, and even though there are competing sounds around them, their voices are distinct because they have been placed close to a microphone in a medium shot. Note that Kane (Welles), both visually and aurally, dominates this scene through his presence in the middle background of each shot.

talking, for example, they appear in medium shots, and their dialogue is naturally the loudest on the sound track; however, they literally have to shout to be heard because of the pitch, loudness, and quality of the competing sounds: the music, the dancing, the crowd noise.

We can say that the sound has its own mise-en-scène here. Although these diegetic, on-screen sounds were recorded directly on the set, some additions were made during the rerecording process. Reversing the ordinary convention of composing the music after the rough cut of a film has been assembled, Bernard Herrmann wrote the music first, and Robert Wise edited the footage to fit the music's rhythm.

Sources and Types

The sound in this scene is diegetic, external, on-screen; was recorded during both production and postproduction; and is diverse in quality, level, and placement. The types include overlapping voices, ordinary dialogue, and singing; music from an on-screen band; sound effects; and ambient noise. Welles's handling of sound dominates this scene: he makes us constantly aware of the sources, the types, and the mix and (unsurprisingly) doesn't use much silence. However, two signs mounted on walls read "SILENCE" and thus, as relics of an earlier period, remind us how quiet these same offices were before Kane took over from the previous editor. Through this visual pun, Welles employs a touch of silence during the loudest sequence in *Citizen Kane*.

Functions

This sound montage

> guides our attention to all parts of the room, making us aware of characters' relative positions (e.g., the contrast between Kane and the others).
> helps define the spatial and temporal dimensions of the setting and the characters' placement within the mise-en-scène (e.g., the sound is loud when the source is closer to the camera).
> conveys the mood and the characters' states of mind (e.g., the sound is frantic and loud and gains momentum until it almost runs out of control, underscoring the idea that these men, Kane and reporters alike, are being blinded and intoxicated by their own success).

Sound creates mood At this party, where spirits are high, almost everyone joins in the act, including Kane, the performers, and Kane's staff of reporters, here pretending as if they were members of the band.

Complex mix of sound In addition to the distinctive voices of the three main characters and the voices of the guests and performers, there is a brass marching band—all of this constituting a sound design and mix that was very advanced for its time.

Who is this man? "Who is this man," a line in Kane's campaign song "There Is a Man," might function as a subtitle for the movie itself and allows Kane—singing, dancing, and mugging his way through the act—to show a lighter side of his many-faceted personality.

> helps represent time (e.g., the sound here is synchronous with the action).

> fulfills our expectations (e.g., of how a party of this kind might sound and of the fact that Kane is continuing on his rapid rise to journalistic and political power).

> creates rhythm beyond that provided by the music (within the changing dramatic arc that starts with a celebration involving all the men and ends with one man's colossal display of ego).

> reveals, through the dialogue, aspects of each main character (e.g., establishes a conflict between Kane and Leland over personal and journalistic ethics, one in which Bernstein predictably takes Kane's side).

> underscores one principal theme of the entire movie (e.g., the song "There Is a Man" not only puts "good old Charlie Kane" in the spotlight—he sings and dances throughout it—but also serves as the campaign theme song when he runs for governor and becomes a dirge after his defeat; at the same time, while the lyric attempts to answer the question "Who is this man?" it has no more success than the rest of the movie).

> arouses our expectations about what's going to happen as the film evolves (e.g., the marching band signals both that the *Inquirer* won over the *Chronicle* and that the *Inquirer* "declares" war on Spain—a war the United States will win).

> enhances continuity with sound bridges (the smooth transitions from shot to shot and scene to scene within the sequence).

Sound effects Welles rarely missed an opportunity to use sound effects expressively, as here, where the bright light of the old-fashioned flash unit not only illuminates the scene but also punctuates his bragging about his acquisition of the *Chronicle* staff: "I felt like a kid in a candy store!"

> provides emphasis (e.g., the sound of the flashlamp when the staff's picture is taken punctuates Kane's bragging about having gotten his candy; after Kane says, "And now, gentlemen, *your complete attention*, if you please," he puts his fingers in his mouth and whistles; the trumpets' blare).

> enhances the overall dramatic effect of the sequence.

This overwhelming sound mix almost tells the story by itself.

Characterization

All the functions named in the previous section are important to this particular sequence and the overall film. In this section, we will look more closely only at how the sound helps illuminate the characters of Charles Foster Kane (Orson Welles), Mr. Bernstein (Everett Sloane), and Jed Leland (Joseph Cotten). Even though their dialogue is primarily a function of the narrative, its vocal delivery brings it to life. Long after you have seen the movie, you remember the characters, what they said, and the voices of those who portrayed them. As one

legacy of his radio experience, Welles planned it that way.

Each of the actors playing these characters has a distinctive speaking voice that is a major part of their characterization. Indeed, their voices are part of the key to our understanding of their characters. The depth and resonance of Welles's voice, coupled with its many colors (or qualities) and capabilities for both nuance and emphasis, enhance his ambiguous portrayal of the character. In several distinct areas, the sound of his voice deepens our understanding of this contradictory figure. It helps Kane flaunt his wealth and his power as the *Inquirer*'s publisher: when he brags to the new reporters about feeling like a "kid in a candy store" and having gotten his candy, his remarks are punctuated by the sound of the photographer's flashlamp. However, this sound may also be interpreted as Welles's way of mocking Kane's bragging.

Kane dominates the table of guests with the announcement that he is going to Europe for his health—"forgive my rudeness in taking leave of you"—but there is in fact nothing physically wrong with him, as we learn when he calls attention to his mania for collection (and wealth) by sarcastically saying, "They've been making statues for two thousand years and I've only been buying for five." This conversation between Kane and Bernstein is directed and acted as if it were a comedy routine on a radio show or in a vaudeville theater between the "top banana" (Kane) and the "straight man" (Bernstein). The implied nature of this exchange is something that 1940s audiences would have instinctively understood.

The sound in this scene helps Kane build on his power, not only as the boss and host of the party— "And now, gentlemen, *your complete attention*, if you please"—but also as the flamboyant and influential publisher: "Well, gentlemen, are we going to declare war on Spain, or are we not?" He's in charge because he's the boss, and the boss's voice also dominates his employees. As he asks this question, the band enters, playing "Hot Time in the Old Town Tonight," and is followed by women dancers carrying toy rifles. When Leland answers, "The *Inquirer* already has," Kane humiliates him by calling him "a long-

ically respectable trivia contest. It has the much more important and complex task of explaining the historical development of a phenomenon on which billions of dollars and countless hours have been spent."[1]

Like other historians, film historians use artifacts to study the past. These artifacts include the various machines and other technology—the cameras, projectors, sound recording devices, etc.—without which there would be no movies. They might also include notes from story conferences, screenplays, production logs, drawings, outtakes, and other objects relevant to the production of a particular movie, as well, of course, as first-person accounts by people involved with the movie, newspaper and magazine articles, and books about the production and the people involved in it. Obviously, the most important artifacts to the film historian are the movies themselves.

Film history includes the history of technologies, the people and industrial organizations that produce the movies, the national cinemas that distinguish one country's movies from another's, the attempts to suppress and censor the movies, and the meanings and pleasure that we derive from them. Gaining knowledge about these and other aspects of film history is pleasurable and interesting in and of itself. But as you graduate from merely watching movies to looking at movies in a critically aware way, your knowledge of film history will also provide you with the perspective and context to understand and evaluate the unique attributes of movies from the past as well as the more complex phenomena of today's movies.

Basic Approaches to Studying Film History

Although there are many approaches to studying film history (including studies of production, regulation, and reception), the beginner should know the four traditional approaches: the aesthetic, technological, economic, and social. In what follows, we describe each approach and cite one or two studies as exemplary models of each.[2]

The Aesthetic Approach

Sometimes called the *masterpiece approach* or *great man approach*, this approach seeks to evaluate individual movies and/or directors using criteria that assess their artistic significance and influence. Ordinarily, historians who take this approach will first define their criteria of artistic excellence and then ask the following questions: What are the significant works of the cinematic art? Who are the significant directors? Why are these movies and these directors important? Historians who take the aesthetic perspective do not necessarily ignore the economic, technological, and cultural aspects of film history—indeed, it would be impossible to discuss many great movies without considering these factors—but they are primarily interested in movies that are not only works of art but are also widely acknowledged masterpieces. The most comprehensive, one-volume international history that takes an aesthetic approach is David A. Cook's *A History of Narrative Film*, 4th ed. (New York: Norton, 2004). Other aesthetic studies are on the auteur theory, which holds that great movies are the work of a single creative mind; one outstanding study in this field is James Naremore's *On Kubrick* (London: BFI, 2007).[3]

---

[1]Robert C. Allen and Douglas Gomery, *Film History: Theory and Practice* (New York: Knopf, 1985), p. 21.

[2]These four traditional categories are covered in Allen and Gomery, chs. 4–7. Jon Lewis and Eric Smoodin, eds., *Looking Past the Screen: Case Studies in American Film History and Method* (Durham, N.C.: Duke University Press, 2007), pp. 4–5, identify four other categories: industrial systems, regulatory systems, reception, and representation.

[3]Film critic Andrew Sarris defines the auteur theory in his *The American Cinema: Directors and Directions, 1929–1968* (New York: Dutton, 1968), pp. 19–37. See also Pauline Kael's famous rebuttal, "Circles and Squares," in *Film Theory and Criticism: Introductory Readings*, ed. Gerald Mast and Marshall Cohen, 2nd ed. (New York: Oxford University Press, 1979), pp. 666–691. Sarris's essay is also included in this anthology (pp. 650–665), but it should be read in the context of his pioneering 1968 study, cited here.

The Technological Approach

All art forms have a technological history that records the advancements in materials and techniques that have affected the nature of the medium. Of all the arts, though, cinema seems to rely most heavily on technology. Historians who chart the history of cinema technology examine the circumstances surrounding the development of each technological advance as well as subsequent improvements. They pose questions such as: When was each invention made? Under what circumstances, including aesthetic, economic, and social, was it made? Was it a totally new idea or one linked to the existing state of technology? What were the consequences for directors, studios, distributors, exhibitors, and audiences? By studying how the major developments (including the introduction of sound, the moving camera, deep-focus cinematography, color film stock, and digital cinematography, processing, and projection) occurred, historians show us how the production of movies has changed and can also evaluate whether or not that change was significant (like widescreen processes) or transitory (like Smell-O-Vision). This approach cuts across artists, studios, movements, and genres to focus on the interaction of technology with aesthetics, modes of production, and economic factors. An excellent example of such a study is David Bordwell, Janet Staiger, and Kristin Thompson, *The Classical Hollywood Cinema: Film Study and Mode of Production to 1960* (New York: Columbia University Press, 1985). For a study of a specific technological subject, see John Belton's *Widescreen Cinema* (Cambridge, Mass.: Harvard University Press, 1992).

The Economic Approach

The motion-picture industry is a major part of the global economy. Every movie released has an economic history of its own as well as a place in the economic history of its studio (policies of production, distribution, and exhibition) and the historical period and country in which it was produced. Historians interested in this subject help us to understand how and why the studio system was founded, how it adapted to changing conditions (economic, technological, social, historical), and how and why different studios took different approaches to producing different movies, how these movies have been distributed and exhibited, and what effect this had on film history. They study how and why the independent system of production superseded the studio system and what effect this has had on production, distribution, and exhibition. They are also concerned with such related issues as management and organization, accounting and marketing practices, and censorship and the rating system. Finally, they try to place significant movies within the nation's economy as well as within the output of the industry in general and the producing studio in particular. Excellent studies include Douglas Gomery's *The Hollywood Studio System: A History* (London: BFI, 2005), Joel W. Finler's *The Hollywood Story*, 3rd ed. (London: Wallflower, 2003), and Tino Balio's *Grand Design: Hollywood as a Modern Business Enterprise, 1930–1939*, History of the American Cinema series, vol. 5 (Berkeley: University of California Press, 1995).

Film as Social History

Because society and culture influence the movies and vice versa, the movies serve as primary sources for studying society. Writing about movies as social history continues to be a major preoccupation of journalists, scholars, and students alike. Historian Ian Jarvie suggests that, in undertaking these studies, we ask the following basic questions: Who made the movies, and why? Who saw the films, how, and why? What was seen, how, and why? How were the movies evaluated, by whom, and why?[4] In addition, those interested in social history consider such factors as religion, politics, and cultural trends and taboos. They ask to what extent, if any, a particular movie was produced to sway public opinion or effect social change. They are also interested in audience composition, marketing, and critical writing and reviewing in the media, from gossip magazines to scholarly books. Overall, they study

[4]This paraphrase of Ian Jarvie comes from Allen and Gomery, p. 154.

the complex interaction between the movies—as a social institution—and other social institutions, including government, religion, and labor. Landmark studies include Robert Sklar's *Movie-Made America: A Cultural History of American Movies*, rev. and updated ed. (New York: Vintage, 1994), and Richard Abel's *Americanizing the Movies and "Movie-Mad" Audiences, 1910–1914* (Berkeley: University of California Press, 2006).

Although some areas in the study of film history may require experience and analytic skills beyond those possessed by most introductory students, you can use your familiarity with film history in writing even the most basic analysis for a class assignment.

Which approach—aesthetic, technological, economic, or social—will we take in this chapter? Where relevant, we will consider them all.

A Short Overview of Film History

Precinema

Before we discuss the major milestones of film history, let's look at some of the key technological innovations that made movies possible.[5] First among these is photography.

Photography   In one sense, movies are simply a natural progression in the history of photography. The word **photography** means, literally, "writing with light" and technically, the static representation or reproduction of light. The concept has its beginnings in ancient Greece. In the fourth century BCE, the Greek philosopher Aristotle theorized about a device that later would be known as the **camera obscura** (Latin for "dark chamber"; Fig. 10.1). In the late fifteenth century, Leonardo da Vinci's drawings gave tangible form to the idea. Both simple and ingenious, the camera obscura may be a box or it may be a room large enough for a viewer to stand

inside. Light entering through a tiny hole (later a lens) on one side of the box or room projects an image from the outside onto the opposite side or wall. An artist might then trace the image onto a piece of paper.

Photography was developed during the first four decades of the nineteenth century by Thomas Wedgwood, William Henry Fox Talbot, and Sir John Herschel in England; Joseph-Nicéphore Niépce and Louis-Jacques-Mandé Daguerre in France; and George Eastman in the United States. In 1802, Wedgwood made the first recorded attempt to produce photographs. However, these were not camera images as we know them, but basically silhouettes of objects placed on paper or leather sensitized with chemicals and exposed to light. These images faded quickly, for Wedgwood did not know how to fix (stabilize) them. Unaware of Wedgwood's work, Talbot devised a chemical method for recording the images he observed in his camera obscura. More important was the significant progress he made toward fixing the image, and he invented the **negative**, or negative photographic image on transparent material, which makes possible the reproduction of the image.

Niépce experimented with sunlight and the camera obscura to make photographic copies of engravings as well as actual photographs from nature. The results of this heliographic (that is, sun-drawn) process—crude paper prints—were not particularly successful, but Niépce's discoveries influenced Daguerre, who by 1837 was able to create a detailed image on a copper plate treated with chemicals—an image remarkable for its fidelity and detail. In 1839, Herschel perfected hypo (short for hyposulfite thiosulfate—that is, sodium thiosulfate), a compound that fixed the image on paper and thus arrested the effect of light on it. Herschel first used the word *photography* in 1839 in a lecture at the Royal Society of London for the Promotion of Natural Knowledge. What followed were primarily technological improvements on Herschel's discovery.

In 1851, glass-plate negatives replaced the paper plates. More durable but heavy, glass was replaced by gelatin-covered paper in 1881. The new gelatin process reduced, from 15 minutes to .001 second, the time necessary to make a photographic exposure,

---

[5]This discussion of early film technologies is necessarily brief. For more on key filmmaking technologies, see Chapter 11, "Filmmaking Technologies and Production Systems."

FIGURE 10.1 Camera Obscura

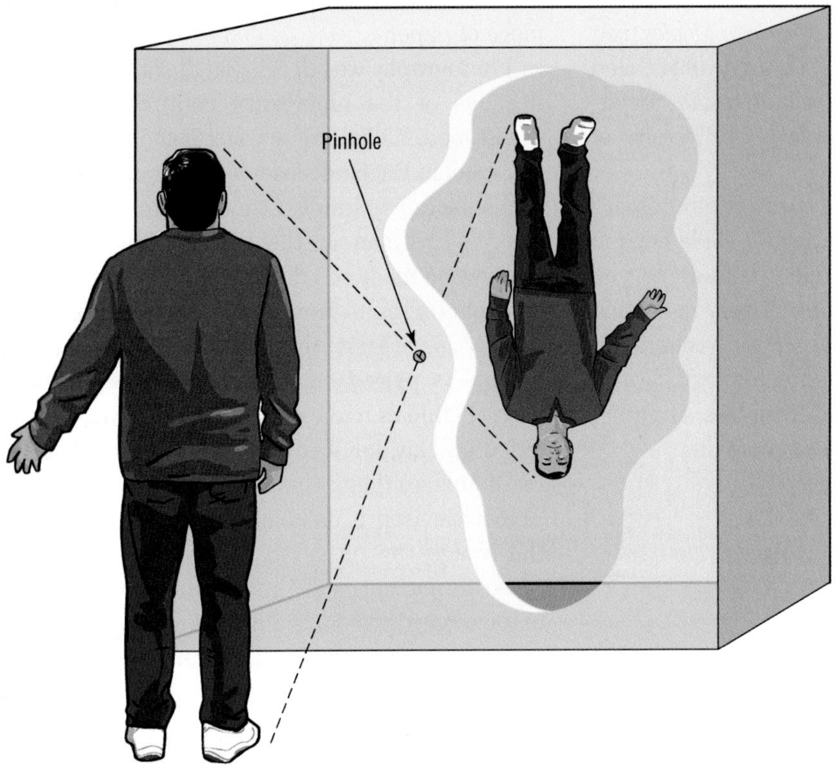

Pinhole

Before the advent of photosensitive film, the camera obscura was used to facilitate lifelike drawing. In this simple schematic, for example, the interior "wall" upon which the upside-down image is projected was usually whitened; an artist could place a piece of drawing paper on the wall and trace the image onto it.

thus making it possible to record action spontaneously and simultaneously as it occurred. In 1887, George Eastman began the mass production of a paper "film" coated with a gelatin emulsion; in 1889, he improved the process by substituting clear plastic (film) for the paper base. Although there have been subsequent technological improvements, this is the photographic film we know today.

This experimentation with optical principles and still photography in the nineteenth century made it possible to take and reproduce photographic images that could simulate action in the image. But simulation was not enough for the scientists, artists, and members of the general public who wanted to see images of life in motion. The intermediary step between still photography and cinematography came with the development of series photography.

Series Photography Series photography records the phases of an action. In a series of still photographs, we see, for example, a man or a horse in changing positions that suggest movement, though the images themselves are static. Within a few years, three men—Pierre-Jules-César Janssen, Eadweard Muybridge, and Étienne-Jules Marey— contributed to its development.

In 1874, Janssen, a French astronomer, developed the **revolver photographique**, or chronophotographic gun, a cylinder-shaped camera that creates exposures automatically, at short intervals, on different segments of a revolving plate. In 1877, Muybridge, an English photographer working in California, used a group of electrically operated cameras (first twelve, then twenty-four) to produce the first series of photographs of continuous motion. On May 4, 1880, using an early projector

[1]

[2]

Series photography Eadweard Muybridge's famous series of photographs documenting a horse in motion were made possible by a number of cameras placed side by side in the structure pictured here [1]. The cameras were tied to individual trip wires. As the horse broke each wire, a camera's shutter would be set off. The result of this experiment—a series of sixteen exposures [2]—proved that a trotting horse momentarily has all four feet off the ground at once (see the third frame). Series photography has been revived as a strategy for creating special effects in contemporary movies.

known as the **magic lantern** and his **zoopraxiscope** (a version of the magic lantern, with a revolving disc that had his photographs arranged around the center), Muybridge gave the first public demonstration of photographic images in motion—a cumbersome process, but a breakthrough.

In 1882, Marey, a French physiologist, made the first series of photographs of continuous motion using the **fusil photographique** (another form of the chronophotographic gun), a single, portable camera capable of taking twelve continuous images. Muybridge and Marey later collaborated in Paris, but each was more interested in using the process for his own scientific studies than for making or projecting motion pictures as such. Marey's invention solved the problems created by Muybridge's use of a battery of cameras, but the series was limited to forty images—a total of 3 or 4 seconds.

The experiments that Janssen, Muybridge, and Marey conducted with various kinds of moving pictures were limited in almost every way, but the technologies needed to make moving pictures on film were in place and awaited only a synthesis.

1891–1903: The First Movies

Who invented the movies?[6] Historic milestones such as this are seldom the result of a few persons working together on a single idea but rather the product of many dreams, experiments, and inventions. Like the making of movies, their invention was the product of collaboration. It did not occur in one moment, but rather took place in four major industrialized countries—the United States, France, England, and Germany—in the years just prior to 1895. Furthermore, in attempting to answer the question, we must distinguish between moving pictures that were projected onto a surface for an audience and those that were not.

In 1891, William Kennedy Laurie Dickson, working with associates in Thomas Edison's research laboratory, invented the **Kinetograph** (the first motion-picture camera) and the **Kinetoscope** (a peephole viewer). The first motion picture made with the Kinetograph, and the earliest complete film on record at the Library of Congress, was Dickson's *Edison Kinetoscopic Record of a Sneeze*

[6]An invaluable history of the invention of the movies, and one on which this section draws, is Charles Musser's *The Emergence of Cinema: The American Screen to 1907*, History of the American Cinema, vol. 1 (New York: Scribner, 1990; repr., Berkeley: University of California Press, 1994).

[1]

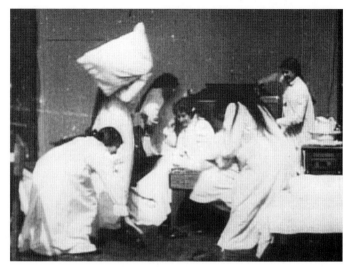

Short records of real life Before narrative or editing, Thomas Edison's first movies (about 30 seconds in length) were simple records of ordinary people and events: a man and woman kissing, a young woman dancing, a man getting a shave and haircut in a barber shop, and a woman and child feeding doves in a barnyard. In *Seminary Girls* (1897), we see young girls having a rare moment of fun in a harmless pillow fight until the school's matron interrupts them. The scene, obviously staged for the stationary camera, was photographed in Edison's first studio, the Black Maria.

[2]

Edison's Kinetograph and the Black Maria These images show Thomas Edison's Black Maria—the first motion-picture "studio"—pictured from the outside [1] and the inside [2]. The interior view shows how awkward and static the Kinetograph was because of both its bulk and its need to be tethered to a power source. In addition, the performers had very little room to move, and the environment was hot and airless. The makeshift quality of the studio, as well as its relatively modest size, is evident from the external view.

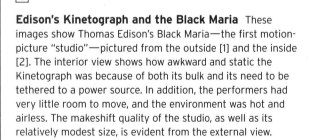

(1894), popularly known as *Fred Ott's Sneeze*, which represents, on Edison and Dickson's part, a brilliant choice of a single, self-contained action for a single, self-contained film of very limited length. Edison's staff made their movies, including *Fred Ott's Sneeze*, inside a crude, hot, and cramped shack known as the **Black Maria**. The Black Maria was

really the first movie studio, for it contained the camera, technicians, and actors. The camera was limited in its motion, able only to move closer to or away from the subject on a trolley. Light was provided by the sun, which entered through an aperture in the roof, and the entire "studio" could be rotated to catch the light. Edison demonstrated the Kinetoscope to various audiences, public and private, and in April 1894, the first Kinetoscope parlor opened in New York City, thus inaugurating the history of commercial movies.

Although the visual image that one saw in the Kinetoscope peephole viewer was moving, it could only be enjoyed by one person at a time. In the same month, the Lathams—Woodville and his two sons, Grey and Otway, former Edison employees—used their movie projector, the Eidoloscope, to show a movie to the press. Although Edison put down the significance of this demonstration, it was in fact the first time an invited audience had seen projected motion pictures in the United States.

Meanwhile, in November in Germany, another pair of brothers, Max and Emil Skladanowsky, projected short films in Berlin. Coincidentally, in France, two brothers (teams of brothers figure significantly in this story), Auguste and Louis Lumière, invented the Cinématographe, a far more sophisticated device than either the Kinetoscope or the Eidoloscope. In December 1895, they used it to project a movie on a screen set up in a small room inside a public café that was converted into a theater. (They had in fact already projected it throughout Europe for small, invited audiences). Although that movie, *Employees Leaving the Lumière Factory* (1895), which the Lumières called an *actualité* (a documentary view of the moment), was only 1 minute in length, it captivated the audience with its depiction of a spontaneous event. The Cinématographe—a hand-cranked device that served as camera, projector, and film printer—was equally amazing. In 1896, Edison unveiled his own projector, the Vitascope, in a New York City theater.

The projection of moving pictures to a paying audience ended the prehistory of cinema and freed it to become the art form of the twentieth century. Aesthetically, the work of the first filmmakers cannot compare in any way with today's movies, yet they managed, in a few years time, to establish the basic types of movies: short narratives, documentary depictions of real life, and experimental movies with special effects that foreshadow today's animation. In addition, they recognized that the movies—like the contemporary steam engine, electricity, and the railroad—would attract paying customers and make them a great deal of money. What they probably did not envision was the power of the movies to shape attitudes and values.

After a few years of experimenting with very short movies, a minute or two in length and hardly more than a novelty, Edison, the Lumière brothers, and other new filmmakers realized that the cinema needed new forms and conventions. It was clear that the movies needed to be less a curiosity, with which the public would soon become tired, and more of a durable and successful commercial entertainment, one that could compete with—and draw from—other popular art forms, such as literature and theater.

Real life as seen through the artists' lens At first glance, Auguste and Louis Lumière's *Children Digging for Clams* (1896) may seem similar to Edison's *Seminary Girls* as a simple record of an ordinary activity. But the differences between them show that the Lumières were artists with a natural sense of style. Not only was it longer (44 seconds) and shot outdoors (with a stationary camera), but it also employs a deep composition. Across the foreground, in a diagonal line, we see the clam-digging children; in the middle ground, we see adults, probably their parents, keeping an eye on them; and in the background, we see other people, the shoreline, and the horizon. As far as composition goes, nothing could be simpler; but by shooting it out of doors in a natural landscape, the Lumières provide an aesthetically pleasing interpretation of an actual event rather than just a documentary record.

Paramount among the early innovators of film form was a Frenchman, Georges Méliès, who in the late 1890s began to make short narrative movies based on the theatrical model of short, sequential scenes shot from a fixed point of view. The only editing within these self-contained scenes were cuts or in-camera dissolves. Rudimentary as these movies were, according to film historian David A. Cook, Méliès was "the cinema's first narrative artist,"[7] famous for innovating many technical and narrative devices. He is best known for his use of special effects—still captivating today—in such

[7]David A. Cook, *A History of Narrative Film*, 4th ed. (New York: Norton, 2004), p. 14.

Méliès the magician Georges Méliès, who was by trade a magician, took naturally to motion pictures, which are, first and foremost, an illusion. He quickly understood that he could make the camera stop and start (what we now call stop-motion photography) and, with this technique, make things vanish and reappear (sometimes in a new form). Like all magicians, he reveled in fooling the public. In *Long Distance Wireless Photography* (1908), Méliès plays the inventor of a process for transmitting photographs from one place to another and dupes his clients. When a man and woman ask for a demonstration, he photographs them and, behind them, projects unflattering images of them. Annoyed at this deception, they try to destroy the studio, but are chased away in a scene of slapstick comedy. Here, Méliès shows a prophetic, but comic, insight into two events that were decades away: the electronic transmission of photographs and television. The action is staged for the camera—just as if it were on a theater stage—and the movie, which is nearly 6 minutes in length, tells a complete story.

The beginnings of cinematic narrative Realizing that they needed to tell stories, the early filmmakers began to develop conventions of cinematic narrative. Among these artists were Georges Méliès in France, G. A. Smith in England, and Edwin S. Porter in the United States. In *Life of an American Fireman* (1903) and *The Great Train Robbery* (1903), Porter broke away from the prevailing step-by-step, one-shot-one-scene editing of Méliès and invented an early form of continuity editing in which he built a scene of shots that seemed chronologically continuous from one shot to the next. We make sense of this, as well as create meaning, by mentally connecting the shots into a logical narrative. Porter also cuts back and forth in time, showing simultaneous events taking place in different locations. For example, the robbers begin their heist by shooting and tying up a telegraph operator at a train station, then board the next train, rob the passengers, uncouple the engine, and head off. As they reach what they think is safety, Porter cuts back to the telegraph office, where (as shown here) a little girl, presumably the operator's daughter, discovers her father and revives him. Porter then cuts directly to a barn dance, where the operator and the little girl report what has happened. Porter then jumps ahead to the outlaws and the final shoot-out, continuing to use ellipsis when necessary to keep the action moving to the conclusion.

landmark films as *A Trip to the Moon* (1902) and *The Impossible Voyage* (1904).

Another early pioneer, Edwin S. Porter, was a director working with Edison, who by 1903 had established a relatively sophisticated approach to narrative filmmaking in such pioneering films as *The Great Train Robbery* (1903; 12 min.), which used multiple camera positions, interior and exterior settings, and crosscutting (intercutting) that made it possible to depict parallel actions occurring simultaneously. He also established the concept that the shot was the basic structural unit of a movie and pioneered the idea of continuity editing.

The Great Train Robbery was the first major milestone in the development of the American narrative film as well as the first "Western."

1908–1927: Origins of the Classical Hollywood Style—The Silent Period

The "silent era" of film history is distinguished by Edwin S. Porter's and D. W. Griffith's developments in narrative form, the crystallization of the classical

Hollywood style, the ascendance of Hollywood as the center of the world's motion-picture industry, the development of movie genres, and early experiments with color and animation.

The "classical Hollywood cinema"[8] refers here to the traditional studio-based style of making motion pictures in both the silent and sound periods. Although the rudiments of the classical style can be seen in the work of Edwin S. Porter, it began its ascendancy with the release of D. W. Griffith's *The Birth of a Nation* (1915) and continues, with various modifications, to identify the cinematic conventions used by most filmmakers today.

The classical Hollywood style is fundamentally built on the principle of "invisibility" that we discussed in Chapter 1. This principle generally includes two parts. The first is that the movie's form (narrative, cinematography, editing, sound, acting, and so forth) should not call attention to itself. That is, the narrative should be as economical and seamless as possible, and the presentation of the narrative should occur in a cinematic language with which the audience is familiar. The second part is the studio system itself, a mode of production that standardized the way movies were produced. Management was vertically organized, meaning that a strong executive office controlled production, distribution, and exhibition; hired all employees, including directors and actors; and assigned work to them according to the terms of their contracts, thus ensuring a certain uniform style for each studio. While we know that such principles were sometimes ignored in practice, they nonetheless serve a purpose in helping us chart the course of stylistic history. Thus, for example, we can understand and appreciate just how radical Orson Welles's approach was in *Citizen Kane* (1941) when he deliberately called attention to technique and in so doing, challenged the perceived limitations of the classical Hollywood style and the studio system itself.

[8]A concept popularized by film scholars David Bordwell, Kristin Thompson, and Janet Staiger, in *The Classical Hollywood Cinema: Film Style and Mode of Production to 1960* (New York: Columbia University Press, 1985).

By 1907, a small film effort started in and around Hollywood, lured by the favorable climate and variety of natural scenery. While its founders were nearly all uneducated immigrants, their business practices were consistent with the ruthless tactics of other Gilded Age entrepreneurs. D. W. Griffith made his first movie there in 1910; in 1911, the first studio was built, and by 1912, some fifteen film studios were operating; by 1914, the American film industry was clearly identified with Hollywood. As a forward-looking sign of this growth, the industry invested heavily in movie theaters, some of which were dubbed "palaces" for their imposing architecture, lavish interiors, and seating for hundreds, sometimes thousands, of people. It also established other "firsts," including trade journals, movie fan magazines, movie reviews in general-circulation newspapers, the star system, and a film censorship law.

During this period, filmmakers began to replace short films (generally one reel in length) with feature-length movies (four or more reels). The term "feature" came to mean major works that stood out on a program that might include shorter films as well. In these early days, the length of one reel was 10–16 minutes, depending on the speed of projection. The longer format not only permitted filmmakers to tackle more complicated narratives but also placed an emphasis on the quality of the production, including mise-en-scène, cinematography, acting, and editing. The growing middle class audience liked longer narratives and more polished productions and was willing to pay more to see such movies. Accordingly, producers could book them for extended runs and, of course, make more money. The transformation of the nickelodeon into the movie palace—which exceeded in splendor any legitimate theater and thus had an attraction all its own—further established the cinema as a serious artistic endeavor. Thus, with changes in a film's length, content, quality, and exhibition, came the first major restructuring of the movie industry. The second was to come with the advent of sound and the third with the development of the independent system of production. Thus the movies took on the modern production system and the cinematic conventions that, however much they have changed, we know today.

The first multiple-reel movies included J. Stuart Blackton's *The Life of Moses* (1909, 5 reels), D. W. Griffith's *Enoch Arden* (1911, 34 min.), *The Loves of Queen Elizabeth* (1912, directed by Henri Desfontaines and Louis Mercanton, 44 min.), a film from France, and such Italian epics as *The Crusaders* (1911, 4 reels, director unknown), *Dante's Inferno* (1911, 5 reels, director unknown), Enrico Guazzoni's *Quo Vadis?* (1913, 120 min.), and Giovanni Pastrone's *Cabiria* (1914, 181 min.). In 1914, clearly the turning point, Edwin S. Porter released *Tess of the Storm Country* (1914, 80 mins.) and directed an astonishing 20 features before retiring from film directing the next year. Cecil B. DeMille, another industry founder, began his feature film career with *The Squaw Man* (1914, 74 mins.) and made 14 features in 1915 alone. Griffith's *Judith of Bethulia* (61 min.) was released in 1914 and *The Birth of a Nation* (187 min.) in 1915.

In terms of their social impact, the silent movies made during this period established trends that continue today. They appealed to all socioeconomic levels and stimulated the popular imagination through their establishment and codification of narrative genres and character stereotypes, particularly those that reinforced prejudices against Native Americans, African Americans, and foreigners in general. Their depiction of certain types of behavior considered immoral provoked calls for censorship, which would become an even bigger problem in the next decade and on into today and raised issues concerning movie content and violence. Although most jobs in the film industry remained male-dominated for the next fifty years, at least acting jobs for women were plentiful from the beginning. Two female directors were at work— Lois Weber and Alice Guy Blaché—and the African American actor Bert Williams starred in his first movie in 1915.

The movie director was central to the development of the art of the motion picture in these early years. D. W. Griffith would soon emerge as the most important of these figures, and *The Birth of a Nation* would become known as one of the most important and controversial movies ever made. While its racist content is repugnant, its form is technically brilliant. Griffith, who borrowed freely from other early filmmakers, was an intuitive and innovative artist, and in this legendary movie we see him perfecting and regularizing (if not inventing) a style that included a dazzling set of technical achievements: the 180-degree system; cutting between familiar types of shots (close-up, medium shot, long shot, extreme long shot, and soft-focus shot); multiple camera setups, accelerated montage, and panning and tilting; and the exploitation of camera angles, in-camera dissolves and fades, the flashback, the iris shot, the mask, and the split screen. He also placed a high value on using a full symphonic score and, more important, developing screen acting by training actors for the special demands of the silent cinema. The longest (3 hours) and most expensive ($110,000) American movie yet made, *The Birth of a Nation* attracted enormous audiences, garnered the critics' praise, and earned, within five years of its opening, approximately $15 million. However, the social and political stance of its story had another impact.

Born in Kentucky, Griffith, who was in sympathy with the antebellum South, tells his story by distorting history and reaffirming the racist stereotypes of his time and background. The movie provoked controversy and riots and was banned in many Northern states. Yet this profoundly American epic, a work of vicious propaganda, is also a cinematic masterpiece that garnered international prestige for American silent movies. Unfortunately—for the future history of the movies—it demonstrated how a manipulative movie could appeal to the public's worst prejudices and make a fortune as a result. Although Griffith made other films, including such silent masterpieces as *Intolerance* (1916), *Broken Blossoms* (1919), *Way down East* (1920), *Orphans of the Storm* (1921), and *Dream Street* (1921)—a very early but unsuccessful attempt to add recorded voices to a movie—his career was virtually finished by 1931.

The most successful American silent feature movies were epics (Erich von Stroheim's *Greed*, 1924), melodramas (King Vidor's *The Big Parade*, 1925), and comedies. Comedy in particular was a major factor in Hollywood's early success. There were gifted comic actors (Buster Keaton, Charles Chaplin, Roscoe "Fatty" Arbuckle, Harold Lloyd,

The first female director Among early filmmakers, Alice Guy Blaché stands out as the first female director in film history. Born in France, where she worked with the Gaumont Film Company, she came to the United States shortly after 1907, founding her own studio and making dozens of narrative films, most of which are lost. *Making an American Citizen* (1912; 16 min.) is unremarkable in its theatrical staging and acting but is well photographed and edited. What's most important is its outspoken feminist message. It tells the story of Ivan and his wife, new Russian emigrants. Ivan believes in the Old World custom of wife abuse. In this shot, a well-dressed New Yorker threatens Ivan when he catches him beating his wife (note the Statue of Liberty in the background). This and other encounters with liberated American males (including a judge who sentences him to prison) convince him to love and respect his wife. With the happy ending, he is, as the title card proclaims, "Completely Americanized." Guy Blaché was not only ahead of her time as a film director, but also highly optimistic in her views about American male-female relationships.

The Birth of a Nation The turning point in D. W. Griffith's great epic (1915) comes in the middle of the movie, as the title card says: "And then, when the terrible days were over and a healing time of peace was at hand . . . came the fated night of April 14, 1865." The scene is Ford's Theatre in Washington, D.C., where a gala performance is being held to celebrate General Robert E. Lee's surrender. In this shot, President and Mrs. Abraham Lincoln enter and greet the enthusiastic audience. Moments later, he is assassinated, ending Part I, "War," and opening Part II, "Reconstruction," a saga of Southern white racism that is the most controversial part of the movie.

Stan Laurel and Oliver Hardy), innovative directors (Mack Sennett and Hal Roach), and such enduring silent movies (shorts, series, and features) as Chaplin's *The Gold Rush* (1925) and Keaton's *The General* (1926).

Other notable films produced in this period include Robert J. Flaherty's *Nanook of the North* (1922), regarded as the first significant documentary film. The art of animation progressed in the hands of such artists as Otto Messmer (the Felix the Cat series), Walt Disney, who made his first cartoons in 1922, and Max and Dave Fleischer, who experimented with color and sound in the early 1920s and whose most endearing character was Betty Boop. Benefiting from Griffith's enormous influence, other filmmakers made improvements in design, lighting, cameras and lenses, the use of color, special effects, and editing equipment. Nothing, of course, would be more important than the experiments with sound that led to the complete transformation of the movie industry after 1927. In the meantime, however, international developments were influencing film history.

1919–1931: German Expressionism

During part of the period just discussed, Eastern and Western Europe were engulfed in chaos. The First World War (1914–18), in which many millions of people died, pitted the United Kingdom, Russia, Italy, and the United States against Germany, Austria-Hungary, the Ottoman Empire, and Bulgaria. (The

A great silent movie challenges the American dream
King Vidor was one of several important directors working in the early 1920s who learned his art from D. W. Griffith. In *The Crowd* (1928), Vidor dared—in the Roaring Twenties, a period of relative prosperity before the stock-market crash of 1929—to make a social critique of the American dream of opportunity and getting ahead. It tells the tragic story of a man who refuses to conform in the New York business world, suggested by the office environment pictured here, which reduces him and other employees to nonentities. The story seems to end with the promise of future happiness for the man and his wife, but it's really ambiguous, leaving us to use our own values and experiences to come to grips with the characters' fate. In the silent-movie period, exhibitors were sometimes offered the choice of alternate endings, particularly for movies with a controversial conclusion. Vidor shot seven different endings for *The Crowd* and offered two of them to the theater owners. (Here we refer to what the director called the "realistic" ending.)

United States, isolationist and opposed to the war, did not enter the conflict until 1917.) In March 1917, the Russian Revolution overthrew Czar Nicholas II. These events changed the world order.

By the end of the war, Germany had suffered a humiliating defeat. But a new democratic government emerged, known unofficially as the Weimar Republic. Seeking to revitalize the film industry and create a new image for the country, the government subsidized the film conglomerate known as UFA (Universum-Film AG), whose magnificent studios, the largest and best equipped in Europe, enabled the German film industry to compete with those of other countries as well as to attract filmmak-

ers from around the world. This led to Germany's golden age of cinema, which lasted from 1919 to Adolf Hitler's rise to power in 1933. Its most important artistic component was the German Expressionist film, which flourished from 1919 to 1931.

German film artists entered the postwar period determined to reject the cinematic past and enthusiastically embrace the avant-garde. Expressionism had flourished in Germany since the early twentieth century in painting, sculpture, architecture, music, literature, and theater. After the war, it reflected the general atmosphere in postwar Germany of cynicism, alienation, and disillusionment. German Expressionist film presents the physical world on the screen as a projection, or expression, of the subjective world, usually that of the film's protagonist. Its chief characteristics are distorted and exaggerated settings; compositions of unnatural spaces; the use of oblique angles and nonparallel lines; a moving and subjective camera; unnatural costumes, hairstyles, and makeup; and highly stylized acting. The classic examples are Robert Wiene's *The Cabinet of Dr. Caligari* (1920), Paul Wegener and Carl Boese's version of *The Golem* (1920), F. W. Murnau's *Nosferatu, a Symphony of Horror* (1922)—the first vampire film—and *The Last Laugh* (1924), Fritz Lang's *Metropolis* (1927) and *M* (1931), G. W. Pabst's *Pandora's Box* (1929), and Josef von Sternberg's *The Blue Angel* (1930).

The most famous expressionist film, and the one traditionally cited as the epitome of the style, is Wiene's *The Cabinet of Dr. Caligari*. What we remember most about this disturbing, complicated story of fantasy and horror told by a madman is its design. The floors, walls, and ceilings of the interior sets are sharply angled; windows admit no natural light, though shafts of illusionistic light and shadow are painted on the walls and floors of the sets; dim staircases seem to lead nowhere; the calligraphy of the titles is bizarre, as is the color tinting—blue, sepia, rose, and green (in the 1996 restored DVD edition). All this differentiates night from day and underscores the different moods. The exterior sets are equally artificial, with buildings, piled on top of one another, jutting upward at strange angles.

German Expressionist film was a short-lived but unforgettable phenomenon, disappearing within

[1]

[2]

Inside *The Cabinet of Dr. Caligari* In Robert Wiene's eerie, foreboding movie (1920), Dr. Caligari (Werner Krauss) operates a carnival attraction featuring a somnambulist (sleepwalker) named Cesare (Conrad Veidt); the "cabinet" in the title refers not only to the type of early freak show called a "cabinet of curiosities" but also to the coffinlike box in which Cesare "sleeps" until Caligari awakens him and orders him to commit murders. The title card shown here [1], written in exaggerated letters, speaks in a folksy tone while echoing the graphics of the movie's painted settings. The power of these settings is evident when we see [2] Dr. Caligari (*left*) attempting to rouse Cesare (*right*), who is presumably "asleep" while standing upright in Caligari's cabinet.

ten years of its establishment. There are aesthetic, political, economic, and social reasons for this. Even though it gave birth to the horror-film genre, in terms of aesthetics German audiences did not crave a steady diet of such films. As far as politics goes, because it emphasized the inner rather than the outer world, Hitler (now rising to power) saw it as a revolt against the traditional values that he sought to preserve. With their lavish studio settings, expressionist films were expensive to make. Furthermore, foreign films were taking an increasing share of the German market, prompting the German film industry to copy them in order to hold its market share. When the government tightened control of UFA, it became clear that Hitler would curtail freedom of expression when he came to power in 1933. Thus, many great German filmmakers were lured to the United States, stimulating the aesthetics of Hollywood production for decades to come. Soon, certain tendencies of the expressionist look became evident in Hollywood's psychological dramas, horror movies, and most notably, the film noir. To quote film historians Gerald Mast and Bruce F. Kawin, "It is difficult to imagine the history of American cinema without this infusion of both visual imagery and thematic commentary from Weimar Germany."[9]

1918–1930: French Avant-Garde Filmmaking

In the 1920s, Paris was the world's center of avant-garde experimentation in painting, literature, drama, music, and film. It was a time when the philosophical approaches of surrealism, cubism, dadaism, and expressionism led to an explosion of artistic styles and movements. The French Avant-Garde film movement included both intellectuals and artists who took their inspiration not only from Karl Marx and Sigmund Freud, but also from the experimental French filmmakers who preceded them in the earliest years of the movies: Georges Méliès, Ferdinand Zecca, Max Linder, Émile Cohl, Jean Durand, and Louis Feuillade, pioneering

[9]Gerald Mast and Bruce F. Kawin, *A Short History of the Movies*, 10th ed. (New York: Pearson/Longman, 2008), p. 193.

[1]

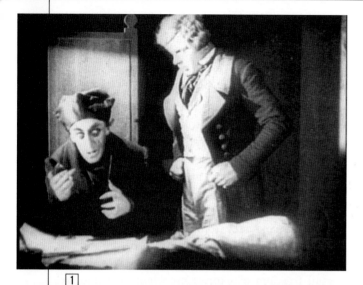

[2]

Dr. Caligari's influence Although Robert Wiene's _The Cabinet of Dr. Caligari_ (1920) is traditionally cited as the best example of German Expressionism, expressionist elements figure strongly in F. W. Murnau's _Nosferatu, a Symphony of Horror_ (1922), the first of many film adaptations of the Dracula story, and _The Last Laugh_ (1924), a charming fable about social justice. Their narratives could not be more different, yet they are linked by their reliance on expressionist design. In contrast to _Dr. Caligari_, where the expressionism relies mostly on graphic effects, those in _Nosferatu_ rely primarily on cinematic effects: low camera angles (as seen in shot [1]), makeup and costume design, lighting, and editing create an eerie mise-en-scène. And even though the vampire figure is truly scary (Nosferatu is played by the memorable Max Schreck, who, pictured here with Gustav von Wangenheim as the real-estate agent, looks like a rat), the movie also manages to make him a sympathetic human being. Far more sympathetic—and far more realistic—is the principal character of _The Last Laugh_, an unnamed hotel porter played equally memorably by Emil Jannings. Here, expressionism can be seen in the mise-en-scène and actor's movements as well as in the composition, play of light and shadow, and exaggerated costume [2], all of which are subtler than what we see in either _Dr. Caligari_ or _Nosferatu_. _The Last Laugh_ is also important for its impressive use of the moving camera and the camera's subjective point of view.

its perceptions, dreams, or hallucinations. Dadaist and surrealist cinema attacks normal narrative conventions by eliminating causality, emphasizing chance and unexpected occurrences, and creating strange and shocking relationships among images. The result is a visual world that appears to be neurotic, unnatural, and illogical, resisting analysis and conclusion by the viewer. And because it emphasizes free association over conventional cinematic language, it attracted painters who were visual artists first and filmmakers second. (Although dada preceded surrealism, they coexisted in the 1920s to such an extent that the two words are often used interchangeably to describe works that demonstrate these characteristics.) In France, the major filmmakers working in these movements include the American-born Man Ray (_Emak-Bakia_, 1926); Jean Epstein, whose _The Fall of the House of Usher_ (1928), inspired by one of Edgar Allan Poe's most famous tales, includes dreamy, impressionistic visual effects (including slow motion, out-of-focus shots, multiple exposures, and distortions); René Clair (_Entr'acte_, 1924); Fernand Léger (_Ballet_

artists who influenced the course of avant-garde and experimental filmmaking around the world.

The French movies that we will discuss tend to fit into one of three different types: (1) short dadaist and surrealist films of an anticonventional, absurdist nature; (2) short naturalistic psychological studies; or (3) feature-length films that also emphasize pure visual form.

Dada and surrealism were two European movements in the arts that sought, provocatively and irreverently, to shock the viewer with surprises and unexpected juxtapositions. Specifically, they attempted to re-create the free play of the mind in

mécanique, 1924); and Germaine Dulac, one of the cinema's first female artists, whose *The Seashell and the Clergyman* (1928) is one of the two acknowledged masterpieces of surrealist cinema.

The other masterpiece is *An Andalusian Dog* (1929), created by two Spanish artists working in Paris: painter Salvador Dalí and filmmaker Luis Buñuel. Here, the logic is that of a dream, with its visual effects including an opening sequence in which we see a razor slitting a woman's eyeball (for an image of this famous shot, see page 78). While Dali soon returned to painting his surrealist masterpieces (including his version of Leonardo's *Mona Lisa* with his own face replacing hers), Buñuel became one of the very few major directors to continue making surrealist feature movies, including *Viridiana* (1961), *Belle de Jour* (1967), and *The Discreet Charm of the Bourgeoisie* (1972). The second type of French Avant-Garde filmmaking in the 1920s consists of psychological studies that emphasize naturalism, the idea that an individual's fate is determined by heredity and environment, not free will. This becomes very powerful in a film such as *Rien que les heures* (1926), by the Brazilian-born Alberto Cavalcanti. A multilayered study of Paris over the course of a day, the film employs cinematic effects, including bold wipes, freeze-frames, double exposures, and split screens. It also reflects the influence of Soviet Montage in its juxtapositions and linkages of shots, some through contrast, others through irony, and still others unrelated. The overall impression of this film (which fits into a small, impressive category of films known as "city symphonies") is that of a mosaic: the images relate only when they are considered in connection to the whole picture. Also impressive are Dimitri Kirsanoff's *Ménilmontant* (1926) and Marcel L'Herbier's *L'Argent* (1928).

All of the films discussed so far in this section in one way or another emphasize visual form for its own sake, have a comparatively short duration, and for the most part were made independently of the French film industry. There was, however, another type of French Avant-Garde filmmaking of the 1920s that includes narrative (often feature-length) movies that are far more ambitious in their scope, length, and overall visual effect. These

Surrealism on film Inspired by Edgar Allan Poe's famous story, Jean Epstein's *The Fall of the House of Usher* (1928) remains captivating with its complex psychological themes, haunting exteriors and interiors, and overall dreamlike quality. In this image, Madeleine Usher (Marguerite Gance) returns from the tomb in which she was buried alive by her brother, Sir Roderick Usher (Jean Debucourt), who dies from fright when she falls upon him.

Turning of *The Wheel* While the movies have always been fascinated by trains, Abel Gance's *The Wheel* (1923) is obsessed with them. Its extraordinary mise-en-scène is a world surrounded by locomotives, tracks, smoke, and railroad workers. This highly melodramatic story contains elements that remind us of classical tragedy, and its sweeping vision of life is matched by a vividly avant-garde style, creating an unforgettable milestone in French cinema.

include Abel Gance's *The Wheel* (1923), which embodies naturalistic philosophy and reflects Griffith's editing style, and *Napoléon* (1927), an almost 6-hour epic of astonishing cinematic beauty and power; Jean Cocteau's *The Blood of a Poet* (1930); Jean Vigo's *À propos de Nice* (1930); René Clair's *An Italian Straw Hat* (1928); and the strangely powerful films of Danish-born Carl Theodor Dreyer, particularly his formalist masterpiece *The Passion of Joan of Arc* (1928). These films, especially the short ones, which are often screened in film history courses, offer an excellent introduction to the diverse art of the French silent movie in the 1920s.

1924–1930: The Soviet Montage Movement

The Soviet Montage movement represents, with the German Expressionist film movement, one of the twin high points of cinematic experimentation, innovation, and achievement in the years between the end of the First World War in 1918 and the coming of sound in 1927. After the Bolshevik (Communist) Revolution of October 1917, led by Vladimir Ilyich Lenin, the challenge was to reunify a shattered nation. Lenin famously proclaimed that cinema would be the most important of the arts in this effort and valued the movies' power to both attract and indoctrinate audiences. He nationalized the film industry and established a national film school to train filmmakers to make propaganda films in a documentary style. Between 1917 and 1929, the Soviet government supported the kind of artistic experimentation and expression that is most effectively seen in the work of four directors: Dziga Vertov, Lev Kuleshov, Sergei Eisenstein, and Vsevolod I. Pudovkin. What they all share in varying degrees is a belief in the power of montage (they adopted the French word for "editing") to fragment and reassemble footage so as to manipulate the viewer's perception and understanding.

Vertov was the first great theorist and practitioner of the cinema of propaganda in documentary form. In 1922, the year of Robert J. Flaherty's *Nanook of the North*, Vertov launched *kino-pravda* (literally, "film truth"). He was influenced by the spirit of Flaherty and the Lumières, which focused

A day in the life of the Russians Dziga Vertov's *The Man with the Movie Camera* (1929) is about life (how the Russians live) and movies (how they are made) and, on first viewing, does not seem to distinguish between the two. In this image, we see the real subject: the man with the movie camera. As a record of human life, it is the prototypical movie. Vertov shows us how to frame reality and movement: through the human eye and the camera eye, or through windows and shutters. But to confound us, he also shows us—through such devices as the freeze-frame, split screen, stop-action, slow motion, and fast motion—how the cinematographer and editor can transform the movements of life into something that is unpredictable. He not only proves that the camera has a life of its own, but also reminds us of the editor, who is putting all of this footage together. Reality may be in the control of the artist, his camera, and its tricks but it also finds definition within the editor's presentation and ultimately the viewer's perception.

on everyday experiences, as well as by the avant-garde pursuit of innovation. Vertov is best known today for *The Man with the Movie Camera* (1929). Kuleshov, a legendary teacher who was influenced by the continuity editing in Griffith's *Intolerance* (1916), built significantly on Griffith's ideas. As a result, he became less interested in how editing helps to advance the narrative than in how it can create nonliteral meaning and thus more interested in discontinuity rather than continuity. Among his many feature-length films is *The Extraordinary Adventures of Mr. West in the Land of the Bolsheviks* (1924). Pudovkin took a third approach to montage, one based on the idea that a film was not shot, but rather built up from its footage. This is reflected in his film *Mother* (1926), which uses extensive crosscutting of images, such as a sequence of shots showing a prison riot intercut with shots of ice breaking up on a river (a reference to Griffith's *Way down East* [1920]). Because his approach emphasized the continuity of the film, where the shots are connected like the links in a chain, it is called *linkage*.

In the first two decades after the birth of the movies, two pioneering geniuses tower above all other filmmakers: D. W. Griffith and Sergei Eisenstein. While they share several notable characteristics—chiefly, inventing new modes of cinematic expression and producing epic historical movies—they are very different artists. Griffith was an American, a capitalist in his entrepreneurial production activities, and a Southern sentimentalist at heart. Unlike Eisenstein, he was self-taught (there were no film schools in the United States until the 1930s); he was not an intellectual, and he was influenced primarily by English literature and theater, in which he worked as an actor and director before turning to film. He did not write theory, but rather produced movies that exemplified his concepts.

By contrast, Eisenstein, a Russian Orthodox Christian, was also a Marxist intellectual whose propaganda movies were financed by the Soviet government. He studied to be an engineer, but after the 1917 revolution joined an avant-garde theater group, where he was shaped by many powerful influences, including the theory and practice of world-famous directors Konstantin Stanislavsky and Vsevolod Meyerhold, by Marx and Freud, and by contemporary German, Russian, and American movies, including those of Griffith. From these varied sources, he developed his own theories of how an aesthetic experience can influence a viewer's psychological and emotional reactions. Unlike Griffith, Eisenstein was a modernist with a commitment to making cinema an art independent from the other forms of creative expression. His films, few in number, are stirring achievements: *Strike* (1925), *The Battleship Potemkin* (1925), *October* (*Ten Days That Shook the World*, 1928), *Alexander Nevsky*

Eisenstein's battle spectacle: *Alexander Nevsky*
Sergei Eisenstein's *Alexander Nevsky* (1938) stands out among Eisenstein's other movies, concerned chiefly with the class wars, for its emphasis on nationalism and patriotism. Focusing on Alexander Nevsky, a Russian prince who defended Russia's northwest territories against invading Teutonic hordes in the thirteenth century, the movie's parallels to contemporary events (i.e., the threat of invasion of Russia by Nazi Germany) were unmistakable. But the movie is far more than a political parable. The movie's set piece—the "Battle on the Ice" sequence, choreographed to Sergei Prokofiev's stirring score—has influenced many other movie battle scenes (e.g., battles in the *Star Wars* saga), particularly in its massing of forces, brutal warfare, and defining costumes. Noteworthy is Eisenstein's reversal of traditional iconography: throughout, as in this image, the bad guys (the Teutons) are in white, while the Russian forces are in black.

(1938; codirected by Dmitri Vasilyev), *Ivan the Terrible, Parts I and II* (1944, 1958), and *Que Viva México* (1930–32, uncompleted and unreleased).

Eisenstein regarded film editing as a creative process that functioned according to the dialectic propounded by Karl Marx, as well as the editing concepts of Griffith and Kuleshov. In theory, Eisenstein viewed the process of historical change as a perpetual conflict of opposing forces, in which a primary force (thesis) collides with a counterforce (antithesis) to produce a third force (synthesis), a new contradiction that is more than the sum of its parts and that will become the basis of a new conflict. In filmmaking practice, one shot (thesis) collides with another shot of opposing content (antithesis) to

The beginnings of a revolution In the first part of *Battleship Potemkin* (1925), Sergei Eisenstein steadily builds a case for the crew members' discontent with their lot—a discontent that will lead to violent revolt. Among other things, the sailors are unhappy with the ship's food. In this image, they examine a slab of the rotten meat they are forced to eat: "We've had enough rotten meat. It's not fit for pigs." Although the meat is crawling with maggots, the ship's doctor tells them that it will be edible if they just wash it off.

produce a new idea (synthesis). The result emphasizes a dynamic juxtaposition of individual shots that not only calls attention to each of these shots but also forces the viewer to reach conclusions about the interplay between them. This "montage of attractions," as Eisenstein called it, presents arbitrarily chosen images (some of them independent of the action) to create the maximum psychological impact. Thus conditioned, viewers would have in their consciousness the elements that would lead them to the overall concept that the director wanted to communicate. Artfully handled, of course, this is manipulation of the highest order, propaganda created to serve the Soviet state. The purest, most powerful example of this approach to filmmaking is *Battleship Potemkin* (1925).

Eisenstein's *Battleship Potemkin* is one of the fundamental landmarks of cinema. Indeed, it has become so popular from screenings in film-studies courses that, over the years, its ability to surprise has diminished. Nevertheless, it is essential to know why it is important to film history. The movie depicts two events—the 1905 workers' mutiny on the *Potemkin* and the subsequent slaughter of ordinary citizens on the Odessa Steps—and, through its dramatic reenactment of those events, provides a successful example of revolution against oppression. Overall, the film's classic five-part structure emphasizes the need for unity in such struggles, but it is the "Odessa Steps" sequence that most people remember, even though its impact may lessen when seen out of context, as it so often is. The sequence, set in Odessa on the wide steps that lead from the town to the harbor, depicts czarist troops brutally killing ordinary citizens, who are celebrating the successful mutiny on the *Potemkin*. Indeed, although the mass is the protagonist, it is the individual faces that we remember. The movie's brutal form (jump cuts and montage editing) perfectly matches the brutality of the massacre. Many directors have been influenced by Eisenstein's theory of montage; some pay homage to the "Odessa Steps" sequence, and others spoof it.

Battleship Potemkin is a great film not only because of its individual elements—the depth of Eisenstein's humanity, the historical and social significance of its story, the formal perfection of its rhythm and editing, and its worldwide influence—but also because of the synergy by which each of these elements is enhanced by the others.

1927–1947: Classical Hollywood Style in Hollywood's Golden Age

The golden age of Hollywood, the most powerful and prolific period of film history yet, included the transition from silent to sound production, consolidation of the studio system, exploitation of familiar genres, imposition of the Motion Picture Production Code, changes in the look of movies, and the economic success of feature-length narrative films. Yet it was less a movement than a force, for in this period, the movies became inextricably linked with the development of American culture and society. From this point forward, the movies defined America, and America defined itself through the movies. (The formidable technological and organizational challenges that enabled these achievements are covered in Chapter 11.)

Populism and popcorn Frank Capra's *Mr. Deeds Goes to Town* (1936), *Mr. Smith Goes to Washington* (1939), and *Meet John Doe* (1941) are often described as a populist trilogy. Indeed, they are emblematic of populism in their belief that ordinary people have the right and power to struggle against the privileged elite. *Mr. Smith Goes to Washington* offers a very sentimental vision of America, filled with stereotypes. Yet it was very successful with the American public, which was dissatisfied with Washington at the end of the Great Depression. In this image, Smith (James Stewart) finishes his filibuster before the U.S. Senate by pleading with his fellow senators to stand up and fight the corruption that is preventing the realization of his dream to finance a national camp for boys. Considering the national situation, this is a small issue indeed. And while it is almost impossible to imagine a similar incident paralyzing Washington today, it gives hope that the common man still has a voice in the direction of our country.

"Wait a minute. You ain't heard nothin' yet!" While these are not the first words we hear Jack Robin (Al Jolson) speak in *The Jazz Singer* (1927; director: Alan Crosland), they are the most memorable. Imagine the excitement of the 1927 audience hearing—for the first time—actors speaking in a movie. This is the highly melodramatic story of a young Jewish boy, Jakie Rabinowitz, who does not want to follow in his father's footsteps and become a cantor; instead, he becomes Jack Robin, a famous "jazz singer" in Broadway shows. It's a classic show-business movie, and Jolson, the country's biggest star in the 1920s, gracefully sings, whistles (image), and dances his way through it. His performance of several songs in blackface makeup may lead us today to make assumptions about Jolson's attitudes about race. Those assumptions should be tempered, however, by an acknowledgment that Jolson was a prominent leader in the fight against show-biz segregation and was influential in promoting the careers of African American actors, singers, songwriters, and writers.

None of this could have been achieved without the efficiency of the studio system, which standardized the way movies were produced. It provided a top-down organization with management controlling everything, especially the employees, who regardless of their status were treated as employees, not artists, and whose careers were subject to the strict terms of their contracts. The transition to sound began in 1926 with the production of some short as well as feature films with recorded sound, and earlier experimental "talkies" were well known back to 1900. But once audiences saw Al Jolson—who in his prime was known as "the world's greatest entertainer"—in Alan Crosland's *The Jazz Singer* (1927), with its synchronized music score and a few

sequences of synchronized sound, they wanted more. Its appeal was probably due less to the few moments of sound than to Jolson's exciting screen persona and his unexpected vocal ad-libbing. The first all-talking film was a routine gangster melodrama, Brian Foy's *The Lights of New York* (1928). Once the conversion to sound was completed in 1930, weekly attendance at the movies and box-office receipts had increased by 50 percent, again proving the Hollywood principle that profits derive from giving the public what it wants. Between 1927 and 1941 (when film production was reduced sharply due to wartime considerations), Hollywood produced over 10,000 movies, an average of 744 each year (compared to 607 produced in 2006).

Screwball comedy The genre of screwball comedy—popular during the Great Depression in the 1930s because it offered an escape from reality—continues to exist today (for example, in movies such as Joel and Ethan Coen's *Intolerable Cruelty* [2003] or George Clooney's *Leatherheads* [2008]), but without the wit or sting of the original. Its principal characteristics include stories of mistaken identity, often involving a person of the working class who accidentally (or not so accidentally) meets with someone from the upper class and, contrary to all expectations, becomes romantically involved; rapid, witty dialogue; and farcical—even fantastic—rags-to-riches plot situations. Mitchell Leisen's *Easy Living* (1937) easily fits the bill. Its script by Preston Sturges, a master of the genre, begins when tycoon John Ball (Edward Arnold), who resents his wife's buying a new sable coat, throws it from his penthouse roof. It lands on Mary Smith (Jean Arthur), an office worker, who is riding on the top of a Fifth Avenue double-decker bus (behind her, the man in the turban is a classic bit of screwball incongruity). Seeing the coat, people assume she is rich, and she quickly learns to enjoy that illusion as she is enticed into a world of glamour and falls improbably in love with John Ball, Jr. (Ray Milland).

The genres dominated production: screwball comedies, musicals, gangster movies, historical epics, melodramas, newspaper and horror movies, Westerns, and biographies. Many of these movies were forgettable, but the remaining ones are some of Hollywood's most important, influential, and memorable creations.

While the moguls ran a tight, highly profitable business within their fortresslike studio walls, outside there were calls for censorship, which, if not answered, threatened those profits. During the early 1920s, after several years of relatively frank portrayals of sex and violence on-screen (a period in which the industry also suffered a wave of scandals), Hollywood faced a credible threat of censorship from state governments and boycotts from Catholic and other religious groups. In 1922, in response to these pressures, Hollywood producers formed a regulatory agency called the Motion Picture Producers and Distributors of America (MPPDA, later the Motion Picture Association of America, or MPAA), headed by Will Hays. Originally conceived of as a public-relations entity to offset bad publicity and deflect negative attention away from Hollywood, the Hays Office (as the agency was commonly known) in 1930 adopted the Motion Picture Production Code, a detailed set of guidelines concerning acceptable and unacceptable subject matter. Nudity, adultery, homosexuality, gratuitous or unpunished violence, and religious blasphemy were among the many types of content that the code strongly discouraged. Perhaps even more significant, the code explicitly stated that art can influence, for the worse, the morality of those who consume it (an idea that Hollywood has been reconsidering ever since).

Adherence to the Motion Picture Code remained fundamentally voluntary until the summer of 1934, when Joseph Breen, a prominent Catholic layman, was appointed head of the Production Code Administration (PCA), the enforcement arm of the MPPDA. After July 1, 1934, all films would have to receive an MPPDA seal of approval before being released. For at least twenty years, the Breen Office rigidly controlled the general character and the particular details of Hollywood storytelling. After a period of practical irrelevance, the code was officially replaced in 1968, when the MPAA adopted the rating system that remains in use today.

Movies produced during Hollywood's golden age were made to be entertaining and successful at the box office, and the result was a period of stylistic conformity, not innovation. If an idea worked once, it usually worked again in a string of similar movies. The idea was to get the public out of the house and into the theater, give people what they wanted (entertainment, primarily), and thus help them forget the Depression and the anxieties caused

Censorship threatens the release of _Baby Face_ The forces that wanted to censor the movies would have found plenty to dislike in Alfred E. Green's _Baby Face_ (1933). Indeed, the released version would not have received a Breen Office seal of approval after July 1, 1934. It tells the story of Lily Powers (Barbara Stanwyck), who sleeps her way from her father's rough Pittsburgh speakeasy to Wall Street and then, floor by floor, up to the executive suite, the camera following her conquests by panning up the side of the obviously phallic building. At each new floor, she gets a better job and a more powerful lover. Lily's a Depression-era stereotype: a calculating, relentless "gold digger." And at a time when interracial friendships in the movies were virtually taboo, the industry's critics would have been further annoyed by Lily's keeping her African American friend and coworker by her side through her adventures. Eventually, she is in deeper than she thinks: one lover murders another (a married man) and then commits suicide (in this image, she has just discovered the two bodies). The movie ends when yet another lover attempts suicide but recovers with Lily looking on, not knowing what's coming next. Because the Motion Picture Production Code was not yet fully in power, the studio tried to get away with this version, but the New York State Censorship Board rejected it, so it trimmed one lascivious male's gaze; some of Lily's seduction scenes; a reference to Friedrich Nietzsche's philosophy, which improbably prompted Lily's rise to power; and a potentially offensive reference to African American food preferences. Finally, it added a new ending: after the last lover recovers from his suicide attempt, Lily returns the money and jewels he's given her, helps him to restore his reputation in the banking world, and then they both move to Pittsburgh where, presumably, they will live happily ever after. This new ending conformed with the code's principle that movies should endorse morality, not exploit it for entertainment purposes.

The golden age at its popular best: _Gone with the Wind_ Many people think of _Gone with the Wind_ (1939; director: Victor Fleming) as _the_ enduring symbol of the golden age of Hollywood. Its romantic story is told against the sweep of the Civil War, its cast is formidable, its mise-en-scène and music are memorable, and it was the first movie to dominate the Oscars. Furthermore, it has won every award imaginable, and while it isn't a great movie in purely cinematic terms, it is a great crowd-pleaser, as attested to by its periodic theatrical revivals and television screenings. It also reflects the highest possible production values for its time—the studio system at its best—a tribute to the extraordinary commitment of its producer, David O. Selznick, who maintained tight, demoralizing control over every aspect of production. For example, the process of casting Scarlett O'Hara, which was not typical of Hollywood at the time (or at any time), involved a two-year process in which Selznick tested nearly twenty-five major Hollywood and Broadway actors. Ironically, this quintessentially American role went to Vivien Leigh (_left_), a British actress virtually unknown in the American film industry.

by the events leading up to the Second World War. The values stressed in these movies were heroism, fidelity, family life, citizenship, community, and of course, fun. Movies with important ideas were most often softened with comic touches and happy endings. So despite the large output, it is hard to find more than a few movies in Hollywood's golden age that stretched cinematic conventions, challenged prevailing social concepts, or provoked new ways of looking at the world. Hollywood during the golden age was not Europe, with its passion for the avant-garde, the revolutionary, or the film as art; few of

Cinematic innovation in *Citizen Kane* *Citizen Kane* (1941; director: Orson Welles) is marked by brilliant innovations that changed cinematic language forever. Among these is deep-focus cinematography, pioneered by Gregg Toland, which permits action on all three planes of the image. Here, the action is focused both on the foreground and background. As Signor Matiste (Fortunio Bononova, *standing second from left*) becomes increasingly frustrated in his efforts to train the voice of Susan Alexander Kane (Dorothy Comingore), her husband, Charles Foster Kane (Orson Welles), standing in the background, registers his impressions of the rehearsal. Husband, wife, and vocal coach are all participating in a long take, making cutting between them unnecessary. However, Kane will soon make it clear—however small he may look in this image—that he, not Matiste, is in charge of his wife's singing career. She, of course, has nothing to say about it. This is only one of Kane's egotistical mistakes that help to ruin their mutual careers and marriage.

those factors were part of the predominant American movie culture before the Second World War.

In terms of cinematic style, narrative and editing conventions adapted to the challenges of sound production, and there were significant innovations in design, cinematography, lighting, acting, and editing, some related to sound, others not. Black-and-white film remained the industry standard through the early 1950s, despite some interesting feature movies in Technicolor, eventually to become the new industry standard. Other technological advancements during the golden age included improvements in lighting, makeup, and film stock. While the predominant cinematographic style of the 1930s was soft-focus, the new lighting and film stock made it

easier to achieve greater depth of focus, which created the illusion of perspective.

That was all to change with the release of *Citizen Kane* in 1941, some forty-six years after the invention of motion pictures; Orson Welles's film revolutionized the medium and has since been considered the most important movie ever made. There are many reasons for that, but what maintains its reputation is Welles's genius as an artist and his vision of a new kind of cinema. He was twenty-four when he began the project, his first movie. While the story of newspaper magnate Charles Foster Kane rests firmly in the biopic genre, Welles tells it with a complex plot consisting of nine sequences (each of which uses a different tone and style), five of which are flashbacks. Including the omniscient camera, there are seven narrators—not all of whom are reliable—who, taken together, provide a modern psychological portrait of a megalomaniac. Released just seven months before the U.S. declared war in December 1941, this was a radical film for Hollywood. And while the movie is open to various interpretations (the Freudian interpretation of young Charlie's relationship to his mother remaining very influential), *Citizen Kane* carries a strong antifascist message. It warns against Kane's arrogant abuse of the First Amendment right of freedom of speech and press, one of the many evils that Americans, reading their own newspapers, associated with Hitler.

Citizen Kane was also radical in its handling of the prevailing cinematic language of its time. We see this in the astonishing complexity and speed of the narrative. It may not seem so radical today, but that is only because it influenced the structure and pace of nearly every significant movie that came after it. In the other elements of cinematic form, Welles was equally innovative. The stark design of the film is heavily influenced by German Expressionism, as seen in the size, height, and depth of the rooms and other spaces at Xanadu. Through deep-space composition, lighting, deep-focus cinematography, and long takes, cinematographer Gregg Toland achieved the highest degree of cinematic realism yet seen. In contrast to the prevailing soft look of 1930s movies, *Citizen Kane* has a hard finish. The omniscient, probing, and usually moving camera, emphasizing its voyeuristic role, goes directly to the heart of each scene. For the most part, the editing is conventional, most often taking place within the long takes (and thus within the camera). Welles avoids such avant-garde techniques as Soviet Montage, for example, unless he wants to call attention to the editing, as he does in the "News on the March" sequence and the pans and swipes that create the passing of time during the famous breakfast-table sequence. Before going to Hollywood, Welles revolutionized American radio broadcasting, and his sound design for *Kane* creates an aural realism equivalent to the movie's visual realism. He frequently uses overlapping sound, which, like the deep-space composition, bombards us with a lightning mix of information that challenges us to choose what to listen to (just as in real life). The film is also much louder than the typical movie of the time, which is another innovation, and the bravado of its dialogue, sound effects, and music puts it in your ears as well as in your face. Bernard Herrmann's musical score was spare, modernist, and completely ahead of its time. In the film's acting, Welles called on his stage and radio experiences to break another Hollywood convention. Actors did not normally rehearse their lines except in private or for a few minutes with the director before shooting, but Welles rehearsed his cast for a month before shooting began, thus enabling his ensemble of actors to handle long passages of dialogue in the movie's distinctive long takes. And the performances, including Welles as Kane, are unforgettable.

Although *Citizen Kane* has been enormously influential on filmmakers around the world—Martin Scorsese said that Welles influenced more young people to become film directors than anyone else in film history—and references to its unique style have been quoted in dozens of other films, Welles's overall style has never been fully imitated. Even after repeated viewings, its tantalizing story, courageous political stance, provocative ambiguity, and razzle-dazzle style continue to exert their hold.

✴ 1942–1951: Italian Neorealism

With German Expressionism, Soviet Silent Realism, and the French New Wave movements, Italian Neorealism stands as one of the most vital movements in the history of world cinema. Developed during the Second World War, neorealism rose to prominence after the war and then flourished for a relatively short period before ending abruptly. Benito Mussolini, the Fascist dictator who ruled Italy from 1922 to 1943, believed, as did Lenin, in the propaganda power of film. To revive the lackluster film industry, he instituted government subsidies and control, banned American movies, established a national film school, and constructed vast new studios. Although the Italian movies produced during his regime were commercially successful (audiences had no choices), they were artistically inferior to what the French were producing before the war. Mussolini was driven from power in 1943 and executed in 1945, thus providing an opportunity for revitalizing the Italian cinema.

In 1942, Cesare Zavattini, a prolific Marxist screenwriter, launched what came to be known as the neorealist movement, influenced its style and ideology, and led a group of young filmmakers to make film history. The group was influenced not only by Zavattini but also by French poetic realism, a movement that consisted of filmmakers seeking freedom in the increasingly repressive French society of the 1930s, and by two contemporary Italian films: Luchino Visconti's *Ossessione* (1943) and Roberto Rossellini's *Rome, Open City* (1945). Rossellini's film more clearly exhibits every characteristic of neorealism and became the standard for the films that followed.

In cinema, as well as the other visual arts, realism, often an elusive concept, is nothing more or less than the depiction of subjects as they appear to the artist in everyday life, without adornment or interpretation. In the postwar period's neorealism, this definition adhered, but the movement was revolutionary because it deliberately broke with the Fascist past and adopted an ideology that reflects Marxist, Christian, and humanist values. The neorealist filmmakers placed the highest value on the lives of ordinary working people; decried such postwar conditions as widespread unemployment, poverty, child labor, government corruption, and inadequate housing (the results of Fascist rule); and focused on the struggle for a decent life in the postwar world. Politically, neorealism is antiauthoritarian,

An early influence on neorealism Luchino Visconti's *Ossessione* (1943) represents a transition between the lackluster Italian cinema of the pre-Second World War period and the brief but significant flowering of neorealism. It represents the older traditions in several ways: it uses professional actors, is based on an American novel, and is known mainly for its torrid love story. Soon after the two lovers—Giovanna (Clara Calamai), an unhappily married woman, and Gino (Massimo Girotti), a drifter—first meet, they become obsessively involved with one another. *Ossessione* foreshadows neorealism in its depiction of the daily routines of ordinary people, its focus on rural Italy, and its consistent use of long shots to preserve real time and emphasize how the setting constrains the characters from becoming independent. Mostly, though, its austere realism, in form and content, influenced the neorealist filmmakers. The film was remade in the United States twice, both times as *The Postman Always Rings Twice* (1946, director: Tay Garnett; 1981, director: Bob Rafelson).

skeptical of the Catholic Church, antibureaucratic, and socialist. But overall, because it does not have an inherent political purpose, it is traditionally regarded more as a style than an ideology.

Stylistically, its characteristics are specific. Despite the lavish production facilities available at the large studios that Mussolini built (or perhaps because of them), the neorealists sought simplicity in their working methods. They used actual locations rather than studio sites, nonprofessional actors, a documentary visual style that included shooting in the streets with natural light and lightweight cameras, the use of long takes to preserve real time, and the use of deep-space cinematogra-

phy to maintain the look of the actual spaces in which shooting occurred. All of these characteristics broke with the prevailing cinematic conventions in Italy.

The most indispensable neorealist films are Vittorio De Sica's *Shoeshine* (1946), *The Bicycle Thieves* (1948; also known as *The Bicycle Thief*), and *Umberto D.* (1952), which marks the end of the movement; Cesare Zavattini wrote the screenplays for all of these. *The Bicycle Thieves*, the movement's masterpiece, which is set in Rome two years after the end of the war, recounts three consecutive days in the life of Antonio Ricci (Lamberto Maggiorani), a laborer, Maria (Lianella Carell), his wife, and Bruno (Enzo Staiola), his son, who looks about eight years old but nonetheless works twelve hours a day at a gas station. It is a simple but powerful story. Antonio is out of work but, at the beginning of the movie, is offered a job (hanging movie posters) on the condition that he has a bicycle. Because his bicycle is in a pawnshop, his wife substitutes the family linen at the pawnshop so that he can reclaim his bicycle and take the job. On his first morning at work, the bicycle is stolen. His friends help him search for it, but they have no luck. When Antonio spots the thief, the Mafia protects that man. Social forces such as the church and fortunetellers cannot help him. Faced with a practical dilemma, he too becomes a bicycle thief (hence the movie's title) and is caught and publicly humiliated. It ends with Antonio in exactly the same dilemma as the moment the film began. This, then, is the story of a good man caught in a seemingly hopeless world, told with insightful observation and compassion. Its ending, true to the neorealist credo, is ambiguous.

The stylistic characteristics of neorealism—the long takes, the actual locations, the spare dialogue, and so on—allow De Sica to show reality without necessarily interpreting it. Nonetheless, he took complete control over the setting, cinematography, lighting, acting, and sound. Even though it is a sound film, much of its power is its relative silence, particularly its lack of voices. Like many films made before the coming of sound, it demonstrates the intensity of silent acting. One definition of a "classic" movie is that it can mean different things to different people at different times in their lives.

The Bicycle Thieves: a neorealist masterpiece During the three-day chronicle that comprises the plot of *The Bicycle Thieves* (1948; director: Vittorio De Sica)—which recounts the story of Antonio Ricci's (Lamberto Maggiorani) desperate search for his dignity—Bruno (Enzo Staiola), his son, is the one person who stands by him. Through hardship after hardship, their shared bond of love and faith is challenged but never broken. Bruno gives his father the courage to survive through one heartbreaking moment after another, and although the movie ends ambiguously, there is no question that father and son will remain friends. In this image, we see Bruno waving good-bye to his father as they both begin their workday. When director De Sica cast Staiola, an unknown boy from the streets, in this part, he found a natural actor who gave the world an unforgettable performance.

The Bicycle Thieves is such a powerful film because of the director's spare style, humanist treatment of the story, and his willingness to trust his viewers to make up their own mind about what it means.

Although neorealist films were innovative, they were not popular with Italians (who preferred the more upbeat American movies) and consequently not successful at the box office (economic success was not one of the movement's primary goals). Critics, furthermore, thought that the films gave a false, even sentimental, portrayal of Italian society, one inconsistent with a country eager for prosperity and change. The government discouraged the neorealists' interest in social problems by subsidizing instead domestic films that focused on the new

prosperity of the postwar society and implementing taxes and quotas on foreign movies.

By 1952 the movement was finished, yet it had an enormous impact on later Italian and world cinema. In fact, a handful of neorealist films helped to rekindle a greater awareness among filmmakers worldwide of the need to observe real life and to abandon, insofar as possible, the make-believe world of the movie studio. The movement also helped to launch the careers of many great Italian directors, including De Sica, Rossellini, Visconti, Federico Fellini, Michelangelo Antonioni, and Pietro Germi and influenced Italian directors who were not directly involved in the movement, including Pier Paolo Pasolini, Bernardo Bertolucci, Ermanno Olmi, and Paolo and Vittorio Taviani. Filmmakers as different as Satyajit Ray in India and Martin Scorsese in the United States regarded neorealism as the principal inspiration in beginning their careers. Today you'll see its influence in such different movies as Jean-Pierre and Luc Dardenne's *L'Enfant* (2005), John Carney's *Once* (2006), and even Matt Reeves's *Cloverfield* (2008).

1959–1964: French New Wave

After the Second World War, France, which had been occupied by the Nazis between 1940 and 1944, faced a unique set of problems, both foreign and domestic. Abroad, it was engaged in two wars with French-controlled territories: the French Indochina War (1946–54), which ended in a divided but independent Vietnam, and the Algerian War of Independence (1954–62), which led to Algeria's independence from France. At home, in addition to the challenges facing President Charles de Gaulle's government in dealing with myriad social, political, racial, ethnic, and cultural differences produced in part by the twin forces of collaboration and resistance during the Nazi occupation, everywhere there were calls for change coming from students, artists, intellectuals, and philosophers, particularly the existentialists, who called for a new world in which individuals would be more responsible for their actions. The French New Wave was born within this broad context.

The origins of the New Wave were influenced by several movements. The first was the French cinema itself, including the 1930s cinematic style known as *poetic realism*, a term that applied to those movies that treated everyday life with a moody sensitivity to mise-en-scène as well as the more contemporary films of Jean-Pierre Melville. The second was the philosophy of Jean-Paul Sartre, the leading figure in French philosophy in the postwar period, who believed that contemporary artists should rebel against the constraints of society, traditional morality, and religious faith; should accept personal responsibility for their actions; and should thus be free to create their own world. His existentialist views helped shape the new French cinema's depiction of modern human beings, while his Marxist views helped form its interpretations of society and history. Finally, the movement learned much from film critic and director Alexandre Astruc, who declared that a filmmaker should use the camera as personally as the novelist uses a pen, thus giving inspiration to the idea of the movie director as auteur.

Other influences on the French New Wave include Italian Neorealism, the contemporaneous British Free Cinema (discussed on page 462), and contemporary developments in the French documentary film. While the Italians and the British offered models of how to make narrative films that told real stories about real people, *cinéma vérité* evolved in France in the early 1960s as a documentary style (the name, which means "film truth," pays homage to Dziga Vertov's *kino-pravda*—"film truth"—work in the Soviet Montage movement). Among other things, it advocated using the lightweight, portable filmmaking equipment that enhanced a filmmaker's mobility and flexibility. Stylistically, its films had a rough, intimate look that often reflected the informality of the filmmaking process. Filmmakers appeared on-screen, cameras jiggled, framing was often informal, scenes were generally unscripted, and continuity was provided primarily through lots of close-ups and sound tracks that continued under the shots. Later, such stylistic innovations would characterize many New Wave movies.

Film theorist André Bazin, known as the father of the New Wave, synthesized these concepts into the coherent model on which the New Wave was established. This interaction of intellect and creativity recalls the origins of several movements you've already encountered: the German, Soviet, and French film movements of the 1920s. Bazin cofounded *Cahiers du cinéma,* which became the leading French film journal of the time, and in his capacity as editor, he became the intellectual and spiritual mentor of the New Wave. His followers included *Cahiers'* contributors, many of whom would become directors: Jean-Luc Godard, François Truffaut, Claude Chabrol, Jacques Rivette, and Eric Rohmer. Others went directly into filmmaking: Chris Marker, Alain Resnais, Agnès Varda, and Louis Malle. (There were other major directors in postwar France who were not directly involved in the New Wave movement, including Jean Cocteau, Robert Bresson, Jean Renoir, Jacques Tati, Jacques Becker, and Max Ophüls.) Bazin's central tenets were realism, mise-en-scène, and authorship (the director's unique style). For him, the most distinctive nature of a movie was its form rather than its content. Accordingly, he encouraged his followers to see as many films as possible, looking particularly at the relationship between the director and the material. In viewing these films, great and otherwise, the young critics and would-be filmmakers developed a particular fascination with those Hollywood films that seemed to prove what Bazin, following Astruc, was saying about the director-as-author. They recognized that most directors of Hollywood films had little say over most aspects of production, but they believed that through his style, particularly the handling of mise-en-scène, a great director could undermine studio control and transform even the most insignificant Western or detective story into a work of art.

Obviously, the New Wave was based on a theory that advocated a change in filmmaking practices. Truffaut's 1954 *Cahiers* essay "A Certain Tendency of the French Cinema" elaborated on the auteur concept and started a critical controversy that has not yet abated.[10] The issue remains: is it the direc-

---

[10]See François Truffaut, "A Certain Tendency of the French Cinema," in *Movies and Methods: An Anthology*, ed. Bill Nichols, 2 vols. (Berkeley: University of California Press, 1976), I, pp. 224–237.

tor or the entire collaborative team, including the director—that makes a movie? Truffaut idolized directors who made highly personal statements in their films—including Jean Renoir, Jean Cocteau, and Max Ophüls in France, and Orson Welles, Alfred Hitchcock, Howard Hawks, Fritz Lang, John Ford, Nicholas Ray, and Anthony Mann in Hollywood—so his answer was clear: the director was the primary "author" of the work. In another influential *Cahiers* essay, "The Evolution of the Language of Cinema," Bazin described mise-en-scène by stressing that everything we see on the screen has been put there by the director for a reason.[11]

The New Wave directors excelled at demonstrating that cinematic form is more important than content; their films were self-reflexive, focusing attention on them *as* movies and diverting our attention away from their narratives. In this, they manipulate our perceptions and keep an aesthetic and psychological distance between us and their movies. The style, substance, and achievements of the French New Wave directors had an invigorating effect on world cinema, and their movies remain very popular. Among their most important films are Jean-Luc Godard's *Breathless* (1960), François Truffaut's *The 400 Blows* (1959), Claude Chabrol's *The Butcher* (1970), Jacques Rivette's *Celine and Julie Go Boating* (1974), Eric Rohmer's *My Night at Maud's* (1969), Chris Marker's *La Jetée* (1962), Alain Resnais's *Last Year at Marienbad* (1961), Agnès Varda's *Cleo from 5 to 7* (1962), and Louis Malle's *Murmur of the Heart* (1971). Although the movement was finished by 1964, many of these directors continued to make films.

If one movie symbolizes the fresh, innovative spirit of the New Wave it is Godard's *Breathless* (1960), for it offers a comprehensive catalog of the movement's stylistic traits: rapid action, use of handheld cameras, unusual camera angles, elliptical editing, direct address to the camera, acting

French New Wave: beginnings Among the first New Wave movies were François Truffaut's *The 400 Blows* (1959) and Jean-Luc Godard's *Breathless* (1960). Truffaut's protagonist, Antoine Doinel (Jean-Pierre Léaud), is a boy in his early teens who, as we see him here [1], has just escaped from a juvenile detention center; Godard's Michel Poiccard (Jean-Paul Belmondo) is a man in his early thirties who is preparing to steal a car and will shortly murder a policeman [2]. Antoine is just a boy prankster facing an unknown future, but Michel is a dangerous criminal whom the police will soon recognize and shoot in cold blood as he attempts to flee capture. Noteworthy is that Truffaut wrote the original treatment of *Breathless* and, after his great success with *The 400 Blows*, made a gift of it to Godard, suggesting that he submit it as the idea for his own first film.

[11]Among Bazin's essays, students should know "The Myth of Total Cinema," "The Evolution of the Language of Cinema," and "Theater and Cinema," in André Bazin, *What Is Cinema?* ed. and trans. Hugh Gray, 2 vols. (Berkeley: University of California Press, 1967–71), I, pp. 17–22, 23–40, 76–124.

that borders on the improvisational, anarchic politics, and an emphasis on the importance of sound, especially words. It is not any one of these techniques that defines the filmmaker's style, but rather the imagination and energy with which

Hitchcock's influence on the New Wave Alfred Hitchcock's movies were greatly admired by New Wave directors. Claude Chabrol, who carefully studied the movies of the master of suspense and surprise, is noted also for movies that combine romance with gory murders. In *The Butcher* (1970), thought by many to be his masterpiece, a group of schoolchildren accompany Hélène (Stéphane Audran), their teacher, to see a magnificent cave that contains prehistoric drawings. Afterward—in the image here—as they enjoy their picnic lunch, blood drips onto one girl's bread from a fresh corpse on a cliff above. When Hélène sees the body, she suspects that it is yet another woman who has been victimized by the local butcher, a man with whom the teacher has a platonic relationship. After that, the suspense—the effect of which Chabrol learned well from Hitchcock—becomes almost unbearable.

Time and mortality in the New Wave Agnès Varda, one of the very few women in the New Wave movement, was a unique force in shaping it. Her experiments in the handling of cinematic time influenced such contemporaries as Jean-Luc Godard and Alain Resnais. And her concern with the cinematic perception of women is beautifully realized in *Cleo from 5 to 7* (1962). It follows two hours in the life of Cléo (Corinne Marchand), a pop singer who wanders aimlessly around Paris while waiting for the results of a biopsy. Told in near-real time, she grapples with such issues as the meaning of friendship, her work, and mortality. Just before going to the hospital to meet her doctor—fearing that she has cancer—Cléo drops her purse; picking up the pieces, she interprets her broken mirror as an omen of death. To call attention to Cléo's ordeal of killing time, Varda titles each episode and indicates its precise running time (here, translated into English): "Chapter 11—CLÉO from 6:04 to 6:12."

he uses them. *Breathless*, a movie that asserts Godard's personality and ideology, virtually defines what is meant by an auteur film. It tells a conventional crime story in an unconventional manner, rejecting the traditional cinematic values of unity and continuity in favor of discontinuity and contrast. Godard called his work a cinema of "reinvention," meaning that he generally kept all kinds of cinematic language in mind as he created his own. Consequently, by employing the iris-out, Godard not only offers homage to D. W. Griffith but also reminds modern audiences of a seldom-used visual device. Dedicating the film to Monogram Pictures (one of Hollywood's "B" or "Poverty Row" studios), Godard evokes the Hollywood film noir through allusions, direct and indirect, to tough films with tough leading men. He also pays homage to French film director Jean-Pierre Melville, a major influence on the New Wave, by casting him in the movie and patterning the role of his leading male charac-

ter on the model in Melville's *Bob le flambeur* (1956). Finally, Godard includes allusions to writers, composers, and painters. Through this broad range of intertextual reference, or pastiche (making one artwork by mixing elements from others), Godard audaciously links his low-budget film noir with the works of some of the greatest artists of all time.

Most important, though, is Godard's editing, which is central to the telling of this narrative. Here, working in the radical tradition started by Eisenstein and his contemporaries—collision between and among images—Godard consciously and deliberately manipulates the images with such editing techniques as jump cuts and nondiegetic inserts. Thus he deliberately avoids such devices as crosscutting—which traditional directors would have used in cutting between the good guys and bad guys in the film's chase scenes—and the familiar sequence—made up of an establishing shot, long shot, medium shot, and close-up, generally in that order—to set the time and place of an action. The restless rhythm of the editing is perfectly suited to the restless mood of the story and the indecisiveness of the movie's two major characters.

While the term *New Wave* began with the French, its spirit soon spread internationally. These efforts were significantly bolstered in many of the countries discussed below by the establishment of state-supported filmmaking schools and film societies, as well as the availability of lightweight filmmaking equipment. In the United States, the New Wave influence was noticeable early on in Arthur Penn's *Bonnie and Clyde* (1967) and recently in Wes Anderson's *The Royal Tenenbaums* (2001) and Michel Gondry's *Eternal Sunshine of the Spotless Mind* (2004), to cite but three examples.

Many of the techniques pioneered by the French New Wave filmmakers have become commonplace, especially in today's independent cinema, so that Godard's films from the early 1960s still look very modern, and the unusually stylized treatment of time and subjectivity in a film like Alain Resnais's *Last Year at Marienbad* remains cutting-edge to this day, confusing and alienating many viewers used to traditional cinematic conventions.

1947–Present: New Cinemas in Great Britain, Europe, and Asia

World War II, fought mainly in Europe and Asia but involving virtually every country in the world, was the most destructive war in history, killing between 40 million to 50 million people, displacing millions of others from their homes or countries, destroying many historic cities, shattering economies, and leaving the specter of the Holocaust to redefine the concept of a civilized world. It was impossible for many countries to return to normal, even though the victory over fascism held the promise of establishing a new and more just society.

How did filmmakers react to the war? They all knew that whatever they did with their movies, the international landscape had changed utterly and that they must acknowledge the horrors, postwar challenges, and hopes for the future. For some filmmakers, it was an opportunity to express their nation's identity through what we call a *national cinema*. While this term is used generally to describe the films identified by and associated with a specific country—for example, through financing, language, or culture—it remains a subject of debate among film scholars and critics.

In the following pages, we differentiate between two kinds of countries: (1) those that resumed filmmaking pretty much as usual after the war, albeit with a different perspective, audience, and set of responsibilities (e.g., Canada, Australia, New Zealand, Ireland, Italy, Sweden, Spain, Russia and the Soviet Union, Hungary, the former Czechoslovakia and former Yugoslavia, Romania, Bulgaria, and many countries in Central and Latin America, Asia, Africa, and the Middle East), and (2) those that established the new wave movements we discuss below: Great Britain, Denmark, Germany, Japan, and China. Today, new cinemas are also emerging in Albania, Bosnia, Slovenia, Serbia, Hungary, Estonia, Turkey, and the Czech Republic. (We emphasize the new wave movements because they represent pockets of resistance to dominant filmmaking traditions that revitalized the cinemas of their respective countries with a distinctive stylistic effect).

In making this simple distinction and in choosing to discuss the new wave movements, we do not overlook the profound achievements of such British and European directors as Ingmar Bergman, Andrzej Wajda, Michelangelo Antonioni, Satyajit Ray, David Lean, or Federico Fellini, to name only a few—artists whose work significantly altered the psychological and imaginative landscape of postwar filmmaking—or more recent directors—such as Jane Campion, Pedro Almodóvar, Abbas Kiarostami, or Ousmane Sembene—whose films, despite the fact that they don't fall within a definable movement or trend, are widely recognized as modern masterpieces.

Like the original new wave of directors in France, each of the movements described below attempted to (1) make a clean break with the cinematic past, (2) inject new vitality into filmmaking, and (3) explore cinema as a subject in itself.

England and the Free Cinema Movement

The British Free Cinema movement, which developed between 1956 and 1959, like the work of Dziga Vertov and the Italian Neorealists, rejected prevailing cinematic conventions; in so doing, they also rejected a cinema and obstinately class-bound society, turned their cameras on ordinary people and everyday life, and proclaimed their freedom to make films without worrying about the demands of producers and distributors or other commercial considerations. Because the films of the Free Cinema movement were entirely the expression of the people who made them, they serve as another manifestation of the growing postwar movement in Europe toward a new cinema of social realism. Its primary effect was a small but impressive body of documentary films, including Lindsay Anderson's *Every Day Except Christmas* (1957), an affectionate look at the people who make the Covent Garden market such a tradition; Karel Reisz's *We Are the Lambeth Boys* (1958), an attempt to understand working-class youth; and Tony Richardson and Karel Reisz's *Momma Don't Allow* (1955), an admiring view of the emerging British pop culture in the mid-1950s. After the war, the British class system began its slow disintegration, and Anderson understood the inherent challenges facing the country as well as the role that movies might play in the transition, when he defined his approach to filmmaking: "I want to make people—ordinary people, not just Top People—feel their dignity and their importance, so that they can act from these principles. Only on such principles can confident and healthy action be based."[12]

This sentiment and Free Cinema movies helped to inspire the British New Cinema of the 1960s, an almost unique situation in which the documentary form was the catalyst for a revived spirit in narrative filmmaking. Memorable socialist-realist films were outspoken on the subjects of gender, race, and economic disparities among the classes, including

***Victim*: the first major movie about gay rights** The British Free Cinema dealt courageously with controversial issues of class, race, gender, and sexual orientation. Basil Dearden's *Victim* (1961) was the first commercial British film to show that homosexuality existed at every level of contemporary society. At the time, homosexual acts between consenting adults were illegal in Great Britain, and gays suffered widespread discrimination and blackmail. In *Victim*, Dirk Bogarde gave a moving performance as Melville Farr, a distinguished lawyer who is exposed by a blackmailing ring for having had an emotional, but nonsexual, gay affair before he married. In this image, he sees the photograph that triggered the blackmail. Outraged by the widespread injustices against homosexuals, he agrees to help the police by giving evidence in court, knowing that sensational newspaper publicity could ruin his career. Bogarde, then one of England's major stars, was lauded for his personal courage in helping to break a social barrier, and *Victim* was instrumental in changing the social and legal climate. In 1967, Great Britain legalized homosexual acts between consenting adults.

Jack Clayton's *Room at the Top* (1959), Karel Reisz's *Saturday Night and Sunday Morning* (1960), Basil Dearden's *Victim* (1961), Tony Richardson's *The Loneliness of the Long Distance Runner* (1962), Lindsay Anderson's *if . . . .* (1968), Joseph Losey's *The Servant* (1963), Richard Lester's *A Hard Day's Night* (1964), and Ken Loach's *Kes* (1969).

Denmark and the Dogme 95 Movement

Postwar Danish cinema is noted primarily for the Dogme 95 movement, founded in 1995 by three directors, including Lars von Trier, the one best known outside Denmark. The movement was

[12]Lindsay Anderson, qtd. in Richard M. Barsam, *Nonfiction Film: A Critical History,* rev. and exp. ed. (Bloomington: Indiana University Press, 1992), p. 252.

based on the Dogme 95 manifesto of ten rules (known as "The Vow of Chastity"), with which participating directors were required to affirm their compliance. These are

1. Shooting must be done on location. Props and sets must not be brought in (if a particular prop is necessary for the story, a location must be chosen where this prop is to be found).
2. The sound must never be produced apart from the images or vice versa. (Music must not be used unless it occurs where the scene is being shot).
3. The camera must be hand-held. Any movement or immobility attainable in the hand is permitted. (The film must not take place where the camera is standing; shooting must take place where the film takes place).
4. The film must be in colour. Special lighting is not acceptable. (If there is too little light for exposure the scene must be cut or a single lamp be attached to the camera).
5. Optical work and filters are forbidden.
6. The film must not contain superficial action. (Murders, weapons, etc. must not occur.)
7. Temporal and geographical alienation are forbidden. (That is to say that the film takes place here and now.)
8. Genre movies are not acceptable.
9. The film format must be Academy 35mm.
10. The director must not be credited.[13]

This statement of principles brought considerable attention to the country's cinema with such movies as von Trier's *The Idiots* (1998), *Breaking the Waves* (1996), *Dancer in the Dark* (2000), *Dogville* (2003), and *The Five Obstructions* (2003). These rules were rigid, and directors often broke their vows, as seen in such Dogme films as Harmony Korine's *Julien Donkey-Boy* (1999), Lone Scherfig's *Italian for Beginners* (2000), Martin Rengel's *Joy*

[13]http://www.dogme95.dk/the_vow/vow.html.

Breaking the rules in *Breaking the Waves* Even though the Dogme rules are rigid, Lars von Trier's *Breaking the Waves* (1996) demonstrates that a director can subvert them to facilitate production. Although the cinematographer used the requisite handheld camera, many of the scenes were shot not in real locations, but in studio settings. The story takes place in the past, not the here and now, and contrary to Dogme rules, contains nondiegetic music. Furthermore, von Trier takes full credit for his role as director. Nonetheless, a major reason for seeing it is the astonishing performance by Emily Watson as Bess, a simple, childlike woman. When her husband, seriously injured in an oil-rig accident, fears that their sex life has ended, he encourages her to have sexual relations with other men. However, she believes, from voices that she hears, that what she is doing is God's wish. These voices—if, indeed, she hears them—often come to her in a deserted church.

Ride (2001), and Susanne Bier's *Open Hearts* (2002). The Dogme movement—clearly as bold, if not as significant, as the French New Wave—influenced some avant-garde directors in Europe and the United States, and its emphasis on freedom is relevant to filmmakers with access to digital video, home computers, and advanced editing software.

Germany and *Das neue Kino*

Following the Second World War and until 1990 (when it was reunified as the German Democratic Republic), Germany was split into a western and eastern part. In West Germany, the Federal Republic reestablished independent film production, even though German audiences preferred Hollywood movies; in East Germany, film production remained under Soviet control, and little of significance was produced.

In 1962, a movement called *das neue Kino* (the New German Cinema) was born, flourishing until the 1980s. Its founders, a group of young writers and filmmakers, recognized that any attempt to revive the German cinema must deal with two large issues: the Nazi period and the brutal break that it made in the German cultural tradition; and the reemergence of postwar Germany as a divided country, the western part of which was known, like Japan at the same time, as an "economic miracle." In addition, they knew the Italian, French, and British New Cinemas that preceded them and had a genuine affection for established genres in Hollywood, particularly melodrama. Like all serious radical groups, it issued a manifesto:

> The collapse of the conventional German film finally removes the economic basis for a mode of filmmaking whose attitude and practice we reject. With it the new film has a chance to come to life. . . .
>
> We declare our intention to create the new German feature film.
>
> This new film needs new freedoms. Freedom from the conventions of the established industry. Freedom from the outside influence of commercial partners. Freedom from the control of special interest groups.
>
> We have concrete intellectual, formal, and economic conceptions about the production of the new German film. We are as a collective prepared to take economic risks.
>
> The old film is dead. We believe in the new one.[14]

This 1962 document (known as the Oberhausen Manifesto)—fusing economic, aesthetic, and political goals—sought to create a new cinema free from historical antecedents, one that could criticize bourgeois German society and expose viewers to new modes of looking at movies. A short list of the early work of the most significant directors includes Volker Schlöndorff's *Young Torless* (1966); Alexander Kluge's *Artists under the Big Top: Perplexed* (1968); and Margarethe von Trotta's *The German Sisters/Marianne and Juliane* (1981; von Trotta is perhaps the most important of a large group of female directors) Rainer Werner Fassbinder's *The Marriage of Maria Braun* (1979), *Fear of Fear* (1975), and *Berlin Alexanderplatz* (1980; a television series, released theatrically in a 15½-hour version, the longest narrative movie ever made); Wim Wenders's *The Goalie's Anxiety at the Penalty Kick* (1972), *The American Friend* (1977), and *Paris, Texas* (1984); and Werner Herzog's *Even Dwarfs Started Small* (1970), *Aguirre: The Wrath of God* (1972), *Heart of Glass* (1976), and *Nosferatu the Vampire* (1979). Ultimately, the movement sparked a renaissance in German filmmaking by encouraging the production of quality films that created considerable excitement in the international cinema community. Its bold treatments of such contemporary issues as sexuality, immigration, and national identity have had a significant influence on filmmakers worldwide.

Japan and Postwar Filmmaking

The movies were popular in Japan as early as 1896, a year after they were invented in the West, and the Japanese film industry flourished—albeit with a highly stylized form of filmmaking that owed a great deal to Japanese literary and theatrical traditions as well as something to Western cinematic traditions—until World War II.

When the war ended in 1945, much of the country lay in ruins and was under occupation by the Allied powers. As the film industry began to revive, it was strongly influenced by such Hollywood masters as John Ford, Howard Hawks, and Orson Welles. However, filmmakers were limited, both by the occupying powers and by a film industry scarce of money, to making films that extolled the freedoms made possible by democracy, particularly the emancipation of women. The three Japanese directors most familiar in the West are Akira Kurosawa, Kenji Mizoguchi, and Yasujiro Ozu. Mizoguchi and Ozu began their directing careers in the 1920s, but it was not until 1950 that Kurosawa launched the golden age of Japanese filmmaking with *Rashomon*.

To Western viewers, Akira Kurosawa is the most recognizable Japanese director, both for the quality of his work and the fact that he, among his contemporaries, was most familiar with the conventions of

[14]For the full text and list of signatories, see http://web.uvic .ca/geru/439/oberhausen.html.

Das neue Kino and Hollywood German New Wave filmmakers had a genuine affection for Hollywood genres, including film noir. In Wim Wenders's *The American Friend* (1977), a crime thriller and neo-noir (shot in color), the title refers to the character of Tom Ripley, played by the American actor Dennis Hopper, shown here. Also appearing in the movie are two distinctly American movie directors: Nicholas Ray (who directed Hopper in *Rebel without a Cause* [1955]) and Samuel Fuller (*Pickup on South Street* [1953]). Although the film was shot mostly in Germany, some scenes were photographed in New York City.

In the Realm of the Senses: sex and violence When Nagisa Oshima's most provocative movie, *In the Realm of the Senses* (1976), was released, it was banned (or cut) in many parts of the world. It explores various sexual activities, including the power dynamics between a man and a woman obsessed with one another, and ends in one of the most disturbingly violent incidents in movie history. This image, a comparatively tame moment, depicts eroticism in eating, where actor Tatsuya Fuji is playfully fed a rare mushroom by his lover. The overall movie is based on a true story involving death-obsessed eroticism and is widely thought to be pornography.

Hollywood filmmaking, especially the work of John Ford. However, aside from familiar cinematic technique, his films are thoroughly Japanese in their fatalistic attitude toward life and death. He initiated the postwar rebirth of Japanese cinema with *Rashomon* (1950), which tells a single story—the rape of a woman—from four different points of view. Kurosawa shows us that we all remember and perceive differently and that truth is relative to those telling their stories. With this profound statement on the power of cinema, he produced a body of work that is notable for its interest in Japanese tradition, especially the samurai culture of medieval Japan, and for its spectacle, action, and sumptuous design. As John Wayne represented John Ford's idea of the ideal hero, so did Toshiro Mifune for Kurosawa, who used him in 16 of his films. In addition to *Rashomon*, there are many other masterpieces among his 30 films: *Ikiru* (1952), *Seven Samurai* (1954), *Throne of Blood* (1957), his version of Shakespeare's *Macbeth*, *Yojimbo* (1961), *Kagemusha* (1980), and *Ran* (1985), his stylized version of Shakespeare's *King Lear*. In creating these works, Kurosawa was a classic auteur, involved in every phase of filmmaking.

If Kurosawa is the master of the samurai as well as contemporary social problem films, then Kenji Mizoguchi, a sublime artist, is the master of mise-en-scène, pictorial values, the long shot, and the moving camera. His stories are about place as much as anything else, and his films, no less than Kurosawa's, have had worldwide influence. Although they are much less known in the United States than they deserve to be, that may be due to the fact that were less influenced by Western filmmaking conventions than Kurosawa's were. Unlike Kurosawa, he had a flourishing career before the war. Mizoguchi's films are highly regarded for their treatment of women. Indeed, his major concerns are women's social, psychological, and economic positions (or lack of them), the differences between women and

Kurosawa's *Ran*: "A scroll of hell" *Ran*, Kurosawa's adaptation of Shakespeare's *King Lear*, pushes the play to extremes. The word "ran" literally means "turmoil" or "chaos" and it suggests rebellion, riot, or war. Kurosawa's *Ran* is full of blood, violence, suffering, and death, qualities depicted in the 12th- and 13th-century Japanese scrolls known as "scrolls of hell," the term Kurosawa used to describe the movie itself. The director has transformed King Lear's three daughters into the three sons of powerful warlord Hidetora Ichimonji. Lady Kaede, the wife of Taro, one of the sons, is a lethal schemer who wants her husband to become leader of the clan. She fails, however, and at the end, she is confronted by a clan loyalist, who tells her, "Vixen . . . you have destroyed the house of Ichimonji, now you should know the shallowness and stupidity of a woman's wisdom." But Kaede has the last word: "It is not shallow or stupid. I wanted to see this castle burn and the House of Ichimonji ruined by the long grudge of my family. I wanted to see all this." We do not see Kaede beheaded, but in this spectacular image, her spattered blood is running down the wall. A maid crouches to the left and the assailant stands at the right; Kaede's body is on the floor. The image resembles a Japanese scroll; overall, it is framed by pots of flowers in the middle ground; in the background, the gruesome composition is framed by sliding doors. Ironically, the dripping blood recalls various abstract modern paintings.

men, male-female relations, and the idea that a man can be saved by a woman's love. These themes characterize his greatest postwar movies: *The Life of Oharu* (1952), *Ugetsu* (1953), *Sansho the Bailiff* (1954), and *Street of Shame* (1956).

Of these three directors, the films of Yasujiro Ozu are considered by the international film community as the most Japanese in their modes of expression and values. Like Mizoguchi, he began his career long before World War II. His best films are concerned not with the traditional world of the samurai but with contemporary family life; indeed, the values of the lower-middle-class families who are the staple of his movies represent a microcosm of postwar society. And since most of them take place within the family home, their look is influenced by Japanese domestic customs and architecture. Because the Japanese often sit on the floor and thus make eye contact with others at that level, Ozu placed his camera similarly, pulling Western audiences immediately into a different world. His compositions are very formal and his camera seldom moved; his editing consisted primarily of cuts rather than, say, fades or dissolves. Unlike Kurosawa, he did not seek to create Western-style continuity. Furthermore, his distinctive style included the use of offscreen space, meaning that his compositions force our eyes to consider the world outside the frame and as a result, heighten our sense of a movie's reality. Like Kurosawa, he was an auteur, infusing his movies with a distinct style unlike any other. While that style might at first seem austere or rigid, the subject of his films is anything but. Many western viewers find them difficult to watch and understand due to the differences in culture. Notable among his 54 films are *Late Spring* (1949), *Early Summer* (1951), *The Flavor of Green Tea over Rice* (1952), *Tokyo Story* (1953), *Early Spring* (1956), *Floating Weeds* (1959), and *An Autumn Afternoon* (1962).

Between the 1950s and 1970s, there arose an extreme new movement (*Nubero Bagu*) that was significantly influenced by the French New Wave in its emphasis on upsetting cinematic and social conventions. Its representative directors were Hiroshi Teshigahara, Yasuzo Masumura, and Nagisa Oshima, among others, and their movies are full of brutality and nihilism. Oshima is, perhaps, the best known of the group, a provocative filmmaker whose work is often compared to the work of Jean-Luc Godard. His movies include *Cruel Story of Youth* (1960), full of violent passion, *In the Realm of the Senses* (1976), a disturbing exploration of human sexuality, and *Merry Christmas, Mr. Lawrence* (1983), a film about intercultural communication in a Japanese prisoner-of-war camp that established Oshima's international reputation as a director who could also communicate across cultures. Also well known in the United States is the work of the experimental

Painterly composition in Mizoguchi's *Sansho the Bailiff* Nothing could be further from the color and chaos of Kurosawa's *Ran* than the calm compositions of Kenji Mizoguchi's *Sansho the Bailiff*. After her husband is banished to a distant province, an aristocratic woman named Tamaki (Kinuyo Tanaka), her lone servant, and her children are forced to wander from place to place. In this image, the wife (*center right*), who cannot find shelter elsewhere, builds a shelter of branches and reeds under the spreading limbs of a tree, with the servant and children helping her. The black-and-white composition of this image shows why Mizoguchi is revered as a master of mise-en-scène. The tree is theatrically perfect, as is the light through the upper branches of the tree, on the mother and daughter, and on the grasses at the right and left of the image. This pictorially pleasing image gives no hint of what's to come: the children are sold into slavery and Tamaki is exiled to an island where she is forced to become a prostitute. Despite the loss of her daughter and her other hardships, Tamaki perseveres; finally, blind and alone, she is reunited with her son. Overall, the movie demonstrates Mizoguchi's interest in issues of freedom and women's place in society.

filmmaker Nobuhiko Obayashi, who is best known for *House* (1977). This stylistically bizarre horror film demonstrates a strong familiarity with French, British, and Italian cinema of the 1960s as well as Japanese film history and silent film tradition. Although a short-lived movement, the Japanese New Wave—along with the postwar filmmakers of China—influenced the style and content of the New American Cinema (discussed on pages 472–477).

China and Postwar Filmmaking

After the Second World War, film production resumed in the People's Republic of China (often referred to as mainland China) as well as in two distinct political entities: Taiwan (the Republic of China), which asserts its independence from the People's Republic, and Hong Kong (a British colony until 1997, when it was transferred by treaty to the People's Republic). The People's Republic, a vast

Unique camera placement in Ozu's *Tokyo Story* Set in postwar Japan, this unforgettable movie tells a familiar and touching story about Shukichi (Chishu Ryu, *left*) and Tomi Hirayama (Chieko Higashiyama, *middle*), two elderly parents who visit their children in Tokyo only to find that they are in the way. However, Noriko (Setsuko Hara, *right*), the couple's widowed daughter-in-law, who is less busy, cheerfully takes charge of entertaining them. In this image, their first meeting, the three are traditionally seated on the floor, where the low placement of Ozu's static camera (*behind and to the left of* Noriko) provides us with Noriko's perspective. The image, with its deep-space composition, permits us to see the rooms behind this group. While it's a simple story, and Ozu observes it with calm detachment, its ending reminds us of the oneness of humanity, helping to make it an international success.

***Farewell My Concubine*: sex and politics** The Beijing Opera, one of China's major cultural treasures, forms the backdrop for two major contemporary Chinese movies, including Hark Tsui's *Peking Opera Blues* (1986). Chen Kaige's *Farewell My Concubine* (1993) tells the lengthy, complicated story of two of the opera's male actors, whose happiness together onstage and off is threatened by a prostitute. The turbulence of this personal story is mirrored by the political upheavals of the period from the 1920s to Mao's Cultural Revolution, and the movie was banned in China, not because of its treatment of politics, but because of its homosexual subject matter. The Beijing Opera is known for its lavish productions, exotic costumes, and stylized makeup as well as for its ancient tradition of using males to play the female roles.

country with the world's largest population, is ostensibly Communist. Taiwan, an island off the southern coast of China, has a democratic government that desires independence even in the face of mainland China's threats of reunification. And Hong Kong, a small island near China's south coast, is, by terms of the treaty by which it reunified with the People's Republic, a limited democracy with considerable sovereignty compared to the other regions of China. The tripartite Chinese film industry is thus clearly affected by these circumstances of history, ideology, and geography.

The People's Republic Postwar government-subsidized filmmaking here has reflected the shifting ideological climate that developed after the 1949 Communist Revolution. Since 1976—with the death of Party Chairman Mao Ze-dong and Premier Zhou Enlai—filmmakers have focused less on party doctrines and become more concerned with individuals, and the Chinese film industry has become more oriented to the Western market. The most important directors are Chen Kaige, Yimou Zhang, and Tian Zhuangzhuang, each of whom has managed, within a repressive society, to make films about traditionally taboo subjects. Among their best-known movies are Chen's *Farewell My Concubine* (1993), about an extramarital love triangle; Yimou's *Raise the Red Lantern* (1991), which, among other subjects, is concerned with the struggle for women's rights; and Tian's *The Horse Thief* (1986), a brilliant study of China's ethnic minorities.

But the Chinese movies that are most popular and influential outside China—the action movies inspired by various martial arts—are produced in Hong Kong and, to a lesser extent, Taiwan.

Hong Kong The Hong Kong martial-arts action movies stem from a venerable tradition in Chinese film history that, through the 1920s to the 1970s, shifted between two basic styles: wuxia (or wushu) and kung fu, both of which combine, to varying degrees, these disparate elements: an intricate, sometimes incomprehensible, melodramatic plot; philosophical codes of honor based on mystical beliefs; spectacular violence; brilliantly choreographed fight sequences; the conflict between cops and gangsters; speeding vehicles; and lavish production values. Their formal characteristics include spectacular studio settings and natural locations, saturated colors, moody lighting, constant motion (slow and fast), disjointed editing techniques, and extensive computer manipulation of images and motion.

Between the late 1970s and early 1980s, a New Wave of Hong Kong cinema emerged in the work of such directors as Ann Hui, Yim Ho, Hark Tsui, Allen Fong, Patrick Tam, Clifford Choi, Dennis Yu, and others. Although many of these artists were trained in U.S. or U.K. film schools, they made movies that dealt with local experiences in a distinctly individual style. Remarkably, they worked in both mainstream cinema and television. This movement also stimulated change in the film industries of the People's Republic and Taiwan. Important early titles are Yim Ho's *The Extras* (1978), Ann Hui's *The Boy from Vietnam* (1978), Hark Tsui's *The Butterfly Murders* (1979), Patrick Tam's *A Spectrum of Multiple Stars: Wang Chuanru** [*sic*] (1975), Alex Cheung's *The First Step: Facing Death* (1977), and Allen Fong's *Father and Son* (1981).

During this time, the film culture in Hong Kong expanded to include popular film clubs and academic programs in film studies and filmmaking. However, the strong personal style of the New Wave movies clashed with the prevailing commercial nature of the island's cinema; by 1985, the New Wave spirit had become diluted, and the movement was absorbed into the mainstream cinema. Important titles from this period include Hark Tsui's *Peking Opera Blues* (1986), Allen Fong's *Just Like Weather* (1986), Ringo Lam's *City on Fire* (1987), John Woo's *A Better Tomorrow* (1986), and Kar Wai Wong's *Ashes of Time* (1994). Superstar performers like Bruce Lee, Jackie Chan (also a writer and director), Yun-Fat Chow, and Jet Li were an equally vital component of the success of these movies, one reason that they all went to Hollywood. Hong Kong directors who have worked in Hollywood include John Woo and Sammo Hung.

Bands of bloody brothers *A Better Tomorrow* (1986), directed by John Woo, is considered a classic example of Hong Kong cinema: violent action depicted in brilliantly choreographed scenes. The image here, from the movie's spectacular conclusion, exemplifies Woo's style: bright colors, gymnastic feats, dozens of blazing guns, exploding firestorms, blood galore, overwrought male bonding, and a certain sly humor that suggests a surreal world. Woo was influenced by such action directors as Sergio Leone and Sam Peckinpah (see *The Wild Bunch*, page 475) and in turn was widely influential on both Chinese and American directors, including Quentin Tarantino, Robert Rodriguez, and the Wachowski brothers.

While the Hong Kong New Wave was short-lived, it stimulated cinematic innovations throughout China, encouraged the movement of directors between television and mainstream cinema, introduced new genres, and tackled formerly taboo subjects. The influence between Hong Kong and Hollywood has gone both ways, with the Chinese learning from such action directors as Sam Peckinpah and Sergio Leone and then influencing such Hollywood directors as Quentin Tarantino (*Reservoir Dogs*, 1992, and the *Kill Bill* movies, 2003–4), Robert Rodriguez (*Desperado*, 1995), Sam Raimi (*A Simple Plan*, 1998), the Wachowski brothers (*The Matrix* trilogy, 1999–2003), Brett Ratner (the *Rush Hour* films, 1998–2007), and Rob Minkoff (*The Forbidden Kingdom,* 2008). Action choreographer Yuen Woo-ping played a major role in many of these movies.

Taiwan By following European models, particularly the Italian Neorealist movement, postwar Taiwanese cinema developed independently of Hong Kong and the People's Republic. In contrast to the action movies of earlier decades, it was concerned with realistic depictions of ordinary people. Excellent examples are Hsiao-hsien Hou's *A City of Sadness* (1989) and *Flight of the Red Balloon* (2007), Edward Yang's *Taipei Story* (1985), Tsai Mingliang's *Vive l'amour* (1994), and Stan Lai's *The Peach Blossom Land* (1992). The first films of Ang Lee, the most familiar Taiwanese director—*The Wedding Banquet* (1993) and *Eat Drink Man Woman* (1994)—were so successful in the West that Lee went to Hollywood, where he showed an affinity for Western literature and themes and made, among other films, *Sense and Sensibility* (1995), *The Ice Storm* (1997), *Brokeback Mountain* (2005), and *Lust, Caution* (2007). In between, he returned to Taiwan to make *Crouching Tiger, Hidden Dragon* (2000), a spectacularly beautiful martial-arts action movie in the venerable Chinese tradition.

Postwar Chinese filmmaking was too diverse, aesthetically and politically, to represent a unified movement such as the French New Wave, but its movies—particularly the Hong Kong action movies—have spoken in a distinct visual language across cultural and linguistic barriers and have had a dynamic effect on filmmaking worldwide, especially in the United States.

India

Despite the worldwide success of *Slumdog Millionaire* (2008), an Anglo-Indian production, and the fact that the Indian film industry—producing more than 1,200 feature movies and an even larger number of documentaries every year—is the world's largest, Indian films are little known in the United States except in cities with a large Indian population. Indeed, in terms of annual film production, India ranks first, followed by Hollywood and China. India, a vast country with some 16 official languages, is a regional cinema that speaks to its many different audiences in social, political, cinematic, and linguistic terms it can understand. Thus a social protest film made in Chennai, in the South, might never be seen by those who live in Bombay, who not only speak a different dialect but seemingly prefer the lavish musicals made by Bollywood,

Flying warriors: *Crouching Tiger, Hidden Dragon* The films of Taiwan-born Ang Lee are known for their diversity (comedies, melodramas, traditional Chinese martial action), their ability to provoke discussion (e.g., *Brokeback Mountain* [2005]), and their almost universal acclaim. *Crouching Tiger, Hidden Dragon* (2000) has it all: a traditional intrigue-filled story about a legendary sword, magnificent exterior and interior settings, beautiful costumes, a love story, and astonishing swordplay. It is a fantastic feat of movie magic, distinguished by the exquisite choreography and special effects that give the illusion of its principal characters in flight. In this image, two female principals, Jade Fox (Cheng Pei-pei) and Jen (Zhang Ziyi) engage in a deadly battle.

as the Mumbai film industry is known. When Indian films are screened theatrically in the United States, the audiences are typically Indians, who understand the culture in which the movie was made and the language spoken in it. For others who want to learn more about this vast, diverse body of filmmaking, there are annual Indian (and South Asian) film festivals in such U.S. cities as New York, Boston, Chicago, and San Francisco, among others. In these settings, the films are likely to be dubbed into English or have English subtitles.

The one exception to this is director Satyajit Ray, the dominating figure in Indian cinema as it is known in the West. He was always unique among Indian filmmakers and, to the moviegoing public in the West, the only Indian director whose name they recognize. In that respect, he very much resembles Akira Kurosawa; both were instinctive filmmakers who made powerful and personal films with recurring themes. Ray and Kurosawa, two of the most individually unique filmmakers the world has ever produced, greatly admired each other's work. Of Ray, Kurosawa said, "Not to have seen the cinema of Ray means existing in the world without seeing the sun or the moon."

Ray was a Bengali, born in the Indian state of West Bengal, the capital of which is Kolkata (Calcutta). The principal influences on his cinematic style come from the literature and art of Bengali culture as well as from four great filmmakers: Vittorio DeSica, Akira Kurosawa, Jean Renoir, and John Ford. This helps to explain why his films are very Indian in content but the least Indian in their cinematic form. The most formative influence was Italian Neorealism, *The Bicycle Thieves* (1949) in particular. It convinced Ray to make a film about everyday Indian life exactly as DeSica had made his; the characteristics of this approach are discussed earlier in this chapter. The result was not one but three films, a trilogy known as the Apu trilogy for the name of its central character: *Pather Panchali* (*Song of the Little Road*, 1955), *Aparajito* (*The Unvanquished*, 1956), and *Apar Sansar* (*The World of Apu*, 1959). As a chronicle of a family, and particular Apu's growth from a boy to a man, they are unparalleled in their humanistic insight and wonder at the natural world. (Note: both Indian

The eye as symbol of consciousness in *Pather Panchali* Director Satyajit Ray is known for his attention to the details in the lives of ordinary people and for the subtle, detached angle with which he views them in his movies. His "Apu" trilogy, of which *Pather Panchali* is the first, recounts a series of small, but significant, episodes in the life of Apu, who lives with his impoverished family in a Bengali village. The trilogy spans the years from his childhood through his early twenties, but here he is a boy of six or seven. Near the beginning of the movie, Apu's sister Durga tries to awaken him so that he can get ready for school. She shakes him, but he does not budge, but then poking her figners through a hole in his blanket, she tenderly pries open a closed eye. We would be wrong to think that Ray will henceforth see things from Apu's point of view, for we are seeing the opening of Apu's consciousness of the world around him. He is an curious boy, delighted by everything he sees and hears—traveling entertainers, a freight train, a pond—and he also learns about life and death, realizing that his father is incapable of supporting the family and witnessing the death of his aged aunt. Careful, connected observation characterizes both Apu and his creator.

and English titles are given because of the variant ways in which they are cited.) For these reasons, as well as for their cinematography and acting, they were recognized worldwide as landmarks of modern cinema. Ray, a true auteur, wrote, produced, and directed all three films; he even scored the music.

In all, Ray made some 34 films, most of which were successful both in India and worldwide. Besides the Apu trilogy, they include *Jalsaghar*

(*The Music Room*, 1958), *Devi* (*The Goddess*, 1960), *Charulata* (*The Lonely Wife*, 1964), *Shatranj-ke-Khilari* (*The Chess Players*, 1977), *Ghare-Baire* (*The Home and the World*, 1984), and *Agantuk* (*The Stranger*, 1992).

Ray's work represented the beginnings of a "new Indian cinema," or Parallel Cinema, meaning that it exists alongside the mainstream commercial industry. Leading this movement were Ritwik Ghatak and Mrinal Sen, like Ray, Bengalis; unlike Ray, Marxists. Western audiences are familiar with their work, primarily because of their political views, and Ghatak, in particular, influenced several young Marxist directors. Ghatak's most distinctive works are *Ajantrik* (*Pathetic Fallacy*, 1958) and *Jukti Takko Aar Gappo* (*Reason, Debate and Story*, 1974). Sen, the more prolific and experimental of the two, is best known for *Bhuvan Shome* (*Mr. Shome*, 1969), *Parasuram* (*Man With the Axe*, 1978), *Kharji* (*The Case Is Closed*, 1982), *Khandaar* (*The Ruins*, 1983), and *Antareen* (*The Confined*, 1993). Shyam Benegal's reputation as the most commercially successful director in the Parallel Cinema is largely due to his quartet of socially conscious films: *Ankur* (*The Seedling*, 1973), *Nishant* (*Night's End*, 1975), *Manthan* (*The Churning*, 1976), and *Bhumika* (*The Role*, 1977). He created a large body of documentaries, including two biographies: *Satyajit Ray, Filmmaker* (1985) and *Nehru* (1985).

The 20 regional cinemas of India—separate industries in virtually every major state that make movies in their own language—are marked by a vibrant diversity of aesthetic styles and political commitments. In the 1980s, for example, there was a resurgence of the Malayalam cinema of the state of Kerala, including films that appealed to an international audience, particularly Shaji N. Karun's *Piravi* (1989) and Rajiv Anchal's *Guru* (1997). Similar commercial success, both inside and outside India, has been made by some Tamil and Oriya films as well as by such commercial Hindi directors as Mira Nair, Nagsh Kukunoor, Nandita Das, and Sudhir Mishra. Bollywood has developed a new genre called Mumbai noir, urban films by such directors as Anurag Kashyap (*Black Friday*, 2004) and Deva Katta (*Prasthanam*, 2010). Finally, with such films as Homi Adajama's *Being Cyrus* (2005) and Sooni Taraporevala's *Little Zizou* (2009), the English-language cinema continues to be a part of India's multilanguage film industry.

1965–1995: The New American Cinema

Twenty years after the end of the Second World War, the United States faced political, cultural, and social challenges that were unprecedented in its history. It was now the most powerful and influential country in the world yet locked with the Soviet Union in a "cold war." It was also a period of anti-Communist vehemence, the Korean War, the beginnings of the feminist, gay/lesbian/transgender, and environmental movements; the Vietnam War and resolute antiwar and civil-rights movements. There was also an unusually high level of violence, including the assassinations of President John F. Kennedy in 1963 and Senator Robert F. Kennedy and the Reverend Martin Luther King, Jr. in 1968; the killing of four Kent State University students, who were protesting the Vietnam War, by the Ohio National Guard in 1970; assassination attempts on Presidents Gerald Ford and Ronald Reagan and Pope John Paul II; and terrorist attacks on the World Trade Center in 1993 and an Oklahoma City courthouse in 1995. Other major events included the U.S. landing on the moon, the beginnings of a vibrant popular music culture, the Watergate crisis and the resignation in disgrace in 1974 of President Richard M. Nixon, the emergence of the AIDS virus, and the collapse of the Soviet Union in 1991.

Against such a fast-moving, turbulent background, it is not surprising that a New American Cinema emerged. The "new" Hollywood encompasses too many transitions from the "old" Hollywood to be simply called a movement. In terms of the changes that affected the American film industry—and the resulting ripples that spread throughout the international film community—the term *phenomenon* is both more accurate and appropriate. These changes were hastened by the collapse of the old studio system, which was replaced by scattered enterprises known as "independent filmmakers." This had both negative and positive implications.

The negative factors included declining audiences, caused in part by competition from television; the escalating costs of producing films independently rather than in the studios, where the permanent physical and human support structure was very cost-effective; and the forced retirement or relocation of studio personnel. However, these were outweighed by the positive factors. The new Hollywood adapted conventions of classical genres to conform to new modes of expression and meet audience expectations, abandoned the code for a new rating system, and did more shooting on location; the result was a more authentic look for the movies. Furthermore, while the studios retained their names and kept their production facilities open to ensure the smoothness of the established preproduction/production/postproduction matrix, they have changed ownership frequently over the years. Movies are now made in complex deals involving the studios and independent production companies headed by individual producers, many of whom invested capital in their own work. The "star machine" collapsed as well, ushering in decades of new talent whose careers, which once would have been meticulously planned and monitored, were now subject to market forces. Marketing of movies remained a precise tool, carefully adapted to meet the needs of new audiences. One of the positive effects of this transition was the increase in audience members who, because of college film-study classes and an overall greater awareness of film, had a better understanding of cinematic conventions than their parents and were attracted to films by a new breed of American directors, also trained in university film schools. With the old labor-dominated system gone, producers could hire artists from anywhere in the world, and American production was greatly enhanced by their contributions. Finally, to seal the death of the "old" Hollywood, New York and other cities in the United States and Canada emerged as thriving centers of film production.

Unlike the French New Wave, the New American Cinema was not born in theory but rather out of the more practical need to adapt to the values of its time. However, like the French New Wave, the prevailing spirit was innovation. But with so many

Stranger Than Paradise: a milestone in the New American Cinema Jim Jarmusch's *Stranger Than Paradise* (1984) did more than any other movie to define the New American Cinema. It tells a distinctly American story; it was made in a fresh, easy style clearly influenced by American movies as well as the new waves in European and Asian cinema; and it was produced by a film-school graduate using funds from various sources, both American and foreign. Although unusual in production, form, and content, this art film was surprisingly successful at the box office. It is a distinctly marginal effort, but in winning the Cannes Film Festival prize for best first feature, it encouraged independent filmmakers and the reception of their work. *Stranger Than Paradise* was shot in a series of long takes, which are structured into three stages of a journey undertaken by three offbeat travelers. They are Willie (John Lurie), a hipster living in New York City; his cousin Eva (Eszter Balint), who comes from Hungary to visit him and their aunt in Ohio; and Willie's friend Eddie (Richard Edson). Eva's visit to New York is the first stage; the second, which takes place a year later, recounts a trip that Willie and Eddie make to Cleveland to visit Eva and the aunt; and the third stage follows them to the "paradise" of Florida. Their travels through the bleak landscape, shot in washed-out black and white, ultimately show that they are going nowhere, but they have a good time, and so do we. Here, we see the trio in Florida—(*left to right*) Eddie, Eva, and Willie—putting on their new sunglasses so they can look like "real tourists."

auteurs—some from the old Hollywood and some from film schools—no single defining style emerged. Indeed, there was a range of styles, resulting in personal, highly self-reflexive films; edgy, experimental, low-budget movies; movies that played homage to great European directors; and, of course, those that still adhered to the conventions of the golden age. Thus diversity and quality are the only links among such directors as Woody Allen, Robert Altman, Tim Burton, John Cassavetes, Joel and Ethan Coen, Francis Ford Coppola, Brian De Palma, Clint

[1]

[2]

Femmes fatales in the New American Cinema Faye Dunaway stars in two of the most important movies of the New American Cinema: Arthur Penn's *Bonnie and Clyde* (1967) and Roman Polanski's *Chinatown* (1974). As Bonnie Parker, she participates fully in a bank robbery with two other members of the fearless, violent Barrow gang: (*left to right*) Buck Barrow (Gene Hackman) and Clyde Barrow (Warren Beatty) [1]. In *Chinatown* [2], she plays Evelyn Mulwray, the neurotic, scheming liar who tries to outwit J. J. Gittes (Jack Nicholson, *pictured left*). In both cases, thanks in part to the rising feminist movement, these characters are at least as equal to their male counterparts as they can be. But Dunaway is also beautiful and seductive, preserving the role of the classic film-noir femme fatale.

Eastwood, George Roy Hill, Jim Jarmusch, Diane Keaton, Stanley Kubrick, Spike Lee, Sidney Lumet, David Lynch, Terrence Malick, Gordon Parks, Sam Peckinpah, Roman Polanski, John Sayles, Paul Schrader, Martin Scorsese, Steven Spielberg, and Gus Van Sant. Typical of Hollywood, males outnumber females. But that ratio is changing, and

reversing the Hollywood tradition, women as well as African American, Hispanic, and Asian directors have begun to write and direct movies.

Their guiding principle was not to discard cinematic conventions, but to adapt them to the new audience. In terms of content, the most noticeable changes were in the predominance of sex and violence and in the nature of the protagonists, both male and female. To quote film historians Bruce F. Mast and Gerald Kawin, "In most cases, the protagonists . . . were social misfits, deviates, or outlaws; the villains were the legal, respectable defenders of society. The old bad guys became the good guys; the old good guys, the bad guys."[15] In a further twist of traditional gender roles, the female protagonists in two of the most distinctive movies of the period, Arthur Penn's *Bonnie and Clyde* (1967) and Roman Polanski's *Chinatown* (1974)—both insightful analyses of America in the 1930s—were as evil as, if not more evil than, the men. Although sex and violence still dominate U.S. movies, there is a large, appreciative audience for films that tackle the other serious issues that were formerly the province primarily of foreign movies that played only in small "art houses."

In terms of form, the strongest influences were such contemporary directors as Ingmar Bergman, Michelangelo Antonioni, Orson Welles, Jean-Luc Godard, and François Truffaut. Plots became more complex in structure and embodied new storytelling techniques. For example, Penn's *Bonnie and Clyde* (1967), which tells the story of two notorious bank robbers that could have been taken from a 1930s Hollywood model, was easily read by the audience as a comic/tragic parable of violent, amoral dissent against an authoritarian social order. Its style reflects not only the director's experience as a Hollywood veteran but also the dynamic of Eisenstein's montage and the surprise of Kurosawa's slow-motion violence.

Stories became palpably more sexual and violent in such movies as Penn's *Bonnie and Clyde* (1967), Dennis Hopper's *Easy Rider* (1969), Peter Bogdanovich's *The Last Picture Show* (1969), Sam Peckinpah's *The Wild Bunch* (1969), Bob Rafelson's

[15]Mast and Kawin, p. 517.

[1]

[2]

[3]

faced, overdressed anarchist." Even though he says this humorously, he uses the tone of his voice, as well as his words, to humiliate his subordinate.

The song about "good old Charlie Kane"—here the excuse for more of Welles's vocal theatrics—later becomes his political campaign theme, so the sound in this scene connects us with later scenes in which we hear this musical theme again. By participating in the singing and dancing, Kane continues to call "complete attention" (his words) to himself. Through both visual and aural imagery, Kane remains in the center of the frame for most of the scene, either directly on-screen himself or indirectly reflected in the windows. His voice dominates all the other sounds in this scene because it always seems to be the loudest.

Leland and Bernstein are different from one another in family background, education, level of sophistication, and relationship to Kane, and their conversation about journalistic ethics establishes another major difference: these characters' voices are also quite different from Kane's voice. Leland has the soft patrician voice of a Virginia gentleman, while Bernstein's voice reflects his New York immigrant-class upbringing. Leland gently questions Kane's motives in hiring the *Chronicle*'s staff and wonders why they can change their loyalties so easily, but the pragmatic Bernstein bluntly answers, "Sure, they're just like anybody else. . . . They got work to do, they do it. Only they happen to

Sound aids characterization in *Citizen Kane*
[1] Standing at opposite ends of the banquet table, Bernstein (*background*) and Kane (*foreground*) banter back and forth as if they were a comedy duo. [2] Welles dominates the scene with sound. Putting his fingers between his lips, Kane gets the attention of his guests and loudly calls for their "complete attention." [3] Bernstein (*left*) and Leland (*right*) join in the singing of "There Is a Man," but Leland, now disillusioned with Kane, sings only to be polite.

be the best in the business." Their reading of these lines embodies one of the movie's major themes: journalistic ethics. Even their singing sets them apart. Bernstein sings as if he's having a good time, but Leland seems to sing only to show his good manners. Their differences, including the differences in their voices, ultimately determine their future relationship with Kane.

Themes

Sound serves many functions in this scene, including the development of several major themes and concerns:

1. *Kane's youthful longings fulfilled.* A major strand of the narrative conveys Kane's lifelong bullying of others, mania for buying things, and egomania as a reaction to being abandoned by his parents at an early age. Here he begins the scene by addressing the new reporters and likening his acquisition of the *Chronicle* staff to a kid who has just gotten all the candy he wants. This statement is punctuated by the sound of a flashbulb.

2. *Kane's ruthless ambition.* The mix of burlesque dancing, loud music, and serious conversation about ethics only underscores Kane's determination to do whatever is necessary to attain his goals.

3. *Kane's disregard for ethics and principles and his relation with his two closest associates.* Kane's domination of the scene is made personal by his humiliation of Leland (throwing his coat at Leland, as if Leland were a lackey) and teasing of Bernstein ("You don't expect me to keep any of those promises, do you?"), a further reference to the "Declaration of Principles" that Kane flamboyantly writes and prints on the first page of the *Inquirer*. The dialogue in this scene (and those scenes that precede and follow it) further clarifies the relationships among Kane, Bernstein, and Leland.

The care and attention that Welles and his colleagues enthusiastically gave to the sound design of this scene was virtually unprecedented in 1941 and was seldom equaled until the 1970s. In giving this rowdy party the appearance of a real event, not

Analyzing Sound

By this point in our study of the movies, we know that sound (like everything else in a movie) is manufactured creatively for the purposes of telling a story. As you attempt to make more informed critical judgments about the sound in any movie, remember that what you hear in a film results from choices made by directors and their collaborators during and after production, just as what you see does. This chapter has provided a foundation for understanding the basic characteristics of film sound and a vocabulary for talking and writing about it analytically. As you screen movies in and out of class, you'll now be able to thoughtfully appreciate and describe how the sound in any movie either complements or detracts from the visual elements portrayed on-screen.

Screening Checklist: Sound

✔ As you analyze a shot or scene, carefully note the specific sources of sound in that shot or scene.

✔ Also keep notes on the types of sound that are used in the shot or scene.

✔ Note carefully those moments when the sound creates emphasis by accentuating and strengthening the visual image.

✔ Does the sound in the shot, scene, or movie as a whole help develop characterization? If so, how does it do so?

✔ In the movie overall, how is music used? In a complementary way? Ironically? Does the use of music in this movie seem appropriate to the story?

✔ Do image and sound complement one another in this movie, or does one dominate the other?

✔ Does this film use silence expressively?

✔ In this movie, do you hear evidence of a comprehensive approach to sound—one, specifically, in which the film's sound is as expressive as its images? If so, explain why you think so.

something staged for the cameras, the sound—along with the visual design, mise-en-scène, acting, and direction, of course—plays a major role in depicting a crucial turning point in the narrative.

Questions for Review

1. What is sound design? What are the responsibilities of the sound designer?
2. Distinguish among recording, rerecording, editing, and mixing.
3. What is the difference between diegetic and nondiegetic sources of sound?
4. What are the differences between sounds that are internal and external? on-screen and offscreen?
5. Is a movie limited to a certain number of sound tracks?
6. How do ambient sounds differ from sound effects? How are Foley sounds different from sound effects?
7. Can the music in a movie be both diegetic and nondiegetic? Explain.
8. How does sound call our attention to both the spatial and temporal dimensions of a scene?
9. Cite an example of sound that is faithful to its source and an example that is not.

10. What is a sound bridge? What are its functions?

Movies Described or Illustrated in This Chapter

Accatone (1961). Pier Paolo Pasolini, director.
Aguirre: The Wrath of God (1972). Werner Herzog, director.
Alexander Nevsky (1938). Sergei Eisenstein, director.
Alien (1979). Ridley Scott, director.
American Beauty (1999). Sam Mendes, director.
Apocalypse Now (1979). Francis Ford Coppola, director.
Applause (1929). Rouben Mamoulian, director.
The Assassination of the Duke de Guise (1908). André Calmettes and Charles Le Bargy, directors.
Badlands (1973). Terrence Malick, director.
Ballast (2008). Lance Hammer, director.
Barry Lyndon (1975). Stanley Kubrick, director.
The Birds (1963). Alfred Hitchcock, director.
Black Hawk Down (2001). Ridley Scott, director.
The Bourne Supremacy (2004). Paul Greengrass, director.
Bride of Frankenstein (1935). James Whale, director.
Le Cercle Rouge (1970). Jean-Pierre Melville, director.
Citizen Kane (1941). Orson Welles, director.
A Clockwork Orange (1971). Stanley Kubrick, director.
Cold Mountain (2003). Anthony Minghella, director.
The Crying Game (1992), Neil Jordan, director.
Delicatessen (1991). Jean-Pierre Jeunet and Marc Caro, directors.

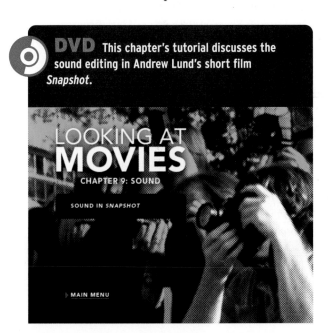

DVD This chapter's tutorial discusses the sound editing in Andrew Lund's short film *Snapshot*.

Double Indemnity (1944). Billy Wilder, director.

Dreams (1990). Akira Kurosawa, director.

Dr. Strangelove or: How I Learned to Stop Worrying and Love the Bomb (1964). Stanley Kubrick, director.

The Empire Strikes Back (1980). Irvin Kershner, director.

The English Patient (1996). Anthony Minghella, director.

Fail-Safe (1964). Sidney Lumet, director.

The Lord of the Rings: The Fellowship of the Ring (2001). Peter Jackson, director.

Gabrielle (2005). Patrice Chéreau, director.

The Ghost and Mrs. Muir (1947). Joseph L. Mankiewicz, director.

The Grapes of Wrath (1940). John Ford, director.

Hallelujah! (1929). King Vidor, director.

Hamlet (1948). Laurence Olivier, director.

The Hours (2002). Stephen Daldry, director.

The Ice Storm (1997). Ang Lee, director.

Inception (2010). Christopher Nolan, director.

Jaws (1975). Steven Spielberg, director.

The Killing (1956). Stanley Kubrick, director.

Laura (1944). Otto Preminger, director.

Lolita (1997). Adrian Lyne, director.

Love Me Tonight (1932). Rouben Mamoulian, director.

M (1931). Fritz Lang, director.

The Magnificent Ambersons (1942). Orson Welles, director.

Magnolia (1999). Paul Thomas Anderson, director.

A Man Escaped (1956). Robert Bresson, director.

The Man Who Wasn't There (2001). Joel Coen, director.

The Matrix (1999). Andy Wachowski and Larry Wachowski, directors.

Me and You and Everyone We Know (2006). Miranda July, director.

Mean Streets (1973). Martin Scorsese, director.

The Mission (1986). Roland Joffé, director.

My Darling Clementine (1946). John Ford, director.

My Life as a Dog (1985). Lasse Hallström, director.

The Night of the Hunter (1955). Charles Laughton, director.

No Country for Old Men (2007). Joel Coen and Ethan Coen, directors.

North by Northwest (1959). Alfred Hitchcock, director.

Once (2006). John Carney, director.

Once upon a Time in the West (1968). Sergio Leone, director.

Pather Panchali (1955). Satyajit Ray, director.

The Player (1992). Robert Altman, director.

Providence (1977). Alain Resnais, director.

Raging Bull (1980). Martin Scorsese, director.

The Red Desert (1964). Michelangelo Antonioni, director.

Reservoir Dogs (1992). Quentin Tarantino, director.

Run Lola Run (1998). Tom Tykwer, director.

The Shining (1980). Stanley Kubrick, director.

The Silence before Bach (2007). Pere Portabella, director.

Slumdog Millionaire (2008). Danny Boyle and Loveleen Tandan, directors.

Spartacus (1960). Stanley Kubrick, director.

The Sweet Hereafter (1997). Atom Egoyan, director.

There's Something about Mary (1998). Bobby Farrelly and Peter Farrelly, directors.

There Will Be Blood (2007). Paul Thomas Anderson, director.

The 39 Steps (1935). Alfred Hitchcock, director.

The Tragedy of Othello: The Moor of Venice (1952). Orson Welles, director.

Trouble in Paradise (1932). Ernst Lubitsch, director.

The Truman Show (1998). Peter Weir, director.

Uncle Boonmee Who Can Recall His Past Lives (2010). Apichatpong Weerasethakul, director.

War of the Worlds (2005). Steven Spielberg, director.

We Don't Live Here Anymore (2004). John Curran, director.

Westfront 1918 (1930). G. W. Pabst, director.

Wild Strawberries (1957). Ingmar Bergman, director.

Winter's Bone (2010). Debra Granik, director.

The Wizard of Oz (1939). Victor Fleming, director.

You, the Living (2007). Roy Andersson, director.

Young Frankenstein (1974). Mel Brooks, director.

CHAPTER TEN

Film History

What Is Film History?

In just over a hundred years, the cinema, like the classical art forms that have preceded it—architecture, fiction, poetry, drama, dance, painting, and music—has developed its own aesthetics, conventions, influence, and, of course, history. Broadly defined, film history traces the development of moving images from early experiments with image reproduction and photography through the invention of the movies in the early 1890s and subsequent stylistic, financial, technological, and social developments in cinema that have occurred up to now. To get some idea of the scope and depth of that record, you might browse through a comprehensive history of film, such as the ten-volume History of American Cinema series (University of California Press). Such comprehensive histories take many years, and often the efforts of many people, to get written. Because of this, most film historians don't undertake such massive projects. Most people who practice film history instead focus their energies on studying specific moments, movements, and phenomena. Jeanine Basinger's *The Star Machine* (New York: Knopf, 2007), for example, provides a masterful account of how the Hollywood studio system during a very specific era (the so-called "golden age") created its stars. C. S. Tashiro's *Pretty Pictures: Production Design and the History of Film* (Austin: University of Texas Press, 1998) limits its scope to focus on one aspect of film production—production design—even as it ranges widely over the full chronology of film history. In both broad and specific studies, the film historian is interested equally in change—those developments that have altered the course of film history—and stability—those aspects that have defied change. Film history is not, to quote film historians Robert C. Allen and Douglas Gomery, "a list of film titles or an academ-

A major turning point in film history Billy Wilder's *Sunset Boulevard* (1950) is a haunting film noir about film history. Norma Desmond (Gloria Swanson), an aging silent-movie star who (in the 1950s) still represents the glamour and allure of the silent era, hopes to revive her career in the sound era with the help of Joe Gillis (William Holden), an aspiring screenwriter. Her fantasies are apparent in one of her most famous (and unintentionally funny) lines: "I am big. It's the movies that got small." Unfortunately, she isn't big anymore, and the movies just kept getting bigger and better after the conversion to sound, one of the major turning points in film history. All Desmond has left is her dreams, and *Sunset Boulevard* is all the more poignant because Gloria Swanson herself was actually one of the greatest stars of the silent era.

The Wild Bunch: blood bath and beyond[16] The New American Cinema ushered in a wave of movies as famous for good stories and superb filmmaking as they were for sex and violence. Director Sam Peckinpah, nicknamed "Bloody Sam," is noted for a string of graphically violent movies, including *The Wild Bunch* (1969), *Straw Dogs* (1971), and *Bring Me the Head of Alfredo Garcia* (1974). His brand of stylized violence reflects the influence of Arthur Penn's *Bonnie and Clyde* (1967) and in turn influenced many Hong Kong action movies as well as a host of American directors whose films include violent action—Martin Scorsese, Brian De Palma, and Francis Ford Coppola. At the conclusion of *The Wild Bunch*, the American gang of the title attempts to claim one of its men from Mapache, a Mexican rebel leader; when Mapache kills the man, this provokes one of the bloodiest battles in movie history. In an impressively choreographed gunfight between the rebel army and the gang members, most are killed, including the gang's leader, Pike (William Holden), who, manning a vicious machine gun, is struck by a gun fired by a boy and dies in blood-drenched action.

Five Easy Pieces (1970), and Terrence Malick's *Badlands* (1973). While continuity editing remained the norm, there was an increased use of such techniques as jump cuts, split screens, slow and fast motion, simulated "grainy" documentary footage, and a mixture of color and black-and-white footage. Stanley Kubrick's *2001: A Space Odyssey* (1968) used very long takes and an absence of editing that calls attention to itself to introduce us to outer space, where time shifts in unfamiliar ways.

Cinematography also adapted as more films were shot on location rather than soundstages and the old Hollywood ideal of visual perfection gave way to a depiction of recognizable actuality. A new generation of cinematographers—including Néstor Almendros, John Alonzo, Conrad Hall, Geoffrey Unsworth, Haskell Wexler, Gordon Willis, and Vilmos Zsigmond,

to name but a few—brought a familiarity with European techniques in framing, lighting, camera movement, shot duration, and, especially, an experimental approach to color. Under the particular influence of such directors as Coppola and Lucas, there was also major experimentation with sound design, multichannel sound recording and reproduction, including the Dolby Digital system, and the replacement of orchestral-type scores with popular music, the sounds and lyrics of which often more directly underscore a movie's action. Finally, in terms of acting, there was a seismic shift from the highly groomed stars of the studio system to a large influx of new actors and a definite reliance on naturalistic acting styles.

In addition to these new directions in the narrative film, there were important advances in the documentary film—notably in Direct Cinema, essentially an American adaptation of *cinéma vérité* (by such filmmakers as Robert Drew, Albert and David Maysles, and Don Alan Pennebaker)—and in

[16] "Blood Bath and Beyond" is the title of A. O. Scott's review in the *New York Times* of Quentin Tarantino's *Kill Bill: Vol. 1*, (October 10, 2003).

experimental films by such artists as Andy Warhol, Ken Jacobs, Bruce Baillie, Carolee Schneemann, Stan Brakhage, and Hollis Frampton. Of late, feature-length animated films have thrived as never before. All of these have had a liberating influence on mainstream filmmaking.

In terms of industry economics and practices, there were many new independent producers, a new financing system by which actors independently arranged their contracts and compensation, a new rating system, and the ability of consumers to rent, buy, or stream movies for home screenings. Combined, these had an impact on production, distribution, exhibition, and profits.

The New American Cinema is significant for these many changes, both large and small, that have transformed the complete structure of the American film industry. Such redefinition and reorganization constitutes a new era—comparable in many ways to the golden age—one dependent on tradition, eager for innovation, adapting to new audiences, and always keeping its eye on the bottom line.

Film history presents an impressive record of achievement, ranging from the first modest efforts to record images on film to the sophisticated movies of today. Even as photography has remained the basis of cinema, in a little more than one hundred years film artists, technicians, and business persons have proved themselves flexible enough to meet, with innovative responses, each challenge facing the medium. When audiences demanded movies with stories as complex as those

[1]

[2]

Documentary and experimental films as pure cinema Both Albert and David Maysles's *Grey Gardens* (1975) [1] and Stan Brakhage's *Dog Star Man* (1962-64) [2] stand out in their respective fields—documentary and experimental films—as superb examples of cinematic form. *Grey Gardens* is a candid, intimate, and often funny look into the lives of two extraordinary women who live together: Mrs. Edith Beale ("Big Edie") and her unmarried daughter, Edith ("Little Edie"). The filmmakers (directors-as-editors) let the film's content shape its form. The women constantly bicker and disagree with one another, so the editing pattern, which juxtaposes one woman with the other, creates a line between them and their views of the past and the present. It is left to the audience to put the pieces together and decide the nature of this power struggle. *Dog Star Man*, like *Grey Gardens*, does not fit a categorical mold, although it is considered a classic experimental film. Stan Brakhage's techniques include superimposing four sequences at once—a kind of visual juxtaposition, similar to that used by the director-editors of *Grey Gardens* in creating multiple meanings—and cutting into the frame to add new material to it. Both movies are pure cinema: work that explores the meaning and experiments with potential of the medium, challenging our perceptions. Films such as these also help us to understand that the work of Stanley Kubrick, another maverick director, is also pure cinema. They involve, to quote the title of one of Brakhage's films, "the act of seeing with our own eyes."

in the novel and theater, the industry developed the full-length narrative film. When the public wanted to hear actors speak as they did on the stage, the industry was transformed with sound recording. And so it goes with other innovations: color film stock, images with greater width and depth, genres to please virtually any audience, and a star system that created every conceivable type of actor. At the same time, there were major improvements in the techniques of cinematography, editing, special effects, acting, and sound recording, as well as new cameras, lenses, film stocks, lighting equipment, and editing devices. Today's artists continue to create new techniques, technologies, and cinematic conventions. They work not just in Hollywood, London, Paris, or Berlin but also in Calcutta, Tokyo, Hong Kong, and Moscow—indeed, in virtually every country and culture in the world. The result—a cinematic language that is universally understood—means that the films of Satyajit Ray, Ingmar Bergman, Steven Soderbergh, Michelangelo Antonioni, or Andrei Tarkovsky speak to an international audience.

The historical development of film is a dynamic process that has created an art form that is constantly evolving. As you will see in the next chapter, the systems of production have kept pace with this aesthetic evolution. In this short history of the movies, we emphasize the films that explore every aspect of this language and in many cases are regarded as cinematic masterpieces. However, not all movies are masterpieces. Film artists—like novelists, painters, or composers—also produce work that is mediocre, films that, despite their weaknesses, please vast audiences and produce the profits that make the film industry a vital part of the world's economy. The history of the movies reveals, among many other things, that art and commerce can coexist.

Analyzing Film History

From this short history of the movies, we can reach several conclusions. First, the movies—in their formal qualities, modes of expression, technologies, and audiences—have changed radically in the course of a little more than hundred years. Second, in many cases, the artists, technicians, and businesspeople responsible for these changes adapted or perfected the achievements of previous filmmakers in order to reach the next level of development. Third, working in different countries and cultures, they produced an art that spoke to a diverse audience in a cinematic language that was universally understood. While there are obviously other common threads unifying the complex course of film history, these should encourage you—when you become excited about a particular movie—to learn more about its place in film history (if it's an older film) or to be alert to a contemporary movie's explicit or implicit connection to other eras of film history and/or particular movies in that history. As you continue to look at movies, whether in class or on your own, you will see the rewards of appreciating, say, a 1927 masterpiece for what it is, where it came from, and how it influenced subsequent film history rather than thinking of it merely as an "old" movie. Likewise, you will also be able to appreciate the latest release for what it is, identifying how those who made it were influenced by past masters as well as what they contributed that seems new. With this approach, you'll understand that there are no "old" or "new" movies, just a continuum of innovation and tradition composed of those movies that we treasure and others that we'd rather forget.

Screening Checklist: Film History

✔ As you study a particular film (or film artist, style, or movement), learn as much as you can about its historical context: the year in which it was made/released; the country of origin; why, if relevant, that year was important to that country's history, and how, if relevant, the movie deals with the events of that period; the means of production (e.g., studio, independent, government-sponsored); the audience for which it was intended; its reception by the public and critics alike. Isolate and identify the movie as closely as you can within this overall context.

✔ Also learn about the film's aesthetic context: Was it made as part of a particular film movement (e.g., Italian Neorealism), or does it break from the prevailing tradition of the period? If it is representative of a movement, how does it measure up against the movement's ideals and achievements? Is it part of a "national cinema" with its own aesthetic, political, and cultural values? Or is it part of the international movement of surrealist films?

✔ Learn something about its director's overall body of work. Is he regarded as an auteur? If so, how is this movie similar to, or different from, his other films? If the director's work is characterized by varying stylistic approaches, is this movie a recognizable example of his style or a break from that tradition? Since you may not have time to see many of the director's movies, compare the movie you are considering with their most famous movie.

✔ Similarly, following the above approach, you may want to study the history of another creative artist in the historical context of a particular genre. A few suggestions are Hayao Miyazaki's anime style within the history of animation, Preston Sturges's screenplays for 1930s screwball comedies, Freddie Young's cinematography for the historical epics directed by David Lean, Ann Roth's approach to designing costumes for period movies, Walter Murch's sound designs for the movies of Francis Ford Coppola, or the production design of films about the Civil War from D. W. Griffith's *The Birth of a Nation* (1915) to Anthony Minghella's *Cold Mountain* (2003).

✔ When an historic event has inspired various movies (e.g., the Great Depression, the Vietnam War, Watergate), you have a rich opportunity to analyze and understand those cinematic interpretations. First, you should understand the complexity of this (and any) historic event by taking notes on how different historians have treated it—in other words, to understand that all historical accounts are themselves interpretations of events. This will establish a context for determining the scope, thoroughness, and effectiveness of the movies inspired by the event.

✔ Have you found that a particular movie has made important innovations in cinematic language or in the use of technology? If so, what are they? Who was principally responsible for them (e.g., the director, sound designer, cinematographer)? Was this a momentary blip on history's screen, or did it become a permanent part of cinematic technique or language? Can you name a specific innovation and its influence on a particular director or movie?

✔ If your movie was the product of a particular Hollywood studio, find out if that studio had a unified style for most of its movies or encouraged its directors to use different styles. If the former, how well does the movie evoke that style? If the latter, how is it different? And did it influence subsequent studio productions?

✔ Many independent movies, those made in the poststudio years, are characterized, on one hand, by adhering to the traditional aspects of cinematic language and, on the other, by making recognizable breaks from tradition. If your movie fits into this category, how "independent" is its director? Is he someone who works solely to fulfill his own vision (e.g., Stanley Kubrick), a maverick who works within the much looser configuration of the New American Cinema (e.g., Clint Eastwood), or a trailblazer who tackles edgy subjects in a bid for new audiences (e.g., Quentin Tarantino)?

✔ Are you interested in the interaction between a movie's ideology and its marketing? If so, choose a movie such as Gus Van Sant's *Milk* (2008)—about the beginnings of the gay-rights movement—and (following the analytical model of Jason Reitman's *Juno* [2007] in Chapter 1), identify its ideology, determine the audiences for which it was produced, and how it was marketed and received. In this, you might provide a context of other films on gay issues, including, among others, Basil Dearden's *Victim* (1961), John Schlesinger's *Midnight Cowboy* (1969), William Friedkin's *Boys in the Band* (1970), Jonathan Demme's *Philadelphia* (1993), and Ang Lee's *Brokeback Mountain* (2005).

Questions for Review

1. What is meant by the term *film history*? Why is a knowledge of it invaluable in looking at movies and analyzing them?

2. What are the four traditional approaches to film history? What are the specific concerns of each?

3. What stylistic movements made cinematic innovations that, as a result, changed the course of film history?

4. The simplest approach to film history is to divide it into the eras of silent and sound production. What was the general state of filmmaking in each of these periods, and how and why does that explain the way movies were made?

5. What (a) was the state of moviemaking in the golden age of the American studio system in the late 1930s, and (b) what film(s) besides Orson Welles's *Citizen Kane* (1941) had a profound effect on filmmakers following its release? What effect(s) did they have?

6. What are the principal differences between the following sets of stylistic movements: (a) German Expressionism and Soviet silent montage; (b) the classical Hollywood style and the New American Cinema; and (c) Italian Neorealism and the French New Wave?

7. The term *New Wave* is used to describe many film movements after the Second World War. What are several of these movements, and what general stylistic characteristics do they have in common?

8. Who, in your understanding, are three of the most innovative and influential directors in film history? What are their contributions?

9. Of the historic events occurring since the invention of the movies, which were most influential in providing subject matter for the movies? Discuss at least two events and identify two movies for each event.

10. From the "prehistory" of the movies, what are the key technological innovations that made the movies possible? Who were three important inventors or innovators, what did they accomplish, and in what countries did they work?

Movies Described or Illustrated in This Chapter

The Adventures of Dollie (1908). D. W. Griffith, director.

Aguirre: The Wrath of God (1972). Werner Herzog, director.

Alexander Nevsky (1938). Sergei Eisenstein, director; Dmitri Vasilyev, codirector.

The American Friend (1977). Wim Wenders, director.

An Andalusian Dog (1929). Salvador Dalí and Luis Buñuel, directors.

An Autumn Afternoon (1962). Yasujiro Ozu, director.

A propos de Nice (1930), Jean Vigo, director.

L'Argent (1928). Marcel L'Herbier, director.

Artists under the Big Top: Perplexed (1968). Alexander Kluge, director.

Ashes of Time (1994). Kar Wai Wong, director.

Baby Face (1933). Alfred E. Green, director.

Badlands (1973). Terrence Malick, director.

Ballet mécanique (1924). Fernand Léger, director.

Battleship Potemkin (1925). Sergei Eisenstein, director.

Belle de Jour (1967). Luis Buñuel, director.

Berlin Alexanderplatz (1980). Rainer Werner Fassbinder, director.

A Better Tomorrow (1986). John Woo, director.

The Bicycle Thieves (1948). Vittorio De Sica, director.

The Big Parade (1925). King Vidor, director.

The Birth of a Nation (1915). D. W. Griffith, director.

The Blood of a Poet (1930). Jean Cocteau, director.

The Blue Angel (1930). Josef von Sternberg, director.

Bonnie and Clyde (1967). Arthur Penn, director.

The Boy from Vietnam (1978). Ann Hui, director.

Breaking the Waves (1996). Lars von Trier, director.

Breathless (1960). Jean-Luc Godard, director.

Bring Me the Head of Alfredo Garcia (1974). Sam Peckinpah, director.

Brokeback Mountain (2005). Ang Lee, director.

Broken Blossoms (1919). D. W. Griffith, director.

The Butcher (1970). Claude Chabrol, director.

The Butterfly Murders (1979). Hark Tsui, director.

The Cabinet of Dr. Caligari (1920). Robert Wiene, director.

Celine and Julie Go Boating (1974). Jacques Rivette, director.

Children Digging for Clams (1896). Auguste Lumière and Louis Lumière, directors.

Chinatown (1974). Roman Polanski, director.

Citizen Kane (1941). Orson Welles, director.

A City of Sadness (1989). Hsiao-hsien Hou, director.

City on Fire (1987). Ringo Lam, director.

Cleo from 5 to 7 (1962). Agnès Varda, director.

Cloverfield (2008). Matt Reeves, director.

Crouching Tiger, Hidden Dragon (2000). Ang Lee, director.

The Crowd (1928). King Vidor, director.

Cruel Story of Youth (1960). Nagisa Oshima, director.

Dancer in the Dark (2000). Lars von Trier, director.

Desperado (1995). Robert Rodriguez, director.

The Discreet Charm of the Bourgeoisie (1972). Luis Buñuel, director.

Dog Star Man, Parts I–IV (1962–64). Stan Brakhage, director.

Dogville (2003). Lars von Trier, director.

Dream Street (1921). D. W. Griffith, director.

Early Spring (1956). Yasujiro Ozu, director.

Easy Living (1937). Mitchell Leisen, director.

Easy Rider (1969). Dennis Hopper, director.

Eat Drink Man Woman (1994). Ang Lee, director.

Edison Kinetoscopic Record of a Sneeze (1894). Thomas A. Edison, director.

Emak-Bakia (1926). Man Ray, director.

Employees Leaving the Lumière Factory (1895). Auguste Lumière and Louis Lumière, directors.

L'Enfant (2005). Jean-Pierre Dardenne and Luc Dardenne, directors.

Entr'acte (1924). René Clair, director.

Eternal Sunshine of the Spotless Mind (2004). Michel Gondry, director.

Even Dwarfs Started Small (1970). Werner Herzog, director.

Every Day Except Christmas (1957). Lindsay Anderson, director.

The Extras (1978). Yim Ho, director.

The Extraordinary Adventures of Mr. West in the Land of the Bolsheviks (1924). Lev Kuleshov, director.

The Fall of the House of Usher (1928). Jean Epstein, director.

Farewell My Concubine (1993). Chen Kaige, director.

Father and Son (1981). Allen Fong, director.

The First Step: Facing Death (1977). Alex Cheung, director.

Five Easy Pieces (1970). Bob Rafelson, director.

The Five Obstructions (2003). Lars von Trier, director.

Flight of the Red Balloon (2007). Hsiao-hsien Hou, director.

Forbidden Kingdom (2008). Rob Minkoff, director.

The 400 Blows (1959). François Truffaut, director.

The General (1926). Buster Keaton, director.

The German Sisters/Marianne and Juliane (1981). Margarethe von Trotta, director.

The Goalie's Anxiety at the Penalty Kick (1972). Wim Wenders, director.

The Gold Rush (1925). Charles Chaplin, director.

The Golem (1920). Paul Wegener and Carl Boese, directors.

Gone with the Wind (1939). Victor Fleming, director.

The Great Train Robbery (1903). Edwin S. Porter, director.

Greed (1924). Erich von Stroheim, director.

Grey Gardens (1975). Albert Maysles, David Maysles, Muffie Meyer, and Ellen Hovde, directors.

A Hard Day's Night (1964). Richard Lester, director.

Heart of Glass (1976). Werner Herzog, director.

The Horse Thief (1986). Tian Zhuangzhuang, director.

The Ice Storm (1997). Ang Lee, director.

The Idiots (1998). Lars von Trier, director.

if . . . . (1968). Lindsay Anderson, director.

In the Realm of the Senses (1976). Nagisa Oshima, director.

Intolerable Cruelty (2003). Joel Coen and Ethan Coen, directors.

Intolerance (1916). D. W. Griffith, director.

Italian for Beginners (2000). Lone Scherfig, director.

An Italian Straw Hat (1928). René Clair, director.

Ivan the Terrible: Part I (1944). Sergei Eisenstein, director.

Ivan the Terrible: Part II (1958). Sergei Eisenstein, director.

The Jazz Singer (1927). Alan Crosland, director.

La Jetée (1962). Chris Marker, director.

Joy Ride (2001). Martin Rengel, director.

Julien Donkey-Boy (1999). Harmony Korine, director.

Junebug (2005). Phil Morrison, director.

Just Like Weather (1986). Allen Fong, director.

Kes (1969). Ken Loach, director.

Kill Bill: Vol. I (2003). Quentin Tarantino, director.

Kill Bill: Vol. II (2004). Quentin Tarantino, director.

The Last Laugh (1924). F. W. Murnau, director.

The Last Picture Show (1969). Peter Bogdanovich, director.

Last Year at Marienbad (1961). Alain Resnais, director.

Leatherheads (2008). George Clooney, director.

Life of an American Fireman (1903). Edwin S. Porter, director.

The Loneliness of the Long Distance Runner (1962). Tony Richardson, director.

Long Distance Wireless Photography (1908). Georges Méliès, director.

Lust, Caution (2007). Ang Lee, director.

M (1931). Fritz Lang, director.

Making an American Citizen (1912). Alice Guy Blaché, director.

The Man with the Movie Camera (1929). Dziga Vertov, director.

March of the Penguins (2005). Luc Jacquet, director.

The Marriage of Maria Braun (1979). Rainer Werner Fassbinder, director.

The Matrix trilogy (1999–2003). Larry Wachowski and Andy Wachowski, directors.

Meet John Doe (1941). Frank Capra, director.

Ménilmontant (1926). Dimitri Kirsanoff, director.

Merry Christmas, Mr. Lawrence (1983). Nagisa Oshima, director.

Metropolis (1927). Fritz Lang, director.

Momma Don't Allow (1955). Tony Richardson and Karel Reisz, directors.

Mother (1926). Vsevolod Pudovkin, director.

Mr. Deeds Goes to Town (1936). Frank Capra, director.

Mr. Smith Goes to Washington (1939). Frank Capra, director.

Murmur of the Heart (1971). Louis Malle, director.

My Night at Maud's (1969). Eric Rohmer, director.

Nanook of the North (1922). Robert J. Flaherty, director.

Napoléon (1927). Abel Gance, director.

Nosferatu the Vampyre (1979). Werner Herzog, director.

Nosferatu, a Symphony of Horror (1922). F. W. Murnau, director.

October (Ten Days That Shook the World) (1928). Sergei Eisenstein, director.

Once (2006). John Carney, director.

Open Hearts (2002). Susanne Bier, director.

Orphans of the Storm (1921). D. W. Griffith, director.

Ossessione (1943). Luchino Visconti, director.

Pandora's Box (1929). G. W. Pabst, director.

Paris, Texas (1984). Wim Wenders, director.

The Passion of Joan of Arc (1928). Carl Theodor Dreyer, director.

Pather Panchali (1955). Satyajit Ray, director.

The Peach Blossom Land (1992). Stan Lai, director.

Peking Opera Blues (1986). Hark Tsui, director.

The Postman Always Rings Twice (1946). Tay Garnett, director.

The Postman Always Rings Twice (1981). Bob Rafelson, director.

Que Viva México (1930–32). Sergei Eisenstein, director.

Raise the Red Lantern (1991). Yimou Zhang, director.

Ran (1985). Akira Kurosawa, director.

Rashomon (1950). Akira Kurosawa, director.

Reservoir Dogs (1992). Quentin Tarantino, director.

Rien que les heures (1926). Alberto Cavalcanti, director.

Rome, Open City (1945). Roberto Rossellini, director.

Room at the Top (1959). Jack Clayton, director.

The Royal Tenenbaums (2001). Wes Anderson, director.

Rush Hour (1998). Brett Ratner, director.

Rush Hour 2 (2001). Brett Ratner, director.

Rush Hour 3 (2007). Brett Ratner, director.

Sansho the Bailiff (1954). Kenji Mizoguchi, director.

Saturday Night and Sunday Morning (1960). Karel Reisz, director.

The Seashell and the Clergyman (1928). Germaine Dulac, director.

Seminary Girls (1897). Thomas A. Edison, director.

Sense and Sensibility (1995). Ang Lee, director.

The Servant (1963). Joseph Losey, director.

Shoeshine (1946). Vittorio De Sica, director.

A Simple Plan (1998). Sam Raimi, director.

A Spectrum of Multiple Stars: Wang Chuanru* (1975). Patrick Tam, director.

Stranger Than Paradise (1984). Jim Jarmusch, director.

Straw Dogs (1971). Sam Peckinpah, director.

Strike (1925). Sergei Eisenstein, director.

Sunset Boulevard (1950). Billy Wilder, director.

Taipei Story (1985). Edward Yang, director.

Tokyo Story (1953). Yasujiro Ozu, director.

A Trip to the Moon (1902). Georges Méliès, director.

2001: A Space Odyssey (1968). Stanley Kubrick, director.

Ugetsu (1953). Kenji Mizoguchi, director.

Victim (1961). Basil Dearden, director.

Viridiana (1961). Luis Buñuel, director.

Vive l'amour (1994). Tsai Ming-liang, director.

Way down East (1920). D. W. Griffith, director.

We Are the Lambeth Boys (1958). Karel Reisz, director.

The Wedding Banquet (1993). Ang Lee, director.

The Wheel (1923). Abel Gance, director.

The Wild Bunch (1969). Sam Peckinpah, director.

Young Torless (1966). Volker Schlöndorff, director.

CHAPTER ELEVEN

Filmmaking Technologies and Production Systems

After reading this chapter, you should be able to

✔ explain the key technological milestones that laid the foundation for the invention of the movies.

✔ understand the basic nature of the three filmmaking technologies: film, video, and digital.

✔ understand the challenges and benefits involved in converting the film industry to digital technology in the areas of production, distribution, and exhibition.

✔ make a clear distinction between the three basic phases of making a movie: preproduction, production, and postproduction.

✔ explain the studio system, its organization, and its decline.

✔ explain the independent system, its current prominence, and how it differs from the studio system.

✔ understand the varieties of financing in the film industry.

✔ understand how movies are marketed and distributed.

The Whole Equation

The art of the movies—the primary concern of this book—is inseparable from its business, methods, filmmaking technologies, and production systems. In his novel *The Last Tycoon*, F. Scott Fitzgerald attempted to explain how Hollywood works:

> You can take Hollywood for granted like I did, or you can dismiss it with the contempt we reserve for what we don't understand. It can be understood too, but only dimly and in flashes. Not half a dozen men have ever been able to keep the whole equation of pictures in their heads.[1]

In fact, however, that equation is simple: moviemaking is, above all, a moneymaking enterprise.[2]

In the movie industry, costs and profits are measured in hundreds of millions of dollars. Today the average Hollywood film costs about $64 million to produce and an additional $35 million to market. Thus, with the average movie costing about $100 million, the individuals and financial institutions that invest in the production of films, and the producers and studios in whom they invest, care first about money (ensuring the safety and potential return of their investments) and second—often a distant second—about art. They focus on movies as commodities and, for that reason, often consider release dates, distribution, and marketing as more important than the products themselves. In view of this reality, it is all the more impressive, then, that the movie industry produces a small number of films each year that can be appreciated, analyzed, and interpreted as genuine works of art rather than simply as commercial products to be consumed.

Because movie production involves a much more complicated and costly process than do most other artistic endeavors, very few decisions are made lightly. Unlike some arts—painting, for example—in which the materials and the process are relatively inexpensive, every decision in filmmaking has significant financial ramifications. Painters may paint over pictures many times without incurring steep costs, and thus their decisions can be dictated almost entirely by artistic inspiration. Movies, in contrast, involve a constant tug-of-war between artistic vision and profitability.

A great movie generally requires two key ingredients: a good script and a director's inspiration, vision, intelligence, and supervision (but not necessarily control) of all aspects of the film's production. Because the director plays the paramount role in the production process and in most cases has final authority over the result, we ordinarily cite a film in this way: Tamara Jenkins's *The Savages* (2007). But although movie history began with staunchly individual filmmakers, movies have been carried

[1] F. Scott Fitzgerald, *The Last Tycoon: An Unfinished Novel* (New York: Scribner's, 1941), p. 3.

[2] David Thomson takes a nonfiction approach to defining the equation in *The Whole Equation: A History of Hollywood* (New York: Knopf, 2005).

forward through the years by teamwork. From the moment the raw film stock is purchased through its exposure, processing, editing, and projection, filmmakers depend on a variety of technology, technicians, and craftspeople. And no matter how clear filmmakers' ideas may be at the start, their work will change considerably, thanks to technology and teamwork, between its early stages and the final version released to the public.

Although many movie directors—working under such pressures as producers' schedules and budgets—have been known for taking their power all too seriously (being difficult on the set, throwing tantrums, screaming at and even physically assaulting members of the cast and crew, and raging at the front office), moviemaking is essentially a collaborative activity.[3] Even then, as film scholar Jon Lewis observes, "what ends up on the screen is not only a miracle of persistence and inspiration but also the result of certain practical concessions to the limitations of the studio system."[4]

Film production is complicated by the cost-effective, standard practice of shooting movies out of chronological order. This means that the production crew shoots the film not in the order that preserves narrative continuity but in an order that allows the most efficient use of human and financial resources. During production, a script supervisor stays as close to the director as possible, for this person is an invaluable source of factual information about the shooting. The script supervisor records all details of continuity from shot to shot, ascertaining that costumes, positioning and orientation of objects, and placement and movement of actors are consistent in each successive shot and, indeed, in all parts of the film. Overall, the pattern of production includes securing and developing a story with audience appeal; breaking the story into units that can be shot most profitably; shooting; establishing through editing the order in which events will appear on-screen; and then adding the sound, music, and special effects that help finish the movie. Today, however, because the use of a video assist camera permits a director to review each take immediately after shooting, it is much easier to match details from shot to shot.

The process once took place in the vast, factory-like studios that dominated Hollywood and other major film-production centers around the world. Today it happens in the self-contained worlds of individual production units, which often operate in leased studio facilities. The differences between these two modes of production are, in a sense, reflected in movies' production credits. In older films, all the (brief) production credits generally appear at the beginning, with the names of the leading actors sometimes repeated in (and constituting) the closing credits. Today opening credits vary widely, but closing credits are lengthy and often include several hundred people, accounting for virtually every person who worked on a film or had something to do with it (e.g., caterers, animal handlers, accountants). Collective-bargaining agreements between producers and various labor unions—representing every person who works on a union production—impose clear definitions of all crewmembers' responsibilities as well as the size and placement of their screen credits. These credits properly and legally acknowledge people's contributions to films.[5]

This chapter provides an introduction to the history of motion-picture technologies and production systems, showing that Hollywood is very much a product of its past. Today's Hollywood reflects how well the industry has adapted to the challenges of changing content, technologies, audiences, and exhibition opportunities. It remains one of the world's largest industries, and the impact of American

[3]Insights into the long hours and hard work that go into movie production are provided in movies about making movies, which show us that, in a world of large egos, collaboration can be a myth and that many things go wrong on most movie sets. See "For Further Viewing" at the end of this chapter for a list of such films. See also Rudy Behlmer and Tony Thomas, *Hollywood's Hollywood: The Movies about the Movies* (Secaucus, N.J.: Citadel, 1975).
[4]Jon Lewis, *Whom God Wishes to Destroy—: Francis Coppola and the New Hollywood* (Durham, N.C.: Duke University Press, 1995), p. 4.

[5]Because nonunion crews make many independent films, these conventions of the division of labor and screen credit do not necessarily apply to independent films. Often on such films, crew members may be relatively inexperienced, not yet qualified for union membership, or unwilling to play several roles in return for the experience and screen credit. Government agencies and volunteer individuals or organizations may also be credited for their contributions.

movies is felt around the globe. Today, however, it confronts another major issue—the question of an all-out conversion from film to digital technology—one that will be decided almost entirely on the relationship between costs and profits, the only equation.

In order to understand certain aesthetic judgments made by film producers, directors, and their collaborators, you should be familiar with the fundamentals of how a movie is made—in particular, with the three filmmaking technologies (film, video, and digital) and the three phases of the moviemaking process (preproduction, production, and postproduction).

Film, Video, and Digital Technologies: An Overview

Looking at movies is more about what is on the screen than the technology that is unique to this art form. And since that technology is far less complicated than you might think, knowing something about it should further enhance your understanding of how movies are made. Motion-picture technology—and the production systems it serves—has developed in a simple, straight line since the early 1890s until recently. The three stages in this technological development are film, video, and digital.

Film Technology

When we refer to film technology, we mean that film stock is the medium on which the image is recorded. Film is an **analog** medium in which the camera (1) creates an image by recording through a camera lens the original light given off by the subject and (2) stores this image on a roll of negative film stock. That stock, coated with an emulsion which contains silver crystals, yields an image that closely resembles what the human eye sees. We call it *analog* because the image is analogous, or proportional, to the input. To state it another way, once it is processed (or "developed"), the negative image (on the negative stock) becomes a positive image (on positive stock); the first image is analogous to the second.

Even though video and digital technology have emerged recently, film remains the dominant technology. Unlike the newer technologies, film involves a mechanical system that moves this film stock through several machines: a camera, a processor, and a projector. These three machines bring images to the screen in three distinct stages, and light plays a vital role throughout.

In the first stage, **shooting**, the camera exposes film to light, allowing that radiant energy to burn a negative image onto each frame. In the second stage, **processing**, the negative is developed into a positive print that the filmmaker can then screen in order to plan the editing, a process that produces the final print. In the third stage, **projecting**, the final print is run through a projector, which shoots through the film a beam of light intense enough to reverse the initial process and project a large image on the movie screen. (This account greatly condenses the entire process to emphasize, at this point, only the cycle of light common to all three stages.)

Projecting a strip of exposed frames at the same speed—traditionally 16 frames per second (fps) for silent film, 24 fps for sound—creates the illusion of movement. Silent cameras and projectors were often hand-cranked, and so the actual speed of the camera, which then had to be matched by the projectionist, might vary from 12 to 24 fps. Cameras and projectors used for making and exhibiting professional films are powered by electric motors that ensure a perfect movement of the film (Figure 11.1). As digital technology replaces this mechanical process, it is changing the equipment and media on which the images are captured, processed, and projected, but the role of light remains the same essential component.

A movie film's **format** is the gauge, or width, of the film stock and its perforations (measured in millimeters) and the size and shape of the image frame as seen on the screen (Figure 11.2). Formats extend from Super 8mm through 70mm and beyond into such specialized formats as IMAX (ten times bigger than a conventional 35mm frame and three times bigger than a standard 70mm frame). The format chosen depends on the type of film

FIGURE 11.1   The Motion-Picture Camera

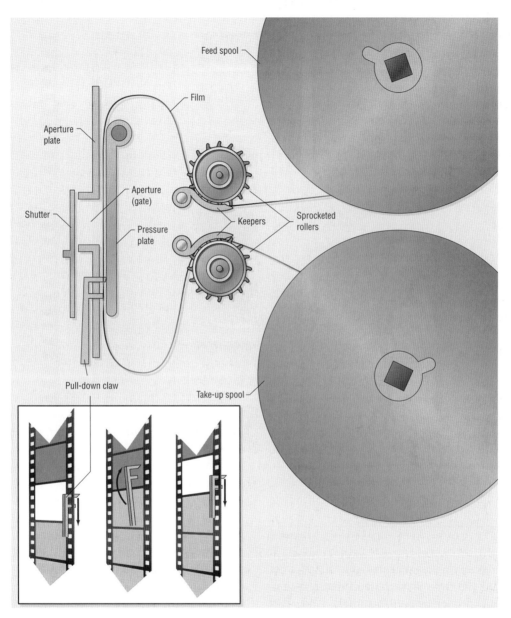

The motion-picture camera moves unexposed film from one storage area, called the **feed spool** (or, in professional cameras today, the portion of the magazine that stores unexposed film), along the **sprocketed rollers**, which control the speed of the film as it moves through the camera and toward the lens, which focuses the image on the film as it is exposed. The **aperture** (or gate) is essentially the window through which each frame of film is exposed. The **shutter**—a mechanism that shields the film from light while each frame is moved into place—is synchronized with the motion of the **pull-down claw**, a mechanism used in both cameras and projectors to advance the film frame by frame. The pull-down claw holds each frame still for the fraction of a second that the shutter allows the aperture to be open so that the film can be exposed. The **take-up spool** (or, again, the portion of the magazine that stores exposed film) winds the film after it has been exposed.

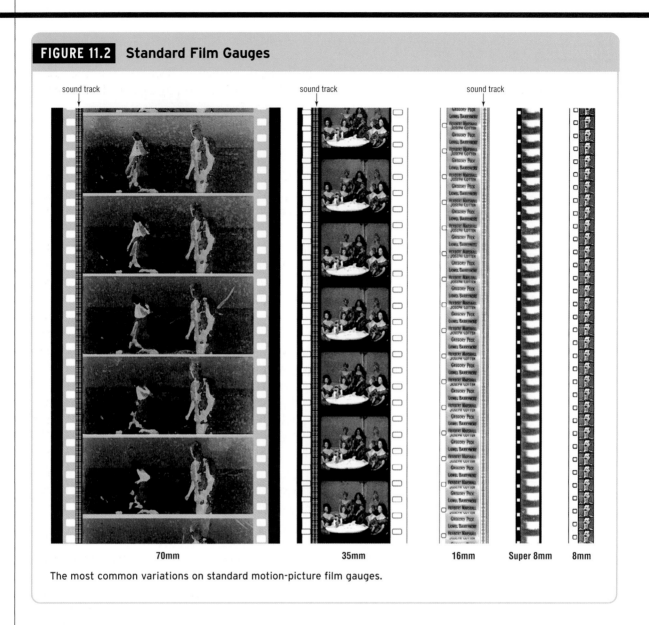

70mm   35mm   16mm   Super 8mm   8mm

The most common variations on standard motion-picture film gauges.

being made, the financing available to support the project, and the overall visual look that the film-maker wants to achieve. For example, a low-key, fairly low-budget, and intimate narrative film (such as Phil Morrison's *Junebug* [2005]) might be shot in 16mm or 35mm format, but an action-filled, broad, and expensive nonfiction film (such as Luc Jacquet's *March of the Penguins* [2005]) might require a 70mm or IMAX format. The **film-stock length** is the number of feet (or meters) or the number of reels being used in a particular film. The **film-stock**

speed (or *exposure index*), the degree to which it is light-sensitive, ranges from very fast, at which it requires little light, to very slow, at which it requires a lot of light. Film is also categorized into black-and-white and color stock.

In traditional film production, cinematographers control the photographic image with their choice of stock; the amount and color of the lighting of each shot, the **exposure** (the length of time that the film is exposed to light), and the opening of the lens aperture (this regulates the amount of light that passes through the lens onto the surface of the film); the **resolution** (the capacity of the camera lens, film stock, and processing to provide fine detail in an image); the instructions provided to the processing laboratory, including special effects; and in the postproduction effort, possible involvement in the editing process.

Professional motion-picture photography is a complex, time-consuming, and expensive process, but many filmmakers think it's worth it because it is the only way they can achieve the rich "look" that we traditionally associate with the movies. However, as we shall discuss below, film and digital images are now virtually indistinguishable, one factor spurring the momentum with which the entire process of making feature movies is moving toward a conversion to digital technology.

Video Technology

Although television was feasible in 1931, it was not until after the Second World War that the U.S. television industry began its rapid growth and transformation of American culture. The word *video* is used to describe the visual and audio components of television, but its technology, before today's digital revolution, also played a noteworthy role in moviemaking after the 1950s. Unlike the photographic image, the video image consists of **pixels** (short for "picture elements"), the small dots that make up the image on a video screen. Think of these pixels as being similar to the individual pieces that constitute a jigsaw picture puzzle—alone, they are meaningless, but arranged in order on a table, they form a picture. When electronic technology puts these pixels together, they make up the picture that is recorded on videotape (later, digital videotape) and that we see on a video monitor. Newspaper and magazine photographs are similarly composed of thousands of dots (each containing a bit of information), which our eyes see as a total photograph. However, the low picture quality of video images never matched the quality of images shot on film, and editing videotape was actually more difficult than editing film. Video's only strengths were that the stock was cheap and did not need processing.

Even though video technology became highly digitized (and today continues to be used in amateur filmmaking, low-budget documentary production, and other areas), it is rarely used by the film industry to make feature-length movies.

Digital Technology

Digital technology involves an electronic process that creates its images through a numbered system of pixels (which we can think of as the binary numbers 0 and 1). Unlike the analog image, these do not have a physical relationship to the original. Indeed, they are not exactly images but rather thousands of digits stored on a **flash card** or a computer hard drive. These digits are reconstructed into visual images each time the movie is edited or shown and, unlike film stock, can be manipulated endlessly. For example, filmmakers can make many different versions of any scene in search of the perfect arrangement or timing of shots as well as adjust and manipulate the light, color, and quality of the image. Furthermore, digital technology is easier to use than film technology. It uses less light than film technology, and like video, there is no processing involved. Overall, digital is much more versatile, easier, and (beyond the initial investment in new equipment) cheaper to work with than film. Film is fragile and disintegrates over time; digital copies (such as DVDs) can be scratched, but compared to a film print, they are easily duplicated and virtually indestructible under normal conditions.

Although clearly superior to video, digital technology's image resolution was not comparable to film's fine-grained resolution until very recently. But as computer technology has progressed rapidly after the turn of the century, new, lightweight, and more affordable digital cameras (such as the Red One) are beginning to match the resolution of 35mm film stock so that the projected image is virtually indistinguishable from film. And ironically, digital technology is also being used to save and restore damaged or decaying film prints, a major benefit for the study of film history. But to give you an idea of the competition by manufacturers for the film industry's business, concurrent improvements are also being made in film cameras, stock, and processing and printing technologies. This can only mean that the race to determine which technology will dominate movie production—film or digital—has not yet been won.

Film versus Digital Technology

Before we proceed, let's summarize the strengths and weaknesses of both technologies. Film stock is a physical thing; digital is virtual representation. Film stock runs through a mechanical device and is subjected to a chemical reaction when light from the lens strikes silver-nitrate crystals (or whatever) on the stock, which must be kept locked away from light and must be processed by a lab and edited on a work print (which allows the editor to see only one version of any scene or sequence at any one time). Digital takes that same light from the lens and processes it through a sensor chip into pixels, which were traditionally put on various types of tape but increasingly are now recorded directly onto a flash card (much like the USB devices you use to move files between computers) or directly onto a computer hard drive. It doesn't have to go through a laboratory for processing and can be manipulated with complete freedom on the computer. Editors can adjust colors, clean up glitches or mistakes, and make an infinite number of versions of any cut, sequence, or scene for comparative purposes. Practically speaking, it's like the difference between writing a paper with a typewriter and writing it with a computer's word-processing program.

What is the current state of digital production, distribution, and exhibition of films? So far, Hollywood has used digital systems to produce less than 1 percent of the movies released (excluding animated features), including George Lucas's *Star Wars: Episode 1—The Phantom Menace* (1999), Michael Mann's *Collateral* (2004), and David Fincher's *Zodiac* (2007). What's in play here is not just the studios' reluctance to pay the costs of buying new equipment and installing new facilities or modifying existing ones—studios can rent digital or analog cameras for about the same price—but also opposition from the filmmakers, distributors, and exhibitors. Some directors—including James Cameron, David Fincher, George Lucas, David Lynch, Robert Rodriguez, and Lars von Trier—have claimed that celluloid film is dead and that future filmmaking will be an all-digital medium. Yet many others prefer film technology, at least in the production stage. They will insist on retaining that option, even though the movies they produce on film will most likely be transferred to digital media for exhibition. Several directors—including Tim Burton, Martin Scorsese, Ridley Scott, Oliver Stone, and Quentin Tarantino—have said that they will continue to shoot on film. They are dedicated to film's particular aesthetic: its film grain, its depth of color and shadow, even its imperfections. Andrew Stanton, the director of *WALL-E* (2008), revealed that Pixar, the studio that produced it, uses sophisticated software to put defects into their high-tech digital images: barrel distortion (lenses make things bend), shallow depth of field (limited image depth in focus), lens flares (light reflecting inside the lens mechanism), and film grain. How ironic it is that digital technicians are now going to such trouble to re-create imperfections that camera technicians have worked so long and hard to minimize or eliminate.

On the other hand, virtually 100 percent of all feature films are digitally edited, showing that all filmmakers are convinced by the efficiency and flexibility of the available editing technology. That's understandable, considering that digital-editing suites are reasonably priced. In distribution and exhibition (getting the movie to the theaters and up on the screens), there has been measurable progress in converting theaters (far less than the 100 percent editing figure but more than the 1 percent production figure). As you might expect, the key factors are economic. The major obstacle is the cost of converting a theater's projection and sound systems, estimated at anywhere from $75,000 to $150,000 or more per screen (remember that a single multiplex can have 12 or more screens, and the projector for each would need converting). As of late 2012, 30,000 of the nation's 40,000 screens had been converted to digital projection, leaving the remainder, mostly small town or seasonal theaters, as they are or in some stage of transition.

However, a recent development indicates that the industry is making major progress in speeding up conversion and lowering its costs. In March 2009, the AMC theater chain announced an agreement with Sony to provide digital movie projectors to their 4,628 screens in five countries. These projectors will be installed between 2009 and 2012 at an estimated cost of some $60,000 per theater.[6]

Clearly, while theater owners are less willing to upgrade than studios might be, there is a substantial potential for distributors and exhibitors to realize great savings as a result of digital conversion. These savings would occur in distribution costs, the availability of a wider range of content for the audiences, and significant control of movie piracy. In contrast to traditional methods of distributing movies to movie theaters, digital distribution seems cost-effective. In traditional film-distribution processes, new film prints, costing around $1,200, must be made for each theater (and must also be replaced regularly because a print deteriorates as it runs through a projector). If this movie were distributed to 5,000 screens (out of the 40,000 total in the United States), that cost would be $6 million, not including the cost of shipping the bulky, heavy cans that contain these 35mm film prints. By contrast, downloading a digital copy of a film to a theater's computer system (which could simply be a hard drive costing under $100) costs virtually nothing. Converting to digital projection (also called *digital cinema*) could save the film industry $1 billion a year or more. The advent of the DVD and the home theater system was once regarded as a threat to the future of the movie theater. However, since both theater admissions and the number of movie screens have, according to the latest available information, remained stable since 2006, it seems highly likely that the development of digital technology will give us the options of looking at movies at home, in theaters, or both.

Digitally equipped theaters are able to offer more than feature films, including sports, entertainment, cultural events, and independent movies that might not otherwise seem profitable but which could be more or less subsidized for short runs in a multiplex. Such an expanded range of content can be particularly valuable in areas where there are no alternative theaters and few cultural opportunities. Finally, with digital distribution, a blockbuster movie could be released and screened simultaneously in all areas of the United States, even around the world, thus maximizing the audience. Such instantaneous, widespread exposure might curtail the market for pirated copies made surreptitiously inside a theater by a thief using a camcorder and then duplicated in cheap copies sold on the streets. However, the industry also fears that digital exhibition will foster the theft and subsequent pirating of the digital release prints themselves. Furthermore, digital technology is changing so rapidly that long-term preservation of digital movies will remain problematic until stable standards can be established. By contrast, the 35mm film format was very rapidly standardized in the 1890s within a few years of the technology's invention and has remained stable, with various improvements, until today.

Finally, the motion-picture industry is traditionally very conservative about investing money that will diminish profits, is not uniformly convinced about the relative strengths and weaknesses of digital technology, and perhaps as a result of these factors, has yet to take a united position in the conversion to digital technology the way it did in undertaking the conversion to sound in the late 1920s. The distributors and exhibitors have the most to lose because they realize the competitive power of such alternative ways of delivering movies as direct downloading to homes and, as a result, have made significant progress in converting theaters. The battle over film versus digital technology is not over. But it seems that the conversion to digital is no longer a matter of if but rather of when.[7]

How a Movie Is Made

The making of a movie, whether by a studio or by an independent producer (as we'll discuss later) and whether it is shot on film, video, or a digital

---

[6]http://www.nytimes.com/2009/03/30/technology/companies/30sony.html?_r=1&scp=4&sq=sony%204k%20digital%20movie%20projector&st=cse.

[7]Producers, distributors, and exhibitors incur additional costs when a movie is made and shown in the increasingly popular 3-D format.

medium, proceeds through three basic phases: preproduction, production, and postproduction.

Preproduction

The first stage, **preproduction**, consists of planning and preparation. It takes as long as necessary to get the job done—on average, a year or two. Initially, filmmakers develop an idea or obtain a script they wish to produce. They may secure from a publisher the rights to a successful novel or buy a writer's "pitch" for a story. The opening segment of the late Robert Altman's *The Player* (1992) provides a comic view of the start of a studio executive's typical day. The executive, Griffin Mill (Tim Robbins), has the responsibility of listening to initial pitches from writers and recommending to his boss the ones he likes. Moving blithely through a world of business politics, intrigue, and power games, he hears from people with and without appointments, losers, hangers-on, hacks, and even experienced authors. Everyone he meets wants to be a screenwriter, and everyone wants to cast Julia Roberts. The pitches are, for the most part, desperate attempts to make a new movie out of two previously successful ones, as when one scriptwriter—who cannot even agree with her partner on what they're talking about—summarizes a proposal as "*Out of Africa* meets *Pretty Woman*." The final pitch before the credits end, about a "political thriller," serves as a transition to the thriller at the heart of Altman's film. One of Hollywood's most inventive and successful independent directors, Altman clearly knew the territory well enough to satirize it.

Once the rights to producing a story have been contracted and purchased, the producers can spend months arranging the financing for a production. The ease with which they accomplish this, and the funds that they secure, will largely depend on the film they offer to their backers and its projected financial returns. As we'll see, a director may spend another month or more discussing the script with the screenwriter and the key people responsible for design, photography, music, and sound. Another two or three months may be spent rewriting the script. Throughout the preproduction period, the producers continually estimate and reestimate the budget. The final budget, which should cover all foreseeable expenses, also reflects their marketing strategy. As one example, the producers of *Inception* (2010) allocated a production budget of $160 million and an advertising budget of $100 million, a shrewd calculation considering the movie was not only a major box-office success but was also nominated for an Academy Award for best picture. During this process of previsualization, before the cameras start to roll, the director and the chief collaborators decide how they want the film to look, sound, and move. At least two to three weeks more can be devoted to organizational issues and details such as scheduling studio space and scouting locations, obtaining permissions to use those locations, and arranging for the design and construction of sets, costumes, and properties. Just before shooting begins, another two weeks will probably be devoted to rehearsals with the cast and crew.

Up to this point, almost a year has elapsed—assuming that all has gone smoothly. Though the entire process of making a movie may seem straightforward, this description does not take into account the inevitable delays, the continuing difficulties in pulling together the financial package, and the countless details that must be attended to. For example, a film made at the peak of the Hollywood studio system would have been carefully planned, budgeted, and supervised by the producer in the front office, whether it was shot in a studio or on location. Daily reports to and from the set ensured that everyone knew, to the minute and to the dollar, the progress and the cost.

Orson Welles extensively composed and planned the shots of his first film, *Citizen Kane* (1941), which was photographed entirely in the RKO studio and miraculously (considering Welles's later reputation as a spendthrift independent director) was completed in less than a year, almost within the allotted budget. By contrast, Francis Ford Coppola, already a highly experienced director by the time he made *Apocalypse Now* (1979), began without a clear plan of what he wanted to achieve, worked as an independent producer with financing from United Artists, and shot the film in a foreign country under very difficult conditions, ultimately exposing 115 hours of film for every hour actually used. During the four years it took to complete the film, he spent more than twice his original budget.

In making a film, meticulous preparation is everything, and key people take the time to think out alternatives and choose the one that seems best for the film. Thorough planning does not stifle further creativity or improvisation during production but rather encourages it, because planning makes the alternatives clear. Director Sidney Lumet emphasizes the logistics:

> Someone once asked me what making a movie was like. I said it was like making a mosaic. Each setup is like a tiny tile [a *setup*, the basic component of a film's production, consists of one camera position and everything associated with it]. You color it, shape it, polish it as best you can. You'll do six or seven hundred of these, maybe a thousand. (There can easily be that many setups in a movie.) Then you literally paste them together and hope it's what you set out to do. But if you expect the final mosaic to look like anything, you'd better know what you're going for as you work on each tiny tile.[8]

Production

Production, the actual shooting, can last six weeks to several months or more. Although the producer and director continue to work very closely together, the director ordinarily takes charge during the shooting. The director's principal activities during this period are conducting blocking and lighting rehearsals on the set with stand-ins, followed by rehearsals with the cast; supervising the compilation of the records that indicate what is being shot each day and informing cast and crew members of their assignments; placing and, for each subsequent shot, replacing cameras, lights, microphones, and other equipment; shooting each shot as many times as necessary until the director is satisfied and calls "print"; reviewing the results of each day's shooting (called *rushes* or *dailies*) with key creative personnel and cast; and reshooting as necessary.

Every director works differently. Ordinarily, however, the director further breaks down the shooting script into manageable sections, then sets a goal of shooting a specified number of pages a day (typically, three pages is a full day's work). This process depends on the number of setups involved. Most directors try to shoot between fifteen and twenty setups a day when they're in the studio, where everything can be controlled; for exterior shooting, the number of setups varies. In any event, everyone involved in the production works a full day—usually from about 8:00 a.m. to about 6:00 p.m. (depending on their jobs and contracts), five days a week, with overtime when necessary. When complicated makeup and costuming are required, the actors may be asked to report for work early enough to finish that preparation before the crew is due to report. After each day's shooting, or as soon thereafter as the processing laboratory can deliver them, the director and others review the rushes. (Movies shot digitally or with a video assist camera can be reviewed immediately, allowing retakes to be made with the same setup or a different one.)

At a recent movie shoot in a Manhattan store, which was closed for the night to give the crew maximum access, any observer would have seen why it takes longer than one might expect to complete even the simplest shot. By actual count, forty crew members were there to support the director and four actors, who were ready to work. After the first setup was blocked, rehearsed, and lit, the director made three takes. This process took three hours. However, the rest of the day's schedule was abandoned because the lighting that had been brought in for the shoot failed. Why? The gaffer, the chief electrician, had neglected to ensure that the store's electrical capacity could support it. By the time generators were located and trucked to the site, two hours had been lost. Of course, any one of a dozen problems—human and technical—could have kept the director and crew from meeting their schedule.

During production, the number of people required to film a particular shot depends on the needs of that shot or, more precisely, on the overall scene in which the shot occurs. Many factors determine the size of the crew for any shot or scene, including the use of studio or exterior locations, day or night shooting, shooting on an uncrowded

---

[8]Sidney Lumet, *Making Movies* (New York: Knopf, 1995), p. 58.

exterior location or a crowded city street, camera and lighting setups, and the extent of movement by the camera and the actors. For example, a scene that involves two people in a simple interior setting, with a basic camera and lighting setup, may require a minimal crew, while a scene involving many people in an exterior setting, with several camera positions and carefully choreographed movement, normally requires a large crew. The creation of artificial weather (rain, wind, or snow) and the use of animals or crowds—all expensive factors—require additional personnel. Shooting on exterior locations is usually more expensive than shooting in a studio because it involves transportation and food, sometimes requires hotel accommodations, and depends to a considerable extent on the weather.

To better understand what's involved in shooting, we'll look briefly at the production of Robert Zemeckis's *Cast Away* (2000). The movie features Tom Hanks as Chuck Noland, a FedEx systems engineer based in Memphis, Tennessee. While he is en route from Moscow to the Far East, his plane crashes in the ocean, and Chuck, the only survivor, washes ashore on a desert island. After sustaining himself physically, emotionally, and spiritually for four years, Chuck builds a raft and attempts to return to civilization. Overwhelmed by the elements and near death, he is picked up by a freighter and returned to Memphis, where he faces yet another emotional challenge.

In making *Cast Away*, the production crew faced daunting physical and logistical problems. Their largest challenge was to make the most efficient use of human, financial, and physical resources. The film, which cost $85 million to produce, was shot on soundstages in Hollywood as well as on actual locations in Texas, Tennessee, Russia, and the Fiji island of Monuriki in the South Pacific; the task of planning the overall production schedule was relatively routine, however. Although the largest part of the film's three-part structure is set on Monuriki and features only one actor (Hanks), the cast actually includes nearly sixty other actors. The credits list another 123 members of the production crew, most involved in the creation of the visual and special effects.

When shooting on Monuriki, the crew had to endure real winds, storms, and floods, and when nature would not cooperate with their shooting schedule, they had to create their own bad weather. Furthermore, their work depended on the tides and available sunlight (Chuck would not have had artificial light on the island). The airplane crash was simulated in Hollywood, where considerable shooting was done underwater, and the scenes of Chuck's attempted escape by raft were shot on the ocean as well as in the perilous surf off another Fiji island. After one month's shooting on Monuriki, capturing footage that established Chuck's overall challenge, the crew took a yearlong hiatus while Hanks lost the fifty pounds he had gained to portray Chuck in the early part of the film. This change helped create the illusion that Chuck had spent four years on the island. Meeting these challenges as successfully as the filmmakers did (while maintaining visual consistency within the footage) was central to maintaining the film's verisimilitude.

Postproduction

When the shooting on a film has been completed, **postproduction** begins. Postproduction consists of three phases: editing, preparing the final print, and bringing the film to the public (marketing and distribution). In brief, editing consists of assembling the visual images and sound recordings, adding the musical score and sound effects, adding the special effects, assembling the sound tracks, and doing any necessary dubbing. Preparing the final print consists of timing the color print, a process of inspecting each shot of a film and assigning color corrections and printer light values to maintain consistency of brightness and color from shot to shot; completing the first combined picture and sound print, in release form, of a finished film; possibly previewing the film; then possibly making changes in response to the comments of preview audiences. Bringing the film to the public consists of determining the marketing and advertising strategies and budgets, setting the release date and number of theaters, finalizing distribution rights and ancillary rights, and finally exhibiting the film.

In your study of movies, keep in mind that the art of the movies has been influenced not only by changes in technology and cinematic conventions but also by changes in the production process. Thus the Hollywood studio-system process that created F. W. Murnau's *Sunrise: A Song of Two Humans* (1927) was very different from the independent production process that created Ang Lee's *Brokeback Mountain* (2005). The history of Hollywood production systems can be easily understood as comprising three basic periods: the studio system, the independent system, and a system today that manages to combine them. Let's look more closely at each of them.

The Studio System
Organization before 1931

The studio system's roots go back to the first decade of the twentieth century and the pioneering attempts of men such as Thomas Edison, Carl Laemmle, Thomas H. Ince, and D. W. Griffith to make, distribute, and exhibit movies. In 1905, Laemmle began to distribute and exhibit films, but by 1909 his efforts were threatened by the Motion Picture Patents Company (MPPC—not to be confused with the Motion Picture Production Code), a protective trade association (or trust) controlled by Edison, which sought both to control the motion-picture industry completely and to eliminate competition by charging licensing fees on production and projection equipment. However, widespread resistance to the MPPC encouraged competition and laid the groundwork for both the studio and independent systems of production. The U.S. government broke the MPPC monopoly in 1915.

Between 1907 and 1913, a large number of movie production companies in New York and New Jersey migrated to various spots in warmer climates, including Florida, Texas, and New Mexico, but eventually the main companies settled in southern California in and around Hollywood. They did so to take advantage of the year-round good weather, the beautiful and varied scenery, the abundant light for outdoor shooting, and the geographic distance from the greedy MPPC;[9] soon they had a critical mass of both capital and talent on which to build an industry. By 1915, more than 60 percent of the American film industry, employing approximately 15,000 workers, was located in Hollywood.

The early studios relied on a system dominated by a central producer, a person in charge of the well-organized mass production system that was necessary for producing feature films. This system of central production began in 1912 and was the dominant practice by 1914. At his Hollywood studio, Inceville, Thomas H. Ince was the first studio head to insist that the authority and responsibilities of the producer, as executive head of a movie production, were distinctly different from those of the director. Before 1931, typical Hollywood studios were dominated by central producers such as Irving Thalberg at Metro-Goldwyn-Mayer, Adolph Zukor at Paramount, and Harry and Jack Warner at Warner Bros. These men—known as moguls, a reference to the powerful Muslim Mongol (or Mogul) conquerors of India—controlled the overall and day-to-day operations of their studios. Executives in New York, generally called the "New York office," controlled the studios financially; various personnel at the studios handled the myriad details of producing films. Central producers, such as Thalberg, supervised a team of associate supervisors (not yet called producers), each of whom had an area of specialization (sophisticated comedies, Westerns, etc.). The associate supervisors handled the day-to-day operations of film production, but the central producer retained total control.

By the late 1920s, the film industry had come to see that the central-producer system encouraged quantity over quality and that less-than-stellar movies did not draw audiences into theaters. As a result, the industry sought a new system, one that would value both profits and aesthetic value.

[9]This peculiar mixture of art, geography, and economics is the subject of Allen J. Scott's *On Hollywood: The Place, the Industry* (Princeton, N.J.: Princeton University Press, 2005).

Organization after 1931

In 1931, the film industry adopted the producer-unit system, an organizational structure that typically included a general manager, executive manager, production manager, studio manager, and individual production supervisors.[10] Each studio had its own configuration, determined by the New York office. The producer-unit system as it functioned at MGM in the 1930s illustrates the structure. (Figure 11.3 indicates the basic form and responsibilities of the producer-unit system. Note that the titles of these team members are generic; the actual titles varied with each studio.)

The general manager, Irving Thalberg, who had been supervising MGM's production since 1924, continued this work in the new unit. At the time, MGM's annual output was some fifty films. Reporting directly to Thalberg was a staff of ten individual unit production supervisors, each of whom was responsible for roughly six to eight films per year; the actual number varied widely because of the scope and shooting schedules of different productions. Each producer, who usually received screen credit with that title, was able to handle various types of movies. Such flexibility also enabled the general manager to assign these producers according to need, not specialization. This producer-unit management system (and its variations) helped create an industry that favored standardization, within which workers were always striving for the ideal relationship between "cost" and "quality."

The system produced movies that had a predictable technical quality, often at the cost of stylistic sameness, or what we call the studio "look"; it resulted in an overall output that inevitably—since hundreds of films were produced each year—valued profitability above all else. Yet although it could be stifling, standardization allowed for creative innovation, usually under carefully controlled circumstances. To help ensure such creativity, unit producers received varied assignments.

Let's look at a typical year for two of Thalberg's individual unit production supervisors: Hunt Stromberg and Bernard Hyman.[11] (During this period, MGM had no female producers.[12])

In 1936, a busy year for MGM, the studio released five movies for which Stromberg received screen credit as producer, including W. S. Van Dyke's *After the Thin Man* (comic murder mystery), William A. Wellman's *Small Town Girl* (romantic comedy), Robert Z. Leonard's *The Great Ziegfeld* (musical biopic), Clarence Brown's *Wife vs. Secretary* (romantic comedy), and W. S. Van Dyke's *Rose-Marie* (musical). In other words, Stromberg produced two musicals, two romantic comedies, and the second of four *Thin Man* movies.

Bernard Hyman, a Thalberg favorite among the MGM unit producers, produced four films that year, some of which were released in 1936 and some in 1937: W. S. Van Dyke's *San Francisco* (1936; a musical melodrama about the 1906 earthquake starring Clark Gable and Jeanette MacDonald), George Cukor's *Camille* (1936; a romantic melodrama starring Greta Garbo and Robert Taylor), Clarence

---

[10]The material in this section was drawn from David Bordwell, Janet Staiger, and Kristin Thompson, *The Classical Hollywood Cinema: Film Style and Mode of Production to 1960* (New York: Columbia University Press, 1985), pts. 2 and 5; Thomas Schatz, *The Genius of the System: Hollywood Filmmaking in the Studio Era* (1988; repr., New York: Holt, 1996), pts. 2 and 3; Joel Finler, *The Hollywood Story*, 3rd ed. (New York: Wallflower, 2003), pt. 2; and Douglas Gomery, *The Hollywood Studio System: A History* (London: British Film Institute, 2005).

[11]In late 1932, because of his own ill health and Mayer's growing dislike of his power, Thalberg took a break, returning in 1933 not as general manager but as a unit producer. The production staff, answerable directly to Mayer, also included David O. Selznick (Mayer's son-in-law) and Walter Wanger, both of whom had left their jobs as central producer at, respectively, RKO and Columbia. And both soon left MGM: Wanger in 1934 to become an independent producer, Selznick in 1935 to found Selznick International Pictures, where he produced a series of major films that were successful artistically and commercially, including Victor Fleming's *Gone with the Wind* (1939).

[12]Good accounts of women in Hollywood include Rachel Abramowitz, *Is That a Gun in Your Pocket: Women's Experience of Power in Hollywood* (New York: Random House, 2000); Ally Acker, *Reel Women: Pioneers of the Cinema, 1896 to the Present* (New York: Continuum, 1991); Jeanine Basinger, *A Woman's View: How Hollywood Spoke to Women, 1930–1960* (New York: Knopf, 1993); and Cari Beauchamp, *Without Lying Down: Frances Marion and the Powerful Women of Early Hollywood* (New York: Scribner, 1997).

General Manager
Irving Thalberg

Thalberg supervised the overall production of some fifty films each year: his responsibilities included selecting the property, developing the script (either by himself or in collaboration with writers), selecting the actors and key production people, editing the film, and supervising marketing. Thus, without ever leaving his office to visit the set, he could be intimately involved in every phase of every production at the studio. He generally received screen credit as "producer."

Executive Manager

Responsible for the studio's financial and legal affairs, as well as daily operations.

Production Manager

Responsible for all pre- and postproduction work; key liaison among the general manager, studio manager, and individual production supervisors.

Studio Manager

Responsible for the support departments (research, writing, design, casting, cinematography, marketing research, etc.) representing almost three hundred different professions and trades.

Individual Unit Production Supervisors

Ten men (e.g., Hunt Stromberg and Bernard Hyman), each responsible for the planning and production of the six to eight individual films per year to which they were assigned by the general manager and production manager, often called *associate* or *assistant producers* and sometimes given screen credit as such. Each producer was sufficiently flexible to be able to handle various types of movies.

Brown's *Conquest* (1937; a romantic historical epic about Napoleon and Countess Marie Walewska, his Polish mistress, starring Greta Garbo and Charles Boyer), and Jack Conway's *Saratoga* (1937; a romantic comedy starring Clark Gable and Jean Harlow). The first three were lavish productions; *Saratoga* was a bread-and-butter movie featuring two of MGM's most popular stars.

Although Hyman regularly produced fewer films each year than Stromberg, both were members of Thalberg's inner group. Reliable if not particularly imaginative (exactly what Thalberg liked in his subordinates), these producers made movies that enhanced MGM's reputation for producing quality films, kept its major stars in the public eye, and satisfied the studio's stockholders. That's what the studio system was all about. Finally, these producers were forerunners of what today we call a *line producer*, the person responsible for supervising the daily operations of a film production.

The Hollywood studio system established the collaborative mode of production that dominated

TABLE 11.1	Structure of the Studio System until 1950		
Major Studios	**Minor Studios**	**Most Significant "B" (Poverty Row) Studios**	**Most Significant Independent Producers**
1. Paramount	1. Universal Studios	1. Republic Pictures	1. Samuel Goldwyn Productions
2. Metro-Goldwyn-Mayer	2. Columbia Pictures	2. Monogram Productions	2. David O. Selznick Productions
3. Warner Bros.	3. United Artists	3. Grand National Films	3. Walt Disney Studios
4. 20th Century Fox		4. Producers Releasing Corporation	
5. RKO		5. Eagle-Lion Films	

American filmmaking during its golden age, concurrently influencing the mode of film production worldwide. The studio system also established an industrial model of production through which American filmmaking became one of the most prolific and lucrative enterprises in the world. Furthermore, although its rigidity ultimately led to its demise after some forty years, the system contained within itself the seeds—in the form of the independent producers that would replace it—to sustain American film production until the present day.

Organization during the Golden Age

By the mid-1930s, Hollywood was divided into four kinds of film production companies: majors, minors, "B" studios, and independent producers (Table 11.1).[13] The five major studios—Paramount, MGM, Warner Bros., 20th Century Fox, and RKO—were all vertically integrated companies, meaning that they followed a top-down hierarchy of control, with the ultimate managerial authority vested in their corporate officers and boards of directors. These managers were in turn responsible to those who financed them: wealthy individuals (e.g., Cornelius Vanderbilt Whitney or Joseph P. Kennedy), financial institutions (e.g., Chase National Bank in New York or Bank of America in California), corporations related to or dependent on the film industry (e.g., RCA, manufacturers of sound equipment used

in movie production), and stockholders (including studio executives and ordinary people who purchased shares on the stock market). Controlling film production through their studios and, equally important, film distribution (the marketing and promotion of a film) and exhibition (the actual showing of a motion picture in a commercial theater) through their ownership of film exchanges and theater chains, they produced "A" pictures, meaning those featured at the top of the double bill (ordinarily, for the price of a single admission, moviegoers enjoyed almost four hours of entertainment: two feature films, a cartoon, a short subject, and a newsreel).

The three minor studios—Universal, Columbia, and United Artists—were less similar. Universal and Columbia owned their own production facilities but no theaters, and thus depended on the majors to show their films. By contrast, United Artists (UA)—founded in 1919 by Mary Pickford, Charles Chaplin, Douglas Fairbanks, and D. W. Griffith—was considered a "studio" even though it was essentially a distribution company established by these artists to give them greater control over how their movies were distributed and marketed. During the 1930s, however, UA was distributing the work of many other outstanding producers, directors, and actors. Although UA declined during the 1940s, it was revived in the 1950s and today is part of MGM.

The five B studios (sometimes called the *poverty row studios* because of their relatively small budgets) were Republic Pictures, Monogram Productions, Grand National Films, Producers Releasing Corpo-

[13]See David A. Cook, *A History of Narrative Film*, 4th ed. (New York: Norton, 2004), pp. 239–255.

ration, and Eagle-Lion Films. Their B movies filled in the bottom half of double bills.

The most important independent producers in the 1930s, when independent production was still a relatively unfamiliar idea, were Hollywood titans Samuel Goldwyn, David O. Selznick, and Walt Disney. Each producer owned his own studio but released pictures through his own distribution company, one of the majors, or United Artists. Disney produced his classic animated films, such as *Pinocchio* (1940), at the Walt Disney studios and released them through his own distribution company, Buena Vista Productions. Goldwyn produced such major pictures as William Wyler's *The Best Years of Our Lives* (1946), which he released through RKO. In 1936, Selznick left MGM to establish Selznick International Pictures. In 1940, three of his films—Victor Fleming's *Gone with the Wind* (1939), Alfred Hitchcock's *Rebecca* (1940), and Gregory Ratoff's *Intermezzo* (1939)—together earned some $10 million in net profits, more than all the films of any of the majors, each of which produced roughly fifty-two films that year. Although he released his films through the major studios, including MGM, Selznick's prestige pictures and remarkable profits established the independent producer as a dominant force in Hollywood for the next sixty years and beyond.

The **producer** guides the entire process of making the movie from its initial planning to its release and is chiefly responsible for the organizational and financial aspects of the production, from arranging the financing to deciding how the money is spent. The studio system was dominated by producers who, in turn, depended on directors who were under studio contract to direct a specific number of films in each contract period.

The work of the **director** is to determine and realize on the screen an artistic vision of the screenplay; cast the actors and direct their performances; work closely with the production designers in creating the look of the film, including the choice of locations; oversee the work of the cinematographer and other key production personnel; and in most cases, supervise all postproduction activity, including the editing. Although some studio system directors—Alfred Hitchcock, John Ford, and Vincente Minnelli,

for example—could be involved completely from preproduction through postproduction, most were expected to receive a script one day and begin filming shortly thereafter. They were seasoned professionals capable of working quickly and were conversant enough with various genres to be able to handle almost any assignment.

The career of Edmund Goulding, who directed thirty-eight movies, exemplifies very clearly the work of a contract director. After starting in silent films in 1925 and directing several films at Paramount Pictures, Goulding made an auspicious start as a director at MGM with *Grand Hotel* (1932), an all-star blockbuster. He followed that with *Blondie of the Follies* (1932), a comedy featuring Marion Davies; the melodrama *Riptide* (1934), starring Norma Shearer; and *The Flame Within* (1935), also a melodrama. From MGM Goulding moved to Warner Bros., where, as a contract director, he made *That Certain Woman* (1937), *Dark Victory* (1939), and *The Old Maid* (1939), all starring Bette Davis; *The Dawn Patrol* (1938), a World War I action film; *'Til We Meet Again* (1940), a wartime romance; and *The Constant Nymph* (1943), a romantic drama.

After World War II, Goulding moved to 20th Century Fox, where the declining quality of the movies he was assigned truly reflects the challenges facing a contract director. Starting with *The Razor's Edge* (1946; a quasi-philosophical movie nominated for an Oscar as Best Picture of 1946) and *Nightmare Alley* (1947), a melodramatic film noir, he went on to direct *We're Not Married!* (1952), an episodic comedy featuring Marilyn Monroe; *Teenage Rebel* (1956), a drama; and for his last film, *Mardi Gras* (1958), a teenage musical starring Pat Boone. Goulding made the most of the challenges inherent in such variety. He was also popular with actors and noted for his screenwriting, which accounts for some of the gaps between pictures (most contract directors were expected to make three or four movies per year). Goulding was also noteworthy as an openly gay man who successfully pursued his career at a time when most Hollywood gays and lesbians remained in the closet.[14]

[14]See William J. Mann, *Behind the Screen: How Gays and Lesbians Shaped Hollywood, 1910–1969* (New York: Viking, 2001).

The actual, physical studios, called "dream factories" by anthropologist Hortense Powdermaker, were complex operations.[15] If you were fortunate enough to get past a studio's high walls and through its guarded gates, you would find yourself in a vast, industrial complex. MGM, for example, the largest studio, covered 117 acres, over which 10 miles of paved streets linked 137 buildings. There were 29 soundstages—huge air-conditioned and sound-proofed production facilities, the largest of which had a floor area of nearly 1 acre. The studio was a self-contained community with its own police and fire services, hospital, film library, school for child actors, railway siding, industrial section capable of manufacturing anything that might be needed for making a movie, and vast backlot containing sets representing every possible period and architecture. In the average year, MGM produced fifty full-length feature pictures and one hundred shorts. Depending on the level of production, the workforce consisted of 4,000 to 5,000 people. The other major studios had smaller but similar operations.

The Decline of the Studio System

Fostered by aggressive competition and free trade, the studio system grew to maturity in the 1930s, reached a pinnacle of artistic achievement and industrial productivity in the 1940s, and then declined at the beginning of the 1950s. We can see this trajectory clearly by looking at the actual number of films produced and released by American studios during that downward swing. As Table 11.2 indicates, the average number of films annually produced and released in the United States from 1936 to 1940 was 495; from 1941 to 1945, the war years, that number fell to 426; in the immediate postwar period, 1946–1950, it fell even further, to 370. In 1951, the total number of U.S. films was 391, the highest it would be until 1990, when 440 films were released. In looking at these data, remember that the total film releases in any one year usually

[15]See Hortense Powdermaker, *Hollywood, the Dream Factory: An Anthropologist Looks at the Movie-Makers* (Boston: Little, Brown, 1950).

TABLE 11.2 Feature Films Produced and Released in the United States, 1936–1951	
Year	Number of Feature Films Released
1936	522
1937	538
1938	455
1939	483
1940	477
1941	492
1942	488
1943	397
1944	401
1945	350
1946	378
1947	369
1948	366
1949	356
1950	383
1951	391

Source: Joel Finler, *The Hollywood Story*, (New York: Crown, 1988), p. 280.
Note: These figures do not include foreign films released in the United States.

reflect two kinds of production: those begun in that year and those begun earlier. In any case, one thing is clear: total Hollywood production between 1936 and 1951 fell by 25 percent.

By the mid-1930s, in fact, the system had reached a turning point as a result of three intertwined factors. First, the studios were victims of their own success. The two most creative production heads—Darryl F. Zanuck, who dominated production at 20th Century Fox from 1933 until 1956, and Irving Thalberg, who supervised production at MGM from 1923 until his death in 1936—had built such highly efficient operations that their studios could function exceptionally well, both stylistically and financially, without the sort of micromanaging that characterized David O. Selznick's style at Selznick

International Pictures. In a very real sense, these central producers and others had made themselves almost superfluous.

Second, several actions taken by the federal government signaled that the studios' old ways of doing business would have to change. President Franklin D. Roosevelt's plan for the economic revitalization of key industries—the 1933 National Industrial Recovery Act—had a major impact on Hollywood. On the one hand, it sustained certain practices that enabled the studios to control the marketing and distribution of films to their own advantage; on the other, it fostered the growth of the labor unions, perennially unpopular with the studio heads, by mandating more thoroughgoing division of labor and job specialization than Hollywood had yet experienced. In 1938, however, the federal government began trying to break the vertical structure of the major studios—to separate their interlocking ownership of production, distribution, and exhibition—an effort that finally succeeded in 1948.

Third, the studios began to reorganize their management into the producer-unit system. Each studio had its own variation on this general model, each with strengths and weaknesses. Although the resulting competition among the units increased the overall quality of Hollywood movies, the rise of the unit producer served as a transition between the dying studio system and the emergence of the independent producer.

Three additional factors further undercut the studio system. The first was a shift in the relations between top management and creative personnel that loosened the studios' hold on the system. From the mid-1930s on, actors, directors, and producers sought better individual contracts with the studios—contracts that would give them and their agents higher salaries and more control over scripts, casting, production schedules, and working conditions. For example, in the early 1950s actor James Stewart had an agreement whereby he would waive his usual salary for appearing in two films (then $200,000 per picture) in exchange for 50 percent of the net profits. Equally significant, these profits would extend through the economic life of the film, whether it was shown on a theater screen, broadcast on television, or distributed via other formats.

The second factor was World War II, which severely restricted the studios' regular, for-profit operations (they were also making movies that supported government initiatives, such as films instructing people how to cope with food rationing or encouraging them to buy war bonds). As noted already, the production of feature films fell precipitously during the war. Because many studio employees (management and labor alike) were in the armed services and film stock was being rationed to ensure the supply needed by armed-services photographers, there were fewer people and materials to make films. Thus, even though audiences went to the movies in record numbers, fewer films were available for them to see.

The third blow to the studio system was the rise of television, to which Hollywood reacted slowly. When the federal government made the studios divest themselves of their theater holdings, it also blocked their plans to replicate this dual ownership of production and distribution facilities by purchasing television stations. At first, the major studios were not interested in television production, leaving it to the minors and to such pioneering independents as Desilu Productions (Desi Arnaz and Lucille Ball, producers). By 1955, though, the majors were reorganizing and retooling what remained of their studios to begin producing films for television. Some efforts were more successful than others, but even more profitable was the sale both of their real estate—on which the studios were built—for development and of the valuable films in their vaults for television broadcasting. Universal Studios had the best of both worlds, continuing to use part of its vast property at the head of the San Fernando Valley for film and television production and devoting the rest to a lucrative theme park dedicated to showing how movies are made.

The Independent System

Through the 1930s and 1940s, the independent system of production—sometimes called the *package-unit system*—coexisted with the studio system, as it continues to do with a much different set of studios. The package-unit system, controlled by a producer unaffiliated with a studio (independents such as Samuel Goldwyn, David O. Selznick, Walt Disney, and others), is a personalized concept of film production that differs significantly from the industrial model of the studio system. Based outside the studios but heavily dependent on them for human and technical resources, the package-unit system governs the creation, distribution, and exhibition of a movie (known as the *package*). The independent producer does what a movie producer has always done: chooses the right stories, directors, and actors to produce quality films.

Depending on many factors, the producer may also choose to be involved in creative responsibilities, ranging from developing the property, revising the screenplay, assembling the key members of the production team, supervising the actual production (including the editing), and marketing and distributing the finished product. Consider the career of Sam Spiegel, one of the most successful independent producers; his movies included John Huston's *The African Queen* (1951), Elia Kazan's *On the Waterfront* (1954), David Lean's *The Bridge on the River Kwai* (1957) and *Lawrence of Arabia* (1962), Joseph L. Mankiewicz's *Suddenly, Last Summer* (1959), and Elia Kazan's *The Last Tycoon* (1976), inspired by the life of his fellow producer Irving Thalberg. Spiegel would have agreed with the successful Hollywood producer who said, "Since I control the money, I control the process."[16] Although that attitude may seem arrogant, it makes excellent business sense to a producer responsible for films like Spiegel's—which were characterized by high costs, high artistic caliber, and high profits.

The producer's team may include an **executive producer, line producer**, and **associate** or **assistant producers**. These variations on the overall title of producer reflect the changes that have occurred since the studio system collapsed and, in different ways, reinvented itself. By the nature of film production, titles must be flexible enough to indicate greater or fewer responsibilities than those listed here. Unlike the members of the craft unions—cinematographers or editors, for example—whose obligations are clearly defined by collective-bargaining agreements, producers tend to create responsibilities for themselves that match their individual strengths and experiences.

At the same time, the comparative freedom of independent filmmaking brings new benefits. Creative innovation is both encouraged and rewarded; actors, writers, and directors determine for themselves not only the amounts of compensation but also the ways in which they receive it; and though the overall number of movies produced each year has decreased, the quality of independently produced films has increased considerably from year to year. Whereas the producer helps transform an idea into a finished motion picture, the director visualizes the script and guides all members of the production team, as well as the actors, in bringing that vision to the screen.

The director sets and maintains the defining visual quality of the film, including the settings, costumes, action, and lighting—those elements that produce the total visual impact of the movie's image, its look and feel. When a film earns a profit or wins the Oscar for Best Picture, the producer takes a large share of the credit and accepts the award (true under the studio system also), but the director usually bears artistic responsibility for the success or failure of a movie. When a film loses money, the director often is saddled with the major share of the blame.

Because creativity at this high level resists rigid categorization, we cannot always neatly separate the responsibilities of the producer and the director. Sometimes one person bears both titles; other times the director or the screenwriter may have initiated the project and later joined forces with the producer to bring it to the screen. But whatever the arrangement, both the producer and the director are involved completely in all three stages of production.

A quick snapshot of a few differences between the studio and independent systems will give you an idea of how moviemaking has changed. At first, each studio's facilities and personnel were permanent and capable of producing any kind of picture, and the studio owned its own theaters, guaranteeing a mar-

[16]Robert Simonds, qtd. in Bernard Weinraub, "What Makes Boys Laugh?: A Philosophy Major Finds the Golden Touch," *New York Times* (July 23, 1998), sec. E, p. 5.

ket for its product. Now, by contrast, an independent producer makes one film at a time, relying on rented facilities and equipment and a creative staff assembled for that one film. Even figuring for those cost-saving elements, the expenses can be staggering.

Moviemaking entails various kinds of "costs." In both the old and the new American film industry, the total cost of a film is what it takes to complete the postproduction work and produce the release negative as well as one or two positive prints for advance screening purposes. But this "total cost" does not include the cost of marketing or of additional prints for distribution, so it is useful only for the special purposes of industry accounting practices. You will generally see this figure referred to as the negative cost of a movie, where *negative* refers to the costs of producing the release negative.

For example, Orson Welles made *Citizen Kane* (1941) at RKO in four and a half months and completed postproduction in another three months; the cost of the release negative was $840,000 (approximately $11 million in 2006 dollars). Today the production stage of a feature film takes at least one year, with the release negative costing an average of $64 million. The average marketing costs per movie of $30 million bring that to a total cost of approximately $100 million. (Unlike expenses calculated today, the costs of the release negative of *Citizen Kane* included marketing and distribution, elements that were then simpler and less costly.)

James Cameron's *Titanic* (1997) cost $200 million, making it the most expensive movie produced to that time, and Steven Spielberg's *Saving Private Ryan* (1998) cost $65 million, a relatively low figure for such an epic film. The use of the most advanced special effects raised the costs of *Titanic*, but for *Saving Private Ryan* the costs remained low because both Spielberg and the star of the film, Tom Hanks, received only minimal fees up front rather than their usual large salaries. According to a clause in their contracts, each man was guaranteed 17.5 percent of the studio's first-dollar gross profit, meaning that thirty-five cents of every dollar earned on the film went to Spielberg and Hanks.

A similar arrangement applied to Spielberg's *Minority Report* (2002), which reportedly cost more than $100 million to make and earned more than three times that in worldwide box office returns and selling 4 million DVDs in the first few months of its initial release.[17] With this movie, Spielberg and his star, Tom Cruise, also stood to make up to 17.5 percent of every dollar earned; thus, it is conservatively estimated that each man earned $55 million once the revenues from all ticket receipts, DVD and video sales, promotional products, and sales of movie rights were computed. As in any other industry, costs and revenues are controlled by supply and demand. As costs increase for making the kind of blockbuster films that return sizable revenues, producers make fewer films, forcing people who work in the industry to become financially creative in negotiating the contracts that preserve their jobs.

Labor and Unions

Before the industry was centralized in Hollywood, movie production was marked by conflicts between management and labor. Strikes led to the formation of guilds and unions, which led to the division of labor; that development, as much as anything, led a hodgepodge of relatively small studios to prosper and grow into one of the world's largest industries. In 1926, the major studios and unions stabilized their relations through the landmark Studio Basic Agreement, which provided the foundation for future collective bargaining in the industry.[18]

Workers in the industry formed labor unions for the standard reasons: they sought worker representation, equity in pay and working conditions, safety standards, and job security. For example, the Screen Actors Guild, established in 1933, is the nation's premier labor union representing actors. In the 1940s, it fought the attempt of the studio system to break long-term engagement contracts; today, it faces new challenges in protecting artists'

[17]http://cn.wikipedia.org/wiki/Minority_Report_(film) (accessed April 26, 2009).
[18]An excellent account of the power of labor unions in Hollywood, including the pervasive presence of organized crime, is Connie Bruck's *When Hollywood Had a King: The Reign of Lew Wasserman, Who Leveraged Talent into Power and Influence* (New York: Random House, 2003).

rights amid the movie industry's conversion to digital production. In addition, because of the uniquely collaborative nature of their jobs, industry workers needed a system that guaranteed public recognition of their efforts. Contracts between the labor unions and the studios covered the workers' inclusion in screen credits. Executive managers often had similar contracts.

In any manufacturing enterprise, division of labor refers to breaking down each step in that process so that each worker or group of workers can be assigned to and responsible for a specialized task. Although this system was designed to increase efficiency in producing steel, cars, and the like, it was applied very successfully in the film industry. Indeed, Hollywood has often been compared to Detroit. Both of these major industrial centers are engaged in the mass production of commodities. Detroit's output is more standardized, though manufacturer and model differentiate the automobiles that roll off the assembly line.

Like automobile manufacturers, each studio during the studio era specialized in certain kinds of films in its own distinctive style (e.g., MGM excelled in musicals; Warner Bros., in films of social realism); but unlike the Detroit product, each film was a unique creative accomplishment, even if it fit predictably within a particular genre such as film noir. For the most part, each studio had its own creative personnel under contract, though studios frequently borrowed talent from each other on a picture-by-picture basis. Once a studio's executive management—board of directors, chairman, president, and production moguls—determined what kinds of films would most appeal to its known share of the audience, the studio's general manager (here titles varied among studios) developed projects and selected scripts and creative personnel consistent with that choice.

In Hollywood, the activities in the three phases of making a movie—preproduction, production, and postproduction—are carried out by two major forces: management and labor. Management selects the property, develops the script, chooses the actors, and assigns the key production people; but the actual work of making the film is the responsibility of labor (the artists, craftspeople,

and technicians belonging to labor unions). Members of management receive the highest salaries; the salaries of labor depend on the kind and level of skills necessary for each job. Such a division of labor across the broad, collaborative nature of creating a film shapes the unavoidable interaction between the work rules set by union contracts and the standards set by professional organizations.

Professional Organizations and Standardization

Beyond the labor unions, other organizations are devoted to workers in the motion-picture industry, including the American Society of Cinematographers (founded in 1918; chartered in 1919), the Society of Motion Picture and Television Engineers (1916) and the American Cinema Editors (1950), which set and maintain standards in their respective professions. These organizations engage in the activities of a traditional professional organization: conducting research related to equipment and production procedures; standardizing that equipment and those procedures; meeting, publishing, consulting with manufacturers in the development of new technologies; promulgating professional codes of conduct; and recognizing outstanding achievement with awards. Although they do not represent their membership in collective bargaining, as do labor unions, they voice opinions on matters relevant to the workplace. Membership in these societies has its distinctions. For example, members of the American Cinema Editor are nominated and elected on the basis of their professional achievements and commitment to the craft of editing. Membership entitles them to place "ACE" after their name in a movie's credits.

In 1927, the industry established the Academy of Motion Picture Arts and Sciences, which seeks, among its stated objectives, to improve the artistic quality of films, provide a common forum for the various branches and crafts of the industry, and encourage cooperation in technical research. Since ancient times, *academy* has been defined as a society of learned persons organized to advance science, art, literature, music, or some other cultural or intellectual area of endeavor. Although profits, not artistic merit, are the basic measure of success in the movie industry, using the word *academy* to describe the activities of this new organization suited early moviemakers' strong need for social acceptance and respectability.

A masterful stroke of public relations, the Academy is privately funded from within the industry and is perhaps best known to the public for its annual presentation of the Academy Awards of Merit, or Oscars, as they are commonly known. Membership in the Academy is by invitation only. Now numbering around 5,800, members fall into sixteen categories: actors, art directors, cinematographers, directors, documentary, executives, film editors, makeup artists and hairstylists, music, producers, public relations, short films and feature animation, sound, visual effects, members-at-large, and writers. Members in each category make the Oscar nominations and vote to determine the winners. All voting members are also eligible to vote for the Best Picture nominees.

Currently, Academy members award Oscars for the "best" in these 24 categories: Actor in a Leading Role, Actor in a Supporting Role, Actress in a Leading Role, Actress in a Supporting Role, Animated Feature, Animated Short Film, Art Direction, Cinematography, Costume Design, Director, Documentary Feature, Documentary Short Subject, Film Editing, Foreign Language Film, Live Action Short Film, Makeup and Hairstyling, Original Score, Original Song, Picture, Sound Editing, Sound Mixing, Visual Effects, Writing—Adapted Screenplay, and Writing—Original Screenplay. In addition, the Academy has the option to present honorary awards, scientific and technical awards, special-achievement awards, and the Jean Hersholt Humanitarian Award and Irving G. Thalberg Memorial Award. Various attempts to add the following new categories have not been approved: Casting, Stunt Coordination, and Title Design.

Financing in the Industry

The pattern for financing the production of motion pictures, much like the establishment of labor practices, developed in the industry's early years.

Within the two decades after the invention of the movies, there were two major shifts: first from individual owners of small production companies (e.g., Edison and Griffith) to medium-sized firms, and then to the large corporations that not only sold stock but also relied heavily on the infusion of major capital from the investment community. Because prudent investors have traditionally considered producing films to be a risky business, the motion-picture industry recognized that it would need efficient management, timely production practices, and profitable results to attract the capital necessary to sustain it. As Hollywood grew, its production practices became more and more standardized. Today, producers aggressively seek the support of a newer breed of investors.

From the beginning, however, the vertical organizational structure of the studios was challenged by independent producers. Although the studios dominated the distribution and exhibition of films (at least until 1948, when the federal government broke that monopoly), the independents did have access to many movie theaters and could compete successfully for the outside financing they required. The early success of independent producers—such as David O. Selznick in gaining the financing for such major undertakings as *Gone with the Wind* (1939)—demonstrates not only their individual strengths but also the viability and possible profitability of their alternative approach to the studio system.

No rule governs the arranging of financing—money may come from the studio, the producer, the investment community, or (most probably) a combination of these—just as no one timetable exists for securing it. By studying the production credits of films, you can see just how many organizations may back a project. For example, Figure 11.4 lists, in the order of their appearance on the screen, the opening credits of Bill Condon's *Gods and Monsters* (1998). Universal Studios released the film, which involved the financial as well as creative input of six entities: Lionsgate Films, Showtime, Flashpoint, BBC Films, Regent Entertainment, and Gregg Fienberg. Separate title screens identify two line producers, three co-executive producers, two executive producers, and two more executive producers. Finally, a "Produced By" screen credit lists

FIGURE 11.4 **Producers' Credits on *Gods and Monsters***

UNIVERSAL
[Title superimposed over company logo]

LIONSGATE FILMS
SHOWTIME and FLASHPOINT
in association with
BBC FILMS
Present

A
REGENT ENTERTAINMENT
PRODUCTION

in association with
GREGG FIENBERG

A
BILL CONDON
FILM

Next, separate titles list the principal members of the cast, film title, and major members of the production crew.

LINE PRODUCERS
JOHN SCHOUWEILER
&
LISA LEVY

CO-EXECUTIVE PRODUCERS
VALORIE MASSALAS
SAM IRVIN
SPENCER PROFFER

EXECUTIVE PRODUCERS
CLIVE BARKER
AND
STEPHEN P. JARCHOW

EXECUTIVE PRODUCERS
DAVID FORREST
BEAU ROGERS

PRODUCED BY
PAUL COLICHMAN
GREGG FIENBERG
MARK R. HARRIS

three more names. Each person receiving credit as a producer was affiliated with one of the six entities listed at the beginning of the film and may also have had some creative responsibility beyond their financial and organizational concerns.

Some producers will have enough start-up financing to ensure that the preproduction phase can proceed with key people on the payroll; others will not be able to secure the necessary funds until they present investors with a detailed account of anticipated audiences and projected profits. Whether a movie is produced independently (in which case it is usually established as an independent corporation) or by one of the studios (in which case it is a distinct project among many), financial and logistical control is essential to making progress and ultimately completing the actual work of production as well as to holding down costs. Initial budgets are subject to constant modification, so budgeting, accounting, and auditing are as important as they would be in any costly industrial undertaking.

In the old studio system, the general manager, in consultation with the director and key members of the production team, determined the budget for a film, which consisted of two basic categories: direct costs and indirect costs. Direct costs included everything from art direction and cinematography to insurance. Indirect costs, usually 20 percent of the direct costs, covered the studio's overall contribution to "overhead" (such items as making release prints from the negative, marketing, advertising, and distribution). Table 11.3 shows the summary budget for Michael Curtiz's *Casablanca* (1942), including a line-item accounting for each major expense. Direct costs were 73 percent of the total budget.

Today, in the independent system, budgeting is done differently. Usually the producer or a member of the producer's team prepares the budget with the assistant director. The total cost of producing the completed movie generally breaks down into a ratio of 30 percent to 70 percent between above-the-line costs (the costs of the preproduction stage, producer, director, cast, screenwriter, and literary property from which the script was developed) and below-the-line costs (the costs of the production

and postproduction stages and the crew).[19] Categorizing costs according to where they are incurred in the three stages of production is a change from the studio-system method. Costs also vary depending on whether union or nonunion labor is being used. In some cases, producers have little flexibility in this regard, but usually their hiring of personnel is open to negotiation within industry standards. Finally, we must always remember that no matter what approach is taken to making movies, movie-industry accounting practices traditionally have been as creative as, if not more creative than, the movies themselves.

Marketing and Distribution

After screening a movie's answer print (the first combined print of the film, incorporating picture, sound, and special effects) for executives of the production company as well as for family, friends, and advisers, the producer may show it to audiences at previews. Members of preview audiences are invited because they represent the demographics of the audience for which the film is intended (e.g., female teenagers). After the screening, viewers are asked to complete detailed questionnaires to gauge their reactions. At the same time, the producer may also have chosen a smaller focus group from this audience and will meet with them personally after the screening to get their reactions firsthand. After analyzing both the questionnaires and the responses of the focus group, the person in charge of the final cut—either the producer or the director—may make changes in the film. Although this procedure is presumably more "scientific" than that employed in previous years by the studios, it reflects the same belief in designing a film by the numbers. Since most major movies are intended as entertainment for the largest, broadest audience possible, the strategy makes business sense. Films intended to appeal to smaller, more

[19]An excellent source of information on current budgeting practices is Deke Simon with Michael Wiese, *Film and Video Budgets*, 4th ed. (Studio City, Calif.: Michael Wiese Productions, 2006).

TABLE 11.3 Summary Budget for *Casablanca*

	Subtotals	Totals	Grand Totals
DIRECT COSTS			**$638,222**
Story		$67,281	
Story	$20,000		
Continuity and treatment (writers, secretaries, and script changes)	$47,281		
Direction		$83,237	
Director: Michael Curtiz	$73,400		
Assistant Director: Lee Katz	$9,837		
Producer: Hal Wallis		$52,000	
Cinematography		$11,273	
Camera operators and assistants	$10,873		
Camera rental and expenses	$400		
Cast		$217,603	
Cast salaries: talent under contract to studio, including Humphrey Bogart, Sydney Greenstreet, Paul Henreid, and others	$69,867		
Cast salaries: outside talent, including Ingrid Bergman, Claude Rains, Dooley Wilson, Peter Lorre, and others	$91,717		
Talent (extras, bits, etc.)	$56,019		
Musicians (musical score, arrangers, etc.)		$28,000	
Sound expenses		$2,200	
Sound operating salaries		$8,000	
Art department		$8,846	
Wardrobe expenses		$22,320	
Makeup, hairdressers, etc.		$9,100	
Electricians		$20,755	
Editors' salaries		$4,630	
Special effects		$7,475	
Negative film stock		$8,000	
Developing and printing		$10,500	
Property labor		$10,150	
Construction of sets		$18,000	
Standby labor		$15,350	
Striking (dismantling sets and storing props)		$7,000	
Property rental and expenses		$6,300	
Electrical rental and expenses		$750	
Location expenses		$1,252	
Catering		$1,200	
Auto rental expenses and travel		$5,000	

TABLE 11.3 (continued)

	Subtotals	Totals	Grand Totals
Insurance		$2,800	
Miscellaneous expenses		$3,350	
Trailer (preview)		$2,000	
Stills		$850	
Publicity		$3,000	
INDIRECT COSTS			$239,778
General studio overhead (35%)	$223,822		
Depreciation (2.5%)	$15,956		
GRAND TOTAL COST (release negative)			$878,000

Source: Adapted from Joel Finler, *The Hollywood Story* (New York: Crown, 1988), p. 39.

homogeneous audiences must attract them through publicity generated by media coverage, festival screenings and awards, and audience word of mouth.

Today's movie audiences are composed primarily of young people, whose preferences are reflected in the following list of the fifty highest-grossing films worldwide. The list in Table 11.4, which is not adjusted for such factors as ticket-price inflation, population size, or ticket purchasing trends, necessarily gives more weight to recent films (in this case, those made since 1977).

The mode of production determines how the activities in this final phase of postproduction are accomplished. Under the studio system, in the days of vertical integration, each studio or its parent company controlled production, distribution, and exhibition. Independent producers, however, have never followed any single path in distributing films. A small producer without a distribution network has various options, which include renting the film to a studio (such as Paramount) or to a producing organization (such as United Artists or Miramax) that will distribute it. These larger firms can also arrange for the film to be advertised and exhibited.

Deciding how and where to advertise, distribute, and show a film is, like the filmmaking process itself, the work of professionals. During the final weeks of postproduction, the people responsible for promotion and marketing make a number of weighty decisions. They determine the release date (essential for planning and carrying out the advertising and other publicity necessary to build an audience) and the number of screens on which the film will make its debut (necessary so that a corresponding number of release prints can be made and shipped to movie theaters). At the same time, they finalize domestic and foreign distribution rights and ancillary rights, contract with firms who make videotapes and DVDs, schedule screenings on airlines and cruise ships, and for certain kinds of films, arrange marketing tie-ins with fast-food chains, toy manufacturers, and so on.

The model for distributing and exhibiting a movie depends on the product itself. For example, there are exclusive and limited releases (a first-run showing in major cities, often used to gauge public response before a wider release), key-city releases (a second-tier release that further measures public response), and wide and saturated releases on hundreds or thousands of screens in the major markets as good reviews and word of mouth builds public awareness and demand. In addition, based on the mode of release, there are complex formulas for establishing the rental cost of a print (or digital download),

TABLE 11.4 Highest-Grossing Films Worldwide

Rank	Title	Year	Worldwide gross in billions (USD)
1	Avatar	2009	$2,782,275,172
2	Titanic	1997	$1,843,201,268
3	Harry Potter and the Deathly Hallows—Part 2	2011	$1,326,916,310
4	Transformers: Dark of the Moon	2011	$1,119,219,561
5	The Lord of the Rings: The Return of the King	2003	$1,119,110,941
6	Pirates of the Caribbean: Dead Man's Chest	2006	$1,066,179,725
7	Toy Story 3	2010	$1,063,171,911
8	Pirates of the Caribbean: On Stranger Tides	2011	$1,039,571,802
9	Alice in Wonderland	2010	$1,024,299,904
10	The Dark Knight	2008	$1,001,921,825
11	Harry Potter and the Philosopher's Stone	2001	$974,755,371
12	Pirates of the Caribbean: At World's End	2007	$963,420,425
13	Harry Potter and the Deathly Hallows—Part 1	2010	$955,417,476
14	Harry Potter and the Order of the Phoenix	2007	$939,885,929
15	Harry Potter and the Half-Blood Prince	2009	$934,416,487
16	The Lord of the Rings: The Two Towers	2002	$925,282,504
17	Star Wars Episode I: The Phantom Menace	1999	$924,317,558
18	Shrek 2	2004	$919,838,758
19	Jurassic Park	1993	$914,691,118
20	The Lion King	1994	$899,251,267
21	Harry Potter and the Goblet of Fire	2005	$896,911,078
22	Spider-Man 3	2007	$890,871,626
23	Ice Age: Dawn of the Dinosaurs	2009	$886,686,817
24	Harry Potter and the Chamber of Secrets	2002	$878,979,634
25	The Lord of the Rings: The Fellowship of the Ring	2001	$870,761,744
26	Finding Nemo	2003	$867,893,978
27	Star Wars Episode III: Revenge of the Sith	2005	$848,754,768
28	Transformers: Revenge of the Fallen	2009	$836,303,693
29	Inception	2010	$823,576,195
30	Spider-Man	2002	$821,708,551
31	Independence Day	1996	$817,400,891
32	Shrek the Third	2007	$798,958,162
33	Harry Potter and the Prisoner of Azkaban	2004	$796,688,549
34	E.T. the Extra-Terrestrial	1982	$792,910,554
35	Indiana Jones and the Kingdom of the Crystal Skull	2008	$786,636,033
36	Spider-Man 2	2004	$783,766,341
37	Star Wars	1977	$775,398,007
38	2012	2009	$769,304,749

TABLE 11.4 (continued)

Rank	Title	Year	Worldwide gross in billions (USD)
39	*The Da Vinci Code*	2006	$758,239,851
40	*Shrek Forever After*	2010	$752,600,867
41	*The Chronicles of Narnia: The Lion, the Witch and the Wardrobe*	2005	$745,011,272
42	*The Matrix Reloaded*	2003	$742,128,461
43	*Up*	2009	$731,342,744
44	*The Twilight Saga: New Moon*	2009	$709,711,008
45	*Transformers*	2007	$709,709,780
46	*The Twilight Saga: Eclipse*	2010	$698,491,347
47	*Forrest Gump*	1994	$677,387,716
48	*The Sixth Sense*	1999	$672,806,292
49	*Kung Fu Panda 2*	2011	$661,580,941
50	*Ice Age: The Meltdown*	2006	$655,388,158

Source: Adapted from http://en.wikipedia.org/wiki/List_of_highest-grossing_films (accessed October 2011).

ticket prices, length of run, up-front guarantees, and box-office grosses. The latter do not reflect what a theater or studio earns, but rather what the public spends to see a film. What part of a movie's gross goes to the producers, investors, and those (directors, writers, actors, etc.) who have a share of the gross included in their contracts remains one of Hollywood's most mysterious dealings.

In a further attempt to create new revenue streams for studios and new viewing options for consumers, Hollywood is planning to bring movies to homes at the same time (or close to it) that they are released in theaters. Such distribution practices are not yet proven to be economically or technically feasible, and in any event, are likely to throw the current method of theatrical distribution into turmoil. But as Netflix, for example, has significantly raised its prices for mail-order DVDs and encouraged its subscribers to stream videos at home, we have already begun to make major changes in the way, time, cost, and place that we look at movies.

Some or all of this activity is responsive to the voluntary movie-rating system administered by the Motion Picture Association of America (MPAA), the trade association of the industry (Table 11.5).

Because the rating helps determine the marketing of a film and thus the potential size of its audience, it is very important.[20] The release of Stanley Kubrick's last film, *Eyes Wide Shut* (1999), provides an excellent example of how a studio might try to influence the rating decision. Featuring top box-office stars Tom Cruise and Nicole Kidman, *Eyes Wide Shut* is a complex movie about sexual realities and fantasies—not for everyone and certainly not for younger viewers. Because Kubrick died just after preparing a cut of the film, we do not know whether the released version represents his complete vision for it. However, we do know that Warner Bros. digitally obscured an orgy scene to avoid an NC-17 rating (no children under seventeen admitted), and some have suggested that the studio also tried to remove other material that might have proved offensive and thus harmful to the box office. *Eyes Wide Shut* was eventually rated R (for strong sexual content, nudity, language, and some drug-related material); after opening strong, it proved a financial disappointment.

[20]Kirby Dick's documentary *This Film Is Not Yet Rated* (2006) provides valuable insight into the workings of the rating system.

TABLE 11.5 MPAA Movie-Rating System

Rating Category	Explanation
G: General Audience	All ages admitted. Specifically: no material is thought to be unsuitable for children. Contains a minimum of violence, as well as no strong language, nudity, sex scenes, or drug-use content.
PG: Parental Guidance Suggested	Some material may not be suitable for children. Specifically: may contain some profanity, violence, or brief nudity, but no drug-use content.
PG-13: Parents Strongly Cautioned	Some material may be inappropriate for children under 13. Specifically: may contain nudity but not sexually oriented nudity. May contain harsher profanity but not if used in a sexual context. May contain violence but only if not too rough or persistent.
R: Restricted	Children under 17 must be accompanied by parent or adult guardian. Specifically: may include strong language, violence, nudity, and drug abuse.
NC-17: No One 17 and under Admitted	No children admitted. Specifically: may contain excessive "violence, sex, aberrational behavior, drug abuse or any other element that most parents would consider too strong and therefore off-limits for viewing by their children."

Source: Motion Picture Association of America, 1990, www.mpaa.org/FlmRat_Ratings.asp (accessed April 2009).

Once initial marketing and distribution decisions have been made, all that remains is to show the film to the public, analyze the reviews in the media and the box-office receipts of the first weekend, and make whatever changes are necessary in the distribution, advertising, and exhibition strategies to ensure that the movie will reach its targeted audience.

Production in Hollywood Today

The production system in Hollywood today is an amalgam of (1) a studio system that differs radically from that of the golden age described earlier and (2) independent production companies, many of which are "small picture" or "prestige" (nongenre) divisions of the larger studios. The term *studio system* no longer means what it once did: a group of vertically integrated, meticulously organized factories, with large numbers of contract employees in the creative arts and crafts. Today there is no "system," and the studios exist to make and release movies, one at a time. In addition, now that almost every studio has its own prestige "indie" division, very few producers are truly independent.

Table 11.6 summarizes this new arrangement. In 2005, there were seven studios and some thirty independent production companies; altogether they produced 398 films and grossed $8.5 billion. With the exception of Sony and DreamWorks, the major studios have been in business since the 1920s.[21]

[21]Columbia Pictures, a minor studio founded in 1924, is now owned by Sony Pictures. See Benjamin M. Compaine and Douglas Gomery, *Who Owns the Media?: Competition and Concentration in the Mass Media Industry*, 3rd ed. (Mahwah, N.J.: Erlbaum, 2000), especially Chapter 6. The biggest surprise on the list is that MGM, a victim of continual corporate reorganization, has dropped from its place as Hollywood's largest studio to the bottom of the list of large independent producers. Also noteworthy is the departure of Harvey and Bob Weinstein from Miramax, which remains under the ownership of Disney, to found a new production outfit, The Weinstein Company.

TABLE 11.6 Hollywood Studios and Independent Production Companies Today

MAJOR STUDIOS

Major studios and owners

20th Century Fox (News Corporation)

Warner Bros. Pictures (Time Warner Inc.)

Columbia Pictures (Sony Corporation of America)

Universal Pictures (NBC Universal)

Walt Disney Pictures (Walt Disney Company)

Paramount Pictures

INDEPENDENT PRODUCTION COMPANIES

Large independents and studio owners (where applicable)

DreamWorks (Reliance ADA Group)

New Line Cinema (Time Warner Inc.)

Miramax (Walt Disney Pictures)

Lionsgate

Focus Features (Universal Pictures)

Warner Independent Pictures (Warner Bros. Entertainment)

Fox Searchlight Pictures (20th Century Fox)

The Weinstein Company

Sony Pictures Classics (Sony Pictures)

MGM

Medium-size independents and studio owners (where applicable)

Paramount Classics (Paramount)

Samuel Goldwyn Films

THINKfilm

Magnolia Pictures

IFC Films

Newmarket Films

Picturehouse

Wellspring Media

Fine Line Features (subsidiary of New Line Cinema)

Small independent production companies and distributors

Strand Releasing

Palm Pictures

Zeitgeist Films

Empire Pictures

Kino International

Milestone

The Cinema Guild

(continued)

TABLE 11.6 (continued)

TLA Releasing

Koch Lorber Films

First Run Features

Percentage of total grosses

Major studios	80%
Independent producers	20%

Source: Material adapted and expanded from "Bulls & Bears," *Film Comment* 42, no. 2 (March/April 2006). Updated with data from 2010.

However, the major studios accounted for 80 percent of that gross income, a percentage that would be even greater if the grosses of their smaller, independent production units were included. Not reflected in Table 11.6, but nonetheless very significant, is the fact that, in 2006, females were the top business or creative executives at five of these seven studios, burying forever the idea that Hollywood is a man's world.

Dominating the market worldwide, the major studios continue to define the nature of movie production in the United States. When one of these smaller studios has a larger corporate owner, the parent firm is usually the distributor. In addition, countless independent producers must distribute their movies through the "big six" studios if they want the largest possible audience and the maximum profits on their investments.[22]

To get a better sense of how this arrangement works today, consider Table 11.7, which shows how the nine Oscar nominees for Best Picture of 2011 were produced and released. All five were independent productions involving multiple coproduction deals. As for distribution, only Tony Gilroy's *Michael Clayton* was distributed by a major studio; Paul Thomas Anderson's *There Will Be Blood* was distributed by the "prestige" division of Paramount; and the other three were distributed by large independent production companies.

Today the American film industry is healthy but changing, as the following brief discussion shows.[23] Although movie theater attendance dropped about 10 percent between 2004 and 2005, rentals and sales of videotapes and DVDs during that period increased. (On average, U.S. residents have attended at least five movies per year between 2000 and 2004.) The industry employed close to 200,000 people in production and related services alone, with another 141,000 people employed in the theaters and rental stores.

As for the ratings, there has been a distinct shift in the past few years toward a more lenient approach, provoking children's advocates and critics of the rating system to condemn the increase of violent and sexually explicit content in movies rated PG or PG-13. The MPAA ratings of the top five grossing movies of 2011 were as follows:

1. David Yates's *Harry Potter and the Deathly Hallows, Part 2*: rated PG-13 for some sequences of intense action violence and frightening images.
2. Michael Bay's *Transformers: Dark of the Moon*: rated PG-13 for intense prolonged sequences of sci-fi action violence, mayhem and destruction, and for language, some sexuality and innuendo.

[22]Compaine and Gomery, *Who Owns the Media?*, p. 373.

[23]This discussion is based on 2004 statistics supplied by the Motion Picture Association of America (MPAA); Table 11.6 is based on 2010 data.

TABLE 11.7 Production and Distribution Data for the 2011* Oscar Nominees for Best Picture

Title	Producers[a]	Number of Coproduction Companies	U.S. Distributor
The Artist	Thomas Langmann	10	Weinstein Company
The Descendants	Jim Burke, Alexander Payne, and Jim Taylor	2	Fox Searchlight Pictures
Extremely Loud & Incredibly Close	Scott Rudin	3	Warner Bros. Pictures
The Help	Brunson Green, Chris Columbus, and Michael Barnathan	6	Walt Disney Studios Motion Pictures
Hugo	Graham King and Martin Scorsese	3	Paramount Pictures
Midnight in Paris	Letty Aronson and Stephen Tenenbaum	5	Sony Pictures Classics
Moneyball	Michael De Luca, Rachael Horovitz, and Brad Pitt	5	Columbia Pictures
The Tree of Life	Sarah Green, Bill Pohlad, Dede Gardner, and Grant Hill	4	Fox Searchlight Pictures
War Horse	Steven Spielberg and Kathleen Kennedy	5	Touchstone Pictures

[a] Names recognized by the Academy of Motion Picture Arts and Sciences for legal and award purposes; thus, this table does not include the names of the executive, associate, and line producers.

* 2011 (as recognized by the Academy) is the year these films were released; the 84th Annual Academy Awards, where these films were nominated, however, took place in 2012.

3. Bill Condon's *The Twilight Saga: Breaking Dawn, Part 1*: rated PG-13 for disturbing images, violence, sexuality/partial nudity, and some thematic elements.
4. Todd Phillips's *The Hangover, Part 2*: rated R for pervasive language, strong sexual content including graphic nudity, drug use, and brief violent images.
5. Rob Marshall's *Pirates of the Caribbean: On Stranger Tides*: rated PG-13 for sexual content/nudity, language, and some violence.

None of the five films that attracted the largest audiences of the year were deemed suitable for the entire family. Their PG-13 and R ratings place large responsibilities on parents who are concerned with the movies their children see.

3-D Movies: Gimmick or Trend of the Future?

Although 3-D production and exhibition is a major issue facing movie producers today, it is not a new process. In 1900, the Lumière brothers experimented with it; in 1922, *The Power of Love* (Nat G. Deverick and Harry K. Fairall, directors) became the first full-length film in 3-D; and the fascinating timeline of 3-D projection will show you that while we often associate 3-D with the 1950s, it has been a part of motion picture history ever since. In the past, several first-rate directors and stars have been associated with 3-D, including Alfred Hitchcock's *Dial M for Murder* (1954) with Ray Milland and Grace Kelly; Curtis Bernhardt's *Miss Sadie Thompson* (1953) with Rita Hayworth; John Farrow's *Hondo* (1953) with John Wayne, and George Sidney's *Kiss*

Me Kate (1953), the M-G-M musical with Kathryn Grayson and Howard Keel.

In 2011, some 38 feature movies were released in 3-D, with roughly 30 scheduled for 2012. This 2011 number is made all the more significant by the presence of movies by three of cinema's most important directors: Martin Scorsese's *Hugo*, Steven Spielberg's *The Adventures of Tintin*, and Francis Ford Coppola's *Twixt*. And the overall development has been spurred by the highest grossing movie to date—James Cameron's *Avatar* (2009)—which was released in some areas in 3-D. Its appeal throughout history, and indeed to the youngest audiences today, is in action, fantasy, science-fiction, horror movies, and in the live and recorded filming of sports events; 3-D helps increase the excitement and audience involvement in what is on the screen.

Stereoscopy is the technical name for 3-D. In simple terms, stereoscopic cinematography creates the illusion of actual depth in the image by making the foreground appear to stand out in relief, distinct from the middle and backgrounds. Although presenting 3-D movies to large audiences still presents great challenges, astonishing successes have been made, particularly with the IMAX 3-D system enhanced with the IMAX 3-D sound system.

The challenges facing a more stable situation in 3-D production are consumer rebellion against it, the conversion of production and exhibition facilities, and its suitability for a wider range of genres. The history of 3-D production is one of peaks and valleys, suggesting that it appears as a gimmick from time to time, and then disappears when the public is tired of it. Indeed, there is today something of a consumer rebellion against the high price of admission tickets (in 2011, that could be from $10 to $18 depending on the city), the bothersome glasses, and the dimly lit screens. In the United States, this situation is troubling, but internationally, where movies make 70 percent of their total box-office income, 3-D is still a new phenomenon that is so far accepted by noncomplaining audiences. The production of 3-D movies is hampered by a cumbersome two-camera process, and the goal—should 3-D production expand—is to develop a stereoscopic camera that has the look and feel of a typical production camera. Likewise, exhibition of 3-D movies is limited by the number of screens retrofitted for the process; the conversion of a nondigital theater costs about $70,000 per screen, and due to the unpredictable future of 3-D, financing is scarce.

Finally, there is the question of the suitability of the process for making movies that reach a broader, older audience, movies that tell stories that are not wholly dependent upon action and violence, that develop subtler moods, and that do not need to make key moments as visually noticeable as they are in today's 3-D blockbusters. Looking at some of the most successful "serious" movies of 2011—including *Black Swan*, *The King's Speech*, *The Social Network*, *True Grit*, and *Winter's Bone*—it's not easy to imagine how they might be enhanced in a 3-D format.

Even though 70 percent of U.S. opening weekend ticket sales for Tim Burton's *Alice in Wonderland* (2010) were for 3-D tickets and 43 percent of opening weekend sales for *Harry Potter and the Deathly Hallows: Part 2* (2011) were for 3-D tickets, it's still an open question whether 3-D movies are here to stay.

Foreign Influences on Hollywood Films

Hollywood is under considerable pressure to make movies that sell to foreign audiences. In 2011, foreign ticket sales accounted for 68 percent of the roughly $32 billion global film market, up 10 percent from a decade ago. Among the various ways studios try to enhance the appeal of their movies is to collaborate with local producers, hire more foreign actors in blockbusters, rewrite scripts to enhance a story's global appeal, and concentrate on producing the action movies that are the most successful. American comedies in general, and romantic comedies in particular, don't sell as well abroad as they do at home. The challenge is to create movies that audiences will actually want to watch.

G.I. Joe: The Rise of Cobra (2009), directed by Stephen Sommers, is a good example of a movie tailored to appeal to domestic and foreign audiences alike. Initially, producers were concerned that a movie with an American military theme might flop overseas, especially at a time of European and Asian opposition to the American military presence in Iraq and Afghanistan. They concentrated on the universal appeal of the science-fiction story—as well as the overall appeal of the G. I. Joe franchise in toys, comic books, and cartoon series—and filled out the cast with foreign stars. In addition to such well-known American actors as Channing Tatum, Joseph Gordon-Levitt, Rachel Nichols, and Dennis Quaid, the cast included Lee Byung-hun Lee from Korea, Adewale Akinnuoye-Agbaje and Christopher Eccleston from the United Kingdom, Karolína Kurková from the Czech Republic, Saïd Taghmaoui from France, and Gerald Okamura from Hawaii. It was a gamble that paid off, and *G.I. Joe* earned slightly more abroad than at home. A 2012 sequel, *G. I. Joe 2: Retaliation*, will also feature an international cast.

Foreign audiences for American movies are growing. From Europe to Asia, there has been a major increase in building movie theaters. In China, for example, 35,000 new screens are scheduled to open in the next five years. While the Chinese film industry is thriving, it cannot produce enough movies to fill the new screens; furthermore, American movies, like *Avatar* and *Alice in Wonderland*, have attracted large Chinese audiences. The IMAX Corporation has opened 66 theaters in the past three years, 25 of them in Asia, and is also taking the IMAX format on the road in portable theaters, erected under movable domes, equipped with IMAX screens. There has also been some discussion about creating different releases of a single movie for different geographic regions. Other major foreign markets for American movies are in Russia, Japan, and South Korea.

While it's too early to say whether foreign forces will continue to have an impact on movie production, it's clear that in today's global economy Hollywood will do whatever it can to sell the maximum number of tickets to audiences abroad.

Maverick Producers and Directors

Hollywood has always had its maverick producers and directors, people who refuse to conform to the accepted way of making movies. Today's most successful maverick, independent producers are Scott Rudin, Jerry Bruckheimer, and Brian Grazer. Among directors, there is a do-it-yourself trend exemplified by John Sayles and Robert Rodriguez, both of whom work entirely outside the Hollywood system. Sayles not only writes, directs, and edits his films, but also finances them with income earned as a scriptwriter and script doctor. His films, which reflect a strong moral and political sensibility, include *Lone Star* (1996) and *Sunshine State* (2002). Rodriguez, who has his own studio in Texas, produces, directs, and sometimes writes the script as well as the musical score and does the special effects. His films (e.g., *Sin City*, 2005, which he codirected with Frank Miller, and *Spy Kids*, 2001) attract large audiences, garner solid critical reviews, and are very profitable, but their semi-improvised look reflects the fact that they are made on comparatively low budgets and fast schedules. Mel Gibson is another maverick director who does it himself while overtly bucking the system. *The Passion of the Christ* (2004), which he produced, wrote, and directed, ranks twenty-eighth on the list of all-time, worldwide box-office successes.

Other mavericks include Steve Buscemi, Francis Ford Coppola, Spike Lee, George Lucas, and Martin Scorsese, each of whom has long held considerable control over the making of his films. Steven Soderbergh, who works inside the Hollywood system and is responsible for such box-office hits as *Haywire* and *Contagion* (both 2001), also experiments with movies made and distributed outside the system, such as *Bubble* (2005). In either mode, he produces and directs, and he often shoots and edits his movies as well. Many filmmakers working in other countries, where Hollywood conventions are less restrictive or nonexistent, flourish as mavericks. Among them are Jean-Pierre Dardenne and Luc Dardenne, French brothers who produced, wrote, and directed the critically acclaimed, documentary-style *L'Enfant* (2005); and Michael Haneke, the German who wrote and directed *Funny Games* (2007), a shot-for-shot English-language remake of his own German-language horror film *Funny Games* (1997).

Thinking about Filmmaking Technologies and Production Systems

Understanding and appreciating what can, and has been, achieved in a particular movie is closely linked to understanding the technology and production systems that existed at the time it was made. Major—sometimes revolutionary—advances in technology and production systems (the how and where movies are made) have generally been made when a director or producer asks for a stylistic effect for which neither technique nor technology currently exist. Sometimes, the response is "That's impossible" or "That's not the way we do things here." Fortunately, though, such requests throw down challenges to the artists and technicians working on the movie. For example, even though Orson Welles had never made a movie before *Citizen Kane*, he knew what he wanted and was sufficiently enthusiastic and persuasive to convince his crew to improve existing technologies (e.g., in deep-focus cinematography) or invent new ones (e.g., in sound recording). The result, of course, radically changed the prevailing conventions of

moviemaking. But even *Citizen Kane*, revolutionary as it was, has its weaknesses. Take, for example, the special effects used throughout the movie. Although the effects represent the state of the art in 1940, they are not seamlessly integrated into the images and so, in contrast to what we see today, are clumsy. Understanding what could (and could not) be achieved at a particular time in film history helps us to understand the current state of film art and the opportunities (and limitations) available to filmmakers. Keeping this perspective is vital today as we watch the film industry making its first steps toward what most experts agree will be an almost total conversion to digital technologies. Yesterday's movies are being digitally remastered in order to restore the visual depth and sparkle of the original 35mm prints, and while those movies today that are being shot digitally do not necessarily improve the image, they are challenging our visual perception and thus the way we look at movies.

Screening Checklist: Filmmaking Technologies and Production Systems

✔ In studying a particular movie, learn as much as you can about the prevailing cinematic conventions and state of the filmmaking art at the time it was made. In particular, do some research on the major creative personnel to determine if any of them are known for particular innovations. For example, if you are studying the influence of F. W. Murnau's *Sunrise: A Song of Two Humans* (1927) on Hollywood conventions, it's important to know his key role in the development of the German expressionist film as well as his pioneering use of the moving camera.

✔ Movies made during the height of the studio system in Hollywood and those made in the independent system that followed are often quite similar in their look. However, the studio system had some space for mavericks, the independent system relies heavily on traditional methods of moviemaking, and the production system in place today is very much a hybrid of the two. In studying a movie, try to determine the extent to which the production system affected its production. You might, for example, examine such related aspects as design, lighting, and cinematography.

✔ Today, we have seven major studios (six of which are carryovers from the golden age) as well as one relative newcomer (DreamWorks). Take a

close look at a movie by one studio that was produced near the beginning of that studio's history, and then compare it to another made more recently. From this comparative viewing, what can you say about how and to what extent that studio has changed from its beginnings?

✔ An interesting way to gain insight into the production of an independent movie is to examine its financing, particularly the nature and investment of each producer and/or production company. This and other related information can be found in such publications as the *Wall Street Journal*, *Variety*, and the *Hollywood Reporter* as well as online at IMDbPro (www.pro.imdb.com). From this information, you can see the hierarchy of financial influences behind the film and pose questions about how this might have affected the movie's content and form.

✔ The conversion to digital technology is a key factor in the overall future of the production, distribution, and exhibition systems of the international film industry. As such, a study of the challenges, costs, and implications of just one of these areas is an excellent subject for your further study, perhaps even a term paper. One way to look at this phenomenon is in the context of the conversion to sound in the late 1920s and early 1930s.

Questions for Review

1. What are the key technological milestones that laid the foundation for the invention of the movies?
2. How do the three filmmaking technologies—film, video, and digital—differ from each other?
3. What are the strengths and weaknesses of film, video, and digital technology?
4. Why are some filmmakers less than enthusiastic about digital technology?
5. What are the challenges and benefits involved in converting the film industry to digital technology in the areas of production, distribution, and exhibition?
6. How was the studio system organized in the golden age, and what factors contributed to its decline?
7. In what major ways does the independent system differ from the studio system?
8. What are the principal activities in each of the three basic phases of making a movie: preproduction, production, and postproduction?
9. How is a movie financed, and why are today's movies so expensive to make?
10. How are movies marketed and distributed? Have these aspects changed between the studio and independent systems?
11. Who were three major Hollywood producers—in both the studio and independent systems—and what are the similarities among them?

Studyspace **Go to wwnorton.com/movies to test and expand your knowledge of the key concepts in this chapter.**

Movies Described or Illustrated in This Chapter

The African Queen (1951). John Huston, director.

After the Thin Man (1936). W. S. Van Dyke, director.

Apocalypse Now (1979). Francis Ford Coppola, director.

The Artist (2011). Michel Hazanavicius, director.

The Best Years of Our Lives (1946). William Wyler, director.

Blondie of the Follies (1932). Edmund Goulding, director.

The Bridge on the River Kwai (1957). David Lean, director.

Brokeback Mountain (2005). Ang Lee, director.

Bubble (2005). Steven Soderbergh, director.

Camille (1936). George Cukor, director.

Casablanca (1942). Michael Curtiz, director.

Cast Away (2000). Robert Zemeckis, director.

Citizen Kane (1941). Orson Welles, director.

Collateral (2004). Michael Mann, director.

Conquest (1937). Clarence Brown, director.

The Constant Nymph (1943). Edmund Goulding, director.

Dark Victory (1939). Edmund Goulding, director.

The Da Vinci Code (2006). Ron Howard, director.

The Dawn Patrol (1938). Edmund Goulding, director.

The Descendants (2011). Alexander Payne, director.

L'Enfant (2005). Jean-Pierre Dardenne and Luc Dardenne, directors.

Eyes Wide Shut (1999). Stanley Kubrick, director.

Extremely Loud & Incredibly Close (2011). Stephen Daldry, director.

The Flame Within (1935). Edmund Goulding, director.

Funny Games (1997; remake, 2007). Michael Haneke, director.

G. I. Joe: The Rise of Cobra (2009). Stephen Sommers, director.

Gods and Monsters (1998). Bill Condon, director.

Gone with the Wind (1939). Victor Fleming, director.

Grand Hotel (1932). Edmund Goulding, director.

The Great Ziegfeld (1936). Robert Z. Leonard, director.

The Help (2011). Tate Taylor, director.

Hugo (2011). Martin Scorsese, director.

Inception (2010). Christopher Nolan, director.

Intermezzo (1939). Gregory Ratoff, director.

The Last Tycoon (1976). Elia Kazan, director.

Lone Star (1996). John Sayles, director.

Mardi Gras (1958). Edmund Goulding, director.

Midnight in Paris (2011). Woody Allen, director.

Minority Report (2002). Steven Spielberg, director.

Moneyball (2011). Bennett Miller, director.

Nightmare Alley (1947). Edmund Goulding, director.

The Old Maid (1939). Edmund Goulding, director.

On the Waterfront (1954). Elia Kazan, director.

The Passion of the Christ (2004). Mel Gibson, director.

Pirates of the Caribbean: Dead Man's Chest (2006). Gore Verbinski, director.

The Player (1992). Robert Altman, director.

The Razor's Edge (1946). Edmund Goulding, director.

Rebecca (1940). Alfred Hitchcock, director.

Rose-Marie (1936). W. S. Van Dyke, director.

San Francisco (1936). W. S. Van Dyke, director.

Saratoga (1937). Jack Conway, director.

The Savages (2007). Tamara Jenkins, director.

Saving Private Ryan (1998). Steven Spielberg, director.

Sin City (2005). Robert Rodriguez, director.

Small Town Girl (1936). William A. Wellman, director.

Spy Kids (2001). Robert Rodriguez, director.

Star Wars: Episode I—The Phantom Menace (1999). George Lucas, director.

Suddenly, Last Summer (1959). Joseph L. Mankiewicz, director.

Sunrise: A Song of Two Humans (1927). F. W. Murnau, director.

Sunshine State (2002). John Sayles, director.

Teenage Rebel (1956). Edmund Goulding, director.

That Certain Woman (1937). Edmund Goulding, director.

'Til We Meet Again (1940). Edmund Goulding, director.

Titanic (1997). James Cameron, director.

The Tree of Life (2011). Terrence Malick, director.

WALL-E (2008). Andrew Stanton, director.

War Horse (2011). Steven Speilberg, director.

We're Not Married! (1952). Edmund Goulding, director.

Wife vs. Secretary (1936). Clarence Brown, director.

Zodiac (2007). David Fincher, director.

For Further Viewing

You can learn more about moviemaking, especially about the long hours and hard work that go into production, from the following movies, which are about making movies or are set within the film industry:

The Bad and the Beautiful (1952). Vincente Minnelli, director.

The Big Knife (1955). Robert Aldrich, director.

Contempt (1963). Jean-Luc Godard, director.

Day for Night (1973). François Truffaut, director.

The Day of the Locust (1975). John Schlesinger, director.

Ed Wood (1994). Tim Burton, director.

8½ (1963). Federico Fellini, director.

The Extra Girl (1923). F. Richard Jones, director.

Frances (1982). Graeme Clifford, director.

Full Frontal (2002). Steven Soderbergh, director.

The Goddess (1958). John Cromwell, director.

Gods and Monsters (1998). Bill Condon, director.

In a Lonely Place (1950). Nicholas Ray, director.

Inside Daisy Clover (1965). Robert Mulligan, director.

Jeanne Eagels (1957). George Sidney, director.

The Last Tycoon (1976). Elia Kazan, director.

The Legend of Lylah Clare (1968). Robert Aldrich, director.

Living in Oblivion (1995). Tom DiCillo, director.

Mommie Dearest (1981). Frank Perry, director.

The Player (1992). Robert Altman, director.

Show People (1928). King Vidor, director.

Singin' in the Rain (1952). Stanley Donen and Gene Kelly, directors.

Stand-In (1937). Tay Garnett, director.

The Star (1952). Stuart Heisler, director.

A Star Is Born (1937). William A. Wellman, director.

A Star Is Born (1954). George Cukor, director.

State and Main (2000). David Mamet, director.

Sunset Boulevard (1950). Billy Wilder, director.

Two Weeks in Another Town (1962). Vincente Minnelli, director.

What Ever Happened to Baby Jane? (1962). Robert Aldrich, director.

What Price Hollywood? (1932). George Cukor, director.

Further Viewing

Now that you've learned the basics of film "language" and have gotten a taste of film history and film production, you're probably eager to see more movies. In addition to the lists of movies at the end of each chapter, the following "best" lists should provide you with a lifetime of viewing options.

Academy Award Winners for Best Picture

The following is a list of all "Best Picture"[1] Academy Award winners, from the first year of the award through 2011. Although the Academy of Motion Picture Arts and Sciences is organized by crafts—for example, cinematographers vote for the cinematography awards, film editors vote for the editing awards, and so on—all Academy members vote for the Best Picture award.

[1] The phrase *Best Picture* was not always the designation that the Academy reserved for this award. In 1928 and 1929, the designation was *Outstanding Picture*; from 1930 to 1940, *Outstanding Production*; from 1941 to 1943, *Outstanding Motion Picture*; from 1944 to 1961, *Best Motion Picture*; and since 1962, *Best Picture*.

Year of Award	Title	Director(s)
1927/28	*Wings*	William A. Wellman
1928/29	*The Broadway Melody*	Harry Beaumont
1929/30	*All Quiet on the Western Front*	Lewis Milestone
1930/31	*Cimarron*	Wesley Ruggles
1931/32	*Grand Hotel*	Edmund Goulding
1932/33	*Cavalcade*	Frank Lloyd

Year of Award	Title	Director(s)
1934	*It Happened One Night*	Frank Capra
1935	*Mutiny on the Bounty*	Frank Lloyd
1936	*The Great Ziegfeld*	Robert Z. Leonard
1937	*The Life of Emile Zola*	William Dieterle
1938	*You Can't Take It with You*	Frank Capra
1939	*Gone with the Wind*	Victor Fleming
1940	*Rebecca*	Alfred Hitchcock
1941	*How Green Was My Valley*	John Ford
1942	*Mrs. Miniver*	William Wyler
1943	*Casablanca*	Michael Curtiz
1944	*Going My Way*	Leo McCarey
1945	*The Lost Weekend*	Billy Wilder
1946	*The Best Years of Our Lives*	William Wyler
1947	*Gentleman's Agreement*	Elia Kazan
1948	*Hamlet*	Laurence Olivier
1949	*All the King's Men*	Robert Rossen
1950	*All about Eve*	Joseph L. Mankiewicz
1951	*An American in Paris*	Vincente Minnelli
1952	*The Greatest Show on Earth*	Cecil B. DeMille
1953	*From Here to Eternity*	Fred Zinnemann
1954	*On the Waterfront*	Elia Kazan
1955	*Marty*	Delbert Mann
1956	*Around the World in 80 Days*	Michael Anderson
1957	*The Bridge on the River Kwai*	David Lean
1958	*Gigi*	Vincente Minnelli
1959	*Ben-Hur*	William Wyler
1960	*The Apartment*	Billy Wilder
1961	*West Side Story*	Robert Wise and Jerome Robbins
1962	*Lawrence of Arabia*	David Lean
1963	*Tom Jones*	Tony Richardson
1964	*My Fair Lady*	George Cukor
1965	*The Sound of Music*	Robert Wise
1966	*A Man for All Seasons*	Fred Zinnemann
1967	*In the Heat of the Night*	Norman Jewison
1968	*Oliver!*	Carol Reed
1969	*Midnight Cowboy*	John Schlesinger
1970	*Patton*	Franklin J. Schaffner
1971	*The French Connection*	William Friedkin
1972	*The Godfather*	Francis Ford Coppola
1973	*The Sting*	George Roy Hill
1974	*The Godfather: Part II*	Francis Ford Coppola

Year of Award	Title	Director(s)
1975	*One Flew over the Cuckoo's Nest*	Milos Forman
1976	*Rocky*	John G. Avildsen
1977	*Annie Hall*	Woody Allen
1978	*The Deer Hunter*	Michael Cimino
1979	*Kramer vs. Kramer*	Robert Benton
1980	*Ordinary People*	Robert Redford
1981	*Chariots of Fire*	Hugh Hudson
1982	*Gandhi*	Richard Attenborough
1983	*Terms of Endearment*	James L. Brooks
1984	*Amadeus*	Milos Forman
1985	*Out of Africa*	Sydney Pollack
1986	*Platoon*	Oliver Stone
1987	*The Last Emperor*	Bernardo Bertolucci
1988	*Rain Man*	Barry Levinson
1989	*Driving Miss Daisy*	Bruce Beresford
1990	*Dances with Wolves*	Kevin Costner
1991	*The Silence of the Lambs*	Jonathan Demme
1992	*Unforgiven*	Clint Eastwood
1993	*Schindler's List*	Steven Spielberg
1994	*Forrest Gump*	Robert Zemeckis
1995	*Braveheart*	Mel Gibson
1996	*The English Patient*	Anthony Minghella
1997	*Titanic*	James Cameron
1998	*Shakespeare in Love*	John Madden
1999	*American Beauty*	Sam Mendes
2000	*Gladiator*	Ridley Scott
2001	*A Beautiful Mind*	Ron Howard
2002	*Chicago*	Rob Marshall
2003	*The Lord of the Rings: The Return of the King*	Peter Jackson
2004	*Million Dollar Baby*	Clint Eastwood
2005	*Crash*	Paul Haggis
2006	*The Departed*	Martin Scorsese
2007	*No Country for Old Men*	Ethan Coen and Joel Coen
2008	*Slumdog Millionaire*	Danny Boyle and Loveleen Tandan
2009	*The Hurt Locker*	Kathryn Bigelow
2010	*The King's Speech*	Tom Hooper
2011	*The Artist*	Michel Hazanavicius

Source: Academy of Motion Picture Arts and Sciences, http://awardsdatabase.oscars.org (accessed April 17, 2009).

The list goes by the years the films were released, not necessarily the year in which they won the award. For example, the 84th Annual Academy Awards were held in 2012 but awarded films from 2011.

Sight & Sound: Top Ten Best Movies of All Time

Every ten years since 1952, the editors of *Sight & Sound*—the official publication of the British Film Institute—have asked some 200 film critics and directors from around the world to choose the top ten feature films made anytime, anywhere in the world. The results are separated into two lists—one derived from the responses by film critics and one from the responses by directors. The following are the results from the most recent poll, published in 2012.

Rank	Year of Release	Title	Director(s)
		THE CRITICS' CHOICES	
1	1958	*Vertigo*	Alfred Hitchcock
2	1941	*Citizen Kane*	Orson Welles
3	1953	*Tokyo Story*	Ozu Yasujirô
4	1939	*The Rules of the Game*	Jean Renoir
5	1927	*Sunrise: A Song of Two Humans*	F. W. Murnau
6	1968	*2001: A Space Odyssey*	Stanley Kubrick
7	1956	*The Searchers*	John Ford
8	1929	*The Man With the Movie Camera*	Dziga Vertov
9	1927	*The Passion of Joan of Arc*	Carl Dreyer
10	1963	*8½*	Federico Fellini
		THE DIRECTORS' CHOICES	
1	1953	*Tokyo Story*	Ozu Yasujirô
2	1968	*2001: A Space Odyssey*	Stanley Kubrick
2	1941	*Citizen Kane*	Orson Welles
4	1963	*8½*	Federico Fellini
5	1976	*Taxi Driver*	Martin Scorsese
6	1979	*Apocalypse Now*	Francis Ford Coppola
7	1972	*The Godfather*	Francis Ford Coppola
7	1958	*Vertigo*	Alfred Hitchcock
9	1974	*Mirror*	Andrei Tarkovsky
10	1949	*The Bicycle Thieves*	Vittorio De Sica

Source: British Film Institute, www.bfi.org.uk/sightandsound (accessed August 3, 2012).

American Film Institute:
One Hundred Greatest American Movies of All Time

The following list was created by a panel of over 1,500 screenwriters, directors, actors, producers, cinematographers, editors, executives, film historians, and critics assembled by the American Film Institute (AFI) in 1996 in honor of cinema's first one hundred years. The panel was given a list of 400 films nominated by the AFI, and asked to select and rank the 100 best American films from that list. All of these films were made during the first hundred years of cinema (1896–1996), so no films made after 1996 are included.

Rank	Year of Release	Title	Director(s)
1	1941	*Citizen Kane*	Orson Welles
2	1942	*Casablanca*	Michael Curtiz
3	1972	*The Godfather*	Francis Ford Coppola
4	1939	*Gone with the Wind*	Victor Fleming
5	1962	*Lawrence of Arabia*	David Lean
6	1939	*The Wizard of Oz*	Victor Fleming
7	1967	*The Graduate*	Mike Nichols
8	1954	*On the Waterfront*	Elia Kazan
9	1993	*Schindler's List*	Steven Spielberg
10	1952	*Singin' in the Rain*	Gene Kelly and Stanley Donen
11	1946	*It's a Wonderful Life*	Frank Capra
12	1950	*Sunset Blvd.*	Billy Wilder
13	1957	*The Bridge on the River Kwai*	David Lean
14	1959	*Some Like It Hot*	Billy Wilder
15	1977	*Star Wars*	George Lucas
16	1950	*All about Eve*	Joseph L. Mankiewicz
17	1951	*The African Queen*	John Huston
18	1960	*Psycho*	Alfred Hitchcock
19	1974	*Chinatown*	Roman Polanski
20	1975	*One Flew over the Cuckoo's Nest*	Milos Forman
21	1940	*The Grapes of Wrath*	John Ford
22	1968	*2001: A Space Odyssey*	Stanley Kubrick
23	1941	*The Maltese Falcon*	John Huston
24	1980	*Raging Bull*	Martin Scorsese
25	1982	*E.T. the Extra-Terrestrial*	Steven Spielberg
26	1964	*Dr. Strangelove*	Stanley Kubrick
27	1967	*Bonnie and Clyde*	Arthur Penn
28	1979	*Apocalypse Now*	Francis Ford Coppola
29	1939	*Mr. Smith Goes to Washington*	Frank Capra
30	1948	*The Treasure of the Sierra Madre*	John Huston

Rank	Year of Release	Title	Director(s)
31	1977	*Annie Hall*	Woody Allen
32	1974	*The Godfather: Part II*	Francis Ford Coppola
33	1952	*High Noon*	Fred Zinnemann
34	1962	*To Kill a Mockingbird*	Robert Mulligan
35	1934	*It Happened One Night*	Frank Capra
36	1969	*Midnight Cowboy*	John Schlesinger
37	1946	*The Best Years of Our Lives*	William Wyler
38	1944	*Double Indemnity*	Billy Wilder
39	1965	*Doctor Zhivago*	David Lean
40	1959	*North by Northwest*	Alfred Hitchcock
41	1961	*West Side Story*	Robert Wise and Jerome Robbins
42	1954	*Rear Window*	Alfred Hitchcock
43	1933	*King Kong*	Ernest B. Schoedsack and Merian C. Cooper
44	1915	*The Birth of a Nation*	D. W. Griffith
45	1951	*A Streetcar Named Desire*	Elia Kazan
46	1971	*A Clockwork Orange*	Stanley Kubrick
47	1976	*Taxi Driver*	Martin Scorsese
48	1975	*Jaws*	Steven Spielberg
49	1937	*Snow White and the Seven Dwarfs*	(no director credited)
50	1969	*Butch Cassidy and the Sundance Kid*	George Roy Hill
51	1940	*The Philadelphia Story*	George Cukor
52	1953	*From Here to Eternity*	Fred Zinnemann
53	1984	*Amadeus*	Milos Forman
54	1930	*All Quiet on the Western Front*	Lewis Milestone
55	1965	*The Sound of Music*	Robert Wise
56	1970	*M*A*S*H*	Robert Altman
57	1949	*The Third Man*	Carol Reed
58	1940	*Fantasia*	James Algar et al.
59	1955	*Rebel without a Cause*	Nicholas Ray
60	1981	*Raiders of the Lost Ark*	Steven Spielberg
61	1958	*Vertigo*	Alfred Hitchcock
62	1982	*Tootsie*	Sydney Pollack
63	1939	*Stagecoach*	John Ford
64	1977	*Close Encounters of the Third Kind*	Steven Spielberg
65	1991	*The Silence of the Lambs*	Jonathan Demme
66	1976	*Network*	Sidney Lumet
67	1962	*The Manchurian Candidate*	John Frankenheimer
68	1951	*An American in Paris*	Vincente Minnelli
69	1953	*Shane*	George Stevens

Rank	Year of Release	Title	Director(s)
70	1971	*The French Connection*	William Friedkin
71	1994	*Forrest Gump*	Robert Zemeckis
72	1959	*Ben-Hur*	William Wyler
73	1939	*Wuthering Heights*	William Wyler
74	1925	*The Gold Rush*	Charles Chaplin
75	1990	*Dances with Wolves*	Kevin Costner
76	1931	*City Lights*	Charles Chaplin
77	1973	*American Graffiti*	George Lucas
78	1976	*Rocky*	John G. Avildsen
79	1978	*The Deer Hunter*	Michael Cimino
80	1969	*The Wild Bunch*	Sam Peckinpah
81	1936	*Modern Times*	Charles Chaplin
82	1956	*Giant*	George Stevens
83	1986	*Platoon*	Oliver Stone
84	1996	*Fargo*	Joel Coen
85	1933	*Duck Soup*	Leo McCarey
86	1935	*Mutiny on the Bounty*	Frank Lloyd
87	1931	*Frankenstein*	James Whale
88	1969	*Easy Rider*	Dennis Hopper
89	1970	*Patton*	Franklin J. Schaffner
90	1927	*The Jazz Singer*	Alan Crosland
91	1964	*My Fair Lady*	George Cukor
92	1951	*A Place in the Sun*	George Stevens
93	1960	*The Apartment*	Billy Wilder
94	1990	*Goodfellas*	Martin Scorsese
95	1994	*Pulp Fiction*	Quentin Tarantino
96	1956	*The Searchers*	John Ford
97	1938	*Bringing Up Baby*	Howard Hawks
98	1992	*Unforgiven*	Clint Eastwood
99	1967	*Guess Who's Coming to Dinner*	Stanley Kramer
100	1942	*Yankee Doodle Dandy*	Michael Curtiz

Source: American Film Institute, www.afi.com/tvevents (accessed April 17, 2006).

Entertainment Weekly:
One Hundred Greatest Movies of All Time

Following publication of the American Film Institute's list, many critics and pundits criticized it for its omissions and the order of its rankings. Among the alternative lists that were published soon after the AFI's was *Entertainment Weekly*'s *100 Greatest Movies of All Time*, published in book form in 1999. The list was selected from 500 choices nominated by *Entertainment Weekly*'s editors. In addition to correcting whatever omissions the *Entertainment Weekly* editors perceived in AFI's listing of top American movies, the list also included movies made outside the United States.

Rank	Year of Release	Title	Director(s)
1	1972	*The Godfather*	Francis Ford Coppola
2	1941	*Citizen Kane*	Orson Welles
3	1942	*Casablanca*	Michael Curtiz
4	1974	*Chinatown*	Roman Polanski
5	1980	*Raging Bull*	Martin Scorsese
6	1960	*La dolce vita*	Federico Fellini
7	1974	*The Godfather: Part II*	Francis Ford Coppola
8	1939	*Gone with the Wind*	Victor Fleming
9	1959	*Some Like It Hot*	Billy Wilder
10	1952	*Singin' in the Rain*	Gene Kelly and Stanley Donen
11	1960	*Psycho*	Alfred Hitchcock
12	1954	*The Seven Samurai*	Akira Kurosawa
13	1956	*The Searchers*	John Ford
14	1964	*Dr. Strangelove*	Stanley Kubrick
15	1925	*The Gold Rush*	Charles Chaplin
16	1977	*Star Wars*	George Lucas
17	1954	*On the Waterfront*	Elia Kazan
18	1962	*Lawrence of Arabia*	David Lean
19	1958	*Vertigo*	Alfred Hitchcock
20	1982	*E.T. the Extra-Terrestrial*	Steven Spielberg
21	1950	*All about Eve*	Joseph L. Mankiewicz
22	1948	*Bicycle Thieves*	Vittorio De Sica
23	1937	*Snow White and the Seven Dwarfs*	(no director credited)
24	1938	*Bringing Up Baby*	Howard Hawks
25	1916	*Intolerance*	D. W. Griffith
26	1968	*2001: A Space Odyssey*	Stanley Kubrick
27	1940	*The Grapes of Wrath*	John Ford
28	1950	*Sunset Boulevard*	Billy Wilder
29	1994	*Pulp Fiction*	Quentin Tarantino
30	1939	*Mr. Smith Goes to Washington*	Frank Capra

Rank	Year of Release	Title	Director(s)
31	1941	*The Maltese Falcon*	John Huston
32	1939	*The Wizard of Oz*	Victor Fleming
33	1962	*Jules and Jim*	François Truffaut
34	1924	*Sherlock, Jr.*	Buster Keaton
35	1940	*The Philadelphia Story*	George Cukor
36	1963	*8 ½*	Federico Fellini
37	1986	*Blue Velvet*	David Lynch
38	1975	*Nashville*	Robert Altman
39	1936	*Swing Time*	George Stevens
40	1993	*Schindler's List*	Steven Spielberg
41	1976	*Taxi Driver*	Martin Scorsese
42	1986	*Aliens*	James Cameron
43	1933	*Duck Soup*	Leo McCarey
44	1959	*North by Northwest*	Alfred Hitchcock
45	1957	*The Seventh Seal*	Ingmar Bergman
46	1957	*The Bridge on the River Kwai*	David Lean
47	1933	*King Kong*	Ernest B. Schoedsack and Merian C. Cooper
48	1967	*Bonnie and Clyde*	Arthur Penn
49	1957	*Sweet Smell of Success*	Alexander Mackendrick
50	1944	*Double Indemnity*	Billy Wilder
51	1945	*Children of Paradise*	Marcel Carné
52	1975	*Jaws*	Steven Spielberg
53	1956	*Invasion of the Body Snatchers*	Don Siegel
54	1958	*Touch of Evil*	Orson Welles
55	1967	*The Graduate*	Mike Nichols
56	1946	*It's a Wonderful Life*	Frank Capra
57	1969	*The Wild Bunch*	Sam Peckinpah
58	1939	*The Rules of the Game*	Jean Renoir
59	1941	*The Lady Eve*	Preston Sturges
60	1977	*Annie Hall*	Woody Allen
61	1938	*The Adventures of Robin Hood*	William Keighley and Michael Curtiz
62	1944	*Henry V*	Laurence Olivier
63	1960	*Breathless*	Jean-Luc Godard
64	1973	*Mean Streets*	Martin Scorsese
65	1949	*The Third Man*	Carol Reed
66	1946	*Notorious*	Alfred Hitchcock
67	1980	*Airplane!*	David Zucker, Jerry Zucker, and Jim Abrahams
68	1935	*Bride of Frankenstein*	James Whale

Rank	Year of Release	Title	Director(s)
69	1970	*The Conformist*	Bernardo Bertolucci
70	1991	*Beauty and the Beast*	Gary Trousdale and Kirk Wise
71	1942	*To Be or Not to Be*	Ernst Lubitsch
72	1931	*M*	Fritz Lang
73	1946	*Great Expectations*	David Lean
74	1957	*Funny Face*	Stanley Donen
75	1982	*Tootsie*	Sydney Pollack
76	1962	*The Manchurian Candidate*	John Frankenheimer
77	1925	*Battleship Potemkin*	Sergei Eisenstein
78	1949	*White Heat*	Raoul Walsh
79	1934	*It's a Gift*	Norman Z. McLeod
80	1922	*Nosferatu*	F. W. Murnau
81	1989	*Do the Right Thing*	Spike Lee
82	1955	*Diabolique*	Henri-Georges Clouzot
83	1946	*The Best Years of Our Lives*	William Wyler
84	1966	*Blow-Up*	Michelangelo Antonioni
85	1962	*To Kill a Mockingbird*	Robert Mulligan
86	1955	*Rebel without a Cause*	Nicholas Ray
87	1930	*L'âge d'or*	Luis Buñuel
88	1968	*The Producers*	Mel Brooks
89	1987	*Wings of Desire*	Wim Wenders
90	1953	*Pickup on South Street*	Samuel Fuller
91	1945	*Mildred Pierce*	Michael Curtiz
92	1927	*Sunrise: A Song of Two Humans*	F. W. Murnau
93	1981	*The Road Warrior*	George Miller
94	1940	*The Shop around the Corner*	Ernst Lubitsch
95	1953	*Tokyo Story*	Yasujiro Ozu
96	1992	*The Last of the Mohicans*	Michael Mann
97	1993	*The Piano*	Jane Campion
98	1991	*The Silence of the Lambs*	Jonathan Demme
99	1974	*Swept Away*	Lina Wertmüller
100	1974	*Celine and Julie Go Boating*	Jacques Rivette

Source: *Entertainment Weekly's 100 Greatest Movies of All Time*, www.filmsite.org/ew100.html (accessed April 17, 2006).

The Village Voice:
One Hundred Best Films of the Twentieth Century

The following list was published in the January 4, 2000, issue of *The Village Voice*, a free weekly newspaper based in New York City. The list was compiled from the results of a poll administered by the editors of the *Voice* in which 50 of the best-known film critics at the time were asked to list their top ten movies of all time. Individual responses were collated, and the following list of 100 films is the result.

Rank	Year of Release	Title	Director(s)
1	1941	*Citizen Kane*	Orson Welles
2	1939	*The Rules of the Game*	Jean Renoir
3	1958	*Vertigo*	Alfred Hitchcock
4	1956	*The Searchers*	John Ford
5	1929	*The Man with a Movie Camera*	Dziga Vertov
6	1927	*Sunrise: A Song of Two Humans*	F. W. Murnau
7	1934	*L'Atalante*	Jean Vigo
8	1928	*The Passion of Joan of Arc*	Carl Theodor Dreyer
9	1966	*Au hasard Balthazar*	Robert Bresson
10	1950	*Rashomon*	Akira Kurosawa
11	1968	*2001: A Space Odyssey*	Stanley Kubrick
12	1972	*The Godfather*	Francis Ford Coppola
13	1955	*Pather Panchali*	Satyajit Ray
14	1915	*The Birth of a Nation*	D. W. Griffith
15	1939	*The Wizard of Oz*	Victor Fleming
16	1946	*It's a Wonderful Life*	Frank Capra
17	1943	*Ordet*	Gustaf Molander
18	1916	*Intolerance*	D. W. Griffith
19	1976	*Jeanne Dielman, 23 Quai du Commerce, 1080 Bruxelles*	Chantal Akerman
20	1960	*Psycho*	Alfred Hitchcock
21	1974	*Chinatown*	Roman Polanski
22	1931	*M*	Fritz Lang
23	1954	*The Seven Samurai*	Akira Kurosawa
24	1953	*The Earrings of Madame de…*	Max Ophüls
25	1942	*The Magnificent Ambersons*	Orson Welles
26	1956	*A Man Escaped*	Robert Bresson
27	1919	*Broken Blossoms*	D. W. Griffith
28	1924	*Greed*	Erich von Stroheim
29	1953	*Ugetsu monogatari*	Kenji Mizoguchi
30	1949	*The Third Man*	Carol Reed
31	1974	*The Godfather: Part II*	Francis Ford Coppola

Rank	Year of Release	Title	Director(s)
32	1927	*The General*	Buster Keaton and Clyde Bruckman
33	1957	*The Seventh Seal*	Ingmar Bergman
34	1976	*Taxi Driver*	Martin Scorsese
35	1955	*The Night of the Hunter*	Charles Laughton
36	1953	*Tokyo Story*	Yasujiro Ozu
37	1948	*Bicycle Thieves*	Vittorio De Sica
38	1931	*City Lights*	Charles Chaplin
39	1933	*King Kong*	Ernest B. Schoedsack and Merian C. Cooper
40	1927	*Metropolis*	Fritz Lang
41	1962	*My Life to Live*	Jean-Luc Godard
42	1924	*Sherlock, Jr.*	Buster Keaton
43	1972	*Aguirre: The Wrath of God*	Werner Herzog
44	1933	*Duck Soup*	Leo McCarey
45	1950	*Sunset Boulevard*	Billy Wilder
46	1975	*Barry Lyndon*	Stanley Kubrick
47	1959	*The 400 Blows*	François Truffaut
48	1928	*Steamboat Bill, Jr.*	Charles F. Reisner
49	1963	*Contempt*	Jean-Luc Godard
50	1925	*The Gold Rush*	Charles Chaplin
51	1959	*North by Northwest*	Alfred Hitchcock
52	1966	*Hold Me While I'm Naked*	George Kuchar
53	1966	*The Rise of Louis XIV*	Roberto Rossellini
54	1955, 1957, 1958	The "Apu" trilogy (*Pather Panchali*, *The Unvanquished*, and *The World of Apu*)	Satyajit Ray
55	1958	*Touch of Evil*	Orson Welles
56	1974	*A Woman under the Influence*	John Cassavetes
57	1941	*The Lady Eve*	Preston Sturges
58	1970	*The Conformist*	Bernardo Bertolucci
59	1942	*The Palm Beach Story*	Preston Sturges
60	1962	*The Man Who Shot Liberty Valance*	John Ford
61	1959	*Pickpocket*	Robert Bresson
62	1963	*An Actor's Revenge*	Kon Ichikawa
63	1980	*Berlin Alexanderplatz*	Rainer Werner Fassbinder
64	1990	*Close Up*	Abbas Kiarostami
65	1964	*The Gospel According to St. Matthew*	Pier Paolo Pasolini
66	1962	*La jetée*	Chris Marker
67	1936	*Modern Times*	Charles Chaplin
68	1927	*October*	Grigori Aleksandrov and Sergei Eisenstein

Rank	Year of Release	Title	Director(s)
69	1950	*Los Olvidados*	Luis Buñuel
70	1946	*Paisan*	Roberto Rossellini
71	1970	*Performance*	Nicolas Roeg and Donald Cammell
72	1985	*Shoah*	Claude Lanzmann
73	1952	*Singin' in the Rain*	Gene Kelly and Stanley Donen
74	1967	*Two or Three Things I Know about Her*	Jean-Luc Godard
75	1952	*Umberto D*	Vittorio De Sica
76	1915	*Les vampires*	Louis Feuillade
77	1950	*All about Eve*	Joseph L. Mankiewicz
78	1955	*All That Heaven Allows*	Douglas Sirk
79	1925	*Battleship Potemkin*	Sergei Eisenstein
80	1946	*Notorious*	Alfred Hitchcock
81	1965	*Pierrot le fou*	Jean-Luc Godard
82	1975	*Fox and His Friends*	Rainer Werner Fassbinder
83	1974	*The Texas Chainsaw Massacre*	Tobe Hooper
84	1902	*A Trip to the Moon*	Georges Méliès
85	1967	*Wavelength*	Michael Snow
86	1958	*Ashes and Diamonds*	Andrzej Wajda
87	1970	*Beyond the Valley of the Dolls*	Russ Meyer
88	1953	*The Golden Coach*	Jean Renoir
89	1975	*Salo*	Pier Paolo Pasolini
90	1974	*Celine and Julie Go Boating*	Jacques Rivette
91	1966	*Masculine-Feminine*	Jean-Luc Godard
92	1922	*Nosferatu*	F. W. Murnau
93	1977	*Star Wars*	George Lucas
94	1982	*Blade Runner*	Ridley Scott
95	1935	*Bride of Frankenstein*	James Whale
96	1962	*Jules and Jim*	François Truffaut
97	1988	*Landscape in the Mist*	Theo Angelopoulos
98	1973	*Mean Streets*	Martin Scorsese
99	1943	*Shadow of a Doubt*	Alfred Hitchcock
100	1977	*Suspiria*	Dario Argento

Source: Village Voice Media, www.filmsite.org/villvoice.htm (accessed April 17, 2006).

Glossary

Words set in **boldface** within definitions are also defined in the glossary.

A

AC   See **assistant cameraperson**.

ADR   See **automatic dialogue replacement**.

additive color systems   In early film-making, techniques used to add color to black-and-white images, including hand-coloring, stenciling, tinting, and toning. Compare **subtractive color systems**.

aerial-view shot   Also known as *bird's-eye-view shot*. An **omniscient-point-of-view shot** that is taken from an aircraft or extremely high crane and implies that the observer can see all.

alienation effect   Also known as *distancing effect*. A psychological distance between audience and stage for which, according to German playwright Bertolt Brecht, every aspect of a theatrical production should strive by limiting the audience's identification with **characters** and events.

ambient sound   Sound that emanates from the ambience (background) of the **setting** or environment being filmed, either recorded during **production** or added during **postproduction**. Although it may incorporate other types of film sound—**dialogue**, **narration**, **sound effects**, **Foley sounds**, and music—ambient sound does not include any unintentionally recorded noise made during production.

amplitude   The degree of motion of air (or other medium) within a sound wave. The greater the amplitude of the sound wave, the harder it strikes the eardrum, and thus the louder the sound. Compare **loudness**.

analog   Film is an analog medium in which the camera creates an image by recording through a camera **lens** the original light given off by the the subject and stores this image on a roll of **negative film stock**. Opposite of **digital**.

animated film   Also known as *cartoon*. Drawings or other graphical images placed in a **series photography**—like sequence to portray movement. Before computer graphics technology, the basic type of animated film was created through drawing.

animatronics   Basically, a mechanized puppet programmed or remotely controlled by computers or humans. Existing prior to digital special effects, it is used to create human figures or animals that do not exist, action that is too risky for real actors or animals, or action that is too fantastic to be possible in real life.

antagonist   The character, creature, or force that obstructs or resists the **protagonist**'s pursuit of their **goal**.

anti-hero   An outwardly unsympathetic **protagonist** pursuing a morally objectionable or otherwise undesirable **goal**.

antirealism   A **treatment** that is against or the opposite of **realism**. However, realism and antirealism (like realism and fantasy) are not strict polarities.

aperture   Also known as *gate*. The camera opening that defines the area of each **frame** of film exposed.

apparent motion   The movie projector's tricking us into perceiving separate images as one continuous image rather than a series of jerky movements. Apparent motion is the result of such factors as the **phi phenomenon** and **critical flicker fusion**.

art director   The person responsible for transforming the **production designer's** vision into a reality on the screen, assessing the staging requirements for a production, and arranging for and supervising the work of the members of the art department.

aspect ratio   The relationship between the **frame**'s two dimensions: the width of the image related to its height.

assistant cameraperson (AC)   Member of the **camera crew** who assists the **camera operator**. The *first AC* oversees everything having to do with the camera, **lenses**, supporting equipment, and the material on which the movie is being shot. The *second AC* prepares the **slate** that is used to identify each **scene** as it is being filmed, files camera reports, and feeds **film stock** into magazines to be loaded into the camera.

associate (or assistant) producer Person charged with carrying out specific responsibilities assigned by the **producer, executive producer**, or **line producer**.

asynchronous sound Sound that comes from a source apparent in the image but that is not precisely matched temporally with the actions occurring in that image.

auteurism A **film theory** based on the idea that the **director** is the sole "author" of a movie. The application of auteurism frequently takes two forms: a judgment of the whole body of a film director's work (not individual films) based on style, and a classification of great directors based on a hierarchy of directorial styles.

automatic dialogue replacement (ADR) **Rerecording** done via computer—a faster, less expensive, and more technically sophisticated process than rerecording that is done with actors.

avant-garde film See **experimental film**.

axis of action An imaginary line connecting two figures in a scene that defines the 180-degree space within which the camera can record shots of those figures. See **180-degree system**.

B

backlight Lighting, usually positioned behind and in line with the subject and the camera, used to create highlights on the subject as a means of separating it from the background and increasing its appearance of three-dimensionality.

backstory A fictional history behind the cinematic narrative that is presented onscreen. Elements of the backstory can be hinted at in a movie, presented through narration, or not revealed at all.

best boy First assistant electrician to the **gaffer** on a movie **production set**.

bird's-eye-view shot See **aerial-view shot**.

bit player An actor who holds a small speaking part.

Black Maria The first movie studio—a crude, hot, cramped shack in which Thomas Edison and his staff began making movies.

blimp A soundproofed enclosure somewhat larger than a camera, in which the camera may be mounted to prevent its sounds from reaching the microphone.

blocking The actual physical relationships among figures and settings. Also, the process during rehearsal of establishing those relationships.

boom A polelike mechanical device for holding the microphone in the air, out of camera range, that can be moved in almost any direction.

C

cameo A small but significant role often played by a famous actor.

camera crew Technicians that make up two separate groups—one concerned with the camera, the other concerned with electricity and lighting.

camera obscura Literally, "dark chamber." A box (or a room in which a viewer stands); light entering (originally through a tiny hole, later through a **lens**) on one side of the box (or room) projects an image from the outside onto the opposite side or wall.

camera operator The member of the **camera crew** who does the actual **shooting**.

cartoon See **animated film**.

casting The process of choosing and hiring actors for a movie.

catalyst The event or situation during the exposition stage of the **narrative** that sets the rest of the narrative in motion. Also known as the **inciting incident**.

causality The relationship between cause and effect; compare **narrative**.

cel A transparent sheet of celluloid or similar plastic on which drawings or lettering may be made for use in animation or titles.

celluloid roll film Also known as *motion picture film* or *raw film stock*. A material for filming that consists of long strips of perforated cellulose acetate on which a rapid succession of **frames** can be recorded. One side of the strip is layered with an emulsion consisting of light-sensitive crystals and dyes; the other side is covered with a backing that reduces reflections. Each side of the strip is perforated with sprocket holes that facilitate the movement of the stock through the sprocket wheels of the camera, the processor, and the projector.

CGI Computer-generated imagery. Compare **in-camera effect** and **laboratory effect**.

character An essential element of film **narrative**; any of the beings who play functional roles within the **plot**, either acting or being acted on. Characters can be **flat** or **round**; major, minor, or marginal; **protagonists** or **antagonists**.

characterization The process of developing a character in a movie. Characterization is the collaborative result of the creative efforts of the actor, the screenwriter, and the director.

character role An actor's part that represents a distinctive **character** type (sometimes a stereotype): society leader, judge, doctor, diplomat, and so on.

chiaroscuro The use of deep gradations and subtle variations of lights and darks within an image.

chronophotographic gun See **revolver photographique**.

cinematic conventions Accepted systems, methods, or customs by which movies communicate. Cinematic conventions are flexible; they are not "rules."

cinematic language The accepted systems, methods, or conventions by which the movies communicate with the viewer.

cinematic time The passage of time within a movie, as conveyed and manipulated by editing.

cinematography The process of capturing moving images on film or some other medium.

climax The highest point of conflict in a conventional narrative; the **protagonist**'s ultimate attempt to attain the **goal**.

closed frame An approach to framing a shot that implies that neither characters nor objects may enter or leave the frame—rendering them hemmed in and constrained. Compare to *open frame*.

close-up (CU) A **shot** that often shows a part of the body filling the **frame**—traditionally a face, but possibly a hand, eye, or mouth.

color   As related to sound, see **quality**.

colorization   The use of digital technology, in a process similar to hand-tinting, to "paint" colors on movies meant to be seen in black and white.

composition   The organization, distribution, balance, and general relationship of stationary objects and figures, as well as of light, shade, line, and color, within the frame.

content   The subject of an artwork. Compare **form**.

content curve   In terms of cinematic duration, the point at which we have absorbed all we need to know in a particular shot and are ready for seeing the next shot.

continuity editing   A style of **editing** (now dominant throughout the world) that seeks to achieve logic, smoothness, sequential flow, and the temporal and spatial orientation of viewers to what they see on the screen. Continuity editing ensures the flow from **shot** to shot; creates a rhythm based on the relationship between cinematic space and **cinematic time**; creates filmic unity (beginning, middle, and end); and establishes and resolves a problem. In short, continuity editing tells a **story** as clearly and coherently as possible. Compare **discontinuity editing**.

costumes   The clothing worn by an actor in a movie (sometimes called *wardrobe*, a term that also designates the department in a studio in which clothing is made and stored).

cover shot   See **master shot**.

coverage   The use of a variety of shots of a scene—taken from multiple angles, distances, and perspectives—to provide the director and editor a greater choice of editing options during postproduction.

crane shot   A **shot** that is created by movement of a camera mounted on an elevating arm (crane) that, in turn, is mounted on a vehicle that, if **shooting** requires it, can move on its own power or be pushed along tracks.

crisis   A critical turning point in a story in which the protagonist must engage a seemingly insurmountable obstacle.

critical flicker fusion   A phenomenon that occurs when a single light flickers on and off with such speed that the individual pulses of light fuse together to give the illusion of continuous light. See also **apparent motion**.

crosscutting   Also called *parallel editing*. Editing that cuts between two or more lines of action, often implied to be occurring at the same time but in different locations.

CU   See **close-up**.

cut   A direct change from one **shot** to another; that is, the precise point at which shot A ends and shot B begins; one result of **cutting**.

cutting   In the process of pre-digital editing, the use of scissors to cut shots out of a roll of film before *splicing* them together with glue to form a continuous whole.

cutting on action   Also known as *match-on-action* cut. A **continuity editing** technique that smoothes the transition between **shots** portraying a single action from different camera angles. The editor ends the first shot in the middle of a continuing action and begins the subsequent shot at approximately the same point in the matching action.

D

dailies   Also known as *rushes*. Usually, synchronized picture/sound work prints of a day's **shooting** that can be studied by the **director**, editor, and other crew members before the next day's shooting begins.

decor   The color and textures of the interior decoration, furniture, draperies, and curtains of a **set**.

deep-focus cinematography   The process of rendering the figures on all planes (background, middle-ground, and foreground) of a deep-space composition in focus.

deep-space composition   An approach to composition within the frame that places figures in all three planes (background, middle-ground, and foreground) of the frame, thus creating an illusion of depth. Deep-space composition is often, though not always, shot with deep-focus cinematography.

depth of field   The distance in front of a camera and its **lens** in which objects are in apparent sharp focus.

design   The process by which the *look* of the **settings**, **props**, lighting, and actors is determined. **Set** design, **decor**, prop selection, lighting **setup**, **costuming**, makeup, and hairstyle design all play a role in shaping the overall design.

dialogue   The lip-synchronous speech of **characters** who are either visible onscreen or speaking offscreen, say from another part of the room that is not visible or from an adjacent room.

diegesis (adj. **diegetic)**   The total world of a **story**—the events, **characters**, objects, **settings**, and sounds that form the world in which the story occurs.

diegetic element   An element—event, **character**, object, **setting**, sound—that helps form the world in which the **story** occurs. Compare **nondiegetic element**.

diegetic sound   Sound that originates from a source within a film's world. Compare **nondiegetic sound**.

digital   An electronic process that creates its images through a numbered system of **pixels** (which we can think of as the binary numbers 0 and 1) that are stored on a **flash card** or a computer hard drive.

digital animation   Animation that employs computer software to create the images used in the animation process (as opposed to **analog** techniques that rely on stop-motion photography, hand-drawn **cels**, etc.).

digital format   A means of storing recorded sound, made possible by computer technology, in which each sound wave is represented by combinations of the numbers 0 and 1.

direct address   A form of **narration** in which an on-screen **character** looks and speaks directly to the audience.

direct cinema   An approach to **documentary filmmaking** that employs an unobtrusive style in an attempt to give viewers as truthful and "direct" an experience of events as possible.

director   The person who (a) determines and realizes on the screen an artistic vision of the screenplay; (b) **casts** the actors and directs their performances; (c) works closely with the production **design** in creating the look of the film, including the choice of locations; (d) oversees the work of the cinematographer and other key **production** personnel; and, (e) in most cases, supervises all **postproduction** activity, especially the **editing**.

discontinuity editing   A style of editing—less widely used than continuity editing, often but not exclusively in experimental films—that joins shots A and B in ways that upset the viewer's expectations and cause momentary disorientation or confusion. The juxtaposition of shots in films edited for discontinuity can often seem abrupt and unmotivated, but the meanings that arise from such discordant editing often transcend the meanings of the individual shots that have been joined together.

dissolve Also known as *lap dissolve*. A transitional device in which **shot** B, superimposed, gradually appears over shot A and begins to replace it at midpoint in the transition. Dissolves usually indicate the passing of time. Compare **fade-in/fade-out**.

distancing effect See **alienation effect**.

documentary film A film that purports to be nonfictional. Documentary films take many forms, including instructional, persuasive, and propaganda. Compare *narrative film*.

dolly A wheeled support for a camera that permits the cinematographer to make noiseless moving **shots**.

dolly in Slow movement of the camera toward a subject, making the subject appear larger and more significant. Such gradual intensification is commonly used at moments of a **character's** realization and/or decision, or as a **point-of-view shot** to indicate the reason for the character's realization. See also **zoom-in**. Compare **dolly out**.

dolly out Movement of the camera away from the subject that is often used for *slow disclosure*, which occurs when an edited succession of images leads from A to B to C as they gradually reveal the elements of a **scene**. Each image expands on the one before, thereby changing its significance with new information. Compare **dolly in**.

dolly shot Also known as *traveling shot*. A **shot** taken by a camera fixed to a wheeled support called a **dolly**. When the dolly runs on tracks (or when the camera is mounted to a crane or an aerial device such as an airplane, a helicopter, or a balloon) the shot is called a *tracking shot*.

double-system recording The standard technique of recording film sound on a medium separate from the picture; this technique allows both for maximum quality control of the medium and for the many aspects of manipulating sound during **postproduction editing**, **mixing**, and synchronization.

down shot See **high-angle shot**.

dubbing See **rerecording**.

duration A quantity of time. In any movie, we can identify three specific kinds of duration: *story duration* (the time that the entire narrative arc—whether explicitly presented on-screen or not—is implied to have taken), *plot duration* (the time that the events explicitly shown on-screen are implied to have taken), and *screen duration* (the actual time that has elapsed to present the movie's plot, i.e., the movie's running time).

Dutch-angle shot Also known as *Dutch shot* or *oblique-angle shot*. A **shot** in which the camera is tilted from its normal horizontal and vertical positions so that it is no longer straight, giving the viewer the impression that the world in the **frame** is out of balance.

Dutch shot See **Dutch-angle shot**.

E

ECU See **extreme close-up**.

editing The process by which the editor combines and coordinates individual **shots** into a cinematic whole; the basic creative force of cinema.

ellipsis In filmmaking, generally an omission of time—the time that separates one **shot** from another—to create dramatic or comedic impact.

ELS See **extreme long shot**.

ensemble acting An approach to acting that emphasizes the interaction of actors, not the individual actor. In ensemble acting, a group of actors work together continuously in a single **shot**. Typically experienced in the theater, ensemble acting is used less in the movies because it requires the provision of rehearsal time that is usually denied to screen actors.

establishing shot A shot whose purpose is to briefly establish the viewer's sense of the setting of a scene—the relationship of figures in that scene to the environment around them. This shot is often, but not always, an *extreme long shot*. See **master shot** and **extreme long shot**.

executive producer Person responsible for supervising one or more **producers**, who in turn are responsible for individual movies.

experimental film Also known as *avant-garde film*, a term implying a position in the vanguard, out in front of traditional films. Experimental films are usually about unfamiliar, unorthodox, or obscure subject matter and are ordinarily made by independent (even underground) filmmakers, not studios, often with innovative techniques that call attention to, question, and even challenge their own artifice.

explicit meaning Everything that a movie presents on its surface. Compare **implicit meaning**.

exposition The images, action, and **dialogue** necessary to give the audience the background of the **characters** and the nature of their situation, laying the foundation for the rest of the **narrative**.

exposure Exposing the recording media (film or digital media) in a camera to light to produce a latent image on it, the quality of which is determined primarily by the source and amount of light. The cinematographer can further control that image by the choice of lens and film stock, use of filters, and the aperture that regulates the amount of light passing through the lens. Normally, it is desirable to have images that are clear and well-defined, but sometimes the story requires images that are over-exposed (very light) or under-exposed (dark or dense).

exposure index See **film stock speed**.

external sound A form of **diegetic sound** that comes from a place within the world of the **story**, which we and the **characters** in the **scene** hear but do not see. Compare **internal sound**.

extra An actor who, usually, appears in a nonspeaking or crowd role and receives no screen credit.

extreme close-up (ECU, XCU) A very close **shot** of a particular detail, such as a person's eye, a ring on a finger, or a watch face.

extreme long shot (ELS, XLS) A **shot** that is typically photographed far enough away from the subject that the subject is too small to be recognized, except through the context we see, which usually includes a wide view of the location, as well as general background information. When it is used to provide such informative context, the extreme long shot is also referred to as an *establishing shot*.

eye-level shot A **shot** that is made from the observer's eye level and usually implies that the observer's attitude is neutral toward the subject being photographed.

eye-line match cut An editing transition that shows us what a particular character is looking at. The cut joins two shots:

[1], the character's face, with his/her eyes clearly visible, then [2], whatever the character was looking at. When the second shot is of another character looking back at the character in the first shot, the resulting reciprocal eye-line match cut, and the cuts that follow, establish the two characters' proximity and interaction, even if only one character is visible on-screen at any one time.

F

factual film A **documentary film** that, usually, presents people, places, or processes in a straightforward way meant to entertain and instruct without unduly influencing audiences. Compare **instructional film, persuasive film**, and **propaganda film**.

fade-in/fade-out Transitional devices in which a **shot** fades in from a black field on black-and-white film or from a color field on color film, or fades out to a black field (or a color field). Compare **dissolve**.

familiar image Any image that a **director** periodically repeats in a movie (with or without variations) to help stabilize the **narrative**.

fast motion Cinematographic technique that accelerates action on-screen. It is achieved by filming the action at a rate less than the normal 24 frames per second (fps). When the shot is then played back at the standard 24 fps, cinematic time proceeds at a more rapid rate than the real action that took place in front of the camera. Compare *slow motion*.

feed spool The storage area for unexposed film in the movie camera.

fiction film See **narrative film**.

fidelity The faithfulness or unfaithfulness of a sound to its source.

figure Any significant thing that moves on the screen—person, animal, object.

fill light Lighting, positioned at the opposite side of the camera from the **key light**, that can fill in the shadows created by the brighter key light. Fill light may also come from a **reflector board**.

film criticism Evaluating a film's artistic merit and appeal to the public. Film criticism takes two basic forms: reviews written for a general audience and appearing in the popular media, and essays published in academic journals for a scholarly audience. Compare **film theory**.

film speed See **film stock speed**.

film stock Celluloid used to record movies. There are two types: one for black-and-white films, the other for color. Each type is manufactured in several standard **formats**.

film-stock length The number of feet (or meters) of **film stock** or the number of reels being used in a particular film.

film-stock speed Also known as *film speed* or *exposure index*. The rate at which film must move through the camera to correctly capture an image; very fast film requires little light to capture and fix the image; very slow film requires a lot of light.

film theory Evaluating movies from a particular intellectual or ideological perspective. Compare **film criticism**.

first AC See **assistant cameraperson**.

first-person narration Narration by an actual **character** in the movie. Compare **voice-over narration**.

flashback A device for presenting or reawakening the memory of the camera, a **character**, the audience—or all three—in which the action **cuts** from the **narrative** present to a past event, which may or may not have already appeared in the movie either directly or through inference. Compare **flashforward**.

flash card A fast, portable, shock-resistant memory card, housed in a small plastic or metal case, that is used as a storage medium in such battery-powered devices as **digital** cameras, mobile phones, and portable digital assistants.

flash-forward A device for presenting the anticipation of the camera, a **character**, the audience—or all three—in which the action **cuts** from the **narrative** present to a future time, one in which, for example, the **omniscient** camera reveals directly or a character imagines, from his or her **point of view**, what is going to happen. Compare **flashback**.

flat character A relatively uncomplicated **character** exhibiting few distinct traits. Flat characters do not change significantly as the story progresses.

floodlight A lamp that produces soft (diffuse) light. Compare **focusable spotlight**.

focal length The distance from the optical center of a **lens** to the focal point (the film **plane** that the cameraperson wants to keep in focus) when the lens is focused at infinity.

focusable spotlight A lamp that produces hard, mirrorlike light that can be directed to precise locations. Compare **floodlight**.

Foley sound A sound belonging to a special category of **sound effects**, invented in the 1930s by Jack Foley, a sound technician at Universal Studios. Technicians known as Foley artists create these sounds in specially equipped studios, where they use a variety of **props** and other equipment to simulate sounds such as footsteps in the mud, jingling car keys, or cutlery hitting a plate.

form The means by which a subject is expressed. The form for poetry is words; for drama, it is speech and action; for movies, it is pictures and sound; and so on. Compare **content**.

formal analysis Film analysis that examines how a **scene** or **sequence** uses formal elements—narrative, mise-en-scène, cinematography, editing, sound, and so on—to convey **story**, mood, and meaning.

format Also called *gauge*. The dimensions of a **film stock** and its perforations, and the size and shape of the image **frame** as seen on the screen. Formats extend from Super 8mm through 70mm (and beyond into such specialized formats as IMAX), but they are generally limited to three standard gauges: Super 8mm, 16mm, and 35mm.

frame A still photograph that, recorded in rapid succession with other still photographs, creates a motion picture.

framing The process by which the cinematographer determines what will appear within the borders of the moving image (the **frame**) during a **shot**.

freeze-frame Also known as *stop-frame* or *hold-frame*. A still image within a movie, created by repetitive printing in the laboratory of the same **frame** so that it can be seen without movement for whatever length of time the filmmaker desires.

frequency The speed with which a sound is produced (the number of sound waves produced per second). The speed of sound remains fairly constant when it passes through air, but it varies in different media and in the same medium at different temperatures. Compare **pitch**.

full-body shot See **long shot**.

fusil photographique A form of the chronophotographic gun (see **revolver photographique**)—a single, portable camera capable of taking twelve continuous images.

FX See **special effects**.

G

gaffer The chief electrician on a movie **production set**.

gate See **aperture**.

gauge See **format**.

generic transformation The process by which a particular **genre** is adapted to meet the expectations of a changing society.

genre The categorization of **narrative films** by **form**, **content**, or both. Examples of genres are musical, comedy, biography, Western, and so on.

goal A narratively significant objective pursued by the **protagonist**.

graphic match cut A match cut in which the similarity between shots A and B is in the shape and form of the figures pictured in each shot. The shape, color, or texture of the two figures matches across the edit, providing continuity.

grip All-around handyperson on a movie **production set**, most often working with the **camera crews** and electrical crews.

group point of view A point of view captured by a **shot** that shows what a group of **characters** would see, but at the group's level, not from the much higher **omniscient point of view**. Compare **single character's point of view**.

H

harmonic content The wavelengths that make up a sound. Compare **quality**.

high-angle shot Also known as *high shot* or *down shot*. A **shot** that is made with the camera above the action and that typically implies the observer's sense of superiority to the subject being photographed. Compare **low-angle shot**.

high-key lighting Lighting that produces an image with very little contrast between darks and lights. Its even, flat illumination expresses virtually no opinions about the subject being photographed. Compare **low-key lighting**.

high shot See **high-angle shot**.

hold-frame See **freeze-frame**.

hub A major event in a **plot**; a branching point in the plot structure that forces a **character** to choose between or among alternate paths. Compare **satellite**.

I

ideological meaning Meaning expressed by a film that reflects beliefs on the part of filmmakers, **characters**, or the time and place of the movie's **setting**. Ideological meaning is the product of social, political, economic, religious, philosophical, psychological, and sexual forces that shape the filmmakers' perspectives.

imaginary line See **180-degree system**.

implicit meaning An association, connection, or inference that a viewer makes on the basis of the given (explicit) meaning conveyed by the **story** and **form** of a film. Lying below the surface of **explicit meaning**, implicit meaning is closest to our everyday sense of the word *meaning*.

improvisation 1. Actors' extemporization—that is, delivering lines based only loosely on the written script or without the preparation that comes with studying a script before rehearsing it. 2. "Playing through" a moment—that is, making up lines to keep **scenes** going when actors forget their written lines, stumble on lines, or have some other mishap.

in-camera effect A **special effect** that is created in the **production** camera (the regular camera used for **shooting** the rest of the film) on the original **negative**. Examples of in-camera effects include **montage** and **split screen**. Compare **laboratory effect** and **CGI**.

inciting incident The narrative event that presents the protagonist with a **goal** that sets the rest of the narrative in motion. Also known as the **catalyst**.

insert, insert shot A shot, containing visual detail—an object or figure not from the scene—that is inserted between one shot and another to establish a story point, or to provide additional information or dramatic emphasis. For example, shot #1 might be an establishing shot of a room (giving us the place); shot #2 (the insert), might be a close-up of a clock photographed on a wall (giving us the time); and shot #3 would logically return us to the room.

insert titles, intertitles Words—printed or hand-written—inserted into the body of a film (e.g., "The day after" or "Saturday morning"); in common usage today, but used extensively in silent movies.

instructional film A **documentary film** that seeks to educate viewers about common interests, rather than persuading them with particular ideas. Compare **factual film**, **persuasive film**, and **propaganda film**.

intercutting Editing technique that juxtaposes two or more distinct actions to create the effect of a single scene.

interior monologue One variation on the mental, subjective **point of view** of an individual **character** that allows us to see a character and hear that character's thoughts (in his or her own voice, even though the character's lips don't move).

internal sound A form of **diegetic sound** in which we hear the thoughts of a **character** we see onscreen and assume that other characters cannot hear them. Compare **external sound**.

iris 1. A circular cutout made with a **mask** that creates a **frame** within a frame. 2. An adjustable diaphragm that limits the amount of light passing through the **lens** of a camera.

iris-in/iris-out See **iris shot**.

iris shot Optical **wipe** effect in which the wipe line is a circle; named after the **iris** of a camera. The *iris-in* begins with a small circle, which expands to a partial or full image; the *iris-out* begins with a large circle, which contracts to a smaller circle or total blackness.

J

jump cut The removal of a portion of a film, resulting in an instantaneous advance in the action—a sudden, perhaps illogical, often disorienting **ellipsis** between two **shots**.

K

key light Also known as *main light* or *source light*. The brightest light falling on a subject.

kinesis The aspect of **composition** that takes into account everything that moves on the screen.

Kinetograph The first motion-picture camera.

Kinetoscope A peephole viewer, an early motion-picture device.

L

laboratory effect A **special effect** that is created in the laboratory through **processing** and printing. Compare **in-camera effect** and **CGI**.

lap dissolve See **dissolve**.

leading role See **major role**.

lens The piece of transparent material in a camera that focuses the image on the film being exposed. The four major types of lenses are the **short-focal-length lens**, the **middle-focal-length lens**, the **long-focal-length lens**, and the **zoom lens**.

lighting ratio The relationship and balance between illumination and shadow—the balance between key light and fill light. If the ratio is high, shadows are deep; the result is called *low-key lighting*; if the ratio is low, shadows are faint or non-existent and illumination is even; the result is called *high-key lighting*.

line of action See **180-degree system**.

line producer The person, usually involved from **preproduction** through **postproduction**, who is responsible for the day-to-day management of the **production** operation.

long-focal-length lens Also known as *telephoto lens*. A **lens** that flattens the space and depth of an image and thus distorts perspectival relations. Compare **middle-focal-length lens**, **short-focal-length lens**, and **zoom lens**.

long shot (LS) Also known as *full-body shot*. A **shot** that shows the full human body, usually filling the **frame**, and some of its surroundings.

long take Also known as *sequence shot*. A **shot** that can last anywhere from one minute to ten minutes. (Between 1930 and 1960, the average length of a shot was 8–11 seconds; today it's 6–7 seconds, signifying that directors are telling their stories with a tighter pace.)

looping See **rerecording**.

loudness The volume or intensity of a sound, which is defined by its **amplitude**. Loudness is described as either *loud* or *soft*.

low-angle shot Also known as *low shot*. A **shot** that is made with the camera below the action and that typically places the observer in a position of inferiority. Compare **high-angle shot**.

low-key lighting Lighting that creates strong contrasts; sharp, dark shadows; and an overall gloomy atmosphere. Its contrasts between light and dark often imply ethical judgments. Compare **high-key lighting**.

low shot See **low-angle shot**.

LS See **long shot**.

M

magic lantern An early movie projector.

main light See **key light**.

main role See **major role**.

major character One of the main **characters** in a movie. Major characters make the most things happen or have the most things happen to them. Compare **minor character** and **marginal character**.

major role Also known as *main role, featured role,* or *leading role*. A role that is a principal agent in helping move the **plot** forward. Whether **movie stars** or newcomers, actors playing major roles appear in many **scenes** and—ordinarily, but not always—receive screen credit preceding the title. Compare **minor role**.

marginal character A **minor character** that lacks both definition and screen time.

mask An opaque sheet of metal, paper, or plastic (with, for example, a circular cutout, known as an **iris**) that is placed in front of the camera and admits light through that circle to a specific area of the **frame**—to create a frame within a frame.

master shot Also known as a *cover shot*. A shot that covers the action of a scene in one continuous take. Master shots are usually composed as *long shots* so that all of the characters in the scene are on-screen during the action of the scene. Editors rely on the master shot to provide *coverage* so that, if other shots of the scene's action (medium shots, close ups, etc.) fail to provide useable footage of certain portions of the scripted scene, the director won't need to reshoot the scene.

match cut A **cut** that preserves continuity between two **shots**. Several kinds of match cuts exist, including the **eye-line match cut**, the **graphic match cut**, and the **match-on-action cut**.

match-on-action cut Also called *cutting on action*. A **match cut** that shows us the continuation of a character's or object's motion through space without actually showing us the entire action. This is a fairly routine editorial technique for economizing a movie's presentation of movement.

MCU See **medium close-up**.

mechanical effect A **special effect** created by an object or event mechanically on the **set** and in front of the camera.

mediation An agent, structure, or other formal element, whether human or technological, that transfers something, such as information in the case of movies, from one place to another.

medium close-up (MCU) A **shot** that shows a **character** from the middle of the chest to the top of the head. A medium close-up provides a view of the face that catches minor changes in expression, as well as some detail about the character's posture.

medium long shot (MLS) Also known as *plan américain* or American shot. A **shot** that shows a **character** from the knees up and includes most of a person's body.

medium shot (MS) A **shot** showing the human body, usually from the waist up.

Method acting Also known as simply *the Method*. A naturalistic acting style, loosely adapted from the ideas of Russian **director** Konstantin Stanislavsky by American directors Elia Kazan and Lee Strasberg, that encourages actors to speak, move, and gesture not in a traditional stage manner, but in the same way they would in their own lives. An ideal technique for representing convincing human behavior, Method acting is used more frequently on the stage than on the screen.

middle-focal-length lens Also known as *normal lens*. A **lens** that does not distort perspectival relations. Compare **long-focal-length lens**, **short-focal-length lens**, and **zoom lens**.

minor character A supporting **character** in a movie. Minor characters have fewer traits than **major characters**, so we know less about them. They may also be so lacking in definition and screen time that we can consider them **marginal characters**.

minor role Also known as *supporting role*. A role that helps move the **plot** forward (and thus may be as important as a **major role**), but that is played by an actor who does not appear in as many **scenes** as the featured players do.

mise-en-scène Also known as *staging*. The overall look and feel of a movie—the sum of everything the audience sees, hears, and experiences while viewing it.

mixing The process of combining different **sound tracks** onto one composite sound track that is synchronous with the picture.

MLS See **medium long shot**.

montage 1. In France, the word for **editing**, from the verb *monter*, "to assemble or put together." 2. In the former Soviet Union in the 1920s, the various forms of editing that expressed ideas developed by theorists and filmmakers such as Sergei Eisenstein. 3. In Hollywood, beginning in the 1930s, a **sequence** of **shots**, often with superimpositions and optical effects, showing a condensed series of events.

motion capture An elaborate process in which the movements of objects or actors dressed in special suits are recorded as data that computers subsequently use to render the motion of **CGI** characters on-screen. Also known as mocap, performance capture, or motion tracking.

motion picture film See **celluloid roll film**.

motif A recurring visual, sound, or **narrative** element that imparts meaning or significance.

movie star A phenomenon, generally associated with Hollywood, comprising the actor and the **characters** played by that actor, an image created by the studio to coincide with the kind of roles associated with the actor, and a reflection of the social and cultural history of the period in which that image was created.

moving frame The result of the dynamic functions of the **frame** around a motion-picture image, which can contain moving action but can also move and thus change its viewpoint.

MS See **medium shot**.

N

narration The act of telling the story of the film. The primary source of a movie's narration is the camera, which narrates the story by showing us the events of the narrative on-screen. When the word "narration" is used to refer more narrowly to *spoken* narration, the reference is to commentary spoken by either an offscreen or on-screen voice. When that commentary is not spoken by one of the characters in the movie, it is *omniscient*. When spoken by a character within the movie, the commentary is *first-person narration*.

narrative A cinematic structure in which **content** is selected and arranged in a cause-and-effect **sequence** of events occurring over time.

narrative film Also known as *fiction film*. A movie that tells a **story**—with **characters**, places, and events—that is conceived in the mind of the film's creator. Stories in narrative films may be wholly imaginary or based on true occurrences, and they may be realistic, unrealistic, or both. Compare nonfiction film.

narrator Who or what tells the story of a film. The primary narrator in cinema is the camera, which narrates the film by showing us events in the movie's narrative. When referring to the more specific action of voice-narration, the narrator may be either a character in the movie (a *first-person narrator*) or a person who is not a character (an *omniscient narrator*).

negative A negative **photographic** image on transparent material that makes possible the reproduction of the image.

nondiegetic element Something that we see and hear on the screen that comes from outside the world of the **story** (including background music, titles and credits, and **voice-over narration**). Compare **diegetic element**.

nondiegetic sound Sound that originates from a source outside a film's world. Compare **diegetic sound**.

nonsimultaneous sound Sound that has previously been established in the movie and replays for some narrative or expressive purpose. Nonsimultaneous sounds often occur when a character has a mental flashback to an earlier voice that recalls a conversation, or to a sound that identifies a place, event, or other significant element of the narrative. Compare *simultaneous sound*.

normal lens See **middle-focal-length lens**.

normal world In a narrative screenplay, the state of the character and setting before the **inciting incident**.

O

oblique-angle shot See **Dutch-angle shot**.

obstacles Events, circumstances, and actions that impede a **protagonist**'s pursuit of the **goal**. Obstacles often originate from an **antagonist** and are central to a narrative conflict.

offscreen sound A form of sound, either **diegetic** or **nondiegetic**, that derives from a source we do not see. When diegetic, it consists of **sound effects**, music, or vocals that emanate from the world of the **story**. When nondiegetic, it takes the form of a musical score or **narration** by someone who is not a **character** in the story. Compare **onscreen sound**.

offscreen space Cinematic space that exists outside the **frame**. Compare **onscreen space**.

omniscient Providing a third-person view of all aspects of a movie's action or **characters**. Compare **restricted**.

omniscient point of view The most common point of view portrayed in movies. An omniscient POV allows the camera to travel freely within the world of the film, showing us the narrative's events from a god-like, unlimited perspective that no single character in the film could possibly have. Compare *character POV* and *group POV*.

on location Shooting in an actual interior or exterior location away from the studio. Compare **set**.

180-degree rule See **180-degree system**.

180-degree system Also known as the *180-degree rule*. The fundamental means by which filmmakers maintain consistent **screen direction**, orienting the viewer and ensuring a sense of the cinematic space in which the action occurs. The system depends on three factors working together in any scene: (1) the action in a scene must move along a hypothetical line that keeps the action on a single side of the camera; (2) the camera must shoot consistently on one side of that line; and (3) everyone on the production set—particularly the director, cinematographer, editor, and actors—must understand and adhere to this system.

on-screen sound A form of **diegetic sound** that emanates from a source that we both see and hear. Onscreen sound may be **internal sound** or **external sound**. Compare **offscreen sound**.

on-screen space Cinematic space that exists inside the **frame**. Compare **offscreen space**.

open frame A **frame** around a motion-picture image that, theoretically, **characters** and objects can enter and leave. Compare **closed frame**.

option contract During the classical Hollywood era, an actor's standard seven-year contract, reviewed every six months: if the actor had made progress in being assigned roles and demonstrating box-office appeal, the studio picked up the option to employ that actor for the next six months and gave the actor a raise; if not, the studio dropped the option and the actor was out of a job.

order The arrangement of **plot** events into a logical sequence or hierarchy. Across an entire **narrative** or in a brief section of it, any film can use one or more methods to arrange its plot: chronological order, cause-and-effect order, logical order, and so on.

outtake Material that is not used in either the rough cut or the final cut, but is cataloged and saved.

overlapping sound Also known as a *sound bridge*. Sound that carries over from one **shot** to the next before the sound of the second shot begins.

P

pan shot The horizontal movement of a camera mounted on the gyroscopic head of a stationary tripod; like the **tilt shot**, the pan shot is a simple movement with dynamic possibilities for creating meaning.

parallel editing Also called *crosscutting* and *intercutting*, although the three terms have slightly different meanings. The intercutting of two or more lines of action that occur simultaneously, a very familiar convention in chase or rescue **sequences**. See also **crosscutting** and **intercutting**. Compare **split screen**.

persistence of vision The process by which the human brain retains an image for a fraction of a second longer than the eye records it.

persuasive film A **documentary film** concerned with presenting a particular perspective on social issues, or with corporate and governmental injustice. Compare **factual film, instructional film,** and **propaganda film**.

phi phenomenon The illusion of movement created by events that succeed each other rapidly, as when two adjacent lights flash on and off alternately and we seem to see a single light shifting back and forth. This cognitive phenomenon is part of the reason we see movies as a continuous moving images, rather than a successive series of still images.

photography Literally, "writing with light"; technically, the recording of static images through a chemical interaction caused by light rays striking a sensitized surface.

pitch The level of a sound, which is defined by its **frequency**. Pitch is described as either *high* or *low*.

pixels Short for "picture elements," these are the small dots that make up the image on a video screen. The dots (denoted by the binary numbers 0 and 1) are meaningless in themselves; but when they are arranged in order, like the pieces in a jigsaw puzzle, they form a picture.

plan américain See **medium long shot**.

plane Any of three theoretical areas—foreground, middle ground, and background—within the **frame**. See also **rule of thirds**.

plot The specific actions and events that the filmmakers select and the order in which they arrange those events and actions to effectively convey on-screen the movie's narrative to a viewer. Compare *narrative* and *story*.

plot duration The elapsed time of the events within a **story** that a film chooses to tell. Compare **screen duration** and **story duration**.

plot point Significant events that turn the **narrative** in a new direction.

point of view (POV) The position from which a film presents the actions of the **story**; not only the relation of the **narrator**(s) to the story but also the camera's act of seeing and hearing. The two fundamental types of cinematic point of view are **omniscient** and **restricted**.

point-of-view editing The process of editing different shots together in such a way that the resulting sequence makes us aware of the perspective or POV of a particular character or group of characters. Most frequently, it starts with an objective shot of a character looking toward something outside of the frame and then cuts to a shot of the object, person, or action that the character is supposed to be looking at.

postproduction The third stage of the production process, consisting of **editing**, preparing the final print, and bringing the film to the public (marketing and distribution). Postproduction is preceded by **preproduction** and **production**.

POV See **point of view**.

preproduction The initial, planning-and-preparation stage of the production process. Preproduction is followed by **production** and **postproduction**.

prime lens A **lens** that has a fixed **focal length**. The **short-focal-length**, **middle-focal-length**, and **long-focal-length** lenses are all prime lenses; the **zoom lens** is in its own category.

processing The second stage of creating motion pictures in which a laboratory technician washes exposed film (which contains a **negative** image) with processing chemicals. Processing is preceded by **shooting** and followed by **projecting**.

process shot Live **shooting** against a background that is front- or rear-projected on a translucent screen.

producer The person who guides the entire process of making the movie from its initial planning to its release and is chiefly responsible for the organizational and financial aspects of the **production**, from arranging the financing to deciding how the money is spent.

production The second stage of the production process, the actual **shooting**. Production is preceded by **preproduction** and followed by **postproduction**.

production designer A person who works closely with the **director**, **art director**, and director of **photography**, in visualizing the movie that will appear on the screen. The production designer is both an artist and an executive, responsible for the overall **design** concept, the *look* of the movie—as well as individual **sets**, locations, furnishings, **props**, and **costumes**—and for supervising the heads of the many departments (art, costume design and construction, hairstyling, makeup, wardrobe, location, etc.) that create that look.

production value The amount of human and physical resources devoted to the image, including the style of its lighting. Production value helps determine the overall style of a film.

projecting The third stage of creating motion pictures, in which edited film is run through a projector, which shoots through the film a beam of light intense enough to project a large image on the movie-theater screen. Projecting is preceded by **shooting** and **processing**.

propaganda film A **documentary film** that systematically disseminates deceptive or distorted information. Compare **factual film**, **instructional film**, and **persuasive film**.

properties Also known as *props*. Objects used to enhance a movie's mise-en-scène by providing physical tokens of narrative information.

props See **properties**.

protagonist The primary **character** whose pursuit of the **goal** provides the structural foundation of a movie's story. Compare **antagonist**.

pull-down claw Within the movie camera and projector, the mechanism that controls the intermittent cycle of **shooting** and **projecting** individual **frames** and advances the film frame by frame.

pull focus See **rack focus**.

Q

quality Also known as *timbre*, *texture*, or *color*. The complexity of a sound, which is defined by its **harmonic content**. Described as *simple* or *complex*, quality is the characteristic that distinguishes a sound from others of the same **pitch** and **loudness**.

R

rack focus Also known as *select focus*, *shift focus*, or *pull focus*. A change of the point of focus from one subject to another within the same **shot**. Rack focus guides our attention to a new clearly focused point of interest while blurring the previous subject in the shot.

raw film stock See **celluloid roll film**.

realism An interest in or concern for the actual or real; a tendency to view or represent things as they really are. Compare **antirealism**.

real time The actual time during which something takes place. In real time, **screen duration** and **plot duration** are exactly the same. Many **directors** use real time within films to create uninterrupted "reality" on the screen, but they rarely use it for entire films. Compare **cinematic time**, **stretch relationship**, and **summary relationship**.

reflector board A piece of lighting equipment, but not really a lighting instrument, because it does not rely on bulbs to produce illumination. Essentially, a reflector board is a double-sided board that pivots in a *U*-shaped holder. One side is a hard, smooth surface that reflects hard light; the other is a soft, textured surface that reflects softer **fill light**.

reframing A movement of the camera that adjusts or alters the **composition** or **point of view** of a shot.

repetition The number of times that a **story** element recurs in a **plot**. Repetition signals that a particular event has noteworthy meaning or significance.

rerecording Also known as *looping* or *dubbing*. The replacing of **dialogue**, which can be done manually (that is, with the actors watching the footage, synchronizing their lips with it, and rereading the lines) or, more likely today, through computerized **automatic dialogue replacement** (ADR). (*Dubbing* also refers to the process of replacing dialogue in a foreign language with English, or the reverse, throughout a film.)

reshoot To make additional **takes** of a **shot** in order to meet the **director**'s standards or as supplemental material for **production** photography.

resolution The concluding narrative events that follow the **climax** and celebrate or otherwise reflect upon story outcomes.

restricted Providing a view from the perspective of a single **character**. For example, restricted **narration** reveals information to the audience only as a specific character learns of it. Compare **omniscient**.

reverse-angle shot A **shot** in which the angle of **shooting** is opposite to that of the preceding shot.

revolver photographique Also known as *chronophotographic gun*. A cylinder-shaped camera that creates exposures automatically, at short intervals, on different segments of a revolving plate.

rising action The development of the action of the **narrative** toward a **climax**. Compare **falling action**.

rough-draft screenplay Also known as *scenario*. The next step after a **treatment**, the rough-draft screenplay results from discussions, development, and transformation of an outline in sessions known as **story conferences**.

round character A complex **character** possessing numerous, subtle, repressed, or contradictory traits. Round characters often develop over the course of a story.

rule of thirds A principle of **composition** that enables filmmakers to maximize the potential of the image, balance its elements, and create the illusion of depth. A grid pattern, when superimposed on the image, divides the image into horizontal thirds representing the foreground, middle ground, and background **planes** and into vertical thirds that break up those planes into additional elements.

rushes See **dailies**.

S

satellite A minor **plot** event in the **diegesis**, or world, of the **narrative** but detachable from it (although removing a satellite may affect the overall texture of the narrative). Compare **hub**.

scale The size and placement of a particular object or a part of a **scene** in relation to the rest—a relationship determined by the type of **shot** used and the placement of the camera.

scenario See **rough-draft screenplay**.

scene A complete unit of **plot** action incorporating one or more **shots**; the **setting** of that action.

scope The overall range of a **story**.

score music Nondiegetic music that is typically composed and recorded specifically for use in a particular film, and is used to convey or enhance meaning and emotion.

screen direction The direction of a **figure**'s or object's movement on the screen.

screen duration The amount of time that it has taken to present the movie's plot on-screen, i.e., the movie's running time. Compare *plot duration* and *story duration*.

screen test A filming undertaken by an actor to audition for a particular role.

script supervisor The member of the crew who is responsible for ensuring continuity throughout the filming of a movie. Although script supervisors once had to maintain detailed logs to accomplish this task, today they generally rely on the **video assist camera** for this purpose.

second AC See **assistant cameraperson**.

select focus See **rack focus**.

sequence A series of edited **shots** characterized by inherent unity of **theme** and purpose.

sequence shot See **long take**.

series photography The use of a series of still photographs to record the phases of an action, although the actions within the images do not move.

set A constructed space used as the setting for a particular shot in a movie. Sets must be constructed both to look authentic and to photograph well. Compare *on location*.

setting The time and space in which a **story** takes place.

setup One camera position and everything associated with it. Whereas the **shot** is the basic building block of the film, the setup is the basic component of the film's **production**.

shift focus See **rack focus**.

shooting The first stage of creating motion pictures, in which images are recorded on previously unexposed film as it moves through the camera. Shooting is followed by **processing** and **projecting**.

shooting angle The level and height of the camera in relation to the subject being photographed. The five basic camera angles produce **eye-level shots**, **high-angle shots**, **low-angle shots**, **Dutch-angle shots**, and **aerial-view shots**.

shooting script A guide and reference point for all members of the **production** unit, in which the details of each **shot** are listed and can thus be followed during filming.

short-focal-length lens Also known as *wide-angle lens*. A **lens** that creates the illusion of depth within a **frame**, albeit with some distortion at the edges of the frame. Compare **long-focal-length lens**, **middle-focal-length lens**, and **zoom lens**.

shot One *uninterrupted* run of the camera. A shot can be as short or as long as the **director** wants, but it cannot exceed the length of the **film stock** in the camera. Compare **setup**.

shot/reverse shot One of the most prevalent and familiar of all **editing** patterns, consisting of **parallel editing** (**crosscutting**) between **shots** of different **characters**, usually in a conversation or confrontation. When used in **continuity editing**, the shots are typically **framed** over each character's shoulder to preserve **screen direction**.

shutter A camera device that shields the film from light at the **aperture** during the film-movement portion of the intermittent cycle of **shooting**.

simultaneous sound Sound that is **diegetic** and occurs onscreen. Compare **nonsimultaneous sound**.

single character's point of view A **point of view** that is captured by a **shot** made with the camera close to the line of sight of one **character** (or animal or surveillance camera), showing what that person would be seeing of the action. Compare **omniscient point of view** and **group point of view**.

slate The board or other device that is used to identify each **scene** during **shooting**.

slow motion Cinematographic technique that decelerates action on-screen. It is achieved by filming the action at a rate greater than the normal 24 frames per second (fps). When the shot is then played back at the standard 24 fps, cinematic time proceeds at a slower rate than the real action that took place in front of the camera. Compare *fast motion*.

sound crew The group that generates and controls a movie's sound physically, manipulating its properties to produce the effects that the **director** desires.

sound design A state-of-the-art concept, pioneered by director Francis Ford Coppola and film editor Walter Murch, combining the crafts of **editing** and **mixing** and, like them, involving both theoretical and practical issues. In essence, sound design represents advocacy for movie sound (to counter some people's tendency to favor the movie image).

sound effect A sound artificially created for the **sound track** that has a definite function in telling the **story**.

soundstage A windowless, soundproofed, professional **shooting** environment that is usually several stories high and can cover an acre or more of floor space.

sound track A separate recording tape occupied by one specific type of sound recorded for a movie (one track for vocals, one for **sound effects**, one for music, etc.).

source light See **key light**.

special effects (SPFX, FX) Technology for creating images that would be too dangerous, too expensive, or, in some cases, simply impossible to achieve with traditional cinematographic materials. The goal of special-effects **cinematography** is generally to create **verisimilitude** within the imaginative world of even the most fanciful movie.

speed See **film-stock speed**.

SPFX See **special effects**.

splicing In pre-digital editing, the act of gluing or taping together shots together to form a continuous whole. See **cutting**.

split screen A method, created either in the camera or during the **editing** process, of telling two **stories** at the same time by dividing the screen into different parts. Unlike **parallel editing**, which **cuts** back and forth between **shots** for contrast, the split screen can tell multiple stories within the same **frame**.

sprocketed rollers Devices that control the speed of unexposed film as it moves through the camera, printer, or projector.

staging See **mise-en-scène**.

stakes In a conventional **narrative**, that which is at risk as a consequence of the **protagonist**'s pursuit of the **goal**.

stand-in An actor who looks reasonably like a particular **movie star** (or at least an actor playing a **major role**) in height, weight, coloring, and so on, and who substitutes for that actor during the tedious process of preparing **setups** or taking light readings.

Stanislavsky system A system of acting, developed by Russian theater **director** Konstantin Stanislavsky in the late nineteenth century, that encourages students to strive for **realism**, both social and psychological, and to bring their past experiences and emotions to their roles. This system influenced the development of **Method acting** in the United States.

Steadicam A camera suspended from an articulated arm that is attached to a vest strapped to the cameraperson's body, permitting the operator to remain steady during "handheld" shots. The Steadicam removes jumpiness and is now often used for smooth, fast, and intimate camera movement.

stock See **film stock**.

stop-frame See **freeze-frame**.

stop-motion cinematography A technique that allows the **camera operator** to stop and start the camera in order to facilitate changing the subject while the camera is not **shooting**. Frequently used for claymation and other forms of physical animation.

story In a movie, all the events we see or hear on the screen, and all the events that are implicit or that we infer to have happened but that are not explicitly presented. Compare **diegesis**, **narrative**, and **plot**.

storyboard A **scene**-by-scene (sometimes **shot**-by-shot) breakdown that combines sketches or photographs of how each shot is to look and written descriptions of the other elements that are to go with each shot, including **dialogue**, sound, and music.

story conference One of any number of sessions during which the **treatment** is discussed, developed, and transformed from an outline into a **rough-draft screenplay**.

story duration The amount of time that the entire narrative arc of a movie's story—whether explicitly presented on-screen or not—is implied to have taken to occur. Compare *plot duration* and *screen duration*.

stream of consciousness A literary style that gained prominence in the 1920s in the hands of such writers as Marcel Proust, Virginia Woolf, James Joyce, and Dorothy Richardson and that attempted to capture the unedited flow of experience through the mind.

stretch relationship A time relationship in which **screen duration** is longer than **plot duration**. Compare **real time** and **summary relationship**.

stuntperson A performer who doubles for another actor in **scenes** requiring special skills or involving hazardous actions, such as crashing cars, jumping from high places, swimming, or riding (or falling off of) horses.

subplot A subordinate **sequence** of action in a **narrative**, usually relevant to and enriching the **plot**.

subtractive color systems Adopted in the 1930s, this technique involved shooting three separate black-and-white negatives through three light filters, each representing a primary color (red, green, blue). Certain color components were subtracted (or removed) from each of the three emulsion layers, creating a positive image in natural color. Compare **additive color systems**.

summary relationship A time relationship in which **screen duration** is shorter than **plot duration**. Compare **real time** and **stretch relationship**.

supporting role See **minor role**.

surprise A taking unawares that is potentially shocking. Compare **suspense**.

suspense The anxiety brought on by partial uncertainty: the end is certain, but the means are not. Compare **surprise**.

swish pan A type of transition between two or more **scenes** made by moving the camera so rapidly that it blurs the moment of transition, thus suggesting (1) that the two actions are happening simultaneously, as in Billy Wilder's *Some Like It Hot* (1959; editor: Arthur P. Schmidt), where a swish pan separates an amorous scene involving Tony Curtis and Marilyn Monroe from a scene of Jack Lemmon, dressed as a woman, dancing with Joe E. Brown; or (2) that several years have elapsed between the scenes that comprise the breakfast-table **sequence** of Orson Welles's *Citizen Kane* (1941; editor: Robert Wise).

synopsis See **treatment**.

T

take An indication of the number of times a particular **shot** is taken (e.g., shot 14, take 7).

take-up spool A device that winds the film inside the movie camera after it has been exposed.

telephoto lens See **long-focal-length lens**.

texture As related to sound, see **quality**.

theme A shared, public idea, such as a metaphor, an adage, a myth, or a familiar conflict or personality type.

third-person narration Narration delivered from outside of the **diegesis** by a **narrator** who is not a character in the movie.

three-point system Perhaps the best-known lighting convention in feature filmmaking, a system that employs three sources of light—**key light**, **fill light**, and **backlight**—each aimed from a different direction and position in relation to the subject.

three-shot A **shot** in which three characters appear; ordinarily, a **medium shot** or **medium-long shot**.

tilt shot The vertical movement of a camera mounted on the gyroscopic head of a stationary tripod. Like the **pan shot**, the tilt shot is a simple movement with dynamic possibilities for creating meaning.

timbre See **quality**.

tracking shot See **dolly shot**.

traveling shot See **dolly shot**.

treatment Also known as *synopsis*. An outline of the action that briefly describes the essential ideas and structure for a film.

two-shot A **shot** in which two **characters** appear; ordinarily a **medium shot** or **medium long shot**.

typecasting The **casting** of actors because of their looks or "type" rather than for their acting talent or experience.

V

variable-focal-length lens See **zoom lens**.

verisimilitude A convincing appearance of truth; movies are verisimilar when they convince you that the things on the screen—people, places, and so on, no matter how fantastic or **antirealistic**—are "really there."

video assist camera A tiny device, mounted in the viewing system of the film camera, that enables a **script supervisor** to view a **scene** on a video monitor (and thus compare its details with those of surrounding scenes, to ensure visual continuity) before the film is sent to the laboratory for **processing**.

viewfinder On a camera, the little window that the cameraperson looks through when taking a picture; the viewfinder's frame indicates the boundaries of the camera's **point of view**.

voice-over narration Narration heard concurrently and over a **scene** but not synchronized to any **character** who may be talking on the screen. It can come from many sources, including a third person (who is not a character) bringing us up-to-date, a first-person narrator commenting on the action, or, in a **nonfiction film**, a commentator. Compare **first-person narration** and **third-person narration**.

W

walk-on A role even smaller than a **cameo**, reserved for a highly recognizable actor or personality.

wardrobe See **costumes**.

wide-angle lens See **short-focal-length lens**.

widescreen Any **aspect ratio** wider than 1.33:1, the standard ratio until the early 1950s.

wipe A transitional device between **shots** in which shot B wipes across shot A, either vertically or horizontally, to replace it.

Although (or because) the device reminds us of early eras in filmmaking, **directors** continue to use it.

X

XCU See **extreme close-up**.

XLS See **extreme long shot**.

Z

zoom in A **shot** in which the image is magnified by movement of the camera's **lens** only, without the camera itself moving. This magnification is the essential difference between the zoom in and the **dolly in**.

zoom lens Also known as *variable-focal-length lens*. A **lens** that is moved toward and away from the subject being photographed, has a continuously variable **focal length**, and helps **reframe** a **shot** within the **take**. A zoom lens permits the **camera operator** during **shooting** to shift between wide-angle and telephoto lenses without changing the focus or **aperture** settings. Compare **long-focal-length lens**, **middle-focal-length lens**, and **short-focal-length lens**. See also **prime lens**.

zoopraxiscope An early device for exhibiting moving pictures—a revolving disk with photographs arranged around the center.

Further Reading

Chapter 1: Looking at Movies

Theory and Aesthetics

Aitken, Ian. *European Film Theory and Cinema: A Critical Introduction.* Bloomington: Indiana University Press, 2001.

Andrew, J. Dudley. *The Major Film Theories: An Introduction.* New York: Oxford University Press, 1976.

Arnheim, Rudolf. *Art and Visual Perception: A Psychology of the Creative Eye.* Rev. ed. Berkeley: University of California Press, 1974.

———. *Film as Art.* Berkeley: University of California Press, 1957.

Bazin, André. *What Is Cinema?* Trans. Hugh Gray. 2 vols. Berkeley: University of California Press, 1967–1971.

Beardsley, Monroe. *Aesthetics: Problems in the Philosophy of Criticism.* New York: Harcourt Brace, 1958.

Beaver, Frank Eugene. *Dictionary of Film Terms: The Aesthetic Companion to Film Art.* New York: Peter Lang, 2006.

Benjamin, Walter. "The Work of Art in the Age of Mechanical Reproduction." In *Film Theory and Criticism: Introductory Readings.* 791–811. Ed. Leo Braudy and Marshall Cohen. 6th ed. New York: Oxford University Press, 2004.

Bordwell, David. *Poetics of Cinema.* New York: Routledge, 2008.

Braudy, Leo, and Marshall Cohen, eds. *Film Theory and Criticism: Introductory Readings.* 7th ed. New York: Oxford University Press, 2009.

Burch, Noël. *Life to Those Shadows.* Ed. and trans. Ben Brewster. Berkeley: University of California Press, 1990.

———. *Theory of Film Practice.* Trans. Helen R. Lane. Princeton: Princeton University Press, 1981.

Carroll, Noël. *Theorizing the Moving Image.* New York: Cambridge University Press, 1996.

Collins, Jim, Hilary Radner, and Ava Preacher Collins, eds. *Film Theory Goes to the Movies.* New York: Routledge, 1993.

Frampton, Daniel. *Filmosophy.* London: Wallflower, 2006.

Gombrich, E. H. *Art and Illusion: A Study in the Psychology of Pictorial Representation.* 2nd rev. ed. New York: Bollingen Foundation, 1961.

Henderson, Brian. *A Critique of Film Theory.* New York: Dutton, 1980.

Iser, Wolfgang. *How to Do Theory.* Malden, Mass: Blackwell, 2006.

Konigsberg, Ira. *The Complete Film Dictionary.* 2nd ed. New York: Penguin, 1997.

Kracauer, Siegfried. *Theory of Film: The Redemption of Physical Reality.* New York: Oxford University Press, 1960.

Lehman, Peter, ed. *Defining Cinema.* New Brunswick, N.J.: Rutgers University Press, 1997.

Mast, Gerald. *Film/Cinema/Movie: A Theory of Experience.* New York: Harper & Row, 1977.

Metz, Christian. *Film Language: A Semiotics of the Cinema.* Trans. Michael Taylor. New York: Oxford University Press, 1974.

Panofsky, Erwin. "Style and Medium in the Motion Pictures." In *Film Theory and Criticism: Introductory Readings.* 289–302. Ed. Leo Braudy and Marshall Cohen. 6th ed. New York: Oxford University Press, 2004.

Ray, Robert B. *How a Film Theory Got Lost and Other Mysteries in Cultural Studies.* Bloomington: Indiana University Press, 2001.

Simpson, Philip, Andrew Utterson, and K. J. Shepherdson, eds. *Film Theory: Critical Concepts in Media and Cultural Studies.* 4 vols. New York: Routledge, 2004.

Wollen, Peter. *Signs and Meaning in the Cinema*. 3rd ed. Bloomington: Indiana University Press, 1972.

Youngblood, Gene. *Expanded Cinema*. New York: Dutton, 1970.

Ways of Looking at Movies

Anderson, Joseph D. *The Reality of Illusion: An Ecological Approach to Cognitive Film Theory*. Carbondale: Southern Illinois University Press, 1996.

Bordwell, David. *Making Meaning: Inference and Rhetoric in the Interpretation of Cinema*. Cambridge, Mass.: Harvard University Press, 1989.

Bywater, Tim, and Thomas Sobchack. *An Introduction to Film Criticism: Major Critical Approaches to Narrative Film*. New York: Longman, 1989.

Carroll, Noël. *Interpreting the Moving Image*. New York: Cambridge University Press, 1998.

———. *The Philosophy of Horror: or, Paradoxes of the Heart*. New York: Routledge, 1990.

Grodal, Torben. *Moving Pictures: A New Theory of Film Genres, Feelings, and Cognition*. New York: Oxford University Press, 1997.

Kawin, Bruce F. *How Movies Work*. Berkeley: University of California Press, 1992.

Palmer, R. Barton. *The Cinematic Text: Methods and Approaches*. New York: AMS Press, 1989.

Perkins, V. F. *Film as Film: Understanding and Judging Movies*. Baltimore: Penguin, 1972.

Plantinga, Carl, and Greg M. Smith, eds. *Passionate Views: Film, Cognition, and Emotion*. Baltimore: Johns Hopkins University Press, 1999.

Smith, Greg M. *Film Structure and the Emotion System*. New York: Cambridge University Press, 2003.

Smith, Murray. *Engaging Characters: Fiction, Emotion, and the Cinema*. New York: Oxford University Press, 1995.

Staiger, Janet. *Media Reception Studies*. New York: New York University Press, 2005.

———. *Perverse Spectators: The Practices of Film Reception*. New York: New York University Press, 2000.

Stokes, Melvyn, and Richard Maltby, eds. *American Movie Audiences: From the Turn of the Century to the Early Sound Era*. London: BFI, 1999.

Formal Analysis

Geiger, Jeffrey, and R. L. Rutsky, eds. *Film Analysis: A Norton Reader*. New York: Norton, 2005.

Chapter 2: Principles of Film Form

Form and Content

Deren, Maya. *An Anagram of Ideas on Art, Form and Film*. Yonkers, N.Y.: Alicat, 1946. Repr. in *The Art of Cinema: Selected Essays*. Ed. George Amberg. New York: Arno, 1972.

Forster, E. M. *Aspects of the Novel*. New York: Harcourt, Brace, 1927.

Form and Expectations

Kozloff, Sarah. *Overhearing Film Dialogue*. Berkeley: University of California Press, 2000.

Realism and Antirealism

Armstrong, Richard. *Understanding Realism*. London: BFI, 2005.

Hochberg, Julian. "The Representation of Things and People." In *Art, Perception and Reality*. 47–94. Ed. E. H. Gombrich. Baltimore: Johns Hopkins University Press, 1972.

Williams, Christopher, ed. *Realism and the Cinema: A Reader*. London: Routledge & Kegan Paul, 1980.

Censorship

Black, Gregory D. *Hollywood Censored: Morality Codes, Catholics, and the Movies*. New York: Cambridge University Press, 1994.

Jacobs, Lea. *The Wages of Sin: Censorship and the Fallen Woman Film, 1928–1942*. Madison: University of Wisconsin Press, 1991.

Lewis, Jon. *Hollywood v. Hard Core: How the Struggle over Censorship Saved the Modern Film Industry*. New York: New York University Press, 2000.

Martin, Olga J. *Hollywood's Movie Commandments: A Handbook for Motion Picture Writers and Reviewers*. New York: Wilson, 1937.

Moley, Raymond. "The Birth of the Motion Picture Code." In *The Movies in Our Midst: Documents in the Cultural History of Film in America*. 317–321. Ed. Gerald Mast. Chicago: University of Chicago Press, 1982.

———. "The Motion Picture Production Code of 1930." In *The Movies in Our Midst: Documents in the Cultural History of Film in America*. 321–333. Ed. Gerald Mast. Chicago: University of Chicago Press, 1982.

Randall, Richard S. *Censorship of the Movies: The Social and Political Control of a Mass Medium*. Madison: University of Wisconsin Press, 1968.

Schumach, Murray. *The Face on the Cutting Room Floor: The Story of Movie and Television Censorship*. New York: Morrow, 1964.

Chapter 3: Types of Movies

General Books on Types and Genres of Movies

Altman, Rick. *Film/Genre*. London: BFI, 1999.

Browne, Nick, ed. *Refiguring American Film Genres: History and Theory*. Berkeley: University of California Press, 1998.

Dixon, Wheeler Winston, ed. *Film Genre 2000: New Critical Essays*. Albany: State University of New York Press, 2000.

Gehring, Wes D., ed. *Handbook of American Film Genres*. New York: Greenwood, 1988.

Grant, Barry Keith. *Film Genre: From Iconography to Ideology*. New York: Wallflower, 2007.

———, ed. *Film Genre Reader*. Austin: University of Texas Press, 1986.

———, ed. *Film Genre Reader II*. Austin: University of Texas Press, 1995.

———, ed. *Film Genre Reader III*. Austin: University of Texas Press, 2003.

———, ed. *Film Genre: Theory and Criticism*. Metuchen, N.J.: Scarecrow, 1977.

Langford, Barry. *Film Genre: Hollywood and Beyond*. Edingburgh: Edinburgh University Press, 2005.

Neale, Steve, ed. *Genre and Contemporary Hollywood*. London: BFI, 2002.

Schatz, Thomas. *Hollywood Genres: Formulas, Filmmaking, and the Studio System*. New York: Random House, 1981.

Solomon, Stanley J. *Beyond Formula: American Film Genres*. New York: Harcourt Brace Jovanovich, 1976.

Warshow, Robert. *The Immediate Experience: Movies, Comics, Theatre and Other Aspects of Popular Culture*. Enl. ed. Cambridge, Mass.: Harvard University Press, 2001.

Types of Movies and Genres

Action Movies

Gallagher, Mark. *Action Figures: Men, Action Films, and Contemporary Adventure Narratives*. New York: Palgrave Macmillan, 2006.

Schneider, Steven Jay, ed. *New Hollywood Violence*. Manchester: Manchester University Press, 2004.

Tasker, Yvonne. *Spectacular Bodies: Gender, Genre, and the Action Cinema*. London: Routledge, 1993.

African American Movies

Bobo, Jacqueline, ed. *Black Women Film and Video Artists*. New York: Routledge, 1998.

Bogle, Donald. *Blacks in American Films and Television: An Encyclopedia*. New York: Garland, 1988.

Bogle, Donald. *Toms, Coons, Mulattoes, Mammies, and Bucks: An Interpretive History of Blacks in American Film*. 4th ed. New York: Continuum, 2001.

Bowser, Pearl, Jane Gains, and Charles Musser, eds. *Oscar Micheaux and His Circle: African-American Filmmaking and Race Cinema of the Silent Era*. Bloomington: Indiana University Press, 2001.

Cripps, Thomas. *Black Film as Genre*. Bloomington: Indiana University Press, 1979.

———. *Slow Fade to Black: The Negro in American Film 1900–1942*. New York: Oxford University Press, 1977, 1993.

Davis, Natalie Zemon *Slaves on Screen: Film and Historical Vision*. Cambridge, Mass.: Harvard University Press, 2000.

Gabbard, Kim. *Jammin' at the Margins: Jazz and the American Cinema*. Chicago: University of Chicago Press, 1996.

Gaines, Jane M. *Fire and Desire: Mixed-Race Movies in the Silent Era*. Chicago: University of Chicago Press, 2001.

Jones, G. William. *Black Cinema Treasures: Lost and Found*. Denton: University of North Texas Press, 1991.

Reid, Mark A. *Black Lenses, Black Voices: African American Film Now*. Lanham, Md.: Rowman & Littlefield, 2005.

Stewart, Jacqueline Najuma. *Migrating to the Movies: Cinema and Black Urban Modernity*. Berkeley: University of California Press, 2005.

Animated Films

Barrier, Michael. *Hollywood Cartoons: American Animation in Its Golden Age*. New York: Oxford University Press, 1999.

Bendazzi, Giannalberto. *Cartoons: One Hundred Years of Cinema Animation*. London: Libbey, 1994.

Clements, Jonathan, and Helen McCarthy. *The Anime Encyclopedia: A Guide to Japanese Animation since 1917*. Rev. ed. Berkeley: Stone Bridge, 2001.

Crafton, Donald. *Before Mickey: The Animated Film 1898–1928*. New ed. Chicago: University of Chicago Press, 1993.

Furniss, Maureen. *Art in Motion: Animation Aesthetics*. Rev. ed. Bloomington: Indiana University Press, 2007.

Grant, John. *Masters of Animation*. New York: Watson-Guptill, 2001.

Holloway, Ronald. *Z Is for Zagreb*. London: Tantivy, 1972.

Kanfer, Stefan. *Serious Business: The Art and Commerce of Animation in America from Betty Boop to Toy Story*. New York: Da Capo Press, 2000.

Laybourne, Kit. *The Animation Book: A Complete Guide to Animated Filmmaking, from Flip-Books to Sound Cartoons to 3-D Animation*. Rev. pbk. ed. New York: Three Rivers, 1998.

Lent, John A., ed. *Animation in Asia and the Pacific*. Bloomington: Indiana University Press, 2001.

Maltin, Leonard. *Of Mice and Magic: A History of American Animated Cartoons*. New York: New American Library, 1980.

McCarthy, Helen. *Anime! A Beginner's Guide to Japanese Animation*. London: Titan, 1993.

———. *The Anime! Movie Guide*. London: Titan, 1996.

———. *Hayao Miyazaki, Master of Japanese Animation: Films, Themes, Artistry*. Berkeley: Stone Bridge, 1999.

Neuwirth, Allan. *Makin' Toons: Inside the Most Popular Animated TV Shows and Movies*. New York: Allworth, 2003.

Noake, Roger. *Animation: A Guide to Animated Film Techniques*. London: Macdonald Orbis, 1988.

Pilling, Jayne, ed. *A Reader in Animation Studies*. London: Libbey, 1997.

Poitras, Gilles. *The Anime Companion: What's Japanese in Japanese Animation?* Berkeley: Stone Bridge, 1999.

Russett, Robert, and Cecile Starr, eds. *Experimental Animation: An Illustrated Anthology*. New York: Van Nostrand Reinhold, 1976.

Wells, Paul. *The Fundamentals of Animation*. Lausanne: AVA, 2006.

Comedy

Cavell, Stanley. *Pursuits of Happiness: The Hollywood Comedy of Remarriage*. Cambridge, Mass.: Harvard University Press, 1981.

Chaplin, Charles. *My Autobiography*. New York: Simon & Schuster, 1964.

Karnick, Kristine Brunovska, and Henry Jenkins, eds. *Classical Hollywood Comedy*. New York: Routledge, 1995.

King, Geoff. *Film Comedy*. London: Wallflower, 2002.

Koszarski, Richard. *An Evening's Entertainment: The Age of the Silent Feature Picture, 1915–1928*. History of the American Cinema, Vol. 3. Berkeley: University of California Press, 1994.

Krutnick, Frank, ed. *Hollywood Comedians: The Film Reader*. New York: Routledge, 2003.

Mast, Gerald. *The Comic Mind: Comedy and the Movies*. 2nd ed. Chicago: University of Chicago Press, 1979.

McDonald, Tamar Jeffers. *Romantic Comedy: Boy Meets Girl Meets Genre*. London: Wallflower, 2007.

Robinson, David. *Buster Keaton*. Bloomington: Indiana University Press, 1969.

Winokur, Mark. *American Laughter: Immigrants, Ethnicity, and 1930s Hollywood Film Comedy*. New York: St. Martin's, 1996.

Sklar, Robert. *Movie-Made America: A Cultural History of American Movies*. Rev. ed. New York: Vintage, 1994.

Disaster Movies

Dixon, Wheeler Winston. *Visions of the Apocalypse: Spectacles of Destruction in American Cinema*. London: Wallflower, 2003.

Keane, Stephen. *Disaster Movies: The Cinema of Catastrophe*. 2nd ed. London: Wallflower, 2006.

Documentary Films

Aitken, Ian. *Encyclopedia of the Documentary Film*. New York: Routledge, 2006.

Aufderheide, Patricia. *Documentary Film: A Very Short Introduction*. New York: Oxford University Press, 2007.

Austin, Thomas, and Wilma de Jong, eds. *Rethinking Documentary: New Perspectives, New Practices*. London: Open University Press, 2008.

Barsam, Richard. *Nonfiction Film: A Critical History*. Rev. and exp. ed. Bloomington: Indiana University Press, 1992.

Chanan, Michael. *The Politics of Documentary*. London: BFI, 2007.

Hogarth, David. *Realer Than Reel: Global Directions in Documentary*. Austin: University of Texas Press, 2006.

Juhasz, Alexandra, and Jesse Lerner, eds. *F Is for Phony: Fake Documentary and Truth's Undoing*. Minneapolis: University of Minnesota Press, 2006.

Nichols, Bill. *Introduction to Documentary*. Bloomington: Indiana University Press, 2001.

———. *Representing Reality: Issues and Concepts in Documentary*. Bloomington: Indiana University Press, 1991.

Plantinga, Carl R. *Rhetoric and Representation in Nonfiction Film*. New York: Cambridge University Press, 1997.

Renov, Michael, ed. *Theorizing Documentary*. New York: Routledge, 1993.

Rothman, William. *Documentary Film Classics*. New York: Cambridge University Press, 1997.

Russell, Patrick. *100 British Documentaries*. London: BFI, 2007.

Tobias, Michael, ed. *The Search for Reality: The Art of Documentary Filmmaking*. Studio City, Calif.: Wiese, 1998.

Experimental Films

Arthur, Paul. *A Line of Sight: American Avant-Garde Film since 1965*. Minneapolis: University of Minnesota Press, 2005.

Berra, John. *Declarations of Independence: American Cinema and the Partiality of Independent Production*. Chicago: Intellect, 2008.

Camper, Fred. "Naming, and Defining, Avant-Garde or Experimental Film." http://www.fredcamper.com/Film/AvantGardeDefinition.html. Accessed April 29, 2009.

Dixon, Wheeler Winston. *The Exploding Eye: A Re-Visionary History of 1960's American Experimental Cinema*. Albany: State University of New York Press, 1997.

Dixon, Wheeler Winston, and Gwendolyn Audrey Foster, eds. *Experimental Cinema: The Film Reader*. New York: Routledge, 2002.

Hagener, Malte. *Moving Forward, Looking Back: The European Avant-Garde and the Invention of Film Culture, 1919–1939*. Amsterdam: Amsterdam University Press, 2007.

Harper, Graeme, and Rob Stone. *The Unsilvered Screen: Surrealism on Film*. London: Wallflower, 2007.

Horak, Jan-Christopher. *Lovers of Cinema: The First American Film Avant-Garde, 1919–1945*. Madison: University of Wisconsin Press, 1995.

Le Grice, Malcolm. *Experimental Cinema in the Digital Age*. London: BFI, 2001.

MacDonald, Scott. *Avant-Garde Film: Motion Studies*. New York: Cambridge University Press, 1993.

———. *A Critical Cinema: Interviews with Independent Filmmakers*. 5 vols. Berkeley: University of California Press, 1988–2006.

Peterson, James. *Dreams of Chaos, Visions of Order: Understanding the American Avant-Garde Cinema*. Detroit: Wayne State University Press, 1994.

Reekie, Duncan. *Subversion: The Definitive History of Underground Cinema*. London: Wallflower, 2007.

Sitney, P. Adams. *Visionary Film: The American Avant-Garde, 1943–1978*. 3rd ed. New York: Oxford University Press, 2002.

Youngblood, Gene. *Expanded Cinema*. New York: Dutton, 1970.

Film Noir

Abbott, Megan E. *The Street Was Mine: White Masculinity in Hardboiled Fiction and Film Noir*. New York: Palgrave Macmillan, 2002.

Bould, Mark. *Film Noir: From Berlin to Sin City*. London: Wallflower, 2005.

Christopher, Nicholas. *Somewhere in the Night: Film Noir and the American City*. New and exp. ed. Emeryville, Calif.: Shoemaker & Hoard, 2006.

Conrad, Mark T., ed. *The Philosophy of Film Noir*. Lexington: University Press of Kentucky, 2006.

Hirsch, Foster. *The Dark Side of the Screen: Film Noir*. 2nd ed. New York: Da Capo, 2001.

———. *Detours and Lost Highways: A Map of Neo-Noir*. New York: Limelight, 2004.

Johnson, Kevin. *The Dark Page: Books That Inspired American Film Noir (1940–1949)*. New Castle, Del.: Oak Knoll, 2007.

Kaplan, E. Ann, ed. *Women in Film Noir*. London: BFI, 1998.

Naremore, James. *More Than Night: Film Noir in Its Contexts*. Updated and exp. ed. Berkeley: University of California Press, 2008.

Porfirio, Robert, Alain Silver, and James Ursini, eds. *Film Noir Reader 3: Interviews with Filmmakers of the Classic Noir Period*. New York: Limelight, 2004.

Silver, Alain, and James Ursini, eds. *Film Noir Reader*. New York: Limelight, 1996.

———. *Film Noir Reader 2*. New York: Limelight, 2004.

———. *Film Noir Reader 4: The Crucial Films and Themes*. New York: Limelight, 2004.

Silver, Alain, and Elisabeth Ward, eds. *Film Noir: An Encyclopedic Reference to the American Style*. 3rd ed. Woodstock, N.Y.: Overlook, 1993.

Telotte, J. B. *Voices in the Dark: The Narrative Patterns of "Film Noir."* Urbana-Champaign: University of Illinois Press, 1989.

Wager, Jans B. *Dames in the Driver's Seat: Rereading Film Noir*. Austin: University of Texas Press, 2005.

Horror Movies

Carroll, Noël. *The Philosophy of Horror: Or, Paradoxes of the Heart*. New York: Routledge, 1990.

Clover, Carol J. *Men, Women, and Chain Saws: Gender in the Modern Horror Film*. Princeton: Princeton University Press, 1992.

Freeland, Cynthia A. *The Naked and the Undead: Evil and the Appeal of Horror*. Boulder, Col.: Westview, 2000.

Grant, Barry Keith, ed. *The Dread of Difference: Gender and the Horror Film*. Austin: University of Texas Press, 1996.

Hardy, Phil, with Tom Milne, Kim Newman, and Paul Willemen, eds. *Horror*. London: Aurum, 1996.

Jancovich, Mark, ed. *Horror, the Film Reader*. New York: Routledge, 2002.

King, Geoff, and Tanya Krzywinska. *Science Fiction Cinema: From Outerspace to Cyberspace.* London: Wallflower, 2000.

Pinedo, Isabel Cristina. *Recreational Terror: Women and the Pleasures of Horror Film Viewing.* Albany: State University of New York Press, 1997.

Tudor, Andrew. *Monsters and Mad Scientists: A Cultural History of the Horror Movie.* Oxford: Blackwell, 1989.

Wells, Paul. *The Horror Genre: From Beelzebub to Blair Witch.* London: Wallflower, 2000.

Movie Makes and Remakes

Forrest, Jennifer, and Leonard R. Koos, eds. *Dead Ringers: The Remake in Theory and Practice.* Albany: State University of New York Press, 2002.

Horton, Andrew, and Stuart Y. McDougal, eds. *Play It Again, Sam: Retakes on Remakes.* Berkeley: University of California Press, 1998.

Zanger, Anat. *Film Remakes as Ritual and Disguise: From Carmen to Ripley.* Amsterdam: Amsterdam University Press, 2006.

Melodramas

Gledhill, Christine, ed. *Home Is Where the Heart Is: Studies in Melodrama and the Woman's Film.* London: BFI, 1987.

Mercer, John, and Martin Shingler. *Melodrama: Genre, Style, Sensibility.* New York: Wallflower, 2004.

Musicals

Altman, Rick. *The American Film Musical.* Bloomington: Indiana University Press, 1987.

———, ed. *Genre, the Musical: A Reader.* London: Routledge & Kegan Paul, 1981.

Barrios, Richard. *A Song in the Dark: The Birth of the Musical Film.* New York: Oxford University Press, 1995.

Cohan, Steven, ed. *Hollywood Musicals, the Film Reader.* New York: Routledge, 2002.

Feuer, Jane. *The Hollywood Musical.* 2nd ed. Bloomington: Indiana University Press, 1993.

Fordin, Hugh. *The World of Entertainment: Hollywood's Greatest Musicals.* Garden City, N.Y.: Doubleday, 1975.

Smith, Susan. *The Musical: Race, Gender and Performance.* London: Wallflower, 2005.

Science-Fiction Films

Hardy, Phil, ed. *Science Fiction.* London: Aurum, 1984.

Luciano, Patrick. *Them or Us: Archetypal Interpretations of Fifties Alien Invasion Films.* Bloomington: Indiana University Press, 1987.

Redmond, Sean, ed. *Liquid Metal: The Science Fiction Film Reader.* London: Wallflower, 2004.

Rose, Mark. *Alien Encounters: The Anatomy of Science Fiction.* Cambridge, Mass.: Harvard University Press, 1981.

Sobchack, Vivian. *Screening Space: The American Science Fiction Film.* 2nd ed. New Brunswick, N.J.: Rutgers University Press, 1997.

Teen Films

Doherty, Thomas. *Teenagers and Teenpics: The Juvenilization of American Movies in the 1950s.* Rev. and exp. ed. Philadelphia: Temple University Press, 2002.

Lewis, Jon. *The Road to Romance and Ruin: Teen Films and Youth Culture.* New York: Routledge, 1992.

Shary, Timothy. *Teen Movies: American Youth on Screen.* London: Wallflower, 2005.

War Movies

DeBauche, Leslie Midkiff. *Reel Patriotism: The Movies and World War I.* Madison: University of Wisconsin Press, 1997.

Doherty, Thomas. *Projections of War: Hollywood, American Culture, and World War II.* New York: Columbia University Press, 1993.

Eberwein, Robert, ed. *The War Film.* New Brunswick, N.J.: Rutgers University Press, 2005.

Isenberg, Michael T. *War on Film: The American Cinema and World War I, 1914–1941.* Rutherford, N.J.: Fairleigh Dickinson University Press, 1981.

Koppes, Clayton R., and Gregory D. Black. *Hollywood Goes to War: How Politics, Profits, and Propaganda Shaped World War II Movies.* New York: Free Press, 1987.

Westerns

Bazin, André. "Evolution of the Western." In *What Is Cinema?* Vol. 2. 149–157. Trans. Hugh Gray. Berkeley: University of California Press, 1971.

Buscombe, Edward, ed. *The BFI Companion to the Western.* London: BFI, 1988.

———. *100 Westerns.* London: BFI, 2006.

Cawelti, John. *The Six-Gun Mystique.* 2nd ed. Bowling Green, Oh.: Bowling Green State University Popular Press, 1984.

Davis, Robert Murray. *Playing Cowboys: Low Culture and High Art in the Western.* Norman: University of Oklahoma Press, 1991.

Frayling, Christopher. *Spaghetti Westerns: Cowboys and Europeans from Karl May to Sergio Leone.* Rev. ed. London: Tauris, 2006.

Hardy, Phil, ed. *The Western.* 2nd ed. London: Aurum, 1991.

Hughes, Howard. *Spaghetti Westerns.* Harpenden, Eng.: Pocket Essentials, 2001.

Kitses, Jim. *Horizons West: Directing the Western from John Ford to Clint Eastwood.* New ed. London: BFI, 2004.

Saunders, John. *The Western Genre: From Lordsburg to Big Whiskey.* London: Wallflower, 2001.

Tompkins, Jane. *West of Everything: The Inner Life of Westerns.* New York: Oxford University Press, 1992.

Wright, Will. *Six Guns and Society: A Structural Study of the Western.* Berkeley: University of California Press, 1975.

Women's Films

Bean, Jennifer M., and Diane Negra, eds. *A Feminist Reader in Early Cinema.* Durham, N.C.: Duke University Press, 2002.

Butler, Alison. *Women's Cinema: The Contested Screen.* London: Wallflower, 2002.

Doane, Mary Ann. *The Desire to Desire: The Woman's Film of the 1940s.* Bloomington: Indiana University Press, 1987.

Kaplan, E. Ann. *Looking for the Other: Feminism, Film, and the Imperial Gaze.* New York: Routledge, 1997.

LaSalle, Mick. *Complicated Women: Sex and Power in Pre-Code Hollywood.* New York: St. Martin's Press, 2000.

Mayne, Judith. *The Woman at the Keyhole: Feminism and Women's Cinema.* Bloomington: Indiana University Press, 1990.

Modleski, Tania. *Loving with a Vengeance: Mass-Produced Fantasies for Women.* 2nd ed. New York: Routledge, 2008.

Mulvey, Laura. *Visual and Other Pleasures*. 2nd ed. New York: Palgrave Macmillan, 2009.

Quart, Barbara Koenig. *Women Directors: The Emergence of a New Cinema*. New York: Praeger, 1988.

Sloan, Jane. *Reel Women: An International Directory of Contemporary Feature Films about Women*. Lanham, Md.: Scarecrow, 2007.

Chapter 4: Elements of Narrative

What Is Narrative?

Abbott, H. Porter. *The Cambridge Introduction to Narrative*. New York: Cambridge University Press, 2002.

Beardsley, Monroe C. *Aesthetics: Problems in the Philosophy of Criticism*. 2nd ed. Indianapolis: Hackett, 1981.

Bordwell, David. *Making Meaning: Inference and Rhetoric in the Interpretation of Cinema*. Cambridge, Mass.: Harvard University Press, 1989.

———. *The Way Hollywood Tells It: Story and Style in Modern Movies*. Berkeley: University of California Press, 2006.

Branigan, Edward. *Narrative Comprehension and Film*. New York: Routledge, 1992.

———. *Point of View in the Cinema: A Theory of Narration and Subjectivity in Classical Film*. New York: Mouton, 1984.

Chatman, Seymour. *Coming to Terms: The Rhetoric of Narrative in Fiction and Film*. Ithaca, N.Y.: Cornell University Press, 1990.

———. *Story and Discourse: Narrative Structure in Fiction and Film*. Ithaca, N.Y.: Cornell University Press, 1978.

Chopra-Gant, Mike. *Cinema and History: The Telling of Stories*. London: Wallflower, 2008.

Fabe, Marilyn. *Closely Watched Films: An Introduction to the Art of Narrative Film Technique*. Berkeley: University of California Press, 2004.

Fell, John L. *Film and the Narrative Tradition*. Norman: University of Oklahoma Press, 1974.

Forster, E. M. *Aspects of the Novel*. New York: Harcourt, Brace, 1927.

Kozloff, Sarah. *Overhearing Film Dialogue*. Berkeley: University of California Press, 2000.

Leitch, Thomas M. *What Stories Are: Narrative Theory and Interpretation*. University Park, Pa.: Pennsylvania State University Press, 1986.

Ryan, Marie-Laure, ed. *Narrative across Media: The Languages of Storytelling*. Lincoln: University of Nebraska Press, 2004.

Scholes, Robert, James Phelan, and Robert Kellogg. *The Nature of Narrative*. Rev. and exp. ed. New York: Oxford University Press, 2006.

Stam, Robert, Robert Burgoyne, and Sandy Flitterman-Lewis. *New Vocabularies in Film Semiotics: Structuralism, Post-Structuralism, and Beyond*. New York: Routledge, 1992.

Thompson, Kristin. *Storytelling in the New Hollywood: Understanding Classical Narrative Technique*. Cambridge, Mass.: Harvard University Press, 1999.

The Screenwriter

Boozer, Jack, ed. *Authorship in Film Adaptation*. Austin: University of Texas Press, 2008.

Desmond, John M., and Peter Hawkes. *Adaptation: Studying Film and Literature*. New York: McGraw-Hill, 2006.

Elliott, Kamilla. *Rethinking the Novel/Film Debate*. New York: Cambridge University Press, 2003.

Field, Syd. *Screenplay: The Foundations of Screenwriting*. Rev. ed. New York: Delta, 2005.

Gerstner, David A., and Janet Staiger, eds. *Authorship and Film*. New York: Routledge, 2003.

Jacobs, Lea. *The Wages of Sin: Censorship and the Fallen Woman Film, 1928–1942*. Madison: University of Wisconsin Press, 1991.

McKee, Robert. *Story: Substance, Structure, Style, and the Principles of Screenwriting*. New York: ReganBooks, 1997.

Welsh, James M., and Peter Lev, eds. *The Literature/Film Reader: Issues of Adaptation*. Lanham, Md.: Scarecrow, 2007.

Wexman, Virginia Wright, ed. *Film and Authorship*. New Brunswick, N.J.: Rutgers University Press, 2003.

Writers Guild of America. *101 Greatest Screenplays*. www.wga.org/subpage_newsevents.aspx?id=1807.

Elements of Narrative

Armes, Roy. *Action and Image: Dramatic Structure in Cinema*. Manchester: Manchester University Press, 1994.

Ivarsson, Jan, and Mary Carroll. *Subtitling*. Simrishamn, Sweden: TransEdit, 1998.

Narration and Narrators

Bordwell, David. *Narration in the Fiction Film* Madison: University of Wisconsin Press, 1985.

Kawin, Bruce F. *Mindscreen: Bergman, Godard, and First-Person Film*. Princeton: Princeton University Press, 1978.

Looking at Narrative: John Ford's *Stagecoach*

Buscombe, Edward. *Stagecoach*. London: BFI, 1992.

Nichols, Dudley. *Stagecoach: A Film by John Ford and Dudley Nichols*. New York: Simon & Schuster, 1971.

Chapter 5: Mise-en-Scène

What Is Mise-en-Scène?: Background and Theory

Andrew, Dudley, ed. *The Image in Dispute: Art and Cinema in the Age of Photography*. Austin: University of Texas Press, 1997.

Bazin, André. "The Virtues and Limitations of Montage." In *What Is Cinema?* Vol. 1. 41–52. Trans. Hugh Gray. Berkeley: University of California Press, 1967.

Bordwell, David. *Figures Traced in Light: On Cinematic Staging*. Berkeley: University of California Press, 2005.

———. *On the History of Film Style*. Cambridge, Mass.: Harvard University Press, 1997.

———. "Widescreen Aesthetics and Mise en Scene Criticism." *The Velvet Light Trap* no. 21 (Summer 1985): 18–25.

Brewster, Ben, and Lea Jacobs. *Theatre to Cinema: Stage Pictorialism and the Early Feature Film*. New York: Oxford University Press, 1997.

Brockett, Oscar G., and Robert R. Findlay. *Century of Innovation: A History of American and European Theatre and Drama since the Late Nineteenth Century*. 2nd ed. Boston: Allyn & Bacon, 1991.

Burch, Noël. *Theory of Film Practice*. Trans. Helen R. Lane. Princeton: Princeton University Press, 1981.

Dalle Vacche, Angela. *Cinema and Painting: How Art Is Used in Film*. Austin: University of Texas Press, 1996.

Dunning, William V. *Changing Images of Pictorial Space: A History of Spatial Illusion in Painting*. Syracuse: Syracuse University Press, 1991.

Eisenstein, Sergei. *Film Form: Essays in Film Theory* [and] *The Film Sense*. Ed. and trans. Jay Leyda. 2 vols. in 1. New York: Meridian, 1957.

———. *Film Essays and a Lecture*. Ed. Jay Leyda. New York: Praeger, 1970.

Farber, Manny. *Negative Space: Manny Farber on the Movies*. Exp. ed. New York: Da Capo, 1998.

Kracauer, Siegfried. *Theory of Film: The Redemption of Physical Reality*. New York: Oxford University Press, 1960.

Meisel, Martin. *Realizations: Narrative, Pictorial, and Theatrical Arts in Nineteenth-Century England*. Princeton: Princeton University Press, 1983.

Nizhny, Vladmir. *Lessons with Eisenstein*. Ed. and trans. Ivor Montagu and Jay Leyda. New York: Hill & Wang, 1962.

Perkins, V. F. *Film as Film: Understanding and Judging the Movies*. Baltimore, Md.: Penguin, 1972.

Turim, Maureen. "Symmetry/Asymmetry and Visual Fascination." *Wide Angle* 4, no. 3 (1980): 38–47.

Vardac, A. Nicholas. *Stage to Screen: Theatrical Method from Garrick to Griffith*. Cambridge: Harvard University Press, 1949.

White, John. *The Birth and Rebirth of Pictorial Space*. 3rd ed. Cambridge, Mass.: Belknap, 1987.

Williams, Christopher, ed. *Realism and the Cinema: A Reader*. London: Routledge & Kegan Paul, 1980.

Wright, Lawrence. *Perspective in Perspective*. London: Routledge & Kegan Paul, 1983.

Production Design

Albrecht, Donald. *Designing Dreams: Modern Architecture in the Movies*. New York: Harper & Row and the Museum of Modern Art, 1986.

Carrick, Edward. *Designing for Films*. London: Studio Publications, 1949.

Corliss, Mary, and Carlos Clarens. "Designed for Film: The Hollywood Art Director." *Film Comment* 14 (May/June 1978): 26–60.

Ettedgui, Peter. *Production Design & Art Direction*. Woburn, Mass.: Focal Press, 1999.

Fischer, Lucy. *Designing Women: Cinema, Art Deco, and the Female Form*. New York: Columbia University Press, 2003.

Frayling, Christopher. *Ken Adam and the Art of Production Design*. London: Faber and Faber, 2005.

Gibbons, Cedric. "The Art Director." In *Behind the Screen: How Films Are Made*. 41–50. Ed. Stephen Watts. London: Barker, 1938.

Heisner, Beverly. *Hollywood Art: Art Direction in the Days of the Great Studios*. Jefferson, N.C.: McFarland, 1990.

———. *Production Design in the Contemporary American Film: A Critical Study of 23 Movies and Their Designers*. Jefferson, N.C.: McFarland, 1997.

Horner, Harry. "The Production Designer." In *Filmmakers on Filmmaking: The American Film Institute Seminars on Motion Pictures and Television*. 2 vols. Vol. I. 149–161. Ed. Joseph McBride. Los Angeles: Tarcher, 1983.

Hudson, Roger. "Three Designers." *Sight & Sound* 34, no. 1 (Winter 1964–65): 26–31.

LoBrutto, Vincent. *By Design: Interviews with Film Production Designers*. Westport, Conn.: Praeger, 1992.

———. *The Filmmaker's Guide to Production Design*. New York: Allworth, 2002.

Lourié, Eugene. *My Work in Films*. San Diego: Harcourt Brace Jovanovich, 1985.

Mandelbaum, Howard, and Eric Myers. *Forties Screen Style: A Celebration of High Pastiche in Hollywood*. New York: St. Martin's, 1989.

Marner, Terence St. John, and Michael Stringer. *Film Design*. New York: Barnes, 1974.

McNamara, Brooks. "The Scenography of Popular Entertainment." *Drama Review* 18, no. 1 (March 1974): 16–24.

Mills, Bart. "The Brave New Worlds of Production Design." *American Film* 7, no. 4 (January/February 1982): 40–46.

Neumann, Dietrich, ed. *Film Architecture: Set Designs from "Metropolis" to "Blade Runner."* New York: Prestel, 1996.

Olson, Robert L. *Art Direction for Film and Video*. 2nd ed. Boston: Focal Press, 1999.

Preston, Ward. *What an Art Director Does: An Introduction to Motion Picture Production Design*. Los Angeles: Silman-James, 1994.

Rizzo, Michael. *The Art Direction Handbook for Film*. Boston: Focal Press, 2005.

Sennett, Robert S. *Setting the Scene: The Great Hollywood Art Directors*. New York: Abrams, 1994.

Surowiec, Catherine A. *Accent on Design: Four European Art Directors*. London: BFI, 1992.

Taylor, John Russell. "Satyajit Ray." In *Cinema, a Critical Dictionary: The Major Film-Makers*. 2 vols. Vol. II. 813–831. Ed. Richard Roud. New York: Viking, 1980.

Whitlock, Cathy and the Art Directors Guild. *Design on Film: A Century of Hollywood Art Direction*. New York: HarperCollins, 2010.

Elements of Design
Setting, Decor, and Properties

Affron, Charles, and Mirella Jona Affron. *Sets in Motion: Art Direction and Film Narrative*. New Brunswick, N.J.: Rutgers University Press, 1995.

Barsacq, Léon. *Caligari's Cabinet and Other Grand Illusions: A History of Film Design*. Rev. and ed. Elliott Stein. Trans. Michael Bullock. Boston: New York Graphic Society, 1976.

Bingen, Stephen, et al. *M-G-M: Hollywood's Greatest Backlot*. Solana Beach, Calif. Santa Monica Press, 2011.

Henderson, Brian. "Notes on Set Design and Cinema." *Film Quarterly* 42, no. 1 (Fall 1988): 17–28.

Higgins, Scott. *Harnessing the Technicolor Rainbow: Color Design in the 1930s*. Austin: University of Texas Press, 2007.

Neumann, Dietrich, ed. *Film Architecture: Set Designs from "Metropolis" to "Blade Runner."* New York: Prestel, 1996.

Pomerance, Murray, ed. *City That Never Sleeps: New York and the Filmic Imagination*. New Brunswick, N.J.: Rutgers University Press, 2007.

Sanders, James. *Celluloid Skyline: New York and the Movies*. New York: Knopf, 2001.

Tashiro, C. S. *Pretty Pictures: Production Design and the History Film*. Austin: University of Texas Press, 1998.

Webber, Andrew, and Emma Wilson, eds. *Cities in Transition: The Moving Image and the Modern Metropolis*. London: Wallflower, 2008.

Costume, Makeup, and Hairstyle

Annas, Alicia. "The Photogenic Formula: Hairstyles and Makeup in Historical Films." In *Hollywood and History: Costume Design in Film*. 52–77. Ed. Edward Maeder. New York: Thames & Hudson, 1987.

Corson, Richard, Beverley Gore Norcross, and James Glavan. *Stage Makeup*. 10th ed. Boston: Pearson, 2009.

Head, Edith, and Jane Kesner Ardmore. *The Dress Doctor*. Boston: Little, Brown, 1959.

Head, Edith, and Paddy Calistro. *Edith Head's Hollywood*. New York: Dutton, 1983.

Kehoe, Vincent J.-R. *The Technique of the Professional Make-up Artist for Film, Television, and Stage*. Boston: Focal Press, 1985.

Landis, Deborah Nadoolman. *Dressed: A Century of Hollywood Costume Design*. New York: Collins Design, 2007.

Leese, Elizabeth. *Costume Design in the Movies: An Illustrated Guide to the Work of 157 Great Designers*. New York: Ungar, 1976.

Maeder, Edward, ed. *Hollywood and History: Costume Design in Film*. New York: Thames & Hudson, 1987.

Moseley, Rachel, ed. *Fashioning Film Stars: Dress, Culture, Identity*. London: BFI, 2005.

Pidduck, Julianne. *Contemporary Costume Film: Space, Place and the Past*. London: BFI, 2004.

Vinther, Janus. *Special Effects Make-up*. New York: Routledge, 2003.

International Styles of Design

Bergfelder, Tim, Sue Harris, and Sarah Street. *Film Architecture and the Transnational Imagination: Set Design in 1930s European Cinema*. Amsterdam: Amsterdam University Press, 2007.

Brunsdon, Charlotte. *London in Cinema: The Cinematic City since 1945*. London: BFI, 2007.

Eisner, Lotte H. *The Haunted Screen: Expressionism in the German Cinema and the Influence of Max Reinhardt*. Trans. Roger Greaves. Berkeley: University of California Press, 1969.

Framing and Composition

Arnheim, Rudolf. *Art and Visual Perception: A Psychology of the Creative Eye*. Rev. ed. Berkeley: University of California Press, 1974.

———. *The Power of the Center: A Study of Composition in the Visual Arts*. New version. Berkeley: University of California Press, 1988.

Braudy, Leo. *The World in a Frame: What We See in Films*. Garden City, N.Y.: Anchor, 1976.

Hochberg, Julian. "The Representation of Things and People." In E. H. Gombrich, Julian Hochberg, and Max Black, *Art, Perception, and Reality*. 47–94. Baltimore, Md.: Johns Hopkins University Press, 1973.

Chapter 6: Cinematography

What Is Cinematography?: General

Andrew, Dudley, ed. *The Image in Dispute: Art and Cinema in the Age of Photography*. Austin: University of Texas Press, 1997.

Astruc, Alexandre. "The Birth of a New Avant-Garde: Le Caméra Stylo." In *The New Wave: Critical Landmarks*. 7–18. Ed. Peter Graham. Garden City, N.Y.: Doubleday, 1968.

Burum, Stephen, ed. *American Cinematographer Manual*. 9th ed. 2 vols. Hollywood: American Society of Cinematographers, 2007.

Campbell, Russell, ed. *Practical Motion Picture Photography*. New York: Barnes, 1970.

Case, Dominic. *Motion Picture Film Processing*. Boston: Focal Press, 1985.

Cheshire, David F. *The Book of Movie Photography: The Complete Guide to Better Moviemaking*. New York: Knopf, 1979.

Coe, Brian. *The History of Movie Photography*. London: Ash & Grant, 1981.

Deren, Maya. "Cinematography: The Creative Use of Reality." In *Film Theory and Criticism: Introductory Readings*. 187–198. Ed. Leo Braudy and Marshall Cohen. 7th ed. New York: Oxford University Press, 2009.

Enticknap, Leo. *Moving Image Technology: From Zoetrope to Digital*. London: Wallflower Press, 2005.

Ettedgui, Peter. *Cinematography*. Woburn, Mass.: Focal Press, 1998.

Kawin, Bruce F. *How Movies Work*. Berkeley: University of California Press, 1992.

Levitan, Eli L. *An Alphabetical Guide to Motion Picture, Television, and Videotape Production*. New York: McGraw-Hill, 1970.

Malkiewicz, J. Kris, and M. David Mullen. *Cinematography: A Guide for Film Makers and Film Teachers*. 3rd ed. New York: Simon & Schuster, 2005.

Mascelli, Joseph V. *The Five C's of Cinematography: Motion Picture Filming Techniques*. Repr., Los Angeles: Silman-James Press, 1998.

Vertov, Dziga. *Kino-Eye: The Writings of Dziga Vertov*. Ed. Annette Michelson. Trans. Kevin O'Brien. Berkeley: University of California Press, 1984.

White, John. *The Birth and Rebirth of Pictorial Space*. 3rd ed. Cambridge, Mass.: Belknap, 1987.

Winston, Brian. *Technologies of Seeing: Photography, Cinematography and Television*. London: BFI, 1996.

Director of Cinematography

Almendros, Néstor. *A Man with a Camera*. Trans. Rachel Phillips Belash. New York: Farrar, Straus, and Giroux, 1984.

Bergery, Benjamin. *Reflections: Twenty-one Cinematographers at Work*. Hollywood: American Society of Cinematographers, 2002.

Burum, Stephen, ed. *American Cinematographer Manual*. 9th ed. 2 vols. Hollywood: American Society of Cinematographers, 1993.

Krasilovsky, Alexis. *Women behind the Camera: Conversations with Camerawomen*. Westport, Conn.: Praeger, 1997.

LoBrutto, Vincent. *Principal Photography: Interviews with Feature Film Cinematographers*. Westport, Conn.: Praeger, 1999.

Maltin, Leonard. *The Art of the Cinematographer: A Survey and Interviews with Five Masters*. Rev. ed. New York: Dover, 1978.

Petrie, Duncan. *The British Cinematographer*. London: BFI, 1996.

Rogers, Pauline B. *Contemporary Cinematographers on Their Art*. Boston: Focal Press, 1998.

Toland, Gregg. "How I Broke the Rules in *Citizen Kane*." In *Focus on Citizen Kane*. 73–77. Ed. Ronald Gottesman. Englewood Cliffs, N.J.: Prentice-Hall, 1971.

Cinematographic Properties of the Shot

Stock

Arnheim, Rudolf. *Film as Art*. Berkeley: University of California Press, 1957.

Basten, Fred E. *Glorious Technicolor: The Movies' Magic Rainbow*. Cranbury, N.J.: Barnes, 1980.

Brakhage, Stan. *Metaphors on Vision*. New York: Film Culture, 1963.

Branigan, Edward. "The Articulation of Color in a Filmic System." *Wide Angle* 1, no. 3 (1976): 20–31.

———. "Color and Cinema: Problems in the Writing of History." *Film Reader* 4 (1979): 16–34.

Dalle Vacche, Angela, and Brian Price, eds. *Color: The Film Reader*. London: Routledge, 2006.

De Grandis, Luigina. *Theory and Use of Color*. Trans. John Gilbert. New York: Abrams, 1986.

Dreyer, Carl. "Color Film and Colored Films." In *Dreyer in Double Reflection*. 168–173. Ed. Donald Skoller. New York: Dutton, 1973.

Durgnat, Raymond. "Colours and Contrasts." *Films and Filming* 15, no. 2 (November 1968): 58–62.

Eisenstein, Sergei. "Color and Meaning." In *Film Form: Essays in Film Theory* [and] *The Film Sense*. 113–153. Ed. and trans. Jay Leyda. New York: Meridian, 1957.

Hertogs, Daan, and Nico de Klerk, eds. *"Disorderly Order": Colours in Silent Film—the 1995 Amsterdam Workshop*. Amsterdam: Stichting Nederlands Filmmuseum, 1996.

Johnson, William. "Coming to Terms with Color." *Film Quarterly* 20, no. 1 (Fall 1966): 2–22.

Mamoulian, Rouben. "Color and Light in Films." *Film Culture* 21 (Summer 1960): 68–79.

Misek, Richard. *A History of Screen Colour* [sic]. London: Wiley-Blackwell, 2010.

Perkins, V. F. *Film as Film: Understanding and Judging Movies*. Baltimore: Penguin, 1972.

Ryan, Roderick T. *A History of Motion Picture Color Technology*. New York: Focal Press, 1977.

Sharits, Paul. "Red, Blue, Godard." *Film Quarterly* 19, no. 4 (Summer 1966): 24–29.

Society of Motion Picture and Television Engineers. *Elements of Color in Professional Motion Pictures*. New York: Society of Motion Picture and Television Engineers, 1957.

Thomas, D. B. *The First Colour Motion Pictures*. London: H.M.S.O., 1969.

Zelanski, Paul, and Mary Pat Fisher. *Color*. Englewood Cliffs, N.J.: Prentice-Hall, 1989.

Lighting

Alton, John. *Painting with Light*. Berkeley: University of California Press, 1995.

Coutard, Raoul. "Light of Day." In *Jean-Luc Godard: A Critical Anthology*. 232–239. Ed. Toby Mussmann. New York: Dutton, 1968.

Ferncase, Richard K. *Film and Video Lighting Terms and Concepts*. Boston: Focal Press, 1995.

Guerin, Frances. *A Culture of Light: Cinema and Technology in 1920s Germany*. Minneapolis: University of Minnesota Press, 2005.

Higham, Charles. *Hollywood Cameramen: Sources of Light*. Bloomington: Indiana University Press, 1970.

Malkiewicz, Kris. *Film Lighting: Talks with Hollywood's Cinematographers and Gaffers*. New York: Prentice-Hall, 1986.

Millerson, Gerald. *The Technique of Lighting for Television and Film*. 3rd ed. Boston: Focal Press, 1991.

———. *The Technique of Lighting for Television and Motion Pictures*. New York: Focal Press, 1972.

Schaefer, Dennis, and Larry Salvato. *Masters of Light: Conversations with Contemporary Cinematographers*. Berkeley: University of California Press, 1984.

von Sternberg, Josef. *Fun in a Chinese Laundry*. New York: Macmillan, 1965.

Lenses

Graham, Arthur. "Zoom Lens Techniques." *American Cinematographer* 44, no. 1 (January 1963): 28–29.

Joannides, Paul. "The Aesthetics of the Zoom Lens." *Sight and Sound* 40, no. 1 (Winter 1970): 40-42.

Kaminsky, Stuart M. "The Use and Abuse of the Zoom Lens." *Filmmakers Newsletter* 5, no. 12 (October 1972): 20–23.

Wees, William C. "Prophecy, Memory, and the Zoom: Michael Snow's Wavelength Re-Viewed." *Ciné-Tracts* nos. 14/15 (Summer/Fall 1981): 78–83.

Framing of the Shot

Barr, Charles. "CinemaScope: Before and After." 140–168. In *Film Theory and Criticism: Introductory Readings*. Ed. Gerald Mast and Marshall Cohen. 2nd ed. New York: Oxford University Press, 1979.

———. "A Letter from Charles Barr." *The Velvet Light Trap* 21 (Summer 1985): 5–7.

Bazin, André. "The Evolution of the Language of Cinema." In *What Is Cinema?* Vol. 1. 23–40. Trans. Hugh Gray. Berkeley: University of California Press, 1967.

———. "Three Essays on Widescreen Film." *The Velvet Light Trap* 21 (Summer 1985): 8–18.

Belton, John. "CinemaScope: The Economics of Technology." *The Velvet Light Trap* 21 (Summer 1985): 35–43.

Carr, Robert E., and R. M. Hayes. *Wide Screen Movies: A History and Filmography of Wide Gauge Filmmaking*. Jefferson, N.C.: McFarland, 1988.

Chisholm, Brad. "Widescreen Technologies." *The Velvet Light Trap* 21 (Summer 1985): 67–74.

Cossar, Harper. *The Evolution of Widescreen Cinema*. Lexington: University of Kentucky Press, 2010.

Katz, David. "A Widescreen Chronology." *The Velvet Light Trap* 21 (Summer 1985): 62–64.

Ogle, Patrick L. "Technological and Aesthetic Influences upon the Development of Deep Focus Cinematography in the United States." *Screen* 13, no. 1 (Spring 1972): 45–72.

Spellerberg, James. "CinemaScope and Ideology." *The Velvet Light Trap* 21 (Summer 1985): 26–34.

Proximity and Depth

Bazin, André. "The Evolution of the Language of Cinema." In *What Is Cinema?* Vol. I. 23–40. Trans. Hugh Gray. Berkeley: University of California Press, 1967.

———. *Orson Welles: A Critical View.* New York: Harper & Row, 1978.

Burch, Noël. *Theory of Film Practice.* Princeton: Princeton University Press, 1981.

Dubery, Fred, and John Willats. *Perspective and Other Drawing Systems.* New York: Van Nostrand Reinhold, 1983.

Dunning, William V. *Changing Images of Pictorial Space: A History of Spatial Illusion in Painting.* Syracuse: Syracuse University Press, 1991.

Nizhny, Vladimir. *Lessons with Eisenstein.* Ed. and trans. Ivor Montagu and Jay Leyda. New York: Da Capo, 1979.

Wright, Lawrence. *Perspective in Perspective.* London: Routledge & Kegan Paul, 1983.

Camera Movement

Lightman, Herb A. "The Fluid Camera." *American Cinematographer* 27, no. 3 (March 1946): 82, 102–103.

Framing and Point of View

Branigan, Edward. *Point of View in the Cinema: A Theory of Narration and Subjectivity in Classical Film.* New York: Mouton, 1984.

Speed and Length of Shot

Bazin, André. "The Ontology of the Photographic Image." In *What Is Cinema?* Vol. I. 9–16. Trans. Hugh Gray. Berkeley: University of California Press, 1967.

Henderson, Brian. "The Long Take." In *A Critique of Film Theory.* 48–61. New York: Dutton, 1980.

Perkins, V. F. "Rope." In *Movie Reader.* 35–37. Ed. Ian Alexander Cameron. New York: Praeger, 1972.

Special Effects

Bizony, Piers. *Digital Domain: The Leading Edge of Digital Effects.* New York: Billboard, 2001.

Bukatman, Scott. *Matters of Gravity: Special Effects and Supermen in the 20th Century.* Durham, N.C.: Duke University Press, 2003.

Culhane, John. *Special Effects in the Movies: How They Do It.* New York: Ballantine, 1981.

Dunn, Linwood G., and George E. Turner, eds. *The ASC Treasury of Visual Effects.* Hollywood: American Society of Cinematographers, 1983.

Finch, Christopher. *Special Effects: Creating Movie Magic.* New York: Abbeville, 1984.

Halas, John, and Roger Manvell. *The Technique of Film Animation.* 4th ed. New York: Focal Press, 1968.

Hamilton, Jake. *Special Effects: In Film and Television.* New York: DK Publishing, 1998.

Harryhausen, Ray. *Film Fantasy Scrapbook.* 3rd ed. San Diego: Barnes, 1981.

Herdeg, Walter, and John Halas. *Film and TV Graphics: An International Survey of Film and Television Graphics.* Zurich: Graphis Press, 1967.

McLean, Shilo T. *Digital Storytelling: The Narrative Power of Visual Effects in Film.* Cambridge, Mass.: MIT Press, 2007.

Netzley, Patricia D. *Encyclopedia of Movie Special Effects.* Phoenix: Oryx Press, 2000.

Pierson, Michele. *Special Effects: Still in Search of Wonder.* New York: Columbia University Press, 2002.

Pinteau, Pascal. *Special Effects: An Oral History.* Trans. Laurel Hirsch. New York: Abrams, 2004.

Rickitt, Richard. *Special Effects: The History and Technique.* New York: Billboard, 2007.

Schechter, Harold, and David Everitt. *Film Tricks: Special Effects in the Movies.* New York: H. Quist, 1980.

Vaz, Mark Cotta, and Craig Barron. *The Invisible Art: The Legends of Movie Matte Painting.* San Francisco: Chronicle, 2002.

Vaz, Mark Cotta, and Patricia Rose Duignan. *Industrial Light & Magic: Into the Digital Realm.* New York: Ballantine, 1996.

Chapter 7: Acting

What Is Acting?

Brandes, D. "Roman Polanski on Acting." *Cinema Papers* no. 11 (January 1977): 226–229.

Braudy, Leo. "Film Acting: Some Critical Problems and Proposals." *Quarterly Review of Film Studies* 1, no. 1 (February 1976): 1–18.

Caine, Michael. *Acting in Film: An Actor's Take on Movie Making.* Rev. exp. ed. New York: NY Applause Theatre Book Publishers, 1997.

Callow, Simon. *Being an Actor.* New York: Picador, 2003.

Campbell, Russell, ed. "The Actor." *The Velvet Light Trap* no. 7 (Winter 1972/73): 1–60.

Dmytryk, Edward, and Jean Porter Dmytryk. *On Screen Acting: An Introduction to the Art of Acting for the Screen.* Boston: Focal Press, 1984.

Eisenstein, Sergei. *Film Form: Essays in Film Theory* [and] *The Film Sense.* Ed. and trans. Jay Leyda. New York: Meridian, 1957.

Kuleshov, Lev. *Kuleshov on Film: Writings.* Ed. and trans. Ronald Levaco. Berkeley: University of California Press, 1974.

Naremore, James. *Acting in the Cinema.* Berkeley: University of California Press, 1988.

Quart, Leonard. "'I Still Love Going to Movies': An Interview with Pauline Kael." *Cineaste* 25, no. 2 (2000): 8–13.

Pudovkin, V. I. *Film Technique and Film Acting.* Ed. and trans. Ivor Montagu. Memorial ed. [rev. and enl.]. New York: Grove, 1970.

Ross, Lillian, and Helen Ross. *The Player: A Profile of an Art.* New York: Simon & Schuster, 1962.

Wexman, Virginia Wright, ed. "Special Issue on Film Acting." *Cinema Journal* 20, no. 1 (Fall 1980).

Wojcik, Pamela Robertson, ed. *Movie Acting, the Film Reader.* New York: Routledge, 2004.

Zucker, Carole, ed. *Making Visible the Invisible: An Anthology of Original Essays on Film Acting.* Metuchen, N.J.: Scarecrow, 1990.

———, ed. "Special Issue on Film Acting." *Post Script: Essays in Film and the Humanities* 12, no. 2 (Winter 1993).

The Evolution of Screen Acting

Affron, Charles. *Lillian Gish: Her Legend, Her Life.* New York: Scribner, 2001.

———. *Star Acting: Gish, Garbo, Davis.* New York: Dutton, 1977.

Allen, Robert C. "The Role of the Star in Film History [Joan Crawford]." In *Film Theory and Criticism: Introductory*

Readings. 606–619. Ed. Leo Braudy and Marshall Cohen. 6th ed. New York: Oxford University Press, 2004.

Allen, Robert C., and Douglas Gomery. *Film History: Theory and Practice.* New York: Knopf, 1985.

Ankerich, Michael G. *Broken Silence: Conversations with Twenty-three Silent Film Stars.* Jefferson, N.C.: McFarland, 1993.

Antonioni, Michelangelo. "Reflections on the Film Actor." *Film Culture* 22–23 (Summer 1961): 66–67.

Balio, Tino. *Grand Design: Hollywood as a Modern Business Enterprise, 1930–1939.* New York: Scribner, 1993.

Barthes, Roland. "The Face of Garbo." In *Film Theory and Criticism: Introductory Readings.* 589–591. Ed. Leo Braudy and Marshall Cohen. 6th ed. New York: Oxford University Press, 2004.

Basinger, Jeanine. *Silent Stars.* New York: Knopf, 1999.

———. *The Star Machine.* New York: Knopf, 2007.

Bean, Jennifer M., and Diane Negra. *Early Women Stars.* Durham, N.C.: Duke University Press, 2001.

Blum, Richard A. *American Film Acting: The Stanislavski Heritage.* Ann Arbor, Mich.: UMI Research Press, 1984.

Cardullo, Bert, Harry Geduld, Ronald Gottesman, and Leigh Woods. *Playing to the Camera: Film Actors Discuss Their Craft.* New Haven: Yale University Press, 1998.

Chaplin, Charles. *My Autobiography.* New York: Simon & Schuster, 1964.

Cole, Toby, and Helen Krich Chinoy, eds. *Actors on Acting: The Theories, Techniques, and Practices of the Great Actors of All Times as Told in Their Own Words.* New York: Crown, 1964.

Coleman, Terry. *Olivier.* New York: Holt, 2005.

deCordova, Richard. "The Emergence of the Star System in America," *Wide Angle* 6, no. 4 (Spring 1985): 4–13.

Dyer, Richard. *Heavenly Bodies: Film Stars and Society.* 2nd ed. New York: Routledge, 2004.

Dyer, Richard, and Paul McDonald. *Stars.* New ed. London: BFI, 1998.

Fischer, Lucy, and Marcia Landy, eds. *Stars, the Film Reader.* New York: Routledge, 2004.

Funke, Lewis, and John E. Booth, eds. *Actors Talk about Acting: Fourteen Interviews with Stars of the Theatre.* New York: Random House, 1961.

Gardner, P. "Bette Davis: A Star Views Directors." *Action* no. 5 (October 1974): 10–17.

Gish, Lillian, with Ann Pinchot. *Lillian Gish: The Movies, Mr. Griffith, and Me.* Englewood Cliffs, N.J.: Prentice-Hall, 1969.

Gledhill, Christine, ed. *Stardom: Industry of Desire.* New York: Routledge, 1991.

Higson, Andrew. "Film Acting and Independent Cinema." *Screen* 27, nos. 3–4 (May–August 1986): 110–132.

Hirsch, Foster. *Acting Hollywood Style: With Photographs from the Kobal Collection.* New York: Abrams, 1991.

———. *A Method to Their Madness: The History of the Actors Studio.* New York: Norton, 1984.

Kael, Pauline. "The Man from Dream City (Cary Grant)." *New Yorker* 51 (July 14, 1975), 40–42 ff.

Kanfer, Stefan. Somebody: The Reckless Life and Remarkable Career of Marlon Brando. New York: Alfred A. Knopf, 2008.

———. Tough Without a Gun: The Life and Extraordinary Afterlife of Humphrey Bogart. New York: Alfred A. Knopf, 2011.

Keane, Marian. "Dyer Straits: Theoretical Issues in Studies of Film Acting." *Post Script: Essays in Film and the Humanities* 12, no. 2 (Winter 1993): 29–39.

McDonald, Paul. *The Star System: Hollywood's Production of Popular Identities.* London: Wallflower, 2000.

Merritt, Russell. "The Griffith-Gish Collaboration: A Tangled Affair." *Griffithiana* 14, nos. 40–42 (October 1991): 101–103.

Morin, Edgar. *The Stars.* Trans. Richard Howard. Minneapolis: University of Minnesota Press, 2005.

Munk, Erika, ed. *Stanislavski and America: An Anthology from the "Tulane Drama Review."* New York: Hill & Wang, 1966.

Olivier, Laurence. *Confessions of an Actor: An Autobiography.* 1982; repr., New York: Penguin, 1984.

———. *On Acting.* New York: Simon & Schuster, 1986.

Phillips, Alastair, and Ginette Vincendeau, eds. *Journeys of Desire: European Actors in Hollywood—a Critical Companion.* London: BFI, 2006.

Stanislavksi, Constantin. *An Actor Prepares.* Trans. Elizabeth Reynolds Hapgood. New York: Theatre Arts, 1936.

———. *Building a Character.* Trans. Elizabeth Reynolds Hapgood. New York: Theatre Arts, 1949.

Strasberg, Lee. *Strasberg at the Actors Studio: Tape-recorded Sessions.* Ed. Robert H. Hethmon. New York: Viking, 1965.

Vineberg, Steven. *Method Actors: Three Generations of an American Acting Style.* New York: Schirmer, 1991.

Walker, Alexander. *Stardom: The Hollywood Phenomenon.* New York: Stein & Day, 1970.

Weis, Elisabeth, ed. *The National Society of Film Critics on the Movie Star.* New York: Viking, 1981.

Yacowar, Maurice. "An Aesthetic Defense of the Star System in Films," *Quarterly Review of Film Studies* 4, no. 1 (Winter 1979): 39–52.

Aspects of Performance

Barr, Tony. *Acting for the Camera.* Boston: Allyn & Bacon, 1982.

Budd, Michael. "Genre, Director, and Stars in John Ford's Westerns: Fonda, Wayne, Stewart, and Widmark." *Wide Angle* 2, no. 4 (1978): 52–61.

Cukor, George. "Dialogue on Film: George Cukor." *American Film* 3, no. 4 (February 1978): 33–48.

McVay, Douglas. "The Art of the Actor." *Films and Filming* 12, no. 10 (July 1966): 19–25.

———. "The Art of the Actor." *Films and Filming* 12, no. 11 (August 1966): 36–42.

———. "The Art of the Actor." *Films and Filming* 12, no. 12 (September 1966): 44–50.

———. "The Art of the Actor." *Films and Filming* 13, no. 1 (October 1966): 26–33.

———. "The Art of the Actor." *Films and Filming* 13, no. 2 (November 1966): 26–33.

Meyerson, Harold. "The Case of the Vanishing Character Actor." *Film Comment* 13, no. 6 (November–December 1977): 6–15.

Prouse, Derek. "Notes on Film Acting." *Sight and Sound* 24, no. 4 (Spring 1955): 174–180.

Rogosin, Lionel. "Interpreting Reality: Notes on the Esthetics and Practices of Improvisational Acting." *Film Culture* no. 21 (Summer 1960): 20–29.

Rosenbaum, Jonathan. "Improvisations and Interactions in Altmanville." *Sight and Sound* 44, no. 2 (Spring 1975): 90–95.

Tomlinson, Doug, ed. *Actors on Acting for the Screen: Roles and Collaborations.* New York: Garland, 1994.

Tucker, Patrick. *Secrets of Screen Acting.* New York: Routledge, 1994.

Wexman, Virginia Wright. "Kinesics and Film Acting: Humphrey Bogart in *The Maltese Falcon* and *The Big Sleep*." *Journal of Popular Film and Television* 7, no. 1 (1978): 42–55.

——. "The Rhetoric of Cinematic Improvisation," *Cinema Journal* 20, no. 1 (Fall 1980): 29–41.

Yacowar, Maurice. "Actors as Conventions in the Films of Robert Altman." *Cinema Journal* 20, no. 1 (Fall 1980): 14–28.

Zucker, Carole. "The Concept of 'Excess' in Film Acting: Notes toward an Understanding of Non-Naturalistic Performance." *Post Script: Essays in Film and the Humanities* 11, no. 2 (Spring 1993): 20–26.

——. "An Interview with Lindsay Crouse," *Post Script: Essays in Film and the Humanities* 12, no. 2 (Winter 1993): 5–28.

How Filmmaking Affects Acting

Balázs, Béla. "The Close-Up." In *Film Theory and Criticism: Introductory Readings*. 304–311. Ed. Leo Braudy and Marshall Cohen. 6th ed. New York: Oxford University Press, 2004.

Salvi, Delia. *Friendly Enemies: Maximizing the Director-Actor Relationship*. New York: Billboard, 2003.

Looking at Acting

Kaplan, E. Ann. "The Case of the Missing Mother: Maternal Issues in Vidor's *Stella Dallas*." In *Feminism and Film*. 466–479. Ed. E. Ann Kaplan. New York: Oxford University Press, 2000.

Smith, Ella. *Starring Miss Barbara Stanwyck*. Rev. ed. New York: Crown, 1985.

Williams, Linda. "'Something Else besides a Mother': *Stella Dallas* and the Maternal Melodrama." In *Feminism and Film*. 479–504. Ed. E. Ann Kaplan. New York: Oxford University Press, 2000.

Chapter 8: Editing

What Is Editing?

Andrew, J. Dudley. *The Major Film Theories: An Introduction*. New York: Oxford University Press, 1976.

Arnheim, Rudolf. *Film as Art*. Berkeley: University of California Press, 1967.

Balázs, Béla. *Theory of the Film: Character and Growth of a New Art*. Trans. Edith Bone. New York: Dover, 1970.

Barsam, Richard. *Nonfiction Film: A Critical History*. Rev. and exp. ed. Bloomington: Indiana University Press, 1992.

Barsam, Richard, ed. *Nonfiction Film: Theory and Criticism*. New York: Dutton, 1976.

Battcock, Gregory. *The New American Cinema: A Critical Anthology*. New York: Dutton, 1967.

Bazin, André. "The Evolution of Film Language" and "The Virtues and Limitations of Montage." In *What Is Cinema?* Vol. I. 23–52. Berkeley: University of California Press, 1967.

Burch, Noël. *Theory of Film Practice*. Trans. Helen R. Lane. Princeton: Princeton University Press, 1981.

Carroll, Noël. *Theorizing the Moving Image*. New York: Cambridge University Press, 1996.

Dmytryk, Edward. *On Film Editing: An Introduction to the Art of Film Construction*. Boston: Focal Press, 1984.

Fairservice, Don. *Film Editing—History, Theory, and Practice: Looking at the Invisible*. Manchester: Manchester University Press, 2001.

Keil, Charlie. *Early American Cinema in Transition: Story, Style, and Filmmaking, 1907-1913*. Madison: University of Wisconsin Press, 2001.

Kuleshov, Lev. *Kuleshov on Film: Writings*. Ed. and trans. Ronald Levaco. Berkeley: University of California Press, 1974.

Metz, Christian. *Film Language: A Semiotics of the Cinema*. Trans. Michael Taylor. New York: Oxford University Press, 1974.

Nilsen, Vladimir. *The Cinema as a Graphic Art (On a Theory of Representation in the Cinema)*. Trans. Stephen Garry. New York: Hill & Wang, 1959.

Nizhny, Vladimir. *Lessons with Eisenstein*. Ed. and trans. Ivor Montagu and Jay Leyda. New York: Hill & Wang, 1962.

Pudovkin, V. I. *Film Technique* [and] *Film Acting*. Ed. and trans. Ivor Montagu. Rev. and enl. ed. New York: Grove, 1960.

The Film Editor

Barsam, Richard. "Discover and Disclose: Helen van Dongen and *Louisiana Story*." In *Filming Robert Flaherty's Louisiana Story: The Helen Van Dongen Diary*. 75–89. Ed. Eve Orbanz. New York: Museum of Modern Art, 1998.

Bordwell, David. *The Cinema of Eisenstein*. Cambridge, Mass.: Harvard University Press, 1993.

Bouzereau, Laurent. *The Cutting Room Floor*. Secaucus, N.J.: Carol, 1994.

Crofts, Stephen, and Olivia Rose. "An Essay towards *Man with a Movie Camera*." *Screen* 18, no. 1 (Spring 1977): 9–58.

Jacobs, Lewis. "D. W. Griffith." In *The Rise of the American Film: A Critical History*. 171–201. New York: Teachers College Press, 1968.

LoBrutto, Vincent. *Selected Takes: Film Editors on Editing*. New York: Praeger, 1991.

Murch, Walter. *In the Blink of an Eye: A Perspective on Film Editing*. 2nd ed. Los Angeles: Silman-James, 2001.

——. "Restoring the Touch of Genius to a Classic [*Touch of Evil*]." *New York Times* (September 6, 1998), sec. 2, pp. 1, 16–17.

Oldham, Gabriella. *First Cut: Conversations with Film Editors*. Berkeley: University of California Press, 1992.

Ondaatje, Michael. *The Conversations: Walter Murch and the Art of Editing Film*. New York: Knopf, 2002.

O'Steen, Sam. *Cut to the Chase: Forty-five Years of Editing America's Favorite Movies*. Studio City, Calif.: Wiese, 2001.

Petrić, Vlada. *Constructivism in Film: The Man with the Movie Camera—a Cinematic Analysis*. New York: Cambridge University Press, 1987.

Prince, Stephen, and Wayne E. Hensley. "The Kuleshov Effect: Recreating the Classic Experiment." *Cinema Journal* 31, no. 2 (Winter 1992): 59–75.

Rosenblum, Ralph, and Robert Karen. *When the Shooting Stops…the Cutting Begins: A Film Editor's Story*. New York: Penguin, 1980.

Schneider, Arthur. *Jump Cut!: Memoirs of a Pioneer Television Editor*. Jefferson, N.C.: McFarland, 1997.

Tsivian, Yuri, Ekaterina Khokhlova, and Kristin Thompson. "The Rediscovery of a Kuleshov Experiment: A Dossier." *Film History* 8, no. 3 (1996): 357–367.

Turim, Maureen. *Flashbacks in Film: Memory and History*. New York: Routledge, 1989.

Continuity Editing

Arijohn, Daniel. *Grammar of the Film Language*. New York: Focal Press, 1976.

Bordwell, David. *The Way Hollywood Tells It: Story and Style in Modern Movies*. Berkeley: University of California Press, 2006.

Gaudreault, André. "Detours in Film Narrative: The Development of Cross-Cutting." *Cinema Journal* 19, no. 1 (Fall 1979): 39–59.

Kepley, Vance, Jr. "Spatial Articulation in the Classical Cinema: A Scene from *His Girl Friday*." *Wide Angle* 5, no. 3 (1983): 50–58.

Jesionowski, Joyce E. *Thinking in Pictures: Dramatic Structure in D. W. Griffith's Biograph Films*. Berkeley: University of California Press, 1987.

Reisz, Karel, and Gavin Millar. *The Technique of Film Editing*. New York: Hastings House, 1973.

Salt, Barry. *Film Style and Technology: History and Analysis*. 2nd ed. London: Starwood, 1992.

Simon, William. "An Approach to Point of View." *Film Reader* 4 (1979): 145–151.

Alternatives to Continuity Editing

Bordwell, David. *The Cinema of Eisenstein*. Cambridge, Mass.: Harvard University Press, 1993.

Curtis, David. *Experimental Cinema*. New York: Universe, 1971.

Eisenstein, Sergei. *Film Essays and a Lecture*. Ed. Jay Leyda. New York: Praeger, 1970.

———. *Film Form: Essays in Film Theory* [and] *Film Sense*. Ed. and trans. Jay Leyda. New York: Meridian, 1957.

Mekas, Jonas. "An Interview with Peter Kubelka." *Film Culture* 44 (Spring 1967): 42–47.

Vertov, Dziga. *Kino-Eye: The Writings of Dziga Vertov*. Ed. Annette Michelson. Trans. Kevin O'Brien. Berkeley: University of California Press, 1984.

Editing Technology and Techniques

Balmuth, Bernard. *Introduction to Film Editing*. Boston: Focal Press, 1989.

Bayes, Steve. *The Avid Handbook*. Boston: Focal Press, 1998.

Bordwell, David, Janet Staiger, and Kristin Thompson. *The Classical Hollywood Cinema: Film Style and Mode of Production to 1960*. New York: Columbia University Press, 1985.

Browne, Steven E. *Nonlinear Editing Basics: Electronic Film and Video Editing*. Boston: Focal Press, 1998.

Case, Dominic. *Film Technology in Post Production*. 2nd ed. Boston: Focal Press, 2001.

Chandler, Gael. *Cut by Cut: Editing Your Film or Video*. Studio City, Calif.: Wiese, 2004.

Crittenden, Roger. *The Thames and Hudson Manual of Film Editing*. New York: Thames & Hudson, 1981.

Dancyger, Ken. *The Technique of Film and Video Editing: Theory and Practice*. 4th ed. Boston: Focal Press, 2007.

Hollyn, Norman. *The Film Editing Room Handbook: How to Avoid the Near-Chaos of the Cutting Room*. 3rd ed. Los Angeles: Lone Eagle, 1999.

Kauffmann, Sam. *Avid Editing: A Guide for Beginning and Intermediate Users*. 4th ed. Boston: Focal Press, 2009.

Kerner, Marvin M. *The Art of the Sound Effects Editor*. Boston: Focal Press, 1989.

Lustig, Milton. *Music Editing for Motion Pictures*. New York: Hastings House, 1980.

McGrath, Declan. *Editing and Post-Production*. Boston: Focal Press, 2001.

Miller, Pat P. *Script Supervising and Film Continuity*. 3rd ed. Boston: Focal Press, 1999.

Ohanian, Thomas A. *Digital Nonlinear Editing: Editing Film and Video on the Desktop*. 2nd ed. Boston: Focal Press, 1998.

Rubin, Michael. *Nonlinear: A Guide to Electronic Film and Video Editing*. 2nd ed. Gainesville, Fla.: Triad, 1992.

Salt, Barry. *Film Style and Technology: History and Analysis*. 2nd ed. London: Starword, 1992.

Stafford, Roy. *Nonlinear Editing and Visual Literacy*. London: BFI, 1995.

Staten, Greg, and Steve Bayes. *The Avid Handbook: Advanced Techniques, Strategies, and Survival Information for Avid Editing Systems*. 5th ed. Boston: Focal Press, 2009.

Thompson, Roy. *Grammar of the Edit*. Boston: Focal Press, 1993.

Walter, Ernest. *The Technique of the Film Cutting Room*. 2nd rev. ed. London: Focal Press, 1973.

Weynand, Diana. *Final Cut Pro for Avid Editors*. 3rd ed. Berkeley: Peachpit, 2008.

Chapter 9: Sound

What Is Sound?

Altman, Rick, ed. *Sound Theory/Sound Practice*. New York: Routledge, 1992.

Bordwell, David, Janet Staiger, and Kristin Thompson. *The Classical Hollywood Cinema: Film Style and Mode of Production to 1960*. New York: Columbia University Press, 1985.

Brophy, Philip. *100 Modern Soundtracks*. BFI Screen Guides. London: BFI, 2004.

Chion, Michel. *Audio-Vision: Sound on Screen*. Ed. and trans. Claudia Gorbman. New York: Columbia University Press, 1994.

Eisenstein, Sergei. *Film Essays and a Lecture*. Ed. Jay Leyda. New York: Praeger, 1970.

———. *Film Form: Essays in Film Theory* [and] *Film Sense*. Ed. and trans. Jay Leyda. New York: Meridian, 1957.

Eyman, Scott. *The Speed of Sound: Hollywood and the Talkie Revolution, 1926–1930*. New York: Simon & Schuster, 1997.

Geduld, Harry M. *The Birth of the Talkies: From Edison to Jolson*. Bloomington: Indiana University Press, 1975.

Gorbman, Claudia. "Annotated Bibliography on Film Sound (Excluding Music)." In *Film Sound: Theory and Practice*. 427–445. Ed. Elisabeth Weis and John Belton. New York: Columbia University Press, 1985.

———. *Unheard Melodies: Narrative Film Music*. Bloomington: Indiana University Press, 1987.

Holman, Tomlinson. *Sound for Film and Television*. 2nd ed. Boston: Focal Press, 2002.

Ivarsson, Jan, and Mary Carroll. *Subtitling*. Simrishamn, Sweden: TransEdit, 1998.

Neale, Steve. *Cinema and Technology: Image, Sound, Colour*. Bloomington: Indiana University Press, 1985.

Sider, Larry, Diane Freeman, and Jerry Sider, eds. *Soundscape: The School of Sound Lectures, 1998–2001*. London: Wallflower, 2003.

Weis, Elisabeth, and John Belton, eds. *Film Sound: Theory and Practice*. New York: Columbia University Press, 1985.

Sound Production

Design

Lastra, James. *Sound Technology in the American Cinema: Perception, Representation, Modernity*. New York: Columbia University Press, 2000.

LoBrutto, Vincent. *Sound-on-Film: Interviews with Creators of Film Sound.* Westport, Conn.: Praeger, 1994.

Madsen, Roy Paul. *Working Cinema: Learning from the Masters.* Belmont, Calif.: Wadsworth, 1990.

Murch, Walter. "Sound Design: The Dancing Shadow." In *Projections 4: Film-makers on Film-making.* 237–251. Ed. John Boorman et al. London: Faber and Faber, 1995.

Pasquariello, Nicholas. *Sounds of Movies: Interviews with the Creators of Feature Sound Tracks.* San Francisco: Port Bridge Books, 1996.

Sonnenschein, David. *Sound Design: The Expressive Power of Music, Voice, and Sound Effects in Cinema.* Studio City, Calif.: Wiese, 2001.

Thom, Randy. "Designing a Movie for Sound." March 13, 1999. www.filmsound.org/randythom. Accessed September 2002.

Weis, Elisabeth. *The Silent Scream: Alfred Hitchcock's Sound Track.* Rutherford, N.J.: Fairleigh Dickinson University Press, 1982.

Whittington, William. *Sound Design and Science Fiction.* Austin: University of Texas Press, 2007.

Recording

Sergi, Gianluca. *The Dolby Era: Film Sound in Contemporary Hollywood.* Manchester: Manchester University Press, 2004.

Editing

Amyes, Tim. *The Technique of Audio Post-Production in Video and Film.* Library of Communication Techniques. Boston: Focal Press, 1990.

Kerner, Marvin M. *The Art of the Sound Effects Editor.* Boston: Focal Press, 1989.

Types of Film Sound
Vocal Sounds

Kozloff, Sarah. *Invisible Storytellers: Voice-Over Narration in American Fiction Film.* Berkeley: University of California Press, 1988.

———. *Overhearing Film Dialogue.* Berkeley: University of California Press, 2000.

Environmental Sounds

Mantell, H. *The Complete Guide to the Creation and Use of Sound Effects for Films, TV and Dramatic Productions.* Princeton: Films for the Humanities, 1983.

Music

Brown, Royal S. *Overtones and Undertones: Reading Film Music.* Berkeley: University of California Press, 1994.

Burt, George. *The Art of Film Music: Special Emphasis on Hugo Friedhofer, Alex North, David Raskin, Leonard Rosenman.* Boston: Northeastern University Press, 1994.

Cooke, Mervyn. *A History of Film Music.* New York: Cambridge University Press, 2008.

———, ed. *The Hollywood Film Music Reader.* New York: Oxford University Press, 2010.

Copland, Aaron. "Film Music." In *What to Listen for in Music.* 152–157. New York: McGraw-Hill, 1957.

Coyle, Rebecca, ed. *Reel Tracks: Australian Feature Film Music and Cultural Identities.* Eastleigh, Eng.: Libbey, 2005.

Dickinson, Kay, ed. *Movie Music: The Film Reader.* New York: Routledge, 2003.

———. *Off Key: When Film and Music Won't Work Together.* New York: Oxford University Press, 2008.

Donnelly, Kevin. *Film and Television Music: The Spectre of Sound.* London, BFI, 2005.

Eisler, Hanns. *Composing for the Films.* New York: Oxford University Press, 1947.

Goldmark, Daniel. *Tunes for 'Toons: Music and the Hollywood Cartoon.* Berkeley: University of California Press, 2005.

Goldmark, Daniel, Lawrence Kramer, and Richard Leppert. *Beyond the Sountrack: Representing Music in Cinema.* Berkeley: University of California Press, 2007.

Hickman, Roger. *Reel Music: Exploring 100 Years of Movie Music.* New York: Norton, 2006.

Hischak, Thomas S. *The Oxford Companion to the American Musical.* New York: Oxford University press, 2008.

Inglis, Ian, ed. *Popular Music and Film.* London: Wallflower, 2003.

Jones, Chuck. "Music and the Animated Cartoon." *Hollywood Quarterly* 1, no. 4 (July 1946): 364–370.

Kalinak, Kathryn. *How the West Was Sung: Music in the Westerns of John Ford.* Berkeley: University of California Press, 2007.

———. *Settling the Score: Music and the Classical Hollywood Film.* Madison: University of Wisconsin Press, 1992.

Karlin, Fred. *Listening to Movies: The Film Lover's Guide to Film Music.* New York: Schirmer, 1994.

Karlin, Fred, and Rayburn Wright. *On the Track: A Guide to Contemporary Film Scoring.* 2nd ed. New York: Routledge, 2004.

Lack, Russell. *Twenty-four Frames Under: A Buried History of Film Music.* London: Quartet, 1997.

London, Kurt. *Film Music.* Trans. Eric S. Bensinger. 1936; repr., New York: Arno, 1970.

MacDonald, Laurence E. *The Invisible Art of Film Music: A Comprehensive History.* New York: Ardsley House, 1998.

Marks, Martin Miller. *Music and the Silent Film: Contexts and Case Studies, 1895–1924.* New York: Oxford University Press, 1997.

Marmorstein, Gary. *Hollywood Rhapsody: Movie Music and Its Makers, 1900 to 1975.* New York: Schirmer, 1997.

Morgan, David. *Knowing the Score: Film Composers Talk about the Art, Craft, Blood, Sweat, and Tears of Writing Music for Cinema.* New York: Harper-Entertainment, 2000.

Newman, William S. *Understanding Music: An Introduction to Music's Elements, Styles, and Forms for Both the Layman and the Practitioner.* 2nd ed. New York: Harper, 1961.

Prendergast, Roy M. *Film Music, a Neglected Art: A Critical Study of Music in Films.* 2nd ed. New York: Norton, 1992.

Romney, Jonathan, and Adrian Wootton, eds. *Celluloid Jukebox: Popular Music and the Movies since the 50s.* London: BFI, 1995.

Russell, Mark, and James Young. *Film Music.* Boston: Focal Press, 2000.

Schelle, Michael. *The Score: Interviews with Film Composers.* Los Angeles: Silman-James, 1999.

Smith, Jeff. *The Sounds of Commerce: Marketing Popular Film Music.* New York: Columbia University Press, 1998.

Sullivan, Jack. *Hitchcock's Music.* New Haven: Yale University Press, 2006.

Thomas, Tony. *Music for the Movies.* 2nd ed. Los Angeles: Silman-James, 1997.

Timm, Larry M. *The Soul of Cinema: An Appreciation of Film Music.* Upper Saddle River, N.J.: Prentice-Hall, 1998.

Wojcik, Pamela Robertson, and Arthur Knight, eds. *Soundtrack Available: Essays on Film and Popular Music.* Durham, N.C.: Duke University Press, 2001.

Silence

Altman, Rick. *Silent Film Sound.* New York: Columbia University Press, 2004.

Walker, Alexander. *The Shattered Silents: How the Talkies Came to Stay.* New York: Morrow, 1979.

Sound in Orson Welles's *Citizen Kane*

Bruce, Graham. *Bernard Herrmann: Film Music and Narrative.* Ann Arbor, Mich.: UMI Research Press, 1985.

Carringer, Robert L. *The Making of "Citizen Kane."* Berkeley: University of California Press, 1985.

Chapter 10: Film History

Film History: Theory and Practice

Allen, Robert C., and Douglas Gomery. *Film History: Theory and Practice.* New York: Knopf, 1985.

Branigan, Edward. "Color and Cinema: Problems in the Writing of History." *Film Reader* 4 (1979): 16–34.

Carnes, Mark C., ed. *Past Imperfect: History According to the Movies.* New York: Holt, 1995.

Gledhill, Christine, and Linda Williams, eds. *Reinventing Film Studies.* New York: Oxford University Press, 2000.

Grainge, Paul, Mark Jancovich, and Sharon Montieth, eds. *Film Histories: An Introduction and Reader.* Toronto: University of Toronto Press, 2007.

Grieveson, Lee, and Haidee Wasson, eds. *Inventing Film Studies.* Durham, N.C.: Duke University Press, 2008.

Guynn, William. *Writing History in Film.* New York: Routledge, 2006.

Hill, John, and Pamela Church Gibson, eds. *The Oxford Guide to Film Studies.* New York: Oxford University Press, 1998.

Hollows, Joanne, Peter Hutchings, and Mark Jancovich, eds. *The Film Studies Reader.* New York: Oxford University Press, 2000.

Hughes-Warrington, Marnie. *History Goes to the Movies: Studying History on Film.* New York: Routledge, 2007.

Lewis, Jon, and Eric Smoodin, eds. *Looking Past the Screen: Case Studies in American Film History and Method.* Durham, N.C.: Duke University Press, 2007.

Polan, Dana. *Scenes of Instruction: The Beginnings of the U.S. Study of Film.* Berkeley: University of California Press, 2007.

World Film History

Barsam, Richard. *Nonfiction Film: A Critical History.* Rev. and exp. ed. Bloomington: Indiana University Press, 1992.

Bordwell, David. *On the History of Film Style.* Cambridge, Mass.: Harvard University Press, 1997.

Cook, David A. *A History of Narrative Film.* 4th ed. New York: Norton, 2004.

———. *Lost Illusions: American Cinema in the Shadow of Watergate and Vietnam, 1970–1979.* History of American Cinema 9. New York: Scribner, 2000.

Dixon, Wheeler Winston. *The Exploding Eye: A Re-visionary History of 1960s American Experimental Cinema.* Albany: State University of New York Press, 1997.

Dixon, Wheeler Winston, and Gwendolyn Audrey Foster. *A Short History of Film.* New Brunswick, N.J.: Rutgers University Press, 2008.

Ellis, Jack C. *A New History of Documentary Film.* New York: Continuum, 2005.

Gaudreault, André. *Film and Attraction: From Cinematography to Cinema.* Trans. Timothy Barnard. Champaign: University of Illinois Press, 2010.

Lanzoni, Rémi Fournier. *French Cinema: From Its Beginnings to the Present.* New York: Continuum, 2002.

Luhr, William, ed. *World Cinema since 1945.* New York: Ungar, 1987.

Mast, Gerald, and Bruce F. Kawin. *A Short History of the Movies.* 10th ed. New York: Pearson/Longman, 2008.

Perry, Ted, ed. *Masterpieces of Modernist Cinema.* Bloomington: Indiana University Press, 2006.

Rees, A. L. *A History of Experimental Film and Video: From Canonical Avant-Garde to Contemporary British Practice.* London: BFI, 1999.

Salt, Barry. *Film Style and Technology.* 2nd ed. London: Starword, 1992.

Sklar, Robert. *Film: An International History of the Medium.* 2nd ed. New York: Abrams, 2002.

Thompson, Kristin, and David Bordwell. *Film History: An Introduction.* 2nd ed. New York: McGraw-Hill, 2003.

American Film History: General

Balio, Tina, ed. *The American Film Industry.* Rev. ed. Madison: University of Wisconsin Press, 1985.

———. *Grand Design: Hollywood as a Modern Business Enterprise, 1930–1939.* History of the American Cinema 5. New York: Scribner, 1993.

Bordwell, David, Janet Staiger, and Kristin Thompson. *The Classical Hollywood Cinema: Film Style and Mode of Production to 1960.* New York: Columbia University Press, 1985.

Bowser, Eileen. *The Transformation of Cinema, 1907–1915.* History of the American Cinema 2. New York: Scribner, 1990.

Cook, David A. *Lost Illusions: American Cinema in the Shadow of Watergate and Vietnam, 1970–1979.* History of the American Cinema 9. New York: Scribner, 2000.

Crafton, Donald. *The Talkies: American Cinema's Transition to Sound, 1926–1931.* History of the American Cinema 4. New York: Scribner, 1997.

Gomery, Douglas. *Shared Pleasures: A History of Movie Presentation in the United States.* Madison: University of Wisconsin Press, 1992.

Hampton, Benjamin B. *A History of the American Film Industry from its Beginnings to 1931,* ed. Richard Griffith. New York: Dover Books, 1970.

Hoberman, J., and Jeffrey Shandler. *Entertaining America: Jews, Movies, and Broadcasting.* Princeton: Princeton University Press, 2003.

Koszarski, Richard. *An Evening's Entertainment: The Age of the Silent Feature Picture, 1915–1928.* History of the American Cinema 3. New York: Scribner, 1994.

Lev, Peter. *Transforming the Screen, 1950–1959.* History of the American Cinema 7. New York: Scribner, 2003.

Lewis, Jon. *American Film: A History.* New York: Norton, 2007.

Lopate, Phillip, ed. *American Movie Critics: An Anthology from the Silents until Now.* Exp. ed. New York: Library of America, 2008.

McCrisken, Trevor B., and Andrew Pepper. *American History and Contemporary Hollywood Film*. New Brunswick, N.J.: Rutgers University Press, 2005.

Mast, Gerald, ed. *The Movies in Our Midst: Documents in the Cultural History of Film in America*. Chicago: University of Chicago Press, 1982.

Monaco, Paul. *The Sixties, 1960–1969*. History of the American Cinema 8. New York: Scribner, 2001.

Musser, Charles. *The Emergence of Cinema: The American Screen to 1907*. History of the American Cinema 1. New York: Scribner, 1990.

Prince, Stephen. *A New Pot of Gold: Hollywood under the Electronic Rainbow, 1980–1989*. History of the American Cinema 10. New York: Scribner, 2000.

Sarris, Andrew. *The American Cinema: Directors and Directions, 1929–1968*. New York: Dutton, 1968.

———. *"You Ain't Heard Nothing Yet": The American Talking Film, History and Memory, 1929–1949*. New York: Oxford University Press, 1998.

Schatz, Thomas. *Boom and Bust: The American Cinema in the 1940s*. History of the American Cinema 6. New York: Scribner, 1997.

Sklar, Robert. *Movie-Made America: A Cultural History of American Movies*. Rev. and updated ed. New York: Vintage, 1994.

Thomson, David. *The Whole Equation: A History of Hollywood*. New York: Knopf, 2005.

Major Stylistic Movements in Film History

The First Movies

Abel, Richard. *Americanizing the Movies and "Movie-Mad" Audiences, 1910–1914*. Berkeley: University of California Press, 2006.

———. *The Ciné Goes to Town: French Cinema, 1896–1914*. Updated and exp. ed. Berkeley: University of California Press, 1998.

———, ed. *Encyclopedia of Early Cinema*. New York: Routledge, 2005.

Abel, Richard. *The Red Rooster Scare: Making Cinema American, 1900–1910*. Berkeley: University of California Press, 1999.

Acker, Ally. *Reel Women: Pioneers of the Cinema, 1896 to the Present*. New York: Continuum, 1991.

Allen, Robert C. *Vaudeville and Film, 1895–1915: A Study in Media Interaction*. New York: Arno, 1980.

Brewster, Ben, and Lea Jacobs. *Theatre to Cinema: Stage Pictorialism and the Early Feature Film*. New York: Oxford University Press, 1997.

Brownlow, Kevin. *The War, the West, and the Wilderness*. New York: Knopf, 1979.

Chanan, Michael. *The Dream That Kicks: The Prehistory and Early Years of Cinema in Britain*. 2nd ed. New York: Routledge, 1996.

Cherchi Usai, Paolo. *Silent Cinema: An Introduction*. London: British Film Institute, 2000.

Cherchi Usai, Paolo, and Lorenzo Codelli, eds. *Before Caligari: German Cinema, 1895–1920*. Pordenone, Italy: Edizioni Biblioteca dell'Immagine, 1990.

Elsaesser, Thomas, ed. *Early Cinema: Space, Frame, Narrative*. London: BFI, 1990.

Fell, John L., ed. *Film before Griffith*. Berkeley: University of California Press, 1983.

Gabler, Neal. *An Empire of Their Own: How the Jews Invented Hollywood*. New York: Crown, 1988.

Hammond, Paul. *Marvellous Méliès*. New York: St. Martin's, 1975.

Hendricks, Gordon. *The Edison Motion Picture Myth*. Berkeley: University of California Press, 1961.

Keil, Charlie, and Shelley Stamp, eds. *American Cinema's Transitional Era: Audiences, Institutions, Practices*. Berkeley: University of California Press, 2004.

Kobel, Peter. *Silent Movies: The Birth of Film and the Triumph of Movie Culture*. Boston: Little, Brown, 2007.

Leyda, Jay, and Charles Musser. *Before Hollywood: Turn-of-the-Century Film from American Archives*. New York: American Federation of the Arts, 1986.

Mahar, Karen Ward. *Women Filmmakers in Early Hollywood*. Baltimore: Johns Hopkins University Press, 2006.

Musser, Charles. *Before the Nickelodeon: Edwin S. Porter and the Edison Manufacturing Company*. Berkeley: University of California Press, 1991.

Rossell, Deac. *Living Pictures: The Origins of the Movies*. Albany: State University of New York Press, 1998.

Youngblood, Denise J. *The Magic Mirror: Moviemaking in Russia, 1908–1918*. Madison: University of Wisconsin Press, 1999.

Classical Hollywood Style: The Silent Period

Balio, Tino, ed. *The American Film Industry*. Rev. ed. Madison: University of Wisconsin Press, 1985.

Bean, Jennifer M., and Diane Negra, eds. *A Feminist Reader in Early Cinema*. Durham, N.C.: Duke University Press, 2002.

Brownlow, Kevin. *The Parade's Gone By*. New York: Knopf, 1968.

Card, James. *Seductive Cinema: The Art of Silent Film*. New York: Knopf, 1994.

Cohen, Paula Marantz. *Silent Film and the Triumph of the American Myth*. New York: Oxford University Press, 2001.

DeBauche, Leslie Midkiff. *Reel Patriotism: The Movies and World War I*. Madison: University of Wisconsin Press, 1997.

Grieveson, Lee, and Peter Krämer, eds. *The Silent Cinema Reader*. London: Routledge, 2004.

Gunning, Tom. *D. W. Griffith and the Origins of American Narrative Film: The Early Years at Biograph*. Urbana: University of Illinois Press, 1991.

Keil, Charlie. *Early American Cinema in Transition: Story, Style, and Filmmaking, 1907–1913*. Madison: University of Wisconsin Press, 2001.

Kobel, Peter, and the Library of Congress. *Silent Movies: The Birth of Film and the Triumph of Movie Culture*. New York: Little, Brown, 2007.

Morey, Anne. *Hollywood Outsiders: The Adaptation of the Film Industry, 1913–1934*. Minneapolis: University of Minnesota Press, 2003.

Negra, Diane, and Jennifer M. Bean, eds. *Early Women Stars*. Special ed. of *Camera Obscura: Feminism, Culture, and Media Studies* 48 (2001).

Pratt, George C. *Spellbound in Darkness: A History of the Silent Film*. Greenwich, Conn.: New York Graphic Society, 1973.

German Expressionism

Barlow, John D. *German Expressionist Film*. Boston: Twayne, 1982.

Budd, Mike, ed. *The Cabinet of Dr. Caligari: Texts, Contexts, Histories*. New Brunswick, N.J.: Rutgers University Press, 1990.

Eisner, Lotte H. *F. W. Murnau*. Berkeley: University of California Press, 1983.

———. *Fritz Lang*. Ed. David Robinson. Trans. Gertrud Mander. New York: Oxford University Press, 1977.

——. *The Haunted Screen: Expressionism in the German Cinema and the Influence of Max Reinhardt.* Trans. Roger Greaves. Berkeley: University of California Press, 1974.

Elsaesser, Thomas. *Weimar Cinema and After: Germany's Historical Imagination.* New York: Routledge, 2000.

Kracauer, Siegfried. *From Caligari to Hitler: A Psychological History of the German Film.* Rev. and exp. ed. Ed. Leonardo Quaresima. Princeton: Princeton University Press, 2004.

Kreimeier, Klaus. *The UFA Story: A History of Germany's Greatest Film Company, 1918–1945.* Trans. Robert Kimber and Rita Kimber. New York: Hill & Wang, 1996.

Myers, Bernard S. *The German Expressionists: A Generation in Revolt.* Concise ed. New York: Praeger, 1966.

Roberts, Ian. *German Expressionist Cinema: The World of Light and Shadow.* London: Wallflower, 2008.

Robinson, David. *Das Cabinet des Dr. Caligari.* London: BFI, 1997.

Scheunemann, Dietrich, ed. *Expressionist Film: New Perspectives.* Rochester, N.Y.: Camden House, 2003.

Willett, John. *Expressionism.* New York: McGraw-Hill, 1970.

——. *The New Sobriety 1917–1933: Art and Politics in the Weimar Republic.* London: Thames & Hudson, 1978.

French Impressionism and Avant-Garde Filmmaking

Abel, Richard. *French Cinema: The First Wave, 1915–1929.* Princeton: Princeton University Press, 1984.

——. *French Film Theory and Criticism: A History/Anthology, 1907–1939.* Vol. I: *1907–1929.* 2 vols. Princeton: Princeton University Press, 1988.

Brownlow, Kevin. *"Napoleon," Abel Gance's Classic Film.* New York: Knopf, 1983.

Clair, René. *Cinema Yesterday and Today.* Ed. R. C. Dale. Trans. Stanley Applebaum. New York: Dover, 1972.

King, Norman. *Abel Gance: A Politics of Spectacle.* London: BFI, 1984.

Soviet Montage

Bordwell, David. *The Cinema of Eisenstein.* Cambridge, Mass.: Harvard University Press,   1993.

Dovzhenko, Alexander. *The Poet as Filmmaker: Selected Writings by Alexander Dovzhenko.* Ed. and trans. Marco Carynnyk. Cambridge, Mass.: MIT Press, 1973.

Eisenstein, Sergei. *Film Essays and a Lecture.* Ed. Jay Leyda. New York: Praeger, 1970.

——. *Film Form: Essays in Film Theory* [and] *Film Sense.* Ed. and trans. Jay Leyda. New York: Meridian, 1957.

——. *Selected Works.* 4 vols. London: BFI, 1988–96. [Vol. I: *Writings, 1922–34,* ed. and trans. Richard Taylor; Vol. II: *Towards a Theory of Montage,* ed. Michael Glenny and Richard Taylor, trans. Michael Glenny; Vol. III: *Writings, 1934–47,* ed. Richard Taylor, trans. William Powell; Vol. IV: *Beyond the Stars: The Memoirs of Sergei Eisenstein,* ed. Richard Taylor, trans. William Powell.]

Kepley, Jr., Vance. *In the Service of the State: The Cinema of Alexander Dovzhenko.* Madison: University of Wisconsin Press, 1986.

Kuleshov, Lev. *Kuleshov on Film: Writings.* Ed. and trans. Ronald Levaco. Berkeley: University of California Press, 1974.

Leyda, Jay. *Kino: A History of the Russian and Soviet Film.* 3rd ed. Princeton: Princeton University Press, 1983.

Lodder, Christina. *Russian Constructivism.* New Haven: Yale University Press, 1983.

Michelson, Annette, ed. *Kino-Eye: The Writings of Dziga Vertov.* Trans. Kevin O'Brien. Berkeley: University of California Press, 1984.

Nilsen, Vladimir. *The Cinema as a Graphic Art (On a Theory of Representation in the Cinema).* Trans. Stephen Garry. New York: Hill & Wang, 1959.

Petrić, Vlada. *Constructivism in Film: The Man with the Movie Camera, a Cinematic Analysis.* Cambridge, Mass.: Cambridge University Press, 1987.

Pudovkin, V. I. *Film Technique and Film Acting.* Ed. and trans. Ivor Montagu. Memorial ed. [rev. and enl.]. New York: Grove, 1960.

Schnitzer, Luda, Jean Schnitzer, and Marcel Martin, eds. *Cinema and Revolution: The Heroic Era of the Soviet Film.* Trans. David Robinson. New York: Hill & Wang, 1973.

Taylor, Richard. *The Politics of the Soviet Cinema, 1917–1929.* New York: Cambridge University Press, 1979.

Taylor, Richard, and Ian Christie, eds. *The Film Factory: Russian and Soviet Cinema in Documents.* Cambridge, Mass.: Harvard University Press, 1988.

——, eds. *Inside the Film Factory: New Approaches to Russian and Soviet Cinema.* London: Routledge, 1994.

Youngblood, Denise J. *Soviet Cinema in the Silent Era, 1918–1935.* Ann Arbor, Mich.: UMI Research Press, 1985.

Classical Hollywood Style in the Golden Age

Basinger, Jeanine. *A Woman's View: How Hollywood Spoke to Women, 1930–1960.* New York: Knopf, 1993.

Dixon, Wheeler Winston, ed. *American Cinema of the 1940s: Themes and Variations.* New Brunswick, N.J.: Rutgers University Press, 2006.

Gomery, Douglas. *The Hollywood Studio System: A History.* London: BFI, 2005.

Hark, Ina Rae, ed. *American Cinema of the 1930s: Themes and Variations.* New Brunswick, N.J.: Rutgers University Press, 2007.

Horne, Gerald. *Class Struggle in Hollywood, 1930–1950: Moguls, Mobsters, Stars, Reds, and Trade Unionists.* Austin: University of Texas Press, 2001.

Maltby, Richard. *Harmless Entertainment: Hollywood and the Ideology of Consensus.* Metuchen, N.J.: Scarecrow, 1983.

Polan, Dana. *Power and Paranoia: History, Narrative, and the American Cinema, 1940–1950.* New York: Columbia University Press, 1986.

Pomerance, Murray, ed. *American Cinema of the 1950s: Themes and Variations.* New Brunswick, N.J.: Rutgers University Press, 2005.

Ray, Robert B. *The ABCs of Classic Hollywood.* New York: Oxford University Press, 2008.

Vasey, Ruth. *The World According to Hollywood, 1918–1939.* Madison: University of Wisconsin Press, 1997.

Italian Neorealism

Armes, Roy. *Patterns of Realism.* New York: Barnes, 1971.

Bondanella, Peter E. *Italian Cinema: From Neorealism to the Present.* 3rd ed. New York: Continuum, 2001.

Brunette, Peter. *Roberto Rossellini.* New York: Oxford University Press, 1987.

Gallagher, Tag. *The Adventures of Roberto Rossellini: His Life and Films*. New York: Da Capo, 1998.

Leprohon, Pierre. *The Italian Cinema*. Trans. Roger Greaves and Oliver Stallybrass. New York: Praeger, 1972.

Liehm, Mira. *Passion and Defiance: Film in Italy from 1942 to the Present*. Berkeley: University of California Press, 1984.

Marcus, Millicent. *Italian Film in the Light of Neorealism*. Princeton: Princeton University Press, 1986.

Overby, David, ed. and trans. *Springtime in Italy: A Reader on Neo-Realism*. London: Talisman, 1978.

Pacifici, Sergio J. "Notes toward a Definition of Neorealism." *Yale French Studies* 17 (Summer 1956): 44–53.

Sitney, P. Adams. *Vital Crises in Italian Cinema: Iconography, Stylistics, Politics*. Austin: University of Texas Press, 1995.

Wagstaff, Christopher. *Italian Neorealist Cinema: An Aesthetic Approach*. Toronto: University of Toronto Press, 2007.

French New Wave

Brody, Richard. *Everything Is Cinema: The Working Life of Jean-Luc Godard*. New York: Metropolitan/ Holt, 2008.

Crisp, Colin. *The Classic French Cinema, 1930–1960*. Bloomington: Indiana University Press, 1993.

Godard, Jean-Luc. *Godard on Godard: Critical Writings*. New York: Viking, 1972.

Graham, Peter, ed. *The New Wave: Critical Landmarks*. Garden City, N.Y.: Doubleday, 1968.

Greene, Naomi. *The French New Wave: A New Look*. London: Wallflower, 2007.

Hayward, Susan. *French National Cinema*. 2nd ed. New York: Routledge, 2005.

Hillier, Jim, ed. *Cahiers du Cinéma, the 1950s: Neo-Realism, Hollywood, New Wave*. Cambridge, Mass.: Harvard University Press, 1985.

———, ed. *Cahiers du Cinéma, 1960–1968: New Wave, New Cinema, Reevaluating Hollywood*. Cambridge, Mass.: Harvard University Press, 1986.

Insdorf, Annette. *François Truffaut*. Rev. ed. New York: Cambridge University, Press, 1994.

McCabe, Colin. *Godard: A Portrait of the Artist at Seventy*. New York: Farrar, Strauss, and Giroux, 2004.

Monaco, James. *The New Wave: Truffaut, Godard, Chabrol, Rohmer, Rivette*. New York: Oxford University Press, 1976.

Mussman, Toby, ed. *Jean-Luc Godard: A Critical Anthology*. New York: Dutton, 1968.

Neupert, Richard. *A History of the French New Wave Cinema*. Madison: University of Wisconsin Press, 2002.

Ostrowska, Dorota. *Reading the French New Wave: Critics, Writers and Art Cinema in France*. London: Wallflower, 2008.

Powrie, Phil, ed. *The Cinema of France*. London: Wallflower, 2006.

Sterritt, David. *The Films of Jean-Luc Godard: Seeing the Invisible*. New York: Cambridge University Press, 1999.

Truffaut, François. *The Films in My Life*. Trans. Leonard Mayhew. New York: Simon & Schuster, 1978.

New Cinemas in Postwar Europe and Asia

Bordwell, David. *Planet Hong Kong: Popular Cinema and the Art of Entertainment*. Cambridge, Mass.: Harvard University Press, 2000.

Charles, John. *The Hong Kong Filmography, 1977–1997: A Complete Reference to 1,100 Films Produced by British Hong Kong Studios*. Jefferson, N.C.: McFarland, 2000.

Cheuk, Pak Tong. *Hong Kong New Wave Cinema (1978–2000)*. Bristol: Intellect, 2008.

Chow, Rey. *Sentimental Fabulations—Contemporary Chinese Films: Attachment in the Age of Global Visibility*. New York: Columbia University Press, 2007.

Dennison, Stephanie, and Song Hwee Lim, eds. *Remapping World Cinema: Identity, Culture and Politics in Film*. London: Wallflower, 2006.

Fu, Poshek, and David Desser, eds. *The Cinema of Hong Kong: History, Arts, Identity*. New York: Cambridge University Press, 2000.

Logan, Bey. *Hong Kong Action Cinema*. London: Titan, 1995.

Nochimson, Martha P. *Dying to Belong: Gangster Movies in Hollywood and Hong Kong*. Malden, Mass.: Blackwell, 2007.

Nowell-Smith, Geoffrey. *Making Waves: New Cinemas of the 1960s*. New York: Continuum, 2008.

Stokes, Lisa Odham, and Michael Hoover. *City on Fire: Hong Kong Cinema*. New York: Verso, 1999.

Stringer, Julian. *Blazing Passions: Contemporary Hong Kong Cinema*. London: Wallflower, 2007.

Tasker, Yvonne, ed. *Fifty Contemporary Filmmakers*. London: Routledge, 2002.

Teo, Stephen. *Hong Kong Cinema: The Extra Dimensions*. London: BFI, 1997.

Yau, Esther C. M., ed. *At Full Speed: Hong Kong Cinema in a Borderless World*. Minneapolis: University of Minnesota Press, 2001.

Zhang, Yingjin. *Chinese National Cinema*. New York: Routledge, 2004.

The New American Cinema

Andrew, Geoff. *Stranger Than Paradise: Maverick Film-makers in Recent American Cinema*. London: Prion, 1998.

Arthur, Paul. *A Line of Sight: American Avant-Garde Film since 1965*. Minneapolis: University of Minnesota Press, 2005.

Biskind, Peter. *Down and Dirty Pictures: Miramax, Sundance and the Rise of Independent Film*. New York: Simon & Schuster, 2004.

———. *Easy Riders, Raging Bulls: How the Sex-Drugs-and-Rock 'n' Roll Generation Saved Hollywood*. New York: Simon & Schuster, 1998.

Friedman, Lester D., ed. *American Cinema of the 1970s: Themes and Variations*. New Brunswick, N.J.: Rutgers University Press, 2007.

Goodwin, Michael, and Naomi Wise. *On the Edge: The Life and Times of Francis Coppola*. New York: Morrow, 1989.

Grant, Barry Keith. *American Cinema of the 1960s: Themes and Variations*. New Brunswick, N.J.: Rutgers University Press, 2008.

Harris, Mark. *Pictures at a Revolution: Five Movies and the Birth of the New Hollywood*. New York: Penguin, 2008.

Hillier, Jim. *The New Hollywood*. New York: Continuum, 1992.

James, David E. *Allegories of Cinema: American Film in the Sixties*. Princeton: Princeton University Press, 1989.

Kashner, Sam, and Jennifer MacNair. *The Bad and the Beautiful: Hollywood in the Fifties*. New York: Norton, 2002.

King, Geoff. *New Hollywood Cinema: An Introduction*. New York: Columbia University Press, 2002.

Levy, Emanuel. *Cinema of Outsiders: The Rise of American Independent Film*. New York: New York University Press, 1999.

Lewis, Jon, ed. *The End of Cinema as We Know It: American Film in the Nineties*. New York: New York University Press, 2001.

——, ed. *The New American Cinema*. Durham, N.C.: Duke University Press, 1998.

McBride, Joseph. *Steven Spielberg: A Biography*. New York: Simon & Schuster, 1997.

McGilligan, Patrick. *Robert Altman, Jumping off the Cliff: A Biography of the Great American Director*. New York: St. Martin's, 1989.

Neale, Steve, and Murray Smith, eds. *Contemporary Hollywood Cinema*. New York: Routledge, 1998.

Pierson, John. *Spike, Mike, Slackers and Dykes: A Guided Tour across a Decade of American Independent Cinema*. New York: Miramax/Hyperion, 1997.

Prince, Stephen, ed. *American Cinema of the 1980s: Themes and Variations*. New Brunswick, N.J.: Rutgers University Press, 2007.

Pye, Michael, and Lynda Myles. *The Movie Brats: How the Film Generation Took over Hollywood*. New York: Holt, Rinehart and Winston, 1979.

Ryan, Michael, and Douglas Kellner. *Camera Politica: The Politics and Ideology of Contemporary Hollywood Film*. Bloomington: Indiana University Press, 1988.

Thompson, Kristin. *Storytelling in the New Hollywood: Understanding Classical Narrative Technique*. Cambridge, Mass.: Harvard University Press, 1999.

Williams, Linda Ruth, and Michael Hammond, eds. *Contemporary American Cinema*. Boston: Open University Press, 2006.

Other Topics in Film History

Race and Ethnicity in American Film History

Bernardi, Daniel, ed. *The Birth of Whiteness: Race and the Emergence of U.S. Cinema*. New Brunswick, N.J.: Rutgers University Press, 1996.

Bogle, Donald. *Toms, Coons, Mulattoes, Mammies, and Bucks: An Interpretive History of Blacks in American Films*. 4th ed. New York: Continuum, 2001.

Bowser, Pearl, and Louise Spence. *Writing Himself into History: Oscar Micheaux, His Silent Films, and His Audiences*. New Brunswick, N.J.: Rutgers University Press, 2000.

Cham, Mbye B., and Claire Andrade-Watkins, eds. *Blackframes: Critical Perspectives on Black Independent Cinema*. Cambridge, Mass.: MIT Press, 1988.

Courtney, Susan. *Hollywood Fantasies of Miscegenation: Spectacular Narratives of Gender and Race*. Princeton: Princeton University Press, 2005.

Cripps, Thomas. *Black Film as Genre*. Bloomington: Indiana University Press, 1978.

——. *Making Movies Black: The Hollywood Message Movie from World War II to the Civil Rights Era*. New York: Oxford University Press, 1993.

——. *Slow Fade to Black: The Negro in American Film, 1900–1942*. New York: Oxford University Press, 1977.

Diawara, Manthia, ed. *Black American Cinema*. New York: Routledge, 1993.

Feng, Peter X. *Identities in Motion: Asian American Film and Video*. Durham, N.C.: Duke University Press, 2002.

Gabbard, Krin. *Black Magic: White Hollywood and African American Culture*. New Brunswick, N.J.: Rutgers University Press, 2004.

George, Nelson. *Blackface: Reflections on African Americans and the Movies*. New York: HarperCollins, 1994.

Guerrero, Edward. *Framing Blackness: The African American Image in Film*. Philadelphia: Temple University Press, 1993.

hooks, bell. *Reel to Real: Race, Sex, and Class at the Movies*. New York: Routledge, 1996.

Jones, G. William. *Black Cinema Treasures: Lost and Found*. Denton: University of North Texas Press, 1991.

Martinez, Gerald, Diana Martinez, and Andres Chavez. *What It Is . . . What It Was!: The Black Film Explosion of the '70s in Words and Pictures*. New York: Miramax/Hyperion, 1998.

Moon, Spencer. *Reel Black Talk: A Sourcebook of 50 American Filmmakers*. Westport, Conn: Greenwood, 1997.

Murray, James P. *To Find an Image: Black Films from Uncle Tom to Super Fly*. Indianapolis: Bobbs-Merrill, 1973.

Noriega, Chon A. *Chicanos and Film: Representation and Resistance*. Minneapolis: University of Minnesota Press, 1992.

Null, Gary. *Black Hollywood: From 1970 to Today*. Secaucus, N.J.: Carol, 1993.

——. *Black Hollywood: The Negro in Motion Pictures*. Secaucus, N.J.: Citadel, 1975.

Reid, Mark A. *Black Lenses, Black Voices: African American Film Now*. Lanham, Md.: Rowman & Littlefield, 2005.

——. *Redefining Black Film*. Berkeley: University of California Press, 1993.

——, ed. *Spike Lee's "Do the Right Thing."* New York: Cambridge University Press, 1997.

Rhines, Jesse Algernon. *Black Film, White Money*. New Brunswick, N.J.: Rutgers University Press, 1996.

Richards, Larry. *African American Films through 1959: A Comprehensive, Illustrated Filmography*. Jefferson, N.C.: McFarland, 1998.

Ross, Karen. *Black and White Media: Black Images in Popular Film and Television*. Cambridge, Mass.: Polity, 1996.

Sampson, Henry T. *Blacks in Black and White: A Source Book on Black Films*. 2nd ed. Metuchen, N.J.: Scarecrow, 1995.

——. *That's Enough, Folks: Black Images in Animated Cartoons, 1900–1960*. Lanham, Md.: Scarecrow, 1998.

Smith, Valerie, ed. *Representing Blackness: Issues in Film and Video*. New Brunswick, N.J.: Rutgers University Press, 1997.

Watkins, S. Craig. *Representing: Hip Hop Culture and the Production of Black Cinema*. Chicago: University of Chicago Press, 1998.

Willis, Sharon. *High Contrast: Race and Gender in Contemporary Hollywood Film*. Durham, N.C.: Duke University Press, 1997.

Yearwood, Gladstone L. *Black Cinema Aesthetics: Issues on Independent Black Filmmaking*. Athens: Center for Afro-American Studies, Ohio University, 1982.

Young, Lola. *Fear of the Dark: 'Race', Gender and Sexuality in the Cinema*. New York: Routledge, 1996.

National Cinemas

Barton, Ruth. *Irish National Cinema*. New York: Routledge, 2004.

Gittings, Christopher E. *Canadian National Cinema: Ideology, Difference and Representation*. New York: Routledge, 2002.

Hake, Sabine. *German National Cinema*. 2nd ed. New York: Routledge, 2008.

Hjort, Mette, and Duncan Petrie, eds. *The Cinema of Small Nations*. Bloomington: Indiana University Press, 2007.

Maingard, Jacqueline. *South African National Cinema*. New York: Routledge, 2007.

Noble, Andrea. *Mexican National Cinema*. New York: Routledge, 2005.

Shaw, Lisa, and Stephanie Dennison. *Brazilian National Cinema*. New York: Routledge, 2007.

Soila, Tytti, Astrid Soderbergh-Widding, and Gunnar, Iversen, eds. *Nordic National Cinemas*. New York: Routledge, 1998.

Street, Sarah. *British National Cinema*. 2nd ed. New York: Routledge, 2009.

Triana-Toribio, Núria. *Spanish National Cinema*. New York: Routledge, 2003.

Women and Film History

Abramowitz, Rachel. *Is That a Gun in Your Pocket?: Women's Experience of Power in Hollywood*. New York: Random House, 2000.

Basinger, Jeanine. *A Woman's View: How Hollywood Spoke to Women, 1930–1960*. New York: Knopf, 1993.

Beauchamp, Cari. *Without Lying Down: Frances Marion and the Powerful Women of Early Hollywood*. New York: Scribner, 1997.

Beckman, Karen. *Vanishing Women: Magic, Film, and Feminism*. Durham, N.C.: Duke University Press, 2003.

Francke, Lizzie. *Script Girls: Women Screenwriters in Hollywood*. London: BFI, 1994.

Mayne, Judith. *Framed: Lesbians, Feminists, and Media Culture*. Minneapolis: University of Minnesota Press, 2000.

Petro, Patrice. *Aftershocks of the New: Feminism and Film History*. New Brunswick, N.J.: Rutgers University Press, 2002.

Rich, B. Ruby. *Chick Flicks: Theories and Memories of the Feminist Film Movement*. Durham, N.C.: Duke University Press, 1998.

Thornham, Sue, ed. *Feminist Film Theory: A Reader*. New York: New York University Press, 1999.

Gay and Lesbian Film History

Aaron, Michele. *New Queer Cinema: A Critical Reader*. New Brunswick, N.J.: Rutgers University Press, 2004.

Benshoff, Harry M., and Sean Griffin. *Queer Images: A History of Gay and Lesbian Film in America*. Lanham, Md.: Rowman & Littlefield, 2006.

———, eds. *Queer Cinema: The Film Reader*. New York: Routledge, 2004.

de Lauretis, Teresa. *Technologies of Gender: Essays on Theory, Film, and Fiction*. Bloomington: Indiana University Press, 1987.

Doty, Alexander. *Flaming Classics: Queering the Film Canon*. New York: Routledge, 2000.

———. *Making Things Perfectly Queer: Interpreting Mass Culture*. Minneapolis: University of Minnesota Press, 1993.

Dyer, Richard. *The Culture of Queers*. New York: Routledge, 2002.

———. *Gays and Film*. Rev. ed. New York: New York Zoetrope, 1984.

———. *Now You See It: Studies in Lesbian and Gay Film*. 2nd ed. New York: Routledge, 2003.

———. *Only Entertainment*. 2nd ed. New York: Routledge, 2002.

Gerstner, David A., ed. *Routledge International Encyclopedia of Queer Culture*. New York: Routledge, 2006.

Gever, Martha, Pratibha Parma, and John Greyson, eds. *Queer Looks: Perspectives on Lesbian and Gay Film and Video*. New York: Routledge, 1993.

Gross, Larry. *Up from Invisibility: Lesbians, Gay Men, and the Media in America*. New York: Columbia University Press, 2001.

Grossman, Andrew, ed. *Queer Asian Cinema: Shadows in the Shade*. New York: Harrington Park, 2000.

Hanson, Ellis, ed. *Out Takes: Essays on Queer Theory and Film*. Durham, N.C.: Duke University Press, 1999.

Holmlund, Chris, and Cynthia Fuchs, eds. *Between the Sheets, in the Streets: Queer, Lesbian, Gay Documentary*. Minneapolis: University of Minnesota Press, 1997.

Lang, Robert. *Masculine Interests: Homoerotics in Hollywood Film*. New York: Columbia University Press, 2002.

Lehman, Peter, ed. *Masculinity: Bodies, Movies, Culture*. New York: Routledge, 2001.

Mann, William J. *Behind the Screen: How Gays and Lesbians Shaped Hollywood, 1910–1969*. New York: Viking, 2001.

Russo, Vito. *The Celluloid Closet: Homosexuality in the Movies*. Rev. ed. New York: Harper & Row, 1987.

Suárez, Juan A. *Bike Boys, Drag Queens and Superstars: Avant-Garde, Mass Culture, and Gay Identities in the 1960s Underground Cinema*. Bloomington: Indiana University Press, 1996.

Tinkcom, Matthew. *Working Like a Homosexual: Camp, Capital, and Cinema*. Durham, N.C.: Duke University Press, 2002.

Tyler, Parker. *Screening the Sexes: Homosexuality in the Movies*. New York: Da Capo. 1993.

Villarejo, Amy. *Lesbian Rule: Cultural Criticism and the Value of Desire*. Durham, N.C.: Duke University Press, 2003.

Waugh, Thomas. *The Fruit Machine: Twenty Years of Writing on Queer Cinema*. Durham, N.C.: Duke University Press, 2000.

———. *Hard to Imagine: Gay Male Eroticism in Photography and Film from Their Beginnings to Stonewall*. New York: Columbia University Press, 1996.

White, Patricia. *Uninvited: Classical Hollywood Cinema and Lesbian Representability*. Bloomington: Indiana University Press, 1999.

Wilton, Tamsin, ed. *Immortal, Invisible: Lesbians and the Moving Image*. New York: Routledge, 1995.

Chapter 11: Film Technologies and Production Systems

Hollywood and Business: The Whole Equation

Balio, Tino, ed. *The American Film Industry*. Rev. ed. Madison: University of Wisconsin Press, 1985.

Behlmer, Rudy, and Tony Thomas. *Hollywood's Hollywood: The Movies about the Movies*. Secaucus, N.J.: Citadel, 1975.

Compaine, Benjamin M., and Douglas Gomery. *Who Owns the Media?: Competition and Concentration in the Mass Media Industry*. 3rd ed. Mahwah, N.J.: Erlbaum, 2000.

Cones, John W. *Film Finance and Distribution: A Dictionary of Terms*. Los Angeles: Silman-James, 1992.

Epstein, Edward Jay. *The Big Picture: Money and Power in Hollywood*. New York: Random House, 2005.

———. *The Hollywood Economist: The Hidden Financial Reality behind the Movies*. Brooklyn, NY: Melville House, 2010.

Fuchs, Daniel. *The Golden West: Hollywood Stories*. Boston: Godine, 2005.

Grainge, Paul. *Brand Hollywood: Selling Entertainment in a Global Media Age*. New York: Routledge, 2008.

Kindem, Gorham, ed. *The American Movie Industry: The Business of Motion Pictures*. Carbondale: Southern Illinois University Press, 1982.

McDonald, Paul, and Janet Wasko, eds. *The Contemporary Hollywood Film Industry*. Malden, Mass.: Blackwell, 2008.

Scott, Allen J. *On Hollywood: The Place, the Industry*. Princeton: Princeton University Press, 2005.

Sedgwick, John, and Michael Pokorny, eds. *An Economic History of Film*. New York: Routledge, 2004.

Simon, Deke, and Michael Wiese. *Film & Video Budgets*. 4th ed. Studio City, Calif.: Wiese, 2006.

Stringer, Julian, ed. *Movie Blockbusters*. New York: Routledge, 2003.

Thomson, David. *The Whole Equation: A History of Hollywood*. New York: Knopf, 2005.

Weinberg, Bernard. "What Makes Boys Laugh: A Philosophy Major Finds the Golden Touch." *New York Times* (July 23, 1998), sec. E, p. 5.

Producers, Directors, and Others Involved in Movie Production

Baker, Barbara. *Let the Credits Roll: Interviews with Film Crew*. Jefferson, N.C.: McFarland, 2003.

Behlmer, Rudy, ed. *Memo from David O. Selznick*. New York: Viking, 1972.

Berg, A. Scott. *Goldwyn: A Biography*. New York: Knopf, 1989.

Bergman, Ingmar. *The Magic Lantern: An Autobiography*. Trans. Joan Tate. New York: Viking/ Penguin, 1988.

Bernstein, Matthew. *Walter Wanger, Hollywood Independent*. Minneapolis: University of Minnesota Press, 2000.

Bogdanovich, Peter. *Who the Devil Made It*. New York: Knopf, 1997.

Brouwer, Alexandra, and Thomas Lee Wright. *Working in Hollywood: 64 Film Professionals Talk about Moviemaking*. New York: Crown, 1990.

Bruck, Connie. *When Hollywood Had a King: The Reign of Lew Wasserman, Who Leveraged Talent into Power and Influence*. New York: Random House, 2003.

Cousins, Mark. *Scene by Scene: Film Actors and Directors Discuss Their Work*. London: Laurence King, 2002.

Custen, George F. *Twentieth Century's Fox: Darryl F. Zanuck and the Culture of Hollywood*. New York: Basic, 1997.

Dmytryk, Edward. *On Screen Directing*. Boston: Focal Press, 1984.

Eyman, Scott. *Lion of Hollywood: The Life and Legend of Louis B. Mayer*. New York: Simon & Schuster, 2005.

Duchovnay, Gerald. *Film Voices: Interviews from "Post Script."* Albany: State University of New York Press, 2004.

Fitzgerald, F. Scott. *The Last Tycoon: An Unfinished Novel*. New York: Scribner, 1941.

Fraser-Cavassoni, Natasha. *Sam Spiegel*. New York: Simon & Schuster, 2003.

Huston, John. *An Open Book*. New York: Knopf, 1980.

Kagan, Jeremy. *Directors Close Up: Interviews with Directors Nominated for Best Film by the Directors Guild of America*. 2nd ed. Lanham, Md.: Scarecrow, 2006.

Katz, Steven D. *Film Directing Shot by Shot: Visualizing from Concept to Screen*. Studio City, Calif.: Wiese, 1991.

Kingdon, Tom. *Total Directing: Integrating Camera and Performance in Film and Television*. Los Angeles: Silman-James, 2004.

Kurosawa, Akira. *Something Like an Autobiography*. Trans. Audie E. Bock. New York: Vintage, 1983.

Lazarus, Paul N., III. *The Film Producer*. New York: St. Martin's, 1992.

Linson, Art. *A Pound of Flesh: Perilous Tales of How to Produce Movies in Hollywood*. New York: Grove, 1993.

———. *What Just Happened?: Bitter Hollywood Tales from the Front Line*. New York: Bloomsbury, 2002.

Lumet, Sidney. *Making Movies*. New York: Knopf, 1995.

Lyman, Rick. *Watching Movies: The Biggest Names in Cinema Talk about the Films That Matter Most*. New York: Times, 2003.

Mackendrick, Alexander. *On Film-making: An Introduction to the Craft of the Director*. Ed. Paul Cronin. London: Faber and Faber, 2004.

Obst, Linda. *Hello, He Lied: And Other Truths from the Hollywood Trenches*. New York: Broadway, 1997.

Rachlin, Harvey. *The TV and Movie Business: An Encyclopedia of Careers, Technologies, and Practices*. New York: Harmony, 1991.

Ray, Satyajit. *Our Films, Their Films*. New York: Hyperion, 1994.

Ross, Lillian. *Picture*. New York: Rinchart, 1952.

Julie Salamon. *The Devil's Candy: The Bonfire of the Vanities Goes to Hollywood*. Boston: Houghton Mifflin, 1991.

Sarris, Andrew. *Interviews with Film Directors*. Indianapolis: Bobbs-Merrill, 1967.

Silver, Alain, and Elizabeth Ward. *The Film Director's Team: A Practical Guide for Production Mangers, Assistant Directors, and All Filmmakers*. 2nd ed. Los Angeles: Silman-James, 1992.

Taub, Eric. *Gaffers, Grips, and Best Boys*. 2nd ed. New York: St. Martin's, 1994.

Tirard, Laurent. *Moviemakers' Master Class: Private Lessons from the World's Foremost Directors*. New York: Faber and Faber, 2002.

Vidor, King. *A Tree Is a Tree: An Autobiography*. New York: Harcourt, Brace, 1953.

von Sternberg, Josef. *Fun in a Chinese Laundry: An Autobiography*. New York: Macmillan, 1965.

Film and Digital Technologies

Allen, Michael. "From *Bwana Devil* to *Batman Forever:* Technology in Contemporary Hollywood Cinema." In *Contemporary Hollywood Cinema*. 109–129. Ed. Steve Neale and Murray Smith. New York: Routledge, 1998.

Allen, Robert C., and Douglas Gomery. *Film History: Theory and Practice*. New York: Knopf, 1985.

Ascher, Steven, and Edward Pincus. *The Filmmaker's Handbook: A Comprehensive Guide for the Digital Age*. 2008 (3rd) ed. New York: Plume, 2007.

Billups, Scott. *Digital Moviemaking: The Filmmaker's Guide to the 21st Century*. 2nd ed. Studio City, Calif.: Wiese, 2000.

Bordwell, David, Janet Staiger, and Kristin Thompson. *The Classical Hollywood Cinema: Film Style and Mode of Production to 1960*. New York: Columbia University Press, 1985.

Campbell, Drew. *Technical Film and TV for Nontechnical People*. New York: Allworth, 2002.

Clark, Barbara, and Susan J. Spohr. *Guide to Postproduction for TV and Film: Managing the Process*. 2nd ed. Boston: Focal Press, 2002.

Dancyger, Ken. *The World of Film and Video Production: Aesthetics and Practices*. Fort Worth: Harcourt Brace College, 1999.

Ebert, Roger, and Gene Siskel. *The Future of the Movies: Interviews with Martin Scorsese, Steven Spielberg, and George Lucas.* Kansas City, Mo.: Andrews and McMeel, 1991.

Enticknap, Leo. *Moving Image Technology: From Zoetrope to Digital.* London: Wallflower, 2005.

Fielding, Raymond, ed. *A Technological History of Motion Pictures and Television: An Anthology from the Pages of the Journal of the Society of Motion Picture and Television Engineers.* Berkeley: University of California Press, 1967.

Hurbis-Cherrier, Mick. *Voice and Vision: A Creative Approach to Narrative Film and DV Production.* Boston: Focal Press, 2007.

Kawin, Bruce F. *How Movies Work.* Berkeley: University of California Press, 1992.

Konigsberg, Ira. *The Complete Film Dictionary.* 2nd ed. New York: Penguin, 1997.

Long, Ben, and Sonja Schenk. *The Digital Filmmaking Handbook.* 3rd ed. Hingham, Mass.: Charles River Media, 2005.

Mamer, Bruce. *Film Production Technique: Creating the Accomplished Image.* 5th ed. Belmont, Calif.: Wadsworth, 2009.

Neale, Stephen. *Cinema and Technology: Image, Sound, Colour.* Bloomington: Indiana University Press, 1985.

Rieser, Martin, and Andrea Zapp, eds. *New Screen Media: Cinema/Art/Narrative.* London: BFI, 2002.

Salt, Barry. *Film Style and Technology: History and Analysis.* 2nd ed. London: Starword, 1992.

Utterson, Andrew, ed. *Technology and Culture, the Film Reader.* London: Routledge, 2005.

Vaz, Mark Cotta, and Patricia Rose Duignan. *Industrial Light & Magic: Into the Digital Realm.* New York: Ballantine, 1996.

The Studio System

Davis, Ronald L. *The Glamour Factory: Inside Hollywood's Big Studio System.* Dallas: Southern Methodist University Press, 1993.

Finler, Joel W. *The Hollywood Story: Everything You Ever Wanted to Know about the American Movie Business but Didn't Know Where to Look.* Rev. ed. New York: Columbia University Press, 2003.

Goldsmith, Ben, and Tom O'Regan. *The Film Studio: Film Production in the Global Economy.* Lanham, Md.: Rowman & Littlefield, 2005.

Gomery, Douglas. *The Hollywood Studio System: A History.* London: BFI, 2005.

Mordden, Ethan. *The Hollywood Studios: House Style in the Golden Age of the Movies.* New York: Knopf, 1988.

Powdermaker, Hortense. *Hollywood, the Dream Factory: An Anthropologist Looks at the Movie-Makers.* Boston: Little, Brown, 1950.

Schatz, Thomas. *The Genius of the System: Hollywood Filmmaking in the Studio Era.* New York: Holt, 1996.

Independent Production

Corman, Roger. *How I Made a Hundred Movies in Hollywood and Never Lost a Dime.* New York: Random House, 1990.

Frolick, Billy. *What I Really Want to Do Is Direct: Seven Film School Graduates Go to Hollywood.* New York: Plume, 1997.

Gaines, Philip, and David J. Rhodes. *Micro-Budget Hollywood: Budgeting (and Making) Feature Films for $50,000 to $500,000.* Los Angeles: Silman-James, 1995.

Goodell, Gregory. *Independent Feature Film Production: A Complete Guide from Concept through Distribution.* Rev. ed. New York: St. Martin's, 1998.

MacDonald, Scott. *A Critical Cinema: Interviews with Independent Filmmakers.* Berkeley: University of California Press, 1988.

Pierson, John. *Spike, Mike, Slackers and Dykes: A Guided Tour across a Decade of American Independent Cinema.* New York: Miramax/Hyperion, 1997.

Polish, Mark, Michael Polish, and Jonathan Sheldon. *The Declaration of Independent Filmmaking: An Insider's Guide to Making Movies outside of Hollywood.* Orlando: Harcourt, 2005.

Rosen, David, and Peter Hamilton. *Off-Hollywood: The Making and Marketing of Independent Films.* New York: Grove Weidenfeld, 1990.

Vachon, Christine, with David Edelstein. *Shooting to Kill: How an Independent Producer Blasts through the Barriers to Make Movies That Matter.* New York: Avon, 1998.

Labor and Unions

Ross, Murray. *Stars and Strikes: Unionization of Hollywood.* New York: Columbia University Press, 1941.

Distribution, Exhibition, and Reception

Austin, Bruce A. *Immediate Seating: A Look at Movie Audiences.* Belmont, Calif.: Wadsworth, 1989.

Compaine, Benjamin M., and Douglas Gomery. *Who Owns the Media?: Competition and Concentration in the Mass Media Industry.* 3rd ed. Mahwah, N.J.: Erlbaum, 2000.

Gomery, Douglas. *Shared Pleasures: A History of Movie Presentation in America.* Madison: University of Wisconsin Press, 1992.

Hark, Ina Rae. *Exhibition, the Film Reader.* New York: Routledge, 2002.

Hayes, Dade, and Jonathan Bing. *Open Wide: How Hollywood Box Office Became a National Obsession.* New York: Miramax/Hyperion, 2004.

Herman, Edward S., and Robert W. McChesney. *The Global Media: The New Missionaries of Corporate Capitalism.* London: Cassell, 1997.

Klinger, Barbara. *Reception: The Film Reader.* London: Routledge, 2009.

Lukk, Tiiu. *Movie Marketing: Opening the Picture and Giving It Legs.* Los Angeles: Silman-James, 1997.

Staiger, Janet. *Media Reception Studies.* New York: New York University Press, 2005.

———. *Perverse Spectators: The Practices of Film Reception.* New York: New York University Press, 2000.

Stokes, Melvyn, and Richard Maltby, eds. *American Movie Audiences: From the Turn of the Century to the Early Sound Era.* London: BFI, 1999.

The Making of . . .

Note: In addition to the books listed here, DVD releases often contain, as supplementary material, a "making of" section.

Auiler, Dan. *"Vertigo": The Making of a Hitchcock Classic.* New York: St. Martin's, 1998.

Behlmer, Rudy. *America's Favorite Movies: Behind the Scenes.* New York: Ungar, 1982.

Carringer, Robert L. *The Making of "Citizen Kane."* Rev. ed. Berkeley: University of California Press, 1996.

Goldner, Orville, and George E. Turner. *The Making of "King Kong": The Story behind a Film Classic*. New York: Ballantine, 1975.

Harmetz, Aljean. *The Making of "The Wizard of Oz": Movie Magic and Studio Power in the Prime of MGM, and the Miracle of Production #1060*. New York: Limelight, 1984.

———. *On the Road to Tara: The Making of "Gone with the Wind."* New York: Abrams, 1996.

———. *Round Up the Usual Suspects: The Making of "Casablanca," Bogart, Bergman, and World War II*. New York: Hyperion, 1992.

Haver, Ronald. *"A Star Is Born": The Making of the 1954 Movie and Its 1985 Restoration*. New York: Knopf, 1988.

Lee, Spike, with Lisa Jones. *"Do the Right Thing": A Spike Lee Joint*. New York: Fireside, 1989.

McClelland, Doug. *Down the Yellow Brick Road: The Making of "The Wizard of Oz."* New York: Bonanza, 1989.

Rebello, Stephen. *Alfred Hitchcock and the Making of "Psycho."* New York: St. Martin's, 1998.

Sammon, Paul M. *Future Noir: The Making of "Blade Runner."* New York: HarperPrism, 1996.

Sayles, John. *Thinking in Pictures: The Making of the Movie "Matewan."* Boston: Houghton Mifflin, 1987.

Permissions Acknowledgments

Chapter One

Still from David Yale's *Harry Potter and the Deathly Hallows: Part 2*. Courtesy of Warner Bros. Pictures/Photofest.

Chapter Two

Still from Terrence Malick's *Tree of Life*. Courtesy of Cottonwood Pictures / The Kobal Collection/Art Resource, NY.

Praxiteles's Hermes with infant Dionysos on his arm. The Archeological Museum, Olympia, Greece. Photo © Erich Lessing/Art Resource, NY.

Alberto Giacometti's Walking Man. Art © Alberto Giacometti Estate/Licensed by VAGA and ARS, New York, NY. Photo: Burnstein Collection/Corbis.

Keith Haring's Self Portrait 1989. In the outdoor exhibition L'Homme qui Marche at the Gardens of the Palais Royal, Paris, March 23-June 18, 2000. Photo © Annebicque Bernard/Corbis Sygma.

The Hon. Frances Duncombe by Thomas Gainsborough. © Geoffrey Clements/Corbis.

Marcel Duchamp's Nude Descending a Staircase, No. 2 Courtesy of the Philadelphia Museum of Art; The Louise and Walter Arensberg Collection.

Chapter Three

Still from Ethan and Joel Coen's *True Grit*. Courtesy of The Kobal Collection/Skydance Productions/Art Resource, NY.

Still from Robert Flaherty's Nanook of the North. Courtesy of The Museum of Modern Art/Film Stills Archive, New York.

Still from Leni Reifenstahl's Triumph of the Will. Courtesy of the Museum of Modern Art/Film Stills Archive, New York.

Still from Fernand Léger's Ballet Mecanique. Courtesy of the Museum of Modern Art/Film Stills Archive, New York.

Chapter Four

Still from Roman Polanski's *The Ghost Writer*. Courtesy of The Kobal Collection/Rp Films/Art Resource, NY.

Chapter Five

Still from Tim Burton's Sweeney Todd: The Demon Barber of Fleet Street. Courtesy of The Kobal Collection/Dreamworks/Warner Bros/GALLO, LEAH/Art Resource, NY.

Still from Guillermo del Toro's Hellboy. Courtesy of The New York Times.

Still from Guillermo del Toro's Hellboy. Courtesy of the Everett Collection.

Still from Robert Wiene's The Cabinet of Dr. Caligari. Courtesy of the Museum of Modern Art/Film Stills Archive, New York.

Still from Yasujiro Ozu's Late Spring. Courtesy of the Museum of Modern Art/Film Stills Archive, New York.

Chapter Six

Still from Tate Taylor's *The Help*. Courtesy of Dreamworks Pictures/The Kobal Collection/Art Resource, NY.

Tracking shot for Victor Fleming's Gone With the Wind. Courtesy of Photofest.

Steadicam used on the set of James Cameron's Titanic. Courtesy of Photofest.

Still from Fritz Lang's Metropolis. Courtesy of the Museum of Modern Art/Film Stills Archive, New York.

Chapter Seven

Still from Tom Hooper's *The King's Speech*. Courtesy of The Weinstein Company/Photofest.

Chapter Eight

Still from Quentin Tarantino's *Inglorious Bastards*. Courtesy of The Kobal Collection/Universal Picture/Art Resource, NY.

Chapter Nine

Still from Kathryn Bigelow's *The Hurt Locker*. Courtesy of First Light Productions/Kingsgatefilms/The Kobal Collection/Art Resource, NY.

Stills from Alfred Hitchcock's The 39 Steps. Courtesy of the Museum of Modern Art/Film Stills Archive, New York.

Chapter Ten

Movie poster from Orson Welle's *Citizen Kane*. Courtesy of RKO/ The Kobal Collection/Art Resource, NY.

Edward Muybridge's horse in motion. Photo courtesy of the Hulton-Deutsch Collection/Corbis.

Interior views of Thomas Edison's Black Maria. Courtesy of the Museum of Modern Art/Film Stills Archive, New York.

Chapter Eleven

Photo of director Zack Snyder and actor Gerard Butler on the set of 300. Courtesy of The Kobal Collection/Warner Bros// Legendary Pictures/Art Resource, NY.

Frame Illustrations by Chapter

Chapter One

Brokeback Mountain, © 2005 Alberta Film Entertainment/ Paramount Pictures; *March of the Penguins*, © 2005 Buena Vista International Film Production France/Participation; *Krrish* © 2006 Film Kraft; *Sweeney Todd* (5 images), © 2007 Dreamworks Pictures; *Juno* (14 images), © 2007 Dancing Elk Productions/ FOX; Superbad, © 2007 Columbia Pictures; *Back to the Future*, © 1985 Universal Pictures; *Juno* (23 images), © 2007 Dancing Elk Productions/FOX; *Way Down East*, © 1920 D. W. Griffith Productions; *The Miracle of Morgan's Creek*, © 1944 Paramount Pictures; *Rosemary's Baby*, © 1968 William Castle Productions; *Knocked Up*, © 2007 Universal Pictures; Waitress, © 2007 Night and Day Pictures; *4 Months 3 Weeks and 2 Days* © 2007 Mobra Films; *Harry Potter and the Sorcerer's Stone*, © 2001 Warner Bros. Pictures; *Harry Potter and the Chamber of Secrets*, © 2002 Warner Bros. Pictures; *Harry Potter and the Prisoner of Azkaban*, © 2004 Warner Bros. Pictures; *Harry Potter and the Goblet of Fire*, © 2005 Warner Bros. Pictures; *Harry Potter and the Order of the Phoenix*, © 2007 Warner Bros. Pictures; Harry Potter and the Half-Blood Prince, © 2009 Warner Bros. Pictures; *Harry Potter and the Deathly Hallows: Part 1*, © 2010 Warner Bros. Pictures; *Harry Potter and the Deathly Hallows: Part 2*, © 2011 Warner Bros. Pictures; *Harry Potter and the Deathly Hallows: Parts 1 and 2 (36 images)*, © 2010 Warner Bros. Pictures.

Chapter Two

Juno (4 images), © 2007 Dancing Elk Productions/ FOX; *Black Hawk Down*, © 2001 Revolution Studios; *The Searchers*, © 1956 C.V. Whitney Pictures/Warner Bros. Pictures; *Bonnie and Clyde* (2 images), © 1967 Tatira-Hiller Productions/ Warner Bros. Pictures; *Way Down East* (4 images), © 1920 D. W. Griffith Productions; *The Silence of the Lambs* (6 images), © 1991 Orion Pictures Corporation; *The New World* (7 images), © 2005 New Line Cinema; *The Grapes of Wrath* (3 images), © 1940 Twentieth Century-Fox Film Corporation; *Atonement* (6 images), © 2007 Working Title Films/Universal Pictures; *The Matrix* (3 images), © 1999 Warner Bros. Pictures; *Gold Rush* (6 images), © 1925 Charles Chaplin Productions; *City of God*, © 2002 O2 Filmes; *The Killer* (8 images), © 1989 Film Workshop; *Donnie Darko* (3 images), © 2001 Pandora Cinema; *l'enfant* © 1987 Rondo Caprioso; Cloverfield, © 2008 Bad Robot; *Employees Leaving the Lumière Factory*, © 1895 Lumière; *A Trip to the Moon*, © 1902 Georges Méliès; *Let the Right One In*, © 2008 EFTI; Kick-Ass, © 2010 Lionsgate; *Jane Eyre*, © 2011 Focus Features.

Chapter Three

Star Wars (5 images), © 1977 Lucas Arts; *Slacker* (6 images), © 1991 Detour Filmproduction; *Mulholland Drive* © 2001 Les Films Alain Sarde; *Syriana*, © 2005 Warner Bros. Pictures; Rango, © 2011 Blind Wink Productions; *Hands Hard Body*, © 1997 Idea Entertainment; *American Movie*, © 1999 Bluemark Productions; *The King of Kong*, © 2007 LargeLab; *Grey Gardens* (2 images), © 1975 Portrait Films; *Exit Through the Gift Shop*, © 2010 Paranoid Pictures; *An Andalusian Dog*, © 1929 Luis Buñuel; *Tribulation 99, Alien Anomalies under America*, © 1992 Other Cinema; *Removed*, © 1999 Naomi Uman; *Borat*, © 2006 Four by Two; *Symbiotictaxiplasm* (2 images), © 1968 Take One Productions; *Tree of Life*, © 2011 Cottonwood Pictures; *Mean Streets*, © 1973 Taplin-Perry-Scorsese Productions; *Goodfellas*, © 1990 Warner Bros. Pictures; *New York, New York*, © 1986 Raymond Depardon; *2001: A Space Odyssey*, © 1968 Metro-Goldwyn-Mayer; *The Godfather*, © 1972 Alfran Productions/Paramount Pictures; *Raising Arizona*, © 1987 Circle Films; *Leaving Las Vegas*, © 1995 Initial Productions; *The Rock*, © 1996 Hollywood Pictures; *White Heat*, © 1949 Warner Bros. Pictures; *Double Indemnity*, © 1944 Paramount Pictures; *Sunset Boulevard*, © 1950 Paramount Pictures; *Brick*, © 2005 Bergman Lustig Productions; *Fargo*, © 1996 PolyGram Filmed Entertainment; *Insomnia*, © 2002 Alcon Entertainment; *Close Encounters of the Third Kind*, © 1977 Columbia Pictures Corporation; *War of the Worlds* © 1953, 2005 Para-mount Pictures; *Avatar*, © 2009 Twentieth Century Fox Film Corporation; *28 Days Later*, © 2002 DNA Films; *The Ring*, © 2002 DreamWorks SKG; *Suspiria*, © 1977 Seda Spettacoli; *Bride of Frankenstein*, © 1935 Universal Pictures; *Butch Cassidy and the Sundance Kid* (2 images), © 1969 Campanile Productions; *The Unforgiven*, © 1992 James Productions; *Dead Man*, © 1995 Pandora Film-production; *My Darling Clementine*, © 1946 Twentieth Century Fox Film Corporation; *Broadway Melody*, © 1929 Metro-Goldwyn-Mayer; *Love Me Tonight*, © 1932 Paramount Pictures; *Dreamgirls* (2 images),

© 2006 DreamWorks SKG; *Mamma Mia!*, © 2008 Universal Pictures; *Dracula*, © 1931 Universal Pictures; *The Twilight Saga: Eclipse*, © 2010 Summit Entertainment; *Buffy the Vampire Slayer*, © 1992 Twentieth Century-Fox Film Corporation; *Serenity*, © 2005 Universal Pictures; *Waltz with Bashir*, © 2008 Bridgit Folman Film Gang; *Motion Painting No. 1*, © 1947 Fischinger Studios; *The Comb*, © 1990 Koninck Studios; *Persepolis*, © 2007 2.4.7. Films; *Polar Express*, © 2004 Castle Rock Entertainment.

Chapter Four

Notorious (5 images), © 1946 Vanguard Films; *Stranger Than Fiction*, © 2006 Columbia Pictures; *The Royal Tenenbaums*, © 2001 Touchstone Pictures; *True Grit*, © 2010 Paramount Pictures; *Funny Games*, © 2007 Celluloid Dreams; *Black Swan*, © 2010 Fox Searchlight Pictures; *Precious* (2 images), © 2009 Lionsgate; *District 9*, © 2009 TriStar Pictures; *Rocky*, © 1976 United Artists; *The Big Lebowski*, © 1998 Working Title Films; *The Social Network* (2 images), © 2010 Columbia Pictures; *127 Hours* (4 images), © 2010 Pathé; *Pulp Fiction* (10 images), © 1994 Miramax FilmsPage; *The Social Network* (5 images), © 2010 Columbia Pictures; The Lives of Others, © 2006 Arte; *The Fighter*, © 2010 Mandeville Films; *Great Expectations (1946)*, © 1946 Cineguild; *Great Expectations (1998)*, © 1998 Art Linson Productions/20th Century Fox; *Citizen Kane*, © 1941 Mercury Productions; *The Usual Suspects*, © 1995 PolyGram Filmed Entertainment; *Memento*, 2000 Newmarket Capital Group; *Gladiator* (2 images), © 2000 DreamWorks SKG; *Raging Bull* (6 images), © 1980 Chartoff-Winkler Productions; *Timecode*, © 2000 Red Mullet Productions; *Some Like it Hot*, © 1959 Ashton Productions; *Blade Runner*, © 1982 The Ladd Company; *The Last Emperor*, © 1987 Yanco Films Limited; *Stagecoach* (23 images), © 1939 Walter Wanger Productions.

Chapter Five

Pan's Labyrinth, © 2006 Estudios Picasso; *Far From Heaven*, © 2002 Clear Blue Sky Productions; *Rear Window* (4 images), © 1954 Paramount Pictures; *Moulin Rouge*, © 2001 Twentieth Century Fox Film Corporation/Bazmark Films; *The Leopard* (8 images), © 1963 Titanus Bros.; *Eyes Wide Shut* (2 images), © 1999 Hobby Films/Warner Bros. Pictures; *Avatar*, © 2009 Twentieth Century Fox Film Corp.; *Sherlock Holmes*, © 2009 Warner Bros. Pictures; *The Social Network*, © 2010 Columbia Pictures; *Cabiria* (3 images), © 1957 Dino de Laurentiis Cinematografica; *Night of the Hunter* (2 images), © 1955 United Artists; *City of God* (3 images), © 2002 O2 Filmes; *Monster*, © 2003 Media 8 Entertainment; *Æon Flux*, © 2005 Paramount Pictures; *Head in the Clouds*, © 2004 Remstar Productions; *North Country*, © 2005 Warner Bros. Pictures; *Alice in Wonderland* (4 images), © 2010 Walt Disney Pictures; *Marie Antoinette*, © 1938 Metro-Goldwyn-Mayer; *The Dark Knight* (2 images), © 2008 Warner Bros. Pictures; *Gone with the Wind*, © 1939 Metro-Goldwyn-Mayer; *The Court Jester*, © 1955 Dena Enterprises/Paramount Pictures; *The Cabinet of Dr. Caligari* (4 images), © 1920 Decla-Bioscop AG; *Suspiria* (2 images), 1929 Seda Spettacoli; *The Last Laugh* (4 images), © 1924 Universum Film; *Queen Kelly*, © 1929 Gloria Swanson Pictures; *The Third Man*, © 1949 London Film Productions; *The Bicycle Thieves*, © 1948 Produzioni De Sica; *The Best Years of Our Lives* (2 images), © 1946 The Samuel Goldwyn Company; *Chinatown* (3 images), © 1974 Paramount Pictures; *Stagecoach* (8 images), © 1939 Walter Wanger Productions; *Crouching Tiger, Hidden Dragon*, 2000 Asia Union Film & Entertainment Ltd.; *2001: A Space Odyssey* © 1968 Metro-Goldwyn-Mayer; *Royal Wedding*, © 1951 Metro-Goldwyn-Mayer; *Forrest Gump*, © 1994 Paramount Pictures; *Sleepy Hollow* (10 images), © 1999 Paramount Pictures; *American Beauty* (17 images), © 1999 DreamWorks SKG

Chapter Six

The Social Network, © 2010 Columbia Pictures; *In Cold Blood*, © 1967 Columbia Pictures Corporation; *Stagecoach*, © 1939 Walter Wanger Productions; *The Searchers*, © 1956 C.V. Whitney Pictures; *The Seventh Seal* (2 images), © 1957 Svensk Filmindustri; *High Noon*, © 1952 Stanley Kramer Productions; *Sweet Smell of Success*, © 1957 Curtleigh Productions; *Barry Lyndon*, © 1975 Peregrine; *Pleasantville*, © 1998 New Line Cinema; *My Darling Clementine*, © 1946 Twentieth Century Fox Film Corporation; *Some Like it Hot*, 1959 Ashton Productions; *Titanic*, © 1997 20th Century Fox Film Corporation; *Sweet Smell of Success*, © 1957 Curtleigh Productions; *Manhattan*, © 1979 Jack Rollins & Charles H. Joffe Productions; *Citizen Kane* (2 images), © 1941 Mercury Productions; *The Scarlet Empress*, © 1934 Paramount Pictures; *THX 1138*, © 1971 American Zoetrope; *Citizen Kane*, © 1941 Mercury Productions; *The Bride of Frankenstein*, © 1935 Universal Pictures; *The Godfather*, © 1972 Alfran Productions; *Dogville* (4 images), © 2003 Zentropa Entertainments; Dr. Strangelove, © 1964 Hawk Films; *Sunset Boulevard*, © 1950 Paramount Pictures; *Barry Lyndon*, © 1975 Peregrine; *The Hurt Locker*, © 2008 Voltage Pictures; *The Devil's Backbone*, © 2001 El Deseo S. A.; *The Book of Eli*, © 2010 Alcon Entertainment/Silver Pictures; *The Graduate*, © 1967 Embassy Pictures Corporation; *Charisma*, © 1999 King Record Co.; *The King's Speech* (7 images), © 2010 The Weinstein Company; *Applause*, © 1929 Paramount Pictures; *Trouble in Paradise*, © 1932 Paramount Pictures; *Notorious*, 1946 Vanguard Films; *Citizen Kane*, © 1941 Mercury Productions; *The Little Foxes* (4 images), © 1941 The Samuel Goldwyn Company; *Badlands*, © 1973 Warner Bros. Pictures; *The Strange Love of Martha Ivers*, © 1946 Hal Wallis Productions; *Days of Heaven*, © 1978 Paramount Pictures; *The Maltese Falcon*, © 1941 Warner Bros. Pictures; *Love Me Tonight*, © 1932 Paramount Pictures; *North by Northwest*, © 1959 Metro-Goldwyn-Mayer; *Do the Right Thing*, © 1989 40 Acres & A Mule Filmworks; *The Shining*, © 1980 Hawk Films; *M* (4 images), © 1931 Nero-Film AG; *Bride of Franken-stein* (2 images), © 1935 Universal Pictures; *Jurassic Park* (2 images) 1993 Universal Pictures; *Citizen Kane* (2 images), © 1941 Mercury Productions; *Gladiator*, © 2000 DreamWorks SKG; *The Grand Illusion*, © 1937 Réalisation d'art cinématographique; *Touch of Evil* (8 images), © 1958 Universal International Pictures; *The Bourne Supremacy*, © 2004 Universal Pictures; *The Birds* (10 images), © 1963 Universal Pictures; *Birth* (4 images), © 2004 New Line Cinema; *Metropolis* © 1927 Universum Film (UFA); *2001: A Space Odyssey*, © 1968 Metro-Goldwyn-Mayer; *Pirates of the Caribbean: Dead Man's Chest*, © 2006 Walt Disney Pictures.

Chapter Seven

The Quiet American, © 1952 Figaro; *I'm Not There*, © 2007 Killer Films; *What's Eating Gilbert Grape?*, © 1993 Paramount Pictures; *Donnie* Brasco, © 1997 Mandalay Entertainment; *Chocolat*, © 2000 Miramax Films; *Broken Blossoms*, © 1919 D.W. Griffith Productions; *Singing in the Rain*, © 1952 Metro-Goldwyn-Mayer; *The Philadelphia*

Story, © 1940 Metro-Goldwyn-Mayer; *A Place in the Sun*, © 1951 Paramount Pictures; *Who's Afraid of Virginia Woolf?*, © 1966 Warner Bros. Pictures; *On the Waterfront*, © 1954 Horizon Pictures; *East of Eden*, © 1955 Warner Bros. Pictures; *Iron Man*, © 2008 Paramount Pictures; *The Letter*, © 1940 Warner Bros. Pictures; *Rabbit Hole*, © 2010 Olympus Pictures; *The Big Trail*, © 1930 Fox Film Corporation; *The Shootist*, © 1976 Dino De Laurentiis Company; *Starman*, © 1984 Columbia Pictures Corporation; *True Grit*, © 2010 Paramount Pictures; *The Social Network*, © 2010 Columbia Pictures; *The Manchurian Candidate*, © 2004 Paramount Pictures; *Monster-In-Law*, © 2005 New Line Cinema; *Imagining Argentina*, © 2003 Multi-video; *Gandhi*, 1982 Columbia Pictures Corporation; *Introducing Dorothy Dandridge*, © 1999 City Entertainment; *The Maltese Falcon*, © 1941 Warner Bros. Pictures; *The Bank Dick*, © 1940 Universal Pictures; *Henry V*, © 1989 British Broadcasting Corporation/BBC; *Knocked Up*, © 2007 Universal Pictures; *Edward Scissorhands*, © 1990 Twentieth Century-Fox Film Corporation; *Taxi Driver*, © 1976 Columbia Pictures Corporation; *Citizen Kane* (8 images), © 1941 Mercury Productions; *The Passion of Joan of Arc*, © 1928 Société générale des films; *Morocco*, © 1930 Paramount Pictures; *Throne of Blood*, © 1957 Toho Company; *The Piano*, © 1993 The Australian Film Commission; *Stella Dallas* (3 images), 1937 The Samuel Goldwyn Company; *Blue Valentine*, © 2010 Incentive Filmed Entertainment/Silverwood Films.

Chapter Eight

Requiem for a Dream (6 images), © 2000 Artisan Entertainment; *Shine a Light*, © 2008 Paramount Classics; *The Thin Red Line* (2 images), © 1998 Fox 2000 Pictures; *They Shoot Horses, Don't They?* (2 images), © 1969 American Broadcasting Company; *Erin Brockovich* (3 images), © 2000 Jersey Films; *Out of Sight* (2 images), © 2000 Jersey Films; *Team America* (5 images), © 2004 Paramount Pictures; *Battleship Potemkin* (8 images), © 1925 Goskino; *Run Lola Run* 6 images), © 1998 X-Filme Creative Pool; *Casablanca* (10 images), © 1942 Warner Bros. Pictures; *Breathless* (12 images), © 1960 Société Nouvelle de Cinématographie/Metro-Goldwyn-Mayer; *The Searchers* (6 images), © 1956 C. V. Whitney Pictures; *Lawrence of Arabia* (2 images), © 1962 Horizon Pictures (II); *Stagecoach* (2 images), © 1939 Walter Wanger Productions; *2001: A Space Odyssey* (3 images), © 1968 Metro-Goldwyn-Mayer; *Now, Voyager* (2 images), © 1942 Warner Bros. Pictures; *Rear Window* (8 images), © 1954 Paramount Pictures; *Night of the Hunter* (4 images), © 1955 Paul Gregory Productions; *Taxi Driver* (4 images), © 1976 Columbia Pictures Corporation; *Cries and Whispers* (3 images), © 1972 Cinematograph AB; *The Tin Drum*, © 1979 Argos Films; *To Die For*, © 1995 Columbia Pictures Corporation; *The 400 Blows* (3 images), © 1959 Les Films du Carrosse; *The Rules of Attraction*, © 2002 Kingsgate Films; *The Birth of a Nation* (6 images), © 1915. D. W. Griffith Productions; *City of God* (9 images), © 2002 O2 Filmes.

Chapter Nine

Inception, © 2010 Warner Bros. Pictures; *Spirited Away*, © 2001 Studio Ghibli; *Apocalypse Now* (3 images), © 1979 Zoetrope Studios;

Mean Streets, © 1973 Taplin-Perry-Scorsese Productions; *Midnight Cowboy* © 1969 Florin Productions; *North by Northwest* (2 images), © 1959 Metro-Goldwyn-Mayer; *Hamlet*, © 1948 Two Cities Films; *Double Indemnity*, © 1944 Paramount Pictures; *Raging Bull*, © 1980 Chartoff-Winkler Productions; *Slumdog Millionaire*, © 2008 Celador Films; *The Tragedy of Othello*, © 1952 Mercury Productions; *Magnolia* (6 images), © 1999 Ghoulardi Film Company; *A Clockwork Orange* (2 images), © 1971 Warner Bros. Pictures; *Winter's Bone*, © 2010 Anonymous Content; *Uncle Boonmee Who Can Recall His Past Lives*, © 2010 Kick the Machine/Illumination Films; *War of the Worlds* (8 images), © 2005 Paramount Pictures; *Once Upon a Time in the West* (2 images), © 1968 Finanzia San Marco; *Apocalypse Now* (6 images), © 1979 Zoetrope Studios; *Me and You and Everyone We Know*, © 2005 IFC Films; *The Man Who Wasn't There* (5 images), © 2001 Good Machine; *Citizen Kane* (9 images), © 1941 Mercury Productions.

Chapter Ten

Sunset Boulevard, © 1950 Paramount Pictures; *Seminary Girls*, © 1897 Edison Manufacturing Company; *Children Digging for Clams*, © 1896 Lumière; *Long Distance Wireless Photography*, © Image Entertainment; *The Great Train Robbery*, © 1908 Edison Manufacturing Company; *Making an American Citizen*, © 1921 Solax Film Company; *Birth of a Nation*, © 1915 D. W. Griffith Productions; *The Crowd*, © 1928 Metro-Goldwyn-Mayer; *The Cabinet of Dr. Caligari* (2 images), © 1920 Decla-Bioscop AG; *Nosferatu*, © 1922 Jofa-Atelier Berlin-Johannisthal; *The Last Laugh*, © 1924 Universum Film (UFA); *The Fall of the House of Usher*, © 1928 Films Jean Epstein; *The Wheel*, © 1923 Films Abel Gance; *The Man with the Movie Camera*, © 1929 VUFKU; *Alexander Nevsky*, © 1938 Mosfilm; Battleship Potemkin, © 1925 Goskino; *Mr. Smith Goes to Washington*, © 1939 Columbia Pictures Corporation; *The Jazz Singer*, © 1927/1952 Warner Bros. Pictures; *Easy Living*, © 1937 Paramount Pictures; *Baby Face*, © 1933 Stable Films; *Gone with the Wind*, © 1939 Selznick International Pictures; *Citizen Kane*, © 1941 Mercury Productions; Ossessione, © 1943 Industrie Cinematografiche Italiane; *The Bicycle Thieves*, © 1948 Produzioni De Sica; *Breathless*, © 1960 Société Nouvelle de Cinématographie/Metro-Goldwyn-Mayer; *The 400 Blows*, © 1959 Les Films du Carrosse; *The Butcher*, © 1970 Les Films de la Boétie; *Cleo from 5 to 7*, © 1962 Ciné Tamaris; *Victim*, © 1961 Allied Film Makers; *Breaking the Waves*, © 1996 Argus Film Produktie; *The American Friend*, © 1977 Filmverlag der Autoren; *In the Realm of the Senses*, © 1976 Argos Films; *Ran*, © 1985 Greenwich Film Productions; *Sansho the Bailiff*, © 1954 Daiei Studios; *Tokyo Story*, © 1953 Shôchiku Eiga; *Farewell My Concubine*, © 1993 Beijing Film Studio; *A Better Tomorrow*, © 1986 Cinema City Film Productions; *Crouching Tiger, Hidden Dragon*, © 2000 Asia Union Film & Entertainment Ltd.; *Pather Panchali*, © 1955 Government of West Bengal; *Stranger Than Paradise*, © 1984 Cinesthesia Productions; *Bonnie and Clyde*, © 1967 Tatira-Hiller Productions; *Chinatown*, © 1974 Paramount Pictures; *The Wild Bunch*, © 1969 Warner Brothers/Seven Arts; *Grey Gardens*, © 1975 Portrait Films; *Dog Star Man*, © 1962 Stant Backhage.

Index

Page numbers in *italics* refer to illustrations and captions; those in **boldface** refer to main discussions of topics.

A

Aardman Animations, 113
ABBA, *107*
Abel, Richard, 435
About Schmidt (Payne), 291
Abrams, J. J., *Super 8,* 66, 85
Abyss, The (Cameron), 281
Academy of Motion Picture Arts and Sciences, 68, 192, 194, 504
Accatone (Pasolini), 405
Ace in the Hole (Wilder), 96
Ackroyd, Barry, *246*
Across the Universe (Taymor), 107, *107*
acting, **287–338**
    analyzing of, *331*
    casting actors and, **310–14,** *312, 313*
    casting factors in, **310–14**
    classical studio era and, **299–392**
    contemporary, **305–9,** *312*
    defined, **288–95**
    early screen styles of, **294–95**
    editing and, **327**
    ensemble, 325–26
    evolution of screen, **294–310**
    filmmaking and, **322–27,** *324, 326, 327*
    framing, composition, lighting, and the long take, **323–26**
    improvisational, 294, *320,* **320–21**
    influence of sound, *297,* **297–99**
    movie actors and, **289–94**
    movie stars and, **299–302,** *302*
    nonnaturalistic, 292
    performances, **327–36,** *329*
    preparing for roles, **316–18,** *317*
    stage vs. screen, 288–89
    Stanislavsky and method acting, **302–4**
    styles, **318–20,** *319*
    subtext and, 303
    technology and, 309–10
    types of actors and, 290–94
    types of roles, **314–16**
action genre, *209*
Actor Prepares, An (Stanislavsky), 303
actors:
    casting of, **310–14,** *312, 313*
    chameleon-type, 290, 292–94
    directors and, **321–22**
    movie, **289–94**
    nonnaturalistic, 292
    personality-type, 290, 291–92
    types of, 290–94

Actors Studio, 303
actualités, *59,* 439
Adajama, Homi, *Being Cyrus,* 472
Adam, Ken, 199
Adamson, Andrew, *Shrek,* 113
Adaptation (Jonze), 345
adaptations:
    for film, *146, 183,* 194, *317*
    literary, 143–45
additive color systems, 234
Adler, Stella, 303
Adrian, *192*
Adventure, The (Antonioni), 200
Adventures of Tintin, The (Spielberg), 516
Æon Flux (Kusama), 188, *189*
aerial-view shot, **263–64,** *277*
Affron, Charles, 300
African Americans:
    actors, 442
    casting of, 311
    movies about, 311, 312–13
African Queen, The (Huston), 307, 502
After Dark, My Sweet (Foley), 96
After the Thin Man (Van Dyke), 496
Agadzhanova, Nina, 151
Agantuk (S. Ray), 472
age and casting, 314
Age of Innocence, The (Scorsese), 197
Agfa film, 235

Aguirre: The Wrath of God (Herzog), 418, 464

Aguirresarobe, Javier, 265

Aibel, Jonathan, 129

Aiello, Danny, 261, *261*

Ajantrik (Ghatak), 472

Akerman, Chantal, 137, 319

Akinnuoye-Agbaje, Adewale, 517

Akira (Otomo), 98

Alcott, John, 236, *236*, 261, 273

Aldrich, Robert, 301
    Kiss Me Deadly, 96
    What Ever Happened to Baby Jane?, 307

Aleksandrov, Grigori, 351, *352*

Alexander (Stone), 269

Alexander Nevsky (Eisenstein and Vasilyev), 172, 195, 405, 449, *449*

Alexie, Sherman, *The Business of Fancydancing*, 314

Alfie (Gilbert), 123, 319

Alfie (Shyer), 319

Alfredson, Tomas, *Let the Right One In*, *59*, 102

Alice in Chains, 408

Alice in Wonderland (Burton), *190*, 211, 292, 516, 517

Alice's Adventures in Wonderland (Carroll), *190*

Alien (R. Scott), 98, 416

alienation effect, 318

Alive (Marshall), 133

All About Eve (Mankiewicz), 302, 307

Alland, William, 146, 241, *241*

Allen, Dede, 368

Allen, Joan, 395

Allen, Robert C., 299, 432

Allen, Woody, 109, 137, 155, 210, *239*, 293, 311, 473
    Annie Hall, 87
    Shadows and Fog, 197
    Vicky Cristina Barcelona, 311

All or Nothing (Leigh), 321

Allures (Belson), 81

Almendros, Néstor, 258, *259*, 475

Almirante-Manzini, Italia, *185*

Almodóvar, Pedro, 265–66, 461
    Broken Embraces, 96
    Volver, 155

Alonso, Lisandro, *Los Muertos*, 325*n*

Alonzo, John, 475

Alonzo, John A., 231

Alphaville (Godard), 97

Altman, Robert, 208, 293, 294, 304, 473, 492
    Gosford Park, 321
    Kansas City, 304
    McCabe & Mrs. Miller, 105
    Nashville, 321
    The Player, 304–5, 315, 416
    Short Cuts, *305*, 321

Alton, John, 227, 242

Alvarado, Trini, *331*

Alvemark, Jan, 421

Amalric, Mathieu, 274

Amazing Grace (Apted), 156

ambient sound, 401

AMC Theaters, 490–91

Amenábar, Alejandro, *The Others*, 102

American Beauty (Mendes), 41, 211, **215–20**, *216–18, 220*, 419

American Cinema Editors, 504

American Federation of Television and Radio Artists (AFTRA), 311

American Film Institute, 307

American Friend, The (Wenders), 464, *465*

American Gangster (R. Scott), 88

American in Paris, An (Minelli), 108, 181

Americanizing the Movies and "Movie-Mad" Audiences, 1910–1914 (Abel), 435

American Movie (Smith), *74*

American Society of Cinematographers, 504

Ames, E. Preston, 181, 182

amplitude, 394

analog, **486**

analysis, 7
    alternative approaches to, 20–22, *21*
    cultural, **22–31**
    formal, 14–20, **22–31**

Anchal, Rajiv, *Guru*, 472

Ancillai, Fausto, 415, *415*

Andalusian Dog, An (Buñuel and Dali), *78*, 79, 447

Anderson, Ken, 143

Anderson, Lindsay:
    Every Day Except Christmas, 462
    if...., 462
    The Whales of August, 307

Anderson, Paul Thomas, *406*, 514
    There Will Be Blood, 200, 404

Anderson, Philip W., 372

Anderson, Wes, 349, 404
    The Darjeeling Limited, 181
    Fantastic Mr. Fox, 112
    The Royal Tenenbaums, 125, *126*, 461

Andersson, Harriet, 370

Andersson, Roy, 202
    You, the Living, 421

Andrei Rublev (Tarkovsky), 172

Andrews, Dana, *203*, 407

Andrews, Michael, 419

Anémic cinéma (Duchamp), 79

Anger, Kenneth, *Scorpio Rising*, 81

animal actors, 316

animated films, **111–15**, *114*, 441, 443
    digital, 111, 112–13, *114*
    hand-drawn, 111, *114*
    motion capture, 113–14
    stop-motion, 111–12

Ankur (Benegal), 472

Annakin, Ken, 156

Ann Arbor Film Festival, 82

Annie Hall (Allen), 87

antagonist, 92, 94, 97, *100*, 103, *103*, 133

Antareen (Sen), 472

antihero, *92*, 94, 129

antirealism, 56–57, 205
    realism and, *56*, **56–60**, *58*, 205, 358

Antonioni, Michelangelo, 200, 201, 208, 457, 461, 474, 477
    The Red Desert, 409

Aparajito (S. Ray), 471

Apar Sansar (S. Ray), 471

Apartment, The (Wilder), 130–31

Apatow, Judd:
    The 40 Year Old Virgin, 109
    Knocked Up, *21*, 22, 109, *319*

aperture, 244, **487**

Apocalypse Now (F. F. Coppola), 202, 343, 390, *394*, 395, 408, 419, *420*, 492

Apocalypse Now Redux (F. F. Coppola), 202, 343

Appaloosa (Harris), 105

apparent motion, 49

Applause (Mamoulian), 107, 252, *254*, 298, 390

Apple, 74–75

À propos de Nice (Vigo), 448

Apted, Michael, 293
    Amazing Grace, 156

"Apu" trilogy (S. Ray), 200, 401, 471–72, *471*

Arbuckle, Roscoe "Fatty," 108, 442
Argento, Dario, *Suspiria, 101, 196*
Arikawa, Sadamasa, 280
Aristotle, 137
Arnaz, Desi, 501
Arnfred, Morton, *The Kingdom,* 102
Arnold, Edward, *452*
Arnold, Jack, *It Came from Outer
    Space,* 98
Arnold, John, 268
Arnold, Lamont, *44*
Arnold, Martin, *Passage à l'acte,* 79
Arnold, Wilfred, 182
Arnulf Rainer (Kubelka), 81
Aronofsky, Darren, 277, *341*
    Black Swan, 127, 128–29, 132, 133,
        207–8, 516
    Sin City, 231
    The Wrestler, 83
Arrested Development, 13, 14
Arriaga, Guillermo, 67
    The Burning Plain, 188
art director, 180–82, 194
    see also production, design in
Arthur, Jean, *452*
Artist, The (Hazanavicius), 299
Artists under the Big Top: Perplexed
    (Kluge), 464
Aseyev, Nikolai, 151
Ashby, Hal, 329, 375
Ashes of Time (Kar), 469
aspect ratio, 248, *249,* 257
Asphalt Jungle (Huston), 96
*Assassination of the Duke de Guise,
    The* (Calmettes and
    Le Bargy), 404
assassination sequence table from
    The Birth of a Nation,
    378–80
assistant producers, 502
associate producers, 502
Astaire, Fred, 105, 209, *210*
Astor, Mary, 260, *260, 315*
Astronomer's Dream, The (Gehr), 81
Astruc, Alexandre, 458
asynchronous sound, 397–98
Atonement (Wright), *48,* 54, 145, 200
Attenborough, Richard, 264, *313,* 314
    Chaplin, 305
    Grey Owl, 314
Atwood, Colleen, 189, *190*
audience awareness, **415–16**
audience expectations, **416,** *417*
auditory point of view, *159*
Audran, Stéphane, *460*

August, John, 155
August, Joseph H., 263
Austen, Jane, 201
auteur theory, 137, 433, 460, 465, 466,
    473
Automatic Dialogue Replacement
    (ADR), 392, *392*
Autumn Afternoon, An (Ozu), 201, 466
Avalanche (Naruse), *325n*
avant-garde films, 67, 68, 76, 81, 82,
    272, 358, 409
    defined, 76
    French, 445–48
    see also experimental films
Avary, Robert, *The Rules of
    Attraction, 375, 375*
Avary, Roger, 146
Avatar (Cameron), 89, *98,* 99, 113,
    179, *179, 310,* 516, 517
Aviator, The (Scorsese), 314
Avildson, John G., *Rocky,* 130, *131*
axis of action, 359, *363*
    see also 180–degree system
Ayers, Lemuel, 182

B

Babel (González Iñárritu), 291
Baby Face (Green), *453*
Bach, Johann Sebastian, 405, 409
background music, 161–62
backlight, 241, *241*
Back Stage, 311
backstory, 143, 148
Back to the Future (Zemeckis), 14
Bacon, Lloyd:
    Footlight Parade, 108
    42nd Street, 108
Badger, Clarence, 191
Badlands (Malick), 123, *258,* 293,
    400, 475
Bagdasarian, Ross, *368*
Baggot, King, *Tumbleweeds,* 105
Bagier, W.L., Jr., 390
Bailey, Pearl, 313
Baillie, Bruce, 476
    Mass for the Dakota Sioux, 81
Balagueró, Jaume, *Rec,* 102
Baldwin, Alec, 125
Baldwin, Craig, *Tribulation 99: Alien
    Anomalies under America,*
    79, *80*
Bale, Christian, *145,* 292
Balint, Eszter, *473*
Balio, Tino, 300, 434

Ball, Alan, 41
Ball, Arthur, 234
Ball, Lucille, 501
Ballad of Little Jo, The (Greenwald),
    105
Ballast (Hammer), 83, 410
Ballet mécanique (Léger and
    Murphy), *77, 79,* 446–47
Ballhaus, Michael, 269, 273
Ball of Fire (Hawks), 331
Bancroft, Anne, 248, *250*
Bancroft, George, 157, *158*
Banderas, Antonio, *312,* 313
Band Wagon, The (Minelli), 108
Bangkok Dangerous (Pang and
    Pang), *91*
Bank Dick, The (Cline), *316*
Bank of America, 498
Banks, Caerthan, 418
Banksy, *Exit Through the Gift Shop, 76*
Bannerjee, Subir, 401
Baquero, Ivana, *173*
Bara, Theda, 191
Baragli, Nino, 354
Barber, Samuel, 419
Barberis, Alberto, 404, *405*
Bardem, Javier, 288, 311, 313
Barker, Clive, *Hellraiser,* 102
barn doors, 237
Barney, Matthew, 82
Barney's Vision (Lewis), 290
Baron, Suzanne, *373*
Baron Cohen, Sacha, *82*
Barry Lyndon (Kubrick), 199, 236,
    236, 245, 322, 396
Barrymore, Drew, 143
Barrymore, Lionel, 295
Barthelmess, Richard, 42, 296, 311
Basinger, Jeanine, 300, *301,* 432
Bass, Saul, *397*
Bassan, Giuseppe, *196*
Bateman, Jason, *11*
Batman (Burton), 211
Batman Forever (Shumacher), 307
Bato, Joseph, *199*
Battisti, Carlo, 328
Battleship Potemkin (Eisenstein), 151,
    155, 351, *352,* 449, 450, *450*
Battles without Honor or Humanity
    (Fukasaku), 93
Bauer, Mary, 347
Baumbach, Noah, *Margot at the
    Wedding, 306,* 307
Bava, Mario, 212
    Black Sunday, 101

Bay, Michael:
    The Rock, 91
    Transformers, 115
    Transformers: Dark of the Moon,
        514
    Transformers: Revenge of the
        Fallen, 403
Bazelli, Bojan, 250
Bazin, André, 161, 256, 309, 349,
    458–59
    "The Evolution of the Language
        of Cinema," 459
BBC Films, 505
Beach, Adam, 314
Beatles, The, *107*
Beatty, Warren, *41, 474*
Beaufoy, Simon, 133
Beaumont, Harry, *The Broadway*
    Melody, 106
Beavers, Louise, 313
Beck, Mat, 279
Becker, Jacques, 458
    Touchez pas au grisbi, 93
Beckert, Hans, 319
Becky Sharp (Mamoulian), 235
Bedard, Irene, 314
Beebe, Roger, *The Strip Mall*
    Trilogy, 82
Beethoven, Ludwig van, *407,* 421, *422*
Before Night Falls (Schnabel), 312
Beijing Opera, 468
Being Cyrus (Adajama), 472
Being John Malkovich (Jonze), 317
Being There (Ashby), 329
Bekmambetov, Timur, *Nightwatch,*
    102
Belle de Jour (Buñuel), 447
Belmondo, Jean-Paul, *361, 459*
Belson, Jordan, *Allures,* 81
Belton, John, 434
Benavente, Michael J., 397
Benchley, Peter, 133
Benegal, Shyam, 472
    Ankur, 472
    Bhumika, 472
    Manthan, 472
    Nehru, 472
    Nishant, 472
    Satyajit Ray, Filmmaker, 472
Ben-Hur (Wyler), 60
Ben Hur: A Tale of the Christ
    (Niblo), 60
Bening, Annette, 41, 215
Benitani, Kenichi, 409
Bennett, Belle, *331*

Bennett, Tony, 412
Bentley, Wes, 41, 217, *218, 220*
Benton, Robert, *The Human Stain,*
    306, 307, 312
Beowulf, 145
Beowulf (Zemeckis), 283
Berenson, Marisa, 322, 396
Berg, Peter, *Hancock,* 188
Berger, Ludwig, 200
Bergfelder, Ulrich, 181
Bergman, Ingmar, 370, *372,* 461,
    474, 477
    Persona, 81
    The Seventh Seal, 231, *232*
    Wild Strawberries, 409
Bergman, Ingrid, 123, *255,* 268, *301*
Berkeley, Busby, 254
Berkey, Craig, 410
Berlin Alexanderplatz (Fassbinder),
    464
Bernhardt, Curtis, 301
    Miss Sadie Thompson, 515
Bernhardt, Sarah, 295
Bernstein, Elmer, 404
Bernstein, Leonard, 404
Berry, Graham, 277
Berry, Halle, 313, *313*
Bertolucci, Bernardo, *157,* 172,
    320, 457
Bertrand, Pierre-André, 398
Best, Ahmed, 309
Best, Eve, 251
best boy, 228
Best Years of Our Lives, The (Wyler),
    203, 228, 326, 499
Bettany, Paul, 319
Better Tomorrow, A (Woo), 469, *469*
Betty Boop, 443
Bewitched (Ephron), 307
Bhumika (Benegal), 472
Bhuvan Shome (Sen), 472
Bicycle Thieves, The (De Sica), 200,
    200, 456, *457,* 471
Bier, Susanne, *Open Hearts,* 463
Bigelow, Kathryn, *The Hurt Locker,*
    133, *246, 387,* 403
Big Heat, The (Lang), 230
Big Lebowski, The (Coen and Coen),
    132, *132,* 133, *308*
Big Parade, The (Vidor), 268, 442
Big Sleep, The (Hawks), 96
Big Trail, The (Walsh), 105, 248, *308*
Big Tree, Chief, 314
Bindler, S.R., *Hands on a Hard Body,* 74
Binoche, Juliet, *292*

biography (biopic) genre, *145,* 156, *157*
Birch, Albert, 398, *417*
Birch, Thora, 41, 215, *218, 220*
Bird, Antonia, *Ravenous,* 108
Bird, Brad:
    The Incredibles, 111, 114–15
    The Iron Giant, 99, 111
    Ratatouille, 111, 181
Birds, The (Hitchcock), 101, 264, 275,
    277, 322, 352, *417*
bird's-eye-view shot, *see* aerial-view
    shot
Birth (Glazer), 278–79, *278,* 326
Birth of a Nation, The (Griffith), 191,
    265, 296, 312, 376, *376,* 381,
    441, 442, *443*
    assassination sequence table,
        378–80
    racism in, 442
Bismuth, Pierre, 146
bit players, 316
Bitzer, G. W., 234, 252
Björklund, Timothy, *Teacher's Pet,* 108
Blaché, Alice Guy, 442, *443*
Black, Dustin Lance, 156
black and white film, **231–34,** 454
    color vs., 230–31, *230, 232*
    moral or ethical implications of,
        231
    in *The Seventh Seal,* 231–32, *232*
    tonality, 233–34, *233*
Black Cat, The (Murnau), 182
Black Cloud (Schroder), 314
Black Friday (Kashyap), 472
Black Hawk Down (Scott), 39, *39,* 408
Blackman, Jeremy, *406*
Black Maria, *438,* **438**
Black Narcissus (Powell and
    Pressburger), 200
Black Pirate, The (Parker), 234
Black Sunday (Bava), 101, 212
Black Swan (Aronofsky), *127,* 128–29,
    132, 133, 207–8, 516
Blackton, J. Stuart, *The Life of*
    Moses, 442
Blade II (del Toro), 13
Blade Runner (R. Scott), 97, 98, 156,
    156, 281
Blair Witch Project, The, (Myrick and
    Sánchez), 102
Blake, Robert, *229*
Blamey, Brian, *407*
Blanchett, Cate, 291, *291*
Bleibtreu, Moritz, 352, *354*
blimp, 255, 297–98

Blochberger, Ludwig, *144*
blocking, 209
Blomkamp, Neill, *District 9,* 99, *130*
Blondie of the Follies (Goulding), 499
Blood of a Poet, The (Cocteau), 448
Blood Wedding (Saura), 108
Bloom, Orlando, 311
Blow (T. Demme), 293
Blue Angel, The (von Sternberg), 444
Blue Sky Studios, 281
Blue Valentine (Cianfrance),
    333–36, *334*
Blue Velvet (Lynch), 130, 202
"B" movies, 93, 99
Boal, Mark, 133
Bob le flambeur (Melville), 460
body actor, **283**
Boese, Carl, *The Golem,* 444
Bogarde, Dirk, 299, *462*
Bogart, Humphrey, 94, 260, *260,*
    315, 322, 328, *357,* 358
Bogdanov, Mikhail, 197
Bogdanovich, Peter, *The Last Picture*
    Show, 474
Bogdanski, Hagen, 228
Boland, Mary, 315
Boles, John, 331
Bollywood, 4, *5,* 470, 472
Bonanova, Fortunio, *454*
Bondarchuk, Sergei, *War and*
    Peace, 197
Bonham Carter, Helena, *6, 190*
Bonnefoy, Mathilde, 351, 352
Bonnie and Clyde (Penn), *41,* 86, 93,
    349, 368, 461, 474, *474, 475*
Bonvillain, Michael, *57,* 272
Book of Eli, The (Hughes and
    Hughes), *250*
boom operator, 391
booms, *297*
Boone, Pat, 499
Boorman, John, 368
Booth, John Wilkes, *380*
Borat: Cultural Learnings of America
    for Make Benefit Glorious
    Nation of Kazakhstan
    (Charles), *82*
Bordwell, David, 434
Born into Brothels (Briski and
    Kauffman), 67–68
Bourne movies (Greengrass), *382*
Bourne Supremacy, The (Greengrass),
    272, *272,* 352, 406
Bow, Clara, 191
Bowden, Mark, *39*

Bowers, David, *Flushed Away,* 113
Bowling for Columbine (Moore), 72
Boyd, Russell, 282
Boyer, Charles, 497
Boyle, Danny, 123, 146
    127 Hours, 133, 135, *135*
    Slumdog Millionaire, 403, *403*
    28 Days Later..., 100, *102*
Boys Don't Cry (Peirce), 344
Boys from Vietnam, The (Hui), 469
Bracco, Lorraine, 273
Braindead, (Jackson), 102
Brakhage, Stan, 476
    Dog Star Man, 81, *476*
Branagh, Kenneth, *209*
    Thor, 85
Brando, Marlon, *241,* 303–4, *303,* 311,
    320, 327, 329
Brandon, Henry, 314
Brandt, Byron, 375
Brannon, Ash, *Toy Story 2,* 309
Braudy, Leo, 205
Brazil (Gilliam), 98, 202
Breakfast at Tiffany's (Edwards), 312
Breakfast with Scot (Lynd), 314
Breaking the Waves (von Trier),
    463, *463*
Breathless (Godard), 87, 351, 358, *361,*
    459–60, *459*
Brecht, Bertolt, 318–19, 320
Breen, Joseph, 452
Breer, Robert, *Fist Fight,* 81
Brennan, Walter, 155, 315
Bresson, Robert, 208, 398, 458
Brick (Johnson), *95*
Bride of Frankenstein, The (Whale),
    101, *102, 195,* 241, *241,* 263,
    263, 415
Bridesmaids (Feig), 109, 134
Bridge on the River Kwai, The (Lean),
    502
Bridges, Jeff, 132, *132,* 292, *308*
Bright, Cameron, 278
Bright Star (Epstein and Friedman),
    156
Bringing Up Baby (Hawks), 399
Bring Me the Head of Alfredo Garcia
    (Peckinpah), *475*
Briski, Zana, *Born into Brothels,* 67
British cinema, **200**
Broadway Melody, The (Beaumont), *106*
Broderick, Matthew, 123
Brody, Adrien, *346*
Brokeback Mountain (A. Lee), *2,*
    110–11, 470, *470,* 495

Broken Blossoms (Griffith), 234, 296,
    296, 311, 442
Broken Embraces (Almodóvar), 96
Broken Flowers (Jarmusch), 90
Brolin, Josh, 288
Bronson, Charles, 355, 415
Brooks, Louise, 297
Brooks, Mel, 280, 419
    The Producers, 109
Brooks, Richard:
    Cat on a Hot Tin Roof, 302
    In Cold Blood, 229
Brosnan, Pierce, 314
Brothers Grimm, The (Gilliam), 202
Broughton, James, *Mother's Day,* 81
Brown, Clarence, 496–97
Brown, Garrett, 273
Brown, Hilyard, 186
Brown, Joe E., *154*
Brown, Royal S., 404, 407
Browning, Tod:
    Dracula, 99, *109*
    Freaks, 101
Bruce, Sally Jane, *186, 370,* 414
Bruckenheimer, Jerry, 517
"B" studios, 460, 498–99
Bubble (Soderbergh), 517
Buck Rogers in the 25th Century
    (Haller), 191
Buena Vista Productions, 499
Buffy the Vampire Slayer, 107
Buffy the Vampire Slayer (Kuzui), *110*
bullet time, *50*
Bullock, Sandra, 143, 309
Buñuel, Luis:
    An Andalusian Dog, 78, 79, 447
    Belle de Jour, 447
    The Discreet Charm of the
        Bourgeoisie, 448
    The Milky Way, 81
    Viridiana, 447
Burch, Noël, 204
Burgess, Don, 281, 283
Burks, Robert, 260, 264, 275, *277*
Burn after Reading (E. Coen), 288
Burning Plain, The (Arriaga), 188
Burns, Ken, 74–75
Burr, Raymond, *368*
Burstyn, Ellen, 303
Burt, Donald Graham, *184*
Burton, Tim, 155, 179, *189, 190,*
    211–15, *215,* 319, *319,* 322,
    404, 473, 490
    Alice in Wonderland, 190, 211, 292,
        516, 517

Burton, Tim (*continued*)
  Charlie and the Chocolate Factory,
    190, 211
  Dark Shadows, 292
  Edward Scissorhands, 292
  Frankenweenie, 112
  Sleepy Hollow, 216
  *Sweeney Todd: The Demon Barber
    of Fleet Street, 6, 171,* 211
Burum, Stephen H., 277
Burwell, Carter, 404, 410, 421
Buscemi, Steve, 517
Bush, George W., 288
Business of Fancydancing, The
    (Alexie), 314
Butch Cassidy and the Sundance Kid
    (Hill), *103,* 110, *110*
Butcher, The (Chabrol), 459, *460*
Butler, Bill, 280
Butterfield 8 (Mann), *302*
Butterfly Murders, The (Hark), 469
Butterworth, Edwin, 280
Büttner, Tilman, 278

C

Caballero, Eugenio, *173,* 182
Cabaret (Fosse), 108
Cabinet of Dr. Caligari, The (Wiene),
    99, *195, 196,* 197, *199,* 234,
    444, *445, 446*
Cabiria (Pastrone), 184, *185,* 191, 442
Cage, Nicolas, *91,* 367
Cagney, James, 92–93, *92,* 103, 193
Cahiers du cinéma, 458–59
Caine, Michael, *289,* 319
Calamai, Clara, *456*
California Indian (Ramos), 314
Calmettes, André, *The Assassination
    of the Duke de Guise,* 404
Cámara, Javier, 265
cameos, 188, 315
camera, *198*
  close-ups and, *326,* **326–27,** *327*
  handheld, 266, **272,** *273*
  vs. human eye, 51, 204
  as narrator, 123
  Steadicam, 185, 266, **272–74,** *273,*
    278
  Technicolor and, 234–35
  tripods and, 266
  video assist, 194
camera angle and height, **259–64,**
    260, 261, 262, 263, 277
camera crew, 228

camera movement, **265–74,** *267, 268,*
    270, 273
camera obscura, **435,** *436*
camera operator, 228
camerapersons, 228
Cameron, James, 143, *238,* 281, 314,
    490, 503
  Avatar, 89, *98,* 99, 113, 179, *179,*
    310, 516, 517
  Terminator movies, 97
Camille (Cukor), 496
Campbell, Martin, *The Green
    Lantern,* 85
Camper, Fred, 76, 81
Campion, Jane, 329, 461
  The Portrait of a Lady, 307
Cannibal! The Musical, (Parker), 107
Canosa, Hans, *Conversations with
    Other Women,* 375
Capote, Truman, *229*
Capote (Miller), 329
Capra, Frank, 293
  It Happened One Night, 109
  Meet John Doe, 109, *451*
  Mr. Deeds Goes to Town, 451
  Mr. Smith Goes to Washington, 451
Capturing the Friedmans (Jarecki), 75
Cardinale, Claudia, 175, *176*
Carell, Lianella, 456
Carey, Harry, 295
Carey, Harry, Jr., 315
Carlini, Carlo, 210
Carlos, Wendy, 389
Carmen Jones (Preminger), 313, *313*
Carney, John, *Once,* 4, 272, 408, 457
Carnival of Souls (Harvey), 101
Caro, Marc, 418
Caro, Niki, *North Country,* 188, *189,* 293
Carpenter, John, *Starman,* 292, *308*
Carpenter, Russell, *238*
Carradine, John, 46, 157, *158, 207*
Carrey, Jim, 109, 421
Carrie (De Palma), 102, 293
Carroll, Diahann, 313, *313*
Carroll, Lewis, *190*
Cars 2 (Lasseter and Lewis), 85
Carter, John R., 419
Carter, Rick, 179
cartoons, 234–35
  see also animated films
Carver, Raymond, 145
Casablanca (Curtiz), *147, 357,* 358,
    507, *508–9*
Casper (Siberling), 281, 282
Cassavetes, John, 321, 473

Cassel, Vincent, 208
Cast Away (Zemeckis), 494
casting, **310–14,** *313*
  of African Americans, 311
  age and, 311, 314
  defined, 310
  ethnicity and, 311
  factors in, **311–14**
  gender and, 311, 314
  of Native Americans, 314
  screen tests in, 311
  stereotypical, 187
Casting Society of America (CSA),
    310
catalyst, 132
  see also inciting incident
Catholic Church, 456
  censorship and, 452
Cat on a Hot Tin Roof (Brooks), *302*
Cat People (Tourneur), 101
causality, *68, 142*
Cavalcanti, Alberto, *Rien que les
    heures,* 447
cel animation, 111
Celine and Julie Go Boating (Rivette),
    459
cels, defined, 46
censorship, 441, 442, 452, *453,* 511
central producers, 495
Cera, Michael, 13, *14*
"Certain Tendency of the French
    Cinema, A" (Truffaut), 458
CGI, *see* computer-generated
    imagery
Chabrol, Claude, 458
  The Butcher, 459, *460*
Chaffey, Don, *Jason and the
    Argonauts,* 112
chambara genre, 108
chameleon-type actors, 290, 292–94
Chan, Jackie, *209,* 469
Chandler, Raymond, 129
Chaney, Lon, 193
Chapin, Billy, *186,* 414
Chaplin, Charles, *52,* 53, 108, 303,
    317, 442, 498
  The Gold Rush, 443
Chaplin (Attenborough), *305,* 314
Chapman, Michael, 277
character roles, 315, *316*
characters:
  development of, 129, *130*
  flat, 160
  goals of, 127, *131*

minor, 160
motivation of, 130
narrative and, **127–31**, *128,* 160
sidekick, 92
sound and, **419,** *420, 421,* **426–28**
in *Stagecoach* (Ford), *158,* 160,
    162–63
types of, 88, **127–31**
Charisma (Kurosawa), *250*
Charles, Larry, *Borat: Cultural
    Learnings of America for
    Make Benefit Glorious
    Nation of Kazakhstan,* 82
Charlie and the Chocolate Factory
    (Burton), 155, *190,* 211
Charlie's Angels (McG), 315
Charlone, César, 187
Charulata (S. Ray), 201, 472
Chase, Borden, 155
Chase Manhattan Bank, 498
Chasney, Jasmine, 345
Chatterjee, Soumitra, 322
Chatwin, Justin, 411
Chaykin, Maury, 418
Chekhov, Anton, 40
Chen, Joan, 313
Cheng Pei-pei, *470*
Chen Kaige, 201
    Farewell My Concubine, 468, *468*
Chereau, Patrice, *Gabrielle,* 410
Cheung, Alex, *The First Step: Facing
    Death,* 469
Chevalier, Maurice, *106,* 260, *261,* 395
Chew, Richard, 372
Cheyenne Autumn (Ford), 314
Chiari, Mario, 210
chiaroscuro, *47, 102,* 186
Chicago (Marshall), 108
Chicago 10 (Morgen), 111
Chieko Higashiyama, *468*
Children Digging for Clams (Lumière
    and Lumière), *439*
Children of Men (Cuarón), 99
China, 467–70
    Hong Kong, 468–69
    People's Republic of, 467–70
    Taiwan, 469–70
Chinatown (Polanski), 96, 199, 204,
    205, 231, 304, 317, 474, *474*
Chinese cinema, 201
Chishu Ryu, *468*
Chocolat (Hallström), *292*
Choi, Cliford, 469
Chopper (Dominik), 156
Chow, Yun-Fat, 54, 314, 469

Christ, Jesus, Harry Potter and,
    25–26, *26*
Christianity, *Harry Potter* movies
    and, 26
chronophotographic gun, **436**
Churchill, Berton, 157, *158, 207*
Churchill, Winston, *25*
Cianfrance, Derek, *Blue Valentine,*
    333–36
Cinderella (Jackson), 143
Cinderfella (Tashlin), 143
cinema:
    compared to live theater, 5
    defined, 3
    of ideas, *84*
    independent filmmakers and,
        472–73
    Indian, 470–72
    international, 461–72
    Parallel Cinema and, 472
    of reinvention, 460
cinematic, conventions, 205, 208,
        238, 240–41, 257, **355–64**
cinematic language, 3, 7–11, 36,
    60–61, *61*
cinematic time, 151, 275
Cinématographe, 439
cinematographer, 226–28
cinematography, **225–86**
    blimp in, 255
    camera movement in, **265–74,**
        267, 268, 270, 273
    camera proximity and, **248–52**
    color in, **242–44**
    computer-generated imagery,
        280–83
    cranes shots in, **269–70**
    deep-focus, 325
    defined, 226
    depth and, **252–59**
    director of photography and,
        226–28
    dolly shot in, *267, 267,* **267–68**
    film stock used in, **229–36,** *233*
    framing in, **248–75,** *263, 264,* 266,
        270, 273, 277
    handheld cameras in, 266, **272,**
        273
    lenses in, **244–47,** *245, 247,*
        254–55, 268–69
    lighting in, **236–44,** *238, 239*
    properties of the shot in, **228–48**
    scale in, *264,* **264–65**
    shot speed and length in, **275–79**
    Technicolor in, 234–35, 255

tracking shot in, 268
types of shots in, *270*
zoom in, 268–69, 271
cinéma vérité, 266, 458, 475
Citizen Kane (Welles), 46, 54, 146, *147,*
    149, 151, *195, 199,* 228, 238,
    239, 241, *241,* 254–55, 267,
    267, 314, **323–26,** *324,* 345,
    346, 418, **423–28,** *424, 425,*
    426, 427, 431, 441, 454, *454,*
    492, 503
    cinematography in, 228
    lighting in, 185
City of God (Meirelles and Lund), 53,
    54, 93, 187, *188,* 358, 376–84,
    381, 382, 383
City of Sadness, A (Hou), 201, 470
City on Fire (Lam), 469
City Streets (Mamoulian), 298*n*
city symphonies, 447
Clair, René, 174, 398
    Entr'acte, 79, 446
    An Italian Straw Hat, 448
    Le Million, 108
Clark, Alfred, 279
Clark, Daniel, *10*
Clarke, Arthur C., 155
Clarke, Shirley, *Skyscraper,* 81
*Classical Hollywood Cinema, The:
    Film Study and Mode of
    Production to 1960*
    (Bordwell, Staiger, and
    Thompson), 434
classical music in film, 397, 404, *407*
Claymation, 113
Clayton, Curtiss, 347, *373,* 375
Clayton, Jack:
    The Innocents, 101
    Room at the Top, 462
Cleo from 5 to 7 (Varda), 459, *460*
Cleopatra (Edwards), 191
Cleopatra (Mankiewicz), 191, *302*
Clift, Montgomery, 304
climax, 135–36, *136*
Cline, Edward, *316*
Clive, Colin, 263
Clockwork Orange, A (Kubrick), 322,
    407
Clooney, George, 288, 314, 348, *349,*
    367
    Good Night, and Good Luck, 231,
        305
    Leatherheads, 452
Cloquet, Ghislain, 210
closed frames, **205–8**

Close Encounters of the Third Kind (Spielberg), *97, 281*

close-up, 5, 51, 252, *252, 278, 326,* **326–27,** *327*

Cloutier, Suzanne, 404, *405*

Cloverfield (Reeves), *57,* 272, 457

Coal Miner's Daughter (Apted), 293

Coates, Anne V., 348, 364, *365,* 367

Cocteau, Jean, 458, 459
  The Blood of a Poet, 448

Cody, Diablo, *11,* 20

Coen, Ethan, 304

Coen, Ethan and Joel, 137, 288, 473
  The Big Lebowski, 132, *132,* 133, *308*
  Intolerable Cruelty, 452
  No Country for Old Men, 410
  Raising Arizona, 91
  True Grit, 40, *65,* 109, *126,* 130, 132, 133, 292, *308,* 516

Coen, Joel, 304, 305, 367, 391, 400, 421, *422*
  Fargo, 95
  The Man Who Wasn't There, 96, 231
  Miller's Crossing, 93

Cohen, Danny, 251

Cohl, Émile, 445

Cold Mountain (Minghella), 191, 200, 307, 390

Collateral (Mann), 291, 490

Collins, Ray, 315

Colonial Expressionism, 214

color, *211, 213,* **242–44**
  additive systems, 234
  vs. black and white, 230–31, *230, 232*
  film production in, *230,* **234–36,** *235, 236*
  film stock and, *235, 236*
  subtractive systems, 234–35
  tinting, 234

color film, *236,* 434, 441

colorization, 230–31

Color Me Kubrick (Cook), 191

Colossal Youth (Costa), 325n

Colpi, Henri, 345

Columbia Pictures, *184,* 496n, 498, 512n

Columbus, Chris:
  Harry Potter and the Chamber of Secrets, 25
  Harry Potter and the Sorcerer's Stone, 25
  Rent, 108

Comb, The (Quay and Quay), *112*

Comédie Française, 295

comedy genre, 93, 108, 442–43
  screwball, *452*
  subgenres of, 109

Comingore, Dorothy, 238, *239,* 267, *454*

composition, 172, **202–10,** *203,* **323–26,** *439*
  deep-space, 252
  defined, 202
  effect on acting, *324*
  framing and, *250,* 255
  rule of thirds in, 257–59

computer-generated imagery (CGI), 113, 114–15, *115,* 184, **280–83,** *310*
  synthespians in, 309, *310*
  "uncanny valley" and, 114, *115*

Conan Doyle, Arthur, *183*

Condon, Bill, 505
  Dreamgirls, 107, 403
  The Twilight Saga: Breaking Dawn, Part 1, 515

conflict, in dramatic structure, *136*

Conner, Bruce, *Marilyn Times Five,* 81

Connery, Sean, 309, 311

Conquest (Brown), 497

Constant Nymph, The (Dean), 499

construct, 143

Contagion (Soderbergh), 517

content:
  defined, 36
  form and, **36–39,** *37, 39*

content curve, 355

continuity, 8, *9,* 194
  sound, **420–21**
  visual, 289, **355–75,** *357*

conventions:
  cinematic, 205, 238, 240–41, 257, **355–64**
  continuity, **355–64**

Conversation, The (F. F. Coppola), 390

Conversations with Other Women (Canosa), 375

Convertino, Michael, 404

Conway, Jack, 497

Cook, Brian W., *Color Me Kubrick,* 191

Cook, David A., 433, 439

Cooley, Stanley, *400*

Coolidge, Martha, *313*

Cooper, Chris, 41, 216, *218,* 290, 305

Cooper, Gary, *233,* 311

Cooper, James Fenimore, 102

Cooper, Merian C., 279
  King Kong, 112

Cooper, Scott, *Crazy Heart, 308*

Copland, Aaron, 404

Copley, Sharlto, *130*

copper plates, 435

Coppola, Carmine, 408

Coppola, Francis Ford, 473, 475, *475,* 517
  Apocalypse Now, 202, 343, 390, *394,* 395, 408, 419, *420,* 492
  Apocalypse Now Redux, 202, 343
  The Conversation, 390
  The Godfather, 53, *242,* 329
  The Godfather movies, 53, 86, *89*
  One From the Heart, 176, 202
  Peggy Sue Got Married, 91
  Rumble Fish, 277
  Tucker: The Man and His Dream, 292
  Twixt, 516

Coppola, Sofia, *Lost in Translation,* 90

Corn is Green, The (Rapper), 307

Corpse Bride (Burton), 404

Corrigan, Lloyd, 235

Cortez, Stanley, 186, 267

Cosby, Bill, 313

Coscarelli, Don, *Phantasm,* 102

Costa, Pedro, *Colossal Youth,* 325n

Costner, Kevin, *Dances with Wolves,* 105, 110, 314

costume, hairstyle and makeup, **188–94,** *189, 190, 192, 193,* 218
  wigs and, 193–94, *193*

Cotten, Joseph, *199,* 316, 423, *424,* 426

Coulouris, George, 323

Counterfeiters, The (Ruzowitzky), 272

Country Girl, The (Seaton), *313*

Court Jester, The (Panama and Frank), *193, 193*

Courtley, Steve, *50*

coverage, 359

Cowan, Jerome, *315*

Cox, Brian, *50*

Cox, John, 398

Coy, Walter, 359, *362*

Crafton, Donald, 298

Craig, Stuart, 179

crane shot, **269–70,** *270*

Craven, Wes:
  A Nightmare on Elm Street, 100
  Scream, 102

Crawford, Joan, 289, 300–301, 314

Crazy Heart (Cooper), *308*

Creadon, Patrick, *Wordplay,* 72

Crews, Laura Hope, 315

Cries and Whispers (Bergman), 370, *372*

Cripple Creek Bar-Room Scene (Edison), 103

crisis, in dramatic structure, 135, *136*, 160–61

Crisp, Donald, 295, 296

Criss Cross (Siodmak), 96

critical flicker fusion, 49

Cromwell, John, *Of Human Bondage*, 306

Cronenberg, David, *The Fly*, 98

Cronenweth, Jeff, *227*

Crosby, Floyd, *233*

Crosland, Alan, *The Jazz Singer*, 106, 451, *451*

crosscutting, 277, 367, 440, 449, 460

Crouching Tiger, Hidden Dragon (A. Lee), 199, 201, *209*, 470, *470*

Crowd, The (Vidor), 207, *444*

Crowe, Russell, 148, *149*, 305, 311, 364

Crowley, Nathan, 176

Cruel Story of Youth (Oshima), 466

Cruise, Tom, *178*, 290–91, 322, 411, *411*, 503, 511

Crusaders, The, 442

Cruz, Penélope, 311

Crying Game, The (Jordan), 263, 405

Cuarón, Alfonso, *146*, *372*, 373
    Children of Men, 99
    Harry Potter and the Prisoner of Azkaban, 25
    Y tu mamá también, 373

Cucaracha, La (Corrigan), 235

Cukor, George, 321, 496
    The Philadelphia Story, *301*
    A Star Is Born, 108

cultural invisibility, 10–11, *11*

Cumberbatch, Benedict, *183*

Cundey, Dean, 264, 281

Curious Case of Benjamin Button, The (Fincher), 283

Curran, John, 404

Currie, Finlay, *146*

Curse of Frankenstein, The (Fisher), 212

Curtis, Simon, *My Week with Marilyn*, 156

Curtis, Tony, *239*

Curtiz, Michael, 173, 193, 301, 507
    Casablanca, *147*, *357*, 358
    Mildred Pierce, 307
    The Private Lives of Elizabeth and Essex, 307
    Yankee Doodle Dandy, 108

Cusack, John, 260

cuts, cutting, 5, 340
    crosscutting and, 367
    director's, 343
    eyeline match, 365, *367*, 370
    graphic match, **365–67**, *366*
    intercutting and, 367
    jump, **368**
    match, **364–67**
    match-on-action, 8, *8*, **364–67**, *366*

Czettel, Rudi, 181

D

DaCosta, Morton, *The Music Man*, 108

dadaist films, 445

D'Agostino, Albert S., 199

Daguerre, Louis-Jacques-Mandeé, 435

Dahl, John, *The Last Seduction*, 96

dailies, 392, 493

Daldry, Stephen, 307, 326, 407
    The Hours, 307

Dalí, Salvador, *An Andalusian Dog*, *78*, 79, 447

Dallwitz, Burkhard, 422

Damon, Matt, 156, *272*, 309, 406

Dancer in the Dark (von Trier), 107, 463

Dances with Wolves (Costner), 105, 110, 314

Dancyger, Ken, 340

Dandridge, Dorothy, 313, *313*

Dangerous (Green), 302

Daniel, Gordon, 419

Daniels, Lee, *Precious: Based on the Novel "Push" by Sapphire*, *128*, 129

Danish cinema, 201

Dante's Inferno, 442

Darcy, Georgine, *368*

Dardenne, Jean-Pierre and Luc, 517
    L'Enfant, *57*, 457
    The Kid with a Bike, 83

Darjeeling Limited, The (Anderson), 181

Dark Days (Singer), 231

Dark Knight, The (Nolan), 111, 176, *192*

Dark Shadows (Burton), 292

Dark Victory (Goulding), 307, 499

Das, Nandita, 472

Das Gupta, Uma, 401

das neue Kino, 463–64, *465*

Dassin, Jules:
    The Naked City, 96
    Rififi, 93

Daves, Delmer, *3:10 to Yuma*, 105

Davidson, Jaye, 405

Davies, Marion, 499

Da Vinci Code, The (Howard), 155

Davis, Bette, 193, 256, *256*, 300, 301–2, 306–8, *306*, 314, 316, 321, 322, 365, *367*, 499

Davis, Don, 404

Davis, Ron, 368

Dawley, J. Searle, 279

Dawn of the Dead (Romero), 102

Dawn Patrol, The (Hawks), 499

Day, Doris, *301*

Day, Richard, 179, 197

Days of Heaven (Malick), 123, 151, 155, 258, *259*

Days of Thunder (T. Scott), 307

Day the Earth Stood Still, The (Wise), 98

Dead Man (Jarmusch), *104*, 105

Deakins, Roger, 231

Dean, James, *303*, 304

Dearden, Basil, *Victim*, 462, *462*

Death Breath (van der Beek), 81

Death of a Salesman (Miller), 51n

Death to the Tinman (Tintori), 83

Debie, Benoît, 275

Debucourt, Roderick, *447*

Decalogue (Kieslowski), 203

décor, **183–87**, *217*, *218*

Decugis, Cécile, 351

deep-focus cinematography, 255–56, 325, 434, 454, *454*

deep-focus sound, 423

deep-space composition, 252, 255–56, *255*, *256*

Delerue, Georges, 404, 408

Delicatessen (Jeunet), 418

Dellaringa, Brandee, 176

Delon, Alain, 175, *176*

del Rio, Dolores, 313

Del Toro, Benicio, 67, 290, 305

del Toro, Guillermo:
    Blade II, 13
    The Devil's Backbone, 13, 108, *247*
    Hellboy, 13
    Hellboy II: The Golden Army, 182, *182*
    Mimic, 13
    Pan's Labyrinth, 13, 173, *173*, 182

DeMille, Cecil B., 182, 279, 279n
    The Squaw Man, 442

Demme, Jonathan, 42, *44, 312*
  The Silence of the Lambs, 53, 102
Demme, Ted, 293
Demy, Jacques, *The Umbrellas of*
    Cherbourg, 105
Dench, Judi, 314
Dencik, Daniel, 351
De Niro, Robert, *146, 152,* 269, 275,
    276, 304, *320,* 321, 322, *371*
De Palma, Brian, 293, 473, *475*
  Carrie, 102
  Scarface, 93
Depp, Johnny, *6, 104,* 128, 189, *190,*
    211, 212, *212, 213, 215,*
    292–93, *292,* 305, 309, 312,
    319–20, *319,* 322
depth, **252–59,** *254–55, 256, 259*
depth of field, 246
Deren, Maya, *Meshes of the*
    Afternoon, 79–81
Dern, Laura, 264, *264*
Desfontaines, Henri, 295
  The Loves of Queen Elizabeth,
    442
De Sica, Vittorio, 200, *200,* 328,
    457, 471
  The Bicycle Thieves, 456, *457,* 471
  Shoeshine, 456
  Umberto D, 456
design, 172, **179–202**
  American Beauty, 216–18, 220
  elements of, **183–94**
  international styles and
    development, **194–202,** *195,*
    198, 200, 201
  sound, **390–91**
Desilu Productions, 501
Desk Set (Lang), 305
Desperado (Rodriguez), 469
Destiny (Lang), 197
Destry Rides Again (Marshall), 105
Detour (Ulmer), 96
Deverick, Nat G., *The Power of Love,*
    515
Devi, Chunibala, 401
Devi (S. Ray), 472
Devil's Backbone, The (del Toro),
    13, *247*
Devine, Andy, 157, *158,* 315
Devo, 404
Dial M for Murder (Hitchcock),
    207, 515
dialogue, **399**
Diamond, I. A. L., 130, *154*

Diary of a Country Priest (Bresson),
    208
Diaz, Cameron, 290
Di Campo, Dino, 389
DiCaprio, Leonardo, *238,* 292, *292,*
    305, 311, 314, *389*
Dick, Philip K., 145, *156*
Dickens, Charles, *146*
Dickerson, Ernest, 261, *261*
Dickson, William Kennedy Laurie,
    437–38
diegesis, 140, 141, 143, 155, *396*
diegetic elements, 140, 141, 143
  in *Stagecoach* (Ford), 161–62
diegetic sound, *396,* **396–97**
Dietrich, Marlene, *240, 301,* 322,
    326, *327*
digital cinematography, 434
digital format, 391
digital technology, **489–91**
digital video discs, *see* DVDs
Dikhtyar, Aleksandr, 197
Dillon, Matt, 347, *372*
dime novels, 102
Dinosaur and the Missing Link, The:
    A Prehistoric Tragedy
    (O'Brien), 112
direct-address narration, 123
direct cinema, 73, 74, *75,* 266, 475–76
direct costs, 507
direction, light, lighting, **238–42**
director, role of, 484–85
director of photography, **226–28**
  see also cinematographer
directors, 499, 502
  actor relationships with, **321–22**
  auteur theory and, 137
  control by, 178–79, *178*
  maverick, **517**
  see also specific directors and films
director's cut, 343
discontinuity, **355–75,** *361*
Discreet Charm of the Bourgeoisie,
    The (Buñuel), 447
Disney, Walt, 143, 235, 443, 499, 502
Disney Studios, 107, 113, 282, 499,
    512*n*
dissolves, **371–72**
distance effect, 318
distribution, film, 498–99
District 9 (Blomkamp), 99, *130*
Di Venanzo, Gianni, 236
Diving Bell and the Butterfly, The
    (Schnabel), 274

D.O.A. (Maté), 96
Do Androids Dream of Electric Sheep?
    (Dick), *156*
Dobbs, Lem, 126
Doctor Zhivago (Lean), 226
documentary films, *4,* 66, 67, **70–75,**
    74, 75, 76, 82–83, *82, 83*
  defined, 71
  see also nonfiction films
Dog Day Afternoon (Lumet), 130
Dogme 95 movement, 84, 201, 351,
    462–63
Dog Star Man (Brakhage), 81, *476*
Dogville (von Trier), 172, 243–44, *243,*
    307, 319, 463
Dolby Digital system, 475
Dolby system, 390
dolly, defined, 267
dolly in, 267
dolly out, 268
dolly shot, 16, *267,* **267–68**
Dominik, Andrew, *Chopper,* 156
Domino (Scott), 82
Donen, Stanley, 209, 298
  On the Town, 108
  Singin' in the Rain, 87, 108, *297*
Donner, Richard:
  The Omen, 102
  Superman, 111
Donnie Brasco (Newell), *292*
Donnie Darko (Kelly), *56,* 99
Don't Look Back (Pennebaker), *291*
Don't Look Now (Roeg), 367
Dorléac, Jean-Pierre, 191
Dorn, Dody, 345
Do the Right Thing (S. Lee), 260–61,
    261, 319
Double Indemnity (Wilder), 47, *94,*
    129, 331, 345, *400*
double-system recording, 392
Douglas, Kirk, *259,* 299
Dovzhenko, Aleksandr, 194, 303
Downey, Robert, Jr., *183, 305,* 311, 314
Downs, Cathy, *105, 414*
downshots, 260
Dracula (Browning), 99, *109*
Drag Me to Hell (Raimi), 102
Dreamgirls (Condon), *107, 403*
Dreams (Kurosawa), 409
Dreams That Money Can Buy
    (Richter), 81
Dream Street (Griffith), 442
DreamWorks, 282, 512
Dreier, Hans, 182, 199

Drew, Robert, 475
Drews, Berta, *372*
Dreyer, Carl Theodor, 208, 278, *326*
  The Passion of Joan of Arc, 448
Dreyfus, Jean-Claude, 418
Dr. Jekyll and Mr. Hyde (Mamoulian), 193, 199
Dr. Strangelove, or: How I Learned to Stop Worrying and Love the Bomb (Kubrick), 109, *245,* 268, 272, 322, 398
Drugstore Cowboy (Van Sant), 277, 347–48
Drums Along the Mohawk (Ford), 235, 314
dubbing, *144,* 392, *392*
Duchamp, Marcel, 57, *58*
  Anémic cinéma, 79
Duel in the Sun (Vidor), 105
Duigan, John, *Head in the Clouds,* 188, *189*
Dulac, Germaine, *The Seashell and the Clergyman,* 447
Dumbo (Sharpsteen), 85
Dunaway, Faye, *41,* 204, 304, *474*
Dunmore, Laurence, 293
Durand, Jean, 445
duration, 16, **149–53,** *152,* 164
  plot, 149, *150,* 151
  plot vs. screen, *150,* 151
  screen, 149, *150,* 151
  of shots, 351
  in *Stagecoach* (Ford), 164
  story, *39,* 149, 151
  story vs. plot, *150*
Dutch-angle shot, *263,* **263**
Duvall, Robert, 304, *420*
Duvall, Shelley, 261, *261,* 394
Duvivier, Julian, 313
DVDs (digital video discs), 509, 511, 514
Dwan, Allan, *The Half-Breed,* 314
Dyer, Richard, 300
Dylan, Bob, 291, *291*
dynamization of space, 51

E

Eagle-Lion Films, 499
early filmmaking, 47–49, 56, 183–85, 233–34, 279, 342, 404
Early Spring (Ozu), 466
Early Summer (Ozu), 466
Earthquake (Robson), 309

Eastman, George, 435, 436
Eastman Color system film, 235
East of Eden (Kazan), *303,* 304
Eastwood, Clint, 104, 315, 326, 473–74
  Million Dollar Baby, 145
  Unforgiven, 103, *104,* 110
Easy Living (Leisen), 182, *452*
Easy Rider (Hopper), 474
Eat Drink Man Woman (A. Lee), 201, 470
Eccleston, Christopher, 517
Eckhart, Aaron, *192*
Edeson, Arthur, 248, 260, *260,* 279
edge lights, 241
Edgerton, Nash, *The Square,* 96
Edison, Thomas A., 103, 234, 437, *438,* 439, *439,* 440, 495, 505
Edison Kinetoscopic Record of a Sneeze (Dickson), 437–38
editing, 5, *8, 9,* 36, 442
  acting and, **327**
  continuity and discontinuity in, **355–75,** *361*
  continuity techniques in, **364–68,** 440, *440*
  defined, **339–86,** 340, *341*
  director's cut in, 343
  dissolves in, **371–72**
  editor's responsibilities in, **344–55**
  ellipsis in, **347–49,** *348, 349,* 367, *440*
  fades-in, **368–70,** *372,* 384
  fades-out, 384
  film editors and, **342–55**
  flashbacks in, *346*
  flash-forwards in, *346*
  freeze-frames in, **373–74,** *374,* 384
  iris shots in, *372,* **372**
  master scene technique in, 359
  master shots and, **359,** *362*
  match cuts in, **364–67,** *366*
  montage in, 129, **349–51,** *350, 352,* 384
  parallel, 42, *43,* **367**
  point of view, **368**
  reverse-angle shots in, 364
  rhythm in, **351–55,** *354*
  screen direction and, **359–64**
  shot/reverse shots, **364**
  of sound, *365, 392,* **392**
  spatial relationships in, **344–45,** *347, 361*
  superimpositions, 384

  temporal relationships in, **345–51**
  transitions in, **368–75**
  wipes in, **372**
Edson, Richard, *473*
Education, An (Scherfig), 128
Edwards, Blake, *Breakfast at Tiffany's,* 312
Edwards, J. Gordon, 191
Edward Scissorhands (Burton), 189, *190,* 211, 292, 319, *319*
Ed Wood (Burton), 211
Egoyan, Atom, 154, 418
  The Sweet Hereafter, 400–401
Eidoloscope, 438, 439
8½ (Fellini), 81
8 Mile (Hanson), 293
Eisenberg, Jesse, 140
Eisenstein, Sergei, 8, 151, 155, 172, 179, 194, 255, 303, 349, 351, 448–50, 474
  Alexander Nevsky, 405, 449, *449*
  Battleship Potemkin, 352, 449, 450, *450*
  Ivan the Terrible, Parts I and II, 449
  montage of attractions, 450
  October (Ten Days that Shook the World), 449
  Que Viva México, 449
  Strike, 449
Ekerot, Bengt, *232*
Elephant (Van Sant), 273
Elephant Man, The (Lynch), 202
Elfman, Danny, 404
Eliot, T. S., 86
Elizabeth (Kapur), 291
Elkind, Rachel, 389
ellipsis, **347–49,** *348, 349,* 367, *440*
  defined, 347
Elswit, Robert, 231
Emak-Bakia (Ray), 79, 446
Eminem, 293
Emperor Jones, The (Murphy), 313
emphasis, sound as, **421–23**
Employees Leaving the Lumière Factory (Lumière and Lumière), *59,* 439
Engel, Tina, *372*
English Patient, The (Minghella), 390
Enigma of Kasper Hauser, The (Herzog), 418
Enoch Arden (Griffth), 442
ensemble acting, 325–26
Enter the Void (Noé), 275

Entr'acte (Clair), 79, 446
environmental sounds, **401–3**
Ephron, Nora, 400
    Bewitched, 307
Epstein, Jean, *The Fall of the House of Usher,* 446, *447*
Epstein, Julius J., *147*
Epstein, Philip G., *147*
Epstein, Robert, *Bright Star,* 156
Erin Brockovich (Soderbergh), 348, *348*
Erman, John, *331*
establishing shots, *207,* 251, 359, *362*
    see also master shots
Estes, Jacob Aaron, 326
Eternal Sunshine of the Spotless Mind (Gondry), 146, 345, 358, 461
E.T. the Extra-Terrestrial (Spielberg), 309
Even Dwarfs Started Small (Herzog), 464
events, **148–49,** *149, 162–63*
    in *Stagecoach* (Ford), 162–64, *162–63*
Ever After (Tennant), 143
Every Day Except Christmas (Anderson), 462
Evil Dead, The (Raimi), 102
Evil Dead II, The (Raimi), 102
"Evolution of the Language of Cinema, The" (Bazin), 459
Execution of Mary Stuart, The (Clark), 279
executive producers, 502
exhibition, film, 498–99
Exit Through the Gift Shop (Banksy), 76
Exorcist, The (Friedkin), 101
expectations:
    and character, *14*
    form and, **39–42,** *41*
    viewer, 13–20
experimental films, 66, 68, **75–82,** *77, 153*
explicitly presented events, 140, *141*
exposure, 488–89
exposure index, **488**
expressionistic films, 195–97, *195,* 443–45
external sound, **398–99**
Extraordinary Adventures of Mr. West in the Land of the Bolsheviks, The (Kuleshov), 448
extras, 315
Extras, The (Ho), 469

extreme close-up (ECU), 252, *252*
extreme long shot, 251, *252*
eye-level shot, **259–60,** *260*
eyeline match cuts, 365, *367, 370*
Eyes Wide Shut (Kubrick), *178,* 291, 307, 322, 511
Eyre, Chris, *Smoke Signals,* 314

F

Facebook, 129, *134,* 142
Faces (Cassavetes), 321
Factor, Max, 192
factual films, **72**
fade in/fade out, 7, **368–70,** *372,* 384
Fail-Safe (Lumet), 398
Fairall, Harry K., *The Power of Love,* 515
Fairbanks, Douglas, *209,* 314, 498
Fairfield, Paula, 423
Faith No More, 408
Falconetti, Maria, 278, *326*
Fall of the House of Usher, The (Epstein), 446, *447*
familiar image, 154
Fancher, Hampton, 156
Fangmeier, Stefen, 282
Fanning, Dakota, 411, *411*
Fantastic Mr. Fox (Anderson), 112
Farenheit 451 (Truffaut), 98
Farewell My Concubine (Chen), 468, *468*
Far From Heaven (Haynes), 173, *174*
Fargo (J. Coen), *95,* 288
Farmer, David, 402
Farmer, Gary, 314
Farrell, Colin, 269
Farrelly, Bobby and Peter, 293, 397
    Stuck on You, 109
Farrow, John, *Hondo,* 515
Fassbinder, Rainer Werner:
    Berlin Alexanderplatz, 464
    Fear of Fear, 464
    The Marriage of Maria Braun, 464
Fast, Cheap & Out of Control (Morris), 75
Fast Five (Lin), 85
fast motion, 277, *448*
Fast Runner, The (Kunuk), 314
Fat City (Huston), *308*
Father and Son (Fong), 469
Favre, Brett, 293
Favreau, Jon:
    Iron Man, 111, 145, 292, *305, 308*
    Iron Man 2, 305

Fax, Jesslyn, *368*
Fear and Loathing in Las Vegas (Gilliam), 202, 293
Fearless Vampire Killers, The (Polanski), 212
Fear of Fear (Fassbinder), 464
featured players, **300**
feature films, 441
Federico, Petrantonio, 400
feed spool, *487*
Fegtè, Ernst, 182
Feig, Paul, *Bridesmaids,* 109, *134*
Felix the Cat (Messmer), 443
Fell, Sam, *Flushed Away,* 113
Fellini, Federico, 200, 210, 236, 328, 457, 461
    8½, 81
Fellowship of the Ring, The (Jackson), 402
Ferguson, Perry, 185, *195*
    The Best Years of Our Lives, 203
Ferran, Pascale, *Lady Chatterly,* 145
Ferrell, Conchata, *348*
Ferrell, Will, 109, *125*
Ferrer, José, 313
Ferretti, Dante, *171,* 197, 200
Ferris Bueller's Day Off (Hughes), 123
Fesler, Bailey, 400, 418, 423, *424*
Fetchit, Stepin, 313
Feuillade, Louis, 445
fiction films, *see* narrative films
fidelity, of sound, **395,** *395*
Field, Syd, *134*
Field, Todd, 329
    In the Bedroom, 293
Fielding, Raymond, 280
Fields, W. C., 108, *316*
Fienberg, Gregg, 505
50 Cent, 293
Figgis, Mike, *153,* 375
    Leaving Las Vegas, 91
Fight Club (Fincher), 182, 329
Fighter, The (Russell), 145
figures, movement of, 202, **209–10**
fill light, 240
Film Acting (Pudovkin), 303
film history, 431–82, *432*
    aesthetic approach, **433**
    approaches to, 433–35
    artifacts of, 433
    auteur theory, 433
    defined, 432–33
    economic approach, 433, **434**

overview, 435–61
    social approach, 433, **434–35**
    technological approach, 433,
        434, **434**
film noir genre, 88, **93–96**, *94, 95,*
    242–43, *432,* 445, 460, *465*
films:
    highest grossing worldwide,
        510–11
    Hollywood and foreign, 516–17
    international, 461–72
    vs. movies, 3
    nonfiction, 194
    principals of, **49–56**
    see also movies
film sound, sources of, *395,* **395–99**
film stock, **229–36,** *486*
    gauges of, 229–30
    length of, **488**
    speed of, 230, **488**
film technology, 486–91
Final Fantasy: The Spirits Within
    (Sakaguchi and
    Sakakibara), 113, 283, 309
financing film production, 498,
    505–7, *506, 508–9*
Fincher, David, 182, 329
    The Curious Case of Benjamin
        Button, 283
    Fight Club, 182
    The Girl with the Dragon Tattoo,
        182, *227*
    Se7en, 182
    The Social Network, 70, 129,
        134, 140–43, *142, 184, 227,*
        310, 516
    Zodiac, 305, 490
Finding Neverland (Forster), 200, 293
Fine, Russell Lee, 277
Finler, Joel W., 434
Finn, Will, *Home on the Range,* 113
Finney, Albert, 319, 348, *348*
Firefly, 110
Firmino da Hora, Leandro, 380
first-person narrators, 123
First Step, The: Facing Death
    (Cheung), 469
Firth, Colin, 251
Fischer, Gunnar, 231–32, *232*
Fischinger, Oskar, *Motion Painting*
    No. 1, 112
Fishburne, Laurence, 313
Fisher, Terence, 212
Fisk, Jack, 200
Fist Fight (Breer), 81

Fitzgerald, F. Scott, 484
Fitzstephens, Jack, 398
Five Easy Pieces (Rafelson), 474–75
Five Obstructions, The (von Trier),
    351, 463
Flaherty, Robert J., *Nanook of the*
    North, 71, *72,* 443, 448
Flame Within, The (Goulding), 499
Flaming Creatures (Smith), 81
flashbacks, 161, 335, 345, *346*
flash card, 489
flash-forward, 161, 345, *346*
Flashpoint, 505
flat characters, 128, *128,* 160
Flavor of Green Tea Over Rice,
    The (Ozu), 466
Fleischer, Dave, 443
Fleischer, Max, 443
Fleming, Tim, 272
Fleming, Victor, 59, 145, 191, 235, *235,*
    269, 394, 404, 496*n,* 499
    Gone with the Wind, 182, *193,* 453
    The Wizard of Oz, 108, 132, 133
Fletcher, Geoffrey, *128*
Fletcher, Robert, 191
Flickr, 82
Flight of the Red Balloon (Hou), 470
Flippen, Jay C., 400
Floating Weeds (Ozu), 466
floodlights, 237
Flowers and Trees (Disney), 235
Flushed Away (Bowers and Fell), 113
Fly, The (Cronenberg), 98
focal length, 244–45
focal planes, 246
focus, lenses and, 245–46, *247*
    rack focus and, *247*
focusable spots, 237
Fogelman, Dan, 129
Fogelson, John, 404
Foley, Jack, 402
Foley, James, *After Dark, My Sweet,* 96
Foley sounds, 392, **401–3,** *402,* 406,
    409, 414–15
Folman, Ari, *Waltz with Bashir,*
    111, *112*
Folsey, George S., 252
Fonda, Henry, 46, 88, 103, *105,* 300,
    314, 315, 371, 398, 401
Fonda, Jane, 314, *346*
Fong, Allen, 469
    Father and Son, 469
    Just Like Weather, 469
Footlight Parade (Bacon), 108
Forbidden Kingdom, The (Minkoff), 469

Forbidden Planet (Wilcox), 98
Ford, John, 88, 137, 179, 201, 207,
    208, 237, *237,* 254, 263,
    308, 321–22, 414, 459, 464,
    471, 499
    Cheyenne Autumn, 314
    Drums Along the Mohawk, 235,
        314
    Fort Apache, 105
    The Grapes of Wrath, 46, *47,* 167,
        228, 401
    The Informer, 230, 263
    The Iron Horse, 105, 314
    The Man Who Shot Liberty Vance,
        105
    My Darling Clementine, 88, *105,*
        205–6, 237, *237,* 371, 398
    The Searchers, 40, 87, 103, 231, *232,*
        314, 327, 359, *362*
    She Wore a Yellow Ribbon, 105,
        231, 314
    Stagecoach, 88, 103, 157–59, 161,
        314, 315, *366*
    3 Godfathers, 103
Ford, Katie, 143
Foreman, Carl, 151
Forest Gump (Zemeckis), 209
form, **36–63,** *40,* 441
    analysis of, 14–20
    and content, **36–39,** *37*
    defined, 36
    and expectations, **39–42**
    principals of film, 46, **49–56**
Forman, Milos, 272
    Hair, 108
format, 486
Forrest Gump (Zemeckis), *210,* 281
Forster, Marc, 293, 314
    Finding Neverland, 200
    Stranger than Fiction, 125
Fort Apache (Ford), 105
Forty Guns (Fuller), 105
42nd Street (Bacon), 108
40 Year Old Virgin, The (Apatow), 109
Fosse, Bob, *Cabaret,* 108
Foster, Jodie, *44,* 317
400 Blows, The (Truffaut), 373, *374,*
    459, *459*
4 months, 3 weeks & 2 days (Mungiu),
    21, 22
Four Sheets to the Wind (Harjo), 314
fourth wall, 318
Fox Grandeur 70mm process, 248
Fox Studios, 282
Foxx, Jamie, 304, 313

Foy, Brian, *The Lights of New York,* 451

Fraker, William, 266

frames, framing, **202–8, 248–75,** *250,* 255, **323–26**

 camera angle and height, **259–64,** *260, 261, 262, 263, 277*

 effects on acting, *324*

 moving frame and, 202

 open and closed, *207*

 point of view and, 202, **274–75**

 and reframing, 202

Frampton, Hollis, 476

 Zorn's Lemma, 81

Franco, James, 133

Frank, Melvin, 193

Frankenstein (Whale), 99, 193, *195,* 197, 211–12, *211*

Frankenstein; or, The Modern Prometheus (Shelley), 96

Frankenweenie (Burton), 112

Franklin, Chester M., *The Toll of the Sea,* 234

Franklin, Sidney, *The Good Earth,* 311

Franzoni, David, 148

Fraser, Brendan, *289*

Freaks (Browning), 101

Frears, Stephen, 172, 260

Fred Ott's Sneeze (Dickson), 438

Freeborn, Stuart, 193

Free Cinema, 458, 462, *462*

Freeman, Morgan, *104,* 290, 304, 313, 317, 411

freeze-frames, 54–56, **373–74,** *374, 384, 448*

French Cancan (Renoir), 108

French "New Wave," *see* New Wave filmmaking

frequency, of sound, 394

Frères, Pathé, 234

Fresh (Yakin), 319

Freud, Sigmund, 445, 449

Freund, Karl, 265

 The Mummy, 99

Fricke, Ron, 277

Friday the 13th movies, 100

Friedberg, Mark, 173, 181

Friedhoff, Günther, 421

Friedkin, William, *The Exorcist,* 101

Friedman, Jeffrey, *Bright Star,* 156

Friedrich, Su, *Sink or Swim,* 77

Fuji, Tatsuya, *465*

Fuji film, 235

Fujimoto, Tak, *258*

Fukasaku, Kinji, *Battles without Honor or Humanity,* 93

Fukunaga, Cary, *Jane Eyre, 61*

Fuller, Samuel, 93

 Forty Guns, 105

 Pickup on South Street, 96, *465*

Funny Games (Haneke), 123, *126,* 517

Fur: An Imaginary Portrait of Diane Arbus (Shainberg), *305, 306,* 307

fusil photographique, **437**

FX, *see* special effects

G

Gable, Clark, 304, 311, 496

Gabrielle (Chereau), 410

gaffer, 228, 391

Gaghan, Stephen, *Syriana, 70*

Gainsborough, Thomas, 57, *58,* 236

Gambon, Michael, *212,* 213

Gance, Abel, 151, 375

 Napoléon, 248, 448

 The Wheel, 447, 448

Gance, Marguerite, *447*

Gandhi (Attenborough), *313,* 314

Gangs of New York (Scorsese), 176

gangster genre, 88, *89,* **90–93,** *92, 93*

Garbo, Greta, 300, 318, 322, 496–97

Garbuglia, Mario, 174

Garcés, Iñigo, *247*

García Bernal, Gael, 373, *374*

García Marquez, Gabriel, 145

Garfield, Andrew, *134,* 142

Garmes, Lee, 326, *327*

Garner, Jennifer, *11*

Garnett, Tay, *The Postman Always Rings Twice,* 96, *456*

Gary, Romain, 156

Gassmann, Remi, 417

Gattaca (Niccol), 99

gauges, film, 229

Gaumont Film Company, *443*

Gaynor, Janet, 297

Gazzara, Ben, 244

Gearty, Eugene, 395, 421, *422*

Gehr, Ernie, *The Astronomer's Dream,* 81

gelatin process, 435–36

General, The (Boorman), 368

General, The (Keaton), 443

generic transformation, 109–10

genre, genre studies, 66, **83–90,** *85,* 108–11, 290, 440, *440*

 defined, 84

 see also specific genres

George, Gladys, 315

German cinema, 195–97, 265

German Expressionism, 443–45

German Sisters, The/Marianne and Juliane (von Trotta), 464

Germi, Pietro, 457

Gerrard, Lisa, 404

Gertie the Dinosaur (McCay), 111

Get Rich or Die Tryin' (Sheridan), 293

Ghare-Baire (S. Ray), 472

Ghatak, Ritwik, 472

 Ajantrik, 472

 Jukti Takko Aar Gappo, 472

Ghosh, Bhupen, 401

Ghost and Mrs. Muir, The (Mankiewicz), 419

Ghost in the Shell (Oshii), 98

Ghost Writer, The (Polanski), *121*

Giacometti, Alberto, 37–39, *38*

Giamatti, Paul, 290

Giant (Stevens), *302,* 304

Gibbons, Cedric, 180*n,* 181, 182, 199

Gibson, Charles, *282*

Gibson, Mel, *209,* 517

Gielgud, John, 400

G.I. Joe: The Rise of Cobra (Sommers), 516

G.I. Joe 2: Retaliation, 517

Gilbert, Lewis, 319

 Alfie, 123

Gillett, Burt, 235

Gilliam, Terry, 202, 293

 Brazil, 98

 Twelve Monkeys, 98–99

Gilroy, Tony, 514

Giovinazzo, Buddy, *No Way Home,* 319

Girl with the Dragon Tattoo, The (Fincher), 182, *227*

Girotti, Massimo, 456

Gish, Dorothy, 295

Gish, Lillian, 42, *43,* 187, 295–97, *296,* 321, *370*

Gladiator (Scott), 60, 148–49, *149, 267, 282,* 404

Glass, Philip, 404, 407

glass-plate negatives, 435

Glazer, Jonathan, 278, *278,* 326

Glazer, Mitch, *146*

Gleason, James, 420

Gleeson, Brendan, 368

Glennon, Bert, 235
Gloria (Cassavetes), 321
*Goalie's Anxiety of the Penalty Kick,
     The* (Wenders), 464
goals, character, 127, *131*
Godard, Jean-Luc, 137, 319, 351, 458,
     460, 466, 474
     Alphaville, 97
     Breathless, 86, 358, *361,* 459–60,
          459
Goddess, The (S. Ray), 201
Godfather, The (F. F. Coppola), 53,
     86, *242,* 329
Godfather, The movies (F. F. Coppola),
     53, *89*
Gods and Monsters (Condon), 505, *506*
Godzilla (Honda), 280
Goldberg, Whoopi, 109
Goldblatt, Stephen, *225,* 281
Gold Diggers of 1933 (LeRoy), 254
Golden, Robert, *370*
Golden Age, Hollywood's, 299–302,
     441, *453*
Goldenberg, William, 364
Golden Compass, The (Weitz), 307
Gold Rush, The (Chaplin), *52,* 53, 443
Goldstein, Robert, 191
Goldwyn, Samuel, 499, 502
Golem, The (Wegener and Boese),
     444
Gomery, Douglas, 432, 434
Gondry, Michel, 146, 345, 358
     *Eternal Sunshine of the Spotless
          Mind,* 461
     The Science of Sleep, 82
Gone with the Wind (Fleming),
     59, 180*n,* 182, 191, *193,* 235,
     235, 269, 313, 404, *453,*
     496*n,* 499, 505
Gong, Li, 313
González Iñárritu, Alejandro:
     21 Grams, 67
     Babel, 291
Good, the Bad, and the Ugly, The
     (Leone), 87
Good Earth, The (Franklin), 311
Goodfellas (Scorsese), *85,* 86, 269,
     273–74, 374, *374*
Good Night, and Good Luck (Clooney),
     231, *305,* 314
Gordon, Seth, *The King of Kong:
     A Fistful of Quarters,* 74
Gordon-Levitt, Joseph, 517
Gore, Al, 72
Gorky, Maxim, 208

Gosford Park (Altman), 321
Gosling, Ryan, 333–36
Gottlieb, Carl, 133
Goulding, Edmund, 499
     Dark Victory, 307
     Grand Hotel, 199
Gowland, Gibson, 297
Graduate, The (Nichols), 248, *250*
*Grand Design: Hollywood as a Modern
     Business Enterprise,
     1930–1939* (Balio), 434
Grand Hotel (Goulding), 199, 499
Grand Illusion (Renoir), 268, *268*
Grand National Films, 498
Grant, Cary, 299–300, *301,* 305, 311,
     397, *397*
Grant, Susannah, 143
Grapes of Wrath, The (Ford), 46, *47,*
     167, 228, 401
graphic match cuts, **365–67,** *366*
Grayson, Kathryn, 515
Grazer, Brian, 517
Grease (Kleiser), 108
Great Depression, 46, 167, *346*
     cinematography and, 235
Great Expectations (Cuarón), *146*
Great Expectations (Lean), *146*
Great Train Robbery, The (Porter),
     103, 279, 440, *440*
Great Ziegfeld, The (Leonard), 496
Greaves, William,
     *Symbiopsychotaxiplasm:
          Take One,* 83
Greed (von Stroheim), 297, 442
Green, Alfred E., 302
     Baby Face, 453
Green, David Gordon, *Pineapple
     Express,* 109
Greene, Graham, 314
Greengrass, Paul, 272, *272,* 352, 406
Green Lantern, The (Campbell), 85
Greenstreet, Sydney, *315*
Greenwald, Maggie, *The Ballad of
     Little Jo,* 105
Greenwood, Jonny, 404
Greenwood, Sarah, *183,* 200
Gregory, Robin, 396
Greno, Nathan, *Tangled,* 129
Grey Gardens (Maysles and Maysles),
     75, 476
Grey Owl (Attenborough), 314
Griebe, Frank, 230
Grier, Pam, 313
Grierson, John, 71
Gries, Tom, *Will Penny,* 105

Griffith, D. W., 42, *43,* 77, 152, 197,
     265, 295–97, 303, 321, 375,
     440–41, 442, *444,* 448–49,
     460, 495, 498, 505
     The Birth of a Nation, 296, 312,
          376, 440–41, 442, *443*
     Broken Blossoms, 234, 296, *296,*
          311, 442
     Dream Street, 442
     Enoch Arden, 442
     Hearts of the World, 296
     Intolerance, 184, *185,* 191, 252, 296,
          442, 448
     Judith of Bethulia, 442
     and Lilian Gish, **295–97,** *296*
     Orphans of the Storm, 442
     Way Down East, 20–22, *21,* 53, 367,
          442, 449
Griffiths, Richard, 213
Grifters, The (Frears), 260
Griggs, Loyal, 279*n*
Grint, Rupert, 23
grips, 228
Grossman, Eugene, 398, 414
group-point-of-view shot, 274
group shot, 252
Group Theatre, 303
Guazzoni, Enrico, *Quo Vadis?,* 442
Guggenheim, Davis, *An Inconvenient
     Truth,* 72
*Guide to Recognizing Your Saints,
     A* (Montiel), *305,* 311
Guinness, Alec, 109, 312, 314, 317
Gunfighter, The (King), 105
Guru (Anchal), 472
Gutiérrez Alea, Tomás, *Memories of
     Underdevelopment,* 4
Gyllenhaal, Jake, *2, 56,* 311

H

Haagensen, Phellipe, 187
Hackman, Gene, 304, *474*
Hagen, Jean, *297*
Haggis, Paul, *In the Valley of Elah,*
     188
Hair (Forman), 108
hairstyle, *see* costume, hairstyle and
     makeup
Half-Breed, The (Dwan), 314
Hall, Allen, *282*
Hall, Charles D., *185, 195,* 197
Hall, Conrad, 219, *229,* 475
Hall, Don, 419
Hall, Philip Baker, *406*

Hallelujah! (Vidor), 390
Haller, Daniel, 191
Haller, Ernest, 235, *235,* 269
Halloween lighting, 101, *102,* 241
Halloween movies, 100
Hallström, Lasse, 326
    Chocolat, 292
    My Life as a Dog, 419
    What's Eating Gilbert Grape, 292
Hamada, Tatsuo, *201*
Hameister, Willy, 234
Hamlet (Kozintsev), 195
Hamlet (Maurice), 295
Hamlet (Olivier), *399*
Hammer, Armie, *310*
Hammer, Lance, *Ballast,* 83, 410
Hammer Studios, 212
Hammett, Dashiell, 93
Hammid, Alexander, *Meshes of the*
    Afternoon, 79
Hampton, Christopher, *312*
Hancock (Berg), 188
handheld cameras, 266, *272,* **272**
Hands on a Hard Body (Bindler), 74
Haneke, Michael, *Funny Games,*
    123, *126,* 517
Hangover, The, Part II, (Phillips),
    109, 515
Hanks, Tom, 209, *210,* 281, 309,
    494, 503
Hansard, Glen, 408
Hanson, Curtis, 293
    L.A. Confidential, 95
    Wonder Boys, 305
Happiness of the Katakuris, The
    (Miike), 108
Hard Day's Night, A (Lester), 462
Hardwicke, Catherine, 404
Hardy, Oliver, 443
Haring, Keith, 37–38, *38*
Harjo, Sterlin, *Four Sheets to the*
    Wind, 314
Hark Tsui, 201, *468,* 469
    The Butterfly Murders, 469
    Peking Opera Blues, 468, 469
Harlan County USA (Kopple), 73–74
Harlow, Jean, 497
harmonic content, 395
Harper, Jessica, *101, 196*
Harris, Ed, *Appaloosa,* 105
Harris, Jon, 372
Harris, Maury, 400
Harris, Richard, 148, *149*
Harrison, Doane, 345

Harris Poll, 309, 311
Harryhausen, Ray, 112
Harry Potter, Jesus Christ and,
    25–26, *26*
Harry Potter and the Chamber of
    Secrets (Columbus), *25*
Harry Potter and the Deathly Hallows:
    Part I (Yates), *25,* 26
Harry Potter and the Deathly Hallows:
    Part II (Yates), *1, 25,* 26, *26,*
    134, 514, 516
Harry Potter and the Goblet of Fire
    (Newell), *25*
Harry Potter and the Half-Blood
    Prince (Yates), *25*
Harry Potter and the Order of the
    Phoenix (Yates), *25*
Harry Potter and the Prisoner of
    Azkaban (Cuarón), *25*
Harry Potter and the Sorcerer's Stone
    (Columbus), *25*
Harry Potter movies, *1, 7,* **22–31,** *23,*
    24–31, 36, 127, 179, 404, 419
    Christianity and, 26
    earnings of, 23
    Hitler and, 23–25, *25*
    mythical analysis of, 25–26
    political analysis of, 23–25, *25*
    World War II and, 23–25, *25*
Hart, William S., 103
Harvey, Herk, *Carnival of Souls,* 101
Hashimoto, Shinobu, 148
Hathaway, Anne, *190*
Havelock-Allan, Anthony, *146*
Hawke, Ethan, *146*
Hawkes, Howard, 464
Hawkes, John, *421*
Hawkesworth, John, *199*
Hawks, Howard, 155, 179, 305, *308,*
    331, 399, 459
    The Big Sleep, 96
    Red River, 105, *110*
    Scarface, 88, 93
Haycox, Ernest, 157–59
Hayden, Sterling, *245*
Hayes, John Michael, 126
Haynes, Todd, 173
    I'm Not There, 54, 291, *291*
Hays, William Harrison, Sr., 452
Hays Office, 452
Haywire (Soderbergh), 517
Hayworth, Rita, 515
Hazanavicius, Michel, *The Artist,* 299
HBO, *True Blood, 109*

Head in the Clouds (Duigan), 188, *189*
Heart of Glass (Herzog), 322, 464
Hearts of the World (Griffith), 296
Heaven (Tykwer), 352
Hecht, Ben, 123
Heckroth, Hein, 200
Hedda Gabler (Ibsen), 51*n*
Hedren, Tippi, 275, *277,* 322
Heil, Reinhold, 405
Heinrichs, Rick, 213
Heist (Mamet), 400
heliographic process, 435
Hellboy (del Toro), 13, 108, 182, *182*
Hellboy II: The Golden Army (del
    Toro), 182, *182*
Hellraiser, (Barker), 102
Helm, Zack, *125*
Help, The (Taylor), *225*
Heman, Roger, Sr., 398, 401, 414
Henabery, Joseph, 376
Henckel von Donnersmarck, Florian,
    The Lives of Others, 144, *228*
Henreid, Paul, 365, *367*
Henry V (Olivier), 317, *317*
Hepburn, Audrey, *301*
Hepburn, Katharine, *301,* 302, 305,
    307, 315
Herman, Lila, 351
Hermes Carrying the Infant Dionysus
    (Praxiteles), 37, *38*
hero, *see* protagonists
Hero (Zhang), 209
Herrmann, Bernard, 397, *397,* 404,
    417, 419, 424, 455
Herschel, John, 435
Herzog, Werner, 137, 322, 418
    Aguirre: The Wrath of God, 464
    Even Dwarfs Started Small, 464
    Heart of Glass, 322, 464
    Invincible, 181
    Nosferatu the Vampire, 464
    Woyzeck, 325*n*
Heston, Charleton, *270,* 271
Heyman, Mark, 128
Hickel, Hal, *282*
high-angle shot, **260,** *261*
high-key lighting, 238, 240–41, *240*
High Noon (Zinnemann), 151, *233*
highshots, 260
Hill, George Roy, 474
    Butch Cassidy and the Sundance
    Kid, 103, 110, *110*
Hill, Hunter, *Lake City,* 294
Hillcoat, John, *The Road,* 188

Hiroshima mon amour (Resnais), 345

Hirsch, Paul, 372

Hirschberg, Lora, *389*

Hirshfeld, Gerald, 280

His Girl Friday (Hawks), 305

historical drama genre, *192*

History of American Cinema, 432

History of Narrative Film,
 A (Cook), 433

Hitchcock, Alfred, *85,* 99, 153, 179,
 182, 197, 200, 208, 264,
 459, *460,* 499

 The Birds, 101, 275, *277,* 322, 352, 417

 Dial M for Murder, 207, 515

 The Lady Vanishes, 200

 North by Northwest, 155, 260, *261,*
  301, 397, *397*

 Notorious, 123, *124,* 125, 208, *255,*
  265, 268, 269, *301*

 Number Seventeen, 182

 Psycho, 41–42, 99, 297, 365, 417

 Rear Window, 126, 174, *175,* 315,
  368, *368*

 Rebecca, 499

 Rope, 151

 Suspicion, 301

 The 39 Steps, 398, *417*

 To Catch a Thief, 301

 Vertigo, 322, 365

Hitch-Hiker, The (Lupino), 96

Hitler, Adolf:

 German Expressionism and, 445

 Harry Potter's Lord Voldemort
  and, 23–25, *25*

 propaganda films and, 73

Ho, Yim, 469

Hoch, Winton C., 231, *232*

Hocks, Richard, 410

Hodge, Adrian, 156

Hodge, John, 123, 146

Hoffe, Monckton, 399

Hoffman, Dustin, 248, *250,* 304,
 314, *396*

Hoffman, Michael, *Restoration, 305*

Hoffman, Philip Seymour, 228, 311,
 329, *406*

Hogarth, William, 212, 236

Højbjerg, Morten, 351

Holden, Stephen, 109

Holden, William, *94, 245, 432, 475*

Holland, Rodney, 396

Hollywood, 79, 82, 93, 149, 184

 African Americans and, 311, 312–13

 comedies, 442–43

film style of, 440–43, 450–55

film systems used in, 234–36

foreign films and, 516–17

Golden Age of, 299–302,
 299–302, 441, 450–55, *453,*
 498, **498–500**

golden age of horror in, 99

musicals, *106*

new, 308, *308,* 472

phases of filmmaking in, 504

studio system, 137, 233, 238, 242,
 310, 315, 321, 451, 472–73,
 485, 509, 512

theme parks and movie sets, 184

see also independent system

Hollywood Ending (Allen), 293

Hollywood production systems:

 best picture nominees (2005), *515*

 contemporary, **512–15**

 decline of studio system, *500,*
  500–501

 financing and, **505–7,** *506, 508–9*

 and Hollywood's Golden Age, *498,*
  498–500

 independent producers and,
  506, 508–9

 independent systems and,
  501–5, *512*

 labor unions and, 503–4

 marketing and distribution,
  507–12, *512*

 maverick producers and
  directors and, **517**

 postproduction and, **494–95**

 production and, **493–94**

 production/distribution data, *515*

 professional organizations and,
  504–5

 studio organization, **495–501,**
  497, 498

 studios and independent
  companies in, *513–14*

Hollywood Reporter, 311

Hollywood Story, The (Finler), 434

Hollywood Studio System, The:
 A History (Gomery), 434

Holm, Ian, 154, 418

Holman, Tomlinson, 391, 415

Holt, Tim, 332

Holt, Willy, 210

Hombre (Ritt), 105

Home and the World, The (S. Ray), 201

Home on the Range (Finn and
 Sanford), 113

Honda, Ishirô, 280

Hondo (Farrow), 515

Hon. Frances Duncombe, The,
 (Gainsborough), 57, *58*

Hong Kong cinema, 201, 468–69

Hong Kong martial arts genre,
 201, *209*

Hooper, Tobe:

 Poltergeist, 102

 The Texas Chain Saw Massacre,
  102

Hooper, Tom, *The King's Speech,*
 66, 156, 251–52, *253,*
 403, 516

Hopkins, Anthony, 288, 312

Hopper, Dennis, 304, *465*

 Easy Rider, 474

Hornby, Nick, 128

Horne, Lena, *313*

horror genre, 81, **99–102,** *100, 101,*
 102, 445

Horror of Dracula (Fisher), 212

Horse Thief, The (Tian), 468

Hou, Hsiao-Hsien, 201

 A City of Sadness, 470

 Flight of the Red Balloon, 470

Houghton, Stanford, 414, 420

Hours, The (Daldry), 307, 326, 407

House (Obayashi), 467

Howard, Byron, *Tangled,* 129

Howard, Ron, *The Missing,* 105

Howard, Tom, 280, *281*

Howe, James Wong, 234, *239*

Howl's Moving Castle (Miyazaki), 113

Hoyde, Ellen, *75*

Hoyt, Harry O., 279

 The Lost World, 112

Hudsucker Proxy, The (Coen), 305

Hughes, Albert, *The Book of Eli, 250*

Hughes, Allen, *The Book of Eli,* 250

Hughes, John, *Ferris Bueller's Day
 Off,* 123

Hugo (Scorsese), 516

Hui, Ann, 201, 469

 The Boys from Vietnam, 469

Human Stain, The (Benton), *306,*
 307, 312

Hume, Alan, 281

Hung, Sammo, 469

Hunte, Otto, 279, *280*

Hunter, Holly, 304, 329, *329,* 367

Hunter, Jeffrey, *40*

Huo, Tingxiao, *209*

Hurd, Earl, 111

Hurt Locker, The (Bigelow), 133, *246, 387, 403*
Hustler, The (Rossen), 304
Huston, Anjelica, 260
Huston, Danny, 278
Huston, John, 204, *205,* 260, *260, 315,* 322, 328, 502
    The African Queen, 307
    Asphalt Jungle, 96
    Fat City, 308
    The Maltese Falcon, 94, 96
    The Misfits, 304
hybridization, **108–11**
hybrid movies, **82–83**
Hyman, Bernard, 496–97
hypo (hyposulfite thiosulfate), 435

I

Ibsen, Henrik, 51*n*
Ice Storm, The (A. Lee), 201, 395, 470
Idiots, The (von Trier), 463
Idziak, Slawomir, 203
if.... (Anderson), 462
Ikiru (Kurosawa), 465
Iliad, The (Homer), 145
illusion of succession, 49
Imagining Argentina (Hampton), *312*
IMAX, 229, 344, 486
    international growth of, 517
    3–D systems, 516
Imitation of Life (Sirk), 173
I'm Not There (Haynes), 54, 291, *291*
iMovie, 75
implied events, 140, *141*
Impossible Voyage, The (Méliès), 440
improvisation, 294, *320,* **320–21**
    defined, 320
in-camera, mechanical, and laboratory effects, **279–80**
in-camera effects, 279, 280
Inception (Nolan), 388, *389,* 492
inciting incident, 132, *136*
In Cold Blood (Brooks), *229*
Inconvenient Truth, An (Guggenheim), 72
Incredibles, The (Bird), 111, 114–15
independent filmmakers, 472–73
independent system, 485, 485*n,* **501–5,** *506,* 508–9, 512, *513–14*
    directors in, 502
    producers in, **501–5**
    see also Hollywood
India, cinema of, 470–72

Indiana Jones and the Last Crusade (Spielberg), 155
Indian cinema, 201
indirect costs, 507
Industrial Light & Magic, 282
Informer, The (Ford), 230, 263
Inglorious Basterds (Tarantino), *339*
Inland Empire (Lynch), 82
Innocents, The (Clayton), 101
Insider, The (Mann), 364
Insomnia (Skjoldbjærg), *95*
instructional films, 72, **72**
intercutting, 367, 440
interior monologue, 398
Intermezzo (Ratoff), 499
internal sound, **398–99,** *399*
international styles of design, **194–202,** *200, 201*
Interpreter, The (Pollack), 307
Interrotron, 75
In the Bedroom (Field), 293, 329
In the Realm of the Senses (Oshima), *465,* 466
In the Valley of Elah (Haggis), 188
Intolerable Cruelty (Coen and Coen), 400, *452*
Intolerance (Griffith), 184, 191, 252, 296, 442, 448
Introducing Dorothy Dandridge (Coolidge), *313*
Invasion of the Body Snatchers (Siegel), 98
Invincible (Herzog), 181
invisibility:
    and cinematic language, **7–11,** *8,* 14
    cultural, 10–11, *11*
    and editing, *8, 9*
    exceptions to, *10*
Invisible Cinema, 82
iPads, 2
Irglová, Markéta, 408
iris, 244
iris-in/iris-out, *372,* **372,** 460
Iron Giant, The (Bird), 99, 111
Iron Horse, The (Ford), 105, 314
Iron Man (Favreau), 111, 145, 292, *305, 308*
Iron Man 2 (Favreau), *305*
Irons, Jeremy, 422
Irréversible (Noé), 147, 148
Irving, Washington, 211
Isfalt, Björn, 419
It (Badger), 191
Italian cinema, 200, *200,* 455–57
Italian for Beginners (Scherfig), 463

Italian Straw Hat, An (Clair), 448
It Came from Outer Space (Arnold), 98
It Happened One Night (Capra), 109
Ito, Kisaku, 201
Ivan the Terrible, Parts I and II (Eisenstein), 195, 449
I Vitelloni (Fellini), 200

J

Jackson, Gemma, 200
Jackson, Peter, 145, 282, 309, 326, 402, 404
    Braindead, 102
    King Kong, 403
    Lord of the Rings movies, 115, 199, 283, 291
Jackson, Samuel L., 305, 313
Jacobs, Ken, 476
Jacquet, Luc, *March of the Penguins, 4,* 488
Jagger, Mick, 344
Jalsaghar (S. Ray), 471–72
Jane Eyre (Fukunaga), *61*
Janney, Allison, 217, *218*
Jannings, Emil, *198,* 297, 446
Jansen, Adolf, 390
Janssen, Pierre-Jules-Césare, 436, 437
Japanese cinema, 201, *201*
Jarecki, Andrew, *Capturing the Friedmans,* 75
Jarmusch, Jim, 474
    Broken Flowers, 90
    Dead Man, 104, 105
    Stranger Than Paradise, 473
Jarvie, Ian, 434
Jason and the Argonauts (Chaffey), 112
Jaws (Spielberg), 133, 260, 280, 415, 419
Jazz Singer, The (Crosland), 106, 451, *451*
Jenkins, George, *The Best Years of Our Lives,* 203
Jenkins, Patty, *Monster,* 188, *189*
Jenkins, Richard, *422*
Jenkins, Tamara, *The Savages,* 311, 484
Jenson, Vicky, *Shrek,* 113
Jessup, Harley, 181
Jesus Christ Superstar (Jewison), 108
Jeunet, Jean-Pierre, 418
Jewison, Norman, 375
    Jesus Christ Superstar, 108

Jezebel (Wyler), 302, 306, *306*
Jindabyne (Lawrence), 145
Joe Strummer and the Mescaleros, 408
Joffé, Roland, 405
Johansson, Scarlett, 311, 421, *422*
Johnny Guitar (Ray), 105
Johns, Glynis, 193, *193*
Johnson, Don, *395*
Johnson, Eric, *145*
Johnson, Joseph MacMillan, 174
Johnson, Rian, *Brick, 95*
Jolie, Angelina, 288
Jolson, Al, 451, *451*
Jones, Arwel, *183*
Jones, Duncan, *Moon, 99*
Jones, Grover, 399
Jones, James, 156
Jones, James Earl, 313
Jones, Jeffrey, 213
Jones, Leslie, *346*
Jonze, Spike, 317, 345
    Where the Wild Things Are, 82
Jordan, Dorothy, 359, *362*
Jordan, Neil, 263, 405
Joyce, James, 80
Joy Ride (Rengel), 463
Judith of Bethulia (Griffith), 442
Jukti Takko Aar Gappo (Ghatak), 472
Julia, Raul, 313
Julia (Zinnemann), 314
Julien Donkey-Boy (Korine), 463
Juliet of the Spirits (Fellini), 236
July, Miranda, *Me and You and Everyone We Know,* 419, *421*
jump cuts, **368,** 450
    defined, 29
Junebug (Morrison), 488
Junge, Alfred, 200
Jungle Book, The (Reitherman), 108
Juno (Reitman), **7–22,** *8, 9, 10, 11, 12, 14, 15, 16–19, 20, 21,* 36–37, *37*
Jurassic Park (Spielberg), 59, 179, 264–65, *264,* 281
Just Like Weather (Fong), 469

K

Kael, Pauline, *186,* 288
Kagemusha (Kurosawa), 465
Kaidan (Kobayashi), 101
Kaminski, Janusz, 274
Kammerspielfilm, 197
Kansas City (Altman), 304
Kapur, Shekhar, *Elizabeth,* 291

Karloff, Boris, 90, 193, 263, 415
Karun, Shaji N., *Piravi,* 472
Kar Wai Wong, *Ashes of Time,* 469
Kasdan, Lawrence, *Silverado,* 105
Kashyap, Anurag, *Black Friday,* 472
Katta, Deva, *Prasthanam,* 472
Kauffman, Ross, *Born into Brothels,* 67
Kaufman, Boris, 275
Kaufman, Charles, 146
    Synecdoche, New York, 82
Kawin, Bruce, 280, 445
Kawin, Gerald, 474
Kaye, Danny, *193*
Kazan, Elia, 303, *303,* 304, 327, 502
    On the Waterfront, 179, 197
    Panic in the Streets, 96
Keaton, Buster, 108, 179, 442
    The General, 443
    The Play House, 375
Keaton, Diane, 53, 210, *239,* 474
Keel, Howard, 515
Keitel, Harvey, 303, 304, 317, *395*
Kelly, Anthony Paul, 42
Kelly, Gene, *297,* 298
    On the Town, 108
    Singin' in the Rain, 87, 108, *297*
Kelly, Grace, *301, 313,* 515
Kelly, Richard, *56*
    Donny Darko, 99
"Ken Burns Effect," 75
Kennedy, Joseph P., 498
Kershner, Irvin, 281
    Star Wars: The Empire Strikes Back, 405
Kes (Loach), 462
Kevan, Jack, 193
key light, 240
Khandaar (Sen), 472
Kharji (Sen), 472
Kiarostami, Abbas, 4, 461
Kick-Ass (Vaughn), *59,* 111
Kidman, Nicole, 243, *243,* 278–79, *278,* 305–6, *306,* 307–8, 322, 326, *372,* 407, 511
Kid with a Bike, The (Dardenne and Dardenne), 83
Kieslowski, Krzysztof, 203, 352
Kill Bill movies (Tarantino), 108, 469
Killer, The (Woo), 54–56, *54,* 201
Killers, The (Siodmak), 96
Killing, The (Kubrick), 400
Kinemacolor, 234
kinesis, 202, **208–11,** *209*
Kinetograph, **437,** *438*
Kinetoscope, **437,** 439

King, Henry, *331*
    The Gunfighter, 105
King, Peter, 193
King, Richard, 388, *406,* 410
King, Stephen, 293
King and I, The (Lang), 108
Kingdom, The, (von Trier and Arnfred), 102
King Kong (Cooper and Schoedsack), 112, 279
King Kong (Jackson), 403
King Lear (Kozintsev), 195
King of Kong, The: A Fistful of Quarters (Gordon), 74
Kingsley, Ben, *313,* 314
King's Speech, The (Hooper), 66, 156, 251–52, *253,* 403, 516
kino-pravda, 448, 458
Kinski, Klaus, 418
Kirk, Mark-Lee, 199
Kirsanoff, Dmitri, *Ménilmontant,* 447
Kiss Me Deadly (Aldrich), 96
Kiss Me Kate (Sidney), 515
Kitano, Takeshi, *Sonatine,* 93
Klein, Saar, *346*
Kleiser, Jeff, 309
Kleiser, Randal, *Grease,* 108
Klimek, Johnny, 405
Klimt (Ruiz), 181
Kline, Kevin, 395
Kloves, Steve, 134
Kluge, Alexander, *Artists under the Big Top: Perplexed,* 464
Knight, Jack T., 389
Knight, Stephen, 156
Knocked Up (Apatow), *21,* 22, 109, *319*
Knoll, John, *282*
Kobayashi, Masaki, *Kaidan,* 101
Koch, Howard, *147*
Kodachrome film, 235
Konisberg, Ira, 280
Konstantin, Leopoldine, *255*
Kopple, Barbara, *Harlan County USA,* 73–74
Korda, Alexander, 200
Korda, Vincent, 182, *199,* 200
Korine, Harmony, *Julien Donkey-Boy,* 463
Koster, Henry, 193
Kotto, Yaphet, 416
Koyaanisqatsi (Reggio), 277
Kozintsev, Grigori, 195
Kramer, Stanley, *On the Beach,* 98

Krampf, Günther, 277
Krasker, Robert, 263
Krauss, Werner, *445*
Krays, The (Medak), 93
Kriemhild's Revenge (Lang), 197
Kroplachev, Georgi, 195
Krrish (Roshan), *5*
Kubelka, Peter, *Arnulf Rainer,* 81
Kubrick, Stanley, 179, 191, 193, 208, 277, 307, 474, *476*
   Barry Lyndon, 199, 236, *236,* 322, 396
   A Clockwork Orange, 322, *407*
   Dr. Strangelove, or: How I Learned to Stop Worrying and Love the Bomb, 109, *245,* 268, 272, 322, 398
   Eyes Wide Shut, 178, 291, 307, 511
   Lolita, 304
   The Killing, 400
   The Shining, 100, 185, 261, *261,* 273, 297, 322, 389, 394, 396
   Spartacus, 60, 257, 405
   2001: A Space Odyssey, 86, *86,* 89, 97, 155, 209, *210,* 280, *281,* 309, 365, *366,* 417, 475
Kuchar, Mike, *Sins of the Fleshapoids,* 81
Kukunoor, Nagsh, 472
Kuleshov, Lev, 194, 303, 340, 345, *347,* 349, 448, 449
   The Extraordinary Adventures of Mr. West in the Land of the Bolsheviks, 448
Kuleshov effect, 345, *347, 381*
Kung Fu Panda (Osborne and Stevenson), *70,* 129
Kung Fu Panda 2 (Yuh), 85
Kung Ming Fan, 54
Kunuk, Zacharias, *The Fast Runner,* 314
Kurková, Karolína, 517
Kurosawa, Akira, 137, 201, 207, 208, 322, 326, 329, *329,* 409, 464–65, 471, 474
   Charisma, 250
   Ikiru, 465
   Kagemusha, 465
   Ran, 465, *466, 467*
   Rashomon, 148, 464, 465
   Seven Samurai, 465
   Throne of Blood, 465
   Yojimbo, 465
Kurosawa, Kyoshi, *Charisma, 250*
Kusama, Karyn, *Æon Flux,* 188, *189*

Kuzui, Fran Rubel, *Buffy the Vampire Slayer, 110*
Kwan, Nancy, 313
Kwei, James Y., 374

L

laboratory, in-camera, and mechanical effects, **279–80**
laboratory effects, 279, 280
labor unions, 485, 485*n,* **503–4**
L.A. Confidential (Hanson), *95*
La Cucaracha (Corrigan), 235
Lady Chatterly (Ferran), 145
Lady Eve, The (Sturges), 399
Lady in the Lake (Montgomery), 275
Lady Vanishes, The (Hitchcock), 200
Laemmle, Carl, 495
Lai, Stan, *The Peach Blossom Land,* 470
La Jetée (Marker), 459
Lake City (Hill and Moore), 294
Lam, Ringo, *City on Fire,* 469
Lamas, Fernando, 313
Lamer, Steven, *258*
Lancaster, Burt, 174, *176*
Lanchester, Elsa, 263, *263*
Landau, Martin, 214, 260, *261*
Land in Anguish (Rocha), 4
Lane, Anthony, 364
Lang, Fritz, 93, 179, 197, 230, *262,* 279, *280,* 319, 444, 459
   M, 390, 444
   Metropolis, 89, 97, 444
   Scarlet Street, 96
Lang, Walter, 305
   The King and I, 108
Langdon, Harry, 108
Langella, Frank, 314, 422
Lansbury, Angela, 314
Lansing, Joi, 271
L'Argent (L'Herbier), 447
Lasseter, John, 59, 113
   Cars 2, 85
   Toy Story 2, 113, 309
Lassie Come Home, 302
Last Emperor, The (Bertolucci), *157,* 172
Last Laugh, The (Murnau), 182, 197, *198,* 265, 297, 444, *446*
Last of the Mohicans, The (Cooper), 102
Last of the Mohicans, The (Mann), 314
Last Orders (Schepisi), 326
Last Picture Show, The (Bogdanovich), 474

Last Seduction, The (Dahl), 96
Last Tango in Paris (Bertolucci), 320
Last Tycoon, The (Fitzgerald), 484
Last Tycoon, The (Kazan), 502
Last Year at Marienbad (Resnais), 81, 459, 461
Late Spring (Ozu), 201, *201,* 466
Latham, Grey, 438
Latham, Otway, 438
Latham, Woodville, 438
Laughton, Charles, 186–87, *370,* 414, 420
Laura (Preminger), 96, 322, 406
Laurel, Stan, 443
Laurel and Hardy, 108
Laurents, Arthur, 151
Lavagnino, Angelo Francesco, 404, *405*
L'Avventura (Antonioni), 200
Law, Jude, *183,* 319
Lawrence, D.H., 145
Lawrence, Marc, 143
Lawrence, Ray, *Jindabyne,* 145
Lawrence of Arabia (Lean), 87, 226, 364, *365,* 502
Lawton, J. F., 143
Leachman, Cloris, 419
Lean, David, *146,* 226, 461, 502
   Lawrence of Arabia, 87, 364, *365*
Leatherheads (Clooney), *452*
Léaud, Jean-Pierre, 322, 374, *374, 459*
Leave Her to Heaven (Stahl), 172
Leaving Las Vegas (Figgis), *91*
Le Bargy, Charles, *The Assassination of the Duke de Guise,* 404
Le Cercle Rouge (Melville), 410
Ledger, Heath, *2, 192*
Le Doulos (Melville), 325*n*
Lee, Ang, 201, *209,* 395, 495
   Brokeback Mountain, 2, 110, *470, 470*
   Crouching Tiger, Hidden Dragon, 199, *470, 470*
   Eat Drink Man Woman, 470
   The Ice Storm, 470
   Lust, Caution, 470
   Sense and Sensibility, 470
   The Wedding Banquet, 470
Lee, Bruce, *209,* 469
Lee, Christopher, 212
Lee, Danny, 54
Lee, Lee Byung-hun, 517
Lee, Rowland V., *195*

Lee, Spike, 260, *261,* 311, 322, 474
   Do the Right Thing, 319
   Malcolm X, 517
"Legend of Sleepy Hollow, The"
   (Irving), 211
Léger, Fernand, *Ballet mécanique,*
   77, 79, 446–47
Lehman, Ernest, 155
Leigh, Janet, 42, *270,* 271, 297, 365
Leigh, Jennifer Jason, 304–5
Leigh, Mike, 321
   Vera Drake, 22
Leigh, Vivien, 191, *193, 453*
Leisen, Mitchell, 182
   Easy Living, 182, *452*
Le Million (Clair), 108, 398
Lemmon, Jack, *154,* 314, 316
L'Enfant (Dardenne and Dardenne),
   57, 457, 517
Lenin, Vladimir Ilyich, 448
Lennon, John, 281
lenses, **244–47,** *245, 247,* 254–56,
   268–69
   defined, 244
   and focus, 245–46, *245*
   images produced by, *245*
   images produced by various, *247*
Leo, Melissa, *145*
Leonard, Robert Z., 496
Leone, Sergio, 354–55, 415, *415,*
   469, *469*
   The Good, the Bad, and the Ugly,
    87
   Once upon a Time in America, 93
   Once Upon a Time in the West, 105
Leopard, The (Visconti), 173, 174–76,
   176
LeRoy, Mervyn, 254
   Little Caesar, 93
Le Samouraï (Melville), 93
Lesnie, Andrew, 282, 283
Lester, Richard, *A Hard Day's*
   Night, 462
Leterrier, François, 398
Leth, Jørgen, 351, 353
Letter, The (Wyler), *306,* 307
Let the Right One In (Alfredson),
   59, 102
Leverett, George, 401
Levine, Ted, 42, *44*
Levinson, Barry, 281
Lewis, Brad, *Cars 2,* 85
Lewis, Cameron, 405
Lewis, Jerry, 143
Lewis, Jon, 485

Lewis, Richard J., *Barney's Vision,* 290
L'Herbier, Marcel, *L'Argent,* 447
Li, Jet, 469
Libatique, Matthew, 231, 277
Libertine, The (Dunmore), 293
Life and Death of Colonel Blimp (Powell
   and Pressburger), 200
Life Aquatic with Steve Zissou, The
   (Anderson), 404
Life is Sweet (Leigh), 321
Life of an American Fireman (Porter),
   440
Life of Moses, The (Blackton), 442
Life of Oharu, The (Mizoguchi), 466
light, lighting, *48,* **185–87,** *188,*
   236–44, *239,* **323–26**
   from above, *242*
   backlight and, 241, *241*
   from below, *241*
   direction of, *237–38,* **238–42,** *239*
   edge lights and, 241
   effect on acting, 323
   and Halloween lighting, 241
   high-key, 238
   and high-key lighting, 240–41, *240*
   and lighting ratio, 240
   low-key, 238
   and low-key lighting, 240–41
   quality of, **238**
   rim lights and, 241
   sources of, *237–38,* **237–38,** *239,*
    240, 241, 242, 243
   three-point system, 238–39,
    240, 244
lighting ratio, 240
Lights of New York, The (Foy), 451
Limey, The (Soderbergh), 8, 126, 348
Lin, Justin, *Fast Five,* 85
Linden, Edward, 279
Linder, Max, 108, 445
Lindley, John, *236*
line producers, 497
linkage, 449
Linklater, Richard:
   A Scanner Darkly, 82, 145
   Slacker, 69
Linney, Laura, 311
Lions Gate Studios, 505
Liotta, Ray, 269, 273
Lipton, Rex, 400
Lisberger, Steven, 280
Little Big Man (Penn), 105, 314
Little Caesar (LeRoy), 93
Little Foxes, The (Wyler), 256, *256,*
   306, 307, 326

Little Shop of Horrors (Oz), 108
Little Zizou (Taraporevala), 472
Litvak, Anatole, 331
Liu, Lucy, 313
Lives of Others, The (Henckel von
   Donnersmarck), *144,* 228
live theater, compared to cinema, 5
Lloyd, Danny, 185, 273
Lloyd, Harold, 108, 442
Lloyd, Phyllida, *Mamma Mia!, 107*
Loach, Ken, *Kes,* 462
location, 183, *184*
Lockwood, Gary, 209, *210*
Logan, Bruce, 280
Logan, John, 148
Lola Montès (Ophüls), 266, 319
Lolita (Kubrick), 304
Lolita (Lyne), 422
Loncraine, Richard, *Richard III, 305*
London Films, 200
Lone, John, *157*
Loneliness of the Long Distance Runner,
   The (Richardson), 462
Lonely Are the Brave (Miller), 105
Lonesome Cowboys (Warhol), 81
Lone Star (Sayles), 517
Long Distance Wireless Photography
   (Méliès), *440*
Longest Day, The (Annakin, Marton,
   and Wicki), 156
long-focal-length lens, 245
long shot, 251, *252*
long take, 151, 277–79, *278,* **323–26,**
   324
Long Voyage Home, The (Ford), 254
looping, 392
Lopez, Jennifer, *312,* 313, 348, *349,* 367
Loquasto, Santo, 197
Lord of the Rings movies (Jackson),
   23, 115, 145, 193, 199, 282,
   283, 291, 309, 326, 404
Lords of Dogtown (Hardwicke), 404
Lorre, Peter, *315,* 318–19
Losey, Joseph, *The Servant,* 462
Los Muertos (Alonso), 325n
Lost Highway (Lynch), 96
Lost in Translation (S. Coppola), 90
Lost World, The (Hoyt), 112, 279
loudness, **394**
Louiso, Todd, *Love Liza,* 228
Love and Death (Allen), 210
Love in the Time of Cholera (Newell),
   145
Lovejoy, Ray, 365, *366*
Love Liza (Louiso), 228

Love Me Tonight (Mamoulian), *106, 107,* 109, 260, *261,* 298n, 395, 418
Lovering, Otho, *366*
Loves of Queen Elizabeth, The (Desfontaines and Mercanton), 442
Lovett, Lyle, 405
Low, Warren, 365
low-angle shot, 7, *8,* **260–63,** *261, 262*
Lower Depths, The (Gorky), 208
Lower Depths, The (Kurosawa), 326
low-key lighting, *102,* 238, 240–41
Loy, Myrna, 321
Lubitsch, Ernst, 182, *254,* 399
    The Merry Widow, 199
    Trouble in Paradise, 109, 390
Lucas, Caryn, 143
Lucas, George, *240,* 281, 282, 309, 344, 372, 475, 517
    Star Wars, 68, 127
    Star Wars: A New Hope, 68, 156
    Star Wars: The Phantom Menace, 490
    THX 1138, 97
Lucas, Marcia, 372
Lucasfilm, 391
Luhrmann, Baz, 176, *176,* 307
    Moulin Rouge!, 108, 307
Luke, Keye, 313
Luketic, Robert, *312*
Lumet, Sidney, 275, 398, 474, 493
    Dog Day Afternoon, 130
Lumière, Auguste and Louis, 56, 72, 194, 439, *439,* 448, 515
Lumière, Louis, *59*
Lund, Kátia, 187, *188,* 358
    City of God, 53, *54,* 93, 376
Lundgren, Siv, 370, *372*
Lupino, Ida, *The Hitch-Hiker,* 96
Lurie, John, *473*
Lust, Caution (A. Lee), 470
Lust for Life (Minelli), 182
Lynch, David, 130, 202, 391, 474, 490
    Inland Empire, 82
    Lost Highway, 96
    Mulholland Dr., 70
Lynd, Laurie, *Breakfast with Scot,* 314
Lyne, Adrian, 422
Lynn, Vera, 398

M

M (Lang), *262,* 319, 390, 444
MacDonald, Jeanette, 260, 395, 496

MacDonald, Joe, *237*
"MacGuffin," 41–42
Mackendrick, Alexander, *233,* 234, *239*
    Sweet Smell of Success, 96
Mackendrick, Alexander, *Sweet Smell of Success,* 322
MacLaine, Shirley, 130, 314
MacMurray, Fred, *94,* 130, 345, *400*
Macy, William H., 290, *406*
Mad Max 2 (Miller), 98
Madonna, 182
Maggiorani, Lamberto, *200,* 456, *457*
magic lantern, 437
magnetic sound recording, 391
Magnificent Ambersons, The (Welles), 199, 267, 326, 400
Magnol, René, 400
Magnolia (Anderson), *406*
Maguire, Tobey, *236,* 311
Mahon, Kevin, *402*
Maielli, Claudio, 415, *415*
Main, Marjorie, 315
Major, Grant, 199
Major Dundee (Peckinpah), 105
major roles, 315
makeup, *see* costume, hairstyle and makeup
Making an American Citizen (Blaché), *443*
Malcolm X (S. Lee), 517
Malick, Terrence, 151, 156, 258, *259,* 265, 293, 400, 474
    Badlands, 123, *258,* 475
    Days of Heaven, 123, 155
    The New World, 42, *45,* 314
    The Thin Red Line, 346
    The Tree of Life, 27, 84, 281
Malkovich, John, 191, 288, 305, 317
Malle, Louis, 458
    Murmur of the Heart, 459
Maltese Falcon, The (Huston), 94, 96, 155, 260, *260, 315,* 328
Mamet, David, 400
Mamma Mia! (Lloyd), *107*
Mamoulian, Rouben, 193, 235, 252, *254,* 260, *261,* 298, 318, 322, 395, 398, 418
    Applause, 107, 390
    Dr. Jekyll and Mr. Hyde, 199
    Love Me Tonight, 106, 107, 109
Manchurian Candidate, The (Frankenheimer), *312*
Manera, Albert, 409
Man Escaped, A (Bresson), 398
Manhattan (Allen), *239*

Mankiewicz, Herman J., 146
Mankiewicz, Joseph L., 191, 302, 502
    All about Eve, 307
    Cleopatra, 302
    The Ghost and Mrs. Muir, 419
    Suddenly, Last Summer, 302
Mann, Aimee, *406*
Mann, Anthony, 242, 459
    Man of the West, 105
    The Naked Spur, 105
    Winchester '73, 105
Mann, Daniel:
    Butterfield 8, 302
    The Teahouse of the August Moon, 312
Mann, Michael, 291
    Collateral, 490
    The Insider, 364
    The Last of the Mohicans, 314
    Public Enemies, 293
Man of a Thousand Faces (Pevney), 193
Man of the West (Mann), 105
Man on Fire (T. Scott), 82
Manthan (Benegal), 472
Mantle, Anthony Dod, 243
Man Who Fell to Earth, The (Roeg), 98
Man Who Knew Too Much, The (Hitchcock), 200
Man Who Shot Liberty Valance, The (Ford), 105
Man Who Wasn't There, The (J. Coen), 96, 231, 421, *422*
Man with the Movie Camera, The (Vertov), 448, *448*
Many Mules, 314
Mara, Rooney, 140
March, Fredric, 193, *203,* 321
Marchand, Corinne, *460*
March of the Penguins (Jacquet), *4,* 488
March of Time, The, 147
Marcoen, Alain, *57*
Mardi Gras (Goulding), 499
Marey, Étienne-Jules, 436, 437
Margot at the Wedding (Baumbach), *306,* 307
Mariano, Rosanna, *372*
Marie Antoinette (Van Dyke), *192,* 193, 199
Marilyn Times Five (Conner), 81
Marker, Chris, 458
    La Jetée, 459
marketing and distribution, **507–12,** *512*
Marks, Owen, 358

Marquand, Richard, 191, 281
Marriage of Maria Braun, The
        (Fassbinder), 464
Marsden, Jason, *392*
Marsh, Mae, 295
Marshall, Frank, *Alive,* 133
Marshall, Garry, 143
        Pretty Woman, 492
Marshall, George, *Destry Rides
        Again,* 105
Marshall, Herbert, 256, *256*
Marshall, Rob:
        Chicago, 108
        *Pirates of the Caribbean: On
                Stranger Tides,* 85, 293, 516
Martelli, Otello, 210
martial arts genre, 201, *209,* 468
Martin, Catherine, 176
Martin, Mardik, *152*
Marton, Andrew, 156
Marvel Comics, 145
Marx, Karl, 445, 449
Marx Brothers, The, 108, 109
mask, *250,* 372
Mason, James, 260, *261*
Mass for the Dakota Sioux (Baillie), 81
Massina, Giulietta, 328
Mast, Bruce F., 474
Mast, Gerald, 445
*Master and Commander: The Far
        Side of the World* (Weir),
        282, 326
master scene technique, 359
master shots, **359,** *362*
Masumura, Yasuzo, 466
match cuts, **364–67,** *366*
        graphic, *366*
match-on-action cuts, **364–67,** *366*
Maté, Rudolph, 278
        D.O.A., 96
Matewan (Sayles), 272
Mathieson, John, *267,* 282
Matras, Christian, 266, *268*
Matrix, The (Wachowski and
        Wachowski), 49, *50,* 59, 176,
        211, 277, 282, 315, 351, 404
Matrix, The movies (Wachowski and
        Wachowski), 25, 53, 97, 469
Matrix I (Whitney), 81
Matrix II (Whitney), 81
Matrix Reloaded, The (Wachowski
        and Wachowski), 405
Matrix Revolutions, The (Wachowski
        and Wachowski), 405
Mattey, Robert A., 280

Matthau, Walter, 304, 314
Mature, Victor, 414
Maumont, Jacques, 400
Maurice, Clément, 295
maverick producers and directors,
        517
Max Factor & Company, 192
Mayer, Carl, 155
Mayer, Louis B., 495, 496*n*
Maysles, Albert, 475
Maysles, Albert and David, *75,*
        475, *476*
McCabe & Mrs. Miller (Altman), 105
McCay, Winsor, *Gertie the Dinosaur,* 111
McConkey, Larry, 273
McDaniel, Hattie, 313
McDormand, Frances, 282
McDowell, Malcolm, 322, *407*
McEwan, Ian, 145
McG, 315
McGarvey, Seamus, *48*
McGivern, Cecil, *146*
McGregor, Ewan, 123, 290
McMurtry, Larry, *2*
McQuarrie, Christopher, *147,* 148
McQueen, Butterfly, 313, 315
McQueen, Steve, 311
Mean Creek (Estes), 326
Me and You and Everyone We Know
        (July), 419, *421*
meaning, 176
        explicit, 12
        implicit, 11, *12*
        interpreting, 176
Means, Russel, 314
Mean Streets (Scorsese), *85, 395*
mechanical, in-camera, and
                laboratory effects, **279–80**
mechanical effects, 279, 280
Medak, Peter, *The Krays,* 93
mediation, 51–53, 57
medium close-up, 252, *252*
medium long shot, 251
medium shot, 251–52, *252*
Meehan, John, 199
Meek, Donald, 157, *158*
Meek's Cutoff (Reichardt), 83, 207
Meet John Doe (Capra), 109, *451*
Meet Me in St. Louis (Minelli), 108, 182
Meet the Fockers (Roach), 404
Meirelles, Fernando, 187, *188,* 358
        City of God, 53, 93, 376
Méliès, Georges, 56, *59,* 194, 234, 279,
        439, *440,* 445
        A Trip to the Moon, 98

melodrama genre, 110
Melville, Jean-Pierre:
        Bob le flambeur, 460
        Le Cercle Rouge, 410
        Le Doulos, 325*n*
        Le Samouraï, 93
Memento (Nolan), 54, 96, 146, 147, 148,
        148, 345
Memories of Underdevelopment
        (Gutiérrez Alea), 4
Mendes, Sam, 41, 211, 215–20, 419
        Road to Perdition, 93
Ménilmontant (Kirsanoff), 447
Menjou, Adolphe, 326
Menke, Sally, *339,* 345
Menyalshchikov, Said, 197
Menzel, Adolf von, 236
Menzies, William Cameron, 180*n,*
        191, 200
        Things to Come, 98, 182
Mercanton, Louis, 295
        The Loves of Queen Elizabeth, 442
Mercer, David, 400
Merry Christmas, Mr. Lawrence
        (Oshima), 466
Merry Widow, The (Lubitsch), 199
Mesa, Matías, 273
Mescall, John J., 241, *241, 263*
Meshes of the Afternoon (Deren and
        Hammid), 79, 81
Messmer, Otto, 443
method acting, 294, **302–4,** *303*
Metro-Goldwyn-Mayer, *see* MGM
Metropolis (Lang), 89, 97, 197, 279,
        280, 444
Metty, Russell, 257, 269
Meyer, Emile, *239*
Meyer, Muffy, *75*
Meyerhold, Vsevolod, 449
MGM (Metro-Goldwyn-Mayer),
        180*n,* 182, 199, 242, 301,
        495–500, 504, 512*n*
Michael Clayton (Gilroy), 514
Micheaux, Oscar, 312–13
microcinema, 82
middle-focal-length lens, 245, *245*
Midler, Bette, *331*
Midnight Cowboy (Schlesinger), *396*
Mifune, Toshiro, 313, 322, 328,
        329, 465
Mighty Joe Young (Schoedsack), 112
Miike, Takashi, *The Happiness of the
        Katakuris,* 108
Mildred Pierce (Curtiz), 173, 301, 307
Miles, Harold, 197, *199*

Milestone, Lewis, 257, *259*
    Ocean's Eleven, 372
Milk (Van Sant), 156
Milky Way, The (Buñuel), 81
Millan, Victor, 271
Milland, Ray, *452,* 515
Miller, Arthur, 51*n,* 303, 304
Miller, Bennett, 329
Miller, David, 301
    Lonely Are the Brave, 105
Miller, Frank, 423, 517
    Sin City, 96, 231
Miller, George, *Mad Max 2,* 98
Miller, Henry, 398
Miller's Crossing (J. Coen), 93
Million Dollar Baby (Eastwood),
    145, 315
Mills, John, *146*
Milner, Victor, *254,* 257, 260
Milton, Franklin, 397, *397*
Mimic (del Toro), 13
Minelli, Vincent, 182, 499
    An American in Paris, 108, 181
    The Band Wagon, 108
    Lust for Life, 182
    Meet Me in St. Louis, 108, 182
Mineo, Sal, 314
Minghella, Anthony, 191
    Cold Mountain, 200, 307, 390
    The English Patient, 390
Minkoff, Rob, *The Forbidden
    Kingdom,* 469
minor characters, 160
Minority Report (Spielberg), 503
minor roles, 315, *315*
*Miracle of Morgan's Creek,
    The* (Sturges), *21, 22*
Miramax, 509, 512*n*
Miranda, Claudio, 283
mise-en-scène, 36, **171–223,** *173, 174,
    175, 176, 199,* 322
    audio/sound, 392, 423–24, *424*
    costume, makeup, and hairstyle
        and, mise-en-scène, design
        and, 172, **179–202**
    framing and, **202–8,** *207*
    production designer and, **180–83**
    staging as, 172, 178
Misfits, The (Huston), 304
Mishra, Sudhir, 472
*Miss Congeniality 2: Armed and
    Fabulous* (Pasquin), 143
Missing, The (Howard), 105
Mission, The (Joffé), 405
Mission Impossible movies, 291

Miss Sadie Thompson (Bernhardt),
    515
Mitchell, Cameron, *Rabbit Hole, 306*
Mitchell, John, 398
Mitchell, Thomas, 157, *158, 366*
Mitchum, Robert, 186, *186, 370,*
    414, 420
mixing sound, **393**
Miyazaki, Hayao, *392*
    Howl's Moving Castle, 113
    Nausicaä, 98
    Spirited Away, 113
Mizoguchi, Kenji, 179, 201, 277,
    464, 465–66
    The Life of Oharu, 466
    Sansho the Bailiff, 466, *467*
    Street of Shame, 466
    Ugetsu, 325*n,* 466
Mizrahi, Isaac, 293
"moguls," 495
Molina, Alfred, 313
Momma Don't Allow (Richardson
    and Reisz), 462
Mo'Nique, *128*
Monogram Pictures, 460
Monogram Productions, 498
monologue, interior, 398
Monopack film, 235
Monroe, Marilyn, *237,* 304, 499
Monster (Jenkins), 188, *189*
Monster-in-Law (Luketic), *312*
Monster's Ball (Forster), *313*
montage:
    sound, 418
    visual, 129, **349–51,** *350, 354,* 380,
        384, 450, 455
    see also Soviet Montage
montage of attractions, 450
Montalban, Ricardo, 313
Móntez, Maria, 313
Montgomery, Robert, *Lady in the
    Lake,* 275
Montiel, Dito, *A Guide to Recognizing
    Your Saints, 305,* 311
Moody, Rick, 201
Moon (Jones), 99
Moore, Julianne, 173, *174,* 305, 407
Moore, Michael:
    Bowling for Columbine, 72
    Farenheit 9/11, 72
    Sicko, 72
Moore, Perry, *Lake City,* 294
Moorehead, Agnes, 323–25, *324*
Moran, Lois, *331*
Moreno, Rita, 313

Morgan, Helen, 298
Morgen, Brett, *Chicago 10,* 111
Mori, Masahiro, 114
Moriarty, Cathy, *152,* 277
Moritz, David, 349
Morning Song Way (Thomas), 314
Morocco (Sternberg), 326, *327*
Morricone, Ennio, 404, 405, 416
Morris, Errol, *Fast, Cheap & Out of
    Control,* 75
Morrison, Phil, *Junebug,* 488
Morrison, Van, "So Quiet in Here,"
    370
Moscow Art Theater, 302, 303
Mother (Pudovkin), 449
Mothersbaugh, Mark, 404
Mother's Day (Broughton), 81
motifs, 20, 81, 215
    see also themes
motion capture, 113–14, **282–83**
Motion Painting No. 1 (Fischinger),
    112
Motion Picture Association of
    America (MPAA), 511, *512*
motion-picture camera, *487*
Motion Picture Patents Company,
    495
Motion Picture Production Code
    (MPPC), 450, **452, 453**
Mottola, Greg, *Superbad,* 13, 109
Moulin Rouge! (Luhrmann), 108, 176,
    176, 307
movement:
    blocking and, 209
    bullet time and, *50*
    of figures, **209–10,** *210*
    illusion in movies of, 5, **47–49,** *50*
movie, defined, 3–5
*Movie-Made America: A Cultural
    History of American Movies*
    (Sklar), 435
movie rating system, *512*
movies:
    apparent motion in, 49
    attendance, 514
    cinematic language in, **60–61**
    as dependent on light, **46–47,** *47*
    feature, 441
    vs. "film," 3
    film form principles in, 46, **49–56**
    form and content in, **36–39,** *37*
    form and expectations in, **39–42**
    highest grossing worldwide,
        510–11
    Hollywood and foreign, 516–17

illusion of movement in, **47–49,** *50*
illusion of succession in, 49
international, 461–72
labor and unions and, **503–4**
length of, 441
the making of, **491–95**
movement in, *50*
narrative in, 39–40
overview, **1–34**
patterns in, **42–46**
persistence of vision in, 49
postproduction of, **494–95**
preproduction of, **492–93**
production of, **493–94**
realism and antirealism in,
        56, **56–60,** 205, 358
space/time manipulation in,
        51, 51*n, 52*
types of, **70–115**
verisimilitude in, **58–60,** *59,* 189,
        202, 205, 211, 279, 358, 392,
        398, 402
see also films; *specific topics*
movie stars, **299–302,** *302*
    what makes, *301*
moving camera, 434
moving frame, 202, 208
Mr. Deeds Goes to Town (Capra), *451*
Mrs. Dalloway (Woolf), 407
Mr. Smith Goes to Washington
        (Capra), *451*
Mühe, Ulrich, *144*
Mulholland Dr. (Lynch), *70,* 202
Mulligan, Carey, 128
Mulligan, Robert, *To Kill a*
        Mockingbird, 79
multiple narrators, *125*
Mumbai noir, 472
Mummy, The (Freund), 99
Mungiu, Cristian, *4 months,*
        3 weeks & 2 days, 21, 22
Munro, Steve, 400, 418
Muraki, Shinobu, 201
Muraki, Yoshiro, 201
Murch, Walter, 343, 351, 390, *394,*
        395, 419, *420*
Murderball (Rubin and Shapiro), 67
Murmur of the Heart (Malle), 459
Murnau, F. W., 155, 179, 182, 197, *198,*
        212, 230, 265, 277, 318, 495
    The Last Laugh, 297, 444, *446*
    Nosferatu, a Symphony of Horror,
        99, 444, *446*
    Sunrise: A Song of Two Humans,
        297

Murphy, Dudley, 313
    Ballet mécanique, 77, 79
Murphy, Eddie, 313
Murphy, Richard, 279
Murray, Bill, 90
Murray, Jack, 359
musical genre, 93, **105–8**
music in film, **403–9,** *406, 407*
Music Man, The (DaCosta), 108
Music Room, The (S. Ray), 172, 201
Mussolini, Benito, movies and,
        455, 456
Muybridge, Eadweard, 436–37, *437*
Myasnikov, Gennadi, 197
My Beautiful Laundrette (Frear), 172
My Darling Clementine (Ford), 88,
        105, 205–6, 237, *237,* 371,
        398, 414
My Dog Skip (Russell), 316
My Life as a Dog (Hallström), 326, 419
My Life in Art (Stanislavsky), 303
My Night at Maud's (Rohmer), 459
Myrick, Daniel, *The Blair Witch*
        Project, 102
Mystic River (Eastwood), 326
My Week with Marilyn (Curtis), 156

N

Nagoyqatsi (Reggio), 277
Nair, Mira, 472
Nakajima, Shozaburo, 201
Nakata, Hideo, *Ringu, 100,* 102
Naked (Leigh), 321
Naked City, The (Dassin), 96
Naked Spur, The (Mann), 105
Nanook of the North (Flaherty), 71–72,
        72, 443, 448
Napoléon (Gance), 151, 248, 375, 448
Naremore, James, 433
narration, 159–60, 400–401, *400*
    auditory point of view as, *159*
    defined, 122
    direct address, 123
narrative, *4,* 36, **66–70,** *68, 82,* 127,
        144, 440–41
    analyzing of, *162–63, 165*
    beginnings of, 439, *440*
    characters and, **127–31,** *128, 158,*
        160, *162–63, 165*
    climax in, 135–36
    conflict in, *136*
    crisis in, 135, *136*
    cultural traditions, *5*
    defined, 3, 39, 122

diegetic and nondiegetic
        elements in, 161–62, 408
dramatic structure in, *136*
duration in, **149–53,** 164
elements of, **131–36**
events in, **148–49,** *149,* 162–64
formula vs. structure, 131
order in, **145–48,** *147,* 161
plot in, 161–64
repetition in, **154–55,** 164
resolution in, 136, *136,* 161
rising action in, 135
scope and, **156–57,** *157,* 166–67
screenwriter and, **136–37**
setting and, 155, *156,* 164–66
setting in, 164–66
Stagecoach analyzed as, **157–67,**
        162–63, 165
stakes in, 134, *136*
story and plot in, **140–45,** *141,* 157,
        161–64
structure in, **131–36**
suspense in, 164
suspense vs. surprise in, **153–54,**
        154
three-act structure and, 160–61
narrative films, 39–40, **70,** 83
narratology, 137, 140
narrators, *126,* 127, 159–60
    camera as, 123
    defined, 122
    first-person, 123
    multiple, *125*
    narration and, **122–27**
    omniscient, 125
    restricted, 126, *127*
    third-person, 125
    voice-over, 72, 74, 95, 123, 125
Naruse, Mikio, *Avalanche, 325n*
national cinema, 461
National Industrial Recovery Act of
        1933, 501
National Velvet, 302
Native American, casting and, 314
Natural Born Killers (Stone), 230, *305*
naturalistic vs. nonnaturalistic
        styles, **318–20,** *319*
Naughton, Bill, 123
Nausicaä (Miyazaki), 98
Navarro, Guillermo, *247*
Nazis:
    in movies, *25,* 41, 123, *124,* 125, 275
    propaganda films and, 73, *73*
Neame, Ronald, *146*
negative, 435

Nehru (Benegal), 472
Neill, Sam, 264, *264*
Neill, Ve, 189
Nelson, Sean, 319, *319*
neorealism, 200, 455–57, 462
Nestor Sextone for President (1988), 309
Netflix, 511
Neuenfels, Benedict, 272
New American Cinema, 368, 472–77, *473, 474, 475*
Newell, Mike:
    Donnie Brasco, 292
    Harry Potter and the Goblet of Fire, 25
    Love in the Time of Cholera, 145
Newman, Paul, 304
Newman, Randy, 404
Newman, Thomas, 419
New Wave filmmaking, 84, 358, 368, 457–61, *459, 460*
New World, The (Malick), 42, *45,* 314
New York New York (Scorsese), *85*
New York State Censorship Board, *453*
Ngor, Haing S., 313
Niblo, Fred, 60
Niccol, Andrew, 309
    Gattaca, 99
Nichols, Dudley, 157–59, 399
Nichols, Mike, 248, *250*
    Who's Afraid of Virginia Woolf?, 302
Nichols, Rachel, 517
Nicholson, Jack, 204, *205,* 261, 290, 291, 292, 297, 302, 304, 317, 322, 394, *474*
Nicholson, William, 148
Nick Cave and The Bad Seeds, "O Children," 27, 28
nickelodeon, 441
Nielson, Connie, 148, 149, *149*
Niépce, Joseph-Nicéphore, 435
Nightmare Alley (Goulding), 499
Nightmare on Elm Street, A (Craven), 100
Night of the Hunter, The (Laughton), 186–87, *186, 370,* 414, 420
Night of the Living Dead (Romero), 101
Night of the Sunflowers, The (Sánchez-Cabezudo), 148
Nightwatch (Bekmambetov), 102
Nighy, Bill, *25, 282*

Nimoy, Leonard, 191
Nishant (Benegal), 472
Nixon (Stone), 288
No Country for Old Men (E. Coen), 288, 410
No Direction Home: Bob Dylan (Scorsese), *291*
Noé, Gaspar, 147
    Enter the Void, 275
    Irréversible, 54
Nolan, Christopher, 146, 147, *148,* 345
    The Dark Knight, 111, 176, *192*
    Inception, 388, *389,* 492
    Memento, 54, 96
Nolan, Jonathan, 146, 147
Nolan, Ken, 39
nondiegetic elements, 141, *141,* 143
    in *Stagecoach* (Ford), 161–62
nondiegetic sound, *396,* **396–97,** *397*
nonfiction films, 194
nonnaturalist actors, 292
nonsimultaneous sound, 397
Noriega, Eduardo, *247*
normal lens, 245
normal world, 131, *132*
Norris, Chuck, 90
Norris, Daran, 349
North by Northwest (Hitchcock), 155, 260, *261, 301, 397, 397*
North Country (Caro), 188, *189,* 294
Northfork (Polish), 176
Nosferatu, a Symphony of Horror (Murnau), 99, 197, *212,* 230, 277, 444, *446*
Nosferatu the Vampyre (Herzog), 418, 464
Notorious (Hitchcock), 123, *124,* 125, 208, *255,* 265, 268, 269, *301*
Novak, Kim, 322, 365
Novick, Ed, *389*
Now, Voyager (Rapper), 307, 365, *367*
No Way Home (Giovinazzo), 319
Noyce, Phillip, *289*
Nuberu Bagu, 466
Nude Descending a Staircase (Duchamp), 57, *58*
Number Seventeen (Hitchcock), 182
Nunn, Bill, 261, *261*

O

Obayashi, Nobuhiko, *House,* 467
Oberhausen Manifesto, 464
Oberst, Walter, *400*

oblique-angle shots, 263
O'Brien, George, 297
O'Brien, Willis, 279
    The Dinosaur and the Missing Link: A Prehistoric Tragedy, 112
obstacles, in plot, 129, *136*
Ocean's Eleven (Milestone), 372
"O Children" song, (Nick Cave and The Bad Seeds), 27, 28
O'Connor, Una, 315
October (*Ten Days that Shook the World*) (Eisenstein), 449
"Odessa Steps" sequence, *see Battleship Potemkin*
Odorama process, 309
O'Farrell, Michael, 423
offscreen sound, **397–98**
offscreen space, **204,** *205, 207*
Of Human Bondage (Cromwell), 306
O'Hara, Karen, *190*
Oingo Boingo, 404
Okamura, Gerald, 517
Okey, Jack, 199
Oklahoma! (Zinnemann), 108
Old Maid, The (Goulding), 499
Olivier, Laurence, *209,* 312, 314, 317, *317,* 321, 329, 398, *399*
Olmi, Ermanno, 457
Olmos, Edward James, 313
Olympiad (Riefenstahl), 351
Omen, The (Donner), 102
omniscient narrators, 125
omniscient point of view, 219, 274
Once (Carney), 4, *272,* 408, 457
Once upon a Time in America (Leone), 93
Once Upon a Time in the West (Leone), 105, 354–55, 415, *415*
O'Neal, Ryan, 322, 396
One Flew Over the Cuckoo's Nest (Forman), 272
One From the Heart (F. F. Coppola), 176, 202
180–degree system, **359–64,** *363,* 442
127 Hours (Boyle), 133, 135, *135*
O'Neil, Barbara, *331,* 332, *332*
On Kubrick (Naremore), 433
on location, 183, *184*
onscreen sound, **397–98**
onscreen space, **204,** *205, 207*
On the Beach (Kramer), 98
On the Town, (Donen and Kelly), 108

On the Waterfront (Kazan), 179, 197, *303*, 304, 327, 502
open and closed frames, *207*
open frames, **205–8**
Open Hearts (Bier), 463
Ophüls, Max, 179, 265, 266, 277, 319, 458, 459
optical sound recording, 391
option contract, 299
order, plot, **145–48**, *147, 148*, 161
Ordinary Heroes (Hui), 201
Orphans of the Storm (Griffith), 442
Osborne, John, 123
Osborne, Mark, *Kung Fu Panda*, *70*, 129
Oscars (Academy Awards), 505
  see also Academy of Motion Picture Arts and Sciences
Oshii, Mamoru, *Ghost in the Shell*, 98
Oshima, Nagisa, 466
  Cruel Story of Youth, 466
  In the Realm of the Senses, *465*, 466
  Merry Christmas, Mr. Lawrence, 466
Óskarsdóttir, Valdis, 345, 358
Ossana, Diana, *2*
Ossessione, (Visconti), 455, *456*
Others, The, (Amenábar), 102
Otomo, Katsuhiro, *Akira*, 98
O'Toole, Peter, 314, 364, *365*
Otterson, Jack, *195*
Otto, Miranda, *346*, 411
Ottosson, Paul, *386*
Outcry, The (Antonioni), 208
Out of Africa (Pollack), 492
Out of Sight (Soderbergh), 348–49, *349*, 367
Out of the Past (Tourneur), 96
Outrage, The (Ritt), 148
outtakes, 392
overlapping sound, 420–21, *422*
Overton, L. E., 398
Ox-Bow Incident, The (Wellman), 105
Oz, Frank, *Little Shop of Horrors*, 108
Ozu, Yasujiro, 179, 201, 208, 464
  An Autumn Afternoon, 466
  Early Spring, 466
  Early Summer, 466
  The Flavor of Green Tea over Rice, 466
  Floating Weeds, 466
  Late Spring, 201, 466
  Tokyo Story, 466, *468*

P

Pabst, G. W.:
  Pandora's Box, 297, 444
  The Three Penny Opera, 108
  Westfront, 390
Pacella, Elio, 415, *415*
Pacific Data Images, 282
Pacino, Al, 53, *89*, 130, *292*, 303, 304, 364
package-unit system, 501–2, *506*, *508–9*
Padre Padrone (Taviani), 400
Page, Ellen, *389*
Paggi, M. M., 395, 418
painting and movies, 212
Palminteri, Chazz, *147*
Panama, Norman, 193
Pandora's Box (Pabst), 297, 444
Pang, Oxide and Danny, *Bangkok Dangerous*, *91*
Pangborn, Franklin, 315, *316*
Panic in the Streets (Kazan), 96
Panofsky, Erwin, 51
pan shot, **266–67**
Pan's Labyrinth (del Toro), 13, 173, *173*, 182
Parallel Cinema, 472
parallel editing, 42, *43*, **367**
Paramount Pictures, 495, 498, 499, 509
Paranormal Activity (Peli), 4, 102
Parasuram (Sen), 472
Paris, Texas (Wenders), 464
Park, Nick, *Wallace and Gromit in The Curse of the Were-Rabbit*, 112
Parker, Albert, 234
Parker, Trey, 349, *350*
  Cannibal! The Musical, 107
  South Park: Bigger, Longer & Uncut, 107
  Team America: World Police, 107
Parks, Gordon, 474
Parks, Rick, 143
Paronnaud, Vincent, *Persepolis*, *114*, 231
Pasolini, Pier Paolo, 457
  Accatone, 405
Pasquin, John, 143
Passage à l'acte (Arnold), 79
Passion of Joan of Arc, The (Dreyer), 208, 278, *326*, 448

Passion of the Christ, The (Gibson), 517
pastiche, 460
Pastrone, Giovanni, 184, *185*, 191
  Cabiria, 442
Pasztor, Beatrix Aruna, 190
Patel, Dev, *403*
Paterson, Owen, 176
Pather Panchali (S. Ray), 200, 401, 471, *471*
patterns, **42–46**, *352*
  and suspense, 42, *44*
Pawnbroker, The (Lumet), 275
Payne, Alexander, 291
Peach, Kenneth, 279
Peach Blossom Land, The (Lai), 470
Peak, Tulé, 187
Pearce, Guy, *148*
Pearson, Richard, 352
Peckinpah, Sam, 368, 469, 474
  Bring Me the Head of Alfredo Garcia, 475
  Major Dundee, 105
  Straw Dogs, 475
  The Wild Bunch, 105, *469*, 474, *475*
Pederson, Con, 280, *281*
Peeping Tom (Powell), 99
Peers, Joan, 298
Peggy Sue Got Married (F. F. Coppola), *91*
Peirce, Kimberly, 344
Peking Opera Blues (Hark), 201, *468*, 469
Peli, Oren, *Paranormal Activity*, 4, 102
Pence, Josh, *310*
Pendowski, Michael, 404
Penn, Arthur, *41*, 314, 349, 368
  Bonnie and Clyde, 86, 93, 461, 474, *474*, *475*
  Little Big Man, 105, 314
Penn, Sean, 67, 290, 312
Pennebaker, Don Alan, 475
  Don't Look Back, 291
Pennies from Heaven (Ross), 108
Peoples, David Webb, 156
People's Republic of China, 467–70
Peploe, Mark, *157*
perceptual characteristics of sound, *393, 394*
Pereira, Hal, 174
Perfect Human, The (Leth), 351
performance, aspects of, **314–22**, *317, 319, 320*

performance capture, **283**

performances, assessing acting, **327–36,** *329*

Peripheral Produce, 82

Perkins, V. F., 181

Persepolis (Satrapi and Paronnaud), *114,* 231

persistence of vision, 49

Persona (Bergman), 81

personality actors, 290, 291–92

persuasive films, 72, **72–73**

Peters, Hans, 182

Pevney, Joseph, 193

Phantasm (Coscarelli), 102

Philadelphia Story, The (Cukor), *301*

Phillips, Todd, *The Hangover, Part II,* 109, 515

phi phenomenon, 49

Phoenix, Joaquin, 148

photography, **435**
    Aristotle and, 435
    director of, **226–28**
    history of, 435–37
    Leonardo Da Vinci and, 435

physical characteristics, of sound, *393, 394*

Pi (Aronofsky), 231

Piano, The (Campion), 329, *329*

Pickford, Mary, 295, 498

Pickup on South Street (Fuller), 96, *465*

Pied Piper of Hamelin, The, 401

Pierce, Jack P., 193

Pierson, Frank, 130

Pike, Kevin, 280

Pineapple Express (Green), 109

Pinkava, Jan, *Ratatouille,* 181

Pinocchio (Disney), 499

Pinter, Harold, 209

Pinto, Freida, *403*

Pioneer Pictures, 235

piracy, 491

Pirates of the Caribbean: At World's End (Verbinski), *282,* 293

Pirates of the Caribbean: Curse of the Black Pearl (Verbinski), 293

Pirates of the Caribbean: Dead Man's Chest (Verbinski), *282,* 293

Pirates of the Caribbean: On Stranger Tides (Marshall), 85, 293, 516

Pirates of the Caribbean movies, 23, 128

Piravi (Karun), 472

pitch, **394**

Pitt, Brad, 283, 292, 329

Pitt, Michael, *126*

Pixar Animation Studios, 282

Pixar Studios, 113, 114, 181, 490

pixels, **489**

Place in the Sun, A (Stevens), *302*

plan américan, 251

planes, focal, 246

Planet of the Apes (Burton), 211

Platoon (Stone), 408, 419

Platt, Louise, 157, *158, 207*

Player, The (Altman), 304–5, 315–16, 416, 492

Play House, The (Keaton), 375

Pleasantville (Ross), *236*

plot:
    causality and, *68, 142*
    defined, 140
    duration in, 149, *150*
    events in, **148–49,** *149*
    explicitly presented events and, 140, *141*
    implied events and, 140, *141*
    obstacles in, 129, *136*
    order in, **145–48,** *147, 148,* 161
    of *Stagecoach* (Ford), 161–64
    story and, **140–45,** *141*

plot duration, 149, *150,* 151

plot points, *134*

Plowright, Joan, 314

Plunkett, Walter, 191

Poe, Edgar Allen, 446, *447*

poetic realism, **458**

point of view (POV):
    auditory, *159*
    editing and, **368**
    framing and, 202, **274–75**
    group, 274
    omniscient, 219, 274
    sound and, **416–18**
    subjective, 219

point-of-view shot, 16, **274–75,** *277*

Poitier, Sidney, 304, 313

Polanski, Roman, 204, *205,* 212, 231, 304, 317, 474
    Chinatown, 96, 199, 474, *474*
    The Ghost Writer, 121
    Rosemary's Baby, 21, 22, 101, 266

Polar Express, The (Zemeckis), 114–15, *115,* 283, 309

Polglase, Van Nest, 185, *195*

Polish, Del, 176

Polish, Michael, *Northfork,* 176

Polito, Jon, *422*

Pollack, Sydney:
    The Interpreter, 307
    Out of Africa, 492
    They Shoot Horses, Don't They?, 346

Polley, Sarah, 401

Poltergeist (Hooper), 102

Polyester (Waters), 309

Polyvision, 375

Pongpas, Jenjir, *409*

Pope, Bill, 277, 282

Porgy and Bess (Preminger), 313

Portabella, Pere, *The Silence before Bach,* 409

Porter, Edwin S., 234, 279, 440, *440*
    The Great Train Robbery, 103
    Tess of the Storm Country, 442

Portman, Natalie, *127,* 128, 208

Portrait of a Lady, The (Campion), 307

Possessed (Bernhardt), 301

Postman Always Rings Twice, The (Garnett), 96, *456*

Postman Always Rings Twice, The (Rafelson), *456*

postproduction, **494–95**

Potente, Franka, 352, *354*

POV, *see* point of view

Poverty Row studios, 460, 498

Powaqqatsi (Reggio), 277

Powdermaker, Hortense, 500

Powell, John, 406

Powell, Michael, 99, 200
    Peeping Tom, 99

Power of Love, The (Deverick and Fairall), 515

Prasthanam (Katta), 472

Praxiteles, 37, *38*

precinema, 435–37

Precious: Based on the Novel "Push" by Sapphire (Daniels), *128,* 129

Preminger, Otto, 93, 179, 265, 313, *313,* 406
    Laura, 96, 322

preproduction, **492–93**

Presley, Elvis, 408

Presley, Robert, 283

Pressburger, Emeric, 200

Pretty Pictures: Production Design and the History of Film (Tashiro), 432

Pretty Woman (Marshall), 143, 492

Prieto, Rodrigo, 269

prime lenses, 246

principle of "invisibility," 441

Private Life of Henry VIII (Korda), 200
Private Lives of Elizabeth and Essex, The (Curtiz), 193, 307
Probyn, Brian, *258*
processing, **486**
process shots, 280
producers, **495–500**, 502–3
    associate or assistant, 502
    central, 495
    executive, 502
    line, 497, 502
    maverick, **517**
    women as, 496
Producers, The (Brooks), 109
Producers, The (Stroman), 109
Producers Releasing Corporation, 498
producer-unit system, **495–98**, *497*
production:
    costs of, 503, 507
    design in, **180–83**, 180*n*
    movie, **493–94**
    sound mixer, 391
    systems, *see* Hollywood production systems
    values, 242
Production Code Administration (PCA), 452
production process, 484
projecting, **486**
Prokofiev, Sergei, 405, *449*
Prometheus, 182
propaganda films, 448, 449, 455
Propellerheads, 405
properties (props), **183–87**
properties of the shot, cinematographic, **228–48**
propoganda films, 72–73, **72–73**
protagonists, 11, 91–92, 94, 97, 100, 103, *103, 104,* **129**
Proulx, Annie, *2,* 110
Proust, Marcel, 80
Prouty, Olive Higgins, 331
Providence (Resnais), 400
proxemics, 210
proximity, **248–52**
Psycho (Hitchcock), 41–42, 99, 297, 365, 417
Public Enemies (Mann), 293
Public Enemy, The (Wellman), 93
Pudovkin, Vsevolod I., 194, 303, 349, 448–49
    Mother, 449

pull-down claw, *487*
Pulp Fiction (Tarantino), *138, 139,* 146, 231, 345
Pursall, David, 156

Q

"Qatsi" trilogy (Reggio), 277
Quaid, Dennis, *174,* 517
Qualen, John, 46
quality, of sound, **395**
Quay, Stephen and Timothy, *The Comb, 112*
Queen Christina (Mamoulian), 318
Queen Elizabeth (Desfontaines and Mercanton), 295
Queen Kelly (von Stroheim), 191, 197, *199*
Que Viva México (Eisenstein), 449
Quiet American, The (Noyce), *289*
Quinn, Anthony, 312
Quo Vadis? (Guazzoni), 442

R

Rabbit Hole (Mitchell), *306*
Rabinowitz, Jay, *341*
rack focus, 246, *246*
Radcliffe, Daniel, 23
Radiohead, 404
Rafelson, Bob:
    Five Easy Pieces, 474–75
    The Postman Always Rings Twice, 456
Rage Against the Machine, 405
Raging Bull (Scorsese), *145, 152,* 277, *402, 403*
Raimi, Sam:
    Drag Me to Hell, 102
    The Evil Dead, 102
    The Evil Dead II, 102
    A Simple Plan, 469
Rainer, Luise, 311
Rains, Claude, 123, *147, 255,* 364
Raise the Red Lantern (Zhang), 201, 468
Raising Arizona (Coen and Coen), *91,* 367
Rake's Progress, A (Hogarth), 212
Raksin, David, 404, 407
Ramos, Timothy Andrew, *California Indian,* 314
Ran (Kurosawa), 201, 465, *466, 467*
Raphaelson, Samson, 399

Rapper, Irving, 365, *367*
    The Corn Is Green, 307
    Now, Voyager, 307
Rashomon (Kurosawa), 148, 464, 465
Ratatouille (Bird and Pinkava), 111, 181
rating system, 70, 511, *512,* 514
Ratner, Brett, *Rush Hour* movies, 469
Ratoff, Gregory, 499
Ravenous (Bird), 108
Ray, Man, *Emak-Bakia,* 79, 446
Ray, Nicholas, 179, 304, 459
    Johnny Guitar, 105
    Rebel without a Cause, 465
Ray, Satyajit, 137, 172, 179, 200–201, 226, 322, 401, 457, 461, 471–72, *471,* 477
    Agantuk, 472
    Aparajito, 471, *471*
    Apar Sansar, 471, *471*
    Charulata, 472
    Devi, 472
    Ghare-Baire, 472
    Jalsaghar, 471–72
    Pather Panchali, 471, *471*
    Shatranj-ke-Khilari, 472
Razor's Edge, The (Goulding), 499
RCA, 498
Rea, Stephen, 263, 405
realism, *57, 58,* 197
    and antirealism, *56,* **56–60,** *58,* 205, 358
    and neorealism, 200, *200*
real time, **150–53,** *153,* 275, 277
real-time relationship, 151, *153*
rear projection, 280
Rear Window (Hitchcock), 126, 174, *175,* 315, 368, *368*
Rebecca (Hitchcock), 499
Rebel Without a Cause (N. Ray), 304, *465*
Rec (Balagueró), 102
recording, 391, 394
Redbourn, Michael, 416
Redbox machines, 2
Red Desert, The (Antonioni), 409
Redford, Robert, 311
Redgrave, Vanessa, 314
Red River (Hawks and Rosson), 105, *110,* 155
Red Shoes, The (Powell and Pressburger), 200
Red Sorghum (Zhang), 201

Reed, Carol, *199, 200,* 263
    The Third Man, 46, 86, 207
Reeves, Keanu, 49, 277
Reeves, Matt, *Cloverfield, 57,* 272,
        457
reflector board, *237, 238, 238*
reframing, 202
Regent Entertainment, 505
Reggio, Godfrey, 277
Reichardt, Kelly:
    Meek's Cutoff, 83, 207
    Wendy and Lucy, 207
Reilly, John C., *406*
Reilly, Kelly, *183*
Reimann, Walter, 197
reinvention, cinema of, 460
Reisz, Karel, 376
    Momma Don't Allow, 462
    *Saturday Night and Sunday
        Morning,* 462
    We Are the Lambeth Boys, 462
Reitherman, Wolfgang, *The Jungle
        Book,* 108
Reitman, Ivan, *Young Adult,* 188
Reitman, Jason, *Juno,* **7–22,**
        36–37, *37*
release negative, 503
Rembrandt (Korda), 200
Removed (Uman), *81*
Rengel, Martin, *Joy Ride,* 463
Rennahan, Ray, 235
Renoir, Jean, 179, 201, 208, 256, 265,
        268, *268,* 458, 459, 471
    French Cancan, 108
Rent (Columbus), 108
repetition, in *Stagecoach* (Ford), 164
repetition of story events, **154–55**
Republic Pictures, 498
Requiem for a Dream (Aronofsky),
        277, *341*
rerecording, 392
Rescued from an Eagle's Nest
        (Dawley), 279
Reservoir Dogs (Tarantino), 93,
        405, 469
Resnais, Alain, 345, 400, 458, *460*
    Last Year at Marienbad, 81,
        459, 461
resolution, 136, *136,* **489**
    in dramatic structure, 161
Restoration (Hoffman), 305
restricted narrators, 126, *127*
reverse-angle shots, 364
revolver photographique, **436**

Reynolds, Debbie, 314
Rezende, Daniel, 358, 376
rhythm:
    in editing, **351–55,** *354*
    and sound, **418–19**
Ricci, Christina, 212, *213, 215*
Richard III (Loncraine), *305*
Richardson, Dorothy, 80–81
Richardson, Miranda, 212
Richardson, Ralph, 314
Richardson, Robert, 239, 343
Richardson, Tony:
    *The Loneliness of the Long Distance
        Runner,* 462
    Momma Don't Allow, 462
    Tom Jones, 123, 319
Richert, William, *Winter Kills, 308*
Richman, Jonathan, 397
Richter, Hans, *Dreams That Money
        Can Buy,* 81
"Ride of the Valkyries, The"
        (Wagner), 419, *420*
Riefenstahl, Leni, 351
    Triumph of the Will, 72–73, *73*
Rien que les heures (Cavalcanti), 447
Rififi (Dassin), 93
Rilla, Wolf, *Village of the Damned,* 98
rim lights, 241
Ring, The (Verbinski), *100,* 250
Ringu (Nakata), *100,* 102
Rinzler, Lisa, 228
Rio (Saldanha), 85
Riptide (Goulding), 499
rising action, 135, *136*
Ritchie, Guy, *183*
    Sherlock Holmes, 305
    Snatch, 372
Ritt, Martin:
    Hombre, 105
    The Outrage, 148
Ritter, Thelma, 304, 315
Rivette, Jacques, 458
    Celine and Julie Go Boating, 459
Rizzo, Gary A., *389*
RKO, 492, 496*n,* 498, 499
Roach, Hal, 443
Roach, Jay, 404
Road, The (Hillcoat), 188
Road to Perdition (Mendes), 93
Robards, Jason, 314, *406*
Robbins, Jerome, *West Side Story,*
        108
Robbins, Tim, 304–5, 412, *413,* 492
Roberts, Julia, 143, 309, 348, *348,* 492

Robeson, Paul, 313
Robinson, Amy, *395*
Robinson, Edward G., 90, 92
Robson, Mark, 309
Rocha, Glauber, *Land in Anguish,* 4
Rock, The (Bay), *91*
Rocky (Avildson), 130, *131*
Rocky Horror Picture Show, The
        (Sharman), 108
Rodat, Robert, 156
Rodis-Jamero, Nilo, 191
Rodrigues, Alexandre, 376
Rodríguez, Alex, 373
Rodriguez, Robert, 423, *469,*
        490, 517
    Desperado, 469
    Sin City, 96, 231
Roeg, Nicolas:
    Don't Look Now, 367
    The Man Who Fell to Earth, 98
Rogen, Seth, *319*
Rogers, Aggie Guerard, 191
Rogers, Ginger, 105
Rohmer, Eric, 319, 458
    My Night at Maud's, 459
Röhrig, Walters, 197
roles:
    preparing for, **316–18,** *317*
    types of, **314–16,** *316*
Rolling Stones, 343–44, *343*
romance genre, 110
Rome, Open City (Rossellini),
        200, 455
Romero, Cesar, 314
Romero, George A.:
    Dawn of the Dead, 102
    Night of the Living Dead, 101
Romney, George, 213
Ronan, Saoirse, *48*
Room at the Top (Clayton), 462
Rooney, Mickey, 312
Roosevelt, Franklin D., 501
Rope (Hitchcock), 151, 151*n*
Rose, Gabrielle, 401
Rose-Marie (Van Dyke), 496
Rosemary's Baby (Polanski), *21,* 22,
        101, 266
Rosenbloom, David, 364
Roshan, Rakesh, *Krrish, 5*
Rosher, Charles, 265
Ross, Gary, 404
    Pleasantville, 236
Ross, Herbert, *Pennies from Heaven,*
        108

Rossellini, Roberto, 200, 457
Rome, Open City, 455
Rossen, Robert, 304
Rosson, Arthur, *Red River,* 105, 109, 155
Rosson, Harold, 235
Roth, Ann, 191
Roth, Tim, 319
rotoscoping, **283**
Roudenko, Vladimir, 375
round characters, 127, *128*
Rouse, Christopher, 352
Rowlands, Gena, 321
Rowlandson, Thomas, 212–13
Royal Tenenbaums, The (Anderson), 125, *126,* 461
Royal Wedding (Donen), 209, *210*
Rózsa, Miklós, 404
Rubell, Paul, 364
Rubin, Henry Alex, *Murderball,* 67
Rudin, Scott, 517
Ruiz, Raoul, *Klimt,* 181
rule of thirds, **257–59,** *258*
Rules of Attraction, The (Avary), 375, *375*
Rumble Fish (F. F. Coppola), 277
Run Lola Run (Tykwer), 230, 351, 352, *354,* 363, 405
Rush, Geoffrey, 251
rushes, 392, 493
Rush Hour movies (Ratner), 469
Rushmore (Anderson), 349
Russell, David O.:
The Fighter, 145
Three Kings, 230
Russell, Harold, *203*
Russell, Jay, 316
Russell, Rosalind, 305
Russell, Vicki, 191
Russian Ark (Sokurov), 278
Russian cinema, 194
Rutherford, Margaret, 314
Rutter, Sharon, 375
Ruzowitzky, Stefan, *The Counterfeiters,* 272
Ryan, Cornelius, 156
Ryan's Daughter (Lean), 226
Ryder, Winston, 389

S

Sabino, Rubens, 187
Sabotage (Hitchcock), 200
Saint, Eva Marie, 260, 327, 397, *397*

St. Matthew Passion (Bach), 405
Saint-Saëns, Camille, 404
Saisaymar, Thanapa, *409*
Sakaguchi, Hironobu, 309
Final Fantasy: The Spirits Within, 113, 283
Sakakibara, Moto, 309
Final Fantasy: The Spirits Within, 113, 283
Sala, Oskar, 417
Saldanha, Carlos, *Rio,* 85
Salomon, Mikael, 281
Sampson, Caleb, 75
Sánchez, Eduardo, *The Blair Witch Project,* 102
Sánchez-Cabezudo, Jorge, *The Night of the Sunflowers,* 148
Sanford, Erskine, 315
Sanford, John, *Home on the Range,* 113
San Francisco (Van Dyke), 496
Sansho the Bailiff (Mizoguchi), 201, 466, *467*
Sarandon, Susan, 290
Saratoga (Conway), 497
Sardo, Giovanni, 400
Sarraute, Anne, 345
Sarrazin, Michael, *346*
Sartre, Jean-Paul, 458
Satrapi, Marjane, *Persepolis, 114,* 231
Saturday Night and Sunday Morning (Reisz), 462
Satyajit Ray, Filmmaker (Benegal), 472
Saura, Carlos, *Blood Wedding,* 108
Savages, The (Jenkins), 311, 484
Savides, Harris, 273, 278, *278*
Saving Private Ryan (Spielberg), 156, 503
Sayles, John, 272, 474, 517
scale, *264,* **264–65**
Scanner Darkly, A (Linklater), 82, 145
Scarface (De Palma), 93
Scarface (Hawks), 88, 93
Scarlet Empress, The (Sternberg), *240*
Scarlet Street (Lang), 96
scenes, 36
Scharff, Stefan, 154
Schepisi, Fred, 326
Scherfig, Lone:
An Education, 128
Italian for Beginners, 463
Schiller, Frederich von, *407*
Schlesinger, John, *396*

Schlöndorff, Volker:
The Tin Drum, 372
Young Torless, 464
Schnabel, Julian:
Before Night Falls, 312
The Diving Bell and the Butterfly, 274
Schnee, Charles, 155
Schneemann, Carolee, 476
Schoedsack, Ernest B., 279
King Kong, 112
Mighty Joe Young, 112
Schoonmaker, Thelma, 374
Schrader, Paul, 93, *152,* 155, *320,* 474
Schreck, Max, 277, *446*
Schroder, Rick, *Black Cloud,* 314
Schubert, Franz, 397
Schüfftan, Eugen, *280*
Schumacher, Joel, *Batman Forever,* 307
Schwartzman, Jason, 349
Schwarzenegger, Arnold, 90, 304
science fiction genre, **96–99,** *97, 98,* 155–56, *156*
Science of Sleep, The (Gondry), 82
scope, **156–57,** *157*
defined, 156
in *Stagecoach* (Ford), 166–67
Scorpio Rising (Anger), 81
Scorsese, Martin, *145, 152,* 155, 265, 322, 455, 457, 474, *475,* 490, 517
The Age of Innocence, 197
The Aviator, 314
Gangs of New York, 176
Goodfellas, 85, 86, 269, 273–74, 374, *374*
Hugo, 516
Mean Streets, 85, 395
New York New York, 85
No Direction Home: Bob Dylan, 291
Raging Bull, 277, 402, 403
Shine a Light, 343–44, *343*
Taxi Driver, 155, 275, *320,* 321, *371*
Woodstock, 344
Scott, Ridley, 490
Alien, 98, 416
American Gangster, 88
Black Hawk Down, 39, *39,* 408
Blade Runner, 97, 98, 156, *156, 281*
Gladiator, 60, 148–49, *149, 267,* 282, 404

Scott, Stephen, 182, *182*
Scott, Tony:
    Days of Thunder, 307
    Domino, 82
    Man on Fire, 82
Scott Pilgrim vs. the World (Wright),
    13, 111
Scream (Craven), 102
screen acting, evolution of, **294–310,**
    442
Screen Actors Guild (SAG), 311, 503
screen direction, **359–64**
screen duration, 149, *150,* 151
screenplay, format, 136–37, *138*
screen tests, 311
screenwriter, **136–37**
    auteur director and, 137
    and screenplay, **136–37**
    as script doctor, 137
screwball comedy, 452, *452*
script doctors, 137
script supervisor, 194, 485
Scrubs, 107
Seabiscuit (Ross), 404
Seagal, Steven, 90
Searchers, The (Ford), *40,* 87, 103, 231,
    232, 314, 327, 359, *362*
Seashell and the Clergyman, The
    (Dulac), 447
Seaton, George, *313*
Seddon, Jack, 156
Seidler, David, 156
Seitz, John F., *245*
Sekula, Andrzej, 231
Self Portrait (Haring), 37–38, *38*
Sellers, Peter, *245,* 322, 329
Selznick, David O., 180*n, 453, 496n,*
    498–99, 500, 502, 505
Selznick International Pictures,
    496*n,* 499, 500–501
Sembene, Ousmane, 461
Seminary Girls (Edison), *438, 439*
Sen, Mrinal:
    Antareen, 472
    Bhuvan Shome, 473
    Khandaar, 472
    Kharji, 472
    Parasuram, 472
Sennett, Mack, 108, 443
Sense and Sensibility (A. Lee), 201,
    470
Sensurround, 309
sequence, 36, 53, 277, *278*
Serenity (Whedon), *110*
series photography, **436–37,** *437*

Serkis, Andy, 309
Serrone, Christopher, 374, *374*
Servant, The (Losey), 462
sets, 183, *184*
    theme park preservation of, 184
Setsuko Hara, *468*
setting, **88,** 164–66, **183–87,** *217,* 440
    narrative and, 155, *156,* 164–66
    in *Stagecoach* (Ford), 164–66,
    165
setup, 228
Se7en (Fincher), 182
Seven Samurai (Kurosawa), 465
Seventh Seal, The (Bergman), 231–32,
    232
Shadows and Fog (Allen), 197
Shah, Naseeruddin, *5*
Shainberg, Steven, *Fur: An*
    Imaginary Portrait of Diane
    Arbus, 305, 306, 307
Shakespeare, William, 145, 209,
    209
Shane, (Stevens), 103
Shanley, John Patrick, 133
Shannon, Harry, 323
Shapiro, Dana Adam, 67
Sharaff, Irene, 191
Sharman, Jim, *The Rocky Horror*
    Picture Show, 108
Sharp, Henry, 234
Sharpsteen, Ben, *Dumbo,* 85
Shatranj-ke-Khilari (S. Ray), 472
Shaw, Robert, 419
Shawn of the Dead, (Wright), 102
Shearer, Douglas, 390, 394
Shearer, Norma, *192,* 194, 499
Sheen, Martin, *258,* 293, *394,* 395,
    400
Sheen, Michael, *190*
Shelley, Mary, 96
Shelly, Adrienne, *Waitress, 21,* 22
Sheridan, Jim, 293
Sherlock Holmes (Ritchie), *305*
Sherlock Holmes stories, *183*
Sherrill, Billy, 405
She Wore a Yellow Ribbon (Ford),
    105, 231, 314
Shields, Jim, 416
Shine a Light (Scorsese), 343–44,
    343
Shining, The (Kubrick), 100, 185,
    261, *261,* 273, 297, 322, 389,
    394, 396
Shirley, Anne, 331, *331*
Shoeshine (De Sica), 200, 456

Shohan, Naomi, 215
shooting, **486**
shooting angle, 259
Shootist, The (Siegel), *308,* 309
Shore, Howard, 404
Short Cuts (Altman), *305,* 321
short-focal-length lens, 244–45, *245,*
    255
shots, 5, 36, *227,* 228, **259–79,** 340
    aerial-view, **263–64,** *277*
    bird's-eye-view, 263–64
    close-up, *326,* **326–27,** *327*
    crane, **269–70,** *270*
    dolly in, 267
    downshots and, 260
    Dutch-angle, *263,* **263**
    eye-level, **259–60**
    freeze-frame, **373–74,** *374*
    ground-level, 382
    group, 252
    high-angle, **260**
    highshots and, 260
    iris, **372**
    low-angle, **260–63,** *262*
    master, **359,** *362*
    moving, 382
    oblique-angle, 263
    overhead, 382
    pan, **266–67**
    point-of-view, **274–75,** *277*
    reverse-angle, 364
    and reverse shots, **364**
    speed/length of, **275–79**
    split-screen, **374–75,** *375*
    three-, 252
    tilt, *267,* **267**
    tracking, 267, *268*
    transitions between, **368–75**
    two-, 252
    types of, 250–52, *252,* 442
    zoom, 268–69, *271*
shots/reverse shots, **364**
Show Boat (Whale), 313
Showtime, 505
Shpinel, Isaac, 195
Shrek (Adamson and Jenson), 113
shutter, *487*
Shyamalan, M. Night, 147
    The Sixth Sense, 102
Shyer, Charles, 319
Siberling, Brad, 281, 282
Sicko (Moore), 72
sidekicks, 92
Sidibe, Gabourey, *128*
Sidney, George, *Kiss Me Kate,* 515

Siegel, Don:
    Invasion of the Body Snatchers, 98
    The Shootist, 308, 309
Siegfried (Lang), 197
Sigel, Newton Thomas, 230
silence:
    sound and, **409–10**
    on sound tracks, *409,* **409–10**
Silence before Bach, The (Portabella),
        409
Silence of the Lambs, The (J. Demme),
        42, *44,* 53, 102
silent era, *432,* 440–43
"Silly Symphony" cartoons (Disney),
        235
Silver, Scott, *145*
Silverado (Kasdan), 105
SImOne (Niccol), 309
Simple Plan, A (Raimi), 469
Simpsons, The, 107
simultaneous sound, 397
Sinatra, Frank, 216
Sin City (Miller and Rodriguez),
        96, 231, 422–23, 517
Sinclair, Kim, 179
Singer, Bryan, 147
    The Usual Suspects, 96, *147,* 148
Singer, Marc, *Dark Days,* 231
Singin' in the Rain (Donen and
        Kelly), 87, 108, *297,* 298
single-character point of view,
        274
Sink or Swim (Friedrich), 77, 79
Sins of the Fleshapoids (Kuchar), 81
Siodmak, Robert:
    Criss Cross, 96
    The Killers, 96
    The Spiral Staircase, 199
Sirk, Douglas, 173
Sixth Sense, The (Shyamalan), 102,
        147
60 Minutes, 73
Sjöström, Victor, 297
Skjoldbjærg, Erik, *Insomnia, 95*
Skladanowsky, Emil, 439
Skladanowsky, Max, 439
Sklar, Robert, 435
Skousen, Camilla, 351
Skyscraper (Clarke), 81
Slacker (Linklater), *69*
Slade, David, *Twilight Saga: Eclipse,
        The, 109*
slapstick comedy, 108
slate, 228
Sledge, Percy, 405

Sleepy Hollow (Burton), *211,* **211–15,**
        212, 213, 215, 216
Sloane, Everett, 423, *424,* 426
slow motion, 275–77, 446, *448,* 474
Slumdog Millionaire (Boyle and
        Tandan), 403, *403,* 470
Smal, Ewa, 203
Smalley, Phillips, 374
Small Town Girl (Wellman), 496
Smith, Chris, *American Movie,* 74
Smith, G.A., *440*
Smith, Jack, *Flaming Creatures,* 81
Smith, Jack Martin, 182
Smith, James, 376
Smith, Lee, 421
Smith, Maggie, 314
Smith, Rose, 376
Smith, Stephen, 281
Smith, Will, 290, 309, 313
Smoke Signals (Eyre), 314
Snatch (Ritchie), 372
Snow, Michael, *Wavelength,* 77, 81
Snyder, Earl, 400
Snyder, Zack:, *483*
socialist-realist films, 462
Social Network, The (Fincher), 70,
        129, *134,* 140–43, *142, 184,*
        227, 310, 516
Société Film d'Art, La (Art Film
        Society), 295
Society of Motion Picture and
        Television Engineers, 504
Soderbergh, Steven, 348, *348, 349,*
        367, 477, 517
    Contagion, 517
    Haywire, 517
    The Limey, 8, 126
Sokurov, Aleksandr, 278
Solaris (Tarkovsky), 98
Some Like It Hot (Wilder), 109, *154,*
        237
Sommers, Stephen, *G.I. Joe: The Rise
        of Cobra,* 516
Sonatine (Kitano), 93
Sondheim, Stephen, *Sweeney Todd:
        The Demon Barber of Fleet
        Street, 6*
songs, in film, 161–62, *406, 407, 408*
Songs from the Second Floor
        (Andersson), 202
Son of Frankenstein (R. Lee), *195*
Sony, 491, 512
"So Quiet in Here" (Morrison), 370
Sorkin, Aaron, *310*
Sörling, Robert, 421

Sorry, Wrong Number (Litvak), 331
Sossamon, Shannyn, *375*
sound, 36, **387–430**
    acting and, *297,* **297–99**
    analyzing of, *425*
    and audience expectations, **416,**
        417
    characteristics of, *393, 394*
    characterization through, **426–28**
    in *Citizen Kane,* **423–28,** *424, 425,*
        426, 427
    continuity and, **420–21**
    defined, 388
    describing film, **393–95**
    diegetic, *408*
    effects, *426*
    emphasis with, **421–23**
    environmental, **401–3**
    Foley, 392, 406, 409
    functions of, *394,* **414–23,** *415, 417,*
        424–26, *425*
    as meaning, *389*
    mixing, **393**
    onscreen vs. offscreen, **397–98**
    pitch, loudness, quality, **395**
    point of view and, *159,* **416–18**
    production, **390–93,** *392*
    rhythm and, **418–19**
    silence and, *409,* **409–10**
    sources of, **395–99,** *396*
    themes and, **428**
    THX technology in, 390
    transition to, 390, *432,* 434
    types of, **399–414,** *400, 402, 406,*
        408
    vocal, **399–401**
    in *War of the Worlds,* **410–14,** *411,*
        412, 413
sound bridge, *365,* 398, 421
sound crew, 390
sound design, **390–91**
sound designer, 391
sound effects, 401–3, *402,* 410
sound era, *432*
    transition to, 450–51, 454
Sound of Music, The (Wise), 108
soundstage, 184
sound track, 390, 393
South Park (Parker and Stone), 349,
        350
South Park: Bigger, Longer & Uncut
        (Parker), 107
Soviet Montage, 358, 448–50, 458,
        474
    see also montage

Spacek, Sissy, *258*, 293–94, 329, 400

space/time manipulation, 51, 51*n*, *52*

Spacey, Kevin, 41, *147*, 215, *216, 220*, 305, 419

Spanish Prisoner, The (Mamet), 400

Sparling, Kent, 410

Spartacus (Kubrick), 60, 257, 405

spatialization of time, 51

spatial relationships in editing, **344–45,** *347, 361*

Spears, Eddie, 314

special effects, *50, 51, 98*
  cinematography and, **279–83,** *280, 281*
  impact on acting, 309–10
  in-camera, 279, *280*
  laboratory, 279, *280*
  mechanical, 279, *280*

Spectrum of Multiple Stars, A: Wang Chuanru (Tam), 469

speed, film, 230
  and length of shot, **275–79**

Spencer, Dorothy, 371

Spencer, Katie, *183*

SPFX, *see* special effects

Spiegel, Sam, 502

Spielberg, Steven, 364, 388, 474
  The Adventures of Tintin, 516
  Close Encounters of the Third Kind, 97, 281
  E.T. The Extra-Terrestrial, 309
  Jaws, 133, 280, 415, 419
  Jurassic Park, 59, 179, 264–65, *264,* 281
  Saving Private Ryan, 156, 503
  War of the Worlds, 97, 179, 291, 388, **410–14,** *411, 412, 413*

Spiral Staircase, The (Siodmak), 199

Spirited Away (Miyazaki), 113, *392*

Spitzig, Ichelle, 176

splicing, 340

split screen, 53, *54, 341,* **374–75,** *375,* 384, *448*

sprocketed rollers, *487*

Spy Kids (Rodriquez), 517

Square, The (Edgerton), 96

Squaw Man, The (DeMille), 442

Staenberg, Zach, 351

Stagecoach (Ford), 88, 103, **157–67,** *158, 159, 162–63, 207,* 231, *232,* 314, 315, *366*
  auditory point of view in, *159*

characters in, *158,* 160, *162–63*

diegetic and nondiegetic elements in, 161–62

duration in, 164

events in, 162–64, *162–63*

order in, 161

plot in, 161–64

repetition in, 164

scope in, 166–67

setting in, 164–66

story in, 161–62

suspense in, 164

"Stage to Lordsburg" (Haycox), 157

staging, 172, 178

Stahl, John M., 172

Staiger, Janet, 434

Staiola, Enzo, *200,* 456, *457*

stakes, 134, *136*

Stalker (Tarkovsky), 98

Stamp, Terrence, 126

stand-ins, 315, *493*

Stanislavsky, Konstantin, 302–3, 318, 449

Stanislavsky system, 302–4, 320

Stanton, Andrew, *WALL-E,* 403, 490

Stanton, Harry Dean, 416

Stanwyck, Barbara, *259,* 293, 300, **330–33,** *331, 332, 453*

Stapleton, Oliver, 260

Star Is Born, A (Cukor), 108

Star Machine, The (Basinger), 300, 432

Starman (Carpenter), 292, *308*

Starr, Beau, 374

Starship Troopers (Verhoeven), 99

star system, 441, 473

Star Trek III: The Search for Spock (Nimoy), 191

Star Wars (Lucas), 68, 156, 281, 345, 372

Star Wars: Attack of the Clones (Lucas), 309

Star Wars: Return of the Jedi (Marquand), 191, 281

Star Wars: Revenge of the Sith (Lucas), 309

Star Wars: The Empire Strikes Back (Kershner), 281, 405

Star Wars: The Phantom Menace (Lucas), 309, 490

Star Wars movies, 23, 25, *68,* 97, 127, 281, 309, *449*

Steadicam, 185, 266, **272–74,** *273,* 278, *382*

Steadicam Ultra 2, *273*

Stealers Wheel, 405

Stefano, Joseph, 42

Steiger, Rod, 275

Steiner, Max, 404

Steinfeld, Hailee, *126*

Steinkamp, Fredric, *346*

Stella (Erman), *331*

Stella Dallas (Vidor), **330–33,** *331, 332,* 334, 336

stereoscopy, 516
  see also 3–D cinematography

Sternberg, Josef von, 179, *240,* 322, 326, *327*

Stevens, Charles, 398

Stevens, George, 304
  Giant, 302
  A Place in the Sun, 302
  Shane, 103
  Swing Time, 108

Stevenson, John, *Kung Fu Panda, 70,* 129

Stewart, James, 126, 174, *175,* 300, 315, 365, 368, *368, 451,* 501

Stewart, James G., 400, 418, 423, *424*

stock, *see* film stock

stock players, **300**

Stoltz, Eric, *138*

Stone, Oliver, 269, 288, 408, 419, 490
  Natural Born Killers, 230, *305*
  W, 288

Stone Temple Pilots, 408

stop-motion animation, 111–12

stop-motion photography, *440, 448*

Storaro, Vittorio, *157*

story, 157–59, 161–62
  backstory and, 143, 148
  causality and, *68,* 142
  construct, 143
  defined, 140
  duration, 149, *150, 152,* 164
  formula, **87**
  and plot, **140–45,** *141*
  of *Stagecoach* (Ford), 157–59, 161–64

storyboard, 202, 213

Strada, La (Fellini), 328

Strange Love of Martha Ivers, The (Milestone), 257, *259*

Stranger than Fiction (Forster), *125*
Stranger Than Paradise (Jarmusch), *473*
Strasberg, Lee, 303
Stravinsky, Igor, 404
Straw Dogs (Peckinpah), *475*
stream of consciousness, 80–81
Streep, Meryl, 302, 407
Streetcar Named Desire, A (Kazan), 304
Street of Shame (Mizoguchi), 466
Streisand, Barbra, 321
stretch relationship, **150–51**
Strike (Eisenstein), 449
Strip Mall Trilogy, The (Beebe), 82
Stroman, Susan, *The Producers,* 109
Stromberg, Hunt, 496, 497
Stromberg, Robert, 179, *190*
structure:
    dramatic, *136*
    narrative, **131–36**
    normal world in, 131, *132,* 160
    three-act, 160–61
    see also form
Struss, Karl, 265
Stuart, Gloria, 315
Stuck on You (Farrelly and Farrelly), 109
Studio Basic Agreement, 503
studio era and acting, **299–302**
studio system, 137, 187, 233, 238, 242, 310, 315, 321, 441, 451, 472–73, 485, **495–501,** *497, 498,* 509, 512, *513–14*
    collapse of, 472–73
    directors in, 499
    organization of, **495–501**
    post-1931, **496–98**
    pre-1931, **495**
    pre-1950, *498*
    producers in, **495–500**
    television and, 501
    see also Hollywood production systems
stunt persons, 315
Sturges, Preston, 399, *452*
    The Miracle of Morgan's Creek, 21, 22
style, acting, **318–20,** *319*
subtext, 303
subtractive color systems, 234–35
Sudden Fear (Miller), 301

Suddenly, Last Summer (Mankiewicz), *302,* 502
summary relationship, 150–51, *152*
Sunrise: A Song of Two Humans (Murnau), 155, 182, 265, 297, 495
Sunset Boulevard (Wilder), *94,* 104, 199, *245,* 299, 314, *432*
Sunshine State (Sayles), 517
Super 8 (Abrams), 66, 85
Superbad (Mottola), 13, *14,* 109
superimpositions, 384
Superman (Donner), 111
supporting players, **300**
supporting roles, 315, *315*
surprise, 153–54, *154*
    vs. suspense, *154*
surrealist films, 446–47, *447*
Suschitzky, Peter, 281
suspense, 153–54, *154,* 164
    patterns and, 42, *44*
    in *Stagecoach* (Ford), 164
    vs. surprise, *154*
Suspense (Smalley and Weber), 374
Suspicion (Hitchcock), *301*
Suspiria (Argento), *101, 196*
Suvari, Mena, 216, *217, 218, 220, 419*
Svankmejer, Jan, *112*
Swain, Mack, 53
Swan, Buddy, 323, *324*
Swank, Hilary, 305, 344
Swanson, Gloria, 191, 197, *199, 245,* 314, *432*
Sweeney Todd: The Demon Barber of Fleet Street (Burton), *6, 171,* 211, 292
Sweeney Todd: The Demon Barber of Fleet Street (Sondheim), *6*
Sweet Hereafter, The (Egoyan), 154, 400–401, 418
Sweet Smell of Success (Mackendrick), 96, *233, 234, 239,* 322
Swing Time (Stevens), 108
swish pans, 384
swordplay, *209*
Sylbert, Richard, 199, 204
Sylwan, Kari, 370
Symbiopsychotaxiplasm: Take One (Greaves), *83*
Synecdoche, New York (Kaufman), 82

synthespians, 309, *310*
    see also computer-generated imagery
Syriana (Gaghan), *70*

T

Tachell, Terri, *130*
Taghmaoui, Saïd, 517
Taipei Story (Yang), 470
Taiwan, 469–70
Taiwan cinema, 201
take, 228
Takemitsu, Toru, 404
take-up spool, *487*
Talbot, William Henry Fox, 435
Tales of Manhattan (Duvivier), 313
Talk to Her (Almodóvar), 265
Tally, Ted, 42
Taloni, Adriano, 400
Tam, Patrick, 469
    A Spectrum of Multiple Stars: Wang Chuanru, 469
Tamai, Masao, 280
Taming of the Shrew, The (Zeffirelli), *302*
Tamsay, Paul, *145*
Tanaka, Kinuyo, *467*
Tandan, Loveleen, *Slumdog Millionaire,* 390, 403
Tangled (Greno and Howard), 129
Tarantino, Quentin, 146, 201, 231, *339,* 345, 405, *469,* 490
    Kill Bill movies, 108, 469
    Pulp Fiction, 138, 139
    Reservoir Dogs, 93, 469
Taraporevala, Sooni, *Little Zizou,* 472
Tarkovsky, Andrei, 172, 477
    Solaris, 98
    Stalker, 98
Tashiro, C.S., 432
Tashlin, Frank, 143
Tati, Jacques, 109, 458
Tatum, Channing, 517
Taviani, Paolo, and Vittorio, *Padre Padrone,* 400, 457
Tavoularis, Dean, 176
Taxi Driver (Scorsese), 155, 275, *320,* 321, *371*
Taylor, Elizabeth, 191, *302,* 314
Taylor, Gilbert, *245,* 268, 272, 281
Taylor, J. O., 279
Taylor, Robert, 496

Taylor, Rod, 275
Taylor, Tate, *The Help,* 225
Taymor, Julie, *Across the Universe,* 107, *107*
Teacher's Pet (Björklund), 108
Teahouse of the August Moon, The (Mann), 312
Team America: World Police (Parker), 107, 349, *350*
Technicolor, *196,* 234–35, 255, 453
Tedeschi, David, 343–44, *343*
Teenage Rebel (Goulding), 499
television, studio systems and, 501
temporal relationships in editing, **345–51**
Ten Commandments, The (De Mille), 279, 279*n*
Tennant, Andy, 143
Tenniel, John, *190*
Terminator 2: Judgment Day (Cameron), 281
Terminator movies (Cameron), 97
Teshigahara, Hiroshi, 466
Tess of the Storm Country (Porter), 442
Tetzlaff, Ted, *255,* 269
Texas Chain Saw Massacre, The (Hooper), 102
Thalberg, Irving, 496–97, 496*n,* *497,* 500, 502
That Certain Woman (Goulding), 499
That Day on the Beach (Yang), 201
themes:
  and movie meaning, 15, **88**
  sound and, **428**
  see also motifs
There's Something About Mary (Farrelly and Farrelly), 293, 397
There Will Be Blood (Anderson), 200, 404, 514
Theron, Charlize, 188, *189,* 292
Thesiger, Ernest, *241, 241,* 263, *263,* 315
They Shoot Horses, Don't They? (Pollack), *346*
Thiault, Jérôme, 418
Thief of Bagdad, The (Powell, Berger and Whelan), 200
Things to Come (Menzies), 98, 182, 200

Thin Man movies (various directors), 496
Thin Red Line, The (Malick), 156, *346*
Third Man, The (Reed), 46, 86, *199,* 200, 207, 263
third-person narrators, 125
39 Steps, The (Hitchcock), 398, *417*
Thomae, Robert, 279
Thomas, Charles Howard, *Morning Song Way,* 314
Thomas Crown Affair, The (Jewison), 375
Thompson, Kristin, 434
Thor (Branagh), 85
Thornton, Billy Bob, 421, *422*
Thou Shalt Not Kill (Kieslowski), 203
3-D cinematography, 252, *282,* 515–16
3 Godfathers (Ford), 103
300 (Snyder), *483*
Three Kings (Russell), 230
Three Little Pigs, The (Disney), 235
Three Penny Opera, The (Pabst), 108
three-point system, lighting, 238–39, *240,* 244
three-shot, 252
3:10 to Yuma (Daves), 105
3 Women (Altman), 293
Throne of Blood (Kurosawa), *209,* 329, 465
Through the Looking Glass (Carroll), *190*
Thulin, Ingrid, 370
Thurman, Uma, *138*
THX 1138 (Lucas), *240,* 97
THX technology, 391
Tian Zhuangzhuang, *The Horse Thief,* 468
tilt shot, *267,* **267**
'Til We Meet Again (Goulding), 499
Timberlake, Justin, *134*
Timecode (Figgis), *153,* 375
Tin Drum, The (Schlöndorff), *372*
tinting, 234
Tintori, Ray, *Death to the Tinman,* 83
Titanic (Cameron), 143, *238,* 314, 503
Title, John, 408
TiVo, 2
T-Men (Mann), 242
To Catch a Thief (Hitchcock), *301*
To Die For (Van Sant), 190, 307, *372, 375*

To Kill a Mockingbird (Mulligan), 79
Tokyo Story (Ozu), 208–9, 466, *468*
Toland, Gregg, 46, 228, 238, *239,* 241, *241,* 254–55, 267, *454*
Tolkien, J. R. R., 145
Toll of the Sea, The (Franklin), 234
Toluboff, Alexander, *207*
Tomasini, George, 352, 365, 367, *368*
Tom Jones (Richardson), 123, 319
tonality, black and white film, 233–34, *233*
tonality, film stock and, *233*
Topsy-Turvy (Leigh), 321
Touchez pas au grisbi (Becker), 93
Touch of Evil (Welles), 96, 269–72, *270,* 277, 316
Tourneur, Jacques:
  Cat People, 101
  Out of the Past, 96
Toy Story (Lasseter, Brannon and Unkrich), 59, 113
Toy Story 2: The Ultimate Toy Box (Lasseter, Brannon and Unkrich), 309
Toy Story movies, 388
tracking shot, 267, 268, *268*
Tracy, Spencer, 305, 314
Tragedy of Othello: The Moor of Venice (Welles), 404, *405*
Trainspotting (Boyle), 123, 146
Transformers (Bay), 115
Transformers: Dark of the Moon (Bay), 514
Transformers: Revenge of the Fallen (Bay), 403
Trasatti, Luciano, 210
Travolta, John, *138,* 146
Treasure of the Sierra Madre, The (Huston), 155
Tree of Life, The (Malick), *27, 84, 281*
Tretyakov, Sergei, 151
Trevor, Claire, 157, *158, 207*
Tribulation 99: Alien Anomalies under America (Baldwin), 79, *80*
tripod, 266
Trip to the Moon, A (Méliès), *59,* 98, 440
Triumph of the Will (Riefenstahl), 72–73, *73*
TRON (Lisberger), 280

Trouble in Paradise (Lubitsch), 109, *254,* 390, 400

True Blood, 82

True Blood (HBO), *109*

True Grit (Coen and Coen), 40, *65,* 109, *126,* 130, 132, 133, 292, *308,* 516

Truffaut, François, 137, 153, 322, 373, *374,* 458–59, 474
"A Certain Tendency of the French Cinema," 458
Farenheit 451, 98
The 400 Blows, 459, *459*

Truman Show, The (Weir), 421

Trumbull, Douglas, 280, *281*

Tsai Ming-liang, *Vive l'amour,* 470

Tumbleweeds (Baggot), 105

Turner, Lana, 299

Twelve Monkeys (Gilliam), 98

20th Century Fox, 242, 498, 499, 500

28 Days Later... (Boyle), *100,* 102

21 Grams (González Iñárritu), 67

Twilight Saga, The: Breaking Dawn, Part 1 (Condon), 515

Twilight Saga, The: Eclipse (Slade), *109*

Twitter, *183*

Twixt (F. F. Coppola), 516

two-shot, 252

2001: A Space Odyssey (Kubrick), 86, *86,* 89, 97, 155, 193, 209, *210,* 280, *281,* 309, 365, *366,* 417, 475

Tykwer, Tom, 351, 352, *354,* 405
Run Lola Run, 230, 363

typecasting, 305

U

Ugetsu (Mizoguchi), 325*n,* 466

Ullmann, Liv, 317, 370, *372*

Ulmer, Edgar G., 182, 197
Detour, 96

Uman, Naomi, *Removed, 81*

Umberto D. (De Sica), 328, 456

Umbrellas of Cherbourg, The (Demy), 105

"uncanny valley," CGI and, 114, *115*

Uncle Boonmee Who Can Recall His Past Lives (Weerasethakul), *409,* 410

Unforgiven (Eastwood), 103, *104,* 110

unions, labor, 485, **503–4**

United Artists, 492, 498, 499, 509

Universal International, 269

Universal Studios, 498, 505

Universum Film AG (UFA), 444, 445

Unkrich, Lee, 309
Toy Story 2, 309

Unsworth, Geoffrey, 280, *281,* 475

Until the End of the World (Wenders), 98

Unvanquished, The (S. Ray), 200, 401

USB devices, 490

Ustinov, Peter, 319

Usual Suspects, The (Singer), 96, 147, *147,* 148

V

vampire movies, *109,* 515

Van Der Beek, James, *375*

van der Beek, Stan, *Death Breath,* 81

Van Dien, Casper, *213*

van Dongen, Helen, 343

Van Dyke, W. S., *192,* 193, 496
Marie Antoinette, 192, 199

Van Enger, Charles, 268

Van Sant, Gus, 277, 307, 347–48, 474
Elephant, 273
Milk, 156
To Die For, 190, 307, *372, 375*

Van Zandt, Philip, 241, *241*

Varda, Agnès, 458

Vardannes, Emilio, *185*

variable-focal-length lens, 245–46

Variety, 311

Vasilyev, Dmitri, 172

Vaughn, Matthew:
Kick-Ass, 59, 111
X-Men: First Class, 85

Veevers, Wally, 280, *281*

Veidt, Conrad, *445*

Vélez, Lupe, 314

Vera Drake (Leigh), 22

Verbinski, Gore, 250
Pirates of the Caribbean: At World's End, 282, 293

Pirates of the Caribbean: Curse of the Black Pearl, 293
Pirates of the Caribbean: Dead Man's Chest, 282, 293
The Ring, 100

Verhoeven, Paul, *Starship Troopers,* 99

verisimilitude, **58–60,** *59,* 189, 201, 205, 211, 230, 279, 358, 392, 398, 402

Vertigo (Hitchcock), 322, 365

Vertov, Dziga, 194, 349, 462
The Man with the Movie Camera, 448, *448,* 458

Viard, Karin, 418

Vicky Cristina Barcelona (Allen), 311

Victim (Dearden), 462, *462*

video assist camera, 194

video technology, **489**

Vidor, King, 268, 330–33, *331,* 398, 442, *444*
Big Parade, The, 442
The Crowd, 207, *444*
Duel in the Sun, 105
Hallelujah!, 390
Stella Dallas, 333, 334, 336

viewfinder, 204

Vigo, Jean, *À propos de Nice,* 448

Village of the Damned (Rilla), 98

villain, *see* antagonist

Vimeo, 82

Viola, Bill, 82

Virgin Queen, The (Koster), 193

Viridiana (Buñuel), 447

Visconti, Luchino, 173, 174–76, *176,* 457
Ossessione, 455, 456

Vitascope, 439

Vitelloni, I (Fellini), 210

Vive l'amour (Tsai), 470

vocal sounds, **399–401**

Vogel, Paul C., 275

Vogt, Tom, 349

voice-over narrators, 72, 74, *75,* 95, 123, 125, 400–401

Voight, Jon, 304, *396*

Voldemort, Lord, Adolf Hitler and, 23–25, *25*

Volver (Almodóvar), 155

von Sternberg, Josef, *The Blue Angel,* 444

von Stroheim, Erich, 179, 191, 197, *245, 268, 268,* 375
   Greed, 297, 442
   Queen Kelly, 197, *199*
von Sydow, Max, *232*
von Trier, Lars, 172, 208, 243, 265, 319, 351, 462, 490
   Breaking the Waves, 463, *463*
   Dancer in the Dark, 107, 463
   Dogville, 307, 463
   The Five Obstructions, 463
   The Idiots, 463
   The Kingdom, 102
von Trotta, Margarethe, *The German Sisters/Marianne and Juliane,* 464
von Wangenheim, Gustav, 277, *446*
"Vow of Chastity, The," 463
Vuh, Popol, 418

W

W (Stone), 288
Wachowski, Andy and Larry, 49, *50,* 59, 277, 281–82, 315, 351, 404
   The Matrix movies, 97, 469, *469*
Wadleigh, Michael, *Woodstock,* 344
Waggner, George, *The Wolf Man,* 99
Wagner, Christian, 82
Wagner, Fritz Arno, *262,* 277
Wagner, Richard, 419, *420*
Wahlberg, Mark, *145*
Waitress (Shelly), *21,* 22
Wajda, Andrzej, 461
Walczak, Diana, 309
Walken, Christopher, 212, *212*
Walker, Roy, 185
Walker, Vernon L., 279
Walking Man II (Giacometti), 37–39, *38*
walk-ons, 316
Wallace & Gromit in The Curse of the Were-Rabbit (Park and Box), 112
Wallace & Gromit movies, 113
Wallach, Eli, 304
WALL-E (Stanton), 403, 490
Walsh, Kay, *146*
Walsh, Raoul, 376
   The Big Trail, 105, 248, *308*
   White Heat, 92, 93

Walt Disney Feature Animation, *see* Disney Studios
Walters, Melora, *406*
Walthall, Henry B., 295
Waltz with Bashir (Folman), 111, *112*
Wanger, Walter, 496*n*
War and Peace (Bondarchuk), 197
wardrobe, 188
   see also costume, hairstyle and makeup
war genre, 93
Warhol, Andy, 476
   Lonesome Cowboys, 81
Warm, Hermann, 197
Warner, Frank, *402, 403*
Warner, Harry and Jack, 495
Warner Brothers, 242, 301, 306, 307, 495, 498, 499, 504, 511
War of the Worlds (H. G. Wells), 411, 423
War of the Worlds (Spielberg), *97,* 179, 291, 388, **410–14,** *411, 412, 413*
War of the Worlds radio drama (Welles), 413
Warrick, Ruth, 151
Washington, Denzel, *250,* 309, *312,* 313, 322
Wasikowska, Mia, *190*
Waters, John, 309
Watling, Leonor, 266
Watson, Alberta, 418
Watson, Emily, *463*
Watson, Emma, 23
Watts, Naomi, 67
Wavelength (Snow), 77, 79, 81
Waxman, Franz, 415
Way Down East (Griffith), 20–22, *21, 42, 43,* 53, 367, 442, 449
Wayne, John, *40,* 90, 104, 157, *158, 207,* 299, *308,* 309, 315, 321, 327, 359, 465, 515
We Are the Lambeth Boys (Reisz), 462
Weaver, Sigourney, 416
Weaving, Hugo, 277
Weber, Billy, *346*
Weber, Lois, 374, 442
Wedding Banquet, The (A. Lee), 201, 470
Wedgwood, Thomas, 435
We Don't Live Here Anymore (Curran), 404

Weerasethakul, Apichatpong, *Uncle Boonmee Who Can Recall His Past Lives, 409,* 410
Wegener, Paul, *The Golem,* 444
Weinstein, Harvey and Bob, 512*n*
Weinstein Company, 512*n*
Weir, Peter, 282, 326, 421
Weis, Elisabeth, 417
Weitz, Chris, *The Golden Compass,* 307
Welles, Orson, 179, 186, 197, 265, 277, 288, 323–26, 423–28, *426,* 464, 503
   Citizen Kane, 46, 54, 146, *147,* 149, 151, 185, *199,* 228, 238, *239,* 267, 314, 345, 346, 418, 423–28, *424, 431,* 441, 454, *454,* 459, 474, 492
   The Magnificent Ambersons, 199, 267, 326, 400
   Touch of Evil, 96, 269–72, *270,* 277, 316
   The Tragedy of Othello, 404, *405*
   War of the Worlds radio drama, 413
Wellman, William A., 496
   The Ox-Bow Incident, 105
   The Public Enemy, 93
Wells, H. G., *War of the Worlds,* 411, 423
Wenders, Wim:
   The American Friend, 464, *465*
   The Goalie's Anxiety of the Penalty Kick, 464
   Paris, Texas, 464
   Until the End of the World, 98
Wendy and Lucy (Reichardt), 207
We're Not Married (Goulding), 499
West, Clare, 191
West, Mae, *301*
western genre, 88, **102–5,** *104, 105,* 110–11, **157–67,** *158, 162–63,* 231, *233*
   subgenres of, 108
Westfront (Pabst), 390
Westmore, Bud, 193
Westmore, George, 191
Westmore, Wally, 193
West Side Story (Robbins and Wise), 108
Wexler, Haskell, 272, 475
Wexman, Virginia Wright, 320

Whale, James, 193, *195,* 197, 211–12, *211,* 241, 263, *263,* 313, 415
  Bride of Frankenstein, 101
  Frankenstein, 99
Whales of August, The (Anderson), 307
What Ever Happened to Baby Jane? (Aldrich), 301, 307
What's Eating Gilbert Grape (Hallström), *292*
Whedon, Joss, *110*
  Serenity, 110
Whelan, Tim, 200
Where the Wild Things Are (Jonze), 82
Whitaker, Forest, 263, 313
White Heat (Walsh), *92,* 93
Whitney, Cornelius Vanderbilt, 498
Whitney, John, *Matrix I,* 81
Who Framed Roger Rabbit (Zemeckis), 281
Who's Afraid of Virginia Woolf? (Nichols), *302*
Wicki, Bernhard, 156
wide-angle lens, 244
Widescreen Cinema (Belton), 434
Wiene, Robert, *195,* 197, *199,* 234
  The Cabinet of Dr. Caligari, 99, *196,* 444, *445, 446*
Wiest, Dianne, 311
Wife vs. Secretary (Brown), 496
wigs, 193–94, *193*
Wilcox, Fred M., *Forbidden Planet,* 98
Wild Bunch, The (Peckinpah), 105, 368, *469,* 474, *475*
Wilde, Hagar, 399
Wilder, Billy, 93, *154,* 197, *237, 245,* 314, 331, 345, *400*
  Ace in the Hole, 96
  The Apartment, 130–31
  Double Indemnity, 47, *94,* 129
  Some Like It Hot, 109
  Sunset Boulevard, 94, 199, 299, *432*
wild recording, 401–2
Wild Strawberries (Bergman), 409
Williams, Bert, 442
Williams, John, 404, 410, *412,* 413, 415, 419
Williams, Michelle, 333–36, *334*

Willis, Bruce, 304, 309
Willis, Gordon, *239, 242,* 475
Will Penny (Gries), 105
Wilson, Ian, 263
Wilson, Thomas F., 14
Winchester '73, (Mann), 105
Wind, The (Sjöström), 297
Winslet, Kate, 314
Winston, Irene, *368*
Winters, Ralph E., 375
Winters, Shelley, 304, 314, 420
Winter's Bone, 516
wipes, **372**
Wise, Robert, 345
  The Day the Earth Stood Still, 98
  The Sound of Music, 108
  West Side Story, 108
Witherspoon, Reese, *236*
With Our King and Queen Through India, 234
Wizard of Oz, The (Fleming), 108, 132, 133, 145, 235, 394
Wladyka, Faith, 335
Wolf Man, The (Waggner), 99
Woman Under the Influence, A (Cassavetes), 321
Wonder Boys (Hanson), *305*
Wong, Anna May, 314
Woo, John, 201
  A Better Tomorrow, 469, *469*
  The Killer, 54–56, *54*
Wood, Natalie, *40,* 327
Wood, Oliver, 272, *272*
Woodstock (Wadleigh), 344
Woolf, Virginia, 80, 407
Wöppermann, Katharina, 181
Wordplay (Creadon), 72
World of Apu, The (S. Ray), 200, 401
World of Glory (Andersson), 202
World War I, 194, 268, 499
World War II, 200, 230, 499, 501
  Harry Potter movies and, 23–25, *25*
  propaganda films in, 73, *73,* 455
Woyzeck (Herzog), 325*n*
Wrestler, The (Aronofsky), 83
Wright, Andrew, 405
Wright, Edgar:
  Scott Pilgrim vs. the World, 13, 111
  Shawn of the Dead, 102
Wright, Joe, *Atonement, 48,* 54, 145, 200
Writers Guild of America, The, *147*

Wuthering Heights (Wyler), 321
Wyler, William, 60, *203,* 228, *256,* 277, 302, 321, 322, 499
  The Best Years of Our Lives, 326
  Jezebel, 306, *306*
  The Letter, 306, 307
  The Little Foxes, 256, *306,* 307, 326
Wynette, Tammy, 405

X

Xena: Warrior Princess, 107
X-Men: First Class (Vaughn), 85

Y

Yakin, Boaz, 319
Yang, Edward, 201
  Taipei Story, 470
Yankee Doodle Dandy (Curtiz), 108
Yates, David:
  Harry Potter and the Deathly Hallows: Part I, 25
  Harry Potter and the Deathly Hallows: Part II, 1, 25, 26, *26,* 134, 514, 516
  Harry Potter and the Half-Blood Prince, 25
  Harry Potter and the Order of the Phoenix, 25
Yellow Earth (Chen), 201
Yenej, Yevgeni, 194
Yeoman, Robert D., 277
Yi, Zhenzhou, 209
Yim Ho, 469
  The Extras, 469
Yip, Tim, 199
Yojimbo (Kurosawa), 465
You, The Living, (Andersson), 42
Young, Freddie, 226–27
Young Adult (Reitman), 188
Young Frankenstein (Brooks), 280, 419
Young Sherlock Holmes (Levinson), 281
Young Torless (Schlöndorff), 464
YouTube, 82
You've Got Mail (Ephron), 400
Yoyotte, Josèphe, 373–74
Y tu mamá también (Cuarón), 373, *374*
Yu, Dennis, 469

Yuen Woo-ping, 469
Yuh, Jennifer, *Kung Fu Panda 2,* 85

Z

Zanuck, Darryl F., 500
Zatorsky, Ernest, 298, 390
Zavattini, Cesare, 455, 456
Zecca, Ferdinand, 445
Zeffirelli, Franco, *The Taming of the Shrew,* 302

Zemeckis, Robert, 209, 281, 309, 494
    Back to the Future, 14
    Beowulf, 283
    The Polar Express, 114, *115,* 283
Zhang, Yimou, 209
    Raise the Red Lantern, 201, 468
Zhang, Ziyi, *209, 470*
Zimmer, Hans, 404, 408
Zinnemann, Fred, 151, *233,* 314
    Oklahoma!, 108
Zodiac (Fincher), *305,* 490

zoom:
    lenses, 268–69
    shots, 268–69, 271
zoom-in shots, 268–69
zoom lens, 245–46, *246,* **268–69**
zoopraxiscope, **437**
Zorn's Lemma (Frampton), 81
Zourdoumis, Leonidas, 277
Zsigmond, Vilmos, 475
Zukor, Adolph, 495
Zumbrunnen, Eric, 345